SQL Server™ 2005
Bible

SQL Server™ 2005
Bible

Paul Nielsen

Wiley Publishing, Inc.

SQL Server™ 2005 Bible

Published by
Wiley Publishing, Inc.
10475 Crosspoint Boulevard
Indianapolis, IN 46256
www.wiley.com

Copyright © 2007 by Wiley Publishing, Inc., Indianapolis, Indiana

Published by Wiley Publishing, Inc., Indianapolis, Indiana

Published simultaneously in Canada

ISBN-13: 978-0-7645-4256-5
ISBN-10: 0-7645-4256-7

Manufactured in the United States of America

10 9 8 7 6 5 4 3 2 1

1B/RW/RQ/QW/IN

For general information on our other products and services or to obtain technical support, please contact our Customer Care Department within the U.S. at (800) 762-2974, outside the U.S. at (317) 572-3993 or fax (317) 572-4002.

Library of Congress Cataloging-in-Publication Data:

Nielsen, Paul.
 SQL server 2005 bible / Paul Nielsen.
  p. cm.
 ISBN-13: 978-0-7645-4256-5 (paper/website)
 ISBN-10: 0-7645-4256-7 (paper/website)
 1. SQL server. 2. Client/server computing. 3. Database management. I. Title.
 QA76.9.C55N55 2006
 005.2'768—dc22
                    2006016151

For Edie, my bride, who is so beautiful to me.

Credits

Executive Editor
Robert Elliott

Development Editors
Mark Cierzniak
Ami Frank Sullivan

Technical Editors
John Mueller
Kevin Lloyd
Chris Shaw

Production Editor
William A. Barton

Copy Editor
Luann Rouff

Editorial Manager
Mary Beth Wakefield

Production Manager
Tim Tate

Vice President and Executive Group Publisher
Richard Swadley

Vice President and Executive Publisher
Joseph B. Wikert

Project Coordinator
Ryan Steffen

Graphics and Production Specialists
Sean Decker
Lauren Goddard
Brooke Graczyk
Jennifer Mayberry
Jill Proll

Quality Control Technician
John Greenough

Media Development Specialists
Angela Denny
Kit Malone
Travis Silvers

Media Development Coordinator
Laura Atkinson

Proofreading and Indexing
Techbooks

About the Author

Paul Nielsen is a hands-on database developer, Microsoft SQL Server MVP, author, and trainer specializing in data architecture and Microsoft SQL Server technologies. Besides holding several certifications, he was the Design-SME (subject matter expert) for the Microsoft Official Course 2784: Tuning and Optimizing Queries Using Microsoft SQL Server 2005.

Paul has been developing datacentric solutions since 1982, and was the Enterprise Data Architect for Compassion International, a SQL Server instructor with Learning Tree, the technical editor for a database magazine, and a U. S. Navy Submariner (Data Systems Tech).

He serves on the PASS (Professional Association for SQL Server) Board of Directors, is active in the Colorado area SQL Server user groups, and organizes the Colorado PASS Camp. For recreation, Paul enjoys scuba diving, playing guitar, and hiking/biking in the Front Range mountains of Colorado. Paul regularly offers public and private workshops in SQL Server development and data architecture, including the popular Advanced Design and Optimization course. For more information visit his website at www.SQLServerBible.com.

About the Co-Authors and Contributors

Hilary Cotter, Microsoft SQL Server MVP and author of Chapter 13, "Using Full-Text Search," and Chapter 39, "Replicating Data," is director of Text Mining and Database Strategy for RelevantNoise, which indexes blogs for business intelligence. He received a degree in mechanical engineering from the University of Toronto, and subsequently studied economics at the University of Calgary and computer science at the University of California (Berkeley). He and his beautiful wife, Miriam, have five children ranging in age from 13 months to six years. Hilary Cotter has a companion volume to this text on merge replication, which is in the works for 2005.

Hilary has worked for Microsoft, Merrill Lynch, UBS-Paine Webber, MetLife, VoiceStream, Tiffany & Co., Pacific Bell, Cahners, Novartis, Petro-Canada, Associated Press, and Johnson and Johnson. You can find Hilary on the Microsoft newsgroups or contact him at hilary.cotter@gmail.com.

Monte Holyfield, author of Chapter 46, "Authoring Reports with Reporting Services," and Chapter 47, "Administering Reports with Reporting Services," is the founder and manager of MJH Software Solutions LLC (www.mjhsoftware.com). He has over 10 years of experience developing custom software and has served in many capacities including solution architect, principal consultant, mentor, and project lead. He is a Microsoft Certified Professional and has successfully leveraged the Microsoft.NET technologies to deliver outstanding solutions to a diverse group of clients. Monte offers a unique combination of technical, analytical, and leadership skills and shares a contagious "can do" attitude. When Monte is not building software, he can most likely be found with his family doing something active such as riding dirt bikes, skiing, windsurfing, or just enjoying the incredible Colorado outdoors.

Kevin Lloyd, Technical Editor, is an experienced SQL Server Developer and Data Architect, Microsoft MCP, consultant and primary member of Data Solutions, LLC. He specializes in data architecture and application integration, data modeling, data quality, and performance tuning. Besides working with SQL Server, he develops C# XML Web Services for SQL Mobile replication. He also enjoys mentoring others in SQL and writing Windows Mobile applications. Kevin has been developing data-centric solutions since 1996 in finance, e-commerce, and government, and has worked or consulted with organizations such as Microsoft Corporation; Frontier Airlines, Inc.; Compassion International, Inc.; and Keane, Inc. He can be reached at kevin@kevndeb.com. When not writing code, he enjoys woodworking, spending time with his family, and traveling.

George Mudrak, author of chapter 4, "Installing SQL Server 2005," Chapter 5, "Client Software Connectivity," and Chapter 54, "Designing High-Performance Data Access Providers," works as an Enterprise Data Architect for Compassion International in Colorado Springs, CO. He has been doing full life-cycle programming in a variety of languages for over 12 years, with his most recent development activities using Microsoft's .NET technologies. He is currently working within the Enterprise Information Architecture and Management (EIM/EIA) realm and has worked at start-ups as well as major corporations. When he's not working, George enjoys spending time with his family, working out, and pursuing hobbies.

John Mueller, primary technical reviewer and co-author of Chapter 34, "Configuring SQL Server," Chapter 35, "Transferring Databases," Chapter 37, "Maintaining the Database," Chapter 38, "Automating Database Maintenance with SQL Server Agent," and Chapter 41, "Administering SQL Server Express," is a freelance author and technical editor. He has writing in his blood, having produced 69 books and over 300 articles to date, with the topics that range from networking to artificial intelligence and from database management to heads-down programming. Some of his current books include a Windows power optimization book, a book on .NET security, and books on Amazon Web Services, Google Web Services, and eBay Web Services. He's currently editor of the .NET electronic newsletter for Pinnacle Publishing. See www.freeenewsletters.com for more information. When John isn't working at the computer, he is likely in his workshop. An avid candle maker and woodworker, he can be found working at a lathe or putting the finishing touches on a bookcase. His website is www.mwt.net/~jmueller.

Darren Shaffer, Microsoft Compact Framework MVP, author of Chapter 26, "Developing for SQL Server Mobile," is the Chief Architect for .NET Solutions at Connected Innovation LLC (www.connectedinnovation.com). Darren is responsible for the design and development of over 25 Compact Framework solutions for Fortune 1000 clients in the past four years. Darren is a frequent speaker at Global Microsoft Events such as MEDC and TechEd. as well as a contributor to MSDN, emphasizing the importance of the .NET Compact Framework, SQL CE/SQL Mobile, and teaching mobile development best practices. Darren moderates the MSDN SQL Mobile forum, and authors a well-traveled blog for .NET junkies at www.dotnetjunkies.com/WebLog/darrenshaffer/default.aspx. A West Point graduate and retired Army Telecommunications Officer, Darren now lives in Colorado with his wife and daughter.

Chris Shaw, technical editor and author of chapter 52, "Providing High Availability" is President of SQL on Call in Colorado Springs, Colorado, for the past 5 years Chris has been working at Premiere Global Services. He has also worked with Yellow Pages Inc, Ford Fairlane Motor Credit, AdminiQuest, Wells Fargo and AT&T Wireless. Chris has published a number of Articles for a number of magazines including SQL Server Magazine and SQL Standard Magazine.

He is a member of Rocky Mountain Microsoft Community Insiders group, is the president of the Colorado Springs SQL Server Users Group, and is one of the organizers of the Colorado PASS Camp. He has also been a guest speaker to a number of other user groups, is a regular speaker at PASS Summits and SQL Connection, and presents web casts with SSWUG; recent presentations include Replication SQL Server 2005, Performance Metrics, and Crisis Management.

Andrew Watt, Microsoft SQL Server MVP, wrote Chapter 33, "InfoPath and SQL Server 2005." Andrew Watt is an independent consultant and experienced computer book author. He has been a Microsoft MVP since 2004.

Michael White has focused on database development and administration since 1992. Concentrating on Microsoft's Business Intelligence (BI) tools and applications since 2000, he has architected and implemented large warehousing and Analysis Services applications, as well as nontraditional applications of BI tools. After many years in corporate IT and consulting, Mike currently works as a software engineer for Wall Street On Demand. He is a strong advocate for the underused BI toolset; currently leads the Boulder (Colorado) SQL Server User Group and is one of the organizers of the Colorado PASS Camp. Mike wrote Chapter 42, "ETL with Integration Services," Chapter 43, "Business Intelligence with Analysis Services," Chapter 44, "Data Mining with Analysis Services," Chapter 45, "Programming MDX Queries," and Chapter 48, "Analyzing Data with Excel and Data Analyzer."

Bill Wunder, Microsoft SQL Server MVP, wrote Chapter 27, "Programming CLR Assemblies within SQL Server," Chapter 29, "Persisting Custom Data Types," and Chapter 30, "Programming with ADO.NET 2.0." Bill's introduction to set based technology began when he was an AS/400 developer in 1993. The query processor at the time was built by an Australian company, LANSA. The 4GL language was called Relational Database Markup Language (RDML). It was an innovative product written in RPG that included commands like SELECT, INSERT, UPDATE and DELETE. Shortly after that introduction he became the DBA for the company's sales force automation application. The database had just been upgraded to SQL Server 4.2.1 running on the Novell OS. He has been working with SQL Server since that time. He began sharing his scripts on the Internet in 1995. He has published over 100 SQL Server related articles at various web sites. He has been a speaker at swynk.com's Back Office Administrators Conferences and Professional Association for SQL Server (PASS) conferences in the US and Europe. He founded and has been a frequent speaker at the Boulder SQL Server Users Group. He received Microsoft's MVP award for his contributions to the SQL Server community in 2004, 2005 and 2006. Today Bill is a working DBA on the Dutch Antilles island of Curaçao. Readers are invited to contact him at bwunder@yahoo.com with any questions or comments.

Contents at a Glance

Contents

Part II: Manipulating Data with Select   115

Part IV: Enterprise Data Management   703

Part V: Business Intelligence   897

Foreword

I first meet Paul a few PASS Summits ago and we now serve together on the PASS Board of Directors. We share a passion for the SQL Server community and that's what I want to write about. Paul and I want to extend an invitation to you to visit your local PASS chapter, attend a PASS camp, and join us at the annual Global Summit, my favorite week of the year. I can guarantee that if you get involved with PASS you'll get more out of it than you put in. This is a great community with plenty of good will and a common desire to help each other grow our skills. Here you'll meet MVPs and authors, fellow DBAs and database developers, the Microsoft SQL Server development team, and friends. So come, get involved, speak up, and let your voice be heard.

Wayne Synder, PASS Director of Vendor Programs
Managing Consultant, Mariner

Acknowledgments

Although many folks assisted me with this book, Ami Sullivan deserves the first thank you for her wonderful work as development editor, moving the words through the process, keeping me on target, and her countless hours. Thank you, Ami.

To my fellow MVPs and SQL Server buddies, Itzik Ben-Gan, Chuck Boyce, Kalen Delaney, Sharon Dooley, Randy Dyess, Fernando Guerrero, Steve Kass, Greg Low, Adam Machanic, Brian Moran, Bill Wunder, Carl Rabeler, Doug McDowell, Pat Wright, and Steve Jones. Without a doubt, the best benefit to being an MVP is participating in the MVP newsgroups.

Applause and kudos to the Colorado SQL Server community leaders, Chris Shaw, Mike White, and Wolfgang Baeck, thanks for all you do. And to the regional Microsoft team, Ani Babaian, David Gollob, Ben Miller, and Ashwin Karuhatty, thank you for supporting the SQL Server community in Colorado.

Chris Shaw spent several hours collaborating on the initial design of the book. Chris, thanks for your ideas—your fingerprint is all over this book.

I am honored to participate with the PASS Board of Directors, Kevin Kline, Guy Brown, Trey Johnson, Joe Webb, Randy Dyess, Rick Heiges, Bill Graziano, Wayne Snyder, Rushabh Mehta, Christopher Stotz, Hyden Richardson, Ed Lehman, Richard Bolesta, and Neil Buchwalter.

To the many readers who submitted suggestions and encouraging words, thank you. I appreciate your e-mails more than you imagine.

Thank you to all those who contributed to the *SQL Server 2000 Bible*. The first edition provided a solid foundation from which to grow.

A hearty thanks to the entire Microsoft SQL Server team for once again building an incredible product that's as much fun to use as it is powerful.

And thank you to my kids, Lauren and David, for putting up with a dad who had no time for exploring or adventure during for the past year; to my friends, who have seen little of me for too many months; and to my bride, for her incredible patience.

Introduction

Welcome to the *SQL Server 2005 Bible*. SQL Server is an incredible database product. It offers an excellent mix of performance, reliability, ease of administration, and new architectural options, yet enables the developer or DBA to control minute details when desired. SQL Server is a dream system for a database developer. If there's a theme to SQL Server 2005, it's new architectural options — SQL Server 2005 opens several new possibilities for designing more scalable and powerful systems. The first goal of this book is share with you the pleasure of working with SQL Server.

Like all books in the Bible series, you can expect to find both hands-on tutorials and real-world practical applications, as well as reference and background information that provides a context for what you are learning. However, to cover every minute detail of every command of this very complex product would consume thousands of pages, so it is the second goal of this book to provide a concise yet comprehensive guide to SQL Server 2005 based on the information I have found most useful in my experience as a database developer, consultant, and instructor. By the time you have completed the *SQL Server 2005 Bible,* you will be well prepared to develop and manage your SQL Server 2005 database.

Some of you are repeat readers of mine (thanks!) and are familiar with my approach from the *SQL Server 2000 Bible*. Even though you might be familiar with my approach and my tone, you will find several new features in this edition, including the following:

- ✦ Coverage of the new architectural options, such as Service Broker, Web Services, XQuery, and Reporting Services

- ✦ More detail on the BI features

- ✦ Ten chapters on selecting data with queries

A wise database developer once showed a box to an apprentice and asked, "How many sides do you see?" The apprentice replied, "There are six sides to the box." The experienced database developer then said, "Users may see six sides, but database developers see only two sides: the inside and the outside. To the database developer, the cool code goes inside the box." This book is about thinking inside the box.

Who Should Read This Book

Whether you are a database developer or a database administrator, whether you are just starting out, have one year of experience or five, this book contains material that will be useful to you. This book is written so that you can learn from my experience and the experience of the co-authors. Each chapter begins with the assumption that you've never seen the topic before, and then progresses through the subject, presenting the information that makes a difference.

The next section describes how the book is divided into different parts. After you read the summaries, you will best know where to start. No matter how you approach it, be sure to read Chapter 1, "The Information Architecture Principle." That chapter describes two key principles upon which the rest of the book is based. Any other chapters you read will be clearer and make more sense once you have internalized both the Information Architecture Principle and optimization theory.

How This Book Is Organized

One of the differences repeat readers will note from prior editions is a slightly different organization. I really got to pull apart the text and draw more or less attention to certain areas of the book as the content and the changes to SQL Server 2005 dictated. Some chapters are only 10 pages long, while others are 30 or more. It was a challenge for me to stop where I did at nearly 1,400 pages! In any event, the book is organized into the following parts and chapters.

Each part is designed to be read sequentially and most chapters build on the previous chapters, but many readers have told me they use the book as a reference. Either way, I hope you find the book useful in your career.

Part I: Laying the Foundation

If SQL Server is the box, and developing is thinking inside the box, then the first part of this book is an introduction to the box. Beginning with the Information Architecture Principle and optimization theory, Part I presents six key topics that lay the foundation for your success with SQL Server:

 ✦ Information Architecture Principle

 ✦ Relational database modeling

 ✦ SQL Server architecture

 ✦ Installation

 ✦ Client software connectivity

 ✦ Management Studio

This isn't the obligatory "introduction to normalization" view of database design. Part I is a current, comprehensive, principle-driven view of information architecture and an introduction to the technologies of SQL Server.

Part II: Manipulating Data with Select

If SQL Server is the box, then Part II is about being one with the box. It begins by exploring the basic logical query flow, and quickly digs deeper into topics such as relational division, correlated subqueries, set-difference queries, and distributed queries. I've devoted ten chapters to the `select` command because understanding the multiple options and creative techniques available with queries is key to becoming a successful SQL Server developer, DBA, or architect.

Please don't assume that Part II is only for beginners. These ten chapters present the core power of SQL. Part VI explores optimization, and it's tempting to go there for optimization ideas. However, the second strategy of optimization theory is using good set-based code, so here are ten chapters on how to optimize your database by writing better queries.

Part III: Developing with SQL Server

If SQL Server is the box, then Part III is all about thinking inside the box, and moving the processing as close to the data as possible. Part III opens with DDL commands (create, alter, and drop), and progresses through nine chapters that dig deeper into Transact-SQL. The conclusion of the T-SQL chapters brings it all together with the data abstraction layer.

SQL Server's list of technologies keeps growing, so the remainder of Part III explores the .NET common language runtime (CLR), SQL Server Mobile, Service Broker, XML, XQuery, Web Services, and InfoPath. Go ahead, unleash the programmer within and have fun. There's a whole world of developer possibilities with SQL Server 2005.

Part IV: Enterprise Data Management

If SQL Server is the box, then Part IV is about keeping the box running smoothly, day after day, because this part is all about the enterprise DBA role.

While SQL Server is more automated than ever before, and Microsoft sometimes makes the error of presenting SQL Server as the database that doesn't require a DBA, the truth is that it takes diligent work to keep a production database up 24 hours a day, 7 days a week, 365 days a year.

Part V: Business Intelligence

If SQL Server is the box, then Part V is about coaxing every secret out of the box. The whole process of analyzing historical and current data both today and in the future is the proactive side of IT, collectively called *business intelligence (BI)*.

In the past three releases of SQL Server, Microsoft has been steadily growing SQL Server's BI services, and SQL Server 2005 brings to fruition years of planning and development. From the enterprise-grade ETL tool to the rich and easy to build cubes, to the slick reporting interface, SQL Server 2005 is more than ready to help you conquer your BI requirements. The chapters in this part show you how.

Part VI: Optimization Strategies

If SQL Server is the box, then Part VI is about making the box fly. This book opens with the Information Architecture Principle, which states that information must be made *readily available*. Optimization theory explains the dependencies between various optimization techniques. This final part puts optimization theory into action with practical optimization strategies.

Part VII: Appendixes

The appendixes provide some lookup information that applies to nearly every chapter: SQL Server specifications and details of the book's sample databases.

How to Use This Book

You should understand some important conventions and icons before embarking on your *SQL Server 2005 Bible* journey.

Conventions and Features

There are many different organizational and typographical features throughout this book designed to help you get the most of the information:

✦ New terms are italicized as they are defined in the text.

✦ When code is referenced within the text, the code words are set in `monospace` type. Sometimes, those same SQL keywords are used as concepts (for example: `inner` join is used both as SQL code and in referring to the concept of a type of join).

✦ Some of the code samples are long. To draw attention to the main point of the code, important keywords in code are highlighted in `bold`.

✦ I'm not fond of page-length query results, so if a result set is particularly long, it is abbreviated with an ellipsis in the listing.

Icons

Whenever the authors want to bring something important to your attention, the information appears in a special type treatment called an *icon*. This book utilizes quite a few icons: Note, Tip, Caution, Cross-Reference, On the Web, New in 2005, Best Practice, and .sys.

Caution   Cautions provide information about things to watch out for, from the simply inconvenient to the potentially hazardous, regarding your data or systems.

Tip   Tips generally are used to provide information that can make your work easier—special shortcuts or methods for doing something easier than the norm.

Note   Notes provide additional, ancillary information that is helpful but somewhat peripheral to the surrounding text.

Best Practice   Best Practice icons indicate recommended ways of doing something, based on lessons I've learned from real-world scenarios and personal experiences.

Cross-Reference   Cross-references direct you to other resources (both within and in addition to this book) that apply to what you're reading about. In several places in this book, material overlaps. For example, when installing SQL Server, one decision involves the authentication mode used for security. Rather than constantly refer you to other parts of the book, I've tried to provide enough information to cover the immediate issue without being redundant. Even so, there are numerous cross-references throughout the book so you can easily locate more detail on any given topic.

On The Web   These icons draw attention to additional information available online, and at the book's website, `www.SQLServerBible.com`.

This icon draws attention to features or improvements that are new to SQL Server 2005.

I'm experimenting with short, free ScreenCasts to augment the printed figures in the book—videos that illustrate how to perform a specific task using SQL Server tools. For example, to watch the sequence to view a deadlock using SQL Server Profiler, detailed in Chapter 49, "Measuring Performance," you can read the sequence and also watch the ScreenCast. To view the ScreenCasts, go to the books website, www.SQLServerBible.com and look for list of ScreenCasts.

SQL Server 2005 has dozens of new system views that expose more information about SQL Server than ever before. These icons highlight this new method of investigating the current state of the server.

What's on the Companion Website

On the publisher-sponsored companion website (www.wiley.com), you will find the following:

✦ Sample code—Each chapter has it's own subfolder on the website, where you'll find all the code output that was discussed in each chapter, organized accordingly.

✦ Errata

On the author-sponsored website (www.SQLServerBible.com) you'll find the preceding and more:

✦ Sample code and sample databases

✦ Errata, updates, and additional articles

✦ SQL Server–related resources and links

✦ Task-specific ScreenCasts

✦ PowerPoint and code from conference and PASS Chapter presentations

✦ Information on workshops

Where to Go from Here

As you begin reading the book, I have three suggestions for you:

1. Visit the website, www.SQLServerBible.com, to download the code, check for updates, and get the latest news about SQL Server.

2. Visit your local PASS Chapter to meet others who are involved in SQL Server and see some great presentations. If fact, I hope to meet you at the Global Summit this fall.

3. If you have questions or just want to share your experience with SQL Server or the book, send me an e-mail: pauln@SQLServerBible.com.

Now, let me introduce you to the Information Architecture Principle, which sets the stage for why we do what we do with our data.

Laying the Foundation

Beginning with the Information Architecture Principle and optimization theory, Part I presents six key topics that lay the foundation for your success with SQL Server.

In his book *Business @ the Speed of Thought,* Bill Gates promoted the concept of a "digital nervous system." His basic premise is that any organization can improve its effectiveness by collecting vital information and making that information available throughout the organization. Every year, the IT profession is getting closer to the vision of ubiquitous information. Database design and technology have both evolved faster since the millennium than at any other time since Dr. Edgar Codd introduced his revolutionary RDBMS concepts three decades earlier. This is truly a time of change.

The next-generation data platform uses client-server, n-tier, and service-oriented architecture (SOA) using XML and Web Services and is a far more extensible and flexible database than that of only a few years ago. Add to all these changes new technologies for performance, availability, and scalability, new tools for business intelligence, and new management tools, throw in a little CLR, and it adds up to an exciting time to be in the business of organizing and delivering information.

Therefore, this first part isn't the obligatory "introduction to normalization" view of database design. Rather, it is a current, comprehensive, principle-driven view of information architecture and an introduction to the technologies of SQL Server.

If SQL Server is the box, and developing is thinking inside the box, then the first part of this book is an introduction to the box.

The Information Architecture Principle

For any complex endeavor, there is value in beginning with a common principle to drive designs, procedures, and decisions. A credible principle is understandable, robust, complete, consistent, and stable. When an overarching principle is agreed upon, conflicting opinions can be objectively measured, and standards can be decided upon that support the principle.

The following principle encompasses the three main areas of information management: database design and development, enterprise data center management, and business intelligence analysis.

Information Architecture Principle: Information is an organizational asset, and, according to its value and scope, must be organized, inventoried, secured, and made readily available in a usable format for daily operations and analysis by individuals, groups, and processes, both today and in the future.

Unpacking this principle reveals several practical implications. First, there should be a known inventory of information, including its location, source, sensitivity, present and future value, and current owner. While most organizational information is stored in IT databases, uninventoried critical data is often found in desktop databases and spreadsheets scattered throughout the organization.

Just as the value of physical assets varies from asset to asset and over time, the value of information is also variable and so must be assessed. The value of the information may be high for an individual or department, but less valuable to the organization as a whole. Information that is critical today might be meaningless in a month, or information that may seem insignificant individually might become critical for organizational planning once aggregated.

If the data is to be made easily available in the future, current designs must be decoupled to avoid locking the data in a rigid, but brittle, database.

Based on the Information Architecture Principle, every data store can be designed or evaluated by seven interdependent data store objectives: simplicity, usability, data integrity, performance, availability, extensibility, and security.

Note   This chapter sets a principle-based foundation for the book, which provides a solid reason for each of the following chapters. However, the principle addresses some advanced database concepts, so if you're new to databases I recommend that you dive right in to Chapter 3, "Exploring SQL Server Architecture," and come back to the database concepts chapters later.

Simplicity vs. Complexity

Underscoring the Information Architecture Principle and the other six data store objectives is a design methodology I jokingly call the *Mortgage-Driven Simplicity Method*. While corporate IT programmers might eventually be terminated if their projects repeatedly fail, the consequences for an independent consultant are much more immediate, and the mortgage must be paid.

As a database consultant, I tend to take on the riskiest database projects — those considered disasters by the client (who had fired the previous consulting firm, or firms, for failure to deliver). In every case, the client originally asks me to finish the last 10 percent, or to optimize a project that didn't quite meet the requirements. What I usually find is a hopeless design.

The primary lesson I've learned from successfully turning around dozens of failed database projects is that the number one reason why software projects fail is not incompetent programmers, but an overly complex design. They fail because the designers were unable, or unwilling, to imagine an elegant solution. I've learned a few lessons from having to pay my mortgage based solely on my ability to deliver databases that performed.

The Mortgage-Driven Simplicity Method states:

> Fear complexity. Continue to collaboratively iterate the design until the design team unanimously agrees that it's the simplest solution possible that meets the requirements.

Complexity

Complexity breeds complexity, and complexity causes several problems. The most common result of complexity is that the project will outright fail. While a complex design may appear to be clever, it seldom meets the requirements. Complexity also makes the solution more difficult for developers to understand and implement, resulting in late projects.

Assuming the project is completed, complexity negatively affects every one of the other six data store objectives (usability, data integrity, performance, availability, extensibility, security). A complex design makes it more difficult to retrieve and update the correct data, which affects both usability and data integrity. Additional components create extra work (additional reads, joins, extra updates) and adds interdependent variables, making tuning more complex, all of which reduce performance.

The complex design potentially creates additional points of failure; and when problems do occur, the complexity obscures the source of the problem, making it difficult or impossible to diagnose and fix, which drives up support costs and limits availability. Compared to a simpler design, complex designs are extremely difficult to modify and adapt to changing requirements. Finally, a complex set of components makes it less likely that data will be correctly secured.

There's a reason why the thesaurus entry for the word "difficult" includes the word "complex."

Simplicity

A simple solution is elegant and appears obvious, but saying that designing a simple solution is easy is like watching the Olympics — masters always make their skill look easy. To quote Dr. Einstein,

"Things should be made as simple as possible — but no simpler."

The "as simple as possible" solution isn't a simpleton answer. The simplest solution that satisfies the requirements may have a level of complexity, but of all the possible designs, it's the simplest. Simplicity is measured as the number of components, technical variables, internal interfaces, and technologies involved in delivering the solution.

Designing a simple solution, in any discipline, is a difficult task that requires every one of the following ingredients:

✦ A complete understanding of the requirements

✦ A broad repertoire of patterns and solutions to draw from

✦ A complete understanding of the technical rules and nuances of the profession

✦ A creative mastery of the profession that knows when and how to push the envelope

✦ A solid understanding of the physical tools and materials used to implement the design and the environment within which the solution must function

✦ Enough trust between the designers that ideas can morph and grow based solely on their merits without personal egos or ownership

✦ The commitment to continue iterating the design for as long as it takes to design an elegant, slam-dunk, simple solution

✦ A healthy fear of complexity

When developing a design, if a few extra hours, or days, of collaboration results in an idea that eliminates a table or process while still meeting the requirements, that's a cause for celebration. Every reasonable reduction in complexity decreases the amount of implementation work and increases the chance of delivering a working product. Every extra dollar spent on design will bring a handsome return during implementation and even more in support costs over the life of the product

Some scoff at naming simplicity as the number one design objective of an inherently complex task like designing a database. From my experience, however, if the design team "gets" simplicity, then there's a good chance the project will be a success. If they don't value simplicity, I wouldn't want to be on that team.

The Usability Objective

The second data store objective is usability. The usability of a data store involves the completeness of meeting the organization's requirements, the suitability of the design for its intended purpose, the effectiveness of the format of data available to applications, and the ease of extracting information. The most common reason a database is less than usable is an overly complex or inappropriate design.

Suitability of Design

Several possible data store design models or types may be selected depending on the data store's scope and purpose.

The scope of the database involves the granularity of use within the organization (individual, department, business unit, company, enterprise) and the temporal nature of the data (for today only, for this fiscal year, forever). The rigor applied in the design and implementation should be proportional to the scope of the data.

Table 1-1 summarizes the data store design types and their suitability for various data store attributes (configuration and requirements).

Table 1-1: Suitability of Data Store Types by Level of Support

Attribute	Relational DBMS	Object DB	O/R DBMS	Generic Pattern	Data Warehouse
Suitable for master data store	●	◖	●	◖	○
Suitable for reference data store	◖	◖	◖	○	●
Data retrieval performance	◖	◖	◖	○	●
Supports schema flexibility	◖	●	●	●	○
Ease of SQL Query/traditional reporting tools	◖	○	◖	○	●
Well-established vendor support	●	○	◖	○	●
Requirement include several "is-a" relationships	○	●	●	○	○
Stores complex data types	◖	●	◖	○	◖
Complex multi-relational associations	◖	◖	●	○	◖
Ease of operations and tuning	◖	◖	●	◖	●
Persisting application objects	○	●	●	◖	○
Preventing data update anomaly	●	○	●	◖	○

○ represents poor support, ◖ represents limited support, and ● represents full support.

Data Store Configurations

An enterprise's data store configuration includes multiple types of data stores, as illustrated in Figure 1-1. There are multiple types of data stores: master data stores, caching data stores, reference data stores, data warehouses, and data marts.

A *master data store*, also referred to as the *operational database,* or *Online Transaction Processing (OLTP) database,* is used to collect first-generation transactional data essential to the day-to-day operation of the organization and unique to the organization. Customer, order, and shipping information are stored in a master data store. An organization might have a master data store to serve each unit or function within the organization.

For performance, master data stores are tuned for a balance of data retrieval and updates. Because these databases receive first-generation data, they are subject to data update anomalies, and benefit from normalization (detailed in the next section).

The master data store is part of Bill Gates' digital nervous system brain. It's the portion that collects all the information from every nerve and organizes the information so that it can be processed by the rest of the brain. The master data store is used for quick responses and instant recognition of the surroundings. For example, by quickly solving an order-handling problem, the master data store serves as the autonomic nervous system, or the reflexes, of an organization.

Caching data stores are optional read-only copies of the master data store, and are used to deliver data by partitioning some of the load off the master data store. A master data store might have multiple caching data stores to deliver data throughout the organization. Caching data stores might reside in a middle tier, or behind a web service. Caching data stores are tuned for high-performance data retrieval.

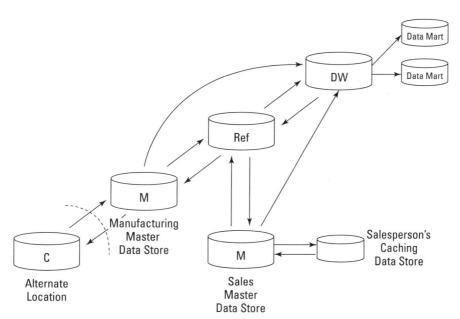

Figure 1-1: A typical organizational data store configuration includes several master data stores feeding a single data warehouse.

Reference data stores are primarily read-only and store generic data that is required by the organization but seldom changes — similar to the reference section of the library. Examples of reference data might be unit of measure conversion factors or ISO country codes. A reference data store is tuned for high-performance data retrieval.

A *data warehouse* collects large amounts of data from multiple master data stores across the entire enterprise using an *Extract-Transform-Load (ETL)* process to convert the data from the various formats and schema into a common format, designed for ease of data retrieval. Data warehouses also serve as the archival location, storing historical data and releasing some of the data load from the operational data stores. The data is also pre-aggregated, making research and reporting easier, thereby reducing errors.

A common data warehouse is essential for ensuring that the entire organization researches the same data set and achieves the same result for the same query — a critical aspect of Sarbanes-Oxley and other regulatory requirements.

Data marts are subsets of the data warehouse with pre-aggregated data organized specifically to serve the needs of one organizational group or one data domain.

The analysis process usually involves more than just SQL queries, and uses data cubes that consolidate gigabytes of data into dynamic pivot tables. Business intelligence (BI) is the combination of the ETL process, the data warehouse data store, and the acts of creating and browsing cubes.

Within Bill Gates' digital nervous system, the data warehouse serves as the memory of the organization. It stores history and is used for data mining such as trend analysis, such as finding out where (and why) an organization is doing well or is failing. The portion of the digital nervous system that is used by an organization for thoughtful musings — slowly turning over a problem and gaining wisdom — is the data warehouse and a BI cube.

Because the primary task of a data warehouse is data retrieval and analysis, the data-integrity concerns present with a master data store don't apply. Data warehouses are designed for fast retrieval and aren't normalized like master data stores. They are designed using a basic star schema or snowflake design. Locks generally don't apply, and the indexing is applied without adversely affecting inserts or updates.

Master Data Stores Design Styles

Database designers are not limited to the relational model. Several database design styles exist from which to choose depending on the requirements of the project.

Relational DBMSs

Relational databases are traditional databases that organize similar or related data into a single table. Relational databases are excellent with stable data schema requirements that include a certain minimum of *is-a* relationships (e.g., a customer is a contact).

Object-Oriented DBMSs

Object-oriented databases align the data structure with object-oriented application design (OOA/D) for the purpose of persisting application objects. OOA/D is based on the concept that an object is an instance of an object class. The class defines the properties and methods of the object, and contains all the code for the object. Each instance of the object can have its own internal variables and can interact with the software world outside the object on its own. Although the terms are different, the basic concept of organizing data is similar, as shown in Table 1-2.

Table 1-2: Comparing Database Terms

Development Style	The Common List	An Item in the List	A Piece of Information in the List
Spreadsheet	Spreadsheet/ worksheet/ named range	Row	Column/cell
Historic information	File	Record	Field
Relational algebra/ logical design	Entity	Tuple (*rhymes with couple*) or Relation	Attribute
SQL/physical design	Table	Row	Column
Object-oriented analysis and design	Class	Object instance	Property

Because the OO DBMSs must store objects, a key criterion for an OO DBMS is that it must be able to store complex objects, such as XML files, or .NET classes.

OO DBMSs are suitable for applications that expect significant schema change, include complex data types, involve several is-a relationships between classes, include complex multi-associations, and require ease of data connectivity with application software.

There are three primary types of object-oriented databases:

✦ An *object-persistence data store (OP DBMS)* is designed to be little more than a repository for object states. All integrity issues are handled by the object-oriented application code, and the database schema is designed to map perfectly with the application's class diagram.

✦ An *object-oriented data store (OO DBMS)* persists application objects and uses metadata (data that describes the way data is organized) to model the object-oriented class structure and enforce object-class integrity.

✦ An *object/relational data store (O/R DBMS)* persists the application objects, and models the class structure within a relational DBMS. O/R DBMSs provide the benefits of OO A/D with the traditional query and reporting ability of relational databases.

Note   For more information about Nordic (New Object Relational Database Design), by the author, visit www.SQLServerBible.com.

Generic Pattern DBMS

The *generic pattern* database, sometimes called the *dynamic-diamond pattern*, illustrated in Figure 1-2, is sometimes used as an OO DBMS physical design within a RDBMS product. This design can be useful when applications require dynamic attributes. A manufacturing material-specifications system, for example, would require different attributes for nearly every material type. To further complicate matters, the attributes that are tracked frequently change depending on the Total Quality Management (TQM) or ISO 9000 process within the company. A purely relational database might use an entity for each material type, requiring constant schema changes to keep current with the material tracking requirements.

Enterprise Architecture

The term *software architecture* takes on varied meanings depending on who's using the term, and their view, or scope, of the world:

✦ When Microsoft refers to architecture they usually mean their .NET Framework or designing any system using multiple Microsoft products together to solve a problem.

✦ *Product architecture* means designing a single application that solves a problem using multiple components.

✦ *Infrastructure architecture* is the design of the network using routers, switches, firewalls, SANs, and servers.

✦ *Data architecture* is the organization and configuration of data stores.

✦ *Enterprise architecture* attempts to manage all of these architectures for an entire organization, and is commonly divided into three areas: infrastructure, application, and data.

How enterprise architecture is accomplished is a subject of much debate. To use the construction industry metaphor, the views on enterprise architecture range from a passive building code committee approving or rejecting plans based on the standards to actively planning the city. While every viewpoint begins with a set of architectural principles, they differ on how those principles are enforced and how much initiative the architecture team used when planning the principles.

The *building code* viewpoint backs away from recommending to a client (those within the organization with the authority to make purchasing decisions) which software or applications they might use. Instead, the architecture team approves or denies client proposals based on the proposal's compliance with the architectural principles and standards. If the proposal doesn't meet the standards, then the client is free to request a variance using a defined procedure (change request). Which applications are built, how they are designed, and who builds them is completely up to the client, not the software architect.

The *zoning board* viewpoint takes the building code view and adds the notion of planning the enterprise's application portfolio. For example, a zoning board style enterprise architect might determine that the organization needs a certain type of application and require the application to be run on the organization's infrastructure, but would leave the actual design or purchase of the application to the clients.

The *city planning* viewpoint is the most aggressive and takes on the role of technical leadership for the organization. As a city planner, the enterprise architect will proactively attempt to forecast the needs of the organization and work with clients to determine a future enterprise portfolio and overall architecture. The architect then works to move the organization toward the future plan by designing or acquiring software, refactoring existing software, and decommissioning software that doesn't conform to the plan. The success factors for this viewpoint are two-fold: The future plan is designed jointly by the clients and the architect; and the future plan is reviewed and updated as the organization and technologies evolve.

The issue of governance is a potential problem. If the architect who originated the principles and standards becomes the enforcer, there is a conflict of interest (lawmaker, law enforcer, judge, and jury). It also places the IT architects in the awkward position of software police, which can lead to division, conflict, and resentment between the IT organization and the enterprise it is trying to serve. The solution is to align the authority with the accountability by moving the architectural principles from the IT architecture office to the executive board. The IT architects recommend principles to the executive board. If the board understands the benefit to the organization and adopts the principles—and the procedures for exemptions—as their own, then IT and the entire organization must all adhere to the principles.

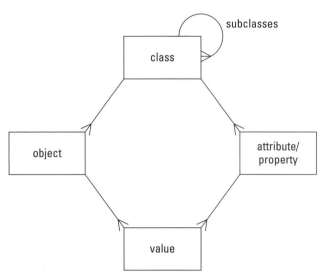

Figure 1-2: The generic pattern is an RDBMS physical schema that is sometimes employed to mimic an OO DBMS.

The class entity drives the database schema. The class entity includes a reflexive relationship to support object class inheritance. As with a hierarchical structure or organizational chart, this relationship permits each object class to have multiple subclasses, and each object class to have one base class. The property entity is a secondary entity to the object entity and enables each object class to contain multiple properties. An object is a specific instance of an object class. As such, it needs to have its own specific values for every property of its object class and all inherited object classes.

Although the result can be impressive, many complications are involved in this process. Many-to-many relationships, which exist in real life, are simulated within object-oriented databases by means of object collections. Properties must meet data-type and validation rules, which must be simulated by the data schema, rather than by SQL Server's built-in data-type and validation rules.

Data Integrity

The ability to ensure that persisted data can be retrieved without error is central to the Information Architecture Principle, and the first problem tackled by the database world. Without data integrity, a query's answer cannot be guaranteed to be correct, consequently, there's not much point in availability or performance.

As data is essentially entities and attributes, data integrity consists of entity integrity and domain integrity, which includes referential integrity and user-defined integrity. Transactional integrity, which deals with how data is written and retrieved, is defined by the ACID principles (atomicity, consistency, isolation, and durability), discussed in a later section, transactional faults, and isolation levels.

Entity Integrity

Entity integrity involves the structure (primary key and its attributes) of the entity. If the primary key is unique and all attributes are scalar and fully dependent on the primary key, then the integrity of the entity is good. In the physical schema, the table's primary key enforces entity integrity. Essentially, entity integrity is normalization.

 Cross-Reference   Normalization is explained in detail in the next chapter, "Relational Database Modeling."

Domain Integrity

In relational theory terms, a domain is a set of possible values for an attribute, such as integers, bit values, or characters. *Domain integrity* ensures that only valid data is permitted in the attribute. Nullability (whether a null value is valid for an attribute) is also a part of domain integrity. In the physical schema, the data type and nullability of the row enforce domain integrity.

Referential Integrity

A subset of domain integrity, *referential integrity* refers to the domain integrity of foreign keys. Domain integrity says that if an attribute has a value, then that value must be in the domain. In the case of the foreign key, the domain is the list of values in the related primary key.

Referential integrity, therefore, is not an issue of the integrity of the primary key but of the foreign key.

The nullability of the column is a separate issue from referential integrity. It's perfectly acceptable for a foreign key column to allow nulls.

Several methods of enforcing referential integrity at the physical-schema level exist. Within a physical schema, a foreign key can be enforced by declarative referential integrity (DRI) or by a custom trigger attached to the table.

User-Defined Integrity

Besides the relational theory integrity concerns, the user-integrity requirements must also be enforced, as follows:

✦ Simple business rules, such as a restriction to a domain, limit the list of valid data entries. Check constraints are commonly used to enforce these rules in the physical schema.

✦ Complex business rules limit the list of valid data based on some condition. For example, certain tours may require a medical waiver. Implementing these rules in the physical schema generally requires stored procedures or triggers.

Some data-integrity concerns can't be checked by constraints or triggers. Invalid, incomplete, or questionable data may pass all the standard data-integrity checks. For example, an order without any order detail rows is not a valid order, but no automatic method traps such an order. SQL queries can locate incomplete orders and help in identifying other less measurable data-integrity issues, including the following:

✦ Wrong data

✦ Incomplete data

✦ Questionable data

✦ Inconsistent data

The quality of the data depends upon the people modifying the data. Data security — controlling who can view or modify the data — is also an aspect of data integrity.

Transactional Integrity

A transaction is a single logical unit of work, such as inserting 100 rows, updating 1,000 rows, or executing a logical set of updates. The quality of a database product is measured by its transactions' adherence to the ACID properties. ACID, you might recall, is an acronym for four interdependent properties: atomicity, consistency, isolation, and durability. Much of the architecture of SQL Server is founded on these properties. Understanding the ACID properties of a transaction is a prerequisite for understanding SQL Server:

✦ The transaction must be *atomic*, meaning all or nothing. At the end of the transaction either all of the transaction is successful or all of the transaction fails. If a partial transaction is written to disk, the atomic property is violated.

✦ The transaction must preserve database *consistency*, which means that the database must begin in a state of consistency and return to a state of consistency once the transaction is complete. For the purposes of ACID, consistency means that every row and value must agree with the reality being modeled, and every constraint must be enforced. If the order rows are written to disk but the order detail rows are not written, the consistency between the `Order` and the `OrderDetail` is violated.

✦ Each transaction must be *isolated,* or separated, from the effects of other transactions. Regardless of what any other transaction is doing, a transaction must be able to continue with the exact same data sets it started with. Isolation is the fence between two transactions. A proof of isolation is the ability to replay a serialized set of transactions on the same original set of data and always receive the same result.

For example, assume Joe is updating 100 rows. While Joe's transaction is under way, Sue deletes one of the rows Joe is working on. If the delete takes place, Joe's transaction is not sufficiently isolated from Sue's transaction. This property is less critical in a single-user database than in a multi-user database.

✦ The *durability* of a transaction refers to its permanence regardless of system failure. Once a transaction is committed it stays committed. The database product must be constructed so that even if the data drive melts, the database can be restored up to the last transaction that was committed a split second before the hard drive died.

The nemesis of transactional integrity is concurrency — multiple users simultaneously attempting to retrieve and modify data. Isolation is less of an issue in small databases, but in a production database with thousands of users, concurrency competes with transactional integrity. The two must be carefully balanced; otherwise, either data integrity or performance will suffer.

SQL Server's architecture meets all the transactional-integrity ACID properties, providing that you, as the developer, understand them, develop the database to take advantage of SQL Server's capabilities, and the DBA implements a sound recovery plan. A synergy exists among

SQL Server, the hardware, the database design, the code, the database-recovery plan, and the database-maintenance plan. When the database developer and DBA cooperate to properly implement all these components, the database performs well and transactional integrity is high.

Transactional Faults

True isolation means that one transaction never affects another transaction. If the isolation is complete, then no data changes from outside the transaction should be seen by the transaction.

The isolation between transactions can be less than perfect in one of three ways: dirty reads, non-repeatable reads, and phantom rows. In addition, transactions can fail due to lost updates and deadlocks.

Dirty Reads

The most egregious fault is a transaction's work being visible to other transactions before the transaction even commits its changes. When a transaction can read another transaction's uncommitted updates, this is called a *dirty read*. The problem with dirty reads is that the data being read is not yet committed, so the transaction writing the data might be rolled back.

Non-Repeatable Reads

A *non-repeatable read* is similar to a dirty read, but a non-repeatable read occurs when a transaction can see the committed updates from another transaction. Reading a row inside a transaction should produce the same results every time. If reading a row twice results in different values, that's a non-repeatable read type of transaction fault.

Phantom Rows

The least severe transactional-integrity fault is a *phantom row*. Like a non-repeatable read, a phantom row occurs when updates from another transaction affect not only the result set's data values, but cause the select to return a different set of rows.

Of these transactional faults, dirty reads are the most dangerous, while non-repeatable reads are less so, and phantom rows are the least dangerous of all.

Lost Updates

A lost update occurs when two users edit the same row, complete their edits, and save the data, and the second user's update overwrites the first user's update.

Because lost updates occur only when two users edit the same row at the same time, the problem might not occur for months. Nonetheless, it's a flaw in the transactional integrity of the database that needs to be prevented.

Deadlocks

A deadlock is a special situation that occurs only when transactions with multiple tasks compete for the same data resource. For example, consider the following scenario:

✦ Transaction one has a lock on data A and needs to lock data B to complete its transaction.

and

✦ Transaction two has a lock on data B and needs to lock data A to complete its transaction.

Each transaction is stuck waiting for the other to release its lock, and neither can complete until the other does. Unless an outside force intercedes, or one of the transactions gives up and quits, this situation could persist until the end of time.

Cross-Reference Chapter 51, "Managing Transactions, Locking, and Blocking," includes walk-through examples of the transactional faults, isolation levels, and SQL Server locking.

Isolation Levels

At the physical level, any database engine that permits logical transactions must provide a way to isolate those transactions. The level of isolation, or the height of the fence between transactions, can be adjusted to control which transactional faults are permitted. The ANSI SQL-92 committee specifies four isolation levels: read uncommitted, read committed, repeatable read, and serializable.

In addition, Microsoft added snapshot isolation to SQL Server 2005. Essentially, snapshot isolation makes a virtual copy, or snapshot, of the first transaction's data, so other transactions do not affect it. This method can lead to lost updates.

The Value of Null

The relational database model represents missing data using the special value of *null*. The common definition of null is "unknown"; however, null can actually represent three subtly different scenarios of missing data:

✦ The column does not apply for this row—for example, if the person is not employed, then any value in the `EmploymentDate` column would be invalid.

✦ The data has not yet been entered, but likely will, such as in a contact row that has the name and phone number, and will hopefully have the address once a sale is made.

✦ The column for this row contains a value of "nothing"—for example, a comment column is valid for every row but may be empty for most rows.

Depending on the type of missing data, some designers use surrogate nulls (blanks, zeroes, or n/a) instead. However, multiple possible values for missing data can create consistency problems when querying data.

The nullability of a column, whether or not the column accepts nulls, may be defined when a column is created. Note that by default, SQL Server does not allow nulls, but the ANSI standard does.

Working with Nulls

Because null has no value, the result of any expression that includes null will also be unknown. If the contents of a bank account are unknown and its funds are included in a portfolio, the total value of the portfolio is also unknown. The same concept is true in SQL, as the following code demonstrates. Phil Senn, a wise old database developer, puts it this way: "Nulls zap the life out of any other value." As proof:

```
SELECT 1 + NULL
```

Result:

```
NULL
```

Another consequence of null's unknown value is that a null is not equal to another null. Therefore, to test for the presence of null, SQL uses the IS NULL syntax.

Both of these behaviors can be overridden. SQL Server will ignore nulls in expression when the connection setting concat_null_yields_null is set to off. The ANSI nulls setting controls whether null can be equal to another null.

Null Controversy

Most database developers design columns that allow nulls when they make sense.

Extreme database purists detest nulls and require that any relational database model not allow nulls. One method of avoiding nulls is to separate any null columns into a separate supertype/subtype table. This method merely replaces a nullable column with a nullable row, which requires a left-outer join to test for the presence of data or retrieve data. The resulting complexity affects not only performance but also data integrity. Instead of retrieving data with a null column, the application developer must be aware of the subtype table and be fluent with left-outer joins. This view focuses on a misguided understanding of a single data store objective, data integrity, at the expense of performance and usability.

Performance

Presenting readily usable information is a key aspect of the Information Architecture Principle. Although the database industry has achieved a high degree of performance, the ability to scale that performance to very large databases with more connections is still an area of competition between database engine vendors.

Because physical disk performance is the most significant bottleneck, the key to performance is reducing the number of physical page reads or writes required to perform a task. The five primary performance factors all seek to reduce the number of physical page reads.

Design

The database schema design can dramatically affect performance. The physical design must consider the query path. An overly complicated design, resulting in too many tables, requires additional joins when retrieving data, and additional writes when inserting or updating data.

Some database schemas discourage set-based processing by requiring that data move from one bucket to another as it's processed. If server-side application code includes several cursors, maybe it's not the fault of the application developer but the database designer.

Set-Based Processing

Relational algebra, the SQL language, and relational database engines are all optimized to work with sets of data. Poorly written code, whether row-by-row cursor-based code, or just poorly written SQL, is a common source of poor performance.

Cross-Reference

Writing excellent set-based queries requires a creative understanding of joins and subqueries, as discussed in Chapter 9, "Merging Data with Joins and Unions," and Chapter 10, "Including Subqueries and CTEs."

A well-written set-based query can perform the entire operation, reading each required page only once, whereas a cursor-based solution will process each row independently. In tests, a simple update operation using cursors takes 70 times as long as the same logic implemented using set-based code.

Indexing

Indexes are the bridge between the query and data. They improve performance by reducing the number of physical page reads required for a table read operation.

✦ *Clustered indexes* group rows together so they can be retrieved in one (or a few) physical page reads, rather than reading from numerous rows scattered throughout the table.

✦ Indexes enable the query optimizer to seek directly at the data rows, similar to how a book index can be used to find the correct page, instead of having to scan the entire table to locate the correct rows. Once the row is determined, the optimizer will perform a bookmark lookup to jump to the data page.

Indexing is a key part of the physical schema design and is considered more of an art than a science, but understanding the database engine's query optimizer and how the index structures work, combined with a knowledge of the database's specific schema and how the queries will be accessing the data, can make index design more exact.

Cross-Reference   Index tuning strategies are discussed in Chapter 50, "Query Analysis and Index Tuning."

Indexes have a downside as well. Although indexes help when reading from the table, they can adversely affect write performance. When a row is inserted or updated, the indexes must be also be kept in synch with the data. Therefore, when a table has multiple indexes, writes to the table will be slower. In other words, there's a tension between designing indexes for reading versus writing. Because an update or delete operation must locate the affected rows, write operations do benefit from frugal indexing. The different indexing requirements of reading versus writing is a major difference between transactional databases and databases designed for reporting or data warehousing.

Partitioning

Partitioning, or spreading the data across multiple disk spindles, is a method of improving the performance of very large databases (VLDs).

Cross-Reference   Chapter 53, "Scaling Very Large Databases," details SQL Server 2005's partitioning features.

Caching

Caching is the means of pre-fetching data from the physical hard drive so the data is in memory when required by a database operation. While caching is the job of the database engine, providing it with enough memory makes a difference.

Availability

The availability of information refers to the information's accessibility when required regarding uptime time, locations, and the availability of the data for future analysis. Recovery, redundancy, archiving, and network delivery all affect availability.

The system requirements drives availability, which is often described in terms of 9s. Five 9s means the system is available 99.999 percent of the required time, as shown in Table 1-3.

Table 1-3: The Chart of Nines

Percent	Uptime	Downtime	Description
99.99999	364d 23h 59m 56s	000d 00h 00m 03s	"7 nines"
99.9999	364d 23h 59m 29s	000d 00h 00m 31s	"6 nines"
99.999	364d 23h 54m 45s	000d 00h 05m 15s	"5 nines"
99.99	364d 23h 07m 27s	000d 00h 52m 33s	"4 nines"
99.95	364d 19h 37m 12s	000d 04h 22m 48s	-
99.9	364d 15h 14m 24s	000d 08h 45m 36s	"3 nines"
99.8	364d 15h 14m 24s	000d 17h 31m 12s	-
99.72603	364d 00h 00m 00s	001d 00h 00m 00s	exactly 1 day
99.5	363d 04h 12m 00s	001d 19h 48m 00s	-
99	361d 08h 24m 00s	003d 15h 36m 00s	"2 nines"
98	357d 16h 48m 00s	007d 07h 12m 00s	-
97	354d 01h 12m 00s	010d 22h 48m 00s	-

Cross-Reference Chapter 36, "Recovery Planning," and Chapter 52, "Providing High Availability," both provide details on SQL Server 2005's availability features.

Redundancy

Redundancy is the identification of possible points of failure and avoiding or reducing the effects of the failure by providing a secondary solution. For some disciplines, redundancy suggests waste, but for data stores, redundancy is a good thing.

A *warm standby server* is a copy of the database on another server ready to go live at a moment's notice. Typically, this method uses log shipping to move the latest transaction to the warm standby server. A *clustered server* is an expensive hardware link between two servers such that when the primary server goes down, the backup server is immediately online.

At some point, the best hardware will fail. If the information is extremely critical to the organization, management may decide that it's too expensive (in lost time to the organization) to restore the database and the transaction log to another server. A solution is to maintain a warm backup server on ready standby so that if the primary server fails, then the warm standby comes online with minimal availability impact.

Recovery

The availability method of last resort is to restore the database and recover the data from backup files. Recovery requires more than just a backup file. The write-ahead transaction log provides a way to recover all transactions committed since the last database backup.

Extensibility

The information architecture principle states that the information must be readily available today and in the future, which requires that the data store is *extensible*, able to be easily adapted to meet new requirements. As an industry, data integrity, performance, and availability are all mature and well understood, so the next major hurdle for the industry to conquer is extensibility.

Two design concepts lead to an extensible system: decoupling the database using an abstraction layer and generalizing entities when possible. Extensibility is also closely related to simplicity. Complexity breeds complexity, and inhibits adaptation.

Abstraction Layer

Many production databases were well designed when they were created, and served their initial purpose remarkably well, for a while. But as changes are required, the development effort becomes increasingly difficult and developers begin to complain about the database. Years later, the development team may still be stuck with a database that no longer serves the purpose but is too difficult to change. The system met the original requirements, but is now extremely expensive to maintain.

The source of the problem is not the database design, but the lack of encapsulation and coupling between the application and the database. An *abstraction layer* is the primary method of decoupling a data store from the application. Without an abstraction layer logically separating the database from the application, any database is destined to become brittle — the slightest change breaks an overwhelming amount of code.

A *data store abstraction layer* is a collection of software interfaces that serve as a gate through which all access to the database must pass. An abstraction layer is essentially a contract between the application code and the database that defines each database call and the parameters. An abstraction layer can be constructed using T-SQL stored procedures, or a software tier. With an abstraction layer in place and enforced, any direct access to the tables via SQL DML commands is blocked.

Cross-Reference Designing and coding a T-SQL–based abstraction layer is explained in Chapter 25, "Creating Extensibility with a Data Abstraction Layer."

An abstraction layer supports extensibility by shielding the application code from schema changes, and vice versa. The implementation of either side of the contract (data store or application code) may be changed without affecting the abstraction layer contract or the other side of the contract.

Generalization

Generalization is the grouping of similar entities into a single entity, or table, so that a single table does more work. The database becomes more flexible because the generalized entities are more likely able to store a new similar entity.

Generalization depends on the idea that there is no single correct normalized schema. For any database problem, several correct solutions are possible. The difference between these solutions is often identifying the problem space's various entities. One view of the entities might identify several specific entities that are technically different but similar. A more generalized view would merge the similar entities, producing a simpler and more compact schema.

Best Practice

I can't overemphasize the importance of generalization. Even more than normalization, this is the technique I depend upon to design simple but flexible schemas. A recent database schema I analyzed used about 80 tables. Using generalization to combine five entities (and associated tables) into one entity, I reduced the schema to 17 tables, and the result was more flexible and powerful than the original. When a database developer brags that he has designed a database with a huge number of tables, I assume that he probably developed a wasteful system.

Security

The final primary database objective based on the Information Architecture Principle is security. For any organizational asset, the level of security must be secured depending on its value and sensitivity. For software, the security begins with the physical security of the data center and the operating system's security. Information security includes three additional components: restricting access to specific data using the database engine's security, identifying the owner of the information, and confirming the veracity of the data by identifying the source, including updates.

Restricted Access

Any production-grade database includes the capability to limit access to the data to individuals or group of individuals. The granularity of restriction may range from simply limiting access to specifying create, select, update, and delete privileges.

Cross-Reference

SQL Server 2005 security, which can be complex, is detailed in Chapter 40, "Securing Databases."

Information Ownership

The owner of the data is the person or organizational group who required the data. This person is typically not the person or process who entered or created the data. The owner is the person who is paying the cost of maintaining the data. For some systems, a single owner may be identified for the entire application. For other systems, each table or row may have an identified owner. For example, all the data within an inventory system may belong to the vice president of manufacturing, while the corporate client contact information may belong to the branch that is serving the contact. Row-level data ownership must be implemented in the schema by adding a `DataOwner` column.

Note Compliance with Sarbanes-Oxley not only requires that data is secure, but that any changes in data ownership and access restrictions are documented.

Audit Trails

Audit trails identify the source and time of creation and any updates. At the minimum level, the audit trail captures the created date/time, and the last updated date/time. The next level of auditing captures the username of the person or process who created or updated the data. A complete audit trail records every historical value. The ability to recreate the data at any given point in time is important for temporal, or time-based, data.

Cross-Reference Chapter 24, "Exploring Advanced T-SQL Techniques," includes methods of creating audit trails.

Optimization Theory and SQL Server

Ask 20 DBAs for their favorite optimization technique or strategy, and you'll likely hear 40 different answers ranging from indexing to adding memory. Is it possible to order this heap of performance ideas? I believe so. Data modeling is essentially puzzling out the pattern of data. So is there is a pattern to the various strategies that can revealed by examining how one strategy affects another?

The first clue is that not all performance strategies perform well or uniformly because there's an inherent dependency between performance strategies that's easily overlooked. For instance, using indexing to improve the performance of a query reduces the duration of a transaction, which facilitates concurrency. So there's some kind of connection between indexing and concurrency. Maybe there's more. Certain performance strategies enable other strategies while some performance strategies have little effect if other strategies have not already been applied.

Optimization Theory addresses these dependencies and provides a framework for planning and developing an optimized data store. Optimization Theory identifies five key optimization strategies (see Figure 1-3). Each strategy has several specific techniques. Each strategy is enabled by its supporting strategy, and no strategy can overcome deficiencies in their supporting strategies.

Schema Design

Schema Design is my number-one performance strategy. Well-designed schemas enable you to develop set-based queries and make it easier to plan effective indexes.

To design an effective schema, you need to do the following:

✦ Avoid overcomplexity.

✦ Select a key carefully.

✦ Handle optional data.

✦ Enforce an abstraction layer.

I believe that the purist logical data modeler is the number-one performance problem in our industry because of the cascading problems caused by his burdensome designs.

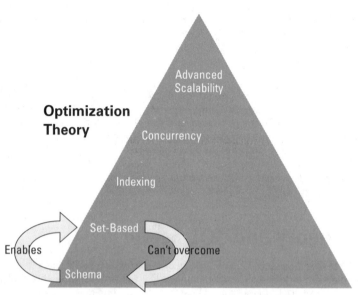

Figure 1-3: Optimization Theory explains that each optimization technique is dependent upon, and enabled by, other optimization techniques.

Queries

SQL is a set-based system, and iterative row-by-row operations actually function as zillions of small single-row sets. Whether the iterations take place as server-side SQL cursors or ADO loops through a record set, iterative code is costly. My number-two performance strategy is to use set-based solutions. But good set-based code can't overcome a clumsy or overly complex schema design.

When deciding where to use iterative code vs. set-based query, use Table 1-4 as a guiding rule of thumb.

Table 1-4: Coding Methods

Problem	Best Solution
Complex business logic	Queries, subqueries, CTEs
Dynamic DDL Generation	Cursors
Demoralizing a List	Multiple assignment variables or cursor
Crosstab	Query with pivot or case expression
Navigating a hierarchy	UDF or CTE
Cumulative totals, running sums	Cursor

Chapter 20, "Kill the Cursor!" explains how to create dramatic performance gains by refactoring complex logic cursors into set-based queries.

Indexing

Indexing is the performance bridge between queries and data and a key performance strategy. An indexing strategy that uses a clustered index to reduce bookmark lookups or group rows to a single data page, uses nonclustered indexes to cover queries and enable seeks, and avoids redundant indexes will speed set-based code. But well-designed indexes can't overcome nonscalable iterative code.

Designing clustered, nonclustered, and covering indexes are explained in detail in Chapter 50, "Query Analysis and Index Tuning."

Concurrency

Locking and blocking is more common a problem than most developers think, and too many DBA solve the problem by lowering the transaction isolation level using `nolock` — and that's dangerous.

Concurrency can be compared to a water fountain. If folks are taking long turns at the fountain or filling buckets, a line may form, and those waiting for the resource will become frustrated. Setting `nolock` is like saying, "Share the water." A better solution is to satisfy the needs with only a sip or to reduce the duration or the transaction. The best way to develop efficient transactions is to design efficient schemas, use set-based code, and index well.

When the schema, queries, and indexes are already reducing the transaction duration, be sure to place only the required logic within logical transactions and be careful with logic inside triggers, since they occur within the transaction. But reducing blocked resources won't overcome an unnecessary table scan.

Advanced Scalability

When the schema, queries, indexes, and transactions are all running smooth, you'll get the most out of SQL Server's high-end scalability features:

✦ Snapshot Isolation

✦ Partition Tables

✦ Index Views

✦ Service Broker

Will you see performance gains by using a performance technique without the enabling technologies in place? Maybe. But you'll see the greatest gains by enabling each layer with its enabling technologies.

Optimization Theory, the idea that there are dependencies between performance technologies, is an evolving concept. For my latest data on Optimization Theory, or my latest Performance Decision presentation, visit www.SQLServerBible.com.

Summary

The Information Architecture Principle is the foundation for database development. The principle unpacks to reveal seven interdependent data store objectives: simplicity, usability, data integrity, performance, availability, extensibility, security. Each objective is important in the design and development of any database.

The first part of this book continues exploring database concepts in the next chapter, which looks at relational database design.

✦   ✦   ✦

Relational Database Modeling

I read *The Time Traveler's Wife,* by Audrey Niffenegger, on my last
trip. Without giving away the plot, it's an amazing sci-fi romance
story. She moves through time conventionally, while he bounces
uncontrollably through time and space, pulled to key events in his life
over and over again. Even though the plot is more complex than the
average novel, I love how Ms. Niffenegger weaves every detail
together into an intricate flow. Every detail fits and builds the characters and the story.

In some ways, a database is like a good story. The plot of the story is
in the data model, and the data represents the characters and the
details. *Normalization* is the grammar and structure of the database.

When two writers tell the same story, each crafts the story differently.
There's no single correct way to tell a story. Likewise, there's no single
correct way to model a database — as long as the database contains
all the information needed to extract the story and it follows the normalized grammar rules, the database will work. A corollary is that just
as some books read better than others, so some database schemas
flow well, while other database designs are difficult to query.

As with writing a novel, the foundation of data modeling is careful
observation and an understanding of reality. Based on those insights,
the data modeler constructs a logical system — a new virtual world —
that models a slice of reality. Therefore, how the designer views reality
and identifies entities and their interactions will influence the design
of the virtual world. Like postmodernism, there's no single perfect
correct representation, only the viewpoint of the author/designer.

The role of the data modeler is arguably the most critical role in any
software project, because the data modeler designs the foundation,
or structure, of the artificial reality that the rest of the code must survive, or die, within. Any feature that involves data persistence must
be designed within the data schema.

The life cycle of a data schema typically spans several generations of
application code, which is a second reason why the data schema is
so critical to the life of the project. The data lives on as applications
come and go. Whereas an application developer must think about the
application being used for two to three years, databases sometimes
live for two to three decades.

From the perspective of the author/designer metaphor, this chapter
explores the basic structures of a relational database: entities, normalization, and relational patterns.

Modeling Reality

Based on the Information Architecture Principle (from Chapter 1), the goal of data modeling is to meet the customer's requirements by defining a data structure that represents certain objects and events in a logical fashion.

The basic data element is a single container for data. Most people know this container as a single cell on a spreadsheet — the intersection of a tuple (row) and an attribute (column). Data modeling is the art of fitting that single unit of data in the right place inside millions of cells so that the entire system of data units is correct, real, and searchable. To be a data modeler is to see every scene, situation, and document from the viewpoint of data elements and a consistent relational design.

Data modeling involves several processes. Designing a data schema isn't purely a sequential process; each step of the design process is dependent on the other steps, and discovery continues throughout the process to some degree. However, the data modeler generally moves among the following processes as the design takes shape:

1. Observation and requirements gathering

2. Logical representation of reality

3. Visible entity identification and design

4. Schema design (secondary and supporting entities)

5. Application-structure design

No schema can model reality perfectly. Each data schema is designed to meet the requirements of the project at a given stage of the project's life cycle. Discerning the actual requirements, balancing the trade-offs between reality and the design, and building a data schema that supports the current version and allows room to grow are skills learned not from a book but from experience.

The purpose of the logical design is to describe entities, relationships, and rules. The physical schema design takes the logical design and implements it within the structure of a particular database management system (DBMS).

Logical vs. Physical Design

I've seen way too much strife over the differences between logical design and physical database schema design. In some organizations these tasks are performed by entirely different teams, who sometime don't even communicate with each other. Some designers insist that the implementation precisely execute the pure logical design. At the other extreme are designers who design directly to the physical schema every time.

The purpose of the logical design is to document the entities and their relationships. It's a communication tool to ensure that the business rules are well understood — nothing more. From that understanding, the design team can create a physical design that meets both the business rules and the performance requirements.

Chapter 17, "Creating the Physical Database Schema," focuses on the physical design.

A mathematical approach to relational database design involves several rules of normalization — rules that govern whether the database design is valid. While designing hundreds of normalized database designs, I have developed an approach to database design that follows the rules of normalization based on the concept of visible and supporting entities. *Visible entities* represent elements users would recognize; *supporting entities* are abstract entities designed by the database modeler to physically support the logical design.

Visible Entities

Visible entities generally represent objects that most people would recognize. Many objects are nouns — people, places, or things, such as a contact, a facility, an item, or an airplane. Visible entities might also represent actions, such as a material being assembled or an order being processed. Typically, a visible object is already represented in a document somewhere.

Some visible objects represent ways in which other primary objects are organized or grouped. For example, clients recognize that groceries fall into several categories — dairy, bread, meats, canned goods, and so on. For another example, purchase orders might be categorized by their priority.

Every Tuple (Row) Is an Island

Each tuple (rhymes with couple) must represent a complete logical thought, and each attribute in the tuple must belong specifically to that tuple and no other.

Every entity is based on the idea that each tuple represents, or models, a single noun or verb. Here's where the experience of data modeling pays off. The key is identifying the unique, yet generic, nouns and verbs. That's what is meant by the term *relational database system*. It's not that entities relate to other entities, but that similar, or related, data is assembled into a single entity.

Only data that describes the object belongs in the entity. Some of the possible attributes, even though they are sometimes listed on paper documents for one object, may actually describe another object. An order form will often include the customer's name and address although the name belongs to the customer and not the order. The address also belongs to the customer. However, if the customer changes his or her address next year, the order should still show the old address. The point is that careful analysis of the objects and their properties is vital to data modeling.

Well-designed entities are generic so they can handle a variety of similar items. For example, a single grocery entity would contain a variety of grocery items, instead of there being an apple entity and a separate beef entity, and so on.

Primary Keys

Every tuple in an entity has to represent a single unique object in reality. In the same way that there can't be two of the same airplane, there can't be two tuples that represent the same airplane. To logically prove that each tuple is unique, one attribute (the primary key) is assigned to be the primary way a specific tuple is referenced for data-modification commands. The logical purpose of the primary key is only to uniquely identify or name the tuple. If you can demonstrate that each object in reality has a single primary key, and vice versa, then you've done your job well.

For an example of a primary key in the physical schema, suppose each customer in the Cape Hatteras Adventures database is identified by his or her Customer ID. Using SQL Server's identity column option, a new integer is automatically generated for each customer row as the row is inserted in the table.

Tables, Rows, Columns

A relational database collects common, or related, data in a single list. For example, all the product information may be listed in one table and all the customers in another table.

A table appears similar to a spreadsheet and is constructed of columns and rows. The appeal of the spreadsheet is its informal development style, which makes it easy to modify and add to as the design matures. In fact, managers tend to store critical information in spreadsheets, and many databases started as informal spreadsheets.

In both a spreadsheet and a database table, each row is an item in the list and each column is a specific piece of data concerning that item. Therefore, each cell should contain a single piece of data about a single item. Whereas a spreadsheet tends to be free-flowing and loose in its design, database tables should be very consistent with regard to the meaning of the data in a column. Because row and column consistency is so important to a database table, the design of the table is critical.

Over the years, different development styles have referred to these columns with various different terms, as listed in Table 2-1.

Table 2-1: Comparing Database Terms

Development Style	The Common List	An Item in the List	A Piece of Information in the List
Spreadsheet	Spreadsheet/ worksheet/ named range	Row	Column/cell
Historic software	File	Record	Field
Relational algebra/ logical design	Entity	Tuple	Attribute
SQL/physical design	Table	Row	Column
Object-oriented design	Class	Object instance	Property

SQL Server developers generally refer to database elements as tables, rows, and columns when discussing the physical schema, and sometimes use the terms entity, tuple, and attribute when discussing the logical design. While the rest of this book will use the physical schema terms, this chapter is devoted to the theory behind the design, so it will use the relational algebra terms (entity, tuple, and attribute).

Identifying Multiple Entities

While each entity must be a proper entity with all attributes dependent on the primary key, a single entity can't model very much. It takes several entities modeled together to represent an entire business function or organizational task.

Additional entities provide multiple additional pieces of information about the primary objects, group the primary objects, and connect them. While developing the logical data model, several types of logical scenarios within the requirements will require multiple entities in the logical model, including the following:

- ✦ Multiple objects

- ✦ Relationships between objects

- ✦ Organizing or grouping objects

- ✦ Consistent lookup values

- ✦ Complex objects

Sometimes the differentiation between objects, lookup values, and grouping objects blurs. As long as all the previous scenarios are considered, the logical data model will be complete.

Multiple Objects

Sometimes what appears to be a single object is in fact a list of multiple objects, as shown in the following examples:

- ✦ In the Cape Hatteras Adventures (CHA) database, a tour may be offered several times. Each time is an event.

- ✦ In the Family database, each person may have several children.

- ✦ An employee time card can include multiple timestamps. The employee time card can be considered a single object, but upon closer examination it's really a list of time events.

- ✦ A daily calendar can include multiple appointments.

Relationships Between Objects

The most common purpose of multiple entities is to describe some type of relationship between two different objects. For example:

- ✦ In the Cape Hatteras Adventures (CHA) sample database, customers participate in tours, and guides lead tours. There are relationships between customers and tours, and between guides and tours.

- ✦ A material can be built from multiple other materials.

- ✦ A health insurance policy can cover multiple family members; this is a relationship between the policy and the family members.

- ✦ For a software-quality tracking system, a software feature can have multiple bugs.

Best Practice

Design the schema for the best query performance for the most probable scenario first, and then design for the exceptions. For example, suppose that 96% of contacts have just one address, 4% have an additional vacation home, and one client has multiple homes on every continent except the Antarctic. Implement the contact table with columns for a single address so 96% of the contacts may be retrieved without a join. Add the alternate addresses using an optional one-to-many table. Use a flag in the contact table to indicate multiple homes so a left-outer join isn't required to check for the possibility of any vacation homes. (Joins are explained in detail in Chapter 9, "Merging Data with Joins and Unions.")

This aspect of the design may take place when designing the logical schema, or the physical schema design may reveal this optimization.

Organizing or Grouping Objects

Objects are sometimes grouped into different categories. These categories should be listed in their own entities. For example:

✦ Customers may be grouped by their customer type in the CHA database.

✦ Materials are grouped by their state (raw materials, works in process, finished goods).

✦ In the Cape Hatteras Adventures sample database, the base camp groups the tours.

Consistent Lookup Values

Object attributes often require consistent lookup values for domain integrity. For example:

✦ The type of credit card used for a purchase

✦ The region for an address

✦ The department code for an item

Complex Objects

Some objects in reality are too complex to model with a single entity. The information takes on more forms than a single primary key and a single tuple can contain. Usually this is because the real-world object includes some form of multiplicity. For example, an order can include multiple order lines. The order lines are part of the order, but the order requires a secondary entity to properly model the multiplicity of the order lines.

Relational Patterns

Once the nouns and verbs are organized, the next step is to determine the relationships among the objects. Each relationship connects two entities using their keys and has the following two main attributes:

✦ **Cardinality:** The number of objects that may exist on each side of the relationship

✦ **Optionality:** Whether the relationship is mandatory or optional

Clients or business analysts should be able to describe the common relationships between the objects using terms such as *includes*, *has*, or *contains*. A customer may place many orders. An order may include many items. An item may be on many orders.

Secondary Entities and Foreign Keys

When two objects relate, one entity is typically the primary entity and the other entity is the secondary entity. One object in the primary entity will relate to multiple objects, or tuples, in the secondary entity, as shown in Figure 2-1.

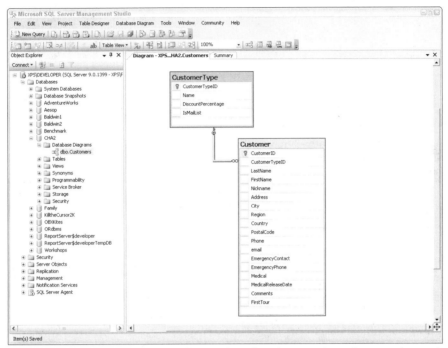

Figure 2-1: A one-to-many relationship consists of a primary entity and a secondary entity. The secondary entity's foreign key connects with the primary entity's primary key.

The role of the foreign key is to hold the primary key's value so the secondary tuple can be matched with the relating primary tuple.

Relationship Cardinality

The cardinality of the relationship describes the number of tuples on each side of the relationship. Either side of the relationship may either be restricted to a single tuple or allowed multiple tuples. The type of key enforces the restriction of multiple tuples. Primary keys enforce the single-tuple restriction, whereas foreign keys permit multiple tuples.

There are several possible cardinality combinations, as shown in Table 2-2. Within this section, each of the cardinality possibilities is examined in detail.

Table 2-2: Relationship Cardinality

Relationship Type	First Entity's Key	Second Entity's Key
One-to-one	Primary entity–primary key–single tuple	Primary entity–primary key–single tuple
One-to-many	Primary entity–primary key–single tuple	Secondary entity–foreign key–multiple tuples
Many-to-many	Secondary entity–foreign key–multiple tuples	Secondary entity–foreign key–multiple tuples

Relationship Optionality

The second property of the relationship is its *optionality*. The difference between an optional relationship and a mandatory relationship is critical to the data integrity of the database.

Some secondary tuples require that the foreign key point to a primary key. The secondary tuple would be incomplete or meaningless without the primary entity. For the following reasons, it's critical in these cases that the relationship be enforced as a mandatory relationship:

✦ An order-line item without an order is meaningless.

✦ An order without a customer is invalid.

✦ In the Cape Hatteras Adventures database, an event without an associated tour tuple is a useless event tuple.

Conversely, some relationships are optional. The secondary tuple can stand alone without the primary tuple. The object in reality that is represented by the secondary tuple would exist with or without the primary tuple. For example:

✦ A customer without a discount code is still a valid customer.

✦ In the OBX Kites sample database, an order may or may not have a priority code. Whether the order points to a valid tuple in the order priority entity or not, it's still a valid order.

Some database developers prefer to avoid optional relationships and so they design all relationships as mandatory and point tuples that wouldn't need a foreign key value to a surrogate tuple in the primary table. For example, rather than allow nulls in the discount attribute for customers without discounts, a "no discount" tuple is inserted into the discount entity and every customer without a discount points to that tuple.

There are two reasons to avoid surrogate null tuples: the design adds work when work isn't required (additional inserts and foreign key checks); and it's easier to locate works without the relationship by selecting where column is not null. The null value is a useful design element. Ignoring the benefits of nullability only creates additional work for both the developer and the database.

Some rare situations call for a complex optionality based on a condition. Depending on a rule, the relationship must be enforced as follows:

✦ If an organization sometimes sells ad hoc items that are not in the item entity, then the relationship may, depending on the item, be considered optional. The `orderdetail` entity can use two attributes for the item. If the `ItemID` attribute is used, then it must point to a valid `item` entity primary key.

✦ However, if the `temext` attribute is used instead, the `ItemID` attribute is left null.

How the optionality is implemented is up to the physical schema. The only purpose of the logical design is to model the organization's objects, their relationships, and their business rules.

Data-Model Diagramming

Data modelers use several methods to graphically work out their data models. The Chen ER diagramming method is popular, and Visio Professional includes it and five others. The method I prefer is rather simple and works well on a whiteboard, as shown in Figure 2-2. The cardinality of the relationship is indicated by a single line or by three lines (chicken feet). If the relationship is optional, a circle is placed near the foreign key.

Figure 2-2: A simple method for diagramming logical schemas

Another benefit of this simple diagramming method is that it doesn't require an advanced version of Visio.

One-to-Many Relationships

By far the most common relationship is a one-to-many relationship. Several tuples in the secondary entity relate to a single tuple in the primary entity. The relationship is between the primary entity's primary key and the secondary entity's foreign key, as illustrated in the following examples:

✦ In the Cape Hatteras Adventures database, each base camp may have several tours that originate from it. Each tour may originate from only one base camp, so the relationship is modeled as one base camp relating to multiple tours. The relationship is made between the `BaseCamp`'s primary key and the `Tour` entity's `BaseCampID` foreign key, as diagrammed in Figure 2-3. Each `Tour`'s foreign-key attribute contains a copy of its `BaseCamp`'s primary key.

Figure 2-3: The one-to-many relationship relates a primary key to a foreign key.

✦ Each customer may place multiple orders. While each order has its own unique `OrderID` primary key, the `Order` entity also has a foreign-key attribute that contains the `CustomerID` of the customer who placed the order. The `Order` entity may have several tuples with the same `CustomerID` that defines the relationship as one-to-many.

✦ A non-profit organization has an annual pledge drive. As each donor makes an annual pledge, the pledge goes into a secondary entity that can store several years' worth of pledges. An entity structure of `donor name, 2001pledge, 2002pledge, 2003pledge` is an amateurish design.

✦ One order may have several order lines. The `Order` primary key is duplicated in the `OrderDetail` entity's foreign key. This constrains each order to a single tuple in the `Order` entity, but allows multiple associated tuples in the `OrderDetail` entity.

One-to-One Relationships

One-to-one relationships connect two entities with primary keys at both entities. Because a primary key must be unique, each side of the relationship is restricted to one tuple.

One-to-one relationships are sometimes used to expand the tuple in one entity with additional, but optional or separate, attributes. For instance, an `Employee` entity can store general information about the employee. However, more sensitive information is stored in a separate entity. While security can be applied on an attribute-by-attribute basis, or a view can project selected attributes, many organizations choose to model sensitive information as two one-to-one entities.

Supertype/Subtype Relationships

A design element that leverages the one-to-one relationship is the supertype/subtype relationship. This relationship connects a single supertype entity with multiple subtype entities to extend the tuple with flexible attributes depending on the type of tuple. The supertype entity has a one-to-one optional relationship with each subtype.

This design is useful when some objects share a majority of attributes but differ in a few attributes, such as customers, vendors, and shippers. All three share name and address attributes, but each has specific attributes. For example, only customers have credit limits and only suppliers have attributes related to purchase orders.

While it's possible to use separate entities for customers and suppliers, a better design is to use a single `Contact` entity to hold the common attributes and separate entities for the attributes unique to customers and suppliers.

If the contact is a customer, additional customer information is stored in the `Customer` entity. If the contact is a supplier, supplier-related information is stored in the `Supplier` entity. All three entities (`Contact, Customer, Supplier`) share the same primary key. One tuple in the `Contact` entity can optionally relate to one tuple in the `Customer` entity, and to one tuple in the `Supplier` entity, as shown in Figure 2-4.

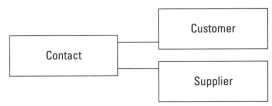

Figure 2-4: A one-to-one relationship relates a primary key to a primary key.

Most supertype/subtype designs permit only a single subtype tuple for each supertype tuple. The contact example, however, could permit a contact to be both a customer and a supplier by adding tuples in each of the subtype entities.

Cross-Reference The supertype/subtype pattern is very similar to the class inheritance concept within object-oriented analysis and design (OOA/D). Therefore, if a database includes several complex supertype/subtype patterns, then the database may be a candidate for an object-oriented style database instead of a relational database. An object/relational DBMS for SQL Server may be downloaded from www.SQLServerBible.com.

Note that there's a performance hit when using this design. Insert operations must insert into two entities, and select operations must join the supertype and subtype entities. Therefore, don't use the supertype/subtype design to categorize tuples; use this design only when several columns are unique to each subtype, and it reduces the workload when selecting only tuples from one of the subtypes.

Many-to-Many Relationships

In a many-to-many relationship, both sides may relate to multiple tuples on the other side of the relationship. The many-to-many relationship is common in reality, as shown in the following examples:

✦ In the OBX Kites sample database, an order may have multiple items, and each item may be sold on multiple orders.

✦ In the Cape Hatteras Adventures sample database, a guide may qualify for several tours, and each tour may have several qualified guides.

✦ In the Cape Hatteras Adventures sample database, a customer may participate in several events, and it is hoped that each tour/event has several customers.

Referr to the previous example in the logical model and you see that the many-to-many relationship between customers and tours is modeled by signifying multiple cardinality at each side of the relationship, as shown in Figure 2-5. The many-to-many relationship is optional because the customer and the tour/event are each valid without the other.

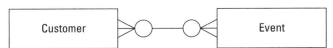

Figure 2-5: The many-to-many logical model shows multiple tuples on both ends of the relationship.

The one-to-one and the one-to-many relationship may be constructed from objects from their organizations that users can describe and understand. In the physical schema, a many-to-many relationship can't be modeled with just the visible objects.

An associative table (see Figure 2-6), sometimes called a resolution or junction table, is required to resolve the many-to-many relationship. This supporting table artificially creates two one-to-many relationships between the two entities.

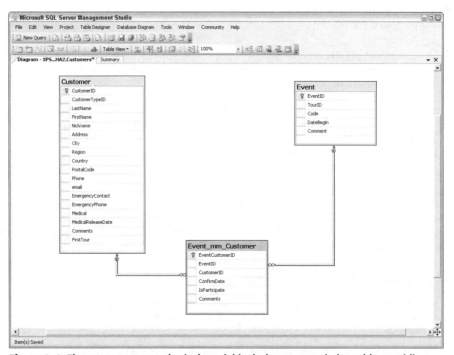

Figure 2-6: The many-to-many physical model includes an associative table providing artificial one-to-many relationships for both tables.

In some cases, additional information may describe the many-to-many relationship. Such information belongs in the resolution entity. For example, in the bill of materials example, the material-to-material relationship might include a quantity attribute in the resolution entity to describe the amount of one material used in the construction of the second material.

The relationship between each primary entity and the resolution entity is mandatory because the relationship is invalid without the primary object. If either the customer or the tour/event were to be deleted, the tuple representing the resolution relationship would become invalid.

Category Entities

Another type of supporting entity is the *category* entity, sometimes called a *lookup table*. These entities provide domain integrity — consistency in terms of the way tuples are organized. An excellent example of this consistency is a state table. Instead of Customer tuples containing inconsistent references in the `Region` attribute to Florida, such as FL, Fl, Fla, and `Florida`, any tuples referencing Florida simply point to the Florida tuple in the state entity. Searching and sorting is faster and easier because of the consistency.

Visible entities typically relate to category entities in a one-to-many relationship. The relationship can be optional or mandatory.

Reflexive Relationships

In some cases a relationship is between two items of the same type, as illustrated in the following common examples:

✦ An organizational chart represents a person reporting to another person.

✦ A bill of materials details how a material is constructed from other materials.

✦ Within the Family sample database, a person relates to his or her mother and father.

These are examples of *reflexive relationships*, most commonly called *recursive relationships,* but also referred to as *unary,* or *self-join* relationships. Because of the way these are diagrammed, it's sometimes informally called an *elephant-ear* relationship.

To use the Family database as an example, each tuple in the `Person` entity represents one person. Each person has both a mother and a father, who are also in the `Person` entity. Therefore, the `MotherID` foreign key and the `FatherID` foreign key point to the mother and father tuples in the same person entity.

Because `PersonID` is a primary key and `MotherID` is a foreign key, the relationship cardinality is one-to-many, as shown in Figure 2-7. One mother may have several children, but each child may have only one mother.

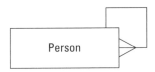

Figure 2-7: The reflexive, or recursive, relationship is a one-to-many relationship between two tuples of the same entity.

A bill of materials is more complex because a material may be built from several source materials, and the material may be used to build several materials in the next step of the manufacturing process. This many-to-many reflexive relationship is illustrated in Figure 2-8.

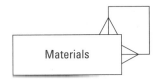

Figure 2-8: The logical schema of a many-to-many reflexive relationship shows multiple cardinality at each end of the relationship.

A resolution entity is required to resolve the many-to-many relationship, just as with the previous many-to-many relationship. In the Material-Specification sample database, the `BillOfMaterials` resolution entity has two foreign keys that both point to the `Material` entity, as shown in Figure 2-9.

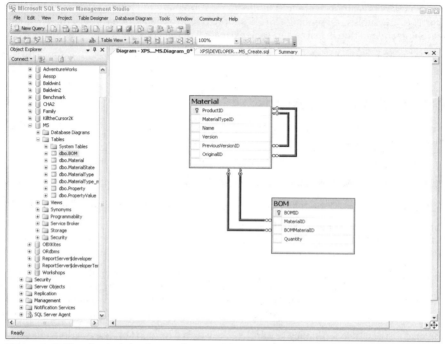

Figure 2-9: The physical database schema of the many-to-many reflexive relationship must include a resolution entity, just like the many-to-many two-entity relationship.

The first foreign key points to the material being built. The second foreign key points to the source material.

Normalization

The most well-known concept of relational database design, normalization, was developed by Dr. E. F. Codd. The purpose of *normalization* is to reduce or eliminate update anomalies that can occur when the same data fact is stored in multiple locations within the database.

Normalization is not the holy grail of database design — it is merely a tool to reduce update anomalies. As such, it is most beneficial for databases that receive first-generation data, such as a transactional database that receives order data. Therefore, databases that are not used for first-generation data (such as reporting databases, data warehouses, or reference data stores) do not necessarily benefit from normalization.

When the industry was moving from a flat-file design to relational data modeling, it was useful to think of normalization as a process that began with a flat file and moved through the normal forms to arrive at a relational design that reduced update anomalies.

Although most database developers are familiar with normalization, the actual working principles of normalization are widely misunderstood. There are three common misunderstandings regarding normalization and database logical schema design:

✦ The most common misconception regarding normalization is believing that more tables means a higher form of normalization. For example, some developers believe that a particular database schema that uses 12 tables in third normal form would use 16 tables if it were designed using fourth normal form.

✦ It is an error to follow the normal forms as if they were a waterfall design process, i.e., beginning with non-normalized design and then correcting for first normal form by eliminating redundant columns, followed by second normal form, and so on.

✦ Another trap is to believe that there is a single correct normalized design for a given problem. A veteran data modeler will be able to see several possible entity configurations and logical schema designs.

Entity/Attribute Design Principles

The key to designing a schema that avoids update anomalies is to ensure that each single fact in real life is modeled by a single data point in the database. There are three principles that define a single data point:

✦ Each database entity must describe one "thing."

✦ There must be a one-to-one relationship between attributes and facts, meaning that every attribute must represent one fact and each fact must be represented by one attribute. To illustrate this principle, a "smart key" that encodes several facts within one attribute violates this principles, as does a design that requires combining two or more attributes to determine a single fact.

✦ Each attribute must describe its entity and not some other related entity.

Normal Forms

Normalization is usually defined in terms of normal forms. Each of the normal forms describes a possible error in designing the entities and attributes, and provides a rule for correcting the error. In this way, the normal forms are similar to how the grammar rules of a written language can identify errors in sentence structure.

When creating the logical design, *normalization* is the mathematical method of evaluating the relational quality of the data model. The opposite of a relational-database model, a flat-file or nonnormalized data model tends to exhibit certain problems with data updates, generally caused by duplicate data. Each progressive form of normalization removes another type of flat-file problem.

A normalized database design has the following advantages over flat-file databases:

✦ Improved data integrity owing to the elimination of duplicate storage locations for the same data

✦ Reduced locking contention and improved multiple-user concurrency

✦ Smaller files

A data model does not begin nonnormalized and then move through the normal forms. Instead, a data modeler usually initially designs the logical schema in at least a third normal form, and may choose to take a portion of the schema to a higher form.

Simplicity and Normalization

Simplicity doesn't mean violating data integrity. The forms of normalization are as basic to database design as grammar is to writing. Good writing doesn't have to break the rules of grammar. In a manner of thinking, the primary principle of Strunk and White's *The Elements of Style* (be concise) is as fundamental to database design as it is to writing.

First Normal Form (1NF)

The first normal form means the data is in an entity format, such that the following three conditions are met:

✦ **Every unit of data is represented within scalar attributes.** A scalar value is a value "capable of being represented by a point on a scale," according to Merriam-Webster.

Every attribute must contain one unit of data, and each unit of data must fill one attribute. Designs that embed multiple pieces of information within an attribute violate the first normal form. Likewise, if multiple attributes must be combined in some way to determine a single unit of data, then the attribute design is incomplete.

✦ **All data must be represented in unique attributes.** Each attribute must have a unique name and a unique purpose. An entity should have no repeating attributes. If the attributes repeat, or the entity is very wide, the object is too broadly designed.

A design that repeats attributes, such as an order entity that includes item1, item2, and item3 attributes to hold multiple line items, violates the first normal form.

✦ **All data must be represented within unique tuples.** If the entity design requires or permits duplicate tuples, that design violates the first normal form.

For an example of the first normal form in action, consider the listing of base camps and tours from the Cape Hatteras Adventures database. Table 2-3 shows base camp data in a model that violates the first normal form. The repeating tour attribute is not unique.

To redesign the data model so that it complies with the first normal form, resolve the repeating group of tour attributes into a single unique attribute, as shown in Table 2-4, and then move any multiple values to a unique tuple. The BaseCamp entity contains a unique tuple for each base camp, and the Tour entity's BaseCampID refers to the primary key in the BaseCamp entity.

Table 2-3: Violating the First Normal Form

BaseCamp	Tour1	Tour2	Tour3
Ashville	Appalachian Trail	Blue Ridge Parkway Hike	
Cape Hatteras	Outer Banks Lighthouses		
Freeport	Bahamas Dive		
Ft. Lauderdale	Amazon Trek		
West Virginia	Gauley River Rafting		

Table 2-4: Conforming to the First Normal Form

Tour Entity		*BaseCamp Entity*	
BaseCampID(FK)	*Tour*	*BaseCampID (PK)*	*Name*
1	Appalachian Trail	1	Ashville
1	Blue Ridge Parkway Hike	2	Cape Hatteras
2	Outer Banks Lighthouses	3	Freeport
3	Bahamas Dive	4	Ft. Lauderdale
4	Amazon Trek	5	West Virginia
	Gauley River Rafting		

Another example of a data structure that desperately needs to adhere to the first normal form is a corporate product code that embeds the department, model, color, size, and so forth within the code. I've even seen product codes that were so complex they included digits to signify the syntax for the following digits.

In a theoretical sense this type of design is wrong because the attribute isn't a scalar value. In practical terms, it has the following problems:

✦ Using a digit or two for each data element means that the database will soon run out of possible data values.

✦ Databases don't index based on the internal values of a string, so searches require scanning the entire table and parsing each value.

✦ Business rules are difficult to code and enforce.

Entities with non-scalar attributes need to be completely redesigned so that each individual data attribute has its own attribute.

The Second Normal Form (2NF)

The *second normal form* ensures that each attribute is in fact an attribute of the entity. It's an issue of dependency. Every attribute must require its primary key, or it doesn't belong in the database.

If the entity's primary key is a single value, this isn't too difficult. Composite primary keys can sometimes get into trouble with the second normal form if the attributes aren't dependent on every attribute in the primary key. If the attribute depends on one of the primary key attributes but not the other, then that is a partial dependency, which violates the second normal form.

An example of a data model that violates the second normal form is one in which the base camp phone number is added to the BaseCampTour entity, as shown in Table 2-5. Assume that the primary key (PK) is a composite of both the BaseCamp and the Tour, and that the phone number is a permanent phone number for the base camp, not a phone number assigned for each tour.

Table 2-5: Violating the Second Normal Form

PK-BaseCamp	PK-Tour	Base Camp Phone Number
Ashville	Appalachian Trail	828-555-1212
Ashville	Blue Ridge Parkway Hike	828-555-1212
Cape Hatteras	Outer Banks Lighthouses	828-555-1213
Freeport	Bahamas Dive	828-555-1214
Ft. Lauderdale	Amazon Trek	828-555-1215
West Virginia	Gauley River Rafting	828-555-1216

The problem with this design is that the phone number is an attribute of the base camp but not the tour, so the phone number attribute is only partially dependent on the entity's primary key. (A more significant problem is that the composite primary key does not uniquely identify the base camp.)

An obvious practical problem with this design is that updating the phone number requires either updating multiple tuples or risking having two phone numbers for the same phone.

The solution is to remove the partially dependent attribute from the entity with the composite keys, and create an entity with a unique primary key for the base camp, as shown in Table 2-6. This new entity is then an appropriate location for the dependent attribute.

Table 2-6: Conforming to the Second Normal Form

Tour Entity		Base Camp Entity	
PK-Base Camp	PK-Tour	PK-Base Camp	PhoneNumber
Ashville	Appalachian Trail	Ashville	828-555-1212
Ashville	Blue Ridge Parkway Hike	Cape Hatteras	828-555-1213
Cape Hatteras	Outer Banks Lighthouses	Freeport	828-555-1214
Freeport	Bahamas Dive	t. Lauderdale	828-555-1215
Ft. Lauderdale	Amazon Trek	West Virginia	828-555-1216
West Virginia	Gauley River Rafting		

The `PhoneNumber` attribute is now fully dependent on the entity's primary key. Each phone number is stored in only one location, and no partial dependencies exist.

The Third Normal Form (3NF)

The *third normal form* checks for transitive dependencies. A *transitive dependency* is similar to a partial dependency in that they both refer to attributes that are not fully dependent on a primary key. A dependency is transient when `attribute1` is dependent on `attribute2`, which is dependent on the primary key.

Just as with the second normal form, the third normal form is resolved by moving the nondependent attribute to a new entity.

Continuing with the Cape Hatteras Adventures example, you assign a guide as the lead guide responsible for each base camp. The `BaseCampGuide` attribute belongs in the `BaseCamp` entity, but it is a violation of the third normal form if other information describing the guide is stored in the base camp, as shown in Table 2-7.

Table 2-7: Violating the Third Normal Form

Base Camp Entity

BaseCampPK	BaseCampPhoneNumber	LeadGuide	DateofHire
Ashville	828-555-1212	Jeff Davis	5/1/99
Cape Hatteras	828-555-1213	Ken Frank	4/15/97
Freeport	828-555-1214	Dab Smith	7/7/2001
Ft. Lauderdale	828-555-1215	Sam Wilson	1/1/2002
West Virginia	828-555-1216	Lauren Jones	6/1/2000

The `DateofHire` describes the guide not the base, so the hire-date attribute is not directly dependent on the `BaseCamp` entity's primary key. The `DateOfHire`'s dependency is transitive in that it goes through the `LeadGuide` attribute.

Creating a `Guide` entity and moving its attributes to the new entity resolves the violation of the third normal form and cleans up the logical design, as demonstrated in Table 2-8.

Table 2-8: Conforming to the Third Normal Form

Tour Entity		LeadGuide Entity	
BaseCampPK	LeadGuide	LeadGuidePK	DateofHire
Ashville, NC	Jeff Davis	Jeff Davis	5/1/99
Cape Hatteras	Ken Frank	Ken Frank	4/15/97
Freeport	Dab Smith	Dab Smith	7/7/2001
Ft. Lauderdale	Sam Wilson	Sam Wilson	1/1/2002
West Virginia	Lauren Jones	Lauren Jones	6/1/2000

Best Practice

If the entity has a good primary key and every attribute is scalar and fully dependent on the primary key, then the logical design is in the third normal form. Most database designs stop at the third normal form.

The additional forms prevent problems with more complex logical designs. If you tend to work with mind-bending modeling problems and develop creative solutions, then understanding the advanced forms will prove useful.

The Boyce-Codd Normal Form (BCNF)

The *Boyce-Codd normal form* occurs between the third and fourth normal forms, and it handles a problem with an entity that might have two sets of primary keys. The Boyce-Codd normal form simply stipulates that in such a case the entity should be split into two entities, one for each primary key.

The Fourth Normal Form (4NF)

The *fourth normal form* deals with problems created by complex composite primary keys. If two independent attributes are brought together to form a primary key along with a third attribute, but the two attributes don't really uniquely identify the entity without the third attribute, then the design violates the fourth normal form.

For example, assume the following conditions:

1. The `BaseCamp` and the base camp's `LeadGuide` were used as a composite primary key.

2. An `Event` and the `Guide` were brought together as a primary key.

3. Because both used a guide, all three were combined into a single entity.

The preceding example violates the fourth normal form.

The fourth normal form is used to help identify entities that should be split into separate entities. Usually this is an issue only if large composite primary keys have brought too many disparate objects into a single entity.

The Fifth Normal Form (5NF)

The *fifth normal form* provides the method for designing complex relationships that involve multiple (three or more) entities. A *three-way* or *ternary* relationship, if properly designed, is in the fifth normal form. The cardinality of any of the relationships could be one or many. What makes it a ternary relationship is the number of related entities.

As an example of a ternary relationship, consider a manufacturing process that involves an operator, a machine, and a bill of materials. From one point of view, this could be an operation entity with three foreign keys. Alternately, it could be thought of as a ternary relationship with additional attributes.

Just like a two-entity many-to-many relationship, a ternary relationship requires a resolution entity in the physical schema design to resolve the many-to-many relationships into multiple artificial one-to-many relationships. However, in this case the resolution entity has three or more foreign keys.

In such a complex relationship, the fifth normal form requires that each entity, if separated from the ternary relationship, remains a proper entity without any loss of data.

The purpose of the relational database is to model reality. Toward that end, the rules and methods of enforcing data integrity are important to both the theory and the practice of developing databases.

One of the keys to enforcing data integrity is educating the owners of the data so that they will value data integrity and "own" not only the job and the project but the data integrity as well. Data integrity seldom occurs by accident. It must be planned for from day one of the project.

One of the most difficult factors in a project's data integrity is legacy data. When legacy data meets relational-data integrity, some serious problems with the legacy data are often revealed.

Best Practice

It's easy for those who were responsible for the legacy system to feel personally threatened by the new project. Getting the legacy developers to feel that they own the data integrity and to participate in the development of the project is far better than presenting the new project so that they are cornered and react defensively. One way to do this is to enable them to set goals and then help them see how best to meet those goals.

Relational Algebra

Relational databases, by their very nature, segment data into several narrow, but long, tables. Seldom does looking at a single table provide meaningful data. Therefore, merging data from multiple tables is an important task for SQL developers. The theory behind merging data sets is *relational algebra*, as defined by E. F. Codd in 1970.

Relational algebra consists of eight relational operators:

✦ **Restrict:** Returns the rows that meet a certain criterion

✦ **Project:** Returns selected columns from a data set

✦ **Product:** Relational multiplication that returns all possible combinations of data between two data sets

✦ **Union:** Relational addition and subtraction that merges two tables vertically by stacking one table above another table and lining up the columns

✦ **Intersection:** Returns the rows common to both data sets

✦ **Difference:** Returns the rows unique to one data set

✦ **Join:** Returns the horizontal merger of two tables, matching up rows based on common data

✦ **Divide:** Returns exact matches between two data sets

In addition, as a method of accomplishing relational algebra, SQL has developed the following:

✦ **Subqueries:** Similar to a join, but more flexible; the results of the subquery are used in place of an expression, list, or data set within an outer query.

In the formal language of relational algebra:

✦ A table, or data set, is a *relation* or *entity.*

✦ A row is a *tuple.*

✦ A column is an *attribute*

Cross-Reference

Relational algebra is put into practice in Chapter 9, "Merging Data with Joins and Unions," and Chapter 10, "Including Subqueries and CTEs."

Summary

Relational theory has been around for over three decades and has become better defined over the years as database vendors compete with extensions, and database theorists further define the problem of representing reality within a data structure. However, E. F. Codd's original work is still the foundation of relational database design and implementation.

Relational database design is a fundamental skill for database developers. To be successful as a developer, you'll need a solid understanding and a repertoire of patterns. The next chapter moves beyond two-dimensional relational databases to 3-D object-oriented databases.

✦　　✦　　✦

Exploring SQL Server 2005 Architecture

I became a reader of J. R. R. Tolkien novels in high school, a few decades before Hollywood brought Middle Earth to the masses. I remember the power of the phrase "and one ring to rule them all." Even though the story revolves around the one ring, there were other rings; and they all must have looked cool and had interesting properties, but the one ring was the strategic ring, the compelling ring. It was the crucible of the story.

Asked at the Get Ready for SQL Server 2005 road shows was the question "Why upgrade to SQL Server 2005?" There were many answers, which boiled down to various new technologies that might provide a payback on the upgrade cost — improved availability and performance, or new business intelligence (BI) tools were popular answers. I agree that any of those improved features might be the deciding factor for a given IT shop.

A Gartner SQL Server 2005 Analysis Report, quoted in *ComputerWeekly*'s August 17, 2004 issue stated, "Yukon (the beta name for SQL Server 2005) is a montage release, lacking a clear focus or vision. Although Microsoft claims that it is delaying the release to ensure greater quality, Gartner believes that the protracted release of Yukon is largely due to the lack of clear focus and direction for SQL Server within Microsoft."

I couldn't disagree more.

Like Tolkien's rings, there are an overwhelming number of incredible new and improved technologies within SQL Server 2005. Is there a single strategic and compelling reason, above other reasons, to move to SQL Server 2005? Is there a one ring of SQL Server 2005?

Many of the cool new features, such as database mirroring, are evolutionary, but not revolutionary. .NET integration is commonly considered to be the most significant new feature of SQL Server 2005. I say, it depends. If .NET is hosted within SQL Server to build faster scalar functions and replace extended stored procedures, then it's only evolutionary. None of these features is the one ring.

Service-oriented architecture (SOA) means designing applications with a standard abstraction layer that can communicate with other SOA-style applications via XML, SOAP, and web services. With the broad acceptance of SOA, the data landscape has dramatically changed since SQL Server 2000 was introduced, and the big-picture, eureka understanding of SQL Server 2005 is that it provides new SOA optimized technologies, enabling it to smoothly blend into this new architectural landscape.

In addition to remaining an excellent database for a traditional client/server or n-tier architecture, SQL Server 2005 extends its technical capabilities to do the following:

✦ Serve XML data as an SOA data store

✦ Serve XML and XSLT directly to web browsers

✦ Store, index, bulk insert, and query XML data natively within the data engine

✦ Serve the enterprise with optimizations specifically targeted at very large databases

To meet these new objectives, the Microsoft SQL development team (in Microsoft buildings 34 and 35) enhanced the existing services and added so many new technologies that it's sure to seem overwhelming or unusual to even longtime SQL Server DBAs.

There are a number of good reasons to upgrade to SQL Server 2005, including improved availability, performance, and a much richer set of BI tools. But the strategic, compelling "one ring" of SQL Server 2005 is that SQL Server provides new architectural options.

SQL Server 2005 is Microsoft's third-generation database server (see Figure 3-1). SQL Server 2005 is more than just one product, more than the database engine, and substantially more than SQL Server 2000. SQL Server 2005 is a broad collection of data-centric services and tools that may be used in concert to build a data solution within a data architecture environment that was difficult or impossible a few years ago.

SQL Server Generations

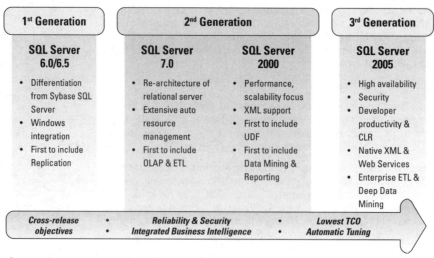

Figure 3-1: SQL Server 2005 is far more than an upgrade. With so many new architectural options available, it is unquestionably a third-generation database platform.

This chapter serves as an overview of SQL Server to help you get the lay of the land and grasp the big picture.

Cross-Reference   If the phrase *SQL Server architecture* invokes the concepts of organizing data pages and indexes, how query plans are cached, and understanding the Query Optimizer, then you'll want to also read Chapter 50, "Query Analysis and Index Tuning."

Data Access Architectures

SQL Server is first and foremost a data server. By itself, SQL Server cannot meet the end user's needs (unless you consider Query Editor to be a client user interface!). If you're new to the client/server model, understanding this pattern is foundational to understanding SQL Server.

The Client/Server Database Model

Technically, the term *client/server* refers to any two cooperating processes. The client process requests a service from the server process, which in turn handles the request for the client. The client process and the server process may be on different computers or on the same computer: It's the cooperation between the processes that is significant, not the physical location.

The term *client/server* applies to many aspects of computing. File servers, print servers, and Internet service providers (ISPs) are all client/server models. File servers provide files, print servers handle print requests, and ISPs handle requests for Internet service. In the area of client/server databases, a database server process handles database requests from the database client process.

Client/Server Databases

In contrast to desktop databases (such as Microsoft Access), which make the clients do all the work, client/server databases are like research librarians who handle a request by finding the information and returning a photocopy. The actual reference materials never leave the watchful eye of the research librarian.

In a client/server database, the database client prepares a SQL request — just a small text message — and sends it to the database server, which in turn reads and processes the request (see Figure 3-2). Inside the server, the security is checked, the indexes are searched, the data is retrieved or manipulated, any server-side code is executed, and the final results are sent back to the client.

All the database work is performed within the database server. If the client requests a data set, the data set is prepared within the server and a copy of the data is sent to the client. The actual data and indexes never leave the server. When the client requests an insert, update, or delete operation, the server receives the SQL request and processes the request internally.

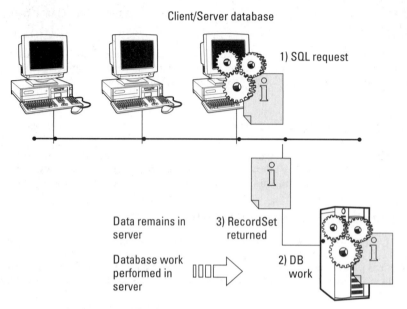

Figure 3-2: Client/server databases perform the work within the server process.

The client/server–database model offers several benefits over the desktop database model:

✦ Reliability is improved because the data is not spread across the network and several applications. Only one process handles the data.

✦ Data integrity constraints and business rules can be enforced at the server level, resulting in a more thorough implementation of the rules.

✦ Security is improved because the database keeps the data within a single server. Hacking into a data file that's protected within the server is much more difficult than hacking into a data file on a workstation.

✦ Performance is improved and better balanced among workstations because half of the workload, the database processing, is being handled by the server, and the workstations are only handling the user-interface half. Because the database server process has single-user rapid access to the data files, and much of the data is already cached in memory, database operations are much faster at the server than in a multi-user desktop-database environment. A database server is serving every user operating a database application; therefore, it's easier to justify the cost of a beefier server.

✦ Network traffic is greatly reduced. Compared to a desktop database's rush-hour traffic, client/server traffic is like a single motorcyclist carrying a slip of paper with all 10 lanes to himself. This is no exaggeration! Upgrading a heavily used desktop database to a well-designed client/server database will reduce database-related network traffic by more than 95 percent.

✦ A by-product of reducing network traffic is that well-designed client/server applications perform well in a distributed environment — even when using slower communications. So little traffic is required that even a 56KB dial-up line should be indistinguishable from a 100baseT Ethernet connection for a .NET-rich client application connected to a SQL Server database.

Client/Server Roles

In a client/server database configuration, each side plays a specific role. If the roles are confused, then the performance and integrity of the client/server database application will suffer.

The database server is responsible for the following:

✦ Processing data modification and retrieval requests

✦ Performing data-intensive processing

✦ Enforcing all database rules and constraints

✦ Enforcing data security

The database client process should be responsible for the following:

✦ Presenting the data to the user in an easily recognizable, inviting, and useful format

✦ Providing an interface to the various tools, data, and reports

✦ Submitting requests to the server

Best Practice

Client/server implementations works best when the data abstraction layer is strongly enforced, meaning that every data access request goes through the data abstraction layer stored procedures. Casual client/server designs that allow applications or reports to directly access the database tables will fail in the long run because the database is no longer extensible. Making changes to the database schema breaks too many other objects so the IT shop becomes paralyzed with fear and chooses to live with the out-of-date design.

N-Tier Design

Often, in a client/server application, more processes are involved besides the database client and the database-server process. Middle tiers are often employed to handle connection handling, connection pooling, and business logic.

A middle tier that handles connections is useful because multiple users can take advantage of a few constantly open connections to the database server. This type of connection, however, affects the way the database server can authenticate individual users. The database-security plan will have to take this into account.

In a situation in which more than one server may be available, a common connection object makes it easier to switch the users from Server A to Server B if Server A should go down. The connection object becomes a single point that could automatically detect the situation and switch to Server B. This type of solution works well with database mirroring.

Placing the business rules and data abstraction layer within a logical tier makes sense for ease of development and maintenance. The question is where to physically locate this logical tier. Some developers argue that the middle-tier logical layer should be in its own server, written in .NET and separate from the database server. I disagree for two reasons:

✦ Business rules and database constraints should be enforced at the database server physical level so they can never be bypassed by any user application or process.

✦ Coding the business rules at the database server level also gives the code faster access to database lookups and improves performance.

The only downsides to coding the business rules within the server are that the programmer must learn server-side programming and the database application is more difficult to port to other database products.

Service-Oriented Architecture

Service-oriented architecture (SOA) is the alternative to client/server data access. Rather than code a custom client/server interface between multiple systems, SOA uses standard HTTP calls and XML, enabling multiple systems to communicate to a system using the same interface.

SOA is useful for large enterprises with several very large systems, but there's an overhead cost for the extensibility. The data is passed and translated between multiple layers. A front-end user GUI using SOA would perform terribly compared to the direct connection of a client/server ADO.NET connection.

I've seen organizations break up a medium-size data application into multiple smaller applications so they can use SOA to communicate between them. This too is a disaster. A web service call to check a foreign key is simply ridiculous.

When to best use SOA web services? They fit well as a secondary data access method to ease communication with other very large systems. Beyond that definition, avoid SOA.

Deploying an SOA data store using SQL Server 2005 is easier with the new HTTP endpoints feature. For details, turn to Chapter 32, "Building an SOA Data Store with Web Services."

SQL Server Services

SQL Server is a more than just a relational database engine; it's a collection of database-related services and components that may be used in concert to build a powerful database back-end solution, as illustrated in Figure 3-3.

Relational Engine

The SQL Server 2005 *relational engine,* sometimes called the *database engine,* is the core of SQL Server. It is the process that handles all the relational database work. SQL is a descriptive language, meaning that SQL describes to the engine only the query to be processed. The engine takes over from there.

SQL Server 2005 supports installation of up to 50 instances of the relational engine on a physical server. Although they share some components, each instance functions as a complete separate installation of SQL Server.

Within the relational engine are several key processes and components, including the following:

✦ SQL Server's Query Optimizer determines how to process the query based on the costs of different types of query-execution operations. The estimated and actual query-execution plans may be viewed graphically, or in XML, using Management Studio (SSMS).

✦ The Buffer Manager analyzes the data pages being used and pre-fetches data from the data file(s) into memory, thus reducing the dependency on disk I/O performance.

✦ The Lazy Writer writes data pages that have been modified in memory to the data file.

✦ The Resource Monitor optimizes the query plan cache by responding to memory pressure and intelligently removing older query plans from the cache.

✦ The Lock Manager dynamically manages the scope of locks to balance the number of required locks with the size of the lock.

✦ SQL Server eats resources for lunch, and for this reason it needs direct control of the available resources (memory, threads, I/O request, etc.). Simply leaving the resource management to Windows isn't sophisticated enough for SQL Server. SQL Server 2005 includes its own OS layer, called SQLOS, which manages all of its internal resources.

On The Web

SQL Server has a long history beginning in 1987 when Sybase created SQL Server for Unix. Since then SQL Server has been through numerous releases and has added new technologies. To read about the history of SQL Server, the various beta code names, and the evolution of the technologies, and to see screen shots of past versions, read the page on SQL Server History online at www.SQLServerBible.com.

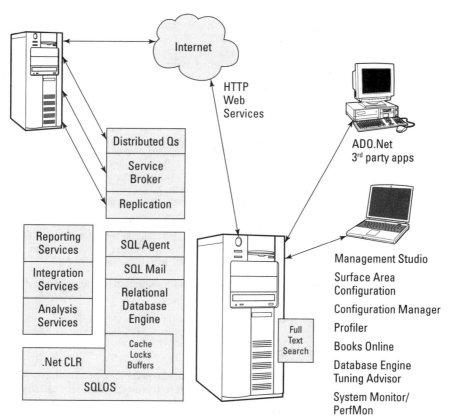

Figure 3-3: SQL Server is a collection of server and client components.

Transact-SQL

SQL Server is based on the SQL standard, with some Microsoft-specific extensions. SQL was invented by E. F. Codd while he was working at the IBM research labs in San Jose in 1971. SQL Server 20050 is entry-level (Level 1) compliant with the ANSI SQL 92 standard. The complete specifications for the ANSI SQL standard are found in five documents that can be purchased from `www.techstreet.com/ncits.html`.

While the ANSI SQL definition is excellent for the common data-selection and data-definition commands, it does not include commands with which to control SQL Server properties, or provide the level of logical control within batches required to develop a SQL Server–specific application. Therefore, the Microsoft SQL Server team has extended the ANSI definition with several enhancements and new commands, and has left out a few commands because SQL Server implemented them differently. The final result is Transact-SQL or T-SQL — the dialect of SQL understood by SQL Server.

Missing from T-SQL are very few ANSI SQL commands (such as foreign key cascade options, nullify, and default), primarily because Microsoft implemented the functionality in other ways. T-SQL, by default, also handles nulls, quotes, and padding differently than the ANSI standard, although that behavior can be controlled. Based on my own development experience, I can say that none of these differences affect the process of developing a database application using SQL Server. T-SQL adds significantly more to ANSI SQL than it lacks.

Understanding SQL Server requires understanding T-SQL. The SQL Server engine understands only one language: Transact-SQL. Every command sent to SQL Server must be a valid T-SQL command. Batches of stored T-SQL commands may be executed within the server as stored procedures. Other tools, such as Management Studio, which provide graphical user interfaces with which to control SQL Server, are at some level converting most of those mouse clicks to T-SQL for processing by the engine.

SQL and T-SQL commands are divided into the following three categories:

✦ **Data Manipulation Language (DML):** Includes the common SQL `select`, `insert`, `update`, and `delete` commands. DML is sometimes mistakenly referred to as *Data Modification Language*; this is misleading, because the `select` statement does not modify data. It does, however, manipulate the data returned.

✦ **Data Definition Language (DDL):** Commands that create and manage data tables, constraints, and other database objects.

✦ **Data Control Language (DCL):** Security commands such as `grant`, `revoke`, and `deny`.

Visual Studio and the CLR

One of the most exciting new features is the incorporation of Visual Studio within SQL Server 2005. While they have been cooperative tools in the past, the integration between Visual Studio 2005 and SQL Server 2005 is tighter than ever before. The two products were developed and launched simultaneously and it shows. Management Studio is a based on the Visual Studio integrated development environment (IDE). But the integration is deeper than just the look and feel of Management Studio. SQL Server 2005's internal operating system, SQLOS, actually hosts the .NET common language runtime (CLR) inside SQL Server.

Assemblies developed in Visual Studio can be deployed and executed inside SQL Server as stored procedures, triggers, user-defined functions, or user-defined aggregate functions. In addition, data types developed with Visual Studio can be used to define tables and store custom data.

Cross-Reference
.NET integration is discussed in Chapter 27, "Programming CLR Assemblies within SQL Server," and Chapter 29, "Persisting Custom Data Types."

There's value in SQLOS hosting the CLR. It means that SQL Server is in control of the CLR resources. It can prevent a CLR problem, shut down and restart a CLR routine that's causing trouble, and ensure that the battle for memory is won by the right player.

By default, the common language runtime is disabled in SQL Server 2005 and must be specifically enabled using the Surface Area Configuration Tool or a T-SQL `set` command. When enabled, each assembly's scope, or ability to access code outside SQL Server, can be carefully controlled.

Service Broker

New in SQL Server 2005, the Service Broker is a managed data queue, providing a key performance and scalability feature by leveling the load over time:

✦ Service Broker can buffer high volumes of calls to an HTTP web service or a stored procedure. Rather than a thousand webs service calls launching a thousand stored procedure threads, the calls can be placed on a queue and the stored procedures can be executed by a few instances to handle the load more efficiently.

✦ Server-side processes that include significant logic or periods of heavy traffic can place the required data in the queue and return to the calling process without completing the logic. The Service Broker will move through the queue calling another stored procedure to do the heavy lifting.

While it's possible to design your own queue within SQL Server, there are benefits to using Microsoft's work queue. SQL Server includes DDL commands to manage Service Broker, and there are T-SQL commands to place on the queue or fetch data from the queue. Information about Service Broker queues are exposed in metadata views, Management Studio, and System Monitor. Most important, Services Broker is well tested and designed for heavy payloads under stress.

Cross-Reference
Service Broker is a key service in building a service-oriented architecture data store. For more information, see Chapter 32, "Building an SOA Data Store with Web Services."

Replication Services

SQL Server data is often required throughout national or global organization, and SQL Server replication is often employed to move the data. Enhanced with new tools for SQL Server 2005, Replication Services can move transactions one-way or merge updates from multiple locations using a publisher, distributor, subscriber topology.

Cross-Reference
Chapter 39, "Replicating Data," explains the various replication models and how to set up replication.

Full-Text Search

Full-Text search has been in SQL Server since version 7, but with each version this excellent tool has been enhanced. SQL queries use indexes to locate rows quickly. By default, indexes index by entire column. Searching for words within the column is a very slow process. Full-Text Search solves this problem by indexing every word within a column.

Once the Full-Text Search has been created for the column, SQL Server queries can search the Full-Text Search indexes and return high-performance in-string word searches.

 Chapter 13, "Using Full-Text Search," explains how to set up and use full text searches within
Reference SQL queries.

The Microsoft Search Service, which performs the Full-Text Search, is actually a component of the operating system that maintains text search capabilities for files. SQL Server leverages the Windows Search Service when performing Full-Text Search. The service may be started or stopped with SQL Server Configuration Manager or from within Windows' Computer Administration/Services.

Notification Services

Initially released in 2003 as an add-on for SQL Server 2000, and enhanced for SQL Server 2005, Notification Services can be programmed to initiate a message based on data changes. The message can be sent to nearly any device, including e-mail, cell phones, and pagers. A typical application for Notification Services would be a transportation ticketing system that automatically notifies passengers of schedule changes or delays.

Server Management Objects

Server Management Objects (SMO) is the set of objects that exposes SQL Server's configuration and management features for programming by .NET front-end code. SMO isn't intended for development of database applications; rather, it's used by vendors when developing SQL Server tools such as Management Studio or a third-party management GUI or backup utility. SMO uses the namespace `Microsoft.SQLServer.SMO`.

 SMO is the replacement for the older SQL-DMO objects found in SQL Server 7 and SQL
2005 Server 2000. SMO is backwardly compatible with SQL Server 7 and SQL Server 2000.

SQL Server Agent

The Server Agent is an optional process that, when running, executes SQL jobs and handles other automated tasks. It can be configured to automatically run when the system boots, or may be started from the SQL Server Configuration Manager or the SQL Server Surface Area Configuration Tool.

 Chapter 38, "Automating Database Maintenance with SQL Server Agent," details SQL agents,
Reference jobs, and mail, as well as the SQL Server Agent.

Distributed Transaction Coordinator (DTC)

The Distributed Transaction Coordinator is a process that handles dual-phase commits for transactions that span multiple SQL Servers. DTC can be started from within Windows' Computer Administration/Services. If the application regularly uses distributed transactions, you should start DTC when the operating system starts.

Cross-Reference Chapter 15, "Working with Distributed Queries," explains dual-phase commitments and distributed transactions.

SQL Mail

The SQL Mail component enables SQL Server to send mail to an external mailbox through SMTP. Mail may be generated from multiple sources within SQL Server, including T-SQL code, jobs, alerts, Integration Services, and maintenance plans.

Cross-Reference Chapter 38, "Automating Database Maintenance with SQL Server Agent," explains how to set up a mail profile for SQL Server and how to send mail.

Business Intelligence Services

Business intelligence (BI) is one area where SQL Server 2005 excels. The growth of BI, and the growth of SQL Server within the BI field, has been phenomenal over the past few years. SQL Server 2005 includes three services designed for business intelligence: Integration Services (IS, sometimes called SSIS for SQL Server Integration Services), Reporting Services (RS), and Analysis Services (AS). All three services are developed using the BI Development Studio and are managed with Management Studio.

Integration Services

Integration Services moves data among nearly any types of data sources and is SQL Server's Extract-Transform-Load (ETL) tool. As shown in Figure 3-4, IS uses a graphical tool to define how data can be moved from one connection to another connection. IS packages have the flexibility to either copy data column for column or perform complex transformations, lookups, and exception handling during the data move. IS is extremely useful during data conversions, collecting data from many dissimilar data sources, or gathering for data warehousing data that can be analyzed using Analysis Services. It even includes tools for fuzzy data scrubbing and bad data collection.

New in 2005 Integration Services is not just an upgrade to SQL Server 2000 Data Transformation Services (DTS). Integration Services is a complete rewrite and truly an enterprise-grade ETL tool. Among the many excellent new features of SQL Server 2005, Integration Services is one of the shining stars.

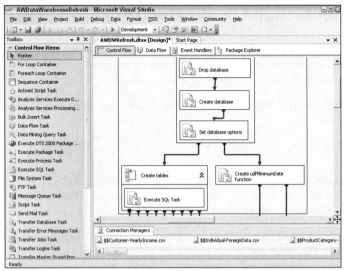

Figure 3-4: Integration Services graphically illustrates the data transformations within a planned data migration or conversion.

Integration Services is very cool. If you have experience with other databases, but are new to SQL Server, this is one of the tools that will most impress you. If any other company were marketing SSIS it would be the flagship product, but instead we find it bundled inside SQL Server without much fanfare and at no extra charge. Be sure to find the time to explore Integration Services.

Cross-Reference Chapter 42, "ETL with Integration Services," describes how to create and execute an SSIS package.

Reporting Services

Reporting Services (RS) for SQL Server 2005 is a full-featured, web-based, managed reporting solution. RS reports can be exported to PDF, Excel, or other formats with a single click, and are easy to build and customize.

Reports are defined graphically or programmatically and stored as .rd files in the Reporting Services databases in SQL Server. They can be scheduled to be pre-created and cached for users, e-mailed to users, or generated by users on-the-fly with parameters. Reporting Services is bundled with SQL Server so there are no end-user licensing issues. It's essentially free although most DBAs place it on its own dedicated server for better performance. If you're still using Crystal Reports, why?

New in 2005 Initially released as an add-on for SQL Server 2000, SQL Server 2005 adds a new web-based Report Builder, acquired from Active Views, which enables power users to build basic reports from preconfigured data models.

Cross-Reference Chapters 46 and 47 deal with authoring and deploying reports using Reporting Services.

Analysis Services

Analysis Services is the service within SQL Server that provides business intelligence or online analysis processing (OLAP). Essentially, Analysis Services enables the developer to define cubes that are similar to Excel pivot tables or Access crosstab queries, but with multiple dimensions. The cubes contain pre-calculated summary, or aggregate, data from very large databases. This enables the user to easily and quickly browse the cube's summarized totals and subtotals without having to query terabytes worth of data (see Figure 3-5).

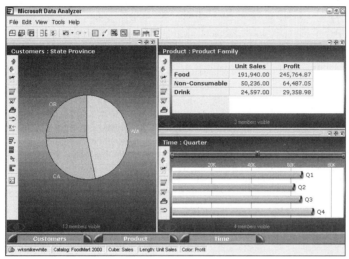

Figure 3-5: Browsing a multidimensional cube within Analysis Services is a fluid way to compare various aspects of the data.

Analysis Services is loaded separately from SQL Server and is considered a high-end data-warehousing feature.

Cross-Reference   Chapters 43, 44, and 45 cover designing cubes, data mining, and programming MDX queries with Analysis Services.

SQL Server 2005 Editions

SQL Server 2005 is available in several editions, which differ in terms of features, hardware, and cost. This section details the various editions and their respective features. Because Microsoft licensing and costs change, check with www.microsoft.com/sql or your Microsoft representative for license and cost specifics.

Cross-Reference   Besides the general descriptions here, Appendix A includes a chart detailing the differences between the multiple editions.

Note   It's easy to confuse *editions* with *versions*. SQL Server 7, SQL Server 2000, and SQL Server 2005 are versions. Editions are the various feature set packages, such as the Developer Edition or the Enterprise Edition, within the versions.

Enterprise (Developer) Edition

This is the high-end edition with the advanced performance and availability features required to support thousands of connections and databases measured by terabytes. To achieve this level of performance you'll want to run Enterprise Edition on a machine with plenty of horse-power — 16 dual-core CPUs, 32 GB of RAM, and a huge SAN sounds nice.

To take advantage of that hardware, Enterprise Edition adds several cool features. These two stand out as worth the cost:

✦ Table partitioning. This is the feature Microsoft exploits to get those amazing TCP benchmark results.

✦ Online, parallel indexing.

The Developer Edition is the same as the Enterprise Edition, with two exceptions. First, the Developer Edition is licensed only for development and testing, so it can't legally be used in a production environment. Second, the Developer Edition runs on workstation versions of Windows, such as Windows NT Workstation, Windows 2000 Professional, and Windows XP Professional. The Developer Edition is included with MSDN Universal or may be purchased separately. When purchased, it is the lowest-cost edition of SQL Server. The street price for Developer Edition is under $50.

Standard Edition

The majority of medium to large production database needs will be well served by the SQL Server 2005 Standard Edition, the workhorse edition of SQL Server. This edition includes all the right features, including Integration Services, Analysis Services, Web Services, database mirroring, and failover clustering.

Note   With multi-core CPUs becoming commonplace in servers, the question is, how does this affect licensing? The good news is that Microsoft is licensing SQL Server by the CPU socket, not the number of CPU cores. This means that a four-way server running dual-core CPUs will function almost as if the server had eight CPUs, but you're only paying for four CPUs' worth of SQL Server licensing.

Standard Edition is perfectly suited for medium-size businesses that need all the primary features and can live without the very high-end high availability features of Enterprise Edition. Although it's limited to four CPUs with multi-core CPUs, it is a lesser limitation than in the past and there's no limit to memory.

I've spoken with several DBAs whose companies have purchased Enterprise Edition, but they're running it on a four-way server with 4 GB of RAM and no clustering or any other high-end feature. Given the performance of today's servers, for most production environments, Standard Edition is the right choice. Don't blow your budget on Enterprise Edition unless you've proven that Standard Edition won't do the job.

With a well-designed four-way server running dual-core CPUs and plenty of RAM, Standard Edition can easily handle 500 concurrent users and a database pushing a terabyte of data.

Best Practice

Unless the advanced features of Enterprise Edition are in high demand, moving to the 64-bit version of Standard Edition and increasing memory is probably a better move than upgrading to Enterprise Edition. There are 64-bit versions of Standard and Enterprise Edition for Intel and AMD processors.

Workgroup Edition

Intended as a departmental database server, Workgroup Edition includes the right mix of features for a small transactional database:

✦ The workhouse database engine supports two CPU sockets, a max of 3 GB of RAM, with no limit on the database size.

✦ Some high-availability features such as log-shipping, but not database mirroring or failover clustering.

✦ Reporting Services, including Report Builder, but not Analysis Services for advanced cubes and BI analysis.

✦ All the programmability of SQL Server 2005, including T-SQL, stored procedures, user-defined functions, full text search, XML, Xquery, Service Broker (subscriber only), and .NET integration; but not web services or notification services.

✦ Admin automation with SQL Server Agent.

✦ Merge and Transactional Replication.

The key feature missing from Workgroup Edition is Integration Services, the rationale being that a workgroup database is likely the source of data that is integrated by other larger databases servers, but it does not pull data from other sources itself. This may be the single factor that drives you to move up to Standard Edition. In my experience, a database of this size does occasionally require moving data even if for an upgrade of an Access database.

I recommend Workgroup Edition for small businesses or departments that don't require extremely high availability or Analysis Services. A server with two dual-core CPUs, 3 GB of RAM, and a well-designed disk subsystem could easily serve 100 busy users with Workgroup Edition.

SQL Server Express Edition

SQL Server Express Edition is not simply a plug-in replacement for the Access Jet database engine. It's a full version of the SQL Server database engine intended to serve as an embedded database within an application. It's completely free — no up front cost, no royalties, no redistributable fees. It's included with MSDN Universal, Office Developer Edition 11, and all the Express development products.

New in 2005

SQL Server Express is the product replacement for MSDE, the free edition of SQL Server 2000. But don't think of SQL Express as MSDE 2005. The user limitation is gone. There's a real administrative user interface,

Express does have some limitations: a maximum database size limit of 4 GB, only one CPU socket (when will AMD ship a 16-core CPU?), and 1 GB of RAM. At this time, Reporting Services is not available with SQL Express, but Microsoft has committed to including RS with SQL Express in the future.

SQL Server Express has its own version of Management Studio and a command-line utility. Chapter 41, "Administering SQL Server Express," covers the specific differences and how to make the most of this edition.

I'd recommend SQL Server Express Edition for any small .NET application that needs a real database. It's more than suitable for applications with up to 25 users and less than 4 GB of data. When Reporting Services ships with Express it will be a MySQL killer for sure.

SQL Server Everywhere Edition

SQL Server /e, originally called Mobile Edition, is technically a different database engine that is fully compatible with SQL Server. Its small footprint of only 1MB of RAM means that it can actually run well on a mobile smart device. Even though it runs a handheld computer, it's a true ACID-compliant database engine.

Because the programmability feature set of SQL Server Everywhere is so different from the full server editions of SQL Server, Chapter 26, "Developing for SQL Server Everywhere," focuses on the specific requirements of developing and deploying a smart client implementation of SQL Server Everywhere.

SQL Server Tools and Components

The following components are client processes for SQL Server used to control, or communicate with, SQL Server.

SQL Server Management Studio

Management Studio is a Visual Studio–esque integrated environment that's used by database administrators and database developers. At its core is a powerful Object Explorer complete with filters and the capability to browse all the SQL Server servers (database engine, Analysis Services, Reporting Services, etc.). Its Query Editor is an excellent way to work with raw T-SQL code and it's integrated with the Solution Explorer to manage projects. Although the interface can look crowded (see Figure 3-6), the windows are easily configurable and can auto-hide.

Chapter 6, "Using Management Studio," discusses the many tools within Management Studio and how to use this flexible development and management interface.

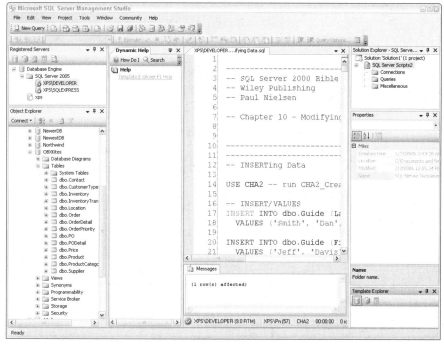

Figure 3-6: Management Studio's full array of windows and tools can seem overwhelming but it's flexible enough for you to configure it for your own purpose.

SQL Server Configuration Manager

This tool is used to start and stop any server, set the start-up options, and configure the connectivity, as shown in Figure 3-7. It may be launched from the Start menu or from Management Studio.

 New in 2005   The Configuration Manager replaces SQL Server 2000's system-tray–based Service Manager and is the network client configuration tool.

Surface Area Configuration Tool

By default, many SQL Server 2005 features are turned off to reduce the exposed surface of SQL Server. While most of these features can be turned on with T-SQL, the Surface Area Configuration tool is the easiest way to configure these features and components.

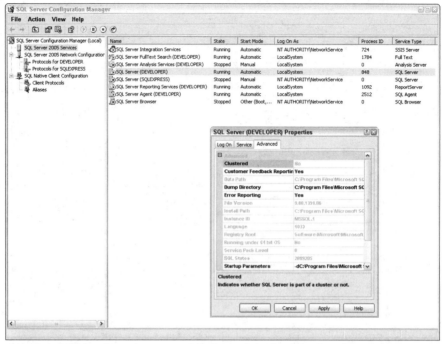

Figure 3-7: The Configuration Manager is the tool used to launch and control SQL Server's many servers.

Business Intelligence Development Studio

Similar to Management Studio, but optimized for BI, this tool is used for developing Integration Services packages, Reporting Services reports, and Analysis Services cubes and data mining.

SQL Integrated Help

The SQL Server documentation team did an excellent job with Books Online (BOL) — SQL Server's mega help on steroids. The articles tend to be complete and include several examples. The indexing method provides a short list of applicable articles. BOL may be opened from Management Studio or directly from the Start menu.

BOL is well integrated with the primary interfaces. Selecting a keyword within Management Studio's Query Editor and pressing Shift+F1 will launch BOL to the selected keyword. The Enterprise Manager help buttons will also launch the correct BOL topic.

Management Studio also includes a dynamic Help window that automatically tracks the cursor and presents help for the current keyword.

Searching returns both online and local MSDN articles. In addition, BOL searches the Codezone Community for relevant articles.

The Community Menu and Developer Center both launch web pages that enable users to ask a question or learn more about SQL Server.

 Microsoft regularly updates BOL. The new version can be downloaded from www.Microsoft.com/sql, and I posted a link to it on www.SQLServerBible.com.

SQL Profiler

SQL Profiler quietly watches SQL Server's traffic and events, recording the selected information to the screen, table, or file. Profiler is great for debugging an application or tuning the database. The Database Tuning Advisor can use the collected data to optimize the database.

Performance Monitor

While Profiler records large sets of details concerning SQL traffic and SQL Server events, Performance Monitor (or System Monitor) is a visual window into the current status of the selected performance counters. Performance Monitor is found within Windows's administrative tools. When SQL Server is installed, it adds the SQL Server counters within Performance Monitor, and SQL Server has a ton of useful performance counters. It's enough to make a network administrator jealous.

 Chapter 49, "Measuring Performance," covers SQL Profiler and Performance Monitor.

Database Tuning Advisor

The Database Tuning Advisor analyzes a batch of queries (from Profiler) and recommends index and partition modifications for performance. The scope of changes it can recommend is configurable and the changes may be applied in part or in whole, at the time of the analysis or later.

 Chapter 50, "Query Analysis and Index Tuning" covers the Database Tuning Advisor.

Command-Line Utilities: SQLCmd, Bulk Copy

These command-line interfaces enable the developer to execute SQL code or perform bulk-copy operations from the DOS prompt or a command-line scheduler. Integration Services and SQL Server Agent have rendered these tools somewhat obsolete, but in the spirit of extreme flexibility, Microsoft still includes them.

Management Studio has a SQLCmd mode that enables you to use the Query Editor as if it were the command-line utility.

SQL Server 2005 Feature Pack

This download includes a couple dozen drivers and code pieces for backward compatibility and compatibility with other systems as well as these other useful tools and utilities:

✦ **SQL Server Upgrade Advisor:** This free downloadable tool analyzes SQL Server 7 or SQL Server 2000 databases and presents a complete report of every issue you should address before or after migrating the database to SQL Server 2005.

✦ **Database Migration Assistant (DMA):** The DMA is more than just a tool; it analyzes the existing database and then makes recommendations about how to migrate, presenting the risks. Currently, DMA only migrates from Oracle to SQL Server, but future DMAs will migrate from other platforms, possibly MySQL and MS Access.

✦ **Best Practices Tool:** The Best Practices Tool analyzes your SQL Server configuration and databases and reports any violations of known best practices. The best practice rules are dynamic, so Microsoft can add to the tool to improve its effectiveness over time.

Note   Microsoft continues to release additional resources, tools, and aids for making SQL Server administration and development more productive. These free utilities are downloadable from `www.Microsoft.com/sql`. AdventureWorks installs with SQL Server, but not by default.

AdventureWorks

AdventureWorks is Microsoft's sample database for SQL Server 2005, replacing Northwind and Pubs. While AdventureWorks has the advantage of being a larger database than the small Northwind and tiny Pubs, it suffers from an overly complex schema and has been met with mixed reviews from the SQL Server training community, earning it the nickname of "AdventureWorst."

On The Web   You can download the scripts to create Northwind and Pubs on SQL Server 2005 from `www.microsoft.com/downloads/details.aspx?familyid=06616212-0356-46a0-8da2-eebc53a68034&displaylang=en`. The specific link is also on `www.SQLServerBible.com`.

In the BI arena, AdventureWorksDW replaces the FoodMart sample and has been well received by the BI community.

Exploring the Metadata

When SQL Server is initially installed, it already contains several system and user objects. Four system databases are used by SQL Server for self-management, two sample user databases are available for experimentation, and every database includes several system objects, including tables, views, stored procedures, and functions.

Within Enterprise Manager, the system objects might be hidden. In the Registered SQL Server Properties page, you can choose what to display using the "Show system database and system objects" option.

System Databases

SQL Server uses four system databases to store system information, track operations, and provide a temporary work area. In addition, the model database is a template for new user databases. These five system databases are as follows:

✦ **Master:** Contains information about the server's databases. In addition, objects in Master are available to other databases. For example, stored procedures in Master may be called from a user database.

✦ **MSDB:** Maintains lists of activities, such as backups and jobs, and tracks which database backup goes with which user database

✦ **Model:** The template database from which new databases are created. Any object placed in the Model database will be copied into any new database.

✦ **Tempdb:** Used for ad hoc tables by all users, batches, stored procedures (including Microsoft stored procedures), and the SQL Server engine itself. If SQL Server needs to create temporary heaps or lists during query execution, it creates them in Tempdb. Tempdb is completely cleared when SQL Server is restarted.

✦ **Reference:** This hidden database is a split off from the Master database, located in the same directory as Master. It serves to make service pack upgrading easier.

Metadata Views

Metadata is data about data. One of Codd's original rules for relational databases is that information about the database schema must be stored in the database using tables, rows, and columns, just like user data. It is this data about the data that makes it easy to write code to navigate and explore the database schema and configuration. SQL Server 2005 has four types of metadata: catalog views, dynamic management views, and system table views:

New in 2005

The metadata features of SQL Server have been completely overhauled and expose significantly more information than previous versions.

✦ **Catalog views** provide information about static metadata — things such as tables, security, and server configuration.

✦ **Dynamic management views (DMVs)** and **functions** yield insight into the current state of the server this millisecond and provide data about things such as memory, threads, stored procedures in cache, and connections.

✦ **Compatibility views** serve as backward compatibility views to simulate the system tables in previous versions of SQL Server.

✦ **Information schema views** are the ANSI SQL 92 standard nonproprietary views used to examine the schema of any database product. The goal of portable database systems is becoming a lost cause and these views are of little practical use for any DBA or database developer who exploits the features of SQL Server.

Summary

SQL Server is indeed a large and complex product that serves the needs of transactional and business intelligence databases. This chapter provided the foundation that's needed for a solid understanding of the big picture concerning SQL Server before diving into its details.

From here, the next few chapters install and configure SQL Server, connect from client applications, and explore Management Studio, the common UI for both SQL Server administrators and database developers.

✦   ✦   ✦

Installing SQL Server 2005

While the actual act of installing SQL Server is relatively easy, knowing the intended users, environment, and uses that the database must meet may not be quite so clear. Additional time spent identifying and answering these and other questions about the environment and use will pay off with a smoother installation.

Although this chapter focuses on the aspects of installing a new SQL Server, some information will be provided on upgrading to SQL Server.

 **New in 2005**   SQL Server 2005 can be used alongside existing SQL Server installations.

Planning Your Installation

Give some thought to the server's hardware. Consider user accounts, including SQL Server's disk configuration, collations, and client access. If a server is being upgraded, take advantage of the Upgrade Advisor Tool, discussed later in this chapter.

Operating System

SQL Server 2005 installs and runs on various operating systems — from Windows XP Home to Windows Server 2003 Enterprise Edition, with the more feature-rich versions running on the higher-end operating systems. Table 4-1 illustrates which editions of SQL Server are compatible with which operating systems.

Security Accounts

Accessing SQL Server requires that a user have an appropriate account for authentication. With Windows Authentication, the SQL Server verifies a user with information from the Windows operating system. The User Management features of Windows provide the capability to enforce access and policies for the users. Alternately, SQL Server can provide the authentication. Whenever possible, use Windows Authentication to control access to the SQL Server.

Table 4-1: Operating System Editions Supported by SQL Server 2005

SQL Server Edition	Windows XP Home Edition (SP 2+)	Windows Server 2003 Web Edition	Windows 2000 Professional (SP 4+)	Windows XP Tablet Edition (SP 2+)	Windows XP Media Edition (SP 2+)	Windows XP Professional (SP 2+)	Windows 2000 Server, Advanced and Datacenter Server (SP 4+)	Windows Small Business Server 2003 Standard and Premium Editions	Windows Server 2003 Standard, Enterprise and Datacenter Editions (SP 1+)
Enterprise / Standard Edition							yes	yes	yes
Workgroup / Evaluation Edition			yes	yes	yes	yes	yes	yes	yes
Developer / Express Edition	yes	yes	yes	yes	yes	yes	yes	yes	yes

Windows Authentication enables user database access to be validated against Windows user management (e.g., logins). This provides a central location to enable, disable, and apply specific security settings related to user logins. These settings would automatically apply to the user account for logging into the database. If an employee leaves the organization, simply disabling the user account also removes access to the database.

Best Practice

Microsoft recommends the use of Windows Authentication for user validation whenever possible.

SQL Server component processes also require Windows login accounts. These can be specified independently during installation by selecting the "Customize for each service account" option. By default, SQL Server, SQL Server Agent, Analysis Server, and SQL Browser share the same login account. Ensure that the assigned Windows login account for each service has the appropriate file and resource permissions. The login account and service relationship is listed in Table 4-2.

Table 4-2: Startup Accounts for SQL Server Services

SQL Server Service Name	Default Account	Optional Accounts
SQL Server	SQL Express on Windows 2000–local system SQL Express on all other operating systems–local service All other editions on all operating systems–domain user	SQL Express–domain user, local system, network service, local service All other editions–domain user, local system, network service
SQL Server Agent	Domain user	Domain user, local system, network service, local service
Analysis Services	Domain user	Domain user, local system, network service, local service
Reporting Services	Domain user	Domain user, local system, network service, local service
Notification Services	N/A	N/A
Integration Services	Windows 2000–local system All other operating systems–network service	Domain user, local system, network service, local service

Continued

Table 4-2 *(continued)*

SQL Server Service Name	Default Account	Optional Accounts
Full Text Search	Same as SQL Server	Domain user, local system, network service, local service
SQL Browser	Domain user	Domain user, local system, network service, local service
SQL Server Active Directory Helper	Network service	Local system, Network service
SQL Writer	Local system	Local system

Note   Creating a specific Windows user account for SQL Server services provides better security and reliability, as the minimal set of permissions can be applied and password resets for users would not impact the service's ability to log in.

If the installation will include servers that will communicate and perform distributed queries or replication, then the login account must be a domain-level account. The domain account must be a member of the Windows Administrators group.

Authentication Mode

SQL Server utilizes two authentication modes for users: SQL Server accounts and Windows accounts. For SQL Server to authenticate, accounts may be created and managed within SQL Server. These accounts are valid only for access to SQL Server and provide no network access. Windows-based accounts are created for access to the network and may be used to provide access to SQL Server. Enabling both methods to access SQL Server is called *mixed mode*. Table 4-3 summarizes the two authentication modes.

Table 4-3: Security-Authentication Modes

Login Method	Windows Authentication Mode	Mixed Mode
Users may authenticate using their Windows User logon	Yes	Yes
SQL Server–specific accounts	No	Yes

When enabling mixed mode, assign a strong password to the administrative account. A strong password typically consists of mixed uppercase and lowercase characters, numeric values, and symbolic values. Leaving the password blank creates a significant security hole.

Cross-Reference   Securing databases is discussed in more detail in Chapter 40, "Securing Databases."

Server Instances

SQL Server 2005 supports up to 50 instances of SQL Server running on the same physical server, including instances of different editions (Enterprise, Standard, or Developer). Multiple instances provide the best value when applied within server-constrained environments and for testing purposes such as compatibility, service pack impacts, replication assessment, and so on. To optimize server performance, start only the necessary instances of SQL Server when testing. Stop the instances once testing is complete. Using multiple instances within a production environment is not recommended due to server performance and availability considerations.

Caution   Using multiple instances of SQL Server to provide multiple databases on the same server negatively affects performance. Each instance requires its own resources as well as CPU cycles to handle requests. While using a hyperthreaded or multi-core processor could mitigate the performance issues to an extent, using a single SQL Server to handle multiple databases is the best solution.

The default location for SQL Server and associated files is as follows:

```
C:\Program Files\Microsoft SQL Server\MSSQL.#
```

The # is the next number in the sequence. SQL Server will take the next available number, with Analysis Server taking the following number. Therefore, if both SQL Server and Analysis Server are installed, the directory structure would look like this:

```
C:\Program Files\Microsoft SQL Server\MSSQL.1   (SQL Server)
C:\Program Files\Microsoft SQL Server\MSSQL.2   (Analysis Server)
```

If just one were installed, it would take the next number in the sequence.

The first installed SQL Server becomes the default instance and has the same name as the server. Each additional instance will be installed as a uniquely named instance, with up to a 16-character name.

Not all installed services are shared among the multiple instances. Table 4-4 shows a list of shared versus instance services. Instance-specific services will have their own installed components.

Table 4-4: Shared SQL Services

Service	Shared	Instance Specific?
Notification Services	Yes	
Data Transformation Services (DTS)	Yes	
SQL Browser	Yes	
SQL Server Active Directory Helper	Yes	
SQL Writer	Yes	
SQL Server		Yes
SQL Server Agent		Yes
Analysis Server		Yes
Report Server		Yes
Full-Text Search		Yes

Hardware Recommendations

The value per dollar for hardware has improved significantly and continues to do so. Overall, hardware is no longer a limiting factor, but wise choices can still improve efficiency. This section provides some design guidelines for planning a server.

Dedicated Server

SQL Server 2005 dynamically manages memory based on its current needs as well as the needs of the operating system and other applications. As other applications are started and consume memory, SQL Server may not have enough memory to perform requested queries from potentially large groups of users, ultimately failing to complete the requests in a timely fashion.

Considering the nearly 24/7 access that databases are meant to provide, it becomes evident that overloading a SQL Server with too many co-resident applications will have a negative impact on performance. Additionally, the more applications running on a server, the higher the risk that an software upgrade or service pack may have side effects that further negatively affect SQL Server performance and reliability.

Having a dedicated SQL Server can mitigate these issues; and in appropriate cases, multiple dedicated servers may be appropriate.

Copious Memory

SQL Server 2005 dynamically acquires and frees memory when needed, continually balancing the memory allocation pool it uses for processing. It is capable of reserving or freeing several megabytes of memory each second.

Standard, Workgroup, Express, and Evaluation editions of SQL Server 2005 still make use of available memory up to the 4 GB limit. Enterprise and Developer editions can utilize more memory through the Address Windowing Extensions (AWE).

Enterprise and Developer editions of SQL Server 2005 can utilize AWE in the following 32-bit operating systems: Windows XP Professional; Windows 2000 Standard Edition; Windows 2000 Advanced Server; Windows 2000 Datacenter Server; Windows Server 2003 Enterprise Edition; and Windows Server 2003 Datacenter Edition.

If the Enterprise or Developer Editions meet the defined business and application needs, then having memory in excess of 4 GB will prove beneficial, as the buffer pool may reside in the AWE-mapped memory space, thus freeing up the lower memory ranges for use. Otherwise, having over 4 GB of memory will not improve SQL Server performance, although still having as much as possible up to 4 GB will improve overall server performance.

Note   To enable AWE, SQL Server 2005 must run under an account that has the Lock Pages in Memory option turned on and the Awe Enabled option set to 1 using `sp_configure`.

Using Multiple CPUs

Traditionally, licensing costs of multi-processor servers have been on a per-socket basis, thus costing several thousands of dollars. Advancements in processor technology such as hyper-threading and multi-core processors provide significant gains in single CPU package servers that perform like single-core multi-package processors.

Intel introduced hyperthreading processor technology in 2002. This technology enables processors to execute multiple threads on a single-core processor while sharing execution resources. Multi-threaded software, such as SQL Server, can execute threads in parallel on a hyperthreaded processor with faster response times. To the operating system, a hyperthreaded processor appears as two processors per physical socket.

Note

While Intel has squeezed performance from a single processor with the introduction of hyperthreading, AMD has taken the route of reducing latency and increasing speed with the introduction of its HyperTransport technology. This technology reduces latency and increases speed of communication between integrated circuits in computers and other electronic devices, including computer peripherals. The HyperTransport technology provides adopters with an aggregate bandwidth of 22.4 GB/sec, representing a 70-fold increase in throughput over legacy PCI buses. While HyperTransport technology is not purely a CPU-based technology, the performance gains deserve mention. CPUs and systems based on this technology experience increased performance on the shear volume of data throughput, and this technology is now supported within AMDs processor lines such as the Opteron, the Athlon 64 /FX processor, dual-core processors, and Semprons.

Both AMD and Intel have released dual-core processors as a first step in multi-core technology. Dual-core processors contain two execution cores within the same physical package. With supporting software, fully parallel execution can occur, as the operating system perceives each core as a distinct processor with its own execution resources. SQL Server licensing continues to be per socket, with Microsoft's view of the multi-core and hyperthreaded processors as a single-socket processor. Therefore, if SQL Server runs on a single processor, then licensing is for one processor; but if the same server were running a four-core or hyperthreaded processor, licensing would still be required for one socket because of the physical packaging. The advantages of multi-core and hyperthreaded processors include not only speed and multi-threading, but also reduced licensing costs, providing substantial savings.

Best Practice

When comparing specs for a new server or upgrading the processor(s), look at either a hyperthreaded processor or a multi-core processor, as the performance gains outweigh single-processor packages for the same SQL Server licensing cost. Give preference to a multi-core processor, as each core has its own execution resources, in contrast to a hyperthreaded processor, which shares the execution resources.

Disk-Drive Subsystems

Small computer system interface (SCSI) devices still dominate the high-end of disk drive services based on throughput. A server that needs to meet high data demands should be based on a SCSI drive. If the server is low throughput with no anticipated growth, a Serial Advanced Technology Attachment (SATA) drive could meet the need. Anticipating the intended use and growth will direct what option should be taken with regard to types of disk drives. Additionally, a variety of manufacturers now provide integrated RAID capability on the motherboards that also support SATA drives.

RAID Disk Subsystems

RAID stands for Redundant Array of Independent/Inexpensive Disks. It is a category of disk drives that utilizes two or more drives in combination for increased performance and fault tolerance. RAID applications will typically be found in high-performance disk systems utilized by servers to improve the persistence and availability of data. Table 4-5 describes the various levels of RAID.

Table 4-5: RAID Levels

RAID Level	Redundancy Percentage	Description
0	0%	*Data striping* — Data is spread out across multiple drives, speeding up data writes and reads. No parity, redundancy or fault tolerance is available.
1	50%	*Data mirroring* — Data is written to two drives and read from either drive, providing better fault tolerance
5	Depends on number of drives (if five drives and last is for parity, then 20%)	Data striping with a parity bit written to one of the drives. Because of the parity bit, any single drive can fail and the disk subsystem can still function. When the failed disk drive is replaced, the disk subsystem can recreate the data on the failed drive it contained. RAID 5 is popular because it offers excellent protection and good speed at the lowest cost.
0+1	50%	*Mirrored striped drives* — Offer the speed of data striping and the protection of data mirroring. This is the most expensive option.

Caution   While software options are available to provide behavior similar to RAID, they are not as efficient as utilizing RAID-specific hardware solutions. The software solutions tie up CPU cycles to perform the RAID activities that could be used for server processing.

Network Performance

Typical motherboards today include built-in network interface cards (NICs) capable of auto switching between 10/100/1000 Mbps. As with any built-in device, these tend to utilize the CPU for required processing, which will affect performance. A variety of manufacturers today offer NIC cards that include onboard possessing, freeing up the tasks from the CPU. This improves overall network and server performance.

Performing the Installation

Once the installation plan has been created and the server is set up to meet the SQL Server requirements, it is time to install the software.

Attended Installations

The SQL Server installation program should automatically launch when the DVD is inserted. If not, browse to the DVD and execute the Setup.exe program.

Note   Antivirus software may initially block execution of the `Splash.hta` file. Allowing this file to run once will continue the setup. If the antivirus software does not allow that option, then disable it for the beginning of the installation.

SQL Server Component Update will install software components required for the SQL Server install to proceed. These components include Windows Installer 2.0, the .NET Framework 2.0, and additional SQL Server setup support files.

System Configuration Check will display the attention status for the requirements, as shown in Figure 4-1. Three status modes are possible: Success, Warning, or Error. Select Report ⇨ View Report to get additional details on errors and warnings.

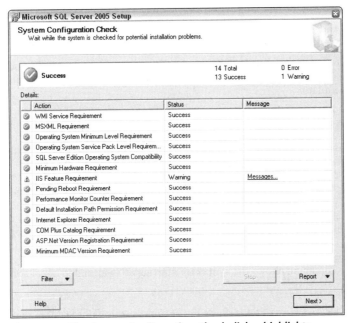

Figure 4-1: The System Configuration Check dialog highlights requirements issues.

To perform an attended installation, execute the following steps:

1. Select the components to install. The Typical, Minimum, and Custom install options found in SQL Server 2000 are not present in the 2005 install. Specific components must be selected. If changes to the subcomponents or program installation path must be made, then the Advanced button provides access to those features.

   During nonclustered installations of SQL Server, the Install as Virtual Server option will be disabled for both the SQL Server Database Services and the Analysis Services. These become available options when installing into a clustered environment.

2. Provide the instance name. If additional servers are being installed, then provide a named instance upon install; otherwise, allowing the default instance to be installed works fine. Click the Installed Instances button to see installed SQL Servers.

3. Choose the Service Account settings. A domain or local system account can be applied either to all services being installed or customized to each selected service.

Note If selecting a local system account for the services, ensure that the account has appropriate privileges.

4. Select the Authentication Mode. When specifying mixed mode, the sa logon password must also be specified. Do not leave this password blank, as that posses a significant security risk.

5. Specify Collation settings and select the desired settings. The selection may be applied to both the SQL Server and Analysis Server or each may be specified independently.

6. Select the Error and Usage Report settings. Checking these boxes allows opting-in to submitting error reports and feature usage data to Microsoft.

7. Click the Install button to begin installation of SQL Server 2005. Any issues that occur during setup will be logged to the installation log files and can be viewed when the installation is complete.

Unattended Installations

SQL Server 2005 continues its tradition of offering the capability to perform an unattended installation based on an .ini configuration file. A well-commented sample .ini file, template.ini, can be found at the root of the SQL Server installation CD. This file contains the [Options] section, which must be customized for the type of installation to perform.

Caution The clear text installation .ini file does not provide any security for logins and passwords that are embedded. Take appropriate measures to restrict access to this file if it contains logins and passwords.

The following example command shows the syntax for starting an unattended installation:

```
setup.exe  /settings  <full path to .ini file>
```

For example, to install an .ini file named mySQLSettings.ini located in a SQLTemp folder, the following command would be executed:

```
Setup.exe  /settings  c:\SQLTemp\mySQLSettings.ini
```

The following command-line switches affect the installation behavior:

✦ /qn performs a silent installation with no dialog boxes

✦ /qb displays only progress dialog boxes.

Once an installation configuration file has been created, it can be used for either an unattended installation or even a remote installation.

Remote Installations

SQL Server 2005 may be installed on a remote network computer. A remote installation could use the same configuration .ini file that an unattended install uses. Three additional values must be present in the remote configuration .ini file, as described in Table 4-6.

Table 4-6: Remote Install Required .ini Options

Option	Description
TargetComputer	The network computer name on which SQL Server will be installed
AdminAccount	The admin user account of the target server where SQL Server will be installed
AdminPassword	The password for the admin user account of the target server

Note   Remote installation can be performed only in a domain environment and not on a workgroup computer.

Installing in a Clustered Environment

When installing SQL Server 2005 within a clustered environment, select the Install as a Virtual Server check box on the Components to Install dialog for either the SQL or Analysis Servers. These options become enabled within a clustered environment only. The install wizard will prompt for additional configuration information related to the install cluster.

Note   SQL Server 2005 may be installed on up to eight cluster nodes.

Ensure that the specified installation account has Administrative rights and that a domain account for the SQL Server services is specified.

Installing Multiple Instances

SQL Server 2005 permits up to 16 instances of SQL Server running on a single physical server. Multiple instances may be useful when third-party vendors insist on differing levels of services packs or for server-level security.

To install additional instances, simply rerun the setup program. Instead of installing the default instance, in the dialog page that asks for the server name, deselect the default instance check box and enter the instance name. There is a cost to running multiple instances; each instance of SQL Server requires its own memory footprint and must compete for resources with the other instances.

Testing the Installation

The best way to test the installation is to connect to the SQL Server instance using SQL Server Management Studio and browse the databases.

If the SQL Server will be accessed programmatically, then additional steps apply. If connecting through ADO.NET, then create a project that imports the `System.Data.SqlClient` namespace and write the appropriate test code for the connection and a sample result set. If the new SQL Native Client must be used for connecting, then install the client DLLs with the `sqlncli.msi` file included on the SQL Server install CD. Once installed, create a Visual Studio project and write the appropriate test code.

Cross-Reference   SQL Native Client (SNAC) is discussed in more detail in Chapter 5, "Client Software Connectivity."

Upgrading from Previous Versions

SQL Server 2005 includes upgrade support for SQL Server 7 and 2000. SQL Server versions 6.5 and earlier do not have upgrade support. They must first be upgraded to SQL Server 2000 and then upgraded to SQL Server 2005. Prior to any upgrade, run the Upgrade Advisor to determine any effects the upgrade may have.

SQL Server 2005 Upgrade Advisor Tool

The SQL Server 2005 Upgrade Advisor Tool examines existing installations of SQL Server 7.0 and SQL Server 2000 for issues that can prevent a smooth upgrade. This includes the Database Engine, Analysis Services, Notification Services, Reporting Services and DTS. Additional information about the Upgrade Advisor and upgrade issues can be accessed from links on the tool's main page. Table 4-7 lists the system requirements for the Upgrade Advisor.

Note   The Upgrade Advisor can be found on the SQL Server installation DVD and installed independently of SQL Server 2005.

Table 4-7: Upgrade Advisor Prerequisites

Prerequisites
Windows 2000 SP4+, Windows XP SP2+ or Windows Server 2003 SP1+
Windows Installer 3.1+
.NET Framework 2.0, included on the SQL Server 2005 media
SQL Server 2000 decision support objects (DSO) for scanning Analysis Services
SQL Server 2000 Client components for scanning DTS packages

The Upgrade Advisor consists of two components: the Analysis Wizard and the Report Viewer. Launch the Analysis Wizard to begin analysis of existing SQL Server installations. Local and remote servers can be configured to auto-detect the server's components. Analysis of one, several, or all of the databases and DTS packages can be performed. Figure 4-2 shows the Upgrade Advisor Progress dialog once the analysis begins.

Caution   The Upgrade Advisor overwrites any prior analysis files for a given server when executed again. If the analysis files must be kept, move them to another location or rename them.

Errors reported by the Upgrade Advisor should be addressed. Launch the Report Viewer to see additional details on the analysis. These details will include when the issue needs to be fixed as well as provide more information on the issue and how to resolve it, as shown in Figure 4-3.

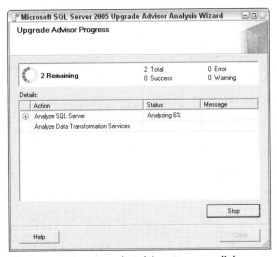

Figure 4-2: The Upgrade Advisor Progress dialog

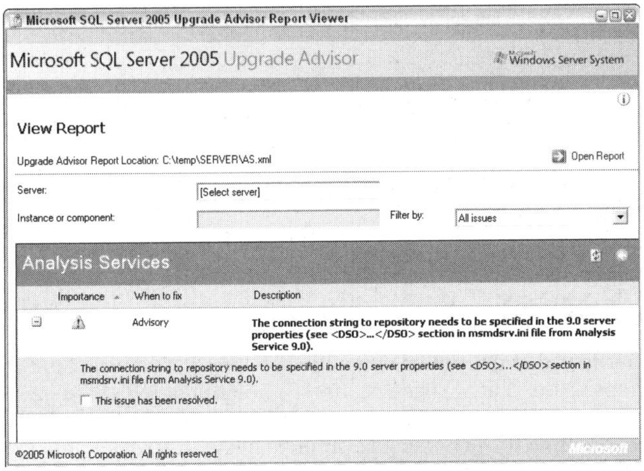

Figure 4-3: The Upgrade Advisor View Report

Several parameters enable refining the list of errors displayed. The server, instance, or component and status of the issues can be selected. The report also supports tracking for resolved issues. Once the issue has been resolved, simply check the "This issue has been resolved" check box.

The report can also be exported to a comma-separated data file by clicking the Export Report link.

Upgrading from SQL Server 2000

The Database Engine, Migration Analysis Services, Reporting Services, Notification Services and Data Transformation Services may all be upgraded to SQL Server 2005. While some of these components may co-reside, others may not. Table 4-8 illustrates how the components may be installed.

Table 4-8: Component Upgrade Types

Server Component	Side-by-Side		Upgraded Migration Required	
Database Engine	Yes	Yes	No	
Migration Analysis Services	Yes	Yes	Yes	
Reporting Services	No	Yes[1]	Yes[2]	
Notification Services	No	No	Yes[3]	
Data Transformation Services		Yes	Yes	Yes

[1] The upgrade is transparent when on a default installation with no modifications.

[2] When installing to a modified/non-default installation. Otherwise, migration is not required.

[3] Migration occurs after the 2005 Database Engine and Notification Services have been installed.

If access to SQL Server 2000 components and data is required, then installing SQL Server 2005 side-by-side with the 2000 installation is the way to go.

Caution   When upgrading SQL 2000 servers, upgrade the client and target database servers first to ensure minimal data failures of the primary servers.

Migrating to SQL Server

During the data life cycle there are distinct points when the conversion to a new database proves beneficial and provides value. During these nexuses, a determination of the new database's features, requirements, value, and business needs must be made. Should enough evidence support the migration, then time-consuming projects begin to translate the data, schemas, and business logic to the new database. Aware of the time and cost inherent in these activities, Microsoft has provided the SQL Server Migration Assistant (SSMA), coinciding with the release of SQL Server 2005, to aid in migrations from alternative databases.

Migration Assistant

The initial release of SSMA includes support for migrating from Oracle to SQL Server 2000. Future releases will continue to expand on the supported databases and conversion.

SSMA provides a significant step forward in determining the complexity of a database project at a fraction of the cost and time associated with traditional determination means. Schema, data, constraint, migration, and validation can be accomplished through the new IDE.

All migrations go through the following phases: assessment, schema conversion, data migration, business logic conversion, validation, integration, and performance analysis.

Assessment

SSMA provides an assessment that includes an estimate on labor required and provides information on what can be migrated automatically versus manually. Approximately 100 statistics are provided to characterize the database and offer insight into the complexity. SSMA also provides an estimate on the hours required to manually accomplish the conversion tasks.

Note   While SSMA provides faster insight into the complexity of the database, it will still take time to identify the complexity of client software at the application and middle-tier levels.

Schema Conversion

Once it's connected to a source Oracle and target SQL database, the IDE displays the various attributes and objects of the databases. The source PL/SQL can be viewed along with the converted T-SQL for comparison. The IDE supports direct editing of the displayed SQL.

Oracle system functions that do not have a counterpart in SQL will be supported through the use of additional UDFs and stored procedures. Constraints, views, and indexes will all convert to their corresponding entities on SQL Server, with data types mapping as illustrated in Table 4-9.

Table 4-9: PL/SQL to T-SQL Data Type Mapping

PL/SQL	T-SQL
Varchar2	Varchar
Char	Char
Number	Numeric
Date	Datetime
Long	Text
Nvarchar2	Nvarchar
Boolean	smallint

Data Migration

The Oracle schema can be automatically converted to the SQL Server schema, and all specified data migrated to the SQL Server database. During migration, the administrator must be aware of possible constraints, triggers and other dependencies that could prevent the record insertions, on a per-table basis, from completing.

Business Logic Conversion

Table 4-10 illustrates the conversions that take place from PL/SQL to SQL Server.

Table 4-10: PL/SQL to T-SQL Conversions

PL/SQL	T-SQL
Outer (+) joins	ANSI-standard outer joins
Hints	Supported hints include First_Rows, Index, Append, Merge_Aj, Merge_Sj, Merge
	Unsupported hints will be ignored.
Boolean	smallint
String parameters with unspecified length	Varchar(8000)
Numeric parameters with unspecified length and precision	Numeric(38,10)
Functions	User-defined functions (UDFs)

Triggers
  Before
  After
  Row-level
  Multiple
	Triggers
	  Instead Of
	  After
	  Emulated using cursors
	  Combined into one

Package functions	UDFs using PackageName_FunctionName convention
Package procedures	Stored procedures using PackageName_ProcedureName convention
Package variables	Emulated with a table and support functions
System functions	System functions or UDFs
If-Elsif. . .Elsif-Else-End	Nested IF statements
NULL	SYSDB.SYS.DB_NULL_STATEMENT
Case	Case
Goto	Goto
Loop with Exit or Exit When	While (1=1) with a Break
While	While
For	While

Cursors
  With parameters
  FOR loop
  Close cursor_name
	Cursors
	  Multiple cursors
	  Cursor with local variables
	  Close cursor_name and
	  Deallocate cursor_name

Return	Return
Comments	Comments

PL/SQL	T-SQL

Variables
  Static
  with %Type
  with %Rowtype
	Variable
	  Resolved at conversion time
	  Group of local variables
	  Group of local variables

Procedure calls	Procedure calls
Function calls	Function calls
Begin Tran Commit Rollback	Begin Tran Commit Rollback
SavePoint	Save Transaction
Exceptions	Emulated in T-SQL

Note   Transactions in SQL Server can be implicit by using SET IMPLICIT_TRANSACTIONS ON, or explicit by using Begin Tran and Commit Tran.

Note   If exceptions are disabled on the target SQL Server, then no exception handling will occur. If exception handling is enabled, then exceptions are converted using IF/GOTO statements and UDFs.

Validation and Integration

The IDE provides a view of the SQL, similar to a code differences tool in which the source and newer versions of code are displayed and support the ability to modify, accept, and/or discard the proposed changes. Additional synchronization options include being able to overwrite the database objects with the current workspace objects, overwrite the workspace objects from the database, and merge objects.

Configuring the Surface Area of SQL Server

Surface area describes the security vulnerability for a given piece of software. The more ways there are to attack the software through services, ports, APIs, scripts, messages, and so on, the larger the surface area and the larger the security risk. By reducing the surface area of an application, the risk is reduced.

Reducing an application's surface area involves identifying and stopping or disabling the unused components, features, and so on. To further this goal with SQL Server 2005, Microsoft has provided the SQL Server Surface Area Configuration Tool to aid in providing more secure installations.

Surface Area Configuration Tool

SQL Server 2005 is "secure by default" and most services are *disabled by default*. The primary configurable surface areas include the Database Engine, Analysis Services, and Reporting Services. The Database Engine and Analysis Services allow for deeper configuration of the services, remote connections, and features.

Once the installation of SQL Server 2005 is complete, run the SQL Server Surface Area Configuration Tool. If upgrading from SQL Server 2000, then the services running in 2000 will be running in 2005. To access the tool, select Microsoft SQL Server 2005 ⇨ Configuration Tools ⇨ SQL Server Configuration Manager.

The initial screen offers some information about the tool and provides a means to configure the services and connections as well as the features of the specified server, local or remote. Figure 4-4 shows the initial form. The server may be changed by selecting the Server Name link located above the configuration options.

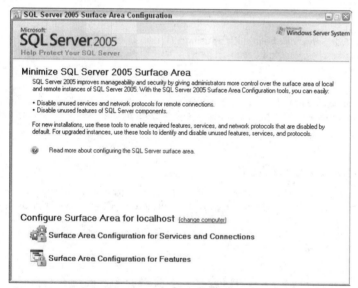

Figure 4-4: The SQL Server 2005 Surface Area Configuration utility provides a means to set up the services, connections, and features of SQL Server 2005.

After looking this utility over, begin configuration of the server by clicking the Services and Connections link for the server.

Surface Area Configuration for Services and Connections

The Services and Connections utility provides one-stop access to the SQL Server services. As shown in Figure 4-5, the various services can be started, stopped, paused, and resumed from this dialog. Additionally, the network connections and the protocols can be specified from this dialog, allowing either local only or remote connections.

Figure 4-5: The Services and Connections configuration utility. Configure the server's connections, service status, and startup type from here.

Table 4-11 shows what services can be configured, depending on what version of SQL Server you installed.

Table 4-11: Service Configurability

Service	Services and Connections	Features
Database Engine	yes	yes
Analysis Services	yes	yes
Reporting Services	yes	yes
Integration Services	yes	
Notification Services	yes	
SQL Server Agent	yes	
Full-text Search	yes	
SQL Server Browser	yes	

Surface Area Configuration for Features

The Surface Area Configuration for Features utility provides management of additional features for the Database Engine, Analysis Services, and Reporting Services.

Database Engine

Configurable features of the Database Engine include the following:

✦ Ad hoc remote queries using OPENROWSET and OPENDATASOURCE. **This feature is disabled by default.**

✦ CLR integration allowing the use of .NET-managed code for stored procedures, triggers, user-defined functions, and types. This feature is disabled by default.

✦ The DAC or dedicated administration connection, a high priority dedicated connection to SQL Server so an administrator can perform diagnostics.

✦ Database mail replaces the deprecated SQL Mail as the mechanism for sending e-mail.

✦ Native XML Web Services allows access to the Database Engine over HTTP using SOAP messages. This feature is disabled by default.

✦ OLE Automation.

✦ Service Broker provides a new queuing mechanism in SQL Server to send messages to other applications or components.

✦ SQL Mail is now deprecated.

✦ Web Assistant consisted of stored procedures that generated HTML. Now deprecated in 2005.

✦ xp_cmdshell to run commands within the operating system. This feature is disabled by default.

Analysis Services

Configurable features of this feature include the following:

✦ Ad hoc data mining queries allow the use of external data sources.

✦ Anonymous connections allow unauthenticated users to connect.

✦ Linked objects allow linking dimensions and measure between instances. This features is disabled by default.

✦ User-defined functions. This feature is disabled by default.

Reporting Services

Configurable features of this feature include the following:

✦ Scheduled events and report delivery provide a service to push reports out. If no subscription functionality is needed, then this feature can be disabled and the reports can be issued on demand.

✦ Web Services and HTTP is used by Reporting Services to deliver reports.

Tip These features are also accessible through the sp_configure stored procedure.

Figure 4-6 shows a sample of the Configuration for Features utility.

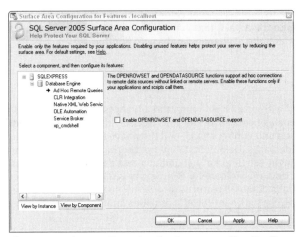

Figure 4-6: The Configuration for Features utility. Configure the various services features from here.

Note   Within the SQL Server Surface Area Configuration Tool, Integration services and SQL Server Browser are not instance aware and keep their own settings.

To improve security, disable features, services, and connections that are not being used.

Best Practice

Command Prompt Utilities

For multiple SQL Server environments, running the Surface Area Configuration Tool on each server would be time-consuming and tedious. Fortunately, the `sac` utility has been provided among the many command prompt utilities that ship with SQL Server 2005. The `sac` utility imports and exports SQL Server 2005 surface area configuration settings. Once one server has been configured, run `sac` to export the surface area settings and apply those settings to other servers. The `sac` utility is located in the `<drive>:\Program Files\Microsoft SQL Server\90\Shared` folder.

Removing SQL Server

To remove SQL Server, use the Add/Remove Programs option in the Windows Control Panel. Each instance of SQL Server is listed separately and may be uninstalled without affecting the other instances. Even with the removal of the default instance, any remaining named instances will continue to function.

User databases will not be deleted by the uninstall and their directory structure remains intact.

Detaching and copying a database to another server prior to removing an instance of SQL Server enables continued access to the data. If that is not possible, backup and restore the database to another server or attach the orphaned database to another server.

Summary

SQL Server 2005 is easy to install with proper planning, and advances in technology aid performance with no impact on licensing costs. With the 2005 release, Microsoft has introduced additional tools to aid in migration and configuration, and they have refined existing tools to assist with the install and upgrade paths. Default installations continue to be straightforward, and a little planning and forethought will help for installations that deviate from the fresh install. Following the "secure by default" philosophy, SQL Server 2005 disables the bulk of its features, especially for fresh installs. Enabled features prior to an upgrade remain enabled once 2005 has been installed. SQL Native Client (SNAC) provides another option to access SQL Server 2005. Chapter 5 discusses SNAC in more detail.

✦　　✦　　✦

Client Software Connectivity

SQL Server 2005 brings SQL Server in line with Microsoft's philosophy of "secure by default" and reduces the surface area of the application. The initial installation allows local access only and no network connections (i.e., traditional client applications will not be able to connect).

Chapter 4, "Installing and Configuring SQL Server" discusses SQL Server surface area configuration as part of the installation process.

The Server Configuration Manager tool installed with SQL Server can nearly always communicate with SQL Server so you can configure the server connectivity options and open the server up for network access.

With network access allowed on the SQL Server, SQL Server provides clients with a new means of accessing functionality and features through the new SQL Server Native Client (SNAC).

Before getting into the SNAC, network access for the new server must be enabled.

Enabling Server Connectivity

When initially installed, SQL Server enables the Shared Memory protocol and disables the remaining protocols. This provides the greatest default security because only applications running locally to the SQL Server can connect.

To broaden SQL Server availability, additional network protocols must be enabled on the server.

Chapter 34, "Configuring SQL Server," discusses SQL Server configuration in detail.

Server Configuration Manager

Network protocols define the common set of rules and formats that computers and applications use when communicating with one another. As mentioned above, the Shared Memory protocol defines how applications must run locally to the server in order to interact with it.

The Named Pipes protocol is an interprocess communications protocol (IPC) that enables a process to communicate with another process, possibly running on a different computer, through the use of shared memory. This protocol typically works well in small and fast local area networks, as it generates additional network traffic during use. In larger and slower networks, TCP/IP works better.

The TCP/IP protocol, or Transmission Control Protocol/Internet Protocol, is widely used today. TCP guarantees the delivery and order of the information sent between computers, while IP defines the format or structure of the data sent. TCP/IP also contains advanced security features that make it attractive to security-sensitive organizations and users. This protocol works well in larger networks and slower networks.

The Server Configuration Manager allows for these various protocols to be enabled and/or disabled as appropriate for the operational environment. The utility may be launched from the Start menu by selecting Start ➪ All Programs ➪ Microsoft SQL Server 2005 ➪ Configuration Tools ➪ SQL Server Configuration Manager. The Server Configuration Manager presents a list of all the available protocols and communication options, as shown in Figure 5-1.

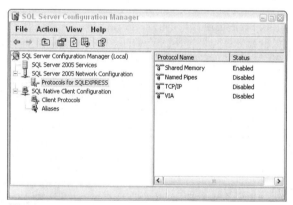

Figure 5-1: The SQL Server Configuration Manager establishes the connectivity protocols used by SQL Server to communicate with clients.

SQL Native Client Connectivity (SNAC)

The SQL Native Client connectivity is managed through the same Server Configuration Manager. SNAC installations will initially default the network protocols to enabling Shared Memory, TCP/IP, and Named Pipes, as shown in Figure 5-2.

If SNAC access is not needed or supported by your organization, disabling the appropriate network protocols will reduce your security risks (surface area).

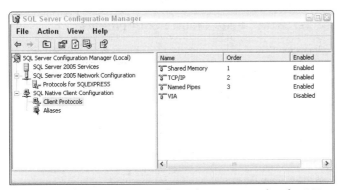

Figure 5-2: The SQL Server Configuration Manager view for SQL Native Client Configuration Client Protocols.

SQL Server Native Client Features

The development community gains access to the new features of SQL Server 2005 through the SQL Server Native Client (SNAC). If the new features are not needed and managed code is a requirement for data access, then ADO.NET will suffice. While a detailed examination of the new features is beyond the scope of this chapter, a summary of each is provided.

Note   ADO.NET is an umbrella label applied to the .NET functionality that supports connections to a variety of data sources. Classes within this library supply the programmatic capability to create, maintain, dispose of, and execute actions against a database.

For developers, Microsoft Data Access Components (MDAC) is compatible with SQL 2005 but will not be enhanced to support the new 2005 Server features.

Note   Because SQL Native Client is a component of SQL Server 2005, it must be installed separately on the development machine and must be included with the application setup. Microsoft has included the `sqlncli.msi` file on the SQL Server installation DVD. This file will install SQL Native Client without requiring the full SQL Server installation DVDs.

Requirements

The software requirements for installing and running SQL Server Native Client are listed in Table 5-1. The operating system will dictate the hardware requirements, including memory, hard disk capacities, CPU, and so on.

Table 5-1: SNAC Installation Requirements

Installer	Operating Systems	Compatible SQL Server
Windows Installer 3.0	Windows XP SP1 or later	SQL Server 7.0 or later supports connectivity.
	Windows 2000 Professional	
	Windows 2000 Server	
	Windows 2000 Advanced Server	
	Windows 2000 Datacenter	
	Windows 2003 Server	
	Windows 2003 Enterprise Server	
	Windows 2003 Datacenter Server	

 Chapter 4, "Installing and Configuring SQL Server," provides details about SQL Server installation requirements.

Database Mirroring

When a database connection is established to a SQL Server 2005 server, the failover partner (i.e., backup server) is automatically identified in a mirrored scenario. This information is used by SNAC to transparently connect to the failover partner if the principal server fails. The failover partner's identity can also be supplied as an optional parameter in the database connection string using the Failover_Partner keyword.

 If the connection to the principal server fails, any current data will be lost; and if a transaction is involved, it will be rolled back. The connection must be closed and reopened to access the failover partner and then any data work must be reapplied. The failover connection is automatic as long as the failover partner's identity is a part of the connection object supplied from either the connection string or a prior successful connection to the server before it went down.

 Chapter 39, "Replicating Data," details another tool used in persisting data.

Asynchronous Operations

There are times when not waiting on a return from the database call is desirable. It is now possible to open and close a database connection without waiting by setting the appropriate property.

Additionally, asynchronous calls returning result sets can be made. In these cases, a valid result set will exist but may still be populating. Therefore, it will be necessary to test the asynchronous status of the result set and process it when it is complete.

Note There are some caveats to performing asynchronous operations such as connection pooled objects and use of the cursor's engine. The asynchronous status is not exposed.

Multiple Active Result Sets (MARS)

SQL Server 2005 provides support for having multiple active SQL statements on the same connection. This capability includes being able to interleave reading from multiple results sets and being able to execute additional commands while a result set is open.

Microsoft guidelines for applications using MARS include the following:

✦ Result sets should be short-lived per SQL statement.

✦ If a result set is long-lived or large, then server cursors should be used.

✦ Always read to the end of the results and use API/property calls to change connection properties.

Note By default, MARS functionality is not enabled. It is turned on through a connection string value — `MarsConn` for the OLE DB provider and `Mars_Connection` for the ODBC provider.

XML Data Types

Much like the current `VarChar` data type that persists variable character values, a new `XML` data type persists XML documents and fragments. This type is available for variable declarations within stored procedures, parameter declarations, and return types and conversions.

 Cross-Reference Chapter 31, "Using XML, Xpath, and Xquery," provides additional information on XML usage.

User-Defined Types

These types are defined using .NET Common Language Runtime (CLR) code. This would include the popular C# and VB.NET languages. The data itself is exposed as fields and properties, with the behavior being exposed through the class methods.

Large Value Types

Three new data types have been introduced to handle values up to $2 \wedge 31\text{-}1$ bytes long. This includes variables, thus allowing for text values in excess of the old 8K limit. The new types and their corresponding old types are listed in Table 5-2.

Table 5-2: New SQL Server 2005 Large Values Types

New Large Data Types	Prior Data Types
varchar(max)	text
nvarchar(max)	ntext
varbinary(max)	image

Handling Expired Passwords

This new feature of SQL Server 2005 enables users to change their expired password at the client without the intervention of an administrator.

A user's password may be changed in any of the following ways:

✦ Programmatically changing the password such that both the old and new passwords are provided in the connection string

✦ A prompt via the user interface to change the password prior to expiration

✦ A prompt via the user interface to change the password after expiration

If the old and new passwords are supplied on the connection string, then ensure that this information has not been persisted in some external file. Instead, build it dynamically to mitigate any security concerns.

Best Practice

Cross-Reference

Chapter 40, "Securing Databases," discusses SQL security in detail.

Snapshot Isolation

The new *snapshot isolation* feature enhances concurrency and improves performance by avoiding reader-writer blocking.

Snapshot isolation relies on the row versioning feature. A transaction begins when the `BeginTransaction` call is made but is not assigned a sequence transaction number until the first T-SQL statement is executed. The temporary logical copies used to support row versioning are stored in `tempdb`.

Note

If `tempdb` does not have enough space for the version store, then various features and operations such as triggers, MARS, indexing, client executed T-SQL and row versioning will fail, so ensure that `tempdb` has more than enough space for anticipated uses.

Summary

SQL Server Configuration Manager now provides the server and SQL Native Client protocol management.

SQL Server 2005 supports new features that enrich the client and programmatic data experience. Developers access these new features through the SQL Server Native Client (SNAC), and are now able to enhance the user experience by providing integrated password changes, improved blocking, and better user interface response with asynchronous calls. In addition, stability increases significantly with the use of mirrored servers and other useful features.

✦　　✦　　✦

Using Management Studio

CHAPTER

6

SQL Server 2005's primary user interface is Management Studio—a powerful set of tools in a Visual Studioesque look and feel that enables the developer or DBA to develop database projects and manage SQL Server with either a GUI interface or T-SQL code. For business intelligence (BI) work with Integration Services, Reporting Services, and Analysis Services, there's a companion tool called SQL Server Business Intelligence Development Studio.

Like many things in life, Management Studio's greatest strength is also its greatest weakness. The number of tasks, tree nodes, and tools within the studios can overwhelm the new user. The windows can dock, float, or become tabbed, so the interface can appear cluttered without any sense of order, as shown Figure 3-6 of Chapter 3.

However, once the individual pages are understood, and the interface options mastered, the studios are very flexible, and interfaces can be configured to meet the specific needs of any database task. Management Studio can even be configured to look almost like SQL Server 2000's Query Analyzer or Enterprise Manager.

Many subsequent chapters in this book will explain how to accomplish tasks using Management Studio or BI Studio, so you won't learn about every feature in this chapter. Instead, this chapter is a navigational guide to the landscape, pointing out the more interesting features along the way.

New in 2005 Management Studio is the natural evolution of SQL Server 2000's Enterprise Manager and Query Analyzer, which it replaces. The Object Explorer and Query Editor tools retain the comfortable feel of their predecessors while adding the flexibility of Visual Studio. For mixed-version environments, Management Studio is backwardly compatible with all of SQL Server 2000, and most of version 7.

A common misconception among new SQL Server DBAs is that Management Studio *is* SQL Server. It's not. Management Studio is a client front-end tool used to manage SQL Server and develop databases. Management Studio sends T-SQL commands to SQL Server, or uses SQL Management Objects (SMOs), just like any other client application. It also inspects SQL Server and presents the data and configuration for viewing. An important feature to organizations with multiple servers is that Management Studio can connect to, or register, multiple instances of SQL Server, reducing the travel required to manage disparate servers.

Note   Much of using Management Studio is obvious to experienced IT professionals, so this chapter highlights the key points as I see them. It does not, however, walk through every menu item. If you are interested in a complete tutorial on using Management Studio, Dale Elizabeth Corey has written a 167-page e-book called *An Introduction to SQL Server 2005 Management Studio*. It's available from `www.SQLServerCentral.com`.

Cross-Reference   It's interesting to watch the commands sent by Management Studio to SQL Server. While Management Studio can generate a script for nearly every action, the actual traffic between SQL Server and its clients may be viewed using SQL Profiler, which is discussed in Chapter 49, "Measuring Performance."

Organizing the Interface

Management Studio includes a wide variety of functionality organized into ten major tools, which may be opened from the View menu, from the standard toolbar, or from the associated hotkey:

- ✦ **Object Explorer** (F8): Used for administering and developing SQL Server 2005 database objects. It's the merger of the best from SQL 2K's Enterprise Manager and Query Analyzer's Object Browser. Very cool.

- ✦ **Summary** (F7): Presents basic information about the selected object as well as several reports.

- ✦ **Registered Servers** (Ctrl+Alt+G): Used to manage the connection to multiple SQL Server 2005 engines. You can register database engines, Analysis Services, Report Servers, SQL Server Mobile, and Integration Services servers.

- ✦ **Template Explorer** (Ctrl+Alt+T): Used to create and manage T-SQL code templates.

- ✦ **Solution Explorer** (Ctrl+Alt+L): Organizes projects and manages source code control.

- ✦ **Properties window** (F4): Displays properties for the selected object.

- ✦ **Bookmarks window** (Ctrl+K, Ctrl+W): Lists current bookmarks from within the Query Editor.

- ✦ **Web Browser** (Ctrl+Alt+R): Used by the Query Editor to display XML or HTML results.

- ✦ **Output window** (Ctrl+Alt+O): Displays messages from Management Studio's integrated development tools.

- ✦ **Query Editor:** The descendant of SQL Server 2000's Query Analyzer, the Query Editor is used to create, edit, and execute T-SQL batches. Query Editor may be opened from the File ➪ New menu by opening an existing query file (assuming you have the .sql file extension associated with Management Studio), by clicking the New Query toolbar button, or by launching a query script from an object in the Object Explorer.

The most commonly used tools — Registered Servers, Summary page, Object Explorer, Template Explorer, and Properties windows — are available on the standard toolbar.

Window Placement

Using the Visual Studio look and feel, any window may float, be docked, be part of a tabbed window, or be hidden off to one side. The current mode may be selected by right-clicking on the window's title bar, selecting the down arrow on the right side of a docked window, or from the Window menu. In addition, grabbing a window and moving it to the desired location will also change the window's mode. Following are the available options:

✦ Setting the mode to **floating** instantly removes the window from Management Studio's window. A floating window behaves like a non-modal dialog box.

✦ Setting the mode to **tabbed** immediately moves the window to a tabbed document location in the center of Management Studio, adding it as a tab to any existing documents already in the location. Drag a tab to change its tab order. Dragging a tab to a side location creates a new tabbed document. Any location (center, right left, top, bottom) can hold several tabbed tools or documents.

A tabbed document area can hold more documents than there is space for to display the tabs. There are two ways to view the hidden tabs. The most obvious way is to scroll horizontally, but the more efficient method is to pull down the list of documents from the Active File arrow in the upper right-hand corner of the tabbed document area.

✦ While a **dockable** window is being moved, Management Studio displays several blue docking indicators, as shown in Figure 6-1. Dropping a window on the arrow will dock it in the selected location. Dropping the window on the center blue spot adds the window to the center location as a tabbed document.

✦ Opening several windows will keep the tools right at hand, but unless you have a mega monitor (and I envy you), the windows will likely use too much real estate. A solution, and one of my favorite new interface features, is **auto-hiding** any window that you want out of the way until the window's tab is clicked. To auto-hide a window, use the View ➪ Auto-Hide menu command or toggle the pin icon in the window's title bar. When the pin is vertical, the window stays open. When the window is unpinned, the window auto-hides. An auto-hidden window must be pinned back to normal before its mode can be changed to floating or tabbed (see Figure 6-1).

Note   To reset Management Studio to its default configuration (Object Explorer, Tabbed Documents, Property Window) use the Window ➪ Reset Window Layout menu command. Fortunately, this command does not reset any custom toolbar modifications.

Ctrl+Tab switches between open windows.

To hide all the docked windows and keep only the tabbed documents in the center visible, use the Window ➪ Auto Hide All menu command.

The flexible positioning of the windows means you can configure the interface to give you access to the tools in whatever way makes you the most comfortable and productive. Personally, I tend to auto-hide the Object Explorer and work with several Query Editors that have been split into two vertical panes.

New in 2005   The windows and dialog boxes within Management Studio are non-modal, fixing one of the most annoying aspects of SQL Server 2000 Enterprise Manager.

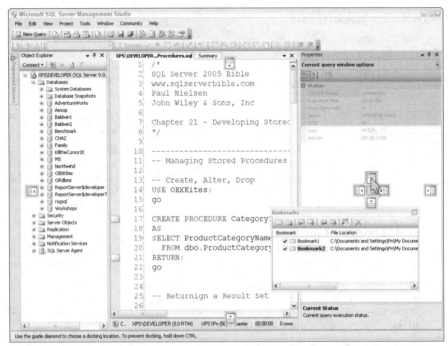

Figure 6-1: Dropping a window on one of the blue docking arrows docks the window to the side of Management Studio. In this figure, the Bookmarks window is about to be docked above the Properties window.

A free ScreenCast demonstrating the various ways to move, dock, and hide Management Studio's windows is available on this book's companion website, `www.SQLServer Bible.com`.

The Context Menu

In keeping with the Microsoft Windows interface standards, the context menu is the primary means of selecting actions or viewing properties throughout Management Studio. The context menu for most object types includes submenus for new objects, and tasks. These are the workhorse menus within Management Studio.

The Summary Page

The ubiquitous Summary page may seem innocent enough but some pretty cool reports are hiding within it. The Summary page is also the place for multiple selection of subnodes.

New in 2005 The Summary page might fill the void left by Enterprise Manager's TaskPad, but the Summary page is significantly improved, and there are gems to be found hidden within the Summary page reports.

Registered Servers

Registered Servers is an optional feature; if you manage only one or a few SQL Servers, then Registered Servers may offer no benefit to you. If, however, you are responsible for many SQL Servers, then Registered Servers is the place to maintain all those connection settings.

Using Registered Servers, connection information can be maintained for connections to the Database Engine, Analysis Services, Reporting Services, SQL Server Mobile Edition Databases, and Integration Services. The toolbar at the top of Registered Services enables selection among the types of services.

The Server context menu, shown in Figure 6-2, can be used to start and stop the service, and to open the registration's Properties page. The menu can also import or export connection information to move registrations between installations of Management Studio.

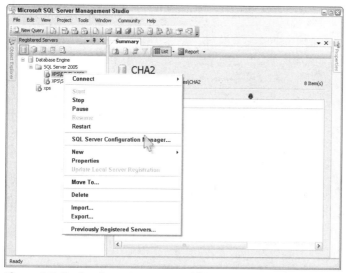

Figure 6-2: Registering a SQL Server within Management Studio so it can connect to the server

Within the Registered Servers tree, servers may be organized by server groups. There's no inherent meaning to these groups — their only purpose is to visually group the servers within the tree.

Object Explorer

A merger of SQL Server 2000's Enterprise Manager and Query Analyzer's Object Browser, Object Explorer offers a well-designed view of all the objects. The top level of the tree lists the connected servers. Object Explorer can connect to a server regardless of whether the server is known by Registered Servers. The benefit of registering the server is that it can be started or stopped using Registered Servers. The server icon color indicates whether or not the server is running.

Navigating the Tree

In keeping with the Explorer metaphor, Object Explorer (see Figure 6-3) is a hierarchical, expandable view of the objects available within the connected servers. A tree is built of roots and nodes. For example, within Windows' My Documents tree, the desktop is the root and all folders or devices expand under the desktop as nodes.

The Database Engine server nodes include databases, server security, server objects, replication, management, notification services, and SQL Server Agent. Most of the tree structure is fixed, but additional nodes are added as objects are created within the server.

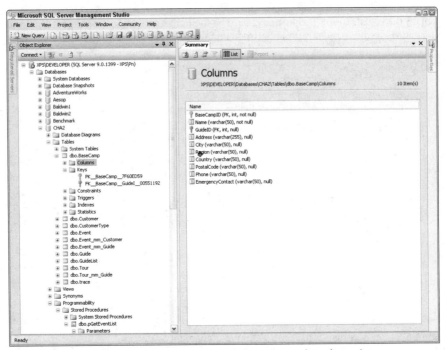

Figure 6-3: Object Explorer's tree structure invites you to explore the various components of SQL Server management and development.

The Databases node contains all the server's databases. When you right-click on a database, the menu includes a host of options and commands. Under each database are standard nodes (see Figure 6-4), which manage the following database objects:

✦ **Database Diagrams:** Illustrates several tables and their relationships. A database may contain multiple diagrams, and each diagram does not need to display all the tables. This makes it easy to organize large databases into modular diagrams.

✦ **Tables:** Used to create and modify the design of tables, view and edit the contents of tables, and work with the tables' indexes, permissions, and publications. Triggers, stored procedures that respond to data-modification operations (insert, update, and delete), may be created and edited here. The only way to launch the Query Designer is from the table listing.

✦ **Views:** Stored SQL statements are listed, created, and edited, and the results viewed, from this node.

✦ **Synonyms:** Alternative names for SQL Server database objects.

✦ **Programmability:** A large section that includes most of the development objects, stored procedures, functions, database triggers, assemblies, types, rules, and defaults.

✦ **Service Broker:** Used to view Server broker queues.

✦ **Storage:** Used to manage non-standard storage such as full-text search, and table partitions.

✦ **Security:** Used to manage security at the database level.

Caution   Because Management Studio and SQL Server are communicating as client and server, the two processes are not always in sync. Changes on the server are often not immediately reflected in Management Studio unless Management Studio is refreshed.

Filtering Object Explorer

Databases can contain numerous objects. To ease navigating these objects, Microsoft has included a filter for portions of the tree that include user-defined objects, such as tables or views. The filter icon is in the Object Explorer toolbar. The icon is only enabled when the top node for a type of user-defined object is selected. For example, to filter the tables, select the tree node and then click on the filter icon or right-click to open the tree's context menu, and select Filter ➪ Filter Settings, also as shown in Figure 6-4.

The Filter Settings dialog box enables you to filter the object by name, schema, or creation date. To remove the filter, use the same context menu, or open the Filter Settings dialog box and choose Clear Filter. Unfortunately, the filter accepts only single values for each parameter. Boolean operators are not permitted.

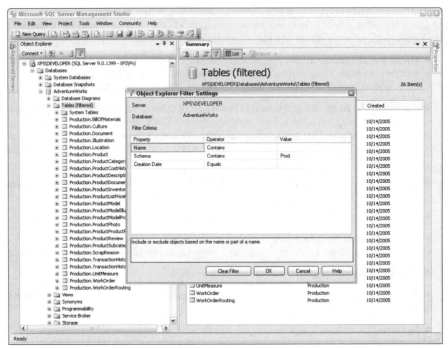

Figure 6-4: The Filter Settings dialog box can be used to limit the number of objects visible in Object Explorer.

The Table Designer

Creating a new table, or modifying the design of an existing table, is easy with the Table Designer. The Table Designer, shown in Figure 6-5, is very similar to MS Access and other database design tool interfaces.

A new table may be created by selecting the table node in the tree and then selecting New Table from the context menu. The design of existing tables may be edited by selecting the table, right-clicking, and selecting Modify from the context menu.

Columns may be individually selected and edited in the top pane. The column properties for the selected column are listed in the bottom pane. Dialog boxes for modifying foreign keys and indexes can be opened using the Table Designer menu or toolbar.

Although I'm a code man myself and prefer Query Editor to the GUI tools, I must admit that the Table Designer page is a clean, straightforward UI, and it generates scripts for every modification.

Cross-Reference The logical design of tables and columns is covered in Chapter 2, "Relational Database Modeling," and the realities of implementing the logical design are discussed in Chapter 17, "Creating the Physical Database Schema."

Figure 6-5: Tables may be created or their designs edited using the Table Designer tool.

Building Database Diagrams

The Database Diagram tool takes the Table Designer up a notch by adding custom table design views (see Figure 6-6) and a multi-table view of the foreign-key relationships. The Database Diagram tool has its own node under each database. Each database may contain multiple diagrams, which makes working with very large databases easier because each module, or section, of the database may be represented by a diagram.

A free ScreenCast on creating the physical schema using the Database Diagram tool may be downloaded or viewed on the book's companion website, www.SQLServerBible.com.

Personally, I like the Database Diagram tool, but some developers think it's clumsy in two areas. The major complaint is that the relationship lines connect the tables without pointing to the primary-key and foreign-key columns. This problem is compounded by another: the frustrating tendency of the lines to become pretzels when tables or lines are moved. Nonetheless, the Database Diagram tool is useful for viewing the schemas of very large databases. In this situation, primary tables often have dozens of connecting lines. If the lines were automatically linked to the primary key, the result would be an unreadable mess.

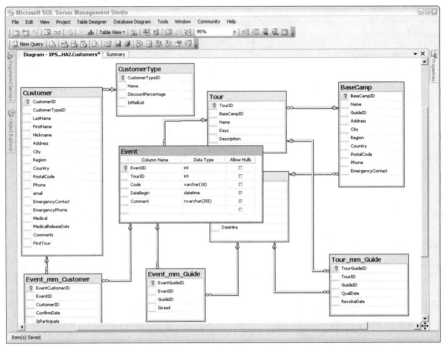

Figure 6-6: The Cape Hatteras Adventures database relationships viewed with the Database Diagram tool. The Event table has been changed to Standard view.

The Query Designer

The Query Designer is a popular tool for data retrieval and modification, even though it's not the easiest tool to find within Management Studio. You can open it in three ways:

✦ Using the Object Explorer, select a table. Using the context menu, choose Open Table. This will open the Query Designer, showing the return from a "select all" query in the results pane. The other panes may now be opened using the Query Designer menu or the toolbar.

✦ When using the Query Editor, the Query Designer may be opened by using the Query Designer button on the toolbar or by using the Query ➪ Design Query menu command.

✦ The Query Designer is integrated within the Query Editor. Highlight a query in the Query Editor, click the Query Designer toolbar button, and Management Studio will open the query within Query Designer. Note that when the Query Designer is opened from the Query Editor, it's a modal dialog box and the results pane is disabled.

Unlike other query tools that alternate between a graphic view, a SQL text view, and the query results, Management Studio's Query Designer simultaneously displays multiple panes (see Figure 6-7), as selected with the view buttons in the toolbar:

✦ **Diagram pane:** Multiple tables or views may be added to the query and joined together in this graphic representation of the select statement's from clause.

✦ **Grid pane:** Lists the columns being displayed, filtered, or sorted

✦ **SQL pane:** The raw SQL select statement may be entered or edited in this pane.

✦ **Results pane:** When the query is executed with the Run button (!), the results are captured in the results pane. If the results are left untouched for too long, Management Studio will request permission to close the connection.

New in 2005

One of my favorite new features in Management Studio is the capability to create and graphically join derived tables within Query Designer's Diagram pane. Way cool!

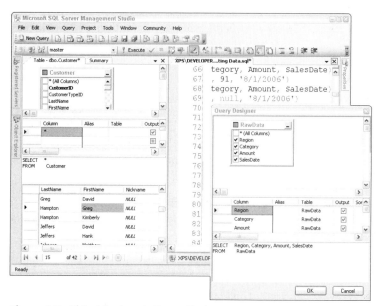

Figure 6-7: Object Explorer's Query Designer

The Query Designer can perform *Data Manipulation Language (DML)* queries — select, insert, update, delete) besides select. Unlike Query Editor, it cannot perform batches or non-DML commands.

The Query Designer may be used to edit data directly in the results pane—a quick-and-dirty way to correct or mock up data. Occasionally, you'll see an error message that says, "Cannot edit data while in Firehose mode." This means that the Query Designer is still retrieving data. Waiting a few seconds to give Management Studio a chance to catch up with SQL Server will normally resolve the error.

Navigating the Query Designer should feel familiar to experienced Windows users. While Books Online lists several pages of keyboard shortcuts, most are standard Windows navigation commands. The one worth mentioning here is Ctrl+0, which enters a null into the result pane.

You can watch a ScreenCast on creating queries using the Query Designer from www .SQLServerBible.com.

Using the Query Editor

The Query Editor carries on the legacy of Query Analyzer, and, for the most part, improves on the favorite old tool.

Connecting to a Server

The Query Editor can maintain multiple open windows and connections within the tabbed document area. In fact, different windows may be connected as different users, which is very useful for testing security.

When Query Editor first opens it will prompt for an initial login. To make further connections, use the File ➪ New Connection menu command. The window title displays the current SQL Server and login user.

New in 2005
Management Studio's Query Editor can open and work with a .sql file even when not connected to a server. Query Analyzer in previous versions of SQL Server had to be connected to a server before a query file could be edited.

Opening a .sql File

There are multiple ways to open a saved query batch file, and one huge trap you want to avoid:

✦ If Management Studio is not open, then double-clicking a .sql file in Windows File Explorer will launch Management Studio, prompt you for a connection, and open the file. Here's the gotcha: If you select multiple .sql files in Windows File Explorer and open them as a group, Windows will launch a separate instance of Management Studio for each file—not a good thing.

✦ If Management Studio is already open, then double-clicking will open the file or selected files into a Query Editor window. Each file will prompt you for a connection.

✦ Multiple .sql files may be dragged from Widows File Explorer and dropped on Management Studio. Each file will open a Query Editor after prompting for a connection.

✦ The most recently viewed files are listed in the Files ➪ Recent Files menu. Selecting a file will open it in the Query Editor window.

✦ The File ➪ File Open menu or toolbar command will open a dialog box to select one or more files.

Executing SQL Batches

As a developer's tool, the Query Editor is designed to execute T-SQL batches, which are collections of multiple T-SQL statements. To submit a batch to SQL Server for processing, use Query ➪ Execute Query, click the Run Query toolbar button, use the F5 key, or press Ctrl+E.

Because batches tend to be long, and it's often desirable to execute a single T-SQL command or a portion of the batch for testing or stepping through the code, the SQL Server team provides you with a convenient feature. If no text is highlighted, the entire batch is executed. If text is highlighted, only that text is executed.

It's worth pointing out that the Parse Query menu command and toolbar button checks only the SQL code. It does not check object names (tables, columns, stored procedures, and so on). This actually is a feature, not a bug. By not including object name–checking in the syntax check, SQL Server permits batches that create objects, and then references them.

The T-SQL batch will execute within the context of a current database. The current database is displayed, and may be changed, within the database combo box in the toolbar.

The results of the query are displayed in the bottom pane. The format may be either text or grid; you can switch using Ctrl+T or Ctrl+D, respectively. The new format will be applied to the next batch execution.

While working with T-SQL code in Query Editor, you can get Books On Line (BOL) keyword help by pressing Shift+F1. Alternately, the dynamic help window in Management Studio will follow your work and display appropriate help topics as you go.

Shortcuts and Bookmarks

Bookmarks are a great way to navigate large scripts. Bookmarks can be set manually, or automatically set using the Find command. Bookmarks work with double control key combinations. For example, holding down the Ctrl key and pressing K and then N moves to the next bookmark. The Ctrl+K keys also control some of the other editing commands, such as commenting code. Bookmarks may also be controlled using the Edit ➪ Bookmarks menu or the bookmark next and previous toolbar buttons. Table 6-1 lists the shortcuts I find especially useful.

Table 6-1: Useful Query Editor Shortcuts

Shortcut	Description
Ctrl+K+K	Add or remove a bookmark
Ctrl+K+A	Enable all bookmarks
Ctrl+K+N	Move to the next bookmark
Ctrl+K+P	Move to the previous bookmark
Ctrl+K+L	Clear all bookmarks
Ctrl+K+C	Comment the selection
Ctrl+K+U	Uncomment the selection

New in 2005   While it's true that these commands are different from the familiar keyboard shortcuts in SQL Server 2000's Query Analyzer, I've come to prefer the flexibility of the Ctrl+K shortcuts.

Viewing Query Execution Plans

One of Query Editor's most significant features is its ability to graphically view query execution plans (see Figure 6-8).

What makes the query execution plans even more important is that SQL is a descriptive language, so it doesn't tell the Query Optimizer exactly how to get the data, but only which data to retrieve. While some performance tuning can be applied to the way the query is stated, most of the tuning is accomplished by adjusting the indexes, which greatly affects how the Query Optimizer can compile the query. The query execution plan reveals how SQL Server will optimize the query, take advantage of indexes, pull data from other data sources, and perform joins. Reading the query execution plans and understanding their interaction with the database schema and indexes is both a science and an art.

Cross-Reference   Chapter 50, "Query Analysis and Index Tuning," includes a full discussion on reading the query execution plan and tuning the underlying indexes.

Query Editor can display either an estimated query execution plan prior to executing the query or the actual plan after the query is run.

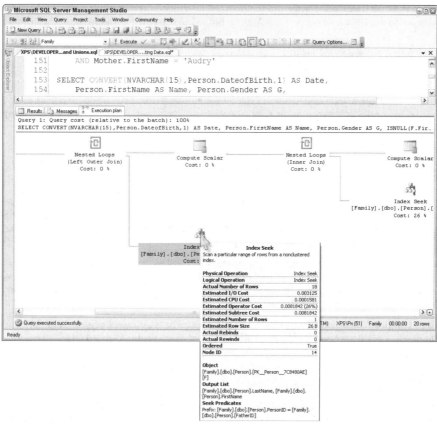

Figure 6-8: Query Editor's ability to graphically display the execution plan of a query is perhaps its most useful feature.

Using the Solution Explorer

The optional Solution Explorer enables you to organize files and connections within projects, similar to the Solution Explorer in Visual Studio. You don't need to use it; File ➪ Open and Save work well without Solution Explorer, but if you work on several database projects then you may find that Solution Explorer helps keep your life organized — or at least your code organized. The Solution Explorer may be found in the View menu, and the Solution Explorer icon may be added to the Standard toolbar using the Customize toolbar.

To use the Solution Explorer for managing query scripts, you must first open a Query Editor window. To create a new project, create the file using the context menu under Scripts.

A new feature in Management Studio, Solution Explorer solves some of the code management headaches that SQL Server 2000 created.

It's possible to integrate Solution Explorer with Visual Studio Source Safe or a third-party version control utility to provide solid document management and version control. For more information, visit the book's website, www.SQLServerBible.com.

Introducing the Templates

Management Studio templates are useful because they provide a starting point when programming new types of code and they help make the code consistent. Templates are managed using the Template Explorer. To use a template, you need to create a new Query Editor window specifying that template.

The templates are simply stored SQL scripts within a directory structure, which means that it's easy to create your own templates or to modify the existing ones. The template directory is specified in the General tab of the Options dialog box. This allows several developers to share a common set of templates on a network drive.

For developers or organizations desiring consistency in their own development styles or standards, I highly recommend taking advantage of Management Studio's templates.

Summary

Management Studio and Query Editor are the two primary DBA and developer interfaces for SQL Server. Mastering the navigation of both these tools is vital to success with SQL Server.

With this understanding of the development interfaces as a foundation, the next part of the book discusses building the database, manipulating data, and coding T-SQL procedures, functions, and triggers.

✦   ✦   ✦

Manipulating Data with Select

Select is the most powerful word in SQL. Because select is so common, it's easy to take it for granted, but no keyword in any programming language I can think of is as powerful and flexible. Select can retrieve, twist, shape, join, and group data in nearly any way imaginable, and it's easily extended with the insert, update, and delete verbs to modify data. SQL Server even extends the select command with XQuery, covered in Chapter 31.

Part II begins by exploring the basic logical query flow, and quickly digs deeper into topics such as relational division, correlated subqueries, set-difference queries, and distributed queries. I've devoted ten chapters to the select command because understanding the multiple options and creative techniques available with queries is key to becoming a successful SQL Server developer, DBA, or architect.

Please don't assume that Part II is only for beginners. These ten chapters present the core power of SQL. Part VI explores optimization, and it may be tempting to go straight there for optimization ideas, but the second strategy of optimization theory is using good set-based code. Therefore, here are ten chapters describing how to optimize your database by writing better queries.

If SQL Server is the box, then Part II is about being one with the box.

Understanding Basic Query Flow

SQL is the romance language of data, but wooing the single correct answer from gigabytes of relational data can seem overwhelming until the logical flow of the query is mastered.

One of the first points to understand is that SQL is a *declarative* language. This means that the SQL query logically describes the question to the SQL Optimizer, which then determines the best method to physically execute the query. As you'll see in the next nine chapters, many ways of stating the query often exist, but each method is usually optimized to the same query-execution plan. This means you are free to express the SQL query in the way that makes the most sense to you. In some cases, one method is considered cleaner or faster than another; I'll point those instances out as well.

SQL queries aren't limited to `select`. The four Data Manipulation Language (DML) commands, `select`, `insert`, `update`, and `delete`, are sometimes taught as four separate and distinct commands. However, I see queries as a single structural method of manipulating data; in other words, it's better to think of the four commands as four verbs that may each be used with the full power and flexibility of the SQL.

Neither are SQL queries limited to graphical interfaces. Many SQL developers who came up through the ranks from Access and who have only built queries using the Access query interface are amazed when they understand the enormous power of the full SQL query.

This chapter builds a basic single table query and establishes the logical query execution order critical for developing basic or advanced queries. With this foundation in place, the rest of Part 3 develops the basic `select` into what I believe is the most elegant, flexible, and powerful command in all of computing.

Understanding Query Flow

One can think about query flow in several different ways. Personally, when I develop SQL code, I imagine the query using the logical flow method, although some developers think through a query using the layout of SQL Server Management Studio's Query Designer. The syntax of the query is in yet another order. To illustrate the declarative nature of SQL, the actual physical execution of the query is optimized in yet a different order.

Syntactical Flow of the Query Statement

In its basic form, the `select` statement tells SQL Server what data to retrieve, including which columns, rows, and tables to pull from, and how to sort the data.

Here's an abbreviated syntax for the `select` command:

```
SELECT *, columns, or expressions
  [FROM table]
    [JOIN table
      ON condition]
  [WHERE conditions]
  [GROUP BY columns]
  [HAVING conditions]
  [ORDER BY Columns];
```

The `select` statement begins with a list of columns or expressions. At least one expression is required — everything else is optional. The simplest possible valid `select` statement is as follows:

```
SELECT 1;
```

The `from` portion of the `select` statement assembles all the data sources into a result set, which is then acted upon by the rest of the `select` statement. Within the `from` clause, multiple tables may be referenced by using one of several types of joins.

The `where` clause acts upon the record set assembled by the `from` clause to filter certain rows based upon conditions.

Aggregate functions perform summation-type operations across the data set. The `group by` clause can group the larger data set into smaller data sets based on the columns specified in the `group by` clause. The aggregate functions are then performed on the new smaller groups of data. The results of the aggregation can be restricted using the `having` clause.

Finally, the `order by` clause determines the sort order of the result set.

A Graphical View of the Query Statement

SQL Server Management Studio includes two basic methods of constructing and submitting queries: Query Designer and Query SQL Editor. Query Designer offers a graphical method of building a query, whereas Query SQL Editor is an excellent tool for ad hoc data retrieval because there are no graphics to get in the way and the developer can work as close to the SQL code as possible.

From SQL Server's point of view, it doesn't matter where the query originates; each statement is evaluated and processed as a SQL statement.

When selecting data using Query Designer, you enter the SQL statements as raw code in the third pane, as shown in Figure 7-1. The bottom pane displays the results in Grid mode or Text mode, and displays any messages. The Object Browser presents a tree of all the objects in SQL Server, as well as templates for creating new objects with code.

Tip   If text is highlighted in the Query Window, QA will execute only that text when you press the Execute Query command button or the F5 key. This is an excellent way to test portions of SQL code.

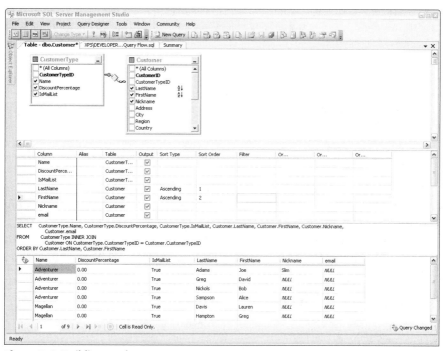

Figure 7-1: Building a select query

Tip   Though it may vary depending on the user-security settings, the default database is probably the Master database. Be sure to change to the appropriate user database using the database selector combo box in the toolbar, or the USE database command.

Logical Flow of the Query Statement

The best way to think through a SQL DML statement is to walk through the query's logical flow. Because SQL is a declarative language, the logical flow may or may not be the actual physical flow that SQL Server's query processor uses to execute the query. Nor is the logical flow the same as the query syntax. Regardless, I recommend thinking through a query in the following order:

1. **From:** The query begins by assembling the initial set of data, as specified in the from portion of the select statement.

2. **Where:** The filter process is actually the where clause selecting only those rows for which the qualification includes the phrase "%First Aid%".

3. **Column Calculations**: Once the rows are available and filtered, they are sorted according to the order by.

Cross-Reference   The construction of SQL expressions is covered in detail in Chapter 8, "Using Expressions and Scalar Functions."

4. **Aggregations:** SQL can optionally perform aggregations on the data set, such as finding the average, grouping the data by values in a column, or turning the result into a pivot table or crosstab.

Cross-Reference   SQL aggregate functions are covered in Chapter 11, "Aggregating Data."

5. **Order By:** Once the rows are available from the from clause and filtered by the where clause, they are sorted according to the order by clause.

6. **Predicate:** After the rows are selected, the calculations are performed, and the data is sorted into the desired order, SQL can restrict the output to the top few rows, or return only specified rows.

As more complexity is added to the SQL select, the flow also becomes more complex. The indexes and tables available to the SQL Server Query Optimizer also affect the *query execution plan.*

As you begin to think in terms of the SQL select statement, rather than in terms of the graphical user interface, understanding the flow of select and how to read the query execution plan will help you think through and debug difficult queries.

Physical Flow of the Query Statement

SQL Server will take the select statement and develop an optimized query execution plan, which is seldom in the execution order you would guess (see Figure 7-2).

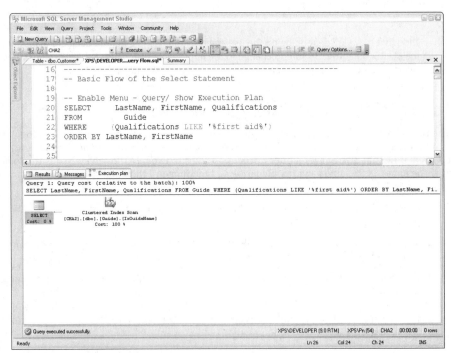

Figure 7-2: The physical execution plan is very different from the syntactical order, or logical understanding, of the query.

From Clause Data Sources

The first component of a typical SQL `select` statement is the `from` clause. In a simple SQL `select` statement, the `from` clause will contain a single table. However, the `from` clause can also contain multiple joined tables, subqueries as derived tables, and views. The maximum number of tables that may be accessed within a single SQL `select` statement is 256.

The `from` clause is the foundation of the rest of the SQL statement. In order for a table column to be in the output, or accessed in the `where` conditions, or in the `order by`, it must be in the `from` clause.

Possible Data Sources

SQL is extremely flexible and can accept data from seven distinctly different types of data sources within the `from` clause:

✦ SQL Server tables.

✦ Subqueries serving as derived tables, also called *subselects* or *in-line views,* are explained in Chapter 10, "Including Subqueries and CTEs."

✦ Common table expressions (CTEs) new to SQL Server 2005 add new features and formatting to the traditional subquery.

✦ Views, or stored `select` statements, can be referenced within the `from` clause as if they were tables. Views are discussed in Chapter 14, "Selecting Data through Views."

✦ Table-valued user-defined functions return rows and columns. See Chapter 22, "Building User-Defined Functions," for more information.

✦ Distributed data sources pull in data from other databases or applications (e.g., Access, Excel, Oracle) using `openquery()` and other functions, as detailed in Chapter 15, "Working with Distributed Queries."

✦ XML data sources using XQuery, as discussed in Chapter 31, "Using XML, SOAP, XPath, and Xquery."

Named Ranges

A table may be assigned a named range, or table alias, within the `from` clause. Once the table has an alias, the table must be referred to by this new name. The keyword `as` is optional and is commonly ignored. The following code accesses the `Guide` table, but refers to it within the query as table `G`:

```
-- From Table [AS] Range Variable
USE CHA2
SELECT G.lastName, G.FirstName
  FROM Guide AS G;
```

You'll find the sample code for every chapter, and the scripts that create and populate the sample databases, on the book's website: www.SQLServerBible.com.

Note In SQL, the use command specifies the current database. It's the code version of selecting a database from the toolbar in Management Studio.

[Table Name]

If the name of a database object, such as a table or column name, conflicts with a SQL keyword, you can let SQL know that it's the name of an object by placing it inside square brackets. The [Order] table in the OBX Kites sample database is a common example of a table name that's also a keyword:

```
USE OBXKites
SELECT OrderID, OrderDate
  FROM [Order];
```

Although it's considered poor practice to include spaces within the names of database objects, some database developers don't follow this guideline. If this is the case, square brackets are required when specifying the database object. The Order Details table in the Northwind sample database illustrates this:

```
USE Northwind
SELECT OrderID, ProductID, Quantity
  FROM [Order Details];
```

Four-Part Table Names

The full and proper name for a table is not just the table name but what is called a *four-part name*:

```
Server.Database.Schema.Table
```

If the table is in the current database, the server and database name are not required. Although it's not required, it's still good practice to specify the table's schema. Typically, the schema is dbo — a holdover from earlier versions when objects were owned by users and dbo represented the database owner.

The use of the four-part name enables the reusability of the query execution plan. Not only is it cleaner programming practice, you also reap performance benefits from specifying the table's owner.

Now that the four-part name has been explained, sample code in this book from here on out will include the owner in the name.

Cross-Reference For more about schemas, scope, and permission issues, see Chapter 40, "Securing Databases." Query plan reuse is discussed in Chapter 50, "Query Analysis and Index Tuning."

Where Conditions

The where conditions filter the output of the from clause and restrict the rows that will be returned in the result set. The conditions can refer to the data within the tables, expressions, built-in SQL Server scalar functions, or user-defined functions. The where conditions can also make use of several possible comparison operators and wildcards, as listed in Table 7-1. In addition, you can specify multiple where conditions with Boolean and, or, and not operators.

Best Practice

One sure way to improve the performance of a client/server database is to let the Database Engine do the work of restricting the rows returned, rather than make the calling application wade through unnecessary data. However, if the database design requires the use of functions within the where clause to locate rows, the function will seriously degrade performance because it is performed on each row. Therefore, well-written where conditions, based on well-planned database designs, are some of the best performance tools available to the SQL Server developer.

Table 7-1: Standard Comparison Operators

Description	Operator	Example
Equals	=	Quantity = 12
Greater than	>	Quantity > 12
Greater than or equal to	>=	Quantity >= 12
Less than	<	Quantity < 12
Less than or equal to	<=	Quantity<= 12
Not equal to	<>, !=	Quantity <> 12 , Quantity != 12
Not less than	!<	Quantity !< 12
Not greater than	!>	Quantity !> 12

Caution

The comparison operators that include an exclamation point are not ANSI standard SQL. <> is portable; ! = is not.

Cross-Reference

In addition to the standard comparison operators, which are no doubt familiar, SQL provides four special comparison operators: between, in, like, and is. The first three are explained in this section. Testing for nulls using the is keyword, and handling nulls, are explained in Chapter 8, "Using Expressions and Scalar Functions."

Best Practice

The best way to find a thing is to look for it, rather than to first eliminate everything it isn't. It's far easier to locate a business in a city than it is to prove that the business doesn't exist. The same is true of database searches. Proving that a row meets a condition is faster than first eliminating every row that doesn't meet that condition. In general, restating a negative where condition as a positive condition will improve performance.

Using the Between Search Condition

The between search condition tests for values within a range. The range can be deceiving, however, because it is inclusive. For example, between 1 and 10 would be true for 1 and 10. When using the between search condition, the first condition must be less than the latter value because in actuality, the between search condition is shorthand for "greater than or equal to the first value, and less than or equal to the second value."

The between search condition is commonly used with dates. The following code sample, also shown in Figure 7-3, locates all events from the Cape Hatteras Adventures sample database occurring during July 2001. The code first uses the CHA2 database and then queries that database:

```
USE CHA2

SELECT EventCode, DateBegin
  FROM dbo.Event
   WHERE DateBegin BETWEEN '07/01/01' AND '07/31/01';
```

Result:

```
EventCode  DateBegin
---------- --------------------------
01-006     2001-07-03 00:00:00.000
01-007     2001-07-03 00:00:00.000
01-008     2001-07-14 00:00:00.000
```

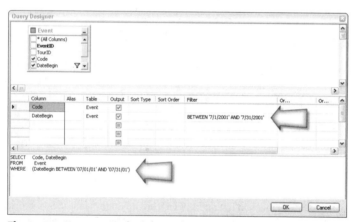

Figure 7-3: You can set the where clause conditions in Management Studio's Query Designer in the Grid or SQL pane.

The previous query returns an accurate result if the dates are stored without a time value. Most applications, however, grab the date and time using SQL Server's GetDate() function, which returns the current server date and time, with the time captured accurate to within three milliseconds. If this is the case, every row has the date and time stored. Therefore, the previous query would miss every row after the time 00:00:00.000 on '07/31/01'. If rows are to be properly selected by full date and time, the end parameter must include the last time for the day. As the next code sample demonstrates, the last time that SQL Server knows about is 12:59:59.998 P.M. The code first creates a sample table for testing, populates it with some sample data, and then queries it to illustrate the issue:

```
CREATE TABLE dbo.DateTest(
  PK INT IDENTITY,
  OrderDate DATETIME
```

```
  )
go
INSERT dbo.DateTest(OrderDate)
  VALUES('1/1/01 00:00')
INSERT dbo.DateTest(OrderDate)
  VALUES('1/1/01 23:59')
INSERT dbo.DateTest(OrderDate)
  VALUES('1/1/01 11:59:59.995 pm')
INSERT dbo.DateTest(OrderDate)
  VALUES('1/2/01');
```

The following query demonstrates the last valid time for the day:

```
SELECT *
  FROM dbo.DateTest
  WHERE OrderDate BETWEEN '1/1/1' AND '1/1/1 11:59:59.998 PM';
```

Result:

```
PK            OrderDate
-----------   -----------------------
1             2001-01-01 00:00:00.000
2             2001-01-01 23:59:00.000
3             2001-01-01 23:59:59.997
```

SQL Server automatically adjusts this query to the next nearest three milliseconds, causing it to return erroneous results:

```
SELECT *
  FROM dbo.DateTest
  WHERE OrderDate BETWEEN '1/1/1' AND '1/1/1 11:59:59.999 PM';
```

Result:

```
PK            OrderDate
-----------   -----------------------
1             2001-01-01 00:00:00.000
2             2001-01-01 23:59:00.000
3             2001-01-01 23:59:59.997
4             2001-01-02 00:00:00.000
```

```
DROP TABLE DateTest;
```

The second query's end time is adjusted to the nearest three-millisecond mark and incorrectly selects any rows for the next day without a time.

The same issue is present with `smalldatetime` data-type columns, which are accurate only to the minute. Selecting `where column <= 11:59:30 PM` rounds up to 12 a.m. the next day.

The following query from the `Family_Queries.sql` script uses the `between` search condition to find mothers who bore children less than nine months after marrying.

Beginning with the `from` clause, the query gathers information about the mother, the marriage, and the children, all from the `person` table. The `where` clause then restricts the results to those with the child's `DateOfBirth` within a certain time frame:

```
SELECT Person.FirstName + ' ' +  Person.LastName AS Mother,
  Convert(Char(12), Marriage.DateOfWedding, 107) as Wedding,
  Child.FirstName + ' ' + Child.LastName as Child,
  Convert(Char(12), Child.DateOfBirth, 107) as Birth
  FROM Person
    JOIN Marriage
      ON Person.PersonID = Marriage.WifeID
    JOIN Person Child
      ON Person.PersonID = Child.MotherID
    WHERE Child.DateOfBirth
      BETWEEN Marriage.DateOfWedding
        AND DATEADD(mm, 9, Marriage.DateOfWedding);
```

Result:

```
Mother              Wedding       Child             Birth
----------------    ------------  ---------------   ------------
Alysia Halloway     Jan 01, 1975  James Halloway    May 24, 1975
```

Using the In Search Condition

The in search condition is similar to the equals comparison operator, but it searches for an exact match from a list. If the value is in the list, the comparison is true. For instance, if region data were entered into the database, the following code finds any Cape Hatteras Adventures base camps in North Carolina or West Virginia:

```
USE CHA2
SELECT BaseCampname
  FROM dbo.BaseCamp
  WHERE Region IN ('NC', 'WV');
```

Result:

```
BaseCampName
-----------
West Virginia
Cape Hatteras
Asheville NC
```

Effectively, the in search condition is the equivalent of multiple equals comparisons "or"ed together:

```
USE CHA2
SELECT BaseCampname
  FROM dbo.BaseCamp
  WHERE Region = 'NC'
    OR Region = 'WV';
```

Result:

```
BaseCampName
-----------
West Virginia
Cape Hatteras
Asheville NC
```

The `in` operator may be combined with `not` to exclude certain rows. For example, `where not in ('NC', 'SC')` would return all rows except those in the Carolinas:

```
USE CHA2
SELECT BaseCampname
  FROM dbo.BaseCamp
  WHERE Region NOT IN ('NC', 'SC');
```

Result:

```
BaseCampName
-----------
FreePort
Ft Lauderdale
West Virginia
```

It's difficult to prove a negative, especially when a null value is involved. Because the meaning of null is "unknown," the value being searched for could be in the list. The following code sample demonstrates how a null in the list will make it impossible to prove that 'A' is not in the list:

```
SELECT 'IN' WHERE 'A' NOT IN ('B',NULL)
```

There's no result because the unknown null value might simply be an "A." Because SQL can't logically prove that "A" is not in the list, the `where` clause returns a false. Anytime a `not in` condition is mixed with a null in the list, every row will be evaluated as false.

Clearly, `in` is very powerful. Although the preceding query used a hard-coded list of states, when combined with a subquery (explained in the next chapter) to generate a dynamic list, `in` solves a world of problems.

Using the Like Search Condition

The `like` search condition uses wildcards to search for patterns within a string. The wildcards, however, are very different from the MS/DOS wildcards with which you may be familiar. Both the SQL and MS/DOS wildcards are shown in Table 7-2.

Table 7-2: SQL Wildcards

Description	SQL Wildcard	MS/DOS Wildcard	Example
Multiple characters	%	*	'Able' LIKE 'A%'
Single character	_	?	'Able' LIKE 'Abl_'
Match in range of characters	[]	n/a	'a' LIKE '[a-g]'
			'a' LIKE '[abcdefg]'
Match not in range of characters	[^]	n/a	'a' LIKE '[^w-z]'
			'a' LIKE '[^wxyz] '

The next query uses the `like` search condition to locate all products that begin with `'Air'` followed by any number of characters:

```
USE OBXKites

SELECT ProductName
  FROM dbo.Product
  WHERE ProductName LIKE 'Air%';
```

Result:

```
ProductName
-------------------
Air Writer 36
Air Writer 48
Air Writer 66
```

The following query finds any product name beginning with a letter between *a* and *d,* inclusive:

```
SELECT ProductName
  FROM Product
  WHERE ProductName LIKE  '[a-d]%';
```

Result:

```
ProductName
--------------------------------------------------------
Basic Box Kite 21 inch
Dragon Flight
Chinese 6" Kite
Air Writer 36
Air Writer 48
Air Writer 66
Competition 36"
Competition Pro 48"
Black Ghost
Basic Kite Flight
Advanced Acrobatics
Adventures in the OuterBanks
Cape Hatteras T-Shirt
```

You can use one of two methods to search for a pattern that contains a wildcard: either enclose the wildcard in square brackets or put an escape character before it. The trick to the latter workaround is that the escape character is defined within the `like` expression.

The following two examples search for the phrase "F-15" in the OBX Kites `product` table. The first query encloses the hyphen, which is normally a wildcard, in square brackets, while the second query defines the ampersand (&) as the escape character:

```
SELECT ProductCode, ProductName
  FROM Product
  WHERE ProductName LIKE '%F[-]15%';
```

```
SELECT ProductCode, ProductName
  FROM Product
  WHERE ProductName LIKE '%F&-15%' ESCAPE '&';
```

Both queries produce the same result:

```
ProductCode      ProductName
----------------  ------------
1013              Eagle F-15
```

Caution   Of the two methods for searching for wildcard characters, the square bracket method is T-SQL-specific and is not ANSI SQL standard. The escape method, however, is both SQL standard and portable.

When using the like operator, be aware that the database collation's sort order will determine both case sensitivity and the sort order for the range of characters. You can optionally use the keyword collate to specify the collation sort order used by the like operator.

Best Practice   While the like operator can be very useful, it can also cause a performance hit. Indexes are based on the beginning of a column, not on phrases in the middle of the column. If you find that the application requires frequent use of the like operator, you should enable full-text indexing—a powerful indexing method that can even take into consideration weighted words and variations of inflections, and can return the result set in table form with ranking for joining. See Chapter 13, "Using Full Text Search," for more details.

Multiple Where Conditions

You can combine multiple where conditions within the where clause using the Boolean logical operators: and, or, and not. As with the mathematical operators of multiplication and division, an order of precedence exists with the Boolean logical operators: and comes first, then or, and then not:

```
SELECT ProductCode, ProductName
  FROM dbo.Product
  WHERE
      ProductName LIKE  'Air%'
    OR
      ProductCode BETWEEN '1018' AND '1020'
    AND
      ProductName LIKE '%G%';
```

Result:

```
ProductCode      ProductName
----------------  ---------------------
1009             Air Writer 36
1010             Air Writer 48
1011             Air Writer 66
1019             Grand Daddy
1020             Black Ghost
```

When you add parentheses, the result of the query is radically changed:

```
SELECT ProductCode, ProductName
  FROM Product
  WHERE
    (ProductName LIKE  'Air%'
  OR
    ProductCode between '1018' AND '1020')
  AND
    ProductName LIKE '%G%';
```

Result:

```
ProductCode      ProductName
----------------  ---------------------
1019             Grand Daddy
1020             Black Ghost
```

While the two preceding queries are very similar, in the first query the natural order of precedence for Boolean operators caused the and to be evaluated before the or. The or included
the Air Writers in the results.

The second query used parentheses to explicitly dictate the order of the Boolean operators.
The or collected the Air Writers and products with a ProductCode of 1018, 1019, or 1020.
This list was then anded with products that included the letter *g* in their names. Only prod-
ucts 1019 and 1020 passed both of those tests.

Best Practice

> When coding complex Boolean or mathematical expressions, explicitly stating your inten-
> tions with parentheses or detailed code reduces misunderstandings and errors based on
> assumptions.

Select...Where

Amazingly, using the where clause in a select statement does not require the use of a from
clause or any table reference at all. A select statement without a from clause operates as a
single row:

```
SELECT 'abc';
```

Result:

```
abc
```

A where clause on a non-table select statement serves as a restriction to the entire select statement. If the where condition is true, the select statement will function as expected:

```
SELECT 'abc' WHERE 1>0;
```

Result:

```
abc
```

If the where condition is false, the select statement is not executed:

```
DECLARE @test NVARCHAR(15) ;
SET @test = 'z';
SELECT @test = 'abc' WHERE 1<0;
SELECT @test;
```

Result:

```
z
```

Functionally, a where clause on a non-table select statement is shorthand for an if condition, such as the one that follows:

```
DECLARE @test NVARCHAR(15);
SET @test = 'z';
IF 1<0
  SELECT @test = 'abc';
SELECT @test;
```

Result:

```
z
```

Ordering the Result Set

Data in a SQL table takes the form of an unsorted list. The primary key's purpose is to uniquely identify the row, not sort the table. Other desktop databases may present the table in the order of the primary key if no order by clause exists. However, it is not good practice to depend on that behavior. If you do not specify an order by clause, the order of the rows in the result set will have no defined meaning.

Having said that, if no order by clause exists, SQL Server will return the rows in the order in which they are fetched. If a table has a clustered index, the rows will likely be returned according to the clustered index. Other logical operations within the query may sort the data to support the logical operation. For example, some joins will sort the data to make the join easier to perform. Therefore, even without an order by clause, the data result may appear to be sorted. Again, if the rows must be in a specific order, the best practice is to specify that order within an order by clause, as demonstrated in Figure 7-4.

SQL can sort by multiple columns, and the sort columns don't have to be columns that are returned by the select, so there's a lot of flexibility in how the columns are specified.

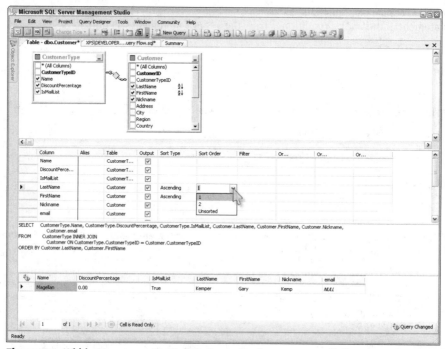

Figure 7-4: Within Management Studio's Query Designer, you can define the sort order by clicking the Ascending or Descending button on the toolbar, or by setting the sort order in the Grid pane.

Specifying the Order by Using Column Names

The simplest way to sort the result set is to completely spell out the order by columns:

```
USE CHA2

SELECT FirstName, LastName
  FROM dbo.Customer
  ORDER BY LastName, FirstName;
```

Result:

```
FirstName      LastName
------------   --------------------
Joe            Adams
Missy          Anderson
Debbie         Andrews
Dave           Bettys
...
```

Note   Order by and the order of columns in the select list are completely independent.

Specifying the Order by Using Expressions

In the case of sorting by an expression, the entire expression can be repeated in the order by clause. This does not cause a performance hit because the SQL Server Query Optimizer is smart enough to avoid recomputing the expression:

```
SELECT LastName + ', ' + FirstName
  FROM dbo.Customer
  ORDER BY LastName + ', ' + FirstName;
```

Result:

```
FullName
----------------------
Adams, Joe
Anderson, Missy
Andrews, Debbie
Bettys, Dave
...
```

Using an expression in the order by clause can solve some headaches. Some database developers store titles in two columns: one column includes the full title, and the duplicate column stores the title stripped of the leading "The." In terms of performance, such denormalization might be a good idea, but using a case expression within the order by clause will sort correctly without duplicating the title.

Cross-Reference
The full syntax for the case expression is covered in the Chapter 8, "Using Expressions and Scalar Functions."

The Aesop's Fables sample database includes a list of titles. If the Title includes a leading "The," then the case expression removes it from the data and passes to the order by:

```
USE Aesop;
SELECT Title, Len(FableText) AS TextLength
  FROM Fable
  ORDER BY
    CASE
      WHEN SubString(Title, 1,3) = 'The'
        THEN SubString(Title, 5, Len(Title)-4)
      ELSE Title
    END;
```

Result:

```
FableName                        TextLength
------------------------------  -----------
Androcles                        1370
The Ant and the Chrysalis        1087
The Ants and the Grasshopper     456
The Ass in the Lion's Skin       465
The Bald Knight                  360
The Boy and the Filberts         435
The Bundle of Sticks             551
The Crow and the Pitcher         491
...
```

Specifying the Order by Using Column Aliases

Alternatively, a column alias may be used to specify the columns used in the order by clause. This is the preferred method for sorting by an expression, because it makes the code easier to read. Note that this example sorts in descending order rather than the default ascending order:

```
SELECT LastName + ', ' + FirstName as FullName
  FROM dbo.Customer
  ORDER BY FullName DESC
```

Result:

```
FullName
-------------
Zeniod, Kent
Williams, Larry
Valentino, Mary
Spade, Sam
...
```

An alias is allowed in the order by clause, but not the where clause, because the where clause is logically executed near the beginning of the query execution, whereas the order by clause is the last logical operation and follows the assembling of the columns and aliases.

Specifying the Order by Using Column Ordinal Position

The ordinal number of the column (column position number) can be used to indicate the order by columns. However, I don't recommend this method. If the columns are changed at the beginning of the select statement, the order by will function differently. Use the ordinal number to specify the sort for complex union queries, which are discussed in Chapter 9, "Merging Data with Joins and Unions." The following query demonstrates sorting by ordinal position:

```
SELECT LastName + ', ' + FirstName AS FullName
  FROM dbo.Customer
  ORDER BY 1
```

Result:

```
FullName
---------------------
Adams, Joe
Anderson, Missy
Andrews, Debbie
Bettys, Dave
...
```

Order by and Collation

SQL Server's collation order is vital to sorting data. Besides determining the alphabet, the collation order also determines whether accents, case, and other alphabet properties are considered in the sort order. For example, if the collation is case sensitive, the uppercase letters are sorted before the lowercase letters. The following function reports the installed collation options and the current collation server property:

```
SELECT * FROM ::fn_helpcollations()
```

Result:

```
name                    description
--------------------    ------------------------
Albanian_BIN            Albanian, binary sort
Albanian_CI_AI          Albanian, case-insensitive,
                        accent-insensitive,
                        kanatype-insensitive, width-insensitive
Albanian_CI_AI_WS       Albanian, case-insensitive,
                        accent-insensitive,
                        kanatype-insensitive, width-sensitive

...
SQL_Latin1_General_CP1_CI_AI
                        Latin1-General, case-insensitive,
                        accent-insensitive,
                        kanatype-insensitive, width-insensitive
                        for Unicode Data, SQL Server Sort Order
                        54 on Code Page 1252 for non-Unicode
                        Data

...
```

The following query reports the current server collation:

```
SELECT SERVERPROPERTY('Collation') AS ServerCollation
```

Result:

```
ServerCollation
------------------------
SQL_Latin1_General_CP1_CI_AS
```

While the server collation setting was determined during setup, the collation property for a database or column can be set using the `collate` keyword. The following code changes the `Family` database collation so that it becomes case sensitive:

```
ALTER DATABASE Family
  COLLATE SQL_Latin1_General_CP1_CS_AS

SELECT DATABASEPROPERTYEX(Family,'Collation')
  AS DatabaseCollation
```

Result:

```
DatabaseCollation
-----------------------------------
SQL_Latin1_General_CP1_CS_AS
```

Not only can SQL Server set the collation at the server, database, and column levels, collation can even be set at the individual query level. The following query will be sorted according to the Danish collation without regard to case or accents:

```
SELECT *
  FROM dbo.Product
  ORDER BY ProductName
    COLLATE Danish_Norwegian_CI_AI
```

Not all queries need to be sorted, but for those that do, the `order by` clause combined with the many possible collations yields tremendous flexibility in sorting the result set.

Select Distinct

The first predicate option in the select command is the keyword distinct, which eliminates duplicate rows from the result set of the query. The duplications are based only on the
output columns, not the underlying tables. The opposite of distinct is all. Because all is
the default, it is typically ignored.

The following code sample demonstrates the difference between distinct and all. Joins are
explained in Chapter 9, "Merging Data with Joins and Unions," but here the join between
tour and event is generating a row each time a tour is run as an event. Because this select
statement returns only the tourname column, it's a perfect example of duplicate rows for the
distinct predicate:

```
SELECT ALL TourName
  FROM Event
    JOIN Tour
      ON Event.TourID = Tour.TourID
```

Result:

```
TourName
-------------------------------------------------
Amazon Trek
Amazon Trek
Appalachian Trail
Appalachian Trail
Appalachian Trail
Bahamas Dive
Bahamas Dive
Bahamas Dive
Gauley River Rafting
Gauley River Rafting
Outer Banks Lighthouses
Outer Banks Lighthouses
Outer Banks Lighthouses
Outer Banks Lighthouses
Outer Banks Lighthouses
Outer Banks Lighthouses
```

With the distinct predicate:

```
SELECT DISTINCT TourName
  FROM Event
    JOIN Tour
      ON Event.TourID = Tour.TourID
```

Result:

```
TourName
-----------------------------------
Amazon Trek
Appalachian Trail
```

```
Bahamas Dive
Gauley River Rafting
Outer Banks Lighthouses
```

While the first query returned 16 rows, the distinct predicate in the second query elimi-nated the duplicate rows and returned only five unique rows.

Note SQL Server's distinct is different from MS Access's distinctrow, which eliminates duplicates based on data in the source table(s), not duplicates in the result set of the query.

Select distinct functions as though a group by clause (discussed in Chapter 11, "Aggregating Data") exists on every output column. Examining the query execution plan for the two previous queries (see Figure 7-5), you can clearly see the distinct as a Stream Aggregate operation, so distinct does require another step in the query execution plan. The performance hit, however, is small (details of the operation reveal that only .000006 percent of the query-execution time is used performing the Stream Aggregate operation); if distinct is logically necessary, you should not avoid it because of its effect on performance.

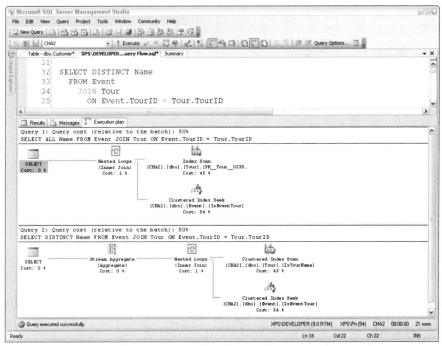

Figure 7-5: Comparing the query execution plan for the two queries reveals the Stream Aggregate operation, which performs the distinct predicate and eliminates duplicate rows.

Ranking

By definition, select works with sets of data. Sometimes, however, it's only the first few rows from the set that are of interest. For these situations, SQL Server includes several ways to filter the results and find the top rows.

Top

As mentioned earlier, SQL Server will return all the rows from the select statement by default. The optional top predicate tells SQL Server to return only a few rows (either a fixed number or a percentage), based upon the options specified, as shown in Figure 7-6.

Top works hand-in-hand with order by. It's the order by clause that determines which rows are first. If the select statement does not have an order by clause, the top predicate still works by returning an unordered sampling of the result set.

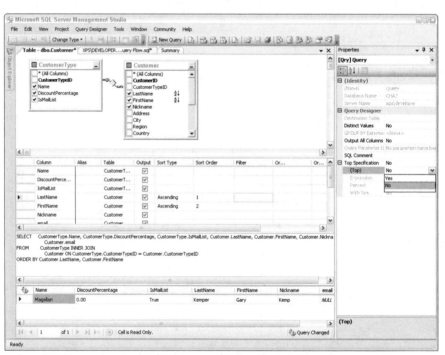

Figure 7-6: The top predicate is set within Management Studio inside the query's Properties page.

The OBXKites sample database is a good place to test the top predicate. The following query finds the top 3 percent of prices in the price table. The price table allows each product to have multiple prices, according to the effective date:

```
SELECT TOP 3 PERCENT Code, ProductName, Price,
    CONVERT(VARCHAR(10),EffectiveDate,1) AS PriceDate
  FROM Product
    JOIN Price ON Product.ProductID = Price.ProductID
  ORDER BY Price DESC
```

Result:

ProductCode	ProductName	Price	PriceDate
1018	Competition Pro 48"	284.9500	05/01/01
1018	Competition Pro 48"	264.9500	05/01/02
1017	Competition 36"	245.9500	05/20/03
1017	Competition 36"	225.9500	05/01/01

The next query locates the three lowest prices in the price table:

```
SELECT TOP 3 Code, ProductName, Price,
    CONVERT(VARCHAR(10),EffectiveDate,1) AS PriceDate
  FROM Product
    JOIN Price ON Product.ProductID = Price.ProductID
  ORDER BY Price
```

Result:

ProductCode	ProductName	Price	PriceDate
1044	OBX Car Bumper Sticker	.7500	05/01/01
1045	OBX Car Window Decal	.7500	05/20/01
1045	OBX Car Window Decal	.9500	05/20/02

The query looks clean and the result looks good, but unfortunately it's wrong. If you look at the raw data sorted by price, you'll actually see three rows with a price of 95 cents. The with ties option solves this problem.

By the very nature of the formatting, computer-generated data tends to appear correct. Testing the query against a subset of data and known results is the best way to check its quality.

Best Practice

The With Ties Option

The with ties option is important to the top predicate. It allows the last place to include multiple rows if those rows have equal values in the columns used in the order by clause. The following version of the preceding query includes the with ties option and correctly results in five rows from a top 3 predicate:

```
SELECT TOP 3 WITH TIES ProductCode,
    ProductName, Price,
    CONVERT(varchar(10),EffectiveDate,1) AS PriceDate
  FROM Product
    JOIN Price ON Product.ProductID = Price.ProductID
  ORDER BY Price
```

Result:

```
ProductCode   ProductName              Price     PriceDate
------------  -----------------------  --------  ----------
1044          OBX Car Bumper Sticker   .7500     05/01/01
1045          OBX Car Window Decal     .7500     05/20/01
1045          OBX Car Window Decal     .9500     05/20/02
1041          Kite Fabric #6           .9500     05/01/01
1042          Kite Fabric #8           .9500     05/01/01
```

Note   If you are moving from Access to SQL Server, be aware that, by default, Access adds the `with ties` option to the `top` predicate automatically.

Caution   Top is a Microsoft T-SQL extension to ANSI SQL and is not portable. If the database must be migrated to another database platform, the use of `top` will become a conversion problem. In contrast, the `rowcount` variable is portable.

New in 2005   SQL Server 2005 introduces several new ranking functions, including `rownumber()`, `rank()`, `denserank()`, and `ntile()`. These new functions may be used as advanced `top` commands. For more information refer to Chapter 8, "Using Expressions and Scalar Functions."

Summary

The heart of SQL is its ability to manipulate data, and the `select` command excels in this area. While this chapter did include a few joins in some of the examples, every technique may be used in a single table join. A wealth of power and flexibility is hidden in the simple `select` command. SQL is declarative—you're only phrasing a question. The Query Optimizer figures out how to execute the query, so you have some flexibility in the development style of the query.

From this foundation, the next nine chapters explore advanced features that add to the power of `select`, incorporating complex expressions, multiple types of joins, subqueries, and groupings. Welcome to the set-based power of SQL.

Using Expressions and Scalar Functions

◆   ◆   ◆   ◆

In This Chapter

Working with expressions and scalar functions

Using logic within a query

Working with nulls, strings, and dates

◆   ◆   ◆   ◆

When my son, David, was younger he built incredible monster trucks and gizmos out of K'NEX construction pieces. If you aren't familiar with K'NEX, do a Google image search and see the wild things kids build with them.

What makes K'NEX cool is that nearly any piece can plug into any other piece. This interconnectivity makes K'NEX flexible. In the same way, the interconnectivity of SQL expressions and functions makes SQL so flexible and powerful.

Expressions can retrieve data from a subquery, handle complex logic, convert data types, and manipulate data. If the secret to being a competent SQL database developer is mastering SQL queries, then wielding expressions and scalar functions is definitely in the arsenal.

An expression is any combination of constants, functions, or formulas that returns a single value. Expressions may be as simple as a hard-coded number, or as complex as a case expression that includes several formulas and functions.

Expressions may be employed in several places within the SQL syntax. Nearly anywhere a value may be used, an expression may be used instead. This includes column values, join on clauses, where and having clauses, and order by columns. Expressions can't be substituted for object names such as table names or column names.

Note   SQL statements are not case-sensitive. The statement will execute whether you use uppercase, lowercase, or mixed case.

Building Expressions

You can construct SQL expressions from a nearly limitless list of constants, variables, operators, and functions, as detailed in Table 8-1. Figure 8-1 illustrates creating an expression using the graphic interface and assigning the column an alias.

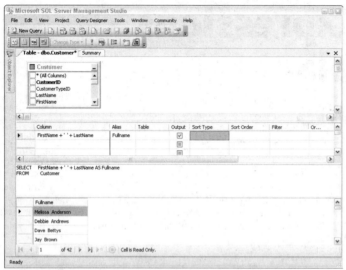

Figure 8-1: Building an expression and assigning an alias with Management Studio's Query Designer

Table 8-1: Building Expressions

Expression Components	Examples
Numeric constants	1, 2, 3
String literals	'LastName', 'Employee: ', 'Life''s Great!'
Dates	'1/6/80', 'Jan 6, 1980', '19800106'
Mathematical operators (in order of precedence)	*, /, % (remainder), +, -
String operator (concatenation)	+
Bitwise operators	and &, or |, exclusive or ^, not ~
Columns	LastName, PrimaryKeyID

Case Expressions	CASE Column1
	  WHEN 1 THEN 'on'
	  ELSE 'off'
	END AS Status

Subqueries	(Select 3)
User-defined variables	@MyVariable
Global variables	ørror
Scalar functions	GetDate(), SysUser()
User-defined functions	dbo.MyUDF()

Cross-Reference Subqueries are covered in Chapter 10, "Including Subqueries and CTEs." Variables are discussed in Chapter 18, "Programming with Transact-SQL." User-defined functions are detailed in Chapter 22, "Building User-Defined Functions."

Operators

While the meaning of many of these expression constants, operators, and expressions is obvious and common to other programming languages, a few deserve special mention:

✦ The Modulo mathematical operator (%) returns only the remainder of the division. The `floor()` (that's "deck" for sailors) and `ceiling()` mathematical functions, which return the integer rounded down or up, are related to it. The `floor()` function is the SQL Server equivalent of the Basic `int()` function:

```
SELECT 15%4 as Modulo,
  FLOOR(1.25) as [Floor], CEILING(1.25) as [Ceiling]
```

Result:

```
Modulo      Floor Ceiling
----------- ----- -------
3           1     2
```

✦ The + operator is used for both mathematical expressions and string concatenation. This operator is different from the MS-DOS symbol for string concatenation, the ampersand (&):

```
SELECT 123 + 456 as Addition,
  'abc' + 'defg' as Concatenation
```

Result:

```
Addition    Concatenation
----------- -------------
579         abcdefg
```

Data from table columns and string literals may be concatenated to return custom data:

```
Select 'Product: ' + ProductName as [Product]
  From Product
```

Result:

```
Product
----------------------------------
Product: Basic Box Kite 21 inch
Product: Dragon Flight
Product: Sky Dancer
...
```

Bitwise Operators

The bitwise operators are useful for binary manipulation. These aren't typically used in transactional databases, but they can prove useful for certain metadata operations. For example, one way to determine which columns were updated in a *trigger,* code that is executed as the result of a data insert, update, or delete (see Chapter 23), is to inspect the `columns_updated()`

function, which returns a binary representation of those columns. The trigger code can test `columns_updated()` using bitwise operations and respond to updates on a column-by-column basis.

Boolean bit operators (`and`, `or`, and `not`) are the basic building blocks of digital electronics and binary programming. While digital-electronic Boolean gates operate upon single bits, these bitwise operators work across every bit of the integer family data type (`int`, `smallint`, `tinyint`, and `bit`) values.

Boolean And

A Boolean "and" (represented by the ampersand character, `&`) returns a value of `true` only if both inputs are true. If either or both are false, the "and" will return a value of `false`, as follows:

```
SELECT 1 & 1
```

Result:

```
1
```

Another "and" example:

```
SELECT 1 & 0
```

Result:

```
0
```

"And"ing two integers is illustrated as follows:

```
--  3 = 011
--  5 = 101
-- AND ---
--  1 = 001

SELECT 3 & 5
```

Result:

```
1
```

Boolean Or

The Boolean "or" operator, the vertical pipe character (`|`), returns `true` if either input is true:

```
SELECT 1 | 1
```

Result:

```
1
```

The following `select` statement combines a set and a cleared bit using the bitwise `or` operator:

```
SELECT 1 | 0
```

Result:

```
1
```

"Or"ing two integers can be illustrated as follows:

```
-- 3 = 011
-- 5 = 101
-- OR  ---
-- 7 = 111

SELECT 3 | 5
```

Result:

```
7
```

Boolean Exclusive Or

The "exclusive or" bitwise operator, the carat (^), returns a value of true if either input is true, but not if both are true. Using it is the same as "or"ing two "and"s, each with a "not" on one input. While that's simple to build in digital electronics, in code the operator is much easier to use, as shown here:

```
SELECT 1^1
```

Result:

```
0
```

A set bit "exclusive or"ed with a cleared bit results in a set bit:

```
SELECT 1^0
```

Result:

```
1
```

Bitwise Not

The last bitwise operator, denoted by the tilde (~), is a bitwise "not" function. Traditionally, the "not" operates on a single bit and is used to alter the input of an "or" or "and" digital gate. This bitwise "not" is a little different. The "not" performs a logical bit reversal for every bit in the expression. The result depends on the data length of the expression. For example, the bitwise "not" of a set bit is a cleared bit:

```
DECLARE @A BIT
SET @A = 1
SELECT ~@A
```

Result:

```
0
```

The bitwise "not" is not suitable for use with Boolean expressions such as if conditions. The following code, for example, is invalid:

```
SELECT  * FROM Product WHERE ~(1=1)
```

Note that the "not" operator also serves as the "one's complement" operator.

Case Expressions

SQL Server's `case` command is a flexible and excellent means of building dynamic expressions. If you're a programmer, no doubt you use the `case` command in other languages. This `case` command, however, is different. It's not used for programmatic flow of control, but rather to logically determine the value of an expression based on a condition, much like the `if()` function in other programming languages.

Like any other expression, a `case` expression won't automatically have a column name. Therefore, as a rule, always provide an alias for any `case` expression.

Best Practice

When programmers write procedural code, it's often because part of the formula changes depending on the data. To a procedural mind-set, the best way to handle this is to loop through the rows and use multiple `if` statements to branch to the correct formula. However, using a `case` expression to handle the various calculations and executing the entire operation in a single query allows SQL Server to optimize the process and is dramatically faster.

Because the `case` expression returns an expression, it may be used anywhere in the SQL DML statement (`Select`, `Insert`, `Update`, `Delete`) where an expression may be used, including column expressions, `join` conditions, `where` conditions, `having` conditions, or in the `order by`.

The `case` statement has two forms, simple and Boolean, described in the following sections.

Simple Case

Gordon 1 877 371 6618

With the simple `case`, the value is presented first and then each test value is listed. However, this `case` is limited in that it can perform only equal comparisons. The `case` expression sequentially checks the `when` conditions and returns the `then` value of the first true `when` condition.

In the following example, based on the OBX Kite Store database, one `customertype` is the default for new customers and is set to `true` in the `isdefault` column. The `case` expression compares the value in the default column with each possible bit setting and returns the character string `'default type'` or `'possible'` based on the bit setting:

```
USE OBXKites
SELECT CustomerTypeName,
    CASE [IsDefault]
      WHEN 1 THEN 'default type'
      WHEN 0 THEN 'possible'
      ELSE '-'
    End as AssignStatus
  From CustomerType
```

Result:

```
CustomerTypeName         AssignStatus
------------------------ ------------
Preferred                possible
Wholesale                possible
Retail                   default type
```

The case expression concludes with an end and an alias. In this example, the case expression evaluates the isdefault column, but produces the AssignStatus column in the SQL select result set.

Boolean Case

The Boolean form of case is more flexible than the simple form in that each individual case has its own Boolean expression. Therefore, not only can each when condition include comparisons other than =, but the comparison may also reference different columns:

```
SELECT
  CASE
    WHEN 1<0 THEN 'Reality is gone.'
    WHEN GetDate() = '11/30/2005'
      THEN 'David gets his driver''s license.'
    WHEN 1>0 THEN 'Life is normal.'
  END AS RealityCheck
```

Following is the result of the query when executed on David's sixteenth birthday:

```
RealityCheck
--------------------------------
David gets his driver's license.
```

As with the simple case, the first true then condition halts evaluation of the case and returns the when value. In this case (Ha! A pun!), if 1 is ever more than 0, the RealityCheck case will accurately report 'reality is gone.' When my son turns 16, the realitycheck will again accurately warn us of his legal driving status. If neither of these conditions is true, and 1 is still greater than 0, all is well with reality and 'Life is normal.'

The point of the preceding code is that the Boolean case expression offers more flexibility than the simple case. This example mixed various conditional checks (<, =, >), and differing data was checked by the when clause.

The Boolean case expression can handle complex conditions, including Boolean and and or operators. The following code sample uses a batch to set up the case expression (including T-SQL variables, which are explained in Chapter 18, "Programming with Transact-SQL"), and the case includes an and and a between operator:

```
DECLARE @b INT, @q INT

SET @b = 2007
SET @q = 25

Select CASE
  WHEN @b = 2007 AND @q BETWEEN 10 AND 30 THEN 1
  ELSE NULL
END AS Test
```

Result:

```
Test
---------
1
```

Working with Nulls

The relational database model represents missing data using *null*. Technically, null means "value unknown." In practice, null can indicate that the data has not yet been entered into the database, or the column does not apply to the particular row.

Because null is unknown, the result of any expression that includes null will also be unknown. If the contents of a bank account are unknown, and its funds are included in a portfolio, the total value of the portfolio is also unknown. The same concept is true in SQL, as the following code demonstrates. Phil Senn, a database developer, puts it this way: "Nulls zap the life out of any other value."

```
SELECT 1 + NULL
```

Result:

```
NULL
```

Because they have such a devastating effect on expressions, some developers detest the use of nulls. They develop their databases so that nulls are never permitted and column defaults supply surrogate nulls (blanks, 0s, or "n/a") instead. Other database developers argue that an unknown value shouldn't be represented by a zero or a blank just to make coding easier. I fall in the latter camp. Nulls are valuable in a database because they provide important information about the status of the data, so it's worth your while to write code that checks for nulls and handles them appropriately.

Testing for Null

Because null is unknown, null is not even equal to null. Going back to the bank account example, if the value of account 123 is unknown and the value of account 234 is unknown, then it's logically impossible to prove that the two accounts are equal. Because the = operator can't check for nulls, SQL includes a special operator, is, to test for equivalence to special values, as follows:

```
WHERE Expression IS NULL
```

The is null SQL search condition is used to test for a null value:

```
IF NULL = NULL
  SELECT '='
ELSE
  SELECT '!='
```

Result:

```
!=
```

The is search condition, however, works as advertised:

```
IF NULL IS NULL
  SELECT 'Is'
ELSE
  SELECT 'Is Not'
```

Result:

```
Is
```

The `is` search condition may be used in the `select` statement's `where` clause to locate rows with null values. Most of the Cape Hatteras Adventures customers do not have a nickname in the database. The following query retrieves only those customers with a null in the `Nickname` column:

```
USE CHA2
SELECT FirstName, LastName, Nickname
  FROM dbo.Customer
  WHERE Nickname IS NULL
  ORDER BY LastName, FirstName
```

Result:

```
FirstName     LastName        Nickname
------------- --------------- ----------------
Debbie        Andrews         NULL
Dave          Bettys          NULL
Jay           Brown           NULL
Lauren        Davis           NULL
...
```

The `is` operator may be combined with `not` to test for the presence of a value by restricting the result set to those rows where `Nickname is not null`:

```
SELECT FirstName, LastName, Nickname
  FROM dbo.Customer
  WHERE Nickname IS NOT NULL
  ORDER BY LastName, FirstName
```

Result:

```
FirstName     LastName        Nickname
------------- --------------- ----------------
Joe           Adams           Slim
Melissa       Anderson        Missy
Frank         Goldberg        Frankie
Raymond       Johnson         Ray
...
```

One exception to the rule that adding a null to a value results in null concerns nulls within columns being added by an aggregate function. Aggregate functions (`Sum()`, `Avg()`, and so on) tend to ignore nulls.

Handling Nulls

When you are supplying data to reports, to end users, or to some applications, a null value will be less than welcome. Often a null must be converted to a valid value so the data may be understood, or so the expression won't fail.

Nulls require special handling when used within expressions, and SQL includes a few functions designed specifically to handle nulls. `Isnull()` and `coalesce()` convert nulls to usable values, and `nullif()` will create a null if the specified condition is met.

To complicate matters further, SQL Server uses three-state logic when dealing with Boolean expressions. Comparing a null with a true will yield null.

Using the IsNull() Function

The most common null-handling function is `isnull()`, which is different from the `is null` search condition. This function accepts a single column or expression, and a substitution value. If the source is a valid value (not null), the `isnull()` function passes the value on. However, if the source is a null, the second parameter is substituted for the null, as follows:

```
IsNull(source_expression, replacement_value)
```

Functionally, `isnull()` is the same as the following `case` expression:

```
CASE
  WHEN source_expression IS NULL THEN replacement_value
  ELSE source_expression
END AS ISNULL
```

The following code sample builds on the preceding queries by substituting the string (`'none'`) for a null for customers without a nickname:

```
SELECT FirstName, LastName, ISNULL(Nickname,'none')
  FROM Customer
  ORDER BY LastName, FirstName
```

Result:

```
FirstName      LastName         Nickname
------------   --------------   ----------------
Joe            Adams            Slim
Melissa        Anderson         Missy
Debbie         Andrews          none
Dave           Bettys           none
...
```

If the row has a value in the `Nickname` column, that value is passed though the `isnull()` function untouched. However, if the nickname is null for a row, then the null is handled by the `isnull()` function and converted to the value `none`.

 Caution   The `isnull()` and `nullif()` functions are T-SQL specific and are not ANSI standard SQL.

Coalesce()

`Coalesce()` is rarely used, perhaps because it's not well known. However, it's a cool function. `Coalesce()` accepts a list of expressions or columns and returns the first non-null value, as follows:

```
Coalesce(expression, expression, ...)
```

`Coalesce()` is derived from the Latin words *co + alescre,* which mean to unite toward a common end, to grow together, or to bring opposing sides together for a common good. The SQL keyword, however, is derived from the alternate meaning of the term—"to arise from the combination of distinct elements." In a sense, the `coalesce()` function brings together multiple, differing values of unknown usefulness, and from them emerges a single valid value.

Functionally, `coalesce()` is the same as the following `case` expression:

```
CASE
  WHEN expression1 IS NOT NULL THEN expression1
  WHEN expression2 IS NOT NULL THEN expression2
  WHEN expression3 IS NOT NULL THEN expression3
  ...
END AS COALESCE
```

The following code sample demonstrates the `coalesce()` function returning the first non-null value. In this case, it's 1+2:

```
SELECT Coalesce(NULL, 1+NULL, 1+2, 'abc')
```

Result:

```
3
```

`Coalesce()` is excellent for merging messy data. For example, when a table has partial data in several columns, the `coalesce()` function can help pull the data together. In one project I worked on, the client had collected names and addresses from several databases and applications into a single table. The contact name and company name made it into the proper columns, but some addresses were in `Address1`, some were in `Address2`, and some were in `Address3`. Some rows had the second line of the address in `Address2`. If the address columns had an address, then the `SalesNote` was a real note. In many cases, however, the addresses were in the `SalesNote` column. Here's the code to extract the address from such a mess:

```
SELECT Coalesce(
    Address1 + str(13)+str(10) + Adress2,
    Address1,
    Address2,
    Address3,
    SalesNote) AS NewAddress
  FROM TempSalesContacts
```

For each row in the `TempSalesContacts` table, the `coalesce()` function will search through the listed columns and return the first non-null value. The first expression returns a value only if there's a value in both `Address1` and `Address2`, because a value concatenated with a null produces a null. Therefore, if a two-line address exists, then it will be returned. Otherwise, a one-line address in `Address1`, `Address2`, or `Address3` will be returned. Failing those options, the `SalesNote` column will be returned. Of course, the result from such a messy source table will still need to be manually scanned and verified.

You won't use the `coalesce()` function every day, but it's a useful tool to have in your developer's bag.

Nullif()

Sometimes a null should be created in place of surrogate null values. If a database is polluted with n/a, blank, or – values where it should contain nulls, you can use the `nullif()` function to replace the inconsistent values with nulls and clean the database.

The `nullif()` function accepts two parameters. If they are equal, it returns a null; otherwise, it returns the first parameter. Functionally, `nullif()` is the same as the following `case` expression:

```
CASE
  WHEN Expression1 = Expression2 THEN NULL
  ELSE Expression1
END AS NULLIF
```

The following code will convert any blanks in the `Nickname` column into nulls. The first statement updates one of the rows to a blank for testing purposes:

```
UPDATE Customer
  SET Nickname = ''
  WHERE LastName = 'Adams'

SELECT LastName, FirstName,
    CASE NickName
      WHEN '' THEN 'blank'
      ELSE Nickname
    END AS Nickname,
    NullIf(Nickname,'') as NicknameNullIf
  FROM dbo.Customer
  WHERE LastName IN ('Adams', 'Anderson', 'Andrews')
  ORDER BY LastName, FirstName
```

Result:

```
LastName     FirstName    Nickname    NicknameNullIf
-----------  -----------  ----------  -------------
Adams        Joe          blank       NULL
Anderson     Melissa      Missy       Missy
Andrews      Debbie       NULL        NULL
```

The third column uses a `case` expression to expose the `blank` value as "blank," and indeed the `nullif()` function converts the `blank` value to a null in the fourth column. To test the other null possibilities, Melissa's `Nickname` was not affected by the `nullif()` function, and Debbie's null `Nickname` value was still in place.

Non-Default Null Behavior

So far, everything in this discussion of nulls is based on SQL Server's default behavior with nulls. However, SQL Server is highly flexible, and the null behaviors may be altered.

By all logic, concatenating a null with a value should produce a null, but that behavior can be changed. The connection setting, `concat_null_yields_null`, determines the outcome of concatenating a value with a null. The connection setting is initially determined by the database default with the same name (`concat_null_yields_null`). Changing the null behavior can be difficult to test because Query Analyzer also has a default set of connection settings, which it applies with every new connection.

The following code sets the database option and the connection option to disable the default behavior:

```
-- set database option
sp_dboption 'CHA2',  CONCAT_NULL_YIELDS_NULL, 'false'
-- examine the database option
SELECT DATABASEPROPERTYEX('CHA2', 'IsNullConcat')
```

Result:

```
0
```

Setting the connection setting:

```
SET CONCAT_NULL_YIELDS_NULL OFF
```

Concatenating a null:

```
SELECT NULL + 'abc'
```

Result:

```
abc
```

Normally, in ANSI SQL (and SQL Server) a comparison to null will yield null. For example, evaluating (1>null) results in a null. However, you can change that behavior by setting ANSI nulls off in the connection. The greatest effect of this change is that nulls may be tested with an equals condition instead of only with an is operator.

As with the previous concatenation option, the connection setting is the one that counts. The following code sample sets the database default option and the connection settings to disable ANSI null behavior:

```
-- set database option
sp_dboption 'CHA2',  ANSI_NULLS, 'false'
-- examine the database option
SELECT DATABASEPROPERTYEX('CHA2','IsAnsiNullsEnabled')
```

Result:

```
0
```

Concatenating a null:

```
SET ANSI_NULLS OFF
```

Testing for a null with an equals sign:

```
SELECT 'true' WHERE (NULL = NULL)
```

Result:

```
true
```

Scalar Functions

Scalar functions return a single value. They are commonly used in expressions within the `select` columns, the `where` clause, or T-SQL code. SQL Server includes dozens of functions, as illustrated in Figure 8-2. This section describes the functions I find most useful.

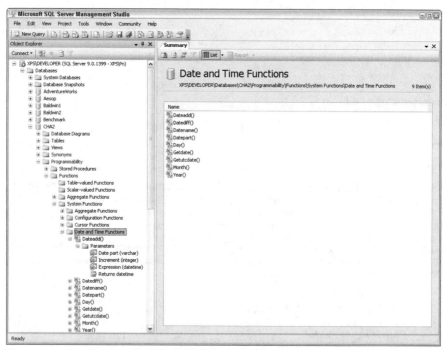

Figure 8-2: Checking out the Object Explorer is the best way to discover all of SQL Server's functions.

Best Practice

Performance is as much a part of the data-schema design as it is a part of the query. Plan on storing the data in the way that it will be searched by a `where` condition, rather than depending upon manipulating the data with functions at query time. While using a function in an expression in a result-set column may be unavoidable, using a function in a `where` condition forces the function to be calculated for every row.

Cross-Reference

With SQL Server 2005 you can develop three types of user-defined functions, as explained in Chapter 22, "Building User-Defined Functions."

User Information Functions

In a client/server environment, it's good to know who the client is. Toward that end, the following four functions are very useful, especially for gathering audit information:

✦ User_name(): Returns the name of the current user as he or she is known to the database. When a user is granted access to a database, the username is different from the server login name that may be assigned.

✦ Suser_sname(): Returns the login name by which the user was authenticated to SQL Server. If the user was authenticated as a member of a Windows user group, this function still returns the user's Windows login name.

✦ Host_name(): Returns the name of the user's workstation.

✦ App_name(): Returns the name of the application connected to SQL Server, as follows:

```
SELECT
  USER_NAME() AS 'User',
  SUSER_SNAME() AS 'Login',
  HOST_NAME() AS 'Workstation',
 APP_NAME() AS 'Application'
```

Result:

```
User    Login            Workstation  Application
------- ---------------- ------------ -------------------
dbo     NOLI\Paul CHA2   NOLI         SQL Query Analyzer
```

Data-Time Functions

Databases must often work with date-time data, and SQL Server includes several useful date-time functions. SQL Server stores both the data and the time in a single data type.

T-SQL includes two functions to return the current datetime:

✦ GetDate(): Returns the current server date and time to the nearest three milliseconds.

✦ GetUTCDate(): Returns the current server date converted to Greenwich Mean Time to the nearest three milliseconds. This is extremely useful for companies that cross time boundaries.

The following four SQL Server date-time functions handle extracting or working with a specific portion of the date or time stored within a datetime column:

Cross-Reference For more information about datetime and other data types, refer to Chapter 17, "Creating the Physical Database Schema."

✦ DateName(date portion, date): Returns the proper name for the selected portion of the datetime value (the portions for datename() and datepart() are listed in Table 8-2):

```
SELECT DATENAME(Year, GetDate()) as Year
```

Result:

```
Year
--------
2001
```

The following code example assigns to Mr. Frank a date of birth and then retrieves the proper names of some of the portions of that date of birth using the datename() function:

```
UPDATE Guide
  SET DateOfBirth = '9/4/58'
  WHERE lastName = 'Frank'
```

Result:

```
SELECT LastName,
    DATENAME(yy,DateOfBirth) AS [Year],
    DATENAME(mm,DateOfBirth) AS [Month],
    DATENAME(dd,DateOfBirth) AS [Day],
    DATENAME(weekday, DateOfBirth) AS BirthDay
  FROM dbo.Guide
  WHERE DateOfBirth IS NOT NULL

LastName   Year   Month         Day   BirthDay
---------  -----  -----------   ----  ----------------
Frank      1958   September     4     Thursday
```

Table 8-2: Datetime Portions Used by Date Functions

Portion	Abbreviation
Year	yy, yyyy
Quarter	qq, q
Month	mm, m
DayofYear	dy, d
Day	dd, d
Week	wk, ww
Weekday	dw
Hour	hh
Minute	mi, n
Second	ss, s
Millisecond	ms

✦ DatePart(date portion, date): Returns the selected portion of the datetime value. The following example retrieves the day of the year and the day of the week as integers:

```
SELECT DATEPART(DayofYear, GetDate()) AS DayCount
```

Result:

```
DayCount
-----------
321
```

```
SELECT DATEPART(dw, GetDate()) AS DayWeek
```

Result:

```
DayWeek
-----------
7
```

The easiest way to get just the date, stripping off the time, is to use a couple of string functions:

```
Select Cast(Char(10), GetDate(), 101) as DateTime
```

✦ DateAdd(date portion, amount, beginning date) and DateDiff(date portion, amount, beginning date): Performs addition and subtraction on datetime data. Databases must often perform addition and subtraction on datetime data. The datediff() and the dateadd() functions are designed expressly for this purpose. The datediff() doesn't look at the complete date but just the date part being extracted.

The following query calculates the number of years and days that my wife, Melissa, and I have been married:

```
SELECT
   DATEDIFF(yy,'1984/5/20', Getdate()) AS MarriedYears,
   DATEDIFF(dd,'1984/5/20', Getdate()) AS MarriedDays
```

Result:

```
MarriedYears MarriedDays
------------ -----------
17           6390
```

The next query adds 100 hours to the current millisecond:

```
SELECT DATEADD(hh,100, GETDATE()) AS [100HoursFromNow]
```

Result:

```
100HoursFromNow
------------------------
2001-11-21 18:42:03.507
```

The following query is based on the Family sample database and calculates the mother's age at the birth of each child using the `datediff()` function:

```
USE Family
SELECT Person.FirstName + ' ' + Person.LastName AS Mother,
    DATEDIFF(yy, Person.DateOfBirth,
    Child.DateOfBirth) AS Age,Child.FirstName
  FROM Person
    JOIN Person Child
      ON Person.PersonID = Child.MotherID
  ORDER By Age DESC
```

The `datediff` function in this query returns the year difference between `Person.DateOfBirth`, which is the mother's birth date, and the child's date of birth. Because the function is in a column expression, it's calculated for each row in the result set:

```
Mother                              Age        FirstName
----------------------------------- ---------- ----------------
Audrey Halloway                      33         Corwin
Kimberly Kidd                        31         Logan
Elizabeth Campbell                   31         Alexia
Melanie Campbell                     30         Adam
Grace Halloway                       30         James
...
```

Best Practice

SQL Server does not include a `date only` data type, but many applications require only the date. To avoid query confusion, strip off the time data and store only the date using a trigger. Triggers are discussed in Chapter 23.

String Functions

Like most modern programming languages, T-SQL includes many string-manipulation functions:

✦ `SubString(string, starting position, length)`: Returns a portion of a string. The first parameter is the string, the second parameter is the beginning position of the substring to be extracted, and the third parameter is the length of the string extracted:

```
SELECT SUBSTRING('abcdefg', 3, 2)
```

Result:

```
cd
```

✦ `Stuff(string, insertion position, delete count, string inserted)`: The inverse of `substring()`, the `stuff()` function inserts one string into another string. The inserted string may delete a specified number of characters as it is being inserted:

```
SELECT STUFF('abcdefg', 3, 2, '123')
```

Result:

```
ab123efg
```

The following code sample uses nested `stuff()` functions to format a U.S. Social Security Number:

```
SELECT STUFF(STUFF('123456789', 4, 0, '-'), 7, 0, '-')
```

Result:

```
123-45-6789
```

✦ `CharIndex(search string, string, starting position)`: Returns the character position of a string within a string:

```
SELECT CHARINDEX('c', 'abcdefg', 1)
```

Result:

```
3
```

The `TitleCase()` user-defined function later in this section uses the `CharIndex()` to locate the spaces separating words.

✦ `PatIndex(%pattern%, string)`: Searches for a pattern, which may include wildcards, within a string. The following code locates the first position of either a c or d in the string:

```
SELECT PATINDEX('%[cd]%', 'abdcdefg')
```

Result:

```
3
```

✦ `Right(string, count)` and `Left(string, count)`: Returns the rightmost or leftmost part of a string:

```
SELECT Left('Nielsen',2) AS '[Left]',
  RIGHT('Nielsen',2) AS [Right]
```

Result:

```
Left  Right
----- ----
Ni    en
```

✦ `Len(string)`: Returns the length of a string:

```
SELECT LEN('Supercalifragilisticexpialidocious') AS Len
```

Result:

```
Len
-----------
34
```

✦ `Rtrim(string)` and `Ltrim(string)`: Removes leading or trailing spaces. While it's difficult to see in print, the three leading and trailing spaces are removed from the following string. I adjusted the column-header lines with the remaining spaces to illustrate the functions:

```
SELECT RTRIM('   middle earth   ') AS [RTrim],
  LTRIM('   middle earth   ') AS [LTrim]
```

Result:

```
RTrim           LTrim
--------------- ---------------
   middle earth middle earth
```

✦ Upper(string) and Lower(string): Converts the entire string to uppercase or lower-case. *Minuscules,* or lowercase letters, were first used in the ninth century to facilitate handwriting. With the advent of the printing press in the fifteenth century, printers manually set the type for each page printed. They stored the letters in cases above the page box. The *uncials* (capital letters) were stored above the minuscules. The terms "uppercase" and "lowercase" stuck. Other than the history, there's not much to know about these two functions, illustrated here:

```
Select UPPER('one TWO tHrEe') as [UpperCase],
  LOWER('one TWO tHrEe') as [LowerCase]
```

Result:

```
UpperCase       LowerCase
-------------   -------------
ONE TWO THREE   one two three
```

✦ Replace(string, string): The replace() function operates as a global search and replace within a string. Using replace() within an update DML command can quickly fix problems in the data, such as removing extra tabs or correcting string patterns. The following code sample removes apostrophes from the LastName column in the OBXKites database's Contact table:

```
USE OBXKites

UPDATE Contact
  SET LastName = 'Adam''s'
  WHERE LastName = 'Adams'

SELECT LastName, REPLACE(LastName, '''', '')
  FROM Contact
  WHERE LastName LIKE '%''%'

UPDATE Contact
  SET LastName = REPLACE(LastName, '''', '')
  WHERE LastName LIKE '%''%'
```

Note   When working with string literals, it's generally difficult to insert a quote into the string without ending the string and causing a syntax error. SQL Server handles this situation by accepting two single quotes and converting them into one single quote within the string:

```
'Life''s Great!' is stored as:  Life's Great!
```

✦ pTitleCase(source, search, replace): T-SQL lacks a function to convert text to title case (first letter of each word in uppercase, and the remainder in lowercase). Therefore, the following user-defined function accomplishes this task:

```
CREATE FUNCTION pTitleCase (
  @StrIn NVARCHAR(1024))
RETURNS NVARCHAR(1024)
AS
  BEGIN
    DECLARE
      @StrOut NVARCHAR(1024),
      @CurrentPosition INT,
      @NextSpace INT,
      @CurrentWord NVARCHAR(1024),
      @StrLen INT,
      @LastWord BIT

    SET @NextSpace = 1
    SET @CurrentPosition = 1
    SET @StrOut = ''
    SET @StrLen = LEN(@StrIn)
    SET @LastWord = 0

    WHILE @LastWord = 0
      BEGIN
        SET @NextSpace =
          CHARINDEX(' ',@StrIn, @CurrentPosition+ 1)
        IF  @NextSpace = 0 -- no more spaces found
          BEGIN
            SET @NextSpace = @StrLen
            SET @LastWord = 1
          END
        SET @CurrentWord =
          UPPER(SUBSTRING(@StrIn, @CurrentPosition, 1))
        SET @CurrentWord = @CurrentWord +
          LOWER(SUBSTRING(@StrIn, @CurrentPosition+1,
                 @NextSpace - @CurrentPosition))
        SET @StrOut = @StrOut +@CurrentWord
        SET @CurrentPosition = @NextSpace + 1
      END
    RETURN @StrOut
  END
```

Running a user-defined function requires including the owner name in the function name:

```
Select dbo.pTitleCase('one TWO tHrEe') as [TitleCase]
```

Result:

```
TitleCase
-----------------------
One Two Three
```

Note   The `pTitleCase` function does not take into consideration surnames with nonstandard capitalization, such as McDonald, VanCamp, or de Jonge. It would be inadequate to hard-code a list of exceptions. Perhaps the best solution is to store a list of exception phrases (Mc, Van, de, and so on) in an easily updateable list. Go to `www.isnotnull.com` to see whether I've updated the function, or if you'd like to submit further enhancements.

On The Web   The code for the `pTitleCase` user-defined function can be downloaded from `www.SQLServerBible.com`.

Soundex Functions

Soundex is a phonetic pattern-matching system created for the American census. Franklin Roosevelt directed the United States Bureau of Archives to develop a method of cataloging the population that could handle variations in the spelling of similar surnames. Margaret K. Odell and Robert C. Russell developed Soundex and were awarded U.S. patents 1261167 (1918) and 1435663 (1922) for their efforts. The census filing card for each household was then filed under the Soundex method. Soundex has been applied to every census since and has been post-applied to census records back to 1880.

The purpose of Soundex is to sort similar-sounding names together, which is very useful for dealing with contact information in a database application. For example, if I call a phone bank and give them my name (Nielsen), they invariably spell it "Nelson" in the contact lookup form, but if the database uses Soundex properly then I'll still be in the search-result list box.

For more information concerning Soundex and its history, refer to the following websites:

✦ `www.nara.gov/genealogy/coding.html`

✦ `www.amberskyline.com/treasuremaps/uscensus.html`

✦ `www.bluepoof.com/soundex/`

Here's how Soundex works. The first letter of a name is stored as the letter, and the following three Soundex phonetic sounds are stored according to the following code:

```
1 - B, F, P, V
2 - C, G, J, K, Q, S, X, Z
3 - D, T
4 - L
5 - M, N
6 - R
```

Double letters with the same Soundex code, A, E, I, O, U, H, W, Y, and some prefixes, are disregarded. Therefore, "Nielsen" becomes "N425" via the following method:

1. The *N* is stored.

2. The *i* and *e* are disregarded.

3. The *l* sound is stored as the Soundex code 4.

4. The *s* is stored as the Soundex code 2.

5. The *e* is ignored.

6. The *n* is stored as the Soundex code 5.

By boiling them down to a few consonant sounds, Soundex assigns "Nielsen," "Nelson," and "Neilson" the same code: N425.

Following are additional Soundex name examples:

✦ Brown = B650 (r—6, n—5)

✦ Jeffers = J162 (ff —1, r—6, s—2)

✦ Letterman = L365 (tt—3, r—6, m—5)

✦ Nelson = N425 (l—4, s—2, n—5)

✦ Nicholson = N242 (c—2, l—4, s—2)

✦ Nickols = N242 (c—2, l—4, s—2)

Using the Soundex() Function

SQL Server includes two Soundex-related functions, `soundex()` and `difference()`. The `soundex(string)` function calculates the Soundex code for a string as follows:

```
SELECT SOUNDEX('Nielsen') AS Nielsen,
   SOUNDEX('Nelson') AS NELSON,
   SOUNDEX('Neilson') AS NEILSON
```

Result:

```
Nielsen NELSON NEILSON
------- ------ -------
N425    N425   N425
```

Note   Other, more refined, soundex methods exist. Ken Henderson, in his book *The Guru's Guide to Transact SQL* (Addison-Wesley, 2000), provides an improved Soundex algorithm and stored procedure. If you are going to implement Soundex in a production application, I recommend exploring his version. Alternately, you can research one of the other refined Soundex methods on the websites listed previously and write your own custom stored procedure.

There are two possible ways to add Soundex searches to a database. The simplest method is to add the `soundex()` function within the `where` clause, as follows:

```
USE CHA2
SELECT LastName, FirstName
  FROM dbo.Customer
  WHERE SOUNDEX('Nikolsen') = SOUNDEX(LastName)
```

Result:

```
LastName        FirstName
--------------  --------------------
Nicholson       Charles
Nickols         Bob
```

While this implementation has the smallest impact on the data schema, it will cause performance issues as the data size grows because the `soundex()` function must execute for every row in the database. A faster variation of this first implementation method pre-tests for names with the same first letter, thus enabling SQL Server to use any indexes to narrow the search, so the `soundex()` function must be performed only for rows selected by the index:

```
SELECT LastName, FirstName
  FROM dbo.Customer
  WHERE SOUNDEX('Nikolsen') = SOUNDEX(LastName)
    AND LastName LIKE 'N%'
```

The first query executes in 37.7 milliseconds on my test server, while the improved second query executes in 6.5 milliseconds. I suspect that the performance difference would increase with more data.

The second implementation method is to write the Soundex value in a column and index it with a clustered index. Because the Soundex value for each row is calculated during the write, the soundex() function does not need to be called for every row read by the select statement. This is the method I would recommend for a database application that heavily depends on Soundex for contact searches.

The OBX Kites sample database demonstrates this method. The pContact_AddNew stored procedure calculates the Soundex code for every new contact and stores the result in the SoundexCode column. Searching for a row, or all the matching rows, based on the stored Soundex code is extremely fast:

First determine the Soundex for "Smith":

```
USE OBXKites
SELECT SOUNDEX('Smith')
-------
S530
```

Knowing the Soundex value for "Smith," the Soundex search is now a fast index seek without ever calling the soundex() function for the row being read during the select statement:

```
SELECT LastName, FirstName, SoundexCode
  FROM Contact
  WHERE SoundexCode = 'S530'
```

Result:

```
LastName      FirstName         SoundexCode
-----------   ---------------   -----------
Smith         Ulisius           S530
Smith         Oscar             S530
```

Using the Difference() Soundex Function

The second SQL Server Soundex function, difference(), returns the Soundex difference between two strings in the form of a ranking from 1 to 4, with 4 representing a perfect soundex match:

```
USE CHA2
SELECT LastName, DIFFERENCE ('Smith', LastName) AS NameSearch
  FROM Customer
  ORDER BY DIFFERENCE ('Smyth', LastName) DESC
```

Result:

```
LastName             NameSearch
--------------------  -----------
```

```
Smythe          4
Spade           3
Zeniod          3
Kennedy         3
Kennedy         3
Quinn           2
...
Kemper          1
Nicholson       0
...
```

The advantage of the difference() function is that it broadens the search beyond the first letters. The problem with the function is that it wants to calculate the Soundex value for both parameters, which prevents it from taking advantage of pre-stored Soundex values.

Data-Type Conversion Functions

Converting data from a one data type to another data type is often handled automatically by SQL Server. Many of those conversions are implicit, or automatic. The exceptions are detailed in Table 8-3.

Table 8-3: Data-Type Conversion Exceptions

From Data Type(s)	To Data Type(s)	Conversion Issue
binary, varbinary	float, real, ntext, text	Conversion not allowed
char, varchar, nchar, nvarchar	binary, varbinary, money, smallmoney, timestamp	Explicit conversion required
nchar, nvarchar	image	Conversion not allowed
datetime smalldatatime	decimal, numeric, float, real, bigint, int, smallint, tinyint, money, smallmoney, bit, timestamp	Explicit conversion required
datetime smalldatatime, decimal, numeric, float, real bigint, int, smallint, tinyint, money, smallmoney, bit	uniqueidentifier, image, ntext, text	Conversion not allowed
decimal, numeric	decimal, numeric	Requires explicit cast to handle numeric precision without data loss
float, real	timestamp	Conversion not allowed
money. smallmoney	char, varchar, nchar, nvarchar	Explicit conversion required
Timestamp	nchar, nvarchar, float, real, uniqueidentifier, ntext, text sql_variant	Conversion not allowed

Continued

Table 8-3 *(continued)*

From Data Type(s)	To Data Type(s)	Conversion Issue
uniqueidentifier	datetime smalldatatime ,decimal, numeric, float, real bigint, int, smallint, tinyint, money, smallmoney, bit, timestamp, image, ntext	Conversion not allowed
Image	char, varchar, nchar, nvarchar, datetime smalldatatime ,decimal, numeric, float, real bigint, int, smallint, tinyint, money, smallmoney, bit, ntext, sql_variant	Conversion not allowed
ntext, text	binary, varbinary, datetime smalldatatime ,decimal, numeric, float, real bigint, int, smallint, tinyint, money, smallmoney, bit, timestamp, uniqueidentifier, image, sql_variant	Conversion not allowed
Ntext	char, varchar	Explicit conversion required
Text	nchar, nvarchar	Conversion not allowed
sql_variant	timestamp, image, ntext, text	Conversion not allowed

---

Those conversions that are explicit require a `cast()` or `convert()` function:

✦ Cast(Input as data type): The ANSI standard SQL means of converting from one data type to another. Even when the conversion can be performed implicitly by SQL Server, using the `cast()` function forces the desired data type.

Cast is actually programmed slightly differently from a standard function. Rather than separate the two parameters with a comma (as most functions do), the data passed to the cast function is followed by the `as` keyword and the requested output data type:

```
SELECT CAST('Away' AS NVARCHAR(5)) AS 'Tom Hanks'
```

Result:

```
Tom Hanks
---------
Away
```

Another example:

```
SELECT CAST(123 AS NVARCHAR(15)) AS Int2String
```

Result:

```
Int2String
---------------
123
```

✦ Convert(datatype, expression, style): Returns a value converted to a different data type with optional formatting. The first parameter of this non-ASNI SQL function is the desired data type to be applied to the expression:

```
Convert (data type, expression[, style])
```

The style parameter refers to the optional date styles listed in Table 8-4. The style is applied to the output during conversion from datetime to a character-based data type, or to the input during conversion from text to datetime. Generally the one- or two-digit style provides a two-digit year, and its three-digit counterpart provides a four-digit year. For example, style 1 provides 01/01/03, while style 101 provides 01/01/2003. The styles marked with an asterisk (*) in Table 8-4 are the exceptions to this rule.

SQL Server also provides numeric formatting styles, but numeric formatting is typically the task of the user interface, not the database.

Table 8-4: Convert Function Date Styles

Style	Description	Format
0/100*	Default	mon dd yyyy hh:miAM (or PM)
1/101	USA	mm/dd/yy
2/102	ANSI	yy.mm.dd
3/103	British/French	dd/mm/yy
4/104	German	dd.mm.yy
5/105	Italian	dd-mm-yy
6/106	-	dd mon yy
7/107	-	mon dd, yy
8/108	-	hh:mm:ss
9 or 109*	Default+milliseconds	mon dd yyyy hh:mi:ss:mmmAM (or PM)
10 or 110	USA	mm-dd-yy
11 or 111	Japan	yy/mm/dd
12 or 112	ISO	yymmdd
13 or 113*	Europe default+milliseconds	dd mon yyyy hh:mm:ss:mmm (24h)
14 or 114	-	hh:mi:ss:mmm (24h)
20 or 120*	ODBC canonical	yyyy-mm-dd hh:mi:ss (24h)
21 or 121*	ODBC canonical + milliseconds	yyyy-mm-dd hh:mi:ss.mmm (24h)
126	ISO8601 for XML use	yyyy-mm-dd Thh:mm:ss:mmm (no spaces)
130	Kuwaiti	dd mon yyyy hh:mi:ss:mmmAM (or PM)
131	Kuwaiti	dd/mm/yy hh:mi:ss:mmmAM (or PM)

* Both styles return dates with centuries.

Best Practice

In a clean client/server design, the server provides the data without formatting and the client application formats the data as required by the user. Unformatted data is more independent than formatted data and can be used by more applications.

The following code demonstrates the `convert()` function:

```
SELECT  GETDATE() AS RawDate,
    CONVERT (NVARCHAR(25), GETDATE(), 100) AS Date100,
    CONVERT (NVARCHAR(25), GETDATE(), 1) AS Date1
```

Result:

```
RawDate                        Date100                  Date1
-----------------------------  -----------------------  ----------
2001-11-17 10:27:27.413        Nov 17 2001 10:27AM      11/17/01
```

Two additional data-type conversion functions provide fast ways to move data between text and numeric:

✦ `Str(number, length, decimal)`: Returns a string from a number:

```
SELECT STR(123,5,2) AS [Str]
```

Result:

```
Str
-----
123.0
```

Server Environment Information

System functions return information about the current environment. This section covers the more commonly used system functions:

✦ `Db_name()`: Returns the name of the current database, as shown in the following example:

```
SELECT GETDATE() AS 'Date',
    DB_NAME() AS 'Database'
```

Result:

```
Date                           Database
-----------------------------  -------
2001-11-15 18:38:50.250        CHA2
```

✦ `GetUTCDate()`: Returns the current Universal Time Coordinate time, or Greenwich Mean Time. This is very useful for consistently recording times for applications that span multiple time zones.

✦ ServerProperty(): Several useful pieces of information about the server may be determined from the serverproperty (property) function, including the following:

- Collation: The collation type

- Edition: Enterprise, Developer, Standard, and so on

- EngineEdition: 1 = Personal or Desktop Engine, 2 = Standard, 3 = Enterprise

- InstanceName: Null if the default instance

- ProductVersion: The version number of the SQL Server

- ProductLevel: "RTM" for the initial release-to-manufacturing version, "SPn" for service packs, "Bn" for beta software

- ServerName: The full server and instance name

For example, the following code returns the engine edition and the product level for my current instance of SQL Server:

```
SELECT
  SERVERPROPERTY ('ServerName') AS ServerName,
  SERVERPROPERTY ('Edition') AS Edition,
  SERVERPROPERTY ('EngineEdition') AS EngineEdition,
  SERVERPROPERTY ('ProductLevel') AS ProductLevel
```

Result:

```
ServerName  Edition              EngineEdition  ProductLevel
----------  -------------------  -------------  ------------
NOLI        Developer Edition    3              SP1
```

Summary

The previous chapter introduced the basic select statement and query flow. This chapter expanded the concept with expressions and calculations that can be inserted in several places within the query, significantly improving its flexibility. In later chapters, you see how expressions can receive data from subqueries and user-defined functions, further increasing the power of the query.

The next chapter continues the progression of adding capability to the query by joining data from multiple data sources.

✦   ✦   ✦

Merging Data with Joins and Unions

In my introduction to this book I said that my purpose was to share the fun of developing with SQL Server. This chapter is it. Making data twist and shout, pulling an answer out of data with a creative query, replacing a few hundred lines of slow looping VB code with a single lightning-fast set-based SQL query — it's all pure fun and covered here.

Relational databases, by their very nature, segment data into several narrow, but long, tables. Seldom does looking at a single table provide meaningful data. Therefore, merging data from multiple tables is an important task for SQL developers. The theory behind merging data sets is *relational algebra*, as defined by E. F. Codd in 1970.

Relational algebra consists of eight relational operators:

✦ **Restrict:** Returns the rows that meet a certain criterion

✦ **Project:** Returns selected columns, or calculated data, from a data set

✦ **Product:** Relational multiplication that returns all possible combinations of data between two data sets

✦ **Union:** Relational addition and subtraction that merges two tables vertically by stacking one table above another table and lining up the columns

✦ **Intersection:** Returns the rows common to two data sets

✦ **Difference:** Returns the rows unique to one data set

✦ **Join:** Returns the horizontal merger of two tables, matching up rows based on common data

✦ **Divide:** The inverse of relational multiplication, returns rows in one data set that match every row in a corresponding data set

In addition, as a method of accomplishing relational algebra, SQL has implemented the following:

✦ **Subqueries:** Similar to a join, but more flexible; the results of the subquery are used in place of an expression, list, or data set within an outer query.

In the formal language of relational algebra:

✦ A table, or data set, is a *relation* or *entity*.

✦ A row is a *tuple*.

✦ A column is an *attribute*.

I'll use these terms throughout this chapter.

Relational theory is now thirty-something and has become better defined over the years as database vendors compete with extensions, and database theorists further define the problem of representing reality within a data structure. However, E. F. Codd's original work is still the foundation of relational-database design and implementation.

 Note   To give credit where credit is due, this entire chapter is based on work of E. F. Codd and C. J. Date. You can find a complete list of recommended resources in the Books page on www.SQLServerBible.com.

This chapter explains the multiple types of joins and unions. The next chapter focuses on simple and correlated subqueries, and uses them to solve relational division problems.

Using Joins

In relational algebra, a *join* is the multiplication of two data sets followed by a restriction of the result so that only the intersection of the two data sets is returned. The whole purpose of the join is to horizontally merge two data sets (usually tables, but it could be a subquery, view, common table expression, or user-defined function) and produce a new result set from the combination by matching rows in one data source to rows in the other data source, as illustrated in Figure 9-1. This section explains the various types of joins and how to use them to select data.

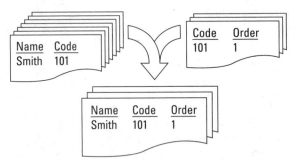

Figure 9-1: A join merges rows from one data set with rows from another data set, creating a new set of rows that includes columns from both. In this diagram, the code, 101, is common to Smith and order number 1, and is used to merge the two original rows into a single result row.

By merging the data using the join, the rest of the SQL `select` statement, including the column expressions, aggregate groupings, and `where` clause conditions, can access any of the columns or rows from the joined tables. These capabilities are the core and power of SQL.

I apologize if this sounds too much like your teenager's math homework, but joins are based on the idea of intersecting data sets. As Figure 9-2 illustrates, a relational join deals with two sets of data that have common values, and it's these common values that define how the tables intersect.

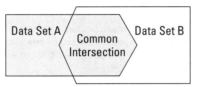

Figure 9-2: Relational joins are based on the overlap, or common intersection, of two data sets.

Note   These set diagrams are a type of Venn diagram. For more information about Venn set diagrams, visit `www.combinatorics.org/Surveys/ds5/VennEJC.html`.

The intersection simply represents the fact that some common attribute can connect a row from the first data set to data in the second data set. The common values are typically a primary key and a foreign key, such as these examples from the OBX Kites sample database:

✦ `ContactID` between the `Contact` and `[Order]` tables

✦ `OrderID` between the `[Order]` and `OrderDetail` tables

✦ `ProductID` between the `Product` and `OrderDetail` tables

SQL includes many types of joins that determine how the rows are selected from the different sides of the intersection. Table 9-1 lists the join types (each is explained in more detail later in this section).

Table 9-1: Join Types

Join Type	Query Designer Symbol	Definition
Inner join		Includes only matching rows
Left outer join		Includes all rows from the left table regardless of whether a match exists, and matching rows from the right table
Right outer join		Includes all the rows from the right table regardless of whether a match exists, and matching rows from the left table

Continued

Table 9-1 *(continued)*

Join Type	Query Designer Symbol	Definition
Full outer join		Includes all the rows from both tables regardless of whether a match exists
ϴ (theta) join		Matches rows using a non-equal condition — the symbol shows the actual theta condition (<>,<=,>=,<>)
Cross join	No join connection	Produces a Cartesian product — a match between each row in data source one with each row from data source two without any conditions or restrictions

Inner Joins

The *inner join* is by far the most common join. In fact, it's also referred to as a *common join*, and was originally called a *natural join* by E. F. Codd. The inner join returns only those rows that represent a match between the two data sets. An inner join is well named because it extracts only data from the inner portion of the intersection of the two overlapping data sets, as illustrated in Figure 9-3.

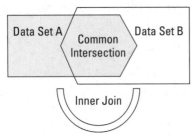

Figure 9-3: The inner join includes only those rows from each side of the join that are contained within the intersection of the two data sources.

Inner joins are easily constructed within Management Studio using the graphical Query Designer tool, as shown in Figure 9-4. Once both tables have been placed in the Diagram pane using the Add Table function, or by dragging the tables from the table list, the join automatically creates the required common joins based on common fields. You must manually remove any joins that you don't wish to use and change joins to other types as needed.

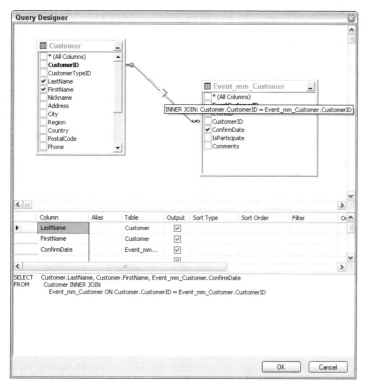

Figure 9-4: Building an inner join within Management Studio's Query Designer

The Query Designer uses a different symbol for each type of join, as shown in Table 9-1. The symbol for an inner join, the *join diamond*, is an accurate illustration of that type of join.

Creating Inner Joins within SQL Code

Within SQL code, joins are specified within the from portion of the select statement. The keyword join identifies the second table, and the on clause defines the common ground between the two tables. The default type of join is an inner join, so the keyword inner is optional:

```
SELECT *
  FROM Table1
    [INNER] JOIN Table2
    ON Table1.column = Table2.column
```

The sample databases and code from this chapter may be downloaded from www.SQLServerBible.com.

Because joins pull together data from two data sets, it makes sense that SQL needs to know how to match up rows from those sets. SQL Server merges the rows by matching a value common to both tables. Typically, a primary key value from one table is being matched with a foreign key value from the secondary table. Whenever a row from the first table matches a row from the second table, the two rows are merged into a new row containing data from both tables.

The following code sample joins the Tour (secondary) and BaseCamp (primary) tables from the Cape Hatteras Adventures sample database. The on clause specifies the common data:

```
USE CHA2

SELECT Tour.Name, Tour.BaseCampID,
    BaseCamp.BaseCampID, BaseCamp.Name
  FROM dbo.Tour
    JOIN dbo.BaseCamp
      ON Tour.BaseCampID = BaseCamp.BaseCampID
```

The query begins with the Tour table. For every Tour row, SQL Server will attempt to identify matching BaseCamp rows by comparing the BasecampID columns in both tables. The Tour table rows and BaseCamp table rows that match will be merged into a new result:

Tour. TourName	Tour. BaseCampID	Basecamp. BaseCampID	Basecamp. BaseCampName
Appalachian Trail	1	1	Ashville NC
Outer Banks Lighthouses	2	2	Cape Hatteras
Bahamas Dive	3	3	Freeport
Amazon Trek	4	4	Ft Lauderdale
Gauley River Rafting	5	5	West Virginia

Number of Rows Returned

In the preceding query every row in both the Tour and BaseCamp tables had a match. No rows were excluded from the join. However, in real life this is seldom the case. Depending upon the number of matching rows from each data source and the type of join, it's possible to reduce or increase the final number of rows in the result set.

To see how joins can alter the number of rows returned, look at the Contact and [Order] tables of the OBX Kites database. The initial row count of contacts is 21, yet when the customers are matched with their orders, the row count changes to 10. The following code sample compares the two queries and their respective results side by side:

```
USE OBXKites
```

```
SELECT ContactCode, LastName          SELECT ContactCode, OrderNumber
  FROM dbo.Contact                       FROM dbo.Contact
  ORDER BY ContactCode                     JOIN dbo.[Order]
```

```
                              ON [Order].ContactID
                                = Contact.ContactID
                              ORDER BY ContactCode
```

Results from both queries:

ContactCode	LastName	ContactCode	OrderNumber
101	Smith	101	1
		101	2
		101	5
102	Adams	102	6
		102	3
103	Reagan	103	4
		103	7
104	Franklin	104	8
105	Dowdry	105	9
106	Grant	106	10
107	Smith		
108	Hanks		
109	James		
110	Kennedy		
111	Williams		
112	Quincy		
113	Laudry		
114	Nelson		
115	Miller		
116	Jamison		
117	Andrews		
118	Boston		
119	Harrison		
120	Earl		
121	Zing		

Only contacts 101 through 106 have matching orders. The rest of the contacts are excluded from the join because they have no matching orders.

Joins can also appear to multiply rows. If a row on one side of the join matches with several rows on the other side of the join, the result will include a row for every match. In the preceding query, some contacts (Smith, Adams, and Reagan) are listed multiple times because they have multiple orders.

Best Practice

Depending on the nullability of the keys and the presence of rows on both sides of the join, joins tend to miss rows because one table or the other produces incorrect data. When retrieving data from multiple tables, it's a best practice to carefully select the correct type of join (inner, left outer, or right outer) for the query, so that every valid row is returned.

ANSI SQL 89 Joins

A join is really nothing more than the act of selecting data from two tables for which a condition of equality exists between common columns. Join conditions in the `on` clause are similar to `where` clauses. In fact, before ANSI SQL 92 standardized the `join...on` syntax, ANSI SQL 89 joins, also called *legacy style joins*, accomplished the same task by listing the tables within the `from` clause and specifying the join condition in the `where` clause. SQL Server includes the ANSI SQL 89 syntax as part of the SQL standard.

The previous sample join between `Contact` and `[Order]` could be written as a legacy join as follows:

```
SELECT Contact.ContactCode, [Order].OrderNumber
  FROM dbo.Contact, dbo.[Order]
  WHERE [Order].ContactID = Contact.ContactID
  ORDER BY ContactCode
```

Personally, I prefer to write joins using the ANSI SQL-92 `join...on` syntax. I believe it's cleaner to specify the join completely within the `from` clause. ANSI 89 joins break up the join so that the joined tables are in the `from` clause and the join condition is in the `where` clause, which seems error-prone to me. However, neither style results in a performance benefit because SQL Server will create the exact same query execution plan regardless of whether the join is constructed using the ANSI standard join or the legacy `where` clause method.

Multiple Table Joins

As some of the examples have already demonstrated, a `select` statement isn't limited to one or two data sources; a SQL Server `select` statement may refer to up to 256 data sources. That's a lot of joins. Because SQL is a declarative language, the order of the data sources is not important. Multiple joins may be combined in multiple paths, or even circular patterns (A joins B joins C joins A). Here's where a large whiteboard and a consistent development style really pay off.

An interesting thing happens when joins across multiple tables are combined with a where-clause restriction (that is, when the joins carry with them the where-clause restriction). A restriction in any one table means that only those rows that meet the restriction condition participate in the join.

The following query (first shown in Figure 9-5 and then worked out in code) answers the question "Who purchased kites?" The answer must involve five tables:

1. The `Contact` table for the "who"

2. The `[Order]` table for the "purchased"

3. The `OrderDetail` table for the "purchased"

4. The `Product` table for the "kites"

5. The `ProductCategory` table for the "kites"

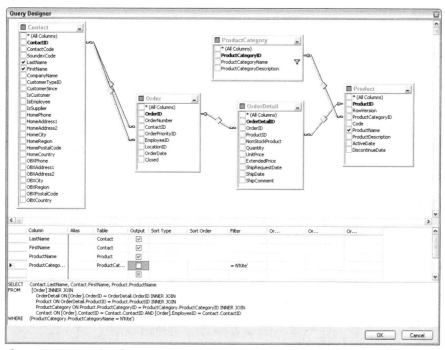

Figure 9-5: Answering the question "Who purchased kites?" using Management Studio's Query Designer

The following SQL select statement begins with the "who" portion of the question and specifies the join tables and conditions as it works through the required tables. The query that is shown graphically in Management Studio (refer to Figure 9-5) is listed as raw SQL in the following code sample. Notice how the where clause restricts the ProductCategory table rows and yet affects the contacts selected:

```
USE OBXKites
SELECT LastName, FirstName, ProductName
  FROM dbo.Contact
    JOIN dbo.[Order]
      ON Contact.ContactID = [Order].ContactID
    JOIN dbo.OrderDetail
      ON [Order].OrderID = OrderDetail.OrderID
    JOIN dbo.Product
      ON OrderDetail.ProductID = Product.ProductID
    JOIN dbo.ProductCategory
      ON Product.ProductCategoryID = ProductCategory.ProductCategoryID
  WHERE ProductCategoryName = 'Kite'
  ORDER BY LastName, FirstName
```

Result:

```
LastName              FirstName               ProductName
------------------    --------------------    ----------------
Adams                 Terri                   Dragon Flight
Dowdry                Quin                    Dragon Flight
...
Smith                 Ulisius                 Rocket Kite
```

Compared with the SQL code generated by Management Studio's Query Designer, the SQL code in the previous query is easier to decipher. While the Query Designer makes queries easier to initially develop, the code is more difficult to read. Sometimes the Query Designer places the on conditions away from the join table, and the formatting is atrocious.

Outer Joins

Whereas an inner join contains only the intersection of the two data sets, an *outer join* extends the inner join by adding the nonmatching data from the left or right data set, as illustrated in Figure 9-6.

Outer joins solve a significant problem for many queries by including all the data regardless of a match. The previous customer-order query demonstrates this problem well. If the requirement is to build a query that lists all customers plus their recent orders, an inner join between customers and orders would miss every customer who had not placed a recent order. This type of error is very common in database applications.

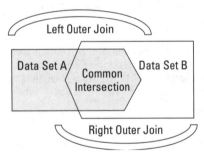

Figure 9-6: An outer join includes not only rows from the two data sources with a match but also unmatched rows from outside the intersection.

Some of the data in the result set produced by an outer join will look just like the data from an inner join. There will be data in columns that come from each of the data sources, but any rows from the outer-join table that do not have a match in the other side of the join will return data only from the outer-join table. In this case, columns from the other data source will have null values.

When building queries using Query Designer, you can change the join type from the default, inner join, to outer join via either the context menu or the properties of the join, as shown in Figure 9-7. The Query Designer does an excellent job of illustrating the types of joins with the join symbol (as previously detailed in Table 7-1).

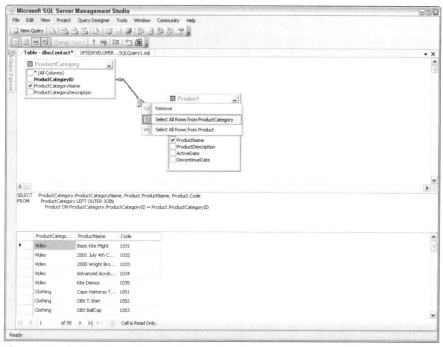

Figure 9-7: The join Properties window displays the join columns, and is used to set the join condition (=, >, <, etc.) and add the left or right side of an outer join (all rows from Product, all rows from OrderDetail).

In SQL code, an outer join is declared by the keywords `left outer` or `right outer` before the `join` (technically, the keyword `outer` is optional):

```
SELECT *
  FROM Table1
    LEFT|RIGHT [OUTER] JOIN Table2
      ON Table1.column = Table2.column
```

Best Practice

Although several keywords in SQL are optional (such as inner and outer) or may be abbreviated (such as proc for procedure), explicitly stating the intent by spelling out the full syntax improves the readability of the code. However, most developers omit the optional syntax.

There's no trick to telling the difference between left and right outer joins. In code, left or right refers to the table that will be included regardless of the match. The outer-join table (sometimes called the *driving table*) is typically listed first, so left outer joins are more common than right outer joins. I suspect any confusion between left and right outer joins is caused by the use of graphical-query tools to build joins, because the left and right refers to the table's listing in the SQL text, and the table's positions in the graphical-query tool are moot.

To modify the previous contact-order query so that it returns all contacts regardless of any orders, changing the join type from inner to left outer is all that's required, as follows:

```
SELECT ContactCode, OrderNumber
  FROM dbo.Contact
    LEFT OUTER JOIN dbo.[Order]
      ON [Order].ContactID = Contact.ContactID
  ORDER BY ContactCode
```

The `left outer join` will include all rows from the `Contact` table and matching rows from the `[Order]` table. The abbreviated result of the query is as follows:

```
Contact.         [Order].
ContactCode      OrderNumber
---------------  -----------
101              1
101              2
...
106              10
107              NULL
108              NULL
...
```

Because contact 107 and 108 do not have corresponding rows in the `[Order]` table, the columns from the `[Order]` table return a null for those rows.

New in 2005 Transact-SQL extended the ANSI SQL 89 join syntax (sometimes called *legacy joins*) with outer joins by adding an asterisk to the left or right of the equals sign in the `where` clause condition. While this syntax worked through SQL Server 2000, it has been removed from SQL Server 2005. ANSI SQL 89 inner joins will still work, but outer joins *require* ANSI SQL 92 syntax.

Outer Joins and Optional Foreign Keys

Outer joins are often employed when a secondary table has a foreign-key constraint to the primary table and permits nulls in the foreign key column. The presence of this optional foreign key means that if the secondary row refers to a primary row, then the primary row must exist. However, it's perfectly valid for the secondary row to refrain from referring to the primary table at all.

Another example of an optional foreign key is an order alert or priority column. Many order rows will not have an alert or special-priority status. However, those that do must point to a valid row in the order-priority table.

The OBX Kite store uses a similar order-priority scheme, so reporting all the orders with their optional priorities requires an outer join:

```
SELECT OrderNumber, OrderPriorityName
  FROM dbo. [Order]
    LEFT OUTER JOIN dbo.OrderPriority
    ON [Order].OrderPriorityID =
      OrderPriority.OrderPriorityID
```

The left outer join retrieves all the orders and any matching priorities. The `OBXKites_Populate.sql` script sets two orders to rush priority:

```
OrderNumber OrderPriorityName
----------- -----------------
1           Rush
2           NULL
3           Rush
4           NULL
5           NULL
6           NULL
7           NULL
8           NULL
9           NULL
10          NULL
```

Reflexive relationships (also called *recursive* or *self-join* relationships) also use optional foreign keys. In the Family sample database, the `MotherID` and `FatherID` are both foreign keys that refer to the `PersonID` of the mother or father. The optional foreign key allows persons to be entered without their father and mother already in the database; but if a value is entered in the `MotherID` or `FatherID` columns, the data must point to valid persons in the database.

Full Outer Joins

A *full outer join* returns all the data from both data sets regardless of the intersection, as shown in Figure 9-8. It is functionally the same as a union distinct operation from a left outer join and a right outer join (unions are explained later in this chapter).

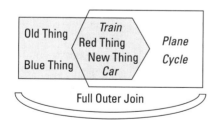

Figure 9-8: The full outer join returns all the data from both data sets, matching the rows where it can and filling in the holes with nulls.

In real life, referential integrity reduces the need for a full outer join because every row from the secondary table should have a match in the primary table (depending on the optionality of the foreign key), so left outer joins are typically sufficient. Full outer joins are most useful for cleaning up data that has not had the benefit of clean constraints to filter out bad data.

The following example is a mock up of such a situation and compares the full outer join with an inner and a left outer join. Table One is the primary table. Table Two is a secondary table with a foreign key that refers to table One. There's no foreign-key constraint, so there may be some nonmatches for the outer join to find:

```
CREATE TABLE dbo.One (
  OnePK INT,
  Thing1 VARCHAR(15)
  )

CREATE TABLE dbo.Two (
  TwoPK INT,
  OnePK INT,
  Thing2 VARCHAR(15)
  )
```

The sample data includes rows that would normally break referential integrity. The foreign key (OnePK) for the plane and the cycle in table Two do not have a match in table One. And two of the rows in table One do not have related secondary rows in table Two. The following batch inserts the eight sample data rows:

```
INSERT dbo.One(OnePK, Thing1)
  VALUES (1, 'Old Thing')
INSERT dbo.One(OnePK, Thing1)
  VALUES (2, 'New Thing')
INSERT dbo.One(OnePK, Thing1)
  VALUES (3, 'Red Thing')
INSERT dbo.One(OnePK, Thing1)
  VALUES (4, 'Blue Thing')

INSERT dbo.Two(TwoPK, OnePK, Thing2)
  VALUES(1,0, 'Plane')
INSERT dbo.Two(TwoPK, OnePK, Thing2)
  VALUES(2,2, 'Train')
INSERT dbo.Two(TwoPK, OnePK, Thing2)
  VALUES(3,3, 'Car')
INSERT dbo.Two(TwoPK, OnePK, Thing2)
  VALUES(4,NULL, 'Cycle')
```

An inner join between table One and table Two will return only the two matching rows:

```
SELECT Thing1, Thing2
  FROM dbo.One
    JOIN dbo.Two
      ON One.OnePK = Two.OnePK
```

Result:

```
Thing1           Thing2
---------------  ---------------
New Thing        Train
Red Thing        Car
```

A left outer join will extend the inner join and include the rows from table One without a match:

```
SELECT Thing1, Thing2
  FROM dbo.One
    LEFT OUTER JOIN dbo.Two
      ON One.OnePK = Two.OnePK
```

All the rows are now returned from table One, but two rows are still missing from table Two:

```
Thing1           Thing2
---------------  ---------------
Old Thing        NULL
New Thing        Train
Red Thing        Car
Blue Thing       NULL
```

A full outer join will retrieve every row from both tables, regardless of a match between the tables:

```
SELECT Thing1, Thing2
  FROM dbo.One
    FULL OUTER JOIN dbo.Two
      ON One.OnePK = Two.OnePK
```

The plane and cycle from table Two are now listed along with every row from table One:

```
Thing1           Thing2
---------------  ---------------
NULL             Plane
New Thing        Train
Red Thing        Car
NULL             Cycle
Blue Thing       NULL
Old Thing        NULL
```

As this example shows, full outer joins are an excellent tool for finding all the data, even bad data. Set difference queries, explored later in this chapter, build on outer joins to zero in on bad data.

Placing the Conditions within Outer Joins

When working with inner joins, a condition has the same effect whether it's in the join clause or the where clause, but that's not the case with outer joins. When the condition is in the join clause, SQL Server includes all rows from the outer table and then uses the condition to include rows from the second table. When the restriction is placed in the where clause, the join is performed and then the where clause is applied to the joined rows. The following two queries demonstrate the effect of the placement of the condition.

In the first query, the `left outer join` includes all rows from table `One` and then joins those rows from table `Two` where `OnePK` is equal in both tables and `Thing1`'s value is `New Thing`. The result is the same rows from table `One`, but fewer rows from table `Two`:

```
SELECT Thing1, Thing2
  FROM dbo.One
    LEFT OUTER JOIN dbo.Two
      ON One.OnePK = Two.OnePK
        AND One.Thing1 = 'New Thing'
```

Result:

```
Thing1           Thing2
---------------  ---------------
Old Thing        NULL
New Thing        Train
Red Thing        NULL
Blue Thing       NULL
```

The second query performs the `left outer join`, producing four rows. The `where` clause then restricts that result to those rows where `Thing1` is equal to `New Thing1`:

```
SELECT Thing1, Thing2
  FROM dbo.One
    LEFT OUTER JOIN dbo.Two
      ON One.OnePK = Two.OnePK
  WHERE One.Thing1 = 'New Thing'
```

Result:

```
Thing1           Thing2
---------------  ---------------
New Thing        Train
```

A Join Analogy

When I teach how to build queries, I sometimes use the following story to explain the different types of joins. Imagine a pilgrim church in the seventeenth century segmented by gender. The men all sit on one side of the church and the women on the other. Now imagine that each side of the church is a database table and the various combinations of people that leave the church represent the different types of joins.

If all the married couples stood up, joined hands, and left the church, that would be an inner join between the men and women. The result set leaving the church would include only matched pairs.

If all the men stood, those who were married held hands with their brides, and they left as a group that would be a left outer join. The line leaving the church would include some couples and some bachelors.

Likewise, if all women and their husbands left the church, that would be a right outer join. All the bachelors would be left alone in the church.

A full outer join would be everyone leaving the church, but only the married couples could hold hands.

Self-Joins

A *self-join* is a join that refers back to the same table. This type of unary relationship is often used to extract data from a *reflexive* (also called a *recursive*) relationship, such as manufacturing databases with bill of materials data (build-from-material to material) and human-resource databases (employee to boss). Think of a self-join as a table being joined with a temporary copy of itself.

The Family sample database uses two self-joins between a child and his or her parents, as shown in the database diagram in Figure 9-9. The mothers and fathers are also people, of course, and are listed in the same table. They link back to their parents and so on. The sample database is populated with five fictitious generations that can be used for sample queries.

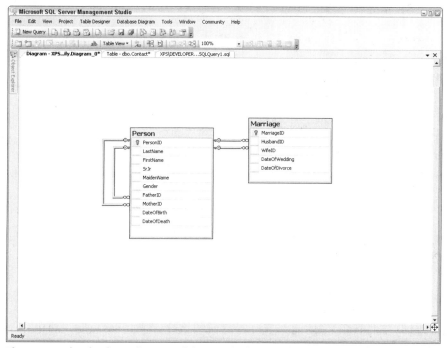

Figure 9-9: The database diagram of the Family database includes two unary relationships (children to parents) on the left and a many-to-many unary relationship (husband to wife) on the right.

The key to constructing a self-join is to include a second reference to the table using a named range or table alias. Once the table is available twice to the select statement, the self-join functions much like any other join. In the following example, The dbo.Person table is referenced using the named range 'Mother':

The following query locates the children of Audry Halloway:

```
USE Family

SELECT Person.PersonID, Person.FirstName,
    Person.MotherID, Mother.PersonID
  FROM dbo.Person
    JOIN dbo.Person Mother
      ON Person.MotherID = Mother.PersonID
  WHERE Mother.LastName = 'Halloway'
    AND Mother.FirstName = 'Audry'
```

The query uses the Person table twice. The first reference without a named range is joined with the second reference, which is restricted by the where clause to only Audry Halloway. Only the rows with a MotherID that points back to Audry will be included in the inner join. Audry's PersonID is 6 and her children are as follows:

```
PersonID     FirstName          MotherID       PersonID
-----------  -----------------  ------------   -----------
8            Melanie            6              6
7            Corwin             6              6
9            Dara               6              6
10           James              6              6
```

While the previous query adequately demonstrates a self-join, it would be more useful if the mother weren't hard-coded in the where clause, and if more information were provided about each birth, as follows:

```
SELECT CONVERT(NVARCHAR(15),Person.DateofBirth,1) AS Date,
    Person.FirstName AS Name, Person.Gender AS G,
    ISNULL(F.FirstName + ' ' + F.LastName, ' * unknown *')
      as Father,
    M.FirstName + ' ' + M.LastName as Mother
  FROM dbo.Person
    Left Outer JOIN dbo.Person F
      ON Person.FatherID = F.PersonID
    INNER JOIN dbo.Person M
      ON Person.MotherID = M.PersonID
  ORDER BY Person.DateOfBirth
```

This query makes three references to the person table: the child, the father, and the mother. The result is a better listing:

```
Date       Name       G   Father              Mother
--------   --------   --- ------------------   ----------------
5/19/22    James      M   James Halloway      Kelly Halloway
8/05/28    Audry      F   Bryan Miller        Karen Miller
8/19/51    Melanie    F   James Halloway      Audry Halloway
8/30/53    James      M   James Halloway      Audry Halloway
2/12/58    Dara       F   James Halloway      Audry Halloway
3/13/61    Corwin     M   James Halloway      Audry Halloway
3/13/65    Cameron    M   Richard Campbell    Elizabeth Campbell
...
```

Cross (Unrestricted) Joins

The *cross join*, also called an *unrestricted join,* is a pure relational algebra multiplication of the two source tables. Without a join condition restricting the result set, the result set includes every possible combination of rows from the data sources. Each row in data set one is matched with every row in data set two — for example, if the first data source has five rows and second data source has four rows, a cross join between them would result in 20 rows. This type of result set is referred to as a *Cartesian product.*

Using the One/Two sample tables, a cross join is constructed in Management Studio by omitting the join condition between the two tables, as shown in Figure 9-10.

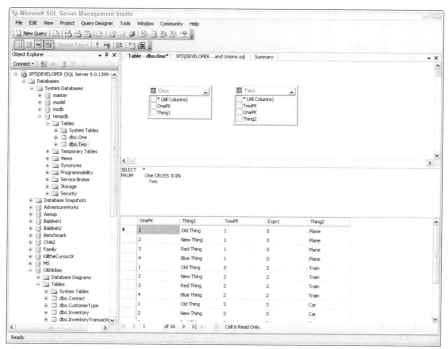

Figure 9-10: A graphical representation of a cross join is simply two tables without a join condition.

In code, this type of join is specified by the keywords cross join and the lack of an on condition:

```
SELECT Thing1, Thing2
  FROM dbo.One
    CROSS JOIN dbo.Two
```

The result of a join without restriction is that every row in table One matches with every row from table Two:

```
Thing1            Thing2
----------------  ----------------
Old Thing         Plane
New Thing         Plane
Red Thing         Plane
Blue Thing        Plane
Old Thing         Train
New Thing         Train
Red Thing         Train
Blue Thing        Train
Old Thing         Car
New Thing         Car
Red Thing         Car
Blue Thing        Car
Old Thing         Cycle
New Thing         Cycle
Red Thing         Cycle
Blue Thing        Cycle
```

Most cross joins are the result of someone forgetting to draw the join in a graphical-query tool; however, they are useful for populating databases with sample data, or for creating empty "pidgin hole" rows for population during a procedure.

Understanding how a cross join multiplies data is also useful when studying relational division, the inverse of a relational multiplication. Relational division requires subqueries, shown in Figure 9-12, so it's explained later in this chapter.

Exotic Joins

Nearly all joins are based on a condition of equality between the primary key of a primary table and the foreign key of a secondary table, which is why the inner join is sometimes called an *equi-join*. But while it's commonplace to base a join on a single equal condition, it is not a requirement. The condition between the two columns is not necessarily equal, nor is the join limited to one condition.

The on condition of the join is in reality nothing more than a where condition restricting the product of the two joined data sets. Where-clause conditions may be very flexible and powerful, and the same is true of join conditions. This reasoning enables the use of three powerful techniques: Θ *(theta) joins, multiple-condition joins,* and *non-key joins.*

Θ (theta) Joins

A theta join (depicted throughout as Θ) is a join based on a non-equal on condition. In relational theory, conditional operators (=, >, <, >=, <=, <>) are called Θ operators. While the equals condition is technically a Θ operator, it is commonly used; only joins that deviate from the equi-join are referred to as Θ join.

The Θ condition may be set within Management Studio's Query Designer using the Join Properties dialog box, as previously shown in Figure 9-7.

Θ joins are often combined with multiple condition joins involving non-key columns. The rest of the code samples in this section all use Θ joins.

Multiple-Condition Joins

If a join is nothing more than a condition between two data sets, it makes sense that multiple conditions are possible at the join. In fact, multiple-condition joins and Θ joins go hand-in-hand. Without the ability to use multiple-condition joins, Θ joins would be of little value.

Join conditions can refer to any table in the from clause, enabling interesting three-way joins. For example:

```
From A
  JOIN B
    ON A.col = B.col
  JOIN C
    ON B.col = C.col
    AND A.col = C.col
```

Non-Key Joins

Joins are not limited to primary and foreign keys. The join can match a row in one data source with a row in another data source using any column, as long as the columns share compatible data types and the data match.

For example, an inventory allocation system would use a non-key join to find products that are expected to arrive from the supplier before the customer's required ship date. A non-key join between the PurchaseOrder and OrderDetail tables with a Θ condition between PO.DateExpected and OD.DateRequired will filter the join to those products that can be allocated to the customer's orders. The following code demonstrates the non-key join (this is not in a sample database):

```
SELECT OD.OrderID, OD.ProductID, PO.POID
FROM OrderDetail OD
  JOIN PurchaseOrder PO
    ON OD.ProductID = PO.ProductID
      AND OD.DateRequired > PO.DateExpected
```

When working with inner joins, non-key join conditions can be placed in the where clause or in the join. Because the conditions compare similar values between two joined tables, I often place these conditions in the join portion of the from clause, rather than the where clause. The critical difference depends on whether you view the conditions as a part of creating the record set the rest of the SQL select statement is acting upon, or as a filtering task that follows the from clause. Either way, the query-optimization plan is identical, so use the method that is most readable and seems most logical to you. Note that when constructing outer joins, the placement of the condition in the join or in the where clause yields different results, as explained in the section on outer joins.

If you look at the Family sample database, you see the question "Who are twins?" uses all three exotic join techniques in the join between person and twin. The join contains three conditions. The `Person.PersonID <> Twin.PersonID` condition is a Θ join that prevents a person from being considered his or her own twin. The join condition on `MotherID`, while a foreign key, is nonstandard because it's being joined with another foreign key. The `DateOfBirth` condition is definitely a non-key join condition. The `where` condition check for `DateOfBirth is not null` simply removes from the query those who married into the family and thus have no recorded parents:

```
SELECT Person.FirstName + ' ' + Person.LastName,
    Twin.FirstName + ' ' + Twin.LastName as Twin,
    Person.DateOfBirth
  FROM dbo.Person
    JOIN dbo.Person Twin
      ON Person.PersonID <> Twin.PersonID
        AND Person.MotherID = Twin.MotherID
        AND Person.DateOfBirth = Twin.DateOfBirth
  WHERE Person.DateOfBirth IS NOT NULL
```

The following is the same query, this time with the exotic join condition moved to the `where` clause. Not surprisingly, SQL Server's Query Optimizer produces the exact same query execution plan for each query:

```
SELECT Person.FirstName + ' ' + Person.LastName AS Person,
    Twin.FirstName + ' ' + Twin.LastName as Twin,
    Person.DateOfBirth
  FROM dbo.Person
    JOIN dbo.Person Twin
      ON Person.MotherID = Twin.MotherID
        AND Person.DateOfBirth = Twin.DateOfBirth
  WHERE Person.DateOfBirth IS NOT NULL
    AND Person.PersonID != Twin.PersonID
```

Result:

```
Person            Twin             DateOfBirth
---------------   --------------   -----------------------
Abbie Halloway    Allie Halloway   1979-08-14 00:00:00.000
Allie Halloway    Abbie Halloway   1979-08-14 00:00:00.000
```

In Microsoft's Northwind database, a non-key join could be created comparing the `Region` columns of the `Customers`, `Shippers`, and `Orders` tables.

The difficult query scenarios at the end of this chapter also demonstrate exotic joins often used with subqueries.

Set Difference

A similar query type that's useful for analyzing the correlation between two data sets is a *set difference query,* which finds the difference between the two data sets based on the conditions of the join. In relational algebra terms, it removes the divisor from the dividend, leaving the difference. This type of query is the inverse of an inner join. Informally, it's called a *find unmatched rows* query.

Set difference queries are great for locating out-of-place data or data that doesn't match, such as rows that are in data set one but not in data set two (see Figure 9-11).

Note The ANSI SQL standard implements the set difference query with the keyword `except`, which SQL Server does not support.

The set difference query is the same as the difference union, except that the difference union is a row-based operation between tables with the same column definitions, whereas a set difference query is concerned only with the columns in the join condition. In a sense, the set difference query is a difference union of only the join-condition columns.

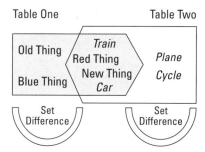

Figure 9-11: The set difference query finds data that is outside the intersection between the two data sets.

Using the One/Two sample tables, the following query locates all rows in table One without a match in table Two, removing set two (the divisor) from set one (the dividend). The result will be the rows from set one that do not have a match in set two.

The outer join already includes the rows outside the intersection, so to construct a set difference query use an outer join with an is null restriction on the second data set's primary key. This will return all the rows from table One that do not have a match in table Two:

```
USE Tempdb

SELECT Thing1, Thing2
  FROM dbo.One
    LEFT OUTER JOIN dbo.Two
      ON One.OnePK = Two.OnePK
  WHERE Two.TwoPK IS NULL
```

Table One's difference is as follows:

```
Thing1            Thing2
----------------  ----------------
Old Thing         NULL
Blue Thing        NULL
```

If you take the theory to a real-world scenario from the OBX Kites sample database, the following code is a set difference query that locates all contacts who have not yet placed an order. The Contact table is the divisor and the set difference query removes the contacts with orders (the dividend). The `left outer join` produces a data set with all contacts and matching orders. The `where` condition restricts the result set to only those rows without a match in the [Order] table:

```
USE OBXKites
SELECT LastName, FirstName
  FROM dbo.Contact
    LEFT OUTER JOIN dbo.[Order]
      ON Contact.ContactID = [Order].ContactID
  WHERE OrderID IS NULL
```

The result is the difference between the `Contact` table and the [Order] table —that is, all contacts who have not placed an order:

```
LastName       FirstName
------------   ----------------
Andrews        Ed
Boston         Dave
Earl           Betty
Hanks          Nickolas
Harrison       Charlie
...
```

The set difference query could be written using a subquery. The `where not in` condition removes the subquery rows (the divisor) from the outer query (the dividend), as follows:

```
SELECT LastName, FirstName
  FROM dbo.Contact
  WHERE ContactID NOT IN
    (SELECT ContactID FROM dbo.[Order])
  ORDER BY LastName, FirstName
```

Either form of the query (`left outer join` or `not in` subquery) works well, with very similar query execution plans, as shown in Figure 9-12.

I often use a modified version of this technique to clean up bad data during conversions. A *full set difference query* is the logical opposite of an inner join. It identifies all rows outside the intersection from either data set by combining a `full outer join` with a `where` restriction that accepts only nulls in either primary key:

```
SELECT Thing1, Thing2
  FROM One
    FULL OUTER JOIN Two
      ON One.OnePK = Two.OnePK
  WHERE Two.TwoPK IS NULL
    OR One.OnePK IS NULL
```

The result is every row without a match in the `One`/`Two` sample tables:

```
Thing1           Thing2
----------------   ----------------
NULL             Plane
NULL             Cycle
Blue Thing       NULL
Old Thing        NULL
```

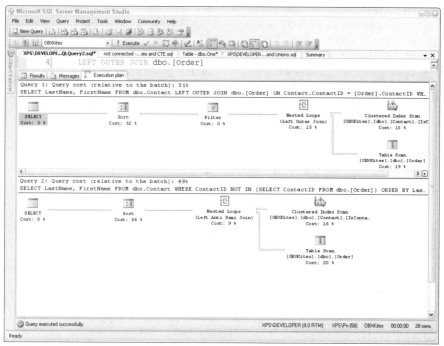

Figure 9-12: The subquery form of the set difference query is optimized to nearly the same query execution plan as the left outer join solution.

Using Unions

The union operation is different from a join. In relational algebra terms, a union is addition, whereas a join is multiplication. Instead of extending a row horizontally as a join would, the union stacks multiple result sets into a single long table, as illustrated in Figure 9-13. These few rules must be followed when constructing a union query:

✦ The column names, or aliases, must be determined by the first select.

✦ Every select must have the same number of columns, and each lineup of columns must share the same data-type family.

✦ Expressions may be added to the select statements to identify the source of the row so long as the column is added to every select.

✦ The union may be used as part of a select into (a form of the insert verb covered in Chapter 16, "Modifying Data") but the into keyword must go in the first select statement.

✦ Whereas the select command will default to all unless distinct is specified, the union is the opposite. By default, the union will perform a distinct; if you wish to change this behavior you must specify the keyword all. (I recommend that you think of the union as "union all" in the same way that the you might think of top as "top with ties.")

✦ The order by clause sorts the results of all the selects and must go on the last select, but it uses the column names from the first select.

Table One

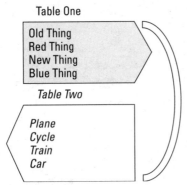

Figure 9-13: A union vertically appends the result of one select statement to the result of another select statement.

In the following union query the order by clause references the Thing1 column in the first select statement:

```
SELECT OnePK, Thing1, 'from One' as Source
   FROM dbo.One
UNION ALL
SELECT TwoPK, Thing2, 'from Two'
   FROM dbo.Two
ORDER BY Thing1
```

The resulting record set uses the column names from the first select statement:

```
OnePK         Thing1             Source
-----------   ----------------   --------
4             Blue Thing         from One
3             Car                from Two
4             Cycle              from Two
2             New Thing          from One
1             Old Thing          from One
1             Plane              from Two
3             Red Thing          from One
2             Train              from Two
```

Unions aren't limited to two tables. The largest I've personally worked with had about 90 tables (I won't try that again anytime soon). As long as the total number of tables referenced by a query is 256 or less, SQL Server handles the load.

Intersection Union

An *intersection union* finds the rows common to both data sets. An inner join finds common rows horizontally, while an intersection union finds common rows vertically. SQL Server doesn't handle intersection or difference unions natively, so they take a little work. To set up the intersection query, these first two statements add rows to table Two so there will be an intersection:

```
INSERT dbo.Two(TwoPK, OnePK, Thing2)
  VALUES(5,0, 'Red Thing')
INSERT dbo.Two(TwoPK, OnePK, Thing2)

SELECT Thing1
  FROM dbo.One
INTERSECT
SELECT Thing2
  FROM dbo.Two
ORDER BY Thing1
```

Result:

```
Thing1
----------------
Blue Thing
Red Thing
```

An intersection union query is similar to an inner join, with every column participating in the on condition. However, an intersection union query will see nulls as common and include the rows in the intersect, whereas an inner join will treat nulls as different and not join two rows with null values.

New in 2005

The intersect and except keywords are new to SQL Server 2005. While the getting the correct results for an intersection or difference union was possible using SQL Server 2000, they required some workaround code. (The workaround code is in the chapter code file if you're interested.)

Difference Union/Except

The *difference union* is similar to the intersection union, but the having restriction permits only those rows found in only one of the two data sets.

A difference union is similar to a set difference query in that it locates all rows that are in one data set but not the other. Whereas a set difference query is interested only in the join conditions (typically the primary and foreign keys) and joins the rows horizontally, a difference union looks at the entire row (or, more specifically, all the columns that participate in the union's select statements) vertically.

SQL Server 2005 uses the ANSI Standard keyword except to execute a difference union:

```
SELECT Thing1
  FROM dbo.One
EXCEPT
```

```
SELECT Thing2
  FROM dbo.Two
ORDER BY Thing1
```

Result:

```
Thing1
----------------
New Thing
Old Thing
```

Summary

Merging data is the heart of SQL, and it shows in the depth of relational algebra as well as the power and flexibility of SQL. From natural joins to correlated subqueries, SQL is excellent at selecting sets of data from multiple data tables. The challenge for the SQL Server database developer is to master the theory of relational algebra and the many T-SQL techniques to effectively manipulate the data. The reward is the fun.

Regardless of the introduction of .NET and the CLR, manipulating data with `select` is still the core technology of SQL Server. While joins are the most natural method of working with relational data, subqueries open numerous possibilities for creative and powerful way to retrieve data from multiple data sources. The next chapter details the many ways subqueries can be used within a query, and introduces common table expressions (CTEs), a new feature to SQL Server.

✦   ✦   ✦

Including Data with Subqueries and CTEs

SQL's real power is reflected by the capability it offers to mix and match multiple methods of selecting data. It's this skill in fluidly assembling a complex query in code to accomplish what can't be done with the GUI tools that differentiates SQL gurus from the wannabes. So without hesitation I invite you to study embedded simple and correlated subqueries, derived tables, and common table expressions, and then apply these query components to solve complex relational problems such as relational division.

Methods and Locations

A *subquery* is an embedded `select` statement within an outer query. The subquery provides an answer to the outer query in the form of a scalar value, a list of values, or a data set, and may be substituted for an expression, list, or table, respectively, within the outer query. The matrix of subquery types and `select` statement usage is shown in Table 10-1. Because a subquery may only contain a `select` query, and not a data-modification query, subqueries are sometimes referred to as *subselects*.

Three basic forms are possible when building a subquery, depending on the data needs and your favored syntax:

✦ **Simple subquery:** The simple subquery can be a stand-alone query and can run by itself. It is executed once, with the result passed to the outer query. Simple subqueries are constructed as normal `select` queries and placed within parentheses.

✦ **Common table expressions (CTEs):** CTEs are a syntactical variation of the simple subquery, similar to a view, which defines the subquery at the beginning of the query using the `with` command. The CTE can then be accessed multiple times within the main query as if it were a view or derived table.

> **New in 2005**
>
> CTEs are introduced in SQL Server 2005 and primarily serve the purpose of building a recursive query, as explained in Chapter 12, "Navigating Hierarchical Data."

✦ **Correlated subquery:** This is similar to a simple subquery except that it references at least one column in the outer query and so it cannot run separately by itself. The outer query runs first and the correlated subquery runs once for every row in the outer query.

Table 10-1: Subquery and CTE Usage

| | *Subquery Returns:* | | |
	Expression	*List*	*Data Set*
Select-Statement Element	*Subquery returns a scalar value*	*Subquery returns a list of values*	*Subquery returns a multi-column data source*
Select (subquery)	The subquery result is used as an expression supplying the value for the column.	X	X
From (data source) as SQ			
This is the only location where a subquery can use a table alias or named range	The subquery's data set is accepted as a derived table source within the outer query.	The subquery's data set is accepted as a derived table source within the outer query.	The subquery's data set is accepted as a derived table source within the outer query.
Where x {=, >, <, >=, <=, <>} (subquery)	The where clause is true if the test value compares true with the subquery's scalar value.	X	X
Where x In (subquery)	The where condition is true if the test value is equal to the scalar value returned by the subquery.	The where condition is true if the test value is found within the list returned by the subquery.	X
Where Exists (Subquery)	The where condition is true if the subquery returns at least one row.	The where condition is true if the subquery returns at least one row.	The where condition is true if the subquery returns at least one row.

Simple Subqueries

Simple subqueries are executed in the following order:

1. The simple subquery is executed once.

2. The results are passed to the outer query.

3. The outer query is executed once.

The most basic simple subquery returns a single (scalar) value, which is then used as an expression in the outer query, as follows:

```
SELECT (SELECT 3) AS SubqueryValue
```

Result:

```
SubqueryValue
--------------
3
```

The subquery (select 3) returns a single value of 3, which is passed to the outer select statement. The outer select statement is then executed as if it were the following:

```
SELECT 3 AS SubqueryValue
```

Of course, a subquery with only hard-coded values is of little use. A useful subquery fetches data from a table, for example:

```
USE OBXKites

SELECT ProductName
  FROM dbo.Product
  WHERE ProductCategoryID
    = (Select ProductCategoryID
        FROM dbo.ProductCategory
        Where ProductCategoryName = 'Kite')
```

To execute this query, SQL Server first evaluates the subquery and returns a value to the outer query (your unique identifier will be different from the one in this query):

```
Select ProductCategoryID
        FROM dbo.ProductCategory
        Where ProductCategoryName = 'Kite'
```

Result:

```
ProductCategoryID
------------------------------------
C38D8113-2BED-4E2B-9ABF-A589E0818069
```

The outer query then executes as if it were the following:

```
SELECT ProductName
  FROM dbo.Product
  WHERE ProductCategoryID
    = 'C38D8113-2BED-4E2B-9ABF-A589E0818069'
```

Result:

```
ProductName
----------------------------------------------------
Basic Box Kite 21 inch
Dragon Flight
Sky Dancer
Rocket Kite
...
```

If you think subqueries seem similar to joins, you're right. Both are a means of referencing multiple data sources within a single query, and many queries that use joins may be rewritten as queries using subqueries.

Best Practice

Use a join to pull data from two data sources that can be filtered or manipulated as a whole after the join. If the data must be manipulated prior to the join, use a subquery.

Common Table Expressions

The common table expression defines what could be considered a temporary view, which can be referenced as a view later in the query. Because CTEs may be used in the same ways that simple subqueries are used, I've included them in the simple subquery heading and will show example code CTEs alongside simple subqueries.

The CTE uses the `with` clause, which defines the CTE. Inside the `with` clause is the name, column aliases, and SQL code for the CTE subquery. The main query can then reference the CTE as a data source:

```
WITH CTEName (parameters)
AS (Simple Subquery)

SELECT...
   FROM CTEName
```

The following example is the exact same query as the preceding subquery, only in CTE format. The name of the CTE is `CTEQuery`. It returns the `ProductionCategoryID` column and uses the exact same SQL `Select` statement as the preceding simple subquery:

```
WITH CTEQuery (ProductCategoryID)
AS (Select ProductCategoryID
        FROM dbo.ProductCategory
        Where ProductCategoryName = 'Kite')
```

Once the CTE has been defined in the `with` clause, the main portion of the query can reference the CTE using its name as if the CTE were any other table source, such as a table or view. Here's the complete example, including the CTE and the main query:

```
WITH CTEQuery (ProductCategoryID)
AS (Select ProductCategoryID
        FROM dbo.ProductCategory
        Where ProductCategoryName = 'Kite')
```

```
SELECT ProductName
  FROM dbo.Product
  WHERE ProductCategoryID
    = (SELECT ProductCategoryID FROM CTEQuery)
```

To include multiple CTEs within the same query, define the CTEs in sequence prior to the main query:

```
WITH CTE1Name (parameters)
AS (Simple Subquery)
WITH CTE2Name (parameters)
AS (Simple Subquery)
SELECT...
  FROM CTE1Name
       JOIN CTE2Name
         ON ...
```

Although CTEs may include complex queries, they come with two key restrictions:

✦ Unlike subqueries, CTEs may not be nested. A CTE may not include another CTE.

✦ CTEs may not reference the main query. Like simple subqueries, they must be self-contained.

Although the CTE syntax may initially appear alien, for very complex queries that reference the same subquery in multiple locations, using a CTE may reduce the amount of code and improve readability.

Best Practice

So far in my testing, I've not seen any performance difference between simple subqueries and CTEs; both are compiled to the same query execution plan.

Using Scalar Subqueries

If the subquery returns a single value it may then be used anywhere inside the SQL select statement where an expression might be used, including column expressions, join conditions, where conditions, or having conditions. Normal operators (+, =, between, and so on) will work with single values returned from a subquery; data-type conversion using the cast() or convert() functions may be required, however.

The example in the last section used a subquery within a where condition. The following sample query uses a subquery within a column expression to calculate the total sales so each row can calculate the percentage of sales:

```
SELECT ProductCategoryName,
    SUM(Quantity * UnitPrice) AS Sales,
    Cast(SUM(Quantity * UnitPrice) /
        (SELECT SUM(Quantity * UnitPrice)
            FROM dbo.OrderDetail) *100 AS INT)
        AS PercentOfSales
  FROM dbo.OrderDetail
    JOIN dbo.Product
      ON OrderDetail.ProductID = Product.ProductID
```

```
      JOIN dbo.ProductCategory
        ON Product.ProductCategoryID = ProductCategory.ProductCategoryID
      GROUP BY ProductCategoryName
      ORDER BY Count(*) DESC
```

The subquery, `select sum(Quantity * UnitPrice) from OrderDetail`, returns a value of 1729.895, which is then passed to the outer query's `PercentageOfSales` column. The result lists the product categories, sales amount, and percentage of sales:

```
ProductCategoryName    Sales            PercentOfSales
---------------------- ---------------- --------------
Kite                   1499.902500      86.70
OBX                    64.687500        3.74
Clothing               113.600000       6.57
Accessory              10.530000        0.61
Material               5.265000         0.30
Video                  35.910000        2.08
```

The following `select` statement is extracted from the `fGetPrice()` user-defined function in the OBXKites sample database. The OBXKites database has a price table that allows each product to have a list of prices, each with an effective date. The OBX Kite store can pre-define several price changes for a future date, rather than enter all the price changes the night before the new prices go into effect. As an additional benefit, this data model maintains a price history.

The `fGetPrice()` function returns the correct price for any product, any date, and any customer-discount type. To accomplish this, the function must determine the effective date for the date submitted. For example, if a user needs a price for July 16, 2002, and the current price was made effective on July 1, 2002, then in order to look up the price the query needs to know the most recent price date using `max(effectivedate)`, where `effectivedate` is = `@orderdate`. Once the subquery determines the effective date, the outer query can look up the price. Some of the function's variables are replaced with static values for the purpose of this example:

```
SELECT @CurrPrice = Price * (1-@DiscountPercent)
  FROM dbo.Price
    JOIN dbo.Product
      ON Price.ProductID = Product.ProductID
  WHERE ProductCode = '1001'
    AND EffectiveDate =
      (SELECT MAX(EffectiveDate)
        FROM dbo.Price
          JOIN dbo.Product
            ON Price.ProductID = Product.ProductID
        WHERE ProductCode = '1001'
          AND EffectiveDate <= '6/1/2001')
```

Calling the function,

```
Select dbo.fGetPrice('1001','5/1/2001',NULL)
```

the subquery determines that the effective price date is `'05/01/2001'`. The outer query can then find the correct price based on the `ProductID` and effective date. Once the `fGetPrice()` function calculates the discount, it can return @CurrPrice to the calling `select` statement:

```
14.95
```

Using Subqueries as Lists

Subqueries begin to shine when used as lists. A single value, commonly a column, in the outer query is compared with the subquery's list by means of the in operators. The subquery must return only a single column; multiple columns will fail.

The in operator returns a value of true if the column value is found anywhere in the list supplied by the subquery, in the same way that where ... in returns a value of true when used with a hard-coded list:

```
SELECT *
  FROM dbo.Contact
  WHERE HomeRegion IN ('NC', 'SC', 'GA', 'AL', 'VA')
```

A list subquery serves as a dynamic means of generating the where ... in condition list:

```
SELECT *
  FROM dbo.Contact
  WHERE Region IN (Subquery that returns a list of states)
```

The following query answers the question "When OBX Kites sells a kite, what else does it sell with the kite?" To demonstrate the use of subqueries, this query will use only subqueries — no joins. All of these subqueries are simple queries, meaning that each can run as a stand-alone query.

The subquery will find all orders with kites and pass those OrderIDs to the outer query. Four tables are involved in providing the answer to this question: ProductCategory, Product, OrderDetail, and Order. The nested subqueries are executed from the inside out, so they read in the following order:

1. The subquery finds the one ProductCategoryID for the kites.

2. The subquery finds the list of products that are kites.

3. The subquery finds the list of orders with kites.

4. The subquery finds the list of all the products on orders with kites.

5. The outer query finds the product names.

```
SELECT ProductName
  FROM dbo.Product
  WHERE ProductID IN
    -- 4. Find all the products sold in orders with kites
    (SELECT ProductID
      FROM dbo.OrderDetail
      WHERE OrderID IN
      -- 3. Find the Kite Orders
      (SELECT OrderID  -- Find the Orders with Kites
        FROM dbo.OrderDetail
        WHERE ProductID IN
          -- 2. Find the Kite Products
          (SELECT ProductID
            FROM dbo.Product
            WHERE ProductCategoryID =
              -- 1. Find the Kite category
              (Select ProductCategoryID
```

```
FROM dbo.ProductCategory
Where ProductCategoryName
    = 'Kite' ) ) ) )
```

Tip You can highlight any of these subqueries and run it as a stand-alone query in a Query window by selecting the subquery and pressing F5.

Subquery 1 finds the `ProductCategoryID` for the kite category and returns a single value.

Subquery 2 uses subquery 1 as a `where` clause expression subquery that returns the kite `ProductCategoryID`. Using this `where`-clause restriction, subquery 2 finds all products of which the `ProductCategoryID` is equal to the value returned from subquery 2.

Subquery 3 uses subquery 2 as a `where` clause list subquery by searching for all `OrderDetail` rows that include any one of the `productIDs` returned by subquery 2.

Subquery 4 uses subquery 3 as a `where` clause list subquery that includes all orders that include kites. The subquery then locates all `OrderDetail` rows for which the `orderID` is in the list returned by subquery 3.

The outer query uses subquery 4 as a `where` clause list condition and finds all products for which the `ProductID` is in the list returned by subquery 4, as follows:

```
ProductName
-------------------------------------------------
Falcon F-16
Dragon Flight
OBX Car Bumper Sticker
Short Streamer
Cape Hatteras T-Shirt
Sky Dancer
Go Fly a Kite T-Shirt
Long Streamer
Rocket Kite
OBX T-Shirt
```

Drat! There are kites in the list. They'll have to be eliminated from the query. To fix the error, the outer query needs to find all the products `where`:

✦ The `ProductID` is `in` order that included a kite

and

✦ The `ProductID` is `not in` the list of kites

Fortunately, subquery 2 returns all the kite products. Adding a copy of subquery 2 with the `not in` operator to the outer query will remove the kites from the list, as follows:

```
SELECT ProductName
  FROM dbo.Product
  WHERE ProductID IN
    -- 4. Find all the products sold in orders with kites
    (SELECT ProductID
      FROM dbo.OrderDetail
```

```
WHERE OrderID IN
-- 3. Find the Kite Orders
(SELECT OrderID  -- Find the Orders with Kites
  FROM dbo.OrderDetail
  WHERE ProductID IN
    -- 2. Find the Kite Products
    (SELECT ProductID
      FROM dbo.Product
      WHERE ProductCategoryID =
        -- 1. Find the Kite category
        (Select ProductCategoryID
          FROM dbo.ProductCategory
          Where ProductCategoryName
            = 'Kite'))))
-- outer query continued
AND ProductID NOT IN
  (SELECT ProductID
    FROM dbo.Product
    WHERE ProductCategoryID =
      (Select ProductCategoryID
        FROM dbo.ProductCategory
        Where ProductCategoryName
          = 'Kite'))
```

Result:

```
ProductName
-------------------------------------------------
OBX Car Bumper Sticker
Short Streamer
Cape Hatteras T-Shirt
Go Fly a Kite T-Shirt
Long Streamer
OBX T-Shirt
```

For comparison purposes, the following queries answer the exact same question but are written with joins. The Product table is referenced twice, so the second reference that represents only the kites has a named range of Kite. As with the previous subqueries, the first version of the query locates all products and the second version eliminates the kites:

```
SELECT Distinct Product.ProductName
  FROM dbo.Product
    JOIN dbo.OrderDetail OrderRow
      ON Product.ProductID = OrderRow.ProductID
    JOIN dbo.OrderDetail KiteRow
      ON OrderRow.OrderID = KiteRow.OrderID
    JOIN dbo.Product Kite
      ON KiteRow.ProductID = Kite.ProductID
    JOIN dbo.ProductCategory
      ON Kite.ProductCategoryID
          = ProductCategory.ProductCategoryID
  Where ProductCategoryName = 'Kite'
```

The only change necessary to eliminate the kites is the addition of another condition to the `ProductCategory` join. Previously, the join was an equi-join between `Product` and `ProductCategory`. Adding a Θ-join condition of `!=` between the `Product` table and the `ProductCategory` table removes any products that are kites, as shown in the following code sample:

```
SELECT Distinct Product.ProductName
  FROM dbo.Product
    JOIN dbo.OrderDetail OrderRow
      ON Product.ProductID = OrderRow.ProductID
    JOIN dbo.OrderDetail KiteRow
      ON OrderRow.OrderID = KiteRow.OrderID
    JOIN dbo.Product Kite
      ON KiteRow.ProductID = Kite.ProductID
    JOIN dbo.ProductCategory
      ON Kite.ProductCategoryID
          = ProductCategory.ProductCategoryID
      AND Product.ProductCategoryID
          != Kite.ProductCategoryID
  Where ProductCategoryName  = 'Kite'
```

These two sets of queries, written using dramatically different syntax, provide the exact same answer. So which is the best query? That's up to you. Depending on complexity, subqueries can be faster because they select fewer rows from step to step. More complex subqueries tend to perform better than large join queries.

Best Practice

SQL is very flexible — there are often a dozen ways to express the same question. Your choice of SQL method should be made first according to your style and to which method enables you to be readable and logically correct, and then according to performance considerations. Slow and correct beats fast and wrong every time.

Here's another example of how a creative subquery can solve a problem. SQL handles finding the top rows from a result set easily, but it's a little trickier to find a middle range of rows. In this day of Web searches that return hundreds of hits, finding rows 101 through 125 is a useful, and frequently required, ability.

This example, based on the OBX Kites Store sample database, finds five products beginning with the 26th product. The subquery finds the first 25 products, which are then skipped by the outer query because of the `where not in` clause:

```
USE OBXKites
SELECT TOP 5 ProductName, ProductID
  FROM dbo.Product
  WHERE ProductID NOT IN
    (SELECT TOP 25 ProductID
       FROM dbo.Product
       ORDER BY ProductID)
  ORDER BY ProductID
```

Result:

```
ProductName            ProductCode
---------------------- ---------------
Handle                 1026
```

```
Third Line Release      1027
High Performance Line   1028
Kite Bag                1029
Kite Repair Kit         1030
```

Using Subqueries as Tables

In the same way that a view may be used in the place of a table within the from clause of a select statement, a subquery in the form of a *derived table* can replace any table, provided the subquery has a named range. This technique is very powerful and is often used to break a difficult query problem down into smaller bite-size chunks.

Using a subquery as a derived table is an excellent solution to the aggregate-function problem. When you are building an aggregate query, every column must participate in the aggregate function in some way, either as a group by column or as an aggregate function (sum(), avg(), count(), max(), or min()). This stipulation makes returning additional descriptive information difficult. However, performing the aggregate functions in a subquery and passing the rows found to the outer query as a derived table enables the outer query to then return any columns desired.

Cross-Reference For more information about aggregate functions and the group by keyword, see Chapter 11, "Aggregating Data."

The question "How many of each product have been sold?" is easy to answer if only one column from the Product table is included in the result:

```
SELECT ProductCode, SUM(Quantity) AS QuantitySold
  FROM dbo.OrderDetail
    JOIN dbo.Product
      ON OrderDetail.ProductID = Product.ProductID
  GROUP BY ProductCode
```

Result:

```
ProductCode      QuantitySold
---------------  ----------------------------------------
1002             47.00
1003             5.00
1004             2.00
1012             5.00
```

The result includes ProductCode, but not the name or description. Of course, it's possible to simply group by every column to be returned, but that's sloppy. The following query performs the aggregate summation in a subquery that is then joined with the Product table so that every column is available without additional work:

```
SELECT Product.ProductCode, Product.ProductName,
    Sales.QuantitySold
  FROM dbo.Product
  JOIN (SELECT ProductID, SUM(Quantity) AS QuantitySold
          FROM dbo.OrderDetail
          GROUP BY ProductID) Sales
    ON Product.ProductID = Sales.ProductID
  ORDER BY ProductCode
```

If you use SQL Server Management Studio's Query Designer, a derived table may be added to the query. Figure 10-1 illustrates the previous query being constructed using the GUI tool.

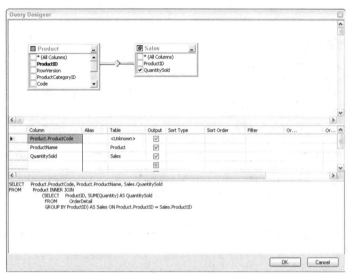

Figure 10-1: Derived tables may be included within Query Designer by using the context menu and selecting Add Derived Table.

The query is fast and efficient, it provides the required aggregate data, and all the product columns can be added to the output columns. The result is as follows:

```
ProductCode ProductName           QuantitySold
----------- --------------------  ------------------
1002        Dragon Flight         47.00
1003        Sky Dancer            5.00
1004        Rocket Kite           2.00
1012        Falcon F-16           5.00
...
```

Another example of using a derived table to solve a problem answers the question "How many children has each mother borne?" from the Family sample database:

```
USE Family
SELECT PersonID, FirstName, LastName, Children
  FROM dbo.Person
    JOIN (SELECT MotherID, COUNT(*) AS Children
            FROM dbo.Person
            WHERE MotherID IS NOT NULL
            GROUP BY MotherID) ChildCount
      ON Person.PersonID = ChildCount.MotherID
  ORDER BY Children DESC
```

The subquery performs the aggregate summation, and the columns are joined with the `Person` table to present the final results, as follows:

```
PersonID    FirstName         LastName          Children
----------- ----------------  ----------------  ----------
6           Audry             Halloway          4
8           Melanie           Campbell          3
12          Alysia            Halloway          3
20          Grace             Halloway          2...
```

Correlated Subqueries

Correlated subqueries sound impressive, and they are. They are used in the same ways that simple subqueries are used, the difference being that correlated subqueries reference columns in the outer query. They do this by referencing the outer query's named range, or table alias, to reference the outer query. This capability to limit the subquery by the outer query makes these queries powerful and flexible. Because correlated subqueries can reference the outer query, they are especially useful for complex `where` conditions.

The capability to reference the outer query also means that correlated subqueries won't run by themselves because the reference to the outer query would cause the query to fail. The logical execution order is as follows:

1. The outer query is executed once.

2. The subquery is executed once for every row in the outer query, substituting the values from the outer query into each execution of the subquery.

3. The subquery's results are integrated into the result set.

If the outer query returns 100 rows, SQL Server will execute the logical equivalent of 101 queries — one for the outer query, and one subquery for every row returned by the outer query. In practice, the SQL Server Query Optimizer will likely figure out a way to perform the correlated subquery without actually performing the 101 queries. In fact, I've sometimes seen correlated subqueries outperform other query plans. If they solve your problem, don't avoid them for performance reasons.

To explore correlated subqueries, the next few queries, based on the Outer Banks Adventures sample database, use them to compare the locations of customers and tour base camps. First, the following data-modification queries set up the data:

```
USE CHA2
UPDATE dbo.BaseCamp SET Region = 'NC' WHERE BaseCampID = 1
UPDATE dbo.BaseCamp SET Region = 'NC' WHERE BaseCampID = 2
UPDATE dbo.BaseCamp SET Region = 'BA' WHERE BaseCampID = 3
UPDATE dbo.BaseCamp SET Region = 'FL' WHERE BaseCampID = 4
UPDATE dbo.BaseCamp SET Region = 'WV' WHERE BaseCampID = 5

UPDATE dbo.Customer SET Region = 'ND' WHERE CustomerID = 1
UPDATE dbo.Customer SET Region = 'NC' WHERE CustomerID = 2
UPDATE dbo.Customer SET Region = 'NJ' WHERE CustomerID = 3
UPDATE dbo.Customer SET Region = 'NE' WHERE CustomerID = 4
UPDATE dbo.Customer SET Region = 'ND' WHERE CustomerID = 5
```

```
UPDATE dbo.Customer SET Region = 'NC' WHERE CustomerID = 6
UPDATE dbo.Customer SET Region = 'NC' WHERE CustomerID = 7
UPDATE dbo.Customer SET Region = 'BA' WHERE CustomerID = 8
UPDATE dbo.Customer SET Region = 'NC' WHERE CustomerID = 9
UPDATE dbo.Customer SET Region = 'FL' WHERE CustomerID = 10
```

This sample set of data produces the following matrix between customer locations and base-camp locations:

```
SELECT DISTINCT Customer.Region, BaseCamp.Region
  FROM dbo.Customer
    JOIN dbo.Event_mm_Customer
      ON Customer.CustomerID = Event_mm_Customer.CustomerID
    JOIN dbo.Event
      ON Event_mm_Customer.EventID = Event.EventID
    JOIN dbo.Tour
      ON Event.TourID = Tour.TourID
    JOIN dbo.BaseCamp
      ON Tour.BaseCampID = BaseCamp.BaseCampID
  WHERE Customer.Region IS NOT NULL
  GROUP BY Customer.Region, BaseCamp.Region
  ORDER BY Customer.Region, BaseCamp.Region
```

Result:

```
Customer    BaseCamp
Region      Region
-------     --------

BA          BA
BA          FL
BA          NC
FL          FL
FL          NC
FL          WV
NC          BA
NC          FL
NC          NC
NC          WV
ND          BA
ND          FL
ND          NC
NE          FL
NE          WV
NJ          FL
NJ          NC
NJ          WV
```

With this data foundation, the first query asks, "Who lives in the same region as one of our base camps?" The query uses a correlated subquery to locate base camps that share the same Region as the customer. The subquery is executed for every row in the Customer table, using the outer query's named range, C, to reference the outer query. If a BaseCamp match exists for that row, the exists condition is true and the row is accepted into the result set:

```
SELECT C.FirstName, C.LastName, C.Region
  FROM dbo.Customer AS C
  WHERE EXISTS
    (SELECT * FROM dbo.BaseCamp AS B
       WHERE B.Region = C.Region)
  ORDER BY LastName, FirstName
```

The same query written with joins requires a `distinct` predicate to eliminate duplicate rows. However, it can refer to columns in every referenced table — something a correlated sub-query within a `where exists` can't do:

```
SELECT DISTINCT C.FirstName, C.LastName, C.Region
  FROM Customer C
    JOIN dbo.BaseCamp B
      ON C.Region = B.Region
  ORDER BY LastName, FirstName
```

The result:

```
FirstName        LastName              Region
---------------  --------------------  --------------------
Jane             Doe                   BA
Francis          Franklin              FL
Melissa          Anderson              NC
Lauren           Davis                 NC
Wilson           Davis                 NC
John             Frank                 NC
```

A more complicated comparison asks, "Who has gone on a tour in his or her home region?"

The answer lies in the `Event_mm_Customer` table — a resolution (or junction) table between the `Event` and `Customer` tables that serves to store the logical many-to-many relationships between customers and events (multiple customers may attend a single event, and a single customer may attend multiple events). The `Event_mm_Customer` table may be thought of as analogous to a customer's ticket to an event.

The outer query logically runs through every `Event_mm_Customer` row to determine whether there `exists` any result from the correlated subquery. The subquery is filtered by the current `EventID` and customer `RegionID` from the outer query.

In an informal way of thinking, the query checks every ticket and creates a list of events in a customer's home region that the customer has attended. If anything is in the list, the `where exists` condition is true for that row. If the list is empty, `where exists` is not satisfied and the customer row in question is eliminated from the result set:

```
USE CHA2
SELECT DISTINCT C.FirstName, C.LastName, C.Region AS Home
  FROM dbo.Customer C
    JOIN dbo.Event_mm_Customer E
      ON C.CustomerID = E.CustomerID
  WHERE C.Region IS NOT NULL
    AND EXISTS
        (SELECT *
          FROM dbo.Event
```

```
          JOIN dbo.Tour
            ON Event.TourID = Tour.TourID
          JOIN dbo.BaseCamp
            ON Tour.BaseCampID = BaseCamp.BaseCampID
        WHERE BaseCamp.Region = C.Region
        AND Event.EventID = E.EventID)
```

The result:

```
FirstName LastName   Home --------- ------------ ------
Francis   Franklin   FL
Jane      Doe        BA
John      Frank      NC
Lauren    Davis      NC
Melissa   Anderson   NC
```

The same query can be written using joins. Although it might be easier to read, the following query took 131 milliseconds compared to only 80 milliseconds taken by the preceding correlated subquery:

```
SELECT Distinct C.FirstName, C.LastName, C.Region AS Home,
    Tour.TourName, BaseCamp.Region
  FROM dbo.Customer C
    JOIN dbo.Event_mm_Customer
      ON C.CustomerID = Event_mm_Customer.CustomerID
    JOIN dbo.Event
      ON Event_mm_Customer.EventID = Event.EventID
    JOIN dbo.Tour
      ON Event.TourID = Tour.TourID
    JOIN dbo.BaseCamp
      ON Tour.BaseCampID = BaseCamp.BaseCampID
      AND C.Region = BaseCamp.Region
      AND C.Region IS NOT NULL
  ORDER BY C.LastName
```

The join query has the advantage of including the columns from the Tour table without having to explicitly return them from the subquery. The join also lists Lauren and Frank twice, once for each in-region tour (and yes, the Amazon Trek tour is based out of Ft. Lauderdale):

```
FirstName LastName   Home  TourName                 Region--------- --
--------- ------ ------------------------ ------Melissa   Anderson   NC
Outer Banks Lighthouses NC
Lauren    Davis      NC    Appalachian Trail        NC
Lauren    Davis      NC    Outer Banks Lighthouses  NC
Jane      Doe        BA    Bahamas Dive             BA
John      Frank      NC    Appalachian Trail        NC
John      Frank      NC    Outer Banks Lighthouses  NC
Francis   Franklin   FL    Amazon Trek              FL
```

Although correlated subqueries can be mind-bending, the flexibility and potential performance gains are worth it. Make sure that the correlated subquery returns the correct answer.

Relational Division

A cross join, discussed previously in this chapter, is relational multiplication — two data sets are multiplied to create a Cartesian product. In theory, all joins are cross joins with some type of conditional restriction. Even an inner join is the relational-multiplication product of two tables restricted to those results that match keys.

Relational division complements relational multiplication just as basic math division complements multiplication. If the purpose of relational multiplication is to produce a product set from two multiplier sets, the purpose of relational division is to divide one data set (the *dividend data set*) by another data set (the *divisor data set*) to find the *quotient data set*, as shown in Figure 10-2. In other words, if the Cartesian product is known, and one of the multiplier data sets is known, relational division can deduce the missing multiplier set.

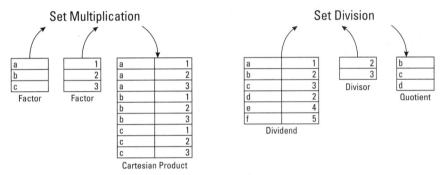

Figure 10-2: Relational division is the inverse of relational multiplication, deducing the quotient set by dividing the dividend set by the divisor set.

While this may sound academic, relational division can be very practical. The classic example of relational division answers the question "Which students have passed every required course?" An *exact relational division* query would list only those students who passed the required courses and no others. A *relational division with a remainder*, also called an *approximate divide,* would list all the students who passed the required courses and include students who passed any additional courses. Of course, that example was both practical and academic.

Relational division is more complex than a join. A join simply finds any matches between two data sets. Relational division finds exact matches between two data sets. Joins/subqueries and relational division solve different types of questions. For example, the following questions apply to the sample databases and compare the two methods:

✦ Joins/subqueries:

- **CHA2:** Who has ever gone on a tour?

- **CHA2:** Who lives in the same region as a base camp?

- **CHA2:** Who has attended any event in his or her home region?

✦ Exact relational division:

- **CHA2:** Who has gone on every tour in his or her home state, but no tours outside it?

- **OBXKites:** Who has purchased every kite but nothing else?

- **Family:** Which women (widows or divorcees) have married the same husbands as each other, but no other husbands?

✦ Relational division with remainders:

- **CHA2:** Who has gone on every tour in his or her home state, and possibly other tours as well?

- **OBXKites:** Who has purchased every kite and possibly other items as well?

- **Family:** Which women have married the same husbands and may have married other men as well?

Relational Division with a Remainder

Relational division with a remainder essentially extracts the quotient while allowing some leeway for rows that meet the criteria but contain additional data as well. In real-life situations this type of division is typically more useful than an exact relational division.

The previous OBX Kites sales question ("Who has purchased every kite and possibly other items as well?") is a good one to use to demonstrate relational division. Because it takes five tables to go from contact to product category, and because the question refers to the join between OrderDetail and Product, this question involves enough complexity that it simulates a real-world relational-database problem.

The toy category will make a good example category because it contains only two toys and no one has purchased a toy in the sample data, so the query will answer the question "Who has purchased at least one of every toy sold by OBX Kites?" (And yes, my kids volunteered to help test this query.)

First, the following data will mock up a scenario in the OBX Kites database. The only toys are ProductCode 1049 and 1050. The OBXKites database uses unique identifiers for primary keys and therefore uses stored procedures for all inserts. The first Order and OrderDetail inserts will list the stored procedure parameters so the following stored procedure calls are easier to understand:

```
USE OBXKites
DECLARE @OrderNumber INT
```

The first person, ContactCode 110, orders exactly all toys:

```
EXEC pOrder_AddNew
   @ContactCode = '110',
   @EmployeeCode = '120',
   @LocationCode = 'CH',
   @OrderDate= '6/1/2002',
   @OrderNumber = @OrderNumber output

EXEC pOrder_AddItem
   @OrderNumber = @OrderNumber,
```

```
      @Code = '1049',
      @NonStockProduct = NULL,
      @Quantity = 12,
      @UnitPrice = NULL,
      @ShipRequestDate = '6/1/2002',
      @ShipComment = NULL

  EXEC pOrder_AddItem
      @OrderNumber, '1050', NULL, 3, NULL, NULL, NULL
```

The second person, `ContactCode` 111, orders exactly all toys — and toy 1050 twice:

```
EXEC pOrder_AddNew
  '111', '119', 'JR', '6/1/2002', @OrderNumber output
EXEC pOrder_AddItem
  @OrderNumber, '1049', NULL, 6, NULL, NULL, NULL
EXEC pOrder_AddItem
  @OrderNumber, '1050', NULL, 6, NULL, NULL, NULL

EXEC pOrder_AddNew
  '111', '119', 'JR', '6/1/2002', @OrderNumber output
EXEC pOrder_AddItem
  @OrderNumber, '1050', NULL, 6, NULL, NULL, NULL
```

The third person, `ContactCode` 112, orders all toys plus some other products:

```
EXEC pOrder_AddNew
  '112', '119', 'JR', '6/1/2002', @OrderNumber output
EXEC pOrder_AddItem
  @OrderNumber, '1049', NULL, 6, NULL, NULL, NULL
EXEC pOrder_AddItem
  @OrderNumber, '1050', NULL, 5, NULL, NULL, NULL
EXEC pOrder_AddItem
  @OrderNumber, '1001', NULL, 5, NULL, NULL, NULL
EXEC pOrder_AddItem
  @OrderNumber, '1002', NULL, 5, NULL, NULL, NULL
```

The fourth person, `ContactCode` 113, orders one toy:

```
EXEC pOrder_AddNew
  '113', '119', 'JR', '6/1/2002', @OrderNumber output
EXEC pOrder_AddItem
  @OrderNumber, '1049', NULL, 6, NULL, NULL, NULL
```

In other words, only customers 110 and 111 order all the toys and nothing else. Customer 112 purchases all the toys as well as some kites. Customer 113 is an error check because she bought only one toy.

At least a couple of methods exist for coding a relational-division query. The original method, proposed by Chris Date, involves using nested correlated subqueries to locate rows in and out of the sets. A more direct method has been popularized by Joe Celko: It involves comparing the row count of the dividend and divisor data sets.

Basically, Celko's solution is to rephrase the question as "For whom is the number of toys ordered equal to the number of toys available?"

The query is asking two questions. The outer query will group the orders with toys for each contact, and the subquery will count the number of products in the toy product category. The outer query's `having` clause will then compare the distinct count of contact products ordered that are toys against the count of products that are toys:

```
-- Is number of toys ordered...
SELECT Contact.ContactCode
  FROM dbo.Contact
    JOIN dbo.[Order]
      ON Contact.ContactID = [Order].ContactID
    JOIN dbo.OrderDetail
      ON [Order].OrderID = OrderDetail.OrderID
    JOIN dbo.Product
      ON OrderDetail.ProductID = Product.ProductID
    JOIN dbo.ProductCategory
      ON Product.ProductCategoryID = ProductCategory.ProductCategoryID
  WHERE ProductCategory.ProductCategoryName = 'Toy'
  GROUP BY Contact.ContactCode
  HAVING COUNT(DISTINCT Product.ProductCode) =
-- equal to number of toys available?
      (SELECT Count(ProductCode)
         FROM dbo.Product
           JOIN dbo.ProductCategory
             ON Product.ProductCategoryID
               = ProductCategory.ProductCategoryID
         WHERE ProductCategory.ProductCategoryName = 'Toy')
```

The result:

```
ContactCode
---------------
110
111
112
```

Exact Relational Division

Exact relational division finds exact matches without any remainder. It takes the basic question of relational division with remainder and tightens the method so that the divisor will have no extra rows that would cause a remainder.

In practical terms it means that the example question now asks, "Who has ordered only every toy?"

If you address this query with a modified form of Joe Celko's method, the pseudocode becomes, "For whom is the number of toys ordered equal to the number of toys available, and also equal to the total number of products ordered?" If a customer has ordered additional products other than toys, the third part of the question eliminates that customer from the result set.

The SQL code contains two primary changes to the previous query. The first change is that the outer query must find both the number of toys ordered and the number of all products ordered. It does this by finding the toys purchased in a derived table and joining the two data sets. The second change is modifying the having clause to compare the number of toys available with both the number of toys purchased and the number of all products purchased, as follows:

```
-- Exact Relational Division
-- Is number of all products ordered...
SELECT Contact.ContactCode
  FROM dbo.Contact
    JOIN dbo.[Order]
      ON Contact.ContactID = [Order].ContactID
    JOIN dbo.OrderDetail
      ON [Order].OrderID = OrderDetail.OrderID
    JOIN dbo.Product
      ON OrderDetail.ProductID = Product.ProductID
    JOIN dbo.ProductCategory P1
      ON Product.ProductCategoryID = P1.ProductCategoryID

    JOIN
        -- and number of toys ordered
        (SELECT Contact.ContactCode, Product.ProductCode
          FROM dbo.Contact
            JOIN dbo.[Order]
              ON Contact.ContactID = [Order].ContactID
            JOIN dbo.OrderDetail
              ON [Order].OrderID = OrderDetail.OrderID
            JOIN dbo.Product
              ON OrderDetail.ProductID = Product.ProductID
            JOIN dbo.ProductCategory
              ON Product.ProductCategoryID =
                    ProductCategory.ProductCategoryID
          WHERE ProductCategory.ProductCategoryName = 'Toy'
        ) ToysOrdered

    ON Contact.ContactCode = ToysOrdered.ContactCode

  GROUP BY Contact.ContactCode

  HAVING   COUNT(DISTINCT Product.ProductCode) =
-- equal to number of toys available?
    (SELECT Count(ProductCode)
      FROM dbo.Product
        JOIN dbo.ProductCategory
          ON Product.ProductCategoryID
            = ProductCategory.ProductCategoryID
      WHERE ProductCategory.ProductCategoryName = 'Toy')

-- AND equal to the total number of any product ordered?
    AND COUNT(DISTINCT ToysOrdered.ProductCode) =
      (SELECT Count(ProductCode)
        FROM dbo.Product
          JOIN dbo.ProductCategory
```

```
        ON Product.ProductCategoryID
          = ProductCategory.ProductCategoryID
     WHERE ProductCategory.ProductCategoryName = 'Toy')
```

The result is a list of contacts containing the number of toys purchased (2), and the number of total products purchased (2), both equal to the number of products available (2):

```
ContactCode
- - - - - - - - - - - - - - -
110
111
```

Summary

While the basic nuts and bolts of subqueries may appear simple, they open a world of possibilities, as they enable you to build complex nested queries that pull and twist data into the exact shape that is needed to solve a difficult problem. As you continue to play with subqueries, I think you'll agree that herein lies the power of SQL. And if you're still developing primarily with the GUI tools, this might provide the catalyst to move you to developing SQL using the query text editor.

The previous chapters established the foundation for working with SQL, covering the select statement, expressions, joins, and unions, while this chapter expanded the select with powerful subqueries and CTEs. If you're reading through this book sequentially, congratulations, you are now over the hump of learning SQL. If you can master relational algebra and subqueries, the rest is a piece of cake.

The next chapter continues to describe the repertoire of data-retrieval techniques with aggregation queries, where using subqueries pays off.

✦   ✦   ✦

Aggregating Data

The Information Architecture Principle in Chapter 1 implies that the asset is information, not just data. Turning raw lists of data and keys into useful information often involves summarizing data and grouping it in meaningful ways. While a certain amount of summarization and analysis can be performed with other tools, such as Reporting Services or Analysis Services, SQL is a set-based language, and a fair amount of summarizing and grouping can be performed very well within the SQL `select` statement.

SQL excels at calculating sums, max values, and averages for the entire data set or for segments of data. In addition, SQL queries can create cross-tabulations, commonly known as *pivot tables*.

New in 2005   While ANSI-92 SQL includes plenty of standard aggregation features, SQL Server 2005 includes the capability to roll your own aggregate functions using the common language runtime. I have no doubt that third-party libraries of custom aggregate functions will appear.

Simple Aggregations

The basic gist of an aggregate query is that instead of returning all the selected rows, SQL Server returns a single row of computed values that summarizes the original data set, as illustrated in Figure 11-1. The types of calculations range from totaling the data to performing basic statistical operations.

It's important to note that in the logical order of the SQL query, the aggregate functions occur following the `from` clause and the `where` filters. This means that the data can be assembled and filtered prior to being summarized without having to use a subquery.

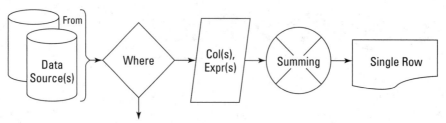

Figure 11-1: The aggregate function produces a single row result from a data set.

Basic Aggregations

SQL includes a set of *aggregate functions*, listed in Table 11-1, which can be used as expressions in the `select` statement to return summary data.

Table 11-1: Basic Aggregate Functions

Aggregate Function	Data Type Supported	Description
sum()	Numeric	Totals all the non-null values in the column.
avg()	Numeric	Averages all the non-null values in the column. Input data type will be returned by avg(), so the input is often converted to a higher precision, such as avg(cast col as a float).
min()	numeric, string, datetime	Returns the smallest number or the first datetime or the first string according to the current collation from the column.
max()	numeric, string, datetime	Returns the largest number or the last datetime or the last string according to the current collation from the column.
count([distinct] *)	Any data type (row-based)	Performs a simple count of all the rows in the result set up to 2,147,483,647. Will not count unique identifiers or blobs.
count_big([distinct] *)	Any data type (row-based)	Similar to the count() function, but the bigint data type can handle up to 2^63-1 rows.

The code examples for this chapter use a small table called `RawData`. The code to create and populate this data set is at the beginning of the chapter's script. You can download the script from www.SQLServerBible.com.

```
CREATE TABLE RawData (
    Region VARCHAR(10),
    Category CHAR(1),
    Amount INT,
    SalesDate DateTime
    )
```

This simple aggregate query counts the number of rows in the table and totals the `Amount` column. In lieu of returning the actual rows from the `RawData` table, the query returns the summary row with the count and total:

```
SELECT
    Count(*) as Count,
    Sum(Amount) as [Sum]
  FROM RawData
```

Result:

```
Count       Sum
----------- -----------
20          946
Warning: Null value is eliminated by an aggregate or
other SET operation.
```

If you're using Management Studio's Query Designer, the query can be converted into an aggregate query using the Group By toolbar button, as illustrated in Figure 11-2. The Group By column is used to select query columns for grouping or aggregate functions. To find the Query Designer, open a table using the Object Explorer.

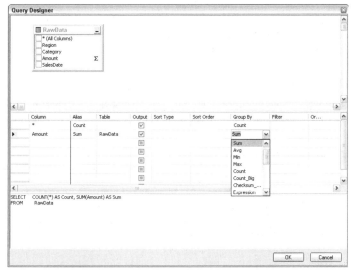

Figure 11-2: Performing an aggregate query within Management Studio's Query Designer

Using the aggregate functions within a `select` statement is pretty straightforward. Here are a few rules to keep in mind while using aggregate functions:

✦ Because SQL is now returning information from a set, rather than building a record set of rows, as soon as a query includes an aggregate function, every column (in the column list, in the expression, or in the `order by`) must participate in an aggregate function. This is logical because if a query returned the total number of order sales, then it could not return a single order number on the same row.

✦ The aggregate (`distinct`) option serves the same purpose as `select distinct` except that it eliminates duplicate values instead of duplicate rows. Therefore, it's of questionable usefulness when used with `sum()` and `avg()`. `Count(distinct *)` is invalid; a column must be specified.

✦ `Count(*)` counts all the rows, but `count(column)` counts all the rows with a value in that column.

✦ Because aggregate functions are expressions, the result will have a null column name. Therefore, use an alias to name the column.

✦ The precision of the aggregate function is determined by the data type precision of the source column. The `Amount` column in the table `RawData` is only an integer data type, so the `avg()` function is calculated as an integer. Converting the data to `numeric(9,5)` can increase the precision of the result:

```
SELECT Avg(amount) as [Integer Avg],
   Avg(Cast((Amount)as Numeric(9,5))) as [Numeric Avg],
   Sum(amount) / Count(*) as [Manual Avg]
   FROM RawData
```

Result:

```
Integer Avg   Numeric Avg   Manual Avg
------------- ------------- -----------------
47            47.300000     39
```

✦ Aggregate queries ignore any null values, so a `sum()` or `avg()` aggregate function will not error out on a null, but simply skip the row with a null. For this reason, a `sum()/count(*)` calculation may provide a different result than an `avg()` function.

Beginning Statistics

Statistics is a large and complex field of study, and while SQL Server does not pretend to replace a full statistical analysis software package, it does calculate standard deviation and variance that is important for understanding the bell-curve spread of numbers.

An average alone is not sufficient to summarize a set of values (in the lexicon of statistics, a "set" is referred to as a *population*). The value in the exact middle of a population is the *mean* (which is different from the average). The difference, or how widely dispersed the values are from the mean, is called the population's *variance*. For example, the populations (1, 2, 3, 4, 5, 6, 7, 8, 9, 10) and (4, 4, 5, 5, 5, 5, 6, 6) both average to 5, but the values in the first set vary widely from the mean, while the second set's values are all close to the mean. The standard deviation is the square root of the variance, and describes the shape of the bell curve formed by the population.

The following query uses the StDevP() and VarP() functions to returns the statistical variance and the standard deviation of the entire population of the RawData table:

```
SELECT
    StDevP(Amount) as [StDev],
    VarP(Amount) as [Var]
  FROM RawData
```

Result:

```
StDevP                VarP
-------------------   --------
24.2715883287435      589.11
```

Note If you need to perform extensive statistical data analysis, I recommend exporting the query result set to Excel and tapping Excel's broad range of statistical functions.

The statistical formulas differ slightly when calculating variance and standard deviation from the entire population versus a sampling of the population. If the aggregate query includes the entire population, use the StDevP() and VarP() aggregate functions, which use the *bias* or *n* method of calculating the deviation.

However, if the query is using a sampling or subset of the population, then use the StDev() and VarP() aggregate functions so SQL Server will use the unbiased or n-1 statistical method. Because group by queries slice the population into subsets, these queries should use StDev() and Var() functions.

Cross-Reference For ranking functions including calculating percentiles, see Chapter 7, "Understanding Basic Query Flow."

Grouping within a Result Set

Aggregate functions are all well and good, but how often do you need a total for an entire table? Most aggregate requirements will include a date range, department, type of sale, region, or the like. That presents a problem. If the only tool to restrict the aggregate function were the where clause, database developers would waste hours replicating the same query, or writing a lot of dynamic SQL queries and the code to execute the aggregate queries in sequence.

Fortunately, aggregate functions are complemented by the group by function, which automatically partitions the data set into subsets based upon the values in certain columns. Once the data set is divided into subgroups, the aggregate functions are performed on each subgroup. The final result is one summation row for each group, as shown in Figure 11-3.

A common example is grouping the sales result by salesperson. A sum() function without the grouping would produce the sum() of all sales. Writing a query for each salesperson would provide a sum() for each person, but maintaining that over time would be a pain. The grouping function automatically creates a subset of data grouped for each unique salesperson, and then the sum() function is calculated for each salesperson's sales. Voilà.

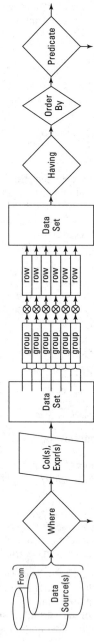

Figure 11-3: The group by clause slices the data set into multiple subgroups.

Simple Groupings

Some groupings use descriptive information for the grouping, so the data used by the group by is the same data you need to see to understand the groupings. These are straightforward, but in a large relational database, they can be rare. For example, the next query groups by the category:

```
SELECT Category,
    Count(*) as Count,
    Sum(Amount) as [Sum],
    Avg(Amount) as [Avg],
    Min(Amount) as [Min],
    Max(Amount) as [Max]
  FROM RawData
  GROUP BY Category
```

Result:

Category	Count	Sum	Avg	Min	Max
X	5	225	45	11	86
Y	11	506	46	12	91
Z	4	215	53	33	83

The first column of this query returns the Category column. While this column does not have an aggregate function, it still participates within the aggregate because that's the column by which the query is being grouped, and it may therefore be included in the result set. Each row in the result set summarizes one category, and the aggregate functions now calculate the row count, sum average, minimum value, and maximum value for each category.

SQL is not limited to grouping by one column. The preceding query is enhanced with the addition of a grouping by ProductCategoryName, as follows:

```
SELECT Year(SalesDate) as [Year], DatePart(q,SalesDate) as [Quarter],
    Count(*) as Count,
    Sum(Amount) as [Sum],
    Avg(Amount) as [Avg],
    Min(Amount) as [Min],
    Max(Amount) as [Max]
  FROM RawData
  GROUP BY Year(SalesDate), DatePart(q,SalesDate)
```

Result:

Year	Quarter	Count	Sum	Avg	Min	Max
2006	1	6	218	36	11	62
2006	2	6	369	61	33	86
2006	3	8	280	70	54	91
2005	4	4	79	19	12	28

For the purposes of a group by, null values are considered equal to other nulls and will be grouped together into a single result row

Aggravating Queries

There are a few aspects of group by queries that can be aggravating when developing applications. Some developers simply avoid aggregate queries and make the reporting tool do the work, but the Database Engine will be more efficient than any client tool. Here are five typical aggravating problems and my recommended solutions.

Including group by Descriptions

The previous aggregation queries all executed without error because every column participated in the aggregate purpose of the query. To test the rule, the following script adds a category table and then attempts to return a column that isn't included as an aggregation function or group by column:

```
CREATE TABLE RawCategory (
  RawCategoryID  CHAR(1),
  CategoryName   VARCHAR(25)
  )

INSERT RawCategory (RawCategoryID, CategoryName)
  VALUES ('X', 'Sci-Fi')
INSERT RawCategory (RawCategoryID, CategoryName)
  VALUES ('Y', 'Philosophy')
INSERT RawCategory (RawCategoryID, CategoryName)
  VALUES ('Z', 'Zoology')

-- including data outside the aggregate function or group by
SELECT Category, CategoryName,
    Sum(Amount) as [Sum],
    Avg(Amount) as [Avg],
    Min(Amount) as [Min],
    Max(Amount) as [Max]
  FROM RawData R
    JOIN RawCategory C
      ON R.Category = C.RawCategoryID
  GROUP BY Category
```

As expected, including region in the column list causes the query to return an error message:

```
Msg 8120, Level 16, State 1, Line 1
Column 'RawCategory.CategoryName' is invalid in the select list
because it is not contained in either an aggregate function or
the GROUP BY clause.
```

There are two solutions for including non-aggregate descriptive columns.

If the query is an ad hoc, run once query, then it's OK to just include the additional columns in the group by clause:

```
SELECT Category, CategoryName,
    Sum(Amount) as [Sum],
    Avg(Amount) as [Avg],
    Min(Amount) as [Min],
    Max(Amount) as [Max]
  FROM RawData R
```

```
      JOIN RawCategory C
        ON R.Category = C.RawCategoryID
    GROUP BY Category, CategoryName
    ORDER BY Category, CategoryName
```

Result:

```
Category  CategoryName    Sum   Avg   Min   Max
--------  --------------  ----- ----- ----- -----
X         Sci-Fi          225   45    11    86
Y         Philosophy      506   46    12    91
Z         Zoology         215   53    33    83
```

The problem with this approach is that it forces SQL Server to actually perform a grouping operation on every column regardless of whether that column is required or not to group the data, which can be an unnecessary performance hit.

For a query used in production, a better solution is to take it to the next level and perform the aggregate function in a subquery and then include the additional columns in the outer query:

```
SELECT sq.Category, CategoryName,
    sq.[Sum], sq.[Avg], sq.[Min], sq.[Max]
  FROM (SELECT Category,
             Sum(Amount) as [Sum],
             Avg(Amount) as [Avg],
             Min(Amount) as [Min],
             Max(Amount) as [Max]
          FROM RawData
          GROUP BY Category ) sq
    JOIN RawCategory C
      ON sq.Category = C.RawCategoryID
  ORDER BY Category, CategoryName
```

The subquery only has to do the work of the aggregate query and group by the category column. To fetch the category name, the result of the subquery is passed to the outer query, which uses a join to include the RawCategory table and access the CategoryName column.

Including All Group By Values

The group by functions occur following the where clause in the logical order of the query. This can present a problem if the query needs to report all the group by column values even though the data needs to be filtered. Although this is a rare request, there is an aggregate query solution that doesn't require outer joins and subqueries. The Group By All option includes all group by values regardless of the where clause. The next query uses this feature to return a 2005 group by row, even though 2005 data is not included in the aggregate calculation:

```
SELECT Year(SalesDate) as Year,
    Count(*) as Count,
    Sum(Amount) as [Sum],
    Avg(Amount) as [Avg],
    Min(Amount) as [Min],
    Max(Amount) as [Max]
  FROM RawData
  WHERE Year(SalesDate) = 2006
  GROUP BY ALL Year(SalesDate)
```

Result:

```
Year    Count   Sum     Avg     Min     Max
------  ------  -----   ------  ------  -----
2005    0       NULL    NULL    NULL    NULL
2006    20      867     54      11      91
```

Nesting Aggregations

Aggregated data is often useful, and it can be even more useful to perform secondary aggregations on aggregated data. For example, an aggregate query can easily `sum()` each category and year/quarter within a subquery, but which category has the max value for each year/quarter? An obvious `max(sum())` doesn't work because there's not enough information to tell SQL Server how to nest the aggregation groupings. Solving this problem requires a subquery to create a record set from the first aggregation, and an outer query to perform the second level of aggregation. For example, the following query sums by quarter and category, and then the outer query uses a `max()` to determine which sum is the greatest for each quarter:

```
Select Y,Q, Max(Sum) as MaxSum
   FROM ( -- Calculate Sums
           SELECT Category, Year(SalesDate) as Y,
              DatePart(q,SalesDate) as Q, Sum(Amount) as Sum
            FROM RawData
            GROUP BY Category, Year(SalesDate),
              DatePart(q,SalesDate)
          ) sq
   GROUP BY Y,Q
   ORDER BY Y,Q
```

Result:

```
Y               Q               MaxSum
-----------     -----------     -----------
2005            4               79
2006            1               147
2006            2               215
2006            3               280
```

Including Detail Descriptions

While it's nice to report the `max(sum())` of 147 for the first quarter of 2006, who wants to manually look up which category matches that sum? The next logical step is including descriptive information about the aggregate data. To add descriptive information for the detail columns, join with a subquery on the detail values:

```
SELECT MaxQuery.Y, MaxQuery.Q, AllQuery.Category, MaxQuery.MaxSum as MaxSum
   FROM (-- Find Max Sum Per Year/Quarter
          Select Y,Q, Max(Sum) as MaxSum
            From ( -- Calculate Sums
                   select Category, Year(SalesDate) as Y,
                      DatePart(q,SalesDate) as Q, Sum(Amount) as Sum
                    from RawData
                    group by Category, Year(SalesDate), DatePart(q,SalesDate)
                  ) sq
```

```
            Group By Y,Q
              ) MaxQuery
    JOIN (-- All Data Query
            Select Category, Year(SalesDate) as Y, DatePart(q,SalesDate) as Q,
                Sum(Amount) as Sum
            From RawData
            Group By Category, Year(SalesDate), DatePart(q,SalesDate)
              ) AllQuery
      ON MaxQuery.Y = AllQuery.Y
       AND MaxQuery.Q = AllQuery.Q
       AND MaxQuery.MaxSum = AllQuery.Sum
    ORDER BY MaxQuery.Y, MaxQuery.Q
```

Result:

```
Y            Q            Category MaxSum
------------ ------------ -------- -----------
2005         4            Y        79
2006         1            Y        147
2006         2            Z        215
2006         3            Y        280
```

While the query appears complex at first glance, it's actually just an extension of the preceding query (in bold with the table alias of `MaxQuery`.)

The last subquery (with the alias of `AllQuery`) finds every the sum of category and year/quarter. Joining `MaxQuery` with `AllQuery` on the sum and year/quarter is used to locate the category and return the descriptive value along with the detail data.

Filtering Grouped Results

Filtering, when combined with grouping, can be a problem. Are the row restrictions applied before the `group by` or after the `group by`? Some databases use nested queries to properly filter before or after the `group by`. SQL, however, uses the `having` clause to filter the groups. At the beginning of this chapter you saw the simplified order of the SQL `select` statement's execution. A more complete order is as follows:

1. The `from` clause assembles the data from the data sources.

2. The `where` clause restricts the rows based on the conditions.

3. The `group by` clause assembles subsets of data.

4. Aggregate functions are calculated.

5. The `having` clause filters the subsets of data.

6. Any expressions are calculated.

7. The `order by` sorts the results.

Continuing with the `RawData` sample table, the following query removes from the analysis any grouping "having" an average of less than 25:

```
SELECT Year(SalesDate) as [Year],
    DatePart(q,SalesDate) as [Quarter],
    Count(*) as Count,
```

```
      Sum(Amount) as [Sum],
      Avg(Amount) as [Avg]
    FROM RawData
    GROUP BY Year(SalesDate), DatePart(q,SalesDate)
    HAVING Avg(Amount) > 25
    ORDER BY [Year], [Quarter]
```

Result:

```
    Year   Quarter   Count   Sum   Avg
    ------ --------- ------- ----- -----
    2006   1         6       218   36
    2006   2         6       369   61
    2006   3         8       280   70
```

Without the `having` clause, the fourth quarter of 2005, with an average of 19, would have been included in the result set. But the `having` clause executed after `group by` and calculation of the aggregate function, serving as a post-aggregate filter.

Generating Totals

While Reporting Services can easily add subtotals and totals without any extra work by the query, it might prove useful to supply the total for a .NET application for display at the bottom of a form or web page. If that's your challenge, then these next three aggregate commands are perfect solutions.

Rollup Subtotals

The `rollup` and `cube` aggregate functions generate subtotals and grand totals as separate rows, and supply a null in the `group by` column to indicate the grand total. `Rollup` generates subtotal and total rows for the `group by` columns. `Cube` extends the capabilities by generating subtotal rows for every `group by` column. A special function called `grouping()` is true when the row is a subtotal or total row. Here I'll demonstrate the `rollup` function.

The `rollup` option, placed after the `group by` clause, instructs SQL Server to generate an additional total row. In this example, the `grouping()` function is used by a `case` expression to convert the total row to something understandable:

```
    SELECT
        CASE Grouping(Category)
          WHEN 0 THEN Category
          WHEN 1 THEN 'All Categories'
        END AS Category,
        Count(*) as Count
      FROM RawData
      GROUP BY Category
        WITH ROLLUP
```

Result:

```
    Category        Count
    -------------- -----------
```

```
X               5
Y               15
Z               4
All Categories  24
```

Adding a second column, Year(SalesDate), to the group by with rollup query will cause SQL Server to calculate subtotals for the second column:

```
SELECT
    CASE Grouping(Category)
      WHEN 0 THEN Category
      WHEN 1 THEN 'All Categories'
    END AS Category,
    CASE Grouping(Year(SalesDate))
      WHEN 0 THEN Cast(Year(SalesDate) as CHAR(8))
      WHEN 1 THEN 'All Years'
    END AS Year,
    Count(*) as Count
  FROM RawData
  GROUP BY Category, Year(SalesDate)
    WITH ROLLUP
```

Result:

```
Category        Year        Count
--------------- ----------- -----------
X               2006        5
X               All Years   5
Y               2005        4
Y               2006        11
Y               All Years   15
Z               2006        4
Z               All Years   4
All Categories  All Years   24
```

Cube Queries

A *cube query* is the next logical progression beyond a rollup query: It adds subtotals for every grouping in a multidimensional manner. Using the same example, the rollup query had subtotals for each category; the cube query adds subtotals for each year:

```
SELECT
    CASE Grouping(Category)
      WHEN 0 THEN Category
      WHEN 1 THEN 'All Categories'
    END AS Category,
    CASE Grouping(Year(SalesDate))
      WHEN 0 THEN Cast(Year(SalesDate) as CHAR(8))
      WHEN 1 THEN 'All Years'
    END AS Year,    Count(*) as Count
  FROM RawData
  GROUP BY Category, Year(SalesDate)
```

```
    WITH CUBE
   ORDER BY IsNull(Category, 'zzz')
```

Result:

```
Category        Year       Count
--------------- ---------- -----------
X               2006       5
X               All Years  5
Y               2005       4
Y               2006       11
Y               All Years  15
Z               2006       4
Z               All Years  4
All Categories  All Years  24
All Categories  2005       4
All Categories  2006       20
```

Computing Aggregates

The compute option is a completely different animal from any other aggregate query. Rather than build an aggregate query, think of the compute clause as an aggregate query tacked on to the end of a normal query. This query will return a normal result set with the detail rows and then add a few rows at the end to report some aggregate information about the same result set. In the following example the entire RawData table is returned, followed by what looks like a second result set with the average and sum:

```
SELECT Category, SalesDate, Amount
  FROM RawData
  WHERE Year(SalesDate) = '2006'
  COMPUTE  Avg(Amount), sum(Amount)
```

Result:

```
Category SalesDate                Amount
-------- ------------------------ -----------
X        2006-01-01 00:00:00.000  11
X        2006-01-01 00:00:00.000  24
...
Y        2006-08-01 00:00:00.000  NULL

avg          sum
-----------  -----------
54           867
```

Compute clauses can even contain their own miniature group by clauses. In this case, all the detail rows are returned divided by the group by, and with subtotals, just like a full-featured report:

```
SELECT Category, SalesDate, Amount
  FROM RawData
  WHERE Year(SalesDate) = '2006'
  ORDER BY Category
```

```
COMPUTE  Avg(Amount), sum(Amount)
  BY Category
```

Result:

```
Category SalesDate               Amount
-------- ----------------------- -----------
X        2006-01-01 00:00:00.000 11
...
X        2006-06-01 00:00:00.000 86

avg         sum
----------- -----------
45          225

Category SalesDate               Amount
-------- ----------------------- -----------
Y        2006-07-01 00:00:00.000 54
Y        2006-07-01 00:00:00.000 63
...
Y        2006-03-01 00:00:00.000 62

avg         sum
----------- -----------
61          427

Category SalesDate               Amount
-------- ----------------------- -----------
Z        2006-04-01 00:00:00.000 33
...
Z        2006-05-01 00:00:00.000 55

avg         sum
----------- -----------
53          215
```

The compute by did a fair job of including subtotals but didn't calculate a grand total. As strange as it seems, to add a grand total, combine both a compute and a compute by:

```
SELECT Category, SalesDate, Amount
  FROM RawData
  WHERE Year(SalesDate) = '2006'
  ORDER BY Category
  COMPUTE avg(Amount), sum(amount)
  COMPUTE sum(Amount)
    BY Category
```

Result:

```
Category SalesDate               Amount
-------- ----------------------- -----------
X        2006-01-01 00:00:00.000 11
...
```

```
X          2006-06-01 00:00:00.000 86

sum
-----------
225

Category SalesDate              Amount
-------- ---------------------- -----------
Y          2006-07-01 00:00:00.000 54
...
Y          2006-03-01 00:00:00.000 62

sum
-----------
427

Category SalesDate              Amount
-------- ---------------------- -----------
Z          2006-04-01 00:00:00.000 33
...
Z          2006-05-01 00:00:00.000 55

sum
-----------
215

avg         sum
----------- -----------
54          867
```

Notice that whereas the other aggregate functions did not supply a column header name and thus needed an alias to identify the column in the result set, the compute function provides a column name.

Building Crosstab Queries

While an aggregate query can group by multiple columns, the result is still columnar and less than perfect for scanning numbers quickly. The cross-tabulation, or crosstab, query pivots one group by column (or dimension) counterclockwise 90 degrees and turns it into the result set's columns, as shown in Figure 11-4. The limitation, of course, is that while a columnar group by query can have multiple aggregate functions, a crosstab query can display but a single measure.

The term *crosstab query* describes the result set, not the method of creating the crosstab, because there are multiple programmatic methods of generating a crosstab query — some better than others. The following sections describe several methods for creating the same result.

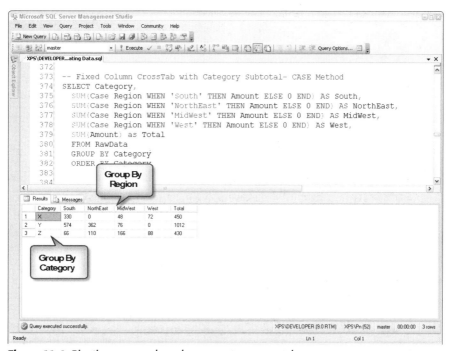

Figure 11-4: Pivoting a group by column creates a crosstab query.

Fixed-Column Crosstab Queries

There are three methods of generating a crosstab query with known, fixed columns using SQL Server 2005. While the columns for every crosstab query may not be known at development time, if the columns can be determined, then there's value in knowing the columns — coding the application forms and reports will be significantly easier with known columns.

Correlated Subquery Method

The first T-SQL method is a common solution, but the performance it offers is poor compared to the other methods and I don't recommend it. However, it is still useful to understand the requirements of creating a crosstab query result set.

The basic idea is that a subquery is executed for every instance of every measure for every pivoted group by column. To walk though this query, visualize each row from the select statement. The first column is the category from the RawData table. The South, NorthEast, Midwest, and West columns are all correlated subqueries that sum() the Amount column filtered by the region and the row's category. If the crosstab query had 1,000 rows and a crosstab column for every week of the year, SQL Server would execute 52,000 subqueries with this method.

The last column adds a subtotal for each category:

```
SELECT R.Category,
   (SELECT SUM(Amount)
     FROM RawData
     WHERE Region = 'South' AND Category = R.Category) AS 'South',
   (SELECT SUM(Amount)
     FROM RawData
     WHERE Region = 'NorthEast' AND Category = R.Category) AS 'NorthEast',
   (SELECT SUM(Amount)
     FROM RawData
     WHERE Region = 'MidWest' AND Category = R.Category) AS 'MidWest',
   (SELECT SUM(Amount)
     FROM RawData
     WHERE Region = 'West' AND Category = R.Category) AS 'West',
   SUM(Amount) as Total
  FROM RawData R
  GROUP BY Category
```

Result:

Category	South	NorthEast	MidWest	West	Total
X	165	NULL	24	36	225
Y	287	181	38	NULL	506
Z	33	55	83	44	215

Case Method

Rather than filter within a correlated subquery for each instance of a measure, this method uses a case expression to filter the data summed by the aggregate so the query engine can process the entire crosstab query as a single set-based operation. That's why this method performs so well and is by far the most popular method of calculating a crosstab query.

To walk through this query, data from the RawData table is not restricted by any where clause. The group by clause partitions the data set by categories. The aggregate functions are then calculated to create a single result row for each category. And here's the trick for this query: The sum() includes a case expression so each column sees only the amount for each region:

```
SELECT Category,
  SUM(Case Region WHEN 'South' THEN Amount ELSE 0 END) AS South,
  SUM(Case Region WHEN 'NorthEast' THEN Amount ELSE 0 END) AS NorthEast,
  SUM(Case Region WHEN 'MidWest' THEN Amount ELSE 0 END) AS MidWest,
  SUM(Case Region WHEN 'West' THEN Amount ELSE 0 END) AS West,
  SUM(Amount) as Total
  FROM RawData
  GROUP BY Category
  ORDER BY Category
```

The result is the same as the correlated subquery method.

Pivot Method

The pivot method deviates from the normal query flow by performing the aggregate function, creating the crosstab results as a data source within the from clause.

SQL Server 2005 includes the new `Pivot` command, designed to ease the creation of crosstab queries. Together with its corollary command, `UnPivot`, these two commands also ease normalizing and denormalizing data.

If you think of pivot as a table-valued function that's used as a data source, it accepts two parameters. The first parameter is the aggregate function for the crosstab's values. The second measure lists the pivoted columns — in this example, the aggregate function sums the `Amount` column, and the pivoted columns are the regions. Because `pivot` is part of the `from` clause, the data set needs a named range or alias:

```
SELECT Category, SalesDate, South, NorthEast, MidWest, West
  FROM RawData
    PIVOT
    (Sum (Amount)
    FOR Region IN (South, NorthEast, MidWest, West)
    ) AS pt
```

Result:

Category	SalesDate	South	NorthEast	MidWest	West
Y	2005-11-01 00:00:00.000	36	NULL	NULL	NULL
Y	2005-12-01 00:00:00.000	15	28	NULL	NULL
X	2006-01-01 00:00:00.000	11	NULL	24	NULL
X	2006-02-01 00:00:00.000	NULL	NULL	NULL	36
Y	2006-02-01 00:00:00.000	47	NULL	NULL	NULL
Y	2006-03-01 00:00:00.000	NULL	62	38	NULL
Z	2006-04-01 00:00:00.000	33	NULL	83	NULL
Z	2006-05-01 00:00:00.000	NULL	55	NULL	44
X	2006-06-01 00:00:00.000	154	NULL	NULL	NULL
Y	2006-07-01 00:00:00.000	117	NULL	NULL	NULL
Y	2006-08-01 00:00:00.000	72	91	NULL	NULL

The result is not what was expected. The `pivot` command used every column. Because the `Amount` and `Region` are specified, it assumed that every remaining column should be used for the group by, and grouped by `Category` and `SalesDate`.

The solution is to use a subquery to select only the columns that should be submitted to the `pivot` command

```
SELECT Category, South, NorthEast, MidWest, West
  FROM (Select Category, Region, Amount from RawData) sq
    PIVOT
    (Sum (Amount)
    FOR Region IN (South, NorthEast, MidWest, West)
    ) AS pt
```

The result is the same as the previous crosstab queries without the unneeded `SalesDate` column.

The final fixed-column crosstab pivot query method is the polished example. Because the pivot is logically part of the `from` clause, it occurs prior to the `where` clause. Therefore, another reason to use a subquery to prepare the data for the `pivot` command is to filter the data or join with other data sources.

The next example filters the data where category = 'z' and adds the category total column so the pivot command creates the same result as the previous case method:

```
SELECT Category, South, NorthEast, MidWest, West,
   IsNull(South,0) + IsNull(NorthEast,0) + IsNull(MidWest,0) +
IsNull(West,0) as Total
   FROM (Select Region, Category, Amount
           From RawData
           Where Category = 'Z') sq
      PIVOT
        (Sum (Amount)
        FOR Region IN (South, NorthEast, MidWest, West)
        ) AS pt
```

The result is the same as the previous correlated subquery and case crosstab queries.

Dynamic Crosstab Queries

The rows of a crosstab query are automatically dynamically generated by the aggregation; however, in every one of the previous crosstab methods, the crosstab columns (region in this example) must be hard-coded in the SQL statement. The only way to create a crosstab query with dynamic columns is to use a SQL batch (possible saved as a stored procedure or user-defined function) to determine the columns at execution time and assemble a dynamic SQL command to execute the crosstab query.

Traditionally, cursors have been used to brute-force through the data, or to assemble the columns so that dynamic SQL can execute the dynamic crosstab query. Using the pivot command with the multiple-assignment variable select (described later in the chapter) makes quick work of a dynamic crosstab query.

Cross-Reference   An Analysis Services cube is basically a dynamic crosstab query on steroids. For more about designing these high-performance interactive cubes, turn to Chapter 43, "Business Intelligence with Analysis Services."

Cursor and Pivot Method

The goal of the cursor is to iterate through the distinct regions and assemble a comma-delimited string in the @RegionColumn variable. Once the trailing comma is removed from @RegionColumn, it's then used as part of a pivot command in a dynamic SQL statement, which is executed using sp_executesql:

```
DECLARE
   @SQLStr NVARCHAR(1024),
   @RegionColumn VARCHAR(50),
   @SemiColon BIT
SET @Semicolon = 0
SET @SQLStr = ''
DECLARE ColNames CURSOR FAST_FORWARD
   FOR
   SELECT DISTINCT Region as [Column]
      FROM RawData
      ORDER BY Region
```

```
    OPEN ColNames
    FETCH ColNames INTO @RegionColumn
    WHILE @@Fetch_Status = 0
      BEGIN
          SET @SQLStr = @SQLStr + @RegionColumn + ', '
          FETCH ColNames INTO @RegionColumn  -- fetch next
      END
    CLOSE ColNames
  DEALLOCATE ColNames
  SET @SQLStr = Left(@SQLStr, Len(@SQLStr) - 1)
  SET @SQLStr = 'SELECT Category, '
      + @SQLStr
      + ' FROM RawData PIVOT (Sum (Amount) FOR Region IN ('
      + @SQLStr
      + ')) AS pt'
  PRINT @SQLStr
  EXEC sp_executesql  @SQLStr
```

The result is the same as the crosstab results in previous examples, but if there were additional regions, they would appear as new columns in the crosstab query.

Cross-Reference Because cursors tend to scale poorly, using a cursor is rarely a good practice, and using a cursor to create a crosstab query is no exception. In my tests, the cursor method performed about ten times slower than the following set-based multiple-assignment-variable method. Nevertheless, for more information about how to code a cursor, see Chapter 20, "Kill the Cursor!"

Multiple Assignment Variable and Pivot Method

This method uses the exact same dynamic SQL string to execute the dynamic crosstab query, but employs a set-based select statement to create the list of regions, instead of a cursor. The select statement appends every region to a comma-delimited list, which is then executed in the same manner as the preceding example:

```
DECLARE @XColumns NVARCHAR(1024)
SET @XColumns = ''
SELECT @XColumns = @XColumns + [a].[Column] + ', '
  FROM
      (SELECT DISTINCT Region as [Column]
        FROM RawData) as a

SET @XColumns = Left(@XColumns, Len(@XColumns) - 1)

SET @XColumns = 'SELECT Category, '
    + @XColumns
    + ' FROM RawData PIVOT (Sum (Amount) FOR Region IN ('
    + @XColumns
    + ')) AS pt'
PRINT @XColumns

EXEC sp_executesql @XColumns
```

The job of the dynamic query code is to assemble the fixed-code crosstab query without specifying the X, or column, values. The subquery returns a list of X values. The recursive select variable appends the values, along with the other text required to build the dynamic crosstab query, to the @XColumns variable. The final set statement builds the completed dynamic SQL string:

The inverse of a crosstab query is the unpivot command, which is extremely useful for normalizing denormalized data. For an explanation of the unpivot command and examples, turn to Chapter 24, "Exploring Advanced T-SQL Techniques."

Summary

SQL Server excels in aggregate functions, with the proverbial rich suite of features; and it is very capable of calculating sums and aggregates to suit nearly any need. From the simple count() aggregate function to the complex dynamic crosstab query and the new pivot command, these query methods enable you to create powerful data analysis queries for impressive reports.

The next chapter examines hierarchical data—to continue the theme of working with the select statement to accomplish increasingly complex tasks.

Navigating Hierarchical Data

CHAPTER

12

No tool is best for every job and as much as I believe SQL is the romance language of data, SQL has a hard time getting along with certain types of data. To put is bluntly, SQL is just plain clumsy at retrieving multiple levels of genealogies or hierarchical data. The lack of an elegant solution becomes obvious when working with family trees, bills of materials, organizational charts, or layers of jurisdictions, or modeling O-O class inheritance.

The problems surrounding hierarchical data involve modeling the data, navigating the tree, selecting multiple generations of ancestors or descendents, or moving portions of the tree to another location. When the requirements demand a many-to-many relationship, such as when many parts may be used within many bills of materials to build multiple other parts, the relationships become even more complex.

This chapter walks you through the various methods of storing and then navigating hierarchical data — from the single-generation reflective join to the cumbersome cursor, and on to the efficient user-defined function.

New in 2005

The ANSI SQL 99 standard (a link to which is provided at this book's website, www.SQLServerBible.com) attempts to deal with hierarchical data (adjacency list pattern) with the introduction of the common table expression, or CTE, which can be used to select multiple levels of data from a hierarchical tree. I may change my mind with time, but at this point the new syntax doesn't feel like SQL and I still prefer the user-defined function method of navigating hierarchical data.

Adjacency List Schema Patterns

The initial problem when working with hierarchical data is how to store the hierarchy, as hierarchies aren't natural to the relational model. There are two primary methods: the adjacency list and the materialized path.

Basic Adjacency List Pattern

By far, the most common schema pattern used to model hierarchical data is the *adjacency list pattern,* informally called *data pairs* or the *self-join pattern,* which stores both the current node's key and its immediate parent's key in the current node row. (For this chapter, I refer to the two data elements in the data pair as *current node* and *parent node*.)

This is the familiar pattern used in the Northwind database's Employees table, which stores the employee's supervisor's EmployeeID in the ReportsTo column, as shown in Figure 12-1.

There's a one-to-many relationship between employees who play the role of supervisor, and employees who report to supervisors. Supervisors may have multiple employees reporting to them, but every employee may have only one supervisor. An employee may both be a supervisor and report to another supervisor.

The ReportsTo column is a foreign key that refers to the EmployeeID column in the same table. The ReportsTo column stores the EmployeeID of the employee's supervisor. The employee is the current node, and the ReportsTo column points to the parent node. The column allows nulls so that the top person of the organization chart can report to no one.

From the supervisor's point of view, his EmployeeID is stored in each of his direct report's rows in the ReportsTo column.

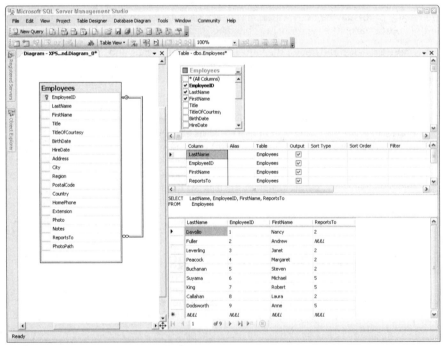

Figure 12-1: The Northwind database's Employees table is a perfect example of an adjacency list pattern storing an organizational chart.

Adjacency List Variations

The basic adjacency list pattern is useful for situations that include only a one-parent-to-multiple-nodes relationship, but it's not sufficient for most serious production database hierarchies. Fortunately, the basic data-pair pattern is easily modified to handle more complex hierarchies. Table 12-1 details the three variations of the adjacency list pattern and when to use each.

Table 12-1: Hierarchical Patterns

Pattern	Solution for
Basic adjacency list or Materialized-Path	Object-oriented classes, simple organizational charts, jurisdictions, species trees
Dual-parent adjacency list or Dual Materialized-Path	Genealogies
Multiple cardinality adjacency list	Bills of materials, complex organization charts

Dual Parents

Biological genealogies (i.e., not considering step-parents) require a method to store both the male and the female parent. This requires two parent ID columns and two foreign keys. The Family sample database uses this model. Because the foreign key references the same table, it must be added following the creation of the table. The following code comes from the script that creates the Family database:

```
CREATE TABLE dbo.Person (
  PersonID INT NOT NULL
    PRIMARY KEY NONCLUSTERED,
  LastName VARCHAR(15) NOT NULL,
  FirstName VARCHAR(15) NOT NULL,
  SrJr VARCHAR(3) NULL,
  MaidenName VARCHAR(15) NULL,
  Gender CHAR(1) NOT NULL,
  FatherID INT NULL,
  MotherID INT NULL,
  DateOfBirth DATETIME  NULL,
  DateOfDeath DATETIME  NULL
  );
go
CREATE CLUSTERED INDEX IxPersonName
  ON dbo.Person (LastName, FirstName);
ALTER TABLE dbo.Person ADD CONSTRAINT
  FK_Person_Father FOREIGN KEY (FatherID) REFERENCES dbo.Person (PersonID);
ALTER TABLE dbo.Person ADD CONSTRAINT
  FK_Person_Mother FOREIGN KEY (MotherID) REFERENCES dbo.Person (PersonID);
```

In the Family database, each person relates to two parent nodes: their biological mother and biological father. Both foreign keys point to the same primary key, as illustrated in Figure 12-2.

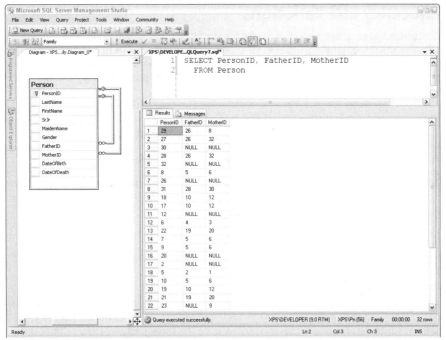

Figure 12-2: The dual-parent adjacency list pattern is useful for genealogies, and is used in the Family sample database.

It might be argued that this pattern violates first normal form because it appears that both the MotherID and FatherID columns hold a PersonID foreign key; but the mother and father relationships are unique, and the gender difference causes each foreign key to actually point to a distinct subset of the person table, which could, and should, be enforced by a trigger.

On The Web

To download and play with these sample databases and several sample queries that explore the variations of the adjacency list pattern, go to www.SQLServerBible.com.

Multiple Cardinalities

When there's a many-to-many relationship between current nodes and parent nodes, an associative table is required, similar to how an associative table is used in any other many-to-many cardinality model. For example, an order may include multiple products, and each product may be on multiple orders, so the order detail table serves as an associative table between the order and the product.

The same type of many-to-many problem commonly exists in manufacturing when designing schemas for bills of materials. For example, part a23 may be used in the manufacturing of multiple other parts, and part a23 itself might have been manufactured from still other parts. In this way, any part is a child or parent of multiple other parts.

To build a many-to-many hierarchical bill of materials, the bill of materials serves as the adjacency table between the current part(s) and the parent parts(s), both of which are stored in the same Parts table, as shown in Figure 12-3.

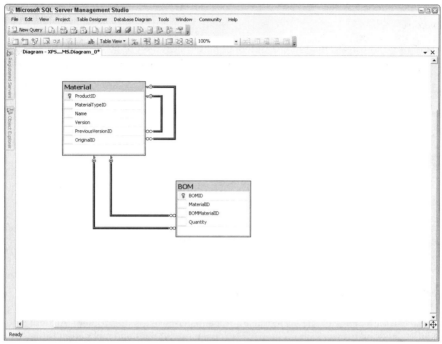

Figure 12-3: The bill of materials schema uses an adjacency table to store which parts are used to manufacture which other parts.

The Materialized-Path Pattern

The Materialized-Path pattern is another excellent method to store and navigate hierarchical data. Basically it stores a denormalized list of the current node's complete ancestry, including every generation of parents down to the current node in the current node row. Using the familiar Northwind `employees` table from SQL Server 2000, the `MaterializedPath` column stores the organizational chart path from the top node to the current node. The `MaterializedPath` column was added here to demonstrate the pattern. A real Materialized-Path solution would not include the `ReportsTo` column:

```
EmployeeID  LastName      FirstName   ReportsTo    MaterializedPath
----------- ------------- ----------- ------------ ----------------
1           Davolio       Nancy       2            21
2           Fuller        Andrew      NULL         2
3           Leverling     Janet       2            23
4           Peacock       Margaret    2            24
5           Buchanan      Steven      2            25
6           Suyama        Michael     5            256
7           King          Robert      5            257
8           Callahan      Laura       2            28
9           Dodsworth     Anne        5            259
```

Continued

Continued

There are pros and cons to the materialized-path pattern. On the positive side, there are several cool ways the hierarchy can be manipulated and analyzed using string functions. A `like` restriction in a `where` clause quickly finds everyone who reports to Mr. Buchanan, without having to navigate the hierarchical layers:

```
Select * from Employees Where Materialixed-Path Like '25_'
```

Result:

```
EmployeeID  LastName       FirstName   ReportsTo    Materialized-Path
----------- -------------- ----------- ------------ -----------------
6           Suyama         Michael     5            256
7           King           Robert      5            257
9           Dodsworth      Anne        5            259
```

Although the materialized-path pattern is interesting, it's limited to the basic hierarchy (one parent per node), which eliminates it as a solution for bills of materials or complex organization charts.

Navigating the Adjacency List

Storing the data in any of the variations of the adjacency list is no problem. Normal inserts, updates, and deletes work fine. The trick is retrieving the data and navigating the hierarchy. The following sections describe multiple solutions — ranging from the absurdly simple to the overly complex. I hope that one is just right for you.

Using a Standard select Statement

Generating a result listing with a single `select` statement is difficult because the number of generations is dynamic, whereas a SQL `select` query requires a known set of tables. A `select` query can handle a fixed number of generations, but when the number of generations isn't known, a pre-coded `select` statement can't handle the flexibility. As an example, the following query returns the grandfather and two generations:

```
USE Family
SELECT
    Person.FirstName + ' ' + IsNull(Person.SrJr,'')
      as Grandfather,
    Gen1.FirstName  + ' ' +  IsNull(Gen1.SrJr,'') as Gen1,
    Gen2.FirstName  + ' ' +  IsNull(Gen2.SrJr,'') as Gen2
  FROM Person
    LEFT JOIN Person Gen1
      ON Person.PersonID = Gen1.FatherID
    LEFT JOIN Person Gen2
      ON Gen1.PersonID = Gen2.FatherID
  WHERE Person.PersonID = 2
```

Result:

```
Grandfather          Gen1                 Gen2
-------------------- -------------------- --------------------
James 1              James 2              Melanie
James 1              James 2              Corwin
James 1              James 2              Dara
James 1              James 2              James 3
```

Alternately, the query could report every parent and every child by joining two instances of the Person table. However, that still doesn't produce a useful tree.

Using a Recursive Cursor

A common programming solution is to navigate the hierarchy using an iterative process to move through the nodes. For T-SQL, that means using the dreaded cursor.

 Cross-Reference For more information about programming cursors (and, more important, avoiding them) turn to Chapter 20, "Kill the Cursor!"

To produce a tree, the cursor examines each child and prints the child indented to the generation level. The cursor does this by selecting all the children of the current person (persons whose MotherID or FatherID matches the current person). Once the cursor is declared and opened, each fetch will print the child and recursively call another instance of the procedure to determine whether the current person has any children. If so, the children will be examined — and so on, and so on.

For every person, the recursive routine is called to check for any children.

The recursive nature of the routine will cause it to run straight down the tree, finding each firstborn child (PK: "5", "8", "15"), followed by finding the siblings of "15" ("16", "29"). To visualize the tree, see the results of the next code example. The recursive routine then moves back up to the siblings of "8" and finds "10." The children of "10" are examined and the firstborn is found to be "19." The recursive routine is called for the children of "19," and "22" and "21" are returned. The recursive routine is called for "22" and "2," but no children are found.

By default, the scope of a cursor extends to any called procedures, but the recursive tree problem requires that each called cursor fetch its own results. Setting the cursor option to local restricts the scope of the cursor and allows a recursive cursor. The option can be set in the cursor declaration or as a database option. The following example demonstrates both methods:

```
ALTER DATABASE Family SET CURSOR_DEFAULT LOCAL
SELECT DATABASEPROPERTYEX('Family', 'IsLocalCursorsDefault')
```

Result:

```
1
```

The following batch creates the ExamineChild procedure, which includes the cursor that tests for children of the current Person row. If children are detected, the stored procedure calls itself recursively:

```
CREATE PROCEDURE ExamineChild
  (@ParentID INT)
AS
```

```
SET Nocount On
DECLARE @ChildID INT,
  @Childname VARCHAR(25)

DECLARE cChild CURSOR LOCAL FAST_FORWARD
  FOR SELECT PersonID,
          Firstname + ' ' + LastName + ' ' + IsNull(SrJr,'')
          as PersonName
        FROM Person
        WHERE Person.FatherID = @ParentID
          OR Person.MotherID = @ParentID
        ORDER BY Person.DateOfBirth
  OPEN cChild
  FETCH cChild INTO @ChildID, @ChildName  -- prime the cursor
  WHILE @@Fetch_Status = 0
    BEGIN
      PRINT
        SPACE(≠tLevel * 2) + '+ '
          + Cast(@ChildID as VARCHAR(4))
          + ' ' + @ChildName
      -- Recursively find the grandchildren
      EXEC ExamineChild @ChildID
      FETCH cChild INTO @ChildID, @ChildName
    END
  CLOSE cChild
DEALLOCATE cChild
```

The recursive `cursor` stored procedure is called, passing to it `PersonID` 2, James Halloway the First. The cursor will locate all of his descendents:

```
EXEC ExamineChild 2
```

Result:

```
+ 5 James Halloway 2
  + 8 Melanie Campbell
    + 15 Shannon Ramsey
    + 16 Jennifer Ramsey
    + 29 Adam Campbell
  + 10 James Halloway 3
    + 19 James Halloway 4
      + 22 Chris Halloway
      + 21 James Halloway 5
    + 18 Abbie Halloway
    + 17 Allie Halloway
  + 9 Dara Halloway
    + 23 Joshua Halloway
    + 24 Laura Halloway
  + 7 Corwin Halloway
    + 14 Logan Halloway
```

Using a `cursor` is an adequate solution to the recursive tree problem when the data set is small, but it fails for large data sets for two reasons. First, SQL Server limits the stored procedure's nesting level to 32 levels deep, so recursive trees with more than 32 levels (less any code used to call the recursive `cursor` code) will fail. The second concern is performance (which is generally the case with any `cursor` solution). Because an iteration is required for each node, it scales linearly. A hierarchy seven levels deep with five million nodes will require five million iterations. A set-based solution could navigate the same hierarchy in seven sets.

Using a Set-Based Solution

The first of three set-based solutions, this batch begins with a single person and stuffs that into the #FamilyTree temp table. Then, the batch steps through each generation and appends every person with a parent in the previous generation to the temp table, using a multi-condition join.

For each person in the #FamilyTree temp table, the FamilyLine column contains the parent's FamilyLine data concatenated with the parent's PersonID. The FamilyLine column provides the data required to sort the tree.

When no new people are found, the `while` condition is no longer satisfied and the batch is complete. Here's the set-based code that makes the cursor obsolete for solving recursive tree problems:

```
CREATE TABLE #FamilyTree (
  PersonID INT,
  Generation INT,
  FamilyLine VarChar(25) Default ''
  )

DECLARE
  @Generation INT,
  @FirstPerson INT

SET @Generation = 1
SET @FirstPerson = 2

-- prime the temp table with the top person(s) in the queue
INSERT #FamilyTree (PersonID, Generation, FamilyLine)
  SELECT @FirstPerson, @Generation, @FirstPerson

WHILE @@RowCount > 0
  BEGIN
    SET @Generation = @Generation + 1

    INSERT #FamilyTree (PersonID, Generation, FamilyLine)
      SELECT Person.PersonID,
             @Generation,
             #FamilyTree.FamilyLine
             + ' ' + Str(Person.PersonID,5)
        FROM Person
          JOIN #FamilyTree
            ON #FamilyTree.Generation = @Generation - 1
              AND
              (Person.MotherID = #FamilyTree.PersonID
                OR
               Person.FatherID = #FamilyTree.PersonID)

  END
```

With the #FamilyTree temp table populated, the following query examines the raw data:

```
SELECT PersonID, Generation, FamilyLine
  FROM #FamilyTree
  Order by FamilyLine
```

Result (abridged):

```
PersonID    Generation  FamilyLine
----------- ----------- -------------------------
2           1           2
5           2           2   5
7           3           2   5   7
14          4           2   5   7   14
...
22          5           2   5   10  19  22
```

Similar to the preceding cursor solution, the next query uses the same space() function to format the result, and it joins with the Person table so it can display the name:

```
SELECT SPACE(Generation * 2) + '+ '
          + Cast(#FamilyTree.PersonID as VARCHAR(4)) + ' '
          + FirstName + ' ' + LastName
          + IsNull(SrJr,'') AS FamilyTree
  FROM #FamilyTree
    JOIN Person
      ON #FamilyTree.PersonID = Person.PersonID
  ORDER BY FamilyLine
```

Result:

```
FamilyTree
------------------------------------------------------
  + 2 James Halloway 1
    + 5 James Halloway 2
      + 7 Corwin Halloway
        + 14 Logan Halloway
      + 8 Melanie Campbell
        + 15 Shannon Ramsey
        + 16 Jennifer Ramsey
        + 29 Adam Campbell
      + 9 Dara Halloway
        + 23 Joshua Halloway
        + 24 Laura Halloway
    + 10 James Halloway 3
        + 17 Allie Halloway
        + 18 Abbie Halloway
        + 19 James Halloway 4
          + 21 James Halloway 5
          + 22 Chris Halloway
```

Using a User-Defined Function

While the set-based solution demonstrated the technique well, encapsulating it within a user-defined function (UDF) greatly improves its reusability.

Cross-Reference This method jumps ahead a bit, using an advanced programming feature of SQL Server to solve the hierarchical problem. For more information about one of my personal favorite features of SQL Server, see Chapter 22, "Building User-Defined Functions."

The advantage of a table-valued user-defined function is that it returns a result set that may be used as a data source with any other normal query. Building a UDF that navigates a hierarchy and returns the result as a table means the hierarchy set can be joined with any other table.

Using the Family database, a UDF could return the descendents of any person in the table, which could then be joined with the Person table to select more information about the ancestors:

```
CREATE FUNCTION dbo.FamilyTree
  (@PersonID CHAR(25))
  RETURNS @Tree TABLE (PersonID INT, LastName VARCHAR(25), FirstName
VARCHAR(25), Lv INT)
AS
BEGIN
  DECLARE @LC INT
  SET @LC = 1
  -- insert the anchor level
  INSERT @Tree
    SELECT PersonID, LastName, FirstName, @LC
      FROM dbo.Person with (NoLock)
      WHERE PersonID = @PersonID

    -- Loop through sub-levels
  WHILE @@RowCount > 0
    BEGIN
      SET @LC = @LC + 1
      -- insert each Generation
      INSERT @Tree
        SELECT Tree.PersonID, Tree.LastName, Tree.FirstName, @LC
          FROM dbo.Person FamilyNode with (NoLock)
            JOIN dbo.Person Tree with (NoLock)
              ON FamilyNode.PersonID = Tree.MotherID
                OR FamilyNode.PersonID = Tree.FatherID
            JOIN @Tree CC
              ON CC.PersonID = FamilyNode.PersonID
          WHERE CC.Lv = @LC - 1
    END
  RETURN
END
```

If we walk through this UDF, we see that it begins by accepting a PersonID as a parameter. This person will serve as the anchor to begin searching the hierarchy. The final result of the function is the list of all the descendents in the hierarchy, starting from the anchor person. The data is stored in the @Tree table variable, which is passed back to the query that called the function. The query can then use the result as a data source within a from clause.

The first step inside the function is to look up the ClassID and add that to the @Classes table variable. The function then iterates through each successive generation until no more descendents are found. With each iteration, it uses a join between the last generation found (stored in the @Tree table) and the person table to find the next generation. This set-based user-defined function offers high performance and scales well:

```
Select * From dbo.FamilyTree(10);
```

Result:

```
PersonID    LastName    FirstName   Lv
----------- ----------- ----------- ----
10          Halloway    James       1
18          Halloway    Abbie       2
17          Halloway    Allie       2
19          Halloway    James       2
22          Halloway    Chris       3
21          Halloway    James       3
```

I've also used this method extensively within my SQL Server object-relational DBMS experiments. You are welcome to download the latest version of the experiment from www.SQLServerBible.com, try it for yourself, and see how this hierarchical UDF solves the problem of class inheritance.

Using Recursive Common Table Expressions

The final solution to navigating the adjacency pairs hierarchy is a recursive common table expression (CTE). Following the same basic logic as code within the user-defined function, the CTE first establishes an anchor, which is then iteratively joined with the rows already identified until no new rows are found.

The basics of building queries that use common table expressions, or CTEs, are explained Chapter 10, "Including Subqueries and CTEs."

The advantage of a recursive CTE is that it uses no procedural code; rather, it uses the new syntax of the CTE. The recursive CTE must use two queries unioned together. The first query serves to select the anchor node. The second query joins with the CTE to select the next generation from the hierarchy. SQL Server continues to execute the second query until there are no new rows. It's the same basic logic as the user-defined function:

```
WITH FamilyTree( LastName, FirstName, PersonID, lv)
AS (
   -- Anchor
     SELECT LastName, FirstName, PersonID, 1
       FROM Person A
       WHERE PersonID = 10

   -- Recursive Call
   UNION ALL
     SELECT Node.LastName,  Node.FirstName,  Node.PersonID, lv + 1
       FROM Person Node
         JOIN FamilyTree ft
           ON Node.MotherID = ft.PersonID
```

```
            OR Node.FatherID = ft.PersonID
    )
SELECT PersonID, LastName, FirstName, lv
  FROM FamilyTree;
```

In this case, the result of the recursive common table expression is identical to the result of the previous user-defined function.

 A walk-through of the recursive CTE is available online at www.SQLServerBible.com.

Of these various solutions to navigating the adjacency pairs hierarchy pattern, the fastest by far is the user-defined query. It performs twice as fast as the recursive CTE, and, depending on the data set, magnitudes faster than the cursor.

Summary

Hierarchical data can present a challenge if you're not armed with patterns and solutions, but knowing the possible patterns and having several navigational methods in your toolset will increase the odds that your next hierarchical data project will be successful.

The next chapter continues with the theme of selecting data, adding the capability to search for words within text using full-text search.

✦   ✦   ✦

Using Full-Text Search

Several years ago I wrote a word search for a large database of legal texts. For word searches, the system parsed all the documents and built a word-frequency table as a many-to-many association between the word table and the document table. It worked well, and word searches became lightning-fast. While I found coding the string manipulation fun, fortunately, you have a choice.

The server versions of Windows include a structured word/phrase indexing system called MS Search. More than just a word parser, MS Full Text Search Engine actually performs linguistic analysis by determining base words and word boundaries, and conjugating verbs for different languages. SQL Server leverages MS Full Text Search Engine on a row and column basis as full-text search catalogs.

ANSI Standard SQL uses the like operator to perform basic word searches and even wildcard searches. For example, the following code uses the like operator to query the Aesop's Fables sample database:

```
-- SQL Where Like
SELECT Title
  FROM Fable
  WHERE Fabletext LIKE '%lion%'
    AND Fabletext LIKE '%bold%'
```

Result:

```
Title
--------------------------------------------------
The Hunter and the Woodman
```

All the code samples in this chapter use the Aesop's Fables sample database. The Aesop_Create.sql script will create the database and populate it with 25 of Aesop's fables. All the code within this chapter is in Ch13.sql.

The main problem with performing SQL Server where...like searches is the slow performance. Indexes are searchable from the beginning of the word, so searching for like 'word%' is fast, but like '%word%' is terribly slow. Searching for strings within a string can't use the b-tree structure of an index to perform a fast index seek so it must perform a table scan instead, as demonstrated in Figure 8-1. It's like looking for all the "Paul"s in the telephone book. The phone book isn't indexed by first name, so each page must be scanned.

With this in mind, Microsoft reengineered one of its search engines (Site Server Search — designed to provide search services for websites) to provide search services for SQL Server 7 (in late 1998). The engine was called MSSearch and it also provided search services to Exchange Content Indexing and SharePoint Portal Server 2001. A different version of MSSearch shipped with the release of SQL Server 2000.

SQL 2005 full-text search (FTS) is the third-generation search component for SQL Server, and this new version is by far the most scalable and feature-rich. SQL 2005 full-text search ships in the Workgroup, Standard, and Enterprise versions of SQL Server.

The search engine that ships with SQL Server 2005 is called MSFTESQL and is disabled by default by the SQL Server Surface Area Configuration Tool. To enable MSFTESQL, launch the SQL Server Surface Area Configuration Tool and select Surface Area Configuration for Services and Components; expand your MSSQLServer instance and drill down on the Full-Text Service node. Configure this service to have a Startup Type of "run automatically."

Basically, full-text indexing builds an index of every significant word and phrase and thus solves the performance problem. In addition, the full-text search engine adds advanced features such as the following:

✦ Searching for one word near another word

✦ Searching with wildcards

✦ Searching for inflectional variations of a word (such as run, ran, running)

✦ Weighting one word or phrase as more important to the search than another word or phrase

✦ Performing fuzzy word/phrase searches

✦ Searching character data with embedded binary objects stored with SQL Server

New in 2005

The most significant improvement in SQL Server 2005's full-text search is raw performance, up to one to two orders of magnitude (10 to 100 times improvement) over SQL 2000 FTS for indexing. But there are many other improvements such as trusted iFilters, improved language support, accent insensitivity, better noise sensitivity, thesaurus support, multi-column queries, support for linked servers, replication support, Backup support/attach/detach databases, Attach and detach with catalogs, indexing of document properties, and improved troubleshooting.

The new search engine (MSFTESQL — an acronym for Microsoft Full-Text Engine for SQL Server) that ships in SQL 2005 has been redesigned from the ground up for optimal performance and is now fully integrated with SQL Server.

Configuring Full-Text Search Catalogs

A *full-text search catalog* is a collection of full-text indexes for a single SQL Server database. Each catalog may store multiple full-text indexes for multiple tables, but each table is limited to only one catalog. Typically, a single catalog will handle all the full-text searches for a database, although dedicating a single catalog to a very large table (one with over a million rows) will improve performance.

Catalogs may index only user tables (not views, temporary tables, table variables, or system tables).

Creating a Catalog with the Wizard

Although creating and configuring a full-text search catalog with code is relatively easy, the task is usually done once and then forgotten. Unless the repeatability of a script is important for redeploying the project, the Full-Text Wizard is sufficient for configuring full-text search.

The wizard may be launched from within Management Studio's Object Explorer. With a table selected, use the context menu and select Full-Text Index ⇨ Define Full-Text Index.

The Full-Text Indexing Wizard works through multiple steps to configure the full-text catalog, as follows:

1. A catalog must belong to a single database.

2. Select the table to add to the catalog.

3. Specify a unique index that MS Full Text Search Engine can use to identify the rows indexed with MS Search. The primary key is typically the best choice for this index; however, any non-nullable, unique, single-column index is sufficient. If the table uses composite primary keys, another unique index must be created to use full-text search.

4. Choose the columns to be full-text indexed, as shown in Figure 13-1. Valid column data types are character data types (`char`, `nchar`, `varchar`, `nvarchar`, `text`, `ntext`, and `xml`) and `image`. (Indexing binary images is an advanced topic covered later in this chapter.) You may need to specify the language used for parsing the words, although the computer default will likely handle this automatically.

   Full-text search can also read documents stored in `image` columns. Using full-text search with embedded blobs (binary large objects) is covered later in this chapter.

Figure 13-1: Any valid columns are listed by the Full-Text Indexing Wizard and may be selected for indexing.

5. Enable change tracking if desired. This will automatically update the catalog when the data changes. If change tracking is not enabled, the catalog must be manually updated.

6. Select a catalog or opt to create a new catalog.

7. Skip creating a population schedule; there's a better way to keep the catalog up to date. (The strategies for maintaining a full-text index are discussed later in the chapter.)

8. Finish.

When the wizard is finished, the catalog is created but still empty. To initially populate the catalog, right-click on the table and select Full-Text Index Table ➪ Enable Full-Text Index and then Full-Text Index Table ➪ Start Full Population from the context menu. This directs SQL Server to begin passing data to MSFTESQL for indexing. Depending on the amount of data in the indexed columns, the population will take a few seconds, a few minutes, or a few hours to complete.

Creating a Catalog with T-SQL Code

To implement full-text search using a method that can be easily replicated on other servers, your best option is to create a SQL script. Creating a catalog with code means following the same steps as the Full-Text Indexing Wizard. A set of system-stored procedures handles configuring and maintaining full-text indexes. The following steps configure a full-text search catalog for the Aesop's Fables sample database:

1. Enable the database for full-text search:

```
USE AESOP
EXEC sp_fulltext_database 'enable'
```

Note　Each of these steps will take a few seconds to complete. SQL Server is the client initiating the process, but it doesn't wait for the conclusion. If the configuration is being written as a script, the wait for delay T-SQL command can insert the required pause.

2. Create the full-text catalog:

```
EXEC sp_fulltext_catalog 'AesopFable', 'create'
```

3. Mark a table for full-text search:

```
EXEC sp_fulltext_table
   'Fable', 'create', 'AesopFable', 'FablePK'
```

4. Add columns to the full-text catalog:

```
EXEC sp_fulltext_column 'Fable', 'Title', 'add'
EXEC sp_fulltext_column 'Fable', 'Moral', 'add'
EXEC sp_fulltext_column 'Fable', 'FableText', 'add'
```

The sp_fulltext_column stored procedure has two other parameters, which specify the word-parsing language and image-indexing information, respectively. The full syntax of the stored procedure is as follows:

```
sp_fulltext_column
   @tabname ='table_name',
   @colname ='column_name',
```

```
@action = 'action',
@language = 'language',
@type_colname ='type_column_name'
```

The action parameter indicates 'add' or 'drop'.

Full-text search can automatically parse the following languages:

- Neutral — 0
- Chinese_Simplified — 0x0804, 2052
- Chinese_Traditional — 0x0404, 1028
- Dutch — 0x0413, 1043
- English_UK — 0x0809, 2057
- English_US — 0x0409, 1033
- French — 0x040c, 1036
- German — 0x0407, 1031
- Italian — 0x0410, 1040
- Japanese — 0x0411, 1041
- Korean — 0x0412, 1042
- Spanish_Modern — 0x0c0a, 3082
- Swedish_Default — 0x041d, 1053
- Thai
- Chinese (Hong Kong SAR, PRC)
- Chinese (Macau SAR)
- Chinese (Singapore)

The language determines the word break points and how the words are parsed for inflections (run, ran, running) and phrases. (Use Neutral for multiple languages or an unsupported language.) The corresponding hex code or integer is passed as a parameter to sp_fulltext_columns. All columns in a table must use the same language.

5. Activate the full-text catalog:

```
EXEC sp_fulltext_table 'Fable','activate'
```

Although the full-text catalog has been defined, it's not yet populated. To initially populate the catalog with code, run the following stored procedure:

```
EXEC sp_fulltext_table 'Fable', 'start_full'
```

Pushing Data to the Full-Text Index

Full-text indexes are off-line indexes maintained by an external service and are updated only when SQL Server passes new data to MS Search. That's both a benefit and a drawback. On one hand, it means that updating the full-text index doesn't slow down large-text updates. On the other hand, it means that the full-text index is not real-time the way SQL Server data are. If a user enters a résumé and then searches for it using full-text search before the full-text index has been updated, the résumé won't be found.

Every full-text index begins empty, and if data already exist in the SQL Server tables, they must be *pushed* to the full-text index by means of a *full population*. A full population re-initializes the index and passes data for all rows to the full-text index. A full population may be performed with Management Studio or T-SQL code. Because the data push is driven by SQL Server, data is sent from one table at a time regardless of how many tables might be full-text indexed in a catalog. If the full-text index is created for an empty SQL Server table, a full population is not required.

Two primary methods of pushing ongoing changes to a full-text index exist:

✦ **Incremental populations:** An incremental population uses a timestamp to pass any rows that have changed since the last population. This method can be performed manually from Management Studio or by means of T-SQL code or scheduled as a SQL Server Agent job (typically for each evening). Incremental population requires a `rowversion` (`timestamp`) column in the table.

Incremental populations present two problems. First, a built-in delay occurs between the time the data are entered and the time the user can find the data using full-text search. Second, incremental populations consolidate all the changes into a single process that consumes a significant amount of CPU time during the incremental change. In a heavily used database, the choice is between performing incremental populations each evening and forcing a one-day delay each time or performing incremental populations at scheduled times throughout the day and suffering performance hits at those times.

✦ **Change tracking and background population:** SQL Server can watch for data changes in columns that are full-text indexed and then send what is effectively a single-row incremental population every time a row changes. While this method seems costly in terms of performance, in practice the effect is not noticeable. The full-text update isn't fired by a trigger, so the update transaction doesn't need to wait for the data to be pushed to the full-text index. Instead, the full-text update occurs in the background slightly behind the SQL DML transaction. The effect is a balanced CPU load and a full-text index that appears to be near real-time.

Best Practice

If the database project incorporates searching for words within columns, using full-text search with change tracking and background population is the best overall way to balance search performance with update performance.

Maintaining a Catalog with Management Studio

Within Management Studio, the full-text search catalogs are maintained with the right-click menu for each table. The menu offers the following maintenance options under Full-Text Index Table:

✦ **Define Full-Text Indexing on Table:** Launches the Full-Text Indexing Wizard to create a new catalog as described earlier in the chapter.

✦ **Edit Full-Text Indexing:** Launches the Full-Text Indexing Wizard to modify the catalog for the selected table.

✦ **Remove Full-Text Indexing from a Table**Drops the selected table from its catalog.

✦ **Start Full Population:** Initiates a data push of all rows from the selected SQL Server table to its full-text index catalog.

✦ **Start Incremental Population:** Initiates a data push of rows that have changed since the last population in the selected table from SQL Server to the full-text index.

✦ **Stop Population:** Halts any currently running full-text population push.

✦ **Change Tracking:** Performs a full or incremental population and then turns on change tracking so that SQL Server can update the index.

✦ **Update Index in Background:** Pushes updates of rows that have been flagged by change tracking to the full-text index as the changes occur.

✦ **Update Index:** Pushes an update of all rows that change tracking has flagged to the full-text index.

Maintaining a Catalog in T-SQL Code

Each of the previous Management Studio full-text maintenance commands can be executed from T-SQL code. The following examples demonstrate full-text catalog-maintenance commands applied to the Aesop's Fables sample database:

✦ Full population:

```
EXEC sp_fulltext_table 'Fable', 'start_full'
```

✦ Incremental population:

```
EXEC sp_fulltext_table 'Fable', 'start_incremental'
```

✦ Remove a full-text catalog:

```
EXEC sp_fulltext_catalog 'AesopFable', 'drop'
```

✦ Change tracking and background updating:

```
EXEC sp_fulltext_table Fable, 'Start_change_tracking'
EXEC sp_fulltext_table Fable,
    'Start_background_updateindex'
```

In addition, T-SQL stored procedures include the following enhanced maintenance features:

✦ **Rebuild:** This command essentially drops and redefines the full-text catalog but does not repopulate the new full-text index. Rebuilding should be followed with a full population. The benefit of rebuilding the catalog is that it automatically reconfigures the table and columns, ensuring that the internal structure of the full-text catalog is clean.

```
EXEC sp_fulltext_catalog 'AesopFable', 'rebuild'
```

✦ **Clean up unused full text catalogs:** This stored procedure removes any vestiges of unused catalogs:

```
EXEC sp_fulltext_service 'clean_up'
```

Throughout SQL Server 2000, the sp_help stored procedure is a welcome means of reporting system information. The full-text search versions of sp_help are as follows:

✦ sp_help_fulltext_catalogs: This system-stored procedure returns information about a catalog, including the current population status:

```
EXEC sp_help_fulltext_catalogs 'AesopFable'
```

Result:

```
                                                NUMBER
                                                FULLTEXT
ftcatid NAME        PATH                 STATUS TABLES
------- ----------- -------------------- ------ ------
5       AesopFable  C:\Program Files     0      1
                    \Microsoft SQL Server
                    \MSSQL\FTDATA
```

The population status column returns the current activity of the catalog as follows:

- 0 - Idle
- 1 - Full population in progress
- 2 - Paused
- 3 - Throttled
- 4 - Recovering
- 5 - Shutdown
- 6 - Incremental population in progress
- 7 - Building index
- 8 - Disk is full. Paused
- 9 - Change tracking

✦ `sp_help_fulltext_tables`: Information about the tables included in the catalog is returned by this variation of `sp_help`:

```
EXEC sp_help_fulltext_tables 'AesopFable'
```

Result (formatted):

TABLE OWNER	TABLE NAME	FULLTEXT KEY INDEX NAME	FULLTEXT KEY COLID	FULLTEXT INDEX ACTIVE	FULLTEXT CATALOG NAME
dbo	Fable	FablePK	1	1	AesopFable

✦ `sp_help_fulltext_columns`: Information about the columns included in the full-text catalog:

```
EXEC sp_help_fulltext_columns 'fable'
```

Result (formatted and truncated):

TABLE_ OWNER	NAME	FULLTEXT COLUMNNAME	BLOBTP COLNAME	LANGUAGE
dbo	Fable	Title	NULL	1033
dbo	Fable	Moral	NULL	1033
dbo	Fable	FableText	NULL	1033

Noise Files

When I built my custom word-search procedure several years ago, one of the optimizations that dramatically improved performance was the exclusion of common words such as a, the, and of. As soon as a word was parsed, the first check was to see if the word was in what I called the "weed list." If it was, the procedure parsed the next word without any handling of the weed word. The time required to parse a legal cite was reduced by more than half, and the size of the word-frequency table was significantly smaller.

Full-text search uses a similar technique by storing lists of ignored words in a *noise file*. Noise words are completely ignored by full-text search; in fact, if a query's search depends on noise words it generates an error.

The decision to include a word in the noise list is made according to its frequency of use and its relative search importance. If a word is very common, it's not a good search candidate and the frequency of its occurrence will hurt performance, so it should be in the noise list.

Alternately, the project may need to search for words in the noise list. For example, if a search for "C language" is important to the database, the letter "C" should be removed from the noise file.

Because noise files are plain-text files, they may be tweaked to meet the needs of certain applications. You must stop MS Full Text Search Engine prior to editing the noise file. Assuming a default installation directory, the copy used by SQL Server's full-text search is located in:

```
C:\Program Files\Microsoft SQL Server
   \MSSQL\FTDATA\noiseENU.txt
```

To test the noise file, stop MS Full Text Search Engine using SQL Server Configuration Manager, add a word to the file, and then try a full-text search for that word. If the query produces the following error, the word was added to the correct noise file:

```
Server: Msg 7619, Level 16, State 1, Line 1
A clause of the query contained only ignored words
```

Word Searches

Once the catalog is created, full-text search is ready for word and phrase queries. Word searches are performed with the `contains` keyword. The effect of `contains` is to pass the word search to MS Full Text Search Engine and await the reply. Word searches can be used within a query in one of two means, `contains` and `ContainsTable`.

The Contains Function

`Contains` operates within the `where` clause, much like a `where in (subquery)`. The parameters within the parentheses are passed to MS Search, which returns a list of primary keys that meet the criteria.

The first parameter passed to MS Full Text Search Engine is the column name to be searched, or an asterisk for a search of all columns from one table. If the `from` clause includes multiple tables, the table must be specified in the `contains` parameter. The following basic full-text query searches all indexed columns for the word "Lion":

```
USE Aesop
SELECT Title
  FROM Fable
  WHERE CONTAINS (Fable.*,'Lion')
```

The following fables contain the word "Lion" in either the fable title, moral, or text:

```
Title
--------------------------------------------------
The Dogs and the Fox
The Hunter and the Woodman
The Ass in the Lion's Skin
Androcles
```

ContainsTable

Not only will full-text search work within the `where` clause, but the `ContainsTable` function operates as a table or subquery and returns the result set from MS Search. This SQL Server feature opens up the possibility of powerful searches.

`ContainsTable` returns a result set with two columns. The first column, `Key`, identifies the row using the unique index that was defined when the catalog was configured.

The second column, `Rank`, reports the ranking of the rows using values from 1 (low) to 1000 (high). There is no high/median/low meaning or fixed range to the rank value; the rank only compares the row with other rows with regard to the following factors:

✦ The frequency/uniqueness of the word in the table

✦ The frequency/uniqueness of the word in the column

Therefore, a rare word will be ranked as statistically more important than a common word.

The same parameters that define the full-text search for `contains` also define the search for `ContainsTable`. The following query returns the raw data from MS Search:

```
SELECT *
  FROM CONTAINSTABLE (Fable, *, 'Lion')
```

Result:

```
KEY          RANK
----------   -----------
3            86
4            80
20           48
14           32
```

The key by itself is useless to a human, but joining the `ContainsTable` results with the `Fable` table, as if `ContainsTable` were a derived table, allows the query to return the `Rank` and the fable's `Title`, as follows:

```
SELECT Fable.Title, FTS.Rank
  FROM Fable
    JOIN CONTAINSTABLE (Fable, *, 'Lion') FTS
    ON Fable.FableID = FTS.[KEY]
  ORDER BY FTS.Rank DESC
```

Result:

```
Title                                       Rank
-----------------------------------------   -----------
Androcles                                   86
```

```
The Butt in the Lion's Skin      80
The Hunter and the Woodman       48
The Dogs and the Fox             32
```

A fourth ContainsTable parameter, top *n* limit, reduces the result set from the full-text search engine much as the SQL select top predicate does. The limit is applied assuming that the result set is sorted descending by rank so that only the highest ranked results are returned. The following query demonstrates the top *n* limit throttle:

```
SELECT Fable.Title, Rank
  FROM Fable
    JOIN CONTAINSTABLE (Fable, *, 'Lion', 2) FTS
    ON Fable.FableID = FTS.[KEY]
  ORDER BY FTS.Rank DESC
```

Result:

```
Title                                 Rank
------------------------------------- -----------
Androcles                             86
The Ass in the Lion's Skin            80
```

The advantage of using the top *n* limit option is that the full-text search engine can pass fewer data back to the query. It's more efficient than returning the full result set and then performing a SQL top in the select statement. It illustrates the principle of performing the data work at the server instead of the client. In this case, MS Full Text Search Engine is the server process and SQL Server is the client process.

Best Practice

Because MS Full Text Search Engine is a separate component from SQL Server, it competes for CPU cycles. Therefore, the addition of a serious full-text search feature to a SQL Server database project is a compelling justification for using a multiple-CPU server. MS Full Text Search Engine is also memory- and Windows–swap-file intensive. A heavily used database that sees regular updates and searches of full-text-enabled columns should run on a stout server.

Advanced Search Options

Full-text search is powerful, and you can add plenty of options to the search string. These options work with contains and ContainsTable.

Multiple Word Searches

Multiple words may be included in the search by means of the or and and conjunctions. The following query finds any fables containing both the word "Tortoise" and the word "Hare" in the text of the fable:

```
SELECT Title
  FROM Fable
    WHERE CONTAINS (FableText,'Tortoise AND Hare')
```

Result:

```
Title
--------------------------------------------------
The Hare and the Tortoise
```

One significant issue pertains to the search for multiple words: While full-text search can easily search across multiple columns for a single word, it searches for multiple words only if those words are in the same column. For example, the fable "The Ants and the Grasshopper" includes the word "thrifty" in the moral and the word "supperless" in the text of the fable itself. But searching for "thrifty and supperless" across all columns yields no results, as shown here:

```
SELECT Title
  FROM Fable
  WHERE CONTAINS (*,' "Thrifty AND supperless" ')
```

Result:

```
(0 row(s) affected)
```

Two solutions exist, and neither one is pretty. The query can be reconfigured so the and con-junction is at the where-clause level rather than within the contains parameter. The problem with this solution is performance. The following query requires two remote scans to the full-text search engine, as shown in Figure 13-2, each of which requires 363 milliseconds of the total 811-millisecond query-execution time:

```
SELECT Title
  FROM Fable
  WHERE CONTAINS (*,'Thrifty')
    AND CONTAINS(*,'supperless')
```

Result:

```
Title
-------------------------------------------------
The Ants and the Grasshopper
```

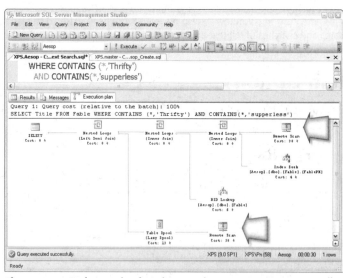

Figure 13-2: Each contains function requires a separate remote call to MS Full Text Search Engine; the result is then scanned by SQL Server.

The other solution to the multiple-column search problem consists of adding an additional column to hold all the text to be searched and duplicating the data from the original columns to a `FullTextSearch` column within an after trigger. This solution is not smooth either. It duplicates data and costs performance time during inserts and updates. The crux of the decision on how to solve the multiple-column is the conflict between fast reads and fast writes — OLAP versus OLTP.

Searches with Wildcards

Because MS Full Text Search Engine is part of the OS and not a SQL Server–developed component, its wildcards use the standard DOS conventions (asterisks and double quotes) instead of SQL-style wildcards.

The other thing to keep in mind about full-text wildcards is that they work only at the end of a word, not at the beginning. Indexes search from the beginning of strings, as shown here:

```
SELECT Title
  FROM Fable
  WHERE CONTAINS (*,' "Hunt*" ')
```

Result:

```
Title
-----------------------------------------------------
The Hunter and the Woodman
The Ass in the Lion's Skin
The Bald Knight
```

If the phrase search includes a wildcard, the wildcard applies to every word in the phrase. For example, the query

```
CONTAINS (*,'He pulled out the thorn*')
```

is the equivalent of the query

```
CONTAINS (*,'He* pulled* out* the* thorn*')
```

Phrase Searches

Full-text search can attempt to locate full phrases if those phrases are surrounded by double quotes. For example, to search for the fable about the boy who cried wolf, searching for "Wolf! Wolf!" does the trick:

```
SELECT Title
  FROM Fable
  WHERE CONTAINS (*,' "Wolf! Wolf!" ')
```

Result:

```
Title
-----------------------------------------------------
The Shepherd's Boy and the Wolf
```

Word-Proximity Searches

When searching large documents, it's nice to be able to specify the proximity of the search words. Full-text search implements a proximity switch by means of the near option. The relative distance between the words is calculated, and, if the words are close enough (within about 30 words, depending on the size of the text), full-text search returns a true for the row.

The story of Androcles, the slave who pulls the thorn from the lion's paw, is one of the longer fables in the sample database, so it's a good test sample.

The following query attempts to locate the fable "Androcles" based on the proximity of the words "pardoned" and "forest" in the fable's text:

```
SELECT Title
  FROM Fable
  WHERE CONTAINS (*,'pardoned NEAR forest')
```

Result:

```
Title
--------------------------------------------------
Androcles
```

The proximity switch can handle multiple words. The following query tests the proximity of the words "lion," "paw," and "bleeding":

```
SELECT Title
  FROM Fable
  WHERE CONTAINS (*,'lion NEAR paw NEAR bleeding')
```

Result:

```
Title
--------------------------------------------------
Androcles
```

The proximity feature can be used with ContainsTable to return a rank from 0–64, which indicates relative proximity. The following query ranks the fables that mention the word "life" near the word "death" in order of proximity:

```
SELECT Fable.Title, Rank
  FROM Fable
    JOIN CONTAINSTABLE (Fable, *,'life NEAR death') FTS
    ON Fable.FableID = FTS.[KEY]
  ORDER BY FTS.Rank DESC
```

Result:

```
Title                                Rank
----------------------------------   -----------
The Serpent and the Eagle            7
The Eagle and the Arrow              1
The Woodman and the Serpent          1
```

Word-Inflection Searches

The full-text search engine can actually perform linguistic analysis and base a search for different words on a common root word. This enables you to search for words without worrying about number or tense. For example, the inflection feature makes possible a search for the word "flying" that finds a row containing the word "flew." The language you specify for the table is critical in a case like this. Something else to keep in mind is that the word base will not cross parts of speech, meaning that a search for a noun won't locate a verb form of the same root. The following query demonstrates inflection by locating the fable with the word "flew" in "The Crow and the Pitcher":

```
SELECT Title
  FROM Fable
  WHERE CONTAINS (*,'FORMSOF(INFLECTIONAL,fly)')
```

Result:

```
Title
--------------------------------------------------
The Crow and the Pitcher
The Bald Knight
```

Note   A nice front-end client program will give the user the option of highlighting the search words in the display of the found documents. Inflection searches will create a difficulty: If the user enters "fly" and the word that was found is "flew," a simple find-and-replace with HTML formatting will miss the found word. The `webhits.dll` script in Index Server can help solve this problem.

Thesaurus Searches

New in SQL 2005 is the capability to do thesaurus lookups for word replacements as well as synonyms. To configure your own thesaurus options, edit the following files found in `C:\Program Files\Microsoft SQL Server\MSSQL.1\MSSQL\Binn\FTERef`.

The thesaurus file for your language will follow the naming convention TS*XXX*.xml, where *XXX* is your language code (for example, ENU for U.S. English, ENG for U.K. English, and so on). You will need to remove the comment lines from your thesaurus file. If you edit this file in a text editor, there are two sections or nodes to the thesaurus file: an *expansion node* and a *replacement node*. The expansion node is used to expand your search argument from one term to another argument. For example, in the thesaurus file, you will find the following expansion:

```
<expansion>
        <sub>Internet Explorer</sub>
        <sub>IE</sub>
        <sub>IE5</sub>
    </expansion>
```

This will convert any searches on "IE" to search on "IE" or "IE5" or "Internet Explorer."

The replacement node is used to replace a search argument with another argument. For example, if you want the search argument *sex* interpreted as *gender*, you could use the replacement node to do that:

```
<replacement>
        <pat>sex</pat>
        <sub>gender</sub>
    </replacement>
```

The pat element (sex) indicates the pattern you want substituted by the sub element (gender).

A FREETEXT query will automatically use the thesaurus file for the language type. Here is an example of a generational query using the Thesaurus option:

```
SELECT * FROM TableName WHERE CONTAINS(*,'FORMSOF(Thesaurus,"IE")')
```

This returns matches to rows containing IE, IE5, and Internet Explorer.

Variable-Word-Weight Searches

In a search for multiple words, the relative weight may be assigned, making one word critical to the search and another word much less important. The weights are set on a scale of 0.0 to 1.0.

The isabout option enables weighting and any hit on the word allows the rows to be returned, so it functions as an implied Boolean or operator.

The following two queries use the weight option with ContainsTable to highlight the difference between the words "lion," "brave," and "eagle" as the weighting changes. The query will examine only the fabletext column to prevent the results from being skewed by the shorter lengths of the text found on the title and moral columns. The first query weights the three words evenly:

```
SELECT Fable.Title, FTS.Rank
  FROM Fable
    JOIN CONTAINSTABLE
    (Fable, FableText,
       'ISABOUT (Lion weight (.5),
       Brave weight (.5),
       Eagle weight (.5))',20) FTS
    ON Fable.FableID = FTS.[KEY]
    ORDER BY Rank DESC
```

Result:

```
Title                               Rank
----------------------------------- --------
Androcles                           92
The Eagle and the Fox               85
The Hunter and the Woodman          50
The Serpent and the Eagle           50
The Dogs and the Fox                32
The Eagle and the Arrow             21
The Ass in the Lion's Skin          16
```

When the relative importance of the word "eagle" is elevated, it's a different story:

```
SELECT Fable.Title, FTS.Rank
  FROM Fable
    JOIN CONTAINSTABLE
    (Fable, FableText,
       'ISABOUT (Lion weight (.2),
       Brave weight (.2),
       Eagle weight (.8))',20) FTS
    ON Fable.FableID = FTS.[KEY]
    ORDER BY Rank DESC
```

Result:

```
Title                               Rank
----------------------------------- -----------
The Eagle and the Fox               102
The Serpent and the Eagle           59
The Eagle and the Arrow             25
Androcles                           25
The Hunter and the Woodman          14
The Dogs and the Fox                9
The Ass in the Lion's Skin          4
```

When all the columns participate in the full-text search, the small size of the moral and the title make the target words seem relatively more important within the text. The next query uses the same weighting as the previous query but includes all columns (*):

```
SELECT Fable.Title, FTS.Rank
  FROM Fable
    JOIN CONTAINSTABLE
    (Fable, *,
       'ISABOUT (Lion weight (.2),
       Brave weight (.2),
       Eagle weight (.8))',20) FTS
  ON Fable.FableID = FTS.[KEY]
  ORDER BY Rank DESC
```

Result:

```
Title                               Rank
----------------------------------- -----------
The Wolf and the Kid                408
The Hunter and the Woodman          408
The Eagle and the Fox               102
The Eagle and the Arrow             80
The Serpent and the Eagle           80
Androcles                           25
The Ass in the Lion's Skin          23
The Dogs and the Fox                9
```

The ranking is relative and is based on word frequency, word proximity, and the relative importance of a given word within the text. "The Wolf and the Kid" does not contain an eagle or a lion, but two factors favor bravado. First, "brave" is a rarer word than "lion" or "eagle" in both the column and the table. Second, the word "brave" appears in the moral as one of only 10 words. So even though "brave" was weighted less, it rises to the top of the list. It's all based on word frequencies and statistics (and sometimes, I think, the phase of the moon!).

Fuzzy Searches

While the `contains` predicate and `ContainsTable`-derived table perform exact word searches, the `freetext` predicate expands on the `contains` functionality to include *fuzzy*, or approximate, full-text searches from free-form text.

Instead of searching for two or three words and adding the options for inflection and weights, the fuzzy search handles the complexity of building searches that make use of all the MS Full Text Search Engine options and tries to solve the problem for you. Internally, the free-form text is broken down into multiple words and phrases, and the full-text search with inflections and weighting is then performed on the result.

Freetext

Freetext works within a where clause just like contains, but without all the options. The following query uses a fuzzy search to find the fable about the big race:

```
SELECT Title
  FROM Fable
  WHERE FREETEXT
    (*,'The tortoise beat the hare in the big race')
```

Result:

```
Title
--------------------------------------------------
The Hare and the Tortoise
```

FreetextTable

Fuzzy searches benefit from the freetext-derived table that returns the ranking in the same way that ContainsTable does. The two queries shown in this section demonstrate a fuzzy full-text search using the freetext-derived table. Here is the first query:

```
SELECT Fable.Title, FTS.Rank
  FROM Fable
    JOIN FREETEXTTABLE
      (Fable, *, 'The brave hunter kills the lion',20) FTS
      ON Fable.FableID = FTS.[KEY]
    ORDER BY Rank DESC
```

Result:

```
Title                               Rank
--------------------------------    ----------
The Hunter and the Woodman          257
The Ass in the Lion's Skin          202
The Wolf and the Kid                187
Androcles                           113
The Dogs and the Fox                100
The Goose With the Golden Eggs      72
The Shepherd's Boy and the Wolf     72
```

Here is the second query:

```
SELECT Fable.Title, FTS.Rank
  FROM Fable
    JOIN FREETEXTTABLE
      (Fable, *, 'The eagle was shot by an arrow',20) FTS
      ON Fable.FableID = FTS.[KEY]
    ORDER BY Rank DESC
```

Result:

```
Title                              Rank
-------------------------------- ----------
The Eagle and the Arrow            288
The Eagle and the Fox              135
The Serpent and the Eagle          112
The Hunter and the Woodman         102
The Father and His Two Daughters   72
```

Binary Object Indexing

SQL Server can store any binary object up to 2GB, which definitely qualifies as a binary large object (blob) in an image column. Full-text search can index words from within those binary objects if the following criteria are met:

✦ Windows must have a filter installed for the object type. SQL Server installs the filters for file types `.doc`, `.xls`, `.ppt`, `.txt`, and `.htm` in the file `offfilt.dll`.

✦ A separate column, `char(3)`, must store the document extension for the blob stored in that row.

✦ The column must be added to the full-text search catalog as a blob search and the document type (for instance, `.txt`, `.doc`, `.xls`) must be stored in an accompanying column.

✦ The full-text search catalog must be populated with full and incremental populations. The Change-tracking and Update-in-the-background options will not support indexing the blobs.

✦ The object must be properly initialized as it is loaded into SQL Server using the Bulk Image Insert program.

Even when full-text search is carefully set up for blobs, this technology is less than perfect, and it takes some tinkering to make it work.

The following stored-procedure call sets up the blob column for full-text search:

```
EXEC sp_fulltext_column
    'Fable','Blob','add',0x0409,'BlobType'
```

The parameters are the same as those for adding a text column, except that the last parameter identifies the column used to specify the blob document type.

SQL Server includes Bulk Image Insert or `BII.exe`, a modified version of the Bulk Copy Program that initializes the blob files and loads them into SQL Server. It's zipped in the file `unzip_util.zip` in the `C:\Program Files\Microsoft SQL Server\80\Tools\DevTools\Samples\utils` directory. Once unzipped, it creates the `bii` subdirectory and unzips the utility files.

The Bulk Image Insert utility copies data from a text file into SQL Server. The text file must be semicolon-delimited (despite the documentation's claim that it must be comma-delimited). Within the text file, an at sign (@) indicates the blob name.

The following sample text file loads the MS Word document `fox.doc` into the Aesop's Fables sample database. The sixth column loads the blobtype and the seventh column points to `fox.doc` (the single line is word-wrapped to fit on the page):

```
Sample.txt:
26; Test Fable; Persistence Pays Off;
                   Try, try again.;doc;@fox.doc
```

After calling the `bii` utility at the command prompt, the utility will move data into the `fable` table from `sample.txt`. The other parameters specify the server name, the database, the user name (using SQL Server users), and the password. The `-v` parameter directs `bii.exe` to report the details of the operation as follows (formatted to fit):

```
>bii "table" in "sample.txt"
        -S"Noli" -D"Aesop" -U"sa" -P"sa" -v
```

Result:

```
BII - Bulk Image Insert Program for Microsoft SQL Server.
Copyright 2000 Microsoft Corporation, All Rights Reserved.
Version: V1.0-1
Started at 2001-12-07 16:28:09.231 on NOLI
Table Noli.Aesop.sa.fable
        FableID int (4)
        Title varchar (50)
        Moral varchar (100)
        FableText varchar (1536)
        BlobType char (3) null
        Blob image (16) null
Inserted 1 rows Read 1 rows 0 rows with errors
   Total Bytes = 19508 inserted 19456 File Bytes
 Total Seconds = 0.02  Kb Per Second = 952.539063
BII - Bulk Image Insert Program for Microsoft SQL Server.
Copyright 2000 Microsoft Corporation, All Rights Reserved.
Version: V1.0-1
Finished at 2001-12-07 16:28:09.332 on NOLI
```

Once the twenty-sixth fable is loaded into the database and the full-text catalog is populated, you can use the following command to search the Word document within SQL Server:

```
EXEC sp_fulltext_table 'Fable', 'start_full'
```

The following query looks for the word "jumped," which is found in the twenty-sixth fable:

```
SELECT Title, BlobType
  FROM Fable
  WHERE CONTAINS (*,'jumped')
```

Result:

```
Title                                   BlobType
--------------------------------------- -----------
Test Fable                              doc
```

Performance

SQL Server 2005's Full-Text Search performance is several orders of magnitude faster than that of SQL Server 2000 and SQL Server 7. However, you still might want to tune your system for optimal performance.

✦ SQL FTS 2005 benefits from a very fast subsystem. Place your catalog on its own controller, preferably its own RAID 10 array. A sweet spot exists for SQL FTS on eight-way servers. To configure your SQL Server for optimal performance, issue the following command:

```
sp_fulltext_service 'resource_usage'
```

✦ After a full or incremental population, force a master merge, which will consolidate all the shadow indexes into a single master index, by issuing the following command:

```
ALTER FULLTEXT CATALOG catalog_name REORGANIZE
```

✦ You can also increase the maximum number of ranges that the gathering process can use. To do so, issue the following command:

```
sp_configure 'max full-text crawl range', 100.
```

✦ You can also change the `'ft crawl bandwidth (max)'` setting. This controls how much memory is dedicated to the population; thus, increasing it has the effect of dedicating more memory to the indexing process but taking available resources away from SQL Server. You can increase this setting by issuing the following command:

```
sp_configure 'ft crawl bandwidth (max)', 1000
```

Summary

SQL Server indexes are not designed for searching for words in the middle of a column. If the database project requires flexible word searches, full-text search is the best tool, even though it requires additional development and administrative work.

This part of this book, "Manipulating Data with Select," deals with managing data, beginning with a description of the basic `select` statement. This chapter explained how to make retrieving data with the `select` statement even better by adding full-text search. The next chapter also addresses the subject of data retrieval, by describing how to store predefined SQL statements as views.

✦ ✦ ✦

Creating Views

A *view* is the saved text of a SQL `select` statement that may be referenced as a data source within a query, similar to how a subquery can be used as a data source — no more, no less. A view can't be executed by itself; it must be used within a query.

Views are sometimes described as "virtual tables." This isn't a completely accurate description because views don't store any data. Like any other SQL query, views merely refer to the data stored in tables.

With this in mind, it's important to fully understand how views work, and the pros and cons of using views, and the best place to use views within your project architecture.

Why Use Views?

While there are several opinions on the use of views, ranging from total abstinence to overuse, the Information Architecture Principle (from Chapter 1) can serve as a guide for the most appropriate use of views. The principle states that "*information . . . must be . . . made readily available in a usable format for daily operations and analysis by individuals, groups, and processes . . .*"

Presenting data in a more useable format is precisely what views do best.

Data within a normalized RDBMS is rarely organized in a readily available format. Building ad hoc queries that extract the correct information from a normalized database is a challenge for most end-users. A well-written view can hide the complexity and present the correct data to the user.

Best Practice

I recommend using views to support ad hoc queries and reports. For occasionally run queries, views perform well even when compared with stored procedures.

Views also help ensure data integrity, because even when users understand joins, they rarely understand when to use an `inner join` versus an `outer join`. Getting that aspect of the join wrong will lead to incorrect results.

Some developers use views as a key component of the data access architecture to isolate the physical schema from dynamic SQL. I still prefer using stored procedures for the abstraction layer because they offer error handling, better transactional control, and the option of programmatic control as discussed in Chapter 25,

"Creating Extensibility with a Data Abstraction Layer." However, views will do the job. I would rather see views directly access a table than allow dynamic SQL to do it.. If your application has a lot of dynamic SQL embedded within a .NET application, using views to build a database abstraction layer may be easier than refactoring the application to call stored procedures.

Based on the premise that views are best used to support ad hoc queries, and not as a central part of the application, here are some ideas for building ad hoc query views:

✦ **Use views to denormalize or flatten complex joins and hide the mysterious keys used to link data within the database schema.** A well-designed view will invite the user to get right to the data of interest.

✦ **Save complex aggregate queries as views.** Because every column must participate in an aggregate function or group by, many complex aggregate queries tend to involve subqueries so they will be able to present non-aggregated columns. Ad hoc query users might be grateful to you for composing these complex queries in advance.

✦ **Use aliases to change cryptic column names to recognizable column names.** Just as the SQL select statement can use column aliases or named ranges (table aliases) to modify the names of columns or tables, these features may be used within a view to present a more readable record set to the user. For example, the column au_lname in the Microsoft Pubs database could use the alias LastName:

```
SELECT au_lname AS LastName FROM Pubs.dbo.Author
```

A view based on the previous select statement would list the author's last name column as LastName instead of au_lname.

✦ **Include only the columns of interest to the user.** When columns that don't concern users are left out of the view, the view is easier to query. The columns that are included in the view are called *projected columns*, meaning that they project only the selected data from the entire underlying table.

✦ **Plan generic, dynamic views that will have long, useful lives.** Single-purpose views will quickly become obsolete and clutter the database. Build the view with the intention that it will be used with a where clause to select a subset of data. The view should return all the rows if the user does not supply a where restriction. For example, the vEventList view returns all the events; the user should use a where clause to select the local events, or the events in a certain month.

If a view is needed to return a restricted set of data, such as the next month's events, then the view should calculate the next month so that it will continue to function over time. Hard-coding values such as = Dec would be poor practice.

The goal when developing views is two-fold — to enable users to get to the data easily and to protect the data from the users. By building views that provide the correct data, you are protecting the data from mis-queries and misinterpretation.

Cross-Reference

Distributed partition views, or *federated databases,* divide very large tables across multiple smaller tables or separate servers to improve performance. The partitioned view then spans the multiple tables or servers, thus sharing the query load across more disk spindles.

Indexed views, included with the Enterprise Edition of SQL Server 2005, are a powerful feature that creates an index over a denormalized set of data as defined by a view. The index may then be applied when executing queries that join across that set of data, regardless of whether the view is in the query, so the name is slightly confusing.

Both of these advanced application views are useful only to solve performance issues for very large (over a terabyte) databases, and are explained in Chapter 53, "Scaling Very Large Databases."

Working with Views

Using the SQL Server Management Studio, views may be created, modified, executed, and included within other queries.

Creating Views Using Management Studio

Because a view is nothing more than a saved SQL select, the creation of a view begins with a working select statement. A SQL select statement, as long as it's a valid SQL select statement (with a few minor exceptions), can be cut and pasted from nearly any other tool into a view.

Within SQL Server Management Studio, views are listed in their own node under each database.

 New in 2005 SQL Server Management Studio offers a much richer environment for working with views, including subqueries, editing the data, saving the graphical layout of tables, and other information about the view.

The New View command in the context menu will launch the Query Designer in a mode that creates views, as shown in Figure 14-1.

Views, Relational Algebra, Abstraction, and Security

One of the basic relational operators is projection—the ability to expose specific columns. One primary advantage of views is their natural capacity to project a predefined set of columns. Here's where theory becomes practical. You can create a view that projects columns on a need-to-know basis and hides columns that are sensitive (e.g., payroll, credit card data), irrelevant, or confusing for the purpose of the view.

SQL Server supports column-level security, and it's a powerful feature. The problem is that ad hoc queries made by users who don't understand the schema very well will often run into the security errors. A recommended solution is to build some of the security into the abstraction layer, which isolates the physical schema from direct data access. The database abstraction layer can be built using views or stored procedures. Either can limit what they project to the outside world to the required columns. Give users security access to select from or execute only the views or stored procedures and restrict access to the physical tables.

For more information on abstraction layers, see Chapter 25, "Hardening the Database with a Data Abstraction Layer," and Chapter 40, "Securing Databases," which details configuring object security.

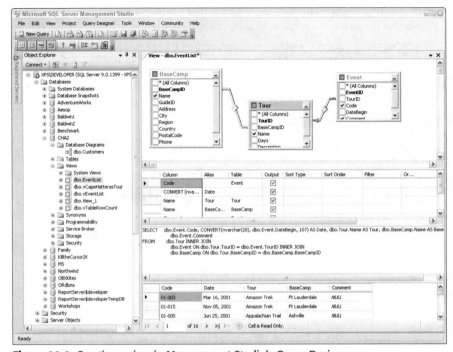

Figure 14-1: Creating a view in Management Studio's Query Designer

The View Designer functions within Management Studio's Query Designer, which is also used to query tables. The actual SQL code for the view is displayed or edited in the SQL pane. Columns may be added to the view by means of the Diagram pane, the Grid pane, or the SQL pane. The Add Table feature, available by context menu or toolbar, can add tables, other views, synonyms, and table-valued functions.

Tables or other views can be added to the new view by means of dragging them to the Diagram pane from the Object Explorer or using the Add Table context menu option.

The Add Derived Tables feature can add a subquery as a data source within the from clause of the view. The SQL for the subquery must be manually entered in the SQL pane.

Cross-Reference For more details on using the Query Designer, refer to Chapter 6, "Using Management Studio."

The Verify SQL Syntax button in the toolbar verifies only the SQL syntax; it does not verify the names of tables, views, or columns in the SQL select statement.

The Save toolbar button actually runs the script to create the view in the database. Note that the view must be a valid, error-free SQL select statement in order to be saved.

Once the view is created, it may be edited within Management Studio by selecting the view and choosing Modify View from the context menu.

To test the view's SQL select statement within Query Designer, use the Execute SQL button or F5.

The view's context menu also includes managing full-text indexing on the view and renaming the view. The view's properties include extended properties and security permissions. Views may be dropped from the database using the context menu or by selecting the view and pressing delete.

Creating Views with DDL Code

Views may be managed using the Query Editor by executing SQL scripts with the Data Definition Language (DDL) commands: create, alter, and drop. The basic syntax for creating a view is as follows:

```
USE CHA2

CREATE dbo.ViewName
AS
SQL Select Statement
```

For example, to create the view vEventList in code, the following command would be executed in a query window:

```
CREATE VIEW dbo.vEventList
AS
SELECT dbo.CustomerType.Name AS Customer,
    dbo.Customer.LastName, dbo.Customer.FirstName,
    dbo.Customer.Nickname,
    dbo.Event_mm_Customer.ConfirmDate, dbo.Event.Code,
    dbo.Event.DateBegin, dbo.Tour.Name AS Tour,
    dbo.BaseCamp.Name, dbo.Event.Comment
    FROM dbo.Tour
        INNER JOIN dbo.Event
            ON dbo.Tour.TourID = dbo.Event.TourID
        INNER JOIN dbo.Event_mm_Customer
            ON dbo.Event.EventID = dbo.Event_mm_Customer.EventID
        INNER JOIN dbo.Customer
            ON dbo.Event_mm_Customer.CustomerID
                = dbo.Customer.CustomerID
        LEFT OUTER JOIN dbo.CustomerType
            ON dbo.Customer.CustomerTypeID
                = dbo.CustomerType.CustomerTypeID
        INNER JOIN dbo.BaseCamp
            ON dbo.Tour.BaseCampID = dbo.BaseCamp.BaseCampID
```

Attempting to create a view that already exists will cause an error. Once a view has been created, the SQL select statement may be easily edited by means of the alter command:

```
ALTER dbo.ViewName
AS
SQL Select Statement
```

The alter command supplies a new SQL select statement for the view.

Here's where the Object Explorer earns its keep. To automatically generate an alter state-ment from an existing view, drill down to the list of views in the Object Explorer and select Script View as ⇨ Alter to ⇨ New Query Editor Windows from the context menu.

Altering a view is preferable to dropping and recreating it, because dropping the view will also drop any security-object permissions that have been established.

To remove a view from the database, use the drop command:

```
DROP VIEW dbo.ViewName
```

Within a script that is intended to be executed several times, the following code can drop and recreate the view:

```
IF EXISTS(SELECT * FROM SysObjects WHERE Name = 'view name')
  DROP VIEW dbo.ViewName
CREATE dbo.ViewName
AS
SQL Select Statement
```

Order By and Views

Views serve as data sources for other queries, and don't support sorting the data within the view. For example, the following code selects data from the vEventList view and orders it by EventCode and name. The order by clause is not a part of vEventList, but is applied to the view by the calling SQL statement:

```
SELECT EventCode, LastName, FirstName, IsNull(NickName,'')
    FROM dbo.vEventList
    ORDER BY EventCode, LastName, FirstName
```

However, T-SQL syntax permits the top predicate in views, and the top predicate is generally useless without an order by. Therefore, if the view includes top 100 percent, it can include an order by:

```
CREATE VIEW dbo.vCapeHatterasTour
    AS
    SELECT TOP 100 PERCENT TourName, BaseCampID
        FROM dbo.Tour

        ORDER BY TourName
```

 New in 2005   In SQL Server 2000, including a top 100 percent in a view would allow the view to include an order by clause. However, in SQL Server 2005, this error was corrected and the order by clause is there only to support the top predicate. Top without a sort order will return only random rows and is of little practical value. Top 100 percent with an order by will not sort the data from a view in SQL Server 2005.

View Restrictions

Although a view can contain nearly any valid select statement, a few basic restrictions do apply:

✦ Views may not include the `select into` option that creates a new table from the selected columns. `Select into` fails if the table already exists and it does not return any data, so it's not a valid view:

```
SELECT * INTO Table
```

✦ Views may not refer to a temporary table (one with a # in the name) or a table variable, because these types of tables are very transient.

✦ Views may not contain `compute` or `compute by` columns. Instead, use standard aggregate functions and groupings. (`Compute` and `compute by` are obsolete and are included for backward compatibility only.)

Executing Views

A view, by itself, cannot be executed. The `select` statement composing the view can be executed, but in that form, technically, the SQL statement is not a view. The SQL statement is a view only once it is stored as a view. A view is useful only as a data source within a query.

That's why SQL Server Management Studio's Open View context menu will automatically generate a simple query, selecting all columns from the view. The initial presentation displays only the results. However, enabling the other Query Designer panes will reveal the query that is selected from the view.

The SQL pane will show the view in the `from` clause of the `select` statement. This is how the view will be referenced by users:

```
SELECT *
  FROM vEventList
```

When views are called from user applications or from ad hoc queries, a `where` condition is typically used to retrieve the correct data from the view. The `where` condition may be entered in the Grid pane or the SQL pane:

```
SELECT * FROM dbo.vEventList WHERE (EventCode = '101')
```

Locking Down the View

Views are designed to control access to data. As such, there are several options that protect the data or the view.

Protecting the Data

The `with check option` causes the `where` clause of the view to check the data being inserted or updated through the view in addition to the data being retrieved. In a sense, it makes the `where` clause a two-way restriction.

This option is useful when the view should limit inserts and updates with the same restrictions applied to the `where` clause.

To understand the need for the `with check` option, it's important to first understand how views function without the `check option`. The following view will generate a list of tours for the Cape Hatteras base camp:

```
ALTER VIEW dbo.vCapeHatterasTour
AS
SELECT TourName, BaseCampID
   FROM dbo.Tour
   WHERE BaseCampID = 2
SELECT * FROM dbo.vCapeHatterasTour


TourName                           BaseCampID
---------------------------------- -----------
Outer Banks Lighthouses            2
```

If the Ashville base camp adds a Blue Ridge Parkway Hike tour and inserts it through the view without the check option, the insert is permitted:

```
INSERT dbo.vCapeHatterasTour (TourName, BaseCampID)
   VALUES ('Blue Ridge Parkway Hike', 1)
(1 row(s) affected)
```

The insert worked and the new row is in the database, but the row is not visible through the view because the where clause of the view filters out the inserted row. This phenomenon is called *disappearing rows*:

```
SELECT * FROM dbo.vCapeHatterasTour


TourName                           BaseCampID
---------------------------------- -----------
Outer Banks Lighthouses            2
```

If the purpose of the view was to give users at the Cape access to their tours alone, then the view failed. Although they can see only the Cape's tours, they successfully modified another base camp's tours.

The with check option would have prevented this fault. The following code will back out the insert and redo the same scenario, but this time the view will include the with check option:

```
DELETE dbo.vCapeHatterasTour
   WHERE TourName = 'Blue Ridge Parkway Hike'
ALTER VIEW dbo.vCapeHatterasTour
   AS
   SELECT TourName, BaseCampID
      FROM dbo.Tour
      WHERE BaseCampID = 2
   WITH CHECK OPTION

INSERT dbo.vCapeHatterasTour (TourName, BaseCampID)
   VALUES ('Blue Ridge Parkway Hike', 1)


Server: Msg 550, Level 16, State 1, Line 1
The attempted insert or update failed because the target view either
specifies WITH CHECK OPTION or spans a view that specifies WITH CHECK
OPTION and one or more rows resulting from the operation did not qualify
under the CHECK OPTION constraint.
The statement has been terminated.
```

This time the insert failed and the error message attributed the cause to the with check option in the view, which is exactly the effect desired.

Some developers will employ views and the with check option as a means of providing row-level security—a technique called *horizontally positioned views*. As in the base camp view example, they will create a view for each department, or each sales branch, and then give users security permission to the view that pertains to them. While this method does achieve row-level security, it also has a high maintenance cost.

Cross-Reference
For the application, row-level security can be designed using user-access tables and stored procedures, as demonstrated in Chapter 27, "Programming CLR Assemblies within SQL Server," but views can help enforce row-level security for ad hoc queries.

Within Management Studio's View Designer, the with check option can be viewed within the View Properties page.

Protecting the View

Three options protect views from data schema changes and prying eyes. These options are simply added to the create command and applied to the view, much as the with check option is applied.

Schema Changes

Database code is fragile and tends to break when the underlying data structure changes. Because views are nothing more than stored SQL select queries, changes to the referenced tables will break the view. Even adding new columns to an underlying table may cause the view to break.

Creating a view with schema binding locks the underlying tables to the view and prevents changes, as demonstrated in the following code sample:

```
CREATE TABLE Test (
    [Name] NVARCHAR(50)
    )
go

CREATE VIEW vTest
WITH SCHEMABINDING
AS
SELECT [Name] FROM dbo.Test
Go

ALTER TABLE Test
    ALTER COLUMN [Name] NVARCHAR(100)

Server: Msg 4922, Level 16, State 1, Line 1
ALTER TABLE ALTER COLUMN Name failed
because one or more objects access this column.
```

Some restrictions apply to the creation of schema-bound views. The select statement must include the owner name for any referenced objects, and select all columns (*) is not permitted.

Within Management Studio's View Designer, the with schema binding option can be enabled within the View Properties page.

Encrypting the View's select Statement

The `with encryption` option is another simulated security feature. When views or stored procedures are created, the text is stored in the `SysComments` system table. The code is therefore available for viewing. The view may contain a `where` condition that should be kept confidential, or there may be some other reason for encrypting the code. The `with encryption` option encrypts the code in `SysComments` and prevents anyone from viewing the original code.

In the following code example, the text of the view is inspected within `SysComments`, the view is encrypted, and `SysComments` is again inspected (as you would expect, the `select` statement for the view is then no longer readable):

```
SELECT Text
    FROM SysComments
    JOIN SysObjects
        ON SysObjects.ID = SysComments.ID
    WHERE Name = 'vTest'
```

The result is the text of the `vText` view:

```
Text
-----------------------------
CREATE VIEW vTest
WITH SCHEMABINDING
AS
SELECT [Name] FROM dbo.Test
```

The following `alter` command rebuilds the view `with encryption`:

```
ALTER VIEW vTest
WITH ENCRYPTION
AS
SELECT [Name] FROM dbo.Test
```

Be careful with this option. Once the code is encrypted, the Query Analyzer Object Explorer can no longer produce a script to alter the view, and will instead generate this message:

```
/****** Encrypted object is not transferable,
and script cannot be generated. ******/
```

In addition, be aware that the encryption affects replication. An encrypted view will not be published.

Application Metadata

The front-end application or data access layer may request schema information, called *metadata,* along with the data when querying SQL Server. Typically, SQL Server will return schema information for the underlying tables, but the `VIEW_METADATA` option tells SQL Server to return schema information about the view, rather than the tables referenced by the view. This prohibits someone from learning about the table's schema and is useful when the view's purpose is to hide sensitive columns.

Updating through Views

One of the main complaints concerning views is that they cannot be updated often. In fact, if the view is much more than a simple `select`, then chances are good that the data can't be updated through the view.

Any of these factors may cause a view to be non-updatable:

Cross-Reference

Of course, the other standard potential difficulties with updating and inserting data still apply. Chapter 16, "Modifying Data," discusses modifying data in more detail.

✦ Only one table may be updated. If the view includes joins, the `update` statement that references the view must attempt to update only one table.

✦ An `instead of` trigger on the view or an underlying table will modify the data-modification operation. The code inside the `instead of` trigger will be executed instead of the submitted data update.

✦ Aggregate functions or `group by`s in the view will cause the view to be non-updatable. SQL Server wouldn't be able to determine which of the summarized rows should be updated.

✦ If the view includes a subquery as a derived table, none of the derived table's columns may be in the output of the view. However, aggregates are permitted in a subquery that is being used as a derived table.

✦ If the view includes the `with check option`, the `insert` or `update` operation must meet the view's `where`-clause conditions.

✦ The `update` or `insert` columns must refer to a single column in the underlying tables. If the same column name appears in two tables, use the designation `table.column` in the column list.

As you can see, it's easy to create a non-updatable view. However, if the project is using views for ad hoc queries and reporting only, updatability isn't a serious issue.

Cross-Reference

One way to work around non-updatable views is to build an `instead of` trigger that inspects the modified data and then performs a legal `update` operation based on that data. Chapter 23, "Creating DML Triggers," explains how to create an `instead of` trigger.

Alternatives to Views

If your development style involves a lot of views, this may have been a depressing chapter. Fortunately, SQL Server 2005 provides several other cool alternatives.

In some cases, stored procedures and functions offer a slight performance benefit over views. In addition, stored procedures do not offer schema binding (a very attractive benefit), whereas views do; however, user-defined functions provide the compiled speed and input parameters of a stored procedure with the schema binding of a view. If you like building modular SQL statements such as views, as I do, you'll find user-defined functions to your liking.

Chapters 18–25 discuss T-SQL, stored procedures, and functions.

If you are using views to support ad hoc queries, as I suggest you do, you may also want to explore providing Analysis Services cubes for those users who need to perform complex explorations of the data. Cubes *pre-aggregate,* or summarize, the data along multiple dimensions. The user may then browse the cube and compare the different data dimensions. For the developer, providing one cube can often eliminate several queries or reports.

Chapter 43, "Business Intelligence with Analysis Services," explains creating cubes.

A related performance issue involving views concerns the locks that views can place on the data. There's nothing inherently wrong with the way views lock the data, and if data is selected through a view and the `select` is immediately completed, then the locks will be immediately dropped. The problem is that users have a tendency to use views to browse data using a front-end application that opens all the data and keeps it open for the length of the browse session. For this reason, views have garnered an undeservedly poor reputation for holding locks. The issue is not the view, but the front-end code or tool. I mention it here in defense of views and to alert you to this potential performance problem.

Nesting Views

Because a view is nothing more than a SQL `select` statement, and a SQL `select` statement may refer to a view as if it were a table, views may themselves refer to other views. Views referred to by other views are sometimes called *nested views*.

The following view uses `vEventList` and adds a `where` clause to restrict the results to those events taking place in the next 30 days:

```
CREATE VIEW dbo.vEventList30days
    AS
    SELECT dbo.vEventList.EventCode, LastName, FirstName
        FROM dbo.vEventList
        JOIN dbo.Event
            ON vEventList.EventCode = Event.EventCode
        WHERE Event.DateBegin
            BETWEEN GETDATE() and GETDATE() + 30
```

In this example, the view `vEventList` is nested within `vEventList30Days`. Another way to express the relationship is to say that `vEventList30Days` depends on `vEventList`. (Within Management Studio the dependencies of an object may be viewed by selecting All Tasks ⇨ Display Dependencies from the context menu for the object.) Figure 14-2 shows the dependencies and the nested view.

Cross-Reference
Another high-end specialized view is a partitioned view, which unions data that has been split into several segmented tables for performance reasons. Partitioned views are explained in Chapter 53, "Scaling Very Large Databases."

Views aren't the only means of nesting `select` statements. Subqueries and common table expressions supply data as if they were tables, or derived tables, and may also be nested within a query, which will encapsulate all the code into a single component and improve performance. The nested view in the preceding code sample could be rewritten as nest-derived tables, as follows (the subquery is the code enclosed in parentheses):

```
SELECT E.EventCode, LastName, FirstName
    FROM
    (SELECT dbo.CustomerType.CustomerTypeName,
        dbo.Customer.LastName, dbo.Customer.FirstName,
        dbo.Customer.Nickname,
        dbo.Event_mm_Customer.ConfirmDate, dbo.Event.EventCode,
        dbo.Event.DateBegin, dbo.Tour.TourName,
        dbo.BaseCamp.BaseCampName, dbo.Event.Comment
    FROM dbo.Tour
        INNER JOIN dbo.Event
```

```
    ON dbo.Tour.TourID = dbo.Event.TourID
INNER JOIN dbo.Event_mm_Customer
    ON dbo.Event.EventID = dbo.Event_mm_Customer.EventID
INNER JOIN dbo.Customer
    ON dbo.Event_mm_Customer.CustomerID
          = dbo.Customer.CustomerID
LEFT OUTER JOIN dbo.CustomerType
    ON dbo.Customer.CustomerTypeID
          = dbo.CustomerType.CustomerTypeID
INNER JOIN dbo.BaseCamp
    ON dbo.Tour.BaseCampID = dbo.BaseCamp.BaseCampID
) E
JOIN dbo.Event
    ON E.EventCode = Event.EventCode
WHERE Event.DateBegin BETWEEN GETDATE()
    and GETDATE() + 30
```

The subquery is given the names range, or table alias, of E. From then on it's referred to by the outer query as E. Granted, this is not a suitable technique for end-user ad hoc queries, but if you're a developer who has been using nested views and you want to tighten up your code, nested derived tables are worth trying.

Cross-Reference Chapter 10, "Including Data with Subqueries and CTEs," explains using subqueries and common table elements.

Nested view

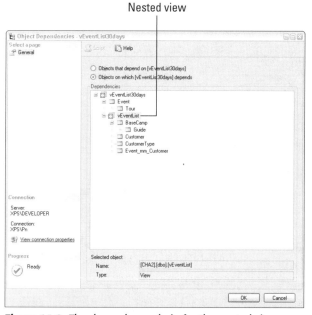

Figure 14-2: The dependency chain for the nested views is easily discerned from the Dependencies dialog boxes for the calling view: vEventList30Days includes the nested view vEventList.

Best Practice

Performance testing has shown that when the data and execution plan are already in the cache, stored procedures are slightly faster than views; however, if the execution plan is not cached (meaning that it has not been executed recently), then views execute faster than stored procedures. Both views and stored procedures test faster than submitting a `select` to SQL Server regardless of what's in the cache. This proves the best practice of using views to support users' ad hoc queries, and stored procedures for the application's data abstraction layer.

Using Synonyms

Views are sometimes employed to hide cryptic database schema names. Synonyms are similar to views, but more limited. Whereas views can project columns, assign column aliases, and build data using joins and subqueries, synonyms can assign alternative names to tables, views, and stored procedures, as shown in Figure 14-3.

While synonyms are very limited compared to views, they do offer a practical application — modifying the object's schema. For databases with extensive use of schema owners other than `dbo`, synonyms can make objects appear to belong to the `dbo` owner and ease query development.

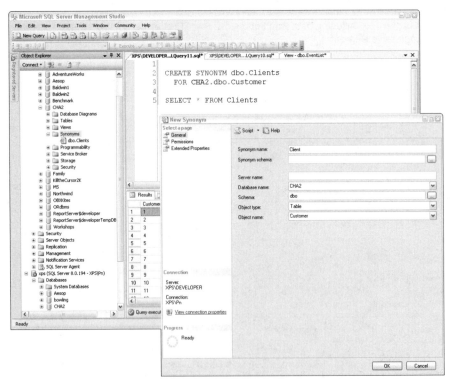

Figure 14-3: Synonyms may be created and managed using Management Studio's Object Explorer.

Summary

Views are nothing more than stored SQL `select` queries. There's no magic in a view. Any valid SQL `select` statement may be saved as a view, including subqueries, complex joins, and aggregate functions.

The previous chapters have discussed retrieving data using the powerful `select` statement. Views store the `select` statement for ad hoc queries. The next chapter continues the discussion of `select`, extending its power beyond the local database with distributed queries.

✦   ✦   ✦

Working with Distributed Queries

Data is seldom in one place. In today's distributed world, most new projects enhance or at least connect to existing data. That's not a problem. SQL Server can read and write data to most other data sources. Heterogeneous joins can even merge SQL Server data with an Excel spreadsheet.

SQL Server offers several methods of accessing data external to the current database. From simply referencing another local database to executing pass-through queries that engage another client/server database, SQL Server can handle it.

Best Practice

While SQL Server can handle the technical problems of querying external data, if the two systems are in fact two separate applications, then directly accessing an external data store will likely violate the principle of encapsulation; and coupling the two data stores reduces the flexibility of the architecture. In many IT shops this practice would not be approved. Instead, the two systems should communicate using XML, SOAP, and SOA, as described in Chapter 1, "The Information Architecture Principle," and Chapter 32, "Building an SOA Data Store with Web Services."

Distributed Query Concepts

Linking to an external data source is nothing more than configuring the name of the linked server, along with the necessary location and login information, so that SQL Server can access data on the linked server.

Linking is a one-way configuration, as illustrated in Figure 15-1. If Server A links to Server B, it means that Server A knows how to access and log into Server B. As far as Server B is concerned, Server A is just another user.

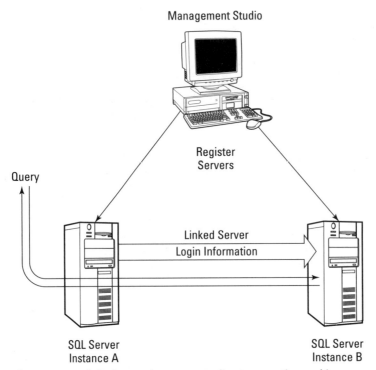

Management Studio

Register
Servers

Query

Linked Server
Login Information

SQL Server
Instance A

SQL Server
Instance B

Figure 15-1: A linked server is a one-way direct connection and is not dependent on Management Studio registering the servers. In this diagram, SQL Server instance A sees SQL Server instance B as a linked server so A can access B's data.

If linking a server is a new concept to you it could easily be confused with registering a server in Management Studio. As illustrated in Figure 15-1, Management Studio is only communicating with the servers as a client application. Linking the servers enables SQL Server instance A to communicate directly with SQL Server instance B.

Links can be established in Management Studio or with T-SQL code. The latter has the advantage of repeatability in case a hasty rebuild is necessary, although building the links in code requires more steps.

A linked server can be a SQL server or any other data source with either an OLE DB provider or ODBC drivers. Distributed queries can select data and modify it (insert, update, delete), according to the features of the OLE DB provider or ODBC driver.

SQL Server queries can reference external data by referring to the pre-configured linked server or specifying the link in the query code.

Note   In this chapter, I refer to the two data sources as *local* and *external*. Other descriptions of distributed queries might refer to the same two servers as local and remote, or sending and receiving.

In a sense, linking to an external data source only moves declaring the link from the query code to a server administration task. Because queries can refer to the named link without concern for the location or security particulars of the link, queries that use linked servers are more portable and easier to maintain than queries that declare the external data source in the query code. If the database is moved to a new server, once the database administrator creates the appropriate links, the queries will work without modification.

In the case of a distributed query, SQL Server is the client process receiving the results from the external data source. Distributed queries can either pull the data into SQL Server for processing or pass the query to the external data source for processing.

Cross-Reference There's more than one way to distribute data. You might want to consider replication (see Chapter 39, "Replicating Data") or setting up a standby server as a reporting server (see Chapter 52, "Providing High Availability").

Accessing a Local SQL Server Database

When you access a second database on a single server, the same SQL Server engine processes the data. Therefore, although the data is outside the local database, the query's not actually a distributed query.

A SQL Server query may access another database on the same server by referring to the table using the database name:

```
Database.Schma.ObjectName
```

Because the database is on the same server, the server name is optional. The schema can refer to a schema or to the user who owns the tables. Typically, the tables are owned by the database owner schema (dbo). If that's the case, then dbo can be assumed:

```
USE CHA2;
SELECT LastName, FirstName
  FROM OBXKites.dbo.Contact;
```

On The Web The code listings in this chapter are also in the ch15.sql script file. In addition, the Cape Hatteras Adventures conversion script (CHA2_Convert.sql) uses distributed queries exclusively to convert the data from Access and Excel to SQL Server.

The previous query is the functional equivalent of this one:

```
SELECT LastName, FirstName
  FROM OBXKites..Contact;
```

Result (abbreviated):

```
LastName        FirstName
------------    ------------
Adams           Terri
Andrews         Ed
...
```

Linking to External Data Sources

SQL Server is also capable of establishing a link to any other data source that is ODBC- or OLE-DB-compatible. The link can be created using Management Studio or T-SQL code.

Linking with Management Studio

A link to another SQL server can be established by means of Management Studio or code. Within Management Studio, linked servers are listed under the Security node, which makes sense because a link is really defining how to log on to another server. Right-click the Security node under the server and select New Linked Server to open the Linked Server Properties form (see Figure 15-2).

Linking to non–SQL Server data sources is covered later in this chapter.

Selecting the Server

In the General tab of the Linked Server Properties form, enter the name of the external SQL server in the Linked Server field, and click the SQL Server button in the Server Type section. To link to a named instance of SQL Server, enter the instance name as ***server\instance*** without square brackets. In Figure 15-2, the linked server is Noli\SQL2.

SQL Server 2000 can link to any other SQL Server 2000 instance, or a SQL Server 7 server, but SQL Server 2000 won't link to a SQL Server 6.5 server without going through an OBDC driver.

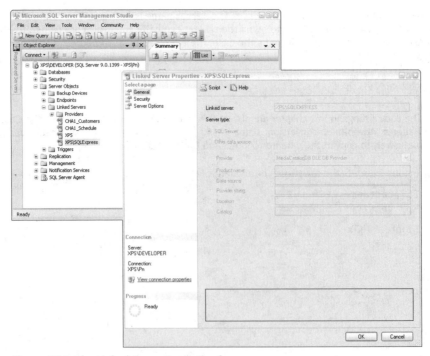

Figure 15-2: The Linked Server Properties form

Configuring the Logins

The whole point of linked servers is to enable local users to run queries that access data from other data sources. If the external data source is SQL Server, it will require some type of user authentication, which is accomplished via mapping logins; and for those local users whose logins are not mapped, via setting the default behavior.

The login map will either pass the user along without translating the login name if the Impersonate option is checked, or translate any user's login to a remote login and password if the Impersonate option is not checked. Of course, on the external server, the login must be a valid login and must have been granted security rights in order for the link to be effective.

The default connection options for a user not mapped are as follows:

✦ **Connection: Not be made:** Restricts the ability to run distributed queries to those users in the user mapping list. If a user not on the user mapping list attempts to run a distributed query, he or she will receive the following error:

```
Server: Msg 7416, Level 16, State 1, Line 1
Access to the remote server is denied
  because no login-mapping exists.
```

✦ **Connection: Be made without using a security context:** This option is for non–SQL Server external data sources and is not useful for SQL Server. SQL Server will attempt to connect as the user SQL without a password. If a user not on the user mapping list attempts to run a distributed query, he or she will receive the following error:

```
Server: Msg 18456, Level 14, State 1, Line 1
Login failed for user 'SQL'.
```

This is the default for Management Studio.

✦ **Connection: Be made using the login's current security context:** When the local SQL server connects to the external SQL Server, it can delegate security, meaning that the local SQL Server will connect to the external SQL Server using the local user's login. Using this method is similar to listing the user and selecting the Impersonate option except that this uses security delegation; and to pass the security context, the login must be the exact same account, not just the same login and password.

The user's rights and roles for the distributed query will be those assigned at the external SQL Server.

To use security delegation, every server must run Windows 2000, and both Kerberos and Active Directory must be enabled.

This is the default when creating the link using T-SQL code.

Best Practice

For most SQL Server–to–SQL Server distributed queries, the local login's security context is the best linked-server security option because it preserves the user's identity and conforms to the SQL Server security plan. If the infrastructure doesn't support Kerberos and Active Directory, then map the users.

✦ **Connection: Be made using this security context:** The final option simply assigns every non-mapped local user to a hard-coded external SQL Server login. While this may be the simplest method, it also allows every local user the same access to the external SQL Server. Using this option should violate any responsible security plan. It would certainly exclude the external SQL Server from achieving C2-level security certification.

Configuring the Options

The third tab in the Linked Server Properties form, Server Options, presents the following options, which control how SQL Server expects to receive data from the external SQL Server:

✦ **Collation Compatibility:** Set this option to `true` if the two servers are using the same collation (character set and sort order).

✦ **Data Access:** If set to `false`, this option disables distributed queries to the external server.

✦ **RPC:** If this option is set to `true`, remote-procedure calls may be made to the external server.

✦ **RPC Out:** If this option is set to `true`, remote-procedure calls may be made from the external server.

✦ **Use Remote Collation:** If this option is set to `true`, distributed queries will use the collation of the external SQL Server, rather than that of the local server.

✦ **Collation Name:** Specifies a collation for distributed queries. This option cannot be chosen if collation compatibility is set.

✦ **Connection Timeout:** The connection timeout in milliseconds.

✦ **Query Timeout:** The distributed query timeout in milliseconds.

Once the link is properly established, a table listing will likely be available in the table node under the linked server. The tables listed will be those of the login's default database. If the default database is the master, and Management Studio is configured in the local server registration to hide system objects, no tables should appear.

Deleting a linked server in Management Studio will also delete all security-login mappings.

Linking with T-SQL

Management Studio handles the connection and the login information in a single form. However, if you choose to establish a linked server with T-SQL code, the server connection and the login information are handled by separate commands.

Establishing the Link

To establish the server link with code, use the `sp_addlinkedserver` system stored procedure. If the link is being made to another SQL Server, and the name of the other SQL Server instance is acceptable as the name for the link, then only two parameters are required: the linked server name and the server product. The following command creates a link to the `SQL2` instance on my test server (`[XPS\Developer]`):

```
-- Note: the author's development sever is named XPS
-- SQL Server Instances:
-- [XPS]                SQL Server 2000 Developer Edition
-- [XPS\Developer]      SQL Server 2005 Developer Edition
-- [XPS\SQLExpress]     SQL Server 2005 Express Edition
-- [XPS\Standard]       SQL Server 2005 Standard Edition

EXEC sp_addlinkedserver
  @server = 'XPS\SQLExpress',
  @srvproduct = 'SQL Server';
```

Note If you run these scripts, you'll need to change the SQL Server instance names to match your configuration.

To link to another SQL Server instance using a linked server name other than the SQL Server instance name, two parameters are added. The `provider` parameter must specify `SQLOLEDB`, and the `@datasrc` (data source) parameter passes the actual SQL Server instance name of the linked server. The `@srvproduct` (server product) parameter is left blank. The `@server` parameter will be the name the linked server will be known by. The example links to the `SQL2` instance on `Noli`, but the linked server will be referred to as `Yonder` in queries:

```
EXEC sp_addlinkedserver
  @server = 'Yonder',
  @datasrc = 'Noli\SQL2',
  @srvproduct = '',
  @provider='SQLOLEDB';
```

The catalog view, `sys.servers`, lists the servers, including linked servers. The system stored procedure, `sp_linkedservers`, also returns information about linked servers:

```
SELECT [Name], Product, Provider, Data_source
  FROM sys.servers
  WHERE Is_Linked = 1;
```

To drop an existing linked server, which only severs the link and does not affect the external server, use the `sp_dropserver` system stored procedure:

```
EXEC sp_DropServer @server = 'Yonder';
```

If any login mappings exist for the linked server, they too will be dropped.

Distributed Security and Logins

In Management Studio, the security issue is broken down into two parts: login mapping and what to do with non-mapped logins. T-SQL uses the `sp_addlinkedsrvlogin` system stored procedure to handle both parts, as follows:

```
sp_addlinkedsrvlogin
  @rmtsrvname = 'rmtsrvname',
  @useself = 'useself', (default True)
  @locallogin = 'locallogin', (default Null)
  @rmtuser = 'rmtuser', (default Null)
  @rmtpassword = 'rmtpassword' (default Null);
```

If the linked server was added using T-SQL instead of Management Studio, then the security option for non-mapped logins is already configured to use the login's current security context.

If the `@locallogin` is `null`, the setting applies to all non-mapped users. The `@useself` option is the same as impersonate.

The following stored procedure call enables the `Noli\Paul` login to access the `Noli\SQL2` server as the `sa` user with the password `secret`:

```
sp_addlinkedsrvlogin
  @rmtsrvname = ' XPS\SQLExpress',
  @useself = 'false',
  @locallogin = 'NOLI\Paul',
```

```
    @rmtuser = 'sa',
    @rmtpassword = 'secret';
```

The next example sets all non-mapped users to connect using their own security context (the recommended option). The local user is null, so this linked server login applies to all non-mapped users. The @useself option is not specified, so the default setting, true, will apply, causing the users to use the local security context:

```
EXEC sp_addlinkedsrvlogin
    @rmtsrvname = 'NOLI\SQL2';
```

The third example will prevent all non-mapped users from executing distributed queries. The second parameter, @useself, is set to false, and the mapping user login and password are left as null:

```
EXEC sp_addlinkedsrvlogin 'NOLI\SQL2', 'false';
```

The catalog view, sys.Linked_Logins, lists the logins. The system stored procedure, sp_helplinkedsrvlogin, also returns information about linked logins:

```
SELECT [Name], Product, Provider, Data_source
   FROM sys.servers  *** Code to be updated  -Paul
   WHERE Is_Linked = 1;
```

To drop a linked server login, use the sp_droplinkedsrvlogin system stored procedure:

```
sp_droplinkedsrvlogin
    @rmtsrvname = 'rmtsrvname', (no default)
    @locallogin = 'locallogin'  (no default);
```

The following code example will remove the Noli\Paul login that's mapped to NOLI\SQL2:

```
EXEC sp_droplinkedsrvlogin
    @rmtsrvname = 'XPS\SQLExpress',
    @locallogin = 'NOLI\Paul';
```

To remove the non-mapped user's default mapping, run the same procedure but specify a null local login, as follows:

```
EXEC sp_droplinkedsrvlogin 'XPS\SQLExpress', NULL;
```

Linked Server Options

The linked server options shown in the Server Options tab of the Linked Server Properties form may be set in code using the sp_serveroption system stored procedure. The procedure must be called once for each option setting:

```
sp_serveroption
    @server = 'server',
    @optname = 'option_name',
    @optvalue = 'option_value';
```

The options are the same as those in the form, with the addition of lazy schema validation, which disables the checking of the table schema for distributed queries. You may want to use lazy schema validation when you're sure of the schema but want to reduce network overhead.

The catalog view, `sys.servers`, returns the linked server's options. The system stored procedure, `sp_helpserver`, also returns information about linked servers:

```
SELECT [Name], Product, Provider, Data_source
  FROM sys.servers
  WHERE Is_Linked = 1;
```

Linking with Non–SQL Server Data Sources

If the external data source isn't SQL Server, SQL Server can likely still access the data. It depends on the availability and the features of the ODBC drivers or OLE DB providers. SQL Server uses OLE DB for external data, and several OLE DB providers are included with SQL Server. If for some reason OLE DB isn't available for the external data source, use the "Microsoft OLE DB Provider for ODBC Drivers" provider. Nearly every data-source type has an ODBC driver.

To set up the linked server, either with code or via Management Studio, a data source (or location) and possibly a provider string to supply additional information are required, in addition to the name of the linked server, the provider name, and the product name. Some common data-source settings are listed in Table 15-1.

Table 15-1: Other Common Data Source Settings

Link to	Provider Name	Product Name	Data Source	Provider String
MS Access	MS Jet 4.0 OLE DB	Access 2003	Database File Location	null
Excel	MS Jet 4.0 OLE DB	Excel	Spreadsheet File Location	Excel 5.0
Oracle	MS OLE Provider for Oracle	Oracle	Oracle System Identifier	null

As two examples of linking to non–SQL Server data sources, the Cape Hatteras Adventures sample database uses distributed queries to pull data from both Access and Excel. The sample database models a typical small business that is currently using Access and Excel to store its customer list and schedule.

Linking to Excel

The code samples used in this section are taken directly from the `CHA2_Convert.sql` script, which moves the data from the old version 1 (Access and Excel) to version 2 (SQL Server). The Cape Hatteras Adventures folks have been keeping their tour schedule in Excel, as shown in Figure 15-3.

Within Excel, each spreadsheet page and named range appears as a table when accessed from an external data provider. Within Excel, the named ranges are set up by means of the Insert ➪ Name ➪ Define menu command. Excel's Define Name dialog box is used to create new named ranges and edit the existing named ranges. The `CHA1_Schedule` spreadsheet has five named ranges (as shown in Figure 15-4), which overlap much like SQL Server views. Each of the five named ranges appears as a table when SQL Server links to the spreadsheet. SQL Server can `select`, `insert`, `update`, and `delete` rows just as if this table were a SQL Server table.

Figure 15-3: Prior to the conversion to SQL Server, the Cape Hatteras Adventures company was managing its tour schedule in the CHA1_Schedule.xls spreadsheet.

Figure 15-4: Tables are defined within the Excel spreadsheet as named ranges. The CHA1_Schedule spreadsheet has five named ranges.

The following code sample sets up the Excel spreadsheet as a linked server:

```
Execute sp_addlinkedserver
  @server = 'CHA1_Schedule',
  @srvproduct =  'Excel',
```

```
@provider = 'Microsoft.Jet.OLEDB.4.0',
@datasrc = 'C:\SQLServerBible\CHA1_Schedule.xls',
@provstr = 'Excel 5.0'
```

Note   Excel spreadsheets are not multi-user spreadsheets. SQL Server can't perform a distributed query that accesses an Excel spreadsheet while that spreadsheet is open in Excel.

Linking to MS Access

Not surprisingly, SQL Server links easily to MS Access databases. SQL Server uses the OLE DB Jet provider to connect to Jet and request data from the MS Access .mdb file.

Because Access is a database, there's no trick to preparing it for linking, as there is with Excel. Each Access table will appear as a table under the Linked Servers node in Management Studio.

The Cape Hatteras Adventures customer/prospect list was stored in Access prior to upsizing the database to SQL Server. The following code from the CHA2_Convert.sql script links to the CHA1_Customers.mdb Access database so SQL Server can retrieve the data and populate the SQL Server tables:

```
EXEC sp_addlinkedserver
  'CHA1_Customers',
  'Access 2003',
  'Microsoft.Jet.OLEDB.4.0',
  'C:\SQLServerBible\CHA1_Customers.mdb';
```

If you are having difficulty with a distributed query, one of the first places to check is the security context. Excel expects that connections do not establish a security context, so the non-mapped user login should be set to no security context:

```
EXEC sp_addlinkedsrvlogin
  @rmtsrvname = 'CHA1_Schedule',
  @useself   = 'false';
```

Developing Distributed Queries

Once the link to the external data source is established, SQL Server can reference the external data within queries. Table 15-2 shows the four basic syntax methods that are available, which differ in query-processing location and setup method.

Table 15-2: Distributed Query Method Matrix

Link Setup	Query-Execution Location	
	Local SQL Server	*External Data Source (Pass-Through)*
Linked Server	Four-part name	Four-part name OpenQuery()
Ad Hoc Link Declared in the Query	OpenDataSource()	OpenRowSet()

Distributed Queries and Management Studio

Management Studio doesn't supply a graphic method of initiating a distributed query. There's no way to drag a linked server or remote table into the Query Designer. However, the distributed query can be entered manually in the SQL pane, as shown in Figure 15-5, and then executed as a query.

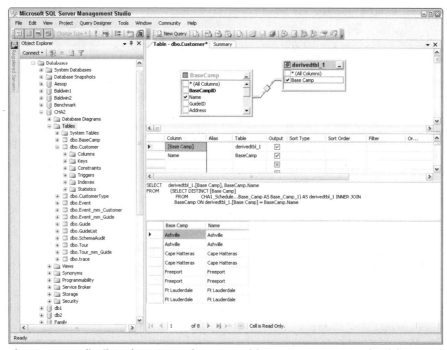

Figure 15-5: A distributed query may be executed from Management Studio if the distributed query source is manually entered in the SQL pane ([XPS].Family.dbo.Person).

Distributed Views

Views are saved SQL `select` statements. While I don't recommend building a client/server application based on views, they are useful for ad hoc queries. Because most users (and even developers) are unfamiliar with the various methods of performing distributed queries, wrapping a distributed query inside a view might be a good idea.

Local-Distributed Queries

A local-distributed query sounds like an oxymoron, but it's a query that pulls the external data into SQL Server and then processes the query at the local SQL Server. Because the processing occurs at the local SQL Server, local-distributed queries use T-SQL syntax and are sometimes called T-SQL distributed queries.

Using the Four-Part Name

If the data is in another SQL Server, a complete four-part name is required:

```
Server.Database.Schma.ObjectName
```

The four-part name may be used in any `select` or data-modification query. On my writing computer is a second instance of SQL Server called `[XPS\Yukon]`. The object's owner name is required if the query accesses an external SQL Server.

The following query retrieves the `Person` table from the `SQL2` instance:

```
SELECT LastName, FirstName
  FROM [XPS\Yukon].Family.dbo.person
```

Result:

```
LastName          FirstName
----------------  ----------------
Halloway          Kelly
Halloway          James
```

When performing an `insert`, `update`, or `delete` command as a distributed query, either the four-part name or a distributed query function must be substituted for the table name. For example, the following SQL code, extracted from the `CHA2_Convert.sql` script that populates the CHA2 sample database, uses the four-part name as the source for an `insert` command. The query retrieves base camps from the Excel spreadsheet and inserts them into SQL Server:

```
INSERT BaseCamp(Name)
  SELECT DISTINCT [Base Camp]
    FROM CHA1_Schedule...[Base_Camp]
    WHERE [Base Camp] IS NOT NULL
```

Tip   If you've already executed `CHA2_Convert.sql` and populated your copy of CHA2, then you may want to re-execute `CHA2_Create.sql` so that you'll start with an empty database.

As another example of using the four-part name for a distributed query, the following code updates the Family database on the second SQL Server instance:

```
UPDATE [Noli\SQL2].Family.dbo.Person
  SET LastName = 'Wilson'
  WHERE PersonID = 1
```

OpenDataSource()

Using the `OpenDataSource()` function is functionally the same as using a four-part name to access a linked server, except that the `OpenDataSource()` function defines the link within the function instead of referencing a pre-defined linked server. While defining the link in code bypasses the linked server requirement, if the link location changes, then the change will affect every query that uses `OpenDataSource()`. In addition, `OpenDataSource()` won't accept variables as parameters.

The `OpenDataSource()` function is substituted for a server in the four-part name and may be used within any DML statement.

The syntax for the `OpenDataSource()` function seems simple enough:

```
OPENDATASOURCE ( provider_name, init_string )
```

However, there's more to it than the first appearance betrays. The `init` string is a semicolon-delimited string containing several parameters (the exact parameters used depend on the external data source). The potential parameters within the `init` string include data source, location, extended properties, connection timeout, user ID, password, and catalog. The `init` string must define the entire external data-source connection, and the security context, within a function. No quotes are required around the parameters within the `init` string. The common error committed in building `OpenDataSource()` distributed queries is mixing the commas and semicolons.

If `OpenDataSource()` is connecting to another SQL Server using Windows, authentication delegation via Kerberos security is required.

A relatively straightforward example of the `OpenDataSource()` function is using it as a means of accessing a table within another SQL Server instance:

```
SELECT FirstName, Gender
  FROM OPENDATASOURCE(
        'SQLOLEDB',
        'Data Source=NOLI\SQL2;User ID=Joe;Password=j'
        ).Family.dbo.Person;
```

Result:

```
FirstName        Gender
---------------- ------
Adam             M
Alexia           F
```

The following example of a distributed query that uses `OpenDataSource()` references the Cape Hatteras Adventures sample database. Because an Access location contains only one database and the tables don't require the owner to specify the table, the database and owner are omitted from the four-part name:

```
SELECT ContactFirstName, ContactLastName
  FROM OPENDATASOURCE(
     'Microsoft.Jet.OLEDB.4.0',
     'Data Source =
        C:\SQLServerBible\CHA1_Customers.mdb'
      )...Customers;
```

Result:

```
ContactFirstName    ContactLastName
------------------  --------------------
Neal                Garrison
Melissa             Anderson
Gary                Quill
```

To illustrate using `OpenDataSource()` in an update query, the following query example will update any rows inside the `CHA1_Schedule.xls` Excel 2000 spreadsheet. A named range was previously defined as `Tours '=Sheet1!$E$5:$E$24'`, which now appears to the SQL query as a table within the data source. Rather than update an individual spreadsheet cell, this query performs an `update` operation that affects every row in which the tour column is equal to `Gauley River Rafting` and updates the `Base Camp` column to the value `Ashville`.

The distributed SQL Server query will use OLE DB to call the Jet engine, which will open the Excel spreadsheet. The `OpenDataSource()` function supplies only the server name in a four-part name; as with Access, the database and owner values are omitted:

```
UPDATE OpenDataSource(
    'Microsoft.Jet.OLEDB.4.0',
    'Data Source=C:\SQLServerBible\CHA1_Schedule.xls;
    User ID=Admin;Password=;Extended properties=Excel 5.0'
    )...Tour
  SET [Base Camp] = 'Ashville'
  WHERE Tour = 'Gauley River Rafting';
```

Figure 15-6 illustrates the query execution plan for the distributed update query, beginning at the right with a Remote Scan that returns all 19 rows from the Excel named range. The data is then processed within SQL Server. The details of the Remote Update logical operation reveal that the distributed update query actually updated only two rows.

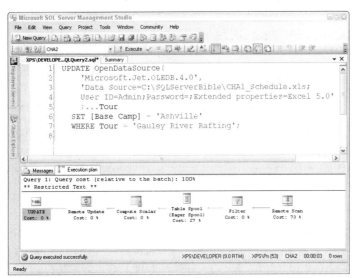

Figure 15-6: The query execution plan for the distributed query using OpenDataSource().

To complete the example, the following query reads from the same Excel spreadsheet and verifies that the update took place. Again, the `OpenDataSource()` function is only pointing the distributed query to an external server:

```
SELECT *
  FROM OpenDataSource(
    'Microsoft.Jet.OLEDB.4.0',
    'Data Source=C:\SQLServerBible\CHA1_Schedule.xls;
    User ID=Admin;Password=;Extended properties=Excel 5.0'
    )...Tour
  WHERE Tour = 'Gauley River Rafting';
```

Result:

```
Base Camp          Tour
----------------   -------------------------
Ashville           Gauley River Rafting
Ashville           Gauley River Rafting
```

Pass-Through Distributed Queries

A pass-through query executes a query at the external data source and returns the result to SQL Server. The primary reason for using a pass-through query is to reduce the amount of data being passed from the server (the external data source) and the client (SQL Server). Rather than pull a million rows into SQL Server so that it can use 25 of them, it may be better to select those 25 rows from the external data source.

Be aware that the pass-through query will use the query syntax of the external data source. If the external data source is Oracle or Access, PL/SQL or Access SQL must be used in the pass-through query.

In the case of a pass-through query that modifies data, the remote data type determines whether the update is performed locally or remotely:

✦ When another SQL Server is being updated, the remote SQL Server will perform the update.

✦ When non–SQL Server data is being updated, the data providers determine where the update will be performed. Often, the pass-through query merely selects the correct rows remotely. The selected rows are returned to SQL Server, modified inside SQL Server, and then returned to the remote data source for the update.

Two forms of local distributed queries exist, one for linked servers and one for external data sources defined in the query, and two forms of explicitly declaring pass-through distributed queries exist as well. OpenQuery() uses an established linked server, and OpenRowSet() declares the link within the query.

Using the Four-Part Name

If the distributed query is accessing another SQL Server, the four-part name becomes a *hybrid distributed query method*. Depending on the from clause and the where clause, SQL Server will attempt to pass as much of the query as possible to the external SQL Server to improve performance.

When building a complex distributed query using the four-part name, it's difficult to predict how much of the query SQL Server will pass through. I've seen SQL Server take a single query and depending on the where clause, the whole query was passed through, each table became a separate pass-through query, or only one table was pass-through.

Best Practice

Of the four distributed-query methods, the best two use the four-part name and the OpenQuery() function, respectively. Both offer the administrative benefit of pre-defined links, making the query more robust if the server configuration changes.

The decision between the four-part name and OpenQuery() will depend on the amount of data, the selection of data, and the performance of the server. I recommend that you test both methods and compare the query execution plans to determine the one that works best in your situation with your data. If both are similar, then use the four-part name to enable SQL Server to automatically optimize the distributed query.

OpenQuery()

For pass-through queries, the OpenQuery() function leverages a linked server, so it's the easiest to develop. It also handles changes in server configuration without changing the code.

The OpenQuery() function is used within the SQL DML statement as a table. The function accepts only two parameters: the name of the linked server and the pass-through query. The next query uses OpenQuery() to retrieve data from the CHA1_Schedule Excel spreadsheet:

```
SELECT *
  FROM OPENQUERY(CHA1_Schedule,
    'SELECT * FROM Tour WHERE Tour = "Gauley River Rafting"');
```

Result:

```
Tour                          Base Camp
-----------------------------  -----------------------------

Gauley River Rafting          Ashville
Gauley River Rafting          Ashville
```

As demonstrated in Figure 15-7, the OpenQuery() pass-through query requires almost no processing by SQL Server. The Remote Scan returns exactly two rows to SQL Server. The where clause is executed by the Jet engine as it reads from the Excel spreadsheet.

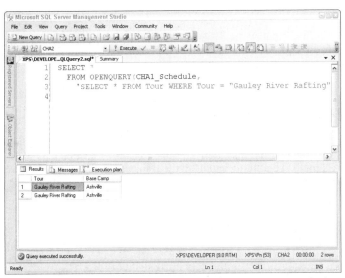

Figure 15-7: The distributed query using OpenQuery() returns only the rows selected by the where clause.

In the next example, the OpenQuery() requests from Jet engine that it extract only the two rows requiring the update. The actual update operation is performed in SQL Server, and the result is written back to the external data set. In effect, the pass-through query is performing only the select portion of the update command:

```
UPDATE OPENQUERY(CHA1_Schedule,
  'SELECT * FROM Tour WHERE Tour = "Gauley River Rafting"')
  SET [Base Camp] = 'Ashville'
  WHERE Tour = 'Gauley River Rafting';
```

OpenRowSet()

The OpenRowSet() function is the pass-through counterpart to the OpenDataSet() function. Both require the remote data source to be fully specified in the distributed query. OpenRowSet() adds a parameter to specify the pass-through query:

```
SELECT ContactFirstName, ContactLastName
  FROM OPENROWSET ('Microsoft.Jet.OLEDB.4.0',
  'C:\SQLServerBible\CHA1_Customers.mdb'; 'Admin';'',
  'SELECT * FROM Customers WHERE CustomerID = 1');
```

Result:

```
ContactFirstName     ContactLastName
-------------------  ----------------------
Tom                  Mercer
```

To perform an update using the OpenRowSet() function, use the function in place of the table being modified. The following code sample modifies the customer's last name in an Access database. The where clause of the update command is handled by the pass-through portion of the OpenRowSet() function:

```
UPDATE OPENROWSET ('Microsoft.Jet.OLEDB.4.0',
  'C:\SQLServerBible\CHA1_Customers.mdb'; 'Admin';'',
  'SELECT * FROM Customers WHERE CustomerID = 1')
  SET ContactLastName = 'Wilson';
```

New in 2005 Bulk operations are supported with OpenRowSet() using SQL Server 2005. This significantly improves performance.

Distributed Transactions

Transactions are key to data integrity. If the logical unit of work includes modifying data outside the local SQL server, a standard transaction is unable to handle the atomicity of the transaction. If a failure should occur in the middle of the transaction, a mechanism must be in place to roll back the partial work; otherwise, a partial transaction will be recorded and the database will be left in an inconsistent state.

Cross-Reference Chapter 51, "Managing Transactions, Locking, and Blocking," explores the ACID properties of a database and transactions.

Distributed Transaction Coordinator

SQL Server uses the Distributed Transaction Coordinator (DTC) to handle multiple server transactions, commits, and rollbacks. The DTC service uses a two-phase commit scheme for multiple server transactions. The two-phase commit ensures that every server is available and handling the transaction by performing the following steps:

1. Each server is sent a "prepare to commit" message.

2. Each server performs the first phase of the commit, ensuring that it is capable of committing the transaction.

3. Each server replies when it has finished preparing for the commit.

4. Only after every participating server has responded positively to the "prepare to commit" message is the actual commit message sent to each server.

If the logical unit of work only involves reading from the external SQL server, the DTC is not required. Only when remote updates are occurring is a transaction considered a distributed transaction.

The Distributed Transaction Coordinator is a separate service from SQL Server. DTC is started or stopped with the SQL Server Service Manager.

Only one instance of DTC runs per server regardless of how many SQL Server instances may be installed or running on that server. The actual service name is msdtc.exe and it consumes only about 2.5 MB of memory.

DTC must be running when a distributed transaction is initiated or the transaction will fail.

Developing Distributed Transactions

Distributed transactions are similar to local transactions with a few extensions to the syntax:

```
SET xact_abort on;
BEGIN DISTRIBUTED TRANSACTION;
```

In case of error, the xact_abort connection option will cause the current transaction, rather than only the current T-SQL statement, to be rolled back. The xact_abort on option is required for any distributed transactions accessing a remote SQL server and for most other OLE DB connections as well.

The begin distributed transaction command, which determines whether the DTC service is available, is not strictly required. If a transaction is initiated with only begin tran, the transaction is escalated to a distributed transaction and DTC is checked as soon as a distributed query is executed. It's considered a better practice to use begin distributed transaction so that DTC is checked at the beginning of the transaction. When DTC is not running, an 8501 error is raised automatically:

```
Server: Msg 8501, Level 16, State 3, Line 7
MSDTC on server 'XPS' is unavailable.
```

The following example demonstrates a distributed transaction between the local SQL Server and the second instance:

```
USE Family;
SET xact_abort on;
BEGIN DISTRIBUTED TRANSACTION;

  UPDATE Person
    SET LastName = 'Johnson2'
    WHERE PersonID = 10;

  UPDATE [Noli\SQL2].Family.dbo.Person
    SET LastName = 'Johnson2'
    WHERE PersonID = 10;

COMMIT TRANSACTION;
```

Rolling back a nested SQL Server local transaction rolls back all pending transactions. However, DTC uses true nested transactions, and rolling back a DTC transaction will roll back only the current transaction.

Monitoring Distributed Transactions

As a separate service installed as part of Windows Server 2003, Distributed Transaction Coordinator activity can be viewed from within the Windows operating system by selecting Control Panel ⇨ Administrative Tools ⇨ Component Services. Component Services provides both a list of current pending distributed transactions (see Figure 15-8) and an overview of DTC statistics (see Figure 15-9).

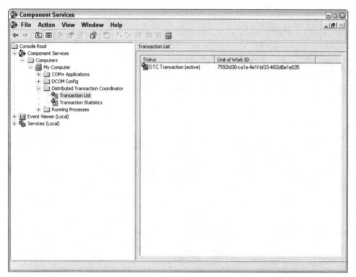

Figure 15-8: Component Services includes a list of current DTC transactions.

If a distributed transaction is having difficulty, it will likely be aborted. However, if the transaction is marked "In Doubt," forcibly committing, aborting, or forgetting the transaction using the context menu in Component Services may resolve the transaction.

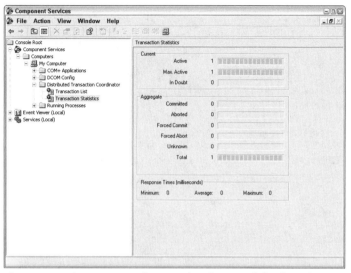

Figure 15-9: The current and accumulated count of distributed transactions as viewed in Component Services. The statistics begin at 0 when DTC is restarted.

Summary

Enterprise data tends to involve multiple platforms and locations. SQL Server's ability to leverage OLE DB and ODBC to perform distributed queries is a key factor in the success of many database projects, and knowing how to build distributed queries well is a necessary component in the database developer's skill set.

Beyond moving data directly with distributed queries, `select` is adept at modifying data. The next chapter moves into the action capabilities of `select`, adding the verbs `insert`, `update`, and `delete` to the power of `select`.

✦   ✦   ✦

Modifying Data

◆ ◆ ◆ ◆

In This Chapter

Inserting data from expressions, other result sets, and stored procedures

Updating data

Deleting data

Avoiding and solving complex data-modification problems

◆ ◆ ◆ ◆

Things change. Life moves on. Because the purpose of a database is to accurately represent reality, the data must change along with reality. For SQL programmers, that means inserting, updating, and deleting rows — using the basic Data Manipulation Language (DML) commands. However, these operations aren't limited to writing single rows of data. Working with SQL means thinking in terms of data sets. The process of modifying data with SQL draws upon the entire range of SQL Server data-retrieval capabilities — the powerful `select`, joins, full-text searches, subqueries, and views.

Best Practice

The SQL `insert`, `update`, and `delete` commands are really verb extensions of the basic `select` command. The full potential of the `select` command lies within each data-modification operation. Even when modifying data, you should think in terms of sets, rather than single rows.

This chapter is all about modifying data within SQL Server using the `insert`, `update`, and `delete` SQL commands. Modifying data raises issues that need to be addressed, or at least considered. Inserting primary keys requires special methods. Table constraints may interfere with the data modification. Referential integrity demands that some `delete` operations cascade to other related tables. This chapter will help you understand these concerns and offer some ways of dealing with them. Because these potential obstacles affect `insert`, `update`, and, to some degree, `delete`, they are addressed in their own sections after the sections devoted to the individual commands.

Cross-Reference

The ACID database properties (Atomic, Consistent, Isolated, and Durable) are critical to the modification of data. For many databases, SQL Server's default transactional control is sufficient. However, misapplied transaction locking and blocking is one of the top four causes of poor performance. Chapter 51, "Managing Transactions, Locking, and Blocking", digs into SQL Server's architecture and explains how data modifications occur within transactions to meet the ACID requirements, and how SQL Server manages data locks.

Data-modification commands may be submitted to SQL Server from any one of several interfaces. This chapter is concerned more with the strategy and use of the `insert`, `update`, and `delete` commands than with the interface used to submit a given command to SQL Server.

Two main interfaces are provided with SQL Server Management Studio for submitting SQL commands: Query Designer and Query Editor. Query Editor, while lacking the visual representation of joins and columns, has a richer set of features for working with T-SQL commands. Query Designer has the advantage of enabling you to build data-manipulation commands both visually and in code, as shown in Figure 16-1. Either interface is suitable for learning data-modification SQL commands, but because Query Editor is better for working with SQL scripts, I recommend you use Query Editor as you work through this chapter.

Cross-Reference   For more details on using Management Studio's Query Designer see Chapter 6, "Using Management Studio."

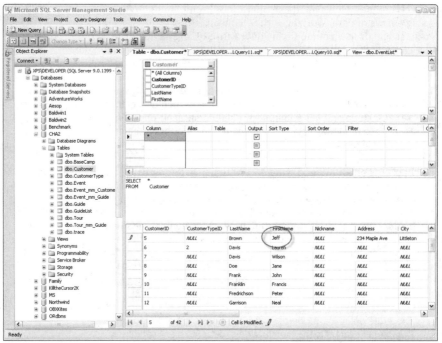

Figure 16-1: Management Studio's Query Designer is well suited to modifying data. Here I've changed the name to "Jeff" in the result pane.

Inserting Data

SQL offers four forms of `insert` and `select`/`into` as the primary methods of inserting data (as shown in Table 16-1). The most basic method simply inserts a row of data, while the most complex builds a data set from a complex `select` statement and creates a table from the result.

Table 16-1: Insert Forms

Insert Form	Description
insert/values	Inserts a single row of values; commonly used to insert data from a user interface
insert/select	Inserts a result set; commonly used to manipulate sets of data
insert/exec	Inserts the results of a stored procedure; used for complex data manipulation
insert default	Creates a new row with all defaults; used for pre-populating pigeonhole data rows
select/into	Creates a new table from the result set of a select statement

Each of these insert forms is useful for a unique task, often depending on the source of the data being inserted.

Cross-Reference   SQL Server complements the SQL insert commands with other tools to aid in moving large amounts of data or performing complex data conversions. The venerable Bulk Copy Wizard and the Copy Database Wizard are introduced in Chapter 35, "Transferring Databases." The Copy Database Wizard actually creates a simple Integration Services package. Chapter 42, "ETL with Integration Services" details IS, a very powerful tool that can move and manipulate large sets of data between/among nearly any data sources.

When inserting new data, primary keys must be generated to identify the new rows. While identity columns and GUIDs both make excellent primary keys, each requires special handling during the insertion of rows. This section covers how to create identity-column values and GUIDs.

Inserting One Row of Values

The simplest and most direct method of inserting data is the insert/values method. Because this form accepts a single set of values, it's limited to inserting data one row at a time. User interfaces tend to accept one row of data at a time, so this is the preferred method for inserting data from a user interface:

```
INSERT [INTO] owner.Table [(columns,...)]
   VALUES (value,...)
```

Building an insert/values statement is pretty straightforward, although you do have a few options. The into keyword is optional and is commonly ignored. The key to building an insert statement is getting the columns listed correctly and ensuring that the data type of the value is valid for the inserted column.

When the values are inserted into a new row, each value corresponds to an insert column. The insert columns may be in any order — the order of the columns within the table is irrelevant — as long as the insert columns and the value columns in the SQL insert command are in the same order.

The file Ch 16-Modifying Data.sql on www.SQLServerBible.com contains all the sample code for this chapter. Additional examples of data-modification statements may be found in any of the sample database "populate" scripts, or in the stored procedures of the OBX Kites sample database.

The following insert commands reference the columns in varying order:

```
USE CHA2

INSERT INTO dbo.Guide (LastName, FirstName, Qualifications)
  VALUES ('Smith', 'Dan', 'Diver, Whitewater Rafting')

INSERT INTO dbo.Guide (FirstName, LastName, Qualifications)
  VALUES ('Jeff', 'Davis', 'Marine Biologist, Diver')

INSERT INTO dbo.Guide (FirstName, LastName)
  VALUES ('Tammie', 'Commer')
```

The following select command verifies the insert:

```
SELECT * FROM dbo.Guide
```

Result (your result may be different depending on the data loaded into the database):

```
GuideID  LastName    FirstName    Qualifications
-------  ----------  -----------  -----------------------------
1        Smith       Dan          Diver, Whitewater Rafting
2        Davis       Jeff         Marine Biologist, Diver
3        Commer      Tammie       NULL
```

Not every column in the table has to be listed, but if a column is listed, then a value has to be available for the insert command. The third insert statement in the previous sample code left off the qualifications column. The insert operation worked nonetheless, and inserted a null into the omitted column.

If the Qualifications column had default constraint, the default value would have been inserted instead of the null. When a column has both no default and a Not Null constraint, and when no value is provided in the insert statement, the insert operation will fail. (There's more information about inserting defaults and nulls in the section "Potential Data-Modification Obstacles" later in this chapter.)

It's possible to explicitly force the insert of a default without knowing the default value. If the keyword DEFAULT is provided in the value-column list, SQL Server will store the default value for the column. This is a good practice because it documents the intention of the code, rather than leave the code blank and assume the default.

Explicitly listing the columns is a good idea. It prevents an error if the table schema changes, and it helps document the insert. However, the insert-column list is optional. In this case, the values are inserted into the table according to the order of the columns in the table (ignoring an identity column). It's critical that every table column receive valid data from the value list. Omitting a column in the value list will cause the insert operation to fail.

You learned earlier that when the columns are explicitly listed within the insert/values command, an identity column can't receive a value. Similarly, the identity column is also ignored in the value list when the columns are assumed. The rest of the values are in the same order as the columns of the Guide table, as follows:

```
INSERT Guide
   VALUES ('Jones', 'Lauren',
      'First Aid, Rescue/Extraction','6/25/59','4/15/01')
```

To view the inserted data, the following select command pulls data from the Guide table:

```
SELECT GuideID, LastName, FirstName, Qualifications
   FROM dbo.Guide
```

Result:

```
GuideID   LastName    FirstName   Qualifications
--------  ----------  ----------- ----------------------------
1         Smith       Dan         Diver, Whitewater Rafting
2         Davis       Jeff        Marine Biologist, Diver
3         Commer      Tammie      NULL
4         Jones       Lauren      First Aid, Rescue/Extraction
```

So far in the sample code, values have been hard-coded string literals. Alternately, the value could be returned from an expression. This is useful when a data type requires conversion, or when data need to be altered, calculated, or concatenated:

```
INSERT dbo.Guide (FirstName, LastName, Qualifications)
   VALUES ('Greg', 'Wilson',
            'Rock Climbing' + ', ' + 'First Aid')
```

The next select statement verifies Greg's insert:

```
Select * FROM dbo.Guide
```

Result:

```
GuideID   LastName    FirstName   Qualifications
--------  ----------  ----------- ----------------------------
1         Smith       Dan         Diver, Whitewater Rafting
2         Davis       Jeff        Marine Biologist, Diver
3         Commer      Tammie      NULL
4         Jones       Lauren      First Aid, Rescue/Extraction
5         Wilson      Greg        Rock Climbing, First Aid
(5 row(s) affected)
```

When the data to be inserted, usually in the form of variables sent from the user interface, is known, inserting using the insert/values form is the best insert method. However, this method isn't very dynamic. If data already exists in the database, the most efficient and flexible method is using the insert/select form.

Inserting a Result Set from Select

Data may be moved and massaged from one result set into a table by means of the insert/select statement. The real power of this method is that the select command can pull data from nearly anywhere and reshape it to fit the current needs. It's this flexibility the `insert/select` statement exploits. Because `select` can return an infinite number of rows, this form can insert an infinite number of rows. The syntax is as follows:

```
INSERT [INTO] owner.Table
  SELECT columns
    FROM data sources
    [WHERE conditions]
```

Cross-Reference

For a comprehensive discussion of the `select` portion of this command, turn to Chapter 7, "Understanding Basic Query Flow" and the rest of Part II, "Manipulating Data with Select."

As with the `insert/values` statement, the data columns must line up and the data types must be valid. If the optional insert columns are ignored, every table column (except an identity column) must be populated in the table order.

The following code sample uses the OBX Kites database. It selects all the guides from the Cape Hatteras Adventures database and inserts them into the OBX Kites `Contact` table. The name columns are pulled from the `Guide` table, while the company name is a string literal (note that the `Guide` table is specified by means of a three-part name, `database.owner.table`):

```
USE OBXKites
-- Using a fresh copy of OBXKites without population


INSERT dbo.Contact (FirstName, ContactCode, LastName, CompanyName)
  SELECT FirstName, LastName, GuideID, 'Cape Hatteras Adv.'
    FROM CHA2.dbo.Guide
```

To verify the insert, the following `select` statement reads the data from the `Contact` table:

```
SELECT FirstName AS First, LastName AS Last, CompanyName
  FROM dbo.Contact
```

Result:

```
First      Last       CompanyName
---------  ---------  -----------------------
Dan        Smith      Cape Hatteras Adv.
Jeff       Davis      Cape Hatteras Adv.
Tammie     Commer     Cape Hatteras Adv.
Lauren     Jones      Cape Hatteras Adv.
Greg       Wilson     Cape Hatteras Adv.

(5 row(s) affected)
```

The key to using the `insert/select` statement is selecting the correct result set. It's a good idea to run the `select` statement by itself to test the result set prior to executing the insert. Measure twice, cut once.

Inserting the Result Set from a Stored Procedure

The `insert/exec` form of the `insert` operation pulls data from a stored procedure and inserts it into a table. Behind these inserts are the full capabilities of T-SQL. The basic function is the same as that of the other insert forms. The columns have to line up between the `insert` columns and the stored-procedure result set. Here's the basic syntax of the `insert/exec` command:

```
INSERT [INTO] owner.Table [(Columns)]
   EXEC StoredProcedure Parameters
```

Be careful, though, because stored procedures can easily return multiple record sets, in which case the `insert` attempts to pull data from each of the result sets, and the columns from every result set must line up with the insert columns.

Cross-Reference

For more about programming stored procedures, refer to Chapter 21, "Developing Stored Procedures."

The following code sample builds a stored procedure that returns the first and last names of all guides from both the Cape Hatteras Adventures database and Microsoft's Northwind sample database from SQL Server 2000. Next, the code creates a table as a place to insert the result sets. Once the stored procedure and the receiving table are in place, the sample code performs the `insert/exec` statement:

```
Use CHA2

CREATE PROC ListGuides
AS
   SET NOCOUNT ON
   -- result set 1
   SELECT  FirstName, LastName
     FROM dbo.Guide
   -- result set 1
   SELECT  FirstName, LastName
     FROM northwind.dbo.employees
   RETURN
```

When the `ListGuides` stored procedure is executed, two result sets should be produced:

```
Exec ListGuides
```

Result:

```
FirstName                      LastName
-----------------------        -----------------------
Dan                            Smith
Jeff                           Davis
Tammie                         Commer
Lauren                         Jones
Wilson                         Greg

FirstName   LastName
----------  --------------------
Nancy       Davolio
Andrew      Fuller
Janet       Leverling
Margaret    Peacock
Steven      Buchanan
Michael     Suyama
```

```
Robert     King
Laura      Callahan
Anne       Dodsworth
```

The following DDL command creates a table that matches the structure of the procedure's result sets:

```
CREATE TABLE dbo.GuideSample
  (FirstName VARCHAR(50),
   LastName VARCHAR(50) )
```

With the situation properly set up, here's the `insert/exec` command:

```
INSERT dbo.GuideSample (FirstName, LastName)
  EXEC ListGuides
```

A `select` command can read the data and verify that 14 rows were inserted:

```
SELECT * FROM dbo.GuideSample
```

Result:

```
FirstName               LastName
-------------------     -------------------
Dan                     Smith
Jeff                    Davis
Tammie                  Commer
Lauren                  Jones
Wilson                  Greg
Nancy                   Davolio
Andrew                  Fuller
Janet                   Leverling
Margaret                Peacock
Steven                  Buchanan
Michael                 Suyama
Robert                  King
Laura                   Callahan
Anne                    Dodsworth
```

`Insert/exec` does require more work than `insert/values` or `insert/select`, but because the stored procedure can contain complex logic, it's the most powerful of the three.

Caution The `insert/exec` and `select/into` forms will not insert data into table variables. Table variables are covered in Chapter 18, "Programming with Transact-SQL."

Creating a Default Row

SQL includes a special form of the `insert` command that creates a new row with only default values. The only parameter of the new row is that the table name, data, and column names are neither required nor accepted. The syntax is very simple, as this code sample shows:

```
INSERT owner.Table DEFAULT VALUES
```

I have never used this form of `insert` in any real-world applications. Nevertheless, if you ever need to pre-populate a table with numerous default rows, `insert default` may be of use.

Creating a Table While Inserting Data

The last method of inserting data is a variation on the `select` command. The `into select` option will take the results of a `select` statement and create a new table containing the results. `Select/into` is often used during data conversions and within utilities that must dynamically work with a variety of source-table structures. The full syntax includes every `select` option. Here's an abbreviated syntax to highlight the function of the `into` option:

```
SELECT Columns
  INTO NewTable
  FROM DataSources
  [WHERE conditions]
```

The data structure of the newly created table might be less of an exact replication of the original table structure than expected because the new table structure is based on a combination of the original table and the result set of the `select` statement. String lengths and numerical digit lengths may change. If the `select/into` command is pulling data from only one table and the `select` statement contains no data-type conversion functions, there's a good chance that the table columns and null settings will remain intact. However, keys, constraints, and indexes will be lost.

`Select/into` is a bulk-logged operation, similar to `bulk insert` and `bulk copy`. Bulk-logged operations may enable SQL Server to quickly move data into tables by skipping the transaction-logging process (depending on the database's recovery model). Therefore, the database options and recovery model affect `select/into` and the other bulk-logged operations. If the database-recovery model is other than full, the `select/into` operation will not be logged.

Cross-Reference For more about `bulk insert` and `bulk copy`, refer to Chapter 19, "Performing Bulk Operations." For details on recovery models refer to Chapter 36, "Recovery Planning."

The following code sample demonstrates the `select/into` command as it creates the new table `GuideList` by extracting data from `Guide` (some results abridged):

```
USE CHA2

-- sample code for setting the bulk-logged behavior
Alter DATABASE CHA2 SET RECOVERY FULL
SP_DBOPTION 'CHA2', 'select into/bulkcopy', 'TRUE'

-- the select/into statement
SELECT *
  INTO dbo.GuideList
  FROM dbo.Guide
  ORDER BY Lastname, FirstName
```

The `sp_help` command can display the structure of a table. Here it's being used to verify the structure that was created by the `select/into` command:

```
sp_help GuideList
```

Result (some columns abridged):

```
Name          Owner     Type           Created_datetime
------------  --------  -------------  -----------------------
```

```
GuideList     dbo      user table    2001-08-01 16:30:02.937


Column_name         Type       Length    Prec  Scale Nullable
----------------    --------   --------   ----- ----- --------
GuideID             int        4          10    0     no
LastName            varchar    50                     no
FirstName           varchar    50                     no
Qualifications      varchar    2048                   yes
DateOfBirth         datetime   8                      yes
DateHire            datetime   8                      yes

Identity           Seed      Increment   Not For Replication
---------------    -------   ---------   -------------------------
GuideID            1         1           0


RowGuidCol
--------------------------
No rowguidcol column defined.


Data_located_on_filegroup
--------------------------
PRIMARY

The object does not have any indexes.

No constraints have been defined for this object.

No foreign keys reference this table.
No views with schema binding reference this table.
```

The following insert adds a new row to test the identity column created by the select/into:

```
INSERT Guidelist (LastName, FirstName, Qualifications)
  VALUES('Nielsen', 'Paul', 'trainer')
```

To view the data that was inserted using the select/into command and the row that was just added with the insert/values command, the following select statement extracts data from the GuideList table:

```
SELECT GuideID, LastName, FirstName
  FROM dbo.GuideList
```

Result:

```
GuideID     LastName      FirstName
---------   ----------    -------------------------
12          Nielsen       Paul
7           Atlas         Sue
11          Bistier       Arnold
3           Commer        Tammie
2           Davis         Jeff
10          Fletcher      Bill
5           Greg          Wilson
4           Jones         Lauren
1           Smith         Dan
```

Developing a Data Style Guide

There are potential data troubles that go beyond data types, nullability, and check constraints. Just as MS Word's spelling checker and grammar checker can weed out the obvious errors but also create poor (or libelous) literature, a database can only protect against gross logical errors. Publishers use manuals of style and style guides for consistency. For example, should Microsoft be referred to as MS, Microsoft Corp., or Microsoft Corporation in a book or article? The publisher's chosen style manual provides the answer.

Databases can also benefit from a data style guide that details your organization's preferences about how data should be formatted. Do phone numbers include parentheses around the area codes? Are phone extensions indicated by "x." or "ext."?

One way to begin developing a style guide is to spend some time just looking at the data and observing the existing inconsistencies. Having done that, try to reach a consensus about a common data style. Picking up a copy of *The Chicago Manual of Style* will also provide some ideas. There's no magical right or wrong style — the goal is simply data consistency.

In this case, the `select/into` command retained the column lengths and null settings. The identity column was also carried over to the new table, although this may not always be the case. I recommend that you build tables manually, or at least carefully check the data structures created by `select/into`.

Select/into can serve many useful functions:

✦ If zero rows are selected from a table, `select/into` will create a new table with only the data schema.

✦ If `select` reorders the columns, or includes the `cast()` function, the new table will retain the data within a modified data schema.

✦ When combined with a `union` query, `select/into` can combine data from multiple tables vertically. The `into` goes in the first `select` statement of a `union` query.

✦ Select/into is especially useful for denormalizing tables. The `select` statement can pull from multiple tables and create a new flat-file table.

Caution

One caveat concerning `select/into` and development style is that the `select/into` statement should not replace the use of joins or views. When the new table is created it's a snapshot in time — a second copy of the data. Databases containing multiple copies of old data sets are a sure sign of trouble. If you need to denormalize data for ad hoc analysis, or to pass to a user, creating a view is likely a better alternative.

Updating Data

Without being overly dramatic, SQL's `update` command is an incredibly powerful tool. What used to take dozens of lines of code with multiple nested loops now takes a single statement. What's even cooler is that SQL is not a true command language — it's a declarative language. The SQL code is only describing to the Query Optimizer what you want to do. The Query Optimizer then develops a cost-based, optimized query execution plan to accomplish the task. It figures out which tables to fetch and in which order, how to merge the joins, and which indexes to use. It does this based on several factors, including the current data-population statistics, the indexes available and how they relate to the data population within the table, and table sizes. The Query Optimizer even considers current CPU performance, memory capacity, and hard-drive performance when designing the plan. Writing code to perform the update row by row could never result in that level of optimization.

Updating a Single Table

The update command in SQL is straightforward and simple. The update command can update one column of one row in a table, or every column in every row in the updated table, but the optional from clause enables that table be a part of a complete complex data source with all the power of the SQL select.

Here's how the update command works:

```
UPDATE dbo.Table
  SET column = value or expression or column,
    column = value...
  [FROM  data sources]
  [WHERE conditions]
```

The update command can update multiple rows, but only one table. The set keyword is used to modify data in any column in the table to a new value. The new value can be a hard-coded string literal, a variable, an expression, or even another column from the data sources listed in the from portion of the SQL update statement.

Cross-Reference   For a comprehensive listing of expression possibilities see Chapter 8, "Using Expressions and Scalar Functions."

The where clause is vital to any update statement. Without it the entire table is updated. If a where clause is present, then every row not filtered out by the where clause is updated. Be sure to check and double-check the where clause. Again, measure twice, cut once.

The following sample update resembles a typical real-life operation and will alter the value of one column for a single row. The best way to perform a single-row update is to filter the update operation by referencing the primary key:

```
USE CHA2

UPDATE dbo.Guide
  SET Qualifications = 'Spelunking, Cave Diving,
First Aid, Navigation'
  Where GuideID = 6
```

The following select statement confirms the preceding update command:

```
SELECT GuideID, LastName, Qualifications
  FROM dbo.Guide
  WHERE GuideID = 6
```

Result:

```
GuideID     LastName                Qualifications
----------- ----------------------  ----------------
6           Bistier                 Spelunking, Cave Diving,
                                      First Aid, Navigation
```

Performing Global Search and Replaces

Cleaning up bad data is a common database developer task. Fortunately, SQL includes a `replace()` function, which when combined with the `update` command can serve as a global search and replace.

In this code sample, which references the Family sample database, every occurrence of "ll" in the `LastName` column is updated to "qua":

```
Use Family

Update Person
   Set LastName = Replace(Lastname, 'll', 'qua')
```

The following `select` statement examines the result of the `replace()` function:

```
Select lastname from Person
```

Result (abbreviated):

```
lastname
----------------
Haquaoway
Haquaoway
Miquaer
Miquaer
Haquaoway
...
```

Referencing Multiple Tables While Updating Data

A more powerful function of the SQL `update` command is setting a column to an expression that can refer to the same column, other columns, or even other tables.

While expressions are certainly available within a single-table update, expressions often need to reference data outside the updated table. The optional `from` clause enables joins between the table being updated and other data sources. Only one table can be updated, but when the table is joined to the corresponding rows from the joined tables, the data from the other columns is available within the `update` expressions.

One way to envision the `from` clause is to picture the joins merging all the tables into a new superwide result set. Then the rest of the SQL statement sees only that new result set. While that is what's happening in the `from` clause, the actual `update` operation is functioning not on the new result set, but only on the declared `update Table`.

Caution

The `update from` syntax is a T-SQL extension and not standard ASNI SQL 92. If the database will possibly be ported to another database platform in the future, use a subquery to update the correct rows:

```
DELETE FROM Table1 a
   WHERE EXISTS (SELECT *
                    FROM Table2 b
                    WHERE
                       EMPL_STATUS = 'A'
                    AND
                       a.EMPLID = b.EMPLID
                 )
```

For a real-life example, suppose all employees will soon be granted a generous across-the-board raise (OK, so it's not a real-life example) based on department, time in the position, performance rating, and time with the company. If the percentage for each department is stored in the Department table, SQL can adjust the salary for every employee with a single update statement by joining the Employee table with the Department table and pulling the Department raise factor from the joined table. Assume the formula is as follows:

```
2 + (((Years in Company * .1) + (Months in Position * .02)
  + ((PerformanceFactor * .5 ) if over 2))
  * Department RaiseFactor)
```

The sample code will set up the scenario by creating a couple of tables, populating them, and testing the formula before finally performing the update:

```
USE Tempdb

CREATE TABLE dbo.Dept (
  DeptID INT IDENTITY NOT NULL PRIMARY KEY NONCLUSTERED,
  DeptName VARCHAR(50) NOT NULL,
  RaiseFactor NUMERIC(4,2)
    )
  ON [Primary]
go

Create  TABLE dbo.Employee (
  EmployeeID INT IDENTITY NOT NULL PRIMARY KEY NONCLUSTERED,
  DeptID INT FOREIGN KEY REFERENCES Dept,
  LastName VARCHAR(50) NOT NULL,
  FirstName VARCHAR(50) NOT NULL,
  Salary INT,
  PerformanceRating NUMERIC(4,2),
  DateHire DATETIME,
  DatePosition DATETIME
    )
  ON [Primary]
go
 -- build the sample data
INSERT dbo.Dept VALUES ('Engineering', 1.2)
INSERT dbo.Dept VALUES ('Sales',.8)
INSERT dbo.Dept VALUES ('IT',2.5)
INSERT dbo.Dept VALUES ('Manufacturing',1.0)
go
INSERT dbo.Employee
  VALUES( 1,'Smith','Sam',54000, 2.0,'1/1/97','4/1/2001' )
INSERT dbo.Employee
  VALUES( 1,'Nelson','Slim',78000,1.5,'9/1/88','1/1/2000' )
INSERT dbo.Employee
  VALUES( 2,'Ball','Sally',45000,3.5,'2/1/99','1/1/2001' )
INSERT dbo.Employee
  VALUES( 2,'Kelly','Jeff',85000,2.4,'10/1/83','9/1/1998' )
INSERT dbo.Employee
  VALUES( 3,'Guelzow','Jo',120000,4.0,'7/1/95','6/1/2001' )
INSERT dbo.Employee
  VALUES( 3,'Anderson','Missy',95000,1.8,'2/1/99','9/1/97' )
```

```
INSERT dbo.Employee
  VALUES( 4,'Reagan','Frank',75000,2.9,'4/1/00','4/1/2000' )
INSERT dbo.Employee
  VALUES( 4,'Adams','Hank',34000,3.2,'9/1/98','9/1/1998' )
```

Assuming 5/1/2002 is the effective date of the raise, this query tests the sample data:

```
SELECT LastName, Salary,
  DateDiff(yy, DateHire, '5/1/2002') as YearsCo,
  DateDiff(mm, DatePosition, '5/1/2002') as MonthPosition,
  CASE
    WHEN Employee.PerformanceRating >= 2
      THEN Employee.PerformanceRating
    ELSE 0
  END as Performance,
  Dept.RaiseFactor AS 'Dept'
  FROM dbo.Employee
  JOIN dbo.Dept
    ON Employee.DeptID = Dept.DeptID
```

Result:

```
LastName   Salary  YearsCo MonthPosition Performance Dept
--------   ------- ------- ------------- ----------- ------
Smith      54000   5       13            2.00        1.20
Nelson     78000   14      28            .00         1.20
Ball       45000   3       16            3.50        .80
Kelly      85000   19      44            2.40        .80
Guelzow    120000  7       11            4.00        2.50
Anderson   95000   3       56            .00         2.50
Reagan     75000   2       25            2.90        1.00
Adams      34000   4       44            3.20        1.00
```

Based on the sample data, the following query tests the formula that calculates the raise:

```
SELECT LastName,
  (2 + (((DateDiff(yy, DateHire, '5/1/2002') * .1)
  + (DateDiff(mm, DatePosition, '5/1/2002') * .02)
  + (CASE
      WHEN Employee.PerformanceRating >= 2
        THEN Employee.PerformanceRating
      ELSE 0
    END * .5 ))
  * Dept.RaiseFactor))/100 as EmpRaise
  FROM dbo.Employee
  JOIN dbo.Dept
    ON Employee.DeptID = Dept.DeptID
```

Result:

```
LastName              EmpRaise
--------------------  -------------------------
Smith                 .041120000
Nelson                .043520000
Ball                  .038960000
Kelly                 .051840000
```

```
Guelzow              .093000000
Anderson             .055500000
Reagan               .041500000
Adams                .048800000
```

With the data in place and the formulas verified, the `update` command is ready to adjust the salaries:

```
UPDATE Employee SET Salary = Salary * (1 +
  (2 + (((DateDiff(yy, DateHire, '5/1/2002') * .1)
  + (DateDiff(mm, DatePosition, '5/1/2002') * .02)
  + (CASE
      WHEN Employee.PerformanceRating >= 2
        THEN Employee.PerformanceRating
      ELSE 0
      END * .5 ))
   * Dept.RaiseFactor))/100 )
  FROM dbo.Employee
  JOIN dbo.Dept
    ON Employee.DeptID = Dept.DeptID
```

The next `select` statement views the fruits of the labor:

```
SELECT FirstName, LastName, Salary
    FROM Employee
```

Result:

```
FirstName    LastName                  Salary
-----------  ------------------------  -----------
Sam          Smith                     56220
Slim         Nelson                    81394
Sally        Ball                      46753
Jeff         Kelly                     89406
Dave         Guelzow                   131160
Missy        Anderson                  100272
Frank        Reagan                    78112
Hank         Adams                     35659
```

The final step of the exercise is to clean up the sample tables:

```
DROP TABLE dbo.Employee
DROP TABLE dbo.Dept
```

This sample code pulls together techniques from many of the previous chapters: creating and dropping tables, `case` expressions, `joins`, and date scalar functions, not to mention the inserts and updates from this chapter. The example is long because it demonstrates more than just the `update` statement. It also shows the typical process of developing a complex `update`, which includes the following:

1. **Checking the available data:** The first `select` joins `employee` and `dept`, and lists all the columns required for the formula.

2. **Testing the formula:** The second `select` is based on the initial `select` and assembles the formula from the required rows. From this data, a couple of rows can be hand-tested against the specs, and the formula verified.

3. **Performing the update:** Once the formula is constructed and verified, the formula is edited into an `update` statement and executed.

The SQL update command *is* powerful. I have replaced terribly complex record sets and nested loops that were painfully slow and error-prone with update statements and creative joins that worked well, and I have seen execution times reduced from minutes to a few seconds. I cannot overemphasize the importance of approaching the selection and updating of data in terms of data sets, rather than data rows.

Deleting Data

The delete command is dangerously simple. In its basic form, it deletes all the rows from a table; and because the delete command is a row-based operation, it doesn't require specifying any column names. The first from is optional, as are the second from and the where conditions. However, although the where clause is optional, it is the primary subject of concern when you're using the delete command. Here's an abbreviated syntax for the delete command:

```
DELETE FROM] owner.Table
  [FROM data sources]
  [WHERE condition(s)]
```

Notice that everything is optional except the actual delete command and the table name. The following command would delete all data from the product table — no questions asked and no second chances:

```
DELETE
  FROM OBXKites.dbo.Product
```

SQL Server has no inherent "undo" command. Once a transaction is committed, that's it. That's why the where clause is so important when you're deleting.

By far, the most common use of the delete command is to delete a single row. The primary key is usually the means of selecting the row:

```
USE OBXKites
DELETE FROM dbo.Product
  WHERE ProductID = 'DB8D8D60-76F4-46C3-90E6-A8648F63C0F0'
```

Referencing Multiple Tables While Deleting

The update command uses the from clause to join the updated table with other tables for more flexible row selection. The delete command uses the exact same technique. What makes it look confusing is that first optional from. To improve readability and consistency, I recommend that you omit the first from in your code.

For example, the following delete statement ignores the first from clause and uses the second from clause to join Product with ProductCategory so that the where clause can filter the delete based on the ProductCategoryName. This query removed all videos from the Product table:

```
DELETE Product
  FROM dbo.Product
  JOIN ProductCategory
    ON Procduct.ProductCategoryID
      = ProductCategory.ProductCategoryID
  WHERE ProductcategoryName = 'Video'
```

Caution   As with the `update` command's `from` clause, the `delete` command's second `from` clause is not an ANSI SQL standard. If portability is important to your project, use a subquery to reference additional tables.

Cascading Deletes

Referential integrity (RI) refers to the fact that no secondary row may point to a primary row unless that primary row does in fact exist. This means that an attempt to delete a primary row will fail if a foreign-key value somewhere points to that primary row.

Cross-Reference   For more information about referential integrity and when to use it, turn to Chapter 2, "Relational Database Modeling," and Chapter 17, "Implementing the Physical Database Schema."

RI will block any delete operation that would violate it. The way around this is to first delete the secondary rows that point to the primary row, and then delete the primary row. This technique is called *cascading the delete* to the lower level. In large databases the cascade might bounce down several levels before working its way back up to the original row being deleted.

Implementing cascading deletes manually is a lot of work. Because foreign-key constraints are checked before triggers, cascading-delete triggers don't work with SQL Server Declared Referential Integrity (DRI) via foreign keys. Therefore, not only will triggers have to handle the cascading delete, but they will have to perform RI checks as well.

Fortunately, SQL Server 2000 offers cascading deletes as a function of the foreign key. Cascading deletes may be enabled via Management Studio (as shown in Figure 16-2) or SQL code.

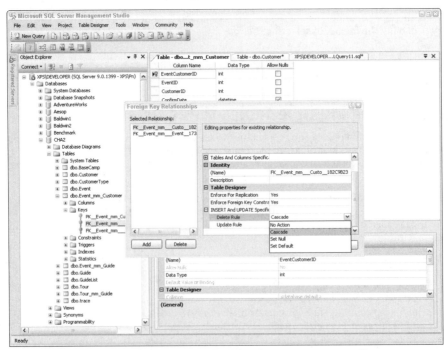

Figure 16-2: Setting foreign keys to cascade delete in Management Studio

The sample script that creates the Cape Hatteras Adventures version 2 database (CHA2_Create.sql) provides a good example of setting the cascade-delete option for referential integrity. In this case, if either the event or the guide is deleted, the rows in the event-guide many-to-many table are also deleted. The on delete cascade foreign-key option is what actually specifies the cascade action:

```
CREATE TABLE dbo.Event_mm_Guide (
  EventGuideID
    INT IDENTITY NOT NULL PRIMARY KEY NONCLUSTERED,
  EventID
    INT NOT NULL
    FOREIGN KEY REFERENCES dbo.Event ON DELETE CASCADE,
  GuideID
    INT NOT NULL
    FOREIGN KEY REFERENCES dbo.Guide ON DELETE CASCADE,
  LastName
    VARCHAR(50) NOT NULL,
  )
  ON [Primary]
```

As a caution, cascading deletes, or even referential integrity, are not suitable for every relationship. It depends on the permanence of the secondary row. If deleting the primary row makes the secondary row moot or meaningless, then cascading the delete makes good sense, but if the secondary row is still a valid row after the primary row is deleted, then referential integrity and cascading deletes would cause the database to break its representation of reality.

For a couple of examples of determining the usefulness of cascading delete from the Cape Hatteras Adventures database, if a tour is deleted, then all scheduled events for that tour become meaningless, as are the many-to-many schedule tables between event and customer, and between event and guide.

Conversely, a tour must have a base camp, so referential integrity is required on the Tour. BaseCampID foreign key. However, if a base camp is deleted, the tours originating from that base camp might still be valid (if they can be rescheduled to another base camp), so cascading a base-camp delete down to the tour is not a reasonable action. If RI is on and cascading deletes are off, a base camp with tours cannot be deleted until all tours for that base camp are either manually deleted or reassigned to other base camps.

Alternatives to Physically Deleting Data

Many developers choose to completely avoid deleting data. Instead, they build systems to remove the data from the user's view while retaining them for safekeeping. This can be done in several different ways:

✦ A logical-delete bit flag in the row may indicate that the row is deleted. This makes deleting or restoring a single row a straightforward matter of setting or clearing a bit. However, because a relational database involves multiple related tables, there's more work to it than that. All queries must check the logical-delete flag and filter out logically deleted rows. In addition, because the rows still physically exist in SQL Server, and the SQL Server referential-integrity system does not know about the logical-delete flag, custom referential integrity and cascading of logical deletes might also be required, depending on how far you want to take the logical-delete system. This method offers fast logical deletes but can slow down selects. Cascading logical deletes can become very complex, and restoring cascaded logical deletes can become a nightmare.

✦ Another alternative to physically deleting rows is to archive the deleted rows in a second table or database. This method is best implemented by a stored procedure that inserts the deleted rows into the archive location and then deletes them from the main production database.

This method offers several advantages. Data is physically removed from the database, so there's no need to artificially modify select queries. Using partitioned views, or a federated database scheme, makes archiving data easier by allowing queries to automatically gather data from multiple databases. Physically removing the data enables SQL Server referential integrity to remain in effect. In addition, the database is not burdened with unnecessary data. Retrieving archived data remains relatively straightforward, although using the archive method requires maintaining an archive location.

See Chapter 53, "Scaling Very Large Databases," for more on partitioned views, and all of Part 5, "Business Intelligence," contains strategies for warehousing and delivering archived data.

✦ The most complete alternative to deleting rows is using a full audit trail of all data modifications. An audit trail is not only useful for viewing a history of updates, but can be used for restoring deleted rows as well. Audit trails have their own cost in terms of complexity, performance, and storage space.

Chapter 24, "Exploring Advanced T-SQL Techniques," explains how to build triggers that perform cascading deletes, manage custom referential integrity, build audit trails, archive data, and logically delete rows.

Returning Modified Data

SQL Server 2005 can optionally return the modified data as a data set for further use. This can be useful when more work must be performed on the modified data, or to return the data to the front-end application to eliminate an extra round-trip to the server.

The capability to return results immediately without issuing another command may initially seem insignificant, but this new T-SQL feature will likely become a favorite for real-world problem solving.

The output clause can access the inserted and deleted virtual tables to select the data to be returned. Normally used only by triggers, inserted and deleted tables contain the before and after views to the transaction. The deleted virtual table stored the old data and the inserted virtual table stored the newly inserted or updated data. The output clause can select all the columns from these tables, or specify individual columns.

For more examples of the inserted and deleted table, turn to Chapter 23, "Creating DML Triggers."

Returning Data from an Insert

The insert command makes the inserted virtual table available. The following example, taken from earlier in this chapter, has been edited to include the output clause. The inserted virtual table has a picture of the new data being inserted and returns the data:

```
USE CHA2;
INSERT dbo.Guidelist (LastName, FirstName, Qualifications)
  OUTPUT Inserted.*
  VALUES('Nielsen', 'Paul','trainer')
```

Result:

GuideID	LastName	FirstName	Qualifications	DateOfBirth	DateHire
7	Nielsen	Paul	trainer	NULL	NULL

Returning Data from an Update

The output clause also works with updates and can return the before and/or after picture of the data. In this example, the deleted virtual table is being used to grab the original value while the inserted virtual table stores the new updated value. Only the Qualifications columns is returned:

```
USE CHA2;
UPDATE dbo.Guide
  SET Qualifications = 'Scuba'
  OUTPUT Deleted.Qualifications as OldQuals ,Inserted.Qualifications as NewQuals
  Where GuideID = 3
```

Result:

OldQuals	NewQuals
NULL	Scuba

Returning Data from a Delete

When deleting data, only the deleted table has any useful data to return:

```
DELETE dbo.Guide
  OUTPUT Deleted.GuideID, Deleted.LastName, Deleted.FirstName
  WHERE GuideID = 3
```

Result:

GuideID	LastName	FirstName
3	Wilson	Sam

Returning Data into a @Table Variable

For T-SQL developers, the output clause can return the data for use within a batch or stored procedure. The data is received into a table variable, which must already have been created. Although the syntax may seem similar to the insert...into syntax, it actually functions very differently.

In this example code, the output clause passes the results to a @DeletedGuides table variable:

```
DECLARE @DeletedGuides TABLE (
  GuideID INT,
  LastName VARCHAR(50),
```

```
   FirstName VARCHAR(50)
   );

DELETE dbo.Guide
  OUTPUT Deleted.GuideID, Deleted.LastName, Deleted.FirstName
  INTO @DeletedGuides
  WHERE GuideID = 2
```

Interim result:

```
(1 row(s) affected)
```

Continuing the batch . . .

```
SELECT * FROM @DeletedGuides
```

Result:

```
(1 row(s) affected)
GuideID     LastName    FirstName
----------- ----------- -----------------
2           Frank       Ken
```

Potential Data-Modification Obstacles

Even assuming that the logic is correct and that the data-modification command is in fact modifying the correct rows with the correct values, plenty can still go wrong. This section surveys several types of potential problems and explains how to avoid them.

As Table 16-2 illustrates, insert and update operations face more obstacles than delete operations because they are creating new data in the table that must pass multiple validation rules. The delete operation only removes data, so it is faced with only a few possible obstacles.

Table 16-2: Potential Data Modification Obstacles

Potential Problem	Insert Operation	Update Operation	Delete Operation
Data Type/Length	X	X	
Primary Key	X	X.	
Foreign Key	X	X	X
Unique Index	X	X	
Not Null and No Default	X	X	
Check Constraint	X	X	
Instead of Trigger	X	X	X
After Trigger	X	X	X
Non-Updatable Views	X	X	X
Views with Check Option	X	X	
Security	X	X	X

Data Type/Length Obstacles

Column data type/length may affect `insert` and `update` operations.

One of the first checks the new data must pass is that of data type and data length. Often, a data-type error is caused by missing or extra quotes. SQL Server is particular about implicit, or automatic, data-type conversion. Conversions that function automatically in other programming languages often fail in SQL Server, as shown in the following code sample:

```
USE OBXKites
INSERT Price (ProductID, Price, EffectiveDate)
    Values ('DB8D8D60-76F4-46C3-90E6-A8648F63C0F0',
            '15.00', 6/25/2002 )

Server: Msg 260, Level 16, State 1, Line 1
Disallowed implicit conversion from data type varchar
to data type money, table 'OBXKites.dbo.Price',
column 'Price'.
Use the CONVERT function to run this query.
```

The problem with the preceding code is the quotes around the new price value, which SQL Server doesn't automatically convert from string to numeric. If this is the problem, using the `cast()` or `convert()` function is the best means of handling the data

Cross-Reference

For more details about data types and tables refer to Chapter 17, "Implementing the Physical Database Schema." Data-type conversion and conversion scalar functions are discussed in Chapter 8, "Using Expressions and Scalar Functions."

Primary Key Obstacles

Primary keys may affect `insert` and `update` operations.

Primary keys, by definition, must be unique. Attempting to insert a primary key that's already in use will cause an error.

Technically speaking, updating a primary key to a value already in use will also cause an error. However, if you are following good design practices the primary key is meaningless to humans, and there should be no reason ever to update a primary key.

Updating a primary key may also break referential integrity, causing the `update` to fail. In this case, however, it's not a primary-key constraint that's the obstacle, but the foreign-key constraint that references the primary key.

Cross-Reference

For more information about the design of primary keys, refer to Chapter 2, "Relational Database Modeling." For details on creating primary keys, refer to 17, "Implementing the Physical Database Schema."

One particular issue related to inserting is the creation of primary-key values for the new rows. SQL Server provides two excellent means of generating primary keys: *identity columns* and *GUIDs*. Each method has its pros and cons, and its rules for safe handling.

Identity columns are SQL Server–generated incrementing integers. SQL Server generates them at the time of the insert and the SQL `insert` statement can't interfere with that process by supplying a value for the identity column.

The fact that identity columns refuse to accept data can be a serious issue if you're inserting existing data whose primary key is already referenced by secondary tables. In the Aesop's Fables sample database, for example, the primary keys are hard-coded into the `insert/value` statements in the populate scripts, much as the primary keys are already known during data conversions.

The solution is to use the `identity_insert` database option. When set to `on` it temporarily turns off the identity column and permits the insertion of data into an identity column. This means that the insert has to explicitly provide the primary-key value. The `identity_insert` option may only be set `on` for one table at a time within a database. The following SQL batch uses the `identity_insert` when supplying the primary key:

```
USE CHA2

-- attempt to insert into an identity column
INSERT dbo.Guide (GuideID, FirstName, LastName)
  VALUES (10, 'Bill', 'Fletcher')
```

Result:

```
Server: Msg 544, Level 16, State 1, Line 1
Cannot insert explicit value for identity column in table
'Guide' when IDENTITY_INSERT is set to OFF.
```

The next step in the batch sets the `identity_insert` option and attempts some more inserts:

```
SET IDENTITY_INSERT Guide On

INSERT Guide (GuideID, FirstName, LastName)
  VALUES (100, 'Bill', 'Mays')

INSERT dbo.Guide (GuideID, FirstName, LastName)
  VALUES (101, 'Sue', 'Atlas')
```

To see what value the identity column is now assigning, the following code re-enables the identity column and inserts another row, and then selects the new data:

```
SET IDENTITY_INSERT Guide Off

INSERT Guide ( FirstName, LastName)
  VALUES ( 'Arnold', 'Bistier')

SELECT GuideID, FirstName, LastName
  FROM dbo.Guide
```

Result:

```
GuideID      FirstName      LastName
-----------  -------------  ------------------------
1            Dan            Smith
2            Jeff           Davis
3            Tammie         Commer
4            Lauren         Jones
5            Greg           Wilson
100          Bill           Mays
101          Sue            Atlas
102          Arnold         Bistier
```

As this code demonstrates, manually inserting a GuideID of "101" sets the identity column's next value to "102."

Another potential problem when working with identity columns is determining the value of the identity that was just created. Because the new identity value is created with SQL Server at the time of the insert, the code causing the insert is unaware of the identity value. The insert works fine; the problem occurs when the code inserts a row and then tries to display the row on a user-interface grid within an application, because the code is unaware of the new data's database-assigned primary key.

SQL Server provides three methods of determining the identity value:

✦ @@identity — This venerable global variable returns the last identity value generated by SQL Server for any table, connection, or scope. If another insert takes place between the time of your insert and the time when you check @@identity, @@identity will return not your insert, but the last insert.

✦ scope_identity() — This system function returns the last generated identity value within the scope of the calling batch or procedure. I recommend using this method, as it is the safest way to determine the identity value you last generated.

✦ ident_current(table) — This function returns the last identity value per table. While this option seems similar to scope_identity(), ident_current() returns the identity value for the given table regardless of inserts to any other tables that may have occurred. This prevents another insert, buried deep within a trigger, from affecting the identity value returned by the function.

Global unique identifiers (GUIDs) make excellent primary keys. With regard to the insertion of new rows, the major difference between identity columns and GUIDs is that GUIDs are generated by the SQL code or by a column default, rather than automatically at the time of the insert. This means that the developer has more control over GUID creation. If a value is inserted into a column with a default, it's no problem: The inserted value is placed into the new row. The default is used only when no value is provided by the insert statement. While GUIDs are a good choice for other reasons as well, the ease of working with a GUID default is certainly a good reason by itself.

Cross-Reference For more about the design issues that pertain to primary keys, and about GUIDs versus identity columns, see Chapter 17, "Implementing the Physical Database Schema."

GUIDs are created by the newid() function. If the default of the primary key is set to NewID(), a new GUID is generated for any new row. In addition, the newid() function may be declared within an insert/values list. The newid() function will even work as an expression in an insert/select that selects multiple rows. Within stored procedures or front-end code, the function may be called and the GUID stored in a variable. The variable is then used in the insert/values statement and inserted into the new row. Any of these options will work well, and they may be combined within an application.

The advantage of predetermining the GUID in code and then sending it with the insert/values command is that the program will then know the primary key of the new row and can continue working with it without having to determine it. The flexibility of the GUID is such that if the situation warrants predetermining the GUID, then that's fine, while if there's no reason to predetermine the GUID, then the default newid() works just as well.

The following sample code demonstrates various methods of generating GUID primary keys during the addition of new rows to the `ProductCategory` table in the OBXKites database. The first query simply tests the `newid()` function:

```
USE OBXKites

Select NewID()
```

Result:

```
5CBB2800-5207-4323-A316-E963AACB6081
```

The next three queries insert a GUID, each using a different method of generating the GUID:

```
--  GUID from Default (the columns default is NewID())
INSERT dbo.ProductCategory
  (ProductCategoryID, ProductCategoryName)
  VALUES (DEFAULT, 'From Default')

-- GUID from function
INSERT dbo.ProductCategory
    (ProductCategoryID, ProductCategoryName)
  VALUES (NewID(), 'From Function')

-- GUID in variable
DECLARE @NewGUID UniqueIdentifier
SET @NewGUID = NewID()

INSERT dbo.ProductCategory
    (ProductCategoryID, ProductCategoryName)
  VALUES (@NewGUID, 'From Variable')
```

To view the results of the previous three methods of inserting a GUID, the following `select` statement is filtered to those rows that are `like 'from%'`:

```
SELECT ProductCategoryID, ProductCategoryName
  FROM dbo.ProductCategory
    WHERE ProductCategoryName LIKE 'From %'
```

Result:

```
ProductCategoryID                    ProductCategoryName
------------------------------------ -----------------------
25894DA7-B5BB-435D-9540-6B9207C6CF8F From Default
393414DC-8611-4460-8FD3-4657E4B49373 From Function
FF868338-DF9A-4B8D-89B6-9C28293CA25F From Variable
```

This `insert` statement uses the `newid()` function to insert multiple GUIDs:

```
INSERT dbo.ProductCategory
    (ProductCategoryID, ProductCategoryName)
    Select NewID(), LastName
      From CHA2.dbo.Guide
```

The following `select` statement retrieves the new GUIDs:

```
SELECT ProductCategoryID, ProductCategoryName
  FROM dbo.ProductCategory
```

Result:

```
ProductCategoryID                    ProductCategoryName
------------------------------------ --------------------
1B2BBE15-B415-43ED-BCA2-293050B7EFE4 Kite
23FC5D45-8B60-4800-A505-D2F556F863C9 Accessory
3889671A-F2CD-4B79-8DCF-19F4F4703693 Video
...
5471F896-A414-432B-A579-0880757ED097 Fletcher
428F29B3-111B-4ECE-B6EB-E0913A9D34DC Atlas
E4B7D325-8122-48D7-A61B-A83E258D8729 Bistier
```

SQL Server provides the flexibility of two excellent candidates for primary key generation. Whether the database relies on identity columns or GUIDs may be based on other factors. Either way, there are multiple methods for inserting new rows. You, as the SQL developer, or DBA, are in control.

Foreign Key Obstacles

Foreign keys may affect `insert`, `update`, and `delete` operations.

A foreign key may block inserts, updates, and deletes. Inserting a new secondary table row with a foreign key value that doesn't match an existing primary key will cause the secondary row insert to fail.

In the following insert example, the `ProductCategoryID` supplied does not exist in the `ProductCategory` table. This causes the foreign-key constraint to block the `insert` operation, as the error message indicates:

```
-- Foreign Key: Insert Obstacle
INSERT Product (ProductID, Code,
    ProductCategoryID, ProductName)
  VALUES ('9562C1A5-4499-4626-BB33-E5E140ACD2AC',
    '999'
    'DB8D8D60-76F4-46C3-90E6-A8648F63C0F0',
    'Basic Box Kite 21"')

Server: Msg 547, Level 16, State 1, Line 1
INSERT statement conflicted with COLUMN FOREIGN KEY
constraint 'FK__Product__Product__7B905C75'.
The conflict occurred in database 'OBXKites',
table 'ProductCategory', column 'ProductCategoryID'.
The statement has been terminated.
```

Note that because every GUID is unique, the GUIDs you will use on your system will be different.

Foreign key constraints can also block updates to either the primary or secondary table. If the primary key is updated and a foreign key is pointed to that primary key, the update will fail.

In the following sample code the update is blocked because the secondary table update is trying to set the foreign key, `ProductCategoryID`, to a value that does not exist in the `ProductCategory` table:

```
-- Foreign Key: Secondary table Update Obstacle
UPDATE Product
  SET ProductCategoryID =
    'DB8D8D60-76F4-46C3-90E6-A8648F63C0F0'
  WHERE ProductID = '67804443-7E7C-4769-A41C-3DD3CD3621D9'

Server: Msg 547, Level 16, State 1, Line 1
UPDATE statement conflicted with COLUMN FOREIGN KEY
Constraint 'FK__Product__Product__7B905C75'.
The conflict occurred in database 'OBXKites',
table 'ProductCategory', column 'ProductCategoryID'.
The statement has been terminated.
```

Updating a primary key to a new value, if foreign keys are pointing to it, has the same effect as deleting a primary-table row with an existing secondary-table row referring to it. In both cases the error is caused not by the primary key but by the foreign key referencing the primary key.

In the following code the error is generated not by the `ProductCategory` table, even though it's the table being updated, but by the `Product` table. This is because the `Product` table has both the foreign key reference constraint and the row that will be violated if the primary key value no longer exists:

```
-- Foreign Key: Primary table Update Obstacle
UPDATE ProductCategory
  SET ProductCategoryID =
    'DB8D8D60-76F4-46C3-90E6-A8648F63C0F0'
  WHERE ProductCategoryID =
    '1B2BBE15-B415-43ED-BCA2-293050B7EFE4'

Server: Msg 547, Level 16, State 1, Line 1
UPDATE statement conflicted with COLUMN REFERENCE constraint
'FK__Product__Product__7B905C75'. The conflict occurred
in database 'OBXKites', table 'Product',
column 'ProductCategoryID'.
The statement has been terminated.
```

For more information about referential integrity in the design of foreign keys, refer to Chapter 2, "Relational Database Modeling." For details about creating foreign keys, refer to Chapter 17, "Implementing the Physical Database Schema."

Unique Index Obstacles

Unique indexes may affect `insert` and `update` operations.

If a column has a unique index (even if it's not a key) attempting to insert a new value, or an update to a new value that's already in use, will fail.

Typically, the entire transaction, including all the inserted or updated rows, will fail. However, there's an index option, `ignore dup key`, that will allow the transaction to succeed with only a warning, and just skip any duplicate rows.

Cross-Reference For more information about creating unique index constraints, refer to Chapter 17, "Implementing the Physical Database Schema" or Chapter 50, "Query Analysis and Index Tuning."

Null and Default Obstacles

Column nullability and defaults may affect `insert` and `update` operations.

An `insert` or `update` operation can send one of four possible values to a table column: data values, `null`, `default`, or nothing at all. The table column can be configured with a default value and nullability. Table 16-3 indicates the result of the operation, according to the column configuration and the new value to be inserted or updated. For example, if the column properties are set so that the column has a default and accept nulls (in the far-right column) and the SQL insert or update sends a null, then the result is an error.

Table 16-3: Data Modifications, Defaults, and Nulls

	Column Properties			
Column Default	no default	no default	has default	has default
Column Nullability:	null	not null	null	not null
SQL Sent	*Result*			
data	data	data	data	data
null	null	error	null	error
default	null	error	default	default
nothing sent	null	most common error	default	default

By far, the most common error in the preceding table is submitting nothing when no default exists and nulls are not permitted.

Cross-Reference For more information about creating defaults and null constraints, refer to Chapter 17, "Implementing the Physical Database Schema." For more information about dealing with nulls when retrieving data, see Chapter 8, "Using Expressions and Scalar Functions."

Check Constraint Obstacles

Check constraints may affect `insert` and `update` operations.

Each table column may have multiple check constraints. These are fast Boolean operations that determine whether the update will pass or fail.

The following check constraint permits Dr. Johnson's insert, but blocks Greg's insert (note that the check constraint is already applied to the database by the `Create_CHA2.sql` script):

```
USE CHA2
go
ALTER TABLE dbo.Guide ADD CONSTRAINT
  CK_Guide_Age21 CHECK (DateDiff(yy,DateOfBirth, DateHire)
    >= 21)
```

The following query inserts Dr. Johnson's data. Because she is 26 years old, her row is accepted by the check constraint:

```
INSERT Guide(lastName, FirstName, Qualifications, DateOfBirth,
DateHire)
  VALUES ('Johnson', 'Mary',
          'E.R. Physician', '1/14/71', '6/1/97')
```

Greg, conversely, is only 19, so his insert is rejected by the check constraint:

```
INSERT Guide (lastName, FirstName,
    Qualifications, DateOfBirth, DateHire)
  VALUES ('Franklin', 'Greg',
    'Guide', '12/12/83', '1/1/2002')


Server: Msg 547, Level 16, State 1, Line 1
INSERT statement conflicted with TABLE CHECK constraint
'CK_Guide_Age21'.
The conflict occurred in database 'CHA2', table 'Guide'.
The statement has been terminated.
```

Cross-Reference For more information about creating check constraints, and their benefits and limitations, refer to Chapter 17, "Implementing the Physical Database Schema."

Instead of Trigger Obstacles

Instead of **triggers may affect** insert, update, **and** delete **operations.**

Triggers are special stored procedures that are attached to a table and fire when certain data-modification operations hit that table. Two types of triggers exist: instead of and after. They differ both in their timing and in how they handle the data-modification operation.

An instead of trigger always causes the insert, update, or delete operation to be canceled. The SQL command submitted to SQL Server is discarded by the instead of trigger; the code within the instead of trigger is executed *instead of* the submitted SQL command, hence the name. The instead of trigger might be programmed to repeat the requested operation so that it looks like it went through, or it could do something else altogether.

The problem with the instead of trigger is that it reports back "one row affected" when in fact nothing is written to the database. There is no error warning because the instead of trigger works properly; however, the operation doesn't go through.

In the following code sample, the InsteadOfDemo trigger causes the insert operation to disappear into thin air:

```
USE CHA2
go

CREATE TRIGGER InsteadOfDemo
ON Guide
INSTEAD OF INSERT
AS
  Print 'Instead of trigger demo'
Return
```

With the instead of trigger in place, the following query inserts a test row:

```
INSERT Guide(lastName, FirstName,
    Qualifications, DateOfBirth, DateHire)
  VALUES ('Jamison', 'Tom',
    'Biologist, Adventurer', '1/14/56', '9/1/99')
```

Result:

```
Instead of trigger demo
(1 row(s) affected)
```

The insert operation appears to have worked, but is the row in the table?

```
SELECT GuideID
  FROM Guide
  WHERE LastName = 'Jamison'
```

Result:

```
GuideID
-----------

(0 row(s) affected)
```

Cross-Reference Building triggers is explained in detail in Chapter 23, "Creating DML Triggers." The flow of data-modification transactions and the timing of triggers are also discussed in Chapter 51, "Managing Transactions, Locking, and Blocking."

Note that the sample code for this chapter drops the InsteadOfDemo trigger before moving on.

After Trigger Obstacles

After triggers may affect insert, update, and delete operations.

After triggers are often used for complex data validation. These triggers can roll back, or undo, the insert, update, or delete if the code inside the trigger doesn't like the operation in question. The code can then do something else, or it can just fail the transaction. However, if the trigger doesn't explicitly rollback the transaction, the data-modification operation will go through as originally intended. Unlike instead of triggers, after triggers normally report an error code if an operation is rolled back.

As Chapter 51, "Managing Transactions, Locking, and Blocking," will discuss in greater detail, every DML command implicitly occurs within a transaction, even if no `transaction begin` command exists. The `after` trigger takes place after the write but before the implicit commit, so the transaction is still open when the `after` trigger is fired. Therefore, a transaction roll-back command in the trigger will roll back the command that fired the trigger.

This code sample creates the `AfterDemo` after trigger on the `Guide` table, which includes `raiserror` and `rollback transaction` commands:

```
USE CHA2

CREATE TRIGGER AfterDemo
ON Guide
AFTER INSERT, UPDATE
AS
   Print 'After Trigger Demo'
   -- logic in a real trigger would decide what to do here
   RAISERROR ('Sample Error', 16, 1 )
   ROLLBACK TRAN
Return
```

With the `after` trigger applied to the `Guide` table, the following `insert` will result:

```
INSERT Guide(lastName, FirstName,
    Qualifications, DateOfBirth, DateHire)
  VALUES ('Harrison', 'Nancy',
    'Pilot, Sky Diver, Hang Glider,
      Emergency Paramedic', '6/25/69', '7/14/2000')
```

Result:

```
After Trigger Demo
Server: Msg 50000, Level 16, State 1,
    Procedure AfterDemo, Line 7
Sample Error
```

A `select` searching for Nancy Harrison would find no such row because the `after` trigger rolled back the transaction.

Cross-Reference For more information on `after` triggers, see Chapter 23, "Creating DML Triggers." Additional trigger strategies are discussed in Chapter 24, "Exploring Advanced T-SQL Programming."

Note that the sample code on the book's CD for this chapter drops the `AfterDemo` trigger so the code in the remainder of the chapter will function.

Calculated Columns

A related issue to non-updateable views involves updating calculated columns. Just like non-updateable views, attempting to write to a calculated column will block the data-modification statement.

Cross-Reference For more details about creating calculated columns, turn to Chapter 17, "Implementing the Physical Database Schema."

Non-Updateable View Obstacles

Non-updateable views may affect `insert`, `update`, and `delete` operations.

Several factors will cause a view to become non-updateable. The most common causes of non-updateable views are aggregate functions (including `distinct`), group bys, and joins. If the view includes other nested views, any nested view that is non-updateable will cause the final view to be non-updateable as well.

The view `vMedGuide`, created in the following sample code, is non-updateable because the `distinct` predicate eliminates duplicates, making it impossible for SQL to be sure of which underlying row should be updated:

```
CREATE VIEW dbo.vMedGuide
AS
SELECT DISTINCT GuideID, LastName, Qualifications
  FROM dbo.Guide
  WHERE Qualifications LIKE '%Aid%'
  OR Qualifications LIKE '%medic%'
  OR Qualifications LIKE '%Physician%'
```

To test the updateability of the view, the next query attempts to perform an `update` command through the view:

```
UPDATE dbo.vMedGuide
  SET Qualifications = 'E.R. Physician, Diver'
  WHERE GuideID = 1
```

Result:

```
Server: Msg 4404, Level 16, State 1, Line 1
View or function 'dbo.vMedGuide' is not updatable
because the definition contains the DISTINCT clause.
```

 Cross-Reference For more about creating views and a more complete list of the causes of non-updateable views, refer to Chapter 14, "Creating Views."

Views with the with check option Obstacles

Views with the `with check option` may affect `insert` and `update` operations.

Views can cause two specific problems, both related to the `with check option`. A special situation called *disappearing rows* occurs when rows are returned from a view and then updated such that they no longer meet the `where` clause's requirements for the view. The rows are still in the database but they are no longer visible in the view.

 Cross-Reference For more about disappearing rows, the `with check option`, and their implications for security, refer to Chapter 14, "Creating Views." SQL Server security roles are discussed in Chapter 40, "Securing Databases."

Adding the `with check option` to a view prohibits disappearing rows, but causes another problem. A view that includes the `with check option` will apply the where-clause condition to both data being retrieved through the view and data being inserted or updated through the view. If the data being inserted or updated will not be retrievable through the view after the insert or update of the operation, the with check option will cause the data-modification operation to fail.

The following code sample modifies the previous view to add the with check option and then attempts two updates. The first update passes the where clause requirements. The second update would remove the rows from the result set returned by the view, so it fails:

```
ALTER VIEW dbo.vMedGuide
AS
SELECT GuideID, LastName, Qualifications
  FROM dbo.Guide
  WHERE Qualifications LIKE '%Aid%'
  OR Qualifications LIKE '%medic%'
  OR Qualifications LIKE '%Physician%'
WITH CHECK OPTION
```

The following queries test the views with check option. The first one will pass because the qualifications include 'Physician', but the second query will fail:

```
UPDATE dbo.vMedGuide
  SET Qualifications = 'E.R. Physician, Diver'
  WHERE GuideID = 1

UPDATE dbo.vMedGuide
  SET Qualifications = 'Diver'
  WHERE GuideID = 1

Server: Msg 550, Level 16, State 1, Line 1
The attempted insert or update failed because the target
view either specifies WITH CHECK OPTION or spans a view
that specifies WITH CHECK OPTION and one or more rows
resulting from the operation did not qualify
under the CHECK OPTION constraint.
The statement has been terminated.
```

Security Obstacles

Security may affect insert, update, and delete operations.

A number of security settings and roles will cause any operation to fail. Typically, security is not an issue during development; however, for production databases, security is often paramount. Documenting the security settings and security roles will help you solve data-modification problems caused by security.

Cross-Reference For more about security and roles, refer to Chapter 40, "Securing Databases."

Best Practice Every data-modification obstacle is easily within the SQL developer's or DBA's ability to surmount. Understanding SQL Server and documenting the database, as well as being familiar with the database schema, stored procedures, and triggers, will prevent most data-modification problems.

Summary

Data retrieval and data modification are primary tasks of a database application. This chapter examined the `insert`, `update`, and `delete` DML commands and how they may be blocked in several ways by the database.

This concludes a ten-chapter study on using the `select` command, and its `insert`, `update`, and `delete` variations, to manipulate data. The next part moves into programming and developing database with SQL Server 2005 using T-SQL, the CLR, and SQL Server's new service-oriented architecture features.

✦   ✦   ✦

Developing with SQL Server

Part II of this book was all about writing set-based queries. This part expands on the `select` command to provide programmable flow of control to develop server-side solutions; and SQL Server has a large variety of technologies to choose from to develop server-side code—from the mature T-SQL language to .NET assemblies hosted within SQL Server.

Part III opens with DDL commands (`create`, `alter`, and `drop`), and progresses through nine chapters that dig deeper into Transact-SQL. The conclusion of the T-SQL chapters brings it all together with the data abstraction layer.

SQL Server's list of technologies keeps growing, so the remainder of Part III explores the .NET common language runtime (CLR), SQL Server Mobile, Service Broker, XML, XQuery, Web Services, and InfoPath. So, unleash the programmer within and have fun. There's a whole world of developer possibilities with SQL Server 2005.

If SQL Server is the box, then Part III is all about thinking inside the box, and moving the processing as close to the data as possible.

Implementing the Physical Database Schema

When I was in the Navy, I learned more from Master Chief Miller than he or I probably realized at the time. One of his theories was that an application was half code and half data. In more than 20 years of developing databases, my experience agrees with the Master Chief.

The data, both the schema and the data itself, is often more critical to the success of a project than the application code. The primary features of the application are designed at the data schema level. If the data schema supports a feature, then the code will readily bring the feature to life; but if the feature is not designed in the tables, then the front-end forms can jump through as many hoops as can be coded and it will never work right.

Optimization theory and strategy is a framework that organizes the dependencies between several popular optimization techniques. This chapter could have been called "Advanced Performance: Step 1."

The logical database schema, discussed in Chapter 2, "Relational Database Modeling," is a purely academic exercise designed to ensure that the business requirements are well understood. A logical design has never stored nor served up any data. In contrast, the physical database schema is an actual data store that must meet the Information Architecture Principle's call to make information "readily available in a usable format for daily operations and analysis by individuals, groups, and processes." The physical schema design team must consider not only data integrity and user requirements, but also performance, agility, query paths, and maintainability as the database is implemented within the nitty-gritty syntax of the particular database platform.

This chapter discusses designing the physical database schema and then focuses on the data-definition language commands `create`, `alter`, and `drop`. These three commands are used to build the physical database schema.

All the code in this chapter and all the sample databases are available for download from the book's website, www.SQLServerBible.com. In addition, you'll find extensive queries using the catalog views that relate to this chapter.

Designing the Physical Database Schema

When designing the physical design, the design team should begin with a clean logical design and/or well-understood and documented business rules, and then brainstorm until a simple, flexible design emerges that performs great.

The actual implementation of the physical design involves six components:

✦ Creating the database files

✦ Creating the tables

✦ Creating the primary and foreign keys

✦ Creating the data columns

✦ Adding data-integrity constraints

✦ Creating indexes (although indexes can be easily added or modified after the physical schema implementation)

Translating the logical database schema into a physical database schema may involve the following changes:

✦ Converting complex logical designs into simpler, more agile table structures

✦ Converting composite primary keys to computer-generated single-column primary keys

✦ Converting the business rules to constraints or triggers

✦ Converting logical many-to-many relationships to two physical one-to-many relationships with an associative, or junction, table

Physical Schema Design Options

Every project team develops the physical database schema drawing from these two disciplines (logical data modeling and physical schema design) in one of the following possible combinations:

✦ A logical database schema is designed and then implemented without the benefit of physical schema development.

This plan is a sure way to develop a slow and unwieldy database schema. The application code will be frustrating to write and the code will not be able to overcome the performance limitations of the design.

✦ A logical database schema is developed to ensure that the business requirements are understood. Based on the logical design, the database development team develops a physical database schema. This method can result in a fast, usable schema.

Developing the schema in two stages is a good plan if the development team is large enough and one team is designing and collecting the business requirements and another team is developing the physical database schema. Make sure that having a completed logical database schema does not squelch the team's creativity as the physical database schema is designed.

✦ The third combination of logical and physical design methodologies combines the two into a single development step as the database development team develops a physical database schema directly from the business requirements. This method can work well providing that the design team fully understands logical database modeling, physical database modeling, and advanced query design.

The key task in designing a physical database schema is brainstorming multiple possible designs, each of which meets the user requirements and ensures data integrity. Each design is evaluated based on its simplicity, performance of possible query paths, flexibility, and maintainability.

Refining the Data Patterns

The key to simplicity is refining the entity definition with a lot of team brainstorming so that each entity does more work — rearranging the data patterns until an elegant and simple pattern emerges. This is where a broad repertoire of database experience aids the design process.

Often the solution is to view the data from multiple angles, finding the commonality between them. Users are too close to the data and they seldom correctly identify the true entities. What a user might see as multiple entities a database design team might model as a single entity with dynamic roles.

Combining this quest for simplicity with some data-driven design methods can yield normalized databases with higher data integrity, more flexibility/agility, and dramatically fewer tables.

Designing for Performance

A normalized logical database design without the benefit of physical database schema optimization will perform poorly, because the logical design alone doesn't consider performance. Issues such as lock contention, composite keys, excessive joins for common queries, and table structures that are difficult to update are just some of the problems a logical design might bring to the database.

Designing for performance is greatly influenced by the simplicity or complexity of the design. Each unnecessary complexity requires additional code, extra joins, and breeds even more complexity.

One particular decision regarding performance concerns the primary keys. Logical database designs tend to create composite meaningful primary keys. The physical schema can benefit from redesigning these as single-column surrogate (computer-generated) keys. The section on creating primary keys later in this chapter discusses this in more detail.

Designing for Extensibility

Maintenance over the life of the application will cost significantly more than the initial development. Therefore, during the initial development process you should consider as a primary objective making it as easy as possible to maintain the physical design, code, and data. The following techniques may reduce the cost of database maintenance:

✦ Use a consistent naming convention.

✦ Avoid data structures that are overly complex, as well as unwieldy data structures, when a simpler data structures will suffice.

✦ Develop with scripts instead of Management Studio.

✦ Avoid non-portable non-ANSI T-SQL extensions, unless your shop is committed to being a Microsoft shop.

✦ Enforce the data integrity constraints from the beginning. Polluted data is a bear to clean up after even a short time of loose data-integrity rules.

✦ Develop the core feature first, and once that's working, then add the bells and whistles.

✦ Document not only how the procedure works, but also why it works.

Responsible Denormalization

Interestingly, the Microsoft Word spell checker suggests replacing "denormalization" with "demoralization." Within a transactional, OLTP database, I couldn't agree more.

Denormalization, purposefully breaking the normal forms, is the technique of duplicating data within the data to make it easier to retrieve.

Cross-Reference

Normalization is described in Chapter 2, "Relational Database Modeling."

For some examples of denormalizing a data structure, including the customer name in an [Order] table would enable retrieving the customer name when querying an order without joining to the Customer table. Or, including the CustomerID in a ShipDetail table would enable joining directly from the ShipDetail table to the Customer table while bypassing the OrderDetail and [Order] tables. Both of these examples violate the normalization because the attributes don't depend on the primary key.

Some developers regularly denormalize portions of the database in an attempt to improve performance. While it can reduce the number of joins required for a query, such a technique can slow down an OLTP database overall because additional triggers must keep the duplicated data in sync, and the data integrity checks become more complex.

Normalization ensures data consistency as new data is entered or data is updated. The recommendation to denormalize a portion of the database therefore depends on the purpose of that data within the database:

✦ If the data is being used in an OLTP manner — that is, the data is original and data integrity is a concern — don't denormalize. Never denormalize original data.

✦ Denormalize aggregate data, such as account balances, or inventory on-hand quantities within OLTP databases, for performance even though such data could be calculated from the inventory transaction table or the account transaction ledge table. These may be calculated using a trigger or a persisted computed column.

✦ If the data is not original and is primarily there for OLAP or reporting purposes, data consistency is not the primary concern. For performance, denormalization is a wise move.

The architecture of the databases and which databases or tables are being used for which purpose are the driving factors in any decision to denormalize a part of the database.

If the database requires both OLTP and OLAP, the best solution might just be to create a few tables that duplicate data for their own distinct purposes. The OLTP side might need its own tables to maintain the data, but the reporting side might need that same data in a single, wide, fast table from which it can retrieve data without any joins or locking concerns. The trick is to correctly populate the denormalized data in a timely manner.

As part of one project I worked on, several analysts entered and massaged data to produce a database that was published quarterly. The published database was static for a quarter and used only for searches — a perfect example of a project that includes both OLTP and OLAP requirements. To improve search performance, a denormalized database was created expressly for reporting purposes. A procedure ran for several hours to denormalize all the data and populate the OLAP database. Both sides of the equation were satisfied.

Cross-Reference Indexed views are basically denormalized clustered indexes. Chapter 53, "Scaling Very Large Databases," discusses setting up an indexed view. Chapters 42, "ETL with Integration Services," and Chapter 43, "Business Intelligence with Analysis Services, include advice on creating a denormalized reporting database and data warehouse.

Creating the Database

The database is the physical container for all database schemas, data, and server-side programming. SQL Server's database is a single logical unit, even though it may exist in several files.

Database creation is one of those areas in which SQL Server requires little administrative work, but you may decide instead to fine-tune the database files with more sophisticated techniques.

The Create DDL Command

Creating a database using the default parameters is very simple. The following Data Definition Language (DDL) command is taken from the Cape Hatteras Adventures sample database:

```
CREATE DATABASE CHA2;
```

The create command will create a data file with the name provided and a .mdf file exten sion, as well as a transaction log with an .ldf extension.

Of course, more parameters and options are available than the previous basic `create` command suggests. By default, the database is created as follows:

- ✦ **Default collation:** Server collation

- ✦ **Initial size:** A data file around 2MB is created when using code, and around 3MB when created using Object Explorer. A transaction log around ½MB is created from code, and around 1MB when using Object Explorer.

- ✦ **Location:** Both the data file and the transaction log file reside in SQL Server's default data directory.

While these defaults might be acceptable for a sample or development database, they are sorely inadequate for a production database. Better alternatives are explained as the `create database` command is covered.

Using the Object Explorer, creating a new database requires only that the database name be entered in the new database form, as shown in Figure 17-1. Use the New Database menu command from the Database node's context menu to open the New Database form.

Cross-Reference   The data file and transaction log file default locations may be configured in the Server properties. Refer to Chapter 34, "Configuring SQL Server," for details.

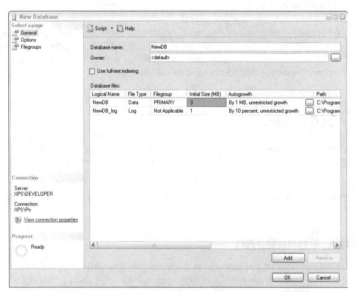

Figure 17-1: The simplest way to create a new database is by entering the database name in Object Explorer's new Database Settings page.

The New Database page includes the several individual pages — the General, Options, and Filegroups pages, as shown in Table 17-1. For existing databases, the Files, Permissions, Extended Properties, Mirroring, and Log Shipping pages are added to the Database Properties page (not shown).

Table 17-1: Database Property Pages

Page	New Database	Existing Database
General	Create new database, setting the name, owner, collation, recovery model, full-text indexing, and data file properties	View (read-only) general properties: name, last back-up, size, collation
Files	n/a	View and modify database owner, collation, recovery model, full-text indexing, and database files
Filegroups	View and modify filegroup information	View and modify filegroup information
Options	View and modify database options such as auto shrink, ANSI settings, page verification method, and single user access	View and modify database options such as auto shrink, ANSI settings, page verification method, and single user access
Permissions	n/a	View and modify server roles, users, and permissions. See Chapter 40, "Securing Databases," for more details.
Extended Properties	n/a	View and modify extended properties
Mirroring	n/a	View and configure database mirroring, covered in Chapter 52, "Providing High Availability"
Transaction Log Shipping	n/a	View and configure database mirroring, covered in Chapter 52, "Providing High Availability"

Database-File Concepts

A database consists of two files (or two sets of files): the data file and the transaction log. The data file contains all system and user tables, indexes, views, stored procedures, user-defined functions, triggers, and security permissions. The write-ahead transaction log is central to SQL Server's design. All updates to the data file are first written and verified in the transaction log, ensuring that all data updates are written to two places.

Caution   Never store the transaction log on the same disk subsystem as the data file. For the sake of the transactional-integrity ACID properties and the recoverability of the database, it's critical that a failing disk subsystem not be able to take out both the data file and the transaction file.

The transaction log contains not only user writes but also system writes such as index writes, page splits, table reorganizations, and so on. After one intensive update test, I inspected the log using Lumigent's Log Explorer and was surprised to find that about 80 percent of all entries represented system activities, not user updates. Because the transaction file contains not only the current information but also all updates to the data file, it has a tendency to grow and grow.

Cross-Reference   Administering the transaction log involves backing up and truncating it as part of the recovery plan, as discussed in Chapter 36, "Recovery Planning." How SQL Server uses the transaction log within transactions is covered in Chapter 51, "Managing Transactions, Locking, and Blocking."

Configuring File Growth

Prior to SQL Server version 7, the data files required manual size adjustment to handle additional data. Fortunately, now SQL Server can automatically grow thanks to the following options (see Figure 17-2):

✦ **Enable Autogrowth:** As the database begins to hold more data, the file size must grow. If autogrowth is not enabled, an observant DBA will have to manually adjust the size. If autogrowth is enabled, SQL Server automatically adjusts the size according to the following growth parameters:

  • **File growth in megabytes:** When the data file needs to grow, this option will add the specified number of megabytes to the file. Growing by a fixed size is a good option for larger data files. Once file growth is predictable, setting this option to a fixed number equal to the amount of growth per week is probably a sound plan.

  • **File growth by percent:** When the data file needs to grow, this option will expand it by the percent specified. Growing by percent is the best option for smaller databases. With very large files, this option may add too much space in one operation and hurt performance while the data file is being resized. For example, adding 10 percent to a 5GB data file will add 500MB; writing 500MB could take a while.

✦ **Maximum file size:** —Setting a maximum size can prevent the data file or transaction log file from filling the entire disk subsystem, which would cause trouble for the operating system.

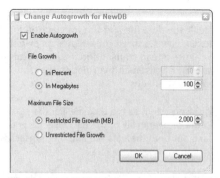

Figure 17-2: With Management Studio's New Database form, NewDB is configured for automatic file growth and a maximum size of 20GB.

The maximum size for a data file is 16 terabytes and log files are limited to 2 terabytes. This does not limit the size of the database because a database can include multiple files.

Automatic file growth can be specified in code by adding the file options to the `create database` DDL command. The file sizes can be specified in kilobytes (KB), megabytes (MB), gigabytes (GB), or terabytes (TB). Megabytes is the default. File growth can be set to a size or a percent. The following code creates the NewDB database with an initial data-file size of 10MB, a maximum size of 2GB, and a file growth of 10MB. The transaction log file is initially 5MB with a maximum size of 1GB and a growth of 10 percent:

```
CREATE DATABASE NewDB
ON
PRIMARY
  (NAME = NewDB,
    FILENAME = 'c:\SQLData\NewDB.mdf',
      SIZE = 10MB,
      MAXSIZE = 2Gb,
      FILEGROWTH = 20)
LOG ON
  (NAME = NewDBLog,
    FILENAME = 'd:\SQLLog\NewDBLog.ldf',
      SIZE = 5MB,
      MAXSIZE = 1Gb,
      FILEGROWTH = 10%);
```

If autogrowth is not enabled, then the files will require manual adjustment if they are to handle additional data. The file size can be adjusted in Management Studio by editing it in the database properties form.

The file sizes and growth options can be adjusted in code with the `alter database` DDL command and the `modify file` option. The following code sets NewDB's data file to manual growth and sets the size to 25MB:

```
ALTER DATABASE NewDB
  MODIFY FILE
    (Name = NewDB,
    SIZE = 25MB,
    MAXSIZE = 2Gb,
    FILEGROWTH = 0);
```

To list the databases using code, query the `sysdatabases` catalog view.

Using Multiple Files

Both the data file and the transaction log can be stored on multiple files for improved performance and to allow for growth. Any additional, or *secondary*, data files have an `.ndf` file extension by default. If the database uses multiple data files, then the first, or *primary*, file will contain the system tables.

While it does not enable control over the location of tables or indexes, this technique does reduce the I/O load on each disk subsystem. SQL Server attempts to balance the I/O load by splitting the inserts among the multiple files according to the free space available in each file. As SQL Server balances the load, rows for a single table may be split among multiple locations. If the database is configured for automatic growth, all of the files will fill up before SQL Server increases the size of the files.

Creating a Database with Multiple Files

To create a database with multiple files using Management Studio, add the filename to the file grid in the Files page of the Database Properties dialog box (see Figure 17-3).

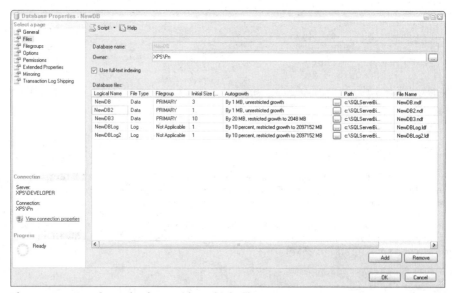

Figure 17-3: Creating a database with multiple files using SQL Server Management Studio

To create a database with multiple data files from code, add the file locations to the create database DDL command using the on option:

```
CREATE DATABASE NewDB
ON
PRIMARY
  (NAME = NewDB,
    FILENAME = 'e:\SQLData\NewDB.mdf'),
  (NAME = NewDB2,
    FILENAME = 'f:\SQLData\NewDB2.ndf')
LOG ON
  (NAME = NewDBLog,
    FILENAME = 'g:\SQLLog\NewDBLog.ldf'),
  (NAME = NewDBLog2,
    FILENAME = 'h:\SQLLog\NewDBLog2.ldf');
```

Result:

```
The CREATE DATABASE process is allocating
   0.63 MB on disk 'NewDB'.
The CREATE DATABASE process is allocating
   1.00 MB on disk 'NewDB2'.
The CREATE DATABASE process is allocating
   1.00 MB on disk 'NewDBLog'.
The CREATE DATABASE process is allocating
   1.00 MB on disk 'NewDBLog2'.
```

sys.

To list the files for the current database using code, query the sysdatabases catalog view.

Modifying the Files of an Existing Database

The number of files for an existing database may be easily modified. If the data is filling the drive, another data file can be added to the database by adding it to the Database Files grid. Add the new filename and location to the database properties file grid in the same way that the files were initially created.

In code, a file can be added to an existing database using the alter database DDL command and the add file option. The file syntax is identical to that which was used to create a new database. The following code adds a third file to the NewDB:

```
ALTER DATABASE NewDB
  ADD FILE
    (NAME = NewDB3,
      FILENAME = 'i:\SQLData\NewDB3.ndf',
      SIZE = 10MB,
      MAXSIZE = 2Gb,
      FILEGROWTH = 20);
```

Result:

```
Extending database by 10.00 MB on disk 'NewDB3'.
```

If a file is no longer desired because the disk subsystem is being retired or designated for another use, one of the data or transaction log files can be deleted by shrinking the file using DBCC ShrinkFile and then deleting it in Management Studio by selecting the file and pressing Delete.

Using T-SQL code, you can remove additional files with the alter database remove file DDL command. The following code removes the data file you added earlier:

```
DBCC SHRINKFILE (NewDB3, EMPTYFILE)
ALTER DATABASE NewDB
  REMOVE FILE NewDB3;
```

Result:

```
DbId FileId CurrentSize MinimumSize UsedPages EstimatedPages
---- ------ ----------- ----------- --------- --------------
12   5      1280        1280        0         0
```

The file NewDB3 has been removed.

Planning Multiple Filegroups

A *filegroup* is an advanced means of organizing the database objects. By default, the database has a single filegroup — the *primary* filegroup. By configuring a database with multiple filegroups, new objects (tables, indexes, and so on) can be created on a specified filegroup. This technique can support two main strategies:

✦ Using multiple filegroups can increase performance by separating heavily used tables or indexes onto different disk subsystems.

✦ Using multiple filegroups can organize the backup and recovery plan by containing static data in one filegroup and more active data in another filegroup.

 An easy way to determine the files and file sizes for all databases from code is to query sysdatabase_files catalog view.

Best Practice

When planning files and filegroups, they benefit most from placing each file on a dedicated disk subsystem. I highly recommend spreading the I/O load over multiple disk spindles.

However, before you dedicate additional disk subsystems for additional data file locations, be sure to cover the needs of the transaction log and tempdb first. Ideally, you should have five disk subsystems (Windows system, apps, and swap file; tempdb; tempdb log; data file; log file) prior to adding any additional data files or filegroups.

Creating a Database with Filegroups

To add filegroups to a database using Management Studio, open the Database Properties page from Object Explorer. On the Filegroups page, add the new logical filegroup. Then, on the Files page, you can add the new file and select the filegroup for the new file in the combo box.

Using T-SQL, you can specify filegroups for new databases using the Filegroups option. The following code creates the NewDB database with two data filegroups:

```
CREATE DATABASE NewDB
ON
PRIMARY
  (NAME = NewDB,
    FILENAME = 'd:\SQLData\NewDB.mdf',
      SIZE = 50MB,
      MAXSIZE = 5Gb,
      FILEGROWTH = 25MB),
FILEGROUP GroupTwo
  (NAME = NewDBGroup2,
    FILENAME = 'e:\SQLData\NewDBTwo.ndf',
      SIZE = 50MB,
      MAXSIZE = 5Gb,
      FILEGROWTH = 25MB)
LOG ON
  (NAME = NewDBLog,
    FILENAME = 'f:\SQLLog\NewDBLog.ndf',
      SIZE = 100MB,
      MAXSIZE = 25Gb,
      FILEGROWTH = 25MB);
```

Modifying Filegroups

You modify filegroups in the same way that you modify files. Using Management Studio, you can add new filegroups, add or remove files from a filegroup, and remove the filegroup if it is empty. Emptying a file group is more difficult than shrinking a file. If there's data in the filegroup, shrinking a file will only move the data to another file in the filegroup. The tables and indexes must be dropped from the filegroup before the filegroup can be deleted.

With Query Editor and T-SQL code, you can add or drop filegroups using the `alter database add filegroup` or `alter database remove filegroup` commands, much as you would use the add or remove file command.

Dropping a Database

A database may be removed from the server by selecting the database in Object Explorer and selecting Delete from the context menu.

In code, you can remove a database with the DDL `drop database` command:

```
DROP DATABASE NewDB;
```

Creating Tables

Like all relational databases, SQL Server is table-oriented. Once the database is created, the next step is to create the tables. A SQL Server database may include up to 2,147,483,647 objects, including tables, so there's effectively no limit to the number of tables you can create.

Designing Tables Using Management Studio

If you prefer working in a graphical environment, Management Studio provides two primary work surfaces for creating tables, both of which you can use to create new tables or modify existing ones:

✦ The Table Designer tool (see Figure 17-4) lists the table columns vertically and places the column properties below the column grid.

✦ The Database Designer tool (see Figure 17-5) is more flexible than the Table Designer form in that it can display foreign-key constraints as connections to other tables.

Cross-Reference   Chapter 6, "Using Management Studio," explains how to launch and navigate these tools.

Each of these tools presents a graphical design of the table. Once the design is complete, Management Studio generates a script that applies the changes to the database. If you're modifying an existing table, often the script must save the data in a temporary table, drop several items, create the new tables, and reinsert the data.

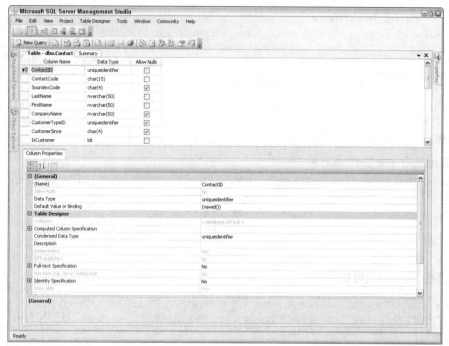

Figure 17-4: Developing the Contact table in the OBXKites sample database using Management Studio's Table Designer

Table Designer displays only the column name and data type (with length), and allows nulls in the column grid. While these are the main properties of a column, I personally find it annoying to have to select each column in order to inspect or change the rest of the properties.

Each data type is explained in detail later in this chapter. For some data types the `length` property sets the data length, while other data types have fixed lengths. Nulls are discussed in the section "Creating User-Data Columns," later in this chapter.

Once an edit is made to the table design, the Save Change Script toolbar button is enabled. This button displays the actual code that the Table Designer will run if the changes are saved. In addition, the Save Change Script button can save the script to a `.sql` file so the change can be repeated on another server.

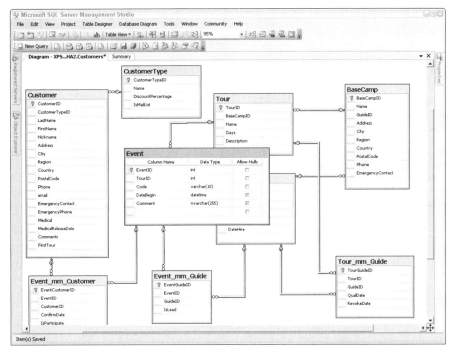

Figure 17-5: Developing the Customer table in the CHA2 sample database using Management Studio's Database Designer

Cross-Reference For more details about using the Table Designer and Database Designer, see Chapter 6, "Using Management Studio."

Working with SQL Scripts

If you are developing a database for mass deployment or repeatable installations, the benefits of developing the database schema in scripts become obvious:

✦ The code is all in one location. Working with SQL scripts is similar to developing an application with VB.Net or C#.

✦ The script may be stored in Solutions or Project using the Solution Explorer. In addition, scripts can be stored in Microsoft SourceSafe or another change-management system.

✦ If a database master script contains all the code necessary to generate the database, then the most current version of the database may be installed without running change scripts or restoring a backup.

✦ An installation that is a fresh new database, as opposed to a backup or detached database, is beneficial for testing because it won't have any residual data.

Working with scripts does have its drawbacks, however:

✦ The T-SQL commands may be unfamiliar and the size of the script may become over-whelming.

✦ If the foreign-key constraints are embedded within the table, the table-creation order is very picky. If the constraints are applied after the tables are created, the table-creation order is no longer a problem; however, the foreign keys are distanced from the tables in the script.

✦ Management Studio database diagrams are not part of the script.

The T-SQL commands for working with objects, including tables, are create, alter, and drop. The following create table DDL command from the Outer Banks Kite Store sample database creates the ProductCategory table. The table name, including the name of the owner (dbo), is provided, followed by the table's columns. The final code directs SQL Server to create the table on the primary filegroup:

```
CREATE TABLE dbo.ProductCategory (
  ProductCategoryID UNIQUEIDENTIFIER NOT NULL
    ROWGUIDCOL DEFAULT (NEWID()) PRIMARY KEY NONCLUSTERED,
  ProductCategoryName NVARCHAR(50) NOT NULL,
  ProductCategoryDescription NVARCHAR(100) NULL
  )
  ON [Primary];
```

To list the tables for the current database using code, query the sysobjects catalog view, filtering for type_desc = 'USER_TABLE'.

For extensive examples of building databases and tables with scripts, you can reference this book's sample databases, which are all developed with scripts and are available on www.SQLServerBible.com.

Schemas

A schema is an object that exists purely to own database objects, most likely to segment a large database into manageable modules, or to implement a segmented security strategy. Typically, and by default, objects are owned by the dbo schema. The schema name is the third part of the four-part name:

```
Server.database.schema.object;
```

In previous versions of SQL Server, objects were owned by users. Or rather, objects were owned by schema-objects that were the same as the user-owners, but no one spoke in those terms. In SQL Server 2005, the concepts of users and schema have been separated. Users may no longer own objects.

If you use custom schemas, other than dbo, every query will have to specify the schema. That's not a bad thing, because using a two-part name improves performance, but always typing a long schema is no fun.

To list the schema for the current database using code, query the `sysschemas` catalog view.

Table and Column Names

SQL Server is very liberal with table and column names, allowing up to 128 Unicode characters and spaces, as well as both uppercase and lowercase letters. Of course, taking advantage of that freedom with wild abandon will be regretted later when typing the lengthy column names and having to place brackets around columns with spaces. It's more dangerous to discuss naming conventions with programmers than it is to discuss politics in a mixed crowd. Nevertheless, here's my two cents.

There is a huge debate over whether table names should be singular or plural. I've seen well-meaning developers ask reasonable questions in the newsgroups and receive a barrage of attacks simply over their table names.

The plural camp believes that a table is a set of rows and as such should be named with a plural name. The reasoning often used by this camp is, "A table of customers is a set of customers. Sets include multiple items, so the table should be named the `Customers` table, unless you only have one customer, in which case you don't need a database."

From my informal polling, however, the singular-name view is held by about three-fourths of SQL Server developers. These developers hold that the customer table is the customer set, rather than the set of customers. A set of rows is not called a *rows set*, but a *row set,* and because tables are generally discussed as singular items, saying, "the `Customer` table" sounds cleaner than "the `Customers` table."

Most (but not all) developers would agree that consistency is more important than the naming convention itself.

Consistency is the database developer's holy grail. The purpose of naming conventions, constraints, referential integrity, relational design, and even column data type is to bring order and consistency to the data we use to model reality. Whenever you're faced with a database decision, asking "Which choice is the most consistent?" is a good step toward a solution.

Best Practice

Personally, I think that developers choose their naming conventions as a way to distance themselves from sloppy designs they've had to work with in the past. Having worked on poorly designed flat-file databases with plural names, I prefer singular names.

If a database is large enough that it will encompass several logical groupings of tables, I prefix a two- or three-letter abbreviation to the table name to make it easier to navigate the database. I've seen a system of numbering modules and tables that I don't recommend. `InvItem` is a good name for the item table in the inventory module. `0207_Item` is too cryptic.

Another issue involving differences in naming is the use of underscores to indicate words within the name. For example, some IT shops insist that the order-detail table be named `ORDER_DETAIL`. Personally, I avoid underscores except in many-to-many resolution tables. Studies have shown that the use of mixed case, such as in the name `OrderDetail`, is easier to read than all lowercase or all uppercase words.

Here are the database-naming conventions I use when developing databases:

✦ Use singular table names with no numbers, and a module prefix if useful.

✦ For many-to-many resolution tables, use `table_mm_table`.

✦ Set all names in mixed case (`MixedCase`) with no underscores or spaces.

✦ For the primary key, use the table name + `ID`. For example, the primary key for the `Customer` table is `CustomerID`.

✦ Give foreign keys the same name as their primary key unless the foreign key enforces a reflexive/recursive relationship, such as `MotherID` referring back to `PersonID` in the Family sample database; or the secondary table has multiple foreign keys to the same primary key, such as the many-to-many reflexive relationship in the Material sample database (`BillofMaterials.MaterialID` to `Material.MaterialID` and `BillofMaterials.SourceMaterialID` to `Material.MaterialID`).

✦ Avoid inconsistent abbreviations.

✦ Use consistent table and column names across all databases. For example, always use `LastName` followed by `FirstName`.

Filegroups

Apart from the columns, the only information you normally supply when creating a table is the name. However, you can create the table on a specific filegroup if the database has multiple filegroups.

The OBX Kites database uses two filegroups for data-organization purposes. All data that is modified on a regular basis goes into the `primary` filegroup. This filegroup is backed up frequently. Data that is rarely modified (such as the order priority lookup codes) go into the `static` filegroup:

```
CREATE TABLE OrderPriority (
  OrderPriorityID UNIQUEIDENTIFIER NOT NULL
    ROWGUIDCOL DEFAULT (NEWID()) PRIMARY KEY NONCLUSTERED,
  OrderPriorityName NVARCHAR (15) NOT NULL,
  OrderPriorityCode NVARCHAR (15) NOT NULL,
  Priority INT NOT NULL
  )
  ON [Static];
```

Creating Primary Keys

The primary and foreign keys are the links that bind the tables into a working relational database. I treat these columns as a domain separate from the user's data column. The design of these keys has a critical effect on the performance and usability of the physical database.

The database schema must transform from a theoretical logical design into a practical physical design, and the structure of the primary and foreign keys is often the crux of the redesign. Keys are very difficult to modify once the database is in production. Getting the primary keys right during the development phase is a battle worth fighting.

Primary Keys

The relational database depends on the primary key—the cornerstone of the physical database schema. The debate over natural (understood by users) versus surrogate (auto-generated) primary keys is perhaps the biggest debate in the database industry.

A physical-layer primary key has two purposes:

✦ To uniquely identify the row

✦ To serve as a useful object for a foreign key

SQL Server implements primary keys and foreign keys as constraints. The purpose of a constraint is to ensure that new data meets certain criteria, or to block the data-modification operation.

A primary-key constraint is effectively a combination of a unique constraint (not a null constraint) and either a clustered or non-clustered unique index.

Creating Primary Keys

In code, you set a column as the primary key in one of two ways:

✦ Declare the primary-key constraint in the `create table` statement. The following code from the Cape Hatteras Adventures sample database uses this technique to create the Guide table and set GuideID as the primary key with a non-clustered index:

```
CREATE TABLE dbo.Guide (
  GuideID INT IDENTITY NOT NULL PRIMARY KEY NONCLUSTERED,
  LastName  VARCHAR(50) NOT NULL,
  FirstName  VARCHAR(50) NOT NULL,
  Qualifications  VARCHAR(2048) NULL,
  DateOfBirth  DATETIME NULL,
  DateHire  DATETIME NULL
  )
  ON [Primary];
```

✦ Declare the primary-key constraint after the table is created using an `alter table` command. Assuming the primary key was not already set for the Guide table, the following DDL command would apply a primary-key constraint to the GuideID column:

```
ALTER TABLE dbo.Guide ADD CONSTRAINT
  PK_Guide PRIMARY KEY NONCLUSTERED(GuideID)
  ON [PRIMARY];
```

Cross-Reference The method of indexing the primary key (clustered vs. non-clustered) is one of the most important considerations of physical schema design. Chapter 50, "Query Analysis and Index Tuning" digs into the details of index pages and explains the strategies of primary key indexing.

To list the primary keys for the current database using code, query the sysobjects and syskey_constraints catalog views.

Natural Primary Keys

A *natural key* reflects how reality identifies the object. People's names, automobile VIN numbers, passport numbers, and street addresses are all examples of natural keys.

There are pros and cons to natural keys:

✦ Natural keys are easily identified by humans. On the plus side, humans can easily recognize the data. The disadvantage is that humans will want to assume meaning into the primary key, often creating "intelligent keys," assigning meaning to certain characters within the key.

Humans also tend to modify what they understand. Modifying primary key values is troublesome. If you use a natural primary key, be sure to enable cascading updates on every foreign key that refers to the natural primary key so that primary key modifications will not break referential integrity.

✦ Natural keys propagate the primary key values in every generation of the foreign keys. In addition, the composite foreign keys tend to grow wide, as they include multiple columns to include every ascending primary key.

The benefit is that it is possible to join from the bottom secondary table to the topmost primary table without including every intermediate table in a series of joins. The disadvantage is that the foreign key become complex and most joins must include several columns.

✦ Natural keys are commonly not in any organized order. This will hurt performance, as new data inserted in the middle of sorted data creates page splits.

Identity Column Surrogate Primary Keys

A *surrogate key* is assigned by computer and typically has no meaning to humans. Within SQL Server, surrogate keys are identity columns or global unique identifiers.

By far, the most popular method for building primary keys involves using an identity column. Like an auto-number column or sequence column in other databases, the identity column generates consecutive integers as new rows are inserted into the database. Optionally, you can specify the initial seed number and interval.

Identity columns offer two advantages:

✦ Integers are easier to manually recognize and edit than GUIDs.

✦ Integers are small and fast. My informal testing shows that integers are about 10 percent faster than GUIDs. Other published tests show integers as 10 to 33 percent faster. However, this performance difference only shows up when you're selecting 1,000 rows. A select statement retrieving a few rows from a large table as a single operation should show no performance difference.

The downside to identity columns is as follows:

✦ Because the scope of their uniqueness is only tablewide, the same integer values are in many tables. I've seen code that joins the wrong tables still return a populated result set because there was matching data in the two tables.

✦ Designs with identity columns tend to add surrogate primary keys to every table in lieu of composite primary keys created by multiple foreign keys. While this creates small, fast primary keys, it also creates more joins to navigate the schema structure.

Identity-column values are generated at the database engine level as the row is being inserted. Attempting to insert a value into an identity column or update an identity column will generate an error unless `set insert_identity` is set to `true`.

Cross-Reference

Chapter 16, "Modifying Data," includes a full discussion of the problems of modifying data in tables with identity columns.

The following DDL code from the Cape Hatteras Adventures sample database creates a table that uses an identity column for its primary key (the code listing is abbreviated):

```
CREATE TABLE dbo.Event (
  EventID INT IDENTITY NOT NULL PRIMARY KEY NONCLUSTERED,
  TourID INT NOT NULL FOREIGN KEY REFERENCES dbo.Tour,
  EventCode VARCHAR(10) NOT NULL,
  DateBegin DATETIME NULL,
  Comment NVARCHAR(255)
  )
  ON [Primary];
```

Setting a column, or columns, as the primary key in Management Studio is as simple as selecting the column and clicking the primary-key toolbar button. To build a composite primary key, select all the participating columns and press the primary-key button.

On The Web

To enable you to experience sample databases with both surrogate methods, the Family, Cape Hatteras Adventures, and Material Specification sample databases use identity columns, and the Outer Banks Kite Store sample database uses unique identifiers. All the chapter code and sample databases may be downloaded from www.SQLServerBible.com.

Using Uniqueidentifier Surrogate Primary Keys

The `uniqueidentifier` data type is SQL Server's counterpart to .NET's global unique identifier (GUID, pronounced GOO-id or gwid). It's a 16-byte hexadecimal number that is essentially unique among all tables, all databases, all servers, and all planets. While both identity columns and GUIDs are unique, the scope of the uniqueness is greater with GUIDs than identity columns, so while they are grammatically incorrect, GUIDs are more unique than identity columns.

GUIDs offer several advantages:

✦ A database using GUID primary keys can be replicated without a major overhaul. Replication will add a unique identifier to every table without a `uniqueidentifier` column. While this makes the column globally unique for replication purposes, the application code will still be identifying rows by the integer primary key only, and therefore merging replicated rows from other servers will cause an error because there will be duplicate primary key values.

✦ GUIDs discourage users from working with or assigning meaning to the primary keys.

✦ GUIDs eliminate join errors caused by joining the wrong tables but returning data regardless, because rows that should not match share the same integer values in key columns.

✦ GUIDs are forever. The table based on a typical integer-based identity column will hold only 2,147,483,648 rows. Of course, the data type could be set to `bigint` or `numeric`, but that lessens the size benefit of using the identity column.

✦ Because the GUID can be generated by either the column default, the `select`-statement expression, or code prior to the `select` statement, it's significantly easier to program with GUIDs than with identity columns. Using GUIDs circumvents the data-modification problems of using identity columns.

The drawbacks of unique identifiers are largely performance based:

✦ Unique identifiers are large compared to integers, so fewer of them fit on a page. The result is that more page reads are required to read the same number of rows.

✦ Unique identifiers generated by `NewID()`, like natural keys, are essentially random, so data inserts will eventually cause page splits, hurting performance. However, natural keys will have a natural distribution (more Smiths and Wilsons, fewer Nielsens and Shaws) so the page split problem is worse with natural keys.

The `Product` table in the Outer Banks Kite Store sample database uses a `uniqueidentifier` as its primary key. In the following script, the `ProductID` column's data type is set to `uniqueidentifier`. Its nullability is set to `false`. The column's `rowguidcol` property is set to `true`, enabling replication to detect and use this column. The default is a newly generated `uniqueidentifier`. It's the primary key, and it's indexed with a non-clustered unique index:

```
CREATE TABLE dbo.Product (
  ProductID UNIQUEIDENTIFIER NOT NULL
    ROWGUIDCOL DEFAULT (NEWSEQUNTIALID())
    PRIMARY KEY CLUSTERED,
  ProductCategoryID UNIQUEIDENTIFIER NOT NULL
    FOREIGN KEY REFERENCES dbo.ProductCategory,
  ProductCode CHAR(15) NOT NULL,
  ProductName NVARCHAR(50) NOT NULL,
  ProductDescription NVARCHAR(100) NULL,
  ActiveDate DATETIME NOT NULL DEFAULT GETDATE(),
  DiscountinueDate DATETIME NULL
  )
  ON [Static];
```

There are two primary methods of generating `Uniqueidentifiers` (both actually generated by Windows), and multiple locations where one can be generated:

✦ The `NewID()` function generates a `Uniqueidentifier` using several factors, including the computer NIC code, the MAC address, the CPU internal ID, and the current tick of the CPU clock. The last six bytes are from the node number of the NIC card.

The versatile `NewID()` function may be used as a column default, passed to an insert statement, or executed as a function within any expression.

✦ `NewsequentialID()` is similar to `NewID()`, but it guarantees that every new `uniquei-dentifier` is greater than any other `uniqueidentifier` for that table.

The `NewsequntialID()` function can be used only as a column default. This makes sense because the value generated is dependent on the greatest `Uniqueidentifier` in a specific table.

The `NewsequentialID()` function is new in SQL Server 2005. Now, `Uniqueidentifiers` can be clustered without the painful page-split problem!

Best Practice

In my opinion, in view of the practical benefits and risks of natural and surrogate keys, some identifiers are actually rigid enough that they will never change, and these are useful natural primary keys. However, if there is any question that the identifier might change or humans may want to modify it, then protect the data from users by using a surrogate primary key. I recommend integer identify columns unless the data will replicated, in which case `uniqueidentifiers` are the answer.

I present a discussion session at SQL Server conferences called "Data Modeling Key Decisions: Pros and Cons" that addresses these issues. I invite you to join me in a lively group to discuss these controversies.

Creating Foreign Keys

A secondary table that relates to a primary table uses a foreign key to point to the primary table's primary key. *Referential integrity (RI)* refers to the fact that the references have integrity, meaning that every foreign key points to a valid primary key. Referential integrity is vital to the consistency of the database. The database must begin and end every transaction in a consistent state. This consistency must extend to the foreign-key references.

Cross-Reference

Read more about database consistency and the ACID principles in Chapter 1, "The Information Architecture Principle," and Chapter 51, "Managing Transactions, Locking, and Blocking."

SQL Server tables may have up to 253 foreign-key constraints. The foreign key can reference primary keys, unique constraints, or unique indexes of any table except, of course, a temporary table.

It's a common misconception that referential integrity is an aspect of the primary key. It's the foreign key that is constrained to a valid primary-key value, so the constraint is an aspect of the foreign key, not the primary key.

Declarative Referential Integrity

SQL Server's *declarative referential integrity (DRI)* can enforce referential integrity without writing custom triggers or code. DRI is handled inside the SQL Server engine, which executes significantly faster than custom RI code executing within a trigger.

SQL Server implements DRI with foreign-key constraints. You can access the Foreign Key Relationships form, shown in Figure 17-6, to establish or modify a foreign-key constraint in Management Studio in two ways:

✦ Using the Database Designer, select the primary-key column and drag it to the foreign-key column. That action will open the Foreign Key Relationships dialog box.

✦ Using the Table Designer, click on the Relationships toolbar button, or select Table Designer ➪ Relationships. Alternately, from the Database Designer, select the secondary table (the one with the foreign key), and choose the Relationships toolbar button, or Relationship from the table's context menu.

There are several options in the Foreign Key Relationships form that define the behavior of the foreign key:

✦ Enforce for Replication

✦ Enforce Foreign Key Constraint

✦ Enforce Foreign Key Constraint

✦ Delete Rule and Update Rule (Cascading delete options are described later in this section)

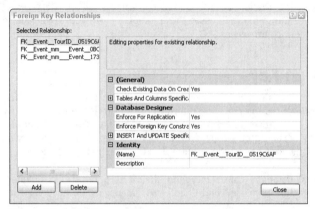

Figure 17-6: Use Management Studio's Foreign Key Relationships form to create or modify declarative referential integrity (DRI).

Within a T-SQL script, you can declare foreign-key constraints by either including the foreign-key constraint in the table-creation code or applying the constraint after the table is created. After the column definition, the phrase `foreign key references`, followed by the primary table, and optionally the column(s), creates the foreign key, as follows:

```
ForeignKeyColumn FOREIGN KEY REFERENCES PrimaryTable(PKID)
```

The following code from the CHA sample database creates the `tour_mm_guide` many-to-many junction table. As a junction table, `tour mm guide` has two foreign-key constraints: one to the `Tour` table and one to the `Guide` table. For demonstration purposes, the `TourID` foreign key specifies the primary-key column, but the `GuideID` foreign key simply points to the table and uses the primary key by default:

```
CREATE TABLE dbo.Tour_mm_Guide (
  TourGuideID INT
    IDENTITY
    NOT NULL
    PRIMARY KEY NONCLUSTERED,
  TourID INT
    NOT NULL
    FOREIGN KEY REFERENCES dbo.Tour(TourID)
    ON DELETE CASCADE,
```

```
GuideID INT
  NOT NULL
  FOREIGN KEY REFERENCES dbo.Guide
  ON DELETE CASCADE,
QualDate DATETIME NOT NULL,
RevokeDate DATETIME NULL
)
ON [Primary];
```

Some database developers prefer to include foreign-key constraints in the table definition, while others prefer to add them after the table is created. If the table already exists, you can add the foreign-key constraint to the table using the alter table add constraint DDL command, as shown here:

```
ALTER TABLE SecondaryTableName
  ADD CONSTRAINT ConstraintName
    FOREIGN KEY (ForeignKeyColumns)
    REFERENCES dbo.PrimaryTable (PrimaryKeyColumnName);
```

The Person table in the Family database must use this method because it uses a reflexive relationship, also called a *unary* or *self-join* relationship. A foreign key can't be created before the primary key exists. Because a reflexive foreign key refers to the same table, that table must be created prior to the foreign key.

This code, copied from the family_create.sql file, creates the Person table and then establishes the MotherID and FatherID foreign keys:

```
CREATE TABLE dbo.Person (
  PersonID  INT NOT NULL PRIMARY KEY NONCLUSTERED,
  LastName  VARCHAR(15) NOT NULL,
  FirstName  VARCHAR(15) NOT NULL,
  SrJr  VARCHAR(3) NULL,
  MaidenName VARCHAR(15) NULL,
  Gender CHAR(1) NOT NULL,
  FatherID INT NULL,
  MotherID INT NULL,
  DateOfBirth  DATETIME  NULL,
  DateOfDeath  DATETIME  NULL
  );
go
ALTER TABLE dbo.Person
  ADD CONSTRAINT FK_Person_Father
    FOREIGN KEY(FatherID) REFERENCES dbo.Person (PersonID);
ALTER TABLE dbo.Person
  ADD CONSTRAINT FK_Person_Mother
    FOREIGN KEY(MotherID) REFERENCES dbo.Person (PersonID);
```

To list the foreign keys for the current database using code, query the sysforeign_key_columns catalog views.

Optional Foreign Keys

An important distinction exists between optional foreign keys and mandatory foreign keys. Some relationships require a foreign key, as with an `OrderDetail` row that requires a valid order row, but other relationships don't require a value—the data is valid with or without a foreign key, as determined in the logical design.

In the physical layer, the difference is the nullability of the foreign-key column. If the foreign key is mandatory, the column should not allow nulls. An optional foreign key allows nulls. A relationship with complex optionality will require either a check constraint or a trigger to fully implement the relationship.

The common description of referential integrity is "no orphan rows"—referring to the days when primary tables were called *parent files* and secondary tables were called *child files*. Optional foreign keys are the exception to this description. You can think of an optional foreign key as "orphans are allowed, but if there's a parent it must be the legal parent."

Cascading Deletes and Updates

A complication created by referential integrity is that RI will prevent you from deleting or modifying a primary row being referred to by secondary rows until those secondary rows have been deleted. If the primary row is deleted and the secondary rows' foreign keys are still pointing to the now deleted primary keys, referential integrity is violated.

The solution to this problem is to modify the secondary rows as part of the primary table transaction. DRI can do this automatically for you. Four outcomes are possible for the affected secondary rows selected in the Delete Rule or Update Rule properties of the Foreign Key Relationships form. Update Rule is meaningful for natural primary keys only:

✦ **No Action:** The secondary rows won't be modified in any way. Their presence will block the primary rows from being deleted or modified.

Use No Action when the secondary rows provide value to the primary rows. You don't want the primary rows to be deleted or modified if secondary rows exist. For instance, if there are invoices for the account, don't delete the account.

✦ **Cascade:** The delete or modification action being performed on the primary rows will also be performed on the secondary rows.

Use Cascade when the secondary data is useless without the primary data. For example, if Order 123 is being deleted, all the order details rows for Order 123 will be deleted as well. If Order 123 is being updated to become Order 456, then the order details rows must also be changed to Order 456 (assuming a natural primary key)

✦ **Set Null:** This option leaves the secondary rows intact but sets the Foreign Key column's value to null. This option requires that the foreign key is nullable.

Use Set Null when you want to permit the primary row to be deleted without affecting the existence of the secondary. For example, if a class is deleted, you don't want a student's rows to be deleted because the student's data is valid independent of the class data.

✦ **Set Default:** The primary rows may be deleted or modified and the foreign key values in the affected secondary rows are set to their column default values.

This option is similar to the Set Null option except that you can set a specific value. For schemas that use surrogate nulls (e.g., empty strings), setting the column default to `' '` and the Delete Rule to `Set Default` would set the foreign key to an empty string if the primary table rows were deleted.

Cascading deletes, and the trouble they can cause for data modifications, are also discussed in the section "Deleting Data" in Chapter 16, "Modifying Data."

Within T-SQL code, adding the `on delete cascade` option to the foreign-key constraint enables the cascade operation. The following code, extracted from the OBXKites sample database's `OrderDetail` table, uses the cascading delete option on the `OrderID` foreign-key constraint:

```
CREATE TABLE dbo.OrderDetail (
  OrderDetailID UNIQUEIDENTIFIER
    NOT NULL
    ROWGUIDCOL
    DEFAULT (NEWID())
    PRIMARY KEY NONCLUSTERED,
  OrderID UNIQUEIDENTIFIER
    NOT NULL
    FOREIGN KEY REFERENCES dbo.[Order]
      ON DELETE CASCADE,
  ProductID UNIQUEIDENTIFIER
    NULL
    FOREIGN KEY REFERENCES dbo.Product,
```

Chapter 24, "Exploring Advanced T-SQL Solutions," shows how to create triggers that handle custom referential integrity and cascading deletes for nonstandard data schemas or cross-database referential integrity.

Creating User-Data Columns

A user-data column stores user data. These columns typically fall into two categories: columns users use to identify a person, place, thing, event, or action, and columns that further describe the person, place, thing, event, or action.

SQL Server tables may have up to 1,024 columns, but well-designed relational-database tables seldom have more than 25, and most have only a handful.

Data columns are created during table creation by listing the columns as parameters to the `create table` command. The columns are listed within parentheses as column name, data type, and any column attributes such as constraints, nullability, or default value:

```
CREATE TABLE TableName (
ColumnName DATATYPE Attributes,
ColumnName DATATYPE Attributes
);
```

Data columns can be added to existing tables using the `alter table add column` command:

```
ALTER TABLE TableName
  ADD ColumnName DATATYPE Attributes;
```

An existing column may be modified with the `alter table alter column` command:

```
ALTER TABLE TableName
  ALTER COLUMN ColumnName
    NEWDATATYPE Attributes;
```

To list the columns for the current database using code, query the `sysobjects` and `syscolumns` catalog views.

Column Data Types

The column's data type serves two purposes:

✦ It enforces the first level of data integrity. Character data won't be accepted into a `datetime` or `numeric` column. I have seen databases with every column set to `nvarchar` to ease data entry. What a waste. The data type is a valuable data-validation tool that should not be overlooked.

✦ It determines the amount of disk storage allocated to the column.

Character Data Types

SQL Server supports several character data types, listed in Table 17-2.

Table 17-2: Character Data Types

Data Type	Description	Size in Bytes
Char(n)	Fixed-length character data up to 8,000 characters long using collation character set	Defined length * 1 byte
Nchar(n)	Unicode fixed-length character data	Defined length * 2 bytes
varchar(n)	Variable-length character data up to 8,000 characters long using collation character set	1 byte per character
varchar(max)	Variable-length character data up to 2GB in length using collation character set	1 byte per character
nvarchar(n)	Unicode variable-length character data up to 8,000 characters long using collation character set	2 bytes per character
nvarchar(max)	Unicode variable-length character data up to 2GB in length using collation character set	2 bytes per character
text	Variable-length character data up to 2,147,483,647 characters in length	1 byte per character
ntext	Unicode variable-length character data up to 1,073,741,823 characters in length	2 bytes per character
sysname	A Microsoft user-defined data type used for table and column names that is the equivalent of nvarchar(128)	2 bytes per character

Unicode data types are very useful for storing multilingual data. The cost, however, is the doubled size. Some developers use `nvarchar` for all their character-based columns, while others avoid it at all costs. I recommend using Unicode data when the database might use foreign languages; otherwise, use `char`, `varchar`, or `text`.

Numeric Data Types

SQL Server supports several numeric data types, listed in Table 17-3.

Table 17-3: Numeric Data Types

Data Type	Description	Size in Bytes
bit	1 or 0	1 bit
tinyint	Integers from 0 to 255	1 byte
smallint	Integers from -32,768 to 32,767	2 bytes
int	Integers from -2,147,483,648 to 2,147,483,647	4 bytes
bigint	Integers from -2^{63} to $2^{63}-1$	8 bytes
decimal or numeric	Fixed-precision numbers up to $-10^{38} + 1$	Varies according to length
money	Numbers from -2^{63} to 2^{63}, accuracy to one ten-thousandths (.0001)	8 bytes
smallmoney	Numbers from -214,748.3648 through +214,748.3647, accuracy to ten thousandths (.0001)	4 bytes
float	Floating-point numbers ranging from -1.79E + 308 through 1.79E + 308, depending on the bit precision	4 or 8 bytes
real	Float with 24-bit precision	4 bytes

Best Practice

When working with monetary values, be very careful with the data type. Using `float` or `real` data types for money will cause rounding errors. The data types `money` and `smallmoney` are accurate to one hundredth of a U.S. penny. For some monetary values, the client may request precision only to the penny, in which case `decimal` is the more appropriate data type.

Date/Time Data Types

SQL Server stores both the date and the time in a single column using the `datetime` and `smalldatetime` data types, described in Table 17-4. The primary differences between the two are accuracy and history. If the column is to hold only the date and will not contain historical data from before the twentieth century, `smalldatetime` is appropriate. If time is included in the requirement, the precision of `smalldatetime` is usually insufficient.

Table 17-4: Date/Time Data Types

Data Type	Description	Size in Bytes
datetime	Date and time values from January 1, 1753, through December 31, 9999, accurate to three milliseconds	8 bytes
smalldatetime	Date and time values from January 1, 1900, through June 6, 2079, accurate to one minute	4 bytes

The Julian calendar took effect on January 1, 1753. Because SQL Server doesn't want to decide which nation's or religion's calendar system to use for data from before 1753, it avoids the issue and simply won't accept any dates prior to 1753. While this is normally not a problem, some historical and genealogy databases require earlier dates. As a workaround, I recommend creating a date column from a char data type and using a trigger or stored procedure to verify the date's formatting and validity upon insertion.

 Caution   Some programmers (non-DBAs) choose character data types for date columns. This can cause a horrid conversion mess. Use the IsDate() function to sort through the bad data.

Other Data Types

Other data types, listed and described in Table 17-5, fulfill the needs created by unique values, binary large objects, and variant data.

Table 17-5: Other Data Types

Data Type	Description	Size in Bytes
timestamp	Database-wide unique random value generated with every update	8 bytes
uniqueidentifier	System-generated 16-byte value	16 bytes
Binary(n)	Fixed-length data up to 8,000 bytes	Defined length
Binary(max)	Fixed-length data up to 8,000 bytes	Defined length
varbinary	Variable-length binary data up to 8,000 bytes	Bytes used
image	Variable-length binary data up to 2,147,483,647 bytes	Bytes used
sql_variant	Can store any data type up to 2,147,483,647 bytes	Depends on data type and length

The timestamp data type, previously known as the rowversion data type, is useful for detecting lost updates, as discussed in Chapter 51: "Managing Transactions, Locking, and Blocking."

The uniqueidentifier is a significant data type and it serves well as a primary key, especially when the database might be replicated. Uniqueidentifiers are discussed in detail in the "Creating Primary Keys" section earlier in this chapter.

Calculated Columns

A calculated column is powerful in that it presents the results of a predefined expression the way a view (a stored SQL select statement) does, but without the overhead of a view. Such a column does not actually store any data; instead, the data is calculated when queried.

Calculated columns also improve data integrity by performing the calculation at the table level, rather than trusting that each query developer will get the calculation correct. They may even be indexed.

The syntax is the opposite of that of a column alias:

```
ColumnName as Expression
```

The OrderDetail table from the OBX Kites sample database includes a calculated column for the extended price, as shown in the following abbreviated code:

```
CREATE TABLE dbo.OrderDetail (
...
  Quantity NUMERIC(7,2) NOT NULL,
  UnitPrice MONEY NOT NULL,
  ExtendedPrice AS Quantity * UnitPrice Persisted,
...
  )
  ON [Primary];
Go
```

New in 2005   Calculated columns may be persisted on the disk with SQL Server 2005. This can significantly improve the performance of calculated columns when used for searches.

Column Constraints and Defaults

The database is only as good as the quality of the data. A constraint is a high-speed data-validation check or business-logic check performed at the database-engine level. Besides the data type itself, SQL Server includes five types of constraints:

- ✦ **Primary-key constraint:** Ensures a unique non-null key
- ✦ **Foreign-key constraint:** Ensures that the value points to a valid key
- ✦ **Nullability:** Indicates whether the column can accept a null value
- ✦ **Check constraint:** Custom Boolean constraint
- ✦ **Unique constraint:** Ensures a unique value

SQL Server also includes the column option:

- ✦ **Column Default:** Supplies a value if none is specified in the insert statement

The column default is referred to as a type of constraint on one page of SQL Server Books Online, but is not listed in the constraints on another page. I call it a column option because it does not constrain user-data entry, nor does it enforce a data-integrity rule. However, it serves the column as a useful option.

Column Nullability

A null value is an unknown value; typically, it means that the column has not yet had a user entry.

Cross-Reference Chapter 8, "Using Expressions and Scalar Functions," explains how to define, detect, and handle nulls.

Whether or not a column will even accept a null value is referred to as the nullability of the column and is configured by the `null` or `not null` column attribute.

New columns in SQL Server default to `not null`, meaning that they do not accept nulls. However, this option is normally overridden by the connection property `ansi_null_dflt_on`. The ANSI standard is to default to `null`, which accepts nulls, in table columns that aren't explicitly created with a `not null` option.

Best Practice Because the default column nullability differs between ANSI SQL and SQL Server, it's best to avoid relying on the default behavior and explicitly declare `null` or `not null` when creating tables.

The following code demonstrates the ANSI default nullability versus SQL Server's nullability. The first test uses the SQL Server default by setting the database `ansi null` option to `false`, and the `ansi_null_dflt_off` connection setting to `on`:

```
USE TempDB;
EXEC sp_dboption 'TempDB', ANSI_NULL_DEFAULT, 'false';
SET ANSI_NULL_DFLT_OFF ON;
```

The `NullTest` table is created without specifying the nullability:

```
CREATE TABLE NullTest(
  PK INT IDENTITY,
  One VARCHAR(50)
  );
```

The following code attempts to insert a null:

```
INSERT NullTest(One)
  VALUES (NULL);
```

Result:

```
Server: Msg 515, Level 16, State 2, Line 1
Cannot insert the value NULL into column 'One',
table 'TempDB.dbo.NullTest';
column does not allow nulls. INSERT fails.
The statement has been terminated.
```

Because the nullability was set to the SQL Server default when the table was created, the column does not accept null values. The second sample will rebuild the table with the ANSI SQL nullability default:

```
EXEC sp_dboption 'TempDB', ANSI_NULL_DEFAULT, 'true';
SET ANSI_NULL_DFLT_ON ON;

DROP TABLE NullTest;

CREATE TABLE NullTest(
  PK INT IDENTITY,
  One VARCHAR(50)
  );
```

The next example attempts to insert a null:

```
INSERT NullTest(One)
  VALUES (NULL);
```

Result:

```
(1 row(s) affected)
```

Unique Constraints

A unique constraint is similar to a unique index or a primary-key constraint. Its purpose is to ensure that every value is a unique value. This option is likely to be used when a column has meaning to a user and is perceived as unique, such as an SSN or ID number.

In Management Studio, a unique constraint is applied in the Index tab of the Table Properties dialog box in the same way that an index is created, except that the unique constraint is selected instead of index.

In code, a unique constraint may be applied to a column by specifying `unique` after the column definition, as follows:

```
CREATE TABLE Employee (
  EmployeeID INT PRIMARY KEY NONCLUSTERED,
  EmployeeNumber CHAR(8) UNIQUE,
  LastName NVARCHAR(35),
  FirstName NVARCHAR(35)
  );
Insert Employee (EmployeeID, EmployeeNumber, LastName, FirstName)
  Values( 1, '1', 'Wilson', 'Bob');

Insert Employee (EmployeeID, EmployeeNumber, LastName, FirstName);
  Values( 2, '1', 'Smith', 'Joe');
```

Result:

```
Server: Msg 2627, Level 14, State 2, Line 1
Violation of UNIQUE KEY constraint 'UQ__Employee__68487DD7'.
Cannot insert duplicate key in object 'Employee'.
The statement has been terminated.
```

To add a unique constraint to an existing table, use the `alter table` DDL command:

```
ALTER TABLE Employee
  ADD CONSTRAINT EmpNumUnique
    UNIQUE (EmployeeNumber);
```

Check Constraints

The check constraint is a fast row-level integrity check. It's basically a small formula that ultimately must return a Boolean `true` or `false`. A check constraint may access any data local to the current row. It can't check other table values or perform lookups. Scalar functions (covered in Chapter 8, "Using Expressions and Scalar Functions") may be included in the check constraint.

A check constraint can contain a user-defined scalar function, covered in Chapter 22, "Building User-Defined Functions," and the function can perform a range of T-SQL code. As a result, calling a user-defined scalar function within a check constraint opens up a world of possibilities, including the possibility for complex lookups. However, complex business-rule checks are more commonly performed within `after` triggers.

Check constraints are useful for ensuring the enforcement of general data-validation rules or simple business rules, such as confirming that a termination date is greater than or equal to the hire date, or that the hire date is greater than the birth date plus 18 years.

A check constraint is significantly faster than a table trigger. If the data-validation rule can be performed by a check constraint, use the check constraint instead of a trigger.

The following code applies the constraint that the `EmployeeNumber` must be other than "1":

```
Drop Table Employee

CREATE TABLE Employee (
  EmployeeID INT PRIMARY KEY NONCLUSTERED,
  EmployeeNumber CHAR(8) CHECK (EmployeeNumber <> '1'),
  LastName NVARCHAR(35),
  FirstName NVARCHAR(35)
  );

Insert Employee (EmployeeID, EmployeeNumber, LastName, FirstName)
  Values( 2, '1', 'Smith', 'Joe');
```

Result:

```
Server: Msg 547, Level 16, State 1, Line 1
INSERT statement conflicted with COLUMN CHECK constraint
'CK__Employee__Employ__5FB337D6'.
The conflict occurred in database 'tempdb',
table 'Employee', column 'EmployeeNumber'.
The statement has been terminated.
```

Use the `alter database` command to add a check constraint to an existing table:

```
ALTER TABLE Employee
  ADD CONSTRAINT NoHireSmith
    CHECK (Lastname <> 'SMITH');
```

Default Option

The default is the value SQL Server will insert into the table if no value is supplied by the `insert` DDL command. Defaults become more important when the column does not permit nulls, because failing to specify a value when inserting into a non-nullable column without a default will cause the insert to be rejected.

The default value may be one of the following:

✦ A valid static numeric or character value, such as `123` or `local`

✦ A scalar system function, such as `GetDate()`or `newID()`

✦ A user-defined scalar function

✦ A null

The default value must be a data type compatible with the column.

If the table is being created using Management Studio, the default is easily specified as one of the column properties.

From code, the default is added as one of the column options as the table is first created, or later as an `alter table add constraint` DDL command.

The following truncated code sample is taken from the `Product` table of the OBX Kite Store sample database. The `ActiveDate` column's default is set to the current date:

```
CREATE TABLE dbo.Product (
...
  ActiveDate DATETIME NOT NULL DEFAULT GETDATE(),
...
    );
```

The same default can be set after the table is created. The following code runs `sp_help` to determine the existing default constraint name, `drop` the constraint, and then reestablish the default constraint using `alter table`:

```
sp_help Product;
```

Result (abbreviated):

```
constraint_type          constraint_name
------------------------ -------------------
DEFAULT on column ActiveDate
                    DF__Product__ActiveD__7F60ED59
```

The `alter table` command removes the existing default constraint:

```
ALTER TABLE Product
  DROP CONSTRAINT DF__Product__ActiveD__7F60ED59
```

The add constraint command re-applies the default:

```
ALTER TABLE Product
  ADD CONSTRAINT  ActiveDefault
  DEFAULT GetDate() FOR ActiveDate;
```

Data Catalog

While SQL Server lacks a formal data-catalog feature, the user-defined data types can serve as a substitute. A user-defined data type is basically a named object with the following additional features:

✦ Defined data type and length

✦ Defined nullability

✦ Predefined rules that may be bound to the user-defined data types

✦ Predefined user-defaults that may be bound to the user-defined data types

For highly normalized databases that don't have the same basic data in different tables, the data-catalog concept may seem irrelevant. However, a good data-type standard within an IT shop is very useful. For example, if every database shares the same specs for a LastName column, coding at all levels becomes easier and less error prone. To create a data catalog of rules, defaults, and user-defined data types, and apply it to multiple databases, the best plan would be to create a DataCatalog.sql script and then run that script in each database, or place them within the Model database.

User-Defined Rules

A rule is similar to a check constraint except it's created independently and then bound to a column. Once a rule is created it may be bound to multiple columns or user-defined data types. The rule consists only of a name and a Boolean expression. The Boolean expression can refer to data using the @ character followed by the name of a data column.

The following code demonstrates creating a rule that tests the birthday column and ensures that future births aren't entered:

```
-- User Defined Rules
CREATE RULE BirthdateRule AS @Birthdate <= Getdate();
```

To apply the rule to a table column or user-defined data type, use the sp_bindrule stored procedure. The first parameter is the name of the rule and the second parameter is the object to which the rule is being bound. This code applies BirthdateRule to the BirthDate column in the Person table:

```
EXEC sp_bindrule
  @rulename = 'BirthdateRule',
  @objname =  'Person.Birthdate';
```

Best Practice

Rules are considered a backward compatibility feature. They are not recommended by Microsoft, and will not be supported in a future version of SQL Server. Check constraints are placed directly on the column, and using them is considered better coding practice than using rules. If you have rules in your database, refactor them as check constraints.

Within Management Studio, rules are created and bound within the Rules node under each database. However, most developers who use rules will want to create them in a reusable script.

User-Defined Default

Defaults are easily created directly in the table definition, although, like rules, they exist primarily for backward compatibility. However, the default object is a named value that may be consistently applied across multiple tables. The defaults may be created and bound to columns in Management Studio in the Defaults node under each database.

The following code creates a user-defined default of the current date. The default is then bound to the Hiredate column:

```
CREATE DEFAULT HireDefault AS Getdate()
go
sp_bindefault 'HireDefault', 'Contact.Hiredate';
```

User-Defined Data Types

A user-defined data type assigns a name to a system data type and nullability setting. The named user-defined data type may then be used like a system data type within any table definition.

The SysName data type is actually a Microsoft-supplied user-defined data type that should be used whenever you are storing system names (table names, column names) in columns.

If you use Management Studio, user-defined data types may be created under the User-Defined Data Type node under each database. User-defined data types may be defined with the sp_addtype system stored procedure by passing the name, data type, and nullability as parameters. The following example creates a user-defined data type, adds a default and a rule, and then binds that rule to a table:

```
EXEC sp_addtype
  @typename = Birthdate,
  @phystype = SmallDateTime,
  @nulltype = 'NOT NULL';
go
EXEC sp_bindefault
  @defname = 'BirthdateDefault',
  @objname = 'Birthdate',
  @futureonly = 'futureonly';

EXEC sp_bindrule
  @rulename = 'BirthdateRule',
  @objname = 'Person.Birthdate';
```

DDL Triggers

A *trigger* is code that executes as the result of some action. DML triggers fire as the result of DML code—an insert, update, or delete. DDL triggers fire as the result of some Data Definition Language (DDL) code—create, alter, or drop. DML triggers respond to data changes, and DDL triggers respond to schema changes. An entire chapter could be written on

DDL triggers. This section is intended to get you over the learning curve and started writing DDL triggers.

New in 2005   DDL triggers are new to SQL Server and are useful for auditing schema-level changes.

DDL triggers can respond to either changes in the database schema or changes at the sever level. Because the triggers can respond to so many types of events and commands, the command that fired the trigger is passed to the trigger in XML using the `EventData()` function.

Cross-Reference   To read about creating DML triggers and their many uses, turn to Chapter 23, "Creating DML Triggers."

Creating and Altering DDL Triggers

DDL triggers are created or altered using syntax similar to working with DML triggers. The location of the trigger, specified by the `on` clause, is either `all server` or `database` — literally, the term is `database`, not the name of the database:

```
CREATE | ALTER TRIGGER TriggerName
ON ALL SERVER | DATABASE
(WITH Option)
FOR | AFTER EventType or EventGroup,...n
AS
Code
```

The options are `encryption` and `execute as`, both of which could prove useful for system-level auditing triggers. There are dozens of events and event groups — one for every DDL type of action that can be executed on the server or database. A few of the more interesting events are listed here; the remainder are in Books Online.

Server-level DDL triggers can respond to the following server events:

✦ Alter Authorization Server

✦ Create | Alter | Drop Database

✦ Create | Alter | Drop Login

✦ Create | Drop Endpoint

✦ Create | Alter | Drop Server Access

Database DDL triggers have these possible events:

✦ Create | Alter | Drop Application Role

✦ Grant | Deny | Revoke Database

✦ Create | Drop Event Notification

✦ Create | Alter | Drop Function

✦ Create | Alter | Drop Index

✦ Create | Alter | Drop Procedure

✦ Create | Alter | Drop Role

✦ Create | Alter | Drop Schema

✦ Create | Alter | Drop Synonym

✦ Create | Alter | Drop Table

✦ Create | Alter | Drop Trigger

✦ Create | Alter | Drop User

✦ Create | Alter | Drop View

✦ Create | Alter | Drop XML Schema Collection

Using Management Studio, database triggers are listed under the database's Programmability node in Object Explorer. Database triggers can be scripted using Object Explorer, but not modified as easily as other programmability objects such as stored procedures. Server triggers are listed under Server Objects in Object Explorer.

To list the database DDL triggers using code, query the `systriggers` and `sysevents` catalog views. Server triggers are found at `sysserver_triggers` and `sysserver_trigger_events`.

To remove the DDL trigger, use the `drop trigger` command:

```
DROP TRIGGER TriggerName
```

EventData()

DDL triggers can respond to so many different events that they need some method of capturing data about the event that caused them to fire. DML triggers have the inserted and deleted logical tables; DDL triggers have the `EventData()` function. This function returns XML-formatted data about the event. The XML schema varies depending on the type of event captured. Note that parts of the XML schema are case sensitive.

Using the `EventData()` function to populate an XML variable, the trigger can use XQuery to investigate the values.

Cross-Reference   For more on XML and working with XQuery, see Chapter 31, "Using XML, XPath and XQuery."

The following sample DDL trigger captures information about any table changes in the CHA2 database and records the changes to an audit table:

```
USE CHA2;

CREATE TABLE SchemaAudit (
  AuditDate DATETIME NOT NULL,
  UserName VARCHAR(50) NOT NULL,
  Object VARCHAR(50) NOT NULL,
  DDLStatement VARCHAR(max) NOT NULL
```

```
    )
go

CREATE TRIGGER SchemaAudit
ON DATABASE
FOR CREATE_TABLE, ALTER_TABLE, DROP_TABLE
AS
DECLARE @EventData XML
SET @EventData = EventData()
INSERT SchemaAudit (AuditDate, UserName, Object, DDLStatement)
SELECT
  GetDate(),
  @EventData.value('data(/EVENT_INSTANCE/UserName)[1]', 'SYSNAME'),
  @EventData.value('data(/EVENT_INSTANCE/ObjectName)[1]', 'VARCHAR(50)'),
  @EventData.value('data(/EVENT_INSTANCE/TSQLCommand/CommandText)[1]',
    'VARCHAR(max)')

GO

CREATE TABLE Test (
  PK INT NOT NULL
  )
GO
DROP TABLE Test
GO
SELECT * FROM SchemaAudit
```

Result:

```
AuditDate                UserName   Object   DDLStatement
----------------------   --------   ------   ------------------------------------
2006-03-07 13:07:24.437  dbo        Test     CREATE TABLE Test (PK INT NOT NULL)
2006-03-07 13:07:24.450  dbo        Test     DROP TABLE Test
```

Enabling and Disabling DDL Triggers

DDL triggers can be turned on and off. This is good because DBAs need an easy way to disable DDL triggers that roll back any schema changes. The following code disables and then
enables the SchemaAudit trigger:

```
DISABLE TRIGGER SchemaAudit
ON Family;

ENABLE TRIGGER SchemaAudit
ON Family;
```

Summary

The logical database schema often requires tweaking in order to serve as a physical schema. It's in the nitty-gritty of the physical-database schema that the logical design takes shape and becomes a working database within the restrictions of the data types, keys, and constraints of the database product. Knowing the table-definition capabilities of SQL Server means that you can implement some project features at the server-constraint level, rather than in T-SQL code in a trigger or stored procedure.

Within Part 4, "Developing with SQL Server," this chapter has provided the code to build the physical schema. From here, the rest of this part continues the development discussion, with several more chapters of T-SQL and then several chapters of .NET and other development technologies.

✦   ✦   ✦

Programming with Transact-SQL

✦   ✦   ✦   ✦

In This Chapter

The basics of T-SQL and batches

Working with local variables

Controlling the flow of the batch

Exploring SQL Server objects with code

Working with temporary tables and table variables

Building dynamic SQL queries

Using multiple assignment variable select statements

Trapping and handling errors

✦   ✦   ✦   ✦

Standard SQL Data Manipulation Language (DML) commands — `select`, `insert`, `update`, and `delete` — only modify or return data. SQL DML lacks both the programming structure to develop procedures and algorithms, and the database-specific commands to control and tune the server. To compensate, each full-featured database product must complement the SQL standard with some proprietary SQL language extension.

Transact-SQL, better known as T-SQL, is Microsoft's implementation of SQL plus its collection of extensions to SQL. The purpose of T-SQL is to provide a set of procedural tools for the development of a transactional database.

T-SQL is often thought of as synonymous with stored procedures. In reality it's much more than that. It may be employed in several different ways within a SQL Server client/server application:

+ T-SQL is used within expressions as part of DML commands (`insert`, `update`, and `delete`) submitted by the client process.

+ T-SQL is used within blocks of code submitted to SQL Server from a client as a batch or script.

+ T-SQL functions are used as expressions within check constraints.

+ T-SQL code is used within batches of code that have been packaged within SQL Server as stored procedures, functions, or triggers.

Truth be told, this book has been covering T-SQL programming since Chapter 7, "Understanding Basic Query Flow." The DML commands are the heart of T-SQL. This chapter merely adds the programmatic elements required to develop server-side procedural code. The language features explained in this chapter are the foundation for developing stored procedures, user-defined functions, and triggers.

Best Practice

Although SQL Server 2005 introduces .NET and the common language runtime to the database development platform, T-SQL remains the best language for tasks that access the database.

Transact-SQL Fundamentals

T-SQL is designed to add structure to the handling of sets of data. Because of this, it does not provide several language features that application development needs. If you do a lot of application programming development, you'll find that T-SQL is in many ways the exact opposite of how you think when programming in VB, C#, Java, or any other structured development language.

T-SQL Batches

A *query* is a single SQL DML statement, and a *batch* is a collection of one or more T-SQL statements. The entire collection is sent to SQL Server from the front-end application as a single unit of code.

SQL Server parses the entire batch as a unit. Any syntax error will cause the entire batch to fail, meaning that none of the batch will be executed. However, the parsing does not check any object names or schemas because a schema may change by the time the statement is executed.

Terminating a Batch

A SQL script file or a Query Analyzer window may contain multiple batches. If this is the case, a batch-separator keyword terminates each batch. By default, the batch-separator keyword is go (similar to how the Start button is used to shut down Windows). The batch-separator keyword must be the only keyword in the line. Any other characters, even a comment, on the same line will neutralize the batch separator.

The batch separator is actually a function of SQL Server Management Studio, not SQL Server. It can be modified in the Query Execution page by selecting Tools ➪ Options, but I wouldn't recommend creating a custom batch separator (at least not for your friends).

Terminating a batch will kill all local variables, temporary tables, and cursors created by that batch.

DDL Commands

Some T-SQL DDL commands, such as `Create Procedure`, are required to be the first command in the batch. Very long scripts that create several objects often include numerous go batch terminators. Because SQL Server evaluates syntax by the batch, using go throughout a long script also helps locate syntax errors.

Switching Databases

Interactively, the current database is indicated in the SQL Editor toolbar and can be changed there. In code, the current database is selected with the use command. Use can be inserted within a batch to specify the database from that point on:

```
USE CHA2
```

It's a good practice to explicitly specify the correct database with the use command, rather than assume that the user will select the correct database prior to running the script.

Executing Batches

A batch can be executed in several ways:

✦ A complete SQL script (including all the batches in the script) may be executed by opening the .sql file with SQL Server Management Studio's SQL Editor and pressing F5, clicking the *! Execute* toolbar button, or selecting Query ⇨ Execute. I have altered my Windows file settings so that double-clicking a .SQL file opens Query Analyzer.

✦ Selected T-SQL statements may be executed within SQL Server Management Studio's SQL Editor by means of highlighting those commands and pressing F5, clicking the *! Execute* toolbar button, or selecting Query ⇨ Execute.

✦ An application can submit a T-SQL batch using ADO or ODBC for execution.

✦ A SQL script may be executed by means of running the SQLCmd command-line utility and passing the SQL script file as a parameter.

✦ The SQLCmd utility has several parameters and may be configured to meet nearly any command-line need.

Cross-Reference For details on running SQLCmd, refer to Chapter 6, "Using Management Studio."

Executing a Stored Procedure

When calling a stored procedure within a SQL batch, the exec command executes the stored procedure with a few special rules. In a sense, because line returns are meaningless to SQL Server, the exec command is serving to terminate the previous T-SQL command.

If the stored-procedure call is the first line of a batch (and if it's the only line, then it's also the first line), the stored-procedure call doesn't require the exec command. However, including the exec command anyway won't cause any problems and prevents an error if the code is cut and pasted later.

The following two system-stored–procedure calls demonstrate the use of the exec command within a batch:

```
sp_help;
EXEC sp_help;
```

This section covered the batch aspects of exec. More information about creative ways to use exec can be found in the "Dynamic SQL" section later in this chapter.

T-SQL Formatting

Throughout this book, T-SQL code has been formatted for readability; this section specifies the details of formatting T-SQL code.

Statement Termination

The ANSI SQL standard is to place a semicolon at the end of each command in order to terminate it. When programming T-SQL, the semicolon is optional. There are a few rules about using the semicolon:

- ✦ Don't place one after a `try end`.

- ✦ Don't place one after an `if` condition.

- ✦ You must place one before any CTE.

Best Practice

As a BestPractice and for improved readability, I recommend using the semicolon. In future versions of SQL Server this may become a requirement, so making the change now may pay off later.

Line Continuation

T-SQL commands, by their nature, tend to be long. Some of the queries in the last chapter, with multiple joins and subqueries, were over a page long. I like that T-SQL ignores spaces and end-of-line returns. This smart feature means that long lines can be continued without a special line-continuation character, which makes T-SQL code significantly more readable.

Other SQL implementations, such as Access, require a semicolon to terminate a SQL query. SQL Server will accept a semicolon, but does not require one.

Comments

T-SQL accepts both ANSI-standard comments and C-style comments within the same batch.

The ANSI-standard comment begins with two hyphens and concludes with an end-of-line:

```
-- This is an ANSI-style comment
```

ANSI-style comments may be embedded within a single SQL command:

```
Select FirstName, LastName      -- selects the columns
   FROM Persons                 -- the source table
   Where LastName Like 'Hal%';  -- the row restriction
```

The SQL Editor can apply or remove ANSI-style comments to all selected lines. Select either Edit ➪ Advanced ➪ Comment Out (Ctrl+K, Ctrl+C) or Edit ➪ Advanced ➪ Remove Comments (Ctrl+K, Ctrl+U), respectively.

C language–style comments begin with /* and conclude with */. These comments are useful for commenting out a block of lines such as a code header or large test query:

```
/*
Order table Insert Trigger
Paul Nielsen
ver 1.0 July 21, 2006
Logic: etc.
ver 1.1: July 31, 2006, added xyz
*/
```

A benefit of C style comments is that a large multi-line query within the comments may be selected and executed without altering the comments.

Debugging T-SQL

When a syntax error is found, the SQL Editor will display the error and the line number of the error within the batch. Double-clicking on the error message will place the cursor on the offending line.

Often the error won't occur at the exact word that is reported as the error. The error location reported is simply how far SQL Server's parser got before it detected the error. Usually the actual error is somewhere just before or after the reported error. Nevertheless, the error messages are generally close.

SQL Server offers a few commands that aid in debugging T-SQL batches.

The `print` command sends a message without generating a result set. I find `print` messages to be useful progress notifications. With Query Analyzer in Grid mode, execute the following batch:

```
Select 3;
Print 6;
```

The result is a record set displayed in the grid with a single row containing 3. The Messages tab displays the following result:

```
(1 row(s) affected)
6
```

It is sometimes useful to slow down the code to check for locks or contention. The `waitfor` command can pause the code for a specified time. When the following batch executes, the output from the batch is displayed after a two-second pause:

```
Print 'Beginning';
waitfor delay '00:00:02';
Print 'Done';
```

Result:

```
Beginning
Done
```

 New in 2005   A key feature that didn't make the SQL Server 2005 release is a T-SQL debugger in Management Studio. Visual Studio 2005 includes a T-SQL debugger, but it's missing from SQL Server 2005. If a debugger is added in a future service pack, I'll post a ScreenCast tutorial on its use on `www.SQLServerBible.com`.

Variables

Every language requires variables to temporarily store values in memory. T-SQL variables are created with the `declare` command. The `declare` command is followed by the variable name and data type. The available data types are identical to those used to create tables, with the addition of the table and the `SQLvariant` data types. Multiple comma-separated variables can be declared with a single `declare` command.

Variable Default and Scope

The scope, or application and duration, of the variable extends only to the current batch. Newly declared variables default to null and must be initialized before they are included in an expression.

The following script creates two test variables and demonstrates their initial value and scope. The entire script is a single execution, even though it's technically two batches (separated by a go), so the results of the three select statements appear at the conclusion of the script:

```
DECLARE  @Test INT,
         @TestTwo NVARCHAR(25);
SELECT @Test, @TestTwo;

SET @Test = 1;
SET @TestTwo = 'a value';
SELECT @Test, @TestTwo ;
Go

SELECT @Test as BatchTwo, @TestTwo;
```

Result of the entire script:

```
----------- -------------------------
NULL        NULL

(1 row(s) affected)


value
----------- -------------------------
1           a value

(1 row(s) affected)

Msg 137, Level 15, State 2, Line 2
Must declare the scalar variable "@Test".
```

The first select returns two null values. After the variables have been initialized they properly return the sample values. When the batch concludes (due to the go terminator), so do the variables. Error message 137 is the result of the final select statement.

Variables are local in scope and do not extend to other batches or to called stored procedures.

Using the Set and Select Commands

Both the set command and the select command can assign the value of an expression to a variable. The main difference between the two is that a select can retrieve data from a data source (e.g., table, subquery, or view) and can include the other select clauses as well (e.g., from, where), whereas a set is limited to retrieving data from expressions. Both set and select can include functions. Use the simpler set command when you only need to assign a function result or constant to a variable and don't need the compiler to consider a data source.

Of course, a `select` statement may retrieve multiple columns. Each column may be assigned to a variable. If the `select` statement retrieves multiple rows, the values from the last row will be stored in the variables. No error will be reported.

The following SQL batch creates two variables and initializes one of them. The `select` statement will retrieve 32 rows, ordered by `PersonID`. The `PersonID` and the `LastName` of the *last person* returned by the `select` will be stored in the variables:

```
USE Family;
Declare @TempID INT,
        @TempLastName VARCHAR(25);
SET @TempID = 99;
SELECT
    @TempID = PersonID,
    @TempLastName = LastName
  FROM Person
  ORDER BY PersonID;
SELECT @TempID, @TempLastName;
```

Result:

```
----------- -------------------------
32 @code last:Campbell
```

Caution

The previous code demonstrates a common coding mistake. Never use a `select` to populate a variable unless you're sure that it will return only a single row, or you're satisfied that only the last row's data will be captured by the variable.

If no rows are returned from the `select` statement, the `select` does not affect the variables. In the following query, there is no person with a `PersonID` of 100, so the `select` statement does not affect the `@TempID` variable:

```
Declare @TempID INT,
        @TempLastName VARCHAR(25);
SET @TempID = 99;
SELECT @TempID = PersonID,
    @TempLastName = LastName
  FROM Person
  WHERE PersonID = 100
  ORDER BY PersonID;
SELECT @TempID, @TempLastName;
```

The final `select` statement reports the value of `@TempID`, and indeed, it's still 99. The first `select` did not alter its value:

```
----------- -------------------------
99 @code last:NULL
```

Conditional Select

Because the `select` statement includes a `where` clause, the following syntax works well, although those not familiar with it may be confused:

```
SELECT @Variable = expression WHERE BooleanExpression;
```

The `where` clause functions as a conditional `if` statement. If the Boolean expression is true the `select` takes place. If not, the `select` is performed, but the `@variable` is not altered in any way because the `select` command has no effect.

Using Variables within SQL Queries

One of my favorite features of T-SQL is that variables may be used with SQL queries without having to build any complex dynamic SQL strings to concatenate the variables into the code. Dynamic SQL still has its place, but the single value can simply be modified with a variable.

Anywhere an expression can be used within a SQL query, a variable may be used in its place. The following code demonstrates using a variable in a `where` clause:

```
USE OBXKites;

DECLARE @ProductCode CHAR(10);
SET @Code = '1001';

SELECT ProductName
  FROM Product
  WHERE Code = @ProductCode;
```

Result:

```
Name
--------------------------------------------------
Basic Box Kite 21 inch
```

Multiple Assignment Variables

A *multiple assignment variable* is a fascinating method that appends a variable to itself using a `select` statement and a subquery.

This section demonstrates a real-world use of multiple assignment variables, but because it's an unusual use of the `select` statement, here it is in its basic form:

```
SELECT @variable = @variable + d.column
  FROM (Derived Table) as d;
```

Each row from the derived table is appended to the variable, changing the vertical column in the underlying table into a horizontal list.

This type of data retrieval is quite common. Often a vertical list of values is better reported as a single comma-delimited horizontal list than as a subreport or another subheading level several inches long. A short horizontal list is more readable and saves space.

The following example builds a list of event dates for the Outer Banks Lighthouses tour offered by Cape Hatteras Adventures in the sample database:

```
USE CHA2;
DECLARE
  @EventDates VARCHAR(1024);
SET @EventDates = '';

SELECT @EventDates = @EventDates
```

```
        + CONVERT(VARCHAR(15), a.d,107 ) + ';  '
          FROM (select DateBegin as [d]
                 from Event
                   join Tour
                     on Event.TourID = Tour.TourID
                 WHERE Tour.[Name] = 'Outer Banks Lighthouses') as a;

    SELECT Left(@EventDates, Len(@EventDates)-1)
      AS 'Outer Banks Lighthouses Events';
```

Result:

```
Outer Banks Lighthouses Events
-----------------------------------------------------------
Feb 02, 2001; Jun 06, 2001; Jul 03, 2001;  Aug 17, 2001;
  Oct 03, 2001; Nov 16, 2001
```

The problem with multiple assignment variables is that the order of the denormalized data isn't guaranteed. Because it's undocumented and considered a kludge, it's not respected in the SQL Server community. Nevertheless, it may prove handy to solve a problem, and I prefer it over a cursor.

Procedural Flow

At first glance it would appear that T-SQL is weak in procedural-flow options. While it's less rich than some other languages, it suffices. The data-handling Boolean extensions — such as exists, in, and case — offset the limitations of if and while.

If

This is your grandfather's if. What's odd about the T-SQL if command is that it determines the execution of *only* the next single statement — one if, one command. In addition, there's no then and no end if command to terminate the if block:

```
IF Condition
  Statement;
```

In the following script, the if condition should return a false, preventing the next command from executing:

```
IF 1 = 0
  PRINT 'Line One';
PRINT 'Line Two';
```

Result:

```
Line Two
```

> **Note**
>
> The if statement is not followed by a semicolon; in fact, a semicolon will cause an error. That's because the if statement is actually a prefix for the following statement; the two are compiled as a single statement.

Begin/End

An if command that can control only a single command is less than useful. However, a begin/end block can make multiple commands appear to the if command as the next single command:

```
IF Condition
  Begin;
    Multiple lines;
  End;
```

I confess: Early one dreary morning a couple of years ago, I spent an hour trying to debug a stored procedure that always raised the same error no matter what I tried, only to realize that I had omitted the begin and end, causing the raiserror to execute regardless of the actual error condition. It's an easy mistake to make.

If Exists()

While the if command may seem limited, the condition clause can include several powerful SQL features similar to a where clause, such as if exists() and if...in().

The if exists() structure uses the presence of any rows returned from a SQL select statement as a condition. Because it looks for any row, the select statement should select all columns (*). This method is faster than checking an @@rowount >0 condition, because the total number of rows isn't required. As soon as a single row satisfies the if exists(), the query can move on.

The following example script uses the if exists() technique to process orders only if any open orders exist:

```
USE OBXKITES;
IF EXISTS(SELECT * FROM [ORDER] WHERE Closed = 0)
  BEGIN;
    Print 'Process Orders';
  END;
```

There is effectively no difference between select * or selecting a column. However, selecting all columns enables SQL Server to select the best column from an index and might, in some situations, be slightly faster.

If/Else

The optional else command defines code that is executed only when the if condition is false. Like if, else controls only the next single command or begin/end block:

```
IF Condition
  Single line or begin/end block of code;
ELSE
  Single line or begin/end block of code;
```

While

The while command is used to loop through code while a condition is still true. Just like the if command, the while command determines only the execution of the following single T-SQL command. To control a full block of commands, the begin/end is used.

Some looping methods differ in the timing of the conditional test. The T-SQL while works in the following order:

1. The while command tests the condition. If the condition is true, while executes the following command or block of code; if not, it skips the following command or block of code and moves on.

2. Once the following command or block of code is complete, flow of control is returned to the while command.

The following short script demonstrates using the while command to perform a loop:

```
Declare @Temp Int;
Set @Temp = 0;

While @Temp <3;
  Begin;
    Print 'tested condition' + Str(@Temp);
    Set @Temp = @Temp + 1;
  End;
```

Result:

```
tested condition       0
tested condition       1
tested condition       2
```

The continue and break commands enhance the while command for more complex loops. The continue command immediately jumps back to the while command. The condition is tested as normal.

The break command immediately exits the loop and continues with the script as if the while condition were false. The following pseudocode (not intended to actually run) demonstrates the break command:

```
CREATE PROCEDURE MyLife()
AS
WHILE Not @@Eyes2blurry = 1
  BEGIN
    EXEC Eat
    INSERT INTO Book(Words)
      FROM Brain(Words)
      WHERE Brain.Thoughts
        IN('Make sense', 'Good Code', 'BestPractice')
    IF @StarTrekNextGen = 'On'
      BREAK
  END
```

Goto

Before you associate the T-SQL goto command with bad memories of 1970s-style spaghetti-BASIC, this goto command is limited to jumping to a label within the same batch or procedure and is rarely used for anything other than jumping to an error handler at the close of the batch or procedure.

The label is created by placing a colon after the label name:

```
LabelName:;
```

The following code sample uses the `goto` command to branch to the `errorhandler:` label, bypassing the `'more code'`:

```
GOTO ErrorHandler;
Print 'more code';
ErrorHandler:;
Print 'Logging the error';
```

Result:

```
Logging the error
```

If you explore the Microsoft-developed system stored procedures, you'll see a few development styles, most of which use `goto` and labels to create a structured procedure.

Examining SQL Server with Code

One of the benefits of using SQL Server is the cool interface it offers to develop and administer the database. Management Studio is great for graphically exploring a database; T-SQL code, while more complex, exposes even more detail within a programmer's environment.

sp_help

`Sp_help`, and its variations, return information regarding the server, the database, objects, connections, and more. The basic `sp_help` lists the available objects in the current database, and the other variations provide detailed information about the various objects or settings.

Adding an object name as a parameter to `sp_help` returns further appropriate information about the object:

```
USE OBXKites;
sp_help price;
```

The result is seven data sets of information about the `Price` table, including the following:

- ✦ Name, creation date, and owner
- ✦ Columns
- ✦ Identity columns
- ✦ Row GUID columns
- ✦ FileGroup location
- ✦ Indexes
- ✦ Constraints

Global Variables

In most programming languages, a global variable is a variable with greater scope — not so in T-SQL. Global variables should be called *system variables*. They are read-only windows into the system status for the current connection and/or batch.

Global variables can't be created. There's a fixed set of global variables, all beginning with two @ signs (listed in Table 18-1). The most commonly used global variables are @@Error, @@Identity, @@NestLevel, and @@ServerName.

Table 18-1: Global Variables

Global Variable	Returns	Scope
@@Connections	The total number of attempted connections since SQL Server started	Server
@@CPU_Busy	The total amount of CPU time, in milliseconds, since SQL Server started	Server
@@Cursor_Rows	The number of rows returned by the last cursor to be opened	Connection
@@DateFirst	The day of the week currently set as the first day of the week; 1 represents Monday, 2 represents Tuesday, and so on. For example, if Sunday is the first day of the week @@DateFirst returns a 7.	Connection
@@DBTS	Current database-wide timestamp value	Database
@@Error	The error value for the last T-SQL statement executed	Connection
@@Fetch_Status	The row status from the last cursor fetch command	Connection
@@Identity	The last identity value generated for the current connection	Connection
@@Idle	The total number of milliseconds SQL Server has been idle since it was started	Server
@@IO_Busy	The total number of milliseconds SQL Server has been performing disk operations since it was started	Server
@@LangID	The language ID used by the current connection	Connection
@@Language	The language, by name, used by the current connection	Connection
@@Lock_TimeOut	The lock timeout setting for the current connection	Connection
@@Max_Connections	The current maximum number of concurrent connections for SQL Server	Server

Continued

Table 18-1 *(continued)*

Global Variable	Returns	Scope
@@Max_Precision	The decimal and numeric maximum precision setting	Server
@@Nestlevel	The current number of nested stored procedures	Connection
@@Options	A binary representation of all the current connection options	Connection
@@Pack_Received	The total number of network communication packets received by SQL Server since it was started	Server
@@Pack_Sent	The total number of network-communication packets sent by SQL Server since it was started	Server
@@Packet_Errors	The total number of network communication–packets errors recognized by SQL Server since it was started	Server
@@ProcID	The stored procedure identifier for the current stored procedure. This can be used with SysObjects to determine the name of the current stored procedure, as follows: SELECT Name FROM SysObjects WHERE id = @@ProcID	Connection
@@RemServer	The name of the login server when running remote stored procedures	Connection
@@RowCount	The number of rows returned by the last T-SQL statement	Connection
@@ServerName	The name of the current server	Server
@@ServiceName	SQL Server's Windows service name	Server
@@SPID	The current connection's server-process identifier—the ID for the connection	Connection
@@TextSize	The current maximum size of BLOB data (text, ntext, or image)	Connection
@@TimeTicks	The number of milliseconds per tick	Server
@@Total_Errors	The total number of disk errors committed by SQL Server since it was started	Server
@@Total_Read	The total number of disk reads by SQL Server since it was started	Server
@@Total_Write	The total number of disk writes by SQL Server since it was started	Server

Global Variable	Returns	Scope
@@TranCount	The number of active transactions for the current connection	Connection
@@Version	The SQL Server edition, version, and service pack	Server

Temporary Tables and Table Variables

Temporary tables and table variables play a different role from standard user tables. By their temporary nature, these objects are useful as a vehicle for passing data between objects or as a short-term scratch-pad table intended for very temporary work.

Local Temporary Tables

A temporary table is created the same way as a standard user-defined table, except the temporary table must have a pound, or hash, sign (#) preceding its name. Temporary tables are actually created on the disk in tempdb:

```
CREATE TABLE #ProductTemp (
ProductID INT PRIMARY KEY
);
```

A temporary table has a short life. When the batch or stored procedure that created it ends, the temporary table is deleted. If the table is created during an interactive session (such as a Query Analyzer window), it survives only until the end of that session. Of course, a temporary table can also be normally dropped within the batch.

The scope of a temporary table is also limited. Only the connection that created the local temporary table can see it. Even if a thousand users all create temporary tables with the same name, each user will only see his or her own temporary table. The temporary table is created in tempdb with a unique name that combines the assigned table name and the connection identifier. Most objects can have names up to 128 characters in length, but temporary tables are limited to 116 so that the last 12 characters can make the name unique. To demonstrate the unique name, the following code creates a temporary table and then examines the name stored in sysObjects:

```
SELECT Name
  FROM TempDB.dbo.SysObjects
  WHERE Name Like '#Pro%';
```

Result (shortened to save space; the real value is 128 characters wide):

```
Name
-------------------------------------------------------------
#ProductTemp_____00000000002D
```

Despite the long name in sysobjects, SQL queries still reference any temporary tables with the original name.

Global Temporary Tables

Global temporary tables are similar to local temporary tables, but have a broader scope. All users can reference a global temporary table, and the life of the table extends until the last session accessing the table disconnects.

To create a global temporary table, begin the table name with two pound signs, (*##TableName*). The following code sample tests to determine whether the global temporary table exists, and creates one if it doesn't:

```
IF NOT EXISTS(
  SELECT * FROM Tempdb.dbo.Sysobjects
    WHERE Name = '##TempWork')
CREATE TABLE ##TempWork(
  PK INT,
  Col1 INT
);
```

When a temporary table is required, it's likely being used for a work in progress. Another alternative is to simply create a standard user table in `tempdb`. Every time the SQL Server is restarted, it dumps and rebuilds `tempdb`, effectively clearing the alternative temporary worktable.

Table Variables

Table variables are similar to temporary tables; in fact, they both exist within `tempdb`. The main difference, besides syntax, is that table variables have the same scope and life as a local variable. They are only seen by the batch, procedure, or function that creates them. They cease to exist when the batch, procedure, or function concludes. Table variables have a few additional limitations:

✦ Table variables may not be created by means of the `select * into` or `insert into @tablename exec` table syntax.

✦ Table variables may not be created within functions.

✦ Table variables are limited in their allowable constraints: no foreign keys or check constraints are allowed. Primary keys, defaults, nulls, and unique constraints are OK.

✦ Table variables may not have any dependent objects, such as triggers or foreign keys.

Table variables are declared as variables, rather than created with SQL DDL statements. When a table variable is being referenced with a SQL query, the table is used as a normal table but named as a variable. The following script must be executed as a single batch or it will fail:

```
DECLARE @WorkTable TABLE (
  PK INT PRIMARY KEY,
  Col1 INT NOT NULL);

INSERT INTO @WorkTable (PK, Col1)
  VALUES ( 1, 101);

SELECT PK, Col1
  FROM @WorkTable;
```

Result:

```
PK          Col1
----------  ----------
1           101
```

Dynamic SQL

The term *dynamic SQL* has a couple of conflicting definitions. Some say it describes any SQL query submitted by a client other than a stored procedure. It's more accurate to say that it describes any SQL DML statement assembled dynamically at runtime as a string and then submitted.

Dynamic SQL is very useful for the following:

✦ Assembling a custom where clause from multiple possible query criteria

✦ Assembling a custom from clause that includes only the tables and joins required to meet the where conditions

✦ Creating a dynamic order by clause, sorting the data differently depending on the user request

Executing Dynamic SQL

The execute command, or exec for short, in effect creates a new instance of the batch as if the code executed were a called stored procedure. While the execute command is normally used to call a stored procedure, it can also be used to execute a T-SQL query or batch:

```
EXEC[UTE] ('T-SQL batch)
  WITH RECOMPILE;
```

The with recompile option forces SQL Server to perform a fresh compile and not reuse any existing query execution plans. If the T-SQL string and its parameters greatly change, the with recompile option will prevent a mismatched query execution plan from performing poorly. However, if the T-SQL string is a similar query, the needless recompile process will slow the execution. Most dynamic SQL procedures create extremely different SQL queries, so the with recompile option is generally appropriate.

For example, the following exec command executes a simple select statement:

```
USE Family;
EXEC ('Select LastName from Person Where PersonID = 12');
```

Result:

```
LastName
----------------
Halloway
```

New in 2005 The security context of executing code should be considered when working with the Execute command. SQL Server 2005 introduces the Execute As syntax to explicitly declare the security context. For more about security contexts and the Execute As syntax, refer to Chapter 40, "Securing Databases."

New to the `Execute` command in SQL Server 2005 is the capability to execute the code at a linked server, instead of only at the local server. The code is submitted to the linked server and the results are returned to the local server:

```
EXEC[UTE] (Code)  AT LinkedServerName
```

sp_excecuteSQL

A newer method of executing dynamic SQL is to use the `sp_executeSQL` system stored procedure. It offers greater compatibility with complex SQL queries than the straight `execute` command. In several situations I have found that the `execute` command would fail to execute the dynamic SQL, but that `sp_executeSQL` worked flawlessly:

```
EXEC Sp_ExecuteSQL
   'T-SQL query',
   Parameters Definition,
   Parameter, Parameter...
```

Concatenating strings is not allowed within `'T-SQL query'`, so parameters fill the need. The query and the definition must be Unicode strings.

Parameters provide optimization. If the T-SQL query has the same parameters for each execution, these parameters can be passed to `sp_executeSQL` so that the SQL query plan can be stored, and future executions are optimized. The following example executes the same query from the `Person` table in the Family database, but this example uses parameters (the N before the parameters is necessary because `sp_executeSQL` requires Unicode strings):

```
EXEC sp_executeSQL
   N'Select LastName
       From Person
       Where PersonID = @PersonSelect',
   N'@PersonSelect INT',
   @PersonSelect = 12;
```

Result:

```
LastName
---------------
Halloway
```

Developing Dynamic SQL Code

Building a dynamic SQL string usually entails combining a `select columns` literal string with a more fluid `from` clause and `where` clause.

Once the SQL string is complete, the SQL statement is executed by means of the `exec` command. The example that follows builds both a custom `from` and `where` clause based on the user's requirements.

Within the batch, the `NeedsAnd` bit variable tracks the need for an `and` separator between `where` clause conditions. If the product category is specified, the initial portion of the `select` statement includes the required joins to fetch the `Product Category` table. The `where` clause portion of the batch examines each possible user criterion. If the user has specified a criterion for that column, the column, with its criterion, is added to the `@SQLWhere` string.

Real-world dynamic SQL sometimes includes dozens of complex options. This example uses three possible columns for optional user criteria:

```
USE OBXKites;

DECLARE
  @SQL NVARCHAR(1024),
  @SQLWhere NVARCHAR(1024),
  @NeedsAnd BIT,

  -- User Parameters
  @ProductName VARCHAR(50),
  @ProductCode VARCHAR(10),
  @ProductCategory VARCHAR(50);

  -- Initialize Variables
SET @NeedsAnd = 0;
SET @SQLWhere = '';

  -- Simulate User's Requirements
SET @ProductName = NULL;
SET @ProductCode = 1001;
SET @ProductCategory = NULL;

  -- Assembly Dynamic SQL

  -- Set up initial SQL Select
IF @ProductCategory IS NULL
  SET @SQL = 'Select ProductName from Product'
ELSE
  SET @SQL = 'Select ProductName
                 from Product
                   Join ProductCategory
                     on Product.ProductCategoryID
                       = ProductCategory.ProductCategoryID';

  -- Build the Dynamic Where Clause
IF @ProductName IS NOT NULL
  BEGIN;
    SET @SQLWhere = 'ProductName = ' + @ProductName;
    SET @NeedsAnd = 1;
  END;

 IF @ProductCode IS NOT NULL
  BEGIN;
    IF @NeedsAnd = 1
      SET @SQLWhere = @SQLWhere + ' and ';
    SET @SQLWhere = 'Code = ' + @ProductCode;
    SET @NeedsAnd = 1;
  END;

IF @ProductCategory IS NOT NULL
  BEGIN;
```

```
   IF @NeedsAnd = 1
      SET @SQLWhere = @SQLWhere + ' and ';
   SET @SQLWhere = 'ProductCategory = ' + @ProductCategory;
   SET @NeedsAnd = 1;
 END;

-- Assemble the select and the where portions of the dynamic SQL
IF @SQLWhere <> ''
  SET @SQL = @SQL + ' where ' + @SQLWhere

Print @SQL
EXEC sp_executeSQL @SQL
  WITH RECOMPILE
```

The results shown are both the printed text of the dynamic SQL and the data returned from the execution of the dynamic SQL statement:

```
Select Name from Product where Code = 1001;

Name
--------------------------------------------------
Basic Box Kite 21 inch
```

Cross-Reference   The dynamic audit-trail method uses a complex dynamic SQL method in its stored procedure. The audit trail is covered in Chapter 24, "Exploring Advanced T-SQL Techniques."

Error Handling

Of course, all robust programming languages provide some method for trapping, logging, and handling errors. In this area, T-SQL has a poor history, but it's making progress. The error handling works well (aside from a few quirks), but some fatal errors cause the code to simply bomb out of T-SQL without giving you the opportunity to test for the error or handle it.

New in 2005   The new Try...Catch command brings SQL Server into the twenty-first century of error trapping. As you upgrade your databases to SQL Server 2005, upgrading the error handling code should be a priority.

Try...Catch

Try...catch is a standard method of trapping and handling errors that .NET programmers have enjoyed for years. The basic idea is that you try to execute a block of code and if there are any errors, you'll catch the error in the catch block of code:

```
BEGIN TRY;
   <code>;
END TRY
BEGIN CATCH;
   <code>;
END CATCH;
```

The T-SQL compiler treats the `end try ... begin catch` combination as a single contiguous command. Any other statements, a batch terminator (`go`), or a statement terminator (`;`) between these two commands will cause an untrapped error. `End try` must be followed immediately with a `begin catch`.

On encountering any error while running the `try` block of code, execution is immediately passed to the `catch` block. If the `try` block of code executes without any error, the `catch` code is never executed, and execution resumes after the `catch` block.

```
BEGIN TRY;
  SELECT 'Try One';
  RAISERROR('Simulated Error', 16, 1);
  Select 'Try Two';
END TRY
BEGIN CATCH
  SELECT 'Catch Block';
END CATCH;
SELECT 'Try Three';
```

Result:

```
---------
Try One

------------
Catch Block

-----------
Try Three

(1 row(s) affected)
```

Walking through this example, SQL Server executes the `try` block until the `raiserror`'s simulated error, which sends the execution down to the `catch` block. The entire `catch` block is executed. Following execution of the `catch` block, execution continues with the next statement, `select 'three'`.

When an error occurs in the `try` block and execution is passed to `catch` block, the error information is also passed to the `catch` block. The information may be examined using the error functions listed in Table 18-2. These functions are designed specifically for the `catch` block. Outside a `catch` block, they will always return a `null` value.

Table 18-2: Catch Functions

Error Function	Returns
Error_Message()	The text of the error message
Error_Number()	The number of the error
Error_Procedure()	The name of the stored procedure or trigger in which the error occurred
Error_Severity()	The severity of the error
Error_State()	The state of the error

These catch functions retain the error information of the error that fired the catch block. They may be called multiple times and still retain the error information. With a catch block, the following select can report the error information:

```
SELECT
  ERROR_MESSAGE() AS [Message],
  ERROR_PROCEDURE() AS [Procedure],
  ERROR_LINE() AS Line,
  ERROR_NUMBER() AS Number,
  ERROR_SEVERITY() AS Severity,
  ERROR_STATE() AS State;
```

Result:

```
Message          Procedure  Line  Number    Severity    State
---------------- ---------- ----- --------- ----------- ---------
Simulated Error  NULL         4    50000      16          1
```

This data can be logged, as shown later in this chapter, or written to an error log table.

Legacy @@Error Global Variable

Historically, T-SQL error handling has been poor at best. The basic error information global variables, such as @@Error and @@rowcount, contain the error status for the previous T-SQL command in the code, with 0 indicating success.

The difficulty is that @@Error is not like other languages that hold the last error in a variable until another error occurs. @@Error is updated for every command, so even testing its value updates it.

The following code sample attempts to update the primary key to a value already in use. This violates the marriage foreign-key constraint and generates an error. The two print commands demonstrate how @@Error is reset by every T-SQL command. The first print command displays the success or failure of the update. The second print command displays the success or failure of the first:

```
USE Family;
UPDATE Person
  SET PersonID = 1
  Where PersonID = 2;
Print @@Error;
Print @@Error;
```

Result:

```
Server: Msg 547, Level 16, State 1, Line 1
UPDATE statement conflicted with COLUMN REFERENCE constraint
  'FK__Marriage__Husband__7B905C75'. The conflict occurred in
  database 'Family', table 'Marriage', column 'HusbandID'.
  The statement has been terminated.
547
0
```

The solution to the last error status problem is to save the error status to a local variable. This method retains the error status so it may be properly tested and then handled. The following batch uses @err as a temporary error variable:

```
USE Family;
DECLARE @err INT;

UPDATE Person
  SET PersonID = 1
  Where PersonID = 2
SET @err = @@Error;

IF @err <> 0
  Begin
    -- error handling code
    Print @err
  End;
```

Result:

```
Msg 547, Level 16, State 1, Line 1
UPDATE statement conflicted with COLUMN REFERENCE constraint
'FK__Marriage__Husban__7B905C75'. The conflict occurred in database
'Family', table 'Marriage', column 'HusbandID'.
The statement has been terminated.
547
```

@@RowCount Global Variable

Another way to determine whether the query was a success is to check the number of rows affected. Even if no error was generated, it's possible that the data didn't match and the operation failed. The @@RowCount global variable is useful for checking the effectiveness of the query.

The reset issue that affects ørror also affects @@RowCount. However, there's no need to store the 0 value.

The following batch uses @@RowCount to check for rows updated. The failure results from the incorrect where clause condition. No row with PersonID = 100 exists. @@RowCount is used to detect the query failure:

```
USE FAMILY;
UPDATE Person
  SET LastName = 'Johnson'
  WHERE PersonID = 100;

IF @@RowCount = 0
  Begin
    -- error handling code
    Print 'no rows affected'
  End;
```

Result:

```
no rows affected
```

Raiserror

To return custom error messages to the calling procedure or front-end application, use the raiserror command. Two forms for raiserror exist: a legacy simple form and the recommended complete form.

The Simple Raiserror Form

The simple form, which dates from the Sybase days, passes only a hard-coded number and message. The severity level is always passed back as 16 — user error severe:

```
RAISERROR ErrorNumber, ErrorMessage;
```

For example, this code passes back a simple error message:

```
RAISERROR 5551212  'Unable to update customer.';
```

Result:

```
Msg 5551212, Level 16, State 1, Line 1
'Unable to update customer.'
```

The Complete Raiserror Form

The improved form incorporates the following four new useful features into the raiserror command:

✦ Specifies the severity level

✦ Dynamically modifies the error message

✦ Uses server-wide stored messages

✦ May optionally log the error to the event log

The syntax for the Windows raiserror adds parameters for the severity level, state (seldom used), and message-string arguments:

```
RAISERROR (
  message or number, severity, state, optional arguments
  ) With Log;
```

Error Severity

Windows has established standard error-severity codes, listed in Table 18-3. The other severity codes are reserved for Microsoft's use.

Table 18-3: Available Severity Codes

Severity Code	Description
10	Status message: Does not raise an error, but returns a message, such as a print statement.
11–13	No special meaning
14	Informational message
15	Warning message: Something may be wrong
16	Critical error: The procedure failed

Adding Variable Parameters to Messages

The error message can be a fixed-string message or the error number of a stored message. Either type can work with optional arguments.

The arguments are substituted for placeholders within the error message. While several types and options are possible, the placeholders I find useful are %s for a string and %i for a signed integer. The following example uses one string argument:

```
RAISERROR ('Unable to update %s.', 14, 1, 'Customer');
```

Result:

```
Msg 50000, Level 14, State 1, Line 1
Unable to update Customer.
```

Stored Messages

The Windows raiserror command can also pull a message from the sysmessages system view. Message numbers 1–50,000 are reserved for Microsoft. Higher message numbers are available for user-defined messages. The benefit of using stored messages is that any messages are forced to become consistent and numbered.

Note that with SysMessages stored messages, the message-number scheme is serverwide. If two vendors or two databases use overlapping messages, then no division exists between databases, and there's no solution beyond recoding all the error handling on one of the projects. The second issue is that when migrating a database to a new server, the messages must also be moved.

The sysMessages table includes columns for the MessageId, Message, Severity and whether the error should be logged. However, the severity of the raiserror command is used instead of the Severity from the SysMessage table, so SysMessage.Severity is moot.

To manage messages in code, use the sp_addmessage system stored procedure:

```
EXEC sp_addmessage 50001, 16, 'Unable to update %s';
```

For database projects that may be deployed in multiple languages, the optional @lang parameter can be used to specify the language for the error message.

If the message already exists, a replace parameter must be added to the system stored procedure call, as follows:

```
EXEC sp_addmessage 50001, 16,
  'Still unable to update %s', @Replace = 'Replace';
```

To view the existing custom messages, select from the sysmessages system view:

```
SELECT *
  FROM sysmessages
  WHERE message_id > 50000;
```

Result:

```
message_id  language_id severity is_event_logged text
----------- ----------- -------- --------------- ----------------------------
50001       1033        16       0               Still unable to update %s
```

To move messages between servers, do either one of the following:

✦ Save the script that was originally used to load the messages.

✦ Use the following query to generate a script that adds the messages:

```
SELECT 'EXEC sp_addmessage, '
    + Cast(message_id as VARCHAR(7))
    + ', ' + Cast(Severity as VARCHAR(2))
    + ', ''' + [text] + ''';'
  FROM sysmessages
  WHERE message_id > 50000;
```

Result:

```
------------------------------------------------------------
EXEC sp_addmessage, 50001, 16, 'Still unable to update %s';
```

To drop a message, use the `sp_dropmessage` system stored procedure with the error number:

```
EXEC sp_dropmessage 50001;
```

Logging the Error

Another advantage of using the Windows form of the `raiserror` command is that it can log the error to the Windows NT Application Event Log and the SQL Server Event Log. The downside to the Application Event Log is that it's stored on individual workstations. While they're great places to log front-end "unable to connect" errors, they're inconvenient places to store database errors.

There are two ways to specify that an event should be logged:

✦ If the stored message is created with the `@with_log = 'with_log'` option, or the "Always log" check box is selected during the addition of a new message with Management Studio the error will be logged.

✦ From the `raiserror` command, the `with log` option causes the current error message to be logged.

The following `raiserror` command writes the error to the event log:

```
RAISERROR ('Unable to update %s.', 14, 1, 'Customer')
   WITH LOG
```

Result:

```
Server: Msg 50000, Level 14, State 1, Line 1
Unable to update Customer.
```

To view errors in the Application Event Log (see Figure 18-1), select Control Panel ➪ Administrative Tools ➪ Event Viewer. The Event Viewer might also be available in a program menu.

SQL Server Log

SQL Server also maintains a series of log files. Each time SQL Server starts, it creates a new log file. Six archived log files are retained, for a total of seven log files. Management Studio's Object Explorer in the Management ➪ SQL Server Logs node lists the logs. Double-clicking a log opens SQL Server's very cool Log File Viewer, shown in Figure 18-2. It's worth exploring, as it has a filter and search capabilities.

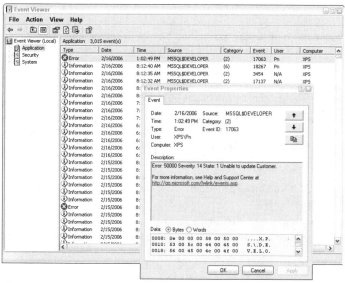

Figure 18-1: A SQL Server raiserror error in the Windows Event Log. Notice that the server and database name are embedded in the error data.

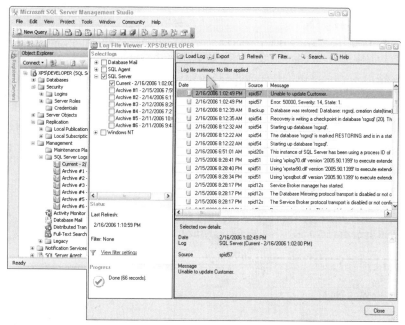

Figure 18-2: Viewing an error in the SQL log using Management Studio

Catch Block

When an error does occur, the typical way to trap and handle the error is to use try/catch blocks. Within the catch block you want to do the following:

1. If the batch is using logical transactions (`begin tran`/`commit tran`), the error handler should roll back the transaction. I recommend rolling back the transaction as the first action so that any locks the transaction might be holding are released.

2. If the error is one that the stored procedure logic detects, and it's not a SQL Server error, raise the error message so the user or front-end application is informed. If it's an error that SQL Server detects, SQL Server will automatically raise the error.

3. Optionally, log the error to an error table.

4. Terminate the batch. If it's a stored procedure, user-defined function, or trigger, terminate it with a `return` command.

The following code sample demonstrates handling errors; if an SQL Server error occurs in the `try` section, control is immediately transferred to the catch block, which can handle the error:

```
Begin Try
    -- T-SQL Code
End Try
Begin Catch
    -- Error handling code
End Catch
```

T-SQL Fatal Errors

If T-SQL encounters a fatal error, the batch will immediately abort without giving you the opportunity to test `@@Error`, handle the error, or correct the situation.

Fatal errors are rare enough that they shouldn't pose much of a problem. Generally, if the code works once it should continue to work unless the schema is changed or SQL Server is reconfigured. The most common fatal errors are those caused by the following:

✦ Data-type incompatibilities

✦ Unavailable SQL Server resources

✦ Syntax errors

✦ SQL Server advanced settings that are incompatible with certain tasks

✦ Missing objects or misspelled object names

For a list of most of the fatal error messages, run the following query:

```
SELECT Error, Severity, Description
  FROM Master.dbo.SysMessages
  WHERE Severity >= 19
  ORDER BY Severity, Error
```

Try...Catch does a good job of handling typical day-to-day user errors, such as constraint-violation errors. Nevertheless, to be safe, front-end application developers should also include error-handling code in their programs.

Summary

T-SQL extends the SQL query with a set of procedural commands. While it's not the most advanced programming language, T-SQL gets the job done. T-SQL batch commands can be used in expressions, or packaged as stored procedures, user-defined functions, or triggers.

The next two chapters continue to discuss T-SQL, including extensions that handle bulk operations and row-based processes. Following the explanation of T-SQL are chapters that package T-SQL batches inside stored procedures, user-defined functions, and triggers.

✦　　✦　　✦

Performing Bulk Operations

Often, the requirement is to load copious amounts of data quickly—whether it's a nightly data load or a conversion from comma-delimited text files. When a few hundred megabytes of data has to get into SQL Server in a limited time frame, a bulk operation is the way to get the heavy lifting done.

XML's popularity may be growing, but its file sizes seem to be growing even faster. XML's data tags add significant bloat to a data file, sometimes quadrupling the file size or more. For very large files, IT organizations are sticking with *CSV* (also know as *comma-delimited*) files. For these old standby files, the best way to insert that data is a bulk operation.

In SQL Server, bulk operations bypass the transaction log and pump data directly to the data file. While this gives bulk operations their speed, the cost of bypassing the transaction log is that it complicates the recovery plan, depending on the recovery model:

✦ **Simple recovery model:** No problem, the transaction log is used for current transactions only.

✦ **Bulk logged recovery model:** No problem, the bulk operation transaction bypasses the log, but then the entire bulk operation's data is still written to the log.

✦ **Full recovery model:** Bulk operations are not recorded to the log, so the log is invalidated. To restart the transaction log recoverability process, following the bulk operation, perform a complete backup and restart the transaction logs.

Cross-Reference

For more details on recovery models and how to set the recovery model, see Chapter 36, "Recovery Planning." Details on the transaction log are covered in Chapter 51, "Managing Transactions, Locking, and Blocking."

Technically, the `select into` syntax is also a bulk logged operation and it too bypasses the transaction log. `Select into` creates a table from the results of a `select` statement and is discussed in Chapter 16, "Modifying Data."

Bulk insert operations are normally one step of an *ETL (extract-transform-load)* nightly process. While developing these processes in T-SQL is perfectly acceptable, Integration Services is a strong alternative and includes bulk operations. For more details about developing Integration Services solutions, see Chapter 42, "ETL with Integration Services."

Best Practice

Bulk insert is extremely fast and I've had good success using it in production environments. My one word of caution is that the data must be clean. Variations in data type, irregular columns, and missing columns will cause trouble.

Bulk operations can be performed by a command prompt using BCP, within T-SQL using the bulk insert command, or using Integration Services.

Bulk Insert

The bulk insert command can be used within any T-SQL script or stored procedure to import data into SQL Server. Basically, the parameters of the command specify the table receiving the data, the file location of the source comma-delimited file, and the options.

To test the bulk insert command, use the Address.csv file that's part of the build script to load the Adventureworks sample database. It's probably already on your hard drive or it can be downloaded from MSDN. The 4 MB file has 19,614 rows of address data—that's small by ETL norms.

The following batch bulk inserts from the address table in the Adventureworks directory into the AWAddress table:

```
Use Tempdb;

CREATE TABLE AWAddressStaging (
  ID INT,
  Address VARCHAR(500),
  City    VARCHAR(500),
  Region  VARCHAR(500),
  PostalCode VARCHAR(500),
  GUID VARCHAR(500),
  Updated DATETIME
  );

BULK INSERT AWAddressStaging
  FROM 'C:\Program Files\Microsoft SQL Server\90\Tools\Samples\
         AdventureWorks OLTP\Address.csv'
  WITH (FIRSTROW = 1,ROWTERMINATOR ='\n');
```

On my Dell XPS notebook the bulk insert completes in less than a half-second.

The first thing to understand about bulk insert is that every column from the source table is simply inserted directly into the destination table using a one-to-one mapping. The first column from the source file is dumped into the first column of the destination table. Each column lines up. If there are too many columns in the destination table, it will fail. If the destination table is short a column, the bulk insert works and the extra data goes into the bit bucket.

Best Practice

Because bulk insert is dependent on the column position of both the source file and the destination table, a BestPractice is to use a view as an abstraction layer between the bulk insert command and the table. If the structure of either the source file or the destination table is altered, modifying the view can keep the bulk insert running without having to change the other object's structure.

Another BestPractice is to bulk insert the data into a staging table, check the data, and then perform the rest of the transformations as you merge the data into the permanent tables.

Cross-Reference

The bulk insert command won't accept a string concatenation or variable in the from parameter, so if you're assembling the string of the file location and the filename, you'll have to assemble a dynamic SQL statement to execute the bulk insert. Building and executing dynamic SQL is covered in Chapter 18, "Programming with Transact-SQL."

Bulk Insert Options

In practice, I've always had to use some options when using bulk insert:

✦ **Field Terminator** specifies the character used to delimit or separate columns in the source file. The default, of course, is a comma, but I've also seen the pipe character (|) used in production.

✦ **Row Terminator** specifies the character that ends a row in the source file. '\n' means end of row and is the typical setting. However, files from mainframes or other systems sometimes don't use a clean end of line. In these cases, use a hex editor to view the actual end of line characters and specify the row terminator in hex. For example, a hex value of '0A' is coded as follows:

```
ROWTERMINATOR = '0x0A'
```

✦ **FirstRow** is useful when specifying whether the incoming file has column headers or not. If the file does have column headers, use this option to indicate that the first row of data is actually the second row of the file.

✦ **TabLock** places an exclusive lock on the entire table, and saves SQL Server the trouble of having to lock the table's data pages being used for just the insert. This option can dramatically improve performance, but at the cost of blocking data readers during the bulk insert. If the bulk insert is part of an ETL into a staging table, then there's no problem; but if it's a bulk insert into a production system with potential users selecting data, this might not be such a good idea.

✦ **Rows per Batch** tells SQL Server to insert *n* number of rows in a single batch, rather than the entire file. Tweaking the batch size can improve performance, and I've found that beginning with 100 and then experimenting to find the best size for the particular set of data works best.

✦ **Max Errors** specifics how many rows can fail before the bulk insert fails. Depending on the business requirement for the data, you may need to set this to zero.

New in 2005

The Errorfile option points to a file that will collect any rows not accepted by the bulk insert operation. This is a great idea and should be used with every bulk insert command in production.

Other options that I've never found I needed in production include Check_Constraints, CodePage, DataFileType, Fire_Triggers, KeepIdentity, KeepNulls, Kilobytes_per_batch, and Order. The BestPractice of bulk inserting into a staging table and then performing the ETL merge into the permanent tables makes these commands less useful.

Bulk insert handles columns in the order they appear in the source comma-delimited file, and the columns must be in the same order in the receiving SQL table. Bulk inserting into a view provides a data abstraction later so that any changes in column order don't break the bulk insert code.

Best Practice

When developing a bulk insert statement, it's generally useful to open the source file using Excel and examine the data. Sorting the data by the columns can help find data formatting anomalies.

BCP

BCP, short for *bulk copy program* (or bulk copy Porsche), is a command-line variation of bulk operations. It differs from bulk insert in that BCP is command-line executed and can import or export data. It uses many of the same options as bulk insert. The basic syntax is as follows:

```
BCP destination table  direction datafile options
```

For the destination, use the complete four-part name (server.database.schema.object). For a complete listing of the syntax, just type BCP at the command prompt.

Because this is an external program, it will need authorization to connect to SQL Server. You have two options: Use the -P password option and hard-code your password into the batch file script, or leave the -P off and it will prompt you to enter a password. Neither is a very good option.

For straightforward ETL operation, I prefer using T-SQL and bulk insert. For complex ETL loads, Integration Services rocks. To be frank, I have little use for automating ETL processes using DOS batch scripts and BCP.

Best Practice

Summary

This chapter built on the previous chapter, "Programming with T-SQL," and explained a specific T-SQL command. Bulk operations provide the additional horsepower needed to import massive amounts of data by ignoring the transaction log and pumping the data directly to the table. The downside is that it complicates the recovery plan. The best way to perform a bulk operation is with the bulk insert T-SQL command or using bulk logged operation in Integration Services.

The next chapter deals with another specific feature of T-SQL and is one of my favorite topics. Join me in killing the cursor!

✦　　✦　　✦

Kill the Cursor!

SQL excels at handling sets of rows. However, the SQL world grew out of the old ISAM files structures, and the vestige of looping through data one row at a time remains in the form of the painfully slow SQL cursor.

While there are legitimate reasons to use a cursor, the most common reason is that programmers with a procedural background feel more comfortable thinking in terms of loops and pointers than set-based relational algebra.

SQL cursors also appear deceptively tunable. Programmers see the long list of cursor options and assume these means the cursor can be tweaked for high performance. The types of cursors have names such as fast forward, dynamic, and scrollable. To quote MSDN, *"Microsoft(r) SQL Server(tm) 2000 implements a performance optimization called a fast forward-only cursor."* The 70-229 SQL Server 2000 Database Design exam even includes a question asking which cursor type is called the firehose cursor. I don't believe there is such a thing. Cursors don't flow, they drip one drop at a time.

The second tier of optimization theory (discussed in Part 6, "Optimization Strategies"), a framework for designing high-performance systems, is developing set-based code, rather than iterative code. While this chapter explains how to iterate through data using a cursor, the emphasis is clearly on strategically exterminating unnecessary cursors and refactoring cursors with set-based code.

Cross-Reference
SQL Server cursors are server-side cursors, which are different from client-side ADO cursors. The SQL Server cursor occurs inside the server before any data is ever sent to the client. Client-side cursors are frequently used to scroll through the rows in an ADO record set within the application to populate a grid or combo box. ADO cursors are covered in Chapter 30, "Programming with ADO.NET 2.0."

Anatomy of a Cursor

A cursor is essentially a pointer to a single row of data. A while loop is used to cycle through the data until the cursor reaches the end of the data set. SQL Server supports the standard ANSI SQL-92 syntax and an enhanced T-SQL cursor syntax, which offers additional options.

The Five Steps to Cursoring

A cursor creates a result set from a `select` statement and then fetches a single row at a time. The five steps in the life of a cursor are as follows:

1. Declaring the `cursor` establishes the type and behavior of the cursor and the `select` statement from which the cursor will pull data. Declaring the `cursor` doesn't retrieve any data; it only sets up the `select` statement. This is the one time that `declare` doesn't require an ampersand. A SQL 92 cursor is declared using `cursorfor`:

```
DECLARE CursorName CURSOR
  FOR Select Statement
  FOR CursorOptions
```

The enhanced T-SQL cursor is very similar:

```
DECLARE CursorName CURSOR CursorOptions
  FOR Select Statement
```

2. Opening the `cursor` retrieves the data and fills the `cursor`:

```
OPEN CursorName
```

3. Fetching moves to the next row and assigns the values from each column returned by the `cursor` into a local variable. The variables must have been previously declared:

```
FETCH [Direction] CursorName INTO @Variable1, @Variable2
```

By default, `Fetch` moves to the `Next` row; however, `fetch` can optionally move to the `Prior`, `First`, or `Last` row in the data set. `Fetch` can even move an `Absolute` row position in the result set, or move forward or backward a `Relative` *n* number of rows. The problem with these options is that row position is supposed to be meaningless in a relational database. If the code has to move to specific positions to obtain a correct logical result, there's a major flaw in the database design.

4. Closing the `cursor` releases the data locks but retains the `select` statement. The cursor can be opened again at this point (`close` is the counterpart to `open`):

```
Close CursorName
```

5. Deallocating the `cursor` releases the memory and removes the definitions of the cursor (`deallocate` is the counterpart to `create`):

```
DEALLOCATE CursorName
```

These are the five basic commands required to construct a cursor. Add a method to manage the iterative loops and the cursor code is complete.

Managing the Cursor

Because a cursor fetches a single row, T-SQL code is required to repeatedly fetch the next row. To manage the looping process, T-SQL offers two cursor-related global variables that provide cursor status information.

The `@@cursor_rows` global variable will return the number of rows in the cursor. If the cursor is populated asynchronously, then `@@cursor_rows` will return a negative number.

Essential to developing a cursor is the @@fetch_status global variable, which reports the state of the cursor after the last fetch command. This information is useful to control the flow of the cursor as it reaches the end of the result set. The possible @@fetch_status values indicate the following:

✦ 0—The last Fetch successfully retrieved a row.

✦ 1—The last Fetch reached the end of the result set.

✦ 2—The last row fetched was not available; the row has been deleted.

Combining @@fetch_status with the while command builds a useful loop with which to move through the rows.

Typically, the batch will prime the cursor with a single fetch followed by a while loop to repeatedly fetch rows from the cursor until the cursor doesn't return any more rows. The top of the cursor loop examines the @@Fetch_Status global variable to determine whether the cursor is done. The following example demonstrates the five cursor steps and managing the iterations using while and @@fetch_status:

```
-- Step 1
DECLARE cDetail CURSOR FAST_FORWARD
  FOR SELECT DetailID
      FROM Detail
        WHERE AdjAmount IS NULL
-- Step 2
OPEN cDetail
-- Step 3 / Priming the Cursor
FETCH cDetail INTO @cDetailID
  EXEC CalcAdjAmount
    @DetailID = @cDetailID,
    @AdjustedAmount = @SprocResult OUTPUT
  UPDATE Detail
    SET AdjAmount  = @SprocResult
    WHERE DetailID = @cDetailID
  WHILE @@Fetch_Status = <>1
    BEGIN
      BEGIN
        EXEC CalcAdjAmount
          @DetailID = @cDetailID,
          @AdjustedAmount = @SprocResult OUTPUT
        UPDATE Detail
          SET AdjAmount  = @SprocResult
          WHERE DetailID = @cDetailID
      END
      -- Step 3 / Iterating through the cursor
      FETCH cDetail INTO @cDetailID  -- fetch next
    END
-- Step 4
CLOSE cDetail
-- 5
DEALLOCATE cDetail
```

Update Cursors

Because the cursor is already iterating through the data set, SQL Server knows which row is the current row. The cursor pointer can be referenced within a SQL DML (Select, Insert, Update, and Delete) command's where clause to manipulate the correct data.

The cursor declare command's for update option enables updating using the cursor. Specific columns may be listed; or, if no columns are listed, then any column may be updated:

```
DECLARE cDetail CURSOR
  FOR SELECT DetailID
      FROM Detail
  WHERE AdjAmount IS NULL
  FOR UPDATE OF AdjAmount
```

Within the cursor loop, after the row has been fetched, a DML command may include the cursor within the where clause using the current of syntax. The following example, from the KilltheCursor.sql script, references the cDetail cursor:

```
UPDATE Detail
  SET AdjAmount = @SprocResult
  WHERE CURRENT OF cDetail
```

Cursor Scope

Because cursors tend to be used in the most convoluted situations, understanding cursor scope is important. The scope of the cursor determines whether the cursor lives only in the batch in which it was created or extends to any called procedures. The scope can be configured as the cursor is declared:

```
DECLARE CursorName CURSOR Local or Global
  FOR Select Statement
```

The default cursor scope is set at the database level with the cursor_default option:

```
ALTER DATABASE Family SET CURSOR_DEFAULT LOCAL
```

The current cursor scope is important to the execution of the procedure. To examine the current default setting, use the database property's examine() function:

```
SELECT  DATABASEPROPERTYEX('Family', 'IsLocalCursorsDefault')
```

Result:

```
1
```

Best Practice

Beyond global and for update, cursors have several additional options that tweak their capability to manage or update data, such as static, keyset, dynamic, and optimistic. I'm not even going to waste the space explaining these other options. The BestPractice is to strategically limit cursors and rely instead on set-based solutions.

Cursors and Transactions

When compared with set-based solutions, cursors seem to have the edge with locking. It's been argued that a million-row set-based update transaction might lock the entire table, whereas performing the same update within a cursor would lock a single row at a time, so while the cursor might take 15 times longer, at least it's not blocking other transactions. You can decide where you fall in this particular debate.

A compromise is to use the `RowNumber()` function with the set-based solution to update batches of rows.

One technique that is sometimes used to improve the performance of cursors is to wrap the entire cursor within a logical transaction. There are pros and cons to this solution. While it will improve the cursor by as much as 50 percent, the penalty is the locking and blocking caused by the transaction.

Cursor Strategies

The key to developing with cursors is to know when to employ a cursor and when to seek a set-based solution. A Google search on cursors will find advice like the following:

> "Don't use a cursor unless you've already spent two weeks searching for a set-based solution, asked all your friends, and posted it on the newsgroups. If three MVPs have given up trying to find a query solution then you can write your cursor."

In that spirit, here are five specific situations that are typically solved using a cursor, and the recommended strategy:

✦ **Complex logic**, with variable formulas and several exceptions, can be difficult to translate into a set-based solution, and this situation is often developed with one of two solutions. The most common is to code all the logic within a cursor loop. Another solution is to create a stored procedure that accepts a single ID, processes a single row, and then returns the calculated value or updates the row.

The recommended solution is to recode the logic as a data-driven query using a `case` expression to handle the variations in the logic. The next section demonstrates this technique.

✦ **Dynamic code iteration**, such as the code generator in my O/R DBMS façade, must construct and execute dynamic DDL code. For this situation, I've not discovered a better solution than a cursor.

✦ **Denormalizing a list** means converting a vertical list of values to a single comma-delimited horizontal list or string. Often, data is better reported as a string than as a subreport or another subheading level several inches long — it's more readable and saves space. While this is often accomplished with a cursor, it is possible to build a set-based solution, as described later in this chapter.

✦ **Building a crosstab query** is one task that's traditionally been viewed as difficult using SQL Server. Building a crosstab query required using a series of `case` expressions. Constructing a dynamic crosstab query required using a cursor.

Chapter 15, "Working with Distributed Queries," demonstrates several methods of building crosstab queries, including the traditional `case`-expression and cursor method and the Pivot keyword, new in SQL Server 2005.

✦ **Navigating a hierarchical tree** can be solved using several set-based methods, although procedural programmers typically approach this task as an exercise in iteratively examining each node.

The recursive CTE query and other high-performance set-based solutions to the tree problem are covered in Chapter 12, "Navigating Hierarchical Data."

Complex-Logic Solutions

A cursor that's wrapped around a complex logic problem is often considered the most difficult cursor to kill. The difficulty arises when the logic includes multiple formulas, variable amounts, and multiple exceptions. This section begins with a working example of a complex-logic cursor and then refactors the cursor's features into various set-based alternatives.

The SQL script `Ch20 KilltheCursor.sql` includes the DDL commands to create the sample database and tables. The script generates random data to any size, and then tests each method from this chapter for performance. A current version of the file may be downloaded from `www.SQLServerBible.com`.

In all, seven solutions are constructed, each of which solves the sample complex-logic problem. At the conclusion of the solutions, they undergo performance tests against a progressively growing set of data.

A Sample Complex-Logic Problem

Imagine a billing situation with multiple billing formulas and multiple exceptions. Here are the business rules for the sample complex-logic cursor.

Variable Formula:

✦ **1 – Normal:** BaseRate * Amount * ActionCode's BaseMultiplier

✦ **2 – Accelerated Rate Job:** BaseRate * Amount * Variable Acceleration Rate

✦ **3 – Prototype Job:** Amount * ActionCode's BaseMultiplier

Exceptions:

✦ If there's an Executive OverRide on the Order, then ignore the Action Code's BaseMultiplier.

✦ If the transaction occurs on a weekend, then multiply the adjusted amount by an additional 2.5.

✦ Premium clients receive a 20% discount to their adjusted rate.

✦ The adjusted rate is zero if the client is a pro bono client.

That's it: three formulas and four exceptions. Typically, that's enough to justify writing a cursor . . . but is it?

The Logic Code

The base logic for the sample cursor is embedded in a stored procedure and a user-defined scalar function. For space purposes, only the stored procedure is listed here, but they share the same logic. Both accept a DetailID and calculate the adjusted amount.

Because the stored procedure operates on a single detail row at a time, it forces a cursor solution that can call the code once for each detail row.

The procedure uses if statements to handle the variable formulas. Another set of if statements handles the exceptions. Although this procedure does feature a variable accelerated rate, as per the requirements, it includes hard-coded values for the exception multipliers:

```
CREATE PROC CalcAdjAmount (
  @DetailID INT,
  @AdjustedAmount NUMERIC(7,2) OUTPUT
  )
AS
SET NoCount ON
-- sproc receives an DetailID
DECLARE
  @Formula SMALLINT,
  @AccRate NUMERIC (7,4),
  @IgnoreBaseMultiplier BIT,
  @TransDate INT,
  @ClientTypeID INT

SELECT @Formula = Formula
  FROM Detail
    JOIN ActionCode
      ON Detail.ActionCode = ActionCode.ActionCode
  WHERE DetailID = @DetailID

SET @IgnoreBaseMultiplier = 0

SELECT @IgnoreBaseMultiplier = ExecOverRide
  FROM [Order]
    JOIN Detail
      ON [Order].OrderID = Detail.OrderID
  WHERE DetailID = @DetailID

-- 1-Normal: BaseRate * Amount * ActionCode's BaseMultiplier
IF @Formula = 1
  BEGIN
    IF @IgnoreBaseMultiplier = 1
      SELECT @AdjustedAmount = BaseRate * Amount
        FROM Detail
          JOIN ActionCode
            ON Detail.ActionCode = ActionCode.ActionCode
        WHERE DetailID  = @DetailID
    ELSE
      SELECT @AdjustedAmount = BaseRate * Amount * BaseMultiplier
```

```
          FROM Detail
            JOIN ActionCode
              ON Detail.ActionCode = ActionCode.ActionCode
          WHERE DetailID  = @DetailID
    END
-- 2-Accelerated: BaseRate * Amount * Acceleration Rate
IF @Formula = 2
  BEGIN
    SELECT @AccRate = Value
      FROM dbo.Variable
        WHERE Name = 'AccRate'

    SELECT @AdjustedAmount = BaseRate * Amount * @AccRate
      FROM Detail
        JOIN ActionCode
          ON Detail.ActionCode = ActionCode.ActionCode
        WHERE DetailID = @DetailID
  END
-- 3-Prototype: Amount * ActionCode's BaseMultiplier
IF @Formula = 3
  BEGIN
    IF @IgnoreBaseMultiplier = 1
      SELECT @AdjustedAmount = Amount
        FROM Detail
          JOIN ActionCode
            ON Detail.ActionCode = ActionCode.ActionCode
          WHERE DetailID = @DetailID
    ELSE
      SELECT @AdjustedAmount = Amount * BaseMultiplier
        FROM Detail
          JOIN ActionCode
            ON Detail.ActionCode = ActionCode.ActionCode
          WHERE DetailID = @DetailID
  END
-- Exception: Weekend Adjustment
SELECT @TransDate = DatePart(dw,TransDate), @ClientTypeID = ClientTypeID
  FROM [Order]
    JOIN Detail
      ON [Order].OrderID = Detail.OrderID
    JOIN Client
      ON Client.ClientID = [Order].OrderID
  WHERE DetailID = @DetailID

IF @TransDate = 1 OR @TransDate = 7
  SET @AdjustedAmount = @AdjustedAmount * 2.5

-- Exception: Client Adjustments
IF @ClientTypeID = 1
  SET @AdjustedAmount = @AdjustedAmount * .8

IF @ClientTypeID = 2
  SET @AdjustedAmount = 0
RETURN
```

SQL-92 Cursor with Stored Procedure

The initial solution is the traditional iterative method — looping through every row, calling a stored procedure for every row, and then updating each row. This is the type of programming that SQL was designed to replace:

```
-- 1
DECLARE cDetail CURSOR
  FOR SELECT DetailID
      FROM Detail
        WHERE AdjAmount IS NULL
  FOR READ ONLY
-- 2
OPEN cDetail
-- 3
FETCH cDetail INTO @cDetailID   -- prime the cursor
  EXEC CalcAdjAmount
    @DetailID = @cDetailID,
    @AdjustedAmount = @SprocResult OUTPUT
  UPDATE Detail
    SET AdjAmount = @SprocResult
    WHERE DetailID = @cDetailID
  WHILE @@Fetch_Status = 0
    BEGIN
      BEGIN
        EXEC CalcAdjAmount
          @DetailID = @cDetailID,
          @AdjustedAmount = @SprocResult OUTPUT
        UPDATE Detail
          SET AdjAmount = @SprocResult
          WHERE DetailID = @cDetailID
      END
      -- 3
      FETCH cDetail INTO @cDetailID   -- fetch next
    END
-- 4
CLOSE cDetail
-- 5
DEALLOCATE cDetail
```

Fast-Forward Cursor with Stored Procedure

The second iterative solution uses a "high-performance" firehose T-SQL cursor. Otherwise, it's essentially the same as the SQL-92 solution:

```
-- 1
DECLARE cDetail CURSOR FAST_FORWARD READ_ONLY
  FOR SELECT DetailID
      FROM Detail
        WHERE AdjAmount IS NULL
-- 2
OPEN cDetail
-- 3
```

```
FETCH cDetail INTO @cDetailID  -- prime the cursor
  EXEC CalcAdjAmount
    @DetailID = @cDetailID,
    @AdjustedAmount = @SprocResult OUTPUT
  UPDATE Detail
    SET AdjAmount  = @SprocResult
    WHERE DetailID = @cDetailID
  WHILE @@Fetch_Status = 0
    BEGIN
      BEGIN
        EXEC CalcAdjAmount
          @DetailID = @cDetailID,
          @AdjustedAmount = @SprocResult OUTPUT
        UPDATE Detail
          SET AdjAmount  = @SprocResult
          WHERE DetailID = @cDetailID
      END
      -- 3
      FETCH cDetail INTO @cDetailID  -- fetch next
    END
-- 4
CLOSE cDetail
-- 5 DEALLOCATE cDetail
```

Fast-Forward Cursor and User-Defined Function

This solution uses a fast-forward cursor to move through the data and, with each row, update the row using the user-defined function to return the correct result:

```
-- 1
DECLARE cDetail CURSOR FAST_FORWARD READ_ONLY
  FOR SELECT DetailID
      FROM Detail
        WHERE AdjAmount IS NULL
-- 2
OPEN cDetail
-- 3
FETCH cDetail INTO @cDetailID  -- prime the cursor
  UPDATE Detail
    SET AdjAmount  = dbo.fCalcAdjAmount(@cDetailID)
    WHERE DetailID = @cDetailID
  WHILE @@Fetch_Status = 0
    BEGIN
        UPDATE Detail
          SET AdjAmount  = dbo.fCalcAdjAmount(@cDetailID)
          WHERE DetailID = @cDetailID
      -- 3
      FETCH cDetail INTO @cDetailID  -- fetch next
    END
-- 4
CLOSE cDetail
-- 5
DEALLOCATE
```

Update Cursor with Stored Procedure

The update cursor solution uses essentially the same logic as the previous cursor solution. The primary difference is that the cursor itself is used to select the correct row by the update statement. The cursor loop still must call the stored procedure one single row at a time:

```
-- 1
DECLARE cDetail CURSOR
  FOR SELECT DetailID
      FROM Detail
  WHERE AdjAmount IS NULL
  FOR Update of AdjAmount
-- 2
OPEN cDetail
-- 3
FETCH cDetail INTO @cDetailID  -- prime the cursor
  EXEC CalcAdjAmount
    @DetailID = @cDetailID,
    @AdjustedAmount = @SprocResult OUTPUT
  UPDATE Detail
    SET AdjAmount = @SprocResult
    WHERE Current of cDetail
  WHILE @@Fetch_Status = 0
    BEGIN
      BEGIN
        EXEC CalcAdjAmount
          @DetailID = @cDetailID,
          @AdjustedAmount = @SprocResult OUTPUT
        UPDATE Detail
          SET AdjAmount = @SprocResult
          WHERE Current of cDetail
      END
      -- 3
      FETCH cDetail INTO @cDetailID  -- fetch next
    END
-- 4
CLOSE cDetail
-- 5
DEALLOCATE cDetail
```

Update Query with User-Defined Function

The update query solution appears surprisingly simplistic, but looks can be deceiving. This solution hides all the logic within the user-defined formula. Although it would appear that SQL Server calls the function for every row of the query, embedding the function within an update DML statement has its benefits. Examining the query execution plan shows that the Query Optimizer incorporates the function's logic within the query plan and generates an excellent set-based solution:

```
UPDATE dbo.Detail
  SET AdjAmount = dbo.fCalcAdjAmount(DetailID)
  WHERE AdjAmount IS NULL
```

Multiple Queries

The sixth solution uses an individual query for each formula and exception. The where clauses of the queries restrict their operation to only those rows that require their respective formula or exception.

This solution introduces a data-driven component. The acceleration rate is supplied from the Variable table using a scalar subquery, and the exceptions are handled using data-driven joins to the ClientType and DayofWeekMultiplier tables:

```
UPDATE dbo.Detail
  SET AdjAmount = BaseRate * Amount
  FROM Detail
    JOIN ActionCode
      ON Detail.ActionCode = ActionCode.ActionCode
    JOIN [Order]
    ON [Order].OrderID = Detail.OrderID
  WHERE (Formula = 1 OR Formula = 3 )AND ExecOverRide = 1
    AND AdjAmount IS NULL

UPDATE dbo.Detail
  SET AdjAmount = BaseRate * Amount * BaseMultiplier
  FROM Detail
    JOIN ActionCode
      ON Detail.ActionCode = ActionCode.ActionCode
    JOIN [Order]
    ON [Order].OrderID = Detail.OrderID
  WHERE Formula = 1 AND ExecOverRide = 0
    AND AdjAmount IS NULL

-- 2-Accelerated  BaseRate * Amount * Acceleration Rate
UPDATE dbo.Detail
  SET AdjAmount = BaseRate * Amount * (SELECT Value
                                        FROM dbo.Variable
                                          WHERE Name = 'AccRate')
  FROM Detail
    JOIN ActionCode
      ON Detail.ActionCode = ActionCode.ActionCode
    JOIN [Order]
    ON [Order].OrderID = Detail.OrderID
  WHERE Formula = 2
    AND AdjAmount IS NULL

-- 3-Prototype    Amount * ActionCode's BaseMultiplier
UPDATE dbo.Detail
  SET AdjAmount = Amount * BaseMultiplier
  FROM Detail
    JOIN ActionCode
      ON Detail.ActionCode = ActionCode.ActionCode
    JOIN [Order]
    ON [Order].OrderID = Detail.OrderID
```

```
    WHERE Formula = 3 AND ExecOverRide = 0
      AND AdjAmount IS NULL

-- Exceptions
-- WeekEnd Adjustment
UPDATE dbo.Detail
  SET AdjAmount = AdjAmount * Multiplier
  FROM Detail
    JOIN [Order]
      ON [Order].OrderID = Detail.OrderID
    JOIN DayOfWeekMultiplier DWM
      ON CAST(DatePart(dw,[Order].TransDate) as SMALLINT) = DWM.DayOfWeek

    -- Client Adjustments
UPDATE dbo.Detail
  SET AdjAmount = AdjAmount * Multiplier
  FROM Detail
    JOIN [Order]
      ON [Order].OrderID = Detail.OrderID
    JOIN Client
      ON [Order].ClientID = Client.ClientID
    Join ClientType
      ON Client.ClientTypeID = ClientType.ClientTypeID
```

Query with Case Expression

The final solution uses a case expression and data-driven values to solve complexity within a single query. The case expression's power derives from the fact that it incorporates flexible logic within a single query.

Data-driven values and formulas are also incorporated into the query using joins to connect the base row with the correct lookup values. Data-driven designs also reduce maintenance costs because values can be easily changed without programming alterations.

In this example, the case expression selects the correct formula based on the values within the ActionCode table. The executive override is hard-coded into the case expression, but with a little work that too could be data driven.

As with the multiple query solution, the acceleration rate and exceptions are data-driven:

```
UPDATE dbo.Detail
SET AdjAmount = DWM.Multiplier * ClientType.Multiplier *
  CASE
    WHEN ActionCode.Formula = 1 AND ExecOverRide = 0
      THEN BaseRate * Amount * BaseMultiplier
    WHEN (ActionCode.Formula = 1 OR ActionCode.Formula = 3 )AND ExecOverRide = 1
      THEN BaseRate * Amount
    WHEN ActionCode.Formula = 2
      THEN BaseRate * Amount * (SELECT Value
                                  FROM dbo.Variable
                                  WHERE Name = 'AccRate')
    WHEN (Formula = 3 AND ExecOverRide = 0)
```

```
      THEN Amount * BaseMultiplier
  END
FROM Detail
  JOIN ActionCode
    ON Detail.ActionCode = ActionCode.ActionCode
  JOIN [Order]
    ON [Order].OrderID = Detail.OrderID
  JOIN Client
    ON [Order].ClientID = Client.ClientID
  Join ClientType
    ON Client.ClientTypeID = ClientType.ClientTypeID
  JOIN DayOfWeekMultiplier DWM
    ON CAST(DatePart(dw,[Order].TransDate) as SMALLINT) = DWM.DayOfWeek
WHERE AdjAmount IS NULL
```

Performance Analysis

To test the performance of these seven different solutions, the `KilltheCursor.sql` script adds data and executes each solution three times. Running through ten iterations reveals performance and scalability of the solutions, as illustrated in Figure 20-1.

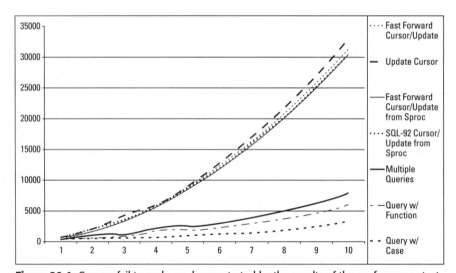

Figure 20-1: Cursors fail to scale, as demonstrated by the results of the performance test.

The slowest performing solution is the update cursor, followed by the other three cursor solutions. All the cursor solutions curve upward, indicating duration growing faster than data — in other words, poor scalability.

The two user-defined function solutions demonstrate well the performance issues with cursors. The user-defined function with a cursor scales linearly with slow performance, while the exact same function when used with a query performs very well.

The highlight of the graph is the flat line representing the query with the case expression solution. Although the code appears complicated and slow, it exhibits the best performance and scalability. The query with case expressions solution even outperforms the multiple queries solution. Why? Because of all the solutions, the query with case expressions solution passes the most control to SQL Server's Query Optimizer.

These tests show cursors running about ten times slower than set-based code and scaling poorly. With some optimizations, the ratio might narrow to only four times variance. However, in real-world scenarios, I've refactored a cursor that ran for seven hours into a set-based solution that ran in three minutes. Tackling complex logic embedded inside a nasty cursor can be mind-numbing, but the payback in performance is huge.

Denormalizing a List Example

The second example of a cursor in action solves a list denormalization problem. The requirement is to produce a comma-delimited string from the list of Outer Banks Lighthouses tour dates.

The cursor locates all dates for the tours. The while loop repeatedly fetches the date and appends each fetched date to the @EventDates local variable. The @SemiColon bit local variable determines whether a semicolon separator is required between the dates. At the end of the batch, the select statement returns the denormalized list of dates:

```
USE CHA2
DECLARE
  @EventDates VARCHAR(1024),
  @EventDate DATETIME,
  @SemiColon BIT

SET @Semicolon = 0
SET @EventDates = ''

DECLARE cEvent CURSOR FAST_FORWARD
  FOR SELECT DateBegin
      FROM Event
        JOIN Tour
          ON Event.TourID = Tour.TourID
          WHERE Tour.[Name] = 'Outer Banks Lighthouses'

  OPEN cEvent
  FETCH cEvent INTO @EventDate   -- prime the cursor

  WHILE @@Fetch_Status = 0
    BEGIN
      IF @Semicolon = 1
        SET @EventDates
          = @EventDates + '; '
            + Convert(VARCHAR(15), @EventDate, 107 )
      ELSE
        BEGIN
          SET @EventDates
```

```
            = Convert(VARCHAR(15), @EventDate,107 )
        SET @SEMICOLON = 1
      END

      FETCH cEvent INTO @EventDate   -- fetch next
    END
  CLOSE cEvent
DEALLOCATE cEvent

SELECT @EventDates
```

Result:

```
------------------------------------------------------------
Feb 02, 2001; Jun 06, 2001; Jul 03, 2001; Aug 17, 2001;
  Oct 03, 2001; Nov 16, 2001
```

A cursor easily solves the problem of denormalizing a list, and for a feature that's rarely used it might suffice. However, the set-based solution using the multiple assignment variable technique offered in the following example is about ten times faster, and should be used for more intensive tasks.

Cross-Reference   For more information about multiple assignment variables, refer to Chapter 18, "Programming with Transact-SQL."

The subquery returns a list to the outer query, which then appends each result to the @EventsDates variable:

```
USE CHA2
DECLARE
  @EventDates VARCHAR(1024)
SET @EventDates = ''

SELECT @EventDates = @EventDates
  + CONVERT(VARCHAR(15), a.d,107 ) + ';  '
      FROM (select DateBegin as [d]
              from Event
                join Tour
                  on Event.TourID = Tour.TourID
        WHERE Tour.[Name] = 'Outer Banks Lighthouses') as a

SELECT Left(@EventDates, Len(@EventDates)-1)
  AS 'Outer Banks Lighthouses Events'
```

Result:

```
Outer Banks Lighthouses Events
------------------------------------------------------------
Feb 02, 2001;  Jun 06, 2001;  Jul 03, 2001;  Aug 17, 2001;
  Oct 03, 2001;  Nov 16, 2001
```

Summary

When an optimization improves performance by a large magnitude of time (hours to minutes, minutes to seconds, etc.), that's when the job is fun. There's no better way to optimize a stored procedure than to find one that has an unnecessary cursor. When you're looking for low-hanging fruit, cursors are about the best you can find.

To quote one of my heroes, Bill Vaughn, "Cursors are evil!" I couldn't agree more. There is no such thing as a firehose cursor; every cursor is slow. Unnecessary cursors made my list of the top five SQL Server performance problems. The very best way to tune a cursor is to replace it with an elegant set-based query.

The next chapter takes everything that has been said about T-SQL in the previous chapters and bundles T-SQL batches into stored procedures.

Developing Stored Procedures

The primary purpose of client/server development is to move the processing as close to the data as possible. Moving data processing from a client application to the server reduces network traffic and improves both performance and data integrity.

One of the most popular methods of moving the processing closer to the data is developing stored procedures, sometimes called *procs*, or *sprocs*. Stored procedures aren't mysterious. All the features of T-SQL queries and batches are in full force. In the same way that a view is a SQL query saved under a view name, a stored procedure is a batch that has been stored with a name so it can be pre-compiled.

Within a client-server database project, code can be created in any of several places. One of the distinctive differences about the various places is how close to the data the code is executed. On the continuum between "close to the data" and "separate from the data," illustrated in Figure 21-1, stored procedures mix the benefits of server-side code with custom programmability.

Processing Continuum

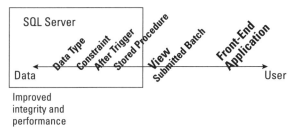

Figure 21-1: On the continuum of processing, the closer the processing is to the data, the better.

As server-side code, stored procedures offer several benefits:

- ◆ Stored procedures are compiled and are the fastest possible means of executing a batch or query.

- ◆ Executing the processing at the server instead of the desktop greatly reduces network traffic.

✦ Stored procedures offer modularity and are an easy means of deploying features and code changes. If the front-end application calls a stored procedure to perform some processing, modifying a stored procedure in a single location upgrades all users.

✦ Stored procedures can be an important component in database security. If all user access goes through stored procedures, direct access to the tables can be denied and all access to the data can be controlled.

To write an efficient stored procedure, don't start with this chapter. A well-written stored procedure is based on a well-written batch (see Chapter 18) consisting of well-written set-oriented SQL queries (see Chapters 7 through 16). This chapter explains how to pull together the batch and wrap it as a stored procedure.

Managing Stored Procedures

The actual management of stored procedures is simple compared to the logic within them. Once you know the basic facts and syntax, managing stored procedures shouldn't present any problems.

Create, Alter, and Drop

Stored procedures are managed by means of the data definition language (DDL) commands: create, alter, and drop.

Create must be the first command in a batch; the termination of the batch ends the creation of the stored procedure. The following example creates a simple stored procedure that retrieves data from the ProductCategory table in the OBXKites database:

```
USE OBXKites;
go

CREATE PROCEDURE CategoryList
AS
SELECT ProductCategoryName, ProductCategoryDescription
  FROM dbo.ProductCategory;
RETURN;
```

As this chapter progresses, more features will be added to the CategoryList example stored procedure.

Dropping a stored procedure removes it from the database. Altering a stored procedure replaces the entire existing stored procedure with new code. When modifying a stored procedure, altering it is preferable to dropping and recreating it, because the latter method removes any permissions.

Of course, stored procedures may be managed completely using Object Explorer. However, I strongly suggest that stored procedures be managed using scripts (.sql files) that may be checked into a version control system.

Returning a Record Set

If a stored procedure is a saved batch, then whatever a batch can do, a stored procedure can do. Just as a batch returns a record set from a SQL select query, a stored procedure will also return a record set from a query.

Referring back to the stored procedure that was created in the preceding section, when the CategoryList stored procedure is executed, the query within the stored procedure returns all rows from the productcategory table:

```
EXEC CategoryList;b
```

Result (abridged):

```
ProductCategoryName    ProductCategoryDescription
---------------------  ----------------------------
Accessory              kite flying accessories
Book                   Outer Banks books
Clothing               OBX t-shirts, hats, jackets
...
```

Compiling Stored Procedures

Compiling a stored procedure is an automatic process. Stored procedures compile and are stored in memory the first time they are executed. Rather more accurately, SQL Server develops query execution plans for the queries and code within the stored procedures, and these query execution plans are stored in memory.

SQL Server uses the Master.dbo.SysCacheObjects table to track compiled objects. To view the compiled stored procedures, run the following query:

```
SELECT cast(C.sql as Char(35)) as StoredProcedure, cacheobjtype,
       usecounts as Count
  FROM Master.dbo.SysCacheObjects C
  JOIN  Master.dbo.SysDatabases D
    ON C.dbid = C.dbid
  WHERE D.Name = DB_Name()
    AND ObjType = 'Proc'
  ORDER BY StoredProcedure;
```

Result (abridged):

```
StoredProcedure                   cacheobjtype        Count  ObjType
--------------------------------  ------------------  -----  --------
CREATE PROCEDURE [dbo].[CleanBatchR Compiled Plan      2      Proc
CREATE PROCEDURE [dbo].[CleanEventR Compiled Plan      1      Proc
CREATE PROCEDURE [dbo].[CleanExpire Compiled Plan      2      Proc
CREATE PROCEDURE [dbo].[CleanExpire Compiled Plan      2      Proc
...
```

A stored procedure's query execution plan can become obsolete while it's in memory. If the data distribution changes radically, or indexes are created or dropped, recompiling the stored procedure will result in improved performance. To manually force a recompile of a stored procedure, use the `sp_recompile` system stored procedure. It flags the stored procedure (or trigger) so that it will be compiled the next time it's executed:

```
EXEC sp_recompile CategoryList;
```

Result:

```
Object 'CategoryList' was successfully marked
   for recompilation.
```

 Cross-Reference For more details about query execution plans and how they're stored in memory, refer to Chapter 50, "Query Analysis and Index Tuning."

Stored Procedure Encryption

When the stored procedure is created, the text of the stored procedure is saved in the `SysComments` table. The text is not stored for the execution of the stored procedures, but only so that it may be retrieved later if the stored procedure needs to be modified.

The `sp_helptext` system stored procedure will extract the original text of the stored procedure:

```
sp_helptext CategoryList;
```

Result:

```
Text
-------------------------------------------
CREATE PROCEDURE  CategoryList
AS
SELECT *
  FROM dbo.ProductCategory
```

If the stored procedure is created with the `with encryption` option, the stored procedure text in `SysComments` is not directly readable. It's common practice for third-party vendors to encrypt their stored procedures. The following `alter` command stores the `CategoryList` procedure with `with encryption` and then attempts to read the code:

```
ALTER PROCEDURE CategoryList
WITH ENCRYPTION
AS
SELECT *
  FROM dbo.ProductCategory;

sp_helptext CategoryList;
```

Result:

```
The text for object 'CategoryList' is encrypted.
```

System Stored Procedures

The basic SQL syntax includes only 10 commands: select, insert, update, delete, create, alter, drop, grant, revoke, and deny. Microsoft performs hundreds of tasks with system stored procedures stored in the master database. To make these procedures available to all databases, special rules govern the scope of system stored procedures. Any procedures beginning with sp_ in the master database can be executed from any database. If a name conflict exists between a system stored procedure and a stored procedure in the local user database, the system stored procedure in the local database is executed.

When creating stored procedures, use a consistent naming convention other than sp_ to name your stored procedures. Using sp_ can only cause name conflicts and confusion. I prefix the names of stored procedures with p, but even no prefix is better than sp_.

Best Practice

Passing Data to Stored Procedures

A stored procedure is more useful when it can be manipulated by parameters. The CategoryList stored procedure created previously returns all the product categories, but a procedure that performs a task on an individual row will require a method for passing the row ID to the procedure.

SQL Server stored procedures may have numerous input and output parameters (up to 2,100 to be exact).

Input Parameters

You can add input parameters that pass data to the stored procedure by listing the parameters after the procedure name in the create procedure command. Each parameter must begin with an @ sign, and becomes a local variable within the procedure. Like local variables, the parameters must be defined with valid data types. When the stored procedure is called, the parameter must be included (unless the parameter has a default value).

The following code sample creates a stored procedure that returns a single product category. The @CategoryName parameter can accept Unicode character input up to 35 characters in length. The value passed by means of the parameter is available within the stored procedure as the variable @CategoryName in the where clause:

```
USE OBXKites;

go
CREATE PROCEDURE CategoryGet
  (@CategoryName NVARCHAR(35))
AS
SELECT ProductCategoryName, ProductCategoryDescription
  FROM dbo.ProductCategory
  WHERE ProductCategoryName = @CategoryName;
```

When the following code sample is executed, the string literal 'Kite' is passed to the stored procedure and substituted for the variable in the where clause:

```
EXEC CategoryGet 'Kite';
```

Result:

```
ProductCategoryName    ProductCategoryDescription
---------------------  -----------------------------------
Kite                   a variety of kites, from simple to
                       stunt, to Chinese, to novelty kites
```

If multiple parameters are involved, the parameter name can be specified or the parameters listed in order. If the two methods are mixed, then as soon as the parameter is provided by name, all the following parameters must be as well.

The next three examples each demonstrate calling a stored procedure and passing the parameters by original position and by name:

```
EXEC StoredProcedure
  @Parameter1 = n,
  @Parameter2 = 'n';

EXEC StoredProcedure n, 'n';

EXEC StoredProcedure n, @Parameter2 = 'n';
```

Parameter Defaults

You must supply every parameter when calling a stored procedure, unless that parameter has been created with a default value. You establish the default by appending an equals sign and the default to the parameter, as follows:

```
CREATE PROCEDURE StoredProcedure (
  @Variable DataType = DefaultValue
    );
```

The following code, extracted from the OBXKites sample database, demonstrates a stored procedure default. If a product category name is passed in this stored procedure, the stored procedure returns only the selected product category. However, if nothing is passed, the null default is used in the where clause to return all the product categories:

```
CREATE PROCEDURE pProductCategory_Fetch2(
  @Search NVARCHAR(50) = NULL
)
-- If @Search = null then return all ProductCategories
-- If @Search is value then try to find by Name
AS
  SET NOCOUNT ON;
  SELECT ProductCategoryName, ProductCategoryDescription
    FROM dbo.ProductCategory
    WHERE ProductCategoryName = @Search
      OR @Search IS NULL;
```

```
IF @@RowCount = 0
  RAISERROR(
    'Product Category ''%s'' Not Found.',14,1,@Search);
```

The first execution passes a product category:

```
EXEC pProductCategory_Fetch 'OBX';
```

Result:

```
ProductCategoryName     ProductCategoryDescription
----------------------  ----------------------------------
OBX                     OBX stuff
```

When pProductCategory_Fetch executes without a parameter, the @Search parameter's default of null allows every row to be seen as true within the where clause, as follows:

```
EXEC pProductCategory_Fetch;
```

Result:

```
ProductCategoryName     ProductCategoryDescription
----------------------  ----------------------------------
Accessory               kite flying accessories
Book                    Outer Banks books
Clothing                OBX t-shirts, hats, jackets
Kite                    a variety of kites, from simple to
                        stunt, to Chinese, to novelty kites
Material                Kite construction material
OBX                     OBX stuff
Toy                     Kids stuff
Video                   stunt kite contexts and lessons,
                        and Outer Banks videos
```

Returning Data from Stored Procedures

SQL Server provides four means of returning data from a stored procedure. A batch can return data via a select statement or a raiserror command. Stored procedures inherit these from batches and add output variables and the return command.

Output Parameters

Output parameters enable a stored procedure to return data to the calling client procedure. The keyword output is required both when the procedure is created and when it is called. Within the stored procedure, the output parameter appears as a local variable. In the calling procedure or batch, a variable must have been created to receive the output parameter. When the stored procedure concludes, its current value is passed to the calling procedure's local variable.

Although output parameters are typically used solely for output, they are actually two-way parameters.

Best Practice

Output parameters are useful for returning single units of data when a whole record set is not required. For returning a single row of information, using output parameters is blazingly faster than preparing a record set.

The next code sample uses an output parameter to return the product name for a given product code from the `Product` table in the OBXKites sample database. To set up for the output parameter:

1. The batch declares the local variable `@ProdName` to receive the output parameter.

2. The batch calls the stored procedure, using `@Prod Name` in the `exec` call to the stored procedure.

3. Within the stored procedure, the `@ProductName` output parameter/local variable is created in the header of the stored procedure. The initial value is `null`.

With everything in place, the process continues. The data path for the `@ProductName` output parameter is as follows:

4. The `select` statement inside the stored procedure sets `@ProductName` to `Basic Box Kite 21 inch`, the product name for the product code "1001."

5. The stored procedure finishes and execution is passed back to the calling batch. The value is transferred to the batch's local variable, `@ProdName`.

6. The calling batch uses the `print` command to send `@ProdName` to the user.

This is the stored procedure:

```
USE OBXKites;
go
CREATE PROC GetProductName (
  @ProductCode CHAR(10),
  @ProductName VARCHAR(25) OUTPUT )
AS
SELECT @ProductName = ProductName
  FROM dbo.Product
  WHERE Code = @ProductCode;
```

This is the calling batch:

```
USE OBXKITES;
DECLARE @ProdName VARCHAR(25);
EXEC GetProductName '1001', @ProdName OUTPUT;
PRINT @ProdName;
```

Result:

```
Basic Box Kite 21 inch
```

Later in this chapter, in "The Complete Stored Procedure" section, is a more complex example taken from the OBXKites sample database that uses an output parameter to pass the order number from the `pOrder_AddNew` stored procedure to the `pOrder_AddItem` stored procedure.

Using the Return Command

A return command unconditionally terminates the procedure and returns a value to the calling batch or client. Technically, a return can be used with any batch, but it can only return a value from a stored procedure or a function.

A return value of 0 indicates success and is the default. Microsoft reserves -99 to -1 for SQL Server use. It's recommended that you use -100 or lower to pass back a failure status.

Use the return value to pass back a success/fail value, but avoid using it to pass back actual data. If you only need to return a value and not a full data set, use an output parameter.

Best Practice

When calling a stored procedure, the exec command must use a local integer variable if the returned status value is to be captured:

```
EXEC @IntLocalVariable = StoredProcedureName;
```

The following basic stored procedure returns a success or failure status, depending on the parameter:

```
CREATE PROC IsItOK (
  @OK VARCHAR(10) )
AS
IF @OK = 'OK'
  RETURN 0
ELSE
  RETURN -100;
```

The calling batch:

```
DECLARE @ReturnCode INT;
EXEC @ReturnCode = IsITOK 'OK';
PRINT @ReturnCode;
EXEC @ReturnCode = IsItOK 'NotOK';
PRINT @ReturnCode;
```

Return:

```
0
-100
```

Path and Scope of Returning Data

Any stored procedure has four possible methods of returning data (select, raiserror, output parameters, and return). Deciding which method is right for a given stored procedure depends on the quantity and purpose of the data to be returned, and the scope of the method used to return the data. The return scope for the four methods is as follows:

✦ return and output parameters are both passed to local variables in the immediate calling procedure or batch within SQL Server.

✦ raiserror and a selected record set are both passed to the end-user client application. The immediate calling procedure or batch is completely unaware of the raiserror or selected record set.

If Query Analyzer executes a batch that calls stored procedure A, which then calls stored procedure B, stored procedure A will not see any `raiserrors` or record sets returned by procedure B, as shown in Figure 21-2.

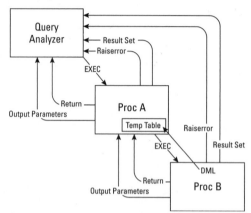

Return Method Scope

Figure 21-2: The path and scope of return methods
differs among the four possible methods of returning
data.

If a stored procedure needs to work with a result set generated by a stored procedure it's calling, a temporary table can be used to pass the data. If the calling procedure creates the temporary table, the scope of the temporary table will make it available within any called
procedures.

In Figure 21-2, procedure B can execute DML statements against any temporary table created
in procedure A. When procedure B is complete, the data is ready for procedure A.

Best Practice

With every returned record set, SQL Server will, by default, also send a message stating the
number of rows affected or returned. Not only is this a nuisance, but I have found in my
informal testing that it can slow a query by up to 17 percent.

Therefore, get into the habit of beginning every stored procedure with the following code:

```
AS
SET NoCount ON
```

There's more about configuring the connection in Chapter 34, "Configuring SQL Server."

Using Stored Procedures within Queries

Stored procedures are typically executed with the exec command or submitted by the client
application. However, a stored procedure can be used within the from portion of a query if
the stored procedure is called from within an openquery() function.

Openquery() is a distributed query function that sends a pass-through query to an external data source for remote execution. When the openquery() function includes a stored procedure, it simply submits the stored procedure to the local server.

Cross-Reference

The openquery() function is explained in more detail in Chapter 15, "Working with Distributed Queries."

Because the result set of the stored procedure is returned via a function being used by a data source in the from clause of the select statement, a where clause can further reduce the output of the stored procedure.

While this technique enables the use of stored procedures within a select statement, it's not as optimized as the technique of passing any row restrictions to the stored procedure for processing within the stored procedure. The only benefit of using openquery() is that it enables a complex stored procedure to be called from within an ad hoc query.

For the purpose of the following code, assume that a linked server connection has been established to the local server with the name NOLI:

```
SELECT * FROM OpenQuery(
  NOLI
  'EXEC OBXKites.dbo.pProductCategory_Fetch')
  WHERE ProductCategoryDescription Like '%stuff%'
```

Result:

```
ProductCategoryName    ProductCategoryDescription
---------------------  ----------------------------------
OBX                    OBX stuff
Toy                    Kids stuff
```

If you need to call complex code within a select statement, using openquery() to call a stored procedure works, but the syntax is a bit bizarre. A better method is to use a case expression or create a user-defined function.

Best Practice

Executing Remote Stored Procedures

Two methods exist for calling a stored procedure located on another server: a four-part name reference and a distributed query. Both methods require that the remote server be a linked server. Stored procedures may only be called remotely; they may not be created remotely.

Cross-Reference

Establishing security links to external data servers is covered in Chapter 15, "Working with Distributed Queries."

The remote stored procedure may be executed by means of the four-part name:

```
server.database.schma.procedurename
```

For example, the following code adds a new product category to the OBXKites database on Noli's (my development server) second instance of SQL Server:

```
EXEC [Noli\SQL2].OBXKites.dbo.pProductCategory_AddNew
   'Food', 'Eatables'
```

Alternately, the OpenQuery() function can be used to call a remote stored procedure:

```
OpenQuery(linked server name, 'exec stored procedure')
```

The next code sample executes the pCustomerType_Fetch stored procedure in the default database for the user login being used to connect to Noli\SQL2. If the default database is incorrect, a three-part name can be used to point to the correct database.

```
SELECT CustomerTypeName, DiscountPercent, [Default]
   FROM OPENQUERY(
      [Noli\SQL2], 'OBXKites.dbo.pCustomerType_Fetch')
```

Result:

```
CustomerTypeName     DiscountPercent Default
-------------------- --------------- -------
Preferred            10              0
Retail               00              1
Wholesale            15              0
```

As with any other distributed query, the Distributed Transaction Coordinator service must be running if the transaction updates data in more than one server.

The Complete Stored Procedure

This section presents a complete stored procedure scenario from the OBXKites sample database. The three stored procedures, pGetPrice, pOrder_AddNew, and pOrder_AddItem, work together to add orders to the database. They demonstrate many features of T-SQL programming and stored procedures. Each of these headings explains the stored procedure and then lists the code.

The code for these three stored procedures and the batch files that call them can be found within the OBXKites_Create.sql and OBXKites_Populate.sql files.

The pGetPrice Stored Procedure

The pGetPrice stored procedure demonstrates parameter defaults, output parameters, error handling, lock timeout, and deadlock handling. It accepts a product code, an optional date, and optional customer-contact code. Using that information, it determines the correct price and returns that price as an output variable.

A contact may be assigned to a customer type, and each customer type may have a standing discount. If the customer's contact code was supplied, the first task of the stored procedure is to locate the discount. If no contact code was supplied, the discount percentage is set to zero.

The OBXKites database uses a price table in which each product may have a different price each day. This method stores a history of prices and enables the store to enter price changes in advance. If pGetPrice is run with a null data parameter, the current date is used. In either case, the procedure must locate the most recent price. To do that it must determine the effective date of the price by finding the max price date that's less than or equal to the required date. Once the effective price date is determined, locating the correct price is easy. pGetPrice uses a subquery to determine the effective date.

Errors are handled by the catch block. If the error is a lock timeout or deadlock, the error handler waits for .25 seconds and goes to the LockTimeOutRetry: label at the beginning of the procedure to try again to gain the lock and complete the procedure. If after five attempts the lock can't be gained, the error handler reports the error and bombs out of the procedure. Here's the actual code:

```
CREATE PROCEDURE pGetPrice(
  @Code CHAR(10),
  @PriceDate DATETIME = NULL,
  @ContactCode CHAR(15) = NULL,
  @CurrPrice MONEY OUTPUT
  )
AS
-- Will return the current price for the product for today or any other date
-- The customer type determines the discount percentage
-- the output parameter, @CurrPrice, will contain the effective price

-- example code for calling this sproc:
-- Declare @Price money
-- EXEC GetPrice '1006', NULL, @Price OUTPUT
-- Select @Price

SET NOCOUNT ON
DECLARE
  @DiscountPercent NUMERIC (4,2),
  @Err INT,
  @ErrCounter INT

SET @ErrCounter = 0
SET @CurrPrice = NULL

LockTimeOutRetry:

BEGIN TRY
  IF @PriceDate IS NULL
    SET @PriceDate = GETDATE()
    -- set the discount percent / if no customer lookup then it's zilch discount
  SELECT @DiscountPercent = CustomerType.DiscountPercent
    FROM dbo.Contact
      JOIN dbo.CustomerType
```

```
            ON contact.CustomerTypeID = CustomerType.CustomerTypeID
         WHERE ContactCode = @ContactCode

      IF @DiscountPercent IS NULL
        SET @DiscountPercent = 0

      SELECT @CurrPrice = Price * (1-@DiscountPercent)
        FROM dbo.Price
          JOIN dbo.Product
            ON Price.ProductID = Product.ProductID
        WHERE Code = @Code
          AND EffectiveDate =
            (SELECT MAX(EffectiveDate)
              FROM dbo.Price
                JOIN dbo.Product
                  ON Price.ProductID = Product.ProductID
              WHERE Code = @Code
                AND EffectiveDate <= @PriceDate)
        IF @CurrPrice IS NULL
          BEGIN
            RAISERROR('Code: ''%s'' has no established price.',15,1, @Code)
            RETURN -100
          END
END TRY

BEGIN CATCH
  SET @Err = @@ERROR
  IF (@Err = 1222 OR @Err = 1205) AND @ErrCounter = 5
    BEGIN
      RAISERROR ('Unable to Lock Data after five attempts.', 16,1)
      RETURN -100
    END
  IF @Err = 1222 OR @Err = 1205 -- Lock Timeout / Deadlock
    BEGIN
      WAITFOR DELAY '00:00:00.25'
      SET @ErrCounter = @ErrCounter + 1
      GOTO LockTimeOutRetry
    END
  -- else unknown error
  RAISERROR (@err, 16,1) WITH LOG
  RETURN -100
END CATCH
```

The pOrder_AddNew Stored Procedure

An order consists of data in two tables, the [Order] table and the OrderDetail table. The [Order] table holds header information and the OrderDetail table contains the products on the order. Initiating an order involves collecting and validating the header information, generating an OrderNumber, and inserting a row in the [Order] table.

The p0rder_AddNew stored procedure accepts the customer-contact code, the employee code for the salesperson responsible for the sale, the location of the sale, and the date of the sale.

Sales are sometimes after the fact, so p0rder_AddNew can't assume the current date is the sales date. If the order date is the default (null), the insert statement uses the current date.

The customer code is also optional. If a customer-contact code is not provided, the default sets it to 0, which is then converted to a ContactID of null. The database schema accepts a null as the customer, recognizing that some sales are anonymous.

Every entry is in human-recognizable codes, but the database uses GUIDs for replication, so the procedure looks up the GUID for the customer, location, and employee, validating the codes during the lookup.

When all the codes are validated, the procedure finds the current order number and increases it by one. The order is finally inserted within the same transaction in which the order number is gathered. This occurs within a serialized transaction to prevent duplicates. (Real-world applications typically have a more complex method of generating an invoice number or order number that handles generating order numbers at multiple sites.)

The procedure uses a similar error-handling scheme as pGetPrice. One notable difference is that the error-detection code within the transaction rolls back the transaction prior to jumping to the error handler.

The last act of the stored procedure is to return the order number as an output variable, permitting the calling batch to use the order number when adding items to the order. The following code creates the p0rder_AddNew stored procedure:

```
CREATE PROC pOrder_AddNew (
  @ContactCode CHAR(15) = 0,
     -- if default then non-tracked customer
  @EmployeeCode CHAR(15),
  @LocationCode CHAR(15),
  @OrderDate DATETIME = NULL,
  @OrderNumber INT OUTPUT
  )
AS
-- Logic:
-- If supplied, check CustomerID valid
  SET NOCOUNT ON
  DECLARE
    @ContactID UNIQUEIDENTIFIER,
    @OrderID UNIQUEIDENTIFIER,
    @LocationID UNIQUEIDENTIFIER,
    @EmployeeID UNIQUEIDENTIFIER,
    @Err INT,
    @ErrCounter INT

  SET @ErrCounter = 0

LockTimeOutRetry:

-- Set Customer ContactID
```

```
   IF @ContactCode = 0
     SET @ContactID = NULL
   ELSE
     BEGIN
       SELECT @ContactID = ContactID
         FROM dbo.Contact
           WHERE ContactCode = @ContactCode
       SET @Err = @@ERROR
         IF @Err <> 0 GOTO ErrorHandler
       IF @ContactID IS NULL
         BEGIN  -- a customer was submitted but not found
          RAISERROR(
            'CustomerCode: ''%s not found',15,1, @ContactCode)
          RETURN -100
         END
     END

-- Set LocationID
  SELECT @LocationID = LocationID
    FROM dbo.Location
    WHERE LocationCode = @LocationCode
  SET @Err = @@ERROR
    IF @Err <> 0 GOTO ErrorHandler
  IF @LocationID IS NULL
    BEGIN  -- Location not found
      RAISERROR(
        'LocationCode: ''%s'' not found',15,1, @LocationCode)
      RETURN -100
    END
  IF EXISTS(SELECT *
                  FROM dbo.Location
                  WHERE LocationID = @LocationID
                    AND IsRetail = 0)
    BEGIN  -- Location not found
      RAISERROR(
        'LocationCode: ''%s'' not retail',15,1, @LocationCode)
      RETURN -100
    END

-- Set EmployeeID
  SELECT @EmployeeID = ContactID
    FROM dbo.Contact
      WHERE ContactCode = @EmployeeCode
  SET @Err = @@ERROR
    IF @Err <> 0 GOTO ErrorHandler
  IF @EmployeeCode IS NULL
    BEGIN  -- Location not found
      RAISERROR(
        'EmployeeCode: ''%s'' not found',15,1, @EmployeeCode)
```

```
        RETURN -100
    END

-- OrderNumber
  SET @OrderID = NEWID()
  SET TRANSACTION ISOLATION LEVEL SERIALIZABLE
  BEGIN TRANSACTION
    SELECT @OrderNumber = Max(OrderNumber) + 1
      FROM [Order]
    SET @OrderNumber =  ISNULL(@OrderNumber, 1)
    SET @Err = @@ERROR
    IF @Err <> 0
      BEGIN
        ROLLBACK TRANSACTION
        GOTO ErrorHandler
      END
  -- All OK Perform the Insert
  INSERT dbo.[Order] (
      OrderID, ContactID, OrderNumber,
      EmployeeID, LocationID, OrderDate )
    VALUES (
      @OrderID, @ContactID,@OrderNumber,
      @EmployeeID, @LocationID, ISNULL(@OrderDate,GETDATE()))
  IF @Err <> 0
    BEGIN
      ROLLBACK TRANSACTION
      GOTO ErrorHandler
    END
  COMMIT TRANSACTION

RETURN -- @OrderNumber already set

ErrorHandler:
  IF (@Err = 1222 OR @Err = 1205) AND @ErrCounter = 5
    BEGIN
      RAISERROR ('Unable to Lock Data after five attempts.', 16,1)
      RETURN -100
    END
  IF @Err = 1222 OR @Err = 1205 -- Lock Timeout / Deadlock
    BEGIN
      WAITFOR DELAY '00:00:00.25'
      SET @ErrCounter = @ErrCounter + 1
      GOTO LockTimeOutRetry
    END
  -- else unknown error
  RAISERROR (@err, 16,1) WITH LOG
  RETURN -100
```

The pOrder_AddItem Stored Procedure

With the order inserted, the third procedure in the set adds items to the order. Sales and inventory have to be flexible, so this procedure has a lot of defaults. The order number and the quantity are the only required parameters. The item is identified by either the product code or a description. The unit price can be either passed to the stored procedure or looked up with the pGetPrice procedure. Lastly, if the item is going to be shipped, a requested ship date and ship comment can be entered. If the ship information is null, the procedure assumes the item was delivered at the time of the sale.

As with the other stored procedures, pOrder_AddItem begins by validating every parameter and fetching the associated GUID to be inserted in the OrderDetail table.

The code that handles the unit price only calls pGetPrice if the unit-price parameter is not null. (The next chapter, Chapter 22, "Building User-Defined Functions," develops an fGetPrice function.) For the purpose of comparison, this procedure also illustrates retrieving the price using the function, but that part of the code is commented out. Here's the code:

```
CREATE PROCEDURE pOrder_AddItem(
  @OrderNumber CHAR(15),
  @Code CHAR(15) = 0, -- if default then non-stock Product
  @NonStockProduct NVARCHAR(256) = NULL,
  @Quantity NUMERIC(7,2),
  @UnitPrice MONEY = 0, -- If Default then lookup the Price
  @ShipRequestDate DATETIME = NULL, --default to Today
  @ShipComment NVARCHAR(256) = NULL -- optional
  )
AS

DECLARE
  @OrderID UNIQUEIDENTIFIER,
  @ProductID UNIQUEIDENTIFIER,
  @ContactCode CHAR(15),
  @PriceDate DATETIME,
  @Err INT,
  @ErrCounter INT

  SET @ErrCounter = 0

LockTimeOutRetry:

-- Fetch OrderID
  SELECT @OrderID = OrderID
    FROM dbo.[Order]
    WHERE OrderNumber = @OrderNumber
  SET @Err = @@ERROR
    IF @Err <> 0 GOTO ErrorHandler

-- Fetch ProductID
  SELECT @ProductID = ProductID
    FROM Product
    WHERE Code = @Code
```

```
    SET @Err = @@ERROR
      IF @Err <> 0 GOTO ErrorHandler

--- Fetch Contact Code / PriceDate
  SELECT @ContactCode = ContactCode, @PriceDate = OrderDate
    FROM dbo.[Order]
      LEFT JOIN Contact
        ON [Order].ContactID = Contact.ContactID
  SET @Err = @@ERROR
    IF @Err <> 0 GOTO ErrorHandler

-- Fetch UnitPrice
  IF @UnitPrice IS NULL
    EXEC pGetPrice
      @Code, @PriceDate, @ContactCode, @UnitPrice OUTPUT
      -- Alternate GetPrice function method
      -- SET @UnitPrice = dbo.fGetPrice (
      --                   @Code,@PriceDate, @ContactCode)
  SET @Err = @@ERROR
    IF @Err <> 0 GOTO ErrorHandler
  IF @UnitPrice IS NULL
    BEGIN
      RAISERROR(
        'Code: ''%s'' has no established price.',15,1, @Code)
      RETURN -1
    END

-- Set ShipRequestDate
  IF @ShipRequestDate IS NULL
    SET @ShipRequestDate = @PriceDate
-- Do the insert
  INSERT OrderDetail(
    OrderID, ProductID, NonStockProduct, Quantity,
    UnitPrice, ShipRequestDate, ShipComment)
  VALUES (
    @OrderID, @ProductID, @NonStockProduct, @Quantity,
    @UnitPrice, @ShipRequestDate, @ShipComment)
  SET @Err = @@ERROR
    IF @Err <> 0 GOTO ErrorHandler

RETURN 0

ErrorHandler:
  IF (@Err = 1222 OR @Err = 1205) AND @ErrCounter = 5
    BEGIN
      RAISERROR (
        'Unable to Lock Data after five attempts.', 16,1)
      RETURN -100
    END
  IF @Err = 1222 OR @Err = 1205 -- Lock Timeout / Deadlock
    BEGIN
```

```
      WAITFOR DELAY '00:00:00.25'
      SET @ErrCounter = @ErrCounter + 1
      GOTO LockTimeOutRetry
   END
-- else unknown error
RAISERROR (@err, 16,1) WITH LOG
RETURN -100
```

Adding an Order

So that you can see the stored procedures in action, the following batch from
OBXKites_Populate.sql illustrates creating two orders. This is the exact code that would
be sent to SQL Server by the front-end application to insert two orders.

The pOrder_AddNew stored procedure creates a new order row and returns the order number
to the calling batch. The calling batch can then create order detail rows using the same order
number by calling the pOrder_AddItem stored procedure. The batch's @OrderNumber local
variable is used to capture the order number from pOrder_AddNew and pass it to each call of
pOrder_AddItem.

The first order explicitly names the parameters. The second order is entered and provides
the parameters by order.

```
DECLARE @OrderNumber INT

--Order 1
EXEC pOrder_AddNew
  @ContactCode = '101',
  @EmployeeCode = '120',
  @LocationCode = 'CH',
  @OrderDate=NULL,
  @OrderNumber = @OrderNumber output

EXEC pOrder_SetPriority @OrderNumber, '1'

EXEC pOrder_AddItem
  @OrderNumber = @OrderNumber,
  @Code = '1002',
  @NonStockProduct = NULL,
  @Quantity = 12,
  @UnitPrice = NULL,
  @ShipRequestDate = '11/15/01',
  @ShipComment = NULL

-- Order 2
EXEC pOrder_AddNew
  '101', '120', 'CH', NULL, @OrderNumber output
EXEC pOrder_AddItem
  @OrderNumber, '1002', NULL, 3, NULL, NULL, NULL
EXEC pOrder_AddItem
  @OrderNumber, '1003', NULL, 5, NULL, NULL, NULL
EXEC pOrder_AddItem
```

```
   @OrderNumber, '1004', NULL, 2, NULL, NULL, NULL
EXEC pOrder_AddItem
   @OrderNumber, '1044', NULL, 1, NULL, NULL, NULL
```

Summary

Using stored procedures is a way to save and optimize batches. Stored procedures are compiled and stored in memory the first time they are executed. No method is faster at executing SQL commands, or more popular for moving the processing close to the data. Like a batch, a stored procedure can return a record set by simply executing a `select` command.

The next chapter covers user-defined functions, which combine the benefits of stored procedures with the benefits of views at the cost of portability.

 ✦   ✦   ✦

Building User-Defined Functions

SQL Server 2000 introduced user-defined functions (UDFs), and the SQL Server community was initially slow to adopt them.

The community discovered that UDFs can be used to embed complex T-SQL logic within a query, and problems that were impossible or required cursors could now be solved with UDFs. The result is that UDFs have become a favorite tool in the toolbox of any serious SQL Server database developer.

The benefits of UDFs can be easily listed:

- ✦ UDFs can be used to embed complex logic within a query.

- ✦ UDFs can be used to create new functions for complex expressions.

- ✦ UDFs offer the benefits of views because they can be used within the `from` clause of a `select` statement or an expression, and they can be schema-bound. In addition, user-defined functions can accept parameters, whereas views cannot.

- ✦ UDFs offer the benefits of stored procedures because they are compiled and optimized in the same way.

The chief argument against developing with user-defined functions has to do with their portability.

UDFs are very proprietary, and any database that uses many UDFs will be difficult or impossible to port to another database platform without a significant redesign. As a result, any user-defined function must be rewritten as a view or stored procedure if the database must be ported to another database platform in the future. To complicate matters further, any client-side code that references a user-defined function within a `select` statement will have to be rewritten and likely redesigned as well.

User-defined functions come in three distinct types (as shown in Figure 22-1):

✦ Scalar functions that return a single value

✦ Updateable inline table functions similar to views

✦ Multi-statement table functions that build a result set with code

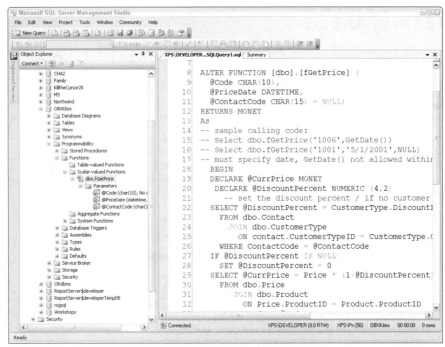

Figure 22-1: Management Studio's Object Explorer lists all the user-defined functions within a database, organized by table-valued and scalar-valued.

New in 2005   User-defined functions are improved in SQL Server 2005 in two significant ways. First, while the CLR isn't the best tool for most server-side code that works with data, for some UDFs the CLR is the best tool. Second, table-valued UDFs may now accept row-by-row parameters, similar to how a correlated subquery works with the outer query, which can solve some of the more difficult query problems.

Scalar Functions

A *scalar function* is one that returns a single specific value. The function can accept multiple parameters, perform a calculation, and then return a single value. These user-defined functions may be used within any expressions within SQL Server, even expressions within check constraints. The value is passed back through the function by means of a `return` command. The `return` command should be the last command in the user-defined function.

The scalar function must be *deterministic*, meaning that it must repeatedly return the same value for the same input parameters. For this reason, certain functions and global variables that return variable data — such as ʘnnections, getdate(), rasd(), newid(), and others — are not allowed within scalar functions.

User-defined scalar functions are not permitted to update the database, but they may work with a local temporary table. They cannot return BLOB (binary large object) data such as text, ntext, or image data-type variables, nor can they return table variables or cursor data types.

Cross-Reference

If the scalar function is calculating a formula, parsing text, or performing some other non-data-access task, the function will perform better if it's written in the CLR instead of T-SQL. For more about programming with the CLR, see Chapter 27, "Programming CLR Assemblies within SQL Server."

Creating a Scalar Function

User-defined functions are created, altered, or dropped with the same DDL commands used for other objects, although the syntax is slightly different to allow for the returned value:

```
CREATE FUNCTION FunctionName (InputParameters)
RETURNS DataType
AS
BEGIN
  Code
  RETURN Expression
END
```

The input parameters include a data-type definition and may optionally include a default value similar to stored procedure parameters (parameter = default). Function parameters differ from stored procedure parameters in that even if the default is desired, the parameter is required to call the function. Parameters with defaults don't become optional parameters. To request the default when calling the function, pass the keyword default to the function.

It's a good idea to include parameter defaults for functions because they keep the function from generating an error if no value is supplied when used as an expression, or if no row is available from a select statement inside the function.

The following user-defined scalar function performs a simple mathematical function. The second parameter includes a default value:

```
CREATE FUNCTION dbo.Multiply (@A INT, @B INT = 3)
RETURNS INT
AS
BEGIN
    RETURN @A * @B
End
go

SELECT dbo.Multiply (3,4)
SELECT dbo.Multiply (7, DEFAULT)
```

Result:

```
-----------
12
21
```

Note Microsoft-developed system functions are stored in the master database and must be called with a prefix of two colons, as in ::fnFunctionName.

For a more complex scalar user-defined function, the fGetPrice stored procedure from the OBXKites sample database returns a single result via an output parameter. The fGetPrice stored procedure or function has to determine the correct price for any given date and for any customer discount. Because it returns a single value, it's a prime candidate for a scalar user-defined function.

The function uses the same internal code as the stored procedure, except that the @CurrPrice is passed back through the final return instead of an output variable. The function uses a default value of null for the contact code. Another difference between the two is that the stored-procedure version of fGetPrice can accept a null default for the data and assume the current date for the sale, whereas user-defined functions must be deterministic and don't allow getdate() within the function, meaning that the date must always be passed to the function. Here is the code for the fGetPrice user-defined scalar function:

```
CREATE FUNCTION fGetPrice (
  @Code CHAR(10),
  @PriceDate DATETIME,
  @ContactCode CHAR(15) = NULL)
RETURNS MONEY
As
BEGIN
  DECLARE @CurrPrice MONEY
   DECLARE @DiscountPercent NUMERIC (4,2)
     -- set the discount percent
     -- if no customer lookup then it's zilch discount
  SELECT @DiscountPercent = CustomerType.DiscountPercent
    FROM dbo.Contact
      JOIN dbo.CustomerType
        ON contact.CustomerTypeID =
            CustomerType.CustomerTypeID
    WHERE ContactCode = @ContactCode
  IF @DiscountPercent IS NULL
    SET @DiscountPercent = 0
  SELECT @CurrPrice = Price * (1-@DiscountPercent)
    FROM dbo.Price
      JOIN dbo.Product
        ON Price.ProductID = Product.ProductID
    WHERE Code = @Code
      AND EffectiveDate =
        (SELECT MAX(EffectiveDate)
            FROM dbo.Price
              JOIN dbo.Product
```

```
                ON Price.ProductID = Product.ProductID
          WHERE Code = @Code
            AND EffectiveDate <= @PriceDate)
    RETURN @CurrPrice
END
```

Calling a Scalar Function

Scalar functions may be used anywhere within any expression that accepts a single value. User-defined scalar functions must always be called by means of at least a two-part name (owner.name). The following script demonstrates calling the fGetPrice() function within OBXKites:

```
USE OBXKites
SELECT dbo.fGetPrice('1006',GetDate(),DEFAULT)
SELECT dbo.fGetPrice('1001','5/1/2001',NULL)
```

Result:

```
--------------------
125.9500
--------------------
14.9500
```

Cross-Reference dbo.GenColUpdated is a user-defined scalar function used within the dynamic audit trail covered in Chapter 24, "Exploring Advanced T-SQL Techniques." The user-defined scalar function dbo.TitleCase is created in Chapter 8, "Using Expressions and Scalar Functions."

Creating Functions with Schema Binding

All three types of user-defined functions may be created with the significant added benefit of schema binding. Views may be schema-bound, but this feature is not available for stored procedures. Schema binding prevents altering or dropping of any object on which the function depends. If a schema-bound function references TableA, columns may be added to TableA, but no existing columns can be altered or dropped, and neither can the table itself.

To create a function with schema binding, add the option after returns and before as during the function creation, as shown here:

```
CREATE FUNCTION FunctionName (Input Parameters)
RETURNS DataType
WITH SCHEMA BINDING
AS
BEGIN;
  Code;
  RETURNS Expression;
END;
```

Schema binding not only alerts the developer that the change will affect an object, it prevents the change. To remove schema binding so that changes can be made, alter the function so that schema binding is no longer included.

Inline Table-Valued Functions

The second type of user-defined function is very similar to a view. Both are wrapped for a stored `select` statement. An inline table-valued user-defined function retains the benefits of a view, and adds compilation and parameters. As with a view, if the `select` statement is updateable, then the function will be updateable.

Creating an Inline Table-Valued Function

The inline table-valued user-defined function has no `begin`/`end` body. Instead, the `select` statement is returned as a `table` data type:

```
CREATE FUNCTION FunctionName (InputParameters)
RETURNS Table
AS
RETURN (Select Statement)
```

The following inline table-valued user-defined function is functionally equivalent to the `vEventList` view created in Chapter 14, "Creating Views."

```
USE CHA2
go
CREATE FUNCTION fEventList ()
RETURNS Table
AS
RETURN(
SELECT dbo.CustomerType.Name AS Customer,
    dbo.Customer.LastName, dbo.Customer.FirstName,
    dbo.Customer.Nickname,
    dbo.Event_mm_Customer.ConfirmDate, dbo.Event.Code,
    dbo.Event.DateBegin, dbo.Tour.Name AS Tour,
    dbo.BaseCamp.Name, dbo.Event.Comment
    FROM dbo.Tour
        INNER JOIN dbo.Event
            ON dbo.Tour.TourID = dbo.Event.TourID
        INNER JOIN dbo.Event_mm_Customer
            ON dbo.Event.EventID = dbo.Event_mm_Customer.EventID
        INNER JOIN dbo.Customer
            ON dbo.Event_mm_Customer.CustomerID
                = dbo.Customer.CustomerID
        LEFT OUTER JOIN dbo.CustomerType
            ON dbo.Customer.CustomerTypeID
                = dbo.CustomerType.CustomerTypeID
        INNER JOIN dbo.BaseCamp
            ON dbo.Tour.BaseCampID = dbo.BaseCamp.BaseCampID)
```

Calling an Inline Table-Valued Function

To retrieve data through `fEventList`, call the function within the `from` portion of a `select` statement:

```
SELECT LastName, Code, DateBegin
  FROM dbo.fEventList()
```

Result (abridged):

```
LastName      Code        DateBegin
------------  ----------  ---------------------------
Anderson      01-003      2001-03-16 00:00:00.000
Brown         01-003      2001-03-16 00:00:00.000
Frank         01-003      2001-03-16 00:00:00.000
```

...

As with stored procedures, a significant performance hit occurs the first time the function is called while the code is being compiled and stored in memory. Subsequent calls are fast.

In comparison to an inline table-valued user-defined function to other SQL Server objects, the performance of an inline function is similar to that of a stored procedure, and about 5–10 percent faster than a view.

Using Parameters

An advantage of inline table-valued functions over views is the function's ability to include parameters within the pre-compiled `select` statement. Views, conversely, do not include parameters, and restricting the result at runtime is typically achieved by adding a `where` clause to the `select` statement that calls the view.

The following examples compare adding a restriction to the view to using a function parameter. The following view returns the current price list for all products:

```
USE OBXKites
go

CREATE VIEW vPricelist
AS
SELECT, Price.Price
  FROM dbo.Price
    JOIN dbo.Product P
      ON Price.ProductID = P.ProductID
  WHERE EffectiveDate =
      (SELECT MAX(EffectiveDate)
         FROM dbo.Price
         WHERE ProductID = P.ProductID
           AND EffectiveDate <= GetDate())
```

To retrieve the current price for a single product, the calling `select` statement adds a `where`-clause restriction when calling the view:

```
SELECT *
  FROM vPriceList
  WHERE = '1001'
```

Result:

```
Code              Price
---------------   ----------------------
1001              14.9500
```

SQL Server internally creates a new SQL statement from vPricelist and the calling select statement's where-clause restriction and then generates a query execution plan.

In contrast, a function allows the restriction to be passed as a parameter to the pre-compiled SQL select statement:

```
CREATE FUNCTION dbo.fPriceList (
  @Code CHAR(10) = Null, @PriceDate DateTime)
RETURNS Table
AS
RETURN(
SELECT Code, Price.Price
  FROM dbo.Price
    JOIN dbo.Product P
      ON Price.ProductID = P.ProductID
  WHERE EffectiveDate =
      (SELECT MAX(EffectiveDate)
        FROM dbo.Price
        WHERE ProductID = P.ProductID
          AND EffectiveDate <= @PriceDate)
      AND (Code = @Code
        OR @Code IS NULL)
  )
```

If the function is called with default code, the price for the entered date is returned for all products:

```
SELECT * FROM dbo.fPriceList(DEFAULT, '2/20/2002')
```

Result:

```
Code              Price
--------------    ---------------------
1047              6.9500
1049              12.9500
...
```

If a product code is passed in the first input parameter, the pre-compiled select statement within the function returns the single product row:

```
SELECT * FROM dbo.fPriceList('1001', '2/20/2002')
```

Result:

```
Code              Price
--------------    --------------
1001              14.9500
```

Correlated User Defined Functions

The apply command, new in SQL Server 2005, may be used with a table-valued user-defined function so that the UDF accepts a different parameter value for each corresponding row being processed by the main query. At least once in SQL Server 2000, I spent a considerable amount of time working around this limitation, and I'm pleased to see this addressed in SQL Server 2005.

There are two forms to the apply command; the most common form, the cross apply, has a confusing name because it operates more like an inner join than a cross join. The cross apply command will join data from the main query with any table-valued data sets from the user-defined function. If no data is returned from the UDF, then the row from the main query is also not returned, as shown in the following example:

```
USE CHA2
go
CREATE FUNCTION fEventList2 (@CustomerID INT)
RETURNS Table
AS
RETURN(
SELECT dbo.CustomerType.Name AS Customer,
   dbo.Customer.LastName, dbo.Customer.FirstName,
   dbo.Customer.Nickname,
   dbo.Event_mm_Customer.ConfirmDate, dbo.Event.Code,
   dbo.Event.DateBegin, dbo.Tour.Name AS Tour,
   dbo.BaseCamp.Name, dbo.Event.Comment
   FROM dbo.Tour
      INNER JOIN dbo.Event
         ON dbo.Tour.TourID = dbo.Event.TourID
      INNER JOIN dbo.Event_mm_Customer
         ON dbo.Event.EventID = dbo.Event_mm_Customer.EventID
      INNER JOIN dbo.Customer
         ON dbo.Event_mm_Customer.CustomerID
            = dbo.Customer.CustomerID
      LEFT OUTER JOIN dbo.CustomerType
         ON dbo.Customer.CustomerTypeID
            = dbo.CustomerType.CustomerTypeID
      INNER JOIN dbo.BaseCamp
         ON dbo.Tour.BaseCampID = dbo.BaseCamp.BaseCampID
   WHERE Customer.CustomerID = @CustomerID
 )

SELECT C.LastName, Code, DateBegin, Tour
  FROM Customer C
    CROSS APPLY fEventList2(C.CustomerID)
  ORDER BY C.LastName
```

Result:

```
LastName        Code        DateBegin                Tour
---------------  ----------  -----------------------  --------------------------
Anderson        01-003      2001-03-16 00:00:00.000  Amazon Trek
Anderson        01-006      2001-07-03 00:00:00.000  Bahamas Dive
Anderson        01-016      2001-11-16 00:00:00.000  Outer Banks Lighthouses
Andrews         01-015      2001-11-05 00:00:00.000  Amazon Trek
Andrews         01-012      2001-09-14 00:00:00.000  Gauley River Rafting
Andrews         01-014      2001-10-03 00:00:00.000  Outer Banks Lighthouses
Bettys          01-013      2001-09-15 00:00:00.000  Gauley River Rafting
Bettys          01-015      2001-11-05 00:00:00.000  Amazon Trek
...
```

The `outer apply` command operates much like a left outer join. With this usage, rows from the main query are included in the result set regardless of whether or not a table-valued data set is returned from the user-defined function.

Multi-Statement Table-Valued Functions

The multi-statement table-valued user-defined function combines the scalar function's ability to contain complex code with the inline table-valued function's ability to return a result set. This type of function creates a table variable and then populates it within code. The table is then passed back from the function so that it may be used within `select` statements.

The primary benefit of the multi-statement table-valued user-defined function is that complex result sets may be generated within code and then easily used with a `select` statement. This enables these functions to be used in place of stored procedures that return result sets.

The new `apply` command may be used with multi-statement user-defined functions in the same way it's used with inline user-defined functions.

Creating a Multi-Statement Table-Valued Function

The syntax to create the multi-statement table-valued function is very similar to that of the scalar user-defined function:

```
CREATE FUNCTION FunctionName (InputParamenters)
RETURNS @TableName TABLE (Columns)
AS
BEGIN
  Code to populate table variable
  RETURN
END
```

The following process builds a multi-statement, table-valued, user-defined function that returns a basic result set:

1. The function first creates a table variable called @Price within the `create function` header.

2. Within the body of the function, two `insert` statements populate the @Price table variable.

3. When the function completes execution, the @Price table variable is passed back as the output of the function.

The fPriceAvg function returns every price in the Price table and the average price for each product:

```
USE OBXKite
go

CREATE FUNCTION fPriceAvg()
RETURNS @Price TABLE
  (Code CHAR(10),
    EffectiveDate DATETIME,
```

```
      Price MONEY)
  AS
    BEGIN
      INSERT @Price (Code, EffectiveDate, Price)
        SELECT Code, EffectiveDate, Price
          FROM Product
            JOIN Price
              ON Price.ProductID = Product.ProductID

      INSERT @Price (Code, EffectiveDate, Price)
        SELECT Code, Null, Avg(Price)
          FROM Product
            JOIN Price
              ON Price.ProductID = Product.ProductID
          GROUP BY Code
      RETURN
    END
```

Calling the Function

To execute the function, refer to it within the `from` portion of a `select` statement. The following code retrieves the result from the `fPriceAvg` function:

```
SELECT *
  FROM dbo.fPriceAvg()
```

Result:

```
Code    EffectiveDate               Price
------  --------------------------  --------
1001    2001-05-01 00:00:00.000     14.9500
1001    2002-06-01 00:00:00.000     15.9500
1001    2002-07-20 00:00:00.000     17.9500
```

Summary

User-defined functions expand the capabilities of SQL Server objects and open up a world of flexibility within expressions and the `select` statement, but at the price of non-portability.

Scalar user-defined functions return a single value and must be deterministic. Inline table-valued user-defined functions are very similar to views, and return the results of a single `select` statement. Multi-statement table-valued user-defined functions use code to populate a table variable, which is then returned.

T-SQL code can be packaged in stored procedures, user-defined functions, and triggers. The next chapter delves into triggers, specialized T-SQL procedures that fire in response to table-level events.

✦   ✦   ✦

Implementing Triggers

Triggers are special stored procedures attached to table events. They can't be directly executed; they fire only in response to an insert, update, or delete event on a table. In the same way that attaching code to a form or control event in Visual Basic or Access causes that code to execute on the form or control event, triggers fire on table events.

Users can't bypass a trigger, and unless the trigger sends a message to the client the end user is unaware of the trigger.

Developing triggers involves several SQL Server topics. Understanding transaction flow and locking, T-SQL, and stored procedures is a prerequisite for developing smooth triggers. Triggers contain a few unique elements, and require careful planning, but provide rock-solid execution of complex business rules and data validation.

Some DBAs oppose the use of triggers because they are proprietary in nature. If the database is ported to another platform, most trigger code will have to be rewritten. Triggers are also accused of hindering performance. In defense of triggers, if a rule is too complex for a constraint, then a trigger is the only other acceptable location for it. A business rule implemented outside the server is not a rule; it's a suggestion. If a trigger is poorly written, it will have a significant negative effect on performance. However, a well-written trigger ensures data integrity and provides good performance.

Trigger Basics

SQL Server triggers fire once per data-modification operation, not once per affected row. This is different from Oracle, which can fire a trigger once per operation, or once per row. While this may seem at first glance to be a limitation, being forced to develop set-based triggers actually helps ensure clean logic as well as fast performance.

Triggers may be created for the three table events that correspond to the three data-modification commands: insert, update, and delete.

SQL Server 2005 has two kinds of transaction triggers: *instead of* triggers and *after* triggers. They differ in their purpose, timing, and effect, as detailed in Table 23-1.

New in 2005 Database triggers fire on data definition language (DDL) commands — Create, Alter, Drop. Because these triggers function at the database schema level, they're covered in Chapter 17, "Implementing the Physical Database Schema."

Table 23-1: Trigger Type Comparison

	Instead of Trigger	*After Trigger*
DML statement	Automatically rolled back	Executed unless the trigger rolls back the transaction
Timing	Before PK and FK constraints	After the transaction is complete, but before it's committed
Number possible per table event	One	Multiple
May be applied to views?	Yes	No
Nested?	Depends on server option	Depends on server option
Recursive?	No	Depends on database option

Transaction Flow

Developing triggers requires understanding the overall flow of the transaction; otherwise, conflicts between constraints and triggers can cause designing and debugging nightmares.

Every transaction moves through the various checks and code in the following order:

1. Identity insert check.

2. Nullability constraint.

3. Data-type check.

4. Instead of trigger execution. If an instead of trigger exists, execution of the DML stops here. Instead of triggers are not recursive. Therefore, if the insert trigger executes a DML command that fires the same event (insert, update or delete), then the instead of trigger will be ignored the second time around.

5. Primary-key constraint.

6. Check constraints.

7. Foreign-key constraint.

8. DML execution and update to the transaction log.

9. After trigger execution.

10. Commit transaction.

11. Writing the data file.

Based on SQL Server's transaction flow, a few points concerning developing triggers are worth noting:

✦ An `after` trigger occurs after all constraints. Because of this, it can't correct data, so the data must pass any constraint checks, including foreign-key constraint checks.

✦ An `instead of` trigger can circumvent foreign-key problems, but not nullability, data type, or identity-column problems.

✦ An `after` trigger can assume that the data has passed all the other built-in data-integrity checks.

✦ The `after` trigger occurs before the DML transaction is committed, so it can roll back the transaction if the data is unacceptable.

Note   For certain applications, event notification may be a better method of handling the data change event.

Cross-Reference   Triggers may be written using the CLR and any .NET language. See Chapter 27, "Programming CLR Assemblies within SQL Server," for more details.

Creating Triggers

Triggers are created and modified with the standard DDL commands, `create`, `alter`, and `drop`, as follows:

```
CREATE TRIGGER TriggerName ON TableName
AFTER Insert, Update Delete
AS
Trigger Code
```

Prior to SQL Server 2000, SQL Server had `after` triggers only. Because no distinction between `after` and `instead of` was necessary, the old syntax created the trigger `for` `insert`, `update`, or `delete`. To ensure that the old after triggers will still work, after triggers can be created by using the keyword `for` in place of `after`.

Triggers may be created with encryption, just like stored procedures. However, the encryption is just as easily broken.

Although I strongly recommend that triggers be created and altered using scripts and version control, you can view and modify triggers using Management Studio's Object Explorer, as shown in Figure 23-1.

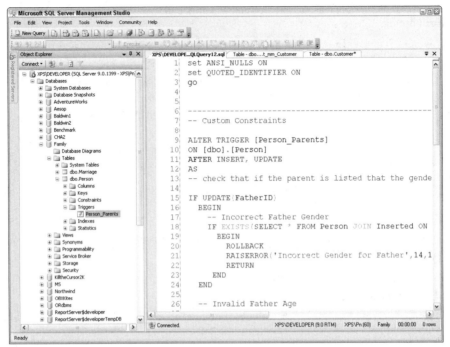

Figure 23-1: Object Explorer will list all triggers for any table, and may be used to modify the trigger using the context menu.

After Triggers

A table may have several after triggers for each of the three table events. After triggers may be applied to tables only.

The traditional trigger is an after trigger that fires after the transaction is complete but before the transaction is committed. After triggers are useful for the following:

✦ Complex data validation

✦ Enforcing complex business rules

✦ Recording data-audit trails

✦ Maintaining modified date columns

✦ Enforcing custom referential-integrity checks and cascading deletes

Best Practice

Use `after` triggers when the transaction will likely be accepted because the work is complete and waiting only for a transaction commit. For this reason, after triggers are excellent for validating data or enforcing a complex rule.

When you are learning a new programming language, the first program written is traditionally a "hello world" application that does nothing more than compile the program and prove that it runs by printing "hello world". The following `after` trigger simply prints `after trigger` when the trigger is executed:

```
USE Family;

CREATE TRIGGER TriggerOne ON Person
AFTER Insert
AS
PRINT 'In the After Trigger';
```

With the after trigger enforced, the following code inserts a sample row:

```
INSERT Person(PersonID, LastName, FirstName, Gender)
  VALUES (50, 'Ebob', 'Bill','M');
```

Result:

```
In the After Trigger

(1 row(s) affected)
```

The `insert` worked and the trigger printed its own version of the "hello world" message.

Instead of Triggers

`Instead of` triggers execute "instead of" (as a substitute for) the submitted transaction, so that the submitted transaction does not occur. It's as if the presence of an `instead of` trigger signals an automatic rollback on the submitted transaction.

As a substitution procedure, each table is limited to only one `instead of` trigger per table event. In addition, `instead of` triggers may be applied to views as well as tables.

Don't confuse `instead of` triggers with `before` triggers or before update events. They're not the same. A before trigger, if such a thing existed in SQL Server, would not interfere with the transaction unless code in the trigger executed a transaction `rollback`.

`Instead of` triggers are useful when it's known that the DML statement firing the trigger will always be rolled back and some other logic executed instead of the DML statement. For example:

✦ When the DML statement attempts to update a non-updateable view, the `instead of` trigger updates the underlying tables instead.

✦ When the DML statement attempts to directly update an inventory table, an `instead of` trigger updates the inventory transaction table instead.

✦ When the DML statement attempts to delete a row, an `instead of` trigger moves the row to an archive table instead.

The following code creates a test `instead of` trigger and then attempts to `insert` a row:

```
CREATE TRIGGER TriggerTwo ON Person
INSTEAD OF Insert
AS
```

```
PRINT 'In the Instead of Trigger'
go

INSERT Person(PersonID, LastName, FirstName, Gender)
  VALUES (51, 'Ebob', '','M')
```

Result:

```
In the Instead of Trigger
```

```
(1 row(s) affected)
```

The result includes the `instead of` trigger's "hello world" declaration and a report that one row was affected. However, selecting `personID` 51 will prove that no rows were in fact inserted:

```
SELECT LastName
  FROM Person
  WHERE PersonID = 51
```

Result:

```
LastName
---------------
(0 row(s) affected)
```

The `insert` statement worked as if one row had been affected, although the effect of the `insert` statement was blocked by the `instead of` trigger. The `print` command was executed instead of the rows being inserted. In addition, the `after` trigger is still in effect, but its `print` message failed to print.

Trigger Limitations

Owing to the nature of triggers (code attached to tables), they have a few limitations. The following SQL commands are not permitted within a trigger:

✦ Create, alter, or drop database

✦ Reconfigure

✦ Restore database or log

✦ Disk resize

✦ Disk init

Disabling Triggers

A user's DML statement can never bypass a trigger, but a system administrator can temporarily disable it, which is better than dropping it and then re-creating it if the trigger gets in the way of a data-modification task.

To temporarily turn off a trigger, use the `alter table` DDL command with the `enable trigger` or `disable trigger` option:

```
ALTER TABLE TableName ENABLE or DISABLE TRIGGER TriggerName
```

For example, the following code disables the `instead of` trigger (`TriggerOne` on the `Person` table):

```
ALTER TABLE Person
   DISABLE TRIGGER TriggerOne
```

To view the enabled status of a trigger, use the `objectproperty()` function, passing to it the object ID of the trigger and the `ExecIsTriggerDisabled` option:

```
SELECT OBJECTPROPERTY(
   OBJECT_ID('TriggerOne'),'ExecIsTriggerDisabled')
```

Listing Triggers

Because triggers tend to hide in the table structure, the following query lists all the triggers in the database. It also examines the `sysobjects` table for `tr` type objects and then joins the `Trigger` table row with the parent object row to report the table name. The query uses a correlated subquery to call the `objectproperty()` function for each row. The result of the correlated subquery is passed to a `case` expression so it can be converted to a string:

```
SELECT SubString(S2.Name,1,30) as [Table],
   SubString(S.Name, 1,30) as [Trigger],
   CASE (SELECT -- Correlated subquery
         OBJECTPROPERTY(OBJECT_ID(S.Name),
            'ExecIsTriggerDisabled'))
      WHEN 0 THEN 'Enabled'
      WHEN 1 THEN 'Disabled'
   END AS Status
   FROM Sysobjects S
      JOIN Sysobjects S2
         ON S.parent_obj = S2.ID
   WHERE S.Type = 'TR'
   ORDER BY [Table], [Trigger]
```

Result:

```
Table           Trigger               Status
-------------   -------------------   --------
Person          Person_Parents        Enabled
Person          TriggerOne            Disabled
Person          TriggerTwo            Enabled
```

Triggers and Security

Only users who are members of the `sysadmin` fixed server role, or are in the `dbowner` or `ddldmin` fixed database roles, or are the table's owners, have permission to create, alter, drop, enable, or disable triggers.

Code within the trigger is executed assuming the security permissions of the owner of the trigger's table.

Working with the Transaction

A DML insert, update, or delete statement causes a trigger to fire. It's important that the trigger have access to the changes being caused by the DML statement so it can test the changes or handle the transaction. SQL Server provides four ways for code within the trigger to determine the effects of the DML statement. The inserted and deleted images contain the before and after data sets, and the updated() and columns_updated() functions may be used to determine which columns were affected by the DML statement.

Determining the Updated Columns

SQL Server provides two methods of detecting which columns are being updated. The update() function returns true for a single column if that column is affected by the DML transaction:

```
IF UPDATE(ColumnName)
```

An insert will affect all columns, and an update will report the column as affected if the DML statement addresses the column. The following example demonstrates the update() function:

```
ALTER TRIGGER TriggerOne ON Person
AFTER Insert, Update
AS
IF Update(LastName)
  PRINT 'You modified the LastName column'
ELSE
  PRINT 'The LastName column is untouched.'
```

With the trigger looking for changes to the LastName column, the following DML statement will test the trigger:

```
UPDATE Person
  SET LastName = 'Johnson'
  WHERE PersonID = 25
```

Result:

```
You modified the LastName column
```

This function is generally used to execute data checks only when needed. There's no reason to test the validity of column A's data if column A isn't updated by the DML statement. However, the update() function will report the column as updated according to the DML statement alone, not the actual data. Therefore, if the DML statement modifies the data from 'abc' to 'abc', the update() will still report it as updated.

The columns_updated() function returns a bitmapped varbinary data type representation of the columns updated. If the bit is true the column is updated. The result of columns_updated() can be compared with integer or binary data by means of any of the bit-wise operators to determine whether a given column is updated.

The documentation states that the columns are represented by bits going from left to right, which is not entirely accurate. The columns are represented by right-to-left bits within l eft-to-right bytes. A further complication is that the size of the varbinary data returned by columns_updated() depends on the number of columns in the table.

The following function simulates the actual behavior of the columns_updated() function. Passing the column to be tested and the total number of columns in the table will return the column bitmask for that column:

```
CREATE FUNCTION dbo.GenColUpdated
  (@Col INT, @ColTotal INT)
RETURNS INT
AS
BEGIN
-- Copyright 2001 Paul Nielsen
-- This function simulates the Columns_Updated() behavior
DECLARE
  @ColByte INT,
  @ColTotalByte INT,
  @ColBit INT

  -- Calculate Byte Positions
  SET @ColTotalByte =    1 + ((@ColTotal-1) /8)
  SET @ColByte = 1 + ((@Col-1)/8)
  SET @ColBit = @col - ((@colByte-1) * 8)

  RETURN Power(2, @colbit + ((@ColTotalByte-@ColByte) * 8)-1)
END
```

This function is used within the dynamic audit-trail trigger/stored procedure by means of performing a bitwise and (&) between columns_updated() and GenColUpdated(). If the bitwise and is equal to GenColUpdated(), then the column in question is indeed updated:

```
Set @Col_Updated = Columns_Updated()
...
Set @ColUpdatedTemp =dbo.GenColUpdated(@ColCounter,@ColTotal)
If (@Col_Updated & @ColUpdatedTemp) = @ColUpdatedTemp
```

Cross-Reference

The dynamic audit-trail trigger code is explained in Chapter 24, "Exploring Advanced T-SQL Techniques." The DynamicAudit.sql script, at www.SQLServerBible.com, applies the code to the Northwind database.

Inserted and Deleted Logical Tables

SQL Server enables code within the trigger to access the effects of the transaction that caused the trigger to fire. The Inserted and Deleted logical tables are read-only images of the data. They can be considered views to the transaction log.

The Deleted table contains the rows before the effects of the DML statement and the Inserted table contains the rows after the effects of the DML statement, as shown in Table 23-2.

Table 23-2: Inserted and Deleted Tables

DML Statement	Inserted Table	Deleted Table
Insert	Inserted rows	Empty
Update	Rows in the database after the update	Rows in the database before the update
Delete	Empty	Rows to be deleted

The Inserted and Deleted tables have a very limited scope. They are visible only within the trigger. Stored procedures called by the trigger will not see the Inserted or Deleted tables.

If the table includes text, ntext, or image data-type columns, those columns may not be accessed in the Inserted or Deleted tables. Attempting to access them will cause an error.

The following example uses the Inserted table to report any new values for the LastName column:

```
ALTER TRIGGER TriggerOne ON Person
AFTER Insert, Update
AS
SET NoCount ON
IF Update(LastName)
  SELECT 'You modified the LastName column to '
    + Inserted.LastName
  FROM Inserted
```

With TriggerOne implemented on the Person table, the following update will modify a LastName value:

```
UPDATE Person
  SET LastName = 'Johnson'
  WHERE PersonID = 32
```

Result:

```
---------------------------------------------------
You modified the LastName column to Johnson
 (1 row(s) affected)
```

Developing Multi-Row Enabled–Triggers

Many triggers I see in production are not written to handle the possibility of multiple-row insert, update, or delete operations. They take a value from the Inserted or Deleted table and store it in a local variable for data validation or processing. This technique checks only the last row affected by the DML statement, a serious data integrity flaw. I've also seen databases that use cursors to step though each affected row. This is the type of slow code that gives triggers a bad name.

Because SQL is a set-oriented environment, every trigger must be written to handle DML statements that affect multiple rows. The best way to deal with multiple rows is to work with the Inserted and Deleted tables with set-oriented operations.

A join between the Inserted table and the Deleted or underlying table will return a complete set of the rows affected by the DML statement. Table 23-3 lists the possible join combinations for creating multi-row–enabled triggers.

Table 23-3: Multi-Row–Enabled FROM Clauses

DML Type	FROM Clause
Insert	FROM Inserted

Update	FROM Inserted
	  JOIN Deleted
	    ON Inserted.PK = Deleted.PK

Insert, Update	FROM Inserted
	  LEFT OUTER JOIN Deleted
	    ON Inserted.PK = Deleted.PK

Delete	FROM Deleted

The following trigger sample alters TriggerOne to look at the inserted and deleted tables:

```
ALTER TRIGGER TriggerOne ON Person
AFTER Insert, Update
AS
SELECT D.LastName + ' changed to ' + I.LastName
  FROM Inserted I
    JOIN Deleted D
      ON I.PersonID = D.PersonID;
GO

UPDATE Person
  SET LastName = 'Carter'
  WHERE LastName = 'Johnson'
```

Result:

```
- - - - - - - - - - - - - - - - - - - - - - - - - - - - - - - - - -
Johnson changed to Carter
Johnson changed to Carter
(2 row(s) affected)
```

The following after trigger, extracted from the Family sample database, enforces a rule that the FatherID must not only point to a valid person (that's covered by the foreign key), but that the person must be male:

```
CREATE TRIGGER Person_Parents
ON Person
AFTER INSERT, UPDATE
AS
IF UPDATE(FatherID)
  BEGIN
    -- Incorrect Father Gender
    IF EXISTS(
        SELECT *
          FROM Person
            JOIN Inserted
              ON Inserted.FatherID = Person.PersonID
          WHERE Person.Gender = 'F')
      BEGIN
        ROLLBACK
        RAISERROR('Incorrect Gender for Father',14,1)
        RETURN
      END
  END
```

Multiple-Trigger Interaction

Without a clear plan, a database that employs multiple triggers can quickly become disorganized and extremely difficult to troubleshoot.

Trigger Organization

In SQL Server 6.5, each trigger event could have only one trigger, and a trigger could apply only to one trigger event. The coding style that was required to develop such limited triggers lingers on. However, since version 7, SQL Server allows multiple `after` triggers per table event, and a trigger can apply to more than one event. This enables more flexible development styles.

Having developed databases that include several hundred triggers, I recommend organizing triggers not by table event, but by the trigger's task. For example:

✦ Data validation

✦ Complex business rules

✦ Audit trail

✦ Modified date

✦ Complex security

Cross-Reference   These tasks are covered in more detail in Chapter 24, "Exploring Advanced T-SQL Techniques."

Nested Triggers

Trigger nesting refers to whether or not a trigger that executes a DML statement will cause another trigger to fire. For example, if the Nested Triggers server option is enabled, and a trigger updates `TableA`, and `TableA` also has a trigger, then any triggers on `TableA` will also fire, as demonstrated in Figure 23-2.

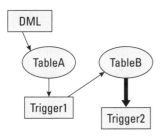

Figure 23-2: The Nested Triggers configuration option enables a DML statement within a trigger to fire additional triggers.

By default, the Nested Triggers option is enabled. The following configuration command is used to enable trigger nesting:

```
EXEC sp_configure 'Nested Triggers', 1
Reconfigure
```

If the database is developed with extensive server-side code, it's likely that a DML will fire a trigger, which will call a stored procedure, which will fire another trigger, and so on.

SQL Server triggers have a limit of 32 levels of recursion. For safety reasons it is useful to test the trigger-recursion level within the trigger. The `Trigger_NestLevel()` function returns the level of nesting. When the limit is reached, SQL Server generates a fatal error.

Recursive Triggers

A recursive trigger is a unique type of nested `after` trigger. If a trigger executes a DML statement that causes itself to fire, it's a recursive trigger, as shown in Figure 23-3. If the database recursive triggers option is off, the recursive iteration of the trigger won't fire.

A trigger is considered recursive only if it directly fires itself. If the trigger executes a stored procedure that then updates the trigger's table, that is an indirect recursive call, which is not covered by the recursive-trigger database option.

Recursive triggers are enabled by means of the `alter database` command:

```
ALTER DATABASE DatabaseName SET RECURSIVE_TRIGGERS ON | OFF
```

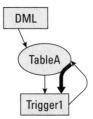

Figure 23-3: A recursive trigger is a self-referencing trigger—one that executes a DML statement that causes itself to be fired again.

An example of a useful recursive trigger is the ModifiedDate trigger. This trigger writes the current date and time to the modified column for any row that's updated. Using the OBX Kites sample database, the script first adds a Created and Modified column to the product table:

```
USE OBXKites

ALTER TABLE dbo.Product
  ADD
    Created DateTime Not Null DEFAULT GetDate(),
    Modified DateTime Not Null DEFAULT GetDate()
```

The trigger first prints the TriggerNest() level. This is very helpful for debugging nested or recursive triggers. The first if statement prevents the Created and Modified date from being directly updated by the user. If the trigger is fired by a user, then the nest level is 1.

The first time the trigger is executed the update is executed. Any subsequent executions of the trigger return because the trigger nest level is greater than 1. This prevents runaway recursion. Here's the trigger DDL code:

```
CREATE TRIGGER Products_ModifiedDate ON dbo.Product
FOR UPDATE
AS
SET NoCount ON

PRINT Trigger_NestLevel()

If Trigger_NestLevel() > 1
Return

If (Update(Created) or Update(Modified))
    AND Trigger_NestLevel() = 1
Begin
  Raiserror('Update failed.', 16, 1)
  Rollback
  Return
End

-- Update the Modified date
UPDATE Product
```

```
    SET Modified = getdate()
    FROM Product
      JOIN Inserted
        ON Product.ProductID = Inserted.ProductID
```

To test the trigger, the next update command will cause the trigger to update the Modified column. The select returns the Created and Modified date and time:

```
UPDATE PRODUCT
    SET [Name] = 'Modified Trigger'
    WHERE Code = '1002'

SELECT Code, Created, Modified
    FROM Product
    WHERE Code = '1002'
```

Result:

```
Code    Created                  Modified
------  -----------------------  -----------------------
1002    2002-02-18 09:48:31.700  2002-02-18 15:19:34.350
```

Note   Recursive triggers are required for replicated databases.

Instead of and After Triggers

If a table has both an instead of trigger and an after trigger for the same event, the following sequence is possible:

1. The DML statement initiates a transaction.

2. The instead of trigger fires in place of the DML.

3. If the instead of trigger executes DML against the same table event the process continues.

4. The after trigger fires.

Multiple after Triggers

If the same table event has multiple after triggers, they will all execute. The order of the triggers is less important than it may at first seem.

Every trigger has the opportunity to rollback the transaction. If the transaction is rolled back, all the work done by the initial transaction and all the triggers are rolled back.

Nevertheless, it is possible to designate an after trigger to fire first or last in the list of triggers. I recommend doing this only if one trigger is likely to roll back the transaction and, for performance reasons, you want that trigger to execute before other demanding triggers. Logically, however, the order of the triggers has no effect.

The sp_settriggerorder system stored procedure is used to assign the trigger order using the following syntax:

```
sp_settriggerorder
  @triggername = 'TriggerName',
  @order = 'first' or 'last' or 'none',
  @stmttype = 'INSERT' or 'UPDATE' or 'DELETE'
```

The effect of setting the trigger order is not cumulative. For example, setting TriggerOne to first and then setting TriggerTwo to first does not place TriggerOne in second place. In this case, TriggerOne returns to being unordered.

Summary

Triggers are a key feature in client/server databases. It's the trigger that enables the developer to create complex custom business rules that are strongly enforced at the database-engine level. SQL Server 2005 has two types of triggers: instead of triggers and after triggers.

The last four chapters have presented T-SQL programming and how to package the code within stored procedures, user-defined functions, and triggers. The next chapter draws on all of these chapters to present ideas for advanced server-side code.

✦   ✦   ✦

Exploring Advanced T-SQL Solutions

As the logical schema is implemented, many business rules and entity relationships are implemented as constraints. However, some of the business rules may be too complex to implement as constraints. These rules may be implemented either in the front-end application, in a middle tier, or in the database server. Of these three possible locations, the database server offers absolute compliance. There's no guarantee that future users will access the data solely through the current middle-tier object or front-end application.

Implementing business rules at the database-server level using T-SQL in triggers, stored procedures, and functions offers the same compelling benefits as constraints:

◆ The rules are absolute, and may not be ignored or bypassed by any DML (Data Manipulation Language — Select, Insert, Update, Delete) request.

◆ The rules are as close to the data as possible, improving data-access speed and reducing network round-trips.

Constraints, triggers, and stored procedures stand watch over the integrity of the data.

The past several chapters have discussed specific techniques for developing server-side code. A recurring theme in these chapters has been that processing should be moved as close to the data as possible. This chapter draws on all those techniques and suggests methods for developing databases that benefit from server-side code.

The methodology of the server-side–code database provides a stored procedure for every data-access requirement of the front-end application, and implements all business rules in the server in either stored procedures or triggers. While this method is development-intensive, it provides several benefits:

◆ All access is through a consistent programmer interface.

◆ All database code is compiled and optimized.

◆ Security is improved.

◆ All actions, even reads, may be audited.

✦ Complex rules and processing are removed from the front-end application.

✦ Query errors are eliminated.

Complex Business Rule Validation

The common solution to implementing data validation is check constraints; however, check constraints (*sans* user-defined functions) are limited to the current row.

Complex data validation deals with two concerns:

✦ Data validation that requires the access of data other than the current row, thus eliminating a check constraint as a possible means of implementing data validation

✦ Data validation that must be dynamic, based on requirements that vary by installation, company, department, or some other data, or just varying over time. Data-validation routines that can pull the requirements from a configuration table enable the local administrator to alter the data requirements without physically changing the schema.

Complex data validation is best implemented within a trigger. Triggers are powerful, flexible, and 100 percent enforced. A user's DML statement cannot bypass a trigger.

The basic tactic when constructing a trigger to enforce complex data validation is to check for the existence of any data in the inserted table that does not meet the rule, and, if any is found, to roll back the transaction. It's important that the trigger test for invalid data. If the trigger tested for the existence of valid data and some rows of a multi-row update were valid but some were not, then the trigger would let the bad in with the good.

Alternately, if the existence of invalid data is simply too difficult to code, the trigger could compare the @@Rowcount of the transaction with the count() of valid data in the Inserted table, but checking for invalid data will typically be faster and easier.

As an example of a need for complex data validation, the following business rule is from the Cape Hatteras Adventures database: *Any lead guide for a tour event must be qualified as a guide for that tour.*

Guides are assigned to the event in the Event_mm_Guide table, so the trigger will check data being inserted into the Event_mm_Guide table.

To check for data that violates the rule, a select statement joins the triggers' Inserted table with the event table to determine the TourID, and then joins with the Tour_mm_Guide table so the guide's qualifications can be checked. Notice that the Event_mm_Guide table is not required in the join; the Inserted table has the required data. The select is then restricted to any rows in which the guide is the lead guide, and in which either the qualification date has not yet occurred or the qualification has been revoked.

If this select statement returns any rows, the insert or update DML operation will be rolled back and an error raised to the client software. Here's the code:

```
USE CHA2

CREATE TRIGGER LeadQualified ON Event_mm_Guide
AFTER INSERT, UPDATE
AS
```

```
SET NoCount ON
IF EXISTS(
  SELECT *
    FROM Inserted
      JOIN dbo.Event
        ON Inserted.EventID = Event.EventID
      LEFT JOIN dbo.Tour_mm_Guide
        ON Tour_mm_Guide.TourID = Event.TourID
        AND Inserted.GuideID = Tour_mm_Guide.GuideID
    WHERE
      Inserted.IsLead = 1
      AND
        (QualDate > Event.DateBegin
      OR
        RevokeDate IS NOT NULL
      OR
        QualDate IS NULL )
      )
  BEGIN
    RAISERROR('Lead Guide is not Qualified.',16,1)
    ROLLBACK TRANSACTION
  END
```

The following two queries test the complex rule validation method by attempting to schedule a qualified guide and an unqualified guide. First, John Johnson is scheduled to lead a Gauley River Rafting trip:

```
INSERT Event_mm_Guide (EventID, GuideID, IsLead)
  VALUES (10, 1, 1)
```

Result:

```
Lead Guide is not Qualified.
```

When Ken Frank is scheduled for the class 5 rapids of the Gauley River, the trigger allows the insert:

```
INSERT Event_mm_Guide (EventID, GuideID, IsLead)
  VALUES (10, 2, 1)
```

Result:

```
(1 row(s) affected)
```

Complex Referential Integrity

Implementing declarative referential integrity via foreign-key constraints is definitely the right way to implement referential integrity.

That said, it's useful to see the code for a *standard* referential-integrity trigger before building a *complex* referential-integrity trigger. The code for a basic referential-integrity trigger would perform a set difference query joining the secondary table's foreign key and the primary table's primary key to locate any foreign-key values in the Inserted table that don't have a match in the primary table. In this example, `TableB` has a foreign key that points to `TableA`. Note that this generic code doesn't apply to any specific database:

```
CREATE TRIGGER RICheck ON Tour
AFTER INSERT, UPDATE
AS
SET NoCount ON
IF Exists(SELECT *
             FROM Inserted
               LEFT OUTER JOIN BaseCamp
                 ON Inserted.BaseCampID
                     = BaseCamp.BaseCampID
               WHERE BaseCamp.BaseCampID IS NULL)
   BEGIN
     RAISERROR
       ('Inappropriate Foreign Key: Tour.BaseCampID', 16, 1)
     ROLLBACK TRANSACTION
     RETURN
   END
```

The following code attempts to assign the "Amazon Trek" tour to `BaseCampID` 99. Because there is no base camp "99," the referential integrity trigger will block the update:

```
UPDATE Tour
   SET BaseCampID = 99
   WHERE TourID = 1
```

Indeed, the result is that the trigger raises an error:

```
Inappropriate Foreign Key: Tour.BaseCampID
```

However rare, some creative, advanced physical-data schemas require referential integrity that can't be enforced by the standard foreign-key constraint. These schemas tend to involve multiple-way relationships.

An example of complex referential integrity is from an MRP II system I worked on. The system could allocate a product to fill an order detail from either an inventory item or a purchase-order detail. One of the designs we experimented with allowed the `Allocation` table to use two foreign keys. The first foreign key pointed to the `OrderDetail` row and handled the `Product` requirement. The second foreign key pointed to the fulfillment source, which could be *either* a `PurchaseOrderDetail` GUID or an `InventoryItem` GUID. Because the foreign-key column could relate to either the purchase order or an inventory item, a standard foreign-key constraint would not do the job.

To implement the complex referential integrity, a trigger on the `Allocation` table checked for either a valid `PurchaseOrderDetailID` or a valid `InventoryItemID` using a set difference query that checked for any rows in the `Inserted` table with a `SourceID` that was in neither the `Inventory` table nor the `PurchaseOrderDetail` table:

```
CREATE TRIGGER AllocationCheck ON Allocation
AFTER INSERT, UPDATE
AS
SET NoCount ON
-- Check For invalid Inventory Item
IF Exists(SELECT *
             FROM Inserted I
```

```
              LEFT OUTER JOIN InventoryItem
                ON I.SourceID = InventoryItem.InventoryItemID
              LEFT OUTER JOIN PurchaseOrderDetail
                ON I.SourceID = PurchaseOrderDetail.PODID
            WHERE Inventory.InventoryID IS NULL
              AND PurchaseOrderDetail.PODID IS NULL)
    BEGIN
      RAISERROR
        ('Invalid product allocation source', 16, 1)
      ROLLBACK TRANSACTION
      RETURN
    END
```

Alternately, having two foreign keys in the allocation table — one pointing to the inventory-item table and one pointing to the purchase-order-detail table — could also solve the same problem with a less creative approach. The twist is that one, and only one, of the two foreign keys must be null — similar to a logical exclusive or. A standard check constraint could handle that requirement:

```
ALTER TABLE Allocation
  ADD CONSTRAINT AllocationSourceExclusive CHECK
    (PurchaseOrderID IS NULL AND InventoryID IS NOT NULL)
      OR
    (PurchaseOrderID IS NOT NULL AND InventoryID IS NULL)
```

The choice between the two complex referential-integrity methods should be made based on the ease of selecting the correct information and the comfort level of the developers. Both methods would require extensive use of left outer joins and the coalesce() function when calculating product allocation.

Row-Level Custom Security

SQL Server is excellent at vertical security (tables and columns) but it lacks the ability to dynamically check row-level security. Views, with check option, can provide a hard-coded form of row-level security, but basing a database on views used in this manner would create a performance and maintenance headache.

Enterprise databases often include data that is sensitive on a row level. Consider these four real-life business-security rules:

✦ Material data, inventory-cost data, and production scheduling are owned by a department and should not be available to those outside that department. However, the MRP system contains materials and inventory tracking for all locations and all departments in the entire company.

✦ HR data for each employee must be available to only the HR department and an employee's direct supervisors

✦ A companywide purchasing system permits only lumber buyers to purchase lumber, and only hardware buyers to purchase hardware.

✦ Each bank branch should be able to read any customer's data file, but only edit those customers who frequent that branch.

A row-based security solution is to develop the database using server-side code. This is a good idea for the following reasons:

✦ A security table can contain the list of users and their departments, or branch read and write rights.

✦ A security procedure checks the user's rights against the data being requested and returns a status of approved or denied.

✦ The fetch procedure checks the security procedure for permission to return the data.

✦ Triggers call the security procedure to check the user's right to perform the DML statement on the requested rows.

To demonstrate this design, the following topics implement row-level security to the OBXKites database. Each employee in the Contact table can be granted read, write, or administer privileges for each location's inventory and sales data. With this row-based security scheme, security can be checked by means of a stored procedure, function, NT login, or trigger.

The Security Table

The Security table serves as a many-to-many associative table (junction table) between the Contact and Location tables. The security levels determine the level of access:

0 or no row: 0 access

1: Read access

2: Write access

3: Admin access

Alternately, three-bit columns could be used for read, write, and administer rights, but the privileges are cumulative, so an integer column seems appropriate.

Creating the Table

The security table has two logical foreign keys. The foreign key to the location table is handled by a standard foreign-key constraint; however, the reference to the contact table should only allow contacts who are flagged as employees, so a trigger is used to enforce that complex referential-integrity requirement. The security assignment is meaningless without its contact or location, so both foreign keys are cascading deletes. A constraint is applied to the security-level column to restrict any entry to the valid security codes (0-3), and another constraint ensures that a contact may have only one security code per location:

```
USE OBXKites

CREATE TABLE dbo.Security (
  SecurityID UniqueIdentifier NOT NULL
    Primary Key NonClustered,
  ContactID UniqueIdentifier NOT NULL
    REFERENCES Contact ON DELETE CASCADE,
  LocationID UniqueIdentifier NOT NULL
    REFERENCES Location ON DELETE CASCADE,
  SecurityLevel INT NOT NULL DEFAULT 0
  )
```

The following three commands add the constraints to the Security table:

```
CREATE TRIGGER ContactID_RI
ON dbo.Security
AFTER INSERT, UPDATE
AS
SET NoCount ON
IF EXISTS(SELECT *
            FROM Inserted
              LEFT OUTER JOIN dbo.Contact
                ON Inserted.ContactID = Contact.ContactID
              WHERE Contact.ContactID IS NULL
                OR Contact.IsEmployee = 0 )
  BEGIN
    RAISERROR
      ('Foreign Key Constraint: Security.ContactID', 16, 1)
    ROLLBACK TRANSACTION
    RETURN
  END

ALTER TABLE dbo.Security
  ADD CONSTRAINT ValidSecurityCode CHECK
    (SecurityLevel IN (0,1,2,3))

ALTER TABLE dbo.Security
  ADD CONSTRAINT ContactLocation UNIQUE
    (ContactID, LocationID)
```

Because OBXKites uses GUIDs for primary keys, it's easier to use stored procedures to enter data. The chapter script (ch27 - Advanced T-SQL Solutions.sql) on the book's website (www.SQLServerBible.com) has stored procedures similar to those used previously in this chapter to enter data into the security table. The chapter script also includes sample data.

Security Fetch

In order for the Security table to be viewed, the first procedure created is pSecurity_Fetch. This procedure returns all the row-based security permissions or it can be restricted to returning those permissions for a single user or a single location:

```
CREATE PROCEDURE pSecurity_Fetch(
  @LocationCode CHAR(15) = NULL,
  @ContactCode CHAR(15) = NULL )
AS
SET NoCount ON
SELECT Contact.ContactCode,
       Location.LocationCode,
       SecurityLevel
    FROM dbo.Security
      JOIN dbo.Contact
        ON Security.ContactID = Contact.ContactID
      JOIN dbo.Location
        ON Security.LocationID = Location.LocationID
```

```
      WHERE (Location.LocationCode = @LocationCode
              OR @LocationCode IS NULL)
        AND (Contact.ContactCode = @ContactCode
              OR @ContactCode IS NULL)
```

Assigning Security

Row-based security permissions are set by adding or altering rows in the Security table, which serves as a junction between contact and location. In keeping with the theme of server-side code, this stored procedure assigns a security level to the contact/location combination. There's nothing new about this procedure. It accepts a contact code and location code, converts the codes into GUID IDs, and then performs the insert:

```
CREATE PROCEDURE pSecurity_Assign(
  @ContactCode VARCHAR(15),
  @LocationCode VARCHAR(15),
  @SecurityLevel INT
  )
AS
  SET NOCOUNT ON
  DECLARE
    @ContactID UNIQUEIDENTIFIER,
    @LocationID UNIQUEIDENTIFIER

  -- Get ContactID
  SELECT @ContactID = ContactID
    FROM dbo.Contact
    WHERE ContactCode = @ContactCode
  IF @@ERROR <> 0 RETURN -100
  IF @ContactID IS NULL
    BEGIN
      RAISERROR
        ('Contact: ''%s'' not found', 15,1,@ContactCode)
      RETURN -100
    END

  -- Get LocationID
  SELECT @LocationID = LocationID
    FROM dbo.Location
    WHERE LocationCode = @LocationCode
  IF @@ERROR <> 0 RETURN -100
  IF @LocationID IS NULL
    BEGIN
      RAISERROR
        ('Location: ''%s'' not found', 15,1,@LocationCode)
      RETURN -100
    END

  -- Insert
  INSERT dbo.Security (ContactID,LocationID, SecurityLevel)
    VALUES (@ContactID, @LocationID, @SecurityLevel)
  IF @@ERROR <> 0 RETURN -100
  RETURN
```

With the pSecurity_Fetch and pSecurity_Assign stored procedures created, the following batch adds some test data. The first two queries return some valid data for the test:

```
SELECT ContactCode
  FROM Contact
  WHERE IsEmployee = 1
```

Result:

```
ContactCode
---------------
118
120
119
```

The next query returns valid locations:

```
SELECT LocationCode FROM Location
```

Result:

```
LocationCode
---------------
CH
Clt
ElC
JR
KH
W
```

Based on this data, the next four procedure calls assign security:

```
EXEC pSecurity_Assign
  @ContactCode = 118,
  @LocationCode = CH,
  @SecurityLevel = 3

EXEC pSecurity_Assign
  @ContactCode = 118,
  @LocationCode = Clt,
  @SecurityLevel = 2

EXEC pSecurity_Assign
  @ContactCode = 118,
  @LocationCode = Elc,
  @SecurityLevel = 1

EXEC pSecurity_Assign
  @ContactCode = 120,
  @LocationCode = W,
  @SecurityLevel = 2
```

The following two commands test the data inserts using the pSecurity_Ffetch procedure. The first test examines the security settings for the 'W' location:

```
EXEC pSecurity_Fetch @LocationCode = 'W'
```

Result:

```
ContactCode     LocationCode     SecurityLevel
---------------  ----------------  -------------
120             W                3
```

The next batch examines the security setting for "Dave Boston" (contact code 118):

```
EXEC pSecurity_Fetch @ContactCode = '118'
```

Result:

```
ContactCode     LocationCode     SecurityLevel
---------------  ----------------  -------------
118             Clt              2
118             CH               3
118             ElC              1
```

The row-based security schema includes several constraints. The following commands test those constraints using the stored procedures:

Testing the unique constraint:

```
EXEC pSecurity_Assign
  @ContactCode = 120,
  @LocationCode = W,
  @SecurityLevel = 2
```

Result:

```
Server: Msg 2627, Level 14, State 2,
  Procedure pSecurity_Assign, Line 35
Violation of UNIQUE KEY constraint 'ContactLocation'.
Cannot insert duplicate key in object 'Security'.
The statement has been terminated.
```

Testing the valid security-code check constraint:

```
EXEC pSecurity_Assign
  @ContactCode = 118,
  @LocationCode = W,
  @SecurityLevel = 5
```

Result:

```
Server: Msg 547, Level 16, State 1,
  Procedure pSecurity_Assign, Line 35
INSERT statement conflicted with COLUMN CHECK constraint
  'ValidSecurityCode'. The conflict occurred in database
  'OBXKites', table 'Security', column 'SecurityLevel'.
The statement has been terminated.
```

Testing the employees-only complex-business-rule trigger:

```
Select ContactCode FROM Contact WHERE IsEmployee = 0
EXEC pSecurity_Assign
  @ContactCode = 102,
```

```
  @LocationCode = W,
  @SecurityLevel = 3
```

Result:

```
Foreign Key Constraint: Security.ContactID
```

Testing the contact foreign-key constraint, which is first checked by the stored procedure:

```
EXEC pSecurity_Assign
  @ContactCode = 999,
  @LocationCode = W,
  @SecurityLevel = 3
```

Result:

```
Server: Msg 50000, Level 15, State 1, Procedure pSecurity_Assign, Line
19

Contact: '999' not found
```

Testing the location-code foreign-key constraint. It's also checked within the stored procedure:

```
EXEC pSecurity_Assign
  @ContactCode = 118,
  @LocationCode = RDBMS,
  @SecurityLevel = 3
```

Result:

```
Server: Msg 50000, Level 15, State 1, Procedure pSecurity_Assign, Line
30
Location: 'RDBMS' not found
```

Handling Security-Level Updates

The pSecurity_Assign procedure used in the previous examples handles new security assignments, but fails to accept adjustments to an existing security setting.

The following alteration to the procedure checks whether the security combination of contact and location is already in the Security table, and then performs the appropriate insert or update. Security permissions may be created or adjusted with the new version of the procedure and the same parameters. Here's the improved procedure:

```
ALTER PROCEDURE pSecurity_Assign(
  @ContactCode CHAR(15),
  @LocationCode CHAR(15),
  @SecurityLevel INT
  )
AS
  SET NOCOUNT ON
  DECLARE
    @ContactID UNIQUEIDENTIFIER,
    @LocationID UNIQUEIDENTIFIER
  -- Get ContactID
  SELECT @ContactID = ContactID
```

```
      FROM dbo.Contact
      WHERE ContactCode = @ContactCode
  IF @ContactID IS NULL
    BEGIN
      RAISERROR
        ('Contact: ''%s'' not found', 15,1,@ContactCode)
      RETURN -100
    END
  -- Get LocationID
  SELECT @LocationID = LocationID
    FROM dbo.Location
    WHERE LocationCode = @LocationCode
  IF @LocationID IS NULL
    BEGIN
      RAISERROR
        ('Location: ''%s'' not found', 15,1,@LocationCode)
      RETURN -100
    END
  -- IS Update or Insert?
  IF EXISTS(SELECT *
              FROM dbo.Security
              WHERE ContactID = @ContactID
                AND LocationID = @LocationID)
    -- Update
    BEGIN
      UPDATE dbo.Security
        SET SecurityLevel = @SecurityLevel
        WHERE ContactID = @ContactID
          AND LocationID = @LocationID
      IF @@ERROR <> 0 RETURN -100
    END

  -- Insert
  ELSE
    BEGIN
      INSERT dbo.Security
        (ContactID,LocationID, SecurityLevel)
        VALUES (@ContactID, @LocationID, @SecurityLevel)
      IF @@ERROR <> 0 RETURN -100
    END
  RETURN
```

The following script tests the new procedure's ability to modify a security permission for a contact/location combination. The first command modifies contact 120's security for location W:

```
EXEC pSecurity_Assign
  @ContactCode = 120,
  @LocationCode = W,
  @SecurityLevel = 2

EXEC pSecurity_Fetch
  @ContactCode = 120
```

Result:

```
ContactCode     LocationCode     SecurityLevel
--------------- ---------------- -------------
120             W                2
```

The following two commands issue a new security permission and edit an existing security permission. The third command fetches the security permissions for contact code 120:

```
EXEC pSecurity_Assign
  @ContactCode = 120,
  @LocationCode = CH,
  @SecurityLevel = 1

EXEC pSecurity_Assign
  @ContactCode = 120,
  @LocationCode = W,
  @SecurityLevel = 3

EXEC pSecurity_Fetch
  @ContactCode = 120
```

Result:

```
ContactCode     LocationCode     SecurityLevel
--------------- ---------------- -------------
120             W                3
120             CH               1
```

The Security-Check Stored Procedure

The security-check stored procedure is central to the row-based security system. It's designed to return a true or false for a security request for a user, a location, and a requested security level.

The procedure selects the security level of the user for the given location and then compares that value with the value of the requested security level. If the user's permission level is sufficient, a 1 (indicating true) is returned; otherwise, a 0 (for false) is returned:

```
CREATE PROCEDURE p_SecurityCheck (
  @ContactCode CHAR(15),
  @LocationCode CHAR(15),
  @SecurityLevel INT,
  @Approved BIT OUTPUT )
AS
SET NoCount ON

DECLARE @ActualLevel INT

SELECT @ActualLevel = SecurityLevel
  FROM dbo.Security
    JOIN dbo.Contact
      ON Security.ContactID = Contact.ContactID
```

```
       JOIN dbo.Location
         ON Security.LocationID = Location.LocationID
     WHERE ContactCode = @ContactCode
       AND LocationCode = @LocationCode

IF    @ActualLevel IS NULL
      OR
         @ActualLevel < @SecurityLevel
      OR
         @ActualLevel = 0
   SET @Approved = 0
ELSE
   SET @Approved = 1

RETURN 0
```

The following batch calls the p_SecurityCheck procedure and uses the @OK local variable to capture the output parameter. When testing this from the script OntheWeb, try several different values. Use the pSecurity_Fetch procedure to determine possible parameters. The following code checks whether contact code 118 has administrative privileges at the Charlotte warehouse:

```
DECLARE @OK BIT
EXEC p_SecurityCheck
   @ContactCode = 118,
   @LocationCode = Clt,
   @SecurityLevel = 3,
   @Approved   = @OK OUTPUT
SELECT @OK
```

Result:

```
0
```

The Security-Check Function

The security-check function includes the same logic as the pSecurity_Check stored procedure. The advantage of a function is that it can be used directly within an if command without a local variable being used to store the output parameter. The function uses the same three input parameters as the stored-procedure version and the same internal logic, but it returns the approved bit as the return of the function, rather than as an output parameter. Here's the function's code:

```
CREATE FUNCTION dbo.fSecurityCheck (
  @ContactCode CHAR(15),
  @LocationCode CHAR(15),
  @SecurityLevel INT)
RETURNS BIT
BEGIN
DECLARE @ActualLevel INT,
  @Approved BIT

SELECT @ActualLevel = SecurityLevel
```

```
      FROM dbo.Security
        JOIN dbo.Contact
          ON Security.ContactID = Contact.ContactID
        JOIN dbo.Location
          ON Security.LocationID = Location.LocationID
      WHERE ContactCode = @ContactCode
        AND LocationCode = @LocationCode

  IF @ActualLevel IS NULL
    OR @ActualLevel < @SecurityLevel
    OR @ActualLevel = 0
    SET @Approved = 0
  ELSE
    SET @Approved = 1

  RETURN @Approved
  END
```

The next batch demonstrates how to call the function to test security within a stored procedure. If the function returns a 0, the user does not have sufficient security and the procedure terminates:

```
-- Check within a Procedure
IF dbo.fSecurityCheck( 118, 'Clt', 3) = 0
  BEGIN
    RAISERROR('Security Violation', 16,1)
    ROLLBACK TRANSACTION
    RETURN -100
  END
```

Using the NT Login

Some applications are designed so that the user logs in with the application, and the row-based security code so far has assumed that the username is supplied to the procedures. However, if the SQL Server instance is using NT authentication, the security routines can use that identification.

Rather than request the contact code as a parameter, the security procedure or function can automatically use suser_sname(), the NT login, to identify the current user. The login name (domain and username) must be added to the Contact table. Alternately, a secondary table could be created to hold multiple logins per user. Some wide-area networks require users to log in with different domain names according to location, so a ContactLogin table is a good idea.

The following function is modified to check the user's security based on his or her NT login and a ContactLogin table. The first query demonstrates retrieving the login within T-SQL code:

```
SELECT suser_sname()
```

Result:

```
--------------
NOLI\Paul
```

The following code creates the secondary table to store the logins:

```
CREATE TABLE dbo.ContactLogin(
  ContactLogin UNIQUEIDENTIFIER
    PRIMARY KEY NONCLUSTERED DEFAULT NewId(),
  ContactID UniqueIdentifier NOT NULL
    REFERENCES dbo.Contact ON DELETE CASCADE,
  NTLogin VARCHAR(100) )
```

With the table in place, a simple `insert` will populate a single row using my login so the code can be tested:

```
INSERT CONTACTLOGIN (ContactID, NTLogin)
  SELECT ContactID, 'NOLI\Paul'
    FROM dbo.Contact
    WHERE ContactCode = 118
```

Check the data:

```
SELECT ContactCode, NTLogin
  FROM dbo.Contact
    JOIN ContactLogin
      ON Contact.ContactID = ContactLogin.ContactID
```

Result:

```
ContactCode      NTLogin
---------------  --------------
118              Paul/NOLI
```

The security-check function is modified to join the `contactlogin` table and to restrict the rows returned to those that match the NT login name. Because the contact code is no longer required, this `select` can skip the contact table and join the `Security` table directly with the `ContactLogin` table:

```
CREATE FUNCTION dbo.fSecurityCheckNT (
  @LocationCode CHAR(15),
  @SecurityLevel INT)
RETURNS BIT
BEGIN
DECLARE @ActualLevel INT,
  @Approved BIT

SELECT @ActualLevel = SecurityLevel
  FROM dbo.Security
    JOIN dbo.Location
      ON Security.LocationID = Location.LocationID
    JOIN dbo.ContactLogin
      ON Security.ContactID = ContactLogin.ContactID
  WHERE NTLogin = suser_sname()
    AND LocationCode = @LocationCode

IF @ActualLevel IS NULL
  OR @ActualLevel < @SecurityLevel
  OR @ActualLevel = 0
```

```
      SET @Approved = 0
   ELSE
      SET @Approved = 1

   RETURN @Approved
   END
```

To test the new function, the following batch will repeat the security check performed in the last section, but this time the user will be captured from the NT login instead of being passed to the function:

```
IF dbo.fSecurityCheckNT('Clt', 3) = 0
   BEGIN
      RAISERROR('Security Violation', 16,1)
      ROLLBACK TRANSACTION
      RETURN -100
   END
```

The function did not return an error, so I'm allowed to complete the procedure.

The Security-Check Trigger

The security-check stored procedure and function both work well when included within a stored procedure, such as the fetch, addnew, update, or delete procedures mentioned in the beginning of this chapter; but to implement row-based security in a database that allows access from views, ad hoc queries, or direct table DML statements, you must handle the row-based security with a trigger. The trigger can prevent updates, but will not be able to check data reads. If row-based security is a requirement for reads, all reads must go through a stored procedure.

The following trigger is similar to the security-check function. It differs in that the trigger must allow for multiple orders with potential multiple locations. The joins have to match up [Order] rows and their locations with the user's security level for each location. The join can go directly from the ContactLogin table to the Security table. Because this is an insert and update trigger, any security level below 2 for any order being written will be rejected and a security-violation error will be raised. The rollback transaction command will undo the original DML command that fired the trigger:

```
CREATE TRIGGER OrderSecurity ON [Order]
AFTER INSERT, UPDATE
AS
IF EXISTS (
SELECT *
  FROM dbo.Security
    JOIN dbo.ContactLogin
      ON Security.ContactID = ContactLogin.ContactID
    JOIN Inserted
      ON Inserted.LocationID = Security.LocationID
  WHERE NTLogin = suser_sname()
    AND SecurityLevel < 2 )
  BEGIN
    RAISERROR('Security Violation', 16,1)
    ROLLBACK TRANSACTION
  END
```

Auditing Data Changes

Data auditing is added to a database to increase its data-integrity level. A full data-audit trail can provide a lot of detailed information, including the following:

✦ All data changes to a row since it was inserted

✦ All data changes made by a specific user last week

✦ All data changes from a certain workstation during lunch

✦ All data changes made from an application other than the standard front-end application

Data-audit trails solve significant problems for DBAs as well as users. My consulting firm once developed a legal compliance/best-practices document-management system for a Fortune 100 company, and its law firm was populating the database with regulatory laws. The law firm fell behind on its schedule and claimed that it was unable to enter data for two weeks because of software problems. When we provided a list of the more than 70,000 column-level data changes made during those two weeks from the data-audit trail, the claim vanished.

I've seen published methods of auditing data that add a few columns to the table, or duplicate the table, to store the last change. Neither of these methods is worthwhile. A partial audit, or a last-value audit, is of no real value. A data-audit trail must permanently record the data changes; otherwise, anyone who understands the system can just make another change and erase the original values.

The Audit Table

The Audit table's purpose is to provide a single location in which to record data changes for the database. The following audit-trail table can store all non-BLOB changes to any table. The Operation column stores an I, U, or D, depending on the DML statement:

```
CREATE TABLE dbo.Audit (
   AuditID UNIQUEIDENTIFIER RowGUIDCol  NOT NULL
     CONSTRAINT DF_Audit_AuditID DEFAULT (NEWID())
     CONSTRAINT PK_Audit PRIMARY KEY NONCLUSTERED (AuditID),
   AuditDate DATETIME NOT NULL,
   SysUser VARCHAR(50) NOT NULL,
   Application VARCHAR(50) NOT NULL,
   TableName VARCHAR(50)NOT NULL,
   Operation CHAR(1) NOT NULL,
   PrimaryKey VARCHAR(50) NOT NULL,
   RowDescription VARCHAR(50) NULL,
   SecondaryRow   VARCHAR (50) NULL,
   [Column] VARCHAR(50) NOT NULL,
   OldValue VARCHAR(50) NULL,
   NewValue VARCHAR(50) NULL
   )
```

The PrimaryKey column stores the pointer to the row that was modified, and the RowDescription column records a readable description of the row. These two columns allow the audit trail to be joined with the original table or viewed directly. The PrimaryKey column is important because it can quickly find all changes to a single row regardless of how the description has changed over time.

The Fixed Audit Trail Trigger

The brute-force method of auditing data uses a trigger on every table, which examines every column using the updated() function and writes any changes to the audit table.

The insert statement joins the Inserted and Deleted tables to correctly handle multiple-row inserts and updates. The join is a left outer join so that an insert operation, with only rows in the Inserted table, can still be recorded. The join is also restricted with a theta join condition so that when a multiple-row update only affects some of the rows for a given column, only those rows that are actually changed are recorded to the audit trail.

For an example of a fixed audit-trail trigger, the following code audits the Product table for the OBXKites database:

```
CREATE TRIGGER Product_Audit
ON dbo.Product
AFTER Insert, Update
NOT FOR REPLICATION
AS

DECLARE @Operation CHAR(1)

IF EXISTS(SELECT * FROM Deleted)
 SET @Operation = 'U'
ELSE
 SET @Operation = 'I'

IF UPDATE(ProductCategoryID)
    INSERT dbo.Audit
      (AuditDate, SysUser, Application, TableName, Operation,
       PrimaryKey, RowDescription, SecondaryRow, [Column],
       OldValue, NewValue)
      SELECT GetDate(), suser_sname(), APP_NAME(), 'Product',
         @Operation, Inserted.ProductID, Inserted.Code,
          NULL, 'ProductCategoryID',
          OPC.ProductCategoryName, NPC.ProductCategoryName
        FROM Inserted
          LEFT OUTER JOIN Deleted
            ON Inserted.ProductID = Deleted.ProductID
            AND Inserted.ProductCategoryID
                <> Deleted.ProductCategoryID
          -- fetch ProductCategory Names
          LEFT OUTER JOIN dbo.ProductCategory OPC
            ON Deleted.ProductCategoryID
                = OPC.ProductCategoryID
          JOIN dbo.ProductCategory NPC
            ON Inserted.ProductCategoryID
                = NPC.ProductCategoryID

IF UPDATE(Code)
    INSERT dbo.Audit
      (AuditDate, SysUser, Application, TableName, Operation,
       PrimaryKey, RowDescription, SecondaryRow, [Column],
```

```
          OldValue, NewValue)
      SELECT GetDate(), suser_sname(), APP_NAME(),
          'Product', @Operation, Inserted.ProductID,
          Inserted.Code, NULL, 'Code',
          Deleted.Code, Inserted.Code
        FROM Inserted
        LEFT OUTER JOIN Deleted
          ON Inserted.ProductID = Deleted.ProductID
            AND Inserted.Code <> Deleted.Code

  IF UPDATE(ProductName)
      INSERT dbo.Audit
        (AuditDate, SysUser, Application, TableName, Operation,
        PrimaryKey, RowDescription, SecondaryRow, [Column],
        OldValue, NewValue)
      SELECT GetDate(), suser_sname(), APP_NAME(),
          'Product', @Operation,
          Inserted.ProductID, Inserted.Code, NULL, 'Name',
          Deleted.ProductName, Inserted.ProductName
        FROM Inserted
          LEFT OUTER JOIN Deleted
            ON Inserted.ProductID = Deleted.ProductID
              AND Inserted.ProductName <> Deleted.ProductName

  IF UPDATE(ProductDescription)
      INSERT dbo.Audit
        (AuditDate, SysUser, Application, TableName, Operation,
        PrimaryKey, RowDescription, SecondaryRow, [Column],
        OldValue, NewValue)
      SELECT GetDate(), suser_sname(), APP_NAME(), 'Product',
          @Operation, Inserted.ProductID, Inserted.Code,
          NULL, 'ProductDescription',
          Deleted.ProductDescription,
          Inserted.ProductDescription
        FROM Inserted
          LEFT OUTER JOIN Deleted
            ON Inserted.ProductID = Deleted.ProductID
              AND Inserted.ProductDescription
                <> Deleted.ProductDescription

  IF UPDATE(ActiveDate)
      INSERT dbo.Audit
        (AuditDate, SysUser, Application, TableName, Operation,
        PrimaryKey, RowDescription, SecondaryRow, [Column],
        OldValue, NewValue)
      SELECT GetDate(), suser_sname(), APP_NAME(), 'Product',
          @Operation, Inserted.ProductID, Inserted.Code,
          NULL, 'ActiveDate',
          Deleted.ActiveDate, Inserted.ActiveDate
        FROM Inserted
          LEFT OUTER JOIN Deleted
```

```
                    ON Inserted.ProductID = Deleted.ProductID
                       AND Inserted.ActiveDate != Deleted.ActiveDate

   IF UPDATE(DiscontinueDate)
       INSERT dbo.Audit
           (AuditDate, SysUser, Application, TableName, Operation,
            PrimaryKey, RowDescription, SecondaryRow, [Column],
            OldValue, NewValue)
           SELECT GetDate(), suser_sname(), APP_NAME(), 'Product',
               @Operation, Inserted.ProductID, Inserted.Code,
               NULL, 'DiscontinueDate',
               Deleted.DiscontinueDate, Inserted.DiscontinueDate
           FROM Inserted
               LEFT OUTER JOIN Deleted
                   ON Inserted.ProductID = Deleted.ProductID
                       AND Inserted.DiscontinueDate
                           != Deleted.DiscontinueDate
```

With the fixed audit-trail trigger installed, the following batch exercises it by inserting and updating product data using both DML statements and the previously created stored procedures. The first trigger test uses the pProduct_AddNew procedure:

```
EXEC pProduct_AddNew 'Kite', 200, 'The MonstaKite',
  'Man what a big Kite!'

SELECT TableName, RowDescription, [Column], NewValue
  FROM dbo.Audit
```

Result:

```
TableName RowDescription
                  Column                    NewValue
--------- ----- ---------------------- --------------------Product
200    ProductCategoryID       Kite
Product   200   Code                   200
Product   200   Name                   The MonstaKite
Product   200   ProductDescription     Man what a big Kite!
Product   200   ActiveDate             Mar  1 2002  1:35PM
Product   200   DiscontinueDate        NULL
```

The trigger is the right place to implement an audit trail because it will catch all the changes, even those made directly to the table with DML commands. This example is a non-stored procedure direct DML update. The audit trail can show the original value as well as the new value:

```
UPDATE dbo.Product
  SET ProductDescription = 'Biggie Sized'
  WHERE Code = 200
```

The following query pinpoints the data history of the ProductDescription column for product 200:

```
SELECT AuditDate, OldValue,  NewValue
  FROM dbo.Audit
```

```
WHERE TableName = 'Product'
  AND RowDescription = '200'
  AND [Column] = 'ProductDescription'
```

Result:

```
AuditDate                    OldValue           NewValue
-------------------------    ----------------   -------------
2002-03-01 13:35:17.093      NULL               Man what a
                                                big Kite!
2002-03-01 15:10:49.257      Man what a         Biggie Sized
                             big Kite!
```

Rolling Back from the Audit Trail

If the audit system is complete, all the changes for a given row since its creation are easily listed for the user. From this list, the user can select a data modification and roll it back. Once an audit-trail row is selected, rolling back the change is simply a matter of submitting an update statement based on the data in the audit trail.

The following code demonstrates rolling back a change from the audit table. The pAudit_RollBack stored procedure accepts an Audit table primary key and from that builds a dynamic SQL update DML command for the correct table, row, column, and rollback value:

```
CREATE PROCEDURE pAudit_RollBack (
  @AuditID UNIQUEIDENTIFIER)
AS
SET NoCount ON

DECLARE
  @SQLString NVARCHAR(4000),
  @TableName NVARCHAR(50),
  @PrimaryKey NVARCHAR(50),
  @Column NVARCHAR(50),
  @NewValue NVARCHAR(50)

SELECT
  @TableName = TableName,
  @PrimaryKey = PrimaryKey,
  @Column = [Column],
  @NewValue = OldValue
  FROM dbo.Audit
  WHERE AuditID = @AuditID

SET @SQLString =
  'UPDATE ' + @TableName
    + ' SET ' + @Column + ' = ''' + @NewValue +''''
    + ' WHERE ' + @TableName + 'ID = ''' + @PrimaryKey + ''''

EXEC sp_executeSQL @SQLString
Return
```

With the procedure in place, the following script simulates the logic needed to roll back an update. The original product description value for product 200 was "Man what a big Kite," and during testing of the fixed audit-trail trigger it was changed to "Biggie Sized." The script finds the audit-trail row for that change and passes the GUID to pAudit_RollBack, which rolls back the previous change:

```
DECLARE @AuditRollBack UNIQUEIDENTIFIER

SELECT @AuditRollBack = AuditID
  FROM dbo.Audit
  WHERE TableName = 'Product'
    AND RowDescription = '200'
    AND OldValue = 'Man what a big Kite!'

EXEC pAudit_RollBack @AuditRollBack

SELECT ProductDescription
  FROM dbo.Product
  WHERE Code = 200
```

Result:

```
ProductDescription
--------------------------
Man what a big Kite!
```

This procedure reverses a single specific change. The procedure could be modified to roll back a row to a certain point in time by selecting the history of the row from the audit trail and then looping through each change in a descending order.

Auditing Complications

Besides the additional development time, adding auditing can present several complications.

Best Practice

Develop the entire database and prove that the data schema is correct prior to implementing a data-audit trail. Changes to the data schema are more complex once audit-trail triggers are in place.

Auditing Related Data

The most significant complication involves auditing related data such as secondary rows. For example, a change to an OrderDetail row is actually a change to the order. A user will want to see the data history of the order and see all changes to any of the data related to the order. Therefore, a change to the OrderDetail table should be recorded as a change to the [Order] table, and the line number of the order detail item that was changed is recorded in the SecondaryRow column.

Recording foreign key changes is another difficult aspect of a full audit trail. A user does not want to see the new GUID or identity value for a foreign-key update. If the order-ship-method foreign key is changed from "Slow Boat" to "Speedy Express," the audit-trail trigger should look up the foreign key and record a readable value. In the Product_Audit sample fixed audit-trail trigger, changes to the ProductCategoryID column write the product category name to the Audit table.

Date Created and Date Modified

When you are using a full data-audit trail, the row's creation date and last-modified date can easily be derived from the audit table. In reality, when an application displays the created and modified date for a table in a large user-interface grid, I strongly recommend denormalizing the row's created and modified dates and storing the columns directly in the audited table.

Cross-Reference   Chapter 23, "Creating DML Triggers," includes a trigger that updates the created and modified columns while preventing problems with recursion.

Auditing Select Statements

Data-audit triggers are limited to auditing insert, update, and delete DML statements. To audit data reads, implement the read audit in the fetch stored procedure. Use SQL Server security to limit access to the table so that all reads must go through a stored procedure or a function.

Data Auditing and Security

Another concern for those creating a full data-audit history is the security of the data-audit trail. Anyone who has read rights to the audit table will be able to effectively see all the data from every audited table. If users will have the capability to see the data history for a given row, use a stored procedure to fetch the audit data so that security can be persevered.

Data Auditing and Performance

A full data-audit trail will add some level of overhead to the system. A single row insert to a 20-column-wide table will add 20 inserts to the audit table. To reduce the performance impact of the audit trail, do the following:

✦ Limit the indexes on the audit table.

✦ Locate the audit table on its own filegroup and disk subsystem. A separate filegroup will make backups easier as well.

✦ Using the fixed audit trigger, limit the auditing to those columns that require such a high level of data integrity.

The Dynamic Audit-Trail Trigger and Procedure

Having spent several months writing fixed audit-trail triggers for a project with hundreds of tables, I felt driven to develop a dynamic auditing system.

The dynamic audit trail is implemented with small triggers on every table. All the trigger does is copy the Inserted and Deleted tables to temporary tables and pass a few variables to a stored procedure where the real work is done. It examines the Columns_Updated binary value, determines the right value to use instead of nulls, and generates a dynamic SQL statement to write the audit trail.

That's the catch: To execute a dynamic SQL statement, sp_execSQL is required and it functions as a nested T-SQL batch. The scope of the Inserted and Deleted tables is limited to the trigger—they aren't available to any called stored procedure or dynamic SQL statement. That's why the temporary tables are used to pass the changes to the stored procedure and then to the dynamic SQL. The temporary table's scope includes called stored procedures and execs, and that makes the dynamic audit trigger possible.

Every method has its trade-off. On the pro side, this trigger/stored procedure/dynamic SQL method is extremely easy to implement. It works with nearly any table. The limitations of this version of the dynamic audit trigger are as follows:

✦ It uses a temporary table to pass the `Inserted` and `Deleted` tables to the stored procedure, so it isn't the fastest method possible. In addition, the temporary tables are created using a `select ... into` syntax, which causes further performance and locking issues.

✦ The current dynamic audit trail doesn't automatically audit related data or secondary tables. Nor does it audit tables with composite primary keys.

✦ It doesn't audit any tables with BLOB columns (`image`, `text`, or `ntext`) because these can't be selected from the `Inserted` and `Deleted` tables.

Because of these limitations, use the dynamic audit-trail method for tables that aren't updated frequently, during the early life stages of a database, or for databases that have acceptable performance when the dynamic audit trail is enabled. For high performance, it's better to employ the fixed audit trigger and brute-force through the columns. However, the fixed audit trigger involves significantly more code and maintenance.

With those disclaimers, here is the code for the dynamic audit trail:

```
/*
Dynamic Audit Trigger Table and Code
Paul Nielsen  www.IsNotNull.com
This sample script adds the dynamic audit trigger to
Northwind Customers and Products table.

Version 1.1 - Aug 6, 2001
*/

USE Northwind
----------------------------------------------------------
-- Create the table to store the Audit Trail

IF Exists (SELECT * FROM sysobjects WHERE NAME = 'Audit')
  DROP TABLE Audit

Go
CREATE TABLE dbo.Audit (
  AuditID UNIQUEIDENTIFIER ROWGUIDCOL  NOT NULL
    CONSTRAINT DF_Audit_AuditID DEFAULT (NEWID())
    CONSTRAINT PK_Audit PRIMARY KEY NONCLUSTERED (AuditID),
  AuditDate DATETIME NOT NULL,
  SysUser VARCHAR(50) NOT NULL,
  Application VARCHAR(50) NOT NULL,
  TableName VARCHAR(50)NOT NULL,
  Operation CHAR(1) NOT NULL,
  PrimaryKey VARCHAR(50) NOT NULL,
--   RowDescription VARCHAR(50) NULL,
  SecondaryRow   VARCHAR(50) NULL,
  [Column] VARCHAR(50) NOT NULL,
```

```
    OldValue VARCHAR(50) NULL,
    NewValue VARCHAR(50) NULL
    )

GO


-------------------------------------------------------------
-- Create function to simulate the Columns_Updated() value

IF EXISTS (SELECT *
              FROM sysobjects
              WHERE NAME = 'GenColUpdated')
    DROP FUNCTION GenColUpdated
Go

CREATE FUNCTION dbo.GenColUpdated
  (@Col INT, @ColTotal INT)
RETURNS INT
AS
BEGIN
-- Copyright 2001 Paul Nielsen
-- This function simulates Columns_Updated()
DECLARE
  @ColByte INT,
  @ColTotalByte INT,
  @ColBit INT

  -- Calculate Byte Positions
  SET @ColTotalByte =    1 + ((@ColTotal-1) /8)
  SET @ColByte = 1 + ((@Col-1)/8)
  SET @ColBit = @col - ((@colByte-1) * 8)

  -- gen Columns_Updated() value for given column position
  RETURN
    POWER(2, @colbit + ((@ColTotalByte-@ColByte) * 8)-1)
END
go


-------------------------------------------------------------
-- Create the Dynamic Audit Stored Procedures

IF EXISTS (SELECT * FROM SysObjects WHERE NAME = 'pAudit')
  DROP PROC pAudit
Go

CREATE PROCEDURE pAudit (
  @Col_Updated VARBINARY(1028),
  @TableName VARCHAR(100),
  @PrimaryKey SYSNAME)
AS
-- dynamic auto-audit trigger/stored procedure
```

```sql
-- Copyright 2001 Paul Nielsen
SET NoCount ON
DECLARE
  @ColTotal INT,
  @ColCounter INT,
  @ColUpdatedTemp INT,
  @ColName SYSNAME,
  @BlankString CHAR(1),
  @SQLStr NVARCHAR(1000),
  @ColNull NVARCHAR(50),
  @SysUser NVARCHAR(100),
  @ColumnDataType INT,
  @IsUpdate BIT,
  @tempError INT

 SET @SysUser = suser_sname()
 SET @BlankString = ''

-- Initialize Col variables
SELECT @ColCounter = 0
SELECT @ColTotal = Count(*)
  FROM SysColumns
    JOIN SysObjects
      ON SysColumns.id = SysObjects.id
  WHERE SysObjects.name = @TableName

-- Set IsUpdated Flag
IF EXISTS(SELECT * FROM #tempDel)
  SELECT @IsUpdate = 1
ELSE
  SELECT @IsUpdate = 0

-- Column Updates
WHILE ((SELECT @ColCounter) != @ColTotal)
  -- run through some columns
  BEGIN
    SELECT @ColCounter = @ColCounter + 1
    SET @ColUpdatedTemp
        = dbo.GenColUpdated(@ColCounter,@ColTotal)

  -- bitwise AND between updated bits
  -- and the selected column bit
  IF (@Col_Updated & @ColUpdatedTemp) = @ColUpdatedTemp
    BEGIN
      SET @ColNull = null
      SELECT
         @ColName = SysColumns.[name],
           -- get the column name & Data Type
         @ColumnDataType = SysColumns.xtype
       FROM SysColumns
         JOIN SysObjects
```

```
                    ON SysColumns.id = SysObjects.id
            WHERE SysObjects.[NAME] = @TableName
              and SysColumns.ColID = @ColCounter
        IF @ColName NOT IN ('Created', 'Modified')
          BEGIN
            -- text columns
            IF  @ColumnDataType IN
               ( 175, 239, 99, 231, 35, 231, 98, 167 )
              SET @ColNull =  ''''''
            -- numeric + bit columns
            ELSE IF  @ColumnDataType IN
               (  106, 62, 56, 60, 108, 59, 52, 122, 104 )
              SET @ColNull = '0'
            -- date columns
            ELSE IF  @ColumnDataType IN ( 61, 58 )
              SET @ColNull =  '''1/1/1980'''
            -- uniqueidentifier columns
            ELSE IF  @ColumnDataType IN ( 36 )
              SET @ColNull =  ''''''

            IF @ColNull IS NOT NULL
              BEGIN
                IF @IsUpdate = 1
-- had to adjust indenting
SET @SQLStr =
  ' Insert Audit(TableName, PrimaryKey, SysUser, [Column],'
  +' AuditDate, Application, OldValue, NewValue,Operation)'
  +' Select '''+ @TableName + ''',
  #tempIn.['+ @PrimaryKey + '],
  ''' + @SysUser + ''', ' +
  '''' + @ColName + ''', GetDate(), App_Name(),' +
  ' IsNull(convert(nvarchar(100),
     #tempDel.[' + @ColName + ']),''<null>''), ' +
  ' IsNull(convert(nvarchar(100),
     #tempIn.[' + @ColName +    ']),''<null>''),''U''' +
  ' From #tempIn' +
  ' Join #tempDel' +
  ' On #tempIn.['+ @PrimaryKey + ']
    = #tempDel.['+ @PrimaryKey + ']' +
  ' AND isnull(#tempIn.' + @ColName +    ',' + @ColNull + ')
    != isnull(#tempDel.' + @ColName +    ',' + @ColNull + ')'
  + ' Where Not (#tempIn.[' + @ColName + '] Is Null
    and #tempDel.[' + @ColName + ']  Is Null)'

ELSE -- Insert
  SET @SQLStr =
  ' Insert Audit(TableName, PrimaryKey, SysUser, [Column],'
  +' AuditDate, Application, OldValue, NewValue,Operation)'
  +' Select '''+ @TableName + ''',#tempIn.['+ @PrimaryKey
  + '], ''' + @SysUser + ''', ' +
  '''' + @ColName + ''', GetDate(), App_Name(),' +
```

```
  ' Null, ' +
  ' IsNull(convert(nvarchar(100),
  #tempIn.[' + @ColName +']),''<null>''),''I''' +
  ' From #tempIn' +
  ' Where Not (#tempIn.[' + @ColName + '] Is Null)'

EXEC sp_executesql  @SQLStr
SET @TempError = @@Error
IF @TempError <> 0
  BEGIN
    -- turn rollback on only if you want a
    -- failure to record audit to cancel
    -- the data modification operation
    -- Rollback
    RAISERROR ('Audit Trail Error', 15, 1)
  END
END END END END RETURN
Go


-------------------------------------------------------------
-- sample Table Triggers
-- this will need to be added to every table
-- and the Table and Primary Key settings

-- Products Trigger

IF EXISTS (SELECT *
            FROM sysobjects
            WHERE NAME = 'Products_Audit')
  DROP TRIGGER Products_Audit
Go

CREATE TRIGGER Products_Audit
ON dbo.Products
AFTER Insert, Update
NOT FOR REPLICATION
AS
-- Dynamic Audit Trail Code Begin
-- (c)2001 Paul Nielsen
DECLARE
  @Col_Updated VARBINARY(1028),
  @TableName VARCHAR(100),
  @PrimaryKey SYSNAME

SET NoCount ON

-- Set up the Audit data
-- set to the table name
SET @TableName = 'Products'
-- set to the column to identify the row
SET @PrimaryKey = 'ProductID'
```

```
SET @Col_Updated = Columns_Updated()
SELECT * INTO #TempIn FROM Inserted
SELECT * INTO #TempDel FROM Deleted

-- call the audit stored procedure
EXEC pAudit @Col_Updated, @TableName, @PrimaryKey

Go
-------------------------------------------------------------
-- Customer Trigger

IF EXISTS (SELECT *
             FROM SysObjects
             WHERE [NAME] = 'Customers_Audit')
  DROP TRIGGER Customers_Audit
Go

CREATE TRIGGER Customers_Audit
ON dbo.Customers
AFTER Insert, Update
NOT FOR REPLICATION
AS
-- Dynamic Audit Trail
-- (c)2001 Paul Nielsen
DECLARE
  @Col_Updated VARBINARY(1028),
  @TableName VARCHAR(100),
  @PrimaryKey SYSNAME
SET NoCount ON
SET @TableName = 'Customers'
SET @PrimaryKey = 'CustomerID'
SET @Col_Updated = Columns_Updated()
SELECT * INTO #TempIn FROM Inserted
SELECT * INTO #TempDel FROM Deleted
EXEC pAudit @Col_Updated, @TableName, @PrimaryKey
```

The sample script, `DynamicAudit.sql`, downloadable from `www.SQLServerBible.com`, includes several test inserts and updates as well as example queries for retrieving data from the audit table and joining the audit table with the products table.

Transaction-Aggregation Handling

Stored procedures are excellent for maintaining denormalized aggregate data. A common example of this is an inventory system that records all transactions in an inventory-transaction table, calculates the inventory quantity on hand, and stores the calculated quantity in the inventory table for performance.

To protect the integrity of the inventory table, the following logic rules should typically be implemented with triggers:

✦ The inventory table should not be updateable by any process other than the inventory transaction table triggers. Any attempt to directly update the inventory table's quantity should be recorded as a manual adjustment in the inventory-transaction table.

✦ Inserts in the inventory-transaction table should write the current on-hand value to the inventory table.

✦ The inventory-transaction table should not allow updates.

The OBXKites database includes a simplified inventory system. To demonstrate transaction-aggregation handling, the following triggers implement the required rules.

The first script creates a sample valid inventory item for test purposes:

```
USE OBXKites

DECLARE
  @ProdID UniqueIdentifier,
  @LocationID UniqueIdentifier

SELECT @ProdID = ProductID
  FROM dbo.Product
  WHERE Code = 1001
SELECT @LocationID= LocationID
  FROM dbo.Location
  WHERE LocationCode = 'CH'

INSERT dbo.Inventory (ProductID, InventoryCode, LocationID)
  VALUES (@ProdID,'A1', @LocationID)

SELECT Product.Code, InventoryCode, QuantityOnHand
  FROM dbo.Inventory
    JOIN dbo.Product
      ON Inventory.ProductID = Product.ProductID
```

Result:

```
Code              InventoryCode   QuantityOnHand
----------------  ---------------  ---------------
1001              A1               0
```

The Inventory-Transaction Trigger

The inventory-transaction trigger performs the aggregate function of maintaining the current quantity-on-hand value in the Inventory table. With each row inserted into the InventoryTransaction table, the trigger updates the Inventory table. The join between the Inserted image table and the Inventory table enables the trigger to handle multiple-row inserts:

```
CREATE TRIGGER InvTrans_Aggregate
ON dbo.InventoryTransaction
AFTER Insert
AS
```

```
UPDATE dbo.Inventory
  SET QuantityOnHand
    = Inventory.QuantityOnHand + Inserted.Value
  FROM dbo.Inventory
    JOIN Inserted
      ON Inventory.InventoryID = Inserted.InventoryID

Return
```

The next batch tests the `InvTrans_Aggregate` trigger by inserting a transaction and observing the inventory transaction and the inventory tables:

```
INSERT InventoryTransaction (InventoryID, Value)
  SELECT InventoryID, 5
    FROM dbo.Inventory
    WHERE InventoryCode = 'A1'

INSERT InventoryTransaction (InventoryID, Value)
  SELECT InventoryID, -3
    FROM dbo.Inventory
    WHERE InventoryCode = 'A1'

INSERT InventoryTransaction (InventoryID, Value)
  SELECT InventoryID, 7
    FROM dbo.Inventory
    WHERE InventoryCode = 'A1'
```

The following query views the data within the `InventoryTransaction` table:

```
SELECT InventoryCode, Value
  FROM dbo.InventoryTransaction
    JOIN dbo.Inventory
      ON Inventory.InventoryID
        = Inventorytransaction.InventoryID
```

Result:

```
InventoryCode    Value
---------------- ------
A1               5
A1               -3
A1               7
```

The `InvTrans_Aggregate` trigger should have maintained a correct quantity-on-hand value through the inserts to the `InventoryTransaction` table. Indeed, the next query proves the trigger functioned correctly:

```
SELECT Product.Code, InventoryCode, QuantityOnHand
  FROM dbo.Inventory
    JOIN dbo.Product
      ON Inventory.ProductID = Product.ProductID
```

Result:

```
Code            InventoryCode    QuantityOnHand
--------------- ---------------- --------------
1001            A1               9
```

The Inventory Trigger

The quantity values in the Inventory table should never be directly manipulated. Every quantity adjustment must go through the InventoryTransaction table. However, some users will want to make manual adjustments to the Inventory table. The gentlest solution to the problem is to use server-side code to perform the correct operations regardless of the user's method. Therefore, the inventory trigger has to redirect direct updates intended for the Inventory table to the InventoryTransaction table, while permitting the InvTrans_Aggregate trigger to update the Inventory table.

As a BestPractice, the trigger must accept multiple-row updates. The goal is to undo the original DML update command while keeping enough of the data to write the change as an insert to the InventoryTransaction table.

Rolling back the DML update won't work because that would obliterate the data within the Inserted and Deleted images, as well as any inserts to a temporary table created within the trigger. Neither can the values be stored in local variables because a single variable couldn't handle a multiple-row update.

The solution is to undo the original DML update command by writing the pre-update values from the Deleted table back into the Inventory table. Then the difference between the Deleted table QuantityOnHand and the Inserted table QuantityOnHand can be written to the InventoryTransaction table as a manual adjustment.

The trigger logic is executed only if the QuantityOnHand column is updated and the trigger is being called by a user's DML statement. If the Inventory table's QuantityOnHand column is being updated by the InvTrans_Aggregate trigger, the NestLevel() will be higher than 1. Here's the Inventory table side of the Inventory - InventoryTransaction table trigger solution:

```
CREATE TRIGGER Inventory_Aggregate
ON Inventory
AFTER UPDATE
AS
-- Redirect direct updates
If Trigger_NestLevel() = 1 AND Update(QuantityOnHand)
  BEGIN
    UPDATE Inventory
      SET QuantityOnHand = Deleted.QuantityOnHand
      FROM Deleted
        JOIN dbo.Inventory
          ON Inventory.InventoryID = Deleted.InventoryID

    INSERT InventoryTransaction
      (Value, InventoryID)
      SELECT
        Inserted.QuantityOnHand - Inventory.QuantityOnHand,
        Inventory.InventoryID
        FROM dbo.Inventory
          JOIN Inserted
            ON Inventory.InventoryID = Inserted.InventoryID
  END
```

To demonstrate the trigger, the following update attempts to change the quantity on hand from 9 to 10. The new Inventory_Aggregate trigger traps the update and resets the quantity on hand back to 9, but it also writes a transaction of +1 to the InventoryTransaction table. (If the transaction table had transaction type and comment columns, the transaction would be recorded as a manual adjustment by user X.) The InventoryTransaction table's InvTrans_Aggregate trigger sees the insert and properly adjusts the Inventory.QuantityOnHand to 10:

```
-- Trigger Test
Update dbo.Inventory
  SET QuantityOnHand = 10
  Where InventoryCode = 'A1'
```

Having performed the manual adjustment, the following query examines the InventoryTransaction table:

```
SELECT InventoryCode, Value
  FROM dbo.InventoryTransaction
    JOIN dbo.Inventory
      ON Inventory.InventoryID
        = Inventorytransaction.InventoryID
```

Sure enough, the manual adjustment of 1 has been written to the InventoryTransaction table:

```
InventoryCode    Value
---------------  ----------------------------------
A1               5
A1               -3
A1               7
A1               1
```

As the adjustment was being inserted into the InventoryTransaction table, the InvTrans_Aggregate trigger posted the transaction to the Inventory table. The following query double-checks the QuantityOnHand for inventory item 'A1':

```
SELECT Product.Code, InventoryCode, QuantityOnHand
  FROM dbo.Inventory
    JOIN dbo.Product
      ON Inventory.ProductID = Product.ProductID
```

Result:

```
Code             InventoryCode   QuantityOnHand
---------------  --------------- ---------------
1001             A1              10
```

Logically Deleting Data

To further increase data integrity, many database developers prohibit the physical deletion of data. Instead, they enable the logical deletion of data. The most common method is to use a delete flag bit column. When the user deletes a row in the front-end application, a trigger actually marks the row as deleted by setting the delete flag to true. A logical delete flag can be implemented in several ways:

✦ The front-end application can set the delete flag to true.

✦ The delete stored procedure can set the delete flag to true.

✦ An instead of trigger can trap the delete DML command and set the delete flag instead of physically deleting the row.

Note   A logical delete flag is not as advanced as it seems. dbase III used a delete flag to mark rows as deleted until the file compress command purged the deleted rows.

The capability to logically delete data is a cool high-end feature that is desirable in mature databases. I would caution you, however, to let logical deletions be among the last features you implement because they can be very time-consuming and can open a huge can of worms as database changes break the logical delete system. Here, my goal is to demonstrate a single-table logical delete system, and to explain the problems with logically deleted data and suggest some strategies to work around those problems.

Logical Delete Triggers

An instead of trigger implements the logical delete system at the table level and ensures that it's always enforced. The trigger has two goals: converting physical deletes into logical deletes, and enabling some method of physically deleting the row.

This trigger allows the sa user to physically delete any row, so there is some method of physically purging the database. An instead of trigger will not recursively fire, so the delete DML command within the trigger will execute. The first command alters the Product table and adds the IsDeleted bit flag:

```
ALTER TABLE Product
  ADD IsDeleted BIT NOT NULL DEFAULT 0

CREATE Trigger Product_LogicalDelete
On dbo.Product
INSTEAD OF Delete
AS

IF (suser_sname() = 'sa')
  BEGIN
    PRINT 'physical delete'
    DELETE FROM dbo.Product
      FROM dbo.Product
        JOIN Deleted
          ON Product.ProductID = Deleted.ProductID
  END
ELSE
  BEGIN
    PRINT 'logical delete'
    UPDATE Product
```

```
        SET IsDeleted = 1
        FROM dbo.Product
          JOIN Deleted
            ON Product.ProductID = Deleted.ProductID
    END
```

To test the logical delete trigger, the next query deletes from the Product table while I'm logged in as Noli\Paul:

```
DELETE Product
  WHERE Code = '1053'
```

Result:

```
logical delete
```

To following select views the logical deleted flag:

```
SELECT Code, IsDeleted
  FROM dbo.Product
    WHERE Code = 1053
```

Result:

```
Code              IsDeleted
---------------   ---------
1053              1
```

Having reconnected as the sa user, I again issued the same delete command:

```
DELETE dbo.Product
  WHERE Code = '1053'
```

Result:

```
physical delete

(1 row(s) affected)


(1 row(s) affected)
```

The first (1row(s) affected) result is the DML delete statement. Even though it was intercepted by the Instead Of trigger and the initial delete was ignored, it is still reported as an affected row. The second (1row(s) affected) result is the delete statement within the Product_LogicalDelete trigger. This delete was effective and physically deleted the row.

Undeleting a Logically Deleted Row

Prior to being physically deleted by the sa user, the row can easily be undeleted by updating the IsDeleted column back to false. If the row-based custom security method described earlier in this chapter is implemented, an after update trigger could test that the user has administrative privileges to the row to update the IsDeleted column to 0.

Filtering Out Logically Deleted Rows

An issue with a logical delete system is that every `select` statement must consider the `IsDeleted` flag; otherwise, deleted data may erroneously affect the result. The best way to ensure that the front-end application retrieves only current and correct data is to use stored procedures for fetching data.

The problem is that when the user issues an ad hoc query, there's no guarantee that he or she is aware of the `IsDeleted` flag or that every query is correct. A solution is to create views or, better still, table-valued user-defined functions for data retrieval, and to limit the users to those views or functions using SQL Server security.

Cascading Logical Deletes

This is where logically deleting data becomes a potential nightmare. If a primary row is physically deleted, the secondary rows that have no meaning without the primary row should also be deleted. Should logical deletes cascade as well?

If an order is logically deleted, the associated order-detail rows must be logically deleted either in the write or in every future read. Both methods have problems.

Cascading during the Read

If an order is logically deleted, its order-detail rows must be excluded from any calculations that are considering open order details. One possible method is to join the order table and include `order.isdeleted` in the `where` clause. This can become very complex as logical deletes cascade through multiple levels. From my experience, implementing cascading logical deletes in the read end of the process can kill performance as the number of tables, joins, and `where` conditions multiply exponentially to cover all the logical delete combinations.

Cascading during the Write

If the secondary rows are logically deleted during the primary table's logical delete operation, the advantage is that the secondary rows are already marked for deletion, so the read operation won't have to check the primary table for logically deleted rows. The problem is determining whether the logically deleted secondary row has been logically deleted itself or because its primary row was logically deleted.

It's possible to use two flags, one for the row logical `delete`, and one for a cascade logical `delete`. In keeping with the saying that today's solution is tomorrow's problem, even this causes headaches. Assume an order is logically deleted, and the logical `delete` is cascaded to the order-detail table. One of the order-detail rows points to a product that has been logically deleted. When the order is undeleted and the order-detail rows are undeleted, the order-detail row that was logically deleted because of the product logical `delete` should stay logically deleted.

There are two possible solutions. The first solution is to add a logical cascade `delete` flag for each foreign-key relationship for a table. This makes the code less than generic and potentially very messy, so I don't like this solution.

The second solution is to use a single logical `delete` cascade flag, but to build a very comprehensive undelete system that examines every primary-table relationship before undeleting a row. While this method entails the most work, it's the best solution.

Logical Deletes and Referential Integrity

Implementing a complete logical `delete` method also creates a potential referential-integrity problem. It would violate referential integrity to refer to a row that has been logically deleted. However, SQL Server's declarative referential integrity does not consider whether the row is logically deleted, only if it's physically in the table.

A database with a logical `delete` system requires a complex referential-integrity trigger that not only determines whether the primary key value exists in the primary table, but also checks the row's `IsDeleted` bit flag.

Degrees of Inactivity

A system that incorporates logical deletions often also includes some other measure of row inactivity, such as an active flag or a retired flag. These flags enable the user to mark a row as less significant without deleting the data. For example, an R&D lab is most concerned with the current formulae or material revisions, so its researchers don't want to wade through thousands of obsolete formula revisions. However, they don't want to delete the data either. Marking a formula inactive serves to hide it, but the user can still select the inactive data if desired.

Archiving Data

Old data is often no longer required for day-to-day activities, and can be safely archived or moved to a separate database location. The easiest way to archive data yet keep it easily available to the user is to move it to a separate table with an identical structure within the same database or within another database.

Archiving data is a good alternative to logically deleting it. The issues of referential integrity and cascading logical deletes are no longer problems if logically deleted data is moved to an archive.

A stored procedure can easily perform the move by inserting the data into the archive table and deleting it from the current table:

```
CREATE PROCEDURE pProduct_Archive (
  @Code CHAR(15) )
AS
SET NoCount ON

BEGIN TRANSACTION

INSERT Product_Archive
  SELECT *
    FROM dbo.Product
    WHERE Code = @Code
IF @@ERROR <> 0
  BEGIN
    ROLLBACK TRANSACTION
```

```
        RETURN
    END

DELETE dbo.Product
    WHERE Code = @Code
IF @@ERROR <> 0
    BEGIN
        ROLLBACK TRANSACTION
    END

COMMIT TRANSACTION
RETURN
```

The stored procedure will likely have to move more than just one table's rows. For example, archiving an order involves both the [Order] table and the OrderDdetail table.

 Partitioned views, discussed in Chapter 53, "Scaling Very Large Databases," are an excellent means of retrieving a combination of both current and archived data.

Summary

I love T-SQL. It's the romance language of data. In this chapter, we've pushed T-SQL to solve many complex data issues. Complex business rules and processing are best implemented as server-side code. Only when the rule is implemented in the server is it 100 percent enforced. A rule implemented outside the server isn't a rule, it's a suggestion. Server-side code is excellent for insert, update, delete, and fetch procedures, complex business rules, complex referential integrity, data-audit trails, and logical deletions.

The next chapter continues to build on the theme of developing with T-SQL with even more practical applications. Walking through some of the data abstraction layer of the OBXKites sample database, Chapter 25 is the capstone of T-SQL development.

✦   ✦   ✦

Creating Extensibility with a Data Abstraction Layer

It's a common morass. The data schema was designed several years or decades ago and while everyone in the IT organization wants to improve the design, it's just too risky and expensive because there are too many direct connections to the data tables. The greatest software cost is not development, but maintenance; and for the database, dynamic SQL statements that directly access the tables are the greatest cost of maintenance. Like dominoes, any change to the schema will cause a ripple effect of broken code, reports, and DTS packages. The simple `select` statement has robbed the database of any hope for extensibility and made the database brittle. The strength of SQL—its ability to easily query the data—becomes its weakness. The answer is an *abstraction layer*.

There are abstraction layers all around us—any common interface that hides the complexity and details of the implementation below the surface is an abstraction layer. A good example of an everyday abstraction layer is the standard driver controls of a car. The steering wheel works as expected without an understanding of the actual linkages to the front wheels. The brake pedal slows the car without the driver understanding how the brake system works. The same is true for the accelerator, the turn signals, the headlights, and so on. The common interface serves as an abstraction of the actual mechanical workings of the automobile.

To prevent or cure a brittle database, use a data abstraction layer—a single entry point to the data that serves as a logical change buffer. It's applying the principle of encapsulation to the database such that any access to the database is accomplished using an agreed upon contract. The database schema or server-side code can be modified or improved so long as the data access contract remains constant. A well-designed data abstraction layer and a flexible generalized database schema are the two keys to building an extensible database.

The information architecture principle described in Chapter 1 supports the concept of a data abstraction layer. The principle claims that data must be made available both now and in the future. If the database is intended to survive into the future, and many databases long outlive their original application UI, then the database must be extensible. The best way to ensure extensibility is with a data abstraction layer.

Pundits find it trendy to claim that client server or n-tier database architectures don't work, and that the answer is service-oriented architecture (SOA). I don't believe that's always true. Building databases without enforcing a data abstraction layer didn't work, but client-server, n-tier, or SOA architectures can work if the design includes a data abstraction layer.

The data abstraction layer can physically exist in either the database, using stored procedures, views and functions, or in an application layer, using .NET and ADO. Don't mix the two, however.

Personally, I prefer building the data abstraction layer within the database for two reasons: First, this places the data validation code and any lookups as close to the data as possible. Second, it ensures that no foreign code can bypass the data abstraction layer and access the data. However, I understand that others disagree and that's OK, so long as there *is* a data abstraction layer.

Generally speaking, the data abstraction layer will need an interface for each of the following tasks:

✦ Inserting data

✦ Updating data

✦ Deleting data

✦ Fetching single rows and lists for every user-recognizable object

Best Practice

When designing the data abstraction layer, avoid using a CRUD matrix approach — CRUD being a list of create, retrieve, update, and delete functions for every table. A data abstraction layer — that is, a set of sprocs for every table — will tend to lock in the schema to that set of sprocs. Instead, design the data abstraction layer as a set of logical contracts that deal with business entities and tasks, even though the contract may involve multiple underlying tables. For example, design a single interface that will involve the inventory, order, and shipping tables.

This chapter walks through some stored procedures from the OBXKites data abstraction layer.

The AddNew Stored Procedure

The addnew stored procedure handles inserting new rows into the database. The stored procedure's main tasks are to validate the data, convert any codes to foreign keys, and perform the insert operation. The addnew procedure might also handle lock-timeout issues. Here's the code for the sample stored procedure from the OBXKites database:

```
CREATE PROCEDURE pProduct_AddNew(
  @ProductCategoryName NVARCHAR(50),
  @Code CHAR(10),
```

```
  @Name NVARCHAR(50),
  @ProductDescription NVARCHAR(100) = NULL
  )
AS
  SET NOCOUNT ON
  DECLARE
    @ProductCategoryID UNIQUEIDENTIFIER

  SELECT @ProductCategoryID = ProductCategoryID
    FROM dbo.ProductCategory
      WHERE ProductCategoryName = @ProductCategoryName
  IF @@Error <> 0 RETURN -100

  IF @ProductCategoryID IS NULL
    BEGIN
      RAISERROR ('Product Category: ''%s'' not found',
        15,1,@ProductCategoryName)
      RETURN -100
    END

BEGIN TRY
  INSERT dbo.Product (ProductCategoryID, Code, ProductName, ProductDescription)
    VALUES (@ProductCategoryID, @Code, @Name, @ProductDescription )
END TRY
BEGIN CATCH
    RAISERROR ('Unable to insert new product', 15,1)
    RETURN -100
END CATCH
```

To test the procedure, the following command passes product code "999," thus inserting
product code "999" in the Product table:

```
EXEC pProduct_AddNew
  @ProductCategoryName = 'OBX',
  @Code = '999',
  @Name = 'Test Kit',
  @ProductDescription
        = 'official kite testing kit for contests.'
```

To make sure the insert worked, the following select string returns product code "999":

```
SELECT ProductName, ProductCategoryName
  FROM dbo.Product
    JOIN ProductCategory
      ON Product.ProductCategoryID
          = ProductCategory. ProductCategoryID
    WHERE Code = '999'
```

Result:

```
Name                ProductCategoryName
----------------    ----------------------
Test Kit            OBX
```

The Fetch Stored Procedure

The `fetch` stored procedure retrieves the data. A sophisticated fetch procedure can accept various parameters and respond with a single row, filtered rows, or all rows, depending on the requirement and the parameters, so multiple `fetch` procedures are not necessary for various scopes of data. The null default is used in the `where` clause to effectively nullify the criterion if the parameter is not supplied.

This stored procedure also handles lock-timeout and deadlock issues using the techniques covered in Chapter 51, "Managing Transactions, Locking, and Blocking." The following sample `fetch` stored procedure retrieves product information for the OBXKites database:

```
CREATE PROCEDURE pProduct_Fetch(
  @ProductCode CHAR(15) = NULL,
  @ProductCategory CHAR(15) = NULL )
AS
SET NoCount ON

SELECT Code, ProductName, ProductDescription, ActiveDate,
    DiscontinueDate, ProductCategoryName, [RowVersion] --,
--      Product.Created, Product.Modified
  FROM dbo.Product
    JOIN dbo.ProductCategory
      ON Product.ProductCategoryID
          = ProductCategory.ProductCategoryID
  WHERE ( Product.Code = @ProductCode
              OR @ProductCode IS NULL )
    AND ( ProductCategory.ProductCategoryName
          = @ProductCategory
              OR @ProductCategory IS NULL )
  IF @@Error <> 0 RETURN -100

RETURN
```

The following command executes the `pProduct_Fetch` stored procedure and retrieves data for all the products when called without any parameters:

```
EXEC pProduct_Fetch
```

Result (columns and rows abridged):

```
Code    Name                           Modified
-----   ------------------------       -----------------------
1001    Basic Box Kite 21 inch         2002-02-18 09:48:31.700
1002    Dragon Flight                  2002-02-18 15:19:34.350
1003    Sky Dancer                     2002-02-18 09:48:31.700
...
```

With a `@ProductCode` parameter, the `fetch` stored procedure returns only the selected product:

```
EXEC pProduct_Fetch
  @ProductCode = '1005'
```

Result (columns abridged):

```
Code   Name                              Modified
-----  --------------------------------  -----------------------
1005   Eagle Wings                       2002-02-18 09:48:31.700
```

The second parameter causes the stored procedure to return all the products within a single product category:

```
EXEC pProduct_Fetch
  @ProductCategory = 'Book'
```

Result (rows and columns abridged):

```
Code   Name                              Modified
-----  --------------------------------  -----------------------
1036   Adventures in the OuterBanks      2002-02-25 17:13:15.430
1037   Wright Brothers Kite Designs      2002-02-25 17:13:15.430
1038   The Lighthouses of the OBX        2002-02-25 17:13:15.430
1039   Outer Banks Map                   2002-02-25 17:13:15.430
1040   Kiters Guide to the Outer Banks   2002-02-25 17:13:15.430
```

The Update Stored Procedure

The update stored procedure accepts the primary method of identifying the row (in this case the product code) and the new data. Based on the new data, it performs a SQL DML update statement.

Cross-Reference   Updates are vulnerable to lost updates, as discussed in Chapter 51, "Managing Transactions, Locking, and Blocking." You can work around the lost update problem with timestamps or minimal updates. Each technique is demonstrated in this section with a sample stored procedure.

The first example procedure handles lost updates by checking the rowversion timestamp column. Each time the row is updated, SQL Server automatically updates the rowversion value. If the rowversion is different, the row must have been updated by another transaction, and the rowversion condition in the where clause prevents the update.

Update with RowVersion

This version of the update procedure updates all the columns of the row, so all the parameters must be supplied even if that column is not being updated. The procedure assumes that the rowversion column was selected when the data was originally retrieved.

If the rowversion value differs from the one retrieved during the select, the update fails to take place. The procedure determines that using the @@rowcount global variable and reports the error to the calling object.

As a sample update procedure, here's the code for the pProduct_Update_RowVersion stored procedure from the OBXKites database:

```
CREATE PROCEDURE pProduct_Update_RowVersion (
```

```
  @Code CHAR(15),
  @RowVersion Rowversion,
  @Name VARCHAR(50),
  @ProductDescription VARCHAR(50),
  @ActiveDate DateTime,
  @DiscontinueDate DateTime )
AS
SET NoCount ON

UPDATE dbo.Product
  SET
    ProductName = @Name,
    ProductDescription = @ProductDescription,
    ActiveDate = @ActiveDate,
    DiscontinueDate = @DiscontinueDate
  WHERE Code = @Code
    AND [RowVersion] = @RowVersion

  IF @@ROWCOUNT = 0
    BEGIN
    IF EXISTS ( SELECT * FROM Product WHERE Code = @Code)
      BEGIN
        RAISERROR ('Product failed to update because
          another transaction updated the row since your
          last read.', 16,1)
        RETURN -100
      END
    ELSE
      BEGIN
        RAISERROR ('Product failed to update because
          the row has been deleted', 16,1)
        RETURN -100
      END
    END
  RETURN
```

To test the timestamp version of the `update` stored procedure, the `pProduct_Fetch` procedure will return the current timestamp for product code "1001":

```
EXEC pProduct_Fetch 1001
```

Result (columns abridged):

```
Code      Name                          RowVersion
--------  ----------------------------  ------------------------
1001      Basic Box Kite 21 inch        0x0000000000000077
```

The `pProduct_Update_Rowversion` stored procedure must be called with the exact same `rowversion` value to perform the update:

```
EXEC pProduct_Update_Rowversion
  1001,
  0x0000000000000077,
```

```
'updatetest',
'new description',
'1/1/2002',
NULL
```

The procedure updates all the columns in the row, and in the process, the rowversion column is reset to a new value.

Minimal-Update

The second version of the update stored procedure demonstrates the minimal-update method of minimizing lost updates. By updating only the specific column requiring update, you reduce the chance of overwriting another user's update significantly. The column-level update is like a surgical strike, hitting only where it's needed and reducing collateral damage.

The stored procedure does not use dynamic SQL to build a custom update, although that could easily be done. However, dynamic SQL executes using the security profile of the user and not the stored procedures, and it introduces a recompile issue that causes performance to suffer. These problems may make using dynamic SQL within production stored procedures an unhealthy choice.

The minimal-update procedure simply performs a single-column update for each parameter provided to the stored procedure:

```
CREATE PROCEDURE pProduct_Update_Minimal (
  @Code CHAR(15),
  @Name VARCHAR(50) = NULL,
  @ProductDescription VARCHAR(50) = NULL,
  @ActiveDate DateTime = NULL,
  @DiscontinueDate DateTime = NULL )

AS
SET NoCount ON

IF EXISTS (SELECT * FROM dbo.Product WHERE Code = @Code)
  BEGIN
    BEGIN TRANSACTION
    IF @Name IS NOT NULL
      BEGIN
        UPDATE dbo.Product
          SET
            ProductName = @Name
          WHERE Code = @Code
        IF @@Error <> 0
          BEGIN
            ROLLBACK
            RETURN -100
          END
      END

    IF @ProductDescription IS NOT NULL
      BEGIN
```

```
        UPDATE dbo.Product
          SET
            ProductDescription = @ProductDescription
          WHERE Code = @Code
        IF @@Error <> 0
          BEGIN
            ROLLBACK
            RETURN -100
          END
      END

    IF @ActiveDate IS NOT NULL
      BEGIN
        UPDATE dbo.Product
          SET
            ActiveDate = @ActiveDate
          WHERE Code = @Code
        IF @@Error <> 0
          BEGIN
            ROLLBACK
            RETURN -100
          END
      END

    IF @DiscontinueDate IS NOT NULL
      BEGIN
        UPDATE dbo.Product
          SET
            DiscontinueDate = @DiscontinueDate
          WHERE Code = @Code
        IF @@Error <> 0
          BEGIN
            ROLLBACK
            RETURN -100
          END
      END
    COMMIT TRANSACTION
  END
ELSE
  BEGIN
    RAISERROR
      ('Product failed to update because the row has
          been deleted', 16,1)
    RETURN -100
  END
RETURN
```

When the minimal-update stored procedure is being called, only the columns requiring update are needed. The procedure first determines whether the row exists; once that check is complete, the parameters that were passed to the procedure are updated in the table. In the following example, the product description for product code "1001" is updated:

```
EXEC pProduct_Update_Minimal
  @Code = '1001',
  @ProductDescription = 'a minimal update'
```

The pProduct_Fetch procedure can test the minimal-update procedure:

```
EXEC pProduct_Fetch 1001
```

Result (abridged):

```
Code       Name              ProductDescription
---------  ----------------  ------------------------
1001       updatetest 2      a minimal update
```

The Delete Stored Procedure

The delete stored procedure executes the delete DML command. This procedure can be the most complex stored procedure, depending upon the level of data-archival and logical deletion. This sample delete procedure taken from the OBXKites database transforms the @ProductCode into a @ProductID, verifies that the product does in fact exist, and then deletes it:

```
CREATE PROCEDURE pProduct_Delete(
  @ProductCode INT
)
AS
  SET NOCOUNT ON
  DECLARE @ProductID UniqueIdentifier

  SELECT @ProductID = ProductID
    FROM Product
    WHERE Code = @ProductCode
  If @@RowCount = 0
    BEGIN
      RAISERROR
        ('Unable to delete Product Code %i
          - does not exist.', 16,1, @ProductCode)
      RETURN
    END
  ELSE
    DELETE dbo.Product
      WHERE ProductID = @ProductID
  RETURN
```

To test the pProduct_Delete stored procedure, the following stored procedure attempts to call a product. Because there is no product code "99," the error trapping raises the error:

```
EXEC pProduct_Delete 99
```

Result:

```
Unable to delete Product Code 99 - does not exist.
```

Cross-Reference   While this delete stored procedure was straightforward, deleting data is potentially one of the more complex tasks for the data abstraction layer, depending on what needs to be done with the old data. For strategies on logically deleting and archiving data, turn to Chapter 24, "Exploring Advanced T-SQL Solutions."

Summary

The data abstraction layer is a key component of your database architecture plan and it plays a major role in determining the future extensibility and maintenance costs of the database. Even when it seems that the cost of developing a data abstraction layer and refactoring the existing application code to hit the data abstraction layer instead of tables might seem expensive, savvy IT or product managers understand that in the long run it will save money and their job.

The next chapter continues the discussion of developing databases, moving into the hand-held world with SQL Server Mobile.

✦   ✦   ✦

Developing for SQL Server Everywhere

Developing applications for the Windows Mobile platform has reached an unprecedented level since the introduction of the .NET Compact Framework in 2003. For the first time, a developer with basic programming skills could use the familiar Visual Studio development environment to create, test, and deploy robust mobile applications. In practice, most enterprise mobile applications require a reliable and secure data repository on the mobile device as well as a way to synchronize mobile data with enterprise servers.

Consider a typical warehouse in which workers perform receiving, storing, picking, and shipping of products or materials. The warehouse supervisor sits down at a terminal at the beginning of each shift, printing out receiving schedules, pick-lists, and inventory levels retrieved from a back-end database server. The success of the warehouse depends on workers cross-checking their activities throughout the day against these print-outs. This process is clearly open to errors, process failures, and even fraud. To automate this process and put the information required to perform warehouse activities into the hands of the workers who need it, the warehouse plans to deploy a Windows Mobile application. Warehouse workers are always on the move, driving forklifts, shifting between loading docks as trucks arrive and depart, and pushing pallet jacks from station to station. To keep all of these highly mobile workers in sync with each other and with back-end servers, the mobile application needs to have frequent connectivity to these back-end servers and be able to track the data that is modified by each worker. It would be tempting to create a .NET Compact Framework application that directly accesses the back-end SQL Server, but during a proof of concept, it becomes apparent that as the mobile application tries to interact with the database, the high cinderblock walls in the warehouse cause wireless network outages as the workers move from station to station. The solution is to have a local cache of data on the mobile device, which enables the workers to continue their job when network connectivity is not available and provides for safe replication of data between the mobile device and back-end servers when a connection is available. SQL Server 2005 Mobile Edition provides this capability—in the warehouse, on the shop floor, in the oil fields, in a hospital emergency room, and in a myriad of other enterprise mobility scenarios.

Launched with Visual Studio 2005 and SQL Server 2005, Microsoft introduced SQL Server 2005 Mobile Edition (or "SQL Everywhere"). More than just an upgrade to its predecessor SQL CE, SQL Everywhere represents a completely reworked mobile database. It includes a revamped query processor, a new storage engine, support for multiple connections to a single database, and the capability to work with SQL Everywhere databases just like any other data source from within Visual Studio 2005 or SQL Server 2005 Management Studio. This chapter covers the capabilities of SQL Everywhere and walks through typical tasks associated with including it in your enterprise mobile solutions.

Note   As this book was in author review, Microsoft announced planned improvements to SQL Server 2005 Mobile Edition and changed the product name to SQL Server 2005 Everywhere Edition.

An Overview of SQL Server 2005 Everywhere Edition

While SQL Everywhere represents a completely reworked product, there is such a large body of applicable reference material and best-practices documented for its predecessors that a brief look back at the history and evolution of SQL Everywhere is useful.

History

With Visual Studio 2003, the .NET Compact Framework 1.0 and SQL Server 2000, Microsoft introduced a freely distributable relational database for Pocket PC and Windows CE devices called SQL Server 2000 Windows CE Edition (or "SQL CE"). With a footprint of only 1.5MB on the device, SQL CE provided a remarkably rich implementation of the major features of SQL Server 2000. SQL CE included support for a subset of ANSI SQL-92 indexes, joins, an optimizing query processor, and your choice of ADOCE, OLEDB, and ADO.NET programming interfaces. SQL CE also provided two technologies to synchronize mobile data with corporate servers: *remote data access (RDA)* and *merge replication*.

While SQL CE provided a usable relational database for Windows Mobile solutions, it also had some significant limitations, the most notable of which was that a SQL CE database really only existed in the context of a mobile device. You had to create, modify, and maintain a SQL CE database either from code running on the device or from a miniature version of Query Analyzer running on the device. SQL CE also limited database access to a single connection and never quite eliminated the possibility of data corruption, requiring frequent database compaction to repair and maintain the mobile database. For example, with SQL CE, mobile users could perform a reset on their device while a long-running database write was executing and the SQL CE database could be rendered unusable and beyond repair. This was obviously not an ideal situation for administrators tasked with supporting deployments of hundreds of mobile devices in motion across a large geographic region.

Note   As this book was in author review, Microsoft announced planned improvements to SQL Server 2005 Mobile Edition and changed the product name to SQL Server 2005 Everywhere Edition.

Concepts

To understand where SQL Everywhere fits into your enterprise architecture in contrast to more familiar RDBMS products such as SQL Server 2000 or 2005, it is important to understand some foundational concepts. SQL Everywhere provides a compact, feature-rich relational database management system (RDBMS) designed to work with Microsoft Windows Mobile devices. SQL Everywhere is compatible with devices running Pocket PC 2003, Windows Mobile 5, and Windows Mobile 5 Smart Phone Edition. Note that Windows CE.NET 4.2 is not a supported platform for SQL Everywhere at this time, but support is expected with the release of the .NET Compact Framework 2.0 Service Pack 1.

Interestingly, SQL Everywhere is also licensed for Windows XP Tablet PC Edition, but not for any other x86-based platform unless a licensed copy of Visual Studio 2005 or SQL Server 2005 is installed on the same computer. Microsoft views the Tablet PC as the perfect platform for "smart client" applications, and SQL Everywhere as a capable, easy-to-deploy database to accompany these applications.

Note   Microsoft's decision to include Tablet PC as the only x86-based platform for which SQL Everywhere is licensed may seem somewhat odd. After all, isn't SQL Server 2005 Express Edition supposed to be the preferred lightweight database for smart-client applications? Why limit SQL Everywhere licensing to Tablet PC only? With a resounding and unanimous voice, the MVP community is applying pressure on Microsoft to expand the licensing for SQL Everywhere to x86 platforms beyond Tablet PC, based largely on the need for a way to share the same database between mobile devices and desktop applications without the overhead of configuring and managing replication. In addition, the difficulty of replicating a SQL Express database deployed via "click once" along with a smart client application is of such complexity and requires such deep expertise in Remote Management Objects (RMO) programming that SQL Everywhere would represent a logical and easily implemented solution in this scenario.

One compelling feature is the way Microsoft licenses SQL Everywhere. SQL Everywhere can be freely distributed to devices running any of the supported operating systems just mentioned; however, you must purchase SQL Server licensing to leverage remote data access (RDA), merge replication, or to make any other connection to SQL Server from SQL Everywhere. For specifics on SQL Everywhere licensing, see www.microsoft.com/sql/editions/sqlmobile/howtobuy.mspx.

SQL Everywhere's main purpose is to provide a local, on-device database that can serve as either the primary data repository for a mobile application or as an off-line data cache in scenarios where data is being pulled from a server, created/modified on the device, and then pushed back to the server. SQL Everywhere can be integrated into .NET Compact Framework Smart-Device projects using Visual Studio 2005, and offers OLEDBCE support for native applications developed using Visual C++ for Devices within Visual Studio 2005. The major architectural components of SQL Everywhere are shown in Figure 26-1.

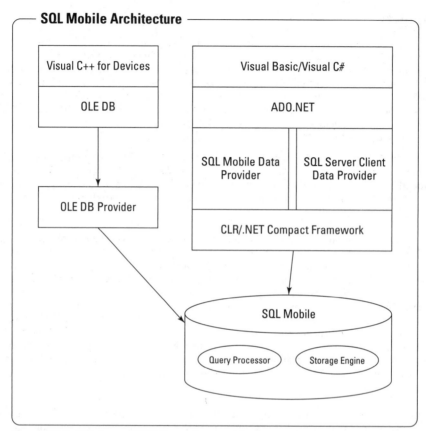

Figure 26-1: SQL Server 2005 Everywhere architecture

As shown in Figure 26-1, the two fundamental components of SQL Everywhere are the *storage engine* and the *query processor,* which can be accessed from both native and managed code. In simple terms, SQL Everywhere's storage engine provides reliable persistent storage; and the query processor provides relational access to that storage. The SQL Everywhere storage engine has been completely rewritten since SQL CE and is now the same underlying storage engine used by the Windows CE.NET Object Store (although you cannot access the Object Store directly through ADO.NET).

The SQL Everywhere query processor is a cost-based, heuristic execution engine that is remarkably efficient given its small footprint on the device. In only about 1.5MB of space on your mobile device, SQL Everywhere provides a large subset of the capabilities of SQL Server 2005 (which has an approximately 38MB minimum footprint!).

> **Note**   *Cost-based* means the query processor considers a variety of query execution plans and chooses the most efficient one. *Heuristic* means that the query processor has the ability to rewrite syntactically equivalent SQL into a statement that produces equivalent results but is known to be more efficient (e.g., an `in` query may be rewritten to use `join` syntax).

SQL Everywhere has powerful relational capabilities that are similar to SQL Server 2005, including the ability to do all of the following:

✦ Create, modify, and delete tables, indexes, constraints

✦ Execute data definition language (DDL) and data manipulation language (DML) commands with a subset of ANSI-92 SQL

✦ Create and guarantee ACID (Atomic, Consistent, Isolated, Durable) transactions

✦ Query information schema views and metadata

✦ Influence query execution with hints, and force join order

As you dive into design and development with SQL Everywhere, the similarities with SQL Server 2000 and SQL Server 2005 make the learning curve seem fairly flat, but there are some important differences to be aware of when getting started with SQL Everywhere:

✦ A SQL Everywhere database is always case insensitive and cannot be made case sensitive.

✦ Only Unicode database types are supported (e.g., `varchar` is not supported in SQL Everywhere, but `nvarchar` is).

✦ Automatic type conversions may occur during remote data access (RDA) and merge replication.

✦ Some SQL Server data types are not supported in SQL Everywhere (e.g., `smallmoney`).

✦ Some data types cannot be included in functions the way they can be in SQL Server. For example, `NTEXT` columns cannot be included in string functions in SQL Everywhere.

✦ Not all of the ANSI-92 SQL specification that SQL Server 2005 implements with T-SQL is supported in SQL Everywhere. For example, subquery capability is limited, many T-SQL built-in functions are omitted, and brackets are not supported as delimiters in SQL syntax.

✦ While many indexes may be defined on a table, the query processor will consider them all and select one and only one index to use in the execution plan.

✦ SQL Everywhere does not process batches of SQL statements — you must submit one statement or command at a time.

✦ There is no transactional or snapshot replication support.

✦ Web-based replication does not require secure transport via SSL, as does replication between SQL Server 2005 and SQL Express.

✦ SQL Everywhere databases are limited to a 4GB maximum size, with the default maximum size automatically set to 128MB.

✦ The degree to which you can make changes to an existing SQL Everywhere database using `ALTER TABLE` is limited to a few basic modifications such as adding or dropping a column or index.

Some features of SQL Server 2005 are not included at all in SQL Everywhere, mostly to keep the memory footprint on the device to a minimum. These missing features include the following:

✦ Triggers

✦ Views

✦ Stored procedures

✦ Connection pooling

✦ Distributed transactions

✦ Encrypted connection strings

This provides a sense of where SQL Everywhere fits into a mobile solution and how it differs from SQL Server. Before you get too concerned about the limitations in the preceding list ("What?! No stored procedures?"), consider that in my experience delivering over two dozen large-scale Windows Mobile solutions that included SQL CE (and more recently SQL Everywhere), no business requirement ever encountered could not be accommodated with this surprisingly powerful little database engine.

As you read the capabilities of SQL Everywhere, you begin to get a sense of how your managed or native mobile application could leverage it as a stand-alone, small footprint mobile database. Taking it a step further, one of the most exciting features of SQL Everywhere are the technologies included with this product that enable you to keep a population of distributed mobile devices synchronized with enterprise database servers.

Out of the box, SQL Everywhere comes with two options for synchronizing data with SQL Server 2000/2005: remote data access (RDA) and merge replication. Figure 26-2 shows the major components of SQL Everywhere's data synchronization architecture, and these components are covered in greater detail later in this chapter.

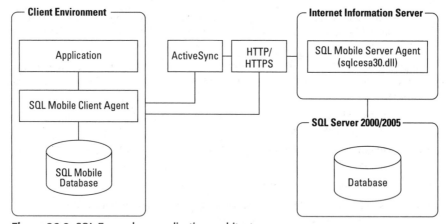

Figure 26-2: SQL Everywhere replication architecture

Note that in either an RDA or merge replication scenario, the gateway through which data synchronization is achieved between SQL Everywhere and SQL Server is always Internet Information Server (IIS) hosting the SQL Server Everywhere Server Agent (an ISAPI DLL). There are situations where a Web Services approach to data synchronization between SQL Everywhere and SQL Server is an excellent alternative, but Microsoft intended RDA and merge replication to cover the most common scenarios.

What's New in SQL Server 2005 Everywhere Edition

SQL Everywhere is more than just an upgrade to SQL CE; in many ways it is a new product. It offers exciting new capabilities as well as new performance characteristics, which are a result of Microsoft reworking the storage engine and the query processor. Here is a summary of the most significant new features that SQL Everywhere brings to Windows Mobile solutions:

✦ Multi-user capability, including multi-user synchronization (SQL CE was a single-user, single-connection database).

✦ A reworked storage engine for increased reliability and performance.

✦ Auto-reuse of empty pages. (SQL CE required frequent compaction to reclaim unused space and recalculate index statistics.)

✦ An improved query processor leverages statistics; and a heuristic, cost-based optimizer.

✦ The new query processor distinguishes between RAM and durable storage on mobile devices.

✦ True ACID database transactions reduce the risks of data loss or corruption due to the transient nature of power and network connectivity inherent in mobile architectures.

✦ Row-level locking, page-level locking, and a variety of new isolation levels.

✦ Visual Studio 2005 integration.

✦ SQL Server 2005 Management Studio integration.

✦ Managed APIs enable asynchronous control of merge replication with progress reporting, and the capability to persist and reuse replication settings and cancel active replications.

✦ Column-level tracking during merge replication, which greatly reduces the amount of data transmitted between SQL Everywhere and SQL Server during replication.

✦ Multiple merge subscriptions in a single SQL Everywhere database.

✦ Named parameters in the Compact Framework 2.0 ADO.NET provider.

✦ The capability to export the execution plan from Query Analyzer 3.0 on the mobile device and view/tune it in SQL Server 2005 Management Studio.

✦ A high-performance SqlCeResultSet, now part of the .NET Compact Framework 2.0 ADO.NET provider, offers an updateable, scrollable cursor that outperforms the SqlCeDataAdapter for loading DataTables and DataSets.

✦ Connect to and manage SQL Everywhere databases resident on a mobile device through ActiveSync.

✦ In-place database compaction (SQL CE required specifying a source and destination database and then renaming the destination database to the source after compaction).

As you can see, Microsoft has invested heavily in making SQL Everywhere increasingly capable as both a relational data store and a data synchronization engine. From a developer's standpoint, the tight integration with Visual Studio 2005 and SQL Server 2005 Management Studio is a welcome relief from working with SQL CE databases programmatically on device. From a performance and reliability standpoint, SQL Everywhere represents a significant leap forward — you can now spend more time solving business problems with your mobile solutions and less time tuning and administering your mobile databases.

Getting Started with SQL Everywhere

If you're ready to take SQL Everywhere for a test drive, this section will lead you through the prerequisite tasks associated with building your first Windows Mobile application with SQL Everywhere. Starting with some important notes on obtaining and installing SQL Everywhere, you will learn to create a SQL Everywhere database using a variety of techniques, upgrade an existing SQL CE 2.0 database to SQL Everywhere, and tour the integration features of SQL Everywhere with both Visual Studio 2005 and SQL Server 2005 Management Studio.

Installing SQL Everywhere

SQL Everywhere is included as an optional installation component of all Visual Studio 2005 versions that have mobile device support (currently the Standard, Professional, and Team System versions). Even if you already have one of these versions of Visual Studio 2005 installed, it's a good idea to visit the SQL Everywhere Downloads page located at www.microsoft.com/sql/editions/sqlmobile/downloads.mspx to check for updates to the Microsoft SQL Server 2005 Everywhere Edition Device SDK. Numerous other downloads are available at this location, including *SQL Everywhere Books Online,* the "IBuySpy" sample application, and the server and replication components you will need to prepare for data synchronization between SQL Everywhere and SQL Server 2000 or 2005. I cannot emphasize enough how important it is to download and become familiar with the SQL Server Everywhere Books Online (BOL) as you begin exploring SQL Everywhere.

After you follow Microsoft's instructions for downloading and installing the Device SDK, make sure you understand its components and where they are located on your development computer.

Development Tools

If you are developing a smart-device application in Visual Studio 2005 using the .NET Compact Framework, you will add a reference to your project to System.Data.SqlServerCe. This namespace provides everything you will need to interact with SQL Everywhere in your application — from simple SQL queries to initiating merge replication or RDA. Installing the Microsoft SQL Server 2005 Everywhere Edition Device SDK places the corresponding System.Data.SqlServerCe assembly with a .dll extension in your Visual Studio 2005 program directory structure at <drive:>\Program Files\Microsoft Visual Studio 8\SmartDevices\SDK\SQL Server\Mobile\v3.0.

If you are a native code developer using Visual C++ to develop your mobile application, once you install the Microsoft SQL Server 2005 Everywhere Edition Device SDK, you will find the required header files — ssceoledb30.h, ca_merge30.h, and ssceerr30.h — in the same location provided previously.

The MSI installer files (i.e., files with the extension *.msi) in this folder are for configuring the SQL Everywhere Server Tools for data synchronization with SQL Server 2000 or 2005. You don't need to install these until you are ready to begin using merge replication or RDA.

Runtime Tools

In order for your Windows Mobile application to leverage SQL Everywhere at runtime on device or in a device emulator, the SQL Everywhere Database Engine (at a minimum) needs to be installed on the device. This engine is packaged into a unit of deployment called a *cabinet file* (better known as a *CAB*). Different CABs are required depending on the Windows Mobile platform and CPU architecture of your target device. Guidance on determining the correct CAB for a given device follows, but before you explore that, you may need to deploy two other CAB files along with the Database Engine CAB: the SQL Everywhere client agent CAB and the SQL Everywhere development utilities CAB. The client agent comes into play when you intend to use merge replication or RDA. The development utilities contain Query Analyzer 3.0 and additional debugging information, and should generally not be deployed with the release version of your mobile application.

CAB files can be copied to your device when connected to your development computer through ActiveSync. They will self-install on the device when opened (simply tap on the CAB filename with the stylus). As a minimum, you must install the Database Engine to use SQL Everywhere on a device. Note that installation of SQL Everywhere is automatic when deploying a Visual Studio 2005 smart device that contains a reference to `System.Data.SqlServerCe`.

Tip   If you are unsure which SQL Everywhere CAB files are required by your mobile application, simply watch the output window in Visual Studio 2005 as you deploy to device; Visual Studio 2005 reports the CAB filenames that it selected as appropriate for your project.

New in 2005   A new feature in Visual Studio 2005 is deploy-time awareness of SQL Everywhere databases, which allows you to control whether a SQL Everywhere database included as content in your project is copied to device always, only if newer, or never.

Choosing the Correct SQL Everywhere CAB Files

Depending on the Windows Mobile OS and device CPU architecture you are targeting, you can find all of the CAB files required by SQL Everywhere by navigating to either `<drive:>\Program Files\Microsoft Visual Studio 8\SmartDevices\SDK\SQL Server\Mobile\v3.0\wce400\armv4` or `<drive:>\Program Files\Microsoft Visual Studio 8\SmartDevices\SDK\SQL Server\Mobile\v3.0\wce500`

The general naming and organizational scheme for these CAB files is first by operating system and then by CPU architecture. Therefore, from the preceding path, choosing "wce500" enables you to drill into the specific folder for your device's CPU (`armv4i`, `mips`, `sh4`, etc.), and from there you will see appropriate files for Windows Mobile 5.0, WindowsCE.NET 5.0, Smartphone 5.0, and so on. This can be a little confusing for new mobile developers, so here are some tips to determine the correct CAB files for your device:

✦ Pocket PC 2003, 2003 Second Edition, and Phone Edition devices are all based on the Windows CE 4 kernel and the ARMV4 CPU architecture (there are some exceptions to this rule, but SQL Everywhere does not support those exceptions).

✦ Windows Mobile 5.0, Windows CE.NET 5.0, and Windows Mobile 5.0 Smartphone Edition are all based on the Windows CE 5 kernel.

✦ If you are unsure of your device's operating system family or CPU architecture, navigate on your device to Start ➪ Settings ➪ System ➪ About.

✦ Remember that you can always deploy to your device or emulator from Visual Studio 2005 and see the CAB filenames that were determined to be correct for your device in the Output Window of Visual Studio 2005 during deployment.

Note   In the mobile world, the unit of deployment on a device is still the CAB. Whether you are installing the Compact Framework, SQL Everywhere, or a Smart Device Setup project, you are copying a CAB file to a device and it self-installs there—that's not going to change anytime soon.

As an example of determining the correct SQL Everywhere CABs for a given device, let's say you have an HP iPaq 4355 running Pocket PC 2003. Pocket PC 2003 is based on the Windows CE 4 kernel, and when you navigate to Start ➪ Settings ➪ System ➪ About on the iPaq, you see that the processor in this device is the Intel(r) PXA 255. This is an ARMV4-compliant CPU architecture (which you can verify at Intel's website), so the correct location in which to find your SQL Everywhere CAB files would be `<drive:>:\Program Files\Microsoft Visual Studio 8\SmartDevices\SDK\SQL Server\Mobile\v3.0\wce400\armv4`. Following are the specific files you would deploy and install on the iPaq 4355:

✦ `sqlce30.ppc.wce4.armv4.CAB`: The SQL Everywhere Database Engine CAB (required)

✦ `sqlce30.dev.ENU.ppc.wce4.armv4.CAB`: The SQL Everywhere development tools CAB (optional)

✦ `sqlce30.repl.ppc.wce4.armv4.CAB`: The SQL Everywhere client agent CAB (optional)

It is also useful to understand the role of each of the specific libraries these CABs will install on your mobile device. In cases where a `SqlCeException` is thrown from your code, the exception message or call stack may include the name of one of these DLLs. Here is a handy quick reference to each SQL Everywhere DLL that can possibly be installed on your mobile device:

✦ SQLCESE30.DLL—storage engine

✦ SQLCEQP30.DLL—query processor

✦ SQLCECA30.DLL—client agent

✦ SQLCESA30.DLL—server agent

✦ SQLCERP30.DLL—replication provider

✦ SQLCEME30.DLL—managed extensions

✦ SQLCEOLEDB30.DLL—OLE-DB provider

✦ SQLCEER30xx.DLL—Error strings localized in locale *xx* where *xx* is one of the following: EN, TW, CN, DE, ES, FR, IT, JA, KO

The next section introduces an important utility included in the SQL Everywhere development-tools CAB called Query Analyzer 3.0. Following the guidelines just outlined, install the appropriate SQL Everywhere Database Engine and development tools CAB files on your mobile device. Keep in mind that the .NET Compact Framework 2.0 is also a requirement if you are planning to develop with managed code.

If you have trouble manually copying and installing these CAB files, simply create a new Smart Device project in Visual Studio 2005. From the Visual Studio 2005 menu, choose File ➪ New ➪ Project ➪ Visual Basic or Visual C# ➪ Smart Device ➪ Pocket PC 2003 ➪ Device Application, and give your project a name. Then add a reference to `System.Data.SqlServerCe` to the project, build the project in DEBUG mode, and deploy to your device or an emulator. This will automatically deploy the correct SQL Everywhere CAB files to your device or emulator. With DEBUG builds, the SQL Everywhere development tools will also be deployed automatically to the device or emulator. Again, you can see the specific CAB files that were deployed to your device in Visual Studio 2005's output window during deployment.

Query Analyzer 3.0

The mobile version of Query Analyzer (formally named Query Analyzer 3.0) is a utility designed to work with SQL Everywhere databases right on the mobile device or device emulator. The following example illustrates the use of Query Analyzer 3.0 to run a query on the IBuySpyStore SQL Everywhere database.

Note   You can find a copy of this SQL Everywhere database in your Visual Studio program directory tree at `<drive:>\Program Files\Microsoft Visual Studio 8\SmartDevices\ SDK\SQL Server\Mobile\v3.0\Northwind.sdf`. To follow the example, simply copy `Northwind.sdf` file onto your mobile device and either start Query Analyzer 3.0 on the device from the device's Start menu, or navigate to the file using File Explorer on the device by tapping on the filename itself with your stylus. Note that Query Analyzer 3.0 can only work with SQL Everywhere databases — it will not connect to or manage a SQL CE 2.0 database. In addition, the older version of Query Analyzer for SQL CE (called Pocket Query Analyzer) will not connect to or manage SQL Everywhere databases. Both versions can be installed on the same device without issue, but when you tap on a SQL Everywhere or SQL CE database file with an extension of *.sdf, whichever version was installed last will attempt to open your database file, which may not yield the results you desire.

Begin this example by ensuring that the Northwind SQL Everywhere database has been copied to your device, as shown in Figure 26-3. It does not matter where on the device's file system you place this file.

Figure 26-3: The Northwind SQL Everywhere database on a Pocket PC 2003 device

Next, tap the Northwind database file on your device to launch Query Analyzer 3.0 and begin working with the database as shown in Figure 26-4.

Figure 26-4: Query Analyzer's 3.0 Objects tab

Note that there are four tabs in the Query Analyzer user interface. The Object tab displays SQL Everywhere databases that are local to your device, and allows you to connect to one of them and drill down to view tables, columns, indexes, and so on. The SQL tab allows you to enter and execute any SQL statement that conforms to SQL Everywhere's implementation of T-SQL. The Grid tab shows the results of your queries; and the Notes tab displays information about the execution of a query, such as the number of rows returned, execution time, or any errors that were encountered.

For this example, on the SQL tab, enter a simple SQL select statement to return all rows in the Northwind Employees table, as shown in Figure 26-5. Once you have entered the query, tap on the green right arrow at the bottom of the screen to execute the query.

Figure 26-5: The SQL tab
in Query Analyzer 3.0

If the query executes successfully, Query Analyzer will automatically switch to the Grid tab
and display the results, as shown in Figure 26-6. If the query fails to execute, the Notes tab
will appear, displaying any error messages that were encountered.

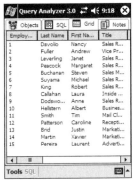

Figure 26-6: The Grid tab
in Query Analyzer 3.0

This is only a brief introduction to Query Analyzer 3.0; many additional useful features are
hiding in this little utility. For example, the ability to create button presets (on the SQL tab)
that run frequently used queries without retyping them, and the ability to perform a limited
amount of schema manipulation on your database (e.g., adding indexes or foreign keys) are
invaluable during the development and validation of your Windows Mobile application.

With any Windows Mobile application that conforms to Microsoft's *Designed for Windows
Mobile* standards, closing Query Analyzer by tapping on the circled X in the upper-right corner of the screen does not actually exit the application, but rather sends it to the background
in the Windows Mobile execution stack. If you are a new mobile developer this may seem
odd, but it enables frequently used programs to stay loaded in memory, which means users
can recall them much faster than restarting the program. This has one very large implication
for us as SQL Everywhere developers in that when Query Analyzer is sent to the background,

a connection to the Northwind database remains open. In order to exit Query Analyzer and close all connections to a SQL Everywhere database, you must tap the Tools ⇨ Exit menu item at the bottom of the Query Analyzer user interface.

Creating a SQL Everywhere Database

Perhaps the first challenge you will face as you endeavor to create a Windows Mobile application that leverages SQL Everywhere will be creating the initial physical database to develop your application around. To overcome this challenge, you have a number of options from which to choose, based on your application requirements and what you are most comfortable with as a developer. SQL Everywhere databases can be created in a variety of ways, including the following:

✦ Programmatically, from either managed or native code

✦ Visually, using Query Analyzer 3.0 on the device

✦ Visually, using Visual Studio 2005

✦ Visually or via scripting/templates, using SQL Server 2005 Management Studio

✦ Automatically, via merge replication

The following sections walk you through a brief explanation and example of each of these techniques.

Create a SQL Everywhere Database with Managed Code

The first option for creating your SQL Everywhere database is to do so in managed code using Visual Studio 2005 and the .NET Compact Framework 2.0. This is an especially useful option in scenarios where you are building and selling mobile applications to a population of users whose network connectivity or frequency of synchronization is not controllable. For example, I created a .NET Compact Framework application a few years ago that enabled physicians to enter all of the medications a patient might be taking and calculate possible drug interactions on their mobile device. The calculation of these interactions was of sufficient complexity that the solution clearly required a relational database on the device. The problem was that I had no control over the network connectivity between a variety of physician devices in a variety of environments and the Internet (to achieve any sort of data synchronization with our servers). The data this mobile application needed was purely read-only on the device, and changed on a quarterly basis. The solution in this case was to simply publish a new version of the Compact Framework application periodically and when first run, drop the old SQL CE database and create a new one programmatically at runtime. The schema of this database and the reference data were deployed along with the mobile application as CSV files, which were removed from the device once loaded into SQL CE. While the physician had to wait two or three minutes the first time she ran a new version of the application, the benefit of never needing to connect to a network and synchronize data far outweighed this minor delay.

Dynamically creating your SQL Everywhere database at runtime and even loading it with an initial set of data from managed code on your device is a useful technique that suits many Windows Mobile solution architectures.

Now it's time to walk through a simple example of creating a SQL Everywhere database in a VB.NET Compact Framework application.

Tip   If you are completely new to using Visual Studio and the .NET Compact Framework to create a Windows Mobile Smart Device application, or you are new to programming with VB.NET or C#, it would be helpful to check out some of the Compact Framework "Getting Started" articles available at `http://msdn.microsoft.com/netframework/programming/netcf/gettingstarted/default.aspx` before attempting the code samples that follow.

When you're ready to dive in, start Visual Studio 2005 and follow these steps:

1. In Visual Studio 2005, select the following menu options: File ➪ New ➪ Project. The New Project dialog appears.

2. In the list of Project types in the left pane of the New Project dialog, expand the node for either Visual Basic or Visual C# depending on your preferred .NET development language, and then expand the Smart Device node.

3. Select the Windows Mobile platform you want to target with your application (Pocket PC 2003, Smartphone 2003, etc.).

4. In the Templates pane on the right side of the New Project dialog, select Device Application.

5. Specify a Name for your project and optionally change the Location and Solution Name at the bottom of the New Project dialog and click the OK button.

6. Visual Studio 2005 will create a new .NET Compact Framework Smart Device application and generate a single form to get you started. The first thing required to make this a SQL Everywhere–compliant application is to add a reference in the project to the SQL Everywhere managed ADO.NET provider, `System.Data.SqlServerCe`.

Follow these steps to add this reference to your Smart Device project:

1. From the Visual Studio 2005 Project menu, choose Add Reference.

2. In the Add Reference dialog that is displayed, scroll down to the System.Data.SqlServer.Ce entry on the .NET tab and select this assembly, as shown in Figure 26-7. If this assembly does not appear in the list, click the Browse tab, navigate to `<drive:>\Program Files\Microsoft Visual Studio 8\SmartDevices\SDK\SQL Server\Mobile\v3.0\System.Data.SqlServerCe.dll`, and select that file. If `System.Data.SqlServerCe.dll` is not present in this location, you do not have SQL Everywhere correctly installed on your development computer. Revisit the section "Installing SQL Everywhere."

3. Finish by clicking OK in the Add Reference dialog.

4. Repeat the preceding three steps and add a reference to `System.Data` as well.

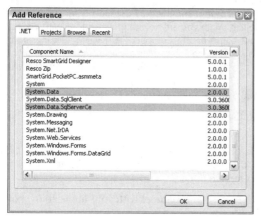

Figure 26-7: Adding a reference to
System.Data.SqlServer.Ce

Now our Smart Device project is ready to work with SQL Everywhere. In the Solution Explorer
pane of Visual Studio 2005, right-click on the form Visual Studio created when the new project
was created (i.e., Form1.vb) and choose the View Code menu item. Modify the code for
Form1.vb to look like the following code example.

Visual Basic.NET Sample

```vbnet
Imports System.IO
Imports System.Data
Imports System.Data.SqlServerCe
Imports System.Text
Imports System.Reflection

Public Class Form1

    Private _sqlMobileDB As String
    Private _connection As String

    Sub New()

        InitializeComponent()

        Dim strAppDir As String =
Path.GetDirectoryName([Assembly].GetExecutingAssembly().GetModules(0).FullyQuali
fiedName)

        Me._sqlMobileDB = strAppDir + Path.DirectorySeparatorChar.ToString() +
"ss2005bible.sdf"
        Me._connection = "Data Source=" & _sqlMobileDB

        CreateDatabase()
        CreateSchema()
```

```vb
        InsertRows()

    End Sub

    Private Sub CreateDatabase()

        If Not System.IO.File.Exists(_sqlMobileDB) Then
            Dim eng As SqlCeEngine = New SqlCeEngine(_connection)
            eng.CreateDatabase()
        End If

    End Sub

    Private Sub CreateSchema()

        Dim sql As String = "CREATE TABLE tb_clients (" & _
                            "clientId int NOT NULL IDENTITY (1, 1) primary key, " & _
                            "clientCode nvarchar(50) NULL, " & _
                            "clientName nvarchar(50) NOT NULL)"

        Dim conn As SqlCeConnection = New SqlCeConnection(_connection)
        conn.Open()

        Dim cmd As New SqlCeCommand(sql, conn)
        cmd.CommandType = CommandType.Text

        Try

            cmd.ExecuteNonQuery()

        Catch sqlex As SqlCeException

            DisplaySQLCEErrors(sqlex)

        Finally

            conn.Close()
            conn.Dispose()

        End Try

    End Sub

    Public Sub InsertRows()

        Dim sql As String = "INSERT INTO tb_clients (clientCode, clientName) " &
                            "VALUES (" & _
                            "'12345', " & _
```

```
                         "'Acme Corporation')"

        Dim conn As SqlCeConnection = New SqlCeConnection(_connection)
        conn.Open()

        Dim cmd As New SqlCeCommand(sql, conn)
        cmd.CommandType = CommandType.Text

        Try

            cmd.ExecuteNonQuery()

        Catch sqlex As SqlCeException

            DisplaySQLCEErrors(sqlex)

        Finally

            conn.Close()
            conn.Dispose()

        End Try


    End Sub

    Public Sub DisplaySQLCEErrors(ByVal ex As SqlCeException)

        Dim errorCollection As SqlCeErrorCollection = ex.Errors
        Dim bld As New StringBuilder()
        Dim inner As Exception = ex.InnerException
        Dim err As SqlCeError

        For Each err In errorCollection

            bld.Append(ControlChars.Lf + " Error Code: " +
err.HResult.ToString())
            bld.Append(ControlChars.Lf + " Message   : " + err.Message)
            bld.Append(ControlChars.Lf + " Minor Err.: " +
err.NativeError.ToString())
            bld.Append(ControlChars.Lf + " Source    : " + err.Source)

            Dim numPar As Integer
            For Each numPar In err.NumericErrorParameters
                If (numPar <> 0) Then
                    bld.Append(ControlChars.Lf + " Num. Par. : " +
numPar.ToString())
                End If
            Next numPar

            Dim errPar As String
```

```
For Each errPar In err.ErrorParameters
    If (errPar <> String.Empty) Then
        bld.Append(ControlChars.Lf + " Err. Par. : " + errPar)
    End If
Next errPar

MessageBox.Show(bld.ToString(), "SQL Everywhere Error")

        Next err

    End Sub

End Class
```

Compile the preceding sample code and then deploy it to either a mobile device connected to your development machine through ActiveSync or to one of the emulators provided with Visual Studio 2005.

This code sample creates a new SQL Everywhere database called `ss2005bible.sdf` in the folder in which the sample application is running (opened with Query Analyzer 3.0), as shown in Figure 26-8.

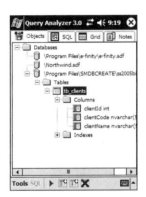

Figure 26-8: A SQL Everywhere database created from managed code

Tap the green arrow at the bottom of the Query Analyzer 3.0 screen to view the row you inserted into the `tb_clients` table.

If you are familiar with ADO.NET programming on the full .NET Framework, you will be pleasantly surprised by just how similar the code in this example is to what you would use to access SQL Server 2000 or 2005 through ADO.NET (e.g., instead of `SqlConnections`, you use `SqlCeConnections`, and `SqlCeCommands` now replaces `SqlCommands`). Note a few things in this example. First, you not only close but dispose of connections to SQL Everywhere when you are done with them. While SQL Everywhere is a multi-user database and supports multiple open connections, the `SqlCeConnections` object is memory intensive on a mobile device. Remember that your code is typically running on a device with limited memory, and garbage collection is a relatively expensive operation in the Compact Framework. In addition to `SqlCeConnection`, be sure to close and dispose of `SqlCeCommands`, `SqlCeDataReaders`, `RemoteDataAccess` and `Replication` objects when they are no longer needed. In addition, note the use of reflection to determine the current directory in which the sample program is running. This is a nice way to keep your SQL Everywhere database in the same folder as your mobile program without hard-coding the path to the database.

The `DisplaySQLCEErrors` method in the code sample is one you will want to add to all of your Smart Device projects that use SQL Everywhere. When you do run into difficulties, this method will provide as much information as possible about the specific error coming from an exception thrown by SQL Everywhere.

Finally, as you bite off more advanced coding tasks with SQL Everywhere, you will find that a single class that exposes an interface to all of the major SQL Everywhere operations (`ExecuteQuery`, `ExecuteNonQuery`, `ExecuteResultSet`, etc.) will be indispensable. There are ports of the Microsoft Enterprise Data Access Application Block freely available for SQL CE that are easily converted to work with SQL Everywhere. An excellent example is available at `www.businessanyplace.net/?p=daabcf`.

Create a SQL Everywhere Database from Query Analyzer 3.0

Another option to create an initial SQL Everywhere database is to use Query Analyzer 3.0 right on your mobile device or emulator. First make sure you have Query Analyzer 3.0 installed on the device, as described earlier in this chapter. Next, run Query Analyzer 3.0 either from the Start menu on your mobile device or by using File Explorer on the device to navigate to `Program Files\SQL Everywhere\locale\isqlw30.exe` and tap on this program. Once Query Analyzer is started, select the Objects tab and click the icon showing a yellow database with green arrow, on the toolbar at the bottom of the screen (see Figure 26-9).

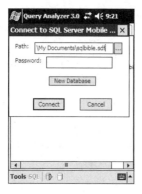

Figure 26-9: Creating a SQL Everywhere database in Query Analyzer 3.0

Note that this same dialog is used both to connect to an existing SQL Everywhere database and to create a new one. Because you are creating a new one, simply type in a path and name for the SQL Everywhere database and tap New Database. The Connect to SQL Everywhere dialog then changes its layout, enabling you to specify sort order and options to password-protect the database and/or encrypt the contents of the database. These topics are covered later in the chapter in the section titled "Security." Just tap the Create button at the bottom of the dialog to finish creating a new SQL Everywhere database with the name and location you specified.

Note By convention, SQL Everywhere databases always have the extension *.sdf, and this file extension is associated with Query Analyzer 3.0 when SQL Everywhere is installed on your mobile device. While you can name a SQL Everywhere database file without an *.sdf extension, you will not be able to tap on the database file and launch Query Analyzer 3.0 without that extension.

Now you can manage the new database you just created on the Objects tab of Query Analyzer 3.0, adding tables, constraints, keys, and indexes, as well as entering SQL on the SQL tab to populate your tables with data.

As you can see, this manual approach is somewhat awkward given the screen size and data input mechanisms of a Windows Mobile device. This technique is useful as a quick way to create a "starter" SQL Everywhere database on the device in the absence of a connection to either a development computer or a merge publication. If the complexity of your target database involves more than a table or two, the other options listed in this section will most likely serve you better.

Create a SQL Everywhere Database with Visual Studio 2005

One of Microsoft's major goals with Visual Studio 2005 was to provide a single development "portal" within which developers can write and test code, work with databases, view servers, work with source-code control libraries, and even view the web pages/RSS feeds of your choosing, without having to leave the familiar world of Visual Studio. One of the most exciting features of Visual Studio 2005 is that it is now SQL Everywhere–enabled. Specifically, from Visual Studio 2005 you can now do the following:

✦ Create, connect to, query, and manage SQL Everywhere databases on the development computer and on an ActiveSync-attached Windows Mobile device

✦ Design SQL Everywhere queries graphically with a visual query designer

✦ Use "drag and drop" to automatically bind data to controls and generate the underlying code to manage those bindings at runtime

✦ Stop worrying about packaging and deploying your SQL Everywhere database along with a Smart Device project — Visual Studio 2005 handles this for you now!

With only enough room to scratch the surface of these features, the following example creates a new SQL Everywhere database from within Visual Studio 2005. Give it a try by starting Visual Studio 2005 and following these steps:

1. Follow steps 1–4 in the previous section, "Create a SQL Everywhere Database with Managed Code," in order to get to the point where you have a blank Smart Device project open and ready to work with in Visual Studio 2005.

2. From the Data menu in Visual Studio 2005, select Add New Data Source and ensure that the yellow Database graphic is selected in the "Where will the application get data from?" panel of the Choose a Data Source Type dialog. Click the Next button.

3. In the Choose Your Data Connection dialog that follows, click the New Connection button. Click the Change button at the top of the Add Connection dialog and select Microsoft SQL Server Mobile Edition as the Data Source. Click OK.

4. Note that in the resulting Add Connection dialog, you can either create a new SQL Everywhere database or connect to an existing one that is located either on the development computer or on a mobile device connected through ActiveSync, as shown in Figure 26-10. Because you are interested in creating a new SQL Everywhere database, just click the Create button in this dialog.

Figure 26-10: Add Connection dialog

5. In the Create New SQL Server 2005 Everywhere Edition Database dialog, either enter or browse to the path in which you want the new SQL Everywhere database to be placed and give it a name such as SS2005BIBLE.SDF, as shown in Figure 26-11. Note that it is fine to leave the password fields blank for this example, but it is a security BestPractice to provide one for a production application, and Visual Studio 2005 will remind you of that when you click the OK button.

Figure 26-11: Create New SQL Server 2005 Everywhere Edition Database dialog

6. When you are warned about not providing a password, click the OK button to continue. You are now returned to the Add Connection dialog, where you can simply click OK to return to the Data Source Configuration Wizard.

7. The SQL Everywhere database you just created is now shown in the field titled "Which data connection should your application use to connect to the database?" Click the Next button to continue the example.

8. Visual Studio 2005 now shows new awareness of SQL Everywhere by warning that if you plan to build and deploy this mobile project including the SQL Everywhere database you just created, then the database needs to be included in the project. This is a nice feature; previous versions of Visual Studio treated a SQL CE database like content, and redeployed the entire database to the mobile device or emulator with each build. When you get the warning, click the Yes button to copy your SQL Everywhere database into the Smart Device project you have created in Visual Studio 2005.

9. The Data Source Configuration Wizard now allows you to create a DataSet composed of one or more SQL Everywhere tables. Because you are creating a new database, there are no tables to select in the Choose Your Database Objects page of the wizard, but had you been connecting to an existing SQL Everywhere database, you could create an ADO.NET DataSet that your Smart Device application could use to interact with the database. One thing you will notice on this page is that even though Visual Studio 2005 knows you are working with a SQL Everywhere database, you see a list of database objects that includes views, stored procedures, and functions, none of which are currently supported by SQL Everywhere. This can be confusing for new mobile developers, so to reiterate: The only database object type you can add to your DataSet are tables.

10. Click the Finish button to complete the Data Source Configuration Wizard.

In Visual Studio 2005's Solution Explorer, you will notice that there is now a copy of the SQL Everywhere database you just created, which has been added to the project with a Build Action of Content and a value for Copy to Output Directory set to Copy if Newer. This is a great new feature in that mobile development is heavy on code/build/deploy iterations, and waiting for the SQL Everywhere database to be deployed each time no longer has to be part of this process.

At this point, you are ready to begin integrating your Smart Device application with SQL Everywhere without ever having left the comfortable world of Visual Studio 2005. To begin exploring Visual Studio 2005's other integration features with SQL Everywhere, choose Server Explorer from the Visual Studio 2005 View menu or choose Show Data Sources from the Data menu in Visual Studio 2005. You can add tables, columns, indexes, and so on, to the new SQL Everywhere database you created, add those objects to one or more DataSets, and even drag these objects onto the Smart Device forms designer and automatically create bindings to DataGrids, ComboBoxes, and other .NET Compact Framework controls. For more information, view the following on-demand webcast located at http://msreadiness.com/WS_abstract.asp?eid=15003229.

Create a SQL Everywhere Database with SQL Server 2005 Management Studio

Just as Visual Studio 2005 is now SQL Everywhere–enabled, SQL Server 2005 Management Studio also allows you to create and manage SQL Everywhere databases in the same familiar way you would manage a SQL Server 2005 database. Microsoft took the SQL Everywhere integration features with SQL Server 2005 Management Studio far beyond what was present in SQL Server 2000 Enterprise Manager and beyond what you just saw in Visual Studio 2005. These points of integration include the following:

✦ SQL Editor support

✦ Capability to create, populate, and modify SQL Everywhere databases

✦ Managed API to execute business logic during merge replication

✦ Support for download-only articles

✦ Support for filtered articles

✦ View graphical query execution plans

✦ Improved wizards to configure replication

✦ Support for SQL Everywhere as a SQL Server Integration Services target

Now it's time to walk through an example of creating a SQL Everywhere database in SQL Server 2005 Management Studio to illustrate some of these new features. Use the following steps to create a brand-new SQL Everywhere database right on the desktop, without involving a mobile device:

1. Start SQL Server 2005 Management Studio.

2. When the Connect To Server dialog appears, choose SQL Server Everywhere as the server type and select New Database from the list of database files.

3. As soon as you choose New Database from the list of database files, a new dialog box is presented that enables you to specify the path and name of the SQL Everywhere database that you want to create, specify the sort order, and add a password to the database. For the database filename, enter `<drive:>\<path>\SS2005BIBLE.SDF`, leave the password fields blank, and click the OK button.

4. SQL Server 2005 Management Studio will warn you that you have not provided a password for this new SQL Everywhere database. For a real application, you should indeed set a password on your database for security purposes. For this walkthrough, click the Yes button on the warning dialog to continue without specifying a password.

5. You should now be back at the Connect to Server dialog, with the values for server type and database file you set previously. To complete this dialog, click the Connect button at the bottom of the dialog, shown in Figure 26-12.

Figure 26-12: Connecting to a SQL Everywhere database in SQL Server 2005 Management Studio

6. In the Object Explorer pane of SQL Server 2005 Management Studio is a new node for the SQL Everywhere database you just created. You'll notice that the Object Explorer provides the same graphical representation of this SQL Everywhere database that it would with a normal SQL Server 2005 database.

At this point, you can right-click on the SQL Everywhere database in Object Explorer, choose New Query, and begin to work with this database just as you would with any other SQL Server. Beyond writing SQL to perform DDL and DML on this database, you can graphically construct the schema of your SQL Everywhere database as well. Try this by right-clicking on the Tables sub-node of the SQL Everywhere database in Object Explorer and choosing New Table. A New Table dialog (see Figure 26-13) enables you to add tables to your database without writing SQL.

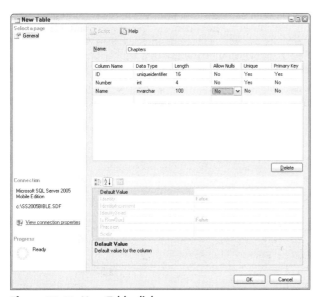

Figure 26-13: New Table dialog

While this walk-through only begins to explore the many things you can do with SQL Everywhere databases in SQL Server 2005 Management Studio, Microsoft has now implemented the SQL Everywhere Books Online with "How To" chapters that illustrate how to perform common database management tasks with managed code, with SQL, and within SQL Server 2005 Management Studio.

Create a SQL Everywhere Database via Merge Replication

To conclude coverage of the available options for creating an initial SQL Everywhere database, there is one last technique that can provide some unexpected side benefits on a large deployment of Windows Mobile devices. One challenge that you will face as you roll out a Windows Mobile application that includes a SQL Everywhere database is managing schema changes that need to be made after deployment. Merge replication offers an option to create a new subscriber database the very first time a Smart Device application replicates with SQL Server. This has some powerful implications, including the following:

✦ Rather than deploy a "starter" SQL Everywhere database with each version of your mobile application, you can have a complete and up-to-date SQL Everywhere database created dynamically on the device the first time your mobile application is executed.

✦ If you need to make significant schema changes or schema changes that cannot automatically be propagated to subscribers in a merge replication relationship with the server, you can have the mobile user upload any changes, delete the SQL Everywhere database on the device, and restart the application. A new SQL Everywhere database with the latest schema is created.

✦ If for some reason a mobile user deletes or damages beyond repair a SQL Everywhere database on the device, a fresh one can be created dynamically without the need to install new files on the device.

✦ If you have an existing server-side database and want to create a SQL Everywhere database that mirrors all or a subset of the schema of the server database, you can publish the server-side articles you wish to include in a SQL Everywhere database, and automatically generate a SQL Everywhere database that subscribes to the server-side publication.

Although merge replication is covered in detail later in this chapter, the following code sample shows the use of the `AddOption.CreateDatabase` capability of SQL Everywhere merge replication.

VB.NET Sample

```
Imports System.Data
Imports System.Data.SqlServerCe

' The code below would be placed in the constructor or Load event of your
' Smart Device project's Startup form/object in order to always replicate
' when your application executes. If the SQL Everywhere database is not found
' locally, one is created while you wait.
Dim repl As SqlCeReplication = GetReplication()
repl.Synchronize()


' All of the replication properties below need to be modified to match your
' merge replication environment.  The values you see in the code are for
' illustration only.
Public Function GetReplication() As SqlCeReplication
    Dim databaseName As String = "\My Documents\SS2005BIBLE.SDF"
Dim connection As String = "Data Source=" & databaseName
    Dim repl As New SqlCeReplication()
    repl.InternetUrl = "http://dellxps/repl/sqlcesa30.dll"
repl.Publisher = "DELLXPS\SQLSERVER"
repl.PublisherDatabase = "Adventureworks"
repl.PublisherSecurityMode = SecurityType.NTAuthentication
repl.Publication = "AW_PUB"
repl.Subscriber = "DDS_PPC"
repl.SubscriberConnectionString = connection
' AddOption.CreateDatabase shown below allows the application to start
' without a SQL Everywhere DB on device, and then create it dynamically upon
' first call to Synchronize()
```

```
            If Not System.IO.File.Exists(databaseName) Then
                repl.AddSubscription(AddOption.CreateDatabase)
            End If
        Return repl
End Function
```

Upgrading an Existing SQL CE 2.0 Database

If you already have a SQL CE 2.0 mobile database that you would like to upgrade to SQL Everywhere, Microsoft provides a command-line utility to perform this upgrade. Note that the upgrade utility runs only on the mobile device and cannot be performed on the desktop.

First, you need to have both the SQL Server CE 2.0 engine and the SQL Everywhere engine installed on the same device. These two products do peacefully coexist side-by-side. Simply install both the SQL CE CAB that is appropriate for your device's CPU architecture and then the corresponding SQL Everywhere CAB on your device, one after the other.

Next, use File Explorer or ActiveSync to copy the `upgrade.exe` file located at `<drive:>\Program Files\Microsoft Visual Studio 8\SmartDevices\SDK\SQL Server\Mobile\v3.0\[platform]\[processor]` onto your device, placing it in the folder containing the SQL CE 2.0 database you wish to upgrade. (Note that there is a corresponding folder for Windows Mobile 5/Windows CE 5.0 devices.)

If you click the `upgrade.exe` file on your device, a reminder of usage is displayed, as shown in Figure 26-14.

Figure 26-14: SQL CE to SQL Everywhere upgrade utility usage

Open the Run menu on the device by pressing and holding the Enter or Action key, click and hold on the clock in the upper-right corner of the screen, release the Enter key, choose Run, and type **upgrade /s [*name of old SQLCE db*] /d [*name of new SQL Everywhere db*]**.

In this example, you upgrade the IBuySpyStore SQL CE 2.0 database to SQL Everywhere by entering the following command into the device's Run menu:

```
upgrade /s IBuySpyStore.sdf /d ibs30.sdf
```

Figure 26-15 shows the resulting `ibs30.sdf` SQL Everywhere database file and a notification that the upgrade succeeded.

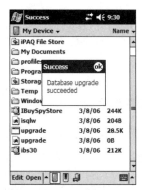

Figure 26-15: SQL
Everywhere upgrade
utility output

Note that your original database is not modified and is left behind after the upgrade completes. If any problems are encountered during the upgrade, a log file with information about those problems is created, which can be opened in Pocket Word and reviewed. In most cases, the resulting upgraded database will be 10–17% smaller than the original (in our example, we went from 276K to 236K). If your original SQL CE database contains any `NTEXT` columns, the resulting database may actually be larger.

Finally, the `upgrade.exe` utility allows you to specify a password for the source database and a flag to encrypt the resulting SQL Everywhere database (these topics are covered in the "Security" section later in this chapter).

Synchronizing Data

So far, you have seen how SQL Everywhere can provide relational persistence capabilities to a Windows Mobile application on device. This section explores how SQL Everywhere can serve as an offline data cache in a synchronization relationship with SQL Server. As previously mentioned, SQL Everywhere includes support for two powerful, yet different, data synchronization technologies: remote data access (RDA) and merge replication. The concept of merge replication may not be new to a SQL Server DBA, but RDA is a technology specific to synchronizing data with mobile devices. This section explains these concepts, as well as one additional option for data synchronization: .NET Web Services.

Before you begin, it is helpful to understand the challenges inherent in synchronizing data to a mobile device. In the simplest scenario, a mobile worker establishes a path of connectivity and pulls a copy of operational data from a server, at which point the worker becomes disconnected while working a shift or driving a route. At the end of the day, any new or changed data needs to make its way back to that server. Sounds simple enough.

What happens, however, if the data on the server changes while the worker is disconnected? To make things more interesting, how can you handle a scenario in which more than one worker pulls the same copy of the data and multiple mobile devices are making changes to that data *while the data is also changing on the server?* Twice per day synchronization is becoming more of an exception than the rule given the growing pervasiveness of wireless networks and wireless-capable devices, so you can't depend on having a window of time during which data will not be changing.

There are many more challenging synchronization scenarios you could consider, but the point is that planning a data synchronization strategy is not as simple as just choosing a technology. Many additional factors are involved in choosing the right strategy for your mobile application, including the degree to which data is logically partitioned across a large population of mobile users; the frequency of device connectivity and synchronization; battery life of the device; the volume of data; network bandwidth; security gateways; and conflict resolution requirements. With this in mind, let's explore which scenarios are best matched with which synchronization technologies.

Remote Data Access

Think of remote data access (RDA) as a pull-push model for data synchronization. RDA allows a mobile application to "pull" all or some of the data in one or more tables from SQL Server to SQL Everywhere and then have SQL Everywhere keep track of changes made to the data in that table. Note that the table must not exist when the RDA pull is initiated — the table and its server-side schema are created in SQL Everywhere each time a pull occurs. Subsequently, the mobile application then "pushes" that table back to the server, and any tracked changes are applied to the SQL Server database. You can perform an RDA pull with change tracking turned off, in which case a subsequent push from that table is not permitted. RDA also provides a mechanism to submit any SQL statement to the server for execution as long as that statement returns no rows. This is an easy way to perform a quick update on the server, bypassing SQL Everywhere entirely.

Using the same synchronization architecture shown in Figure 26-2, the pull and push are orchestrated through the SQL Everywhere Server Agent within IIS. RDA is simpler to get running than merge replication but it requires slightly more code within the mobile application (although the code is highly repeatable and well documented). Note that all aspects of RDA are controlled by the mobile application, programmatically.

RDA is a solid solution for pulling lookup data (e.g., a zip codes table or a customers table) or large amounts of data to populate SQL Everywhere tables. The data is compressed in transit, and transfer performance is generally superior to merge replication. The change tracking capabilities also make it suitable for posting data that originates on the mobile device back to the server, with similar high performance.

There is one major aspect of RDA that you have to factor into your data synchronization architecture regarding the definition of *optimistic concurrency*. RDA uses optimistic concurrency, but with a slightly different definition than you may be used to in the SQL Server world. RDA optimistic concurrency means that when you push your changes back to the server, those changes are applied on the server-side tables *even if the same data on the server has changed* since the RDA pull took place. This is obviously a limitation in mobile application scenarios where the elapsed time from pull to push is long and data is changing on the server and other mobile devices frequently.

Another issue you have to manage with RDA is the incrementing of identity columns when multiple mobile devices are pulling from the same server-side tables. If one mobile user performs a pull and the highest integer identity value on a table at that moment is 32, then the next record that user inserts into the table receives the identity value of 33. Obviously, if a second user performs a pull on the same table, that user can also create a 33 on his device. There is no conflict resolution on the server side for RDA updates to tables, so this can result in synchronization errors, which are returned to you when you execute the push. You can manually manage identity values as each pull is performed, but RDA truly finds its sweet spot where there is no overlap in the data that a mobile user will be modifying or adding across the pool of mobile devices.

Merge Replication

Merge replication can be thought of as a publisher-subscriber model of data synchronization. It is a powerful and complex technology that aspires to accommodate the most challenging of mobile data synchronization scenarios. While RDA is controlled programmatically from within the mobile application, much of the logic that defines your data synchronization rules with merge replication can be implemented on the server. While merge replication actually requires less code on the mobile device, the process of configuring and managing merge replication over time is much more involved than RDA.

Merge replication involves creating a *publication* within SQL Server 2000 or 2005 that defines one or more *articles* (limited to tables, columns, indexes, keys, and constraints in SQL Everywhere replication), which contain data rows that can then be filtered horizontally or vertically. The server is referred to as the *publisher,* and the SQL Everywhere database is referred to as the *subscriber*. A *subscription* to the publication is then added to a SQL Everywhere database and the subscription is synchronized with the publication. This synchronization consists of a bi-directional dialog between the subscriber and the publisher and is designed to handle row changes on both ends of that dialog as well as some basic schema changes.

New in SQL Server 2005 and SQL Everywhere is the introduction of column-level tracking of changes for merge replication. For example, consider a table called SurveyAnswers that is part of a publication. This table consists of 15 columns, one of which is an image column designed to hold a signature or digital picture (possibly a very wide column!). If all that changed in a row since the last synchronization was an `nvarchar` column, only the value in that column is sent to the server. With SQL CE and SQL Server 2000 replication, the entire row, including the image, had to be transmitted to the server.

Large enterprise mobile deployments benefit from merge replication not only as a result of the advanced capabilities of the synchronization itself, but also from the set of administrative tools on the server side. From a corporate data center, an administrator can use Replication Monitor from SQL Server 2005 Management Studio to assess the state of all mobile subscribers, when they last synchronized, the throughput they achieved, and any conflicts that may have occurred during the synchronization. The administrator can also centrally re-initialize any mobile subscription to force that subscriber to take a new *snapshot* of the publication on the server. A snapshot is a representation of the schema of all articles in a publication, scripts to create these articles within SQL Everywhere, and an initial set of data to populate in the SQL Everywhere subscription. The SQL Agent on the server generates snapshots, which the SQL Everywhere Server Agent knows where to find based on configuring the publication for web replication with SQL Everywhere.

For an end-to-end example of creating a Compact Framework application with SQL Everywhere that uses merge replication to SQL Server, see http://msdn.microsoft.com/library/default.asp?url=/library/en-us/dnppcgen/html/desktop_device_tools_sql_mobile.asp.

Web Services

The .NET Compact Framework 2.0 includes strong support for calling Web Services and parsing XML. Designing a custom Web Services–based data synchronization strategy may sound intimidating, but in the right mobile scenarios it can be accomplished without much more effort than is required to set up and configure merge replication. Here are some of the indicators that a Web Services approach might make sense for your mobile architecture:

✦ The data required by and/or created by a specific mobile user can be logically and strongly partitioned from other mobile users. In other words, the possibility of a synchronization conflict is expected to be negligible or you are willing to write code to manage those conflicts.

✦ The use cases that are executed by the mobile application are single-user use cases. In other words, two or more mobile users running the same application are not "teaming up" on a given unit of work. A scenario in which three different workers on the loading dock are all entering data about the same pallet that just arrived is a scenario rich with the possibility of data conflicts.

✦ The payload of data you intend to send back and forth to the server averages less than 1MB.

✦ The typical connectivity scenario between device and server involves the Internet and multiple firewalls and/or proxy servers through which you will need to route data.

✦ You have requirements for a level of control over the exact articles to be published, filters and partitions, date transformations, or administration of the synchronization process that merge replication cannot provide.

✦ You have a server-side database other than SQL Server against which you must synchronize.

If your situation matches any of these scenarios, a Web Services approach to data synchronization may be a good choice. In practice, the most effective Web Services synchronization implementations have all of the following in common:

✦ Uniqueness across all data in the solutions domain is guaranteed, usually by using unique identifiers such as a GUID as the primary key on all synchronized data tables.

✦ The data payload in any single Web Service call from the mobile application is kept under 1MB.

✦ A strategy of "drop and replace" in conjunction with an "outbox" on the device is used to guarantee no dropped sync records. For example, if you have a table called "Orders" into which a mobile user is inserting or updating records, the GUID primary key of each new, modified, or deleted record is placed into a simple table called Orders_Outbox, which has two columns: the GUID of the record from the Orders table that was operated upon, and a DateTime to assist in applying multiple changes to a given record in the correct order.

✦ Some simple web methods are exposed to get and put data from/to SQL Server. The payload in either direction is a DataSet with one or more DataTables that correspond to specific tables in the SQL Everywhere database.

✦ When it is time to synchronize the SQL Everywhere database with the server, a DataSet is created with one DataTable for each of the outboxes described above. Each table is filled with the complete row data from the source table corresponding to the GUIDs in the outbox. This DataSet is sent to the server (a "put") and a DataSet is returned with the same set of DataTables, but this time the tables are filled with the GUIDs of the rows sent and a status code that indicates success or failure. The GUIDs of the records that were successfully posted to the server are deleted from the corresponding outbox. Those that failed remain in the outbox so that they can be re-attempted on a subsequent synchronization.

✦ When pulling data from the server (a "get"), as long as there are no outstanding records in a table's outbox, the table can be truncated and replaced with the results of the Web Service call. For example, you might expose a web method with the signature DataSet GetNamedTable(string TableName, which returns a DataSet with a single DataTable populated with the server-side rows from the requested table. On the mobile device, you would apply these rows to the corresponding SQL Everywhere table using a drop-and-replace approach. It is not uncommon to introduce the additional parameters of filter criteria (used in the server-side WHERE clause) and the concept of an As-Of Date to pull only new or changed records from the server since some specified point in time.

While your specific requirements will dictate the implementation details of a Web Services approach, the generic approach described here can be relatively fast to implement and highly effective.

Packaging and Deployment

Numerous options are available to deploy a mobile application that includes a SQL Everywhere database. The challenge is not only to get SQL Everywhere and any supporting replication libraries onto the device, but also to provide an initial SQL Everywhere database required for the application to run the first time.

Options for deploying SQL Everywhere include the following:

✦ Manually copy the necessary CAB files to each device.

✦ Connect the device to a PC or server through ActiveSync and deploy the mobile application using Visual Studio 2005.

✦ Pull the SQL Everywhere CAB files from an IIS web page using Pocket IE on a connected device.

✦ Use an automated device configuration management tool, such as those available from Odyssey Software or Symbol Technologies.

This section explores all of the options available for deploying a SQL Everywhere database to a population of mobile devices.

Creating the Database Programmatically

While it is the least attractive option in terms of user experience, one option is to program-matically create and populate a SQL Everywhere database on a device at application startup. This is useful in situations where the application may have a small amount of relatively static data. A typical approach to loading the initial data is to read CSV files deployed along with the mobile application and load tables from these CSV files, removing the files when finished.

Deploying a Starter Database with the Mobile Application

Perhaps the most common approach is to create a "starter database" and include it in your Smart Device project as content. The starter database is pre-populated with any static or lookup data and then synchronized at application startup to obtain required operational data.

Creating the Database Dynamically through Merge Replication

Another approach covered earlier in this chapter is to create your database dynamically through merge replication with the `AddOption.CreateDatabase` option set on your replica-tion object. Besides the advantage of a smaller deployment payload, this option allows a new database to be deployed to a device simply by deleting the old one and executing a replica-tion. This is an easy way to propagate publication schema changes that exceed the capabili-ties of the merge replication Propagate Schema Changes option. In limited bandwidth scenarios, this approach may not be an option given the time it might take to create a large database dynamically via merge replication.

Other Approaches

Note a few other miscellaneous approaches to this problem, including the following:

✦ Pull the CAB file containing the SQL Everywhere database to the device using Pocket IE on the Windows Mobile device.

✦ Deploy the SQL Everywhere database on Storage Cards, which can be pre-loaded and provided to mobile users for insertion into their device's card slots.

✦ Implement a custom application update mechanism, such as the MSDN example pro-vided at `http://msdn.microsoft.com/library/default.asp?url=/library/en-us/dnnetcomp/html/AutoUpdater.asp`.

Security

Security is an important consideration in an enterprise mobile application. Mobile devices are particularly prone to being lost, stolen, damaged, or used by someone other than the intended owner. Data synchronization with SQL Everywhere can involve connections to non-secure networks. For these reasons, Microsoft provides a variety of options to protect enter-prise data stored in SQL Everywhere and to secure data as it is being synchronized.

Password Protection

Consider that a SQL Everywhere database is really just a file residing on a mobile client. Assuming that a malicious user has access to either Query Analyzer 3.0 or a custom application that can connect to your database file, a first line of defense to foil that connection is to password-protect your SQL Everywhere databases. Passwords are specified at the time you create your database or can be added or modified after creation during a compact operation on the Database Engine. Passwords can be up to 40 characters in length and include letters, symbols, and digits. Once added, it is impossible to access a SQL Everywhere database without specifying the correct password in your ADO.NET or OLE DB connection string (or by entering it when prompted as you connect using Query Analyzer 3.0).

Caution   Do not forget or misplace the password you assign. There is absolutely no way to access the database or to reset the database so that it doesn't require a password without the original password. SQL Everywhere passwords are not recoverable.

Encryption

A next line of defense to secure your data in a SQL Everywhere database is to encrypt the contents of the database. Like password protection, encryption is added either at database creation time or during a compact operation on the Database Engine. The encryption applied is a 128-bit proprietary Microsoft algorithm. Microsoft keeps the specifics of this top-secret algorithm, which benefits everyone. The great news about SQL Everywhere encryption is that there is almost no performance penalty for encrypting your databases. Expect an average 2 percent degradation across an intensive suite of SELECT, INSERT, and UPDATE operations on a 5MB SQL Everywhere database.

Encryption, combined with a strong password, is your best option to protect SQL Everywhere data, especially when using removable storage cards in your mobile devices.

Secure Data Synchronization

Whether using RDA, merge replication, or your own custom web-services data synchronization strategy, securing data in route during synchronization is imperative. Because these options all involve HTTP transport and IIS as a synchronization gateway, you can leverage the security options in IIS to construct secure synchronization models.

Start by always using SSL and HTTPS for secure transport. To that, add the use of a single separate virtual directory for each mobile application you synchronize with, and configure them to respect the principal of least privilege for each of those individual applications. Using NTFS (versus FAT) on your IIS server provides the additional ability to limit the number and set of subscribers who will access a given virtual directory. Finally, never use anonymous authentication for any production data synchronization with SQL Everywhere.

Additional security checkpoints can be established between IIS, the SQL Everywhere Server Agent, and SQL Server 2005. For detailed coverage of these options, see the topic *Planning Server Security* in the SQL Server 2005 Mobile Edition Books Online.

Tuning, Maintenance, and Administration

Like any relational database in production use, SQL Everywhere requires tuning and maintenance in order to achieve optimal performance and ensure trouble-free operation over time. This section introduces you to the basic concepts of SQL Everywhere performance tuning and walks through the greatly expanded set of methods now available to maintain the health of your mobile databases. While most applications that perform mostly read-only operations on SQL Everywhere can run indefinitely without much attention, the majority of applications that perform intensive data storage, retrieval, and synchronization will require both maintenance and periodic tuning to realize their full potential.

Measuring and Improving Query Performance

While the topic of query performance tuning is much larger than this chapter, real-world experience with SQL Everywhere points to a small set of high-impact performance-tuning recommendations:

✦ Add indexes to your SQL Everywhere tables. Make them useful and selective. For multi-column indexes, put the most selective columns to the left.

✦ Rewrite subqueries to use joins. SQL Everywhere's query processor always rewrites the IN subquery to use a JOIN so that it can consider different execution plans.

✦ Avoid joins of more than five tables.

✦ Use parameterized queries and prepare your SqlCeCommands for repetitive DML tasks such as inserting hundreds of rows into a table.

✦ Return as little data as possible from queries — take only what you need in SQL and in replication.

✦ Use the SqlCeResultSet whenever possible to query or update more than one row.

✦ Consider denormalizing the database when you cannot achieve acceptable performance exhausting other approaches.

✦ Minimize or even eliminate table constraints.

✦ If your SQL Everywhere database will reside on a storage card, research the I/O speed of the card and don't eject the card from the mobile device while the database has open connections.

For more information on these performance tuning tips, visit the SQL Server 2005 Performance site located at http://msdn.microsoft.com/sql/learning/perf/default.aspx.

As part of SQL Everywhere's integration with SQL Server 2005 Management Studio, it is now possible to see a graphical execution plan of any DML query you want to tune for SQL Everywhere. Selecting Display Estimated Execution Plan from the Query menu will display a graphical execution plan and provide the option to store the plan in XML format. This is useful when the location where the poorly performing query is running and the location of the person doing the tuning and analysis are not the same.

SQL Everywhere Maintenance

SQL Everywhere's storage engine has been redesigned to reduce the need for maintenance and the risk of data corruption that were major frustrations with SQL CE. SQL Everywhere database files are divided into 4KB logical units or "pages." As data is stored, indexed, and removed from the database over time, there can be pages that contain unused space as well as pages that are entirely empty in the database. To optimize performance and minimize space on the client device, unused space must be reclaimed, index statistics must be recalculated periodically, and transaction buffers must be purged. SQL Everywhere provides the concepts of AutoShrink, Compaction, and AutoFlush to tend to these tasks.

AutoShrink

AutoShrink is a new feature in SQL Everywhere that automatically reorganizes the pages in a SQL Everywhere database file so that all empty pages are contiguously arranged at the end of the file, truncating them to reclaim space. AutoShrink can be tuned by specifying the `AutoShrink_Threshold` property in your connection string. This property expresses the percentage of free space in the database file to allow before executing AutoShrink. Do not hesitate to set this property to an aggressive value, as the process of AutoShrinking has little impact on processor resources or performance.

If you want to explicitly shrink a SQL Everywhere database, the `SqlCeEngine` object now supports a shrink method that effectively performs an immediate AutoShrink, regardless of the percentage of free space in the database.

Compact

Compact is a `SqlCeEngine` method that provides the capability to reclaim space as well as change database settings such as password, locale ID, and encryption. Unlike AutoShrink, Compact not only reclaims empty pages, it creates an entirely new database, which has the following benefits:

1. All indexes are recreated and statistics recomputed.

2. Table pages are reorganized to be contiguous.

3. Incrementing identity columns are reset so that the next available value is one step value more than the highest value in use.

4. Any changes to the password, encryption, and/or locale ID are applied to the new database.

Here is an example of using the Compact method on a SQL Everywhere database.

Example (C#):

```
string originalDB  = "AWMobile.sdf";
string compactedDB = "AWMobile.sdf.tmp";
SqlCeEngine engine = new SqlCeEngine("Data Source = " + originalDB);
try
{
    engine.Compact("Data Source = " + compactedDB);
    engine.Dispose();
    File.Delete(originalDB);
    File.Move(compactedDB, originalDB);
```

```
}
catch(SqlCeException e)
{
      DisplaySQLErrors(e);
}
finally
{
      engine.Dispose();
}
```

With SQL Everywhere and the new `SqlCeEngine` object in Compact Framework 2.0, Compact can be performed in place, meaning no destination database is specified in the `Data Source` property and the original database is overwritten in place. Therefore, the preceding example becomes the following:

```
string originalDB  = "AWMobile.sdf";
SqlCeEngine engine = new SqlCeEngine("Data Source = " + originalDB);
try
{
   engine.Compact();
   engine.Dispose();
}
catch(SqlCeException e) {}
finally
{
   engine.Dispose();
}
```

AutoFlush

SQL Everywhere supports transactions through both the ADO.NET and OLEDBCE interfaces. A transaction buffer pool contains changes that are pending a transactional commit and subsequent recording to the underlying SQL Everywhere database. The buffer pool ensures that transactions are always written to the database in the order in which they are committed. Transactions can be committed but not yet written to the database due to abnormal program termination or other blocking processes writing their own transactions. The interval at which the buffer pool changes are written to the database can be fine-tuned in SQL Everywhere using the `Flush Interval` property in your connection string. This property specifies the maximum number of seconds that can elapse prior to committed transactions being written to the database.

Repairing a Damaged SQL Everywhere Database

With SQL CE, Microsoft listened as mobile developers reported incidences of corrupted databases. They realized that there was a fundamental flaw in the storage engine for SQL CE on mobile devices that feature transient power supplies and removable storage cards. As previously stated, the storage engine for SQL Everywhere is completely rewritten and was designed with the safety of your mobile data in mind. Every database write is now staged in a shadow copy area as well as being applied to the physical database itself. In this way, upon recovery from a power loss or device reset, SQL Everywhere ensures that all writes happen in the correct order and are not lost. This section covers the new options available to you as a database developer to verify and repair a SQL Everywhere database as part of a regular database maintenance plan.

Verify

Verify is another new SqlCeEngine method that is called to determine the need to perform a repair. Verify recalculates the checksum of all pages in the SQL Everywhere database and compares them to expected values. If this check fails, Verify returns false, signifying the need to execute a repair, described next.

Repair

While SQL Everywhere's storage engine has been rewritten to vastly reduce the possibility of data corruption, the fundamental fact that SQL Everywhere operates on mobile devices presents the need to handle corruption if it does occur. Imagine your SQL Server 2005 database running on a server where a user can (and thinks nothing of) powering off the server throughout the day or pulling the removable drive containing the data file out of the server. SQL Everywhere databases are frequently placed on storage cards in mobile devices — storage cards that can be removed in the middle of a write transaction. Therefore, it's a good idea to Verify your SQL Everywhere databases periodically; and if you get a false return value, call the new Repair method on the SqlCeEngine.

Finally, offering an option beyond compact, Microsoft now also provides two specific repair options that dictate what to do if the Repair method does find corrupted data:

1. RepairOption.DeleteCorruptedRows removes any corrupted rows from the SQL Everywhere database.

2. RepairOption.RecoverCorruptedRows will make an attempt to read from a corrupted page, but it does not guarantee success. In addition, if it does succeed in recovering one or more rows, there is no guarantee that logical corruption might not still exist in the database. Still, just having one more possible option to recover from mobile database corruption is a step in the right direction.

A code snippet illustrating how these methods work together follows. One effective technique for SQL Everywhere database maintenance is to execute code like the following on a weekly basis or every *n* executions of your mobile application.

Example (C#)

```
SqlCeEngine engine = new SqlCeEngine("Data Source = AWMobile.sdf");
if (!engine.Verify())
{
    Cursor.Current = Cursors.WaitCursor;
    engine.Repair(null, RepairOption.RecoverCorruptedRows);
    Cursor.Current = Cursors.Default;
    MessageBox.Show("SQL Everywhere Database has been repaired.");
}
```

Keeping Merge Replication Healthy

Merge replication is a powerful option for SQL Everywhere to SQL Server 2000/2005 data synchronization. While the performance of merge replication can be assessed and audited in the Replication Monitor of SQL Server 2005 Management Studio, there is an understated need to perform periodic maintenance to keep merge replication performing optimally. A number of real-world enterprise-class mobile deployments have seen the performance of merge replication degrade quickly and significantly after only a few days serving 20–30 mobile subscribers.

Following are the top three maintenance and tuning tasks that need to be performed to keep merge replication performing well in your enterprise over time:

1. Defragment all indexes on the `Distribution.MSmerge_*` tables frequently (nightly if possible).

2. Lower the snapshot retention period from the default of 14 days if application usage patterns permit.

3. Increase the number of generations per batch on the server.

Obviously, much more can be done to fine-tune merge replication, but these three tasks are commonly overlooked and can have the most immediate impact on replication performance.

For more information on tuning and maintaining merge replication, see
`www.microsoft.com/technet/prodtechnol/sql/2000/maintain/mergperf.mspx`.

More Information

Listed here are some particularly useful references for SQL Server 2005 Everywhere Edition. While the amount of SQL Everywhere information on MSDN and other websites is building since its introduction, with some exceptions most of the wealth of reference material on MSDN devoted to SQL Server 2000 Windows CE Edition 2.0 is applicable to SQL Everywhere as well.

✦ SQL Server 2005 Everywhere Edition Developer Center:
   `http://msdn.microsoft.com/SQL/2005/mobile/default.aspx`

✦ SQL Server 2005 Everywhere Edition Books Online:
   `http://msdn2.microsoft.com/en-us/library/ms173053(SQL.90).aspx`

✦ MSDN Newsgroup (news.microsoft.com):
   `microsoft.public.sqlserver.ce`

✦ MSDN webcasts:
   `http://msdn.microsoft.com/sql/webcasts/default.aspx`

✦ Many SQL Server 2000 Windows CE Edition topics on MSDN apply to SQL Everywhere:
   `http://msdn.microsoft.com/SQL/SQLCE/default.aspx`

Summary

SQL Server 2005 Everywhere Edition provides a powerful database for enterprise mobile applications. SQL Everywhere provides rich relational database features on device for disconnected clients as well as built-in capabilities for data synchronization with SQL Server in connected scenarios. SQL Everywhere databases can be secured, deployed, and maintained in large enterprise deployments. For database programmers and administrators familiar with SQL Server 2000 or 2005, working with SQL Everywhere is a short learning curve given tight and consistent integration with Visual Studio 2005 and SQL Server 2005 Management Studio.

✦   ✦   ✦

Programming CLR Assemblies within SQL Server

With SQL Server 2005, the .NET Framework's common language runtime (CLR) becomes available within SQL Server. The CLR produces more scalable complex logic and calculations at the database level through stored procedures, functions, triggers, and user-defined aggregations. The CLR also adds the capability to more accurately model the real world that the database supports, with user-defined types. While T-SQL continues to be the optimal data access tool, the CLR should be viewed as a new dimension of flexibility in n-tier datacentric application design. Before CLR integration, it was necessary to either endure the slow computational facilities within T-SQL or move large amounts of data on the wire before crunching to produce a relatively smaller result for ultimate consumption by the application. With CLR integration, the best of both is possible, provided the hardware under the SQL Server and the developer behind the keyboard are both up to the task.

Note   The individual letters of the abbreviation CLR are frequently pronounced "clear" by many developers. Neither the individual letters nor "clear" is more technically correct. Both pronunciations are in use.

SQL Server does not merely use the .NET Framework components provided by the operating system. The CLR used by SQL Server actually runs in the SQL Server memory space. SQL Server manages synchronization and integrity for traditional non-preemptive SQL Server SPIDs and the preemptively scheduled CLR threads. SQL Server can manage both CLR threads and native SPIDs within the context of the same local transaction on the database server.

There are some limitations to what the SQL Server–hosted CLR can do in comparison to the Windows-hosted CLR. Some of the limitations result from the newness of the CLR with the Database Engine; others are by design. In future releases the limitations will decrease and the features will expand. At this time, SQL Server does not support static or shared .NET components that require persistence of state from one reference to that component to the next.

As a simple example, a classic database auto-incrementing value could not be implemented as an in-memory CLR function. This is because static persistence of state between invocations of the CLR function is not permitted. It simply can't remember the last value used each time a function is called. This is very similar to the behavior of a T-SQL function or procedure.

Only a subset of the rich .NET base class libraries are available to the server-side SQL Server–integrated CLR. For example, the `System.Windows.Forms` and `System.Drawing` namespaces cannot be used at the database because the notion of user interface (UI) controls does not exist at the database. Only the available base classes are shown in the dialog used to add references to a CLR integration project in Visual Studio.

In addition, there are a number of limitations to the general .NET object-oriented programming (OOP) model when database objects are defined using CLR integration. These limitations, along with the many empowering features of programming CLR assemblies for use within SQL Server, will be further illuminated in the discussion that follows.

Microsoft recognized that acceptance of this .NET Framework and SQL Server technology integration by the current community of database administrators and server-side T-SQL developers will be a valuable win in gaining early acceptance of this new database feature family. Undoubtedly, they also recognized that many of those same people lack the background and training necessary to adequately lead the way in building database components that can truly exploit the power and flexibility of CLR integration. This chapter is organized to aid administrators and developers in understanding CLR integration.

The chapter opens by introducing the .NET Framework. It then describes how to use Visual Studio to create database components that run in the CLR. Next you'll read a survey of the .NET Framework architecture components intended to support CLR integration. Building on these basics, the chapter provides some example components, which demonstrate each of the new database types that are available with the integration of the CLR into SQL Server 2005. Finally, the chapter provides some considerations for when to use CLR integration components.

.NET Framework Crash Course

The Microsoft .NET Framework is an application services component of the Windows operating system. The .NET Framework's purpose is to provide a safe and robust application development and execution environment in which multiple programming languages share a rich collection of common libraries.

Applications built upon the .NET Framework are created according to industry-standard service-oriented architecture (SOA) protocols such as XML to enable open communication with other application components that may or may not be .NET-based or even running on Windows boxes.

Processes created using the .NET Framework are by default designed not to undermine the integrity of the operating environment should the process fail or attempt an illegal operation.

The .NET Framework holds the promise of heretofore unrealized Windows scalability and performance, though with Version 2.0 the performance remains constrained by the interests of interoperability and integration across the Microsoft software base. For this release, the performance objectives seem to have been to offer performance comparable to existing APIs such as COM and OLE-DB. In the main, these objectives appear to have been realized, and in some cases even eclipsed. In future revisions it is reasonable to expect significant additional performance gains.

The .NET Framework is available to the Windows 2000, Windows 2003, Windows XP, and Windows CE operating systems, as well as future versions of Windows such as Longhorn. Flexible versioning allows different builds of the .NET Framework base class libraries to be available to different applications running on a particular machine at the same time. This is intended to alleviate the rigidity of the previous .dll registration model familiar to many developers.

Assemblies

.NET components called *assemblies* are the basic unit of compilation. Assemblies use a strong naming convention to uniquely identify versions and can reside with the application or in a hierarchy in the windows system environment know as the global assembly cache, or GAC. (Like the CLR acronym, some developers pronounce the individual letters and others use a single Klingon-sounding syllable, "gack," which rhymes with tack.) By default, the common .NET Framework class libraries are located in the GAC. Regardless of the programming language used, all .NET applications can access the same common libraries of the GAC.

.NET applications use a two-stage compilation process. Assemblies are stored in Microsoft's Intermediate Language (IL or MSIL). Usually this is pronounced with the individual letters IL, or sometimes as "missile." While the developer writes code in her favorite .NET language, when the work is compiled the instructions are converted to IL and stored in an assembly. Generally speaking, the generated IL is identical regardless of the programming language used to code the application.

At execution time, the IL is converted to machine instructions by the Just in Time (JIT) compiler of the CLR and loaded into memory. The CLR is smart about when IL is converted to machine code, striving to move instructions to memory only as needed and to move code out of memory when no longer needed. This latter activity is commonly known as *garbage collection*.

All types are validated by the JIT compiler at runtime. Other security, whether by certificate, signing, policy, and so on, is also enforced at execution time. Therein lies the portability magic of the .NET Framework. As long as the operating system can speak IL and the IL is allowed to run locally, the application can run on that machine.

The basic .NET Framework component is a type. A type can be a value or a reference. Value types have the following characteristics:

✦ They include primitives such as integer, char, or Boolean.

✦ They are maintained on the execution stack.

✦ They cannot include fields, methods or properties.

✦ They are uniquely assigned to variables.

Reference types have these characteristics:

✦ They include objects such as class, interface, delegate, array, and enumeration.

✦ They are maintained in a managed object heap separate from the execution stack.

✦ They can include fields, methods, and properties.

✦ They are shared by all variables assigned to the type.

Using CLR integration, the developer can extend a primitive to include fields, methods, and primitives. In doing so, the primitive value type is transformed into a reference type.

Only types that conform to the .NET Framework's common type system (CTS) specification can load and execute in the CLR. These are said to be *managed types*. According to the .NET Framework architecture, all programming languages that comply with the CTS should generate identical managed types. In practice there are some differences between the .NET languages. The Framework provides the common language specification (CLS) to reconcile the language differences. Compliance to the CLS is the shared responsibility of the developer and the compiler. Only if code is CLS compliant is the IL produced guaranteed to be accessible by any other language that produces managed types. Note that only CTS and not necessarily CLS compliance is required for components to run in the CLR. CLS compliance only ensures that components written in other .NET programming languages can properly use the assembly. Furthermore, only the publicly exposed types and members of a component need to be CLS-compliant in order for the assembly to be legitimately CLS compliant.

Tip   The CTS specification, including the CLS, can be found in the .NET Framework SDK documentation available in the Visual Studio 2005 documentation, as well as on the Microsoft website.

The basic unit for compilation, distribution, reuse, versioning, and security in the .NET Framework is the assembly. In object-oriented programming (OOP) terminology, this can be considered the boundary of encapsulation; and indeed the .NET Framework is object oriented. See the following sidebar for some additional references for OOP technology and Microsoft's .NET implementation of OOP technology. An assembly contains the executable code as IL and all metadata resources for one or more types. Much of the metadata is information about the types contained in the assembly. Each assembly also includes a *metadata manifest*. The manifest includes the friendly name and the attributes that comprise the strong name for the assembly, provided of course the assembly was created with a strong name. The manifest also includes the assembly's references. The references are a complete listing of any dependent assemblies for the assembly. From the assembly manifest, the JIT compiler can efficiently convert an assembly's IL to machine instructions as needed.

App Domains

The basic unit of memory workspace of a running .NET application is an *application domain,* commonly called an *app domain*. In theory, a .NET application can discover assemblies either when the application is compiled or when the application is executed, in a manner similar to ActiveX early binding and late binding. In practice, the behavior can be somewhat confusing without a solid understanding of the multi-layered lookup methods used to bring the assemblies of an application into the app domain.

The assembly manifest defines the set of assemblies that the JIT compiler will include in a specific app domain. While many app domains can run in a single process, the app domain is the scope of type safety. A type cannot reference code or resources outside of its app domain unless specific remoting protocol rules have been satisfied that will ensure the integrity of each process. Remoting is a stateful interprocess communication mechanism. It uses a listener on the server to enable clients to create a reference to an object that can exist anywhere outside the client app domain.

Microsoft's Object-Oriented Technology

A thorough introduction to object-oriented programming (OOP) is beyond the scope of the *SQL Server 2005 Bible*. However, it is recognized that many readers are coming from a SQL Server environment in which the closest thing to a real programming language is T-SQL. This sidebar is intended to help any readers with limited experience find additional learning resources on the path to producing rich and powerful OOP code using the .NET Framework.

Readers with little or no OOP background should not be discouraged by the amount of new server-side development technology that accompanies the CLR. Take comfort that understanding how the Database Engine works will continue to be most useful whether database components are compiled in the .NET Framework or loaded as conventional T-SQL objects. Developers more familiar with .NET and developers more familiar with SQL Server now have a better reason than ever to work collaboratively. Whenever possible, server-side developers should consider using CLR integration to learn from front-end and mid-tier programmers, while at the same time sharing with them knowledge about SQL Server's behaviors and internals. Everybody wins.

Readers who want to better understand the fundamentals of OOP may want to consider the classic OOP title *Object-Oriented Programming*, by Peter Coad and Jill Nicola (ISBN 013032616X) or the quick reading *OOP Demystified*, by Jim Koegh and Mario Davidson (ISBN 0072253630).

Readers already comfortable with OOP may want to focus directly on understanding the .NET OOP implementation. For a VB.NET-focused exploration, consider *Building Applications and Components with Visual Basic .NET*, by Ted Pattison and D. Joe Hummel (ISBN 0201734958). Readers more interested in C# programming may want to check out *An Information Systems Approach to Object-Oriented Programming Using Microsoft Visual C# .NET*, by Kyle Lutes, Alka Herriger, and Jack Purdam (ISBN 0619217359).

Of course, the Visual Studio 2005 documentation is also a good place to find additional details on the .NET-specific OOP implementation.

Remoting aside, the assembly manifest metadata of one app domain's assembly must be known before an assembly from another app domain can reference that assembly. This is true regardless of whether the app domains are running in the same process, running different processes on the same operating system instance, or running on different machines in different parts of the world. Essentially, this requires that each of the assemblies that must communicate or share resources across app domains be compiled to IL with a reference to the assembly being referenced in the other app domain. In some cases, remoting between app domains is desirable for performance or security reasons, but the stringent rules are an indication that XML is a more flexible and preferred method of inter-app domain communication than trying to share safe types across app domains in most cases.

Caution　　Remoting, in its simplest terms, is the .NET version of DCOM. Developers may naturally want to pursue the possibility of using remoting to avoid the need to include explicit manifest references to user-defined types defined in SQL Server in application-tier assemblies. In the unlikely event that remoting could actually be used to create references to types inside the SQL Server process, the solution would be very complex, and would by definition expose the SQL Server. It's unlikely that such an approach would be worth the risk or the development effort in most cases.

Applications containing only managed types written using the .NET Framework are said to be *managed code*. Managed code differs from unmanaged code in that the runtime environment for managed code is abstracted from the hardware and operating system into the common language runtime (CLR) environment. It is permissible for a programmer to circumvent this safe mode of execution, especially considering the large body of existing legacy code that will be impractical to rewrite immediately, if at all, into .NET-managed code. For example, unmanaged COM components can be referenced using system supplied primary interop assemblies (PIAs) when available, or other non-COM library functions can be executed using the Platform Invoke mechanism.

Best Practice

A C++ (or, to a limited degree, a C#) programmer can allocate memory and use pointers to reference memory. Unfortunately, this capability to opt out of type safety implies that the door is not completely closed for building applications that can bring the operating environment down. For this reason alone, one of the most important steps to take in protecting the SQL Server is to build and deploy only CLS-compliant type-safe assemblies at the database server.

Cross-Reference

Additional information on primary interop assemblies can be found in Chapter 30, "Programming with ADO .NET 2.0."

It should be evident that .NET code can exist in multiple locations in reference to the application that might use it. This reality affords a good opportunity to highlight a new kind of security facility built into the CLR: *code access security (CAS)*. CAS ensures that all managed code uses safe methods to access types. Like the CLS, it is the duty of the compiler to verify this type safety. It is the responsibility of the developer to write verifiably CAS type-safe code. CAS provides security syntax so developers can declaratively set permissions properties or imperatively create permission objects.

As anticipated by the CAS model, each assembly identifies the permissions it needs in its manifest. Because the assembly manifest is the entry point to the assembly at runtime, the requested permissions for the assembly are checked before any code is executed in that assembly. Reciprocally, secure class libraries ensure that the caller has the necessary permissions to use that class library. CAS goes beyond the traditional user authentication and user permission security model. With CAS, code is making sure that other pieces of code have the correct authority to interact.

It is very important that developers write CAS-aware code. Failure to do so can bring the server down. Fortunately, CLR integration does even more than other .NET code to ensure that the code running within SQL Server is CAS compliant. The CLR runtime environment within SQL Server provides partial classes for the developer that combine with other code behind the scenes to create CLR database components. Within the part of the class that the developer does not manipulate are some important CAS-compliant security instructions.

When SQL Server JITs (Just in Time compiles) the code, it is checked for CAS code security, type safety is verified, and SQL Server permissions are checked. As a .NET database component is coded, it is marked as either SAFE, EXTERNAL ACCESS, or UNSAFE. This establishes the programming model restrictions to be used and determines the CAS declarations and imperatives that will be used by that assembly.

To build CLS-compliant assemblies, the developer must adhere to the CLS rules as spelled out in the document *Common Language Infrastructure, Partition I: Concepts and Architecture,* which can be found in the Tool Developers Guide folder installed with the Microsoft .NET Framework SDK. Even if the developer follows the specification to the letter, a CLS-compliant compiler is also necessary to ensure CLS-compliant assemblies. All Visual Studio 2005 compilers are capable of CLS compliance. CLS compliance should be considered a requirement for CLR integration components simply because there is no way to anticipate the languages that may need to interact with a particular database object. Consider building database-integrated CLR objects using VB.NET and the Visual Studio 2005 to keep the CLS compliance very nearly effortless.

When is VB.NET the better choice for CLS compliance? It is true that the C++ and C# compilers in Visual Studio 2005 are capable of producing CLS-compliant code, as is the VB compiler. For developers new to programming in the .NET Framework, VB.NET is the most likely to help you write CLS-compliant code. VB.NET is intended to be the easiest .NET language to use, and it is targeted at *rapid application development (RAD)* environments. Generally speaking, VB.NET exposes only CLS-compliant instructions. Of course, the choice is ultimately yours; and if you are already familiar with a particular managed language, then using that language may be the better choice. If you are new to programming in the .NET Framework or work primarily in a RAD environment, give strong consideration to developing your database components with VB.NET.

What makes Visual Studio the better choice for a compiler host? The simple answer is all the other features and facilities that Visual Studio offers. The same VB.NET compiler ships with the .NET Framework SDK, so it is technically possible to write VB code using no more than Notepad, and compile it at the command line to produce fully CLS-compliant binaries. Some would even argue that it is necessary to understand how such things work at the lowest level before moving up to an elegant tool such as Visual Studio.

There may be some academic merit to that outlook, but by no means is it necessary to struggle with the unassisted text editor coding or the command-line compiler. Maximum benefit and code quality are enabled from Visual Studio. You may indeed feel a greater connection to the programming language when using the SDK directly, but it's almost certain that developers who jump right into Visual Studio will deploy their first successful .NET database component long before developers who start out with the SDK. For most developers new to the .NET Framework, there are more than enough new concepts to master without adding to the challenge unnecessarily. As you will see, the features of Visual Studio 2005 make it unquestionably the better choice. Before looking more closely at the tools used to build CLR integration types, consider the types that can be built.

Overview of the CLR SQL Server Types

Five kinds of SQL Server objects can be created for SQL Server 2005 using the .NET Framework:

✦ Stored procedures

✦ Functions

✦ Triggers

✦ User-defined types

✦ User-defined aggregations

The first three are extensions to functionality that has been available using T-SQL in previous versions of SQL Server. The T-SQL counterparts for these objects remain available and even improved in SQL Server 2005. Later in this chapter you will see when to use the CLR type and when to use the tried and true T-SQL object. The remaining two database object types that can be created using CLR integration — user-defined types (UDT) and user-defined aggregations (UDAs) — are new in SQL Server 2005. This section of the chapter explores the commonalties among the five CLR SQL Server types, and then the unique characteristics of each are considered.

CLR Integration .NET Type Attributes

Earlier, the concept of a .NET framework app domain was described. In SQL Server the app domain is defined by the object owner. Object owner is a database-scoped principal. This means that the app domain or basic level of code isolation for CLR integration is all objects owned by the same user or role within the current database.

Additional information on principals can be found in Chapter 40, "Securing Databases."

SQL Server CLR objects always include self-describing metadata elements known as *attributes*. Attributes are used throughout the .NET Framework to determine the intention of a particular assembly, class, method, property, events, or type. For example, an attribute can be used to define a method as CLS compliant. Or, looking ahead to the upcoming chapter on using Web Services, an attribute is used to mark a method as a Web Service for objects outside of that method's app domain.

Web Services are discussed in detail in Chapter 32, "Building an SOA Data Store with Web Services."

The SQL Server object type named attributes are more correctly known as .NET Framework custom attributes. The developers of CLR integration at Microsoft created derived class extensions from System.Attribute to interpret these attributes. Custom attributes are evaluated when the type is imported into SQL Server and when the type is JITed into the runtime environment. For SQL Server objects, the custom attributes define which of the five database object types is in the source. The custom attributes also provide all the information SQL Server needs to import the object at deployment. Any relevant custom attributes are also evaluated when the CREATE OBJECT T-SQL statement is executed for that object after it has been imported.

Best Practice

Place custom attribute blocks immediately before the source code being attributed in the source file. The custom attribute block can also be placed at the beginning of the source file if an attribute modifier is specified to define where the attribute will be applied. However, the relationship between the attribute and the code being attributed is not visually obvious for someone maintaining unfamiliar code. SQL Server object templates in Visual Studio 2005 will always use the first method. Each attribute is enclosed in an angle bracket pair ("<", ">") and includes the attribute name followed by a set of required positional parameters and then a list of optional attribute arguments. The attributes for SQL Server objects are nicely self-documenting.

Following are some examples of VB.NET database object type custom attributes as generated by the SQL Server Object templates in Visual Studio 2005:

```
<SqlProcedure()> _

<SqlTrigger(Name:="name", Target:="Table", Event:="FOR UPDATE")> _

<SqlFunction()> _

<Serializable()> _
<SqlUserDefinedType(Format.Native)> _
      <SqlMethod> _
      <SqlFacet> _

<Serializable()> _
<SqlUserDefinedAggregate(Format.Native)> _
```

However, as discussed in greater detail later, setting the argument lists can be technically perplexing. Note that the `SqlProcedure` attribute does not take any arguments and that the other SQL Server type attributes receive default values if not specified.

The template also presents the `Serializable` attribute with the UDT and UDA types. `Serializable` is a system attribute, rather than a custom attribute, that is used at runtime instead of at upload time. Serializable means that the object being attributed can write its state to the database — or some other permanent store — and then later read that exact state back out of the permanent store. Serialization is an important attribute for any UDT or UDA that must be materialized and indexed in the database. Types that are not serialized may not be sorted, and their use may be disqualified in some cases. For example, types not serialized may not be indexed, ordered, grouped, compared or persisted when used as computed columns in the database.

User-defined types may include two attributed members: `SqlMethod`, which inherits from `SqlFunction`, and `SqlFacet`, which is used to describe the return type of the UDT.

The SQL Server object custom attribute serves as a prototype for the constructor of the underlying class for that type. Certainly this is not the only way that attributes are used in the .NET Framework. Recall that instances of the class are created by calling the new method of the class. An explicit call to create a new instance of a stored procedure, for example, is never seen in user code. However, when a CLR stored procedure is created, the CLR will indeed be calling the constructor of the class each time that CLR stored procedure is executed.

Shared Features of SQL Server CLR Types

In fact, the execution environment is worthy of coverage as a common feature of the five SQL Server object types. In the .NET Framework crash course that instantiated this chapter, the mechanical cogs of the CLR were described: Developer code is precompiled into Intermediate Language (IL) that is programming language independent. When code is referenced in the execution environment, a Just in Time (JIT) compiler loads the IL into memory as machine language instructions. The most conventional .NET code would JIT the IL into instructions that a Windows OS would process. CLR integration means that the JIT compiler will read the IL from database tables, rather than from a .dll library file. The compiler creates instructions that SQL Server stores, schedules, and processes in SQL Server memory space. This puts SQL server in the business of not only managing the traditional kernel, data cache, procedure cache, and the already troublesome MemToLeave, but also a fully pre-emptive, potentially processor-intensive compiled execution environment. At first blush, that should scare the bejesus out of every *SQL Server 2005 Bible* reader.

The saving grace is that little will happen when a CLR component is called unless the CLR has been enabled on the SQL Server. By default, CLR is disabled. To enable the CLR execution environment, use the SQL Server Surface Area Configuration Tool or run the T-SQL sp_configure command, as shown here:

```
exec sp_configure 'clr enabled', 1
reconfigure with override
```

Once the CLR is enabled, when a CLR integration component is called, it will be JITed into memory on first use. The machine instructions will remain available in memory until it ages out or the SQL Server service is stopped. The first time an object is instantiated, there is a JIT-related performance penalty. After that initial compile, the object should be available as a binary element of the kernel, much like intrinsic functions and data types.

It may be somewhat unrealistic to expect the CLR to perform comparably to system functions, but it is valid, for example, to expect a CLR date/time-based inline function to perform much more in line with the SQL Server built-in DATETADD() function than will a T-SQL defined inline function used in the where clause of a range query involving many rows. The CLR function will not be quite as fast as the built-in function, though the CLR function will behave and perform much more like the built-in than a T-SQL function in a set-based query context.

Data Types

Before examining the attribute arguments and other unique characteristics of each SQL Server object type, some attention must be given to a significant commonality among them: data types. In a manner no less unlikely than the way the non-yielding SQL Server execution environment hosts the preemptive CLR execution environment, the CLR must also bring together the native SQL Server data types and the .NET Framework data types. Numeric .NET data types are considered value types. Value types are generally managed on the call stack memory space. Character .NET data types are referenced objects and always use memory that is separate from the call stack, in what is known as the *managed object heap.*

Data types that inherit from an object — anything on the managed object heap inherits from the common base class "object" — are impressive. Such types can have members including properties and methods to make manipulation much more flexible than primitive value data types. A value type can be moved or boxed from the call stack to the object heap if it is defined or used as if it had properties, methods, or fields. Boxing may be explicit or implicit.

Tip It is sometimes useful to force a primitive into the managed heap to give it object-like behavior. This is known as *boxing.* Classic database examples in which boxing might occur would be when dates are stored as character literals in the database or when an integral value must be compared to a column containing character data. The thing about boxing is that comparing tens of thousands of rows based on a column that is a reference type in CLR code will degrade performance if the data is actually of a value type. It will not be readily obvious that a particular data access operation is suffering from the side effects of boxing. Typically, issues surrounding boxing will begin to emerge as the community gains some experience with CLR integration and it becomes possible to perceptively identify CLR types that seem to run inexplicably slower than other CLR types. It is possible to look at the IL to establish whether boxing is occurring. Readers interested in pursuing such research are encouraged to investigate the IL disassembler utility, ILDASM.EXE, shipped with Visual Studio 2005.

Data types in CLR code can be challenging. One of the biggest issues is the fact that primitive data types in the .NET Framework are not null aware. In SQL Server, null indicates that an entity attribute has no value; therefore, by ANSI default, it cannot be compared in an equality expression or considered in an aggregation, among other things. Primitive data types in the CLR programming model lack this concept of null. Fortunately, there is a collection of data types available in the `System.Data.SqlTypes` namespace that map directly to the internal SQL Server data type. All of these types implement the `INullable` interface. That doesn't mean the challenges of data type mapping between .NET and SQL Server are eliminated, but it does provide a great deal of help. For example, if you need to compare a database decimal value with a precision greater than 28 to a real-time measurement value stored in a .NET decimal, it will be necessary to convert the .NET decimal to a `SqlDecimal` to avoid a possible exception in the code. In a similar but opposite scenario, a `SqlMoney` value could be overflowed if compared to a .NET decimal value that originated from a provider other than SQL Server.

For the developer writing only in the CAS "SAFE" mode, CLR database components using the types from the `Sytem.Data.SqlTypes` namespace will provide a cleaner connection between CLR integration components and the database. In addition, using the `SqlTypes` for data that originates in the database will make the code inherently faster because the .NET Framework types will be implicitly converted to `SqlTypes` by the CLR when they are sent to the database, and either the `SqlType` or the .NET data type must be explicitly converted for other comparison or assignment operations from one to the other. Table 27-1 lists the native SQL Server data types as enumerated by `System.Data.SqlDBType`, the matching `System.Data.SqlTypes`, and the equivalent intrinsic .NET Framework data types. Comments are included where particular issues have been noted by the author.

Table 27-1: SQL Server/CLR/.NET Data Types

SQL Server Native Data Type	CLR SQL Server Integration Data Type	CLR .NET Framework Data Type	Comments
Bigint	SqlInt64	Int64	
Binary, Varbinary, Varbinary(MAX)	SqlBytes, SqlBinary	Byte[]	
Bit	SqlBoolean	Boolean	
Char, NChar, Nvarchar, NvarChar(MAX), sysname, Varchar, Varchar(MAX)	SqlChars, SqlString	String, Char[]	All character data is Unicode in the .NET Framework.
Datetime, SmallDateTime	SqlDateTime	DateTime	

Continued

Table 27-1 *(continued)*

SQL Server Native Data Type	CLR SQL Server Integration Data Type	CLR .NET Framework Data Type	Comments
Decimal, Numeric	SqlDecimal	Decimal	+/-10^38 +1 in SQL Server and SQLDecimal, .NET decimal range is less: +/7.9228162514264337 593543950335E+28.
Float	SqlDouble	Double	SQL mantissa is scalable, default is float(53).
Image		Byte[], BitMap	All binary objects are streamed in and out of the database as SQLBinary.
Int	SqlInt32	Int32	
Money Smallmoney	SqlMoney	Decimal	SqlMoney range is 2^63, expressed to the one ten thousandth of the currency unit.
Ntext, Text			
Real	SqlSingle	Single	The SQL-92 real equivalent is float(24).
Smallint	SqlInt16	Int16	
SQL_variant	None	Object	
Table		ISqlResultSet	
Timestamp		Byte[]	
Tinyint	SqlByte	Byte	
User Defined Type	None		The UDT assembly must be provided at the client in order for the application to have knowledge of it.
Uniqueidentifier	SqlGuid	Guid	
Xml	SqlXml	None	

.NET Methods That Support CLR Integration

Most of the rich programming structure of the .NET Framework is available to the developer who is building CLR database components through the SqlClient namespace. There is a set of classes in this namespace defined for returning results and messages to the requesting application. Another set of classes is used for database access operations from CLR integration types.

 Cross-Reference Details on System.Data.SqlClient data access are found in Chapter 30, "Programming with ADO.NET 2.0."

Some operations (e.g., bulk loading, MARS, asynchronous execute, SQLNotoficationRequest, and update batching) will be allowed only if the connection is not the in-process local context. While most of the server-side functionality is now integrated into the SqlClient, there are a number of classes for very important objects used for server-side processing in the Microsoft.SqlServer.Server namespace in the System.Data assembly. These classes provide support for specialized activities required only within the in-process context — most notably, explicitly naming the connection as "the current context," delivering results and messages to the requestor or client, and performing data access operations using the in-process connection context.

Tip The vision for CLR integration going into the SQL Server 2005 development cycle appears to have been to encapsulate the CLR integration in-process server-side context in isolation from the SqlClient out-of-process networked execution context. One of the expected benefits of this isolation was that it provided an ability to support server cursors at the server yet avoid the scalability limitations of server API cursors at the client. It eventually emerged that the technology was such that if server cursors were to be supported in CLR integration code, it should also be exposed to the SqlClient namespace. Shortly thereafter, the final realignment emerged, resulting in the assimilation of the in-process server-side execution context into the SqlClient. The fallout for developers from this rather significant change so late in the development process is hundreds of examples are circulating on the Internet and perhaps even in the Microsoft newsgroups that were created before the dust settled on these changes. If sample code is encountered that references the System.Data.SqlServer namespace, it's a safe bet that this code pre-dates the RTM release of SQL Server 2005. It was very late in the .Net Framework 2.0 development cycle that CLR integration components appear in the System.Data.SqlClient namespace. Server-side processing is now a mode within the SqlClient that is set and recognized by the connection string, as shown here:

```
Dim cnSQL As SQLConnection = _
    New SQLConnection("context connection=true")
```

The actual definition for the connection context is found in the Microsoft.SqlServer.Server namespace in Visual Studio 2005.

Developers frequently find advantage in working with example code. Given that the beta cycles for SQL Server 2005 were some of the most public pre-release software development cycles ever, a huge amount of sample code is available that predates the release. The samples remain useful in most cases provided that developers are aware that the namespace references may need some correction before the example code is functional.

The `Microsoft.SqlServer.Server.SqlContext` class is used to set up specialized SQL Server server-side components. Opening a communication protocol to a requesting application or client is done through the `SqlContext.Pipe()` property. This property is used to move result sets and messages from a CLR integration stored procedure and the requesting application. `SqlContext.Pipe()` provides the overloaded `Send` method, which can return a message (discussed in greater detail later in this chapter):

```
pPipe.Send(System.Data.String)
```

an error:

```
pPipe.Send(System.Data.SqlClient.Error)
```

a result set:

```
pPipe.Send(System.Data.Sql.ISqlReader)
```

or a row of data, depending upon the argument provided:

```
pPipe.Send(System.Data.Sql.ISqlRecord)
```

When returning results, `Pipe.Send` can deliver data from an already executed query and build a `DataReader` on a `DataSet` or send a `DataReader` built directly from a forward-only or firehose result set from the database.

Best Practice

The communication pipe is intended primarily for procedures and functions, but it can also be used with triggers. As with T-SQL triggers, sending messages from underneath the data is potentially risky because there is no way to be certain that the message has a chance to be heard.

The `SqlContext` object provides a useful class of information within triggers through the `SqlContext.TriggerContext()` property, which identifies the `Microsoft.SqlServer.Server.TriggerAction` enum that caused a DDL or DML trigger to fire.

One of the great benefits of combining the functionality of the short-lived `System.Data.SqlServer` namespace into the `System.Data.SqlClient` namespace is a reduction in the number of different technologies needed to effectively implement CLR integration. Other than the few members that are now in the `Microsoft.SqlServer.Server` namespace and the small number of connection context restricted features, the tools used to build data access code are the same regardless of whether the code will be deployed at the server or at another application layer.

T-SQL CLR DDL Commands and Catalog Views

Loading CLT types into SQL Server requires the creation of two database objects. In all cases, the assembly that contains the type(s) must first be created; then the CLR type(s) in that assembly are created. Creating the assembly is essentially the act of validating and loading the IL into the `sysassemblies` catalog view. No usable artifacts are created solely by the execution of CREATE ASSEMBLY. The assembly hierarchy consists of the following three views:

✦ `sysassemblies`: Contains one row of metadata for each assembly, including the assembly name and CAS security mode

✦ `sysassembly_files`: Contains the IL binary data for each file in the assembly

✦ `sysassembly_references`: Contains one row for each assembly referenced by the current assembly's manifest

Assemblies

The `CREATE ASSEMBLY` DDL statement provides all the information necessary to populate the catalog view. Multiple versions of a strongly named assembly can exist on the server at the same time. Multiple copies of the same assembly version cannot exist on the SQL Server at the same time. To replace a simply named assembly or a particular version of a strongly named assembly, it is necessary to first drop the existing assembly using `DROP ASSEMBLY`. It is also possible to modify an assembly using `ALTER ASSEMBLY`. The current NT login account must have read access to the UNC file system location where the assembly .dll will be loaded. Even if the development project consists of multiple source files, the `CREATE ASSEMBLY` command requires that only assemblies consisting of one IL file can be loaded into the SQL Server. Delegation is not supported through the `CREATE ASSEMBLY` command. All referenced assemblies and their manifests must be available at the same network location as the assembly or the `create` command will fail.

Tip Always create assemblies for the production SQL Server environment with strong names.

`CREATE ASSEMBLY`, `DROP ASSEMBLY`, and `ALTER ASSEMBLY` are by default granted to `sysadmin` server role members and `db_owner` database role members. Permission to execute any of the commands is grantable to other users. If the CAS security for the assembly is `EXTERNAL_ACCESS`, then the login user creating the assembly must also have `EXTERNAL_ACCESS` permissions:

`GRANT EXTERNAL_ACCESS to <Windows user or group>`

If the assembly security is `unsafe`, only a member of the `sysadmin` server role can create the assembly.

Database Objects

After the assembly is created, any types from that assembly can be created using the `CREATE` DDL commands for the appropriate type. The DDL commands and the catalog views populated include the following:

✦ `CREATE PROCEDURE`: `sysobjects` with type = "PC"

✦ `CREATE FUNCTION`: `sysobjects` with type = "FS" if scalar function, type = "FT" if table-valued function

✦ `CREATE TRIGGER`: `systriggers` with `parent_class` = 0 from DDL triggers and 1 for DML triggers. `sysobjects` also populated with type = "TR" for DML triggers but not populated for DDL triggers

✦ CREATE TYPE: `systypes` with `is_user_type` = 1 and `is_assembly_type` = 1

✦ CREATE AGGREGATE: `sysobjects` with **type** = "AF"

The user creating CLR types in a database must either own the assembly or be granted the REFERENCES permission on the assembly:

```
GRANT REFERENCES ON <assembly name> TO <Windows user or Group>
```

A dynamic management view is available to see the assemblies that have been JITed on the server:

```
sysdm_loaded_assemblies
```

A typical query to determine the assemblies currently used in a database might be written as follows:

```
SELECT a.clr_name
   , USER_NAME(a.principal_id) as [principal]
   , la.load_time
   , a.permission_set_desc
FROM sysdm_clr_loaded_assemblies la
JOIN sysassemblies a
ON la.assembly_id = a.assembly_id
```

Visual Studio 2005 provides GUI functionality that will deploy CLR Integration objects to a specified database. During deployment, both the CREATE ASSEMBLY and DDL CREATE statements are executed behind the scenes. Administrators and developers must also understand how both statements are used to load CLR integration components into the database. It is very unlikely that deploying to production using Visual Studio will be an acceptable practice.

Building Database Types with Visual Studio 2005

CLR stored procedures, functions, and triggers, such as T-SQL stored procedures, functions, and triggers, have more similarities than differences. Generally speaking these CLR types will consist of a single method. Conversely, a UDT or UDA is not at all like a CLR stored procedure, function, or trigger.

The UDT or UDA can be a `struct` or a class. Note that the `struct` is generally preferable because by definition it will be stored on the stack, rather than as a reference type in the object heap. A UDT or UDA written as a class is almost certain to be a reference type and will incur a performance penalty when compared to a `struct`. Whether a `struct` or a class, the UDT or UDA will contain multiple members and must meet a significant number of design criteria. The remainder of this chapter focuses on method-based stored procedure, function, and trigger types.

Cross-Reference   You'll find more information on user-defined types in Chapter 29, "Persisting Custom Data Types."

Creating a CLR Project

The initial steps in creating a CLR integration component with Visual Studio 2005 are almost identical regardless of the component type that will be created. For example, even though by definition a CLR integration project will not require a database connection because it will exist inside the database, when a project is created, Visual Studio will prompt the developer to specify a new or existing database connection. This connection will be used for development and debugging of the component. Be sure to specify the database location where the component is to be unit tested at the time the project is created.

Once a data source is defined, it is possible at any time to right-click on the data source in the Server Explorer to bring up the context menu used to enable debugging for the application, T-SQL objects, and CLR integration types. The user must also have permission to `sp_enable_sql_debug` stored procedure (located in the master database) and ALTER permission on each object being debugged at the database. Note that only database administrators can debug CLR types that employ the `Execute as` clause or use a certificate, and only one type at a time can be debugged on a server. All other CLR threads are frozen on the server during the debugging session. This is probably not ideal for a shared server such as those used for integration testing. CLR debugging is best suited for a unit test environment in which the database server is an instance dedicated to a single developer's use.

Best Practice

CLR integration development and testing requires Visual Studio 2005 and SQL Server 2005. Debugging and collaboration while debugging are not well supported if a shared SQL Server is used. The preferred configuration for a developer creating enterprise-class CLT objects is a workstation with Visual Studio and a full SQL Server Developer Edition on the local machine. Developers working on components for distributed or federated database applications may wish to consider a local workstation with adequate resources to support virtual server instances to adequately model the production environment. Virtual environments are superior to named SQL Server instances to ensure that security considerations are implemented at the initial development stages.

After the development data source is set, the New Project dialog shown in Figure 27-1 appears. Select the database project type under the language that will be used to code the type. Give careful consideration to naming the project at this time. Some shops may elect to keep multiple CLR integration types in a single project, while others may determine that each type should be a separate project. Factors driving this decision include the number of developers, the complexity of the types, and the amount of code reuse between types.

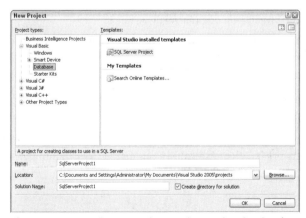

Figure 27-1: Creating a CLR integration project in Visual Studio 2005. After selecting the database type under the desired programming language on the left, select the SQL Server Project template.

Once the project is created, the template for the type to be coded can be added to the project by right-clicking the project name in the Solution Explorer and selecting the Add option or by selecting the project menu option in the main Visual Studio menu. The Solution Explorer context menu is shown in Figure 27-2. Using the Solution Explorer project context menu is convenient because it provides a single location for the most common Visual Studio activities while creating a CLR type. From this context menu, the Properties dialog for the project can be selected to display the Project Designer dialog. Use Project Designer to specify a strong name, set the CAS permission level for the assembly, and set the compile and deployment options for the project.

Whenever an assembly can be used by multiple applications, Microsoft recommends giving that assembly a strong name. A strong name creates a globally unique identity for an assembly or manifest consisting of the textual name, a version number, optional culture information, the public part of a private/public key pair, and a digital signature. Because there is no practical way to prevent multiple applications from using the database and generally it is undesirable to do so, all CLR integration components should be strongly named.

The public/private key pair used for signing is created using the command-line Strong Name Tool—sn.exe. The key pair generated by the Strong Name Tool is stored in a .snk text file if it is in a *cryptographic service provider (CSP)* container. The public-private key-pair file or CSP container can be generated, and signing the assembly can be completed at compile time using the information entered in the Project Designers Signing and Publish tabs. Careful consideration must be given to the signing strategy for the enterprise. In almost all cases a key shared by all components of an application will be desirable. The shop may choose to closely guard the private key and exclusively use delayed assembly signing. In this scenario, the assembly is signed by one of a few trusted persons to ensure that only the desired assemblies are loaded to the production SQL Server.

There are options to Build, Clean, Rebuild, and Deploy from the Solution Explorer context menu. These compiling options are also found under Visual Studio's main menu Build option:

✦ **Build:** This will recompile to IL only those project files and components that have changed since the last build.

✦ **Clean:** This will remove all compiled IL and output files from the project.

✦ **Rebuild:** This will clean the project and compile all files.

✦ **Deploy:** This will build, not rebuild, the project and load the assembly and all types in the assembly into the database specified as the data source for the project.

Run profiler on that data source SQL Server during deploy to see the CREATE ASSEMBLY and CREATE <object> generated by Visual Studio. The deployment option is a powerful development tool that will generate the DROP and CREATE the assembly and the DROP and CREATE type statements on the development SQL Server. It is doubtful that this will provide a useful method to place CLR objects in the production environment in an enterprise setting. To deploy to production environments as solution, create the IL .dlls using the Create menu option and stage the file at a network location. Assemblies can then be loaded into the database using scripted CREATE ASSEMBLY statements.

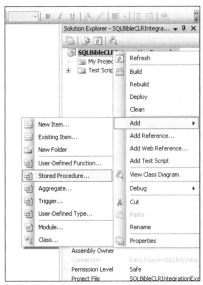

Figure 27-2: Adding a CLR stored procedure to a SQL Server project. The next step is to supply a name for the generated template that includes the custom attributes for a stored procedure and a skeleton for the stored procedure method.

Referring again to Figure 27-2, notice that two kinds of references can be added to the project. The first is a reference to an existing component that will be reused in the current project, and the other is a reference to a Web Service.

Adding a component reference to a CLR integration type provides only a subset of the reference options that are available to other .NET applications. Figure 27-3 shows this reduced list of available .NET common components usable in SQL Server's CLR. References to reusable components created in local projects can also be added by selecting the Projects tab of this dialog. Before local projects are available in the References dialog, the path to the local projects must first be set in the Project Designer.

Referencing an XML Web Service creates a proxy within the project to a `.wsdl` or `.asmx` file. The proxy will enable statement completion while developing the project and enable the CLR integration component to become the client for the specified Web Service. The Web Service definition file can exist on the local server, on the local network, or on the Internet. Once the Web Service is added to the project, the members generated in the proxy can be viewed in the Object Explorer. The potential for consuming Web Services in CLR stored procedures is cool indeed.

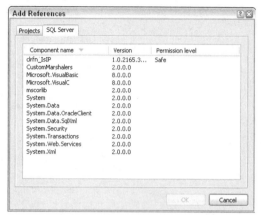

Figure 27-3: Adding a reference to a SQL Server project. Other assembly components in the project space and all available system component assemblies are shown in the dialog box.

Caution   Use care when consuming a Web Service while developing. The generated proxy can execute code on the local machine in the security context of the logged in user at the moment the proxy is opened within the Visual Studio IDE. Depending on what the Web Service does, the local workstation can be overwhelmed by the Web Service's action.

Cross-Reference   See Chapter 31, "Using XML, XPath, and XQuery," and Chapter 32, "Building an SOA Data Store with Web Services," for additional details on using Web Services in SQL Server.

Coding a CLR Stored Procedure

Stored procedures are the most flexible form of the CLR integration types. That's not to say that stored procedures are the easiest or most straightforward of the types. Stored procedures are the most likely object to use EXTERNAL_ACCESS and UNSAFE CAS security. Although in some scenarios it will be useful to look outside of the SQL Server within a function or, even less likely, a trigger, the CLR stored procedure provides a more natural conduit for integration of heterogeneous data stores at the database. The risk of using a function or trigger that becomes involved in a potentially long-running transaction in the preemptive execution environment will be a limiting factor in its usability as a means of interfacing the Database Engine to the outside world. Conversely, .NET Framework stored procedures can easily and safely communicate with the file system.

On The Web   The complete Visual Studio 2005 projects for all the code described here, complete with test scripts, can be downloaded from the *SQL Server 2005 Bible* website, www .SQLServerBible.com.

Consider a CLR stored procedure that serves as a utility to export any data set or collection of data sets from the database to a comma-delimited .csv file. This is a useful example that demonstrates a number of the concepts just discussed. The procedure will do the following:

✦ Read data requiring data access through the connection context

✦ Write to the file system, necessitating EXTERNAL ACCESS CAS security

✦ Provide some informational messaging to the requester, providing an opportunity to use the pipe class

The procedure will accept two arguments:

✦ A valid T-SQL query, function, or stored procedure that returns one or more result sets

✦ A valid filename, including the path

The next code example demonstrates the following parts of the procedure. First, a stored procedure template is created. After adding the stored procedure template to a new database project and adding a reference to the System.IO namespace to the assembly, the stored procedure method can be given an appropriate name and the parameters specified. Next, to access local data, it will be necessary to invoke the in-process connection context. Because the utility procedure must be able to obtain data access by calling a stored procedure, a SQL statement, or perhaps even both, a command object capable of doing both must be provided. Next, it may be useful to report the action about to be completed back to the caller. This is easily accomplished by invoking the SQLPipe and formatting some messages. For example, the input parameters can be sent as informational.

Notice that the stored procedure argument that is declared as a native SqlString type must be converted before it can be used in a .NET operation, whereas the argument declared as a .NET string is usable without conversion. In the latter case, the conversion was done implicitly when the procedure was called, so the cost of the conversion was probably not avoided even if the effort was less for the coder.

Before the SqlConnection can be used it must be opened.

In addition, before the resultant output can be written to a file, a stream to the file must be established. This will be the first use of the System.IO namespace that was added to the assembly previously. Moreover, because the procedure will be using resources outside of the SQL Server context in which it is running, the security mode must be set to EXTERNAL_ACCESS as outlined earlier, and the necessary access rights and permissions in the file system must be specified.

Once the connection is open and the file is ready to receive data, the command can be executed. There are a number of execute methods available for the command. It may be desirable to populate an in-memory DataSet, to stream the results as XML, or even to simply get a scalar value—all of which require the appropriate method. For the CSV utility example, the result will be streamed as a forward-only result set or DataReader using the ExecuteReader method. The ExecuteReader method accepts a CommandBehavior argument that can further tune the result to the requirements at hand. Here, the optional default command behavior is specified and could have been omitted. As an example of other usage, if the requirement for the utility were that only one result set would be processed into the file, rather than *n* number of result sets, then the argument CommandBehavior.SingleResult could have been specified.

When the `DataReader` is executed, the schema for the result sets can easily be identified on-the-fly by creating an untyped in-memory `DataTable` and populating it with a call to the `GetSchemaTable` method of an existing `DataReader`. This method will allow the columns' names to be included in the CSV file.

At last the result set can be sent to the file. Finally, the file stream buffer must be flushed and the stream closed, the `DataReader` must be closed, and the connection closed before the method is ended:

```
Imports System.IO

<Microsoft.SqlServer.Server.SqlProcedure()> _
Public Shared Sub clrusp_ResultToCSVFile(ByVal sTSQL As SqlString, _
                                         ByVal sFile As String)

Dim cnCLR As SqlConnection = New SqlConnection("context connection=true")

Dim qryGetResult As SqlCommand = cnCLR.CreateCommand
qryGetResult.CommandText = CStr(sTSQL)
qryGetResult.CommandType = CommandType.Text

Dim pInfo As SqlPipe = SqlContext.Pipe
pInfo.Send("T-SQL batch to execute: " & CStr(sTSQL))
pInfo.Send("Destination file: " & sFile)

cnCLR.Open()

Dim strmResult As StreamWriter = New StreamWriter(sFile)

Dim sqldrResult As SqlDataReader = _
            qryGetResult.ExecuteReader(CommandBehavior.Default)

Dim sqldrResultSchema As DataTable
sqldrResultSchema = sqldrResult.GetSchemaTable
For Each drRow As DataRow In sqldrResultSchema.Rows
  strmResult.Write(drRow("ColumnName").ToString)
  If CInt(drRow("ColumnOrdinal")) < FieldCount - 1 Then
    strmResult.Write(",", 0, 1)
  Else
    strmResult.Write(vbCrLf, 0, 2)
  End If
Next

If sqldrResult.HasRows Then
  While sqldrResult.Read()
    For i As Int32 = 0 To sqldrResult.FieldCount - 1
      strmResult.Write(sqldrResult.GetSqlValue(i).ToString, 0, _
                       Len(sqldrResult.GetSqlValue(i).ToString))
      If i < sqldrResult.FieldCount - 1 Then
        strmResult.Write(",", 0, 1)
      Else
        strmResult.Write(vbCrLf, 0, 2)
      End If
    Next
  End While
End While
```

```
End If

strmResult.Flush()
strmResult.Close()
sqldrResult.Close()
cnCLR.Close()
```

Of course, a few other things are necessary, such as error handling and processing multiple result sets when they exist. The reader is encouraged to review the full project OntheWebsite.

CLR Functions

A CLR function is less likely to require as much code as a stored procedure. For the same reasons that it is desirable to be concise in a T-SQL function, the CLT function should be narrow in purpose. This will keep transactions as brief as possible and avoid performance degradation that might be hidden in the function's code. A CLR stored procedure could elegantly modify the structure of data within a database, whereas a function should never change the state of the database.

> **Caution** Microsoft has chosen not to restrict functions from making a client-side ADO.NET 2.0 connection from within a CLR function. This means that there is a possibility to change the database state, and there is nothing to prevent such activity from within a function. This possibility flies in the face of everything that is good about CLR functions. Beware of this feature!

Consider how a scalar function might be used to validate an IP address. Such an operation is easy to do with a CLR function that exploits the .NET regular expressions. The function is very powerful because it could be used in DML, in T-SQL stored procedures, or in column check constraints and computed columns.

To create the function simply add an import of the System.Text.RegularExpression namespace to the Visual Studio 2005 Function template, set the function attributes to indicate that the function is deterministic and precise, bang in a couple of lines of code, and deploy the function. This function is useful within a check constraint or an indexed computed column because it will do the necessary string manipulation much faster than a T-SQL equivalent:

```
Imports System.Text.RegularExpression

<Microsoft.SqlServer.Server.SqlFunction _
(DataAccess:=DataAccessKind.None, IsDeterministic:=True, IsPrecise:=True)> _
Public Shared Function clrfn_IsIP(ByVal Value As String) As Boolean
Dim rx As New Regex( _
  "((2[0-4]\d|25[0-5]|[01]?\d\d?)\.){3}(2[0-4]\d|25[0-5]|[01]?\d\d?)", _
      RegexOptions.IgnoreCase _
      Or RegexOptions.IgnorePatternWhitespace)
Return rx.Match(CType(Value, String)).Success
End Function
```

If a function returns a result set rather than a scalar value, the result is a streaming table valued function. The qualifying word here is "streaming." A T-SQL table-valued function will return the entire table before it can be used. This involves a fair amount of memory and tempdb space if the result set is large or the query to produce the result set must consider a large amount of data. The same function written as a streaming CLR function can be consumed as it is created, thereby reducing the memory and `tempdb` requirements dramatically in most cases. Fortunately, table-valued functions do allow the data set to be initialized using the context connection, rather than force the use of a client-side ADO connection. It is worth reiterating: Using a client-side ADO.NET connection, while possible within a function, undermines the role of the function — to efficiently provide data to a non-set-based operation — and should be avoided.

To close this survey of CLR database types, consider the CLR trigger. In SQL Serve 2005, triggers have much new to offer. CLR triggers provide all the functionality available in T-SQL triggers. The trigger can be associated with either a DML or a DDL action. The inserted and deleted tables are available for DML triggers. Event or event groups can be specified for DDL triggers.

The pre-release Books Online trigger example demonstrates the use of regular expressions to perform an e-mail address validation and then some appropriate audit logging. This may be interesting, but it seems more appropriately done as a check constraint and a T-SQL audit trigger. In fact, for most purposes that suggest the possibility of using a CLR trigger, it's more likely that a T-SQL trigger that writes to a Service Broker queue will better serve the administrator and developer. Time will tell, but the CLR trigger may be the least useful of the CLR types. Consider the following DDL CLR trigger that provides the trigger context properties for database-level DDL operations to see how the CLR trigger is formed:

> **Note**
>
> CLR integration triggers may be of interest to those working toward SOX (Sarbanes–Oxley) compliance because the audit activity is compiled and therefore not as susceptible to on-the-fly circumvention or inadvertent modification as a T-SQL trigger. The trigger event context XML also contains a standardized and complete collection of audit information.

```
<Microsoft.SqlServer.Server.SqlTrigger _
    (Name:="clrtr_ddlchanges", _
     Target:="DATABASE", _
     Event:="DDL_DATABASE_LEVEL_EVENTS")> _
Public Shared Sub clrtr_ddlchanges()
    Dim pInfo As SqlPipe = SqlContext.Pipe
    pInfo.Send(SqlContext.TriggerContext.TriggerAction.ToString)
    pInfo.Send(SqlContext.TriggerContext.EventData.Value.ToString)
    pInfo.Send(SqlContext.WindowsIdentity.Name.ToString)
End Sub
```

Informative possibilities, to be sure, but all the information available in this CLR trigger is as easily found in a T-SQL trigger, and the likelihood that a trigger will need to write data to another table is quite high. It would seem that the cost of transition between the database table and the CLR, plus `JITing` the trigger, will be more difficult to justify than either a CLR stored procedure or function, provided of course that the correct reasons are used to determine when a stored procedure, function, or even a trigger would be better written in the CLR or in T-SQL.

The CLR may also be used to create custom aggregate functions similar to `min()`, `max()`, and `sum()`. A complete discussion of developing user-defined aggregate functions is beyond this scope of this book, but you can find examples on the book's website at `www.SQLServerBible.com`.

Using the CLR versus Using T-SQL

Undoubtedly, a minority of SQL Server shops will never enable the CLR. In contrast, some shops will use only CLR programmed components at the database. Neither option is well considered when performance and scalability are fundamental objects of the software being produced.

For most shops, the initial movement into CLT integration will provide the greatest return rate through the transposition of existing problematic user-defined functions and stored procedures into better-performing CLR equivalents. That's not to say that a poorly designed database component can be transformed into a poorly written CLR object and all will be well. Good optimization practices and performance monitoring remain fundamental to good database design. Inadequate design notwithstanding, a handful of obvious existing problems will provide low-hanging fruit for conversion to CLR-based objects:

✦ Existing COM extended stored procedures place the stability of the entire database server at risk. User-defined extended stored procedures should be considered top-priority candidates for conversion to CLR integrated components.

✦ The OLE automation stored procedures have almost as long and notorious a reputation as extended stored procedures for poor error handling, slow performance, memory leaks, and obscurity between the T-SQL layer and the underlying COM environment. The code safety of managed code is an unquestionably attractive alternative to the sp_OA... stored procedures.

✦ Complex business rules and computationally intensive logic in existing stored procedures and functions may be able to benefit from the advantages of compiled code and streaming fast-forward table-valued functions. Array processing at the database server is now possible, as are compiled business-rule-based bucketing aggregations.

✦ Complex business rules and computationally intensive logic currently done by moving large data sets across the wire for processing at the middle tier will be able to process that data at the database server, thereby capitalizing on reduced network I/O patterns.

✦ Existing successful applications that have felt the pain of even relatively simple inline user-defined functions when used in the where clause of a range query that involves many rows will be able to perform almost as well as systems functions — provided they do not require data access.

✦ Parameterized list processing — also known as *tabular cracking* — and other string manipulation and validation operations that currently require iteration and often many lines of code to process a string can be easily and efficiently processed within CLR database types using .NET string data type members and the powerful REGEX (e.g., regular expressions) class.

✦ Security and server stability are at risk when T-SQL is used to access the file system, network resources, or other external data providers through OLEDB interfaces or command-line services. The CLR security model (CAS) affords a valuable layer of security abstraction between the SQL Server and the outside world because it is code based, rather than user based. As an added justification and benefit of using CLR components to interface the SQL and external resources, the CLR provides multiple elegant methods for producing a tabular output usable within the Database Engine from non-tabular data.

It is unlikely that many shops will immediately employ a significant number of user-defined types and user-defined aggregates. These technologies are completely new. In typical fashion, adoption of the new technology will lag behind the adaptation to the new CLR forms of existing database technologies. Most organizations will correctly take a more conservative tack into UDA and UDT implementations because the true potential has yet to be demonstrated by the vendor to the user community. That's not to say that organizations that do make an early investment in UDT and UDA included data models will not reap great advantage from the technology. The next two chapters present some use cases and in-depth implementation details for user-defined aggregates and user-defined types.

T-SQL Is Not Going Away

With or without the CLR, the best way to access relational data is through a set-based query. Set-based queries are expressible only in T-SQL. Sure, it's possible to embed set-based queries in CLR components, but is the cost always justifiable? Will the optimizer get an equal chance to produce the best query plan if all queries are stuffed inside quotes in .NET code, as it is using a T-SQL stored procedure? Will the transparency in such a coding style be adequate to facilitate effective security and code maintenance? The answer to each of these questions will surely prove to be in the negative by-and-large, for all the same reasons that have persisted through the generations of SQL Server concerning why stored procedures are preferred and why dynamic SQL is risky and less maintainable.

What we have with the CLR is a new region of indetermination. Only experience and knowledge of the application will be useful to ultimately establish whether a particular requirement is better serviced at the database server or at an upstream layer. If the database is selected, only experience and knowledge of the application will be useful to determine when a requirement will be best addressed through T-SQL or in the CLR. The trade-off between adding additional load to the database server and reduced network data movement must be carefully weighed. Clearly, the high-volume application stands to lose more by moving all logic to the database server than does a departmental utility application with a known limited load. Just as clearly, the cost of making the wrong decision and putting all logic at the database only to later have the application's utilization expand beyond expectation could be high if it becomes necessary to port T-SQL-based activity to managed code on a different application tier.

Microsoft seems to be telling us that the cost to move CLR integrated code from the database to an application layer will be less. Time will tell. There will be times when executing a data access query from a CLR component is the best choice, just as there will be times when using an old school T-SQL cursor will provide the most desirable query structure. For the most part, the CLR is not a replacement for set-based query processing, just as T-SQL is not the best place to iterate across a record set. Assuming the confidence is high that application logic is correctly hosted at the database, the rule of thumb ought to be use T-SQL when the requirement is to access the relational database, and consider the CLR when you need to accomplish more than straightforward data access in a single query. Building applications at the database with the intention to scale out to additional tiers is a more dubious design decision and will — perhaps dangerously — tilt the options in that rule of thumb more toward using CLR integration types over T-SQL objects.

Summary

This chapter has been a whirlwind tour through the vast expanse of the .NET Framework. Key concepts of the common language runtime (CLR) and Microsoft .NET Framework–style object-oriented programming have been presented to provide a basis for understanding the technical requirements of creating CLR integrated database components. With that foundation, each of the five SQL Server object types that can be created using CLR integration has been introduced. Also described were the new .NET classes used to support CLR integration, along with the new T-SQL DDL commands necessary to manage CLR integration in the enterprise. Pulling all those concepts and tools together, the chapter described how to use Visual Studio 2005 to create and deploy CLR objects into the database. Also presented were some tips on when to consider CLR integration and when to stick with good old T-SQL.

The impact of CLR integration on SQL Server is largely an unknown as SQL Server 2005 is released, but the potential is undeniable.

✦   ✦   ✦

Queueing Data with Service Broker

Service Broker is one of my favorite features of SQL Server 2005. This powerful yet simple work queue system can be used to add asynchronous messaging and work queues to a database abstraction layer to provide high scalability, and is essential in any SOA data store architecture.

If you've ever built a table to hold work to be done, such as orders to be processed by an MRP system, then you've built a work queue. In one application Service Broker is just that — a high-performance, wide-payload work queue integrated into SQL Server with DDL and monitoring capabilities.

Service Broker can also be used to pass messages with guaranteed secure delivery between work queues, which opens up a world of possibilities.

Because Service Broker is essentially just a SQL Server table, it includes all the cool transactional and back-up capabilities inherent to SQL Server. This is what sets Service Broker apart from other queuing technologies such as MSMQ.

The queue contains a single wide column for the message body, which is OK because the message will typically contain a single XML file or fragment or SOAP message as the payload.

New in 2005 The Service Broker technology was added with SQL Server 2005, so this entire chapter is new to SQL Server.

Service Broker is not enabled by default so the first specific step to working with Service Broker is to turn it on using the `alter database` command:

```
ALTER DATABASE AdventureWorks SET ENABLE_BROKER;
```

Configuring a Message Queue

Service Broker uses a messaging or dialog metaphor, but there's much more to Service Broker than just the messages. The Service Broker objects must be defined in the following order:

1. *Message types* define the legal requirements of the message.

2. *Contracts* define the agreement between the initiating service and the target, including the message type, the queue, and the services.

3. *Queues* hold the lists of messages.

4. *Services* communicate with the queue and either send or receive messages as the initiating service or the target service.

Other than defining the message type as XML and naming the objects, there isn't much complexity to setting up a Service Broker database. That's because the data definition language, or DDL, does all the work; and Service Broker is a message-agnostic work queue that's serving as an infrastructure for the messages. There's more work in placing messages on and taking messages off the queue.

Because Service Broker is integrated within SQL Server, the objects are created using the familiar create DDL commands.

The first step to creating a Service Broker queue is to define a message type and a contract that uses that message type:

```
CREATE MESSAGE TYPE HelloWorldMessage
  VALIDATION = WELL_FORMED_XML ;
CREATE CONTRACT HelloWorldContract
  ( HelloWorldMessage SENT BY INITIATOR);
```

The initiator and target queues are also simply created using DDL:

```
CREATE QUEUE [dbo].[TargetQueue] ;
CREATE QUEUE [dbo].[InitiatorQueue] ;
```

Likewise, the initiator and target services are also defined using DDL. Both services are associated with a queue, and the receiving, or target, service specifies that it can receive messages from a contract:

```
CREATE SERVICE InitiatorService
    ON QUEUE [dbo].[InitiatorQueue];
GO

CREATE SERVICE TargetService
    ON QUEUE [dbo].[TargetQueue]
    (HelloWorldContract);
```

With the Service Broker objects created, you'll be able to see them listed under the Object Explorer Service Broker node.

Working with Dialogs

With the Service Broker object created, messages can be placed into the queue or received from the queue. Messages exist as part of a conversation that can be divided into conversation groups.

Sending a Message to the Queue

The following code creates a conversation using a `conversationhandle` GUID. Send places a single message onto a queue within a transaction. The `begin conversation` command opens the conversation and the `send` command actually places the message into the queue:

```
BEGIN TRANSACTION ;

DECLARE @message XML ;
SET @message = N'<message>Hello, World!</message>' ;

DECLARE @conversationHandle UNIQUEIDENTIFIER ;

BEGIN DIALOG CONVERSATION @conversationHandle
    FROM SERVICE [InitiatorService]
    TO SERVICE 'TargetService'
    ON CONTRACT [HelloWorldContract]
    WITH ENCRYPTION = OFF, LIFETIME = 1000 ;

SEND ON CONVERSATION @conversationHandle
  MESSAGE TYPE [HelloWorldMessage]
  (@message) ;

END CONVERSATION @conversationHandle ;

COMMIT TRANSACTION ;
```

To view the message in the queue, select from the queue table as if it were a normal relational table:

```
SELECT CAST(message_body as nvarchar(MAX)) from [dbo].[TargetQueue]
```

Receiving a Message

The `receive` command will retrieve and remove the oldest message from the queue. Use `receive` within a transaction so that if something goes wrong, the receive can be rolled back and the message will still be in the queue.

Service Broker is not a trigger that can code when a message is placed on the queue; some code must run to extract the message. To accomplish this, Microsoft added a new option to the `wait for` command, enabling it to wait for a message in the queue. Without this option, the code would have to run a loop to continuously check for a new message.

The following routine within a stored procedure will wait for a message and then receive the top message from the queue:

```
USE AdventureWorks ;
GO

-- Process all conversation groups.
WHILE (1 = 1)
```

```
BEGIN

DECLARE @conversation_handle UNIQUEIDENTIFIER,
        @conversation_group_id  UNIQUEIDENTIFIER,
        @message_body XML,
        @message_type_name NVARCHAR(128);

BEGIN TRANSACTION ;

-- Get next conversation group.

WAITFOR(
  GET CONVERSATION GROUP @conversation_group_id FROM [dbo].[TargetQueue]),
  TIMEOUT 500 ;

-- If there are no more conversation groups, roll back the
-- transaction and break out of the outermost WHILE loop.

IF @conversation_group_id IS NULL
BEGIN
    ROLLBACK TRANSACTION ;
    BREAK ;
END ;

    -- Process all messages in the conversation group. Notice
    -- that all processing occurs in the same transaction.

    WHILE 1 = 1
    BEGIN

        -- Receive the next message for the conversation group.
        -- Notice that the receive statement includes a WHERE
        -- clause to ensure that the messages received belong to
        -- the same conversation group.

        RECEIVE
          TOP(1)
          @conversation_handle = conversation_handle,
          @message_type_name = message_type_name,
          @message_body =
          CASE
              WHEN validation = 'X' THEN CAST(message_body AS XML)
              ELSE CAST(N'<none/>' AS XML)
          END
        FROM [dbo].[TargetQueue]
        WHERE conversation_group_id = @conversation_group_id ;

        -- If there are no more messages, or an error occurred,
```

```
          -- stop processing this conversation group.

          IF @@ROWCOUNT = 0 OR @@ERROR <> 0 BREAK;

          -- Show the information received.

          SELECT 'Conversation Group Id' = @conversation_group_id,
               'Conversation Handle' = @conversation_handle,
               'Message Type Name' = @message_type_name,
               'Message Body' = @message_body ;


          -- If the message_type_name indicates that the message is an error
          -- or an end dialog message, end the conversation.

          IF @message_type_name =
'http://schemas.microsoft.com/SQL/ServiceBroker/EndDialog'
              OR @message_type_name =
'http://schemas.microsoft.com/SQL/ServiceBroker/Error'
          BEGIN
              END CONVERSATION @conversation_handle ;
          END ;

    END; -- Process all messages in conversation group.

   -- Commit the receive statements and the end conversation statement.

   COMMIT TRANSACTION ;

END ; -- Process all conversation groups.

use tempdb;;
```

Service Broker can handle complex message groups, such as multiple line items of an order that may not appear consecutively in the queue due to other messages being received simultaneously. The conversation group can be used to select out the related messages.

Monitoring Service Broker

While Management Studio has no visibility in the activity of a queue, nor summary page reports for the queue object, you can select directly from the queue or select a count(). In addition, there are database catalog views to shed light on the queue.

To see these demos in action from the Web Service to Service Broker to a stored procedure, and how to monitor Service Broker, view the ScreenCast available online at www .SQLServerBible.com.

Summary

Service Broker is one of those technologies that provides no benefit "out of the box." Unless you take the effort to architect the database using Service Broker, there's no benefit. However, if you do take the time to design the database using Service Broker, you'll see significant scalability benefits as Service Broker queues buffer the work load.

The next chapter continues the progression through SQL Server technologies and discusses ADO.NET 2.0 and its powerful methods for connectivity.

✦   ✦   ✦

Persisting Custom Data Types

U ser-defined types (UDTs) are new in SQL Server 2005. Don't con-fuse them with user-defined data types. SQL Server has pro-vided a user-defined data type of limited utility for some time. This legacy T-SQL extension was primarily an intra-database convenience. There was no support for creating a new data type, merely a conve-nient mechanism for aliasing an existing primitive such as an integer, char, or binary in an effort to provide consistency across the database. It was easier to identify a type relationship in columns in multiple tables and to keep columns of the same purpose in different tables the same length. For example, all such columns could be aliased to the same user-defined data type. However, applications that referenced one of those columns with a user-defined data type would see the column as the underlying native data type. No applica-tions would really care that the user-defined data type had been defined because it had no meaning outside of the local database where it was defined. The user-defined data type was not truly per-sisted through the application layers.

Cross-Reference   User-defined types (UDTs) are one of the five common language runtime (CLR) integration types introduced with SQL Server 2005. A general discussion of CLR integration types in SQL Server 2005 is presented in Chapter 27, "Programming CLR Assemblies within SQL Server."

In SQL Server 2005, as a part of common language runtime (CLR) inte-gration, that story is changing with the introduction of the user-defined type (UDT). The basic premise that a UDT is created from existing primitive types remains true. In addition, the legacy aliased user-defined data type can still be created in T-SQL. The similarities between UDTs and user-defined data types ends there. UDTs have important new capabilities that have meaning beyond the local database. The UDT can include more than one primitive type when implemented in .NET. The type can have any and all of the members of any .NET class, including methods, properties, and fields. Equally important, it is the responsibility of the developer to ensure that the type is made known to all layers of the application that will use it, not merely by the underlying primitive definition but by the UDT's name and structural definition. A reference to the UDT definition must be deployed with all code that will use the UDT, not only at the database layer, but also at all other application layers.

The CLR integration UDT is unlike any database object in SQL Server prior to SQL Server 2005. Stored procedures, functions, and triggers created in the CLR consist of a single method. These methods have T-SQL counterparts; the UDT does not.

A UDT is defined as either a class or a structure. When created as a class, all the functionality of the UDT is encapsulated in that class. Microsoft has issued some discouraging words about not trying to implement business objects as SQL Server UDTs, but in fact a UDT will allow objects to be stored in the database. Perhaps the message from Microsoft is that CLR integration is not yet ready for full-blown business objects in the database or that a UDT will never be able to support the richness of full-blown business objects such as a customer or an order in the database. For that answer, it is necessary to see how the UDT evolves beyond SQL Server 2005.

Likewise, the UDT is not being touted as an array structure even though many of the early examples of the UDT circulating over the Internet during the beta/CTP period for SQL Server 2005 are simple arrays. An array is a repeating data collection that can be easily compared to the rows in a database table. Generally, arrays are smaller than tables and have a lifetime that is limited to the current execution context. If arrays are needed at the database, consider the use of a CLR stored procedure or function, rather than a UDT.

The new possibilities with UDTs will challenge and excite the minds of creative developers, even as it strikes fear in the hearts of traditional database administrators. It is important for everyone to develop a good understanding of the rules and responsibilities that come with the rewards of UDTs in SQL Server 2005. Building upon a fundamental understanding of creating and managing a UDT, there is a certainty of unknown proportions that the UDT is poised to change the relational database as we know it. Like it or not, the door to the object-relational database model is opening.

The bar for T-SQL developers and experienced VB developers adapting to the other CLR integration types is not as high as is the bar for putting a UDT in place. One possible exception is the *user-defined aggregate (UDA)*. It could be argued that the UDA is a special case of the UDT.

Cross-Reference   User-defined aggregates (UDAs) are another of the five common language runtime (CLR) integration types introduced with SQL Server 2005.

The other CLR integration types closely parallel traditional database objects in form and function once they are created in the database. There is no traditional parallel facility for the UDT in SQL Server. All developers will need to understand the following:

✦ The fundamental differences between a class and a structure

✦ The relationship between native database data types and .NET types

✦ How to support the database null in the .NET Framework

✦ How to debug and deploy a CLR integration type within the database

✦ How the UDT database dependency relationship differs from the other CLR integration types

✦ The need to deploy the type in all application layers that will reference the type

Even the most experienced application programmers will need to acquire adequate T-SQL expertise to functionally test the new type and—even in cases where the choice is made to implement a UDT as a class, rather than a structure—fully exercise the structure and members of the type. Conversely, the seasoned T-SQL developer will need to understand fundamental .NET Framework programming and concepts from delegation to serialization fundamental to the CLR.

Creating CLR Integration User-Defined Types

Coding a UDT requires the creation of a complete class or structure. With the other CLR integration types, much of the code is abstracted from the developer, who must implement only a partial class that will usually require coding only a single method. To be sure, the requirements to define and deploy a UDT include those required to create any other class. In addition, there is a considerable list of additional requirements for creating, testing, and using a UDT. It's very important to get the design considerations for a UDT right because the UDT will affect — and need to be maintained at — multiple layers in the application. Making changes is not as elegant as getting things right from the start. Debugging and testing a UDT adds a layer of data dependencies and a layer of .NET .dll dependencies beyond the CLR type that require special treatment. Deploying a UDT requires a complete understanding of the .NET Framework architecture. In many enterprise situations, manipulation of the global assembly cache (GAC), or alternately, an unprecedented coupling of the application layers and the database layer, is mandatory.

Most developers will use Visual Studio 2005 Professional or Team System to create UDTs. The Standard and Express Editions do not provide complete debugging functionality for CLR integration components. It is also possible to develop and deploy a UDT using the .NET SDK. The SDK uses the same language-specific compilers as Visual Studio 2005. Once compiled, a UDT assembly is loaded into SQL Server 2005 using the CREATE ASSEMBLY and CREATE TYPE T-SQL DDL statements, regardless of the toolset used to write and compile the type. The real value of using the Visual Studio 2005 IDE lies in the development and debugging process. Using Visual Studio 2005, the developer can create and control test scripts that allow the full set of deployment issues to be avoided until the type is ready for integration testing. For this reason alone it is recommended that developers new to CLR integration and the .NET Framework use the Visual Studio 2005 IDE, rather than attempt to learn both the .NET SDK and the .NET Framework. The time saved and the improved quality of the code produced will easily justify the cost of a Visual Studio 2005 license.

Cross-Reference   All versions of SQL Server 2005 support CLR integration. To determine which Database Engine version is best for a production or pre-production use such as development, match the SQL Server version used with the other database requirements for the environment. A discussion of the features for each version of SQL Server can be found in Chapter 3, "Exploring SQL Server Architecture."

Regardless of whether the .NET Software Development Kit (SDK) or Visual Studio 2005 is used, several requirements must be understood and a design decision must be made before a UDT can be successfully created. Will the type be a class or a structure? How will the type satisfy the SQL Server 2005 coding contract? Which code access security (CAS) mode will the type require? What method will be used to sign the assembly? How will deployment to all application layers be managed?

Cross-Reference   .NET assembly signing options and CAS security are discussed in greater detail in Chapter 27, "Programming CLR Assemblies within SQL Server."

Caution

Failure to carefully consider these questions can create a precarious web of dependencies that are difficult to unravel. For example, in the database, a type cannot be changed while it is in use in a table; and in the application layer, the structure of the type must exactly match the structure in use in the database. Making a change in a UDT might require that the data in the UDT column be preserved and the column dropped (because there is no ALTER TYPE command), a new type definition uploaded to the database, the data moved into a new column, and the application reference to the type be updated before the application can resume. Clearly, it is a repair involving several changing parts. Application failure is likely if any one part fails to be correctly modified.

Satisfying the Requirements

Creating and using CLR integration UDTs requires SQL Server 2005 and the .NET Framework Version 2. UDT implementation is not backwardly compatible. UDTs cannot be used or referenced by any previous version of SQL Server or applications running any previous version of the .NET Framework. UDTs can exist in .NET applications without being manifest at the database, although the requirements are slightly different. While remotely similar to the VB6 type that could be declared within a procedure, and the legacy SQL Server alias type object that was restricted to one primitive element that is required to be a native SQL Server type, the CLR integration UDT must be declared as a VB.NET structure or class.

The reasons for using a structure for most UDTs are found in the underpinnings of the .NET Framework. The structure is a value type, and the class is a reference type. The structure is allocated from the call stack, and the class is allocated from the object heap. This seemingly minor difference creates some interesting behavioral differences between the structure and the class. Taken together, those behavioral differences translate to more work for the CLR in comparing and assigning reference types or classes. Table 29-1 lists some differences between a structure and a class in the .NET Framework.

Table 29-1: Comparing VB.NET Structures and Classes

	Structure	*Class*
Declaration Type	Value	Reference
Memory Allocation	Program Stack	Object Heap
Minimum Number of Members	1	0
Required Number of Protected Members	1	0
Constructor	Default constructor not allowed. Members initialized to default values.	Default constructor required (used to create a New instance)
Access Model Restrictions	Yes — Protected not allowed	No
Events	Only Shared (Static in C#) Sub can be event handler	Any method can be event handler
Inherits From	Inherits only from System.ValueType	Inherits from any class except System.ValueType
Inheritable	No — Sealed	Yes unless explicitly declared NotInheritable

	Structure	*Class*
Polymorphism	Boxing (conversion to reference type) required to implement interface	Inheritance-based object heap programming contract supports interfaces
Lifetime	Cannot live independently	Alive while reachable
Garbage Collection	No — Instances are copies, not references. Relies on container class for garbage collection.	Yes — Finalized when no active references remain
Assignment	Copy on Assignment (By Value)	Object Cloning (By Reference)
Assign Nothing	Members can be accessed	Members not available
Change Isolation	Instance isolated	Change affects other references
Equality	Member by member test	Equals method used to compare objects

Some reasons to implement a UDT as a class, rather than a structure, include the following:

✦ **Controlling lifetime:** It may be advantageous for one process to create an instance of a UDT and for other processes to continue to reference the UDT long after the creator process has finished. For example, a batch control header or lineage identification structure could be held in memory for the duration of a batch run or iteration.

✦ **Polymorphism:** Even though SQL Server is not inheritance aware, if a UDT is derived from multiple base classes, then inheritance via interfaces may be used in the derived UDT class. In such cases, the overhead of the structure on the stack may far exceed the overhead of a class in the heap, so the value type will be *boxed*. Boxing results in a copy of the value being maintained both on the program stack and in the object heap.

✦ **Inheritance:** If the programming model had reason to create a base UDT from which multiple other types would be derived, then this could only be accomplished using a class type. The structure does not support inheritance.

✦ **Underlying object types in UDT:** If a UDT member is a reference type such as a string, then referring to that member will require the creation of an object on the object heap. If created as a structure, then the UDT would be created on the stack, but it would include a reference to that member object. A little-used member that can be initialized to "nothing" may be better kept in a value type structure. A regularly used member is less likely to realize any benefit from a value type that exists on the program stack.

✦ **Use of COM:** It's a bit of a stretch, but in the event that a UDT implements an `Interop` assembly to some legacy code that is valuable to the organization, careful examination of the behavior of the type when created as a structure or a class will be necessary. For example, where a non-blittable variable is marshaled by the `Interop` assembly, the documentation warns to expect problems. (Non blittable variables are those that experience indeterminate or incorrect conversion between the .NET Framework and COM.) Such types include strings, arrays, objects, classes, and value types. That doesn't leave many other native data types, so it is fairly safe to assume that if the use of COM is planned in a type, then the type should be created as a class.

The other important requirement considerations are easily discussed in the context of the Visual Studio 2005 User-Defined Type template.

Coding a CLR UDT with Visual Studio

Some of the requirements illuminated by the template represent decision points, while others are necessary for all types. Moving from top to bottom through the template-generated code, this section explores the requirements and coding differences necessary to achieve the desired behaviors by building on a sample data type.

The sample data type used will be an Internet Protocol version 4 (IPv4) address. This is the most common addressing scheme in use on the Internet today. The IPv4 address is traditionally represented as four integral values, each in the range 0 to 255 to represent a byte, separated by a point, as in 192.168.1.1. Currently, most networks assign one or more IPv4 addresses to each node to support the open-system interconnection (OSI) transport and network layers. The Internet uses *domain name system (DNS)* names assigned to IPv4 addresses. It is common to need to represent IPv4 addresses in the database, but somewhat problematic to ensure data integrity of IPv4 values in previous releases of SQL Server. Typically, the IP address would simply be stored as a string, and validation would be assumed to have happened at another layer of an application that was interested in the IP address as a data-entity attribute. With the SQL Server 2005 UDT, it is readily possible to accept only valid IP addresses at the database through the use of .NET regular expressions. Furthermore, it is now possible to reference the System.Net namespace from the members of the UDT.

The complete Visual Studio 2005 solution for the UDTs discussed in this chapter can be downloaded from the *SQL Server Bible 2005* website at www.SQLServerBible.com. In the downloadable solution are working examples of the IPv4 UDT implemented in three ways:

✦ As a structure in its simplest form, as shown below

✦ As a structure with a user defined format

✦ As a class

Consider how a UDT can be developed to create an IPv4 UDT. In the bare-bones structure type UDT shown, the elements of the UDT can be seen. First notice the system assemblies that must be included in all UDTs:

```
Imports System
Imports System.Data
Imports System.Data.Sql
Imports System.Data.SqlTypes
Imports Microsoft.SqlServer.Server
Imports System.Text.RegularExpressions

' need IsByteOrdered set true if the UDT will be an index column
<Serializable()> _
<Microsoft.SqlServer.Server.SqlUserDefinedType(Format.Native, _
IsByteOrdered:=True)> _
Public Structure IPType1
    Implements INullable

    Private Shared ReadOnly _parser As _New _
```

```vbnet
Regex("\A((2[0-4]\d|25[0-5]|[01]?\d\d?)\.){3}(2[0-4]\d|25[0-5]|[01]?\d\d?)")
  Private Const _NULL As String = "NULL_IP"
  Private m_Null As Boolean
  Private m_OctetA As Byte
  Private m_OctetB As Byte
  Private m_OctetC As Byte
  Private m_OctetD As Byte

  Public Overrides Function ToString() As String
    If Me.IsNull Then
      Return _NULL
      ' could also use
      'Return Nothing
    Else
      Return Me.m_OctetA.ToString() & "." & _
      Me.m_OctetB.ToString() & "." & _
      Me.m_OctetC.ToString() & "." & _
      Me.m_OctetD.ToString()
    End If

End Function

  Public ReadOnly Property IsNull() As Boolean Implements INullable.IsNull
    Get
      Return m_Null
    End Get
End Property

  Public Shared ReadOnly Property Null() As IPType1
    Get
      Dim h As IPType1 '= New IPType1
      h.m_Null = True
      Return h
    End Get
End Property

  Public Shared Function Parse(ByVal s As SqlString) As IPType1

    If s.IsNull Or s.Value = _NULL Then
      ' database determines if a column can be null
      Return Null
    End If
    ' constructor not required for a structure
    ' It is allowed but not necessary
    ' each member will get the default value so each octet
    ' of the IP address will be initialized to 0 (default byte value)
    Dim u As IPType1 '= New IPType1

    'need a .NET string to parse and split
    Dim str As String = Convert.ToString(s)
    Dim m As Match = _parser.Match(str)
```

```vb
  If m.Success Then

    Dim arr() As String = str.Split(CType(".", Char))
    u.OctetA = CType(arr(0), Byte)
    u.OctetB = CType(arr(1), Byte)
    u.OctetC = CType(arr(2), Byte)
    u.OctetD = CType(arr(3), Byte)
    Return u

  Else
    Throw New ArgumentException("Invalid IP v4 Address")
    '        Return Nothing
  End If

End Function

'results in 0.0.0.0 = null
Public Property OctetA() As Byte
  Get
    OctetA = m_OctetA
  End Get
  Set(ByVal value As Byte)
    m_OctetA = value
  End Set
End Property

Public Property OctetB() As Byte
  Get
    OctetB = m_OctetB
  End Get
  Set(ByVal value As Byte)
    m_OctetB = value
  End Set
End Property

Public Property OctetC() As Byte
  Get
    OctetC = m_OctetC
  End Get
  Set(ByVal value As Byte)
    m_OctetC = value
  End Set
End Property

Public Property OctetD() As Byte
  Get
    OctetD = m_OctetD
  End Get
  Set(ByVal value As Byte)
    m_OctetD = value
  End Set
```

```
   End Property

   <SqlMethod(IsDeterministic:=True, IsPrecise:=True)> _
   Public Function GetCSubNet() As String
     GetCSubNet = m_OctetC.ToString + "." + m_OctetD.ToString
   End Function
End Structure
```

If it is necessary to include additional functionality, then other namespaces from those available for CLR integration projects should also be included in the Imports list, and a reference to the assembly should be set for the Visual Studio project. For example, regular expressions, Windows Management Instrumentation (WMI), and many network services can be accessed by CLR integration types through the system-provided .NET namespaces. To make use of regular expressions add the following statements:

```
Imports System.Text.RegularExpressions
```

Next, the class or structure is declared. Several important aspects of the declaration of the type vary, depending on whether the type will be class-based or structure-based. First, any attributes required for the type are stated. Next, the type is scoped and named. For a class that will inherit from another class, the inheritance is specified. Note that a class can inherit from only one other class, and a structure cannot inherit. If the class will implement any interfaces, the interface implementations are listed after the inheritance. Finally, the class or structure is closed with an `End Class` or `End Structure` statement. All members of the type must occur between the declaration statement and the end statement.

Now consider the elements of the class or structure declaration statement in greater detail.

The `Serializable` attribute provides metadata support to aid in presenting the data state of the UDT into a stream of bytes that can be transported and consumed by other components as well as packing the stream for storage into the data type. The `Serializable` attribute is not required for a UDT although it is obviously valid in most cases. Of course, serialization helps define how the stream of bytes will be deserialized back to the data members of the UDT from a stream. In general, serialization is concerned with serializing all fields of the UDT into a binary stream or an XML stream. No properties are required for the `Serializable` attribute — it simply must be specified and then any serialization interfaces and methods needed are implemented in the body of the structure or class.

Cross-Reference A discussion of using custom attributes for CLR integration types in SQL Server 2005 is presented in Chapter 27, "Programming CLR Assemblies within SQL Server."

The `SqlUserDefinedType` attribute is a specialized or custom attribute used only for a SQL Server UDT. As noted in Chapter 27, the compiler uses this attribute when the assembly is compiled to IL. It also affects the assembly manifest as well as being used by SQL Server when the assembly is loaded into the SQL Server. This attribute is quite powerful and includes four properties. You must specify the format property that defines the storage format of the type. The template provides `Format.Native` as a default. This format should provide the most compatibility and performance with the least amount of additional coding. If columns of the type being created will have indexes built on them, it is also necessary to set the `IsByteOrdered` property. The other format options include the very useful `Format.UserDefined` and the relatively uninteresting `Format.Unknown`.

If a UDT is defined as a class using the native format, then the `StructLayout` attribute must also be specified to ensure the COM compatibility. This is done by adding the `InteropServices` namespace and providing a value for the `LayoutKind` property of the `StructLayout`. Possible `LayoutKind` options are `Auto`, `Explicit`, and `Sequential`, although for most CLR integration UDTs `Sequential` will be used. Basically, `Auto` tells the system to decide the physical layout of the UDT's fields, `Explicit` allows the programmer to define the layout, and `Sequential` instructs the code to lay out the fields in the order in which they are sent. By default, the compilers in Visual Studio use the `Sequential` layout.

The namespace is imported:

```
Imports System.Runtime.InteropServices
```

The `LayoutKind.Sequential` property is included with the other custom attributes:

```
<System.Runtime.InteropServices.StructLayout(LayoutKind.Sequential)> _
```

The scope of a structure is used to define access to the type. In VB.NET, the access levels may be set by specifying any of the modifiers: `Public`, `Private`, `Friend`, `Protected`, or `ProtectedFriend`. There are similar scoping modifiers for other .NET programming languages. In order for a UDT to be available outside of the application domain — recall from Chapter 27 that an application domain in SQL Server is analogous to a database schema — the access scope should be set as `Public`:

```
<Serializable()> _
<Microsoft.SqlServer.Server.SqlUserDefinedType(Format.Native,
IsByteOrdered:=True)> _
Public Structure IPType1
    Implements INullable
```

Unlike a class, the structure cannot inherit from another structure. However, like a class, the structure can shadow — or hide and completely override — another programming element that has the exact same name, by using the `Shadows` modifier.

Cross-Reference See Chapter 27, "Programming CLR Assemblies within SQL Server," for additional resources about understanding and working with the .NET Framework.

A class can inherit from another class. This means that in addition to the access modifiers and the `Shadows` modifier, two additional modifiers are available for the class-based type that define the inheritance scope of the class:

✦ `MustInherit` requires that the class can only be inherited, and prohibits instances of the class from being created

✦ `tInheritable` prevents all other classes from inheriting from the type

If you were creating a master type from which multiple types would be based and you did not want the base type to be implemented in SQL Server, then the class could be modified with `MustInherit`. If concerns about security or performance warrant the prevention of other types from being derived by a class-based UDT, then the class could be modified with `NotInheritable`.

If the type is declared as a class, it can inherit from one base class. To derive from another class in VB.NET, the `Inherits` keyword (along with the base class name) is provided immediately after the type is named. It is necessary to include a reference to the assembly where the base class is found if it is not in the current assembly, and the namespace for the base class must be included in the Imports section at the top of the file. While the type is able to derive from a base class, note that SQL Server is not aware of the inheritance. If derived members are to be used, then they must be explicitly included in the current class.

When SQL Server is not involved, the members of the base class are implicitly available in any derived class. However, SQL Server CLR integration base class inheritance is powerless at this time. SQL Server requires that no public members be overridden, and no implicit inheritance is recognized by the CLR that runs in SQL Server. These mutually effacing requirements render classic inheritance a non-event with CLR integration at this time. Look for this limitation to change considerably as the object-relational look and feel of CLR integration continues to evolve. In the meantime, implementing interfaces rather than inheriting from a base class to derive functionality from other classes will be a much more developer-friendly proposition.

```
<Serializable()> _
<Microsoft.SqlServer.Server.SqlUserDefinedType(Format.Native,
IsByteOrdered:=True)> _
<System.Runtime.InteropServices.StructLayout(LayoutKind.Sequential)> _
Public Class IPType3
  Implements INullable
```

To that end, the last thing to do in the class declaration statement is to name the interfaces that will be used by the type. The class can implement multiple interfaces. The UDT will always need to implement `INullable` from the `System.Data.SQLTypes` namespace. This interface exposes the `IsNull` member property that enables the .NET Framework to function in the database where null is a possible value of any data type.

Other interfaces that are implemented by the native SQL Server data types include `IComparable` and `IXMLSerializable`. `IComparable` is an interface from the `System` namespace that serves to add comparison support for .NET. The interface enables the developer to define how an instance of a UDT will be evaluated in an expression. `IXMLSerializable` is an interface from the `System.XML` namespace that provides serialization and deserialization support between the storage structure to XML streams through the overrideable `ReadXML` and `WriteXML` member methods. Another interface that will be interesting in UDT solutions that are used in remoting and internal organizational situations is `IBinarySeralize`, from the `Microsoft.SQLServer.Server` namespace. The `Read` and `Write` member methods of this interface must be implemented when the `UserDefined` serialization format is used:

```
<Serializable()> _
<Microsoft.SqlServer.Server.SqlUserDefinedType(Format.UserDefined, _
  IsByteOrdered:=True, _
  IsFixedLength:=True, _
  MaxByteSize:=4, _
  Name:="IPv4")> _
Public Structure IPType2
  Implements INullable, IComparable, IBinarySerialize, IXMLSerializable
```

Recall that the serialization format will normally be specified as `Native` in the UDT `SQLUserDefinedType` attribute. The `UserDefined` serialization format is useful in cases where the UDT structure or class includes property members that do not correspond to native SQL Server numeric or date data types. In addition, when the format is `UserDefined`, the `IsByteOrdered` property ID is required and the `MaxByteSize` for the UDT must be specified, in the range 1 to 8,000. This size limitation is imposed by SQL Server. The 8K limit should help clarify why business objects are not good candidates for UDTs at this time.

The Read and Write methods necessary for UserDefined serialization seem to be somewhat mystifying due to the lack of a clear explanation in the documentation. Unfortunately, this may lead some developers — in particular, those developers trying to find their way from T-SQL to .NET programming — to lock into native serialization to avoid what they don't understand. This may actually be a good thing for infrequently used UDTs that are used as an aid to implementing business rules. However, native serialization may be a restricting factor for the UDTs where performance is most important. For example, consider how useful it may be to sort a geo-spatial coordinate according to geographical attributes such as continent, country, state, and township. Similarly, consider how useful it might be to serialize IPv4 values by octet, rather than as a string. Native serialization does not lend itself to such custom sorting needs. The UserDefined serialization provides a lot of flexibility in how data can be moved and stored.

Visual Studio's documentation provides a much better discussion of serialization than is found in the SQL Server CLR integration documentation. Unfortunately, even the Visual Studio documentation requires readers to make a conceptual stretch to apply the general discussion of serialization in the .NET Framework as it applies to complex business objects to the specialized SQL Server UDT that requires only the Read and Write methods and where business object complexity is discouraged. Serialization is nothing more than encoding the values of all member fields of a structure or class instance into a positional stream of bits for a transport or copy operation. It is somewhat obscure to recognize that all the fields, public and private, need to be loaded and sent on the stream, although it is only necessary for the developer to explicitly serialize enough of the member fields to allow the state of the instance to be exactly recreated when the stream is deserialized at the other end of the transport or copy operation.

In the IP address examples available for this chapter, one of the types uses UserDefined serialization. The four-byte private fields must be always presented in the exact same sequence in order to ensure that the same IP address is always expressed. The consequences of misordering the IP octets or dropping one in transport and trying to use the incomplete or incorrect data are obvious to anyone with a rudimentary exposure to TCP/IP networking. Serialization will guarantee the order and quality of the data between the database and the client. In the Read member method, it is necessary only to load the fields into the BinaryReader. Then, in the Write method, the fields must be deserialized from a BinaryWriter in the exact same order used in the Read method:

```
Public Sub Read(ByVal r As System.IO.BinaryReader) _
                    Implements IBinarySerialize.Read
  m_OctetA = r.ReadByte()
  m_OctetB = r.ReadByte()
  m_OctetC = r.ReadByte()
  m_OctetD = r.ReadByte()
End Sub
Public Sub Write(ByVal w As System.IO.BinaryWriter) _
                    Implements IBinarySerialize.Write
  w.Write(m_OctetA)
  w.Write(m_OctetB)
  w.Write(m_OctetC)
  w.Write(m_OctetD)
End Sub
```

In the snippets shown here, the IP octets are specified in order from A through D. This is not technically necessary as long as the order of the fields in the Read method is the same as the order of the fields in the `Write` method. This flexibility is demonstrated in the downloadable code, as is an implementation of `IComparable`.

Testing and Debugging the UDT

Before a UDT can be adequately exercised, a successfully compiled assembly must be deployed to a SQL Server. In addition, the most likely functional test scenarios will involve creating a table and issuing a well-designed battery of DML to verify that the newly deployed UDT works as desired within the database context.

Visual Studio provides a very useful "Test Scripts" project-level component for this phase of development. There are three significant advantages to using the project over deploying a UDT to a test SQL Server — even a Developer Edition SQL Server on the same environment where Visual Studio is deployed — and testing from the SQL Server Management Studio (SSMS) query tool or even the SQLCMD command-line utility. One is that the developer's attention can be exclusively focused on testing the functionality. When test scripts are used in the project, the UDT can be deployed and redeployed during development simply by using the Visual Studio Deploy option from the Debug menu. When SSMS or another tool outside of the Visual Studio IDE is used, it is also necessary to manually ensure that that tool has a reference to the most recently compiled version of the UDT. The second advantage is that stepping through the code from the test T-SQL script into the CLR code is fully supported only from the Visual Studio IDE. The third advantage is that the test script will be versioned in SourceSafe along with the other components of the project.

It is useful to include DDL to create and drop any tables and views referenced in the test script within that script. This will save the time spent browsing to the table or view in the Server Explorer to remove the objects before changes to the type can be deployed during development.

Performance Considerations

Optimization of CLR code is not nearly as bountiful of an effort as performance tuning in T-SQL code. While the developer lore is full of stories of turning a 30-hour T-SQL stored procedure into a 10-minute query by refactoring, CLR integration UDTs are not likely to provide such heroic opportunities, mostly because when done even close to correctly and appropriately, there is little likelihood that any more than a few more CPU cycles can be squeezed from the code that underlies a UDT. When the implementation is incorrect, there are some performance traps that remain, which can be avoided by the wary developer. For example, if a UDT implements a method that requires `EXTERNAL_ACCESS` security and the result of that member method is persisted in a data set when the UDT value is added to a table, then it should be understood that there is no way to control what might happen during retrieval of the external data value. It's very possible that a perception of slow database I/O can be the result of network latencies or unresponsive external data sources accessed from the .NET code of a UDT class.

Consider a method from the example code for this chapter of a user-defined IP address data type that uses the `System.Net` namespace to resolve the provided IP address to a server name using the DNS class:

```
<SqlMethod(IsDeterministic:=False)> _
Public Function GetDNSName() As String
  If Not (Me.IsNull) Then
```

```
      GetDNSName = _NULL
    Else
      Try
      GetDNSName = Dns.GetHostEntry(IPAddress.Parse(Me.ToString)).HostName
        Catch ex As Sockets.SocketException
          GetDNSName = "Socket Error: " & ex.SocketErrorCode.ToString
        End Try
    End If
End Function
```

Caution   As a general design point, beware of the power of CLR integration. Suppose this method was called each time an IP address was inserted into a table. The machine name could be persisted as a computed column in this way. Several calamities could inadvertently extend the duration of the insert transaction beyond acceptable limits. Many unexpected and unpredictable events beyond the control of the CLR running within a SQL Server can occur. Network latency problems or DNS conflicts could create an unacceptable contention level at the table. All the inserts can do is to suffer through the slowness. Furthermore, in a high insert rate scenario where the IP addresses being added to a table cannot be resolved to a host name, the overhead of handling the SocketException for each value inserted can also create the perception of slowness at the database. In other words, the power of CLR Integration can easily lead to undesirable issues that must be anticipated when designing and using the UDT.

As with any other data column, a column that employs a UDT can provide improved performance if indexed. A UDT column can be indexed as long as it can be sorted in binary order. A heterogeneous UDT — one containing a mixture of native types — will result in a more useful index if the order of deserialization of the member fields is carefully considered. Consider a UDT with integral and character fields. If the character field is most interesting to search, and the most likely column for where clause search argument (SARG) expressions, it stands to reason that the character field should be laid down first when the data value is serialized to storage. Computed columns derived from UDT class members can also be indexed, provided the member is attributed with the IsDeterministic property.

One other issue that has been discussed already in terms of structural differences is value semantics verses reference semantics. Recall that a UDT created as a structure is a value type and by definition lives on the program stack, whereas a UDT created as a class inherits from Object and therefore lives in the object heap memory space. In most situations the performance costs for this difference will not be significant. In the example code for this chapter, provided OntheWebsite, a performance test is provided that does an equal number of inserts of the same values into a UDT structure (value semantics), a UDT class (reference semantics) using native serialization, a UDT class using a UserDefined serialization, and a native varchar column. No meaningful difference was detected between the various data types in terms of insert performance. Regardless, it is useful to be aware of the difference when tuning a CLR UDT and to fully evaluate the costs of each when designing a UDT.

Additional performance considerations for using CLR integration UDTs will emerge as adoption of this technology finds its way into SQL Server–based applications. In concert with this discovery process, Microsoft will undoubtedly introduce refinements to the UDT model to further improve UDT performance behavior.

CLR Integration UDT Deployment Details

There are at least three ways to work with a UDT in the development environment. During development and functional unit testing, the Visual Studio 2005 IDE can be used to execute the T-SQL DDL, and queries can be used to test the UDT as previously described. Once the new type is ready for consumption by other developers in tables and server-side code (e.g., T-SQL tables and views and CLR or T-SQL procedures, functions, triggers, and aggregates), the UDT assembly can be deployed to the local folder of each client tool that will be used in the development effort — including SQL Server Management Studio (SSMS). When the UDT is ready for general consumption in the development environment, it can be deployed to the GAC or the client application workspace of all client applications that will reference the new UDT.

The ability to use different versions of a type at the same time in a database can be a boon or a boondoggle. Proper management and planning is critical to ensure that everyone is testing with the appropriate client-side libraries. Inside the database the problems aren't as potentially messy as they are in the client space. It would be entirely possible for four developers using the SSMS on their local workstation to be testing with references to four different versions of a type while only one version exists in the database. All that is necessary is that each of the developers copy the .dll for the type into the application executable folder of any .NET application at different times.

For SSMS, the default location to place the .dll on the machine where SSMS is running is `C:\Program Files\Microsoft SQL Server\90\Tools\Binn\VSShell\Common7\IDE`.

This will provide a reference to the UDT for queries executed from that SSMS. Unmanaged OLE-DB connections, such as the SQLDMD utility, and ODBC connections, such as the osql utility, will recognize instances of the UDT only as binary data.

In general, the `REFERENCES` SQL Server permission is necessary to use a UDT. If the UDT is used in a CLR integration or T-SQL procedure, function, or trigger as a local variable or parameter, then the `EXECUTE` permission is also necessary.

Strongly Named Assemblies and the GAC

Applications that reference a particular assembly will try to use that exact assembly down to the name, version, and signature. If the assembly does not use a strong name, the application may not care about the assembly's version. This complicates assembly deployment because it is all too possible to miss the update of an assembly at some places in a service-oriented architecture, resulting in the assembly for a UDT in the database not being a valid match to the assembly being referenced by that service node. To make this hidden problem even riskier, as long as the public structure and name of the type referenced by .NET application code matches the public structure and the name of the type in the database, an application can operate as though it has full and accurate knowledge of the type in the database. This seems all too similar to the .dll hell that the .NET Framework was supposed to avoid.

While reverse engineering and disassembly exploits have long been a potential risk for all programming languages and environments, the .NET Framework actually provides a tool for IL disassembly. Fortunately, the .NET Framework security model holds no premise that obscuring the code from external view is a necessary part of the security model. Assembly signing and authentication are the keys to .NET assembly security. Assemblies can be signed by a very secure, private key/public key set intended to prevent the introduction of assembly components that might compromise an application. Such assemblies can only reference assemblies — outside of the `System` namespace, of course — that are signed with the same key pair. Signing is necessary for all assemblies placed in the GAC.

Microsoft suggests that when an assembly will be shared by more than one application on a machine, the assembly ought to be placed in the GAC. It is more secure and easier to ensure that an assembly in the GAC is locked down to administrator-only access. It is also possible to run multiple versions of the same assembly side by side from the GAC. Conversely, if even one assembly from an application is placed in the GAC, then deployment of the application is complicated by the requirement to use the Windows Installer 2.0 or the Global Assembly Cache Tool to move the assembly into the GAC of each application node that will use the UDT. Assemblies deployed with the application in the application folder can be moved or migrated using xcopy-based promotion and rollout tactics. Additionally, developers can be in control of which assemblies belong with their application if the assemblies are not deployed to the GAC. The security requirements of the organization must be considered in order to determine when to deploy to the GAC and when to deploy to the application folder.

Creating Strongly Named .NET Assemblies

It is important to understand how to create a strongly named assembly when working with UTDs that will be deployed to the GAC. There are three aspects to a strong name: the assembly's identity, a public key, and a private key. The private key is also known as a *digital signature*. All aspects of a strong name can be managed using Visual Studio 2005.

The assembly identity can be viewed and modified on the Application tab of the Project Designer. The Project Designer shown in Figure 29-1 is accessed through the Project menu's `<project name>` properties . . . item or through the Project's properties from the context menu (found by a right mouse-click on the project name in the Solution Explorer).

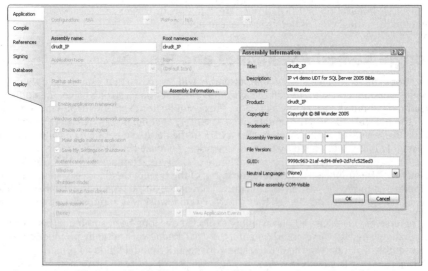

Figure 29-1: The assembly identity. The assembly's name, the version information, and the culture settings (such as language) establish the assembly's identity.

The key pair needed to complete the strong name can be generated using the Strong Name Tool (`sn.exe`). Access the tool by launching the Visual Studio Command Prompt. The Strong Name Tool has a number of functions. As with other command-line-based tools, help information can be displayed by typing

```
sn /?
```

at the command prompt. Figure 29-2 show the commands for creating a public/private key pair and deploying the key to the solution folder of a project.

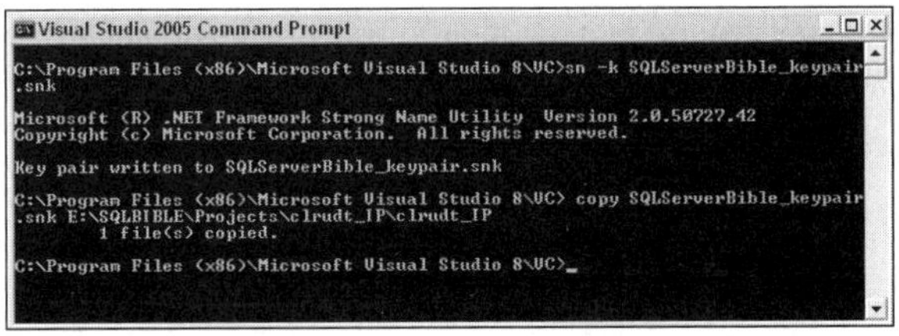

Figure 29-2: Creating a public/private key pair used to create a strong name for an assembly. The example is shown on a 64-bit operating system, but the same procedure is used for 32-bit systems.

Once the key is deployed to the project folder, the Project Designer can be used to include the key file in the assembly, as shown in Figure 29-3.

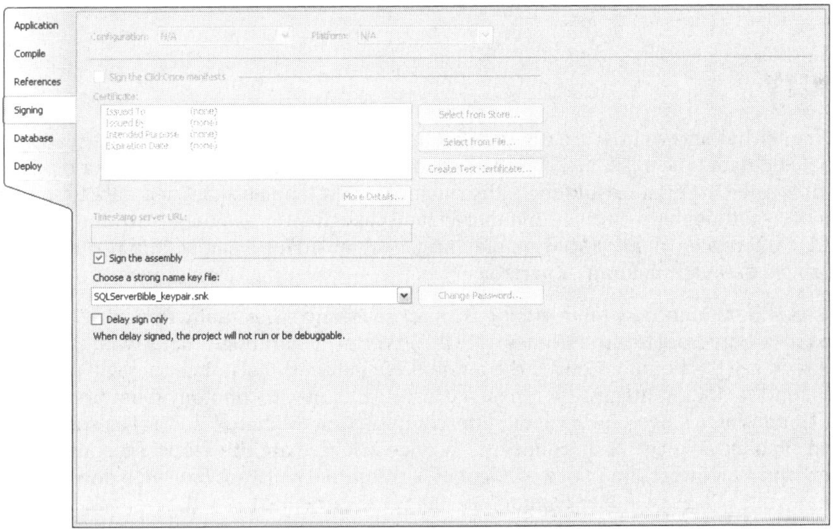

Figure 29-3: Add a key to an assembly using the Project Designer.

The strong name information will be included in the assembly's manifest. There is a command-line tool that can be used to add the key to the assembly: the Assembly Linker (al.exe). This tool does the same work as the Signing tab of the Project Designer, but it requires the assembly's .dll as an argument. The Project Designer is much more user friendly. Working with the .dll means the developer cannot use the Visual Studio Deploy option during development.

Inline attributes in the assembly's code can also be used to specify the key file, as shown here:

```
<Assembly:AssemblyKeyFileAttribute("SQLServerBible_keypair.snk")>
```

An organization's security policies may require more complex strong name implementation practices. For example, an organization may not expose the digital signature (private key part) to developers. In this case, development and testing of the UDT at the database might be completed without a strong name. When the UDT is ready for widespread deployment, a security officer or signing authority might add the key before the UDT is deployed to an integrated environment. The advantages to such a practice include protecting intellectual property and preventing malicious or untested code from entering a production environment.

Maintaining the UDT

Be prepared for an unprecedented level of detail when making a change to a UDT that has already found its way to production systems. Changing the structural definition of a UDT requires that the type is dropped and then recreated. Preserving the existing data and ensuring that it fits the new structure appropriately will require care and testing. Identifying the application code and hosts that need to be updated simultaneously with the database change is an exercise in cooperation and communication unlike anything necessary in traditional database development.

Summary

This chapter has shown how greatly the CLR integration UDT differs from the already familiar user-defined data type alias. In SSMS they are differentiated as user-defined data types and UDTs presented in separate folders in the database view. The user-defined data type remains a possibility although its days are numbered, and this chapter has demonstrated that the .NET UDT offers a far richer and wide-reaching mechanism for encapsulating complex data into a single database column or variable.

Microsoft will undoubtedly meet great customer resistance to actually removing the user-defined data type from future releases of SQL Server — even though that's what Books Online insists they will do. Equally likely is the amount of customer resistance that will prevent a rapid adoption of CLR integration types. A great deal of new technology must first be assimilated. There is also a need for a vastly different approach to change control as software development slips into the age of disconnected service-oriented architectures. Disconnected systems and CLR integration pose challenges for iterative software life-cycle development unlike any the SQL Server user community has yet experienced.

At some point, usable migration and change strategies will emerge. As that is evolving, data architects and developers will recognize the value of small objects in the database; and, as a prediction, Microsoft will respond to user pressures and expand the feature set so that the size and complexity of the object in the database will expand beyond the 8K limit. Sound familiar?

Eventually, usability and functionality will compel most development shops to unlock the potential of CLR integration UDTs in their applications and begin the inevitable march into the object-relational database world.

Programming with ADO.NET 2.0

Unless data can be moved in and out of the database, there is no need for the database, the database administrator, or the database developer. In this chapter, the focus moves away from the database and into the application layer to examine one of the most important and useful SQL Server data access technology genealogies: the ActiveX Data Objects (ADO) family. The newest member, ADO.NET 2.0, is a suite of managed technologies capable of interacting with many Relational Database Management Systems (RDBMS). Of course, SQL Server 2005 is a close relative to ADO.NET 2.0 in the family of Microsoft technologies. It is reasonable — and correct — to expect that they share a special relationship. As you will see, the underlying interface between ADO.NET application code and SQL Server is optimized.

The chapter covers ADO and ADO.NET, with special attention given to the new concepts and features introduced in ADO.NET version 2.0. The first new bit of information to learn is that the technologies are not mutually exclusive. Both ADO and ADO.NET are available to the Visual Studio 2005 programmer. Both have a place in the programmer's toolkit, and it will prove useful to know how ADO and ADO.NET technologies differ. This chapter compares and contrasts ADO and ADO.NET as an aid in making good development decisions. It also illuminates the fundamental shift that occurs between ADO.NET 1.*x* and ADO.NET 2.0 because these sweeping changes are keys to getting the most not only from SQL Server 2005, but also from previous releases of SQL Server.

Cross-Reference Understanding the .NET Framework and object-oriented programming (OOP) is fundamental to using ADO.NET. A brief introduction and additional references for those seeking a more in-depth study of the .NET Framework and fundamental OOP concepts can be found in Chapter 27, "Programming CLR Assemblies within SQL Server."

This chapter provides information on the Visual Studio 2005 IDE features that aid in developing and debugging data access solutions that employ ADO and ADO.NET. There isn't room to discuss all the similarities between Visual Studio and SQL Server Management Studio (MANAGEMENT STUDIO), though they are many and welcome. This chapter covers only Visual Studio's capabilities to aid in the development of ADO and ADO.NET data access methods within applications.

Cross-Reference Readers new to Visual Studio will find much of the material in Chapter 6, "Using Management Studio," and in Part 5, "Business Intelligence," of interest as a good introduction to the user interface shared between SQL Server 2005 and Visual Studio 2005.

An Overview of ADO.NET

In keeping with the Microsoft data access tradition, ADO.NET 2.0 builds upon the existing data access technology base. Since the introduction of SQL Server v1.1, this tradition has shown some common threads of evolution. Each generation has made creating a connection between the application and the data easier than the last, and each has provided greater flexibility and improved features. The improvements have consistently moved in step with leading contemporary design goals, such as host-based computing, client/server, n-tier, service-oriented architecture (SOA), or web services, at any given time in the evolution. Each iteration of the data access technology has attempted to repair the problems of its predecessors in important areas, such as support for referential integrity, performance, and application stability.

With each release of SQL Server, the oldest surviving data access technologies tend to be left behind as newer technologies are integrated. Only rarely are data access changes revolutionary. SQL Server 2005 is no exception. With this release, the DB-Library API is being left behind.

Tip It is true that DB-Library is deprecated with SQL Server 2005 and considered an obsolete Microsoft Data Access Component (MDAC) library. Microsoft does not provide support or the tools necessary to do any DB-Library application development. If possible, DB-Library applications should be updated. However, there is a way to continue using legacy applications written with this old API with SQL Server 2005. Simply copy the DB-Library DLL (`ntwdblib.dll`) from the installation media of a previous version of SQL Server on client machines. The file can be copied to the DB-Library application directory or to a valid location in the `%PATH%` environment string.

The original or "classic" ADO is showing its age and vulnerability. It is not supported by the new SQL Native Client (SNAC or SQLNCLI). Microsoft documentation tends to use the awkward SQLNCLI acronym to refer to this new API. Microsoft folks in presentation and the user community in general are much more likely to use the SNAC (pronounced like "snack") acronym.

ADO will be shipped with the Microsoft Data Access Component (MDAC) libraries. Furthermore, ADO will be able to access SQL Server 2005 databases. However, the new features of SQL Server 2005 will not be available with ADO. New applications should not be written with ADO. Instead, plan how applications now using ADO and the underlying Component Object Model (COM) technology will be upgraded or replaced. In a future release of SQL Server, ADO and COM will no longer be supported.

This chapter describes the steps to undertake to begin preparing for that eventuality. The installed base of ADO-based applications is simply too large for ADO to change or disappear at this time or any time soon. Certainly, the BestPractice is to develop new applications under the service-oriented architecture (SOA) model using ADO.NET 2.0, but it's still necessary to understand both ADO and previous ADO.NET technologies in addition to ADO.NET 2.0 in order to support and maintain existing applications while building the next generation of applications.

ADO brought unprecedented speed and flexibility in data access and data manipulation to the Windows development platform. Beginning with ADO and the COM-based OLE DB interfaces that ADO employs, developers acquired the ability to access heterogeneous data sources — from documents to databases — with a single consistent methodology. ADO abstracted the powerful yet complex COM components and OLE DB interfaces to a simple and friendly object model that enabled large numbers of programmers and web developers to build successful applications.

ADO

Even today, ADO remains a COM-based data access technology. It's important to realize that Object Linking and Embedding components (COM-based OLE DB) have been around since the earliest days of the Microsoft Windows platform. Much has changed since that time. Most notably, the COM specifications were published, and more recently data access has moved away from the OS layer and into the common language runtime (CLR) space. However, much remains the same. As fast as the database world is changing, it took a very long time for that early vision of OLE and COM to be accepted by the developer community, and only then did it reach maturity. It is hoped that the software life cycle for .NET will not be as steep or as long and will enjoy a much longer ride at apogee. While Microsoft is making assurances that the COM binary standard will be around through the next version of the Windows OS, Vista, the likelihood that it will begin descending into obscurity sometime thereafter is real. The movement toward XML-based data transfer is safely beyond critical mass. This leaves COM and the original ADO to play only a legacy role.

As one convincing signal of that progression, with ADO.NET 2.0, Microsoft is recommending that the high-level ADO data access implementation of COM be accessed only through the ADO primary interop assembly (PIA) (`ADODB.dll`). Figure 30-1 shows how this assembly exposes the unmanaged COM components into the managed .NET environment. The ADO code will remain essentially ADO code, but through the PIA it will be managed by the CLR, rather than at the operating system layer. This will not mandate large changes in legacy implementations of ADO, though some changes will be necessary. Nor will it mean that current ADO implementations will be much different than before when written in .NET. It will still be necessary to specify a valid OLE DB data provider in the ADO connection string, for example, and to understand the interfaces and requirements of each of those data providers. Conversely, constructors and garbage collection, security, and runtime type checking (courtesy of the .NET Framework) come into play.

Application problems could result in operating system instability in this model. With SQL Server 2005, ADO uses the `adodb.dll` PIA to provide continued support for ADO application code while realizing the safety of a managed .NET Framework client. The SQL Native Client (SNAC) is optimized for SQL Server access because it communicates directly through the Network services.

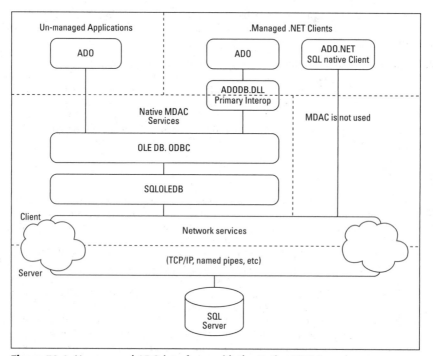

Figure 30-1: Unmanaged ADO interfaces with the Native MDAC services to access the database

Migrating code to ADO.NET 2.0 is the development goal. To ease the transition, use the provided primary interop assembly. For example, a phased approach to upgrading applications to ADO.NET can be pursued. A reasonable scenario is to first migrate ADO applications to the adodb.dll, requiring minimal code changes. Applications gradually become modified to move state away from the database and into .NET data sets or XML streams. Once state is possible at the client, the door is open for caching and data maintenance at the client, as well as disconnected service-oriented architectures. The result is more reliable applications.

Tip   Thoughtful planning is necessary in moving ADO applications to the .NET Framework. Microsoft has done a good job of making topics regarding moving from ADO to ADO.NET available on the Internet. Microsoft's journal for developers, *MSDN,* published a very useful two-part article by John Papa, "Migrating from ADO to ADO.NET," in July 2004 and August 2004. These articles and many other articles from this informative and in-depth magazine are available online at http://msdn.microsoft.com/msdnmag/default.aspx at no cost to the reader. The URL to part one of "Migrating from ADO to ADO.NET" is http://msdn.microsoft.com/msdnmag/issues/04/07/DataPoints/default.as px. The URL for part two is http://msdn.microsoft.com/msdnmag/issues/04/08/ DataPoints/default.aspx. Readers can also find very useful information about moving from ADO to ADO.NET by searching the Microsoft Developer's Network (MSDN) online library at http://msdn.microsoft.com/library/default.asp. Finally, be sure to consult SQL Server Books Online when planning a migration from ADO to ADO.NET. The Books Online article "Updating an Application to SQL Native Client from MDAC" lists many potential problems that can be avoided if identified early in the migration design.

Since ADO's introduction, it hasn't been necessary to be an advanced COM or OLE DB programmer to support, maintain, and enhance existing ADO-based applications. It will continue to be useful to have a high level of insight into COM and OLE DB to support and debug many ADO issues. Most ADO experience and knowledge can be useful when working with ADO.NET. After all, ADO is the basis on which ADO.NET is built. Likewise, OLE DB is the foundation of ADO. Understanding OLE DB can also prove useful when working with ADO or ADO.NET.

OLE DB

The key to OLE DB is found in the consumer and provider metaphor used to describe the technology. OLE DB is a method for connecting data from data providers to applications that consume the data. Well-defined steps must be completed in order to create some common ground between the variety of data providers and the consumer. OLE DB is a COM CoType or related group of COM interfaces that is described in a discoverable hierarchy, qualified by properties and controlled by events. Generally, OLE DB tries to deliver rows and columns of data to consumers. Some providers are not well suited to such descriptions. The CoType hierarchy provides a ladder on which different types of data can ascend from unknown sources to the consumer, beginning at different rungs on the ladder yet coalescing at the point of delivery, known as the CoCreateInstance CoType. Each rung of this conceptual ladder can be thought of as a consumer of the rung below and a provider to the rung above. These transitions are collectively known as *interfaces*. All interfaces inherit from the primordial IUnknown interface. This shows how the components are useful and reusable in that each CoType is similar in form even if very different in function. This is easily borne out if the structural similarities among the ADO objects are considered. At the simplest level, each has properties and methods, and participates in a member hierarchy.

 Readers desiring more details on CoTypes and OLE DB in general might want to consult the "Introduction to OLE DB Programming" located in the MSDN library at http://msdn.microsoft.com/library/default.asp?url=/library/en-us/oledb/htm/oledbpart1_introduction_to_ole_db.asp. CoTypes are discussed throughout this multi-chapter conceptual reference.

The number of OLE DB CoTypes is fairly large. What is useful and quite powerful in OLE DB is the ability to express and transfer all provided data to the consumer in the simple terms of a data value, its length, and distinguishing properties such as a status. Ideally, the status is good data (DBPROPSTATUS_OK), but the status may also indicate a null value or an indication that the value is bad and by what criteria it is deemed bad among other states.

OLE DB, as with all of the COM components, is not programming language dependent. This makes it an ideal low-level architecture for the high-level languages that are used to implement ADO. The low-level specifications are able to remain the same while the ADO object model can be expressed in VB, C#, scripting languages such as VBScript and JScript, and languages capable of entering the low-level specification space, such as C++. OLE DB is a rich programming solution designed to enable database technology to handle data from database and non-database sources in record sets or streams. ADO makes OLE DB available and useful to developers in a way that makes meeting those overarching deadlines and delivery schedules possible. That said, it is not the final data access solution.

Caution   If a programmer specifies an invalid memory location and the compiler does not check type safety, memory leaks and access violation can occur, which will undermine the stability of the application and the database. Memory leaks occur when a memory location is allocated by an application but never returned to the pool of free memory when the application no longer needs that location. Access violations occur when code attempts to read or write to an address that is already in use by another thread of execution. The Visual Studio 2005 C++ compiler cannot verify that memory references are not lost or invalid, so C++ does not protect the programmer from introducing potentially severe defects into application code. The VB.NET compilers, and, to a slightly lesser extent, the C# compilers, as well as the Windows Scripting Host, offer much better protection from such corruptions of memory. The PEVerify tool included in the .NET Framework 2.0 SDK can be used to identify type-safe IL code. The tool is not useful for identifying the location and type of any type-safety defect in the programmer's code.

ADODB Primary Interop Assembly

COM and .NET are compatible technologies. .NET assemblies can be used in COM application code and COM components can be used in .NET code. .NET assemblies can be marshaled by COM wrappers. The COM wrapper must implement the core set of COM interop assemblies. An interop assembly is essentially metadata — or type definitions — for the COM components expressed in managed code.

For additional details on the interoperability of COM and .NET components, see the Microsoft Patterns and Practices white paper "Microsoft .NET/COM Migration and Interoperability" at http://msdn.microsoft.com/library/default.asp?url=/library/en-us/dnbda/html/cominterop.asp.

A primary interop assembly is designated by the original owner of a COM object. The PIA is the recommended interop assembly to be used in the .NET Framework when exposing a COM object in managed code. Microsoft provides such a digitally signed PIA for ADO in Visual Studio .NET: adodb.dll. Microsoft recommends that only this assembly be used for ADO when used in .NET code. As shown in Figure 30-2, the reference for the adodb primary interop assembly is selected from the list of .NET references when adding to a Visual Studio project, rather than adding a reference to the ADO component on the COM tab of the Add Reference dialog.

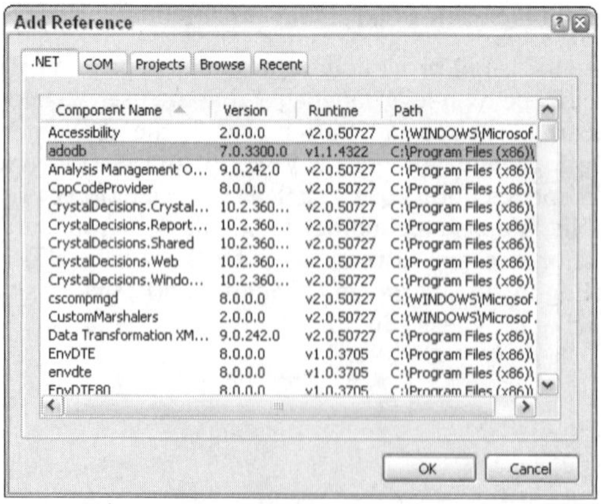

Figure 30-2: Selecting the adodb.dll as a .NET reference in a Visual Studio project

One final consideration when using ADO in Visual Studio 2005 and with ADO.NET 2.0 is that the SNAC does not provide ADO support. This means that the ADO application will rely on MDAC components to access SQL Server. ADO.NET is supported in the SNAC and shouldn't require coordination with the complex web of MDAC libraries and components.

MDAC is becoming a part of the various Microsoft operating systems and will no long be versioned or released apart from the operating systems. A specially installed MDAC is not used in any of the examples in this chapter. The MDAC drivers used are those provided with Windows XP SP2, Windows XP x64, Windows Server 2003 R2 Standard, and Windows Server 2003 R2 Enterprise x64 editions. It is unlikely that Microsoft will announce any future versioned releases to the MDAC libraries. Perhaps the best place to monitor MDAC changes in the future will be in OS releases, service packs, and patch documentation. Similarly, MDAC version compatibly should be verified through regression testing anytime a Microsoft provided change is applied to the operating system.

SNAC is a completely separate API from MDAC. The SNAC is designed to simplify the task of keeping SQL Server clients updated in lock-step with the server. When SQL clients must rely on MDAC components, an update to MDAC is necessary to ensure client and database compatibility can cause problems and failures for other application components running on the client. It follows that MDAC changes necessary for other application components can create problems with the SQL Server connectivity. With SNAC, the SQL client is contained in a single .dll file. The risks of introducing a SNAC change to the application server are low compared to the risks of introducing an MDAC change.

On The Web

Another place to watch for changes to MDAC and SNAC is the Data Access and Storage Developer Center at http://msdn.microsoft.com/data/default.aspx. One informative document that can be found there is the current Microsoft "Data Access Technologies Road Map" vision at http://msdn.microsoft.com/data/mdac/default.aspx?pull=/library/en-us/dnmdac/html/data_mdacroadmap.asp.

The ADO Object Model

Thus far, this chapter has provided a handle on ADO's place in the .NET world and ADO's OLE DB infrastructure as well as how to implement ADO in the .NET Framework. Now consider where ADO fits — or more appropriately doesn't fit — into the ADO.NET grand scheme. One of the design goals of ADO.NET has been to provide all the capabilities of good old ADO. At a minimum, ADO is the role model for ADO.NET. ADO.NET 1.x came up a bit short in meeting the design features of ADO, so the adoption of .NET was impeded in the data access space. With the ADO.NET 2.0 release and SQL Server 2005, the full feature set of ADO is combined with the independence and safety of the .NET Framework and the promise of XML. Not that there isn't some work to be done before ADO is completely bested by the new kid, especially in terms of performance. Understanding this progression from ADO to ADO.NET 2.0 is best accomplished by comparing the object models of the two. To adequately complete the comparison, consider the features and components of the ADO object model. This will build a foundation for reviewing what is new and what is improved in ADO.NET as the chapter progresses.

ADO isn't just a wrapper over OLE DB. It provides real value to the developer and has several advantages over previous database-access methods. The following list describes those advantages originated by ADO:

✦ **Independently created objects:** With ADO it is no longer necessary to thread through a hierarchy of objects. The developer creates only the objects needed, thus reducing memory requirements while increasing application speed and decreasing the lines of code needed.

✦ **Batch updating:** Instead of sending one change to the server, they can be collected in local memory and sent at one time. Using this feature improves application performance (because the data provider can perform the update in the background) and reduces network load.

✦ **Stored procedures:** These procedures reside on the server as part of the database manager. They are used to perform specific tasks on the data set. ADO uses stored procedures with in/out parameters and return values.

✦ **Multiple cursor types:** Cursors point to the data currently in play and can be manifested as client-side and server-side cursors.

> **Cross-Reference**
>
> It's important to distinguish between application code cursors and T-SQL cursors. Client-side application cursors have little of the performance and contention issues of T-SQL cursors. Server-side cursors, particularly when updateable, can negatively impact the database almost to the degree that T-SQL cursors can be problematic. See Chapter 20, "Kill the Cursor!" for more information on cursors.

✦ **Returned row limits:** This enables information retrieval limited to the amount of data actually needed to meet the user's request.

✦ **Multiple record-set objects:** Works with multiple record sets returned by stored procedures or batch processing.

✦ **Free threaded objects:** This feature enhances web server performance by enabling the server to perform multiple tasks.

Like all OLE DB components, ADO uses COM. ADO provides a dual interface: a program ID of ADODB for local operations and a program ID of ADOR for remote operations. The ADO library itself is free-threaded, even though the registry shows it as using the apartment-threaded model. The thread safety of ADO depends on the OLE DB provider that is used. In other words, if a Microsoft provider such as the Open Database Connectivity (ODBC) OLE DB provider is used, then no problems should be expected. If a third-party OLE DB provider is used, then it may be necessary to check the vendor documentation before assuming that ADO is thread-safe (a requirement for using ADO over an Internet or intranet connection).

> **Note**
>
> Open Database Connectivity (ODBC) is a technology for connecting applications to databases that has been in use longer than OLE DB. Unlike OLE DB, ODBC is designed for connecting only to RDBMS sources. The ODBC driver is included in the SNAC, however.

A small set of objects is used to work with ADO. Table 30-1 lists these objects and describes how to use them. Most of these object types have a counterpart in predecessor technologies that Microsoft has introduced, although the level of ADO-object functionality is much greater than that offered by previous technologies and, as demonstrated next, the potential usability for more recent technologies such as ADO.NET and XML transcends even ADO.

Table 30-1: ADO-Object Overview

Object	Description
Connection	A connection object defines the connection with the OLE DB provider. Use this object to perform tasks such as beginning, committing, and rolling back transactions. There are also methods for opening or closing the connection and for executing commands.
Error	ADO creates an error object as part of the connection object. The error object provides additional information about errors raised by the OLE DB provider. A single error object can contain information about more than one error. Each object is associated with a specific event, such as committing a transaction.
Command	A command object performs a task using a connection or recordset object. Even though commands can be executed as part of the connection or recordset object, the command object is much more flexible and enables the definition output parameters.
Parameter	The parameter object defines a single parameter for a command. A parameter modifies the result of a stored procedure or query. Parameter objects can provide input, output, or both.
Recordset	The recordset contains the result of a query, and a cursor for choosing individual elements within the returned table.
Record	A record is a single row of data. It can stand alone or be derived from a record set.
Field	A field object contains a single column of data contained in a record or recordset object. In other words, a field can be thought of as a single column in a table; it contains one type of data for all the records associated with a record set.
Stream	When a data provider is not able to easily express the value and length of the data as a record set with discrete fields, as is the case for large text, BLOB, or document data, the data may be sent to the consumer via the stream object.
Property	Some OLE DB providers will need to extend the standard ADO object. Property objects represent one way to do this. A property object contains attribute, name, type, and value information.

There are also four object collections in ADO: Errors, Parameters, Fields, Properties. Note that these collections are containers for child objects in the ADO model. There are no collections at the root of the object model and the model never gets more than two levels deep. The structure is consistent and simple, always with the following progression:

Parent Object ➪ Collection of dependent objects ➪ Child Object.

OLE DB Data Providers

Even when ADO is used through the provided .NET primary interop assembly, all data access will occur through one of the available OLE DB COM data providers. A *data provider* manages the connection between the client and the DBMS using a number of objects. Of course, this means that a data provider requires a source of information and has to define the specifics for creating that connection. Generally, a provider is database specific or provides a means for configuring a specific database. Figure 30-3 shows a typical list of database providers. Some of the providers on the list are quite specialized.

Figure 30-3: A typical list of database providers

The source of an OLE DB object is known as a provider. Consequently, ADO also relies on data providers as a source of data. Even in this day of the .NET Framework, the number of OLE DB providers—each specialized to a particular data source—is greater than at any time in the past. One nice thing about OLE DB is that the same provider works with any Visual Studio programming language.

Generally, especially for SQL Server developers, it's better to use the SQL Server–specific provider. Even though other general-purpose providers will work, Microsoft has optimized the SQL Server provider for use with SQL Server. The performance advantages of using the SQL Server provider over using a general-purpose provider are well known.

Tip

To find out which OLE DB providers are available on a particular machine, create an new text file and rename it to include an extension of "udl" (e.g., `temp.udl` —the name is not important, only the extension). Open the file to see a dialog similar to the one shown in Figure 30-3 showing all the OLE DB providers installed locally on that Windows family computer.

Mapping Data Types

When working exclusively within SQL Server, the problem with data types amounts to choosing the right type for a given data-storage need. However, when moving the data from the DBMS through a data provider to a client, several layers of transition occur. For some DBMSs this is an extreme problem because the general providers supplied with OLE DB don't support many special data types. For all providers, the cost of data type conversions as data propagates through those layers is significant. These problems of data typing are additional reasons to use the SQL Server–specific OLE DB data providers when working with ADO.

When using data found in a SQL Server table in a client application, the provider must map the data from a type that SQL Server understands to a type that the client application will understand. Fortunately for SQL Server developers, the ADO mapping for the SQLOLEDB provider is relatively straightforward. Table 30-2 shows how the SQL Server provider maps ADO data types. One problem occurs when ADO uses the same data type to represent two or three SQL Server data types when the application requires subtle differences to appear in the user interface. The complete set of SQL Server 2005 data types are exposed in the SQL Native Client. ADO is only aware of the SQL Server 2000 data types and will not be able to handle the new types, such as XML or a varchar(max), discussed later in this chapter.

Table 30-2 shows the SQL Server 2005 data types and the equivalent ADO data types, along with the data type conversion that the NET Framework will conduct for each ADO data type.

Table 30-2: SQL Server to ADO/ADO.NET Data Mapping

SQL Server Data Type	ADO Data Type (.NET Framework Data Type)	Notes
Bigint	adBigInt (int64)	The bigint data-type value ranges from -2^63 (-9,223,372,036,854,775,807) through 2^63-1 (9,223,372,036,854,775,807). This value is only available for SQL Server 2000, but the OLE DB provider will still try to send it to SQL Server 7.0 and older systems, and data loss will result. Use the adBigInt type only when necessary and then with caution.
Binary	adBinary (byte[])	ADO uses the same data-type equivalence for both binary and timestamp.
Bit	adBoolean (Int16)	While this data transfer always works, conceptual differences exist between the two. For example, a bit can have values of 1, 0, or NULL, while an adBoolean always has either a true or false value.
Char	adChar (string)	ADO uses the same data-type equivalence for char, varchar, and text data types. The .NET Framework uses Unicode (UTF-16) to represent all character data.
Datetime	adDBTimeStamp (DateTime)	The default precision for the Datetime datatype in SQL Server is 3.33 milliseconds.

Continued

Table 30-2 *(continued)*

SQL Server Data Type	ADO Data Type (.NET Framework Data Type)	Notes
Decimal	adNumeric (Decimal)	ADO uses the same data-type equivalence for both decimal and numeric data types.
Float	adDouble (Double)	
Image	adVarbinary (byte[])	This data type can be so large that it won't fit in memory. The lack of memory can cause provider errors and possibly only a partial retrieval. When this happens, the developer must write a custom routine to retrieve the data in pieces. ADO uses the same data-type equivalence for image, tinyint, and varbinary.
Int	adInteger (Int32)	
Money	adCurrency (Decimal)	ADO uses the same data-type equivalence for money and smallmoney.
Nchar	adWChar (string)	ADO uses the same data-type equivalence for nchar, ntext, nvarchar, and sysname. The .NET Framework uses Unicode (UTF-16) to represent all character data.
Ntext	adWChar (string)	This data type can be so large that it won't fit in memory. The lack of memory can cause provider errors and possibly a partial retrieval. When this happens, the developer must write a custom routine to retrieve the data in pieces. ADO uses the same data-type equivalence for nchar, ntext, nvarchar, and sysname. The .NET Framework uses Unicode (UTF-16) to represent all character data.
Numeric	adNumeric (decimal)	ADO uses the same data-type equivalence for both decimal and numeric data types.

SQL Server Data Type	ADO Data Type (.NET Framework Data Type)	Notes
Nvarchar	adWChar (string)	ADO uses the same data-type equivalence for nchar, ntext, nvarchar, and sysname. The .NET Framework uses Unicode (UTF-16) to represent all character data.
NvarChar(MAX)	None (string)	SQL Server 2005 provides the same data-type equivalence for what was previously Nvarchar if less than or equal to 8 KB, and text if greater than 8 KB. The .NET Framework uses Unicode (UTF-16) to represent all character data.
Real	adSingle (Single)	
Smalldatetime	adTimeStamp (DateTime)	
Smallint	adSmallInt (Int16)	
Smallmoney	adCurrency (Decimal)	ADO uses the same data-type equivalence for money and smallmoney.
sql_variant	adVariant (object)	This data type can contain any of a number of primitive data types, such as smallint, float, and char. It can't contain larger data types such as text, ntext, and image. The adVariant type maps to the OLE DB DBTYPE_VARIANT data type and is only usable with SQL Server 2000. Be careful when using this data type because it can produce unpredictable results. Even though OLE DB provides complete support for it, ADO doesn't.
Sysname	adWChar (string)	ADO uses the same data-type equivalence for nchar, ntext, nvarchar, and sysname. The .NET Framework uses Unicode (UTF-16) to represent all character data.

Continued

Table 30-2 *(continued)*

SQL Server Data Type	ADO Data Type (.NET Framework Data Type)	Notes
Text	adChar (string)	This data type can be so large that it won't fit in memory. The lack of memory can cause provider errors and possibly a partial retrieval. When this happens, the developer must write a custom routine to retrieve the data in pieces. ADO uses the same data-type equivalence for char, varchar, and text data types. The .NET Framework uses Unicode (UTF-16) to represent all character data.
Timestamp	adBinary (byte[])	ADO uses the same data-type equivalence for both binary and timestamp.
Tinyint	adTinyInt (byte)	
Uniqueidentifier	adGUID (Guid)	The data provider supports a string GUID, not a true GUID. This means that when an actual GUID is needed, the code must explicitly convert it into a GUID data structure.
Varbinary	adVarbinary (byte[])	ADO uses the same data-type equivalence for image and varbinary.
Varbinary(MAX)	none (byte[])	SQL Server 2005 provides the same data-type equivalence for what was previously varbinary if less than or equal to 8KB, and image if greater than 8 KB.
Varchar	adChar (string)	ADO uses the same data-type equivalence for char, varchar, and text. The .NET Framework uses Unicode (UTF-16) to represent all character data.
Varchar(MAX)	None (string)	SQL Server 2005 provides the same data-type equivalence for what was previously varchar if less than or equal to 8 KB, and text if greater than 8 KB. The .NET Framework uses Unicode (UTF-16) to represent all character data.

The comments in Table 30-2 touch upon the most significant problems that can occur in the mapping of data between ADO and SQL Server. It is important to also consider data-conversion errors. According to Microsoft, all nondirect data translations are subject to data loss. For example, neither the provider nor SQL Server will complain if an eight-byte number is converted into a four-byte number, but obviously there is a potential for data loss. In addition, some types cannot be converted to other types. For example, it's impossible to convert an adBinary data type into an adSmallInt data type. In this situation, the development environment would complain. The sort order of SQL character data types is by default different from the sort order of .NET data types.

The .NET Framework adds another level of conversion and potential conversion errors to the ADO implementation. ADO data types are specified within ADO Objects. The .NET Framework will convert those data types to valid .NET data types implicitly when they are used outside of the ADO objects in the code. This conversion should happen without the need for explicit data conversion type casting, although it is good programming practice to always ensure that data is always of the type expected. The developer must remain vigilant for data type conversion problems when programming ADO, even in the .NET Framework. Using the .NET data types that support null values may provide relief for conversion problems with many applications. There seems to be no perfect solution to this problem short of environment coding standards that mandate consistent BestPractice programming techniques for all programmers in the environments, and rigorous testing.

To avoid unexpected data type conversions at assignment, ADO data types can be assigned using explicit casting to the desired data type.

Best Practice

ADO and Scripting

ADO often appears in scripts of various types. Because ADO relies on COM technology, any scripting language capable of creating an object can probably use ADO to retrieve data from a database. Using scripts to perform small tasks makes sense because they can easily be modified if necessary and they are quick to write. Be aware that scripting facilities such as the Windows Script Component can be created and referenced from VB.NET or C#, and the Windows Scripting Host runs ADO as a COM component only. Interoperability with .NET does not apply.

Recall from the discussion in Chapter 27, "Programming CLR Assemblies within SQL Server," that .NET code is compiled to IL. Because the compilation to IL must happen at some point before runtime, the concept of late binding is not available to .NET code. Conversely, script-based ADO, such as when used in the Windows Scripting Host 5.6, a SQL Server 2000 DTS ActiveX script step, or a pre .NET ASP page, requires late binding. Late binding simply means that the COM object referenced is created at runtime and is identifiable by the use of the CreateObject() function. Therefore, in order to use ADO in scripts, MDAC must be installed on any machine that will execute scripts. In contrast, ADO.NET will be fully supported by the SQL Native Client and will not require MDAC. This important new distinction with ADO.NET 2.0 is covered in greater detail later in this chapter.

Of course, scripting languages don't provide the robust interactive environment found in programming languages such as C# or Visual Basic or even ASP.NET. It may be necessary to restrict the use of scripts to small tasks such as calling on a stored procedure to perform some task automatically or to retrieve the result of a data query for onscreen display.

Microsoft makes a point of demonstrating the flexibility of ADO with several languages, including Java, JavaScript, VBScript, and the new XML-based Windows Script Component available in Visual Studio 2005.

ADO.NET

It's somewhat confusing that ADO.NET inherits the ADO part of its name from the original ADO. ADO is the acronym for ActiveX Data Objects. ActiveX is a clear signal that the topic is IUnknown and COM. IUnknown is the prototype for all COM classes. In its raw form it indicates that the calling module needs to know nothing about a called object and the caller will still be able to statefully interact with the called module. While deep down in the bowels of .NET there still exists COM programmability, the whole point of the .NET Framework and the common language runtime (CLR) is the shift away from the limitations of the COM code execution environment and toward consistency in the object-oriented class model. IUnknown means there is no need to know anything about a class in order to instantiate and use the class. The .NET Framework portends that the system assemblies and the base classes will be reliably consistent types. In short, there is little that is COM-based ADO in ADO.NET from a technical perspective.

Only from a functional perspective is ADO.NET a natural progression from ADO. A new technology was required to overcome the limitations of ADO performance and scalability — a technology that provided the developer with a variety of execution options. ADO.NET was designed to both overcome ADO limitations and leverage the developer's ADO skills. The basic objects of ADO are found in ADO.NET. Commands executed on connections to data providers are used in ADO.NET with only slight differences from the commands executed on connections to data providers used with ADO. However, with ADO.NET, developers have greater control over how the data will be retrieved and manipulated. Execution can be asynchronous and batched. Results can be elegantly stored and manipulated at the application, disconnected from the database. Alternately, results can as easily be streamed as binary data or as XML.

Many developers labor under the misconception that ADO.NET is simply the upgrade to ADO. ADO was developed to support client/server applications and presupposes that the user and the data will both remain connected to the application for the lifetime of an execution cycle. At the risk of oversimplifying the difference, ADO held state in the data source and ADO.NET is built to be able to maintain state disconnected from the database. One advantage for .NET is that there is no requirement that the database remain connected to the application for the complete execution cycle. In part, this design goal is realized because XML technology is fundamental to ADO.NET. To a larger degree, state is managed in the ADO.NET application layer by the local application cache known as the DataSet class. In ADO.NET 2.0, state management is further extended with asynchronous command execution and *Multiple Active Result Sets (MARS)*.

The following sections describe ADO.NET objects, keeping ADO objects in perspective, and point out the new features in the ADO.NET 2.0 release. In other words, the discussion will build on the ADO information presented earlier in this chapter as ADO.NET concepts are introduced. ADO.NET is a managed object model with functional abilities much like the classic ADO, yet designed to enable more scalable applications, particularly in the disconnected environments found in many n-tier, SOA, web services, and ASP.NET applications.

The ADO.NET Object Model

The ADO.NET object model is different from the object model used by ADO. The model is more complex yet undeniably richer.

The most striking difference is the in-memory data cache known as the DataSet. This ADO.NET object can be divided into two components: the DataSet and the data provider. The DataSet is a special object that contains one or more tables. The data in the DataSet is retrieved from the data source through the provider and stored in the application work space. The data can be manipulated and constrained at the application. The DataSet is a disconnected subset of the data from the data source defined by the provider properties. The data provider properties include the Connection, Command, DataReader, and DataAdapter objects. Each of these objects also has capabilities not found in an ADO provider. For example, a DataAdapter can actually handle more than one connection and one set of rules. As with many managed objects, enumerators are used to access the various objects within these main objects in application code.

✦ **Data provider:** Contains the classes that create the connection, issue commands, handle the data reader, and provide data-adapter support. The connection provides the conduit for database communications. The command enables the client to request information from the database server through the data adapter. In addition to providing data, the data adapter also enables the client cache to synchronize or update back to the data source. The data reader is a one-way, read-only method of viewing data in ADO. The data adapter provides the real-time connection support normally associated with live data connections.

✦ **Dataset:** The representation of information within the database. It contains two collections: DataTableCollection and DataRelationCollection. The DataTableCollection contains the columns and rows of the table, along with any constraints imposed on that information. The DataRelationCollection contains the relational information used to create the dataset.

Table 30-3 provides an overview of the most frequently used ADO.NET data classes.

Table 30-3: ADO.NET 2.0 Class Overview

Class Type	Description
Connection	Creates the physical connection between the DBMS and a DataAdapter, DataReader, or factory. The Connection object also includes logic that optimizes the use of connections within the distributed-application environment.
ProviderFactory	New in ADO.NET 2.0. Each .NET provider implements a ProviderFactory class, each of which derives from the common base class DBProviderFactory. The factory class includes methods for creation of provider-specific ADO.NET components in a generic code style. The idea behind the ProviderFactory is to enable the developer to write generic code that can use a provider determined at runtime. The possible providers a factory can use are stored in the machine.config file.
Command	Defines an action to perform on the DBMS, such as adding, deleting, or updating a record. The DataAdapter includes the command objects required to query, delete, insert, and edit records.
Parameter	A parameter to a command
Error	The error or warning information returned from the database. For SQL Server this includes the error number, severity, and the text for the error.
Exception	The application exception when ADO.NET 2.0 encounters an error. The Error class is created by the Exception class. The Exception class is used in ADO.NET 2.0 try-catch error handling.

Continued

Table 30-3 *(continued)*

Class Type	Description
DataAdapter	Translates the data from the data provider source into the in-memory DataSet or DataReader. The DataAdapter performs all queries, translates data from one format to another, and performs table mapping. One DataAdapter can manage one database relation. The result collection can have any level of complexity. The DataAdapter is also responsible to issuing requests for new connections and terminating connections after it obtains the data.
DataReader	Provides a live connection to the database. However, it only provides a means of reading the database. In addition, the DataReader cursor works only in the forward direction. This is the object to use to perform a fast retrieval of a local table when there is no need to update the database. The DataReader blocks subsequent DataAdapters and associated Connection objects, so it's important to close the DataReader immediately after using it.
DataSet	Contains a local copy of the data retrieved by one or more DataAdapters. The DataSet uses a local copy of the data, so the connection to the database isn't live. A user makes all changes to the local copy of the database, and then the application requests an update. (Updates can occur in batch mode or one record at a time.) The DataSet maintains information about both the original and the current state of each modified row. If the original row data matches the data on the database, the DataAdapter makes the requested update. If not, the DataAdapter returns an error, which the application must handle. DataSets may be typed or untyped in ADO.NET 2.0. DataSets are defined in the System.Data namespace, they are not provider specific. Only the DataAdapter classes are associated with the provider.
Transaction	New in ADO.NET 2.0. The ADO.NET transaction is by default a lightweight transactional container for a single data source. If the ADO code enlists another data source in the transaction, the transaction will transparently escalate to a distributed or multi-phase transaction, with no additional coding required by the developer.

Note Visual Studio 2005 provides a TableAdapter class, which is a single-table data collection that can be used in application code much like an ADO.NET 2.0 DataSet. The TableAdapter is significantly easier for the developer to create and manipulate than the underlying ADO.NET 2.0 data components when only one table is needed at the application. The TableAdapter is not derived from the System.Data.DataSet class as are all other DataSets. In fact, TableAdapters are not even part of the .NET Framework. They are a level of abstraction provided by Visual Studio 2005. All TableAdapters inherit from System.Component .ComponentModel. This means they are fully integrated with the Visual Studio tools, such as the Data Grid. In addition, the base class for a TableAdapter can be any of the .NET providers that expose a DataTable class. The base class is specified when the TableAdapter is created. TableAdapters are type-safe and include all properties and methods necessary to connect to a data source, retrieve the table's data, and update the data source. More information about the TableAdapter can be found in the MSDN white paper "TableAdapters in Visual Studio 2005," located at http://msdn.microsoft.com/library/default.asp?url=/library/en-us/dnvs05/html/tableadapters.asp.

Managed Providers

Four managed providers are included in ADO.NET 2.0:

✦ **OracleClient:** The Microsoft provider for the Oracle database. This provider requires that the Oracle client be installed.

✦ **OleDb:** The bridge provider for using OLE DB providers in ADO.NET

✦ **SqlClient:** The Microsoft provider for SQL Server 7.0 and later. Just as the OLE DB provider directly connects SQL Server and ADO, the SQLClient uses a private protocol for direct connection to SQL Server from ADO.NET.

✦ **SqlServerCe:** The Microsoft provider for SQL Server CE mobile edition

As noted above, the `OracleClient` provider requires the co-installation of the Oracle client. The OleDb.NET provider relies upon MDAC components for some functionality. `SQLClient` and `SqlServerCe` are contained in the SQL Native Client library.

> **Note** ADO.NET 1.1 included an Odbc managed provider. The namespace for this managed provider is no longer supported in ADO.NET 2.0. The SQL Native Client does include an ODBC driver. This will provide support for existing ODBC applications. However, the removal of the `System.Data.ODBC` namespace in ADO.NET 2.0 seems to signal the end of the ODBC API as a mainstream data access API.

While ADO.NET 1.*x* used the shared MDAC architecture, it did not have a single object that was instantiated to create a command, a data reader, or a data adapter. It supported several per-provider class-specific objects contained in different libraries that performed these tasks. It was necessary for the developer to select the namespace appropriate to the application. The selected namespace aligned with a specific provider.

When working with SQL Server, that meant using the objects that Microsoft had optimized for native SQL Server use, including `SqlConnection`, `SqlCommand`, `SqlDataReader`, and `SqlDataAdapter`.

These provider-specific classes are still supported. When the data source is SQL Server, the provider-specific classes will be optimized and therefore are preferred. Better performance should be expected from any of the per-provider classes. In addition, there is a common base class alternative with ADO.NET 2.0 that should receive consideration for use on new projects. In an environment that must support multiple RDBMS data sources, the common class may require fewer lines of code than duplicating the same logic with each provider. However, the likelihood that coding with the common base class will require some per-provider customizations is quite high.

Table 30-4 shows a cross-reference of `System.Data.Common` classes and the provider-specific classes available for each of the class types listed previously in Table 30-2.

> **Note** When working with other RDBMS data sources in ADO.NET 1.1, the developer had to use a separate but parallel set of ADO.NET provider classes for each provider. Included with the .NET Framework 1.1 were the classes of the `System.Data.OleDb` namespace, the `System.Data.Odbc` namespace, and the `OracleClient` namespace. Developers could also write custom providers, and third-party sources made other provider namespaces available. The same Interfaces used by Microsoft to create the included provider classes can be used to create custom providers.

Table 30-4: ADO.NET 2.0 Class Reference by Namespace

Class Type (from Table 30-3)	System.Data. Common	System.Data. SQLClient	System.Data. OracleClient	System.Data. OleDb
Connection	DbConnection	SqlConnection	OracleConnection	OleConnection
ProviderFactory	DbProviderFactory	SqlClientFactory	OracleClientFactory	OleDbFactory
Command	DbCommand	SqlCommand	OracleCommand	OleCommand
Parameter	DbParameter	SqlParameter	OracleParameter	OleParameter
Error	None	SqlError	None	OleError
Exception	DbException	SqlException	OracleException	OleException
DataAdapter	DbDataAdapter	SqlDataAdapter	OracleDataAdapter	OleDataAdapter
DataReader	DbDataReader	SqlDataReader	OracleDataReader	OleDataReader
Transaction	DbTransaction	SqlTransaction	OracleTransaction	OleTransaction

In ADO.NET 2.0, the `System.Data.Common` namespace introduces a base class to write provider-independent (often termed *generic*) code using a common base class shared among all providers. The provider is defined and accessed through the `DbProviderFactory` class in this model. The provider components are `DbConnection`, `DbCommand`, `DbDataReader` and `DbDataAdapter`. The factory model creates the capability to specify not only the connection string, but also the provider in the application's configuration file, the registry, another structure, or even user input readable at the time the connection class is instantiated. It is called a factory because of the capability to construct instances of provider-specific classes automatically. The factory-created classes are inherited by a factory class in the `SQLClient` or any other provider-specific classes. In theory, the result is simplified and provider-agnostic code from the developer's perspective.

In many cases it may be possible to achieve that coding objective with the `System.Data.Common` classes. Applications that must be able to run on multiple database platforms are prime candidates for generic ADO.NET. In reality, each specific provider needs extensions to the base model, so the base class is probably not completely usable by any .NET providers without some references to provider-specific classes in the developer's code. Consequently, common base class coding may be more complex than using the provider-specific namespaces at this time. Undoubtedly, the common base class usability will continue to evolve in future releases of ADO.NET. It is conceivable that the provider-specific classes derived from the common base class model may even fall out of favor in the future. For now, it may be wise for all but the most adventurous developers to proceed with some caution into the generic coding model.

For additional details on the common base class and the `DBPProviderFactory`, see the MSDN white papers "Generic Coding with the ADO.NET 2.0 Base Classes and Factories," by Bob Beauchemin, at `http://msdn.microsoft.com/library/default.asp?url=/library/en-us/dnvs05/html/vsgenerics.asp`, and "Writing Generic Data Access Code in ASP.NET 2.0 and ADO.NET 2.0," by Dr. Shahram Khosravi, at `http://msdn.microsoft.com/library/default.asp?url=/library/en-us/dnvs05/html/vsgenerics.asp`.

The managed-database providers for ADO.NET incorporate a certain level of intelligence not found in the ADO version of the same providers. For example, the .NET providers make better use of database connections. They make and break connections as necessary to ensure optimal use of server and client resources. The differences between an unmanaged and a managed provider can easily be categorized into four areas:

✦ **Object Access Technique:** An unmanaged provider will use a COM progID to access the required objects. When working with a managed provider, the application relies on a `command` class. The `command` class may still access the COM progID, but the `command` class hides the details of the access from the developer, which makes development faster and less error-prone. It also enables streamlining of the SQL client data access and allows the possibility that the ADO.NET code will have the same look and feel regardless of whether the underlying access is via a COM ProgID or not.

✦ **Data Result Handling:** The unmanaged provider relies on the `Parameter` objects of the `Command`, along with the `Recordset` and `Stream` objects provided by ADO, to present the data within the application. The managed equivalents include the `Parameter`, `DataSet`, `DataTable`, and `DataReader` classes, along with the `ExecuteReader`, `ExecutePageReader`, `ExecuteNonQuery`, and `ExecuteScalar` methods of the `command` class and the XML stream. The unmanaged COM interface will always incur the overhead of converting SQL data types to COM data types. The managed providers have the distinct advantage here again because of the XML-based transport stream.

✦ **Data Updates:** Because the unmanaged environment uses a live connection, resources are in constant use and the user must have a connection to the database. In addition, the developer spends plenty of time creating the commands by hand. The managed environment uses connections only as needed to actually transfer data, so resource usage is more efficient and the user doesn't need a connection at all times. As shown later in the chapter, the managed environment also provides other automation techniques, including the `CommandBuilder` method.

✦ **Data-Transfer Format:** The unmanaged environment uses binary data transfer. The managed-data provider relies solely on XML for data transfer in ADO.NET 1.*x*. Distributed applications in ADO.NET 2.0 can also be transferred using binary serialization, with a remarkable improvement in size and throughput over XML in cases where remoting is appropriate. Remoting provides improved performance and interoperability in interprocess communication between .NET applications. If either the source or target of a data transfer is not a .NET application, then XML will provide a standards-based method to transfer data, which will require much less code and therefore lower maintenance cost than unmanaged transfer methods.

The differences in data-transfer methods between the managed XML and unmanaged data providers requires close examination. The XML data-transfer format used by a managed provider is better suited to SOA and the Internet because it enables data transfer through firewalls that normally block binary data transfers. However, XML is a bulkier data-transfer method and isn't secure. In the past, it may have been enticing to use ADO for local database needs and ADO.NET for distributed applications because of the obvious size and performance penalties inherent in XML and the illusory security value of binary over ASCII bits flying over the private network. The ADO.NET 2.0 binary serialization option provides a performance advantage to remote streams and thereby helps reduce the often poorly founded temptation to continue to support both ADO and ADO.NET.

SQL Native Client

With SQL Server 2005 and ADO.NET 2.0, access to SQL Server does not rely on MDAC. Instead, the `SQLClient` is contained in a single .dll known as the SQL Native Client. The SQL Native Client is expected to resolve the well-known consistency issues in the distribution of updates through the massive MDAC file set, and improve security by limiting the number of interfaces — or surface area — exposed. The proprietary .NET to SQL Server access protocols, as well as OLE DB and ODBC interfaces to SQL Server and the traditional native interfaces to SQL Server, are contained in the SQL Native Client.

It would be ideal if only the SQL Native Client were required to access SQL Server. Unfortunately, that ideal remains elusive. Only SQL Server 7.0 and later are supported by the SQL Native Client. SQLXML is not integrated in the SQL Native Client. In all likelihood many .NET Framework applications will have dependencies on both MDAC and the SQL Native Client. After all, one of the selling points for .NET is heterogeneous data sources. The monolithic SQL Native Client should simplify maintenance and security of the contained interfaces but it does not appear that there will be a noticeable difference in how applications interact with SQL Server. Similarly, it is likely that ODBC, OleDB, and in particular ADO, access will continue to be problematic to whatever extent the SQL Native Client is dependent on MDAC components.

Cross-Reference

SQLXML is updated to version 4.0 in SQL Server 2005. While not integrated into the SQL Native Client provider, SQLXML is supported in the .NET Framework through the OLE DB-based SQLXMLOLED provider. Additional information on SQLXML, including details on .NET programming with SQLXML, can be found in Chapter 31, "Using XML, XPath, and XQuery."

Data Types

ADO.NET uses XML to move data from the database to the application. This is not XML as in the XML data type, but XML as in the actual carrier of all SQL data, just as TDS is the native binary carrier of SQL data from SQL Server. XML can support all data types without prejudice because XML is a stream of bits. Visual Studio applications, conversely, rely on managed data types to represent onscreen data. In other words, XML adds yet another translation layer to the mix. ADO.NET moves the data in and out of the database on an XML stream. Then it must unpackage the XML stream into the desired flavor of relational data results at the application. All of the data restrictions, oddities, and problems that were discussed in the ADO section also apply to the data provided to the application by ADO.NET. Consequently, developers must consider the same problems, such as data loss and compatibility problems, during development.

Fortunately, the managed environment provides good marshaling for data types used in database management. Using ADO.NET may introduce a small performance penalty to transport the inherently bloated XML stream and to package and unpackage that stream. However, it is unlikely that the managed environment will introduce data-translation problems. In fact, the expectation is that in the near future, ADO.NET's XML-based I/O performance will be as good as ADO's binary transport method. ADO.NET uses .NET Framework data types, rather than define its own data types, as was the case with ADO. This should immediately help curb the proliferation of data type conversion errors at runtime.

One particularly compelling reason to favor ADO.NET over ADO, even in the short term, is ADO.NET's better support for the new SQL Server data types, such as `XML`, `VARCHAR(MAX)`, `VARBINARY(MAX)`, and any CLR user-defined data types

Cross-Reference Refer to Table 27-1 in Chapter 27, "Programming CLR Assemblies within SQL Server," for a full mapping of data types between SQL Server 2005 and the .NET Framework.

The XML data type that can be stored in SQL Server 2005 should not to be confused with the XML stream that ADO.NET uses to transport data. The XML data type is supported by the System.Data.SQLTypes SqlXml data type in ADO.NET 2.0. The XML data type can be used to store XML documents and XML document fragments. ADO.NET 2.0 supports reading this data type through the XMLDataReader method. Unlike other SQL Server 2005 data types, XML is not validated in ADO.NET but at the SQL server. This means that the XML data type has some risk of raising errors during the DataAdapter's update method—when changes are sent back to the database—that would not be expected for other primitive data types. SQLXML 4.0 provides the richest client-side support for the XML data type, including its own set of Data Access components. Recall that SQLXML 4.0 is not provided as part of ADO.NET 2.0.

CLR user-defined data types deserve a special mention here. In order to use a CLR user-defined data type (UDT) in .NET code, a structurally consistent version of the assembly that defines the data type must be available not only on the database server, but also on the application server. There is a small amount of flexibility in the requirements. It is not necessary that the assembly be a strongly named match on the server and at the application, only that the structure of the type be identically defined at both locations. This requirement makes sense. The system-defined primitive data types, int, char, bit, and so on, must exist at both locations. The difference lies in the logistics required to keep a custom feature such as the UDT synchronized at all tiers, compared to the comparatively static primitive types. A UDT that is used only on the SQL Server is likely to be of little real value, and a UDT that is deployed in a production environment is likely to be somewhat fragile because of this awkward requirement. Careful deployment planning is necessary when using UDTs in ADO.NET 2.0 applications.

Cross-Reference For a complete discussion on creating and deploying CLR user-defined data types, see Chapter 29, "Persisting Custom Data Types."

DataAdapters and DataSets

Until this point in the chapter, ADO and ADO.NET have been shown to be very different technologies despite the similarities in their names and a common purpose. The core of ADO is the Recordset. To modify data through a record set it is necessary to either use a server API cursor that stays in the database or write code that sends updates back to the database once the changes are identified. Both methods have proven to be fragile because of concurrency and contention issues, and both can require a hefty chunk of code. To work with multiple Recordsets, it is necessary to create multiple connections and to juggle the Recordsets in code or pull multiple Recordsets from the database as a collection and work with them one at a time. Either method has proven to be rigid and can require a hefty chuck of often repetitive code.

Thc primary in-memory data store of ADO.NET is the DateSet. The DataAdapter is used to connect the data source and the in-memory data store. In ADO.NET 2.0, the DataSet is more powerful than ever.

The DateSet is disconnected from the database to reduce contention in the database and therefore open the door to highly scalable applications. The code required to either fill the DateSet from the database or update the database from the DateSet is minimal.

The DataAdapter populates the DateSet with a stream of data from the database, and handles any inserts, updates, or deletes that must be propagated back to the database.

DateSet queries can reference multiple DataTables within the DateSet, and enforcement of defined relationships and data types occurs seamlessly at the moment data is modified in the DateSet.

Index optimizations in ADO.NET 2.0 have enabled the size of the DateSet cache to increase significantly, and performance has improved considerably over ADO.NET 1.x. A DataSet populated with a relatively small amount of data may not realize benefits from these index optimizations. As the DataSet grows larger, the optimizations become more important.

Note Visual Studio 2005 is well integrated with ADO.NET 2.0 classes. ADO.NET is already a remarkably easy to use technology. Many features of the Visual Studio UI simplify ADO.NET usage even further. For examples, a DateSet can be bound to a control simply by dragging and dropping the dataset on the control at design time. In addition, using the DataAdapter Wizard and the DateSet Wizard at design time will produce a typed dataset and the code to populate it.

Using the CommandBuilder method will automatically create the update, insert, and delete commands that the DataAdapter will use to maintain the database based upon the select statement used to fill the DateSet: one line of code to generate three database operations.

Binary serialization functionality in ADO.NET 2.0 also allows those larger DateSets to be propagated out of the database and between tiers of the application much faster. This feature is most useful in .NET remoting situations whereby different components of the same application do not suffer the penalties of complexity regarding being able to decode the binary data stream.

By default, the DataReader class uses a read-only, forward-only cursor. The DataReader object is able to offer a connected behavior or to enable disconnected mode operation for applications. A user can download data from the company database while using an Internet (or other) connection. In the disconnected mode, the data is then available for viewing offline (but not for direct modification at the database because the connection to the database is lost). While perhaps more interesting for the DataReader per se than the DataTable, ADO.NET 2.0 also provides methods to easily morph a DataTable into a DataReader using GetTableReader or to fill a DataTable from a DataReader or a database-connected DataAdapter. Increased flexibility and reduction in lines of code required by these refinements to the DataTable class are two more reasons to consider ADO.NET over ADO.

One drawback to programmatically making a DateSet from a DataReader is that the DateSet will not be typed. One advantage of typed data sets is an opportunity for better performance by not forcing any more implicit data-conversion layers or any more complex translations than necessary in .NET. Another advantage is more readable code. For example, to locate and use a column in a DataTable of an untyped DateSet, the code would look like the following:

```
City = dsOrder.Tables[n].Rows[n].ItemArray.GetValue(1).ToString()
```

Using an ADO.NET typed DateSet, the code is considerably friendlier:

```
City = dsOrder.Invoice[0].Name;
```

Clearly, the reference to the typed DataSet is more concise.

An ADO `Recordset` object has the advantage of requiring less code to access an individual value. In addition, note that the field can be accessed by name when using a `Recordset` object — the `DateSet` or stand-alone `DataTable` offers an integer item indexed value that must be derived from the field's position within the data result. The typed dataset is the readability winner hands down. Using ADO.NET offers other significant advantages that may not be readily identified if an "ADO is better" attitude is allowed to cloud the picture.

ADO.NET 2.0 also provides Multiple Active Result Set (MARS) for SQL Server 2005 only. MARS is easily understood as a mechanism for pooling sessions in a similar manner to how connections have been pooled for quite some time in ADO technologies. While there are still many reasons to create multiple connections, in some cases, such as where multiple queries must maintain transactional consistency, a MARS connection can provide transactional consistency and performance benefits without the need for a two-phase transaction riding on multiple connections. Select statements can be interleaved as desired when the provider is MARS-enabled. When inserts, updates, or deletes occur on a MARS-enabled connection, serialization of DML and select statements will occur. The MARS behavior is not enabled by default in SQL Server 2005. To enable the functionality specify `MultipleActiveResultSets` `=true` in the connection string.

> **Note** Even though MARS is not enabled by default, overhead is involved in all connections in order to support MARS. Microsoft has stated that setting `MultipleActiveResultSets =False` will not eliminate this MARS-related overhead. Possibly the only reason to ever set MARS off is to ensure an error condition when more than one query is submitted on a connection.

ADO does provide remote-connectivity features, but like all other COM-based technologies, it uses the Distributed Component Object Model (DCOM) as the basis for data exchange across a remote network. This means that the connection-port number changes often and that the data itself is in binary form. One benefit of this approach is that few crackers and hackers have the knowledge required to peek at the data (assuming they can unscramble it after locating it). The disadvantages include an inability to leverage ADO.NET 2.0–specific features, the high technical cost of transferring binary data, and web server firewall support. Good firewall design keeps ports closed and restricts binary data.

 On The Web Simply stated, DCOM is COM when the components must communicate on the network. With DCOM, the components use RPC to communicate. In practice, security and integration with the network protocol stack render DCOM a different technology than COM, even though they serve a similar purpose. Readers seeking more details on DCOM should refer to Microsoft's 1996 white paper titled "DCOM Technical Overview," at `http://msdn.microsoft.com/library/default.asp?url=/library/en-us/dndcom/html/msdn_dcomtec.asp`.

ADO.NET gets around the firewall problems by using XML to transfer the data using HyperText Transport Protocol (HTTP) or some other appropriate data transfer technology. The data is in ASCII format and relies on a single port for data transfers. There are a number of other tools in the developer's toolkit that ride above ADO.NET to better secure XML on the wire, such as SSL encryption and signing, certificate exchange, and the self-contained Web Services Security protocol in environments where text on the wire is a security issue.

A host of additional enhancements are available in ADO.NET 2.0. It would be prudent for the developer community to pay attention to whether actual behavior matches expectations. Some enhancements are made possible by the new features of SQL Server 2005 and are covered throughout the book. Some of the more interesting .NET enhancements include:

✦ Automatic transaction escalation from a local transaction to a distributed transaction at the point where multiple data sources become involved in an open transaction.

✦ Improved `DataTable` indexing, expected to deliver great performance improvement for large result sets.

✦ `DataSet` updates can be sent to the database in batches by specifying a value greater than 0 for the `SQLDataADapter.UpdateBatchSize` property.

✦ Better enumeration of available data sources. For example, the `SqlClient` is supposed to be able to find all available SQL Servers on the network.

✦ Improved connection pooling control, which includes the capability both to set the bounds for the number of connections in a pool and to drain the pool of all existing connections.

✦ ADO.NET 2.0–based Bulk-Insert API allows fast bulk insert of data from a `DataTable` or a `DataReader`.

✦ ADO.NET 2.0 can be the output for an Integration Services package.

✦ A notification method to inform dependent mid-tier layers that data has changed in the database. This will prove useful in high-volume n-tier settings where data sets are cached and the underlying data is unpredictably volatile. A `SqlDependency` is bound to a `SqlCommand`. Then the application performs a very lightweight polling of a Service Broker queue for notification of changed data using the `SQLNotificationRequest` method.

✦ The capability to execute asynchronously. The capability to emit worker threads and continue processing on the main thread is not new, but the capability for ADO.NET to enlist and manage asynchronous workers is. The connected query methods now support the typical .NET `begin...end` code structure for asynchronous operations (e.g., `BeginExecuteNonQuery...EndExecuteNonQuery`). Note that WinForms do not support ADO.NET 2.0 asynchronous queries. Asynchronous execution is off by default. To enable, specify `"Asynchronous Processing=true"` in the connection string.

✦ SQL Server performance metrics are exposed in the programming interface as properties of the connection.

Cross-Reference   Four important extensions to ADO.NET can be used in server-side CLR on SQL Server: `SQLContext`, `SqlPipe`, `SqlTriggerCOntext`, and `SqlDataRecord`. These are described in some detail in Chapter 27, "Programming CLR Assemblies within SQL Server."

ADO.NET in Visual Studio 2005

There was some concern within the SQL Server DBA community when Microsoft announced that SQL Server's Enterprise Manager would be moving into Visual Studio. That seems to have been a misunderstanding. SQL Server Management Studio (MANAGEMENT STUDIO) has found its way into the common Visual Studio graphical interface, but they remain separate products sharing little more than a common look and feel.

A complete description of the Visual Studio Integrated Development Environment (IDE) is beyond the scope of this chapter. Fortunately, details of the IDE are well covered in the Microsoft Visual Studio documentation. This section examines the IDE components that are particularly important for the development of successful applications that use ADO.NET 2.0.

Server Explorer

It's a smart bet that each ADO.NET 2.0 project will begin with the Server Explorer. The programmer will either add a data connection or select an existing data connection when an ADO.NET 2.0 project is created. A new data connection can be defined using the Data Source Configuration Wizard from the Data menu item or in Server Explorer by selecting Add Connection from the context menu of the Data Connections icon.

In addition to managing database connections, Server Explorer provides other useful database tools. Database metadata diagramming, access, and generation capabilities are available to the developer from Server Explorer. While the database components exposed by Server Explorer do not provide support identical to Management Studio's Object Explorer they are quite similar. In some cases, Server Explorer is better than Management Studio. For example, not only can database objects be created, viewed, and modified from Server Explorer, but typed DataSets and DataTables can be created just by dropping tables from Server Explorer onto the DataSet at design time.

Programming purists might object to this easy drag-and-drop approach to coding, but developers shouldn't discount the real performance and consistency benefits of typed data sets, which are often derided in part because of the tedium and precision required to code a typed DataSet. Developers and DBAs with a shortage of time and a wealth of workload will appreciate the help. Everyone stands a much improved chance of meeting those ever-shortening project due dates when the Visual Studio helpers are used.

Note   Server Explorer functionality is accessible programmatically through the ServiceController namespace. This can provide elegant, high-level access to automation actions such as starting and stopping services.

Debugging ADO.NET

Interactively debugging application code in Visual Studio is straightforward and elegant. ADO.NET code is specialized to the data source. It is of unquestionable benefit to be able to include not only the application code, but also T-SQL code executing on the data source in the debugging session. Getting the debugger to step into T-SQL code is somewhat painful. To be able to step into database code while debugging an application in Visual Studio, all of the following conditions must be met:

✦ Allow SQL/CLR Debugging must be enabled on the data connection in Server Explorer.

✦ Enable SQL Server Debugging must be checked on the Debug tab of the project's Properties dialog in Solution Explorer.

✦ Visual Studio's Remote Components Setup must have been run on the SQL Server machine if the SQL Server is not running on the same OS instance as Visual Studio.

✦ Additionally, if SQL Server and Visual Studio are not on the same computer, and either SQL Server or Visual Studio are running on Windows XP with the Internet firewall, the firewall must be configured to allow remote debugging. On the Visual Studio machine, this would involve adding devenv.exe to the white list and opening port 135. On the SQL Server machine, sqlservr.exe must be added and port 135 opened.

✦ If server-side CLR components are to be debugged, it is necessary to install and configure the Visual Studio Remote Debug Monitor on the SQL Server 2005 machine.

✦ If the remote SQL Server is a SQL Server 7 or SQL Server 2000 instance, it is necessary to configure DCOM on the SQL Server to allow remote debugging using the `dcomcnfg.exe` utility. The procedure varies by operating system. Refer to the DCOM documentation or to the Microsoft Visual Studio documentation for complete details.

✦ The Visual Studio documentation on debugging is outstanding. Complete information on how to use the debugging tools, including what is installed on a SQL Sever when remote debugging is enabled, is available.

Debugging T-SQL code will cause all managed connections on the database server instance to stop while the developer is stepping through a stored procedure or function. All resource locks will also persist according to the normal concurrency configuration for the SQL Server. Essentially, this means that debugging T-SQL code on a busy SQL Server is to be avoided. By extension, it should almost go without saying that using the Visual Studio debugger on a production SQL Server is sure to cause more problems than it might solve.

Application Tracing

Once the application has been moved to production, tools such as Server Explorer and the Visual Studio debugger facilities are of little use. There are runtime tools such as the Windows debugger and SQL Profiler that can identify problems that inevitably surface only in the production environment. SQL Profiler is an excellent tool for performance tuning and troubleshooting at the SQL Server. Many readers may be familiar with the ODBC runtime tracing capability. While ODBC trace is exceptionally verbose and anything but lightweight, it identifies error conditions and connectivity problems down to the application statement level. Furthermore, it is possible to employ ODBC trace even in the production environment when necessary without risking the gridlock that is unavoidable. Visual Studio languages have offered various types of debug build-only assertion capabilities for some time. The .NET Framework offers a diagnostics alternative that is usable in both debug and release builds in the `System.Diagnostics.Trace` namespace.

It's up to developers to instrument their application by adding trace points during development. By default, every .NET application domain — the basic unit of isolation in the CLR — contains a `DefaultTraceListener`, and can contain other listeners in its collection. Normally the role of the trace listener is to direct trace output to a file or the event log. A .NET application developer can define trace points at method calls or even metrics such as performance counters throughout the application's code.

Trace switches can also be defined by the developer to produce various levels of trace output during runtime, depending on the value of the trace switch. Trace switches can be set at runtime within the `app.config` file. Under favorable run conditions, tracing can be disabled. If problems occur, tracing can be enabled at a level appropriate for capturing information for a given problem.

Among the large body of information available on the Internet about trace instrumentation with the .NET Framework is a very good MSDN magazine article by Jon Fancet, "Powerful Instrumentation Options in .NET Let You Build Manageable Apps with Confidence," at `http://msdn.microsoft.com/msdnmag/issues/04/04/InstrumentationinNET/`, and an excellent MSDN white paper by Bob Beauchemin, "Tracing Data Access," at `http://msdn.microsoft.com/library/default.asp?url=/library/en-us/dnvs05/html/vsgenerics.asp`.

With ADO.NET 2.0, trace instrumentation is extended by Microsoft to include built-in trace points in the ADO.NET assemblies, the SQL Native Client .dll, and the other .NET providers. By all accounts, the aim is to integrate this trace facility with the `System.Diagnostics` `.Trace` class tracing capabilities. Unfortunately, as of this writing, that integration is not yet realized, and the method for capturing this trace information is not documented.

Application Building Basics

This discussion of ADO.NET 2.0 would not be complete without a look at the code techniques that have been covered thus far in this chapter. This section of the chapter provides code that uses the `adodb.dll` .NET primary interop assembly to interact with SQL Server, code that uses the `SqlClient` to perform equivalent operations, and code that demonstrates access through the SQL Native Client using the common base classes. As stated previously, the ADO and ADO.NET technologies are fundamentally different technologies yet do similar work. The code is presented to show how different interactions with the database are completed by each technology.

Little space will be given here in matters of graphical interface design, XML or remoting in the .NET Framework. Windows Forms design, ASP.NET, SOA, and remoting are extensive subjects that must require more space than the *SQL Server 2005 Bible* can allocate. Instead, shown here are the methods needed to move data in and out of the data source and how to work with the ADO.NET components. The purpose is to see how easily and elegantly data can be moved in and out of the data access layer. What is done with that data above the data access layer is best left to the developer's imagination.

With that said, the coding style used here is intended only to permit a straightforward view of a particular method. How ADO.NET is used in .NET Framework programming depends largely on usage requirements and the established coding practices within a given development environment.

The first activity in any ADO.NET project is to connect to the data source(s) that will be used to develop the project using the Server Explorer.

Sample code for this chapter is available on the SQL Server 2005 Bible website at www.SQLServerBible.com. The code uses a console application to show the techniques that follow.

Connecting to SQL Server

The easiest way to create a connection is to run the Data Source Configuration Wizard. From the Visual Studio Data menu, launch the wizard by selecting Add New Data Source or view the data sources associated with an existing application project by selecting the Show Data Sources menu option.

It is easy to programmatically define a connection string. The connection string is a set of name-value pairs. One slight confusion in defining a connection string is that they can be somewhat different for each .NET provider, and the ADO connection is different still.

Tip

With the .NET Framework 2.0, connection strings are more flexible than in the past. For example, an `ADODB.dll` provider connection string or a SNAC connection string will allow the SQL Server to be called a "Data Source" or a "Server."

It is possible to define the connection string based on values stored in the file system or the registry or specified by a user. If the common base class is used, it is possible to define both the provider used and the connection string in the `app.config` file.

Data Adapters

The Data Source Configuration Wizard offers opportunities to specify tables, views, stored procedures, and functions that are to be used to create the `DataSet` and to create a typed `DataSet`. Alternately, the `DataSet` can be added and specified by adding a data set to the project in Solution Explorer. Using this method, the Dataset Designer will be opened for the project.

The Dataset Designer allows either the toolbox or Server Explorer to be used to source and identify the application's `DataSet`. The `DataSet` Designer tool is another great way to ensure that only typed data sets are created. The programming purist can even type out the definition for a typed data set if so desired, although there seems to be scant justification for this technique.

Recall that a typed `DataSet` can prevent runtime data conversion errors from sneaking into the code. If the intention is to use an untyped `DataSet`, there is no reason to use the Dataset Designer. All that is necessary is to declare a new, empty `DataSet` in-line, before it is filled from the specified `DataAdapter`:

```
'populate an untyped dataset from a SqlDataAdapter
Dim daScrapReasons As SqlDataAdapter = _
        New SqlDataAdapter(sSQLScrapReasons, cnADONET2)

'create an untyped dataset
Dim dsWOWithScrap As New DataSet

'fill the DataSet from the Adapter
daScrapReasons.Fill(dsWOWithScrap, "ScrapReason")
```

If the developer opts for the typed data set, then the Table Adapter Configuration Wizard can be used to create a Table Adapter for each table in the specified `DataSet`. The wizard is launched from the context menu of the Dataset Designer design surface. Within this wizard, the programmer can select database tables or specify queries and stored procedures from which to populate the table adapter(s). Once the table population is defined, the wizard will willingly create the `INSERT`, `UPDATE`, and `DELETE` SQL commands that will be executed when the `DataAdapter.Update` method is called on the data set. These commands can be viewed and edited as desired in the Properties pane of the adapter. The code generated by the design surface can also be viewed. Editing this code is not recommended, as changes may cause incorrect behavior. Any custom changes will be lost if the DataSet or TableAdapter is regenerated by the wizard.

DataReaders and Recordsets

ADO `Recordsets` can be processed as Server API cursors or as client cursors. On the client side, the `Recordsets` can be used after the database connection is closed, but it is completely up to the developer to determine if and how the data can be modified and propagated back to the database:

```
'A record set from an ADO server side cursor
Dim rsADOWOWithScrap As New ADODB.Recordset
rsADOWOWithScrap.CursorLocation = CursorLocationEnum.adUseServer

rsADOWOWithScrap.Open(sSQLWOWithScrap, cnADO,_
                    CursorTypeEnum.adOpenForwardOnly, _
                    LockTypeEnum.adLockReadOnly)
'A disconnected recordset from an ADO client cursor
Dim cmdADOWOWithScrap1 As New ADODB.Command
Dim rsADOWOWithScrap1 As New ADODB.Recordset
cmdADOWOWithScrap1.CommandText = sSQLWOWithScrap
cmdADOWOWithScrap1.CommandType = _
                    CommandTypeEnum.adCmdText
rsADOWOWithScrap1.CursorType = _
                    CursorTypeEnum.adOpenStatic
rsADOWOWithScrap1.LockType = _
                    LockTypeEnum.adLockBatchOptimistic
rsADOWOWithScrap1.CursorLocation = _
                    CursorLocationEnum.adUseClient
cmdADOWOWithScrap1.ActiveConnection = cnADO
rsADOWOWithScrap1 = cmdADOWOWithScrap1.Execute
```

The ADO.NET `DataReader` is a forward-only client cursor. It can be loaded into a `DataTable` if needed. The `DataAdapter` includes methods to insert, update, and delete data from the DataSet's `DataTable` back to the database.

Streams

Data can be streamed in and out of the database as XML or in binary format. Streams can be somewhat difficult to work with because of their transient nature. Generally, a stream can be consumed once and then it disappears:

```
Dim bfBINWOWithScrap As New Binary.BinaryFormatter
Dim msXMLWOWithScrap As New MemoryStream()
Dim msBINWOWithScrap As New MemoryStream()

'get XML streamfrom dataset
bfBINWOWithScrap.Serialize(msXMLWOWithScrap, _
                    dsBINWOWithScrap)
```

Typically, XML streams are used in .NET Framework AppDomains and to move data in service-oriented settings. Binary streams are most frequently used in scenarios where remoting between AppDomains is appropriate. Intimate knowledge of the data is necessary to serialize (i.e., meaningfully write to disk) a binary stream. The XML stream includes metadata information and can be serialized by any receiver that is able to manipulate XML.

Asynchronous Execution

In some cases, a query or procedure needs time to execute at the database, and the application can do other useful work while the query completes. In spite of the somewhat restrictive rules regarding when asynchronous execution can be used, the capability provides increased flexibility, as shown in the following code:

```
Dim rdrAsyncScrapCountInit As IAsyncResult = _
              cmdScrapCount.BeginExecuteReader

'do some other work

Dim rdrAsyncScrapCount As SqlDataReader = _
    cmdScrapCount.EndExecuteReader(rdrAsyncScrapCountInit)
```

The database connection will support only one asynchronous query at a time. This means that from the application or mid-tier, multiple connections might be required. From server-side CLR, asynchronous queries are not supported in ADO.NET 2.0.

Using a Single Database Value

An application is often interested in a single column or perhaps a few columns from a single row. With ADO, the options are to execute a query and return the value into a `Recordset` that is one-column wide and one row long, or to execute a command with output parameters defined in the command's parameters collection. The single value or single row into a `Recordset` is well known to be the least scalable because of the overhead required to build and tear down the `Recordset` repeatedly. Therefore, in ADO, the preference should always go to using the parameters collection:

```
paramscrapWOCount = _
    cmdScrapWOByProduct.CreateParameter("ScrapWOCount", _
                         DataTypeEnum.adInteger, _
                         ParameterDirectionEnum.adParamOutput)
cmdScrapWOByProduct.Parameters.Append(paramscrapWOCount)
cmdScrapWOByProduct.Parameters.Item("ProductName").Value = sProductName
```

With ADO.NET, the options are greater and the preference is less obvious. The value can be returned into a `DataTable` of one row in length. This method could be advantageous in some scenarios where the data point is used in concert with other `DataTables` in the `DataSet`. In addition, the `ExecuteWithNoQuery` method could be used to populate variables via the parameters collection when multiple columns from a single row are of interest, or the `ExecuteScalar` method could be used for cases when only a single value will be needed:

```
Dim iScrapWOCount As Integer = _
    cmdScrapCount.ExecuteScalar()
```

or

```
cmdScrapCountByProduct.Parameters.Add("@ScrapWOCount", _
                         SqlDbType.Int).Direction = _
                         ParameterDirection.Output
cmdScrapCountByProduct.ExecuteNonQuery()
```

Data Modification

When a change is made to data in the .NET application, the change must be moved to the database. This can be done within a pessimistic concurrency model or an optimistic concurrency model. The concurrency model is actually a mechanism to aid the developer in deciding whether to use a disconnected ADO.NET `DataClass` (under the optimistic concurrency model) or a connected method (under the pessimistic model) to read and write to the database.

Note	The pessimistic concurrency model is useful when data is bulk loaded or when DML queries (INSERT, UPDATE, or DELETE SQL statements) or input parameters are used within an ExecuteNonQuery statement. The optimistic concurrency model is useful when it is desirable for the application to take specific steps such as retrying or writing to a failure log when a data modification operation fails.

Updating a dataset requires nothing more than value assignment within .NET. Any or all rows in a DataSet can be inserted, deleted, or updated. When a data row is changed within a DataSet, the row is marked as changed. Running the Update method of the DataAdapter will cause the Insert, Update, and Delete commands defined in the DataAdapter to be executed on the database using the DataAdapter's data. It is possible that another user has changed a data point between the time it was read to a DataAdapter and the time that data was written back to the database. In such a case, if the insert fails, the code must determine whether a concurrency error has occurred. This is typically done with a timestamp column or by comparing the original values in the dataset with the current values in the database when an update method is executed. It is the developer's responsibility to determine the correct resolution for such concurrency collisions.

In ADO.NET 1.1 the insert, update and delete commands processed by the Update method could be automatically generated by the Table Adapter Configuration Wizard. The generated statements would compare every column of the table in the DataSet with the corresponding database column using a .NET currency option named CompareAllSearchableValues. The resulting statements were unruly, performed poorly, and made it difficult to detect and resolve collisions. The preferred method is to use stored procedures even for the commands in the DataAdapter. With ADO.NET 2.0, stored procedures can be created using the wizard, although they are not particularly good procedures. Different concurrency options other than CompareAllSearchableValues can also be specified. Alternatives include CompareRowVersion, which checks for changes in the primary key and the row version, and OverwriteChanges, which checks only the primary key to determine if a collision has occurred. The options are getting better, but the preferred method is still to write custom SQL commands for DataAdapters and to use stored procedures, rather than embed SQL statements in the application code.

Binding to Controls

In the true spirit of reducing lines of code, the only thing necessary to bind data to a control in Visual Studio 2005 is to drag the data component onto the control and voila! A bound data control is created. In order to make things look nice, it is almost a certainty that more layout design will be needed, but that takes us out of ADO.NET programming and into the business of form design.

Summary

ADO and ADO.NET have been compared in this chapter. The advantages and limitations of one over the other have been discussed at some length. Admittedly, the bias has been one in favor of ADO.NET. While it was perhaps less compelling to use ADO.NET 1.x than good old ADO in some scenarios, this chapter has tried to show that in fact ADO.NET 2.0 offers the most complete high-level data access technology from Microsoft to date.

✦　　　✦　　　✦

Using XML, XPath, and XQuery

T he Internet is moving from being a vehicle primarily for e-mail and data presentation (web pages) into a phase that also includes high-performance data connectivity using service-oriented architecture and XML. With XML becoming ubiquitous, data architects must decide what role XML will play within their database designs. Fortunately, SQL Server 2005 provides the technical options to accommodate nearly any architectural choice.

During the "Get Ready for SQL Server 2005 Road Show," in the fall of 2005, when I presented the new XML capabilities, the most common question was, "Why do I want XML in my database?" No one in the SQL Server community is suggesting that the XML will replace relational data, but there may be situations when it makes sense to store some XML data, such as when XML documents are received, handled, and then discarded. When the data is semi-structured, meaning that the format of the data changes frequently over time or source, then a fluid XML document may be more efficient than fixed relational data.

On The Web

For an introduction to XML, XML Schema, and XST, download the `XMLPrimer.pdf` file from the book's web site, `www.SQLServerBible.com`. Sample code from this chapter, plus additional XML code samples, are available in the file `ch31.sql`.

New in 2005

SQL Server 2000 had first-generation XML capabilities to publish to the Web and work with XML data. SQL Server 2005's XML capabilities are revolutionary compared to SQL Server 2000. The Database Engine itself now natively supports the XML data and XQuery.

When XML data is received by SQL Server, there are three possible options for storing the data:

✦ Store the XML as XML using the XML data type. If the XML structure is fluid, this is likely the best choice.

✦ Decompose the XML and store as relational data using `OpenXML`. If the XML data is already a part of the relational schema, or the data must be available for easy reporting, then decomposing the data into relational tables is the best choice.

✦ The last option is to store the XML as large text. With the new XML features of SQL Server 2005, this is never the best choice.

XML Data Type

As a native SQL Server data type, the XML data type can be used in any of the following ways:

✦ Declared as a local T-SQL variable

✦ Used as a parameter for stored procedures and user-defined functions

✦ Returned from a user-defined function

✦ Created as a table column data type

The XML data type can store complete XML documents or XML fragments up to 2GB in length. A fragment could be one order and the order details lines, while a full document would be all customer data with every order and all order details lines.

The XML data must be well-formed (syntactically correct) XML, and optionally can be validated using an XML Schema collection.

There are several way cool advantages to using the XML data type. The data engine actually separates the XML elements and attributes and then stores just the data as binary data, as VarBinary(max). The XML paths (tags) are stored as tokens that point to the actual data. This significantly reduces the storage size, improves performance, and enables the data engine to use XML indexes and navigate the data using XQuery.

Casting and Converting

Because XML is so new, here are the basic rules for converting data to and from XML. Any character data can be inserted into XML and XML nodes.

XML data type can be cast to other related character types:

✦ Char, VarChar

✦ NChar, NVarChar

✦ VarBinary(Max)

✦ SQL_Variant (first converting to VarChar)

XML data types can be cast from, but not to, text or ntext.

XML Type Limitations

Because XML is stored differently than relational data and because of its nested format, there are a few other restrictions to working with XML:

✦ XML types cannot be treated like character types.

✦ No equality comparisons, e.g., =, >, < (except is null and is not null).

✦ No order by or group by.

✦ No built-in scalar functions except isnull() and coalesce().

✦ Cannot be used as a key column or in a unique constraint.

✦ Cannot be declared with collate.

XML Schema Collections

The risk of using XML is that it's so fluid and flexible that without some constraints, there may be anything in the data. It's the same problem as the comment column, which stores everything from address changes to order notes to birth dates and employee gripes.

The solution is to define an optional XML Schema Definition (XSD) namespace and bind the XML column or variable to the XSD. The XSD Schema can be defined to accept an entire XML document or a fragment.

The first step is to create the XSD as part of the XML Schema collection in the database. Once the schema is created the XML variable or column that refers to the schema can be created . Here, the XSD called ItemSchema is added to the schema in the XMLearn sample database:

```
CREATE DATABASE XMLearn
USE XMLearn

CREATE XML SCHEMA COLLECTION ItemSchema AS N'
  <xsd:schema xmlns:xsd="http://www.w3.org/2001/XMLSchema"
    xmlns="resume-schema"
    targetNamespace="resume-schema"
    elementFormDefault="qualified">
  <xsd:element name="Item" type="ItemType"/>
  <xsd:complexType name="ItemType" mixed="true">
   <xsd:sequence>
    <xsd:element name="SKU" type="xsd:string" minOccurs="1"/>
    <xsd:element name="Size" type="xsd:string" minOccurs="1"/>
    <xsd:element name="Color" type="xsd:string" minOccurs="1"/>
   </xsd:sequence>
  </xsd:complexType>
  </xsd:schema>'
```

> **sys.** To view the installed schemas, query the `sysxml_schema_collections` system view.

With the XSD schema installed in the XML Schema collection, XML variables or columns can be created that bind to the XSD Schema:

```
CREATE TABLE XMLGeneric (
  ID INT IDENTITY NOT NULL PRIMARY KEY,
  Data XML (SchemaName)
  )
```

The XSD schema can also be defined using Management Studio. The column properties include the XSD schema namespace, which can be used to select the XSD from the Schema Collection.

> **Note** SQL Server 2005 does not support the older document type definitions (DTDs) and uses XSDs exclusively.

XML Indexes

A significant advantage to using the XML data type is that the XML nodes themselves can be indexed. XML indexes benefit XQuery queries but are not used when you retrieve XML using relational queries. Based on my testing, these indexes perform very well. Creating XML indexes is a multiple-step operation involving primary and secondary indexes.

A Primary XML index must be created first. It binds the XML nodes to the relational clustered index and enables creating the XML-specific indexes:

```
CREATE [ PRIMARY ] XML INDEX index_name
    ON <object> ( xml_column_name )
    [ USING XML INDEX xml_index_name
        [ FOR { VALUE | PATH | PROPERTY } ][ ; ]
```

The table must have a clustered index, and the clustered index cannot be modified while the XML indexes are in place.

Once the Primary is in place, secondary XML indexes (such as those following) can be created to improve XQuery performance:

✦ **Value:** Indexes the data values for searching by value

✦ **Path:** Indexes the XML node names for searching the XML structure

✦ **Property:** Optimizes name/value pair predicates

Querying XML Data

When data is stored directly in XML data columns, you can use XPath and XQuery to retrieve the data, insert data, or update data. XQuery is relatively new and still a work in progress.

If you've used XPath, then you're on your way to using XQuery. Almost all valid XPath statements are also XQuery statements, and XPath is used to select values in XQuery FLWOR expressions.

I believe a 1,000-page book would be required to cover XQuery and merging XQuery with relational select queries. One thing's for certain: As data technologies evolve, XML and XQuery are part of the future of any data-oriented career.

XPATH

XPath is a feature of XML. It adds result restriction and aggregation capabilities to XML while navigating through the XML hierarchy to access any node (element, attribute, or piece of text) within the XML document. The XPath code may be added to the XSL style sheet or to other XML queries to filter the data. The most applicable use of XPath for SQL Server is in templates.

XPath must first identify the node. Identifying a node is very similar to the column name within a SQL select statement's where clause. For example, to navigate to the event element under the tour element, use the following structure:

```
/Tours/Tour/Event
```

The preceding example uses absolute location. The node location may also be selected by means of relative location, so that a portion of the XSL that's working with child data may select a parent node for the filtering process.

To navigate down the hierarchical XML tree to an attribute, use the @ sign, as follows:

```
/Tours/Tour/@Name
```

Once the correct node is identified, XPath has several filtering features to select the correct data. For the execution of a where = filter, the criteria are specified after the node in square brackets. The file, CHA2_Events_XPath.xsl, includes the following XPath code:

```
/Tours/Tour/@Name ['Gauley River Rafting']
```

The following code uses the query function to retrieve XPath data within a relational query:

```
SELECT Customer, OrderDetail.query(
   '/Items[1]/Item[1]/SKU')
   FROM XMLOrders
```

FLWOR Queries

The FLWOR query is the heart of XQuery. FLWOR is an acronym for For-Let-Where-Order By-Return, the syntax of the query. It's similar to the basic flow of the select query but designed to iterate through XML hierarchical data.

The For clause corresponds to the from clause in SQL. Because XQuery was designed by application XML folks and not database folks, the For actually means For-Each and literally means to iterate though all the elements, which reveals the non-set-based thinking of XML.

The Let clause is used for a variable assignment that can then be used later in the XQuery. In SQL Server 2005, Let is not supported.

Where is similar to the SQL where clause. It restricts the XML elements and attributes selected.

The Order By clause is also intuitive to SQL developers.

The Return clause is the XQuery twist. This creative syntax is used to configure, or mold, the formatting of the XML returned from the XQuery.

```
SELECT Customer, OrderDetail.query(
   'for $i in /Items/Item
   where $i/Quantity = 2
   return $i/SKU')
   FROM XMLOrders
```

XQueries are used within query functions, as shown in the next section.

Merging XQuery with Select

SQL Server XQuery is slightly different from the XQuery standard. This is because the XQuery standard is written to select data from an XML file, whereas the XQuery methods in SQL Server are designed to integrate within a select statement.

The `exist` method simply tests for the existence of an XML node, similar to the SQL "if exists" (select...) syntax:

```
SELECT Customer
  FROM XMLOrders
  WHERE OrderDetail.exist(
  '/Items/Item[SKU = 234]')=1
```

The `exist` method will return a 1 if true, or 0 if false. Result:

```
Name
------
Sam
```

The `value` method actually returns a value from the XQuery. It's limited to returning only a scalar value, similar to a subquery that returns a scalar value:

```
SELECT Customer,OrderDetail.value(
  '/Items[1]/Item[1]/SKU[1]', 'VARCHAR(25)')
  FROM XMLOrders
```

The `query` method allows a full XQuery to return data within the relational select query:

```
SELECT Customer, OrderDetail.query(
  'for $i in /Items/Item
  return $i/SKU')
  FROM XMLOrders
```

The `nodes` method is probably the most useful XQuery method because it actually returns a rowset that can be joined with relational data within a select query.

The final XQuery method, `modify`, is used to modify values within an XML data variable or column. The modify method must be used with an `update` query and can modify using `insert`, `delete`, or `replace`:

```
UPDATE XMLOrders
  SET OrderDetail.modify(
    'insert
    <Items SKU = "678" Quantity = "2"/>
     into /Items[1]'
    )
  WHERE OrderID = 1


UPDATE XMLOrders
  SET OrderDetail.modify(
    'delete /Items/Item[1]'
    )
  WHERE OrderID = 1
```

Decomposing XML SQL Server

When dealing with XML data, one option is to decompose the data and store it in relational tables. Toward that end, SQL Server 2005 enables you to create and read XML data from within a `select` statement.

Reading XML into SQL Server

Applications read XML using a parser that in turn exposes the XML data within the Document Object Model, or DOM. This W3C-established standard is an object-oriented representation of an XML document. The XML document, and each element, attribute, and text within the document, becomes a DOM object. DOM is very powerful and may be used within object-oriented code to create, read, or modify an XML document.

SQL Server uses the Microsoft XML parser and DOM to read an XML document in a two-stage process:

1. The `sp_xml_preparedocument` stored procedure reads the XML document using the MSXML parser and creates the DOM objects internal to SQL Server. The DOM object is identified by an integer returned by the stored procedure.

2. `OpenXML` is used as a data source within an SQL DML statement. `OpenXML` identifies the DOM object using the integer returned from `sp_xml_preparedocument`.

The following code sample first sets the sample XML data into the @XML SQL Server local variable. SQL Server then reads data into SQL using the preceding two stages, as follows:

1. When the `sp_xml_preparedocument` stored procedure is executed, the DOM is created. The DOM ID is received as an output parameter from the stored procedure and stored in the @iDOM variable.

2. The `Select` statement refers to the `OpenXML` system function as a data source. It accepts three parameters:

   - The integer ID of the internal DOM object, which was stored in the @iDOM variable

   - The `rowpattern` of the XML document, which `OpenXML` used to identify the element structure of the XML data. In this case, the `rowpattern` is `'/Tours/Tour/Event'`.

   - The XML configuration flag, which determines how the elements and attributes are interpreted by `OpenXML` according to Table 31-1.

3. The `OpenXML`'s `With` option forces a column matching for the result set passed back from `OpenXML`. A column is defined by its XML name, data type, and optional XML `element` location.

Table 31-1: OpenXML Configuration Flags

Flag Value	Setting	Description
0	Default	Defaults to attribute-centric
1	Attribute-centric	`OpenXML` looks for attributes
2	Element-centric	`OpenXML` looks for elements
8	Combined	`OpenXML` looks for attributes and then looks for elements

The batch closes with the sp_removedocument system stored procedure, which releases the DOM from memory:

```
DECLARE
  @iDOM int,
  @XML VarChar(8000)

Set @XML = '
<?xml version="1.0" encoding="UTF-8"?>
<Tours>
  <Tour Name="Amazon Trek">
    <Event Code="01-003" DateBegin="2001-03-16T00:00:00"/>
    <Event Code="01-015" DateBegin="2001-11-05T00:00:00"/>
  </Tour>
  <Tour Name="Appalachian Trail">
    <Event Code="01-005" DateBegin="2001-06-25T00:00:00"/>
    <Event Code="01-008" DateBegin="2001-07-14T00:00:00"/>
    <Event Code="01-010" DateBegin="2001-08-14T00:00:00"/>
  </Tour>
  <Tour Name="Bahamas Dive">
    <Event Code="01-002" DateBegin="2001-05-09T00:00:00"/>
    <Event Code="01-006" DateBegin="2001-07-03T00:00:00"/>
    <Event Code="01-009" DateBegin="2001-08-12T00:00:00"/>
  </Tour>
  <Tour Name="Gauley River Rafting">
    <Event Code="01-012" DateBegin="2001-09-14T00:00:00"/>
    <Event Code="01-013" DateBegin="2001-09-15T00:00:00"/>
  </Tour>
  <Tour Name="Outer Banks Lighthouses">
    <Event Code="01-001" DateBegin="2001-02-02T00:00:00"/>
    <Event Code="01-004" DateBegin="2001-06-06T00:00:00"/>
    <Event Code="01-007" DateBegin="2001-07-03T00:00:00"/>
    <Event Code="01-011" DateBegin="2001-08-17T00:00:00"/>
    <Event Code="01-014" DateBegin="2001-10-03T00:00:00"/>
    <Event Code="01-016" DateBegin="2001-11-16T00:00:00"/>
  </Tour>
</Tours>'

-- Generate the internal DOM
EXEC sp_xml_preparedocument @iDOM OUTPUT, @XML

-- OPENXML provider.
SELECT *
  FROM OPENXML (@iDOM, '/Tours/Tour/Event',8)
         WITH ([Name] VARCHAR(25) '../@Name',
               Code VARCHAR(10),
               DateBegin DATETIME
              )
EXEC sp_xml_removedocument @iDOM
```

Result (abridged):

```
Name                    Code      DateBegin
------------------      --------  -------------------------
Amazon Trek             01-003    2001-03-16 00:00:00.000
Amazon Trek             01-015    2001-11-05 00:00:00.000
Appalachian Trail       01-005    2001-06-25 00:00:00.000
Appalachian Trail       01-008    2001-07-14 00:00:00.000
...
```

Creating XML with SQL Server 2005

SQL Server 2005 can produce XML documents directly from queries. The `for XML` optional `select` suffix directs SQL Server to format the query-data result as an XML document, rather than as a standard SQL result set.

Note   The XML output appears as a single-column result. By default, the Query Analyzer `maximum size per column` is set too low to view the XML result set. It may be changed to its maximum setting of 8192 in the Results tab of the Options dialog, opened from Tools ⇨ Options.

The `for XML` suffix generates the XML data, but not the declaration section or the `root` element. The application will need to wrap the data from SQL Server correctly to create a result set that qualifies as a well-formed XML document.

For XML Raw

The `For XML` suffix has three modes: `raw`, `auto`, and an `elements` option. The `For XML Raw` mode simply dumps the result-set rows to an XML document without generating any hierarchical structure. Each SQL row becomes an XML `row` element:

```
SELECT Tour.Name, Event.Code, Event.DateBegin
  FROM Tour
  JOIN Event
    ON Tour.TourID = Event.TourID
  FOR XML RAW
```

Result (abridged):

```
<row Name="Amazon Trek" Code="01-003"
  DateBegin="2001-03-16T00:00:00"/>
<row Name="Amazon Trek" Code="01-015"
  DateBegin="2001-11-05T00:00:00"/>
<row Name="Appalachian Trail" Code="01-005"
  DateBegin="2001-06-25T00:00:00"/>
<row Name="Appalachian Trail" Code="01-008"
  DateBegin="2001-07-14T00:00:00"/>
<row Name="Appalachian Trail" Code="01-010"
  DateBegin="2001-08-14T00:00:00"/>
...
```

For XML Auto

The auto mode determines any hierarchies within the data structure and generates a much more usable XML document. The earlier sample XML document at the beginning of this chapter was produced with the following query:

```
SELECT Tour.Name, Event.Code, Event.DateBegin
  FROM Tour
  JOIN Event
    ON Tour.TourID = Event.TourID
  FOR XML AUTO
```

The elements option causes the for XML auto mode to generate elements instead of attributes. The following variation of the sample XML document uses the elements option to generate elements exclusively:

```
SELECT Tour.Name, Event.Code, Event.DateBegin
  FROM Tour
  JOIN Event
    ON Tour.TourID = Event.TourID
  FOR XML AUTO, ELEMENTS
```

Result (abridged):

```
<Tour>
  <Name>Amazon Trek</Name>
  <Event>
    <Code>01-003</Code>
    <DateBegin>2001-03-16T00:00:00</DateBegin>
  </Event>
  <Event>
    <Code>01-015</Code>
    <DateBegin>2001-11-05T00:00:00</DateBegin>
  </Event>
</Tour>
<Tour>
  <Name>Appalachian Trail</Name>
  <Event>
    <Code>01-005</Code>
    <DateBegin>2001-06-25T00:00:00</DateBegin>
  </Event>
  <Event>
    <Code>01-008</Code>
    <DateBegin>2001-07-14T00:00:00</DateBegin>
  </Event>
  <Event>
    <Code>01-010</Code>
    <DateBegin>2001-08-14T00:00:00</DateBegin>
  </Event>
</Tour>
  ...
```

Cross-Reference SQL Server Integration Services also supports importing and exporting XML data. For more details on SSIS, turn to Chapter 42, "ETL with Integration Services."

Summary

Whether or not you agree with the idea of storing XML within the database, XML is here to stay, and it is a critical technology for any database professional. Service-oriented architecture is based in part on the concept of self-describing XML documents. XQuery is emergent as a key technology to work with XML data. XML is no longer just a verbose replacement for comma-delimited data; it is the ***common language*** of data interoperability.

The next chapter continues this discussion of using XML within SQL Server by exploring Web Services and SOAP wrappers as a method of transporting XML.

✦　　✦　　✦

Building an SOA Data Store with Web Services

Service-oriented architecture (SOA) is all the rage. Attend any architectural conference and a majority of the sessions are about some aspect of SOA. SQL Server 2005 has numerous evolutionary advances, but the primary revolutionary change is its new SOA capability.

Essentially, service-oriented architecture is a software design philosophy that emphasizes encapsulation of business functionality within an application, and applications are loosely coupled using a common method of communication:

✦ *Application encapsulation* means that the interface, or contract, between the two applications is rock solid; neither communicating application needs to know about the internal functionality of the other application, and implementation changes within the application won't affect the other application.

✦ A *common interface* means that any application can request data from any other application using the same protocols. Typically, this means Web Services and native Simple Object Access Protocol (SOAP)/XML as the preferred method of communicating between SOA-enabled applications.

SQL Server 2005 includes a set of technologies geared specifically for SOA architectures:

✦ Native HTTP endpoints and SOAP

✦ Service Broker — By their nature, SOA applications must scale well; that's a primary requirement. To achieve the scalability, SQL Server 2005 includes Service Broker, an asynchronous internal message queue that's designed to handle wide payloads.

✦ XML data type and XQuery

✦ .NET as an enabling technology within SQL Server 2005

To build an SOA data store, begin by defining the contract, or interface, that the application must support. In practical terms, that means defining the messages and parameters that will be received via Web Services. Then you create the stored procedure that will receive the message and the Web Service that will listen for the message.

Best Practice

With multiple possible methods of connecting to the database, which should you choose? ADO or Web Services. As a rule of thumb, use direct "pedal to the metal" ADO for .NET clients that are connecting over a local network. However, if you need to connect through a firewall over the Internet, then Web Services is your solution. If you need connectivity from both local and remote users, consider using Web Services for both depending on the payload and performance. Web Services will be slightly slower even over the local network because of the multiple layers and translations, but writing the data access layer once will be easier to maintain.

This chapter introduces SQL Server 2005 endpoints and describes how to configure the endpoint. However, the Web Service is only half of the picture. To fully understand Web Services, you also need to see the .NET application that consumes, or uses, the Web Service.

ScreenCast

For a complete demo of communicating via Web Services from .NET, watch the ScreenCast and download the Web Service sample application from `www.SQLServerBible.com`.

HTTP Listening

As you probably know, Hypertext Transport Protocol, or HTTP, is used through the Internet to request and deliver HTML pages to browsers. Web Services technology takes that to the next level by using HTTP to request and deliver information messages between systems.

An *endpoint* is listening node, or address, used to receive the HTTP Web Service requests. A Web Service server may host multiple endpoints, and each endpoint may include multiple methods or types of messages that it can process.

A Web Service is the endpoint along with the associated application code and the definition of the data exchange — so, yes, the endpoint is the Web Service, but it's more than just the endpoint. A Web Service is a smart endpoint.

Note

To actually consume data from the Web Service you'll have to write some code. Visual Studio includes sample code to consume a Web Service. Using just a browser, you can view a WSDL, but you can't execute a method or select data from SQL Server Web Service.

About HTTP.sys

Previously, to build a Web Service for SQL Server data, it required building several layers: IIS, .NET code, a message queuing system, and ADO to connect to SQL Server at the back end. All those layers affected performance.

A better way to build a Web Service is to leverage the high-performance HTTP listener built into the new generation of operating systems. At the kernel level of Windows Server 2003, Windows XP, and probably Windows Vista, is the HTTP.sys process, which listens to HTTP requests. SQL Server 2005 uses HTTP.sys endpoints.

Caution Windows Server 2003 uses IIS 6.0, which uses HTTP.sys as it's listening service, so there's no conflict between listening with IIS and SQL Server simultaneously. However, Windows XP SP2 still uses IIS 5.1, which listens by itself without using HTTP.sys This means that if you are trying to build a Web Service using Windows XP, then either IIS must be disabled or the port configurations must be adjusted to avoid a conflict between IIS and HTTP.sys both listening on the default port 80.

Implicit Endpoints

There are two methods to create an endpoint using SQL Server 2005: implicit and explicit. The implicit method using the `create endpoint` DDL command enables SQL Server to control the creation of the endpoint and is the recommended method:

```
CREATE ENDPOINT sql_endpointtest
STATE = STARTED
AS HTTP(
    PATH = '/sql',
    AUTHENTICATION = (INTEGRATED),
    PORTS = (CLEAR),
    SITE = '*' , CLEAR_PORT = 20000
    )
FOR SOAP (
    WEBMETHOD 'http://tempUri.org/'.'GetSqlInfo'
            (name='master.dbo.xp_msver',
             SCHEMA=STANDARD),
    WSDL = DEFAULT,
    SCHEMA = STANDARD ,
    DATABASE = 'master'
    );
```

There are two sections to the `create endpoint` command: the transport, which defines how the endpoint will listen, and the payload, which details the methods and the messages.

The transport section of the `create endpoint` command, beginning with the keyword `as`, configures the endpoint path, authentication method, and ports. In the preceding example, the transport method is HTTP (as opposed to TCP/IP).

The `ports` can be configured as `clear` or secured (`SSL`). Clear ports need the port number defined with the `Clear_Port` option.

The payload section defines the content of the endpoint, typically `For SOAP`. This section also defines the web methods, the WSDL type, and the schema and database.

The method section is critical — it's what connects the endpoint with a stored procedure or service broker queue. In the preceding sample, the method calls a stored procedure. A single endpoint can, and typically does, include multiple methods.

Explicit Endpoints

The alternative to allowing SQL Server to create the connection between SQL Server and HTTP.sys is to specifically configure, or hard code, SQL Server's connection to HTTP.sys using an explicit endpoint. I recommend using the implicit endpoints and letting SQL Server manage the communication with HTTP.sys

Configuring HTTP.sys

HTTPcfg is also excellent for examining the processes that are listening on HTTP.sys and for controlling the listening connection. When HTTPcfg refers to ACL, it means Access Control List. It's a command-line tool included with Windows Server 2003, but you must download a copy for use with Windows XP. It's also included with the MSFT Service toolkit, `windowsxp-kb838079-supporttools-enu.exe`.

You can download it from the Microsoft downloads page.

WSDL

The Web Service Description Language, or WSDL (pronounced "wisdell"), is a standard feature built into nearly every Web Service and is used by clients to discover the methods and messages available from a given Web Service. SQL Server and HTTP.sys provide WSDL out of the box in three flavors: default, simple, and custom. The default is rather verbose, but is likely the best option.

Once you've created the endpoint, test that it's up and running. The easiest way is to request a WSDL from the Web Service. In Internet Explorer, use the URL `http://server:port/path?wsdl`, as shown in Figure 32-1.

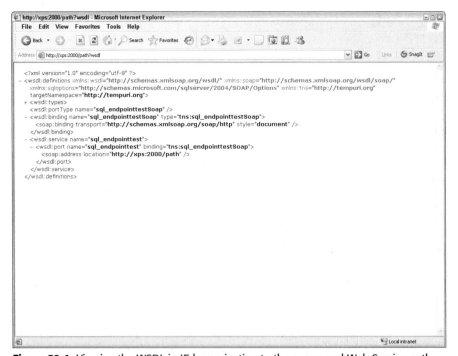

Figure 32-1: Viewing the WSDL in IE by navigating to the server and Web Service path

The simple WSDL option presents a tighter, brief version of the WSDL.

To create a custom WSDL, there's a system stored procedure that returns the default WSDL, which can be called within your custom WSDL stored procedure to generate a basic WSDL. You then free the default WSDL or append additional information as your SOA architecture requires.

Endpoint Security

The primary concern when passing data over the Internet is security. SQL Server 2005 Web Services is doubly secure because access is authenticated at the transport level by HTTP.sys and then again by SQL Server 2005. Neither layer permits anonymous access.

The HTTP Transport authentication can be configured as Basic, Digest, or Integrated (NTLM, Kerberos).

The SQL Server credentials are sent in the SOAP package created by the consuming application. Because this can be encrypted, no credentials need be sent in the clear. When you're using mixed logins and the SOAP package is authenticating to SQL Server using SQL logins, it's important to use secure sockets to encrypt the data.

Summary

While most data access to SQL Server will continue to be with ADO.NET, I believe that Web Services is a significant architectural option that deserves to be understood and used where it makes sense. Although there is an overhead cost to using Web Services and they can be more difficult to configure than ADO, Web Services offer excellent security, smooth interoperability, and flexible deployment over the Internet.

The next chapter broadens the connectivity options even further with InfoPath, Microsoft's technology for bringing data to the office. Whether it's a good idea architecturally, I'll let you decide, but either way it's a technology worth understanding.

✦   ✦   ✦

InfoPath and SQL Server 2005

Among the essential tasks of applications accessing SQL Server 2005 are retrieving information from the database and displaying it effectively to information workers, and supporting information workers in storing business information.

These important tasks are typically achieved using forms. Many people who work with information spend significant parts of each working day filling in forms. Some of the data collected in or displayed in those forms originates in SQL Server databases. In a business context with rapidly changing information needs, the ability to flexibly create and adapt business forms is important.

There are several approaches to creating forms to use with data stored in SQL Server, including Windows forms and web forms. Microsoft's InfoPath 2003 provides an alternative way to create forms, one that can retrieve data from SQL Server and submit data to SQL Server.

This chapter presents an introduction to InfoPath 2003, describing several of its features and how it can be used with SQL Server.

Overview of InfoPath 2003

InfoPath 2003 is a graphical authoring tool that is used to create XML-based forms. With InfoPath, it is easy to create many types of forms, yet it has more complex functions. InfoPath 2003 is available as part of Microsoft Office 2003 Professional Enterprise Edition or as a stand-alone product. It provides a way for users who are unfamiliar with XML to create XML-based forms using straightforward drag-and-drop techniques. One of the data sources that InfoPath can use is SQL Server.

> **Note** Everything in this chapter describes the features and behavior of InfoPath Service Pack 1. Service Pack 1 added many features that were not included in the initial product release of InfoPath 2003.

In InfoPath, a designer or developer creates a *form template*. An information worker opens a form template as a form on which data is entered. The form can be saved locally to a server (for later submission) or submitted directly to a server. Unlike traditional web forms, which submit name-value pairs to a server, InfoPath submits a well-formed XML document.

Note   A form template has a .xsn file extension. A locally saved XML document created from a form template has a .xml file extension.

On The Web   At the time of writing, a trial version of InfoPath 2003 is available from www.microsoft .com/office/infopath/prodinfo/trial.mspx.

Automatic Data Validation

One of the significant benefits of InfoPath 2003 is that the data is validated on the client before the XML document (created from the form template) is submitted to the server. Validation is carried out using the W3C XML Schema technology. There is no need to write custom JScript or JavaScript code.

Validation takes place immediately when the user navigates away from a form control. Different visual cues are provided to indicate missing data that is required, and data that is present but invalid.

If a form contains invalid data, then it is not possible for a user to submit that data to the server; the error in the data must be corrected before the data can be submitted to the server. However, a partially completed form or a form that contains invalid data can be saved locally for later addition of missing data or correction of invalid data. After any missing data has been entered into the form and/or all validation errors have been corrected, the form can be submitted.

Offline Form Completion

In a world where increasing numbers of employees spend significant amounts of time outside the office and disconnected from the Internet, using forms technologies that require a connection becomes unrealistic. InfoPath provides a practical solution for this intermittently connected scenario.

When the user is connected to the server — for example, before a business trip — a *form template* can be downloaded. One or more blank forms can be saved locally from the form template. In a sales scenario, the salesperson can save a form for recording data for each customer visit without having to connect to the Internet while filling in the form. Later, when the salesperson has Internet or other network connectivity, the data on all the relevant forms can be submitted to the server.

Conditional Formatting

InfoPath 2003 supports conditional formatting of individual form controls or collections of form controls in a *section*. Conditional formatting is the formatting of parts of a form depending on the data entered into the form. Conditional formatting controls display parts of the form. It does not depend on whether or not the data entered is valid.

One use of conditional formatting is to conceal form controls that are not applicable to a particular situation. Paper-based forms have to be laid out in a way that enables the collection of all data that might be relevant. Inevitably, in some situations the person completing the form has to indicate that a part of the form is not applicable. In an InfoPath form, it can improve the user experience if only relevant form controls are displayed. For example, in a health questionnaire in InfoPath, it makes no sense to display questions about pregnancies if the user's gender is male. The questions relating to pregnancy can be displayed only when female gender has been indicated when the user fills in the form. Similarly, in a sales form, conditional formatting might be used to show sales that are below quota in red.

Conditional formatting can also be used to highlight information that is particularly interesting, or of concern, or which requires early action. For example, if an InfoPath form is used to record the results of an on-site safety inspection, then values that are close to safety limits could be highlighted in one color and values that are outside safety limits could be highlighted in another color.

Security in InfoPath 2003

InfoPath 2003 uses the Internet Explorer security model as the basis for its security. This makes sense because an InfoPath form template can be downloaded from a web server or e-mailed to a user. Because those types of form delivery imply the possibility of malicious code being contained in a form template, InfoPath forms typically run in a cached location that does not have full access to system resources on the user's machine.

If you are unfamiliar with the Internet Explorer security model, you might want to look at an article located at http://msdn.microsoft.com/library/default.asp?url=/library/en-us/ipsdk/html/ipsdkFormSecurityModel_HV01083562.asp.

However, InfoPath also includes the concept of a *fully trusted form,* sometimes abbreviated to *trusted form.* A fully trusted form is installed specifically on the user machine. Typically, a trusted form is installed explicitly using Microsoft Windows Installer (MSI) before the user can be granted additional permissions. Trusted forms are displayed in the Custom Installed Forms section of the InfoPath user interface.

Cached InfoPath forms are uniquely identified by a URL or URN. Trusted forms are identified by a URN. For forms in which the URL that identifies a form is in the same domain as the user's machine, the form may be in the Intranet zone. If the URL is in a different domain than the user's machine, then some aspects of form behavior are not available, in order to protect against malicious code. Cached forms that are identified by a URN will have been installed using, for example, a Microsoft Windows Installer. Such forms are treated as though they resided in the Local Machine zone and therefore have full access to the user's machine.

The need to install fully trusted forms can seem clumsy, but because a fully trusted form has full permissions on the user's machine, it is important that the user thinks carefully before installing a fully trusted InfoPath form.

Following are some of the specific security features of InfoPath:

✦ **Protecting form template design:** This provides limited protection of the form template design. The user cannot change the form design when filling in a form, but the user can alter the form template by opening it in design mode. The form template created would have a different URL.

✦ **Digital signatures:** Information entered into a form can be digitally signed. This provides assurance that a form has been signed and indicates who signed it.

✦ **Using trusted forms can be disabled:** This provides a way to prevent users from running forms that have full access to their machine resources.

InfoPath Object Model

InfoPath has an object model that is exposed to programmers. The object model reflects the hierarchy of nodes in the XML document that InfoPath will submit and the containing form template. Because an InfoPath form can be used in various scenarios, it is important that some properties and methods are exposed only when the form is fully trusted.

Scripting and .NET Code

The original release of InfoPath 2003 supported scripting in the Microsoft Script Editor using JScript and VBScript code. Service Pack 1 provides improved support for .NET-based programming.

Note

Microsoft has released an Office Solution Accelerator to assist with Sarbanes-Oxley compliance. InfoPath is one of the Office 2003 products supported. For further information about the Office Solution Accelerator, visit `http://msdn.microsoft.com/office/understanding/SOX/default.aspx`.

Creating a Form Template

Creating a form template is the first design step. Several options are available. The following description relates to the creation of a form template that connects to a SQL Server database.

To create a form template, carry out the following steps:

1. Start InfoPath 2003.

2. Select File ➪ Design a Form, as shown. The Design a Form task pane opens. By default, it is positioned at the right of the screen.

3. In the Design a Form task pane, select the New from Data Connection option. The Data Connection Wizard opens.

4. In the Data Connection Wizard screen, select the default option, Database (Microsoft SQL Server or Microsoft Office Access only).

5. In the next screen of the Data Connection Wizard, click the Select Database button.

6. In the Select Data Source window, click New SQL Server Connection.odc. Then click Open.

7. In the Connect to Database Server screen, enter the name of the SQL Server machine to which you want to connect.

8. Select the authentication method that you want to use. Two options are available: Windows Integrated Security and SQL Authentication. If you select the latter, you need to supply a username and password to enable connection to the database.

9. Click Next. The Select Database and Table window opens.

10. From the drop-down menu, select the database to which you want to connect. In the example shown in Figure 33-1, the connection is to the pubs sample database.

The pubs database is a SQL Server 2000 sample database. It can be downloaded from www.microsoft.com/downloads/details.aspx?FamilyId=06616212-0356-46A0 -8DA2-EEBC53A68034&displaylang=en.

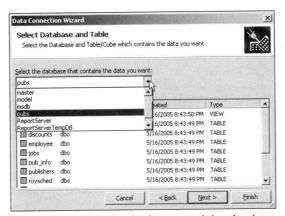

Figure 33-1: Select the database containing the data you want.

11. Once the desired database has been selected, the views and tables contained in the database are displayed in the lower part of the Select Database and Table window. You may then select a table to connect to. In the example shown in Figure 33-2, the authors table in the dbo schema is selected.

In the Data Connection Wizard, there is a reference to "Owner," rather than the SQL Server 2005 notion of schema. This is because InfoPath 2003 was released when SQL Server 2000 was the most current version. InfoPath has no specific knowledge of SQL Server 2005 schemas.

12. Click Next. The Save Data Connection and Finish window is displayed. Review the default filename for the data connection and edit it if desired. Enter a description for the data connection and click Finish. Data connections are stored in Office Data Connection files with an .odc file extension. Another screen in the Data Connection Wizard is displayed, as shown in Figure 33-2. Notice that InfoPath displays the authors table as authors.dbo, rather than the expected form in SQL Server 2005 of dbo.authors.

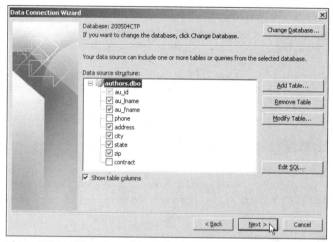

Figure 33-2: Select the columns in the table.

13. You now have several options depending on the query you want to create:

✦ If you click the Change Database button, you are offered the option of changing the data connection. You either repeat the process of creating a new data connection or use a different pre-existing data connection.

✦ If you click the Add Database button, you can select another table, which is in a child relationship to the parent table already selected.

14. You can then proceed to specify a relationship between the parent table and the child table, using the Edit Relationship dialog:

✦ If you click the Remove Database button, then the selected parent database is removed. To replace it, click the Add Database button and select it again or select an alternative database.

✦ If you click the Modify Database button, then you can sort the data to be retrieved from the selected database by the values in up to three columns. The check box in the lower part of the dialog controls whether or not you can retrieve multiple records from the table to be displayed in the form.

✦ If you click the Edit SQL button, you can see the T-SQL statement that InfoPath has created and can, with care, edit it if appropriate. The T-SQL statement can be tested using the Test SQL Statement button.

Caution   InfoPath supports only a limited range of relatively simple T-SQL queries. When editing the T-SQL created by the wizard, be careful not to create a query that InfoPath cannot cope with.

Either by editing the T-SQL or using the graphical interface, it is possible to create queries that InfoPath cannot handle. This will often cause the submit functionality to be disabled. Note that the dialog incorrectly uses the term "database" to refer to the server on which SQL Server is located.

Apart from the many-to-one relationship situation, submit functionality can also be disabled in the following situations:

✦ The user doesn't have permissions to alter data in the relevant table(s).

✦ A stored procedure was used to query the data.

✦ The query uses a data type such as `image`, `text`, and `ntext`, which InfoPath doesn't support.

For now, assume that you don't want to take any of the options listed in the preceding bullet points.

15. Click the Next button. On the next screen it is important to observe whether or not submit functionality is enabled.

16. Click Finish. The InfoPath design mode for a skeletal form view is displayed. Notice the Data Source task pane to the right of the screen. The Data source section contains folders for query fields and data fields. The query fields are used when retrieving data from the database. The data fields are used when submitting data to the database. The simplest way to design a form view that contains both query and submission functionality is to drag the folder from the Data source area to the corresponding area in the main part of the design surface. When you drag the data source, you will be offered two options: Section with Controls or Section. Choose Section with Controls.

17. Edit the placeholder text to "Authors Form." Click in the subtitle to delete it. Edit the labels for the controls so that they appear similar to Figure 33-3.

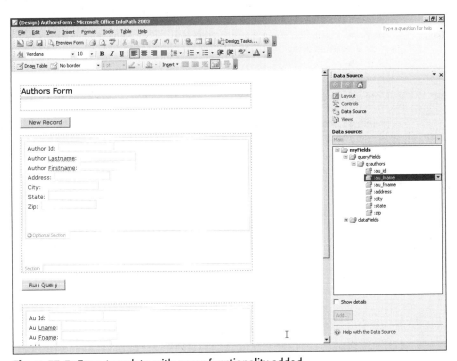

Figure 33-3: Form template with query functionality added

18. Save the form template as `AuthorsForm.xsn`.

19. Click the Preview Form button in the toolbar. In the preview mode, type **Gringlesby** in the Author Lastname text box. Click the Run Query button. The data for Burt Gringlesby is displayed in the form controls in the lower part of the screen.

If there were multiple records for the chosen last name, then they would all be displayed in the lower part of the form view.

Other Features of InfoPath

InfoPath supports layout tables to produce a more precise layout than the simple example shown earlier. To access the layout tables, click Layout in the Data Source task pane.

To see the full range of form controls that InfoPath supports, click Controls in the Data Source task pane. The form controls available include text boxes, check boxes, buttons, sections, and so on.

Each form control has many associated properties. To access the properties of a text box, such as the one used in the example, right-click in the control in design mode and select Textbox Properties from the context menu. The Text Box Properties dialog will appear.

The Text Box Properties dialog enables you to add validation or rules to the form control.

The sample form template created earlier in this chapter has a single view. In a typical InfoPath form template, multiple views would be created. For example, separate views might be created to query the database and to add new or amended information to the database.

Note   For more information about InfoPath 2003, you can simply use the InfoPath Help task pane, accessible using the keyboard shortcut Ctrl+F1.

Note   More convenient and speedy are the individual help files. General InfoPath help is located at `C:\Program Files\Microsoft Office\Office 11\1033\InfMain.chm`. The programmer's reference is located at `C:\Program Files\Microsoft Office\Office 11\1033\InfRef.chm`.

Summary

This chapter serves as a good introduction to InfoPath and its relationship to SQL Server. It described the basics of the product, as well as how to create a form template. This chapter concludes the part on developing with T-SQL. The next part covers Enterprise Data Management.

✦   ✦   ✦

Enterprise Data Management

Part IV is about the enterprise DBA role.

The project isn't done when the production database goes live. A successful database requires preventive maintenance (tune-ups) and corrective maintenance (diligent recovery planning).

The Information Architecture Principle introduced in Chapter 1 presented that idea *that information . . . must be . . . secured, and made readily available for daily operations by individuals, groups, and processes, both today and in the future.*

While SQL Server is more automated than ever before, and Microsoft sometimes makes the error of presenting SQL Server as the database that doesn't require a DBA, the truth is that it takes diligent work to keep a production database up 24 hours a day, 7 days a week, 365 days a year.

If SQL Server is the box, then Part IV is about keeping the box running smoothly, day after day.

Configuring SQL Server

SQL Server has a plethora of configuration options. The difficulty in mastering them lies in the fact that they are spread across three levels:

✦ Server-level options generally configure how the server works with hardware, and determine the database defaults.

✦ Database-level options determine the behavior of the database and set the connection-level defaults.

✦ Connection-level options determine the current behaviors within the connection or current procedure.

Several of the configuration options overlap or simply set the default for the level immediately below. This chapter pulls these three configuration levels into a single unified understanding of how they relate and affect each other.

Setting the Options

Whether you choose to adjust the properties from Management Studio's graphical tool or from code is completely up to you, but not every property is available from Management Studio using the graphical interface or queries. While the graphical interface has the advantages of being easy to use and walks you through easy to understand dialogs that prompt for the possible options in a pick and choose format, it lacks the repeatability of a T-SQL script run as a query.

sys.

To view miscellaneous information about the computer system for use while configuring SQL Server, select `sysdm_os_sys_info` from the dynamic management view.

Configuring the Server

The server-level configuration options control serverwide settings, such as how SQL Server interacts with hardware, how it multi-threads within Windows, and whether triggers are permitted to fire other triggers. When configuring the server, keep in mind the goals of configuration — consistency and performance.

Graphically, many of the server options may be configured within the Server Properties page, which you can open by right-clicking a server in the console tree and choosing Properties from the context menu. The General tab in Management Studio's SQL Server Properties (Configure) dialog box (see Figure 34-1) reports the versions and environment of the server.

Figure 34-1: The General page of Management Studio's Server Properties dialog

The same information is available to code. For example, the version may be identified with the @@Version global variable:

```
Select @@Version
-----------------------------------------------------------------
Microsoft SQL Server 2005 - 9.00.1399.06 (Intel X86)
   Oct 14 2005 00:33:37
   Copyright (c) 1988-2005 Microsoft Corporation
   Developer Edition on Windows NT 5.1 (Build 2600: Service Pack 2)
```

Note Many of the configuration properties do not take effect until SQL Server is restarted. For this reason, the General tab in the SQL Server Properties (Configure) dialog box will display the current running values.

Within code, many of the server properties are set by means of the sp_configure system stored procedure. When executed without any parameters, this procedure reports the current settings, as in the following code (word-wrap adjusted to fit on the page):

```
EXEC sp_configure
```

Result (using the standard options):

name run_value	minimum	maximum	config_value	run_value
allow updates	0	1	0	0
clr enabled	0	1	0	0
cross db ownership chaining	0	1	0	0
default language	0	9999	0	0
max text repl size (B)	0	2147483647	65536	65536
nested triggers	0	1	1	1
remote access	0	1	1	1
remote admin connections	0	1	0	0
remote login timeout (s)	0	2147483647	20	20
remote proc trans	0	1	0	0
remote query timeout (s)	0	2147483647	600	600
server trigger recursion	0	1	1	1
show advanced options	0	1	0	0
user options	0	32767	0	0

The extended stored procedure, xp_msver, reports additional server and environment properties:

```
EXEC xp_msver
```

Result:

Index	Name	Internal_Value	Character_Value
1	ProductName	NULL	Microsoft SQL Server
2	ProductVersion	589824	9.00.1399.06
3	Language	1033	English (United States)
4	Platform	NULL	NT INTEL X86
5	Comments	NULL	NT INTEL X86
6	CompanyName	NULL	Microsoft Corporation
7	FileDescription	NULL	SQL Server Windows NT
8	FileVersion	NULL	2005.090.1399.00
9	InternalName	NULL	SQLSERVR
10	LegalCopyright	NULL	(c) Microsoft Corp. All rights reserved.
11	LegalTrademarks	NULL	Microsoft(r) is a registered trademark of Microsoft Corporation. Windows(TM) is a trademark of Microsoft Corporation
12	OriginalFilename	NULL	SQLSERVR.EXE
13	PrivateBuild	NULL	NULL
14	SpecialBuild	91684864	NULL
15	WindowsVersion	170393861	5.1 (2600)
16	ProcessorCount	1	1
17	ProcessorActiveMask	1	00000001
18	ProcessorType	586	PROCESSOR_INTEL_PENTIUM
19	PhysicalMemory	1023	1023 (1073201152)
20	Product ID	NULL	NULL

The ServerProperty system function is yet another means of determining information about the server. The advantage of this method is that the function may be used as an expression within a select statement. The following example uses the ServerProperty function to return the SQL Server instance edition:

```
SELECT ServerProperty('Edition')
```

Result:

```
Developer Edition
```

Configuring the Database

The database-level options configure the current database's behavior regarding ANSI compatibility and recovery.

Most database options can be set in Management Studio within the Database Properties page, which may be found by right-clicking a database in the console tree and choosing Properties from the context menu. The Options tab is shown in Figure 34-2.

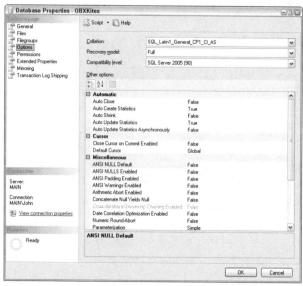

Figure 34-2: Management Studio's Database Properties Option page can be used to configure the most common database properties.

The database configuration options can be set using code and the sp_dboption system stored procedure. When executed without any parameters, this procedure lists the available database settings:

```
EXEC sp_dboption
```

Result:

```
Settable database options:
------------------------------------
ANSI null default
ANSI nulls
ANSI padding
ANSI warnings
arithabort
auto create statistics
auto update statistics
autoclose
autoshrink
concat null yields null
cursor close on commit
db chaining
dbo use only
default to local cursor
merge publish
numeric roundabort
offline
published
quoted identifier
read only
recursive triggers
select into/bulkcopy
single user
subscribed
torn page detection
trunc. log on chkpt.
```

Configuring the Connection

Many of the connection-level options configure ANSI compatibility or specific connection-performance options.

Connection-level options are very limited in scope. If the option is set within an interactive session, the setting is in force until it's changed or the session ends. If the option is set within a stored procedure, the setting persists only for the life of that stored procedure.

To view session statistics, select `sysdm_db_session_space_usage` from the dynamic management view. You can also view file space usage statistics using the `sysdm_db_file_space_usage` view, page and row count information for each partition using the `sysdm_db_partition_stats` view, and page allocation and deallocation activity by task using the `sysdm_db_task_space_usage` view.

The connection-level options are typically configured by means of the `set` command. The following code configures how SQL Server handle `nulls` within this current session:

```
Set Ansi_nulls Off
```

Result:

```
The command(s) completed successfully.
```

Connection properties can also be checked by means of the `SessionProperty()` function:

```
Select SessionProperty ('ANSI_NULLS')
```

Result:

```
0
```

Management Studio sets several connection options when it makes a connection to the server. You can access these properties by clicking the View Connection Properties link in the Properties dialog boxes for objects such as the server and databases. Figure 34-3 shows an example of the Connection Properties dialog box accessed from the Server Properties dialog.

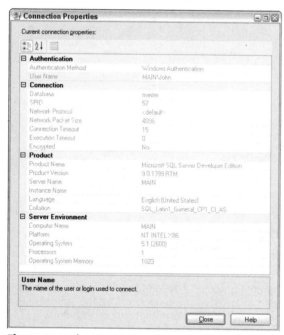

Figure 34-3: The Connection Properties dialog can be used to view the connection-level options for the current session.

To view operational session statistics, select `sysdm_exec_sessions` from the dynamic management view.

Configuration Options

Because so many similar configuration options are controlled by different commands and at different levels (server, database, connection), this section organizes the configuration options by topic, rather than command or level.

Displaying the Advanced Options

Before you can work with many of the SQL Server options, you must configure the server to display them. To perform this task, you must turn on the advanced options using the following code:

```
EXEC sp_configure 'show advanced options', 1
RECONFIGURE
```

After you set the advanced option display on, you can use the sp_configure command to display a list of all of the stored procedures:

```
EXEC sp_configure
```

Result (with advanced options enabled):

name	minimum	maximum	config_value	run_value
Ad Hoc Distributed Queries	0	1	0	0
affinity I/O mask	-2147483648	2147483647	0	0
affinity mask	-2147483648	2147483647	0	0
Agent XPs	0	1	1	1
allow updates	0	1	0	0
awe enabled	0	1	0	0
blocked process threshold	0	86400	0	0
c2 audit mode	0	1	0	0
clr enabled	0	1	0	0
cost threshold for parallelism	0	32767	5	5
cross db ownership chaining	0	1	0	0
cursor threshold	-1	2147483647	-1	-1
Database Mail XPs	0	1	0	0
default full-text language	0	2147483647	1033	1033
default language	0	9999	0	0
default trace enabled	0	1	1	1
disallow results from triggers	0	1	0	0
fill factor (%)	0	100	0	0
ft crawl bandwidth (max)	0	32767	100	100
ft crawl bandwidth (min)	0	32767	0	0
ft notify bandwidth (max)	0	32767	100	100
ft notify bandwidth (min)	0	32767	0	0
index create memory (KB)	704	2147483647	0	0

in-doubt xact resolution	0	2	0	0
lightweight pooling	0	1	0	0
locks	5000	2147483647	0	0
max degree of parallelism	0	64	0	0
max full-text crawl range	0	256	4	4
max server memory (MB)	16	2147483647	2147483647	
2147483647				
max text repl size (B)	0	2147483647	65536	65536
max worker threads	128	32767	0	0
media retention	0	365	0	0
min memory per query (KB)	512	2147483647	1024	1024
min server memory (MB)	0	2147483647	0	0
nested triggers	0	1	1	1
network packet size (B)	512	32767	4096	4096
Ole Automation Procedures	0	1	0	0
open objects	0	2147483647	0	0
PH timeout (s)	1	3600	60	60
precompute rank	0	1	0	0
priority boost	0	1	0	0
query governor cost limit	0	2147483647	0	0
query wait (s)	-1	2147483647	-1	-1
recovery interval (min)	0	32767	0	0
remote access	0	1	1	1
remote admin connections	0	1	0	0
remote login timeout (s)	0	2147483647	20	20
remote proc trans	0	1	0	0
remote query timeout (s)	0	2147483647	600	600
Replication XPs	0	1	0	0
scan for startup procs	0	1	1	1
server trigger recursion	0	1	1	1
set working set size	0	1	0	0
show advanced options	0	1	1	1
SMO and DMO XPs	0	1	1	1
SQL Mail XPs	0	1	0	0
transform noise words	0	1	0	0
two digit year cutoff	1753	9999	2049	2049
user connections	0	32767	0	0
user options	0	32767	0	0
Web Assistant Procedures	0	1	0	0
xp_cmdshell	0	1	0	0

Start/Stop Configuration Properties

The startup configuration properties, described in Table 34-1, control how SQL Server and the processes are launched.

Table 34-1: Start/Stop Configuration Properties

Property	Level*	Graphic Control	Code Option
AutoStart SQL Server	S	Management Studio, Configuration Manager, or Services Console	-
AutoStart SQL Server Agent	S	Management Studio, Configuration Manager, or Services Console	-
AutoStart MS DTC	S	Services Console	-
Show Advanced Options	S	-	EXEC sp_configure 'show advanced options'
Scan for startup procs	S	-	EXEC sp_configure 'scan for startup procs'

* The configuration level refers to Server, Database, or Connection.

Startup Parameters

You use the startup parameters with the SQL Server services. The startup parameters are similar to the parameters passed to a program when it is started from the DOS command line. You must stop the SQL Server service to use the parameters, and you enter them in the Start Parameters field on the General tab, shown in Figure 34-4.

Figure 34-4: Add startup parameters to the SQL Server service to change its behavior.

Simply type the parameters you want to use and restart the service. Besides the standard master database–location parameters, two parameters are particularly useful:

✦ -m—Starts SQL Server in single-user mode and is required to restore or rebuild a lost master database. While the database is in single user mode, avoid Management Studio.

✦ -x—Disables tracking of CPU and cache-hit statistics for maximum performance.

To track any performance counter on the system, select sysdm_os_performance_coun-ters from the dynamic management view. You can also view a complete list of all of the modules loaded on the system by selecting sysdm_os_loaded_modules from the dynamic management view.

Additional startup parameters are as follows:

✦ -d—Used to include the full path of the Master file

✦ -e—Used to include the full path of the Error file

✦ -c—Starts SQL Server so that it is not running as a Windows service

✦ -f—Used to start up with a minimal configuration

✦ -g—Specifies virtual memory (in MB) available to SQL Server for extended stored procedures

✦ -n—Disables logging to the Windows application log

✦ /Ttrace#—Enables trace-specific flags by trace flag number

Startup Stored Procedures

Two additional server properties are not exposed on Management Studio's Server Properties page but are available from code. SQL Server can be configured to scan for a startup stored procedure every time the SQL Server starts—similar to how Microsoft DOS operating systems scan for the autoexec.bat file when they boot up. There's no fixed name for a startup procedure, and there may be multiple startup procedures. To create a startup stored procedure, run the sp_procoption system stored procedure to mark a startup stored procedure. So you can further control the startup procedure, the server property scan for startup procs turns the startup procs feature on or off:

```
EXEC sp_configure 'scan for startup procs', 1
RECONFIGURE
```

Memory-Configuration Properties

SQL Server can either dynamically request memory from the operating system or consume a fixed amount of memory. These settings can be configured on the SQL Server Properties Memory tab, shown in Figure 34-5, or from code by means of the sp_configure stored procedure.

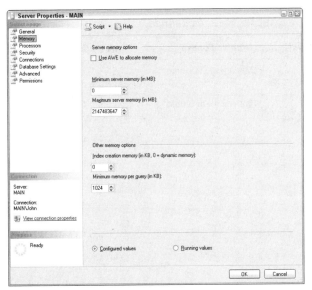

Figure 34-5: Memory page of Management Studio's SQL Server Properties dialog

SQL Server provides a wealth of memory-related information that you can obtain from the dynamic management views. Select `sysdm_os_memory_cache_clock_hands` to return the status of each hand for a specific cache clock, `sysdm_os_memory_clerks` to obtain a set of all currently active memory clerks, and `sysdm_os_memory_objects` to retrieve a list of all memory objects allocated by SQL Server. The `sysdm_os_memory_pools` view returns a row for each object that SQL Server stores. You can also obtain cache health statistics by selecting `sysdm_os_memory_cache_counters`, `sysdm_os_memory_cache_entries`, and `sysdm_os_memory_cache_hash_tables`.

The memory-configuration properties, listed in Table 34-2, control how SQL Server uses and allocates memory.

Table 34-2: Memory-Configuration Properties

Property	Level*	Graphic Control	Code Option
Dynamic Memory Minimum	S	Management Studio	`EXEC sp_configure 'min server memory'`
Dynamic Memory Maximum	S	Management Studio	`EXEC sp_configure 'max server memory'`
Fixed Memory Size	S	Management Studio	`EXEC sp_configure 'min server memory'` and `EXEC sp_configure 'max server memory'`

Continued

Table 34-2 *(continued)*

Property	Level*	Graphic Control	Code Option
Reserve Physical Memory for SQL Server	S	Management Studio	EXEC sp_configure 'set working set size'
Minimum Query Memory	S	Management Studio	EXEC sp_configure 'min memory per query'
AWE Enabled	S	-	EXEC sp_configure 'AWE Enabled'
Index Create Memory	S	-	EXEC sp_configure 'index create memory'
Locks	S	-	EXEC sp_configure 'locks'
Max Text Repl Size	S	-	EXEC sp_configure 'max text repl size'
Open Objects	S	-	EXEC sp_configure 'open objects'

* The configuration level refers to Server, Database, or Connection.

Dynamic Memory

If SQL Server is set to dynamic memory, then SQL Server's memory footprint can grow or be reduced as needed within the minimum and maximum constraints based on the physical memory available and the workload. SQL Server will try to maintain its requirement and 4 to 10MB extra memory. The goal is to have enough memory available while avoiding Windows having to swap pages from memory to the virtual-memory support file (pagefile.sys).

The minimum-memory property prohibits SQL Server from reducing memory below a certain point and hurting performance, but it doesn't set the initial memory footprint. The minimum simply means that once SQL Server has reached that point, it will not reduce memory below it.

The maximum-memory setting prevents SQL Server from growing to the point where it contends with the operating system, or other applications, for memory. If the maximum is set too low performance will suffer.

Microsoft Search Engine, used by SQL Server for full-text searches, is also memory-intensive. If you are doing a significant amount of full-text searching, be sure to leave plenty of memory available for Search Engine. The official formula from Microsoft is

> Total virtual memory – (SQL Server maximum virtual memory + virtual memory requirements of other services) ≥ 1.5 times the physical memory

For example, for a server that has 192MB of physical memory, allowing 96MB for SQL Server and 64MB for Search Engine, the total virtual memory must be greater than 288MB (physical memory times 1.5) plus 160MB (SQL Server and MS Search planning memory), for a total of 448MB required virtual memory. Because the server has 192MB of physical memory, the virtual-memory support file must be at least 252MB to meet the requirements set by the formula. In other words, the more physical memory in the server, the larger the swap file required.

To view a list of active full-text search catalogs, select `sysdm_fts_active_catalogs` from the dynamic management view. If you need information about the memory pools used as part of a full-text crawl or a full-text crawl range, select `sysdm_fts_memory_pools` from the dynamic management view. When you need statistics about memory buffers belonging to a specific memory pool used as part of a full-text crawl or a full-text crawl range, select `sysdm_fts_memory_buffers` from the dynamic management view instead.

Personally, I run SQL Server configured for dynamic memory with the minimum set to 16MB and the maximum set to the computer's total RAM less 128MB. This reserves a minimum amount of memory for SQL Server and permits SQL Server to grow as needed, but still reserves 128MB for Windows and prevents SQL Server from contending with Windows for memory when running several very huge queries. Depending on your configuration, you may want to leave more for the operating system.

Multiple SQL Server instances do not cooperate when requiring memory. In servers with multiple instances, it's highly possible for two busy instances to contend for memory and for one to become memory-starved. Reducing the maximum-memory property for each instance can prevent this from happening.

From T-SQL code, the minimum- and maximum-memory properties are set by means of the `sp_configure` system stored procedure. It's an advanced option, so it can only be changed if the `show advanced options` property is on:

```
EXEC sp_configure 'show advanced options', 1

EXEC sp_configure 'min server memory', 16
```

Result:

```
Configuration option 'min server memory (MB)'
   changed from 0 to 16.
Run the RECONFIGURE statement to install.
```

The following code sets the max-memory configuration:

```
EXEC sp_configure 'max server memory', 128
```

Result:

```
Configuration option 'max server memory (MB)'
   changed from 128 to 128.
Run the RECONFIGURE statement to install.
```

To automatically calculate the maximum memory based on the available physical memory, the following stored procedure examines the result set of `xp_msver` to determine the physical memory and then executes `sp_configure`:

```
CREATE PROC pSetMaxMemory (
  @Safe INT = 64 )
AS
  CREATE TABLE #PhysicalMemory (
    [Index] INT,
    [Name] VARCHAR(50),
    [Internal_Value] INT,
    [Character_Value] VARCHAR(50) )
  DECLARE @Memory INT
```

```
INSERT #PhysicalMemory
    EXEC xp_msver 'PhysicalMemory'
SELECT @Memory =
    (Select Internal_Value FROM #PhysicalMemory) - @safe
EXEC sp_configure 'max server memory', @Memory
RECONFIGURE

go

EXEC pSetMaxMemory  -- sets max memory to physical - 64Mb
EXEC pSetMaxMemory 32 --  sets max memory to physical - 32Mb
```

Reconfigure

After a configuration setting is changed with sp_configure, the RECONFIGURE command causes the changes to take effect. If you don't run RECONFIGURE, the config_value field will still show the change, but the change won't appear in the run_value field, even if you restart the service. Some configuration changes take effect only after SQL Server is restarted.

```
RECONFIGURE

The command(s) completed successfully.
```

Instead of dynamically consuming memory, SQL Server may be configured to immediately request a fixed amount of memory from the operating system. To set a fixed amount of memory from code, set the minimum- and maximum-memory properties to the same value.

Although calculating memory cost, polling the environment, and requesting memory may seem as if they would require overhead, you aren't likely to see any performance gains from switching from dynamic to fixed memory. The primary purpose of using fixed memory is to configure a dedicated SQL Server computer to prevent page-swapping by combining the fixed-memory setting with the next option presented in this chapter.

Regardless of the amount of memory SQL Server is allocated by Windows, the Windows Memory Manager may opt to swap some of the SQL Server pages to the swap file if SQL Server is idle. If SQL Server memory is set to a fixed size, swapping can be prevented by setting Reserve Physical Memory for SQL Server to true.

The SQL Server Reserve Physical Memory property may be set in code with the set working set size option along with the sp_configure system stored procedure:

```
EXEC sp_configure 'set working set size', 1
RECONFIGURE
```

SQL Server must restart in order for the Reserve Physical Memory property change to take effect.

At times, the SQL Server team amazes me with the level of detailed control it passes to DBAs. SQL Server will allocate the required memory for each query as needed. The min memory per query option sets the minimum threshold for the memory (KB) used by each query. While increasing this property to a value higher than the default 1MB may provide slightly better performance for some queries, I see no reason to override SQL Server automatic memory control and risk causing a memory shortage. The following code increases the minimum query memory to 2MB:

```
EXEC sp_configure 'min memory per query', 2048
RECONFIGURE
```

Six additional memory-related properties that are unavailable from Management Studio can be configured from code.

Query Wait

If the memory is unavailable to execute a large query, SQL Server will wait for the estimated amount of time necessary to execute the query times 25 and then time out. During this time, the query will hold any locks, and an undetectable deadlock may occur. If you are seeing this type of behavior, you can hard-code the query's lack-of-memory timeout to a certain number of seconds using the following code:

```
EXEC sp_configure 'query wait', 20
RECONFIGURE
```

This code specifies that every query will either start execution within 20 seconds or time out.

AWE Memory

SQL Server is normally restricted to the standard 3GB physical-memory limit. However, SQL Server Enterprise Edition, when running on Windows 2005 Datacenter, can use up to 64GB of physical memory by configuring SQL Server to address the Address Windowing Extensions (AWE) API. The AWE-enabled property turns on AWE memory addressing within SQL Server:

```
EXEC sp_configure 'AWE Enabled', 20
RECONFIGURE
```

Index Memory

The amount of memory SQL Server uses to perform sorts when creating an index is generally self-configuring. However, you can control it by using sp_configure to hard-code a certain memory footprint (KB) for index creation. For example, the following code fixes the memory used to create an index to 8MB:

```
EXEC sp_configure 'index create memory', 8096
RECONFIGURE
```

To view current low-level I/O, locking, latching, and access method activity for each partition of a table or index in the database, select sysdm_db_index_operational_stats from the dynamic management view. You can view index usage stats by selecting sysdm_db_index_usage_stats, and physical details, such as size and fragmentation stats, by selecting sysdm_db_index_physical_stats from the dynamic management view.

Lock Memory

Excessive locks can bring a SQL Server to its knees both in terms of waiting for locks and in terms of the memory consumed by the locks (96 bytes per lock). By default, SQL Server will begin with 2 percent of its memory reserved for locks and then dynamically allocate memory up to 40 percent of SQL Server's maximum available memory. That should be sufficient. If you are getting errors indicating there isn't enough memory for locks, don't just increase the lock property. There's a problem in the code. The following example disables the dynamic lock-memory allocation and allocates memory for 16,767 locks, consuming a little over 1.5MB of memory:

```
EXEC sp_configure 'locks', 16767
RECONFIGURE
```

Max Open Objects

SQL Server prefers to dynamically control its memory, including the pool used to track the current open objects (tables, views, rules, stored procedures, defaults, and triggers). Each object takes only one allocation unit, even if it is referenced numerous times. SQL Server reuses memory space in the object pool, but if SQL Server is complaining that it has exceeded the number of open objects, then the property can be manually configured. The following code sets the maximum number of open objects to 16,767:

```
EXEC sp_configure 'open objects', 16767
RECONFIGURE
```

Note   You can always discover the minimum and maximum values for a particular property by running the `sp_configure` command with the property, but without the property value. For example, run `EXEC sp_configure 'open objects'` and you'll discover that the `open objects` property can have any value in the range of 0 to 2,147,483,647.

Processor-Configuration Properties

You can use the processor-configuration properties (listed in Table 34-3) to control how SQL Server makes use of symmetrical multi-processor computers for SQL Server.

Table 34-3: Processor-Configuration Properties

Property	Level*	Graphic Control	Code Option
SMP Processors Used	S	Management Studio	`EXEC sp_configure 'affinity mask'`
Maximum Worker Threads	S	Management Studio	`EXEC sp_configure 'max worker threads'`
Boost SQL Server Priority on Windows	S	Management Studio	`EXEC sp_configure 'priority boost'`
Use Windows NT Fibers	S	Management Studio	`EXEC sp_configure 'lightweight pooling'`
Number of processors for parallel execution of queries	S	Management Studio	`EXEC sp_configure 'max degree of parallelism'`
Minimum query plan threshold for parallel execution	S	Management Studio	`EXEC sp_configure 'cost threshold for parallelism'`
Query wait	S	-	`EXEC sp_configure 'query wait'`

* The configuration level refers to Server, Database, or Connection.

The Processors tab (see Figure 34-6) of the SQL Server Properties page determines how SQL Server will make use of symmetrical multi-processor computers. Most of these options are moot in a single-processor server.

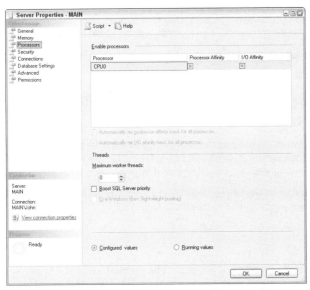

Figure 34-6: The Processors page shows the processors available on the system and enables you to set how SQL Server uses them.

Affinity Mask

In a multi-CPU server, the operating system can move processes to CPUs as the load requires. The SQL Server processor affinity, or the relationship between a task and a CPU, can be configured on a per-CPU basis. By enabling the affinity between SQL Server and a CPU, you make that CPU available to SQL Server, but it is not dedicated to SQL Server. Therefore, while a CPU can't be forced to run SQL Server, it can be segmented from SQL Server.

Best Practice

Because of the overhead involved in switching processes, Windows performance benefits if it can run on one CPU without SQL Server. If the server has eight CPUs or more, I might recommend disabling a single CPU to free Windows processes from competing with SQL Server.

In Management Studio, CPU affinity is configured by means of the check boxes in the Processors tab (refer to Figure 34-6).

In code, the individual CPUs are enabled by setting the `affinity mask` bits using `sp_configure`. Because 3 is 00000011 in base 2, the following code enables processors 0 and 1 in an SMP server:

```
EXEC sp_configure 'affinity mask', 3
RECONFIGURE
```

Note A value of 0 for the affinity mask property indicates that SQL Server uses all of the available processors.

Max Worker Threads

SQL Server is a multi-threaded application, meaning that it can execute on multiple processors concurrently for increased performance. The threads are designed as follows:

✦ A thread for each network connection

✦ A thread to handle database checkpoints

✦ Multiple threads to handle user requests. When SQL Server is handling a small number of connections, a single thread is assigned to each connection. However, as the number of connections grows, a pool of threads handles the connections more efficiently.

Depending on the number of connections and the percentage of time those connections are active (versus idle), making the number of worker threads less than the number of connections can force connection pooling, conserve memory, and improve performance.

From code, the maximum number of worker threads is set by means of the sp_configure stored procedure and the max worker threads option:

```
EXEC sp_configure 'max worker threads', 64
RECONFIGURE
```

 To view information about the connections established to this instance of SQL Server, select sysdm_exec_connections from the dynamic management view. This information includes statistics about each of the databases, connections by both local and remote users, and the details for each connection.

Priority Boost

Different processes in Windows operate at different priority levels, ranging from 0 to 31. The highest priorities are executed first and are reserved for the operating-system processes. Typically, Windows scheduling priority-level settings for applications are 4 (low), 7 (normal), 13 (high), and 24 (real-time). By default, SQL Server installs with a Windows scheduling priority level of 7.

For single CPU servers, or systems running SQL Server along with other foreground applications, a Windows scheduling priority level of 7 is desirable. Boosting the priority in this situation may cause less than smooth operations. However, for dedicated SQL Server multi-CPU servers, the higher Windows scheduling priority level of 13 is recommended. In code, to set the Windows scheduling priority level to 13, the priority boost option is set to 1:

```
EXEC sp_configure 'priority boost', 1
RECONFIGURE
```

Lightweight Pooling

Another useful option for servers with symmetrical multi-processing helps reduce the overhead of frequently switching processes among the CPUs. Enabling the NT fiber threads option creates fewer process threads, but those threads are associated with additional fibers, or lightweight threads, that remain associated with their thread. The smaller number of threads helps reduce process-switching and improve performance. In Management Studio, this option is referred to as Use Windows NT fibers. In code, the configuration option is lightweight pooling:

```
EXEC sp_configure 'lightweight pooling', 1
RECONFIGURE
```

Parallelism

The Enterprise Edition of SQL Server (and the Developer and Evaluation Editions because they are the same edition with different licensing) will execute complex queries using several processors in parallel, instead of serially. That's great for the user running the massive query that aggregates every row in a 20GB database, but what about the other users who are now waiting while one user ties up all the processors? The solution is to limit the number of processors used in a single parallel query and to set the cost threshold (in estimated seconds) required before SQL Server will consider the query a candidate for parallel execution.

Additional overhead is involved in generating a parallel query execution plan, synchronizing the parallel query, and terminating the query, so longer queries benefit the most from parallelism. However, parallel queries are amazingly fast. To determine whether a query is using parallelism, view the query execution plan in Query Analyzer. A symbol shows the merger of different parallel query execution threads.

My recommendation is to enable half of the available processors (remember the affinity mask) minus one for parallel-query execution. For example, if the server has eight processors and seven are available for SQL Server, then set SQL Server to use three processors for parallelism. Because parallel queries can greatly boost performance, depending on your CPU demand, you may want to try actually lowering the cost threshold slightly so more queries will benefit from parallelism.

In code, query parallelism is set by means of the max degree of parallelism and cost threshold for parallelism options. Setting max degree of parallelism to 0 enables all available processors for parallelism:

```
EXEC sp_configure 'max degree of parallelism', 1
EXEC sp_configure 'cost threshold for parallelism', 1
RECONFIGURE
```

Best Practice

While these server-tuning options can affect performance, performance begins with the database schema, queries, and indexes. No amount of server tuning can overcome poor design and development.

Security-Configuration Properties

The security-configuration properties, shown in Table 34-4, are used to control the security features of SQL Server.

Table 34-4: Security-Configuration Properties

Property	Level*	Graphic Control	Code Option
Security Authentication Mode	S	Management Studio	-
Security Audit Level	S	Management Studio	-
StartUp SQL Server Security Account	S	Management Studio	-
C2 Audit Mode	S	-	`EXEC sp_configure 'C2 audit mode'`
Cross Database Ownership Chaining	S	Management Studio	-

* The configuration level refers to Server, Database, or Connection.

The same security-configuration options established during the installation are again presented in the Security tab of the Server Properties page (see Figure 34-7), so the configuration may be adjusted after installation. The authentication model and the SQL Server Windows accounts are exactly the same as in the installation.

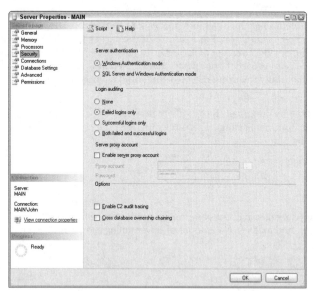

Figure 34-7: Security page of Management Studio's SQL Server Properties dialog

Security-Audit Level

The additional option configures the level of user-login auditing performed by SQL Server. Based on this setting, SQL Server will record every successful or failed user login attempt to either the Windows application log or the SQL Server log.

C2 Security

When configuring SQL Server for C2-level security, enabling the C2 Audit Mode property ensures that SQL Server will refuse to continue if it is unable to write to the security-audit log. The property can be set with the following code and may not be set from within Management Studio:

```
EXEC sp_configure 'C2 audit mode', 1
RECONFIGURE
```

For more information about locking down SQL Server's security, refer to Chapter 40, "Securing Databases."

You can obtain the text for any SQL query by selecting `sysdm_exec_sql_text` from the dynamic management view. You must supply a `sql_handle` value to obtain the query text. The `sysdm_exec_requests` view provides a complete list of every query currently executing on this instance of SQL Server. The output of this view includes the `sql_handle` needed by the `sysdm_exec_sql_text` view.

Connection-Configuration Properties

The connection-configuration properties, shown in Table 34-5, are used to set connection options in SQL Server.

Table 34-5: Connection-Configuration Properties

Property	Level*	Graphic Control	Code Option
Max Concurrent User Connections	S	Management Studio	EXEC sp_configure 'user connections'
Default Connections Options	S	Management Studio	-
Permit Remote Server Connections	S	Management Studio	EXEC sp_configure 'remote access'
Remote Query Timeout	S	Management Studio	EXEC sp_configure 'remote query timeout (s)'
Enforce DTC	S	Management Studio	EXEC sp_configure 'remote proc trans'
Network Packet Size	S	-	EXEC sp_configure 'network packet size'
Remote Login Timeout	S	-	EXEC sp_configure 'remote login timeout'

* The configuration level refers to Server, Database, or Connection.

The Connections tab (see Figure 34-8) sets connection-level properties, including defaults, number of connections permitted, and timeout settings.

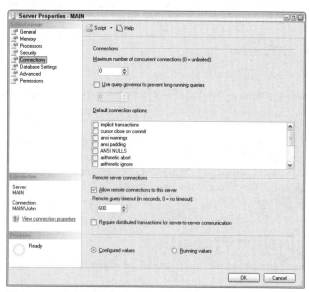

Figure 34-8: Connections page of Management Studio's SQL Server Properties dialog

Maximum Concurrent User Connections

The `Maximum concurrent user connections` option should probably not be set to a given number of users because applications often open several connections to SQL Server. For example, ODBC- and ADO-based applications will open a connection for every connection object in code — possibly as many as one for every form, list box, and/or combo box. Access tends to open at least two connections.

The purpose of this option is to limit the number of connections in a memory-starved server because each connection consumes 40KB. For most servers the default of 0, or unlimited connections, is appropriate.

The maximum number of user connections may be set within code with the `user connections` option:

```
EXEC sp_configure 'user connections', 0
RECONFIGURE
```

To determine the current setting in code, examine the value in the `@@maxconnections` global variable:

```
SELECT @@MAX_CONNECTIONS
```

Result:

```
-----------
32767
```

Remote Access

The remote server's connection properties are used for distributed queries — referencing data from one SQL Server in another. By default, this feature is enabled. To disallow distributed queries from calling the server, disable the check box or set the remote access option to 0:

```
EXEC sp_configure 'remote access', 0
RECONFIGURE
```

Remote Query Timeout

The remote query timeout option sets the number of seconds SQL Server will wait on a remote query before assuming it failed and generating a timeout error. The default value of 10 minutes seems sufficient for executing a remote query:

```
EXEC sp_configure 'remote query timeout', 600
RECONFIGURE
```

Enforce DTC

When updating multiple servers within a transaction (logical unit of work), SQL Server can enforce dual-phase commits using the Distributed Transaction Coordinator.

From code, the Enforce DTC property is enabled by setting the remote proc trans option to 1:

```
EXEC sp_configure 'remote proc trans', 1
RECONFIGURE
```

 Cross-Reference   Transactions are explained in Chapter 51, "Managing Transactions, Locking, and Blocking."

Network-Packet Size and Timeout

Two connection-related properties are available only through code. The network-packet size may be changed from its default of 4KB by means of the network packet size option. The following code sets the network-packet size to 2KB:

```
exec sp_configure 'network packet size', 2048
RECONFIGURE
```

Very rarely should the network-packet size need reconfiguring. Consider this property a fine-tuning tool and use it only when the data being passed tends to greatly exceed the default size, such as large text or image data.

The remote login timeout property is also unavailable from Management Studio. This property sets the maximum wait time to log into a remote data source. The default of 20 can be changed to 30 with the following code:

```
EXEC sp_configure 'remote login timeout', 30
RECONFIGURE
```

Max Large-Data-Replication Size

Although you can't configure it in Management Studio, you can use the following code to configure the maximum size of the text and image data that may be sent via replication:

```
EXEC sp_configure 'max text repl size', 16767
RECONFIGURE
```

SQL Server provides four dynamic management views that are exceptionally helpful when working with replication: `sysdm_repl_articles`, `sysdm_repl_tranhash`, `sysdm_repl_schemas`, and `sysdm_repl_traninfo`.

 The details of replication are discussed in Chapter 39, "Replicating Data."

Server-Configuration Properties

The server-configuration properties, shown in Table 34-6, enable you to set serverwide performance and display properties in SQL Server.

Table 34-6: Server-Configuration Properties

Property	Level*	Graphic Control	Code Option
Default Language for Server Messages	S	Management Studio	`EXEC sp_configure 'default language'`
Allow Changes to System Tables	S	Management Studio	`EXEC sp_configure 'allow updates'`
Query Cost Governor	S	Management Studio	`EXEC sp_configure 'query governor cost limit'`
Two-digit Year Interpreter	S	Management Studio	`EXEC sp_configure 'two digit year cutoff'`
Default Full-text Language	S	-	`EXEC sp_configure 'default full-text language'`

* The configuration level refers to Server, Database, or Connection.

The Advanced tab of Management Studio's Server Properties page (see Figure 34-9) is best left with the default values.

Default Message Language

The default language for server user messages can be set in Management Studio as well as in code:

```
EXEC sp_configure 'default language', 0
RECONFIGURE
```

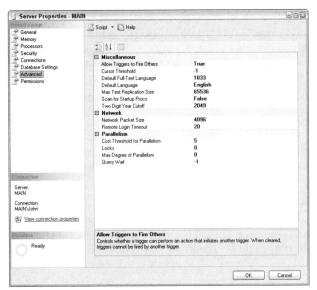

Figure 34-9: Advanced page of Management Studio's SQL Server Properties dialog

Full-Text Search Default Language

The default language for full-text searches can be set only from within code:

```
EXEC sp_configure 'default full-text language', 1033
RECONFIGURE
```

In this case, the value of 1033 refers to English. The server normally sets the correct value for you during installation. You need to change this value only when you need to support something other than the default system language.

On The Web

Many of the language settings in SQL Server rely on a *locale identifier (LCID)*. You can find a list of common LCID values at http://krafft.com/scripts/deluxe-calendar/lcid_chart.htm.

Allowing Changes to System Tables

The "Allow modifications to be made to the system catalogs" server-behavior option enables direct modifications to system tables; it should be avoided. The sp_configure version of this option is allow updates.

I can think of no system-table value that should be directly manipulated, although any change is best made through Microsoft's system stored procedures, or through standard SQL alter commands.

Best Practice

Query Governor Cost Limit

In the same way that a small gas-engine governor controls the top speed of the engine, the query governor limits the maximum number of queries SQL Server will perform according to the estimated query cost. If a user submits a query that exceeds the limit set by the query governor, SQL Server will not execute the query.

The following code sets the max-query plan to 10 seconds for the entire server:

```
EXEC sp_configure 'query governor cost limit', 10
RECONFIGURE
```

In code, however, the query governor can be changed for the current connection. The following code disables the governor within the scope of the current connection/batch:

```
SET QUERY_GOVERNOR_COST_LIMIT 0
```

Personally, I don't use the query governor to limit user-query execution, but if you have a smoothly running database with all application queries running in under one second, and users are now submitting poorly written ad hoc queries that consume unreasonable resources, using the query governor might be a good way to prevent those queries from executing.

Two-Digit-Year Cutoff

The two-digit-year support helps handle Y2K problems by converting a two-digit year to a four-digit year based on the values supplied. If the two-digit year falls after the first value (default 1959), it is interpreted as being in the twentieth century. If it falls before the second value (default 2049), it is interpreted as being in the twenty-first century. For example, 01/01/69 remains 01/01/1969, and 01/01/14 is interpreted as 01/01/2014. The following example sets the two-digit-year cutoff to 41:

```
EXEC sp_configure 'two digit year cutoff', 2041
RECONFIGURE
```

Index-Configuration Properties

The index statistics and fill-factor options, shown in Table 34-7, establish the defaults for new indexes in SQL Server.

Table 34-7: Index-Configuration Properties

Property	Level*	Graphic Control	Code Option
Auto Create Statistics	D	Management Studio	ALTER DATABASE <DB Name> SET auto_create_statistics {ON | OFF}
Auto Update Statistics	D	Management Studio	ALTER DATABASE <DB Name> SET auto_update_statistics {ON | OFF}
Index Fill Factor	S	Management Studio	EXEC sp_configure 'fill factor'

* The configuration level refers to Server, Database, or Connection.

These options do not alter any existing indexes; they only set the defaults for new indexes. You can also view and set the index configuration properties using the sp_autostats command. Query the current settings by providing a table from the current database as follows:

```
sp_autostats 'Categories'
```

Result:

```
Global statistics settings for [Northwind]:
   Automatic update statistics: ON
   Automatic create statistics: ON

settings for table [Categories]

Index Name        AUTOSTATS Last Updated
---------------   --------- -----------------------
[PK_Categories]  ON        2006-02-27 19:29:11.873
[CategoryName]   ON        NULL
```

Change the settings by adding a flag value after the table name. A value of ON enables the automatic features, whereas OFF disables the feature. You can also change the settings for a particular index by adding an index name.

Cross-Reference The details of index creation are discussed in Chapter 17, "Implementing the Physical Database Schema." Index management and tuning is covered in Chapter 50, "Query Analysis and Index Tuning."

Configuring Database Auto Options

Four database-configuration options determine the automatic behaviors of SQL Server databases (see Table 34-8). In Management Studio they are all set in the Options tab of the Database Properties page.

Table 34-8: Index-Configuration Properties

Property	Level*	Graphic Control	Code Option
Auto Close	D	Management Studio	ALTER DATABASE <DB Name> SET auto_close {ON | OFF}
Auto Shrink	D	Management Studio	ALTER DATABASE <DB Name> SET auto_shrink {ON | OFF}
Auto Create Statistics	D	Management Studio	ALTER DATABASE <DB Name> SET auto _create_statistics {ON | OFF}
Auto Update Statistics	D	Management Studio	ALTER DATABASE <DB Name> SET auto _ update _ statistics {ON | OFF}

* The configuration level refers to Server, Database, or Connection.

Auto Close

Auto close directs SQL Server to release all database resources (cached data pages, compiled stored procedures, saved query execution plans) when all users exit and all processes are complete. This frees memory for other databases. While this option will improve performance slightly for other databases, reloading the database will take longer, as will recompiling the procedures and recalculating the query execution plans, once the database is again opened by a user.

If the database is used regularly, do not enable auto close. If the database is used occasionally, then auto close might be appropriate to save memory.

Caution   Many front-end client applications repeatedly open and close a connection to SQL Server. Setting auto close on in this type of environment is a sure way to kill SQL Server performance.

Use the following to set auto close in code:

```
ALTER DATABASE database SET AUTO_CLOSE ON | OFF
```

Auto_Shrink

If the database has more than 25 percent free space, this option causes SQL Server to perform a shrink database operation. This option also causes the transaction log to shrink after it's backed up.

Performing a file shrink is a costly operation because several pages must be moved within the file. This option also regularly checks the status of the data pages to determine whether they can be shrunk.

The default setting is on for Desktop and Personal edition, off for Standard and Enterprise.

Cross-Reference   Shrinking the data and transaction log files is discussed in detail in Chapter 36, "Recovery Planning."

To set the auto shrink option in code, do the following:

```
ALTER DATABASE database SET AUTO_SHRINK ON | OFF
```

Auto Create Statistics

Data-distribution statistics are a key factor in how the Query Optimizer creates query execution plans. This option directs SQL Server to automatically create statistics for any columns for which statistics could be useful.

To set auto create statistics in code, do the following:

```
ALTER DATABASE database SET AUTO_CREATE_STATISTICS ON | OFF
```

Auto Update Statistics

Out-of-date data-distribution statistics aren't very useful. This option keeps the statistics automatically updated. The default for this option is set to on.

To set the auto update statistics option in code, do the following:

```
ALTER DATABASE database SET AUTO_UPDATE_STATISTICS ON | OFF
```

Query and index tuning rely heavily on data-distribution statistics. The strategies involving statistics are explained in Chapter 49, "Measuring Performance."

Cursor-Configuration Properties

The cursor-configuration properties, shown in Table 34-9, are used to control cursor behavior in SQL Server.

Table 34-9: Cursor-Configuration Properties

Property	Level*	Graphic Control	Code Option
Cursor Threshold	S	-	EXEC sp_configure 'cursor threshold'
Cursor Close on Commit	SDC	-	ALTER DATABASE <DB Name> SET cursor_close_on_commit {ON | OFF}
Cursor Default	D	-	ALTER DATABASE <DB Name> SET cursor_default {LOCAL | GLOBAL}

* The configuration level refers to Server, Database, or Connection.

To view statistics about the open cursors in various databases, select `sysdm_exec_cursors` from the dynamic management view.

Cursor Threshold

The `cursor threshold` property sets the number of rows in a cursor set before the cursor keysets are generated asynchronously. Synchronous keysets are faster than other cursor types, but they consume more memory. Every cursor keyset will be generated asynchronously if the `cursor threshold` property is set to 0.

The default of -1 causes all keysets to be generated synchronously, which is OK for smaller keysets. For larger cursor keysets this may be a problem. When you are working with cursors, the following code will permit synchronous cursor keysets for cursors of up to 10,000 rows:

```
EXEC sp_configure 'cursor threshold', 10000
RECONFIGURE WITH OVERRIDE
```

Cursor Close on Commit

This property will close an open cursor after a transaction is committed when set to `on`. If it is set to `off`, then cursors will remain open across transactions until a `close cursor` statement is issued.

To set cursor close on commit in code, do the following:

```
SET CURSOR_CLOSE_ON_COMMIT ON
```

You can also use this alternative:

```
ALTER DATABASE database SET CURSOR_CLOSE_ON_COMMIT ON | OFF
```

Cursor Default

This property will make each cursor local to the object that declared it when set to `local`. When it is set to `global`, the scope of the cursor can be extended outside the object that created it.

To set cursor default in code, do the following:

```
ALTER DATABASE database SET CURSOR_DEFAULT LOCAL | GLOBAL
```

SQL ANSI–Configuration Properties

The SQL ANSI–configuration properties, shown in Table 34-10, are used to set ANSI behavior in SQL Server.

Table 34-10: SQL ANSI–Configuration Properties

Property	Level*	Graphic Control	Code Option
ANSI Defaults	C	-	`SET ANSI_DEFAULTS {ON	OFF}`
ANSI Null Behavior	SDC	Management Studio	`ALTER DATABASE <DB Name> SET ansi_null_Default {ON	OFF}`
ANSI Nulls	SDC	Management Studio	`ALTER DATABASE <DB Name> SET ansi_nulls {ON	OFF}`
ANSI Padding	SC	-	`ALTER DATABASE <DB Name> SET ansi_padding {ON	OFF}`
ANSI Warnings	SDC	-	`ALTER DATABASE <DB Name> SET ansi_warnings {ON	OFF}`
Arithmetic Abort	SC	-	`ALTER DATABASE <DB Name> SET arithabort {ON	OFF}`
Arithmetic Ignore	SC	-	`SET arithignore {ON	OFF}`
Numeric Round Abort	D	-	`ALTER DATABASE <DB Name> SET numeric_roundabort {ON	OFF}`
Null Concatenation	DC	-	`ALTER DATABASE <DB Name> SET concat_null_yields_null {ON	OFF}`

Property	Level*	Graphic Control	Code Option
Use Quoted Identifier	D	-	ALTER DATABASE <DB Name> SET quoted_identifier {ON | OFF}
ANSI SQL 92 Compatibility Flag	C	-	SET fips_flagger {ENTRY | FULL | INTERMEDIATE | OFF}

* The configuration level refers to Server, Database, or Connection.

The connection default properties (there are several) affect the environment of batches executed within a connection. Most of the connection properties change SQL Server behavior so that it complies with the ANSI standard. Because so few SQL Server installations modify these properties, it's much safer to modify them in code at the beginning of a batch if the code depends on a non-Microsoft behavior than to set them at the server or database level.

For example, T-SQL requires a `begin transaction` to start a logical unit of work. Oracle assumes a `begin transaction` is at the beginning of every batch. If you prefer to work with implicit (nonstated) transactions, you're safer setting the implicit transaction connection property at the beginning of your batch than setting it in the server defaults. The server default will affect every batch and may break Microsoft-standard T-SQL code. For these reasons, I recommend leaving the connection properties at the default values, setting them in code if needed.

The SQL ANSI-configuration settings are set with the `alter database` command. For backward compatibility, the `sp_dboption` is also available.

ANSI Null Default

The `ansi_null_default` setting controls the database's default nullability. This default setting is used when a `null` or `not_null` is not explicitly specified when creating a table.

To set this option in code, do the following:

```
ALTER DATABASE database SET ANSI_NULL_DEFAULT ON | OFF
```

ANSI NULLs

The `ansi_nulls` database setting is used to determine comparison evaluations. When set to `on`, any comparison to a null value will evaluate to null. When set to `off`, the comparison of two `null` values will evaluate to `true`.

To set ANSI nulls in code, do the following:

```
ALTER DATABASE database SET ANSI_NULLS ON | OFF
```

ANSI Padding

The `ansi_padding` database setting affects only newly created columns. When set to `on`, data stored in variable data types will retain any padded zeros to the left of variable binary numbers, and any padded spaces to the right or left of variable-length characters. When set to `off`, all leading and trailing blanks and zeros are trimmed.

To set ANSI padding in code, do the following:

```
ALTER DATABASE database SET ANSI_PADDING ON | OFF
```

ANSI Warnings

The `ansi_warnings` database setting is used to handle ANSI errors and warnings. When this setting is `off`, all errors, such as null values in aggregate functions and divide-by-zero errors, are suppressed. When the setting is `on`, the warnings and errors will be raised.

To set ANSI warnings in code, do the following:

```
ALTER DATABASE database SET ANSI_WARNINGS ON | OFF
```

Arithmetic Abort

When set to `on`, the `arithabort` database setting will abort the data process if an arithmetic error occurs, such as data overflow or divide-by-zero. If set to `off`, then only a warning message is passed if an arithmetic error occurs, and the data process is able to proceed.

To set arithmetic abort in code, do the following:

```
ALTER DATABASE database SET ARITHABORT ON | OFF
```

Numeric Round Abort

The `numeric_roundabort` database setting is used to control the behavior of numeric decimal-precision-rounding errors in process. When set to `on`, the process will abort if the numeric-decimal precision is lost in an expression value. When set to `off`, the process will proceed without error, and the result will be rounded down to the precision of the object in which the number is being stored.

To set numeric round abort in code, do the following:

```
ALTER DATABASE database SET NUMERIC_ROUNDABORT ON | OFF
```

Concatenation Null Yields Null

The `concat_null_yields_null` database setting is used to control the behavior of the resultant when concatenating a string with a `null`. When set to `on`, any string concatenated with a `null` will result in a `null`. When set to `off`, any string concatenated with a `null` will result in the original string, ignoring the `null`.

To set numeric round abort in code, do the following:

```
ALTER DATABASE database SET CONCAT_NULL_YIELDS_NULL ON | OFF
```

Use Quoted Identifier

The `quoted_identifier` database setting enables you to refer to an identifier, such as a column name, by enclosing it within double quotes. When set to `on`, identifiers can be delimited by double quotation marks. When set to `off`, identifiers cannot be placed in quotation marks and must not be keywords:

```
ALTER DATABASE database SET QUOTED_IDENTIFIER ON | OFF
```

The default is `off`. This option must be on to create or modify indexed views or indexes on calculated columns.

Trigger Configuration Properties

The trigger configuration properties, shown in Table 34-11, are used to control trigger behavior in SQL Server.

Table 34-11: Trigger Configuration Properties

Property	Level*	Graphic Control	Code Option
Allow Nested Triggers	S	Management Studio	`EXEC sp_configure 'nested triggers'`
Recursive Triggers	D	Management Studio	`ALTER DATABASE <DB Name> SET recursive_triggers {ON	OFF}`

* The configuration level refers to Server, Database, or Connection.

Trigger behavior can be set at both the server and database levels.

Nested Triggers

Triggers can be nested by means of being called in a recursive hierarchy up to a maximum of 32 levels. This is a server-level configuration setting.

To set nested triggers in code, do the following:

```
EXEC sp_configure 'nested triggers', 1
RECONFIGURE
```

Recursive Triggers

A trigger is a small stored procedure that is executed upon an `insert`, `update`, or `delete` operation on a table. If the code in the trigger again inserts, updates, or deletes the same table, the trigger causes itself to be executed again. This recursive behavior is enabled or disabled by the recursive trigger database option.

Cross-Reference

Nested triggers, server properties, and recursive triggers (a database property) are often confused with each other. Refer to Chapter 23, "Creating DML Triggers," for a complete explanation, including coverage of how triggers can call other triggers and how this server property controls trigger behavior.

The default is `off`. Nested triggers, a related option, is a server option. To set the option in T-SQL code, do the following:

```
ALTER DATABASE database SET RECURSIVE_TRIGGERS ON | OFF
```

Database-State-Configuration Properties

The database-state-configuration properties, shown in Table 34-12, are available in SQL Server. These configurations are mostly used when a DBA is performing maintenance on the database.

Table 34-12: Database-State-Configuration Properties

Property	Level*	Graphic Control	Code Option
Database Off-Line	D	-	ALTER DATABASE <DB Name> SET offline
Read-Only	D	Management Studio	ALTER DATABASE <DB Name> SET read_only
Restricted Access — Members of db_owner, dbcreator, or sysadmin	D	Management Studio	ALTER DATABASE <DB Name> SET restricted_user
Restricted Access — Single user	D	Management Studio	ALTER DATABASE <DB Name> SET single_user
Restricted User — Disabled	D	Management Studio	ALTER DATABASE <DB Name> SET multi_user
Compatibility Level	D	Management Studio	EXEC sp_dbcmptlevel <DB Name> {60 | 65 | 70 | 80 | 90}

* The configuration level refers to Server, Database, or Connection.

The state of the database can also be set with the `alter database` command. The `sp_dboption` command is also available for backward compatibility.

Database-Access Level

The database-access-configuration options are used to set the state of the database. When the database is offline, no access to the database is allowed.

To set a database to an `offline` state in code, do the following:

```
ALTER DATABASE database SET OFFLINE
```

The `read_only` database-state settings are used to allow only selects from the database. `read_only` cannot take effect if any users are in the database. To reset the database to a normal read-and-write state, the `read_write` database setting is used.

To set a database to a `read_only` state in code, do the following:

```
ALTER DATABASE database SET READ_ONLY
```

The database restricted access–database state settings are also available. The three restricted access levels are `single_user`, `restricted_user`, and `multi_user` states. These settings control which users are allowed to access the database. The `single_user` setting is appropriate when you are doing database maintenance. The `restricted_user` setting allows database access only to users in the db_owner, dbcreator, and sysadmin roles. The `multi_user` setting is used to set the database in the normal operating state.

To set the database restricted access state in code, do the following:

```
ALTER DATABASE database SET SINGLE_USER
```

Compatibility Level

In SQL Server, the database-compatibility level can be set from 60 (SQL Server version 6.0) to 80 (SQL Server 2005). Setting the database-compatibility level to a level lower than 80 may be necessary if you are upgrading the Database Engine and still need to maintain the behavior of an earlier version of SQL Server.

To set compatibility level in code, do the following:

```
EXEC sp_dbcmptlevel database, 80
```

Recovery-Configuration Properties

The recovery-configuration properties, shown in Table 34-13, are used to set recovery options in SQL Server.

Table 34-13: Recovery-Configuration Properties

Property	Level*	Graphic Control	Code Option
Recovery Model	D	Management Studio	ALTER DATABASE <DB Name> SET RECOVERY {FULL | BULK_LOGGED | SIMPLE}
Torn Page Detection	D	Management Studio	ALTER DATABASE <DB Name> SET TORN_PAGE_DETECTION {ON | OFF}
Backup Timeout	S	-	-
Media Retention	S	-	EXEC sp_configure 'media retention'
Recovery Interval	S	-	EXEC sp_configure 'recovery interval'

* The configuration level refers to Server, Database, or Connection.

The recovery options determine how SQL Server handles transactions and the transaction log, and how the transaction log is backed up.

Recovery Model

SQL Server 2005 uses a recovery model to configure several settings that work together to control how the transaction log behaves regarding file growth and recovery possibilities. The three recovery model options are as follows:

✦ **Simple:** The transaction log contains only transactions that are not yet written to the data file. This option provides no up-to-the-minute recovery.

✦ **Bulk-Logged:** The transaction log contains all DML operations, but bulk insert operations are only marked, not logged.

✦ **Full:** The transaction log contains all changes to the data file. This option provides the greatest recovery potential.

Chapter 36, "Recovery Planning," focuses on recovery planning and operations in detail.

The recovery option can be set in code with the set recovery option.

Torn-Page Detection

Even though SQL Server works with 8KB data pages, the operating system I/O writes in 512-byte sectors. Therefore, it's possible that a failure might occur in the middle of a data-page write, resulting in only some of the 512-byte sectors to be written.

In keeping with the ACID properties of the database, the torn-page detection option instructs SQL Server to toggle a bit on each 512-byte sector with each write operation. If all the sectors were updated, all the torn-page detection bits should be identical. If, upon recovery, any of the bits are different, SQL Server can detect the torn-page condition and mark the database as suspect.

Some argue that this option is not necessary if the server has battery backup and the disk subsystem has battery backup on the cache, but I still use it.

Additional minor recovery options (back-up timeout, media retention, and recovery interval) are all discussed in Chapter 36, "Recovery Planning."

Summary

Configuration options are important for compatibility, performance tuning, and controlling the connection. The configuration options are set at the server, database, and connection level. Most of the options can be set from Management Studio's Database Properties page; nearly all can be configured with code.

Continuing with SQL Server administration tasks, the next chapter focuses on maintaining databases with database-consistency checks.

✦   ✦   ✦

Transferring Databases

T ransferring data may be a mundane task, but SQL Server databases are often developed on one server and deployed on other servers. Without a reliable and efficient method of moving database schemas and whole databases, the project won't get very far.

SQL Server enables multiple means of moving databases. As a database developer or database administrator (DBA), you should have basic skills in the following topics, three of which are covered in this chapter:

- ✦ Copy Database Wizard

- ✦ SQL scripts

- ✦ Detach/attach

- ✦ Backup/restore (covered in Chapter 36, "Recovery Planning")

The keys to determining the best way to move a database are knowing how much of it needs to be moved and whether or not the servers are directly connected by a fast network. Table 35-1 lists the copy requirements and the various methods of moving a database.

✦ ✦ ✦ ✦

In This Chapter

Using the Copy
Database Wizard

Generating SQL scripts

Detaching and
attaching databases

✦ ✦ ✦ ✦

Table 35-1: Database Transfer Methods

Requirement	Copy Database Wizard	SQL Scripts	Detaching Attaching	Backup Restore
Exclusive Access to the Database	Yes	No	Yes	No
Copies Between Disconnected Servers	No	Yes	Yes	Yes
Copies Database Schema	Yes	Yes	Yes	Yes
Copies Data	Yes	No	Yes	Yes
Copies Security	Server logins, database users, security roles, and permissions	Depends on the script	Database users, security roles, and permissions	Database users, security roles, and permissions
Copies Jobs/ User-Defined Error Messages	Yes	Depends on the script	Yes	Yes

Copy Database Wizard

The Copy Database Wizard actually generates a Data Transformation Service package that can copy or move one or more databases from one server to another. If the database is being moved to a server on the same network server, this is the premiere method. This method won't work to copy a database from SQL Server 2005 to an older version of SQL Server. In addition, both source and destination server must have the SQL Server Agent running (it is stopped by default when working with SQL Server 2005). The Copy Database Wizard offers the most flexibility and capability. Its only limitation is that it requires exclusive access to the database. You access the Copy Database Wizard by right-clicking the database you want to copy and choosing Tasks ➪ Copy Database from the context menu. Skip past the Welcome to the Copy Database Wizard page by clicking Next.

Cross-Reference   For more information about starting and stopping SQL Server Agent, refer to Chapter 4, "Installing SQL Server 2005."

On pages 1 and 2 of the functional portion of the Copy Database Wizard, the wizard begins by gathering the name of the source and destination servers and the required security information to log into the server.

On page 3, the wizard asks how you want to transfer the database. Using the detach and attach method is faster, but it requires that SQL Server have additional rights to both source and destination databases, and you must allow exclusive access to both. The detach and attach method works best for large databases. The SQL Management Object (SMO) method doesn't require any special access and users can continue using the source database. However, this method is significantly slower and Microsoft doesn't recommend it for large databases.

On page 4, the wizard displays the default locations for the database files on the destination server. You can also modify the locations here if needed. The wizard will move all the objects and data.

On page 5, the wizard asks you to configure the destination database. You assign the database a name and specify how the Copy Database Wizard reacts when a database with the requested name already exists on the destination. The options are either stopping the transfer or dropping the existing database and creating a new database with the same name.

On page 4 (see Figure 35-1) you can optionally direct the wizard to move the following:

✦ All logins or only those that have access to the database

✦ All or selected non-system stored procedures in the Master database that are used by the database

✦ All or selected SQL Agent jobs (automated and optionally scheduled tasks)

✦ All or selected user-defined error messages (used by the `raiserror` T-SQL command)

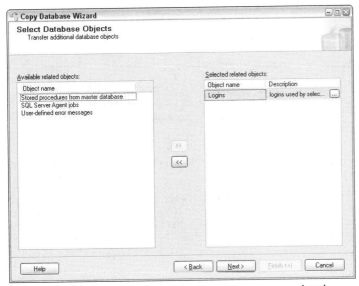

Figure 35-1: The Copy Database Wizard can move server-related information as it moves the database.

Depending on the options selected, the wizard may display additional pages to select the Master database non-system stored procedures, the SQL Server Agent jobs, and the user-defined error messages.

The Configure the Package page shows the package location. You can also provide a name for the package and choose a method for logging errors. The default method uses the Windows event log. It's also possible to send a list of errors to a text file. The wizard will request a file-name when you choose this option.

The Schedule the Package page, shown in Figure 35-2, directs the wizard to either run the Integration Services package once upon completion of the wizard, run it once later, or set it up on a regular schedule.

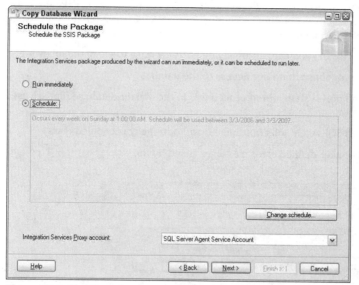

Figure 35-2: The Copy Database Wizard can run the Integration Services package once now, once later, or on a schedule.

When finished, the wizard generates and runs an Integration Services package (see Figure 35-3) and saves it on the destination server.

You can open the generated Integration Services package, shown in Figure 35-4, by selecting the Jobs node under SQL Server Agent in the console tree and then double-clicking on the package. If the name was not edited in the wizard's schedule page, then the name should be CDW followed by the two server names and an integer. The creation date is also listed.

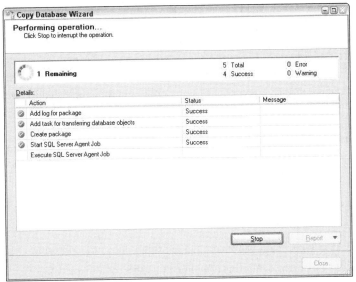

Figure 35-3: When the Copy Database Wizard executes the Integration Services package, it displays its progress as it works its way through the steps.

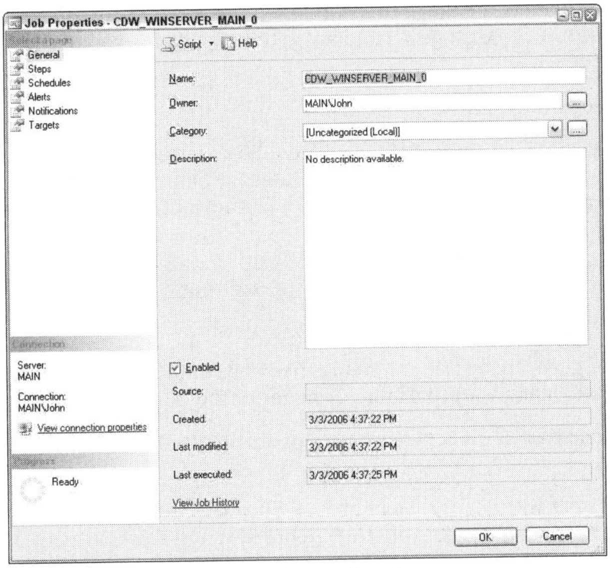

Figure 35-4: The Copy Database Wizard creates an SQL Server Agent job; in this case, it named the job CDW_WINSERVER_MAIN_0.

Working with SQL Script

Of the four methods for moving a database, running a SQL Script, or batch, is the only method that creates a new database. Perhaps it's false logic, but the idea of starting with a fresh installation at a client site, without any residue from test data, is a reassuring thought.

Scripts are smaller than databases. They often fit on a floppy, and they can be edited with Notepad. As an example, the sample databases for this book are distributed by means of scripts.

Scripts are useful for distributing the following:

✦ Database schema (databases, tables, views, stored procedures, functions, and so on)

✦ Security roles

✦ Database jobs

✦ Limited sample data or priming data

Though it's possible, I wouldn't recommend creating a script to move the following:

✦ **Data:** A script can insert rows, but this is a difficult method of moving data.

✦ **Server logins:** A script can easily create server logins, but server logins tend to be domain specific, so this option is useful only within a single domain.

✦ **Server jobs:** Server-specific jobs generally require individualized tweaking. While a script may be useful to copy jobs, they will likely require editing prior to execution.

Scripts may also be used to implement a change to a database. The easiest way to modify a client database is to write a script. The change script can be tested on a backup of the database.

Scripts may be generated in several ways:

✦ The database can be developed initially in Management Studio using a handwritten DDL script. Chapter 17, "Implementing the Physical Database Schema," explains how to create such a script. In addition, the sample databases OntheWebsite are all created using a DDL script. This is my preferred method.

On The Web

The code for this chapter may be downloaded from the book's website at www
.SQLServerBible.com.

✦ Management Studio can generate a script to create the entire database or a change script for schema changes made with the Table Designer or the Database Designer.

✦ Most third-party database-design tools generate scripts to create the database or apply changes.

With a focus on generating scripts with Management Studio, open the Management Studio script generator, select the database in the console tree, right-click, and select Tasks ➪ Generate Scripts.

Skip the Welcome to the Generate SQL Server Scripts page. In Management Studio's Script Wizard, use the Select Database page, shown in Figure 35-5, to choose the objects that should be included in the script.

Figure 35-5: Management Studio can generate scripts for any of the databases within the DBMS.

The Choose Script Options page, shown in Figure 35-6, contains two sets of options. The General options determine script behavior, such as whether Management Studio appends the new script to an existing script file. The Table/View options determine script features, such as whether the script contains code to create foreign keys.

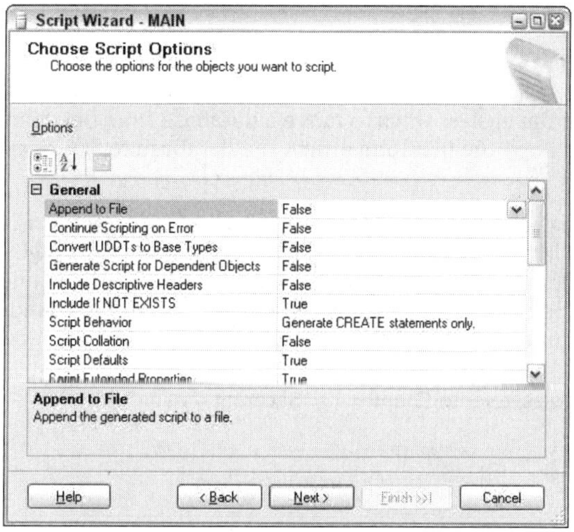

Figure 35-6: Set the script options to match the database features you require and to define the behavior you expect from Management Studio.

The Choose Object Types page contains a list of objects within the selected databases. As a minimum, you'll see an option to script tables.

The pages that follow vary depending on the objects you select. For example, if you choose to script tables, then you'll see a Choose Tables page in which you select the tables you want to script.

Eventually, you'll reach the Output Option page, shown in Figure 35-7. Use the options on this page to select an output method. If you choose the Script to File option, then you'll also need to choose the output filename and output format.

Figure 35-7: Choose an output option that matches the kind of database transfer you want to perform.

Detaching and Attaching

Though it is often overlooked, one of the easiest ways to move a database from one computer to another is to detach the database, copy the files, and attach the database to SQL Server on the destination computer.

For developers who frequently move databases between notebooks and servers, this is the recommended method. Detaching a database effectively deletes the database from SQL Server's awareness, but leaves the files intact. The database must have no current connections and not be replicated if it is to be detached. Only members of the SysAdmins fixed server role may detach and attach databases.

Cross-Reference For more details on the security roles, refer to Chapter 40, "Securing Databases."

Detaching and attaching the database will carry with it any database users, security roles, and permissions, but it will not replicate server logins. These will need to be resolved manually on the destination server. It's best to coordinate security with the network administration folks and leverage their security groups. If the source and destination servers have access to the same network security groups, this will alleviate the security login issues for most installations.

Using Management Studio, right-click the database to be copied and select Tasks ⇨ Detach. The Detach Database dialog box, shown in Figure 35-8, will appear.

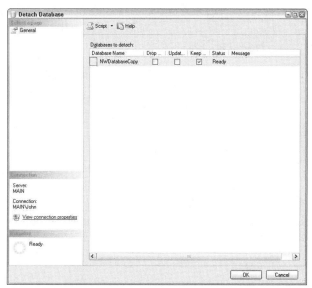

Figure 35-8: The Detach Database feature removes the database from SQL Server's list of databases and frees the files for copying.

Once the file is detached, it will disappear from the list of databases in Management Studio. The files may be copied or moved like regular files.

To reattach the database file, select Databases in the Management Studio console tree and Tasks ⇨ Attach from the action menu or context menu. The Attach Database dialog box, shown in Figure 35-9, simply offers a place to select the file and verify the file locations and names.

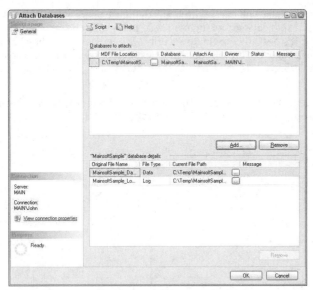

Figure 35-9: The database may be reattached by means of Management Studio's Attach Database tool.

In code, the database is detached by running the `sp_detach_db` system stored procedure. The first parameter is the database to be detached. A second optional parameter simply turns off automatic updating of the index statistics. The following command detaches the OBX Kites sample database:

```
sp_detach_db 'OBXKites'
```

If you wish to reattach a database with code, the counterpart to `sp_detach_db` is the `sp_attach_db` system stored procedure. Attaching a database requires specifying the files' locations as well as the database name, as follows:

```
EXEC sp_attach_db @dbname = 'OBXKites',
    @filename1 = 'e:\SQLData\OBXKites.mdf',
    @filename2 = 'f:\SQLData\OBXKitesStatic.ndf',
    @filename3 = 'g:\SQLLOG\OBXKites.ldf'
```

Summary

When you need to move a database, don't back it up; there are better ways to move it. Choose the right transfer method based on network proximity of the servers and the objects and/or data to be moved.

The next chapter moves on to recovery planning. You'll not only discover techniques for performing a backup, but also work with transaction logs and recovering various data objects, up to an entire server.

✦   ✦   ✦

Recovery Planning

The foundation for this book, the Information Architecture Principle (introduced in Chapter 1), puts into words the reason why there must be a solid recovery plan:

Information is an organizational asset, and, according to its value and scope, must be organized, inventoried, secured, and made readily available in a usable format for daily operations and analysis by individuals, groups, and processes, both today and in the future.

It goes without writing that for information to be "readily available . . . both today and in the future," regardless of hardware failure, catastrophes, or accidental deletion, there has to be a plan B.

Obviously, this is an imperfect world and bad things do happen to good people. Since you're bothering to read this chapter, I'll be honest and agree that doing backups isn't very exciting. In some jobs excitement means trouble, and this is one of them. To a good DBA, being prepared for the worst means having a sound recovery plan that has been tested more than once.

Consistent with the flexibility found in other areas of SQL Server, there are multiple ways to perform a backup, each suited to a different purpose. SQL Server offers three recovery models, which help organize the backup options and simplify database administration.

This chapter discusses the concepts that support the recovery effort, which entail both backup and restoration. It seems foolish to study backup without also learning about how restoration completes the recovery.

Cross-Reference

Recovery planning is not an isolated topic. Transactional integrity (Chapter 1 and Chapter 51) is deeply involved in the theory behind a sound recovery plan. Once the recovery strategy is determined, it's often implemented within a maintenance plan (Chapter 37). Because recovery is actually a factor of availability, the high availability of log shipping and failover servers (Chapter 52) is also a factor in recovery planning.

While backups tend to be boring, restores tend to occur when people are excited. For this reason, it makes sense to be as familiar with restoration as with backup.

Recovery Concepts

The concept of database recovery is based on the D in the transactional-integrity ACID properties—transactional *durability*. Durability means that a transaction, once committed, regardless of hardware failure, must be persistent.

SQL Server accomplishes transactional durability with a write-ahead transaction log. Every transaction is written to the transaction log prior to being written to the data file. This provides a few benefits to the recovery plan:

✦ The transaction log ensures that every transaction can be recovered up to the very last moment before the server stopped.

✦ The transaction log permits backups while transactions are being processed.

✦ The transaction log reduces the impact of a hardware failure because the transaction log and the data file may be placed on different disk subsystems.

The strategy of a recovery plan should be based on the organization's tolerance level, or *pain level*, for lost transactions. Recovery-plan tactics involve choosing among the various backup options, generating a backup schedule, and off-site storage.

SQL Server backup and recovery are very flexible, offering three recovery models from which to choose. The transaction log can be configured, based on your recovery needs, according to one of the following recovery models:

✦ **Simple:** No transaction log backups

✦ **Bulk-logged:** Bulk-logged operations are not logged

✦ **Full:** All transactions are logged

In addition, SQL Server offers five backup options:

✦ **Full:** Complete backup of all data

✦ **Differential:** Backup of all data pages modified since the last full backup

✦ **Transaction log:** Backup of all transactions in the log

✦ **File or filegroup:** Backup of all the data in the file or filegroup

✦ **File differential:** Backup of all data pages modified since the last file or filegroup backup

> **Note**   Backing up the database may not be the only critical backup you have to perform. If the database-security scheme relies on Windows authentication, backing up the Windows users is important as well. The point is that the SQL Server recovery plan must fit into a larger IT recovery plan.

SQL Server backups are very flexible and can handle any backup-to-file ratio. A single backup instance can be spread across several backup files, creating a *backup set*. Conversely, a single backup set can contain multiple backup instances.

Restoration always begins with a full backup. Differential and transaction log backups then restore the transaction that occurred after the full backup.

New in 2005

If you're familiar with performing backups using SQL Server 2000, you'll notice several tweaks and improvements. Features that were seldom used, such as the backup wizards or the backup at a later scheduled date, are gone; and a few new features, such as restoring parts of a damaged file and faster recovery times with Enterprise Edition, are welcome.

Recovery Models

The recovery model configures SQL Server database settings to accomplish the type of recovery required for the database, as detailed in Table 36-1. The key differences among the recovery models involve how the transaction log behaves and which data is logged.

Table 36-1: SQL Server Recovery Models

Recovery Model	Description	Transaction Atomicity	Transaction Durability	Bulk-Copy Operations (Select Into, and Bulk Insert)
Simple	Transaction log is continuously truncated on checkpoints	Yes	No, can restore only to the last full or differential backup	Not logged – high performance
Bulk-Logged	`Select-into` and `bulk-insert` operations are not logged as transactions	Yes	Maybe, can restore only to the last full or differential backup, or to the last transaction-log backup if no bulk-copy operations have been performed	Only marked – high performance
Full	All transactions are logged and stored until transaction-log backup	Yes	Yes, can restore up to the point of recovery	Slower than simple or bulk-logged

While the durability of the transaction is configurable, the transaction log is still used as a write-ahead transaction log to ensure that each transaction is atomic. In case of system failure, the transaction log is used by SQL Server to roll back any uncommitted transactions as well as to complete any committed transactions.

Simple Recovery Model

The simple recovery model is suitable for databases that require that each transaction be atomic, but not necessarily durable. The simple recovery model directs SQL Server to truncate, or empty, the transaction log on checkpoints. The transaction log will keep a transaction until it's confirmed in the data file, but after that point the space may be reused by another transaction in a round-robin style.

Because the transaction log is only a temporary log, there's no need for transaction-log backups. This recovery model has the benefit of keeping the transaction log small, at the cost of potentially losing all transactions since the last full or differential backup. Choosing the simple recovery model is the equivalent of setting the `truncate log on checkpoint` database option to `true` in SQL Server 7.0 or later.

A recovery plan based on a simple recovery model might perform full backups once a week and differential backups every weeknight, as shown in Figure 36-1. The full backup copies the entire database, and the differential backup copies all changes that have been made since the last full backup.

Simple Recovery Model
    Backup Plan

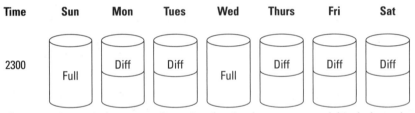

Figure 36-1: A typical recovery plan using the simple recovery model includes only full and differential backups.

When restoring from a simple recovery plan:

1. Restore the most recent full backup.

2. Restore the most recent (optional) single differential backup.

The Full Recovery Model

The full recovery model offers the most robust recovery plan. Under this model all transactions, including bulk-logged operations, are fully logged in the transaction log. Even system functions such as index creation are fully logged. The primary benefit of this model is that every committed transaction in the database can be restored right up to the point when failure occurred.

Best Practice

For production databases, I recommend the full recovery model. While it will run on a single drive system, the transaction log should be located on a fault-tolerant disk subsystem separate from the data files to ensure a high level of transactional durability.

The trade-off for this high level of transactional integrity is a certain amount of performance:

✦ Bulk-logged and select-into operations will be slower. If the database doesn't import data using these methods, this is a moot point.

✦ The transaction log will be mammoth. If copious drive space is available, this too is a moot point.

✦ Backing up and restoring the transaction log will take longer than it does with the other recovery models. However, in a crisis, restoring all the data will likely be more important than quickly restoring partial data.

The full recovery model can use all five types of database backups. A typical backup schedule is illustrated in Figure 36-2.

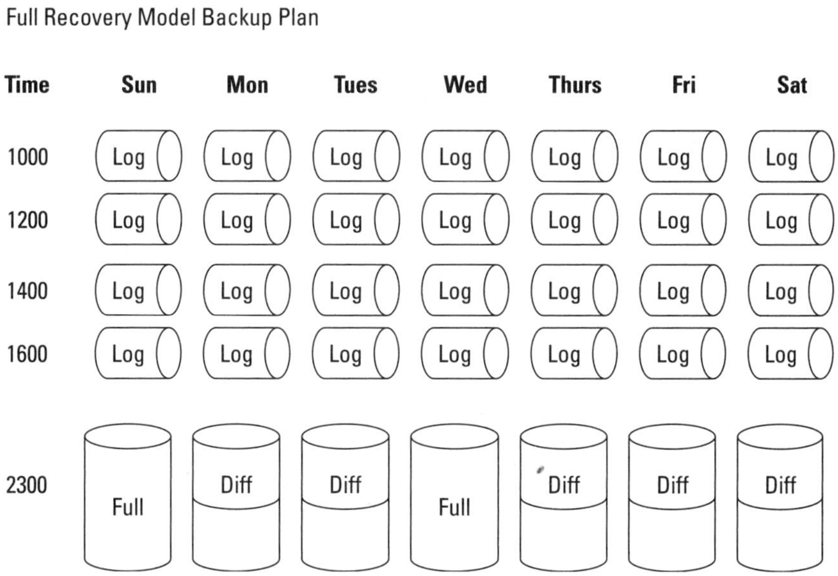

Full Recovery Model Backup Plan

Time	Sun	Mon	Tues	Wed	Thurs	Fri	Sat
1000	Log	Log	Log	Log	Log	Log	Log
1200	Log	Log	Log	Log	Log	Log	Log
1400	Log	Log	Log	Log	Log	Log	Log
1600	Log	Log	Log	Log	Log	Log	Log
2300	Full	Diff	Diff	Full	Diff	Diff	Diff

Figure 36-2: A typical recovery plan using the full recovery model, using full, differential, and transaction-log backups.

A full-recovery backup plan will typically do a full database backup twice a week, and differential backups every other night. The transaction log is backed up throughout the day, from as little as two times to as often as every 15 minutes.

When restoring from the full-recovery model, do the following:

1. Back up the current transaction log.

Note

If the disk subsystem containing the transaction log is lost, the database is marked suspect by SQL Server and it is not possible to back up the current transaction log. In this case, the best recovery option is to restore to the last transaction-log backup. Other reasons for a database being marked suspect would be that the database file itself has been removed or renamed, or the database is currently offline.

2. Restore the most recent full backup.

3. Restore the most recent single differential backup, if one has been made since the last full backup.

4. Restore, in sequence, all the transaction-log backups made since the time of the last full or differential backup. If the last backup was a full backup, then restoring it is sufficient. If the last backup was a differential backup, you will need to restore the most recent full backup before restoring the most recent differential.

The Management Studio restore form (discussed in the section "Performing the Restore with Management Studio," later in this chapter) automatically helps you choose the correct set of backups, so it's not as complicated as it sounds.

Bulk-Logged Recovery Model

The bulk-logged recovery model is similar to the full recovery model except that the following operations are not logged:

✦ Bulk inserts (BCP)

✦ Select * into table DML commands

✦ Writetext and updatetext BLOB operations

✦ Create index (including indexed views)

Because this recovery model does not log these operations they run very fast. The transaction log only marks that the operations took place and tracks the *extents* (a group of eight data pages) that are affected by the bulk-logged operation. When the transaction log is backed up, the extents are copied to the transaction log in place of the bulk-logged marker.

The trade-off for bulk-logged operation performance is that the bulk-logged operation is not treated as a transaction. While the transaction log itself stays small, copying all affected extents to the transaction-log backup can make the log-backup file more than mammoth.

Because bulk-logged operations are not logged, if a failure should occur after the bulk-logged operation but before the transaction log is backed up, the bulk-logged operation is lost and the restore must be made from the last transaction log. Therefore, if the database is using the bulk-logged recovery model, every bulk-logged operation should be immediately followed by a transaction-log backup.

This model is useful only when the database sees a large number of bulk-logged operations, and if it's important to increase their performance. If the database is performing adequately during bulk-logged operations in the full recovery model, bypass the bulk-logged recovery model.

Note that the simple recovery model does not log bulk-copy operations either.

Using this setting is essentially the same as setting the `Select Into/Bulkcopy` database option to `true`.

Setting the Recovery Model

The model system database's recovery model is applied to any newly created database. The full recovery model is the default for the Standard and Enterprise Editions. The Personal and Desktop editions use the simple recovery model as their default, but you can change the default by setting the recovery model for the model system database.

Using Management Studio, you can easily set the recovery model on the Options tab of the Database Properties dialog box. Select the database and right-click to get to the Database Properties dialog.

In code, the recovery model is set with the `alter database` DDL command:

```
ALTER DATABASE DatabaseName SET Recovery Option;
```

The valid options are `Full`, `Bulk_Logged`, and `Simple`. The following code sets the CHA2 sample database to the full recovery model:

```
USE CHA2;
ALTER DATABASE CHA2 SET Recovery Full;
```

I recommend explicitly setting the recovery model in the code that creates the database.

The current recovery model for every database can be determined from code using the `sys.database` catalog view:

```
SELECT [name], recovery_model_desc
  FROM sysdatabases;
```

Modifying Recovery Models

While a database is typically set to a single recovery model, there's nothing to prevent you from switching between recovery models during operation to optimize performance and suit the specific needs of the moment.

It's perfectly valid to run during the day with the full recovery model for transaction durability, and then to switch to bulk-logged during data imports in the evening.

During recovery it's the full, differential, and transaction-log backups that count. The recovery operation doesn't care how they were made.

Because the simple recovery model does not permanently log the transactions, care must be taken in switching to or from the simple recovery model:

+ If you are switching to simple, the transaction log should be backed up prior to the switch.

+ If you are switching from simple, a full database backup should be performed immediately following the switch.

Backing Up the Database

The actual process of performing a backup presents as many options as the underlying concepts present.

Backup Destination

A backup may copy the data to any one of two possible destinations:

✦ **Disk subsystem:** A backup can be performed either to a local disk (preferably not the same disk subsystem as the database files) or to another server's disk drive by using the Universal Naming Convention (UNC). The SQL Server account must have write privileges to the remote drive in order to save the backup file.

Best Practice

I strongly recommend backing up to a disk file on another server and then copying the backup flies to tape or DVD (for small databases) using the organization's preferred IT backup method. This method is the fastest for SQL Server, and it enables the IT shop to continue using a familiar single-tape backup-software technique. If this creates a network bottleneck, use a dedicated network connection or backbone between the SQL Server and the file server.

✦ **Tape:** SQL Server can back up directly to most tape-backup devices.

Note

Several companies offer a third-party backup for SQL Server that uses named pipes. While you may find third-party backup useful, I encourage you to become familiar with SQL Server's built-in recovery methods before making the decision to use it.

A disk- or tape-backup file is not limited to a single backup event. The file may contain multiple backups and multiple types of backups.

Backup Rotation

If the backup file is being copied to tape, then *media retention* or *rotation*, and the off-site media-storage location, become important.

A common technique is to rotate a set of five tapes for the weekly backups and another set of six tapes for the remaining daily backups. The weekly tapes would be labeled Sunday1, Sunday2, and so on, and the daily tapes would be labeled Monday, Tuesday, Wednesday, Thursday, Friday, and Saturday.

Palindromes also represent a great method for rotating backup tapes. A *palindrome* is a word, phrase, or number that's the same backward or forward, such as "kayak" or "drab as a fool, aloof as a bard." Some numbers when reversed and added to themselves will create a palindrome; for example, 236 + 632 = 868. Palindromes have a rich history: In ancient Greece they inscribed "Nipson anomemata me monan opsin," meaning "wash the sin as well as the face," on fountains.

Using four tapes labeled A through D, a backup rotation might be ABCDCBA ABCDCBA . . . .

Alternately, the palindrome method can be implemented so that each letter represents a larger interval, such as A for daily, B for weekly, C for monthly, and D for quarterly.

Rotating backup tapes off site is an important aspect of recovery planning. Ideally, a contract should support an off-site recovery site complete with server and workstations.

Performing Backup with Management Studio

The first backup must be a full database backup to begin the backup cycles.

You can perform a database backup from Management Studio, selecting the database to be backed up. From the database context menu, or from the database Summary Page, select Tasks ➪ Backup to open the Back Up Database form, shown in Figure 36-3.

Figure 36-3: The Back Up Database form has two pages — one to set up the backup and an options page.

The backup source is configured in the General page:

✦ **Database:** The database to be backed up. By default this is the current database in Management Studio.

✦ **Backup:** The type of backup: full, differential, or transaction-log. If the database is set to the simple recovery model, transaction-log will not be available. For full or differential backups, the whole database or selected files and filegroups can be backed up.

The rest of the Back Up Database form specifies the destination:

✦ **Name:** The required name of the backup.

✦ **Description:** Optional additional information about the backup.

✦ **Expiration Date:** SQL Server will prevent another backup from overwriting this backup until the expiration date.

✦ **Destination:** Sets the destination tape file or disk file. If the current destination is incorrect, delete it and add the correct destination.

✦ **Contents:** Displays the backups already in the selected destinations.

The Options page presents the following options:

✦ **Append to existing backup set or Overwrite all existing backup sets:** Determines whether the current backup will be added to the backup file or whether the backup media should be initialized and a new series of backups placed in them. Optionally, SQL Server can check the expiration date of the sets to be overwritten.

✦ **Verify backup upon completion:** Despite the name, this option does not compare the data in the backup with the data in the database, nor does it verify the integrity of the backup. It simply confirms that the backup sets are complete and that the file is readable. Nevertheless, I always use this option.

✦ **Eject tape after backup:** Directs the tape to eject, which helps prevent other backups from overwriting the backup file.

✦ **Remove inactive entries from the log:** This is the Management Studio equivalent of truncating the transaction log. Once the transaction log has been successfully backed up, it's common to remove transactions that were backed up so the log doesn't need to increase in size.

✦ **Check media set name and backup set expiration:** Tests the backup media to ensure that they're the correct media

✦ **Backup set will expire:** Sets an expiration date for the backup. This establishes a protective waiting period for the backup, to prevent it from being overwritten before the date specified.

✦ **Initialize and labels:** Directs SQL Server to initialize and label the tape.

Backing Up the Database with Code

The backup command offers a few more options than Management Studio, and using the backup command directly is useful for assembling SQL Server Agent jobs by hand, rather than with the Maintenance Plan Back Up Database Task.

Without all the options and frills, the most basic backup command is as follows:

```
BACKUP DATABASE Databasename
  TO DISK = 'file location'
  WITH
    NAME = 'backup name'
```

The following command backs up the CHA2 database to a disk file and names the backup CHA2Backup:

```
BACKUP DATABASE CHA2
  TO DISK = 'e:\Cha2Backup.bak'
  WITH
    NAME = 'CHA2Backup'
```

Result:

```
Processed 200 pages for database 'CHA2',
  file 'CHA2' on file 1.
Processed 1 pages for database 'CHA2',
  file 'CHA2_log' on file 1.
BACKUP DATABASE successfully processed 201 pages
  in 0.316 seconds (5.191 MB/sec).
```

The backup command has a few important options that deserve to be mentioned first:

✦ Tape (Backup To:): To back up to tape instead of disk, use the to tape option and specify the tape-drive location:

```
TAPE = '\\.\TAPE0'
```

✦ Differential: Causes the backup command to perform a differential backup instead of a full database backup. The following command performs a differential backup:

```
BACKUP DATABASE CHA2
   TO DISK = 'e:\Cha2Backup.bak'
   WITH
      DIFFERENTIAL,
      NAME = 'CHA2Backup'
```

✦ To back up a file or filegroup, list it after the database name. This technique can help organize backups. For example, for backup purposes, the OBX Kites sample database is designed to place static tables in one filegroup and active tables in the primary filegroup.

✦ Password: If the backup is being made to an unsecured tape, a password is highly recommended. This password is for the specific backup instance.

The backup command has numerous additional options:

✦ Description: Identical to the Description field within Management Studio.

✦ ExpireDate: Identical to Management Studio; prevents the backup from being overwritten before the expiration date.

✦ RetainDays: The number of days, as an integer, before SQL Server will overwrite the backup.

✦ Stats = %: Tells SQL Server to report the progress of the backup in the percentage increment specified; the default increment is 10 percent.

✦ BlockSize: Sets the block size of the backup. For disk backups it's not needed; for tape drives it is probably not needed, but available to solve problems if required for compatibility. For disk backups, the default Windows block size is used automatically, which is typically 4096 bytes on a drive over 2GB in size. If a backup to disk will later be copied to a CD/RW, try a block size of 2048.

✦ MediaName: Specifies the name of the media volume. This option serves as a safety check: If the backup is being added to the media, the name must match.

✦ MediaDescription: Writes an optional media description.

✦ MediaPassword: Creates an optional media password that applies to the entire medium (disk file or tape). The first time the medium is created the password can be set. If the password is specified when the medium is created, it must be specified every subsequent time the backup medium is accessed to add another backup or to restore.

✦ Init/NoInit: Initializes the tape or disk file, thus overwriting all existing backup sets in the medium. SQL Server will prevent initialization if any of the backups in the medium have not expired or still have the number of retaining days. NoInit is the default.

✦ NoSkip/Skip: This option "skips" the backup-name and backup-date checking that normally prevents overwriting backups. Noskip is the default.

The last options apply only when backing up to tape:

✦ NoFormat/Format: Will format the tape (not the disk drive!) prior to the backup. Format automatically includes skip and init.

✦ Rewind/NoRewind: Directs SQL Server to rewind the tape. The default is to rewind.

✦ UnLoad/Load: Automatically rewinds and unloads the tape. This is the default until the user session specifies load.

✦ Restart: If a multi-tape backup fails in the middle of the backup (a tape breaks, for example), the Restart option will continue the backup sequence in midstream without having to go back to the first tape. This option can save time, but be sure to run a restore verifyonly (see next topic) after the backup to be sure.

Verifying the Backup with Code

Management Studio's backup includes an option to verify the backup, and the T-SQL Backup command does not. Management Studio actually calls the T-SQL restore verifyonly command after the backup to perform the verification:

```
RESTORE VERIFYONLY
    FROM DISK =  'e:\Cha2Backup.bak'
```

Result:

```
The backup set is valid.
```

The verification has a few options, such as *Eject tape after backup*. Most of these verification options are for tapes and are self-explanatory.

Working with the Transaction Log

Sometimes it seems that the transaction log has a life of its own. The space within the file seems to grow and shrink without rhyme or reason. If you've felt this way, you're not alone. This section should shed some light on why the transaction log behaves as it does.

Inside the Transaction Log

The transaction log contains all the transactions for a database. If the server crashes the transaction log, both transactions that have been written are used for recovery by rolling back uncommitted partial transactions and by completing any transactions that were committed but not written to the data file.

Virtually, the log can be imagined as a sequential list of transactions sorted by date and time. Physically, however, SQL Server writes to different parts of the physical log file in virtual blocks without a specific order. Some parts might be in use, making other parts available, so the log reuses itself in a loose round-robin fashion.

The Active and Inactive Divide

The transactions in the transaction log can be divided into two groups (see Figure 36-4):

✦ **Active transactions** are uncommitted and not yet written to the data file.

✦ **Inactive transactions** are all those transactions before the earliest active transaction.

Transaction Log

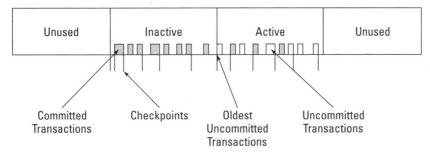

Figure 36-4: The inactive transactions are all those prior to the oldest active transaction.

Because transactions are of varying duration, and are committed at different times, it's very likely that committed transactions are in the active portion of the log. The active portion does not merely contain all uncommitted transactions, but all transactions since the start of the oldest uncommitted transaction. One very old uncommitted transaction can make the active portion appear unusually large.

Transaction Checkpoints

Understanding how SQL Server uses checkpoints in the transaction log is important to understanding how the transaction log is backed up and emptied. Checkpoints calculate the amount of work that must be done to recover the database.

A checkpoint automatically occurs under any of the following conditions:

✦ When an alter database command changes a database option

✦ When the server is shut down

✦ When the number of log entries exceeds the estimated amount of work required by the server's recovery interval configuration option

✦ If the database is in the simple recovery model or log-truncate mode, when the transaction log becomes 70 percent full

Checkpoints may be manually initiated with a checkpoint command. Checkpoints perform the following activities:

✦ Marks the checkpoint spot in the transaction log

✦ Writes a checkpoint-log record, including the following:

• The oldest active transaction

• The oldest replication transaction that has not been replicated

• A list of all active transactions

• Information about the minimum work required to roll back the database

✦ Writes to disk all dirty data pages and log pages

Basically, a checkpoint gets everything up to date as best it can and then records the current state of the dividing line between active and inactive in the log.

Backing Up the Transaction Log

Performing a transaction log backup is very similar to performing a full or differential backup, with a few notable differences.

The T-SQL command is as follows:

```
BACKUP LOG CHA2
  TO DISK = 'e:\Cha2Backup.bak'
  WITH
    NAME = 'CHA2Backup'
```

Result:

```
Processed 1 pages for database 'CHA2',
  file 'CHA2_log' on file 9.
BACKUP LOG successfully processed 1 pages
  in 0.060 seconds (0.042 MB/sec).
```

The same media options apply to the transaction log backup that apply to the database backup; in addition, two options are transaction-log specific. The `no_truncate` option is for backing up the transaction log during a recovery operation, and the `norecovery`/`standby` option is for running a standby server. Both are covered in more detail later in this chapter in the section "Recovering with T-SQL Code."

The transaction log may not be backed up if any of the following conditions exist:

✦ The database is using a simple recovery model.

✦ The database is using a bulk-logged recovery model, a bulk-logged operation has been executed, and the database files are damaged.

✦ Database files have been added or removed.

In any of these cases, perform a full database backup instead.

Truncating the Log

Updates and deletes might not increase the size of a data file, but to the transaction log every transaction of any type is simply more data. Left to its own devices, the transaction log will continue to grow with every data modification.

The solution is to back up the inactive portion of the transaction log and then remove it. By default, backing up the transaction log will also truncate the log (refer to Figure 36-3).

If, for example, the disk is full, the transaction log might need to be truncated without the database being backed up. There's no way to just truncate the log without performing a backup. With T-SQL, however, the transaction log can be truncated with either `Backup...NoLog` or `Backup...TruncateOnly` (the two are synonymous):

```
BACKUP LOG CHA2
  WITH TRUNCATE_ONLY
```

Caution   If the transaction log is manually truncated and then backed up, there will be a gap in the transaction-log sequence. Any transaction-log pickups after the gap will not be restored. A full backup is recommended to restart the backup sequencing.

The Transaction Log and Simple Recovery Model

When the database is using a simple recovery model, the transaction log ensures that each committed transaction is written to the data file, and that's it. When the transaction log is 70 percent full SQL Server will perform a checkpoint and then truncate the log, so the free space of the transaction log will fluctuate but the minimum is the size of the active portion of the transaction log.

Recovery Operations

There are any number of reasons to restore a database, including the following:

✦ A disk subsystem has failed.

✦ A sleepy programmer forgot a `where` clause in a SQL `update` statement and updated everyone's salary to minimum wage.

✦ The server melted into a pool of silicon and disk platters.

✦ A large import worked, but with yesterday's data.

The best reason to restore a database is to practice the backup/restore cycle, and to prove that the recovery plan works. Without confidence in the recovery, there's little point in doing backups.

Detecting the Problem

If a problem with a database file does exist, Management Studio shows the database as unavailable, and looking in the logs reveals the problem, as shown in Figure 36-5.

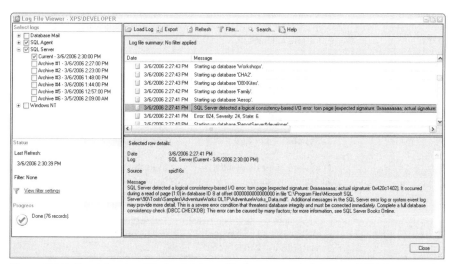

Figure 36-5: The AdventureWorks database file is corrupted. (I stopped SQL Server and mangled the header of the file using a hex editor.) Management Studio shows the database without a tree. Further down the console tree are the SQL Server logs.

To further investigate a problem, check the SQL Server log. In Management Studio, the log can be viewed under Management ➪ SQL Server Logs. SQL Server writes errors and events to an error log file in the \error directory under the MSSQL directory. SQL Server creates a new file every time the server is started. The six previous versions of the file are saved in the same directory. Some errors may also be written to the Windows Application Event Log.

Recovery Sequences

The two most important concepts about recovering a database are as follows:

✦ A recovery operation always begins by restoring a full backup and then restores any additional differential or transactional backups. The restore never copies only yesterday's work. It restores the entire database up to a certain point.

✦ There's a difference between restore and recover. A *restore* copies the data back into the database and leaves the transactions open. *Recovery* is the process of handling the transactions left open in the transaction log. If a database-recovery operation requires that four files be restored, only the last file is restored with recovery.

Only logins who are members of the SysAdmins fixed server role can restore a database that doesn't currently exist. SysAdmins and db_owners can restore databases that do currently exist.

The actual recovery effort depends on the type of damage and the previous recovery plans. Table 36-2 is a comparative listing of recovery operations.

Table 36-2: Recovery Sequences

Recovery Model	Damaged Database File	Damaged Transaction Log
Simple	1) Restart server. 2) Restore full backup. 3) Restore latest differential backup (if needed).	Restart the server. A new 1MB transaction log will be automatically created.
Full or Bulk-Logged	1) Back up current transaction log with no_truncate option*. 2) Restore full backup. 3) Restore latest differential backup (if needed). 4) Restore all the transaction-log backups since the last differential or full backup. All committed transactions will be recovered.	1) Restore full backup. 2) Restore latest differential backup (if needed). 3) Restore all the transaction-log backups since the last differential or full backup. Transactions made since the last backup will be lost.

If the database is using the bulk-logged recovery model and a bulk-insert operation occurred since the last transaction-log backup, the backup will fail. Transactions that occurred after the transaction-log backup will not be recoverable.

Performing the Restore with Management Studio

As with the backup command, there are numerous ways to launch the restore form within Management Studio:

✦ Select the database to be backed up. From the context or Action menu select All Tasks ⇨ Backup Restore to open the SQL Server Restore database form.

✦ Select Tasks ⇨ Restore ⇨ Database to open the SQL Server Restore database form.

✦ Select Databases in the console tree, right-click, and select Restore Database from the context menu.

The Restore Database form, shown in Figure 36-6, does a great job of intelligently navigating the potential chaos of the backup sequences, and it always offers only legal restore options.

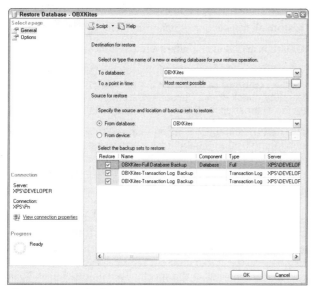

Figure 36-6: Only the correct sequence of restoring from multiple backup files is possible from Management Studio's Restore Database form.

The selection you make at the top of the form is the name of the database after the restore.

The Restore Database form can restore database backups, file backups, or backups from a device (i.e., a tape drive). The Restore Wizard will present a hierarchical tree of backups, while the filegroups or file restore lists the files and must be manually restored in the correct order.

The "Show backups of database" option is used to select the first backup in the database-backup sequence to restore. Based on the sequence selected, the grid displays a hierarchical tree of the possible backup sequences:

✦ Full database backups are represented by gold hard-drive symbols at the highest level of the tree.

✦ Differential backups are represented by blue hard-drive symbols at the second level of the tree.

✦ Transaction-log backups are represented by notebook symbols at the lowest level of the tree.

Depending on the full and differential backups selected, only certain differential and transaction-log backups may be chosen.

The process of one full backup, the second differential backup, and the following 15 transaction-log backups can be correctly sequenced by selecting the final transaction log to be restored. Restoring the 17 backup files is performed with a single click of the OK button.

If one of the backup files being restored is a transaction log, the Point in Time Restore option becomes available because only a transaction log can restore only some of the transactions.

The point-in-time restore will restore all transactions committed before the time selected.

The Options tab of the Restore Database dialog box offers a few significant options:

✦ The "Overwrite the existing database" option disables a safety check that prevents Database A backup from being restored as Database B and accidentally overwriting an existing Database B. The safety check doesn't prohibit Database A backup being restored over Database A, so in most cases this option is moot.

✦ Because it is very possible that the database is being restored to a different file location than the original backup, the Option tab includes a way to assign new file locations.

✦ The Recovery State option enables you to ship the log to a warm standby server. For a normal restore, the option should be left operational.

✦ If only certain files or filegroups are being restored, the Restore: File or File Groups option enables you to select the files or filegroups you wish to restore.

✦ If the backup history, stored in msdb, is not available — because the server is being rebuilt or the database is being restored to a different server — then the Restore: From Device option can be used to manually select the specific backup disk file and backup instance within the file.

New in 2005

SQL Server 2005 is able to restore partial data pages. This can be very beneficial in instances when one page of a five-terabyte database page becomes corrupted. While I'm glad Microsoft included this feature, I believe its practical use is extremely rare, and it can cause more problems than it creates. If you have a database file error, you're much better off taking the time to do a proper restore than trying to piece together lost pages, so this capability isn't covered here.

Restoring with T-SQL Code

Database backup is a regularly scheduled occurrence, so if SQL Server's built-in Maintenance Plan Wizard isn't to your liking, it makes sense to write some repeatable code to perform backups and set up your own SQL Server Agent jobs.

However, unless the backup plan is only a full backup, it's impossible to know how many differential backups or transaction-log backups need to be restored; and because each backup file requires a separate restore command, it's impossible to script the recovery effort beforehand without writing a lot of code to examine the msdb tables and determine the restore sequence properly.

The restore command will restore from a full, differential, or transaction-log backup:

```
RESTORE DATABASE (or LOG) DatabaseName
   Optional-File or Filegroup PARTIAL
   FROM BackUpDevice
   WITH
     FILE = FileNumber,
     PASSWORD = Password,
     NORECOVERY or RECOVERY or STANDBY = UnDoFileName,
     REPLACE,
     STOPAT datetime,
     STOPATMARK = 'markname'
     STOPBEFOREMARK = 'markname'
```

To restore a full or differential backup use the restore database command; otherwise, use the restore log for a transaction log. To restore a specific file or filegroup, add its name after the database name. If the file or filegroup is the only data being restored, add the partial option.

A backup set often contains several backup instances. For example, a backup set might consist of the following:

1: Full backup

2: Differential backup

3, 4, 5, 6: Transaction-log backups

7: Differential backup

8, 9: Transaction-log backups

The with file option specifies the backup to restore. If it's left out of the command, the first backup instance is restored.

The recovery/norecovery option is vital to the restore command. Every time a SQL Server starts, it automatically checks the transaction log, rolling back any uncommitted transactions and completing any committed transactions. This process is called *recovery*, and it's a part of the ACID properties of the database.

Therefore, if the restore has the norecovery option, SQL Server restores the log without handling any transactions. Conversely, recovery instructs SQL Server to handle the transactions. In the sequence of the recovery operation, all the restores must have the norecovery option enabled, except for the last restore, which must have the recovery option enabled.

Deciding between `recovery` and `norecovery` is one of the complications involved in trying to write a script to handle any possible future recovery operation.

If the recovery operation includes a transaction-log restore, the recovery can stop before the end of the transaction log. The options `stopat` and `stopatmark` will leave the end of the transaction log unrestored. The `stopat` accepts a time, and the `stopatmark` restores only to a transaction that was created with a named mark. The `stopbeforemark` option restores everything up to the beginning of the marked transaction.

Cross-Reference Chapter 23, "Creating DML Triggers," details SQL Server transactions and how to create marked transactions.

The following script demonstrates an example of a restore sequence that includes a full backup and two transaction-log backups:

```
-- BackUp and recovery example

CREATE DATABASE Plan2Recover;
```

Result:

```
The CREATE DATABASE process
   is allocating 0.63 MB on disk 'Plan2Recover'.
The CREATE DATABASE process
   is allocating 0.49 MB on disk 'Plan2Recover_log'.
```

Continuing:

```
USE Plan2Recover;

CREATE TABLE T1 (
   PK INT Identity PRIMARY KEY,
   Name VARCHAR(15)
   );
Go
INSERT T1 VALUES ('Full');
go
BACKUP DATABASE Plan2Recover
   TO DISK = 'e:\P2R.bak'
   WITH
     NAME = 'P2R_Full',
     INIT;
```

Result:

```
Processed 80 pages for database 'Plan2Recover',
   file 'Plan2Recover' on file 1.
Processed 1 pages for database 'Plan2Recover',
   file 'Plan2Recover_log' on file 1.
BACKUP DATABASE successfully processed 81 pages
   in 0.254 seconds (2.590 MB/sec).
```

Continuing:

```
INSERT T1 VALUES ('Log 1');
go
BACKUP Log Plan2Recover
  TO DISK = 'e:\P2R.bak'
  WITH
    NAME = 'P2R_Log';
```

Result:

```
Processed 1 pages for database 'Plan2Recover',
  file 'Plan2Recover_log' on file 2.
BACKUP LOG successfully processed 1 pages
  in 0.083 seconds (0.055 MB/sec).
```

Continuing:

```
INSERT T1 VALUES ('Log 2');
go
BACKUP Log Plan2Recover
  TO DISK = 'e:\P2R.bak'
  WITH
    NAME = 'P2R_Log';
```

Result:

```
Processed 1 pages for database 'Plan2Recover',
  file 'Plan2Recover_log' on file 3.
BACKUP LOG successfully processed 1 pages
  in 0.057 seconds (0.008 MB/sec).
```

Continuing:

```
SELECT * FROM T1;
```

Result:

```
PK          Name
----------- ----------------
1           Full
2           Log 1
3           Log 2
```

At this point the server is hit with a direct bolt of lightning and all drives are fried, with the exception of the backup files. The following recovery operation goes through the full backup and the two transaction-log backups. Notice the `norecovery` and `recovery` options:

```
-- NOW PERFORM THE RESTORE
Use Master;
RESTORE DATABASE Plan2Recover
  FROM DISK = 'e:\P2R.bak'
  With FILE = 1, NORECOVERY;
```

Result:

```
Processed 80 pages for database 'Plan2Recover',
   file 'Plan2Recover' on file 1.
Processed 1 pages for database 'Plan2Recover',
   file 'Plan2Recover_log' on file 1.
RESTORE DATABASE successfully processed 81 pages
   in 0.089 seconds (7.392 MB/sec).
```

Continuing:

```
RESTORE LOG Plan2Recover
   FROM DISK = 'e:\P2R.bak'
   With FILE = 2, NORECOVERY;
```

Result:

```
Processed 1 pages for database 'Plan2Recover',
   file 'Plan2Recover_log' on file 2.
RESTORE LOG successfully processed 1 pages
   in 0.009 seconds (0.512 MB/sec).
```

Continuing:

```
RESTORE LOG Plan2Recover
   FROM DISK = 'e:\P2R.bak'
   With FILE = 3, RECOVERY;
```

Result:

```
Processed 1 pages for database 'Plan2Recover',
   file 'Plan2Recover_log' on file 3.
RESTORE LOG successfully processed 1 pages
   in 0.044 seconds (0.011 MB/sec).
```

To test the recovery operation:

```
USE Plan2Recover;
Select * from T1;
```

Result:

```
PK          Name
----------- ---------------
1           Full
2           Log 1
3           Log 2
```

As this script shows, it is possible to recover using T-SQL, but in this case Management Studio beats code as the best way to accomplish the task.

System Databases Recovery

So far, this chapter has dealt only with user databases, but the system databases are important to the recovery operation as well. The master database contains key database and security information, and the MSDB database holds the schedules and jobs for SQL Server, as well as the backup history. A complete recovery plan must include the system databases.

Master Database

The master database, by default, uses the simple recovery model. Using only full backups for the master database is OK; it's not a transactional database.

Backing Up the Master Database

The master database is backed up in the same manner as user databases.

Be sure to back up the master database when doing any of the following:

✦ Creating or deleting databases

✦ Modifying security by adding logins or changing roles

✦ Modifying any server or database-configuration options

Because the MSDB database holds a record of all backups, back up the master database and then the MSDB.

Recovering the Master Database

If the master database is corrupted or damaged, SQL Server won't start. Attempting to start SQL Server with the Service Manager will have no effect. Attempting to connect to the instance with Management Studio will invoke a warning that the server does not exist or that access is denied.

The only solution is to start SQL Server in single-user mode (using the -m parameter) and then restore the master database as you would a user database.

MSDB System Database

Like the master database, the msdb database, by default, uses the simple recovery model.

Because the msdb database contains information regarding the SQL Server Agent jobs and schedules, as well as the backup history, it should be backed up whenever you do the following:

✦ Perform backups

✦ Save DTS packages

✦ Create new SQL Server Agent jobs

✦ Configure SQL Server Agent mail or operators

✦ Configure replication

✦ Schedule tasks

The msdb database is backed up in the same way that a user database is backed up.

To restore the msdb database you do not need to put the server in single-user mode, as you do with the master database. However, it's still not a normal restore, because without a current msdb, Management Studio is not aware of the backup history. Therefore, the msdb backup can't be chosen as a backup database but must be selected as a backup device.

The Contents button can be used to check the disk device for specific backups. If several backup instances are in the backup device, the Contents dialog box can be used to select the correct backup. It then fills in the file number in the restore form.

Performing a Complete Recovery

If the server has completely failed and all the backups must be restored onto a new server, this is the process to follow:

1. Build the Windows server and restore the domain logins to support Windows authentication.

2. Install SQL Server and any service-pack upgrades.

3. Put SQL Server in single-user mode and restore the master database.

4. Restore the msdb database.

5. If the model database was modified, restore it.

6. Restore the user databases.

Best Practice

Performing a flawless recovery is a "bet your career" skill. I recommend taking the time to work through a complete recovery of the production data to a backup server. The confidence it will build will serve you well as a SQL Server DBA.

Summary

The recovery cycle begins with the backup of the databases. The ability to survive hardware failure or human error is crucial to the ACID properties of a database. Without the transaction's durability, the database can't be fully trusted. Because of this, recovery planning and the transaction log provide durability to committed transactions.

The recovery cycle transfers data from the past to the present. In the next chapter, you'll learn how to secure the database.

✦   ✦   ✦

Maintaining the Database

T he Database Consistency Checker (DBCC) commands are at the heart of database maintenance, even since the earliest versions of SQL Server. However, thanks to Microsoft's zero-maintenance initiative, SQL Server 2005 is now easier to maintain than ever before. Not only are many of the traditional database maintenance duties no longer required, but the Maintenance Plan Wizard can set up a custom set of SQL Server Agent jobs that execute an excellent database maintenance plan.

DBCC Commands

Microsoft SQL Server's primary command for database maintenance is the Database Consistency Checker (DBCC) command and its 34 options.

The first DBCC command to become familiar with is the DBCC help command, which returns the syntax with all the options for any DBCC command:

```
DBCC Help ('CheckDB');
```

Result:

```
CheckDB [('database_name'
  [, NOINDEX | REPAIR])]
  [WITH NO_INFOMSGS[, ALL_ERRORMSGS]
  [, PHYSICAL_ONLY]
  [, ESTIMATEONLY][, TABLOCK]]
DBCC execution completed. If DBCC printed
  error messages,contact your system
  administrator.
```

All DBCC commands report their activity or errors found, and then conclude with the standard execution-completed statement, including the puzzling request to report any error to the system administrator. You are the database pro. If you're running DBCC, you're the best person to handle it.

Note   Several obsolete DBCC commands and options are included for backward compatibility only. These are not included in this chapter. For example, the DBCC `ROWLOCK` command is no longer needed because SQL Server 2005 performs row locking automatically.

On The Web   You can find a complete list of deprecated (outdated or no longer accessible) DBCC commands at `http://msdn2.microsoft.com/en-US/library/ms144262.aspx`.

Database Integrity

DBCC `CheckDB` performs several consistency checks on the internal physical structure of the database. It's critical for the health of the database that the physical structure is correct. DBCC `CheckDB` checks things such as index pointers, data-page offsets, the linking between data pages and index pages, and the structural content of the data and index pages. If a hardware hiccup has left a data page half-written, DBCC `CheckDB` is the best means of detecting the problem:

```
DBCC CheckDB ('OBXKites');
```

Result (abridged):

```
DBCC results for 'OBXKites'.
DBCC results for 'sysobjects'.
There are 114 rows in 2 pages for object 'sysobjects'.
DBCC results for 'sysindexes'.
There are 77 rows in 3 pages for object 'sysindexes'.
...
DBCC results for 'ProductCategory'.
There are 8 rows in 1 pages for object 'ProductCategory'.
DBCC results for 'Product'.
There are 55 rows in 1 pages for object 'Product'.
CHECKDB found 0 allocation errors
    and 0 consistency errors in database 'OBXKites'.
DBCC execution completed. If DBCC printed error messages,
    contact your system administrator.
```

Note   The results you see could vary from those displayed in the book depending on your SQL Server configuration and any changes you have made to the database.

Two options simply determine which messages are reported, without altering the functionality of the integrity check: `all_errormsgs` and `no_infomsgs`. The `estimate_only` option returns the estimated size of the `tempdb` required by `CheckDB`.

If the database is large, the `noindex` option can be used to skip checking the integrity of all user-table non-clustered indexes. For additional time savings, the `Physical_Only` option performs only the most critical checks on the physical structure of the pages. Use these options only when time prevents a complete `CheckDB` or when the indexes are about to be rebuilt.

To list the system tables for the current database using code, query the `sysobjects` catalog view, filtering for `type_desc = ' SYSTEM_TABLE'`. You can do the same for other object types, including user tables (`USER_TABLE`), constraints (`PRIMARY_KEY_CONSTRAINT`, `DEFAULT_CONSTRAINT`, `CHECK_CONSTRAINT`, `UNIQUE_CONSTRAINT`, and `FOREIGN_KEY_CONSTRAINT`), stored procedures (`SQL_STORED_PROCEDURE`), triggers (`SQL_TRIGGER`), and views (`VIEW`). You can also discover special SQL Server features such as internal tables (`INTERNAL_TABLE`) and queues (`SERVICE_QUEUE`).

Repairing the Database

If an error is found, DBCC can attempt to repair it. This is a separate operation from the normal integrity checks because the database must be placed in single-user mode with the `sp_dboption` command before a `DBCC CheckDB` can be executed with the `Repair_Rebuild` option. Make sure you return `sp_dboption` to its previous state when you're done:

```
EXEC sp_dboption OBXKites, 'Single_user', 'True';
DBCC CheckDB ('OBXKites', Repair_Rebuild);
GO
EXEC sp_dboption OBXKites, 'Single_user', 'False';
GO
```

Result (abridged):

```
DBCC results for 'OBXKites'.
Service Broker Msg 9675, State 1: Message Types analyzed: 14.
Service Broker Msg 9676, State 1: Service Contracts analyzed: 6.
Service Broker Msg 9667, State 1: Services analyzed: 3.
...
DBCC results for 'OrderPriority'.
There are 1 rows in 1 pages for object "OrderPriority".
DBCC results for 'ProductCategory'.
There are 8 rows in 1 pages for object "ProductCategory".
CHECKDB found 0 allocation errors and 0 consistency errors in
   database 'OBXKites'.
DBCC execution completed. If DBCC printed error messages,
   contact your system administrator.
```

DBCC offers three repair modes, each performing a more radical surgery on the internal structure than the last:

✦ `Repair_Fast`: The simplest repair mode repairs non-clustered index keys and does not touch the data pages.

✦ `Repair_Rebuild`: The mid-level repair method performs a complete check and rebuild of all non-clustered indexes and index pointers. Again, this method doesn't write to any data pages.

✦ `Repair_Allow_Data_Loss`: This, the most severe, option performs all the index repairs and rebuilds the data-page allocations and pointers, and removes any corruption found in the data pages. Because it updates the data-page structure, some data loss is possible.

Best Practice

Run a DBCC CheckDB every day and after any hardware malfunction. If an error is detected, run the Repair_Rebuild repair mode to attempt to repair the database before using the Repair_allow_data_loss option to perform a full data-page repair. This is not the best option for very large databases (VLDBs) with high-availability needs. In this case, you may want to schedule a check weekly during low points in usage.

Multi-User Concerns

Improved with SQL 2005, DBCC CheckDB can now be executed while users are in the database, and it will multithread using all CPUs. However, CheckDB is very processor and disk intensive, so run it when the database has the fewest users.

New in 2005

You can now run the DBCC CHECKALLOC, DBCC CHECKTABLE, or DBCC CHECKCATALOG commands at the same time that you run DBCC CHECKDB.

DBCC CheckDB will normally use schema locks while it is checking the database if DBCC is run while users are in the database. The TabLock option reduces the lock granularity to only a table-shared lock. DBCC CheckDB will run less efficiently, but the database concurrency will be higher, thus allowing users to perform their work:

```
DBCC CheckDB ('OBXKites') With TabLock;
```

Result (abridged):

```
DBCC results for 'OBXKites'.
DBCC CHECKDB will not check SQL Server catalog or Service Broker
    consistency because a database snapshot could not be created
    or because WITH TABLOCK was specified.
DBCC results for 'syssysrowsetcolumns'.
There are 654 rows in 6 pages for object "syssysrowsetcolumns".
DBCC results for 'syssysrowsets'.
...
DBCC results for 'ProductCategory'.
There are 8 rows in 1 pages for object "ProductCategory".
CHECKDB found 0 allocation errors and 0 consistency errors in
    database 'OBXKites'.
DBCC execution completed. If DBCC printed error messages,
    contact your system administrator.
```

Note

Whenever you use the TabLock option, you'll see an additional output line stating "DBCC CHECKDB will not check SQL Server catalog or Service Broker consistency because a database snapshot could not be created or because WITH TABLOCK was specified." This is an informational message; don't worry about it. However, when you see this message without the TabLock option, you'll want to verify that you have all of the required services started.

Object-Level Validation

DBCC CheckDB performs a host of database structural-integrity checks. It's possible to run these checks individually. As an advantage, each of these commands provides more detailed information about its specific database object. For that reason, it's best to run DBCC CheckDB for the daily database-maintenance plan and use these object-specific versions for debugging.

If the database requires repair, always use the full CheckDB over one of the lesser versions:

✦ DBCC CheckAlloc ('database'): A subset of CheckDB that checks the physical structure of the database. The report is very detailed, listing the extent count (64KB or eight data pages) and data-page usage of every table and index in the database.

✦ DBCC CheckFileGroup ('filegroup'): Similar to a CheckDB but for a specific filegroup only.

✦ DBCC CheckTable ('table'): Performs multiple parallel checks on the table.

✦ DBCC CleanTable ('database', table'): Reclaims space from a varchar, nvarchar, text, or ntext column that was dropped from the table. This option actually updates the database and is not included in CheckDB unless the maximum-repair option is being used. Therefore, CleanTable might be a useful option to include in the daily maintenance plan if the database experiences regular text updates.

Data Integrity

Above the physical-structure layer of the database is the data layer, which can be verified by the following DBCC options. These three data-integrity DBCC commands are not automatically executed by the DBCC CheckDB command. They should be executed independently:

✦ DBCC CheckCatalog ('database'): Checks the integrity of the system tables within a database, ensuring referential integrity among tables, views, columns, and data types. While it will report any errors, under normal conditions no detailed report is returned. DBCC CheckCatalog won't repair any errors. If an error is found, rebuild the table or database from a script and move any data that is still recoverable from the old table to the new table. If no errors are found, nothing of interest is reported.

✦ DBCC CheckConstraints ('table','constraint'): Examines the integrity of a specific constraint, or all the constraints for a table. It essentially generates and executes a query to verify each constraint, and reports any errors found. As with CheckCatalog, if no issues are detected, nothing is reported.

✦ DBCC CheckIdent ('table'): Verifies the consistency of the current identity-column value and the identity column for a specific table. If a problem exists, the next value for the identity column is updated to correct any error. If the identity column is broken, the new identity value will violate a primary key or unique constraint and new rows cannot be added to the table.

The following code demonstrates the usage of the DBCC CheckIdent command:

```
Use CHA2;
DBCC CheckIdent ('Customer');
```

Result:

```
Checking identity information: current identity value '127',
    current column value '127'.
DBCC execution completed. If DBCC printed error messages,
    contact your system administrator.
```

Index Maintenance

Indexes provide the performance bridge between the data and SQL queries. Because of data inserts and updates, indexes fragment, the data-distribution statistics become out of date, and the fill factor of the pages can be less than optimal. Index maintenance is required to combat these three results of normal wear and tear and to prevent performance reduction.

Cross-Reference Chapter 17, "Implementing the Physical Database Schema," contains information on index creation.

Database Fragmentation

As data is inserted into the data pages and index pages, the pages fill to 100 percent. At that point, SQL Server performs a page split, creating two new pages with about 50 percent page density each. While this solves the individual page problem, the internal database structure can become fragmented.

To demonstrate the DBCC commands that affect fragmented tables and indexes, a table large enough to become fragmented is required. The following script builds a suitable table and a non-clustered index. The clustered primary key is a GUID, so row insertions will occur throughout the table, generating plenty of good fragmentation:

```
USE Tempdb;

CREATE TABLE Frag (
  FragID UNIQUEIDENTIFIER NOT NULL DEFAULT NewID(),
  Col1 INT,
  Col2 CHAR(200),
  Created DATETIME DEFAULT GetDate(),
  Modified DATETIME DEFAULT GetDate()
  );

ALTER TABLE Frag
  ADD CONSTRAINT PK_Frag
  PRIMARY KEY CLUSTERED (FragID);

CREATE NONCLUSTERED INDEX ix_col
  ON Frag (Col1);
```

The following stored procedure will add 100,000 rows each time it's executed:

```
CREATE PROC Add100K
AS
SET nocount on;
DECLARE @X INT;
SET @X = 0;
  WHILE @X < 100000
    BEGIN
      INSERT Frag (Col1,Col2)
        VALUES (@X, 'sample data');
      SET @X = @X + 1;
    END
GO
```

The following batch calls Add100K several times and populates the Frag table (be patient, the query can require several minutes to execute):

```
EXEC Add100K;
EXEC Add100K;
EXEC Add100K;
EXEC Add100K;
EXEC Add100K;
```

DBCC ShowContig (table, index) reports the fragmentation details and the density for a given table or index. With half a million rows, the Frag table is very fragmented and most pages are slightly more than half full, as the following command shows:

```
DBCC ShowContig (frag) WITH ALL_INDEXES;
```

In the following result, Index 1 is the clustered primary-key index, so it's also reporting the data-page fragmentation. Index 2 is the non-clustered index:

```
DBCC SHOWCONTIG scanning 'Frag' table...
Table: 'Frag' (1227255527); index ID: 1, database ID: 2
TABLE level scan performed.
- Pages Scanned................................: 22056
- Extents Scanned..............................: 2772
- Extent Switches..............................: 22055
- Avg. Pages per Extent........................: 8.0
- Scan Density [Best Count:Actual Count].......: 12.50%
  [2757:22056]
- Logical Scan Fragmentation ..................: 99.24%
- Extent Scan Fragmentation ...................: 12.63%
- Avg. Bytes Free per Page.....................: 2542.0
- Avg. Page Density (full).....................: 68.59%
DBCC SHOWCONTIG scanning 'Frag' table...
Table: 'Frag' (1227255527); index ID: 2, database ID: 2
LEAF level scan performed.
- Pages Scanned................................: 2748
- Extents Scanned..............................: 348
- Extent Switches..............................: 2721
- Avg. Pages per Extent........................: 7.9
- Scan Density [Best Count:Actual Count].......: 12.64%
  [344:2722]
- Logical Scan Fragmentation ..................: 98.07%
- Extent Scan Fragmentation ...................: 99.14%
- Avg. Bytes Free per Page.....................: 3365.3
- Avg. Page Density (full).....................: 58.42%
DBCC execution completed. If DBCC printed error messages,
    contact your system administrator.
```

DBCC IndexDefrag defragments the index pages of both clustered and non-clustered indexes. It will organize the nodes for faster performance, compact the index, and reestablish the fill factor for an index:

```
DBCC IndexDefrag (DatabaseName, TableName, IndexName);
```

Performing the DBCC IndexDefrag operation is similar to rebuilding an index, with the distinct advantage that defragmenting an index is performed in a series of small transactions that do not block users from performing inserts and updates.

The next two commands defrag both indexes:

```
DBCC IndexDefrag ('Tempdb', 'Frag', 'PK_Frag');
```

Result:

```
Pages Scanned Pages Moved Pages Removed
------------- ----------- -------------
22033          15194       6852
```

```
DBCC IndexDefrag ('Tempdb', 'Frag', 'ix_col');
```

Result:

```
Pages Scanned Pages Moved Pages Removed
------------- ----------- -------------
2748           1610        1134
```

A DBCC ShowContig command examines the index structure after the defragmenting of the index. Both the logical-fragmentation and page-density problems created by the insertion of half a million rows are resolved:

```
DBCC ShowContig (frag) WITH ALL_INDEXES;
```

Result:

```
DBCC SHOWCONTIG scanning 'Frag' table...
Table: 'Frag' (1227255527); index ID: 1, database ID: 2
TABLE level scan performed.
- Pages Scanned................................: 15204
- Extents Scanned..............................: 1915
- Extent Switches..............................: 1925
- Avg. Pages per Extent........................: 7.9
- Scan Density [Best Count:Actual Count].......: 98.70%
  [1901:1926]
- Logical Scan Fragmentation ..................: 0.60%
- Extent Scan Fragmentation ...................: 15.25%
- Avg. Bytes Free per Page.....................: 38.9
- Avg. Page Density (full).....................: 99.52%
DBCC SHOWCONTIG scanning 'Frag' table...
Table: 'Frag' (1227255527); index ID: 2, database ID: 2
LEAF level scan performed.
- Pages Scanned................................: 1614
- Extents Scanned..............................: 205
- Extent Switches..............................: 207
- Avg. Pages per Extent........................: 7.9
- Scan Density [Best Count:Actual Count].......: 97.12%
  [202:208]
- Logical Scan Fragmentation ..................: 1.05%
- Extent Scan Fragmentation ...................: 99.02%
- Avg. Bytes Free per Page.....................: 41.5
- Avg. Page Density (full).....................: 99.49%
DBCC execution completed. If DBCC printed error messages,
    contact your system administrator.
```

At this point, you have a couple of objects in the `tempdb` database that you'll want to clean up. Use the following code to perform the task:

```
DROP TABLE Frag;
GO
DROP PROCEDURE Add100K;
GO
```

Index Statistics

The usefulness of an index is based on the data distribution within that index. For example, if 60 percent of the customers are in New York City, selecting all customers in NYC will likely be faster with a table scan than with an index seek. However, to find the single customer from Delavan, Wisconsin, the query definitely needs the help of an index. The Query Optimizer depends on the index statistics to determine the usefulness of the index for a particular query.

The statistics appear as indexes in some listings with names beginning with _WA_Sys or heed_.

`DBCC Show_Statistics` reports the last date the statistics were updated and the basic information about the index statistics, including the usefulness of the index. A low density indicates that the index is very selective. A high density indicates that a given index node points to several table rows and may be less useful than a low-density index.

The following code demonstrates the `Update Statistics` command:

```
use cha2;
exec sp_help customer;
Update Statistics Customer;
```

The procedures `sp_createstats` and `sp_updatestats` will create and update statistics on all tables in a database, respectively.

To view operational index statistics, select `sysdm_db_index_operational_stats` from the dynamic management view. You can also check usage statistics by selecting `sysdm_db_index_usage_stats`, and physical statistics by selecting `sysdm_db_index_physical_stats`. The `sysdm_db_index_operational_stats` and `sysdm_db_index_physical_stats` require that you provide input arguments or NULL values for each of the inputs, such as database ID, object ID, index ID, and partition number.

Index Density

Index density refers to what percentage of the index pages contains data. If the index density is low, SQL Server has to read more pages from the disk to retrieve the index data. The index's *fill factor* refers to what percentage of the index page contains data when the index is created or defragmented, but the index density will slowly alter during inserts, updates, and deletes.

The `DBCC DbReIndex` command will completely rebuild the index. Using this command is essentially the equivalent of dropping and creating the index with the added benefit of allowing the user to set the fill factor as the index is recreated. In contrast, the `DBCC IndexDefrag` command will repair fragmentation to the index's fill factor but will not adjust the target fill factor.

The next command recreates the indexes on the `Frag` table and sets the fill factor to 98 percent:

```
DBCC DBReIndex ('Tempdb.dbo.Frag','',98)
```

Cross-Reference Index density can affect performance. Chapter 37, "Maintaining the Database," includes more information on planning the best index fill factor.

Database File Size

SQL Server 7.0 moved beyond SQL Server 6.5's method of allocated space with fixed-size files called *devices*. Since SQL Server 7.0, data and transaction logs can automatically grow as required. File size is still an area of database-maintenance concern. Without some intervention or monitoring, the data files could grow too large. The following commands and DBCC options deal with monitoring and controlling file sizes.

To view database file size information, select `sysdm_db_file_space_usage` from the dynamic management view.

Monitoring Database File Sizes

Three factors of file size should be monitored: the size of the database files and their maximum growth size, the amount of free space within the files, and the amount of free space on the disk drives.

The current and maximum file sizes are stored within the `sysfiles` system table:

```
Select name, size, maxsize from sysfiles;
```

Result:

```
name        size    maxsize
---------   ------- ---------
CHA2        280     -1
CHA2_log    96      268435456
```

To detect the percentage of the file that is actually being used, use the `sp_spaceused` system stored procedure. The DBCC `Updateusage` command ensures that the index-usage information is accurate:

```
DBCC Updateusage ('tempdb');
EXEC sp_spaceused;
```

Result:

```
database_name       database_size       unallocated space
-----------------   ----------------    -----------------
Tempdb              210.56 MB           73.44 MB

reserved     data           index_size      unused
----------   ------------   -------------   ----------------
138368 KB    122168 KB      14504 KB        1696 KB
```

To view session space usage, select `sysdm_db_session_space_usage` from the dynamic management view.

To determine the size and percentage of free space within the transaction log, use the DBCC SQLPerf(LogSpace) command:

```
DBCC SQLPerf (LogSpace)
```

Result (abridged):

```
Database Name   Log Size (MB)   Log Space Used (%)    Status
-------------   -------------   ------------------    --------
master          3.3671875       33.207657             0
tempdb          0.7421875       59.473682             0
model           0.4921875       63.194443             0
...
OOD             0.484375        72.278229             0
MS              0.7421875       37.302631             0

DBCC execution completed.
   If DBCC printed error messages,
   contact your system administrator.
```

To monitor the amount of free space on the server's disk drives, use the xp_fixeddrives procedure:

```
Xp_fixeddrives
```

Result:

```
drive MB Free
----- -------
C     429
F     60358
```

Cross-Reference   For more information about configuring the data and transaction log files for autogrowth and setting the maximum file sizes, refer to Chapter 17, "Implementing the Physical Database Schema."

Shrinking the Database

Unless the database is configured to automatically shrink in the background, the file space that is freed by deleting unused objects and rows will not be returned to the disk operating system. Instead, the files will remain at the largest size to which the data file may have grown. If data is regularly added and removed, constantly shrinking and growing the database would be a wasteful exercise. However, if disk space is at a premium, a large amount of data has been removed from the database, and the database is not configured to automatically shrink, the following commands may be used to manually shrink the database. The database can be shrunk while transactions are working in the database.

Note   Using auto shrink during the day, when users are accessing the database, will definitely affect performance. Normally, you'll want to use auto shrink after working hours.

DBCC ShrinkDatabase can reduce the size of the database files by performing two basic steps:

1. Packing data to the front of the file, leaving the empty space at the end of the file

2. Removing the empty space at the end of the file, reducing the size of the file

These two steps can be controlled with the following options:

✦ The `notruncate` option causes `DBCC ShrinkDatabase` to perform only step 1, packing the database file but leaving the file size the same.

✦ The `truncateonly` option eliminates the empty space at the end of the file, but does not first pack the file.

✦ The target file size can be set by specifying the desired percentage of free space after the file is shrunk. Because autogrowth can be an expensive operation, leaving some free space is a useful strategy. If the desired free space percentage is larger than the current amount of free space, this option will not increase the size of the file.

The following command shrinks OBXKites and leaves 10 percent free space:

```
DBCC ShrinkDatabase ('OBXKites', 10);
```

Result:

```
DBCC SHRINKDATABASE: File ID 3 of database ID 12 was skipped
   because the file does not have enough free space to reclaim.
DbId   FileId      CurrentSize MinimumSize UsedPages   EstimatedPages
------ ----------- ----------- ----------- ----------- ---------------
12     1           216         152         184         184


(1 row(s) affected)

DBCC execution completed. If DBCC printed error messages,
   contact your system administrator.
```

The results show that not all of the files had space to reclaim. The command tells you which files it did change by displaying the old and new statistics. `DBCC ShrinkDatabase` affects all the files for a database, whereas the `DBCC ShrinkFile` command shrinks individual files.

 Cross-Reference The database can be configured to automatically shrink the files. See Chapter 34, "Configuring SQL Server," for more information.

Shrinking the Transaction Log

When the database is shrunk, the transaction log is also shrunk. The `notruncate` and `truncateonly` options have no effect on the transaction log. If multiple log files exist, SQL Server shrinks them as if they were one large contiguous file.

A common problem is a transaction log that grows and refuses to shrink. The most likely cause is an old open transaction. The transaction log is constructed of virtual logs partitions. The success or failure of shrinking the transaction log depends on the aging of transactions within the virtual logs and log checkpoints. SQL Server can only shrink the transaction log by removing data older than the oldest transaction within the structure of the virtual logs.

To verify that an old transaction has a hold on the transaction log, use the `DBCC OpenTran` command:

```
USE OBXKites;

BEGIN TRAN;
UPDATE Product
  SET ProductDescription = 'OpenTran'
```

```
    WHERE Code = '1002';

DBCC OpenTran ('OBXKites');
```

Result:

```
Transaction information for database 'OBXKites'.

Oldest active transaction:
    SPID (server process ID): 57
    UID (user ID) : -1
    Name         : user_transaction
    LSN          : (19:524:2)
    Start time   : Mar  8 2006  4:20:38:890PM
    SID          :
    0x0105000000000000515000000b4b7cd2267fd7c3043170a32eb030000
DBCC execution completed. If DBCC printed error messages,
    contact your system administrator.
```

Based on this information, the errant transaction can be tracked down and the SPID (user connection) can be killed. Management Studio's Current Activity node can provide more information about the SPID's activity. A more drastic option is to stop and restart the server and then shrink the database.

Cross-Reference   The recovery model and transaction log backups both affect how the transaction log grows and automatically shrinks. For more information on these critical issues, refer to Chapter 36, "Recovery Planning."

Now that you've seen an open transaction, let's close it. The following code commits the transaction and verifies there aren't any other open transactions for the database:

```
COMMIT TRAN;

DBCC OpenTran ('OBXKites');
```

Result:

```
No active open transactions.
DBCC execution completed. If DBCC printed error messages,
    contact your system administrator.
```

Miscellaneous DBCC Commands

The remaining seven DBCC commands are used in troubleshooting during testing of stored procedures and triggers:

✦ DBCC DropCleanBuffers: Cleans the memory of any buffered data so that it doesn't affect query performance during testing.

✦ DBCC Inputbuffer (SPID): Returns the last statement executed by a client, as identified by the client's SPID. This command can be executed only by members of the sysadmin server group, for obvious security reasons.

✦ DBCC Outputbuffer (SPID): Returns the results of the last statement executed by a client. Like the DBCC InputBuffer command, this command can only be executed by members of the sysadmin group.

✦ DBCC PinTable (DatabaseID, ObjectID): Tags a table so that once it is in memory it will not be flushed from memory. Avoid pinning a table; it's far better to let SQL Server cache pages in memory as they are needed.

✦ DBCC UnPinTable (DatabaseID, ObjectID): Removes a table from the pin list.

✦ DBCC ProcCache: Reports some basic statistics about the procedure cache as queries and procedures are compiled and stored in memory.

✦ DBCC ConcurrencyViolation: The Desktop and Personal editions of SQL Server are limited to five concurrent users. This command checks how many times that limitation was reached.

Managing Database Maintenance

SQL Server provides a host of database maintenance commands. Fortunately, it also provides the DBA with ways to schedule maintenance tasks.

Planning Database Maintenance

An ideal database maintenance plan includes the following functions in the following order:

✦ **Consistency checks:** DBCC CheckDB and DBCC CleanTable(table) for tables that experience heavy text updates, DBCC CheckCatalog, DBCC CheckConstraints, and DBCC CheckIdent for database structure integrity.

✦ Updating the index statistics.

✦ Defragmenting the database.

✦ Rebuilding the indexes.

✦ **Backups:** A strategic backup plan includes a mix of full, differential, and transaction log backups of the system databases and all significant user databases.

✦ Checking the file sizes and free disk space.

These maintenance tasks can be automated in SQL Server Agent jobs.

Maintenance Plan Wizard

The Maintenance Plan Wizard, built into Management Studio, helps automate a basic maintenance plan and can perform all the required maintenance tasks. All of the maintenance plans appear in the Management\Maintenance Plans folder of Management Studio. Launch the Wizard by right-clicking the Maintenance Plans folder and choosing New Maintenance Plan from the context menu. Type a name for the Maintenance plan in the New Maintenance Plan dialog box and click OK.

Once you assign a name to your maintenance plan, Management Studio opens a new center window that includes the maintenance plan name, a description, the time you want to schedule the maintenance plan, and a list of tasks to perform. Figure 37-1 shows a sample maintenance plan with some tasks already entered.

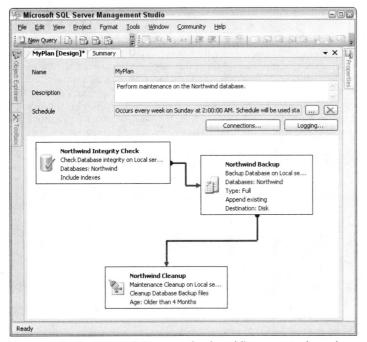

Figure 37-1: Create a maintenance plan by adding some tasks and scheduling a time to perform the tasks.

Adding a Task

A maintenance plan must contain at least one task. Fortunately, it isn't hard to add one to your maintenance plan. Simply drag and drop the appropriate task from the Toolbox, shown in Figure 37-2, to the design area of the maintenance plan. The resulting task will appear as a square (refer to Figure 37-1).

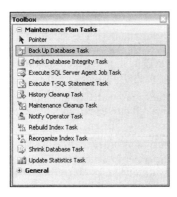

Figure 37-2: Use the Toolbox to add new tasks to your maintenance plan.

The task isn't configured yet. Use the Properties window, shown in Figure 37-3, to configure the task. The content of the Properties window varies by task. For example, when you select a Back Up Database Task, you'll see properties to choose the kind of database, the backup device type, and other information associated with backing up the database. The upper portion of the Properties window contains the name of the selected task. You can choose other tasks using the drop-down list box. The middle of the Properties window contains a list of properties for the selected task. You can organize the properties by category or in alphabetical order. The lower part of the Properties window contains a description for the selected property. Once you have worked with tasks for a while, the description usually provides enough information to help you remember how to use the selected property.

Figure 37-3: Define the task specifics using the Properties window.

Sometimes you may not want to use the Properties window. For example, you might be working with a new task. In this case, you can bypass the Properties window by double-clicking the task. A task-specific window like the one shown in Figure 37-4 for a backup task will appear. Unlike the Properties window, this dialog box displays the task properties in context. In addition, it grays out task elements until you define the correct functionality. For example, when you choose to back up specific databases, the dialog box won't let you perform any other configuration task until you choose one or more databases for the backup.

It's interesting to click View T-SQL when you finish configuring the task. The resulting window displays the T-SQL that the task will use. The Transact SQL (Task Generated) window won't let you edit the command, but seeing how the Maintenance Plan Wizard generates the code can prove helpful when you need to create SQL commands of your own.

You know when a task is complete by the appearance of the square in the design area. Incomplete tasks, those that won't execute correctly, have a red circle with an X through it on the right side of the display.

After you define a task, add the next task in your list. You can add the tasks in any order and place them in any order on screen. Connect the tasks in the order in which you want SQL Server to execute them. Figure 37-1 showed several tasks with one task connected to the next task in the list. The example will check the integrity of the Northwind database first, then back it up, and finally perform some file maintenance

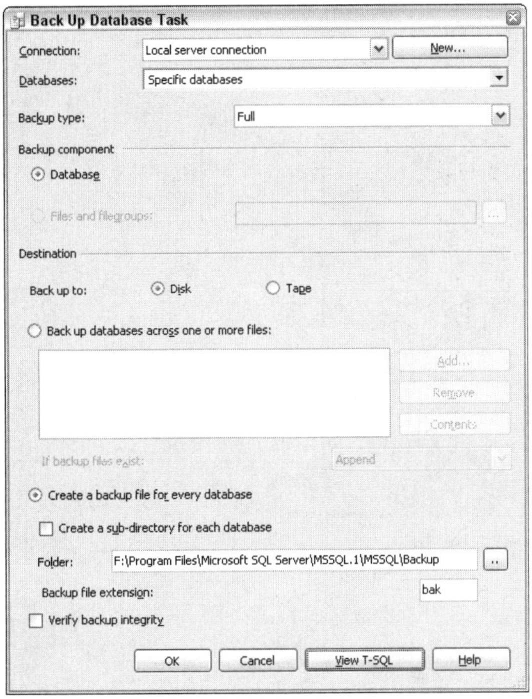

Figure 37-4: In addition to the Properties window, you can use the task-related dialog box for configuration.

Defining the Schedule

You can perform tasks on demand or schedule them to run automatically. Generally, it's a good idea to set standard tasks such as backup to run automatically. Click the ellipsis next to the Schedule field to display the Job Schedule Properties dialog box, shown in Figure 37-5, when you want to change the task schedule.

Select the scheduling requirements for the task. For example, you can set a task to run daily, weekly, or monthly. The dialog box also enables you to select a specific starting time for the task and determine when the scheduling begins and ends. The one form of scheduling that this dialog box doesn't provide is on demand. To set the maintenance task to run on demand, click the red X next to the Schedule field.

Creating New Connections

Depending on your database setup, you might need to create multiple connections to perform a particular task. The Maintenance Plan Wizard always provides a connection to the default instance of the local database. Click Connections to add more connections to the current maintenance plan (any additions won't affect other maintenance plans you create). You'll see the Manage Connections dialog box shown in Figure 37-6.

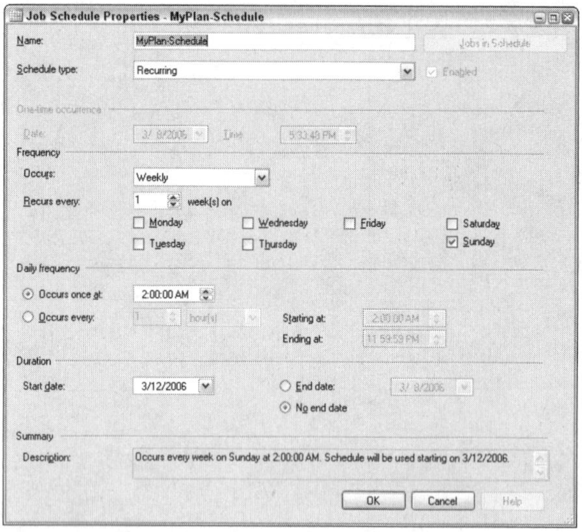

Figure 37-5: Define a schedule that meets the task requirements; use off hours scheduling for tasks that require many resources.

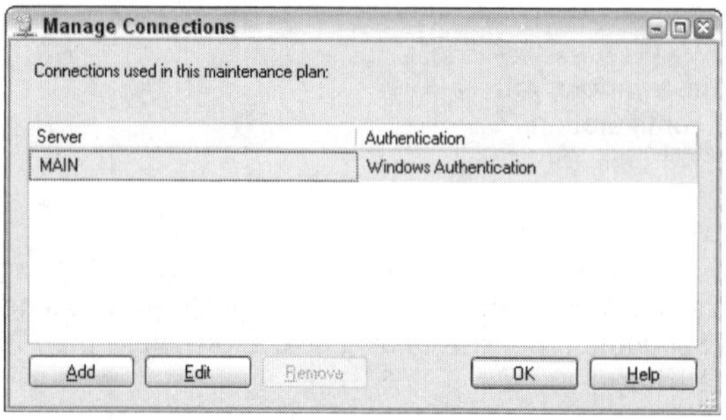

Figure 37-6: Add new connections as needed to perform maintenance tasks.

Click Add in the Manage Connections dialog box to add a new connection. You'll see a New Connection dialog box. A connection consists of three elements: connection name, server name, and server security. Choose a connection name that reflects the server and instance. Using a name such as My Connection isn't particularly helpful when you need to troubleshoot the maintenance task later. You can either type the server and instance name or select it from a list that the Maintenance Plan Wizard provides when you click the ellipses next to the Select or Enter a Server Name field. Finally, choose between Windows integrated or SQL Server security. Click OK to add the new connection to the list.

The Manage Connections dialog box also lets you edit existing connections or remove old connections. When you edit an existing connection, you see a New Connection dialog box in which you can change the logon arguments or the server name for the connection. The wizard grays out the other fields of this dialog box. Simply click Remove to delete a connection you no longer need from the list.

Note

Connection deletion is a one-way process and it happens quite quickly. Make sure you have the correct connection selected before you click Remove because the wizard won't ask for confirmation before deleting the connection.

Logging the Maintenance Progress

Many of the maintenance tasks that you automate using the Maintenance Plan Wizard will execute during off hours, when you're unlikely to be around to monitor the system. Fortunately, you can set maintenance tasks to log and report their actions so that you don't have to watch them every moment. To use this feature, click Logging. You'll see the Reporting and Logging dialog box shown in Figure 37-7.

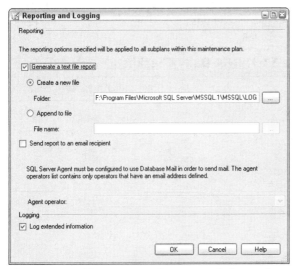

Figure 37-7: Add new connections as needed to perform maintenance tasks.

The features of the Reporting and Logging dialog box let you send the report to a file or your e-mail. The e-mail feature works quite well and saves you the time of searching for the file on the hard drive. However, the text file provides an archive that could prove helpful long after you've deleted the e-mail from your inbox. Once you configure the reporting options, click OK and the maintenance plan will record its actions for you.

You normally want to provide extended information about all maintenance tasks that the system performs without your supervision. Even the smallest piece of information can help you determine where a particular maintenance action went awry.

Best Practice

Command-Line Maintenance

Database maintenance is normally performed within Management Studio or automated with SQL Server Agent. However, maintenance can be performed from the DOS command prompt by means of SQLMaint. This utility has numerous options that can perform backups, update statistics, and run DBCC. Specific information on SQLMaint can be found in SQL Server 2005 Books Online.

SQLMaint may be useful in some situations, such as when using non–SQL Server schedulers or integrating the database maintenance plan with system utilities, such as third-party backups. Nevertheless, I recommend that you stay with SQL Server Agent over SQLMaint unless there's a compelling reason to abandon SQL Server's internal scheduler.

Monitoring Database Maintenance

It's not enough to simply schedule the tasks; they must be monitored as well. In larger installations with dozens of SQL Servers spread around the globe, just monitoring the health of SQL Server and the databases becomes a full-time job. Table 37-1 provides a sample DBA daily checklist that can be used as a starting point for developing a database monitoring plan.

Table 37-1: DBA Daily Checklist

Item	S	M	T	W	T	F
System Databases Backup						
Production User Databases Backup						
SQL Agent, SQL Main, & DTC running						
Database Size, Growth, Disk Free Space						
Batch Jobs Execute OK						
DBCC Jobs Execute OK						
SQL Log Errors						
Replication Log Agent Running						
Replication Distribution Cleanup Job Execute OK						
SQL Server Last Reboot						

Depending on complexity and the number of servers, the DBA daily checklist can be maintained manually with an Excel spreadsheet or tracked in a SQL Server table.

Summary

This chapter covered database maintenance in detail. SQL Server offers a rich set of commands and utilities that can be used to monitor the health of, and perform maintenance on, SQL Server. The Maintenance Plan Wizard is also available to streamline database maintenance. All installations of SQL Server should also include a database maintenance schedule to assist the DBA in keeping track of maintenance performed.

The next chapter explains how to use SQL Agent, which may be used to schedule jobs and create custom maintenance jobs.

✦   ✦   ✦

Automating Database Maintenance with SQL Server Agent

The automation of database maintenance is crucial to ensuring that a database is regularly checked, maintained, and optimized. Automated checking consists of monitoring database size to identify issues before they generate mayhem; maintenance includes frequent backups; and optimization involves tweaking the index configuration for optimal performance. Automation ensures that these activities do not consume too much of your time, so you can focus on more pressing issues (such as improving your golf game, perhaps).

Ideally, you want SQL Server to monitor itself and alert you when it encounters a critical condition. Luckily for you, Microsoft grants this specific wish, because SQL Server 2005 includes a powerful component that can send alerts when specific critical conditions occur. Better still, this same component also enables you to schedule routine maintenance tasks either on a one-time basis or on a recurring basis — for example, once a month or, say, on the first Saturday of every month. SQL Server Agent is the service responsible for processing alerts and running scheduled jobs.

Setting Up SQL Server Agent

Setting up SQL Server Agent is straightforward, as long as you avoid two pitfalls: The first is rather elementary, the second a bit more subtle. We'll cover the easy one first. Because SQL Server Agent is a Windows service, you want to make sure that the service is restarted if anybody reboots the server. (Microsoft sets this service not to start by default when you install SQL Server, so you'll always need to set it to start automatically after an installation.) This is an elementary step, but it is occasionally overlooked (and then, after someone restarts the server, none of the scheduled jobs run and, perhaps even worse, critical alerts go undetected).

Best Practice

The best way to avoid problems with services not restarting is to set them to start automatically. Open the Services console found in the Administrative Tools folder of the Control Panel. Right-click the SQL Server Agent (Instance) service and choose Properties from the context menu. Select Automatic in the Startup Type field and click OK.

The SQL Server Agent service is named SQL Server Agent, with the instance name appearing in parentheses. If more than one SQL Server instance is installed on the server, a SQL Server Agent service will exist for each instance.

As with any service, the SQL Server Agent startup mode can be changed through the Services console in the Control Panel. However, an easier way to accomplish the same goal is to use the SQL Server Configuration Manager found by selecting Start ➪ Programs ➪ Microsoft SQL Server 2005 ➪ Configuration Tools. The SQL Server Configuration Manager appears in Figure 38-1.

Figure 38-1: The SQL Server Configuration Manager dialog enables you to easily change the startup mode of the SQL Server Agent service.

Here are the steps to follow to ensure that the startup mode of the SQL Server Agent service is set to automatic:

1. Open the SQL Server Configuration Manager.

2. Highlight the SQL Server 2005 Services folder.

3. Right-click the service you want to change and choose Properties from the context menu. The service's Properties dialog box will appear.

4. Select the Service tab.

5. Highlight the Start Mode property and choose the new starting mode from the drop-down list box.

6. Click OK to make the change complete.

It is a good idea to take one extra step to ensure that SQL Server Agent (and SQL Server, for that matter) is always running. Here's how to accomplish this:

1. Start SQL Server Management Studio (its default location is Start ➪ Programs ➪ Microsoft SQL Server 2005 ➪ Management Studio).

2. Expand the folders until you find the server you are configuring. If you are working on the actual server you are configuring, the path is `Console Root/Microsoft SQL Server/ SQL Server Group/(local) (Windows NT)`.

3. Expand to see the folders below the server. One of these folders is entitled SQL Server Agent. Right-click the folder and choose Properties from the context menu. Choose the General folder, which offers the options shown in Figure 38-2.

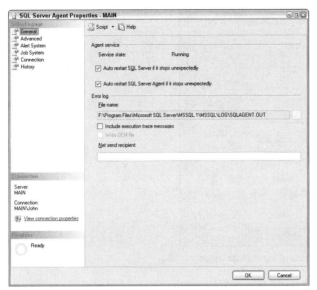

Figure 38-2: The General tab on the SQL Server Agent Properties dialog box enables you to configure how the service runs.

4. Check both of the Auto restart options (refer to Figure 38-2). This will ensure that SQL Server and SQL Server Agent restart when they unexpectedly stop.

The second pitfall to be aware of when setting up SQL Server Agent has to do with security. You have to determine which account will be used to run this service. By default, the SQL Server Agent service runs under the security context of the system account. Because the system account has access to only local resources, you must use a domain account if you want to access network resources in any of the scheduled jobs. You may, for example, want to back up a database to a different server. Typically, you will also need a domain account to enable SQL Server to send e-mail and pager notifications (the steps you need to follow to do this are outlined later in this section). You must also use a domain account for replication to work. You typically configure SQL Server Agent to use a Windows domain account that is a member of the sysadmin role so that you have the necessary permission to run jobs or send notifications.

To change the account used to run the SQL Server Agent service, follow these steps:

1. Open the SQL Server Configuration Manager.

2. Highlight the SQL Server 2005 Services folder.

3. Right-click the SQL Server Agent entry and choose Properties from the context menu. The Properties dialog box will appear.

4. Select the Log On tab. As shown in Figure 38-3, you can choose between one of the built-in accounts or use a specific account. Because this is my development system, I'm using a specific account. Normally you choose between the Local System, Local Service, and Network Service accounts for a production system.

Figure 38-3: Choose a built-in or other account to use for log on purposes.

5. Click OK. A dialog box will inform you that the change in account will require a service restart.

6. Click Yes. The account change will appear as soon as the service restarts.

The final step is to set up the SQL Server Agent mail profile so that the service can send e-mail and pager notifications when alerts occur. This requires setting up and configuring a mail service and letting SQL Server Agent know how to access the mail service. The easiest mail service to use for this purpose is Exchange Server. If you are using Microsoft Exchange as the mail service, here are the steps you must follow:

1. Set up an Exchange mailbox for SQL Server Agent Mail on the Exchange server (normally this is a different server from the database server). Configure this mailbox for the domain account used to run the SQL Server Agent mail service. Be sure to pick a descriptive name for the profile, identifying it as the SQL Server Agent Mail profile. This will help prevent accidental deletion of this important profile.

2. Install MAPI-compliant mail-client software such as Outlook on the database server.

3. Set up a Mail profile for SQL Server Agent using the Mail utility on the Control Panel of the database server. This mail profile should point to the Mail Exchange server and the Exchange mailbox you set up in the first step of this procedure.

Now all that is left to do is to tell SQL Server Agent which mail profile to use when sending e-mail. This is done in the SQL Server Agent Properties dialog, as follows:

1. Click the Alert System tab.

2. In the Mail Session group, check the Enable Mail Profile option. The other options in this group become available.

3. Select the Mail Profile you have set up for this purpose. You can test whether mail has been properly configured by clicking the Test button.

Understanding Alerts, Operators, and Jobs

An alert defines a specific action that will be carried out when a certain condition is met. Such a condition can be set up for a variety of performance counters, including number of connections, database file size, and number of deadlocks per second. A condition can also be tied to an error number or degree of error severity. When acting upon an alert condition, SQL Server Agent can notify one or more operators, run a job, or both.

Operators are the people responsible for handling critical conditions on the database server. As pointed out in the previous section, one of the neat things SQL Server Agent does is send messages to operators to report job status or make them aware of server conditions. Operators can be set up to receive messages via e-mail, pager, or Net Send. You can specify at which times an operator is available to receive messages via pager (for example, 9:00 A.M. to 5:00 P.M., Monday to Friday). You can also suspend notification for a specified operator, such as when the operator is taking time off.

A job is a database task or group of database tasks. Examples of typical jobs are backing up a database, reorganizing the indexes, or executing a Data Transformation Services (DTS) package. SQL Server Agent jobs are also used behind the scenes to implement and schedule a maintenance plan using the Maintenance Plan Wizard in SQL Server Management Studio.

Managing Operators

Just as you need to create logins for the users who will be accessing a SQL Server database, you need to create operators in SQL Server to be able to send alerts to these support people. Creating operators in SQL Server is straightforward. Here's how it works:

1. Start SQL Server Management Studio and find the SQL Server Agent folder below the server you are configuring.

2. Right-click the SQL Server Agent\Operators folder and select New Operator from the context menu. This brings up a dialog box similar to the one shown in Figure 38-4. Choose the General folder as shown in the figure.

3. Type in the name of the operator as well as his or her e-mail address, pager e-mail address, and/or Net Send address, depending on how you want the notification to be sent. If you fill out a pager address you can specify when the operator is available to be paged. If an e-mail address is ambiguous, you should specify a fully qualified e-mail address in square brackets, such as [SMTP:SQLSupport@YourCompany.com]. Alternatively, you can click the button with the ellipsis (. . .) to browse the address book on the database server.

4. Select the Notifications folder and choose the notification method for each alert.

5. Click the Jobs option and set the notification method for each job.

Note   You'll need to revisit the operator configuration every time you create a new alert or job. Make sure you have operators assigned to new alerts and jobs as needed.

If an operator is unavailable to respond to notification, you can temporarily disable this operator by clearing the Enabled checkbox in the General folder. If you do this, make sure that another operator will be notified. Rather than disable an operator, change the e-mail, pager, and Net Send addresses until the operator becomes available again.

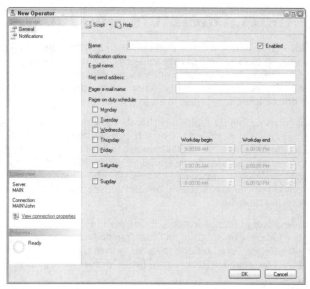

Figure 38-4: The New Operator dialog enables you to specify when an operator is available to receive pager notifications.

Managing Alerts

Depending on how you perform the SQL Server setup, you might not see any default alerts. However, SQL Server does add some default alerts when you install specific product features such as replication. The names of the fourteen replication alerts start with "Replication." Figure 38-5 shows a list of the replication-related alerts. By default, SQL Server disables all of the replication alerts except for the warnings, and the alerts have no operators assigned to them. If you decide to use the replication features, you should also provide operators to receive the alerts so you know when something has gone wrong. The "Managing Operators" section of this chapter details one method you can use to add operators to an alert. The following sections describe how to create your own errors and alerts.

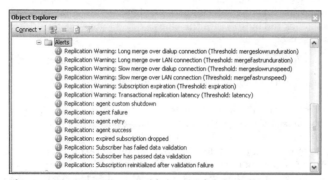

Figure 38-5: SQL Server provides several default alerts when you install replication support.

Creating User-Defined Errors

If you are deploying custom-written applications that use SQL Server as their data store, the application programmers may define their own set of errors. You use the sp_addmessage command to perform this task. As a minimum, you must supply the error number (any value between 50,001 and 2,147,483,647), the severity (a number between 1 and 25), and the message text. The sproc also accepts a language identifier that consists of the name of any language installed on the server, such as English. The default setting is the currently selected language. You must also determine whether you want to write the error message to the Windows event log. The default setting is false in this case. Finally, you can provide an argument to replace an existing message with a new message. If you attempt to create a new message with the same number as an existing number without providing the replace value, the system displays error message 15043, stating "You must specify 'REPLACE' to overwrite an existing message."

To list the error messages supported by SQL Server, query the sys.sysmessages catalog view filtering for error > 50000 when you want to see just the custom error messages. You can also filter the messages by severity and language ID. The mysterious-looking dlevel field has a value of 128 when the error message writes to the Windows event log.

Here's an example of using the sp_addmessage command:

```
sp_addmessage 50001, 1, 'This is a test message.';
```

In this case, the command adds a new message with a message identifier of 50001. The severity level of this message is 1 and the human-readable text is "This is a test message." The system won't write this message to the event log and it will use the current server language. However, suppose you decide to change this message so that it does write to the event log. In this case, you'd change the command to the following:

```
sp_addmessage 50001, 1, 'This is a test message.', 'English', True,
    REPLACE;
```

Notice that the command now has a language specified. The value of True indicates that the system will write the message to the event log. Finally, because you're replacing this message with one that already exists, the command includes the word REPLACE.

As far as alerts are concerned, user-defined and native SQL Server messages are handled uniformly. Specify the error number or severity level, and when an error is raised that matches the alert condition, SQL Server Agent will initiate the specified response. The following section covers how to set up these kinds of alerts.

Creating an Alert

You can create two kinds of alerts. The first is triggered by an error number or by an error of a specified severity. The second is triggered by a SQL Server performance counter. Here is how to set up both kinds of alerts:

1. Start SQL Server Management Studio.

2. Right-click the SQL Server Agent\Alerts folder and choose New Alert from the context menu. You'll see the New Alert dialog box shown in Figure 38-6.

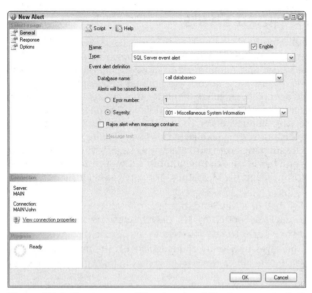

Figure 38-6: An error condition is one of the two events that can trigger an alert.

3. Type a name for your alert. Because an alert can affect one or all databases and define any number of events or conditions, you'll want to name the alert carefully. Use keywords so that the system orders the alert automatically for you. For example, you might use "Event: Northwind: Severity Level 16" as a name.

4. Select the type of alert you want to create. The Type list box enables you to specify which kind of alert you want to create: a SQL Server event alert (triggered by an error number or level of severity), a SQL Server performance-condition alert, or a Windows Management Interface (WMI) event alert. Figure 38-7 shows the changes to make to the New Alert dialog box to create a SQL Server performance-condition alert. In this case, the alert will trigger when the size of the Northwind database log rises above 2,000 KB (or 2MB). You can access any of the SQL Server performance counters using this technique.

5. Configure the alert (what to do in this step depends on the choice you made in previous step):

   a. If you are creating a SQL Server event alert, select the severity or error number you want to monitor. When specifying an error number, you can use the button with the ellipsis to search for an error. If specifying severity, you typically focus on the critical errors, which by default have a severity of 19 or higher. You can either monitor all databases on the server or monitor a specific database. Finally, you can also restrict alerts to messages containing a specific text string by specifying the filter text in the Error Message Contains This Text text box.

   b. If you are creating a SQL Server performance-condition test alert, select the object and counter you want to monitor. Then set the threshold for that counter.

You can specify that the alert occur when the counter falls below, equals, or rises above, the specified value. For some counters, you can specify the instance to which the counter is to be applied. For example, you can monitor the data-file size for either all databases on the server or just one specific database.

c. If you are creating a WMI event alert, you must provide the namespace for the event, such as `\\.\root\Microsoft\SqlServer\ServerEvents\MSSQLSERVER`. In addition, you must provide a query for that namespace. All WMI queries rely on the Windows Management Instrumentation Query Language (WQL).

6. Select the Response tab. Determine the kind of response you want the alert to request. In the Response tab, you can specify one or more operators to be notified, or which job to run, or both. You will learn how to set up jobs in the next section, "Managing Jobs." Of course, the New Operator button brings up the New Operator dialog box discussed in the previous section, "Managing Operators." Typically, you choose to send the error text in an e-mail or a Net Send, but not when you are paging an operator. Three check boxes below the list of operators to be notified let you control when the error text is sent.

7. Select the Options tab. Choose one of the request methods: Email, Pager, or Net Send. In addition to the standard message text, you can also provide special text for this alert. Finally, for recurring alerts, you can specify the delay between responses in minutes and seconds. This is especially important for SQL Server performance-condition alerts, because these conditions tend to exist for a long time and you do not want to flood the operators with multiple alerts for the same condition.

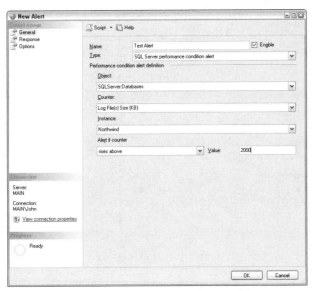

Figure 38-7: A performance condition is one of the two events that can trigger an alert.

Managing Jobs

A job is defined as a series of steps with a specific work flow. You can, for example, specify that step 1 will execute step 2 if it succeeds, but will execute step 3 if it fails. Steps come in two basic types. The first type involves replication. The second can execute Transact-SQL script, ActiveX script (Visual Basic script or JScript), or any operating-system command. The latter are the most frequently used. After each step, you can specify the next action depending on whether the step succeeds or fails. You have four options:

✦ Go to the next step.

✦ Go to step x, where x is the number of any step defined in the job.

✦ Quit the job, reporting success.

✦ Quit the job, reporting failure.

You can also set the number of times you want a step to be attempted in case of failure. You can associate one or more schedules with a job. This enables you to automatically run a job at a specified time. A schedule can specify that a job should run once at a specific time or on a recurring basis. You can also schedule a job to run whenever SQL Server Agent starts or whenever the CPU becomes idle. In the Advanced tab of the SQL Server Agent Properties dialog (see Figure 38-8), you can specify when you consider the CPU to be idle. This involves selecting the level of average CPU usage that the CPU must fall below for a specified time in seconds. Finally, you can also set notifications for completion, success, or failure of a job.

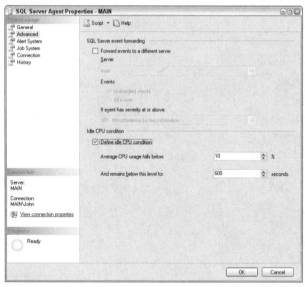

Figure 38-8: Set the conditions that you consider equivalent to CPU idle time.

Best Practice

It's important to realize that your server is never completely idle. Even a well-tuned setup will usually have 2 percent or 3 percent activity. Consequently, setting the Average CPU Usage Falls Below setting to 0 percent means the job will never run. However, nor do you want to set this value so high that it interferes with jobs that must run in the foreground in near real time. Consequently, using a setting between 5 percent and 12 percent normally works best. Likewise, the amount of idle time is important. Using a setting between 360 and 600 seconds works well. However, an administrator for a large system might want to set this value higher to ensure that the server is truly idle, while an administrator for a smaller system might want to use a lower value to maximize use of idle time.

Some wizards create jobs behind the scenes when you use them. Wizards that do so include the Maintenance Plan Wizard, the Backup Wizard, the DTS Import Wizard, and the DTS Export Wizard. Any form of replication also creates jobs behind the scenes.

As with alerts, you create a new job using the New Job dialog box. Here are the steps to follow when using the New Job dialog box. Creating a job involves five distinct steps:

1. Create a job definition.

2. Set each step to execute.

3. Set the next action for each step.

4. Configure a job schedule.

5. Handle completion-, success-, and failure-notification messages.

The following sections walk you through each of these steps. The first section that follows discusses the optional step of creating a job category.

Creating a Job Category

As you will see in the next section, when defining a job, you can assign a category to it. This enables you to group similar jobs together. Here are the steps you can use to manage job categories:

1. Start SQL Server Management Studio and find the Management folder below the server you are configuring.

2. Expand the SQL Server Agent folder.

3. Right-click the Jobs folder and choose Manage Job Categories from the context menu. This brings up the Manage Job Categories dialog box, shown in Figure 38-9.

4. You can create a new job category by clicking Add. This brings up the New Category properties dialog.

5. Type a descriptive name for the category in the Name field.

6. Add jobs to this category by clicking the Show All Jobs check box and selecting the corresponding check box in the Select column of the job list. Jobs that don't have a category assigned automatically appear in the list. Selecting Show All Jobs will also reveal jobs that already have a category assigned.

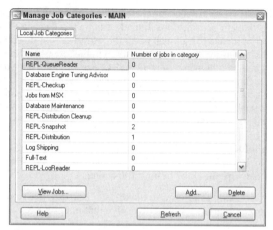

Figure 38-9: The Manage Job Categories dialog enables you to maintain the job categories used when you define a new job.

You can also use the Manage Job Categories dialog box to remove existing job categories. Highlight the job category that you want to delete and click Delete.

In addition, you can see a list of the jobs currently assigned to a particular category. Highlight the job category you want to view and click View Jobs. Add additional jobs to a category by checking the job's entry in the Select column of the New Job Category dialog box.

Creating a Job Definition

The main component of a job definition is the unique name that will be used to refer to the job. You use this unique name, for example, to specify which job to run when an alert is triggered. Here's how you create a job definition:

1. Start SQL Server Management Studio and find the SQL Server Agent folder below the server you are configuring.

2. Expand the SQL Server Agent folder to see the items below it.

3. Right-click the Jobs folder and choose New Job from the context menu. This brings up a New Job dialog box similar to the one shown in Figure 38-10.

4. In the General tab, give the job a unique name (up to 128 characters), select an appropriate category and owner for the job, and type a description of the job. Only administrators can change the owner of an existing job.

> **Note**　Only predefined logins can be used as the owner. If you do not find the login you want to use, exit the job definition by clicking the Cancel button and create a login for the account you want to use. To do this, expand the Security item a few items below the Management item in Management Studio, right-click on Logins, and then select New Login.

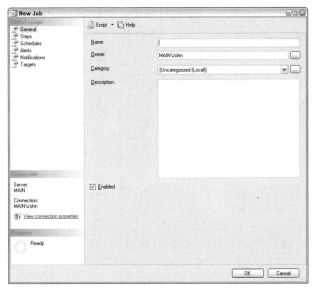

Figure 38-10: You can categorize and assign an owner to a new job in the New Job dialog box.

5. Select the Targets folder. Select the Target Local Server for jobs that run on a single, local machine. If job scheduling across multiple servers is configured, choose Target Multiple Servers and select which server acts as the target server (the server on which the job runs). To run on multiple servers, select Target Multiple Servers and specify the servers on which the job will run.

6. Click Apply to create the job definition. You are now ready for the next steps, as explained in the following sections.

Setting Up the Job Steps

After you have created a job definition, you may want to define what steps need to be performed during the job. You do this by clicking the Steps page (see Figure 38-11) in the Job Properties dialog box. The buttons on this screen are as follows:

✦ *New* creates a new step.

✦ *Insert* inserts a step before the currently highlighted step.

✦ *Edit* modifies the currently highlighted step.

✦ *Delete* deletes the currently highlighted step.

✦ *Move step up* moves the currently highlighted step up one in the list.

✦ *Move step down* moves the currently highlighted step down one in the list.

✦ *Start step* enables you to choose which step is executed first. This first step is indicated by a green flag.

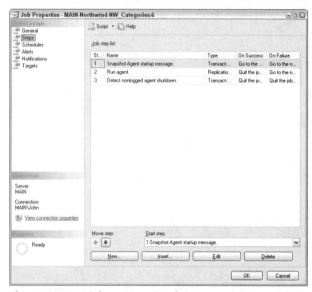

Figure 38-11: A job may consist of one or more steps, which are created in the Steps page.

When you create a new step, you are presented with the New Job Step dialog box, shown in Figure 38-12. All steps require a unique name (up to 128 characters). For the three most common types of steps (Transact-SQL Script, ActiveX script, and operating-system commands), you simply type in the command box the code you want executed. You may also click the Open button to load the code from a file. The Parse button enables you to check the syntax of the command.

After you have entered the code that should run for the step, you can click the Advanced tab (see Figure 38-13) in the New Job Step dialog box to specify what happens after the step executes. You can also specify how many times the step is attempted in case of initial failure, as well as the delay in minutes between the attempts.

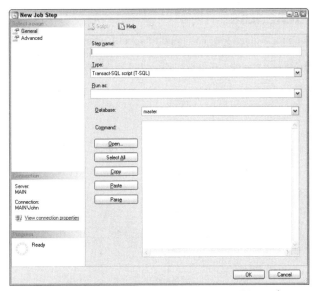

Figure 38-12: A step can execute any Transact-SQL code.

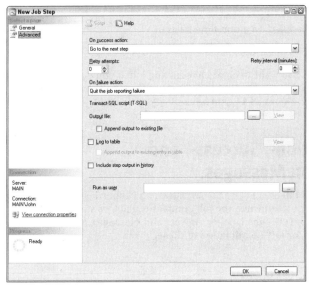

Figure 38-13: Use the Advanced tab to control what happens after a step executes.

Configuring a Job Schedule

After you have entered the steps for a given job, you need to specify when the job is to be executed. You do this in the Schedules tab of the Job Properties dialog box. Clicking the New Schedule button on this tab brings up the New Job Schedule dialog, shown in Figure 38-14.

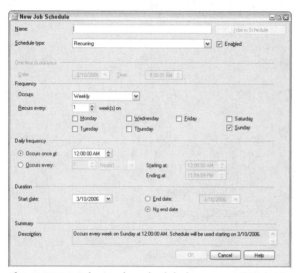

Figure 38-14: Jobs can be scheduled on a one-time basis or on a recurring basis.

For many maintenance tasks, you want to create a recurring job. If you don't like the default (every week on Sunday at 12:00:00 A.M.), you can define how frequently the task is to be repeated. As you can see from Figure 38-14, you have plenty of flexibility in scheduling a recurring job.

Handling Completion-, Success-, and Failure-Notification Messages

Finally, click the Notifications tab (see Figure 38-15) of the Job Properties dialog box to specify the type of notification to be used when the job completes, fails, or succeeds. You can send a message to an operator (via e-mail, pager, or Net Send message), log the related event, automatically delete the step, or any combination of these.

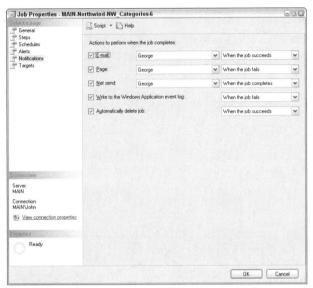

Figure 38-15: You can specify the type of notification to be used when the job completes, fails, or succeeds.

Summary

SQL Server Agent is a powerful ally that will ensure you never forget to perform a crucial maintenance task, and that will alert you when something critical requires your attention. The former goal is achieved through recurring jobs, the latter through alerts.

In this chapter you learned how to set up SQL Server Agent. You learned what alerts, operators, and jobs are, and the steps required to manage them. In short, you should now be fully equipped to use all features of SQL Server Agent to automate crucial maintenance tasks.

✦　　✦　　✦

Replicating Data

In any environment where the database administrator (DBA) has to manage more than one SQL Server, the DBA will sooner or later have to distribute data from one SQL Server to another SQL Server, or another RDBMS. SQL Server has a rich set of options to distribute data; SQL Server 2005 has added several options to the mix. Unlike other RDBMS Microsoft solutions to distribute data, are all free; but their richness and robustness make them invaluable components to any distribution data solution.

Why Replicate Data?

There are several reasons why a DBA might want to replicate data:

✦ Fault tolerance/disaster recovery

✦ Application requirements

✦ Performance gains

✦ Data distribution

Fault Tolerance/Disaster Recovery

Fault tolerance refers to the degree to which a system can withstand errors or problems. Faults generally fall into two categories:

✦ **Local:** These are confined to the server or server enclosure, e.g., hardware failure, OS or SQL Server crash, human actions, and so on.

✦ **Regional:** These are major disruptions such as earthquake, power failure, terrorist attack, and so on.

In general, most clients will be forgiving of a regional event. A client can typically handle a regional event such as the loss of the power grid that also takes their systems offline. However, it's far more difficult to explain to a client that the reason he can't withdraw money from his ATM is because Joe in accounting tripped on the power cord for the server. Clients are less likely to understand a local event that doesn't affect their systems.

Organizations pick a fault-tolerant solution based on how much downtime or data loss they can abide. For instance, most financial institutions can't tolerate the same amount of downtime as, for example, a retail store outlet. A company requiring minimum downtime will pick a high-availability solution, which involves clustering for

protection against local failures, or perhaps even geo-spatial clustering to protect against regional failures. Such a solution would provide automatic failover; in the event of failure (regional or local), clients connecting to one server will be seamlessly redirected to servers running in another location with minimal data loss — if any.

Clustering is a technology that provides automatic failover. Clustering involves grouping two or more servers (called *nodes*) together to act as a single virtual server. The nodes share resources among themselves. Clustering allows for automatic failover. The virtual server will float between nodes; at any one time, one node may be providing resources for the virtual server. If this node experiences hardware failure or goes offline for maintenance, then another node will host the virtual server, with minimal downtime for the clients.

Most financial institutions use hardware data mirroring, using a solution from a vendor such as EMC, Hitachi (HDS), or Veritas, which mirrors the data at the hardware level. Such a solution is more scalable than clustering, and provides for regional fault tolerance and automatic failover. Clustering is limited by the distance between the nodes (typically, a distance that will allow 500 ms. round-trips for pings).

The other solutions for providing fault tolerance are SQL Server 2005 data mirroring, log shipping, and replication. SQL Server 2005 also provides automatic failover, but the high-availability mode increases the commit time of each transaction on the source, and requires a third server in the mix. Data mirroring is not a scalable solution for SQL Servers under significant load.

New in 2005

The data mirroring feature of SQL Server 2005 directly addresses previous complaints that SQL Server 2000 didn't provide a robust reliability model. Using this new feature will greatly enhance the reliability of SQL Server setups and make the data more accessible.

Log shipping is another alternative that provides fault tolerance but not automatic failover. With log shipping, a backup is restored on the destination server, and then log dumps are shipped from the source server to the destination server and applied. While you can dump the transaction log every minute, the practical limit is closer to five minutes, which means log shipping is not as scalable as clustering, hardware data mirroring, or SQL Server data mirroring. However, log shipping does work well if you are trying to synchronize two databases for which you have frequent schema changes.

Replication can also be used for fault tolerance, but with several caveats:

✦ No automatic failover.

✦ Every table must have a primary key if you are using transactional replication. Transactional replication is the best-suited replication type for fault tolerance because it ensures that the replicated data store contains a precise copy of your data.

sys.

To view metadata about transactions being replicated in a transactional publication, select `sysdm_repl_tranhash` from the dynamic management view.

✦ Replication will modify the objects on the destination server, which can sometimes make it unusable for failover — for example, the identity property of columns is removed, primary keys are replaced by unique indexes, the `NOT FOR REPLICATION` property is not used, and declarative referential integrity (DRI) and some of the indexes on the source server are not replicated.

✦ System objects are not replicated.

✦ Changes to primary keys on the source server are not replicated.

To use replication for fault tolerance, you must configure the destination server to account for the preceding factors. Replication does free up your destination database for useful work, and the latency is better than it would be with log shipping.

Application Requirements

Replication is frequently used when applications require data to be consolidated from one or more servers to a central repository; and/or to be transformed as it travels from one server to another. Frequently, DBAs will work in environments where they have a central office with multiple branch offices and they need to consolidate data centrally (often called point-of-sale, or POS, applications), or to distribute data to each branch office. Another example would be sales agents who visit clients, take their orders, and synchronize the orders nightly or when they return to the office one week later (often called field force automation, or FFA, applications). A classic example of this is a delivery fleet that updates their order details using their PDAs (running SQL Server 2005 Mobile Edition) at their delivery locations, after which the order details are replicated over the Internet to their head office (often called field force automation, or FFA, applications). Replication can be used to consolidate data centrally, or to replicate data from one RDBMS server to another; you can replicate from SQL Server to previous versions of SQL Server, Oracle Sybase, DB2, MS Access, and SQL CE (merge replication only). With SQL Server 2005, you can now replicate from Oracle servers to SQL Server. Replication can be used to replicate to the same database.

Performance Gains

Replication is frequently used when you need to move your reporting functionality off your main SQL Server to a separate SQL Server. With replication, as opposed to other data distribution solutions (log shipping, data mirroring, or hardware data mirroring), you can have completely different indexes or even tables on your reporting server and keep both servers in sync with the same data. You can also improve aggregate read performance by replicating the same data to a bank of SQL Servers; instead of having 1,000 users reading a single server, the load is distributed over 10 SQL Servers so that 100 users read a single server, achieving 10 times the read performance. Another example of improving performance using replication is when you have branch offices connecting over the WAN to a head office to connect to the central SQL Server. The latency involved with this network hop can cause the application to crawl; and while a Citrix or Terminal Services solution is ideal for distributed environments like this, frequently the most effective approach is to replicate the data to SQL Servers in the branch offices, and have the users' applications use this database. Then the changes can be replicated centrally. Another interesting approach is to replicate data to worker nodes that will perform batch operations on the data and then replicate it back upon completion. You can get considerable performance improvements by offloading such batch processing to these worker nodes.

Data Distribution

Replication is often used when you need to support a large group of users from multiple servers. Each server contains a copy of the same data, so it doesn't matter which server a user relies on to obtain data. Distributing the data also enhances many of the other reasons for using replication. You obtain fault tolerance by having multiple copies of the data available on a number of machines. Even if one machine experiences downtime, users can still access the data on another machine. Often, this redundancy addresses specific application needs, such as performance or uptime requirements. Finally, by enabling users to access data from a distributed source, the system can enhance performance by accessing the least loaded machine.

Comparing Options for Distributing Data

Because there are many options for distributing data, it is important to understand how they vary in order to determine when replication is the best choice:

✦ **Distributed transactions:** This involves programmatic solutions whereby you apply your transactions on both the source server and the destination server, usually within the confines of a transaction. There is a price to pay in terms of latency for this and it usually involves considerable programming effort. Distributed transactions are used when real-time synchronization is a must; they are typically used in financial transactions.

✦ **Linked servers:** Linked servers are similar to distributed transactions, but typically you access a linked server within the database, as opposed to within your code. The performance costs of using a linked server do not make them scalable. Linked servers also provide access to a wider variety of data sources than SQL Server replication provides. Linked servers are typically used to connect with data sources that replication does not support or which require ad hoc access.

✦ **Triggers:** Triggers can be used to distribute data, but they are best suited to distributing data locally and considerable performance and administrative overhead is associated with their use. Typically, triggers are used for auditing purposes.

✦ **Integration Services** (formerly known as Data Transformation Services, or DTS)**:** IS can distribute data and has a very rich set of features for transforming data as it migrates from the source server to the destination server. In addition, Integration Services can be used to distribute data to a wider variety of data sources than SQL Server replication supports. IS does not track individual transactions, so if you choose to use Integration Services to distribute your data, you will have to replace the entire data set each time, or have some mechanism to determine what has changed on the source server so you can only replicate the changes. Integration Services is typically used with batch processes and not in processes that require minimal latency.

New in 2005 The snapshot isolation feature addresses performance and accessibility complaints users made about SQL Server 2000. By using this feature, you can improve overall performance and make it easier for users to get the data they need.

✦ **Backup/restore:** The previous options are used to distribute individual transactions. Backup/restore involves distributing the entire database. This is only a good solution when customers need copies of the entire database, which they will have to treat as read-only because a subsequent restored backup will overwrite the work done on the last restored copy. Users will have to disconnect from the database while the backup is restored, and there is no capability to migrate any work done on the destination server back to the source server. Nor is there any capability to distribute a portion of the data; you are limited to the entire database.

✦ **Log shipping:** Log shipping can be thought of as a continuous backup restore, which starts with a restore of the backup on the destination server, followed by periodic restores of the transaction logs. These logs must be restored in order, and all logs must be restored. Users will have to go offline as the backup and logs are installed. There is no capability to distribute a portion of the data; you are limited to the entire database. Log shipping does not provide the small latency that replication does, and it does not allow you to send a subset of your data to the destination server. In addition, you cannot massage the data in any way while sending the data from the source server to the destination server.

✦ **Microsoft SQL Server data mirroring:** Data mirroring, new in SQL 2005, will mirror a database between two servers. It requires a third SQL Server (called a *witness*) that will determine when the source server goes offline, and will failover clients to the destination server. Data mirroring uses continuous log shipping under the covers. It works well for mid-size databases under medium load.

✦ **Clustering:** Clustering involves specialized hardware and requires different versions of the OS. Clustering involves sharing a database, SQL Server, or resource between nodes. Clients connect to a virtualized SQL Server, which will connect to an underlying node to access the shared resource. If a resource fails, the virtualized SQL Server/resource will be migrated to the failover node, with little impact on the clients. Clustering is not a data distribution technology, but rather a fault-tolerant solution designed to minimize downtime or provide high availability. Clustering should be used for fault tolerance over replication; it "distributes" an entire SQL server.

✦ **Software data mirroring:** These products install a file system driver that interrupts file activity and replicates this activity to a destination server. These host-based products consume RAM and CPU on the host (source server). They offer similar functionality to hardware data mirroring but they don't offer the same performance (although they come close). An example of a software data mirroring provider is Double-Take.

✦ **Hardware data mirroring:** Hardware data mirroring, offered as hardware products by vendors such as Hitachi Data Systems, EMC, or Veritas, replicate changes that happen on the byte level from one disk array to another array. These solutions make heavy use of caching and tend to be very expensive and complex, but they are required when the cost of downtime is significant.

The preceding list is ordered according to level of granularity. For instance, the first three alternatives distribute data at the transaction level. DTS and replication are performed on an article or table level. Log shipping and data mirroring are performed on a database level. Clustering, and hardware and software data mirroring, mirror servers or disk arrays. These solutions are also ordered according to required skill set for the DBA and expense, although the expense of programming distributed transactions can be considerable.

To view metadata about database objects published as articles in a replication topology, select `sysdm_repl_articles` from the dynamic management view.

Replication can replicate a subset of your tables, columns, or rows. Replication can also replicate partitioned tables, the schema of stored procedures (as well as the execution of a stored procedure), views, indexed views (as an indexed view or as a table that represents the indexed view), user-defined types and functions, full-text indexes, alias data types, schema objects (constraints, indexes, user triggers, extended properties, and collation) and DDL (such as alter table statements, etc.). The latency you will see with a replication solution in a production environment under load is typically under one minute. Replication is a low-cost alternative that offers a high degree of flexibility that the other solutions do not offer.

The Microsoft Model

Microsoft's replication model is based on Sybase's Replication Server (Microsoft SQL Server itself was based on Sybase); however, SQL Server's replication component ships with all versions except for SQL Server 2005 Express and SQL 2005 Mobile Edition, although both of these versions can be subscribers to SQL Server 2005 publications. (SQL Server 2005 Mobile

Edition, the new version of SQL CE, which runs on PDAs or handhelds, can only be a subscriber to merge publications.) The model is based on metaphors from the world of magazine publishing. The following sections explore each of the components. SQL Server 2000 shipped with a code sample that illustrated how to publish from heterogeneous servers to SQL Server. This functionality is still available in SQL Server 2005.

Publisher

A *publisher* is a source server that contains the objects and data you wish to replicate. Typically, the publisher will be a SQL Server 2005 server, but it can also be a SQL 2000 server or an Oracle Server publishing to a SQL 2005 Server. SQL Server ships with a replication provider that enables you to create third-party publishers.

Note   SQL Server 2005 can act as a gateway, so you can publisher from an Oracle server to SQL Server 2005 and then republish to another SQL Server (2000 or 2005) or to heterogeneous subscribers.

Subscriber

The *subscriber* subscribes to, or receives, the objects' schema and their data (called a *subscription*) from the publisher. A subscriber may receive subscriptions from one or more publishers. Subscribers can be SQL Server 2005, SQL Server 2005 Mobile Edition, SQL 2000, or SQL 7 servers. For the most part, subscribers will be read-only, but with certain replication types they can publish data back to the publisher.

Distributor

The *distributor* is an SQL server that distributes the schema, data, and subsequent transactions from the publisher to the subscriber. It also stores historical information about the subscriptions. Normally, the publisher and distributor will be on the same machine, but if you are under significant load, some replication types will benefit by migrating the distributor to a separate server from the publisher. Core to the distributor is the *distribution database,* which is the repository for historical information and replication metadata used by snapshot and transactional replication. A publisher can only use one distribution database. A distributor can provide one or more distribution databases for different publishers; each of these publishers could use their own distribution database, or they could share a single distribution database with other publishers.

Central Publisher

In the most common replication typology, a publisher publishes schema and data to one or more subscribers. Central publishers are most frequently used when you have a central office or repository that is publishing to one or more branch offices, reporting servers, worker nodes, and so on.

Central Subscriber

A central subscriber is typically used when you are consolidating data, perhaps from branch offices centrally, to a reporting server, or in a data warehouse to your central repository. In the central subscriber model, the remote publishers can publish the same articles or different articles to the central subscriber.

Republishing

Republishing refers to situations in which a subscriber also acts as a publisher, publishing the same articles to which it subscribes to other subscribers. This topology can work well when you need to scale out your replicating solution. For instance, you could have a central office, which publishes to regional offices, which in turn publish to local subscribers. For republishing to work well, you must understand how data flows and which server owns the data or has the authoritative source of the data; this will lead to a consistent end-to-end replication solution. If you don't have such control of data flow, duplicate data could be entered at various locations, or you could wind up with data islands, whereby data exists in downstream locations, but not in upstream locations.

Peer-to-Peer

The peer-to-peer model is new in SQL Server 2005. It is similar to bi-directional transactional replication, but bi-directional replication was limited to two nodes. In peer-to-peer replication, two or more SQL Servers replicate to each other using transactional replication. If one of the nodes goes offline or is disconnected from the others nodes participating in the peer-to-peer topology, clients can continue to use this node, and when this node reconnects with the other nodes in the topology, all nodes synchronize to a consistent state. This replication model was designed with the "update anywhere" paradigm in mind, to provide improved read and write performance as well as higher availability by scaling out database activity to multiple nodes. A client may connect to any node involved in a peer-to-peer replication model, make a change, and have that change reflected in all the nodes participating in the peer-to-peer topology. For the peer-to-peer replication model to work successfully, the data should be carefully partitioned to minimize conflicts. A conflict describes any of the following:

✦ Data with the same PK value is inserted in different nodes simultaneously and when the replication process moves this data to the other nodes, a primary key collision takes place.

✦ Data is updated on one node but simultaneously deleted on the other node.

✦ An update or delete statement affects a different number of rows when applied on different nodes. This is an indication that the databases do not have the same data and you have lost database consistency between the two databases.

Article

An article is the smallest unit that you can publish. An article can be any of the following: tables, partitioned tables, stored procedures (Transact-SQL and CLR), stored procedure execution (Transact-SQL and CLR), views, indexed views, indexed views as tables, user-defined types (CLR), user-defined functions (Transact-SQL and CLR), alias data types, full-text indexes, and schema objects (constraints, indexes, user triggers, extended properties, and collation). For views, indexed views, stored procedures and functions, only the schema is replicated, although you can replicate indexed views to tables, and you can replicate the execution of stored procedures. Normally, for logistical or administrative reasons, there is one publication per database, with all articles belonging to the publication. The main scenario in which you might want to put separate articles into different publication is when the publications are of different replication types (e.g., merge and transactional). In SQL 2000, you could split the articles into different publications for two main benefits:

✦ **Improved performance:** The independent agent option in transactional replication can result in two or more parallel streams of data going to a single subscription database.

✦ **Greater reliability:** Replicating large tables can be troublesome. Placing large tables in their own publication enables you to use alternative methods to deploy them, or to recover from failures to them without affecting replication of other articles belonging to different publications.

By default, snapshots are restartable in SQL Server 2005 (if your distribution agent fails to apply the entire snapshot, the next time it is run it will only fill in the missing pieces of the snapshot and not restart from the beginning) and the independent option is enabled by default.

In general, you should at least group your publication by DRI — in other words, by table or data dependencies.

Push Subscriptions

A push subscription is a subscription initiated by the publisher. In other words, the publisher will control when the snapshot and subsequent replication commands are sent to the subscriber. Tracking information and replication metadata is stored at the publisher.

Push subscriptions are used in the following circumstances:

✦ You have a relatively small number of subscribers.

✦ You are replicating over the LAN or WAN; push subscriptions do not work well over the Internet.

✦ You want a central point of administration.

Push subscriptions are the simplest form of subscription to deploy and consequently are the most frequently deployed subscription type.

Pull Subscriptions

A pull subscription is a subscription in which the subscriber controls when it receives the snapshot and data. Using pull subscriptions can lessen the load on your publisher/distributor because the distribution or merge agents will run on the subscriber, making your replication solution much more scalable. Pull subscriptions are suitable in the following circumstances:

✦ You have a large number of subscribers.

✦ You are replicating over unreliable links or the Internet and the subscribers are autonomous, i.e., they will determine when they wish to receive data.

✦ You don't require a central point of administration.

Pull subscriptions need more work to deploy and tend to need more maintenance but are frequently the best choice for larger replication environments.

Replication Types

There are three basic replication types:

✦ Snapshot

✦ Transactional

✦ Merge

Snapshot and transactional replication types are mainly used when the subscribers are read-only; in other words, the changes that you replicate originate on the source only and are replicated to the subscriber. However, two variations to the transactional and snapshot models allow changes that occur on the subscriber to be replicated back to the publisher. Merge replication is designed for bi-directional replication to clients that are frequently offline—for instance, a sales force that takes their laptops to client offices on sales calls, synchronizing periodically while in the field.

Snapshot Replication

Snapshot replication uses the metaphor of a *snapshot* from the world of photography. A snapshot publication provides a "point in time" image of your data and sends it to your destination server. Snapshot replication is ideal in the following scenarios:

✦ The nature of your data is not time dependent and changes infrequently.

✦ The bulk of your data changes at discreet intervals.

✦ The volume of data is not large.

Snapshot replication does not require primary keys on tables it is replicating. Consequently, many DBAs will use it in place of transactional replication, which does require a primary key. Frequently, however, there will be a candidate key on the tables you are replicating with snapshot replication. If you can identify these candidate keys and convert them to primary keys, transactional replication is often a better choice.

Snapshot replication allows you to replicate tables, partitioned tables, stored procedures, stored procedure views, indexed views, indexed views as tables, user-defined types (CLR), user-defined functions (Transact-SQL and CLR), alias data types, full-text indexes, and schema objects. You can also replicate a subset of the tables or views—for instance, a subset of the columns or a subset of the rows. Snapshot replication has two components:

✦ A snapshot agent

✦ A distribution agent

The snapshot agent is what generates the creation scripts and the data for objects you are replicating. The snapshot agent writes these creation scripts and the object's data to a directory in the file system called the *snapshot folder*. Commands are also written to the distribution database, which the distribution agent uses to create the replicated objects on the subscriber using the creation scripts and data found in the snapshot folder. The distribution agent is what distributes the data from the publisher to the subscriber.

Snapshot replication is not as scalable as transactional replication, especially when your bandwidth is limited. Use transactional replication whenever possible, as only the changes will be replicated with transactional replication, whereas with snapshot replication your entire data set will be replicated each time.

Snapshot Replication with Immediate Updating

Snapshot replication with immediate updating allows changes that occur on the subscriber to be replicated via a two-phase commit process using MS's DTC (Distributed Transaction Coordinator) back to the publisher. Changes that occur on the publisher will remain there until the next snapshot is generated by the snapshot agent and distributed by the distribution agent. The commit process will commit the transaction that originated on the subscriber first on the publisher and then back on the subscriber. One of the side effects of this process is that the identity ranges are continually in synchronization between the publisher and the subscriber. This type of snapshot replication is useful used when the majority of the transactions originate on the publisher. Note two drawbacks to using immediate updating:

✦ Increased transaction commit time on the subscriber as the transaction is first committed to the publisher and then the subscriber

✦ If the publisher goes offline or the link between the subscriber and publisher goes down, the transaction will hang on the subscriber for typically 20 or so seconds before being rolled back. The application must be able to gracefully handle such an event.

Note   This option is not available through the wizard, but only through replication stored procedures.

Snapshot Replication with Queued Updating

Snapshot replication with queued updating uses triggers on the replicated subscriber tables to log changes that originate on the subscriber to a queue. This queue is read by a *queue reader agent* that applies the transactions on the publisher. Changes originating on the publisher remain there until the snapshot agent runs again. In SQL 2000 you had the option to use MSMQ (Microsoft Message Queue) or a SQL Server table as your queue. In SQL 2005 you can only use SQL Server to provide the queuing services. Snapshot replication with queued updating is not a good option for more than 10 subscribers. Note that this option is not available through any of the wizards, only through the replication stored procedures.

Snapshot Replication with Immediate Updating and Queued Failover

Snapshot replication with immediate updating and queued failover allows a replication solution using immediate updating to failover to queued replication if you need to bring your publisher offline for maintenance or planned downtime. Note that this option is not available through the wizards, only through the replication stored procedures.

Transactional Replication

Snapshot replication sends the entire data set (or a subset of the rows or columns if you are using filtering) to the subscriber each time a new snapshot is generated. Snapshot replication can provide point-in-time synchronization. After the snapshot is generated and distributed to the subscriber(s), the subscriber becomes increasingly out of sync with the publisher. The subscriber will become synchronized with the publisher the next time the snapshot is generated and distributed. The term for the degree to which the subscriber is out of sync with the publisher is called *latency*. Latency with snapshot replication is typically very large.

Transactional replication uses the transaction log to generate transactions for replication to the subscribers. It is more scalable than snapshot replication because only the transactions or changes are replicated. The latency is much less than with snapshot replication, as changes are continually being applied to the subscriber.

Transactional replication has three components: a snapshot agent to generate the schema, data, and necessary replication metadata to track the replication process, a distribution agent to distribute the snapshot and subsequent commands, and a log reader agent to read the transaction log for the publication database.

Snapshot Agent

The snapshot agent is shared between the snapshot, transactional, and merge replication types. It generates the schema for the objects being replicated, any associated data, and required replication tracking metadata in the form of text and binary files, which it writes to a folder within the default snapshot folder or another specified location. It then writes tracking data to the distribution database, which the distribution agent will read to synchronize the subscriber with the publisher.

Log Reader Agent

The log reader agent polls the transaction logs looking for transactions to replicate to the subscriber. It writes the identifiers for these transactions to a table in your distribution database called `msrepl_transactions`. It breaks down these transactions into singleton commands: one command for each affected row.

Consider a transaction that updates 100 rows on your publisher, such as an update, insert (a select into), or delete. This transaction will be written to the transaction log as a single transaction, and then the log reader will read the transaction and make an entry for this transaction in the distribution database table (`Msrepl_Transactions`). It will then break this transaction down into singleton commands, writing these commands to the distribution database table `MSRepl_Commands` (the reason for this is discussed in the following section). If the command is large, the single command may be written over multiple rows in the distribution database. These commands are stored in binary format but you can read them using the replication stored procedure `sp_browsereplcmds`, which you can find in the distribution databases. By default, the commands that transactional replication uses to synchronize the data originating on the publisher to the subscriber are in the form of stored procedures. You can also optionally use DML statements (`INSERT`, `UPDATE`, `DELETE`), which are necessary if you are replicating to heterogeneous data sources (i.e., non-SQL-Server subscribers).

Note   A singleton is a statement that affects one row.

Once the log reader agent has written this information to the distribution database it places markers in the transaction log indicating that this transaction has been committed to the distribution database. These portions of the log can then be reclaimed if you dump the log and are running the full recovery model or you are running the simple recovery model. Note that transactional replication works with every recovery model you select.

Distribution Agent

The distribution agent distributes the commands in the distribution database to the subscriber. It also removes from the distribution database any commands that have been replicated to all subscribers and are beyond the retention period defined for the distribution database.

The transactional replication process breaks down transactions to singletons so that it can count how many rows are affected by each singleton when it is applied on the subscriber by the distribution agent. If a singleton affects 0 or more than one rows, the replication process will gracefully fail and tell the distribution agent that there is a data consistency problem. This verification process is what ensures that the publisher and subscriber are in a consistent state; in other words, the subscriber will always have the data as the subscriber. The distribution agent applies all the singleton commands (which form the original transaction) in the context of a transaction. If one of these constituent single commands fail, all the singletons that form the transaction will be rolled back. It is in this sense that transactional replication replicates transactionally.

Peer-to-Peer Replication

Peer-to-peer replication, new to SQL Server 2005, is an option with transactional replication. All nodes in a peer-to-peer replication topology subscribe and publish from and to all other nodes. A transaction originating at one node will be replicated to all other nodes, but not replicated back to its originator. This replication model is intended for use in applications that have multiple databases or database servers participating in a scale-out solution. Clients may connect to one of many databases, which typically have the same data. One of the databases or database servers can be removed from the bank of servers participating in the scale-out solution and the load will be distributed among the remaining databases or databases servers. All nodes in a peer-to-peer replication solution contain identical copies of the data.

Peer-to-peer replication addresses concerns that users of SQL Server 2000 had about ensuring that a distributed set of servers remained updated.

Bi-directional Transactional Replication

Bi-directional transactional replication is best used when you are able to partition your replication solution to minimize conflicts or when you know that only one side of your replication solution will be writeable at any one time. Bi-directional transactional replication only works between two nodes, i.e., one publisher-subscriber pair.

Transactional Replication with Immediate Updating

Transactional replication with immediate updating is similar to snapshot replication with immediate updating — only changes occurring on the publisher are replicated to the subscriber, via the distribution agent, every time the distribution agent runs. Changes occurring on the subscriber are replicated back to the publisher via a two-phase commit process implemented using Microsoft's DTC (Distributed Transaction Coordinator). If you choose to use this you must have a very reliable link between your publisher and subscriber. If your link goes down or your publisher becomes unavailable, transactions originating on your subscriber will hang for 20 seconds and then be rolled back.

Transactional Replication with Queued Updating

Transactional replication with queued updating is similar to snapshot replication with queued updating, but changes occurring on the publisher are replicated to the subscriber via the distribution agent every time the distribution agent runs. Changes occurring on the subscriber are replicated back to the publisher via the queue reader agent. Transactional replication with queued updating is best used when the following applies:

✦ The number of changes originating on the subscriber are a small fraction of the changes originating on the publisher.

✦ There are 10 or fewer subscribers.

If both of these conditions are not met your replication solution will not be optimal; you will experience frequent deadlocks while the queue reader is running.

Transactional Replication with Immediate Updating and Queued Failover

Transactional replication with immediate updating is useful when the following applies:

✦ The bulk of your transactions originate on your publisher.

✦ Some of the transactions originate on your subscriber and you want them replicated to your publisher.

✦ There are a small number of subscribers.

✦ You want to be able to take your publisher offline.

In this case, you can use immediate updating with queued failover. You will have to manually modify your subscriptions from immediate updating to queued by issuing the stored procedure call `sp_setreplfailovermode` (with a setting of *queued,* to failover to queued updating, or *immediate,* to fail over to immediate updating when connectivity has been restored).

Transactional Replication over the Internet

Microsoft recommends that when you replicate over the Internet you use a virtual private network (VPN) to provide a highly secure replication solution. If you don't, you will likely have to use pull subscriptions, with anonymous subscribers, and download your snapshot using FTP. If you do use FTP, there is always a chance that hackers will be able to access your snapshot and possibly compromise your server.

VPNs provide an essential service for businesses that need to track data across large distances. In fact, as the presence of the Internet grows even in remote areas, so does the use of VPNs. You can obtain additional information about the inner workings of VPNs at `http://computer.howstuffworks.com/vpn.htm`.

Merge Replication

Merge replication is designed with mobile or frequently offline clients in mind. Changes can be made on the publisher or the subscriber; and when the merge agent runs, these changes are synchronized and both the publisher and subscriber will converge to the same values. Merge replication works by implementing triggers on each table that you are replicating and by using a GUID column with GUID values to uniquely track every row on all the tables being replicated. When a change is made to one of these tables, the change is recorded in a metadata table that contains a list of GUIDs corresponding to the rows that have changed in the database participating in merge replication. When the merge agent runs, it gathers a list of the GUIDS in these metadata tables, which represents the rows in the tables that have changed on the publisher and subscriber. For the rows that have changed on only the publisher or only the subscriber, the merge replication agent will retrieve the rows' values from the underlying table on the publisher or subscriber, and then insert, delete, or update the row where the row is not present, or not updated. If the row has been modified on both sides of the replication solution between merge agent runs, the merge agent will detect this change as a conflict and make a decision based on how you have specified you want conflicts resolved. By default, the publisher will win most conflicts. To change the way conflicts are resolved, you can select the resolver to be used after you create the publication using the New Publication Wizard:

1. Right-click the publication you want to modify and choose Properties from the context menu.

2. Select the Articles folder.

3. Click the Article Properties button, select Select properties of Highlighted Table article or Set properties of All Table articles, and then select the Resolver tab (see Figure 39-1).

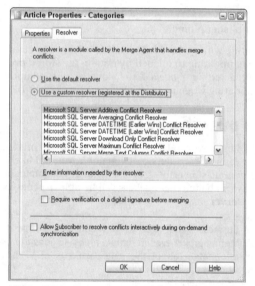

Figure 39-1: Custom resolvers for merge replication

 To view metadata about table columns published by replication, select `sysdm_repl_schemas` from the dynamic management view.

The default is Use the Default Resolver, which means the publisher or subscriber with the highest priority wins. The following options are available:

✦ **Microsoft SQL Server Additive Conflict Resolver:** Values of the column defined in the "Enter information needed by the resolver" text box are summed together for conflicting rows.

✦ **Microsoft SQL Server Averaging Conflict Resolver:** Values of the column defined in the "Enter information needed by the resolver" text box are averaged together for conflicting rows.

✦ **Microsoft SQL Server DATETIME (Earlier Wins) Conflict Resolver:** The row with the earlier value for the column defined in the "Enter information needed by the resolver" text box wins the conflict.

✦ **Microsoft SQL Server DATETIME (Later Wins) Conflict Resolver:** The row with the later value for the column defined in the "Enter information needed by the resolver" text box wins the conflict.

✦ **Microsoft SQL Server Download Only Conflict Resolver:** The data downloaded wins.

✦ **Microsoft SQL Server Maximum Conflict Resolver:** The row with the highest value in the column defined in the "Enter information needed by the resolver" text box wins the conflict.

✦ **Microsoft SQL Server Merge Text Columns Conflict Resolver:** Data in the text column defined in the "Enter information needed by the resolver" text box wins the conflict.

✦ **Microsoft SQL Server Minimum Conflict Resolver:** The row with the highest value in the column defined in the "Enter information needed by the resolver" text box wins the conflict.

✦ **Microsoft SQL Server Priority Conflict Resolver:** The row with the highest priority wins the conflict.

✦ **Microsoft SQL Server Subscriber Always Wins Conflict Resolver:** The subscriber always wins any conflict.

✦ **Microsoft SQL Server Upload Only Conflict Resolver:** The row uploaded from the subscriber wins the conflict.

✦ **Microsoft SQL Server Stored Procedure Conflict Resolver:** The conflict is resolved based on the stored procedure defined in the "Enter information needed by the resolver" text box.

You also have two other options:

✦ Create your own custom resolver using stored procedures or COM-based components.

✦ Use custom logic defined in the `Microsoft.SqlServer.Replication.BusinessLogicSupport` namespace with RMO.

You can also perform column-level tracking, which means that updates are tracked on a column-level basis, so if someone updates a phone number and someone else simultaneously updates the address of the same row, when the merge agent runs it will merge the two columns together without overwriting the data — the new phone number and new address will appear in both the publisher and subscriber. You also have the option of doing interactive conflict resolution for update and delete conflicts. This option is available when you pull the subscription using Windows Synchronization Manager and you enable Windows Synchronization Manager and your publication for interactive conflict resolution. When a conflict is detected, the conflict wizard will be launched and the user on the subscriber machine has the opportunity to resolve the conflict at that time or to select the default conflict resolution selection.

Merge Replication and SQL CE or SQL Mobile Subscribers

SQL Server 2005 enables users of SQL CE or SQL Mobile clients to subscribe to merge publications. SQL 2005 Mobile clients can subscribe to multiple publications, but SQL CE subscribers can only subscribe to a single publication per SQL CE database.

Merge Replication over the Internet

New in SQL Server 2005 is the capability to have your merge subscriptions securely connect over the Internet and synchronize with your merge publisher using HTTPS, through a process called *web synchronization*. You can still replicate across the Internet deploying your subscriptions through FTP but this process is considered insecure.

New in SQL 2005 Replication

The following sections describe what is new in SQL 2005 replication.

Restartable Snapshots

In previous of SQL Server you had to redeploy an entire snapshot from the beginning if your snapshot deployment failed in the last few tables or rows. In SQL Server 2005, when you restart the distribution agent, only the missing parts of the snapshot will be redeployed.

Oracle Publishing

SQL Server 2005 allows you to configure an Oracle RDBMS to publish to a SQL Server 2005 subscriber or distributor. The Configuration Wizard puts triggers on the Oracle tables. These triggers track changes and then send them to the SQL Server 2005 subscribers. You can only enable an Oracle server for transactional or snapshot replication — merge publications are not supported on Oracle sever. The publication is deployed through a script run on the Oracle publisher that allows for easy removal of all replication objects and metadata on the Oracle publisher.

Very Tight Security

SQL Server 2005 has been designed from the ground up to be highly secure. Nowhere is the security effort more visible than in replication. Previously, all replication types used an Admin share from which to download the snapshots. This has been replaced in SQL Server 2005 with a local path (i.e., \Program Files\Microsoft SQL Server\MSSQL.1\Repldata), but you have the option to configure the default snapshot location for a share for pull subscribers who will not be able to access the local path. All replication agents have the ability to run under a security account different from the one under which your SQL Server Agent account runs. This enables you to have the replication agents run under lower security privilege accounts than was possible in SQL Server 2000. Merge replication subscribers can now connect with your web server over HTTPS and synchronize, which is much more secure than the options available in SQL Server 2000.

Peer-to-Peer Replication Model

As mentioned previously, the peer-to-peer transactional replication topology allows you to scale out your high-availability solution to multiple clients for a "write anywhere" model. Instead of having 1,000 users simultaneously accessing one server with considerable horsepower, you would have 10 SQL Servers with identical data divide your 1,000 users over all 10 SQL Servers — i.e., 100 users per SQL Server. Less contention means much better performance, and each of the SQL Servers requires less hardware than the single SQL Server. In the peer-to-peer model, any data change on one node is replicated to all other nodes, so all nodes have exactly the same data. Using this topology, you must ensure that conflicts are minimized by partitioning, or by having all write activity only occur on one node. Otherwise, your distribution agent will fail and your nodes will become progressively out of sync.

To enable a transactional replication to participate in a peer-to-peer topology, create a normal transactional publication (not a transactional publication with updateable subscribers). After your publication is created, right-click on your publication, select Subscription Options, and set Allow Peer to Peer Subscriptions to True. Deploy your subscription to all subscribers. After the subscriptions have been deployed to all subscribers, right-click on your publication and select Configure Peer to Peer Configuration Wizard.

Replicating All DDL

You now have the capability to optionally replicate all `ALTER` statements, including `ALTER TABLE`, `ALTER VIEW`, `ALTER PROCEDURE`, `ALTER FUNCTION`, and `ALTER TRIGGER`.

In prior versions of SQL Server, you frequently had to drop your publications to make schema changes, although in SQL Server 2000 you could make some changes via the replication stored procedures `sp_repladdcolumn` and `sp_repldropcolumn`.

You also have the option of disabling the replication of schema changes by right-clicking on your publication selection properties, and then clicking Subscription Options. Change the Replication Schema Options to False. This option is available in all replication types.

Replicating Full-Text Indexes

SQL Server 2005 allows you to replicate SQL Server full-text indexes. For this to work, you must enable the subscriber database for full-text indexing, and you must specify this property in the article's properties. When you get the articles dialog, click the Article Properties button, click Set Properties of Highlighted Table Article, or Set Properties of All Table articles, and ensure that the Copy Full-Text Indexes option is set to True.

Allowing Anonymous Subscriptions for All Publications

SQL Server 2000 had two types of subscribers: named and anonymous. Named subscribers were used for small numbers of subscribers. Replication metadata would be stored for each subscriber and purged when deployed to each subscriber. Replication metadata was not tracked with anonymous subscribers, and subscriptions were typically the same for each subscriber. A publication would have to be created for a named subscriber or an anonymous subscriber. In SQL Server 2005 all publications can be deployed to named or anonymous subscribers.

Logical Records in Merge Replication

In SQL Server 2000, updates occurring on tables related by DRI and published in merge publication could be applied on the subscriber or publisher out of order. For instance, child records could arrive before the parent record arrived on the publisher. In some cases, the merge agent would fail, requiring a restart. In SQL Server 2005, transactions are replicated as a logical unit called *logical records,* whereby parent records are replicated before child records.

Precomputed Partitions

Precomputed partitions are a feature of merge replication in SQL Server 2005. In SQL Server 2000, when the merge agent ran, it would determine which of the changed rows should be merged with particular subscribers. This process could cause performance degradation. With

SQL Server 2005, you can enable precomputation of the partitions, which means that the selection of rows to be sent to a particular subscriber will be done in advance of the merge agent running. Consequently, the merge agents run faster and with less performance degradation.

Updates to Unique Keys

In SQL Server 2000, an update to a primary key column would be segmented into a delete operation followed by an insert. This could cause problems with cascading deletes on tables. In SQL Server 2005, updates to primary key columns are replicated as update statements, resulting in improved performance.

Custom Conflict Handling through SQL RMO

In SQL Server 2000, you could create COM objects or stored procedures to provide custom logic for handing conflicts with merge replication. In SQL Server 2005, you can create custom logic using RMO with the `Microsoft.SqlServer.Replication.BusinessLogicSupport` namespace. You can also use this object for handling errors and data changes.

Numerous Performance Improvements

Snapshots are now generated by default with the concurrent snapshot option for transactional replication, which means that brief locks are held while the snapshot is generated. In SQL Server 2000, replicated tables would be locked while the snapshot was generated. Agents now auto-sense the network state and reconnect when the link becomes available. Agent failures in SQL Server 2000 due to network failure would require DBA intervention to restart them when the link was available again. There is also improved blob support in merge and updateable subscriptions.

Latency Tokens

One of the most frequently asked questions in transactional replication is, How out of date is my subscriber from my publisher? In other words, how soon after a transaction is applied on the publisher does the transaction get applied on the subscriber? SQL Server 2005's Replication Monitor has a tab called Tracer Tokens for transactional. Clicking the Insert Tracer button on this tab will insert a record on the publisher that enables you to tell how long it takes for the record to be applied on the publisher (see Figure 39-2).

Transactional Parallelism

In SQL Server 2000, all transactional publications from a single database to a particular subscriber would share a distribution agent. For named subscriptions you could enable multiple distribution agents called *independent agents*. With this option you could have two or more parallel streams of data being sent to a subscriber at any one time. This independent agent is the default in SQL 2005, which results in much better transactional replication distribution performance.

Download Only Articles

Also new in SQL Server 2005 is the capability to specify that certain articles are "download only" (data only moves from the publisher to the subscriber). If changes occur to a table that is defined as download only and is published for merge replication, then changes originating on the subscriber will not be merged with the publisher and will stay in the subscriber. Changes occurring on the publisher will be merged with the subscriber.

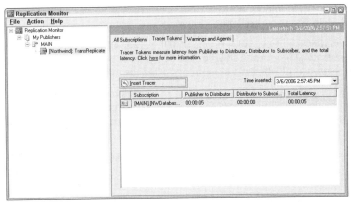

Figure 39-2: Use tracer tokens to monitor the latency of updates between publisher and subscriber.

Replication Monitor

Replication monitor has been completely redesigned, and is now your central point of replication maintenance. Replication Monitor is no longer integrated into Enterprise Manager or SQL Server WorkBench, but rather is a separate management console. You can launch Replication Monitor from the command line by navigating to `\Program Files\Microsoft SQL Server\90\Tools\Binn` and typing **sqlmonitor.exe.** Alternately, you can launch it within Management Studio by right-clicking the Replication folder for your SQL Server and choosing Launch Replication Monitor from the context menu. Replication Monitor, shown in Figure 39-3, is very similar to the Replication Monitor Group present in SQL Server 2000, enabling you to quickly get health checks on all of the SQL Servers you have elected to monitor.

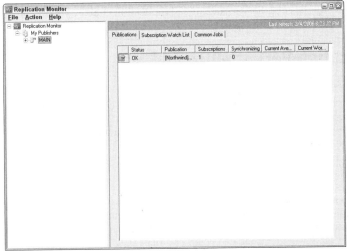

Figure 39-3: The Replication Monitor has been redesigned for ease of use.

In Figure 39-3, the Replication Monitor's current focus is on the SQL Server 2005 instance of the SQL Server called Main. Some of the Replication Monitor's features are as follows:

✦ Greatly improved metrics. Previous versions of SQL Server showed three states of replication jobs: successful, failed, and retrying. The SQL Server 2005 Replication Monitor adds a caution symbol indicating the state of performance problems.

✦ Minimized performance impact of monitoring. In prior versions of SQL Server, replication monitoring could cause locking on replication systems under significant load. The Replication Monitor has been redesigned from the ground up to minimize the performance impact of monitoring.

✦ Greatly improved monitoring of merge replication. The Replication Monitor now provides per-article statistics for merge replication, enabling administrators to quickly pinpoint problem articles.

✦ Tracer tokens for measuring the latency of transactional replication. These tokens allow you to get point-in-time estimates of transactional replication performance and latency estimates.

✦ Warnings when subscriptions are about to expire. Prior versions of SQL Server provided no indication when subscriptions were about to expire. The Replication Monitor in SQL Server 2005 provides warnings when subscriptions are about to expire.

Merge Replication over HTTPS

In prior versions of SQL Server, if you had to replicate over the Internet you were forced to use FTP or a VPN. VPNs tend to be slow and if you are not using Microsoft VPN client (select Start ⇨ Settings ⇨ Network and Dial-up Connections ⇨ Make a New Connection ⇨ Connect to a private network through the Internet), VPNs can be costly. FTP is considered to be an insecure solution because the FTP password travels across the Internet in plain text unless you are using anonymous access, which means anyone can download your snapshot. Connecting over the Internet also means opening port 1433 for inbound connections on your firewall, also considered a security risk. SQL Server 2005 merge replication enables you to configure a web server to allow web synchronizations of clients over the Internet via HTTPS.

Merge Replication Performance and Scalability Improvements

SQL Server 2005 offers many improvements to merge replication scalability and performance. Plain vanilla merge replication performance has increased at least 20 percent, but if you can take advantage of precomputed filtering you can achieve at least a doubling in performance. Articles that are download only can achieve a five-fold increase in performance.

SQL RMO

In SQL Server 2000, you could build publications and subscriptions using SQL DMO or replication stored procedures. SQL Server 2005 adds SQL RMO (Replication Management Objects), which is now the preferred method of creating replication objects (over SQL DMO). SQL RMO can be used in .NET and has smaller overhead than SQL DMO or replication stored procedures.

Simplified Wizards

The replication wizards have been greatly simplified. In SQL Server 2000, is took 52 mouse clicks to deploy the simplest publication to a subscriber. SQL Server 2005 replication wizards have the following advantages:

✦ 40 percent fewer pages (on average)

✦ Greatly simplified dialogs

✦ Improved default values and auto-detection

✦ Less branching

✦ All wizards provide you with the capability to script out the action or to execute it immediately.

✦ The push and pull subscription wizards have been consolidated into a single wizard. The New Subscription Wizard can simultaneously create multiple subscriptions with different properties for a publication. This can greatly decrease the effort of setting up replication for small deployments because you can generate all the subscriptions by running the wizard only once. For larger deployments, you can still generate scripts to ease the administrative overhead.

Initializing a Subscriber

In previous versions of SQL Server you could deploy your snapshot by running the snapshot agent to generate the schema and data in the file system, and then have the distribution or merge agent read these files and recreate the objects you are replicating on the subscriber(s). You also had the option to precreate the subscription database the way you wanted it through a manual process, and then do a no-sync subscription. Creating a subscription manually could involve a lot of work setting constraints and identity columns to NOT FOR REPLICA-TION, and putting the required replication stored procedures in place. Running the snapshot agent each time and sending the snapshot files to the subscriber(s) using the distributor or merge agents could be lengthy processes if your snapshots were large.

With SQL Server 2005 you have several options in addition to having the snapshot agent generate the snapshot and have the distribution or merge agents deploy it.

Backup and Restore

You can use a standard backup and restore procedure to create a subscription database on your subscriber. When you are deploying your subscriber, select the "initialize the subscriber" method.

Copy Database

You can also manually create all objects on the subscriber via the bulk copy program (bcp), DTS, or other data synchronization methods. You will have to do considerable work adding the NOT FOR REPLICATION clause to identity columns and foreign key constraints, and you will need to modify the replication stored procedures.

Dynamic Snapshots

With merge replication you can use dynamic snapshots, which enables you to filter your snapshot based on filtering criteria. This enables you to send to your subscriber only the data that this subscriber will use, as opposed to the entire snapshot.

Configuring Replication

To configure replication in SQL Server 2005, you need to connect to your SQL Server in Management Studio, right-click on the Replication folder, and select Configure Distribution. This will launch the Configure Distribution Wizard. Click Next to advance to the Distributor dialog. This enables you to configure the SQL Server to use a local distributor or a remote Distributor.

Using a Local Distributor

There is no hard-and-fast rule as to when you should use a local distributor versus a remote distributor. With a local distributor, your publisher serves as both publisher and distributor. With a remote distributor, your distributor is on a different SQL Server than your publisher. An indication as to when you should migrate to a remote distributor is when your log reader and distribution agents experience considerable locking.

To configure your SQL Server for a local distributor, select the default option in the Configure Distribution Wizard entitled "YourServerName will act as its own Distributor" and click Next. Accept the default path for your snapshot folder if you are using push subscriptions. If you are using pull subscriptions, share the path `C:\Program Files\Microsoft SQL Server\MSSQL.X\MSSQL\ReplData` and enter in the Snapshot Folder text box for this dialog the path `\\ServerName\ShareName`, where `ServerName` is the name of your publisher and `ShareName` is the name of your share, which maps to `C:\Program Files\Microsoft SQL Server\MSSQL.X\MSSQL\ReplData` and X is the instance name for your SQL Server 2005 instance. Make sure you give read rights to the account under which your distribution agents will run on the pull subscribers. You will have to have created the share in advance. Click Next and accept all the defaults (ideally, you would place your distribution database on a RAID 10 drive array for performance reasons), click Next again, click Next again to enable this server to use this distribution database, click Next to configure this server as a distributor (or to generate a script for this action to run later), and click Next to confirm the changes you are making. Then click Finish.

Your local distributor can act as a distributor for other publishers configured to use this distributor. These other publishers can use the default distribution database on the local distributor, or you can create a separate distributor for them. A publisher can only use a single distribution database and can only be configured to use a single distributor.

Using a Remote Distributor

If your SQL Server is under significant load, you might want to use a remote distributor. If you choose to use a remote distributor you must do the following:

✦ Configure the remote distributor as a distributor.

✦ Configure the publisher to use this distributor. (Connect with the distributor, select Distributor Properties, click Publishers, add the publisher using the Add button, and enter the administrative link password.)

✦ Have the administrative link password.

Ideally, the remote distributor will be on the local LAN and clustered, because if it goes offline your transaction logs on your publishing databases can get very large. If you do decide to select a remote distributor, click the Add button, connect to the distributor, enter the administrative link password, select the Configure Distributor check box (the default), click Next, and then click Finish.

Creating Snapshot Replication Publications

To create snapshot replication publications, connect to your SQL Server using Management Studio, expand the publication folder, and right-click on the Local Publications folder and select New Publication. Click Next in the New Publication Wizard dialog box. Select the database you wish to replicate, and click Next. For the publication type, select Snapshot Publication (this is the default). Click Next to launch the Articles dialog. Select the type of objects you wish to replicate by clicking on them, or expand the object type and select individual objects — for instance, expand tables and select individual tables to replicate.

If you drill down on an individual article, as Figure 39-4 illustrates, you have the option to deselect columns.

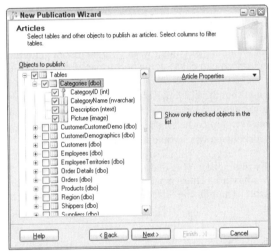

Figure 39-4: You always have the option of choosing the article and individual article columns.

You can choose which columns will not be replicated to the subscriber(s) by deselecting the columns, a process called *vertical filtering* or *vertical partitioning*. The example shown in Figure 39-4 replicates all of the columns, which is the setup you'll normally use.

By clicking on the Article Properties button you can modify the defaults for the articles (for instance, the object owner name, or even the name the article will have when replicated to the subscriber).

After you select each object you wish to replicate, click Next.

Note   You may get a dialog box entitled Article Issues. This dialog box warns you about problems you may have when you deploy your subscription. For instance, you may get a warning if you publish views or stored procedures that you must create the base objects these views or stored procedures reference. You will also get warnings that indexed views are only supported on SQL Server 2000 Enterprise Edition or later.

Clicking Next will launch the Filter Table Rows dialog box. This dialog gives you the opportunity to horizontally filter or partition your tables and views. You can choose to only replicate a portion of the rows — for instance, all rows in which the customer lives in California. To do this, click the Add button and select the table or article you wish to filter. Then click on the particular column that will be used as the basis of your filter. You can select multiple columns by prefacing them with a Boolean clause. For instance, your filter condition could look like this:

```
SELECT <published_columns> FROM [Person].[Address] WHERE [StateProvinceID]
=5 and[ModifiedDate] > getdate() -365
```

The preceding code filters by customers who live in the state of California and whose record has been modified over the past year (assuming a `StateProvinceID` of 5 means California). Your filter can include system functions such as `SUSER()`, `HOST_NAME()`, or `@@ServerName`. Note that `HOST_NAME()` resolves to the node of a cluster and the host agent is initialized. To have this resolve to your subscriber, you should use `@@Servername` and use a pull subscription. If you use a push subscription it will resolve to the publisher or distributor server name.

Clicking Next will launch the Snapshot Agent dialog box. Use this dialog box to schedule when you want your snapshot generated. For example, you might want your snapshot generated during off hours because snapshot generation can cause some performance degradation.

New in 2005

SQL Server 2005 provides better snapshot flexibility. By default, SQL Server 2005 generates any snapshot you create immediately, which means that you don't have to wait for the data to become available. However, this new approach can affect performance, so you can also tell SQL Server to generate the snapshot later when you don't require it immediately.

Click Next to launch the Agent Security dialog box. This dialog enables you to specify which account will be used to generate your snapshot. There is no default; set the account you wish to use. Click the Security Settings button to launch the Snapshot Agent Security dialog box, shown in Figure 39-5.

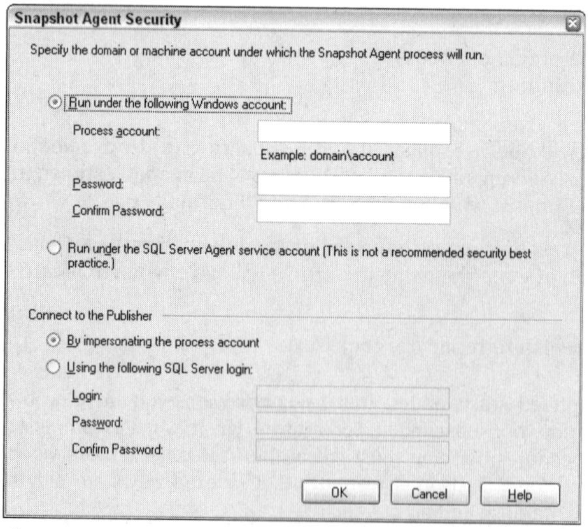

Figure 39-5: Use the Snapshot Agent Security dialog box to set the account for the replication.

Best Practice

Even though it might seem like a good idea to use the SQL Server Agent account for the snapshot, this account normally provides too many rights. Use an account specially designated for use by the snapshot agent. In addition to limiting the potential for security problems, using a separate account also enables you to perform account monitoring so that you can easily detect unwanted activity.

The options are to run the snapshot agent under a Windows account or the SQL Server Agent service account (the default for SQL Server 2000). Some DBAs felt that this gave the snapshot agent too many rights, so in SQL Server 2005 you have the option to select a lower-privilege account to run the snapshot agent under. This account is used when writing the snapshot files to the server running the snapshot share.

You also have the option to select the account your snapshot agent will use to connect to the publisher. In SQL Server 2000 this had to be a system administrator account. In SQL Server 2005 you can use a lower-privilege account. It is recommended that you use a Windows account, as it uses a higher level of encryption than what is available when using a SQL authentication account.

If you do choose to generate the script, the next dialog box will enable you to specify where you want the script file generated. Otherwise, you will get an article summary dialog box in which you can name your publication. You will then get a dialog displaying the status of the creation of your publication.

Next, you must create a subscription to your publication, a topic covered in the section "Creating Subscriptions."

Creating Transactional Replication Publications

Creating transactional replication publications is highly similar to creating snapshot publications. To create a transactional replication publication, connect to your SQL Server using Management Studio, expand the Replication folder, right-click on the Local Publications folder, and select New Publication. In the New Publication Wizard dialog box, click Next. In the Publication Database dialog box, select the database you want to publish. Click Next. This will launch the Publication Type dialog box, in which you should select Transactional Publication. Click Next. You will see a list of the object types you can publish, similar to the one shown earlier in Figure 39-4.

Use this dialog to select which object types you want to replicate. You can replicate all the members of an object type (i.e., all the tables or stored procedures) or you can expand the object type and only replicate some of the objects, e.g., some of the tables. As with snapshot replication, you can choose to vertically filter the objects by drilling down on the table, view, or indexed view, deselecting the column you do not want replicated to the subscriber.

To change the article's properties, click the Article Properties button. The resulting dialog box, shown in Figure 39-6, allows fine-grained control over how the articles are replicated to the subscriber(s).

You have several options, including assigning a different table owner or name on the subscriber (Destination object name or Destination object owner), specifying what happens if the object already exists on the subscriber, and specifying how transactions will be delivered to subscribers.

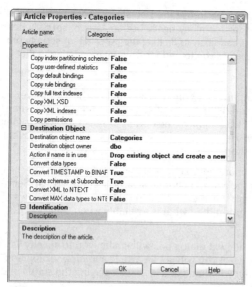

Figure 39-6: Article Properties dialog box

The available options for what happens if the object already exists on the subscriber are as follows:

✦ Drop the existing object and create a new one (the default).

✦ Keep the existing object unchanged.

✦ Delete data. If article has a row filter, delete only data that matches the filter.

✦ Truncate all data in the existing object.

In most cases, you will want to use the first option. If you have a central subscriber, you will probably want to use the third option. If you need to keep an archive, you will probably want the second option. If you need to replicate data to a fixed schema, use the last option — to truncate all data in the existing object.

You have the option to use a system-generated stored procedure with a system-generated name, or to use a system-generated stored procedure using a name of your own choosing (by entering the name you wish to use). You also have the option to choose how the transactions are replicated: using a stored procedure with the CALL format (CALL format replicates all columns whether they are changed or not, an option only available for INSERT and DELETE procedures), XCALL format, or MCALL format (MCALL format replicates only the columns that have been updated, an option only available for UPDATE procedures); using a DML statement (INSERT, UPDATE, or DELETE) without column names, using a DML with column names; or choosing not to have the statements replicated.

Some interesting options are available when replicating other object types. For instance, you have the option to replicate the execution of stored procedures or replicate the indexed view to tables on the subscriber.

After you have selected how you wish your objects to be replicated, click Next. You may get an Articles Issues dialog box. Evaluate the issues described in this dialog and adjust your article properties if necessary. Click Next to launch the Filter Table Rows dialog box.

If you wish to horizontally filter your table articles, click the Add button. You might want to review the information about filtering table articles in "Creating Snapshot Replication Publications." After you have created your filter, click Next. This will launch the Snapshot Agent dialog. Here you have the option to generate the snapshot immediately or schedule it at a later time.

Click Next. This will launch the Agent Security dialog box. Click the Security Settings dialog box. Review the Snapshot Agent Security options, described earlier. There is a check box that allows the log reader agent to inherit the security settings from the account used to generate snapshots. You can also deselect this option and set the security settings manually for the log reader agent. Click Next. The Wizard Actions dialog box will appear. Select whether you want to create the publication immediately, script it for later deployment, or both. Click Next to launch the Complete the Wizard dialog box. You can assign a name to your publication here and review the publication properties summary. Click Next to finish creating your publication. The Creating Publication dialog box will be launched.

For some transactional publications, you may need to modify some of the publication properties because there are no options to make these modifications during the publication creation. To make these modifications, expand the local publications folder and locate the publication you wish to modify. Right-click on it and select properties. There are seven sections:

✦ General

✦ Articles

✦ Filter Rows

✦ Snapshot

✦ FTP Snapshot

✦ Publication Access List

✦ Agent Security

Use the General tab to enter a description of your publication. There is also an option to control what happens if your subscriber is offline for more than a preset period. You have two options: to drop your subscription or to have it expire. If you choose to have your subscription expire, you will need to recreate and redeploy your snapshot. If you choose to have your subscription dropped, you will need to recreate your subscription on the expired subscriber. These options are necessary because the longer your subscriber is offline, the more replication metadata pools in the subscriber. This can cause overall performance degradation on your publisher; and depending on how much data has pooled on the publisher, sometimes it is more efficient to simply redeploy the snapshot.

Use the Articles tab to make changes to the articles that comprise your snapshot. You have the option to add or drop articles from your publication in this tab, or to change your article properties.

The Filter Rows tab enables you to modify existing filters or add new filters to your table articles.

Use the Snapshot tab to control where your snapshot is created (a default location; another location, typically a directory in your ftp site; or both), whether the snapshot in an alternative location is compressed, and scripts to be run before or after the snapshot is deployed on the subscriber. You may want to run a pre-snapshot script to create login accounts on your subscriber, or to enable your subscription database for full-text indexing. The post-snapshot command comes in handy if you want to enable constraints on your subscriber tables, for example.

The FTP Snapshot tab is useful for controlling options your subscribers will use when they connect via FTP to download your snapshot. For instance, you can enable your publication to be pulled via FTP, control whether anonymous authentication will be used, or specify an NT account that will be used when you are not using FTP authentication (note that NT security will not be applied, this account must be a local NT account and not a domain account, and the password will travel across the Internet in plain text), the FTP server name (note that the FTP server does not have to exist on the publisher or distributor), the FTP port to use, and the path from the FTP root (you should enter /ftp here).

The Snapshot tab has several options that control aspects of your distribution agent:

✦ **Independent Distribution Agent:** The default of true means that multiple distribution agents can be spawned on an as-needed basis, servicing a single subscription database. By default in SQL Server 2000, if you have multiple publications in a single publication database, all subscribed to by a single subscription database, then there would be a single distribution agent shared by all publications for that subscription database. With SQL Server 2005, the default is to have multiple distribution agents, which results in multiple streams of data going into your subscription database, and consequently much higher performance.

✦ **Snapshot always available:** This option controls whether a snapshot is generated each time the snapshot agent is run. The default is true. If you have only named subscribers you can set this to false.

✦ **Allow anonymous subscriptions:** This option allows your subscribers to create anonymous or named subscriptions.

✦ **Attachable subscription database:** This option allows you to copy an existing subscription database to another subscriber for fast deployment of your subscriptions. By default this feature is disabled, and it will be deprecated in a future release of SQL Server.

✦ **Allow pull subscriptions:** This option allows subscribers to pull their subscriptions.

✦ **Allow initialization from backup files:** This option allows you to create a backup and then restore the backup on the subscriber. You then need to create your subscription and specify that the snapshot is to be deployed via the backup. To create your subscription you use the sp_addsnapshot command as follows:

```
exec sp_addsubscription @publication = N'test', @subscriber =
'SubscriberServerName',@destination_db = N'awsub', @subscription_type =
N'Push',
@sync_type = N'initialize with backup', @article = N'all',
@update_mode = N'read only', @subscriber_type = 0,
@backupdevicetype='disk',@backupdevicename='c:\adventure.bak'
```

Note Many of the sp_addsubscription command arguments have no defaults. For example, you must define the @publication argument. The example shown in this section provides you with examples of the kind of input you must provide.

✦ **The Allow non-SQL Server Subscribers:** This option allows you to replicate to heterogeneous data sources such as Oracle, Sybase, DB2, and others.

✦ **The allow data transformations section:** This section allows you to run a DTS package to massage your transactions as they go from the publisher to the subscriber. This option is not available in SQL Server 2005, but is available in SQL 2000, so SQL 2005 subscribers can take advantage of it.

✦ **The Schema Replication section:** Select whether you want to replicate DML statements (ALTER TABLE, ALTER VIEW, ALTER PROC, etc.) to your subscribers. The default is true.

✦ **Allow peer-to-peer subscriptions:** This option allows you to enable your publication for deployment in a peer-to-peer environment.

✦ **Allow immediate updating:** This option indicates whether your publication is enabled for immediate updating.

✦ **Allow queued updating:** This option indicates whether your publication is enabled for queued updating.

> If your publication is enabled for immediate updating or queued updating, two other options are available: Report Conflicts Centrally and Conflict Resolution Policy. Report Conflicts Centrally controls whether the conflicts will be reported centrally on the publisher or whether they will merely be logged to the conflict tables on the subscriber. The Conflict Resolution Policy determines what will happen when a conflict occurs: the publisher wins, the subscriber wins, or the publisher wins and the subscription is reinitialized.

The next tab in the Publication Properties is the Publication Access list. It displays a list of which accounts can access the publication. The account under which you configure your distribution and snapshot agents to run must be included in this group.

The final tab in the Publication Properties dialog box is the Agent Security tab, where you can modify the accounts under which your log reader, snapshot, distribution, and queue reader agents run.

This completes our look at creating and administering transactional publications. After you have created your publication you must deploy it to your subscribers.

Creating Bi-directional Transactional Replication Publications

Bi-directional transactional publications are best used when you want bi-directional replication between a single publisher/subscriber pair. You cannot expand this to more than a single publisher/subscriber pair without significant hacking. Merge replication or peer-to-peer replication are better choices when you have multiple nodes on which you wish to establish bi-directional replication. Before you deploy a bi-directional replication solution, you must take care to minimize the chances of conflicts occurring. Ideally, updates will occur only on a single node at any one time — for instance, if you are using bi-directional replication for a disaster recovery implementation where you know only one node will be active at a time. If it is possible that you may have simultaneous updates occurring on both nodes, you should partition your tables by using different identity ranges and increments, or by a location identifier column.

To set up bi-directional transactional replication you need to back up your publication database and restore it on your subscriber. Then modify the columns with the identity property to have different ranges or increments (for instance, you can have a range starting with 1 on the publisher and 2 on the subscriber, and then have an increment of 2; the publisher would have odd values for its identity columns, and the subscriber would have even values). You then need to modify all triggers, constraints, and identity columns for `Not For Replication`. Then, on your publisher, create your publication and do a no sync subscription to your subscriber. Run `sp_scriptpublicationcustomprocs 'PublicationName'` in your publication database to generate the replication stored procedures, and run this script in your subscription database. When you have completed these steps, do the same on your subscriber. Then start your distribution agents if they have not already started.

If you do get conflicts, your distribution agents will fail, probably on primary key violations or data consistency failures (e.g., a row could not be found on the subscriber while applying the command). You will have to enable logging to determine which row is causing the error and manually fix it — probably by deleting the row.

Creating Oracle Publications

To create an Oracle publication you must first create a replication administrative user on your Oracle server. You will find a script to create this account with in `C:\Program Files\Microsoft SQL Server\MSSQL.X\MSSQL\Install\OracleAdmin.sql`. Run this script using PL/SQL and enter the requested information (account name, password, and instance).

Then you must enable your Oracle Server as a publisher. To do this, execute the following steps:

1. Connect with your SQL Server that is going to act as the distributor or perhaps even your distributor/subscriber. You will have to have configured this server as your distributor in advance.

2. Right-click on the Replication folder and select Distributor Properties. Select the Publisher tab.

3. Click the Add button and select Add Oracle Publisher. You will get a dialog box prompting you to log on to your Oracle Server. This dialog box looks very similar to the logon prompt you get when trying to log on to SQL Server via Management Studio. If you don't know your Oracle Server name you can click on the drop-down box for Server Instance and browse for your Oracle Server.

4. Click OK, and then click the Options button.

5. For authentication, select Oracle Standard Authentication, and enter the login and password of the replication admin account created above. Click Remember Password. Then click the Connection Properties tab, which contains two options:

   • Gateway: Use this for high-performance replication solutions.

   • Complete: Use this when you want to transform your data or do row filtering.

6. Make your selection and click Connect.

Now that you have created a replication administrative user on your Oracle server, you can create your Oracle publication. To do so, execute the following steps:

1. Expand the Replication folder and right-click Local Publications.

2. Select New Oracle Publication; then expand the databases in the Replication folder.

3. Right-click the Local Publications folder and then click New Oracle Publication.

4. On the Oracle Publisher dialog box, select the Oracle Server on which you wish to create a publication, and click Next.

5. On the Publication Type dialog box, select Snapshot publication or Transactional publication.

6. Click Next to launch the Articles dialog box. Select the objects you wish to replicate. Notice you also have the option to vertically filter table or view objects here and you can configure data type mappings if necessary.

7. Click Next to launch the Filter Table Rows dialog box. This dialog box is very similar to the Filter Rows dialog box from SQL Server Snapshot and Transactional replication dialogs.

8. Click Next to launch the Snapshot Agent dialog box. Accept the defaults, and click Next to launch the Agent Security dialog box.

9. Configure the accounts under which the log reader and snapshot agents will run. Click Next to launch the wizard's Actions dialog box, and choose whether you wish to script the publication.

10. Click Next for the Publication Summary dialog box. Name your publication, review the publication properties, and click Finish to build your publication. After your publication has been created, create your subscriptions.

Creating Peer-to-Peer Replication Publications

To create peer-to-peer publication, you must first create a normal transactional publication. After you create the normal transactional publication, use the following steps to create a peer-to-peer replication:

1. Right-click the publication that you find in the Replication\Local Publications folder in Management Studio and select Properties. Select the Subscription Options tab shown in Figure 39-7, and ensure that the Allow Peer-to-Peer Subscriptions option is set to True (the default is False).

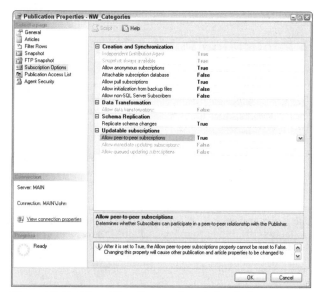

Figure 39-7: Select Allow Peer-to-Peer Subscriptions to enable peer-to-peer replication.

2. Click OK to close the Publication Properties dialog box.

3. Back up your database and deploy your subscriptions using the backup you created.

4. Right-click the publication and choose Configure Peer-to-Peer Topology from the context menu. This step launches the Configure Peer-to-Peer Topology Wizard.

5. Click Next.

6. Select your Publication and click Next.

7. Highlight all of the publishers you want to participate in the peer-to-peer topology.

8. Select the subscriber databases from the drop-down menu and click Next.

9. Configure security for the connection to the distributor and the connection to the publisher in the Log Reader Agent Security dialog box. You will need to do this for each publisher and peer database participating in the peer-to-peer topology.

10. Click Next to launch the Distributor Agent Security dialog box.

11. Configure the accounts you want to use to connect to your distributor and subscriber.

12. Click Next to launch the New Peer Initialization dialog box. You have two options here. The first one is relevant when no changes have been made at the publication database since you configured your subscription. In this case, select "I created the peer database manually, or I restored a backup of the original publication database which has not been changed since the backup was taken." If the publication database has changed since you deployed the subscription, you will need to back up the publication database again. Select "I restored a backup of the original publication database, and the publication database was changed after the backup was taken" and browse to select the backup.

13. Click Next. You'll see a publication summary that describes all of the changes you've made.

14. Review the publication details in the Publication Summary dialog box and click Finish.

Creating Merge Replication Publications

Merge replication is intended for clients who are occasionally or frequently disconnected from the publisher and need to work offline on their offline copies of the database. At periodic intervals they need to synchronize their changes with the publisher (called an *upload*) and receive changes from the publisher (called a *download*). Whenever clients have to work offline from the publisher for any amount of time, the probability of conflicts increases. Merge replication is designed from the ground up to handle such conflicts.

To create a merge publication, connect to the SQL Server that will be your publisher and expand the Replication folder. Right-click on the Local Publications folder and select New Publication. Click Next at the New Publication Wizard dialog box.

You begin by configuring the database options. Select your publication database in the Publication Database dialog box and click Next. For the publication type select Merge Publication. Click Next to launch the Subscriber Types dialog box, shown in Figure 39-8. Select the types of subscribers the publisher will serve.

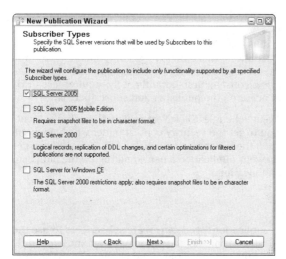

Figure 39-8: Choose the kinds of subscribers the publication will serve.

Now it's time to configure the articles. Click Next to launch the Articles dialog box. Select the types of articles you wish to replicate. Notice here that you cannot replicate the execution of stored procedures or indexed views as tables. However, you can vertically filter tables and views by drilling down into the individual tables and displaying the member columns. Select the columns you wish to replicate. To set article options, click the Article properties button and set properties on highlighted articles or all table articles. The available options are much the same as with snapshot or transactional replication.

Notice that you can control the synchronization direction on a per-article basis. You will get better performance if you configure an article as Download only to Subscriber, allow Subscriber changes, or Download only to Subscriber–prohibit Subscriber changes, rather than bi-directional (the default).

In addition, notice the Identity Range Management features. Automatic Identity Ranges is a method of assigning identity range pools to subscribers and the publisher to avoid primary key conflicts due to the same identity values used simultaneously on the publisher and one or more subscribers. It allows you to set the identity range you wish to use on the publisher, and another range to use on each subscriber. For example, the publisher could have an identity range from 1 to 10,000, and the first subscriber could have an identity range from 10,001 to 10,100. The next subscriber would then have an identity range from 10,101 to 10,200. As the publisher or subscriber's identity value approaches the threshold percent multiplied by the range, SQL Server will increment the range when the merge agent runs. This approach to identity management allows for efficient identity range use.

After you select your publication properties, click Next to launch the Article Issues dialog box. Review the article issues and adjust your publication as needed.

Filtering works somewhat differently than it does for other publications. Click Next to launch the Filter Table Rows dialog box. If you wish to horizontally filter your merge articles, click Add. There will be two options: Add Filter and Automatically Generate Filters. The first option enables you to generate row filters on individual tables. The second option enables you to set the filter on a single table, and will then walk the DRI of all tables, adding filters to related tables. When you create the filter, an option at the bottom of the dialog enables you to specify how many subscriptions will receive data from this table. The second option (A row from this table will only go to one subscription) is the precomputed partition option. It will accumulate more replication metadata during article construction, but ultimately requires less CPU resources to merge transactions that occur on the publisher and subscribers later.

Click Next to define your snapshot agent schedule. Click Next again to launch the Agent Security dialog box, which enables you to set the security context under which your snapshot agent will run. Click Next to launch the Wizard Actions dialog box. You will then get your Publication Summary dialog box. Give your publication a name and review the publication summary. Click Finish to build your publication.

Creating Subscriptions

Once you create and configure some publications, you can create subscribers to use them. To create subscriptions to your publications, connect to your subscriber and expand the Replication folder. Right-click the Local Subscriptions folder and choose New Subscriptions from the context menu. Click Next at the New Subscription Wizard dialog box. You'll see the Publication dialog box shown in Figure 39-9. Select the publisher in the Publisher drop-down menu. Expand the publication database and locate the publication to which you want to subscribe. Notice how each of the subscriptions use an icon that indicates its subscription type. Click on it to give it focus, and then click Next.

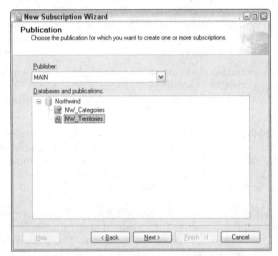

Figure 39-9: Select a publisher and one of the subscriptions from the list.

At this point, you must decide what kind of subscription to create. Select whether you wish to use pull subscriptions or push subscriptions. Use the following to decide:

✦ When you have many subscribers, use pull subscriptions.

✦ When you have subscribers who are not always connected, use pull subscriptions.

✦ If the preceding don't apply, use push subscriptions.

Adding one or more subscribers to the subscription comes next. Click Next to launch the Subscribers dialog box, shown in Figure 39-10. Check the servers you wish to make subscribers of this publication, and in the Subscribers and subscription database section, click on the drop-down menu to select the subscription database. You can also add subscribers that do not appear in this list by clicking the Add Subscriber button.

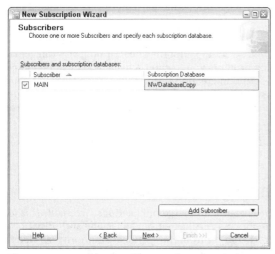

Figure 39-10: Add subscribers to the subscription; each subscriber must have a database to store the replicated data.

Each subscriber will require a security setup. Click the Next button to launch the Distribution Agent Security dialog box. Click the ellipses next to each subscriber and use the Distribution Agent Security dialog box to configure security for each subscriber. Only after you completely configure the security options will the wizard highlight the Next button.

As part of the subscription process, you must determine when the subscriber is available to replicate the data the publisher provides. Click Next to launch the Synchronization Schedule dialog box. In the Agent Schedule drop-down menu, select whether you want the agent to run continuously, on demand (by Windows Synchronization Manager), or on a schedule.

Click Next to launch the Initialize Subscriptions dialog box. Note that if your publication supports updateable subscriptions, you will get the Updateable Subscriptions dialog box before you get Initialize Subscriptions dialog box. In the Commit at Published drop-down menu, select Simultaneously Commit Changes if you wish to use immediate updating, or choose Queue Change and Commit Where Possible if you wish to use queue updating. You will then get a dialog to enter account information for the linked server used by the updateable subscribers. You can create an account to use here or select to use an existing linked server between the subscriber and publisher. Click Next to launch the Initialize Subscriptions dialog box.

If you have deployed your subscription from a backup or have manually created the subscription database with the schema and data of the objects you wish to replicate to, then you can manually move the database. Otherwise, select Immediately if you wish to immediately send the snapshot to the subscriber. Select At First Synchronization if you wish to control when the snapshot will be applied. Click Next to launch the Wizard Actions dialog.

If you are subscribing to a merge publication, you will get a Subscription Type dialog box before the Initialize Subscriptions dialog box. The Subscription Type dialog enables you to set the priority on your subscription as well as the subscription type. If you select a client subscription type, the first subscriber merging with the publisher wins a conflict. If you select a server subscription type, you can select a priority to assign to the subscriber. By assigning different priorities to different servers to which you are replicating, you can control which server will win a conflict. Clicking Next will launch the Initialize Subscriptions dialog box.

This dialog enables you to either immediately create the subscription, script it for later deployment, or both. If you select to immediately create the snapshot, you will get the Subscription Summary dialog box; if you select to script the subscription, you will get the Script File Properties dialog box, which prompts you to enter a name and location indicating where you wish to generate your subscription creation script. Click Finish to create your subscription and/or generate your subscription script. You can check the status of your subscription creation or script creation in the Creating Subscriptions dialog box. Click Close upon completion of the actions.

You may wish to right-click on your subscription in the Local Subscription folder and select View Subscription Status to check on the deployment of your subscription.

Creating Web Synchronizing Subscriptions

SQL Server 2005 supports web synchronization for merge publications. To enable this feature you must decide whether you wish to obtain a certificate from an issuing authority (for example, thawte.com, verisign.com, or cacert.com) or from the certificate authority service that ships as part of the OS. You must install this certificate on your copy of IIS.

Installing the certificate requires access to IIS. Open the Internet Information Services console located in the Administrative Tools folder of the Control Panel and expand the Web Sites folder. Right-click the website you want to use for subscriptions and choose Properties from the context menu. You'll see a Web Site Properties dialog box similar to the one shown in Figure 39-11. Click the Directory Security tab.

Figure 39-11: The Directory Security tab contains options for installing a certificate for your IIS server.

Begin the certificate installation by clicking Server Certificate. You'll see the Web Server Certificate Wizard. Click Next, and then click Create a New Certificate. Click Next and select Prepare the Request Now (if you are using an online certificate authority, select Send the Request Immediately to an Online Certification Authority).Click Next, and in the Name and security settings section, assign a name and a bit length to your certificate. Click Next and set the organization and organization unit. Click Next. Enter the common name that will be your DNS name, or the computer's NetBIOS name. Click Next. In the Geographical Information dialog box enter your country, state/province, and city info. Click Next. Select a name for your certificate file and a path. Click Next, and in the Summary Page dialog box, click Next and then click Finish.

When you choose to use a certificate that you create yourself, begin by opening the Certification Authority console located in the Administrative Tools folder of the Control Panel. Connect to your certificate server, right-click on your Certificate Server, select All Tasks, and select Submit a New Request. Locate the certificate file you made previously and click on it to open it. Next expand the Pending Request folder and right-click on the certificate you find there. Select All Tasks, and Issue. Expand the Issued Certificates folder, right-click on the issued certificate, and select All Tasks and Export Binary Data. Select Save Binary Data to a File and click OK. Select the location where you wish to save the file and accept the certificate name. Click Save.

Return to the Internet Information Services console and click the Server Certificate button. Click Next. Select Process the Pending Request and Install the Certificate. Click Next. Browse to the location of the certificate you created above (it will probably be called Binary Certificate–*X*.tmp, where *X* is an integer). Double-click on it and click Next. Select the SSL port you will be using. Click Next, Next again, and then Finish. Your certificate is installed.

At this point, IIS is ready to use as a subscriber. Connect to your publisher using Management Studio, expand the Replication folder, and expand the Local Publications folder. Right-click on the merge publication you wish enable for web synchronization and select Configure Web Synchronization. You'll see the Configure Web Synchronization Wizard. The following steps explain how to configure the required settings:

1. Click Next. Select the type of clients who will be connecting to your merge publication. You have a choice of standard SQL Server clients or mobile clients.

2. Click Next. You'll see the Web Server dialog box shown in Figure 39-12. Select the name of the web server to which your merge clients will connect. This server does not have to be your SQL Server publisher.

3. Choose an existing virtual directory or select Create a New Virtual Directory in the Web Server dialog box. Generally, you'll want to use a new virtual directory to keep your data separate from other data on the system. When you want to use an existing directory, expand your website, select the existing directory, and click Next. Proceed to step 5. Otherwise, click Next without choosing a directory and proceed to step 4.

4. Type the alias you want to use for the virtual directory in the Virtual Directory Information dialog box. Type a physical path, such as `c:\inetpub\wwwroot`, and click Next. If the physical path does not already exist you will get a prompt asking whether you wish to create it. Click Yes.

Note

If the directory you chose does not already have the SQL Server ISAPI dll required for web synchronization, you will get a prompt to copy the dll. Select Yes.

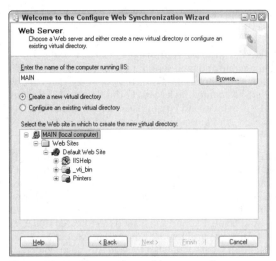

Figure 39-12: Choose the web server settings you want to use for the subscription.

5. Click Next to launch the Authenticated Access dialog box. Select from among three authentication modes: Integrated Windows authentication, Digest authentication for Windows domain servers, or Basic authentication.

Note   You can use Integrated authentication for local LAN or WANS only; it can't be used over the Internet without opening ports that should otherwise be secured. If you choose Integrated Windows authentication, click Next to launch the Directory Access dialog box. If you do use Integrated, ensure that the accounts you will be using to connect to the web server are in the PAL of your publication, and are the accounts your subscriber will use to connect to the Web Server providing web synchronization services.

Best Practice   Always choose Integrated Windows authentication whenever possible for IIS to maintain a high level of security. Use Basic authentication as a last option because it sends the username and password in clear text. Use Digest authentication in conjunction with SSL/HTTPS, and pre-create the accounts you wish to use in the AD. You will need to add the domain name to the realm, and make sure that the accounts you are using to connect to the web server providing web synchronization services are in the PAL of your publication.

6. Click Next to launch the Directory Access dialog box. Enter the names of the accounts your subscriber will use to connect to the web server providing web synchronization services. Ideally, you will add a group to simplify management.

7. Click Next to launch the Snapshot Share Access; this share will be of the form `\\PublisherServerName\ShareName`. This share should map to your alternate snapshot folder, which we will configure later.

8. Click Next for the Web Synchronization Wizard summary. Click Finish. Click Close when the Configure Web Synchronization dialog completes.

Now that your merge publication is configured for web synchronization, right-click it and choose Properties from the context menu. First, you need to configure the snapshot. Click on the Snapshot tab. In the "Put files in the following folder" text box, enter the name of your snapshot folder. This could be a share on your web server; if your SQL Server is hosting your web server, it will be the default snapshot folder location. Make sure this option is checked.

Second, configure the virtual directory used to store the snapshot. Click on the FTP Snapshot and Internet tab, and click "Allow Subscribers to synchronize by connecting to a web server." The web server address will look like this: `https://WebServerName/VirtualDirectoryName`. The Virtual Directory Name will be the virtual directory you created or configured in the Web Server dialog box in the Configure Web Synchronization Wizard dialog box.

Third, check the subscription type to ensure that users can connect to it. Click Subscription Options and ensure that Allow Pull Subscriptions is set to True. Then click on the Publication Access List. Add the account or group you will be using on your subscriber to connect to the web server and publisher.

You're ready to create the web subscription:

1. Right-click Local Subscriptions on your subscriber, and then select New Subscription.

2. Click Next. Select your publisher in the drop-down list. Locate your publication and select it.

3. Click Next. Select "Run each agent at its Subscriber" in the Merge Agent Location dialog box.

4. Click Next. Highlight your subscriber(s). and in the Subscription Database drop-down menu, select your subscriber database.

5. Click Next to launch the Merge Agent Subscriber. Select the account under which your merge agent will run on your subscriber. In the Connect to the Publisher and Distributor field enter the name of the account you entered in the PAL.

6. Click OK and then click Next. In the Synchronization Schedule dialog, select Run on Demand Only or a Schedule. Selecting Run Continuously will probably not work well over the Internet.

7. Click Next to launch the Initialize Subscriptions dialog box. Select whether you want the snapshot generated immediately or at a later time.

8. Click Next. In the Web Synchronization dialog, select Use Web Synchronization.

9. Click Next. Verify that the URL is correct in the Web Server Information dialog box. Enter the name that you wish to use for Basic authentication.

10. Click Next. Ensure that Client is selected in the Subscription type.

11. Click Next. Click Next in the Wizard Actions dialog to generate your snapshot immediately (or optionally script the subscription for later deployment).

12. Click Finish in the Subscription Summary dialog box.

Your snapshot should be applied to your subscriber. You can view its status by right-clicking on the subscription that you see in the Local Subscription folder on your subscriber and selecting View Synchronization Status. You may have to click the Start button to get the most recent status information.

Monitoring Your Replication Solution

All monitoring of your replication topology is now done through the Replication Monitor, which is now a stand-alone component found in \Program Files\Microsoft SQL Server\90\Tools\ Binn\SQLMonitor.exe. You can also launch it by right-clicking on the Replication folder and selecting Launch Replication Monitor. If you expand a publisher in the Replication Monitor, all the publications on that publisher will be displayed. You can right-click on the publisher to do any of the following:

✦ Modify the publisher settings

✦ Remove the publisher

✦ Connect to the distributor

✦ Disconnect from the distributor

✦ Set Agent profiles

✦ Configure replication alerts

You can right-click on the publications for that publisher to do any of the following:

✦ Reinitialize all subscriptions

✦ Generate a snapshot

✦ Modify publication properties

✦ Refresh the publication's status

✦ Validate subscriptions (transactional and merge replication)

The option you will most frequently use here is the Set Agent Profiles option.

Agent Profiles

Replication agents have many switches on them; profiles are groups of switches that provide distinct functions. By default, snapshot replication has a single profile. Transactional replication has five profiles: Continue on data consistency errors (which will cause the distribution agent to skip errors related to primary key violations or rows missing on the subscriber); a default profile; a verbose profile (for debugging); an OLEB streaming profile (used when you are replicating blobs); and a Windows Synchronization Manager profile (when your subscription is controlled via Windows Synchronization Manager). Merge agents have a high-volume server-to-server profile; row count and checksum validation (for validations); row count (for validations); slow link (for slow links such as phone lines); verbose history agent (for debugging); and Windows Synchronization Manager profiles. You can add custom profiles for finer-grained control.

Returning to the Replication Monitor, if you click on a snapshot or merge publication, the right-hand pane of Replication Monitor will display two tabs:

✦ All Subscriptions

✦ Warning and Agents

Optionally, it will also display a third tab for transactional replication publications:

✦ Tracer Tokens

All Subscriptions

The All Subscriptions tab displays all subscriptions and their status, their subscriber and subscription databases, and their last synchronization time. You can filter the subscriptions by clicking the Show button, which displays the following:

✦ All subscribers

✦ The 25 worst performing subscriptions

✦ The 50 worst performance subscriptions

✦ Errors and Warning only

✦ Errors only

✦ Warning only

✦ Subscriptions running

✦ Subscriptions not running

These options allow for a high degree of visibility or filtering of your subscriptions.

Warnings and Agents

The Warnings and Agents tab is shown in Figure 39-13. All agents for this subscription will be displayed in the lower half of this pane. If you right-click on an agent you can do the following:

✦ View details about this agent's history

✦ Start the agent

✦ Modify its properties (which is where you will exercise all the fine-grained control over your agent)

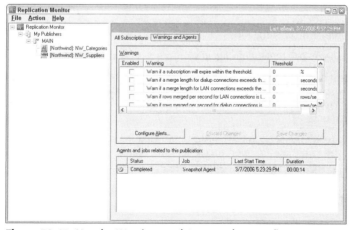

Figure 39-13: Use the Warnings and Agents tab to configure notifications about your agent.

The Warnings and Agents tab has two sections:

✦ Warnings

✦ Agent Status

The Warnings tab is used to raise alerts when a condition is triggered—for instance, when your latency exceeds a certain amount, or your subscription is close to expiration. You enable these warnings by checking the check box. After you have enabled the warnings, you need to configure how these alerts are handled. Click the Configure Alerts button, select the warning, and click the Configure button. You then have the option to enable the alert; raise an alert if the message contains a specific string; execute a job when you receive an alert; send e-mail, a page, or a net send command to an operator; and specify history retention.

The Agent Status tab enables you to view details on your job. You have the option to view agent details, stop and start the agent, select an agent profile, and modify properties of your agent. Selecting properties will launch the Job Properties dialog, shown in Figure 39-14.

Modifying Replication Agent Properties

Whenever you need to modify the default behaviors of your replication agent, you will do it through profiles or by modifying your agent's properties. To modify your agent's properties, locate the subscription whose agent you wish to modify in the Replication Monitor, right-click on it, and select View Details. In the Subscription dialog box, choose Actions ➪ Distribution Agent Properties. The Job Properties dialog box will appear, which contains the following six tabs:

✦ General

✦ Steps

✦ Schedules

✦ Alerts

✦ Notifications

✦ Targets

The General tab enables you to name your job, set the job owner, set the category, describe the category, and enable or disable the job.

The Steps tab is the tab you use to set your agent's properties, as shown in Figure 39-14.

Highlight the Run Agent step and click Edit. In the Command section you can add parameters or modify values of existing parameters. For instance, you could add the `-QueryTimeout 300` parameter, which will cause the replication subsystem to wait for 300 seconds before marking a replication agent suspect.

Use the Schedules tab to set the schedule. The Alerts tab enables you to set alerts, the Notifications tab enables you to notify operators when the replication agent fails, and you use the Targets tab when working with a master job server.

Tracer Tokens

Tracer tokens enable you to inject a tracer into a publication and time how long it takes for this token to be replicated to the distributor and then to the subscriber(s). This will provide you with an instantaneous value for latency.

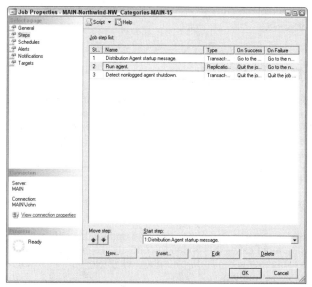

Figure 39-14: Set agent properties by modifying the steps used to start it as needed.

Replication Performance

There are two aspects related to improving replication performance: creating and deploying your snapshot, and distributing your data.

As the size of your initial snapshot grows, deploying your snapshot through a backup/restore offers better performance. If you choose to distribute your snapshot via your merge or distribution agent, make sure you put your subscription database in the select into/bulk copy recovery model for best loading performance.

Here are several tips for transactional replication distribution:

✦ To ensure that your subscriber tables are as lightweight as possible, minimize the use of triggers and indexes.

✦ If the bulk of the write activity that occurs on your publisher occurs as part of a batch, consider replicating the execution of stored procedures. If most of the write activity occurs as part of singleton activity, you will not benefit from replicating the execution of stored procedures.

✦ Change the PollingInterval setting on your distribution agent to 1 s.

Here are several tips for merge replication:

✦ Place indexes on columns that are used in join conditions.

✦ Use precomputed partitions if possible.

✦ Use download-only articles if possible.

To view metadata about each replicated transaction, select `sysdm_repl_traninfo` from the dynamic management view.

Replication Troubleshooting

To troubleshoot replication problems, look in the Replication Monitor for publishers and publications that have a white cross on a red circle. In the All Subscriptions pane, locate the problem subscription and right-click on it and select View Details. At the bottom of the Error Details dialog box you will see the error message in the Last Message of the selected session section. If nothing is displayed, cancel the View Details section, right-click on your failed agent, and select the Verbose Agent profile. Restart your agent. You should get more error details display in the View Details dialog box this time.

Many replication errors are transitory and can be cleared by merely rerunning the distribution or merge agent.

Sometimes, especially when running merge replication or using updateable subscribers, you will find unexpected data loss. In most cases this is due to conflicts. To view these conflicts (and roll them back if you are using merge replication), right-click on your publication in Management Studio and select View Conflicts.

If your data has not made it to the subscriber yet, you might want to check the synchronization status of your subscriber. Right-click on your subscription and select View Synchronization Status.

It is also possible to log the output of the replication agents to log files. To do this use the following switches on your problem agent, and start up your agent again:

```
-OutputVerboseLevel 3 -Output c:\Temp\Out.log
```

Some distribution agent errors can be skipped by using the `-Skiperrors XXX` switch in your distribution agent (where *XXX* is your error number).

There are several other commands you can use to get a window into your replication processes. For instance, `sp_hrowsereplcmds` shows what is in your distribution database. The view `distribution.dbo.MSdistribution_status` shows how many commands have been distributed to your subscribers and how many are awaiting distribution. `Sp_repltran` issued in your publication database shows commands waiting to be picked up by the log reader agent.

Summary

Replication is a method of data distribution, although it is not always the best choice for every data distribution need. This chapter discussed the alternatives as well as the replication types, when to use each type, and how to deploy a replication solution. This chapter covered SQL Server 2005's many new replication features, including how to navigate the new menus for deploying and administrating replication.

✦   ✦   ✦

Securing Databases

When I was a data systems technician in the Navy, I spent almost two years at CSTSC, Combat System Technical School Command, in Mare Island, California. It was good. My class was one of the last groups to be trained on the AN-UYK-7 computer. The CPU was a drawer with about 50 small cards populated with transistors. We learned to troubleshoot the CPU to the logic-gate level. It was very cool. We shared the island with the Crypto-tech school. The sailors in crypto school had it rough; they couldn't carry anything in or out of their school — no notes, no books, nothing. At least we could meet after hours in study groups. I was glad to be on the computer side of the command. Security has never thrilled me, but the Information Architecture Principle clearly states that information must be secured.

It's common practice to develop the database and then worry about security. While there's no point in applying security while the database design is in flux, the project benefits when you develop and implement the security plan sooner rather than later.

Security, like every other aspect of the database project, must be carefully designed, implemented, and tested. Security may affect the execution of some procedures and must be taken into account when the project code is being developed.

A simple security plan with a few roles and the IT users as sysadmins may suffice for a small organization. Larger organizations — the military, banks, or international organizations — will require a more complex security plan that's designed as carefully as the logical database schema.

If security is tightly implemented with full security audits performed by SQL Profiler, the SQL Server installation can be certified at C2-level security. Fortunately, SQL Server's security model is well thought out and, if fully understood, both logical and flexible. While the tactics of securing a database are creating users and roles and then assigning permissions, the strategy is identifying the rights and responsibilities of data access and then enforcing the plan.

**New in
2005**   Security in SQL Server 2005 is enhanced in several ways: Users are replaced with schema as owners, permissions are much more granular, code can be programmed to execute as a specific user, and data can be encrypted.

Maybe you heard that SQL Server 2005 was originally SQL Server 2003. Microsoft spent an extra year doing a security code review on SQL Server. The emphasis on security affects the initial installation. Previous versions of SQL Server installed with a large surface area exposed to possible attacks. Now, SQL Server installs locked down, and you, as the DBA, must enable features before they can be used. Even remote connections are disabled by default.

The new SQL Server Surface Area Configuration Tool is used to enable features and components, thereby controlling the exposed surface area. It's designed to be run after installation. Once configured, the DBA should rarely need to use the tool, which is covered in Chapter 4, "Installing SQL Server 2005."

Security Concepts

The SQL Server security model is large and complex. In some ways it's more complex than the Windows security model. Because the security concepts are tightly intertwined, the best way to begin is to walk through an overview of the model.

SQL Server security is based on the concept of *securables,* objects that can be secured, and *principals,* objects that can be granted access to a securable. Principals are users and roles. Users are assigned to roles, both of which may be granted permission to objects, as illustrated in Figure 40-1. Each object has an owner, and ownership also affects the permissions.

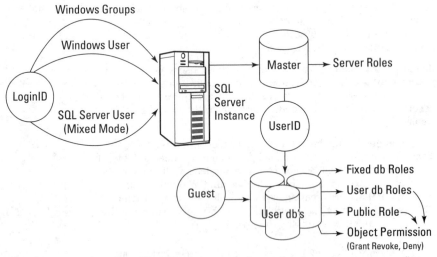

Figure 40-1: An overview of the SQL Server security model shows how users are first authenticated to the server, followed by the databases, and finally the objects within the databases. The circles represent how the user is identified.

Server-Level Security

A user may be initially identified to SQL Server via one of three methods:

✦ Windows user login

✦ Membership in a Windows user group

✦ SQL Server–specific login (if the server uses mixed-mode security)

At the server level, the user is known by his or her `LoginID`, which is either his or her SQL Server login, or his or her Windows domain and user name.

Once the user is known to the server and identified, the user has whatever server-level administrative rights have been granted via fixed server roles. If the user belongs to the `sysadmin` role, he or she has full access to every server function, database, and object in the server.

A user can be granted access to a database, and his or her network login ID can be mapped to a database-specific user ID in the process. If the user doesn't have access to a database, he or she can gain access as the guest user with some configuration changes within the database server.

Database-Level Security

At the database level, the user may be granted certain administrative-level permissions by belonging to fixed database roles.

The user still can't access the data. He or she must be granted permission to the database objects (e.g., tables, stored procedures, views, functions). User-defined roles are custom roles that serve as groups. The role may be granted permission to a database object, and users may be assigned to a database user-defined role. All users are automatically members of the public standard database role.

Object permissions are assigned by means of `grant`, `revoke`, and `deny`. A `deny` permission overrides a `grant` permission, which overrides a `revoke` permission. A user may have multiple permission paths to an object (individually, through a standard database role, and through the public role). If any of these paths is denied, the user is blocked from accessing the object. Otherwise, if any of the paths is granted permission, then the user can access the object.

Object permission is very detailed and a specific permission exists for every action that can be performed (`select`, `insert`, `update`, `run`, and so on) for every object. Certain database fixed roles also affect object access, such as the ability to read or write to the database.

It's very possible for a user to be recognized by SQL Server and not have access to any database. It's also possible for a user to be defined within a database but not recognized by the server. Moving a database and its permissions to another server, but not moving the logins, will cause such orphaned users.

Object Ownership

The final aspect of this overview of SQL Server's security model involves object ownership. Every object is owned by a schema. The default schema is dbo — not to be confused with the dbo role.

New in 2005   In previous versions of SQL Server, objects were owned by users, or, more precisely, every owner was also a schema. There are several advantages in SQL Server 2005. ANSI SQL defines a model of database–schema–objects.

Ownership becomes critical when permission is being granted to a user to run a stored procedure when the user doesn't have permission to the underlying tables. If the ownership chain from the tables to the stored procedure is consistent, then the user can access the stored procedure and the stored procedure can access the tables as its owner. However, if the ownership chain is broken, meaning there's a different owner somewhere between the stored procedure and the table, then the user must have rights to the stored procedure, the underlying tables, and every other object in between.

Most security management can be performed in Management Studio. With code, security is managed by means of the `grant`, `revoke`, and `deny` Data Control Language (DCL) commands, and several system stored procedures.

Windows Security

Because SQL Server exists within a Windows environment, one aspect of the security strategy must be securing the Windows server.

Windows Security

SQL Server databases frequently support websites, so Internet Information Server (IIS) security and firewalls must be considered within the security plan.

Windows security is an entire topic in itself, and therefore outside the scope of this book. If, as a DBA, you are not well supported by qualified network staff, then you should make the effort to become proficient in Windows Server technologies, especially security.

SQL Server Login

Don't confuse user access to SQL Server with SQL Server's Windows accounts. The two logins are completely different.

SQL Server users don't need access to the database directories or data files on a Windows level because the SQL Server process, not the user, will perform the actual file access. However, the SQL Server process needs permission to access the files, so it needs a Windows account. Two types are available:

✦ **Local admin account:** SQL Server can use the local admin account of the operating system for permission to the machine. This option is adequate for single-server installations but fails to provide the network security required for distributed processing.

✦ **Domain user account (recommended):** SQL Server can use a Windows user account created specifically for it. The SQL Server user account can be granted administrator rights for the server and can access the network through the server to talk to other servers.

Cross-Reference   The SQL Server accounts were initially configured when the server was installed. Installation is discussed in Chapter 4, "Installing SQL Server 2005."

Server Security

SQL Server uses a two-phase security-authentication scheme. The user is first authenticated to the server. Once the user is "in" the server, access can be granted to the individual databases.

SQL Server stores all login information within the master database.

SQL Server Authentication Mode

When SQL Server was installed, one of the decisions made was which of the following authentication methods to use:

✦ **Windows authentication mode:** Windows authentication only

✦ **Mixed mode:** Both Windows authentication and SQL Server user authentication

This option can be changed after installation in Management Studio, in the Security page of the SQL Server Properties dialog box, as shown in Figure 40-2.

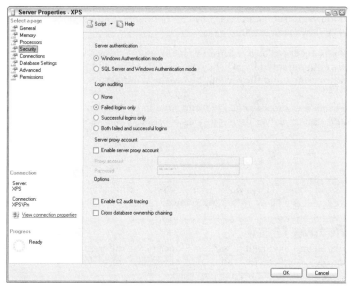

Figure 40-2: Server-level security is managed in the Security tab of the SQL Server Properties dialog box.

From code, the authentication mode can be checked by means of the xp_loginconfig system stored procedure, as follows:

```
EXEC xp_loginconfig 'login mode'
```

Result:

```
name                           config_value
---------------------------    ---------------------------
login mode                     Mixed
```

Notice that the system stored procedure to report the authentication mode is an extended stored procedure. That's because the authentication mode is stored in the registry in the following entry:

```
HKEY_LOCAL_MACHINE\SOFTWARE\Microsoft\
    MicrosoftSQLServer\<instance_name>\MSSQLServer\LoginMode
```

A value for `LoginMode` is 0 is for Windows authentication and 1 for mixed mode.

The only ways to set the authentication mode are to use either Management Studio or RegEdit.

Windows Authentication

Windows authentication is superior to mixed mode because the user does not need to learn yet another password and because it leverages the security design of the network.

Using Windows authentication means that users must exist as Windows users to be recognized by SQL Server. The Windows SID (security identifier) is passed from Windows to SQL Server.

Windows authentication is very robust in that it will authenticate not only Windows users, but also users within Windows user groups.

When a Windows group is accepted as a SQL Server login, any Windows user who is a member of the group can be authenticated by SQL Server. Access, roles, and permissions can be assigned for the Windows group, and they will apply to any Windows user in the group.

Best Practice

If the Windows users are already organized into groups by function and security level, using those groups as SQL Server users provides consistency and reduces administrative overhead.

SQL Server also knows the actual Windows username, so the application can gather audit information at the user level as well as at the group level.

Adding a New Windows Login

Windows users are created and managed in various places in the different Windows versions. In Windows XP classic view, users can be managed by selecting Control Panel ➪ Administrative Tools ➪ Computer Management, as shown in Figure 40-3.

Once the users exist in the Windows user list or the Windows domain, SQL Server can recognize them. To add a new login to SQL Server using Object Explorer, follow these steps:

1. Open the Security ➪ Logins node under the server and use the context menu to select New Login.

2. In the General page of the Login–New dialog (see Figure 40-4), use the Search button to locate the Windows user.

3. You may enter a username or group name or use the Advanced button to search for a user.

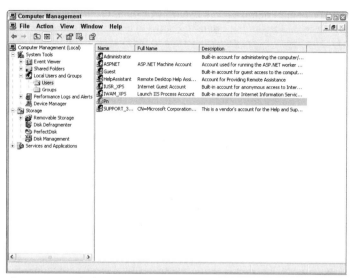

Figure 40-3: Windows users are managed and assigned to Windows groups by means of the Computer Management tool.

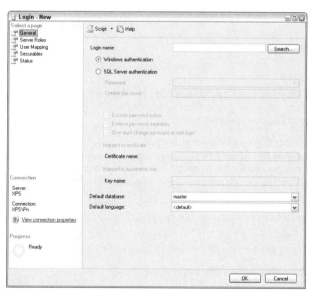

Figure 40-4: The General page of the Login–New dialog is used to create and edit user logins at the server level.

The user may be assigned a default database and language at the bottom of the SQL Server Login Properties dialog. Note that assigning a default database does not automatically grant access to that database. The user may be granted access to databases in the Database Access tab. (Database access is discussed in the next section.)

To use T-SQL code to add a Windows user or group, run the `sp_grantlogin` system stored procedure. Be sure to use the full Windows username, including the domain name, as follows:

```
EXEC sp_grantlogin 'XPS\Joe'
```

To view Windows logins using code, query the `sysserver_principals` catalog view.

The Login–New dialog is also used to manage existing users. To open the Login Permission version of the dialog for an existing user, select the user under the Security ➪ Logins node and use the context menu's Properties command or double-click the user.

Removing a Windows Login

Removing a windows login from SQL Server is simple enough with Management Studio. Select the login in Object Browser and use the context menu to delete the user. Of course, this doesn't delete the user from Windows; it only removes the user from SQL Server.

To remove a Windows user or group from SQL Server, use the `sp_revokelogin` system stored procedure. The Windows user or group will exist in Windows; it just won't be recognized by SQL Server:

```
EXEC sp_revokelogin 'XPS\Joe'
```

Denying a Windows Login

Using the paradigm of `grant`, `revoke`, and `deny`, a user may be blocked for access using `sp_denylogin`. This can prevent a user or group from accessing SQL Server even if he or she could otherwise gain entry from another method.

For example, suppose the Accounting group is granted normal login access, while the Probation group is denied access. Joe is a member of both the Accounting group and the Probation group. The Probation group's denied access blocks Joe from the SQL Server even though he is granted access as a member of the Accounting group, because `deny` overrides `grant`.

To deny a Windows user or group, use the `sp_denylogin` system stored procedure. If the user or group being denied access doesn't exist in SQL Server, then `sp_denylogin` adds and then denies him, her, or it:

```
EXEC sp_denylogin 'XPS\Joe'
```

To restore the login after denying access, you must first grant access with the `sp_grantlogin` system stored procedure.

You can only revoke a login using T-SQL. The feature isn't supported in Management Studio.

Setting the Default Database

The default database is set in the Login Properties form in the General page. The default database can be set from code by means of the `sp_defaultdb` system stored procedure:

```
EXEC sp_defaultdb 'Sam', 'OBXKites'
```

Orphaned Windows Users

When a Windows user is added to SQL Server and then removed from the Windows domain, the user still exists in SQL Server but is considered *orphaned*. Being an orphaned user means even though the user has access to the SQL Server, he or she may not necessarily have access to the network and thus no access to the SQL Server box itself.

The `sp_validatelogins` system stored procedure will locate all orphaned users and return their Windows NT security identifiers and login names. For the following code example, Joe was granted access to SQL Server and then removed from Windows:

```
EXEC sp_validatelogins
```

Result (formatted):

```
SID                                              NT Login
------------------------------------------------ ----------
0x010500000000000515000000FCE31531A931...        XPS\Joe
```

This is not a security hole. Without a Windows login with a matching SID, the user can't log into SQL Server.

To resolve the orphaned user:

1. Remove the user from any database access using `sp_revokedbaccess`.

2. Revoke the user's server access using `sp_revokelogin`.

3. Add the user as a new login.

Security Delegation

In an enterprise network with multiple servers and IIS, logins can become a problem because a user may be logging into one server that is accessing another server. This problem arises because each server must have a trust relationship with the others. For internal company servers, this may not be a problem, but when one of those servers sits in a DMZ on the Internet, you may not want to establish that trust, as it presents a security hole.

Security delegation is a Windows 2005 feature that uses Kerberos to pass security information among trusted servers.

For example, a user can access IIS, which can access a SQL Server, and the SQL Server will see the user as the username even though the connection came from IIS.

A few conditions must be met in order for Kerberos to work:

✦ All servers must be running Windows 2000 or later, running Active Directory in the same domain or within the same trust tree.

✦ The "Account is sensitive and cannot be delegated" option must not be selected for the user account.

✦ The "Account is trusted for delegation" option must be selected for the SQL Server service account.

✦ The "Computer is trusted for delegation" option must be selected for the server running SQL Server.

✦ SQL Server must have a Service Principal Name (SPN), created by `setspn.exe`, available in the Windows 2000 Resource Kit.

Security delegation is difficult to set up and may require the assistance of your network-domain administrator. However, the ability to recognize users going through IIS is a powerful security feature.

SQL Server Logins

The optional SQL Server logins are useful when Windows authentication is inappropriate or unavailable. It's provided for backward compatibility and for legacy applications that are hard-coded to a SQL Server login.

Best Practice

Implementing SQL Server logins (mixed mode) will automatically create an `sa` user, who will be a member of the `sysadmin` fixed server role and have all rights to the server. An `sa` user without a password is very common and the first attack every hacker tries when detecting a SQL Server. Therefore, the BestPractice is disabling the `sa` user and assigning different users, or roles, to the `sysadmin` fixed server role instead.

To manage SQL Server users in Management Studio use the same Login–New dialog used when adding Windows users, but select SQL Server Authentication.

In T-SQL code, use the `sp_addlogin` system stored procedure. Because this requires setting up a user, rather than just selecting one that already exists, it's more complex than adding a `sp_grantlogin`. Only the login name is required:

```
sp_addlogin 'login', 'password', 'defaultdatabase',
  'defaultlanguage', 'sid', 'encryption_option'
```

For example, the following code adds Joe as a SQL Server user and sets his default database to the OBX Kite Store sample database:

```
EXEC sp_addlogin 'Sam', 'myoldpassword', 'OBXKites'
```

The encryption option (`skip_encryption`) directs SQL Server to store the password without any encryption in the `sysxlogins` system table. SQL Server expects the password to be encrypted, so the password won't work. Avoid this option.

The server user ID, or SID, is an 85-bit binary value that SQL Server uses to identify the user. If the user is being set up on two servers as the same user, then the SID will need to be specified for the second server. Query the `sysserver_principals` catalog view to find the user's SID:

```
SELECT Name, SID
  FROM sysserver_principals
  WHERE Name = 'Sam'
```

Result:

```
Name       SID
---------  ----------------------------------------------
Sam        0x1EFDC478DEB52045B52D241B33B2CD7E
```

Updating a Password

The password can be modified by means of the `sp_password` system stored procedure:

```
EXEC sp_password 'myoldpassword', 'mynewpassword', 'Joe'
```

If the password is empty, use the keyword `NULL` instead of empty quotes (`' '`).

Removing a Login

To remove a SQL Server login, use the `sp_droplogin` system stored procedure:

```
EXEC sp_droplogin 'Joe'
```

Removing a login will also remove all the login security settings.

Setting the Default Database

The default database is set in the Login Properties form in the General page, just as it is for Windows users. The default database can be set from code by means of the `sp_defaultdb` system stored procedure:

```
EXEC sp_defaultdb 'Sam', 'OBXKites'
```

Server Roles

SQL Server includes only fixed, predefined server roles. Primarily, these roles grant permission to perform certain server-related administrative tasks. A user may belong to multiple roles.

The following roles are best used to delegate certain server administrative tasks:

✦ *Bulk admin* can perform bulk insert operations.

✦ *Dbcreators* can create, alter, drop, and restore databases.

✦ *Diskadmin* can create, alter, and drop disk files.

✦ *Processadmin* can kill a running SQL Server process.

✦ *Securityadmin* can manage the logins for the server.

✦ *Serveradmin* can configure the serverwide settings, including setting up full-text searches and shutting down the server.

✦ *Setupadmin* can configure linked servers, extended stored procedures, and the startup stored procedure.

✦ *Sysadmin* can perform any activity in the SQL Server installation, regardless of any other permission setting. The `sysadmin` role even overrides denied permissions on an object.

SQL Server automatically creates a user, `'BUILTINS/Administrators'`, which includes all Windows users in the Windows Admins group, and assigns that group to the SQL Server `sysadmin` role. The `BUILTINS/Administrators` user can be deleted or modified if desired.

If the SQL Server is configured for mixed-mode security, it also creates an `sa` user and assigns that user to the SQL Server `sysadmin` role. The `sa` user is there for backward compatibility.

Best Practice

Disable or rename the `sa` user, or at least assign it a password but don't use it as a developer and DBA sign on. In addition, delete the `BUILTINS/Administrators` user. Instead, use Windows authentication and assign the DBAs and database developers to the `sysadmin` role.

A user must reconnect for the full capabilities of the sysadmin role to take effect.

The server roles are set in Management Studio in the Server Roles page of the Login Properties dialog (see Figure 40-5).

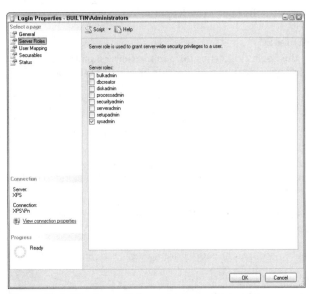

Figure 40-5: The Server Roles page is used to assign server-administrative rights to users. Here, the Windows Admin group is granted the sysadmin role.

In code, a user is assigned to a server role by means of a system stored procedure:

```
sp_addsrvrolemember
   [ @loginame = ] 'login',
   [ @rolename = ] 'role'
```

For example, the following code adds the login XPS\Lauren to the sysadmin role:

```
EXEC sp_addsrvrolemember  'XPS\Lauren', 'sysadmin'
```

The counterpart of sp_addsrvrolemember, sp_dropsrvrolemember, removes a login from a server fixed role:

```
EXEC sp_dropsrvrolemember  'XPS\Lauren', 'sysadmin'
```

To view the assigned roles using code, query the sysserver_principals catalog view to select the members, joined with the sysserver_role_members, and joined again to the sysserver_principals to select the roles.

Database Security

Once a user has gained access to the server, access may be granted to the individual user databases. Database security is potentially complex.

Users are initially granted access to databases by either adding the database to the user or adding the user to the database.

Guest Logins

Any user who wishes to access a database but has not been declared a user within the database will automatically be granted the user privileges of the guest database user if the guest user account exists (refer to Figure 40-1).

The guest user is not automatically created when a database is created. It must be specifically added in code or as a database user. The guest login does not need to be predefined as a server login.

```
EXEC sp_adduser 'Guest'
```

Caution   Be very careful with the guest login. While it may be useful to enable a user to access the database without setting him or her up, the permissions granted to the guest user apply to everyone without access to the database.

The guest user must be removed from a database when guests are no longer welcome.

Granting Access to the Database

Users must be explicitly granted access to any user database. Because this is a many-to-many relationship between logins and database, you can manage database access from either the login side or the database side.

When a login is granted access to the database, the login is also assigned a database user-name, which may be the same as the login name or some other name by which the login will be known within the database.

To grant access to a database from the login side using Object Explorer, use the User Mapping page of the Login Properties form (shown in Figure 40-6).

Note   Many security settings involve multiple objects such as users and databases or roles and object permissions. These settings can be made from either the Login Permissions form or the role or object Properties page.

To grant access from the database point of view, use the New User Context Menu command under the Database ➪ Security ➪ Users node to open the Database User–New form, shown in Figure 40-7. Enter the login to be added in the Login Name field. To search for a login, use the ellipses (...) button. You must enter a name by which the user will be known within the database in the User Name field.

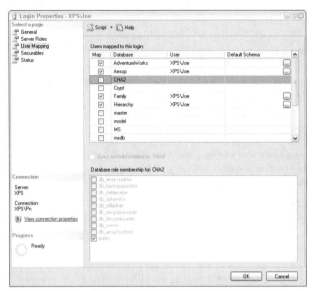

Figure 40-6: You can use the Login Properties form to grant a login access to any database and to assign database roles.

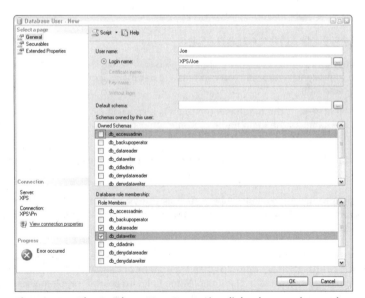

Figure 40-7: The Database User Properties dialog box can be used to add a new user to the database or to manage the current users.

Granting Access Using T-SQL Code

Of course, a stored procedure is available to grant database access to a user: sp_grantdb access. The stored procedure must be issued from within the database to which the user is to be granted access. The first parameter is the server login, and the second is the optional database user name:

```
USE Family
EXEC sp_grantdbaccess 'XPS\Lauren', 'LRN'
```

Lauren now appears in the list of database users as 'LRN'.

To remove Lauren's database access, the system stored procedure sp_revokedbaccess requires her database username, not her server login name:

```
USE Family
EXEC sp_revokedbaccess 'LRN'
```

To query the database user using T-SQL, select from the sysdatabase_principals catalog view.

Fixed Database Roles

SQL Server includes a few standard, or fixed, database roles. Like the server fixed roles, these primarily organize administrative tasks. A user may belong to multiple roles. The fixed database roles include the following:

✦ db_accessadmin can authorize a user to access the database, but not to manage database-level security.

✦ db_backupoperators can perform backups, checkpoints, and dbcc commands, but not restores (only server sysadmins can perform restores).

✦ db_datareaders can read all the data in the database. This role is the equivalent of a grant on all objects, and it can be overridden by a deny permission.

✦ db_datawriters can write to all the data in the database. This role is the equivalent of a grant on all objects, and it can be overridden by a deny permission.

✦ db_ddladmins can issue DDL commands (create, alter, drop).

✦ db_denydatareaders can read from any table in the database. This deny will override any object-level grant.

✦ db_denydatawriters blocks modifying data in any table in the database. This deny will override any object-level grant.

✦ db_owner is a special role that has all permissions in the database. This role includes all the capabilities of the other roles. It is different from the dbo user role. This is not the database-level equivalent of the server sysadmin role; an object-level deny will override membership in this role.

✦ db_securityadmins can manage database-level security — roles and permissions.

Assigning Fixed Database Roles with Management Studio

The fixed database roles can be assigned with Management Studio with either of the following two procedures:

✦ Adding the role to the user in the user's Database User Properties form (see Figure 40-7), either as the user is being created or after the user exists.

✦ Adding the user to the role in the Database Role Properties dialog. Select Roles under the database's Security node, and use the context menu to open the Properties form (see Figure 40-8).

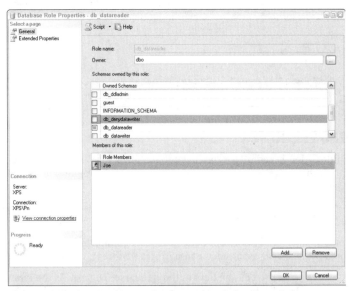

Figure 40-8: The Database Role Properties dialog lists all the users assigned to the current role. Users can be added or removed from the role with the Add and Remove buttons.

Assigning Fixed Database Roles with T-SQL

From code, you can add a user to a fixed database role with the `sp_addrole` system stored procedure.

To examine the assigned roles in T-SQL, query the `sysdatabase_role_members` catalog view joined with `sysdatabase_principal`.

Securables Permissions

The database user can be granted very granular permission to specific securable objects using the Securables page of the Database User form, shown in Figure 40-9.

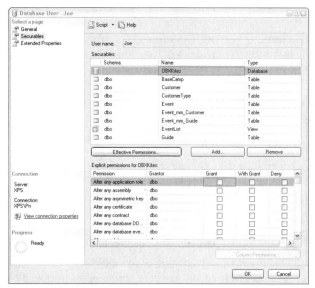

Figure 40-9: The Securables page is used to grant specific permission to individual objects.

The permissions that can be granted depend on the type of object. Even databases are included as a securable object, which presents several database-specific permissions.

Unless you have a compelling reason to manage the permissions on an individual-statement level, it's easier to manage the database administrative tasks using the fixed database roles.

The grant, revoke, and deny commands are detailed in the next section.

Application Roles

An application role is a database-specific role that's intended to allow an application to gain access regardless of the user. For example, if a specific Visual Basic program is used to search the Customer table and it doesn't handle user identification, the VB program can access SQL Server using a hard-coded application role. Anyone using the application gains access to the database.

Caution   Because using an application role forfeits the identity of the user, I strongly advise against using application roles.

Object Security

If the user has access to the database, then permission to the individual database objects may be granted. Permission may be granted either directly to the user or to a standard role and the user assigned to the role. Users may be assigned to multiple roles, so multiple security paths from a user to an object may exist.

Object Permissions

Object permissions are assigned with the SQL DCL commands, grant, revoke, and deny. These commands have a hierarchy. A deny overrides a grant, and a grant overrides a revoke. Another way to think of the DCL commands is that any grant will grant permission unless the user is denied permission somewhere.

Several specific types of permissions exist:

✦ **Select:** The right to select data. Select permission can be applied to specific columns.

✦ **Insert:** The right to insert data.

✦ **Update:** The right to modify existing data. Update rights requires select rights as well. Update permission can be set on specific columns.

✦ **Delete:** The right to delete existing data.

✦ **DRI (References):** The right to create foreign keys with DRI.

✦ **Execute:** — The right to execute stored procedures or user-defined functions.

Object-level permission is applied with the three basic DCL commands, grant, deny, and revoke. Whether security is being managed from Management Studio or from code, it's important to understand these three commands.

Granting object permission interacts with the server and database roles. Here's the overall hierarchy of roles and grants, with 1 overriding 2, and so on:

1. The sysadmin server role

2. Deny object permission

   or the db_denydatareader database role

   or the db_denydatawriter database role

3. Grant object permission

   or object ownership

   or the db_datareader database role

   or the db_datewriter database role

4. Revoke object permission

Best Practice

An easy way to test security is to configure the server for mixed mode and create a SQL Server Login test user. Using Query Analyzer, it's easy to create additional connections as different users—much easier than it is to change the server registration and log into Management Studio as someone else.

If your environment prohibits mixed-mode security, the easiest way to check security is to right-click Management Studio or Query Analyzer and use the Run As command to run as a different user. But this entails creating dummy users on in the Windows domain.

Granting Object Permissions with Code

Setting an object permission is the only security command that can be executed without a system stored procedure being called:

```
GRANT Permission, Permission
  ON Object
  TO User/role, User/role
  WITH GRANT OPTION
```

The permissions may be all, select, insert, delete, references, update, or execute. The role or username refers to the database username, any user-defined public role, or the public role. For example, the following code grants select permission to Joe for the Person table:

```
GRANT Select ON Person TO Joe
```

The next example grants all permissions to the public role for the Marriage table:

```
GRANT All ON Marriage TO Public
```

Multiple users or roles, and multiple permissions, may be listed in the command. The following code grants select and update permission to the guest user and to LRN:

```
GRANT Select, Update ON Person to Guest, LRN
```

The with grant option provides the ability to grant permission for the object. For example, the following command grants Joe the permission to select from the Person table and grant select permission to others:

```
GRANT Select ON Person TO Joe WITH GRANT OPTION
```

The with grant option may only be used when you are managing security with code. Management Studio has no feature for accessing the with grant option.

Revoking and Denying Object Permission with Code

Revoking and denying object permissions uses essentially the same syntax as granting permission. The following statement revokes select permissions from Joe on the Marriage table:

```
REVOKE All ON Marriage TO Public
```

If the permission included the with grant option, then the permission must be revoked or denied with the cascade option so that the with grant option will be removed. The following command denies select permissions from Joe permission on the Person table:

```
DENY Select ON Person TO Joe CASCADE
```

Standard Database Roles

Standard database roles, sometimes called user-defined roles, can be created by any user in the server sysadmin, database db_owner, or database security admin role. These roles are similar to those in user groups in Windows. Permissions, and other role memberships, can be assigned to a standard database role, and users can then be assigned to the role.

Best Practice

The cleanest SQL Server security plan is to assign object permissions and fixed roles to standard database roles, and then to assign users to the roles.

The Public Role

The public role is a fixed role but it can have object permissions like a standard role. Every user is automatically a member of the public role and cannot be removed, so the public role serves as a baseline or minimum permission level.

Caution   Be careful when applying permissions to the public role because it will affect everyone except members of the sysadmin role. Granting access will affect everyone; more important, denying access will block all users except members of the sysadmins role, even object owners, from accessing data.

Managing Roles with Code

Creating standard roles with code involves using the sp_addrole system stored procedure. The name can be up to 128 characters and cannot include a backslash, be null, or be an empty string. By default the roles will be owned by the dbo user. However, you can assign the role an owner by adding a second parameter. The following code creates the manager role:

```
EXEC sp_addrole 'Manager'
```

Result:

```
New role added.
```

The counterpart of creating a role is removing it. A role may not be dropped if any users are currently assigned to it. The sp_droprole system stored procedure will remove the role from the database:

```
EXEC sp_droprole 'Manager'
```

Result:

```
Role dropped.
```

Once a role has been created, users may be assigned to the role by means of the sp_addrolemember system stored procedure. The following code sample assigns Joe to the manager role:

```
EXEC sp_addrolemember 'Manager', Joe
```

Result:

```
'Joe' added to role 'Manager'.
```

Unsurprisingly, the system stored procedure sp_droprolemember removes a user from an assigned role. This code frees Joe from the drudgery of management:

```
EXEC sp_dropRoleMember 'Manager', Joe
```

Result:

```
'Joe' dropped from role 'Manager'.
```

Hierarchical Role Structures

If the security structure is complex, a powerful permission-organization technique is to design a hierarchical structure of standard database roles. For example:

✦ The worker role may have limited access.

✦ The manager role may have all worker rights plus additional rights to look up tables.

✦ The administrator role may have all manager rights plus the right to perform other database-administration tasks.

To accomplish this type of design, follow these steps:

1. Create the worker role and set its permissions.

2. Create the manager role and set its permissions. Add the manager role as a user to the worker role.

3. Create the admin role. Add the admin role as a user to the manager role.

The advantage of this type of security organization is that a change in the lower level affects all upper levels. As a result, administration is required in one location, rather than dozens of locations.

Object Security and Management Studio

Object permissions, because they involve users, roles, and objects, can be set from numerous places within Management Studio. It's almost a maze.

From the Object List

Follow these steps to modify an object's permissions:

1. From an object node (tables, views, stored procedures, or user-defined functions) in the Object Browser, double-click an object or select Properties from the context menu to open the Properties dialog for that object type.

2. Click the Permissions button to open the Object Properties dialog.

As with setting statement permissions in the Database Properties Security tab, you can select grant, with grant, or deny. The object list at the top of the dialog lists all the objects in the database. This list can be used to quickly switch to other objects without backing out of the form to the console and selecting a different object.

The Columns button at the bottom opens the Column Permissions dialog. Select the user and then click the button to set the columns permission for that user. Only `select` and `update` permissions can be set at the column level, because inserts and deletes affect the entire row.

From the User List

From the list of database users in Management Studio, select a user and double-click, or select Properties from the right-click context menu. The Database User Properties dialog is used to assign users to roles.

Clicking the Properties button will open the properties of the selected role.

Clicking the Permissions button will open the Permissions tab of the Database User Properties dialog. This dialog is similar to the Permissions tab of the Database Object Properties dialog.

Unfortunately, the list of objects appears to be unsorted, or only partially sorted, and the grid headers don't re-sort the list of objects. This dialog also desperately needs a `select all` function, and other features such as those in Access's permissions forms.

From the Role List

The third way to control object permissions is from the database role. To open the Database Role Properties dialog, double-click a role in the list of roles, or select Properties from the right-click context menu. The Database Role Properties dialog can be used to assign users or other roles to the role, and to remove them from the role.

The Permissions button opens the permissions dialog box for the role. This form operates like the other permission forms except that it is organized from the role's perspective.

Ownership Chains

In SQL Server databases, users often access data by going through one or several objects. Ownership chains apply to views, stored procedures, and user-defined functions. For example:

✦ A Visual Basic program might call a stored procedure that then selects data from a table.

✦ A report might select from a view, which then selects from a table.

✦ A complex stored procedure might call several other stored procedures.

In these cases, the user must have permission to execute the stored procedure or select from the view. Whether the user also needs permission to select from the underlying tables depends on the ownership chain from the object the user called to the underlying tables.

If the ownership chain is unbroken from the stored procedure to the underlying tables, the stored procedure can execute using the permission of its owner. The user only needs permission to execute the stored procedure. The stored procedure can use its owner's permission to access the underlying tables. The user doesn't require permission to the underlying tables.

Ownership chains are great for developing tight security where users execute stored procedures but aren't granted direct permission to any tables.

If the ownership chain is broken, meaning that there's a different owner between an object and the next lower object, SQL Server checks the user's permission for every object accessed.

In the example,

✦ The ownership chain from dbo.A to dbo.B to dbo.Person is unbroken, so dbo.A can call dbo.B and access dbo.Person as dbo.

✦ The ownership chain from dbo.A to Sue.C to Joe.Purchase is broken because different owners are present. Therefore, dbo.A calls Sue.C using Joe's permissions, and Sue.C accesses Joe.Purchase using Joe's permissions.

✦ The ownership chain from dbo.A through dbo.B to Joe.Person is also broken, so dbo.A calls dbo.B using dbo's permissions, but dbo.B must access Joe.Purchase using Joe's permissions.

A Sample Security Model Example

For a few examples of permissions using the OBXKites database, Table 40-1 lists the permission settings of the standard database roles. Table 40-2 lists a few of the users and their roles.

Table 40-1: OBXKites Roles

Standard Role	Hierarchical Role Structures	Primary Filegroup Tables	Static Filegroup Tables	Other Permissions
IT	sysadmin server role	-	-	-
Clerk	-	-	-	Execute permissions for several stored procedures that read from and update required day-to-day tables
Admin	db_owner database fixed role	-	-	-
Public	-	Select permissions	-	-

Table 40-2: OBXKites Users

User	Database Standard Roles
Sammy	Admin
Joe	
LRN	IT
Clerk Windows group (Betty, Tom, Martha, and Mary)	Clerk

From this security model, the following users can perform the following tasks:

✦ Betty, as a member of the Clerk role, can execute the VB application that executes stored procedures to retrieve and update data. Betty can run select queries as a member of the Public role.

✦ LRN, as the IT DBA, can perform any task in the database as a member of the sysadmin server role.

✦ Joe can run select queries as a member of the public role.

✦ As a member of the Admin role, Sammy can execute all stored procedures. He can also manually modify any table using queries. As a member of the admin role that includes the db_owner role, Joe can perform any database administrative task and select or modify data in any table.

✦ Joe can perform backups, but only LRN can restore from the backups.

C2-Level Security

Organizations that require proof of their database security can investigate and implement C2-level security.

The Department of Defense Trusted Computer System Evaluation Criteria (TCSEC) evaluates computer and database security. The security scale ranges from A (very rare) meaning *verified design*, to D, meaning *minimal protection*. The C2-level security rating, meaning *controlled-access protection*, is required for classified data, IRS data, and most government contracts.

Essentially, C2-level security requires the following:

✦ A unique `loginID` for each user, protected from capture or eavesdropping. The user must be required to log in prior to accessing the database.

✦ A method of auditing every attempt by any user or process to access or modify any data.

✦ The default access to any object is no access.

✦ Access is granted at the discretion of the owner, or by the owner.

✦ Users are responsible for their data access and modifications.

✦ Data in memory is protected from unauthorized access.

For SQL Server's certification, Science Applications International Corporation of San Diego performed the tests as a third-party testing facility for the National Security Agency and the National Institute of Standards and Technology, which jointly run the government's security-certification program. The test took 14 months to complete and was funded by Microsoft.

The 47-page *SQL 2005 C2 Admin and User Guide* may be downloaded from `http://msdn.microsoft.com/library/en-us/secauthz/security/c2_level_security.asp`.

Implementing C2-level security on SQL Server requires the following:

✦ SQL Server 2005 must be running on Windows NT 4 Service Pack 6a.

✦ Merge replication, snapshot replication, federated databases, and distributed databases are not allowed.

✦ Full auditing must be implemented using SQL Profiler.

✦ The C2 security option must be enabled, which shuts down SQL Server if the audit file is not functioning.

✦ Other restrictions on the location and size of the audit file exist.

Views and Security

A popular, but controversial, method of designing security is to create a view that projects only certain columns, or that restricts the rows with a `where` clause and a `with check option`, and then grants permission to the view to allow users limited access to data. Some IT shops require that all access go through such a view. This technique is even assumed in the Microsoft certification tests.

Cross-Reference Chapter 14, "Creating Views," explains how to create a view and use the `with check option`.

Those opposed to using views for a point of security have several good reasons:

✦ Views are not compiled or optimized.

✦ Column-level security can be applied with standard SQL Server security.

✦ Using views for row-level security means that the `with check option` must be manually created with each view. As the number of row-level categories grows, the system requires manual maintenance.

Cryptography

Usually, securing access to the table is sufficient; if not, securing the column will suffice. However, for some information, such as credit card numbers or secret government data, the information's sensitivity warrants further security by encrypting the data stored in the database.

New in 2005 While previous versions of SQL Server did not address data encryption (other than optionally encrypting data during the transport to the client), SQL Server 2005 is better suited to the enterprise environment because it can encrypt data inside SQL Server with passwords, keys, or certificates. All editions of SQL Server support data encryption.

Introduction to Cryptography

Data encryption is basically a scrambling of the data with a secret key to produce an encoded copy of the data called the *cipher data*. Without the key, the data is impossible to unscramble.

Symmetric encryption uses the same key to both encrypt and decrypt the data. While this method is simpler to administer, generally it is considered riskier because more tasks (people) need copies of the key. This may not be a problem when encrypting and decrypting data inside SQL Server.

Asymmetric encryption is considered stronger because one key, a private key, is paired with a second public key. If the data is encrypted with one of those two keys it can be decrypted with the other. In other words, if I encrypt some data using my private key and you already have my public key, then you can decrypt the data. If I've had to share my public key with several partners and I want to ensure that only you can decrypt the data, then we can double the encryption using both our private and public keys. I encrypt using my private key and encrypt it again using your public key. You reverse the order, decrypting with your private key and then my public key.

Note Data can also be encrypted and decrypted using .NET at the middle tier or the front end. This offers the advantage that the database server never sees readable data. Darren Shafer and I used this method for a SQL Server 2000 project storing credit card data. Darren wrote a C# .NET class that employed the `System.Security.Cryptography` class to use a Rinjdael encryption algorithm. It worked great and the data was encrypted from the time it was initially received until the authorized user viewed the report.

Encrypting with a symmetric key produces a smaller data set than using asymmetric keys. One option is to encrypt the data with a symmetric key generated specifically for this set of data and then encrypt the symmetric key using asymmetric keys.

Certificates are similar to keys but are generally issued by an organization, such as VeriSign, to certify that the organization associated with the certificate is legitimate. It's possible to generate local certificates within SQL Server.

The SQL Server-Crypto Hierarchy

SQL Server encryption is based on a hierarchy of keys. At the top of the hierarchy is a unique *service master key* generated by SQL Server for encryption the first time it's needed.

At the next level is the *database master key,* which is a symmetric key SQL Server uses to encrypt private certificates and asymmetric keys. You create a database master key using the `create master key` DDL command. SQL Server then encrypts the database master using the service master key and stores it in both the user database and the master database:

```
CREATE MASTER KEY
  ENCRYPTION BY PASSWORD = 'P@$rw0rD';
```

The password must meet Windows' strong password requirements.

 To view information about the master keys, use the `syssymmetric_keys` and the `sysdatabases.is_master_key_encrypted_by_server` catalog views.

Within the database, and below the database master key in SQL Server's cryptographic hierarchy, are certificates and private keys.

When it comes to actually encrypting data, SQL Server provides four methods:

- ✦ Passphrase
- ✦ Symmetric key
- ✦ Asymmetric key
- ✦ Certificate

Encrypting with a Passphrase

The first method of encrypting data is to use a passphrase, similar to a password but without the strong password requirements, to encrypt the data. The encrypted data will be binary so the example code uses a `varbinary` data type for the `creditcardnumber` column. You should test your situation to determine the required binary length.

The actual encryption is accomplished using the `EncryptbyPassPhrase` function. The first parameter is the passphrase, followed by the data to be encrypted. This example demonstrates encrypting data using the `insert` DML command:

```
CREATE TABLE CCard (
  CCardID INT IDENTITY PRIMARY KEY NOT NULL,
  CustomerID INT NOT NULL,
  CreditCardNumber VARBINARY(128),
```

```
Expires CHAR(4)
);
INSERT CCard(CustomerID, CreditCardNumber, Expires)
  VALUES(1,EncryptbyPassPhrase('Passphrase', '12345678901234567890'), '0808');
```

A normal `select` views the encrypted value actually stored in the database:

```
SELECT *
  FROM CCard
  WHERE CustomerID = 1;
```

Result (binary value abridged):

```
CCardID       CustomerID   CreditCardNumber        Expires
-----------   ------------ --------------------    -------
1             1                     0x01000000C8CF68C        0808
```

To decrypt the credit card data into readable text, use the `decryptbypassphrase` function and `convert` the binary result back to a readable format:

```
SELECT CCardID, CustomerID,
  CONVERT(VARCHAR(20), DecryptByPassPhrase('Password', CreditCardNumber)),
      Expires
  FROM CCard
  WHERE CustomerID = 1;
```

Result:

```
CCardID       CustomerID                           Expires
-----------   ------------ --------------------    -------
1             1            12345678901234567890 0808
```

Sure enough—the data decrypted to the same value previously inserted. If the passphrase was incorrect the result would have been null.

There is one other option to the passphrase encryption method. An *authenticator* may be added to the encryption to further enhance it. Typically, some internal hard-coded value unknown by the user is used as the authenticator to make it more difficult to decrypt the data if it's removed from the database.

The following code sample adds the authenticator to the passphrase encryption. The code, 1, enables the authenticator, and the last parameter is the authenticator phrase:

```
INSERT CCard(CustomerID, CreditCardNumber, Expires)
  VALUES(3,EncryptbyPassPhrase('Passphrase','12123434565678788989',
      1, 'hardCoded Authenticator'), '0808');

SELECT CCardID, CustomerID,
  CONVERT(VARCHAR(20),DecryptByPassPhrase('Passphrase', CreditCardNumber,
      1, 'hardCoded Authenticator')), Expires
  FROM CCard
  WHERE CustomerID = 3;
```

Result:

```
CCardID       CustomerID                           Expires
-----------   ------------ --------------------    -------
2             3            12123434565678788989 0808
```

Encrypting with a Symmetric Key

Using a symmetric key provides an actual object for the encryption, rather than just a human-readable passphrase. Symmetric keys can be created within SQL Server using the `create` DDL command:

```
CREATE SYMMETRIC KEY CCardKey
WITH ALGORITHM = TRIPLE_DES
ENCRYPTION BY PASSWORD = 'P@s$wOrD';
```

Once the keys are created, they are listed in Management Studio's Object Explorer under the database's Security ➪ Symmetric Keys node.

To view information about the symmetric keys using T-SQL, query the `syssymmetric_keys` catalog view.

Keys are objects and can be altered or dropped like any other SQL Server object.

Encryption Algorithms

The algorithm defines how the data will be encrypted using this key. There are nine possible algorithms from which to choose: DES, TRIPLE_DES, RC2, RC4, RC4_128, DESX, AES_128, AES_192, AES_256. They differ in speed and strength.

The Data Encryption Standard (DES) algorithm was selected as the official data encryption method for the U.S. government in 1976, but it can be broken by brute force using today's computers in as little as 24 hours. The triple DES algorithm uses a longer key and is considerably stronger.

The Advanced Encryption Standard (AES), also known as Rijndael (pronounced "Rhine-dahl"), was approved by the National Institute of Standards and Technology (NIST) in November 2001. The 128, 192, or 256 in the algorithm name identifies the bit size of the key. The strongest algorithm in SQL Server's toolbox is the AES_256.

Note   SQL Server leverages Windows' encryption algorithms, so if an algorithm isn't installed on Windows, SQL Server can't use it. AES is not supported on Windows XP or Windows 2000.

Because the symmetric key might be transported in the open to the client, the key itself can also be encrypted. SQL Server can encrypt the key using one, or multiple, passwords, other keys, or certificates. A `key_phrase` can be used to seed the generation of the key.

A temporary key is valid only for the current session and should be identified with a pound sign (#), similar to temporary tables. Temporary keys can use a GUID to help identify the encrypted data using the `indentity_value = 'passphrase'` option.

Using the Symmetric Key

To use the symmetric key, the first step is to `open` the key. This decrypts the key and makes it available for use by SQL Server:

```
OPEN SYMMETRIC KEY CCardKey
  DECRYPTION BY PASSWORD = 'P@s$wOrD';
```

Using the same CCard table created previously, the next code snippet encrypts the data using the CCardKey key. The encryptbykey function accepts the GUID identifier of the key, which can be found using the key_guid() function, and the actual data to be encrypted:

```
INSERT CCard(CustomerID, CreditCardNumber, Expires)
  VALUES(1,EncryptbyKey(Key_GUID('CCardKey'),'11112222333344445555'), '0808');
```

To decrypt the data the key must be open. The decryptbykey function will identify the correct key from the data and perform the decryption:

```
SELECT CCardID, CustomerID,
  CONVERT(varchar(20), DecryptbyKey(CreditCardNumber)) as CreditCardNumber,
    Expires
  FROM CCard
  WHERE CustomerID = 7;
```

Result:

```
CCardID      CustomerID  CreditCardNumber                 Expires
-----------  ----------- ------------------------------   -------
1            7           11112222333344445555             0808
```

It's a good practice to close the key after the transaction:

```
CLOSE SYMMETRIC KEY CCardKey
```

For most applications, you'll want to encrypt the data as it goes into the database, and decrypt it as it is selected. If you want to move the data to another server and decrypt it there, then both servers must have identical keys. To generate the same key on two servers, the key must be created with the same algorithm, identity_value, and key_phrase.

Using Asymmetric Keys

Using asymmetric keys involves encrypting and decrypting with matching private and public keys. Generating an asymmetric key is similar to generating a symmetric key:

```
CREATE ASYMMETRIC KEY AsyKey
  WITH ALGORITHM = RSA_512
  ENCRYPTION BY PASSWORD = 'P@s$wOrD';
```

SQL Server supports RSA_512, RSA_1024, and RSA_2048 as possible asymmetric algorithms. The difference is the bit length of the private key.

Asymmetric keys can also be generated from existing key files:

```
CREATE ASYMMETRIC KEY AsyKey
  FROM FILE  = ' C:\SQLServerBIble\AsyKey.key'
  ENCRYPTION BY PASSWORD = 'P@s$wOrD';
```

Encrypting and decrypting data with an asymmetric key is very similar to using symmetric keys except that the key doesn't need to be open to be used.

Using Certificates

Certificates are typically used to encrypt data over the web for HTTPS endpoints. SQL Server includes certificates for its native HTTP Web Services feature. Certificates are typically obtained from a certificate authority.

Cross-Reference   For information on how to use certificates with HTTP endpoints, see Chapter 32, "Building an SOA Data Store with Web Services."

Preventing SQL Injection

SQL injection is a hacker technique that appends SQL code to a parameter that is later executed as dynamic SQL. What makes SQL injection so dangerous is that anyone with access to the organization's website and who can enter data into a text field can attempt an SQL injection attack. There are several malicious techniques that involve appending code or modifying the where clause. Before learning how to prevent it, it's important to understand how it works, as the following sections explain.

Appending Malicious Code

Adding a statement terminator, another SQL command, and a comment, a hacker can pass code into the execute string. For example, if the parameter passed in is

```
123'; Delete OrderDetail --
```

the parameter, including the delete DDL command, placed within a dynamic SQL string would execute as a batch:

```
SELECT *
  FROM Customers
  WHERE CustomerID = '123'; Delete OrderDetail --'
```

The statement terminator ends the intended code and the delete command looks to SQL Server like nothing more than the second line in the batch. The quotes would normally cause a syntax error, but the comment line solves that problem for the hacker. The result? An empty OrderDetail table.

Other popular appended commands include running xp_commandshell or setting the sa password.

Or 1=1

Another SQL injection technique is to modify the where clause so that more rows are selected than intended.

If the user enters the following string into the user text box:

```
123' or 1=1 --
```

then the 1=1 (always true) condition is injected into the where clause:

```
SELECT *
  FROM Customers
  WHERE CustomerID = '123' or 1=1 --'
```

With every row selected by the SQL statement, what happens next depends on how the rest of the system handles multiple rows. Regardless, it's not what should happen.

Password? What Password?

Another creative use of SQL injection is to comment out part of the intended code. If the user enters the following in the web form:

```
UserName: Joe' --
Password : who cares
```

the resulting SQL statement might read as follows:

```
SELECT USerID
  FROM Users
  WHERE UserName = 'Joe' --' AND Password = 'who cares'
```

The comment in the username causes SQL Server to ignore the rest of the where clause, including the password condition.

Prevention

Several development techniques can prevent SQL injection:

✦ Use Execute As and carefully define the roles so that statements don't have permission to drop tables.

✦ Use DRI referential integrity to prevent deleting primary table rows with dependent secondary table rows.

✦ Never let user input mixed with dynamic SQL in a web form execute as submitted SQL. Always pass all parameters through a stored procedure.

✦ Check for and reject parameters that include statement terminators, comments, or xp_.

✦ Avoid dynamic SQL like the plague that it is.

✦ Test your database using the SQL injection techniques above.

SQL injection is a real threat. If your application is exposed to entry from the Internet and you haven't taken steps to prevent SQL injection, it's only a matter of time before your database is attacked.

Summary

In this era of cybercrime, data security is more important than ever. Security is integral to the Information Architecture Principle. While it's possible to set all the users to sysadmin and ignore security, with a little effort SQL Server security is functional and flexible enough to meet the needs presented by a variety of situations.

The next chapter, "Administering SQL Server Express," concludes this part of the book with specifics about deploying and administering SQL Server Express.

✦   ✦   ✦

Administering SQL Server Express

SQL Server 2005 Express Edition, also called SQL Server Express, or SSE for short, is the low-end version of Microsoft's very popular database program SQL Server. SSE is free to use and redistribute. Any database you create with SSE is directly usable in higher-level versions of SQL Server. Microsoft has taken big steps in making SSE approachable and usable by all types of developers, from beginners to advanced users. The functionality and ease of use packed into SSE make it a very attractive choice for your database application.

SSE is well suited for a limited installation such as a local database setup for a developer. For example, you don't get management software as part of the package; the management software comes as a separate download. In addition, you won't see some features such as Reporting Services in the current version, although Microsoft might add this particular feature in a future version. Unlike other Express products that Microsoft has introduced, SQL Server Express will remain a free download indefinitely.

Because SQL Server Express will typically be repeatedly installed in numerous systems, this chapter details how to create a silent install that can be built into your application installation. In addition, SQL Server Express uses a modified version of SQL Server Management Studio, which is also covered in this chapter.

Note   For more details about deploying applications that use SQL Server Express, I recommend *SQL Server 2005 Express Edition Starter Kit* by Rajesh George and Lance Delano (Wrox, 2006).

On The Web   It pays to keep track of what Microsoft is doing with their various products. The blogs on Microsoft Developer Network (MSDN) are an ideal place to look. For example, Microsoft is currently planning an updated version of SQL Server Express, which you can learn about in the blog at `http://blogs.msdn.com/euanga/archive/2006/02/03/SSEAS_Beta.aspx`. If you want to sign up for the beta of this product, check out the website at `http://blogs.msdn.com/sqlexpress/archive/2006/02/02/ExpressBeta.aspx`.

Installing SQL Server Express

You can use the installation procedure found in Chapter 4 to perform a graphical setup of your copy of SSE. However, you probably won't want users of your applications to go through the graphical installation. A silent background installation works better in these cases to ensure that the user doesn't become mired in details that could ultimately result in an incorrect installation of your application.

Best Practice

The best way to improve user satisfaction is to reduce installation complexity whenever possible. Besides making the user happy, simplified installations improve the chances of getting a good application installation.

Cross-Reference

The installation features of SQL Server Express are similar to those used by SQL Server 2005; SQL Server Express simply has fewer features (such as the lack of Reporting Services). For more information about SQL Server installation, refer to Chapter 4, "Installing SQL Server 2005."

It's easy to obtain your copy of SSE from the Microsoft website at http://msdn.microsoft.com/vstudio/express/sql/. As with the full SQL Server version, you need to download the Northwind and Pubs databases separately at www.microsoft.com/downloads/details.aspx?familyid=06616212-0356-46a0-8da2-eebc53a68034&displaylang=en. You install the databases using the same techniques that you would with SQL Server.

Cross-Reference

For more information about using the Northwind and Pubs databases, refer to Chapter 3, "Exploring SQL Server Architecture."

The file you receive from the Microsoft website, SQLEXPR.EXE, is compressed. You can decompress it using the /X command-line switch. The Choose Directory for Extracted Files dialog box that appears will have the current directory listed. Normally, you'll want to use a new directory to hold the decompressed files so that you don't contaminate the SSE files with other files on your hard drive.

The following sections discuss two methods you can use to take the complexity out of silent installations. The first technique relies on using command-line parameters. This option works best with simple applications or batch files because working at the command line usually limits flexibility by reducing your capability to edit parameters and test them iteratively. When you need more control than a command-line installation allows, you can opt for the second technique, which relies on INI files to configure SSE. Although the INI technique requires more work on your part, it can provide you with an installation better suited to your application's requirements. There isn't any substantial difference between command-line and INI installations from a functionality perspective; either method can result in a full or customized SSE install.

Note

SSE relies on the Microsoft .NET Framework 2.0 for much of its functionality. Even though your development machine likely has this product installed, the application users may not, so you need to verify the presence of the .NET Framework on their system by checking for the \WINDOWS\Microsoft.NET\Framework\v2.0.50727 folder. If the user doesn't have this folder, the latest version of the .NET Framework 2.0 found at www.microsoft.com/downloads/details.aspx?familyid=0856eacb-4362-4b0d-8edd-aab15c5e04f5&displaylang=en can be installed.

Using Command-Line Parameters to Install SSE Silently

The command-line install enables you to use something as simple as a batch file to perform the SSE installation. In fact, you can simply open a command prompt using the Start ⇨ Programs ⇨ Accessories ⇨ Command Prompt shortcut. You perform an SSE setup using the SETUP.EXE file located in the directory you used to store the uncompressed SSE application files. If you want to perform a basic install, all you need to do is type **SETUP** at the command prompt and press Enter. You can achieve the same thing by double-clicking SETUP in Windows Explorer.

Most references you'll see recommend using the Start command to start the SSE setup program. Using Start causes Windows to open a new command window to execute SETUP. Unless you have a specific reason for using a separate command window, you may want to skip this utility. However, before you make a decision, type **Start /?** at the command line and press Enter. You'll see numerous command-line switches you can use to customize the command-line environment for SETUP.EXE. For example, you might want to run the window minimized or bump up the installation priority so it completes faster. The one command-line switch that you always use with the Start command in this case is /WAIT. The /WAIT command-line switch tells Windows to keep the window open until SETUP.EXE completes its tasks. Consequently, a command line using Start would look like this (all of the command-line switches appear on one line, even though they appear on multiple lines in the book):

```
Start /WAIT ["title"] [/Dpath] [/I] [/MIN] [/MAX] [/SEPARATE |
/SHARED] [/LOW | /NORMAL | /HIGH | /REALTIME | /ABOVENORMAL |
/BELOWNORMAL] [/B] SETUP [SSE parameters]
```

Unlike many Windows command-line applications, typing SETUP /? doesn't display a list of options for the SSE SETUP application. The following list describes each of the SSE setup program options:

✦ /qb — Performs a silent installation in which the user can see basic interface features such as the progress bar.

✦ /qn — Performs a silent installation in which the user doesn't see any interface elements at all.

✦ ADDLOCAL=[ALL | Feature List] — Defines which SSE elements to add to the local installation. The ALL option installs all of the features. You can use this parameter to define the initial installation list or features that you want to add to an existing installation. The features appear in a comma-delimited list without any spaces. For example, ADDLOCAL=SQL_Engine,SQL_Data_Files installs the SQL data engine and a place to store the data files. The options must appear as they do in the installation hierarchy shown in Figure 41-1. Consequently, when you want to install the Data Files (SQL_Data_Files) option, you must also install the Database Services (SQL_Engine). The features you can include with the current version of SSE include SQL_Engine, SQL_Data_Files, SQL_Replication, SQL_FullText, Client_Components, Connectivity, and SDK.

Note   Future versions of SSE will likely include additional features, such as Reporting Services (RS_Server), that don't appear in the current version.

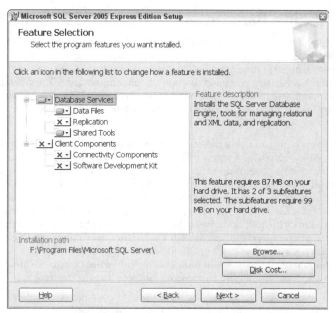

Figure 41-1: Use the ADDLOCAL option command-line to determine which features are available in the Feature Selection page of the installation.

✦ `AGTACCOUNT=Account` and `AGTPASSWORD=Password` — Defines the SQL Server Agent account and password for the SQL Server Agent (Instance) Service. Access the service using the Services console found in the Administrative Tools folder of the Control Panel. The name and password appear on the Log On tab of the Properties dialog box.

✦ `AGTAUTOSTART=[0 | 1]` — Determines whether SQL Server Agent starts automatically. Set the value to 1 to start the service automatically. When you start SQL Server Agent, the system also starts SQL Server, regardless of its automatic start setting.

Note   The full version of SQL Server 2005 supports the `ASACCOUNT` and `ASPASSWORD` parameters to set Analysis Services security. In addition, it supports the `ASAUTOSTART` parameter to control automatic start of Analysis Services. Normally, you'd also need to set the Analysis Services data directory using the `INSTALLASDATADIR` parameter. Analysis Services also uses a default collation that you can modify with the `ASCOLLATION` parameter. Because SSE doesn't support this feature, you can't use these two parameters at the command line.

✦ `COMPANYNAME=Name` — Defines the name of the company registering this product. You must provide this value when working with an INI file, but it's optional when working at the command line.

✦ `DISABLENETWORKPROTOCOLS=[0 | 1 | 2]` — Specifies which network protocols the installation program enables. Use a value of 0 to enable all three network protocols: shared memory, named pipes, and Transmission Control Protocol/Internet Protocol (TCP/IP). A value of 1 is the safest option because it only enables shared memory. No one can use the server remotely when you select the shared memory option. A value of 2 is standard for setups that someone must access from a remote location because it enables both shared memory and TCP/IP.

✦ ERRORREPORTING=[0 | 1]—Enables or disables a feature that sends error reports to Microsoft when catastrophic errors occur during installation. Setup automatically disables error reporting when you don't provide this parameter.

✦ INSTALLDATADIR=Path—Determines the location of the SQL Server data directory.

✦ INSTALLSQLDIR=Path—Determines the location of the SQL Server installation directory. Setup uses a default path of \Program Files\Microsoft SQL Server\.

✦ INSTALLSQLSHAREDDIR=Path—Determines the location of the Integration Services, Notification Services, and Workstation components. Setup uses a default root directory of \Program Files\Microsoft SQL Server\90 and places the various components in subfolders.

✦ INSTANCENAME=Name—Specifies the name of the SSE instance. Each instance (installation) must have a unique name.

Note The full version of SQL Server requires a product identifier—a unique value that identifies a particular installation. Because SSE is free, you don't have to supply this value.

✦ REBUILDDATABASE=1—Changes the Setup application functionality to rebuild the system databases. You can use this feature to change the databases to their default state after they become corrupted or when you need to change the method that SSE uses to collate data. After you rebuild the databases, you must restore the master, model, and msdb databases before you can begin restoring the user databases.

✦ REINSTALLMODE=[O | M | U | S]—Repairs an existing installation to add missing files and replace corrupted files. Setting this parameter to O reinstalls missing files or replaces files when Setup has a newer version to use. Use the M option to rewrite all of the machine-specific registry keys. The U option rewrites all of the user-specific registry keys. Finally, the S option reinstalls all of the shortcuts.

✦ REMOVE=[ALL | Feature]—Uninstalls SQL Server or removes a subset of the functionality it provides. See the ADDLOCAL parameter for a description of product features. You can also use this parameter during an installation to install all features except the one or two features you don't need.

Note The full version of SQL Server 2005 supports the RSACCOUNT and RSPASSWORD parameters to set Report Services security. In addition, it supports the RSAUTOSTART parameter to control automatic start of Analysis Services. The Report Server also requires special configuration that you define using the RSCONFIGURATION parameter. Because SSE doesn't support this feature, you can't use these two parameters at the command line.

Note The full version of SQL Server 2005 includes sample databases that you configure using the SAMPLEDATABASESERVER parameter. Because SSE doesn't include any sample databases, you can't use this parameter at the command line.

✦ SAPWD=Password—Defines the System Administrator (SA) password when using mixed mode security. SSE requires a strong password.

✦ SAVESYSDB=[0 | 1]—Determines whether Setup saves the system databases during an uninstall. You typically use this parameter when you plan to update to a newer version of SQL Server.

✦ SECURITYMODE=SQL — Specifies that SSE uses mixed-mode security. SSE uses Windows security only when this parameter is missing.

✦ SQLACCOUNT=Account and SQLPASSWORD=Password — Defines the SSE account and password for the SQL Server (Instance) Service. Access the service using the Services console found in the Administrative Tools folder of the Control Panel. The name and password appear on the Log On tab of the Properties dialog box.

✦ SQLAUTOSTART=[0 | 1] — Determines whether the SQL Server (Instance) service starts automatically. Set the value to 1 to start the service automatically.

✦ SQLCOLLATION=Settings — Defines the collation settings at the server, database, column, and expression levels. Generally, the default collation works fine unless you have special requirements, such as the need to support multiple languages.

You can discover more about collation in general at http://msdn2.microsoft.com/ en-us/library(d=robot)/ms143508.aspx. The information you need to set Windows collation appears at http://msdn2.microsoft.com/en-us/library(d=robot)/ ms143515.aspx. Information about using binary collations appears at http://msdn2. microsoft.com/en-us/library(d=robot)/ms143350.aspx.

✦ UPGRADE=SQL_Engine — Performs an upgrade of SQL Server, rather than an installation. You must provide the INSTANCE parameter when using this option.

✦ USERNAME=Name — Specifies the name of the individual registering the product. You must provide this value when working with an INI file, but it's optional when working at the command line.

✦ USESYSDB=Path — Specifies the root path to the system databases during an upgrade. Never include the Data folder in the path. For example, if the data appears in the \Program Files\Microsoft SQL Server\MSSQL.1\MSSQL\Data folder, then you would use a root path of \Program Files\Microsoft SQL Server\MSSQL.1\MSSQL.

Using INI Files to Install SSE

The initialization (INI) file installation technique provides access to all of the same features that the command-line installation provides. Consequently, all of the features discussed in the section "Using Command-Line Parameters to Install SSE Silently" also apply to the INI technique. However, the INI technique relies on a different method for defining the installation parameters and requires that you use the following at the command line:

```
SETUP.EXE /settings C:\SQLEXPR\TEMPLATE.INI /qn
```

Unlike the command-line installation, you use the /settings command-line switch to specify the name and location of an INI file. The /qn command-line switch performs the installation without displaying any user interface. You can also use the /qb command-line switch when you want to display a basic interface that include items such as the progress bar.

If you want to create an INI file quickly, use the TEMPLATE.INI file provided as part of the SSE files. You'll find it in the folder you used to decompress the files. The TEMPLATE.INI file contains a wealth of documentation and all of the settings you need to change for the INI file, as shown in Figure 41-2.

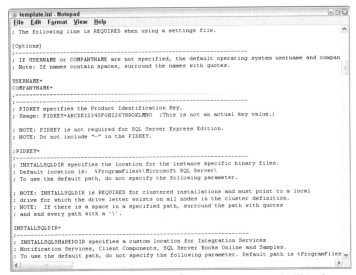

Figure 41-2: Don't start your INI file from scratch; simply fill in the blanks of the TEMPLATE.INI file.

Review the INI file in a little more detail using the code shown in Figure 41-1. Every INI file begins with the [Options] section shown in Figure 41-2. The SSE setup doesn't require any other section names and `SETUP.EXE` ignores any extra sections that you add (or it may display an error message regarding them).

The `TEMPLATE.INI` file contains a wealth of comments. Every comment line starts with a semicolon (;). You can add your own comments as necessary to document company preferences. It's also easy to create entries that you only sometimes need and then comment them out when not needed. Make sure you document these entries so you remember when to use them and when to avoid them.

Simply type in the required value when you do want to use an option, such as `USERNAME` shown at the top of Figure 41-1. Microsoft has included every option that `SETUP.EXE` accepts in `TEMPLATE.INI`, so you can go from the top to the bottom of the file to ensure you don't miss any of the options you need to fill out. The file has also commented out options that SSE doesn't support, such as the `PIDKEY`. You'll find comments for these parameters indicating that SSE doesn't use them.

SQL Server Management Studio Express Edition

SEE doesn't come with a management tool as the full version of SQL Server does; you need to download the management tool separately. SQL Server Management Studio Express Edition (SSMS-EE) is a free download from the Microsoft website at `www.microsoft.com/downloads/details.aspx?FamilyId=82AFBD59-57A4-455E-A2D6-1D4C98D40F6E&displaylang=en`, and is used to manage SSE. SSMS-EE includes the following features:

✦ A single, integrated, easy-to-use GUI for simple database operations

✦ Wizards for managing and creating objects such as databases and tables

✦ The capability to view objects within a database using Object Explorer

✦ A robust query editor that supports multiple result sets

Once you download SSMS-EE, you can install it by double-clicking the Microsoft Installer (MSI) file. You don't need to consider any command-line options in this case.

 New in 2005   SSE supports five users only. If you need to support more than five users, you must use the full version of SQL Server.

SSMS-EE works precisely the same as Management Studio for the full version of SQL Server. Of course, it has limitations based on the limits of SSE. The two big omissions are the lack of a Notifications folder and a SQL Server Agent folder. You'll also find that SSMS-EE lacks entries for features that might appear in future versions of SSE. Nonetheless, in all other ways SSMS-EE works like its bigger brother, which means you can use this product as a training tool for many tasks.

Cross-Reference   For more information about using Management Studio, refer to Chapter 6, "Using Management Studio."

Summary

For some database applications, SQL Server Express is the perfect choice. The limitations don't affect performance and you can install it as a back-end for an application without additional expense. This chapter described how SQL Server Express uses a slimmed-down Management Studio, and how to create a silent install.

✦   ✦   ✦

Business Intelligence

If the Information Architecture Principle stated in Chapter 1 is true, then information is useful not only for daily operations, but also for current and future analysis. Hence, extract, transform, and load (ETL) processes collect data from the daily operations and store it in data warehouses using patterns organized for analysis, rather than daily operations. Cubes, MDX queries, and Reporting Services pull from the data warehouse and present the data for analysis.

This whole process of analyzing historical and current data both today and in the future is the proactive side of IT and is collectively called business intelligence (BI).

In the past three releases of SQL Server, Microsoft has been steadily growing SQL Server's BI services, and SQL Server 2005 brings to fruition years of planning and development. From the enterprise-grade ETL tool and the rich and easy to build cubes to the slick reporting interface, SQL Server 2005 is more than ready to help you conquer your BI requirements.

However, BI, by definition, does not exist in a vacuum. Not only is the data warehouse dependent on numerous operational databases, but the BI toolset frequently includes multiple tools from multiple vendors. While non-SQL Server tools are beyond the scope of this book, this part covers using Excel, the most popular data analysis tool on the planet, as a front end for SQL Server's BI suite.

If you're an old hand at BI, then welcome to SQL Server 2005's sweet BI suite. If you've been around operational data for a while but never had the chance to work on the analysis side, you're in for a treat.

If SQL Server is the box, then Part V is about coaxing every secret out of the box.

ETL with Integration Services

Integration Services is most commonly described as an extract-transform-load (ETL) tool. ETL tools are traditionally associated with preparing data for warehousing, analysis, and reporting, but Integration Services represents a step beyond the traditional role. It is really a robust programming environment that happens to be good at data and database-related tasks.

Many prospective Data Transformation Services (DTS) users have been intimidated by the learning curve, sticking to the Transact-SQL they know instead of investigating a more powerful ETL tool. This has made traditional SQL approaches one of the largest competitors for DTS/Integration Services, but those who investigate Integration Services will find several advantages:

- ✦ Simple, fast methods for moving large quantities of data, minimizing database load and batching data into destination tables to keep blocking and transaction log sizes down.

- ✦ The capability to chain together many tasks, with complete control over ordering, and error and exception handling. Many tasks can be executed in parallel.

- ✦ Connections to read or write most any type of data without special programming or linked server calls.

- ✦ Common data and database management tasks are implemented without the need to write code; .NET scripting environment for other tasks and fully extensible with custom add-ins.

- ✦ Resulting packages are as manageable as the situation requires, with several deployment, configuration, auditing, and logging options.

While careful coding in SQL or other languages can approach the same core functionality, most projects require significant effort and end up with minimal exception handling — often something like "stop and send me an e-mail if there is a problem." One colleague recently received 8,000 e-mails over a two-day period from such a data loading system.

Integration Services enables you to avoid many of the tedious details, providing the opportunity to spend time building applications that can self-heal. It also excels at identifying problems and performing recovery operations within the application itself. Many of the Integration Services features, such as error row redirection, complex precedence constraints, data conversion, and fuzzy lookup, are well suited to the self-healing challenge. There is nothing better than building a system integration application that one seldom even thinks about.

 New in 2005

Integration Services is the successor to the Data Transformation Services (DTS) product available in SQL Server 2000. It shares a few of the basic concepts, but has been completely rewritten from the ground up. Integration Services is available in the Standard and Enterprise Editions of SQL Server 2005.

Design Environment

One of the best ways to understand Integration Services is to understand its design environment. Begin by opening a new Integration Services Project within the Business Intelligence Development Studio. The Integration Services template is located in the Business Intelligence folder. The window that appears should look similar to Figure 42-1.

 Cross-Reference

For more details about working in Business Intelligence Development Studio, see Chapter 6, "Using Management Studio."

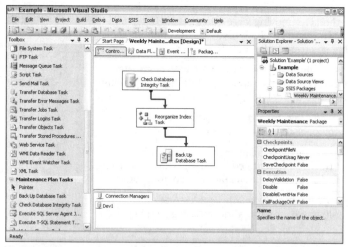

Figure 42-1: The Control Flow tab of Integration Services' design environment

Beyond the ever-present Solution Explorer and Properties panes, several panes and tabs are used in building a package (use the View menu to display any missing panes):

✦ **Connection Managers pane:** Connection Managers are pointers to files, databases, and so on, that are used to provide context for the execution of tasks placed on the design surface. For example, an Execute SQL Task will require a database connection.

✦ **Toolbox:** Provides a list of tasks that can be dragged onto the design surface. The list of available tasks varies depending on the selection of different tabs.

✦ **Control Flow tab:** This is the primary design surface on which tasks are placed, configured, and ordered by connecting tasks with precedence arrows.

✦ **Data Flow tab:** One of the tasks that can be configured on the Control Tab is a Data Flow task, used to move and transform data. The Data Flow tab is used to configure Data Flow tasks; think of it as a properties window on steroids.

✦ **Event Handlers tab:** Events are exposed for the overall package and each task within it. Tasks are placed here to execute for any event, such as `OnError` or `OnPreExecute`.

✦ **Package Explorer tab:** Lists all the package's elements in a single tree view. This can be helpful for discovering configured elements not always obvious in other views, such as event handlers and variables.

The package runs by executing control flow tasks, beginning with tasks that have no incoming precedence constraints (arrows). As each task completes, the next task(s) execute based on the precedence constraints until all tasks are complete. For users of DTS in SQL 7.0 and SQL 2000, this approach to building a package will be familiar, but why the Data Flow tab?

Each data flow is a single task on the Control Flow tab; drill-down (e.g., via a double-click) to view a single data flow's configuration on the Data Flow tab (see Figure 42-2). Note that it does not contain tasks but data sources, destinations, and transformations. The arrows between the boxes are not precedence but data inputs and outputs that determine how data flows from source to destination. Unlike DTS, where transformations happen in a single step as data is being read from a source and written to a destination, Integration Services allows several transformations to be used between reading and writing data. Data flows can come from several sources, and they can be split and merged, and written to several destinations within the confines of a single Data Flow task. Because the transformations occur without reading and writing the database at every step, well-designed data flows can be surprisingly fast.

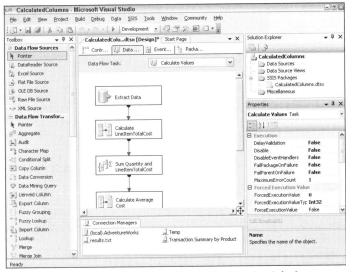

Figure 42-2: The Data Flow tab of Integration Services' design environment

Connection Managers

A *connection manager* is a wrapper for the connection string and properties required to make a connection at runtime. Once the connection is defined, it can be referenced by other elements in the package without duplicating the connection definition, thus simplifying the management of this information and configuration for alternate environments.

New connection managers can be created by right-clicking in the Connection Managers pane or by choosing the New option when configuring a task that requires a connection manager. When right-clicking, notice that several of the more popular connection types are listed directly on the menu, but additional connection types are available by choosing the New Connection option.

Each connection type has both an editor dialog and properties that appear in the Properties pane, both of which vary depending on the connection type. Each of the two lists may contain properties not available in the other. For example, the OLE DB editor is the only location to set the connection timeout, while the delay validation property must be set in the Properties pane.

Variables

As with all proper programming environments, Integration Services provides variables to control execution, pass around values, and so on. Right-click the design surface and choose Variables to show the Variables pane. By default, the Variables pane will display only variables whose scope matches the currently selected object or one of its parents. For example, clicking on the design surface will select the package object and display only the variables scoped at the package level, but selecting a control flow task will show variables for both the selected task and the package (the task's parent). Alternately, the full variable list can be displayed by selecting the Show User Variables button on the pane's toolbar.

The scope of a variable determines where it is visible. Variables with package scope (scope equals the package name) are visible everywhere, whereas variables scoped to a task or event handler are visible only within that object. Variables scoped to a container are visible to the container and any objects it contains.

Create a new variable by first selecting the object to provide the scope and then push the Variable pane's Add Variable toolbar button. Once created, set the variable's name, data type, and value. Note that a variable's scope cannot be changed without deleting and recreating it.

In addition to scope, each variable also has a namespace, which by default is either User or System. The namespace for user-created variables can be changed, but very little (only the occasional value) can be changed for system namespace variables. The namespace is used to fully qualify a variable reference. For example, a variable called MyVar in the user namespace is referred to as User::MyVar.

Variable Usage

Variable values can be manually set via the Variables pane, but their values can also come from a number of other sources, including the following:

✦ Provided at runtime via the /SET switch on the dtexec utility (or equivalent dialog of the dtexecui utility).

✦ Variables values can be entered as expressions, which are evaluated at runtime. Such expressions could include comparing two variable values, calculating a value from other variables, or calculating values based on the current date.

✦ `For` and `Foreach` container tasks can set a variable(s) to contain a simple numeric sequence, each file in a directory on disk, each node in an XML document, and items from other lists and collections.

✦ Query results can provide variable values, either as an individual value or an entire result set.

✦ Scripts can set package variable values as well, but only at the end of execution (values are fixed during execution).

Among the many places for variables to be used, property expressions are among the most useful, as nearly any task property can be determined at runtime based on an expression. This allows variables to control everything from the text of a query to the enabling/disabling of a task.

Expressions

Expressions are used throughout Integration Services to calculate values used in looping, splitting data streams, setting variable values, and setting task properties. The language used to define an expression is a totally new syntax, resembling a cross between C# and Transact-SQL. Fortunately, an Expression Builder is available in many places where an expression can be entered. Some of the key themes include the following:

✦ Variables are referred to by prefixing them with an @, and can be qualified by namespace, making `@[User::foo]` the fully qualified reference to the user variable `foo`. Columns are referred to by their name, and can be qualified by their source name, making `[RawFileSource].[Customer Name]` the fully qualified reference to the Customer Name column read from the `RawFileSource`. Square brackets are optional for names with no embedded spaces or other special characters.

✦ Operators are very C-like, including == (double equal signs) for equality tests, prefix of an exclamation mark for `not` (e.g., `!>` and `!=`), `&&` for logical `AND`, `||` for logical `OR`, and `?` for conditional expressions (think `iif()` function). For example, `@[User::foo] == 17 && CustomerID < 100` returns `true` if the variable `foo` equals 17 AND the CustomerID column is less than 100.

✦ String constants are enclosed in double-quotes, and special characters are C-like backslash escape sequences, like `\n` for new line and `\t` for tab.

✦ The `cast` operator works by describing the target type in parentheses immediately before the value to be converted. For example, `(DT_I4)"193"` will convert the string "193" to a four-byte integer, whereas `(DT_STR,10,1252)@[User::foo]` converts the value of the user variable `foo` to a 10-character string using codepage 1252. The codepage has no default, so everyone will learn the number of their favorite codepage.

A codepage, not to be confused with a locale identifier, maps character representations to their corresponding codes. Two good sources for codepage references are `www.i18nguy.com/unicode/codepages.html` and `www.microsoft.com/typography/unicode/cscp.htm`.

✦ Functions come from the Transact-SQL world, including the familiar date (`GETDATE`, `DATEADD`, `YEAR`), string (`SUBSTRING`, `REPLACE`, `LEN`), and mathematical (`CEILING`, `SIGN`) entries.

Configuring Elements

A large number of elements work together in a functioning Integration Services package, including control flow tasks, task precedence, and data flow components. This section describes the concepts and settings common to each area. Later in this chapter, the functions and unique properties are described for individual elements.

Control Flow

Work flow for both the Control Flow and Event Handler tabs are configured by dragging control flow elements (tasks and/or containers) onto the design surface, configuring each element's properties, and then setting execution order by connecting the items using precedence constraints. Each item can be configured using the overlapping sets of properties in the Properties pane and the Editor dialog. Right-click an item and choose Edit to invoke the Editor, which presents multiple pages (content varies according to the type of task).

All editors include an Expressions page that enables many of the configurable properties to be specified by expressions, rather than static values. Existing expression assignments can be viewed and modified directly on the page, or you can press the ellipsis next to an expression to launch the Expression Builder. Additional expression assignments can be added by clicking the ellipsis in the top line of the expressions page, launching the Property Expressions Editor, shown in Figure 42-3. Choose the property to be set in the left column, and then enter the expression in the right column, pressing the ellipsis to use the Expression Builder if desired.

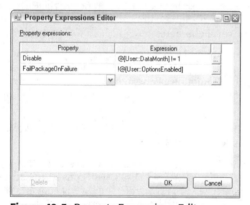

Figure 42-3: Property Expressions Editor

While many of the properties available vary by item, several are available across all items, including packages, containers, and individual tasks. These common properties include the following:

- ✦ **DelayValidation:** Normally, each task in a package is validated before beginning execution to avoid unnecessary partial runs (such as waiting 20 minutes to find out the last step's filename was mistyped). Set this property to true to delay validation until the task actually runs. This option is useful for tasks that reference objects that don't exist when the package starts, but will exist by the time the task executes.

- ✦ **Disable:** When true the task will not execute. Also available from the context menu's disable/enable toggle. Note how disabled tasks display in a darker color.

✦ **DisableEventHandler:** This keeps event handlers from executing for this item. Useful when a parent container has established an event handler that should not apply to this particular item.

✦ Error handling properties are best considered as a group:

- **FailPackageOnFailure:** When set to true, the entire package fails when the individual item fails. The default is false.

- **FailParentOnFailure:** When set to true, the parent container fails when the individual task fails. If a task is not explicitly included in a container (i.e., For Loop, Foreach Loop, or Sequence), then it is implicitly wrapped in an invisible TaskHost container, which acts as the parent. The default is false.

- **MaximumErrorCount:** Maximum number of errors a task or container can see before failing itself. The default is 1.

Given the default settings that apply at the package, container, and task levels, any task that fails will cause its container to fail, which in turn will fail the package, all based on the `MaximumErrorCount`. This is true regardless of any failure branches defined by precedence constraints. Increase the `MaximumErrorCount` on a task to enable error branching to work.

Given this behavior, where do the "FailOn" properties fit in? Consider a container with two tasks, one that is expected to fail in certain cases (call it "Try") and another that will recover from the expected failure (call it "Recover"), but is not itself expected to fail. First, the container's `MaximumErrorCount` must be increased to allow the "Recover" to be reached when "Try" fails. But this has the side effect of ignoring failures in "Recover"! Use the `FailPackageOnFailure` property on "Recover" to stop the entire package when the task fails, or `FailParentOnFailure` to take the failure precedence branch from the container when "Recover" fails.

✦ **LoggingMode:** This property defaults to `UseParentSetting` so that logging can be defined for the entire package at once, but individual items can also be enabled or disabled.

✦ Transactions can be used to ensure that a sequence of operations, such as changes to multiple tables, either succeed or fail together. The following properties control transactions in a package:

- **IsolationLevel:** Specifies the isolation level of a transaction as one of the following: Unspecified, Chaos, ReadUncommitted, ReadCommitted, RepeatableRead, Serializable, or Snapshot. The default is Serializable.

- **TransactionOption:** This property offers three options: NotSupported (the item will not participate in a transaction), Supported (if a parent container requires a transaction this item will participate), and Required (if a parent container has not started a transaction, this container will start one).

Once begun by a parent container, all child items can participate in that transaction by specifying a `TransactionOption` setting of either Supported or Required.

Control Flow Precedence

As described earlier, precedence constraints determine the order in which tasks will execute. Select any task or container to expose its precedence constraint arrow, and then drag that arrow to the task that should follow it, repeating until all items are appropriately related. Any unconstrained task will be run at the discretion of the runtime engine in an unpredictable and often parallel ordering. Each constraint defaults to an "On Success" constraint, which can be adjusted by double-clicking the constraint to reveal the Precedence Constraint Editor, shown in Figure 42-4.

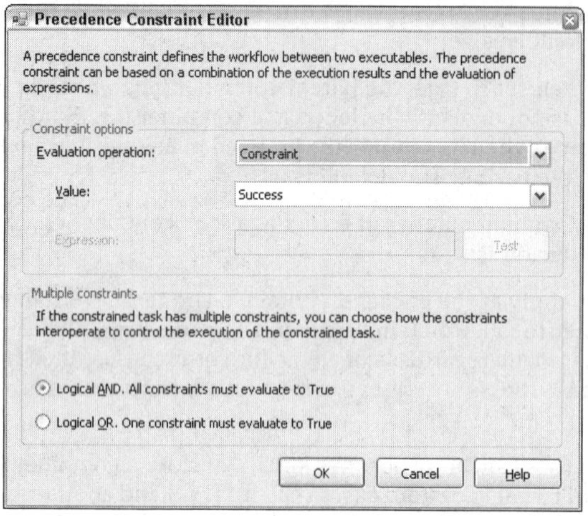

Figure 42-4: Precedence Constraint Editor

The upper half of the editor, labeled "Constraint options," determines when the constraint should fire. It relies on two evaluation operation concepts:

✦ **Constraint:** How the previous item completed: Success, Failure, or Completion (completion being any outcome, either success or failure)

✦ **Expression:** The evaluation of the entered expression, which must resolve to either true or false

These concepts are combined as four separate options: constraint, expression, expression and constraint, expression or constraint — enabling very flexible constraint construction. For example, consider a task that processes a previously loaded table of data and counts the successfully processed rows. The processing task could have two outgoing paths: a success path indicating that the task was successful AND the processed rowcount matches the loaded rowcount, and a failure path indicating that either the task failed OR the rowcounts don't match.

The lower half of the editor, labeled "Multiple constraints," determines how the downstream tasks should deal with multiple incoming arrows. If logical AND is chosen (the default), then all the incoming constraints must fire before the task can execute. If logical OR is chosen, then any incoming constraint firing will cause the task to execute. Logical AND is the most frequently used behavior, but logical OR is useful for work flows that split apart and then rejoin. For example, control can split when an upstream task has both success and failure branches, but the failure branch needs to rejoin the normal processing once the error has been resolved. Using a logical AND at the merge point would require both the success and failure branches to execute before the next task could run, which cannot happen by definition.

The arrows that represent precedence constraints provide visual clues as to the type of constraint. Green arrows denote a success constraint, red a failure constraint, and blue a completion constraint. Constraints that use an expression include an f(x) icon. Logical AND constraints are solid, whereas logical OR constraints are dotted lines.

Data Flow

Unlike other tasks that can be configured in the control flow, a Data Flow task does not show an Editor dialog in response to an edit request. Instead, it switches to the Data Flow tab to view/configure the task details. Each of these components appearing on the design surface can in turn be configured by the Properties pane, a component-specific editor dialog, and for many components an advanced editor as well.

Each data flow must begin with at least one Data Flow source, and generally ends with one or more Data Flow destinations, providing a source and sink for the data processed within the task. Between source and destination any number of transformations may be configured to sort, convert, aggregate, or otherwise change the data.

Out of each source or transformation, a green Data Flow path arrow is available to be connected to the next component. Place the next component on the design surface and connect it to the path before attempting to configure the new component, as the path provides necessary metadata for configuration. Follow a similar process for the red error flow for any component that has been configured to redirect error rows.

Use the Data Flow Path Editor to view/configure paths as necessary, double-clicking on a path to invoke its editor. The editor has three pages:

✦ **General:** For name, description, and annotation options. While the default annotations are usually adequate, consider enabling additional annotations for more complex flows with intertwined paths.

✦ **Metadata:** Displays metadata for each column in the Data Flow path, including the data type and source component. This information is read-only, so adjust upstream components as necessary to make changes, or use a Data Conversion transformation to perform necessary conversions.

✦ **Data Viewers:** Allows different types of Data Viewers to be attached to the path for testing and debugging.

Because a data flow occurs within a single Control Flow task, any component that fails will cause the task to fail.

Event Handlers

Event handlers can be defined for a long list of possible events for any Control Flow task or container. Use them for custom logging, error handling, common initialization code, or a variety of other tasks. If a handler is not defined for a given item when an event fires, Integration Services will search parent containers up to the package level looking for a corresponding event handler and use it instead. It is this "inheritance" that makes event handlers useful, enabling a single handler to be built once and then used repeatedly over many tasks and containers. Once a parent handler has been established, exceptions in the children can be created by setting the child's `DisableEventHandler` property to true, or by giving the child item its own event handler.

To construct an event handler, switch to the Event Handlers tab, and choose the Control Flow item (Executable) in the upper left drop-down list and the event in the upper right list. Then press the hotlink on the design surface to initialize the event. Build the logic within the handler as if it were just another control flow.

Executing a Package in Development

As portions of a package are completed, they can be tested by running the package within the development environment. Right-click a package in the Solution Explorer and choose Execute Package to start the package in debug mode. Packages run in debug mode display progress within the designer environment, with tasks and components changing from white (not yet run) to yellow (running) to green or red (completed with success or failure, respectively).

Caution

There are other convenient methods to execute a package from within Business Intelligence Development Studio, but care should be exercised to ensure that the correct object executes. Selecting Start Debugging from the menu, keyboard (F5), or toolbar can be very convenient, but ensure that the package to be executed has been "Set as Startup Object" by right-clicking on that package in the Solution Explorer. In addition, solutions that contain more than one project may execute unexpected actions (e.g., deploying an Analysis Services database) regardless of startup object/project settings before beginning to debug the selected package. Even in development, inadvertently starting a six-hour data load or stepping on a cube definition can be quite painful.

Once the debug run begins, an Execution Results tab appears displaying the execution trace, including detailed messages and timing for each element of the package. When the package completes, it remains in debug mode to allow variables and state information to be reviewed. To return to design mode, press the Stop button on the Debug toolbar, or choose Stop Debugging from the Debug menu (Shift+F5).

Breakpoints can be set on any task, container, or the package by right-clicking on the object and selecting Edit Breakpoints. The Set Breakpoints dialog (see Figure 42-5) allows a breakpoint to be set on any event associated with that object. PreExecute and PostExecute events are common choices; selecting an object and pressing F9 is a shortcut for toggling the PreExecute event breakpoint. Optionally, a breakpoint can be ignored until the nth execution (Hit count equals), any time at or after the nth execution (Hit count greater than or equal to), or ignored except for the nth, 2nth, etc., hit count (Hit count multiple).

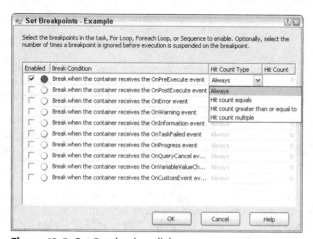

Figure 42-5: Set Breakpoints dialog

While execution is suspended at a breakpoint, use the Locals window to view the current values of variables, and check the Output window for useful messages and warnings, and the Execution Results tab for details on progress across all tasks.

The analog to the breakpoint for data flows is the Data Viewer. Double-click on a data path of interest to add a viewer. Then, during a debug run, package execution will be suspended when the Data Viewer has been populated with data. Press the Go or Detach buttons on the Data Viewer to resume execution.

Breakpoints can also be placed in the code of a Script task. Open the script, set a breakpoint on the line of interest, and Integration Services will stop in the script debugger at the appropriate time.

Integration Services Package Elements

The individual elements that can be used in constructing an Integration Services package are described in detail in this section. For general concepts and common properties, review the earlier sections of this chapter.

Connection Managers

A connection manager is a wrapper for the connection string and properties required to make a connection at runtime. Once the connection is defined, it can be referenced by other elements in the package without duplicating the connection definition, thus simplifying the management of this information and configuration for alternate environments.

Database

Defining database connections through one of the available connection managers requires setting a few key properties:

- ✦ **Provider:** The driver to be used in accessing the database
- ✦ **Server:** The server or filename containing the database to be accessed
- ✦ **Initial Catalog:** Selects the default database in a multi-database source
- ✦ **Security:** Database authentication method and any username/password required

The first choice for accessing databases is generally an OLE DB connection manager using one of the many native providers, including SQL Server, Oracle, Jet (Access), and a long list of other source types. Other database connection managers include the following:

> **Note** The key to most Integration Services packages is speed. ADO.NET has more capabilities, but for the majority of cases, that is not what you are after in IS. Most developers prefer OLE DB for that reason, and because one cannot configure an output using an ADO.NET connection, only an input.

- ✦ **ADO:** Provides ADO abstractions (e.g., Command, Recordset) on top of the OLE DB provider. ADO is not used by Integration Services built-in elements, but would be required by custom tasks written to the ADO interface (e.g., legacy Visual Basic 6.0 code).

- ✦ **ADO.NET:** Provides ADO.NET abstractions (e.g., named parameters, data reader, data set) for the selected database connection. While not as fast as using OLE DB, an ADO.NET connection can execute complex parameterized scripts, provide an in-memory record-set to a Foreach loop, or support custom tasks written using C# or VB.NET.

- ✦ **ODBC:** Allows a connection manager to be configured based on an ODBC DSN. This is useful when OLE DB or .NET providers are not available for a given source (e.g., Paradox).

- ✦ **Analysis Services:** When accessing an existing Analysis Services database, this connection manager is equivalent to an OLE DB connection using the Analysis Services 9.0 provider. Alternately, an undeployed Analysis Services database in the same solution can be referenced — a useful feature for packages being developed in support of a new database. If one of the older OLAP providers is needed for some reason, it can be accessed via the OLE DB connection manager.

- ✦ **SQL Server Mobile:** Allows a connection to mobile database .SDF files.

As individual tasks execute, a connection described by the connection manager is opened and closed for each task. This default setting safely isolates tasks, keeping prior tasks from tweaking the connection of subsequent tasks. Should keeping the same connection between tasks be desired, set the `RetainSameConnection` property to `True`. With appropriate care, this allows a session to be shared between tasks for the manual control of transactions, passing of temp tables, and so on.

Data Source and Data Source Views

Connection managers can also be created based on a data source, which can be very useful to the designer when the package is being developed as part of a project with several packages requiring synchronization of their connection managers. It is also very useful when the source database(s) include a large number of tables or a number of unfamiliar structures.

 Cross-Reference   For more information about data sources and data source views, see Chapter 43, "Business Intelligence with Analysis Services."

Create the connection manager by right-clicking in the Connection Manager pane and choosing New Connection from Data Source, inheriting the connection information from the data source. The data source must be part of the project (not the solution) that contains the package being designed. When setting up tasks to use this connection manager, select it from the list of available connections normally. Or, if one or more data source views have been created, they will be listed as children of the data source with appropriately shorter lists of tables. If a data source view is built up using tables from multiple data sources, only the primary data source's objects are visible when the data source view is selected. Named queries are available for package use, however — a handy feature if a particular view is to be used frequently within a package.

Data source connection managers are entirely a design-time convenience; once deployed, the packages operate as if individual connection managers had been set up without using a data source reference.

File

Remember that every file or folder referenced needs to be available not only at design time, but after a package is deployed as well. Consider using Universal Naming Convention, or UNC, paths for global information or package configurations (see "Maintainable Packages," later in this chapter) to adjust names and locations for specific target servers. UNC is a method of identifying a path so it can be accessed from anywhere on the network a package may be run; it takes the form of \\servername\sharename\path\file.ext. The many file configuration managers are listed here:

✦ **Flat File:** Presents a text file as if it were a table, with locale and header options. The file can be in one of three formats:

- **Delimited:** File data is separated by column (e.g., comma) and row delimiters (e.g., {CR}{LF}).

- **Fixed Width:** File data has known sizes without either column or row delimiters. When opened in Notepad, such a file will appear as if all data is on a single line.

- **Ragged Right:** File data is interpreted using fixed width for all columns except the last, which is terminated by the row delimiter.

Only files that use the delimited format will be able to interpret zero-length strings as null.

✦ **Multiple Flat Files:** Same as the Flat File connection manager, but allows multiple files to be selected, either individually or using wildcards. Data then appears as a single large table to Integration Services elements.

✦ **File:** Identifies a file or folder in the file system without specifying content. Such file pointers are used by several elements with Integration Services, including the File System and FTP tasks for file manipulation and the Execute SQL task to identify the file from which a SQL statement should be read. The usage type (Create file, Existing file, Create folder, Existing folder) ensures that the correct type of file pointer is created.

✦ **Multiple Files:** Same as the file connection manager, but allows multiple files to be selected, either individually or using wildcards.

✦ **Excel:** Identifies a file containing a group of cells that can be interpreted as a table (0 or 1 header rows, data rows below without row or column gaps).

Special

Beyond Database and File connection managers, several other types are provided:

✦ **FTP:** Defines a connection to an FTP server. For most situations, entering the server name and credentials is sufficient to define the connection. This is used with the FTP task to move and remove files or create and remove directories using FTP.

✦ **HTTP:** Defines a connection to a Web Service . Enter the URL of the WSDL for the Web Service in question—for example, http://MyServer/reportserver/reportservice.asmx?wsdl points to the WSDL for Reporting Services on MyServer. Used with the Web Service task to access Web Service methods.

✦ **MSMQ:** Defines a connection to a Microsoft Message Queue; used in conjunction with a Message Queue task to send or receive queued messages.

✦ **SMO:** Specifies the name and authentication method to be used with Database Transfer tasks (Transfer Objects, Transfer Logins, etc.).

✦ **SMTP:** Specifies the name of the Simple Mail Transfer Protocol Server for use with the Send Mail task. Older SMTP server versions may not support all the commands necessary to send e-mail from Integration Services.

✦ **WMI:** Defines a server connection for use with Windows Management Instrumentation tasks, which enable logged and current event data to be collected.

Control Flow Elements

The Control Flow tab provides an environment for defining the overall work flow of the package. The following elements are the building blocks of that work flow.

Containers

Containers provide important features for an Integration Services package, including iteration over a group of tasks and isolation for error and event handling.

In addition to containers, the Integration Services Designer will also create task groups. Define a group by selecting a number of Control Flow items, right-clicking one of the selected items, and choosing Group. This encloses several tasks in a group box that can be collapsed into a single title bar. Note, however, that this group has no properties and cannot participate in the container hierarchy—in short, it is a handy visual device that has no effect on how the package executes.

The containers available are as follows:

✦ **TaskHost:** The TaskHost container is not visible in a package, but implicitly hosts any task that is not otherwise enclosed in a container. Understanding this default container helps understand error and event handler behaviors.

✦ **Sequence:** This simply contains a number of tasks without any iteration features, but provides a shared event and error-handling context, allows shared variables to be scoped to the container level instead of the package level, and enables the entire container to be disabled at once during debugging.

✦ **For Loop:** Provides the advantages of a Sequence container, but runs the tasks in the container as if the tasks were in a C# for loop. For example, given an integer variable `@LoopCount`, assigning the For Loop properties `InitExpression` to `@LoopCount=0`, `EvalExpression` to `@LoopCount<3`, and `AssignExpression` to `@LoopCount=@LoopCount+1` will execute the contents of the container three times, with `@LoopCount` containing the values (0,1,2) on each successive iteration.

✦ **Foreach Loop:** Provides iteration over the contents of a container, but based on various lists of items:

  • **File:** Each file in a wildcarded directory command

  • **Item:** Each item in a manually entered list

  • **ADO:** Each row in a variable containing an ADO recordset or ADO.NET data set

  • **ADO.NET Schema Rowset:** Each item in the schema rowset

  • **Nodelist:** Each node in an XPath result set

  • **SMO:** List of server objects (e.g., jobs, databases, file groups)

Describe the list to be iterated on the Collection page, and then map each item being iterated over to a corresponding variable. For example, a File loop requires a single string variable mapped to index 0, but an ADO loop requires *n* variables for *n* columns, with indexes 0 through n-1.

Control Flow Tasks

Tasks that can be included in control flow are as follows:

✦ **ActiveX Script:** Allows legacy VB and Java scripts to be included in Integration Services. New scripts should use the Script task instead. Consider migrating legacy scripts where possible.

✦ **Analysis Services Execute DDL:** Sends Analysis Services Scripting Language (ASSL) scripts to an Analysis Services server to create, alter, or process cube and data mining structures. Often such scripts can be created using the Script option in SQL Server Management Studio.

✦ **Analysis Services Processing Task:** Identifies an Analysis Services database, a list of objects to process, and processing options

✦ **Bulk Insert:** Provides the fastest mechanism to load a flat file into a database table without transformations. Specify source file and destination table as a minimum configuration. If the source file is a simple delimited file, specify the appropriate row and column delimiters; otherwise, create and specify a format file that describes the layout of the source file. Specifying sort columns that match the clustered key of the target table will minimize table fragmentation. Error rows cannot be redirected, but rather cause the task to fail.

New in 2005

Those familiar with SQL Server 2000's DTS will be tempted to set properties such as `Batchsize` to increase speed and keep the database transaction log size to a minimum, but changing the default values for these settings is not required for Integration Services, and often has the opposite effect of similar settings in DTS.

✦ **Data Flow:** Provides a flexible structure for loading, transforming, and storing data as configured on the Data Flow tab. See the section "Data Flow Components," later in this chapter for the components that can be configured in a Data Flow task.

✦ **Data Mining Query:** Runs prediction queries against existing, trained data mining models. Specify the Analysis Services database connection and mining structure name on the Mining Model tab. On the Build Query tab, enter the DMX query, using the Build New Query button to invoke the Query Builder if desired. The DMX query can be parameterized by placing parameter names of the form `@MyParamName` in the query string. If parameters are used, map from the parameter name (without the @ prefix) to a corresponding variable name on the Parameter Mapping tab. Results can be handled by either sending them to variable(s) on the Result Set tab and/or to a database table on the Output tab:

• Single-row result sets can be stored directly into variables on the Result Set tab by mapping each Result (column) Name returned by the query to the corresponding target variable, choosing the Single Row result type for each mapping.

• Multiple-row result sets can be stored in a variable of type `Object` for later use with a Foreach loop container or other processing. On the Result Set tab, map a single Result Name of 0 (zero) to the object variable, with a result type of Full Result Set.

• Independent of any variable mappings, both single-row and multiple-row result sets can be sent to a table by specifying the database connection and table name on the Output tab.

✦ **Execute DTS 2000 Package:** Allows legacy DTS packages to be executed as part of the Integration Services work flow. Specify the package location, authentication information, and DTS-style Inner/Outer variable mappings. Optionally, once the package is identified, it can be loaded as part of the Integration Services package.

✦ **Execute Package:** Executes the specified Integration Services package, allowing packages to be broken down into smaller, reusable pieces. Invoking a child package does require substantial overhead, so consider the number of invocation per run when considering child packages. For example, one or two child packages per file processed is probably fine, but one package per row processed is probably not. The child package will participate in a transaction if the Execute Package task is configured to participate. Variables available to the Execute Package task can be used by the child package by creating a "parent package variable" configuration in the child package, mapping each parent package variable to a locally defined package variable as needed.

✦ **Execute Process:** Executes an external program or batch file. Specify the program to be run in the `Executable` property, including the extension (e.g., MyApp.exe), and the full path if the program is not included in the computer's `PATH` setting (e.g., `C:\stuff\ MyApp.exe`). Place any switches or arguments that would normally follow the program name on the command line in the `Arguments` property. Set other execution time parameters as appropriate, such as `WorkingDirectory` or `SuccessValue` so Integration Services knows if the task succeeded. The `StandardInputVariable` property allows the text of a variable to be supplied to applications that read from `StdIn` (e.g., `find` or `grep`). The `StandardOutputVariable` and `StandardErrorVariable` properties enable the task's normal and error messages to be captured in variables.

✦ **Execute SQL:** Runs a SQL script or query, optionally returning results into variables. On the General page of the editor, set the `ConnectionType` and `Connection` properties to specify the database the query will run against. `SQLSourceType` specifies how the query will be entered:

  • **Direct Input:** Entered into the `SQLStatement` property by typing in the property page, pressing the ellipsis to enter the query in a text box, pressing the Browse button to read the query from a file into the property, or pressing the Build Query button to invoke the query builder.

  • **File connection:** Specify a file that the query will be read from at runtime.

  • **Variable:** Specify a variable that contains the query to be run.

A query can be made dynamic either by using parameters or by setting the `SQLStatement` property using the Expressions page of the editor. Using expressions is slightly more complicated but much more flexible, as parameter use is limited — only in the `WHERE` clause and, with the exception of ADO.NET connections, only for very simple queries. If parameters are to be used, the query is entered with a marker for each parameter to be replaced, and then each marker is mapped to a variable via the Parameter Mapping page. Parameter markers and mapping vary by connection manager type:

  • **OLE DB:** Write the query leaving a ? to mark each parameter location, and then refer to each parameter using its order of appearance in the query to determine a name: 0 for the first parameter, 1 for the second, and so on.

  • **ODBC:** Same as OLE DB, except parameters are named starting at 1 instead of 0

- **ADO:** Write the query using ? to mark each parameter location, and specify any non-numeric parameter name for each parameter. For ADO, it is the order in which the variables appear on the mapping page (and not the name) that determines which parameter they will replace.

- **ADO.NET:** Write the query as if the parameters were variables declared in Transact-SQL (e.g., SELECT name FROM mytable WHERE id = @ID), and then refer to the parameter by name for mapping.

✦ The ResultSet property (General page) specifies how query results are returned to variables:

- **None:** Results are not captured.

- **Single row:** Results from a singleton query can be stored directly into variables. On the Result Set tab, map each result name returned by the query to the corresponding target variable. As with input parameters, result names vary by connection manager type. OLE DB, ADO, and ADO.NET connections map columns by numeric order starting at 0. ODBC also allows numeric mapping, but starts at 1 for the first column. In addition, OLE DB and ADO connections allow columns to be mapped by column name instead of number.

- **Full result set:** Multiple-row result sets are stored in a variable of type Object for later use with a Foreach loop container or other processing. On the Result Set tab, map a single result name of 0 (zero) to the object variable, with a result type of Full Result Set.

- **XML:** Results are stored in an XML DOM document for later use with a Foreach loop container or other processing. On the Result Set tab, map a single result name of 0 (zero) to the object variable, with a result type of Full Result Set.

✦ **File System Task:** Provides a number of file (copy, delete, move, rename, set attributes) and folder (copy, created, delete, delete content, move) operations. Source and destination files/folders can be specified by either a File connection manager or a string variable that contains the path. Remember to set the appropriate usage type when configuring a File connection manager (e.g., Create folder vs. Existing folder). Set the OverwriteDestination or UseDirectoryIfExists properties to obtain the desired behavior for preexisting objects.

✦ **FTP:** Supports a commonly used subset of FTP functionality, including send/receive/delete files and create/remove directories. Specify the server via an FTP connection manager. Any remote file/path can be specified via either direct entry or a string variable that contains the file/path. A local file/path can be specified via either a File connection manager or a string variable that contains the file/path. Wildcards are accepted in filenames. Use OverWriteFileAtDest to specify whether target files can be overwritten, and IsAsciiTransfer to switch between ASCII and binary transfer modes.

✦ **Message Queue:** Sends or receives queued messages via MSMQ. Specify the message connection, send or receive, and the message type.

✦ **Script:** This task allows Visual Basic .NET code to be embedded in a task. Properties include the following:

- **PrecompileScriptIntoBinaryCode:** Compiles the script when it's saved by the designer and increases the likelihood the script will execute properly in all target environments at the cost of larger package file size.

- **ReadOnlyVariables/ReadWriteVariables:** List the read and read/write variables to be accessed within the script, separated by commas, in these properties. Attempting to access a variable not listed in these properties will result in a run-time error. Entries are case sensitive, so `myvar` and `MyVar` are considered different variables.

- **EntryPoint:** Name of the class that contains the entry point for the script. There is normally no reason to change the default name (ScriptMain). It generates the following code shell:

```
Public Class ScriptMain
    Public Sub Main()
        '
        ' Add your code here
        Dts.TaskResult = Dts.Results.Success
    End Sub
End Class
```

At the end of execution, the script must return `Dts.TaskResult` as either `Dts.Results.Success` or `Dts.Results.Failure` to indicate the outcome of the task. Variables can be referenced through the `Dts.Variables` collection. For example, `Dts.Variables("MyVar").Value` exposes the value of the `MyVar` variable. Be aware that the collection is case sensitive, so referencing `"myvar"` will not return the value of `"MyVar"`. The `Dts` object is an instance of the `ScriptObjectModel` class, which exposes several other useful members, including the `Dts.Connections` collection to access connection managers, `Dts.Events.Fire` methods to raise events, and the `Dts.Log` method to write log entries. See "Interacting with the Package in the Script Task" in SQL Server 2005 Books Online for additional details.

✦ **Send Mail:** Sends a text-only SMTP e-mail message. Specify the SMTP configuration manager and all the normal e-mail fields (To, From, etc.). Separate multiple addresses by commas (not semicolons). The source of the message body is specified by the `MessageSourceType` property as either Direct Input for entering the body as text in the `MessageSource` property, File `Connection` to read the message from a file at runtime, or Variable to use the contents of a string variable as the message body. Attachments are entered as pipe-delimited file specs. Missing attachment files will cause the task to fail.

✦ **Transfer Database:** Copies or moves an entire database from SQL Server 2000 or 2005 to a SQL Server 2005 instance. Choose between the faster `DatabaseOffline` method, which detaches, copies files, and reattaches the databases or the slower `DatabaseOnline`, which uses SMO to create the target database. Identify the source and destination servers via SMO connection managers. For the `DatabaseOnline` method specify the source and destination database names, and the path for each destination file to be created. The `DatabaseOnline` method requires the same information, plus a *network share path* for each source and destination file, as the copy must move the physical files. Specifying UNC paths for the network share path is the most general, but packages that are running on one of the servers can reference local paths for that server. Using the `DatabaseOnline` method requires that any objects the database depends on, such as logins, be in place before the database is transferred.

✦ **Transfer Error Messages:** Transfers custom error messages (a la `sp_addmessage`) from one server to another. Identify the source and destination servers via SMO connection managers and the list of messages to be transferred.

✦ **Transfer Jobs:** Copies SQL Agent jobs from SQL Server 2000 or 2005 to another SQL Server 2005 instance. Identify the source and destination servers via SMO connection managers and the list of messages to be transferred. Any resources required (e.g., databases) by the jobs being copied must be available to successfully copy.

✦ **Transfer Logins:** Copies logins from SQL Server 2000 or 2005 to another SQL Server 2005 instance. Identify the source and destination servers via SMO connection managers and the list of logins to be transferred. The list may consist of selected logins, all logins on the source server, or all logins that have access to selected databases (see the `LoginsToTransfer` property).

✦ **Transfer Master Stored Procedures:** Copies any custom stored procedures from the master database on one server to the master database on another server. Identify the source and destination servers via SMO connection managers, and then select to either copy all custom stored procedures or individually mark the procedures to be copied.

✦ **Transfer Objects:** Copies any database-level object from SQL Server 2000 or 2005 to a SQL Server 2005 instance. Identify the source and destination servers via SMO connection managers and the database on each server. For each type of object, select to either copy all such objects or to individually identify which objects to transfer, and then enable copy options (e.g., `DropObjectsFirst`, `CopyIndexes`, etc.).

✦ **Web Service:** Executes a Web Service call, storing the output in either a file or a variable. Specify an HTTP connection manager and a local file in which to store WSDL information. If the HTTP connection manager points directly at the WSDL file (e.g., `http://MyServer/MyService/MyPage.asmx?wsdl` for the `MyService` Web Service on `MyServer`), then use the Download WSDL button to fill the local copy of the WSDL file; otherwise, manually retrieve and create the local WSDL file. Setting `OverwriteWSDLFile` to true will store the latest Web Service description into the local file each time the task is run.

Once connection information is established, switch to the Input page to choose the service and method to execute, and then enter any parameters required by the chosen method. The Output page provides a choice of output to either a file as described by a File connection manager or a variable. Take care to choose a variable with a data type compatible with the result the Web Service will return.

✦ **WMI Data Reader:** Executes a Windows Management Instrumentation (WQL) query against a server to retrieve event log, configuration, and other management information. Select a WMI connection manager and specify a WQL Query (e.g., `SELECT * FROM win32_ntlogevent WHERE logfile = 'system' AND timegenerated > '20050911'` for all system event log entries since 9/11/2005) from direct input, a file containing a query, or a string variable containing a query. Choose an output format by setting the `OutputType` property to "Data table" for a comma-separated values list, "Property name and value" for one comma-separated name/property combination per row with an extra newline between records, and "Property value" for one property value per row without names. Use `DestinationType` and `Destination` to send the query results to either a file or a string variable.

✦ **WMI Event Watcher:** Similar to a WMI data reader, but instead of returning data, the task waits for a WQL specified event to occur. When the event occurs or the task times out, the SSIS task events `WMIEventWatcherEventOccured` or `WMIEventWatcherEventTimeout` can fire, respectively. For either occurrence, specify the action (log and fire event or log only) and the task disposition (return success, return failure, or watch again). Set the task timeout using the `Timeout` property, with 0 specifying no timeout.

✦ **XML:** Performs operations on XML documents, including comparing two documents (diff), merging two documents, applying diff output (diffgram) to a document, validating a document against a DTD, and performing XPath queries or XSLT transformations. Choose a source document as direct input, a file, or a string variable, and an output as a file or string variable. Set other properties as appropriate for the selected OptionType.

Maintenance Plan Tasks

Maintenance Plan tasks provide the same elements that are used to build maintenance plans for use in custom package development. Tasks use an ADO.NET connection manager to identify the server being maintained, but any database selected in the connection manager is superseded by the databases identified within each Maintenance Plan task. Any questions about what a particular task does can be answered by pressing the View T-SQL button on the maintenance task.

 Cross-Reference For more information about database maintenance, see Chapter 37, "Maintaining the Database."

The available tasks are as follows:

✦ **Back Up Database:** Creates a native SQL backup of one or more databases.

✦ **Check Database Integrity:** Performs a DBCC CHECKDB.

✦ **Execute SQL Server Agent Job:** Starts the selected SQL Agent job via the .sp_start_job stored procedure.

✦ **Execute T-SQL Statement:** A simplified SQL-Server-only statement execution. Does not return results or set variables: use the Execute SQL task for more complex queries.

✦ **History Cleanup:** Trims old entries from backup/restore, maintenance plan, and SQL Agent job history.

✦ **Maintenance Cleanup:** Prunes old maintenance plan, backup, or other files.

✦ **Notify Operator:** Performs an sp_notify_operator, sending a message to selected on-duty operators defined on that SQL Server.

✦ **Rebuild Index:** Issues an ALTER INDEX REBUILD for each table, view, or both in the selected databases.

✦ **Reorganize Index:** Uses ALTER INDEX ... REORGANIZE to reorganize either all or selected indexes within the databases chosen. It optionally compacts large object data.

✦ **Shrink Database:** Performs a DBCC SHRINKDATABASE.

✦ **Update Statistics:** Issues an UPDATE STATISTICS statement for column, index, or all statistics in the selected databases.

Data Flow Components

This section describes the individual components that can be configured within a Data Flow task, including the sources of data for the flow, transforms that change that data, and destinations that receive the transformed data. See the "Data Flow" section earlier in this chapter for general information about configuring a Data Flow task.

Sources

Data Flow sources supply the rows of data that flow through the Data Flow task. Right-clicking a source on the design surface reveals that each source has two different editing options: Edit (basic) and Show Advanced Editor, although in some cases the basic Edit option displays the Advanced Editor anyway. The common steps to configuring a source are represented by the pages of the basic editor:

✦ **Connection Manager:** Specify the particular table, file(s), view, or query that will provide the data for this source. Several sources will accept either a table name or a query string from a variable.

✦ **Columns:** Choose which columns will appear in the data flow. Optionally, change the default names of the columns in the data flow.

✦ **Error Output:** Specify what to do for each column should an error occur. Each type of error can be ignored, cause the component to fail (default), or redirect the problem row to an error output.

The Advanced Editor provides the same capabilities as the basic editor in a different format, plus much finer control over input and output columns, including names and data types. The rows sent to the data flow can also be sorted using the Advanced Editor. On the Input and Output Properties tab, choose the top node of the tree and set the IsSorted property to true. Then select each of the output (data flow) columns to be sorted and enter a SortKeyPosition value, beginning with 1 and incrementing by 1 for each column used for sorting. To sort a column descending, specify a negative SortKeyPosition. For example, giving the Date and Category columns SortKeyPosition values of -1 and 2, respectively, will sort Date descending and Category ascending.

The available sources are as follows:

✦ **OLE DB:** The preferred method of reading database data. It requires an OLE DB connection manager.

✦ **DataReader:** Uses an ADO.NET connection manager to read database data. A direct input query string is required to identify the data to be consumed.

✦ **Flat File:** Requires a Flat File connection manager. Delimited files translate zero-length strings into null values for the data flow when the RetainNulls property is true.

✦ **Excel:** Uses an Excel connection manager and either worksheet or named ranges as tables. A SQL command can be constructed using the Build Query button that selects a subset of rows. Data types are assigned to each column by sampling the first few rows.

✦ **Raw:** Reads a file written by the Integration Services Raw File destination (see the following "Destinations" section) in a preprocessed format, making this a very fast method of retrieving data. Because the data has already been processed once, no error handling or output configuration is required. The input filename is directly specified without using a connection manager.

✦ **XML:** Reads a simple XML file and presents it to the data flow as a table, using either an inline schema (a header in the XML file that describes the column names and data types) or an XSD (XML Schema Definition) file. The XML source does not use a connection manager; instead, specify the input filename and then either an XSD file or indicate that the file contains an inline schema. (Set the UseInlineSchema property to true or select the check box in the basic editor).

✦ **Script:** A script component can act as a source, destination, or transformation of a data flow. Use a script as a source to generate test data or format a complex external source of data. For example, a poorly formatted text file could be read and parsed into individual columns by a script. Start by dragging a script component onto the design surface, choosing Source from the pop-up Select Script Component Type dialog. On the Inputs and Outputs page of the editor, add as many outputs as necessary, renaming them as desired. Within each output, define columns as appropriate, carefully choosing the corresponding data types.

On the Script page of the editor, list the read and read/write variables to be accessed within the script, separated by commas, in the `ReadOnlyVariables` and `ReadWriteVariables` properties, respectively. Leave the `PreCompile` property set at the default `True` unless the size of the package on disk is of concern. Press the Script button to expose the code itself, and note that the primary method to be coded overrides `CreateNewOutputRows`, as shown in this simple example:

```
Public Class ScriptMain
    Inherits UserComponent
    '-- Create 20 rows of random integers between 1 and 100
    Public Overrides Sub CreateNewOutputRows()
        Randomize()
        Dim i As Integer
        For i = 1 To 20
            OutputOBuffer.AddRow()
            OutputOBuffer.RandomInt = CInt(Rnd() * 100)
        Next
    End Sub
End Class
```

This example works for a single output with the default name `Output 0` containing a single integer column `RandomInt`. Notice how each output is exposed as `name+"buffer"` and embedded spaces are removed from the name. New rows are added using the `AddRow` method and columns are populated by referring to them as output properties. An additional property is exposed for each column with the suffix `_IsNull` (e.g., `OutputOBuffer.RandomInt_IsNull`) to mark a value as `NULL`.

Reading data from an external source requires some additional steps, including identifying the connection managers that will be referenced within the script on the Connection Managers page of the editor. Then, in the script, additional methods must be overridden: `AcquireConnections` and `ReleaseConnections` to open and close any connections, and `PreExecute` and `PostExecute` to open and close any record sets, data readers, and so on (database sources only). Search for the "Examples of Specific Types of Script Components" topic in SQL Server Books Online for full code samples and connection manager methods.

Destinations

Data Flow destinations provide a place to write the data transformed by the Data Flow task. Configuration is similar to that of sources, including both Advanced and Basic editors and three common steps to configuration:

✦ **Connection Manager:** Specify the particular table, file(s), view, or query to which data will be written. Several destinations will accept a table name from a variable.

✦ **Columns:** Map the columns from the data flow (input) to the appropriate destination columns.

✦ **Error Output:** Specify what to do should a row fail to insert into the destination: ignore the row, cause the component to fail (default), or redirect the problem row to an error output.

The available destinations are as follows:

✦ **OLE DB:** Writes rows to a table, view, or SQL command (ad hoc view) for which an OLE DB driver exists. Table/view names can be selected directly in the destination or read from a string variable, and each can be selected with or without "fast load." Fast load can decrease runtime by an order of magnitude or more depending upon the particular data set and selected options. Options for fast load are as follows:

- **Keep identity:** When the target table contains an identity column, either this option must be chosen to allow the identity to be overwritten with inserted values (ala SET IDENTITY_INSERT ON), or the identity column must be excluded from mapped columns so that new identity values can be generated by SQL Server.

- **Keep nulls:** Choose this option to load null values instead of any column defaults that would normally apply.

- **Table lock:** Keeps a table-level lock during execution

- **Check constraints:** Enables CHECK constraints (e.g., a valid range on an integer column) for inserted rows. Note that other types of constraints, including UNIQUE, PRIMARY KEY, FOREIGN KEY, and NOT NULL constraints cannot be disabled. Loading data with CHECK constraints disabled will result in those constraints being marked as "not trusted" by SQL Server.

- **Rows per batch:** Specifying a batch size provides a hint to building the query plan, but does not change the size of the transaction used to put rows in the destination table.

- **Maximum insert commit size:** Similar to the BatchSize property of the Bulk Insert task, the maximum insert commit size is the largest number of rows included in a single transaction. When this property is left at its default of 0, the entire data set is loaded in a single transaction.

New in 2005

Those familiar with SQL Server 2000's DTS will be tempted to set properties such as rows per batch and maximum insert commit size to increase speed and keep the database transaction log size to a minimum, but changing the default values for these settings is not required for Integration Services, and often has the opposite effect of similar settings in DTS.

✦ **SQL Server:** This destination uses the same fast-loading mechanism as the Bulk Insert task, but is restricted in that the package must execute on the SQL Server that contains the target table/view. Speed can exceed OLE DB fast loading in some circumstances. Options are the same as those described for the Bulk Insert task.

✦ **DataReader:** Makes the data flow available via an ADO.NET DataReader, which can be opened by other applications, notably Reporting Services, to read the output from the package.

✦ **Flat File:** Writes the data flow to a file specified by a Flat File connection manager. Because the file is described in the connection manager, limited options are available in the destination: Choose whether to overwrite any existing file and provide file header text if desired.

✦ **Excel:** Sends rows from the data flow to a sheet or range in a workbook using an Excel connection manager. Note that an Excel worksheet can handle at most 65,536 rows of data, the first of which is consumed by header information. Strings are required to be Unicode, so any DT_STR types need to be converted to DT_WSTR before reaching the Excel destination.

✦ **Raw:** Writes rows from the data flow to an Integration Services format suitable for fast loads by a raw source component. It does not use a connection manager; instead, specify the AccessMode by choosing to supply a filename via direct input or a string variable. Set the WriteOption property to an appropriate value:

  • **Append:** Adds data to an existing file, assuming the new data matches previously written data.

  • **Create always:** Always start a new file.

  • **Create once:** Create initially and then append on subsequent writes. This is useful for loops that write to the same destination many times in the same package.

  • **Truncate and append:** Keeps the existing file's metadata, but replaces the data.

Raw files cannot handle BLOB data.

✦ **Recordset:** Writes the data flow to a variable. Stored as a record set, the object variable is suitable for use as the source for a Foreach loop or other processing within the package.

✦ **SQL Server Mobile:** Writes rows from the data flow into a SQL Mobile database table. Configure by identifying the SQL Server Mobile connection manager that points to the appropriate .SDF file, and then enter the name of the table on the Component Properties tab.

✦ **Dimension Processing and Partition Processing:** These tasks enable the population Analysis Services cubes without first populating the underlying relational data source. Identify the Analysis Services connection manager of interest and then choose the dimension or partition of interest. Then select a processing mode:

  • **Add/Incremental:** Minimal processing required to add new data

  • **Full:** Complete reprocess of structure and data

  • **Update/Data-only:** Replaces data without updating the structure

✦ **Data Mining Model Training:** Provides training data to an existing data mining structure, thus preparing it for prediction queries. Specify the Analysis Services connection manager and the target mining structure in that database. Use the Columns tab to map the training data to the appropriate mining structure attributes.

✦ **Script:** A script can also be used as a destination, using a similar process to that already described for using a script as a source. Use a script as a destination to format output in a manner not allowed by one of the standard destinations. For example, a file suitable for input to a COBOL program could be generated from a standard data flow. Start by dragging a script component onto the design surface, choosing Destination from the pop-up Select Script Component Type dialog. Identify the input columns of interest and configure the script properties as described previously. After pressing the Script button to access the code, the primary routine to be coded is named after the Input name with a _ProcessInputRow suffix (e.g., Input0_ProcessInputRow). Note the row object passed as an argument to this routine, which provides the input column information for each row (e.g., `Row.MyColumn` and `Row.MyColumn_IsNull`). Connection configuration and preparation is the same as described in the source topic. Search for the "Examples of Specific Types of Script Components" topic in SQL Server Books Online for full code samples and connection manager methods.

Transformations

Between the source and destination, transformations provide functionality to change the data from what was read into what is needed. Each transformation requires one or more data flows as input and provides one or more data flows as output. Like sources and destinations, many transformations provide a way to configure error output for rows that fail the transformation. Many transformations also provide both a basic and advanced editors to configure the component, with normal configurations available from the basic editor when available.

The standard transformations available in the Data Flow task are as follows:

✦ **Aggregate:** Functions rather like a `GROUP BY` query in SQL, generating Min, Max, Average, and so on, on the input data flow. Due to the nature of this operation, Aggregate does not pass through the data flow, but outputs only aggregated rows. Begin on the Aggregations tab by selecting the columns to include and adding the same column multiple times in the bottom pane if necessary. Then, for each column, specify the output column name (Output Alias), the operation to be performed (e.g., Group by, Count ...), and any comparison flags for determining value matches (e.g., Ignore case). For columns being distinct counted, performance hints can be supplied for the exact number (Distinct Count Keys) or an approximate number (Distinct Count Scale) of distinct values the transform will encounter. The scale ranges are as follows:

  - **Low:** Approximately 500,000 values

  - **Medium:** Approximately 5,000,000 values

  - **High:** Approximately 25,000,000 values

  Likewise, performance hints can be specified for the Group By columns by expanding the Advanced section of the Aggregations tab, entering either an exact (Keys) or an approximate (Keys Scale) count of different values to be processed. Alternately, performance hints can be specified for the entire component instead of individual columns on the Advanced tab, along with the amount to expand memory when additional memory is required.

✦ **Audit:** Adds execution context columns to the data flow, allowing data to written with audit information about when and where it came from. Available columns are PackageName, VersionID, ExecutionStartTime, MachineName, UserName, TaskName, and TaskId.

✦ **Character Map:** Allows strings in the data flow to be transformed by a number of operations: Byte reversal, Full width, Half width, Hiragana, Katakana, Linguistic casing, Lowercase, Simplified Chinese, Traditional Chinese, and Uppercase. Within the editor, choose the columns to be transformed, adding a column multiple times in the lower pane if necessary. Each column can then be given a destination of a New column or In-place change (replaces the contents of a column). Then choose an operation and the name for the output column.

✦ **Conditional Split:** Enables rows of a data flow to be split between different outputs depending upon the contents of the row. Configure by entering output names and expressions in the editor. When the transform receives a row, each expression is evaluated in order, and the first one that evaluates to true will receive that row of data. When none of the expressions evaluate to true, the default output (named at the bottom of the editor) receives the row. Once configured, as data flows are connected to downstream components, an Input Output Selection pop-up appears, and the appropriate output can be selected. Unmapped outputs are ignored and can result in data loss.

✦ **Copy Column:** Adds a copy of an existing column to the data flow. Within the editor, choose the columns to be copied, adding a column multiple times in the lower pane if necessary. Each new column can then be given an appropriate name (Output Alias).

✦ **Data Conversion:** Adds a copy of an existing column to the data flow, enabling data type conversions in the process. Within the editor, choose the columns to be converted, adding a column multiple times in the lower pane if necessary. Each new column can then be given an appropriate name (Output Alias) and data type. Conversions between code pages are not allowed. Use the Advanced editor to enable locale-insensitive fast parsing algorithms by setting the `FastParse` property to `true` on each output column.

✦ **Data Mining Query:** Runs a DMX query for each row of the data flow, enabling rows to be associated with predictions, such as the likelihood a new customer will make a purchase or the probability a transaction in fraudulent. Configure by specifying an Analysis Services connection manager, choosing the mining structure and highlighting the mining model to be queried. On the Query tab, press the Build New Query button and map columns in the data flow to the columns of the model (a default mapping is created based on column name). Then specify the columns to be added to the data flow in the lower half of the pane (usually a prediction function) and give the output an appropriate name (Alias).

✦ **Derived Column:** Uses expressions to generate values that can either be added to the data flow or replace existing columns. Within the editor, construct Integration Services expressions to produce the desired value, using type casts to change data types as needed. Assign each expression to either replace an existing column or be added as a new column. Give new columns an appropriate name and data type.

✦ **Export Column:** Writes large object data types (`DT_TEXT`, `DT_NTEXT`, or `DT_IMAGE`) to file(s) specified by a filename contained in the data flow. For example, large text objects could be extracted into different files for inclusion in a website or text index. Within the editor, specify two columns for each extract defined: a large object column and a column containing the target filename. A file can receive any number of objects. Set Append/Truncate/Exists options to indicate the desired file create behavior.

✦ **Fuzzy Grouping:** Identifies duplicate rows in the data flow using exact matching for any data type and/or fuzzy matching for string data types (`DT_STR` and `DT_WSTR`). Configure the task to examine the key columns within the data flow that identify a unique row. Several columns are added to the output as a result of this transform:

- **Input key** (default name `_key_in`): A sequential number assigned to identify each input row.

- **Output key** (default name `_key_out`): The `_key_in` of the row this row matches (or its own `_key_in` if not a duplicate). One way to cull the duplicate rows from the data flow is to define a downstream conditional split on the condition `[_key_in] == [_key_out]`.

- **Similarity score** (default name `_score`): A measure of the similarity of the entire row, on a scale of 0 to one, to the first row of the set of duplicates.

- **Group Output** (default name <column>_clean): For each key column selected, this is the value from the first row of the set of duplicates (i.e., the value from the row indicated by _key_out).

- **Similarity Output** (default name Similarity_<column>): For each key column selected, this is the similarity score for that individual column versus the first row of the set of duplicates.

Within the editor, specify an OLE DB connection manager, where the transform will have permissions to create a temporary table. Then configure each key column by setting its Output, Group Output, and Similarity Output names. In addition, set the following properties for each column:

- **Match Type:** Choose between Fuzzy and Exact Match types for each string column (non-string data types always match exactly).

- **Minimum Similarity:** Smallest similarity score allowed for a match. Leaving fuzzy match columns at the default of 0 enables similarity to be controlled from the slider on the Advanced tab of the editor.

- **Numerals:** Specify whether leading or trailing numerals are significant in making comparisons. The default of Neither specifies that leading and training numerals are not considered in matches.

- **Comparison Flags:** Choose settings appropriate to the type of strings being compared.

✦ **Fuzzy Lookup:** Similar to the Lookup transform, except that when an exact lookup fails, a fuzzy lookup is attempted for any string columns (DT_STR and DT_WSTR). Specify on OLE DB connection manager and table name where values will be looked up, and a new or existing index to be used to cache fuzzy lookup information. On the columns tab, specify a join between the data flow and the reference table, and which columns from the reference table will be added to the data flow. On the Advanced tab, select the similarity required for finding a match: The lower the number the more liberal the matches become. In addition to the specified columns added to the data flow, match metadata is added as follows:

- **_Similarity:** Reports the similarity between all of the values compared.

- **_Confidence:** Reports the confidence level that the chosen match was the correct one compared to other possible matches in the lookup table.

- **_Similarity_<column name>:** Similarity for each individual column.

The Advanced editor allows settings of MinimumSimilarity and FuzzyComparisonFlags for each individual column.

✦ **Import Column:** Reads large object data types (DT_TEXT, DT_NTEXT, or DT_IMAGE) from files specified by a filename contained in the data flow, adding the text or image objects as a new column in the data flow. Configure in the Advanced editor by identifying each column that contains a filename to be read on the Input Columns tab. Then, on the Input and Output Properties tab, create a new output column for each filename column to contain the contents of the files as they are read, giving the new column an appropriate name and data type. In the output column properties, note the grayed-out ID property, and locate the properties for the corresponding input (filename) column. Set the input column's FileDataColumnID property to the output column's ID value to tie the filename and contents columns together. Also set the ExpectBOM property to true for any DT_NTEXT data being read that has been written with byte-order-marks.

✦ **Lookup:** Finds rows in a database table that match the data flow and includes selected columns in the data flow, much like a `JOIN` between the data flow and a table. For example, a product ID could be added to the data flow by looking up the product name in the master table. Configure the basic lookup by identifying the OLE DB connection manager and reference table/view/query that will participate in the lookup. On the Columns tab, map the join columns between the data flow and the reference table by dragging and dropping lines between corresponding columns. Then check the reference table columns that should be added to the data flow, adjusting names as desired in the bottom pane.

The Advanced tab provides an opportunity to optimize memory performance of the Lookup transform. By default, the entire reference table is read into memory at the beginning of the transform to minimize I/O, a practice that can be very slow for larger tables. Check Enable Memory Restrictions to only cache a portion of the table, choosing a cache size appropriate for the number of values likely to be loaded in a single package execution. The SQL statement can also be modified if a more efficient form is available for a data set.

✦ **Merge:** Combines the rows of two sorted data flows into a single data flow. For example, if some of the rows of a sorted data flow are split by an error output or Conditional Split transform, they can be merged again. The upstream sort must have used the same key columns for both flows, and the data types of columns to be merged must be compatible. Configure by dragging two different inputs to the transform and mapping columns together in the editor. See Union All for the unsorted combination of flows.

✦ **Merge Join:** Provides SQL `JOIN` functionality between data flows sorted on the join columns. Configure by dragging the two flows to be joined to the transform, taking care which one is connected to the left input if a left outer join is desired. Within the editor, choose the join type, map the join columns, and choose which columns are to be included in the output.

✦ **Multicast:** Copies every row of an input data flow to many different outputs. Once an output has been connected to a downstream component, a new output will appear for connection to the next downstream component. Only the names of the output are configurable.

✦ **OLE DB Command:** Executes a SQL statement (e.g., `UPDATE` or `DELETE`) for every row in a data flow. Configure by specifying an OLE DB connection manager to use when executing the command, and then switch to the Component Properties tab and enter the SQL statement using question marks for any parameters (e.g., `UPDATE MyTable SET Col1 = ? WHERE Col2=?`). On the Column Mappings tab, associate a data flow column with each parameter in the SQL statement.

✦ **Percentage Sampling:** Splits a data flow by randomly sampling the rows for a given percentage. For example, this could be used to separate a data set into training and testing sets for data mining. Within the editor, specify the approximate percentage of rows to allocate to the Selected output, while the remaining rows are sent to the Unselected output. If a sampling seed is provided, the transform will always select the same rows from a given data set.

✦ **Pivot:** Denormalizes a data flow, similar to the way an Excel pivot table operates, making attribute values into columns. For example, a data flow with three columns, Quarter, Region, and Revenue, could be transformed into a data flow with columns for Quarter, Western Region, and Eastern Region, thus pivoting on Region.

✦ **Row Count:** Counts the number of rows in a data flow and places the result into a variable. Configure by populating the `VariableName` property.

✦ **Row Sampling:** Nearly identical to the Percentage Sampling transform, except that the number of rows to be sampled is entered, rather than the percentage of rows.

✦ **Script:** Start by dragging a script component onto the design surface, choosing Transformation from the pop-up Select Script Component Type dialog. Within the editor, mark the columns that will be available in the script, and indicate which will be ReadWrite versus ReadOnly. On the Inputs and Outputs tab, add any output columns that will be populated by the script above and beyond the input columns.

On the Script page of the editor, list the read and read/write variables to be accessed within the script, separated by commas, in the ReadOnlyVariables and ReadWriteVariables properties, respectively. Leave the PreCompile property set at the default of True unless the size of the package on disk is of concern. Press the Script button to expose the code itself, and note that the primary method to be coded overrides <inputname>_ProcessInputRow, as shown in this simple example:

```
Public Class ScriptMain
    Inherits UserComponent
    Public Overrides Sub Input0_ProcessInputRow(ByVal Row As
InputOBuffer)
        'Source system indicates missing dates with ancient values
        If Row.TransactionDate < #1/1/2000# Then
            Row.TransactionDate_IsNull = True
            Row.PrimeTimeFlag_IsNull = True
        Else
            'Set flag for prime time transactions
            If Weekday(Row.TransactionDate) > 1 _
            And Weekday(Row.TransactionDate) < 7 _
            And Row.TransactionDate.Hour > 7 _
            And Row.TransactionDate.Hour < 7 Then
                Row.PrimeTimeFlag = True
            Else
                Row.PrimeTimeFlag = False
            End If
        End If
    End Sub
End Class
```

This example uses one ReadWrite input (TransactionDate) and one output (PrimeTimeFlag), with the input name left with the default of Input 0. Each column is exposed as a property of the Row object, as is the additional property with the suffix _IsNull to test or set the column value as NULL. The routine is called once for each row in the data flow.

✦ **Slowly Changing Dimension:** Compares the data in a data flow to a dimension table, and, based on the roles assigned to particular columns, maintains the dimension. This component is unusual in that it does not have an editor; instead, a wizard guides the steps of defining column roles and interactions with the dimension table. At the conclusion of the wizard, a number of components are placed on the design surface to accomplish the dimension maintenance task.

✦ **Sort:** Sorts the rows in a data flow by selected columns. Configure by selecting the columns to sort by. Then, in the lower pane, choose the sort type, the sort order, and the comparison flags appropriate to the data being sorted.

✦ **Term Extraction:** Builds a new data flow based on terms it finds in a Unicode text column (DT_WSTR or DT_NTEXT). This is the training part of text mining, whereby strings of a particular type are used to generate a list of commonly used terms, which is later used by the Term Lookup component to identify similar strings. For example, the text of saved RSS documents could be used to find similar documents in a large population. Configure by identifying the column containing the Unicode text to be analyzed. If a list of terms to be excluded has been built, identify the table and column on the Exclusions tab. The Advanced tab controls the extraction algorithm, including whether terms are single words or phrases (articles, pronouns, etc., are never included), scoring algorithm, minimum frequency before extraction, and maximum phrase length.

✦ **Term Lookup:** Provides a "join" between a Unicode text column in the data flow and a reference table of terms built by the Term Extraction component. One row appears in the output data flow for each term matched. The output data flow also contains two columns in addition to the selected input columns: Term and Frequency. Term is the noun or noun phrase that was matched and Frequency is the number of occurrences in the data flow column. Configure the transform by specifying the OLE DB connection manager and table that contains the list of terms. Use the Term Lookup tab to check the input columns that should be passed through to the output data flow, and then map the input Unicode text column to the Term column of the reference table by dragging and dropping between those columns in the upper pane.

✦ **Union All:** Combines rows from multiple data flows into a single data flow, given the source columns are of compatible types. Configure by connecting as many data flows as needed to the component. Then, using the editor, ensure that the correct columns from each data flow are mapped to the appropriate output column.

✦ **Unpivot:** Makes a data flow more normalized by making columns into attribute values. For example, a data flow with one row for each quarter and a column for revenue by region could be turned into a three-column data flow: Quarter, Region, and Revenue.

Maintainable and Manageable Packages

Integration Services enables applications to be created with relatively little effort, which is a great advantage from a development perspective, but can be a problem if quickly developed systems are deployed without proper planning. Care is required to build maintainable and manageable applications regardless of the implementation. Fortunately, Integration Services is designed with many features that support long-term maintainability and manageability.

Designing before developing is especially important when first getting started with Integration Services, as practices established early are often reused in subsequent efforts, especially logging, auditing, and overall structure. Perhaps the key advantage to developing with Integration Services is the opportunity to centralize everything about a data processing task in a single place, with clear precedence between steps, and opportunities to handle errors as they occur. Centralization greatly increases maintainability compared to the traditional "script here, program there, stored procedure somewhere else" approach. Other topics to consider during design include the following:

✦ Identify repeating themes for possible package re-use. Many tasks that repeat the same activities on objects with the same metadata are good candidates for placing in reused subpackages.

✦ Appropriate logging strategies are the key to operational success. When an error occurs, who will be responsible for noticing and how will they know? For example, how will they know whether a package was supposed to run but did not for some reason? What level of logging is appropriate? (More is not always better: too many irrelevant details will mask true problems.) What kinds of environment and package state information will be required to understand why a failure has occurred after the fact?

✦ Auditing concepts may be useful for both compliance and error-recovery operations. What type of information should be associated with data created by a package? If large quantities of information are required, consider adding the details to a *lineage log,* adding only an ID to affected records.

✦ For packages that run on multiple servers or environments, what configuration details change for those environments? Which storage mode (registry, SQL, XML, etc.) will be most effective at distributing configuration data? When possible, use systemwide configurations instead of package-specific ones to simplify the distribution and maintenance of configurations.

✦ Determine how to recover from a package failure. Will manual intervention be required before the package can run again? For example, a package that loads data may be able to use transactions to ensure that rerunning a package will not load duplicate rows.

✦ Consider designing checkpoint restartable logic for long-running packages.

✦ Determine the most likely failure points in a package. What steps will be taken to address a failure (realistically, not theoretically)? Add those steps to the package if possible, using error data flows and task constraints now to avoid labor costs later.

Good development practices help increase maintainability as well. Give packages, tasks, components, and other visible objects meaningful names. Liberal use of annotations to note non-obvious meanings and motivations will benefit future developers as well. Finally, use version-control software to maintain a history of package and related file versions.

Logging

Because many packages are destined for unattended operation, generating an execution log is an excellent method for tracking operations and collecting debug information. Right-click on the package design surface and choose Logging to configure logging for a package. On the Providers and Logs tab, add a provider for each output type that will be logged (multiple are allowed). On the Details tab, specify the events for which log entries will be written; the advanced view (see Figure 42-6) also allows selecting which columns will be included in each event's log entry.

The tree view in the left pane represents the container hierarchy of the package. The check boxes correspond to each object's `LoggingMode` property: Clear for Disabled, a black check for Enabled, and a gray check for `UseParentSetting` (logging settings inherited from the parent). By default, all objects will inherit from the package settings. Highlighting an item in the tree displays the details for that object in the current tab. Note that providers can only be configured for the package, and any object with `UseParentSetting` will have its options grayed out in deference to its parents settings.

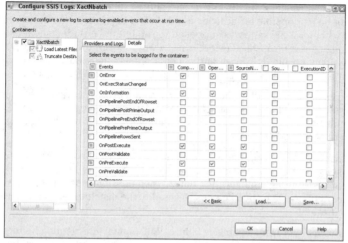

Figure 42-6: Advanced view of the Details tab

The standard log providers are as follows:

✦ **Text File:** Writes a comma-separated-value text file. Configure with an appropriate File connection manager.

✦ **SQL Profiler:** Writes a .TRC file that can be viewed in the Profiler application. This can be a useful option when viewed with other trace or performance information within Profiler. Configure with an appropriate File connection manager.

✦ **SQL Server:** Writes log entries to the dbo.sysdtslog90 table in the database indicated by the associated OLE DB connection manager. Any database can be chosen to host this table. If the table schema does not exist, it will be created on first use.

✦ **Event Log:** Writes log entries to the Windows application event log on the computer that executes the package. No configuration is required.

✦ **XML File:** Writes an .XML file. Configure with an appropriate File connection manager.

The logging configuration Details tab also provides an Advanced mode that allows log data columns to be chosen for each event. Once a useful set of event/column combinations have been constructed, they can be saved as a template and reloaded on other packages.

Package Configurations

Package configurations make it easier to move packages between servers and environments, providing a way to set properties within the package based on environment-specific configurations. For example, the server names and input directories might change between the development and production environments.

Right-click on the package design surface and choose Package Configurations to setup/modify configurations. The list of configurations shown here are applied to the package in the order listed. To add a new configuration, ensure configurations are enabled and press Add to start the Package Configuration Wizard. Choose the desired Configuration Type (storage location). There are essentially three categories to consider:

✦ **Registry & Environment Variable:** These types can hold a single property only.

✦ **XML File & SQL Server Table:** Each of these configuration types can hold any number of property settings.

✦ **Parent Package Variable:** Allows access to the contents of a single variable from the calling package.

Most configuration types allow the storage location to be identified either directly or via an environment variable. The environment variable approach can be useful when the storage location (e.g., file directory) must change between environments. Once the configuration type and location are specified, the Select Properties to Export option enables the properties that will change between environments to be chosen. Complete the wizard by reviewing the selections and giving the configuration a name.

Configurations can be reused between packages if the names of the objects containing the properties to be set are the same between packages. For example, packages that use the same names for their connection managers could share a configuration that sets server or filenames. To share a configuration in a subsequent package, choose the same configuration type, and then specify the same storage location (e.g., XML filename) as the initial package. When prompted by a dialog warning that the configuration already exists, select Reuse Existing.

Checkpoint Restart

Enabling checkpoint restart allows a package to restart without rerunning tasks that already completed successfully. Note the following basic rules about restart points:

✦ Only Control Flow tasks define restart points — a Data Flow task is viewed as a single unit of work regardless of the number of components it contains.

✦ Any transaction in progress is rolled back on failure, so the restart point must retreat to the beginning of the transaction. Thus, if the entire package executes as a single transaction, it will always restart at the beginning of the package.

✦ Any loop containers are started over from the beginning of the current loop.

✦ The configuration used on restart is saved in the checkpoint file and not the current configuration file.

Enable checkpoints by setting the package properties:

✦ **CheckpointFilename:** Name of the file to save checkpoint information in.

✦ **CheckpointUsage:** Set to either IfExists (starts at the beginning of the package if no file, or at the restart point if the checkpoint file exists) or Always (fails if the checkpoint file does not exist).

✦ **SaveCheckPoints:** Set to True.

In addition, the `FailPackageOnFailure` property must be set to True for the package and every task or container that can act as a restart point.

Deploying Packages

The Business Intelligence Development Studio is an excellent environment for designing and debugging Integration Services packages, but it is not an efficient method of routinely executing packages. Without installing a package on a server, it can execute without the development overhead by using dtexec/dtexecui. Run dtexecui from the command line and specify the desired execution options, and then either press the Execute button or switch to the Command Line page to copy the appropriate dtexec command-line switches.

Conversely, installing packages on the target SQL Server(s) makes sense when a package will be reused. Once installed, a package is known to the Integration Services service, which in turn can be connected to SQL Server Management Studio for tracking and monitoring. Integration Services also caches the components executed by packages to reduce startup time.

Installing Packages

Creating a Deployment Utility provides a utility that installs all the packages in a project on a target server. Configure the utility by right-clicking on the project (not the package) in the Solution Explorer and choosing Properties. Navigate to the Deployment Utility page of the resulting dialog and set the value of CreateDeploymentUtility to True. Review the settings for DeploymentOutputPath indicating where the install package will be written relative to the project directory, and the setting of AllowConfigurationChanges, which enables configuration values to be adjusted as part of the install process. Save the property changes, and then choose Build <Project name> from the Build menu to create the install package.

Once the deployment utility has been created, log on to the target server and double-click the package manifest (<project name>.SSISDeploymentManifest) to start the Package Installation to install the packages on the target server.

In addition, individual packages can be installed on a server using SQL Server Management Studio. Log on to the target server and connect the local instance of Integration Services in the Object Explorer. On either the File System or MSDB nodes, right-click and choose Import Package. Note that the source package can be stored either as a file or a SQL Server (msdb) package. Similar functionality is available from the dtutil command-line utility.

Executing Packages

Once installed on the target server, a package can be executed in several ways:

✦ Locate the installed package in SQL Server Management Studio, right-click and choose Run Package, which in turn invokes dtexecui for the selected package.

✦ Run the dtexecui utility, which allows the full array of execution options to be selected. It will also display the command-line switches to use with the dtexec command-line utility.

✦ From a SQL Agent Job step, choose the step type as SQL Server Integration Services Package and the package source as SSIS Package Store.

Choice of execution method and location can have a profound impact on performance and reporting. Execution using dtexec/dtexecui can offload package processing from the SQL Server when run on another server or workstation. These options also default to providing verbose feedback during execution, which can be useful in tracking progress or understanding errors. However, consider network traffic that may be introduced by this scenario. For example, loading a series of data files from a file server to the SQL Server via a workstation can double the network load (every file must move from the file server to the workstation, and then again from the workstation to the SQL Server) compared to running the package on the SQL Server.

Running a package via the SQL Agent will cause the package to execute on the SQL Server, which tends to minimize network load, but this can be a problem if the SQL Server does not have adequate resources to accommodate the often memory-hungry package. In addition, reporting for SQL Agent executions is limited to the logging enabled within the package, which must be configured carefully to ensure that adequate operational and debugging information is captured.

Summary

Integration Services is a capable environment for building applications that move large quantities of data efficiently and sequence multi-step processing with robust error handling. Management features such as easy installation, auditing and logging facilities, and environment-specific configurations make Integration Services applications easy to live with once developed.

Many organizations have written reams of Transact-SQL and programmed custom applications to address tasks that Integration Services handles with ease. For those willing to make a small investment in learning the Integration Services environment, the cost savings and performance gains can be truly stunning.

The best way to get started is to choose a small project and dive in. Like any programming environment, the first application will not be perfect, but soon you'll wonder how you ever lived without Integration Services.

✦　　✦　　✦

Business Intelligence with Analysis Services

Having worked with various organizations and data systems, over time I've noticed a progression of reporting and analysis solutions. First queries are run directly against the online transactional processing (OLTP) database, but this approach conflicts with production use of the database and generally limits access to very few due to security concerns.

Often the next step is to make a nightly copy of the OLTP database for the express purpose of running analytical queries. These attempts at using an OLTP database for online analytical processing (OLAP) are problematic on a number of fronts:

✦ OLTP data structures are optimized for single, atomic transactions, whereas OLAP queries summarize large volumes of data. Thus, queries are painfully slow.

✦ OLTP data may reflect limited history, whereas OLAP tends to be interested in historical trends.

✦ OLTP data structures are understood by a relatively small population of experts in the organization, whereas OLAP is most effective when exposed to the widest possible audience.

A common refinement on querying the OLTP database is to create a new database that contains tables of summary data. When done carefully, this approach can address some speed and history issues, but it is still understood by a relatively small population. Consistent interpretation tends to be a problem as well, because summary tables are often created at different times for different purposes.

These two concepts of consistent interpretation and availability to a wide audience are key strategies for successful OLAP in particular and Business Intelligence (BI) in general. An organization needs to have widely understood data on which to base its business decisions—the only alternatives are rumor and intuition.

This chapter describes the how to use Analysis Services as part of your BI solution, enabling data-based decision-making in your organization.

Data Warehousing

SQL Server 2005 Analysis Services has broadened functionality such that several scenarios do not require a data warehouse for sustainable operation. Nonetheless, it is helpful to understand the concepts of the warehouse when approaching Analysis Services.

Star Schema

The data warehouse is the industry standard approach to structuring a relational OLAP data store. It begins with the idea of dimensions and measures, whereby a dimension is a categorization or "group by" in the data, and the measure is the value being summarized. For example, in "Net Sales by Quarter and Division," the measure is Net Sales and the dimensions are Quarter (time) and Division (organization).

Deciding which dimensions and measures to include in the warehouse should be based on the needs of the business, bringing together an understanding of the types of questions that will be asked and the semantics of the data being warehoused. Interviews and details about existing reports and metrics can help gain a first approximation, but for most organizations a pilot project will be needed to fully define requirements.

Business needs can then provide a basis for building the star or snowflake schema that is the building block of the warehouse (see Figure 43-1).

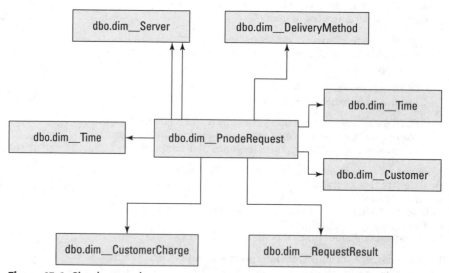

Figure 43-1: Simple star schema

The star schema derives its name from its structure: a central fact table and a number of dimension tables gathered around like the points of a star. Each dimension is connected back to the fact table by a foreign key relationship.

The fact table consists of two types of columns: the keys that relate to each dimension in the star and the measures of interest.

Each dimension table consists of a primary key by which it relates back to the fact table and one or more attributes that categorize data for that dimension. For example, a customer dimension may include attributes for name, e-mail address, and zip code. In general, the dimension will represent a denormalization of the data in the OLTP system. For example, the AdventureWorksDW customer dimension is derived from the AdventureWorks tables Sales.Individual and Person.Contact, and fields parsed from the XML column describing demographics, among others.

Occasionally, it makes sense to limit denormalization by making one dimension table refer to another, thus changing the star schema into a snowflake schema. For example, Figure 43-2 shows how the product dimension has been snowflaked in AdventureWorks' Internet Sales schema. Product category and subcategory information could have been included directly in the product DimProduct table, but instead separate tables have been included to describe the categorizations. Snowflakes are useful for complex dimensions in which consistency issues might otherwise arise, such as the assignments of subcategories to categories in Figure 43-2, or for large dimensions where storage size is a concern.

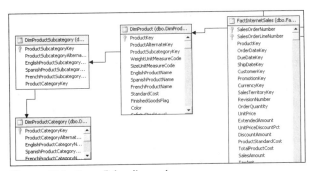

Figure 43-2: Snowflake dimension

Best Practice

Traditionally, snowflake schema have been discouraged because they add complexity and can slow SQL operations, but Analysis Services eliminates the majority of these issues. If a dimension can be made more consistent using a snowflake structure, then do so unless: (1) The procedure required to publish data into the snowflake is too complex or slow to be sustainable or (2) The schema being designed will be used for extensive SQL queries that will be slowed and complicated by the snowflake design.

Consistency

Defining the star schema enables fast OLAP queries against the warehouse, but gaining needed consistency requires following some warehousing rules:

✦ When loading data into the warehouse, null and invalid values should be replaced with their reportable equivalents. This enables the data's semantics to be researched carefully once and then used by a wide audience, leading to a consistent interpretation throughout the organization. Often, this involves manually adding rows to dimension tables to allow for all the cases that can arise in the data (e.g., Unknown, Internal, N/A, etc.).

✦ Rows in the fact table should never be deleted, and no other operations should be performed that will lead to inconsistent query results from one day to the next. Often this leads to delaying import of in-progress transactions.

✦ Avoid using OLTP keys to relate fact and dimension tables, even though it is often very convenient to do so. Consider a star schema containing financial data when the accounting package is upgraded, changing all the customer IDs in the process. If the warehouse relation is based on an identity column, changes in the OLTP data can be accomplished by changes to the relatively small amount of data in the customer dimension. If the OLTP key were used, the entire fact table would need to be converted.

Astute readers will notice that these ideas about consistency are related to ideas about the eventual size of the fact table. In general, fact tables grow such that the only practical operation is to insert new rows — delete and update operations become impractical. In fact, database size estimates can ignore the size of dimension tables and use just the size of the fact tables.

Best Practice

Keeping large amounts of history in the warehouse doesn't imply keeping data forever. Plan for archiving from the beginning by using partitioned fact tables that complement the partitioning strategy used in Analysis Services. For example, a large fact table might be broken into monthly partitions, maintaining two years of history.

Loading Data

Given the architecture of the star/snowflake schema, adding new data begins at the points and moves inward, adding rows to the fact table last in order to satisfy the foreign key constraints. Often, warehouse tables are loaded using Integration Services, but examples are shown here as SQL inserts for illustration.

Loading Dimensions

The approach to loading varies with the nature of the source data. In the fortunate case where the source fact data is related by foreign key to the table containing dimension data, only the dimension data needs to be scanned. This example uses the natural primary key in the source data, product code, to identify rows in the Products staging table that have not yet been added to the dimension table:

```
INSERT INTO Warehouse.dbo.dimProduct (ProductCode, ProductName)
SELECT stage.Code, stage.Name FROM Staging.dbo.Products stage
    LEFT OUTER JOIN Warehouse.dbo.dimProduct dim ON stage.Code=dim.ProductCode
WHERE dim.ProductCode is NULL
```

Often, the source dimension data will not be related by foreign key to the source fact table, so loading the dimension table requires a full scan of the fact data in order to ensure consistency. This next example scans the fact data, picks up a corresponding description from the dimension data when available, or uses "Unknown" as the description when none is found:

```
INSERT INTO Warehouse.dbo.dimOrderStatus (OrderStatusID, OrderStatusDesc)
SELECT DISTINCT o.status, ISNULL(mos.Description,'Unknown')
FROM Staging.dbo.Orders o
  LEFT OUTER JOIN Warehouse.dbo.dimOrderStatus os
    ON o.status=os.OrderStatusID
  LEFT OUTER JOIN Staging.dbo.map_order_status mos
    ON o.status = mos.Number
WHERE os.OrderStatusID is NULL
```

Finally, a source table may contain both fact and dimension data, which opens the door to inconsistent relationships between dimension attributes. The following example adds new product codes that appear in the source data, but guards against multiple product name spellings by choosing one with an aggregate function. Without using MAX here, the query may return multiple rows for the same product code:

```
INSERT INTO Warehouse.dbo.dimProduct (ProductCode, ProductName)
SELECT stage.Code, MAX(stage.Name) FROM Staging.dbo.Orders stage
  LEFT OUTER JOIN Warehouse.dbo.dimProduct dim ON stage.Code=dim.ProductCode
WHERE dim.ProductCode is NULL
```

Loading Fact Tables

Once all the dimensions have been populated, the fact table can be loaded. Dimension primary keys generally take one of two forms: the key is either a natural key based on dimension data (e.g., ProductCode) or it is a surrogate key without any relationship to the data (e.g., the identity column). Surrogate keys are more general and adapt well to data from multiple sources, but each surrogate key requires a join while loading. For example, suppose our simple fact table is related to dimTime, dimCustomer, and dimProduct. If dimCustomer and dimProduct use surrogate keys, the load might look like the following:

```
INSERT INTO Warehouse.dbo.factOrder
  (OrderDate, CustomerID, ProductID, OrderAmount)
SELECT o.Date, c.CustomerID, p.ProductID, ISNULL(Amount,0)
FROM Staging.dbo.Orders o
  INNER JOIN Warehouse.dbo.dimCustomer c on o.CustCode = c.CustomerCode
  INNER JOIN Warehouse.dbo.dimProduct p on o.Code = p.ProductCode
```

Because dimTime is related to the fact table on the date value itself, no join is required to determine the dimension relationship. Measures should be converted into reportable form, eliminating nulls whenever possible. In this case, a null amount, should it ever occur, is best converted to 0.

Best Practice

The extract-transform-load (ETL) process consists of a large number of relatively simple steps that evolve over time as source data changes. Centralize ETL logic in a single location as much as possible, document non-obvious aspects, and place it under source control. When some aspect of the process requires maintenance, this will simplify rediscovering all the components and their revision history. Integration Services and SourceSafe are excellent tools in this regard.

Analysis Services Quick Start

One quick way to get started with both data warehousing and Analysis Services is to let the Business Intelligence Development Studio build the Analysis Services database and associated warehouse tables for you, based on the structures defined in the AdventureWorks sample database. Begin by identifying or creating a SQL Server warehouse database. Then open Business Intelligence Development Studio and create a new Analysis Services project.

Right-click on the Cubes node in the Solution Explorer and choose New Cube to begin the Cube Wizard. On the first page of the wizard, Select Build Method, choose "Build the cube without using a data source," enable the Use a Cube Template option, and choose the template from the list that corresponds to your edition of SQL Server. Work through the rest of the wizard, accepting the defaults except for the Define Time Periods page — pause here long enough to check a few extra time periods (e.g., Year/Quarter/Month) to make the time dimension interesting.

At the Completing the Wizard page, select the Generate Schema Now option to automatically start the Schema Generation Wizard. Work through the remaining wizard pages, specifying the warehouse location and accepting the defaults otherwise. At the end of the Schema Generation Wizard, all the Analysis Services and relational objects are created. Even if the generated system does not exactly meet a current need, it provides an interesting example.

The Cube Wizard allows many customizations of the template-defined structures, or changes can be made to the cube and dimensions within the Analysis Services project manually. The schema can be regenerated by right-clicking the project within the Solution Explorer and choosing Generate Relation Schema at any time.

Even more customized systems can be built by first creating the desired dimensions individually, beginning with templates when possible and manually creating dimensions and attributes when necessary. Then use the Cube Wizard without a template, enter the desired measures, and include the separately created dimensions.

Analysis Services Architecture

New in 2005

While Analysis Services functionality has been part of the SQL Server product since version 7.0, the 2005 release is a full reimplementation of the product. Many of the underlying concepts carry over from previous versions, but the details are different enough that features presented in the remainder of this chapter should be considered new.

Analysis Services builds upon the concepts of the data warehouse to present data in a multidimensional format instead of the two-dimensional paradigm of the relational database. How is Analysis Services multidimensional? When selecting a set of relational data, the query identifies a value via row and column coordinates, while the multidimensional store relies on selecting one or more items from each dimension to identify the value to be returned. Likewise, a result set returned from a relational database is a series of rows and columns, whereas a result set returned by the multidimensional database can be organized along many axes depending upon what the query specifies.

Instead of the two-dimensional table, Analysis Services uses the multidimensional cube to hold data in the database. The cube thus presents an entity that can be queried *via multidimensional expressions (MDX)*, the Analysis Services equivalent of SQL.

Analysis Services also provides a convenient facility for defining calculations in MDX, which in turn provides another level of consistency to the Business Intelligence information stream.

Cross-Reference

See Chapter 45, "Programming MDX Queries," for details on creating queries and calculations in MDX.

Analysis Services uses a combination of caching and pre-calculation strategies to deliver query performance that is dramatically better than queries against a data warehouse. For example, an existing query to summarize the last six months of transaction history over some 130 million rows per month takes a few seconds in Analysis Services, whereas the equivalent data warehouse query requires slightly more than seven minutes.

Unified Dimensional Model

The Unified Dimensional Model (UDM) defines the structure of the multidimensional database.

At the heart of the UDM is a data source view that identifies which relational tables provide data to Analysis Services and the relations between those tables. In addition, it supports giving friendly names to included tables and columns. Based on the data source view, measure groups and dimensions are defined according to data warehouse facts and dimensions. Cubes then define the relations between dimensions and measure groups, forming the basis for multidimensional queries.

Server

The UDM is hosted as part of the Analysis Services server, as shown in Figure 43-3.

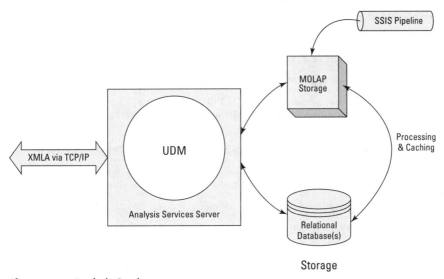

Figure 43-3: Analysis Services server

Data can be kept in a Multidimensional OLAP (MOLAP) store, which generally results in the fastest query times, but requires pre-processing of source data. Processing normally takes the form of SQL queries derived from the UDM and sent to the relational database to retrieve underlying data. Alternately, data can be sent directly from the Integration Services pipeline to the MOLAP store.

In addition to storing measures at the detail level, Analysis Services can store pre-calculated summary data called *aggregations*. For example, if aggregations by month and product line are created as part of the processing cycle, queries that require that combination of values do not have to read and summarize the detailed data, but can use the aggregations instead.

Data can also be left in the relational database, or ROLAP store, which generally results in the fastest processing times at the expense of query times. Without aggregations, queries against a ROLAP store cause the equivalent SQL to be executed as needed. Aggregations can be pre-calculated for ROLAP, but doing so requires processing all the detailed data, so MOLAP is the preferred option. A relational database in this context is not limited to SQL Server, but may be any data source for which an OLE DB provider exists.

A compromise between the speed of MOLAP storage and the need for preprocessing, called *proactive caching,* serves queries out of MOLAP storage when possible, but queries the relational database to retrieve the latest data not yet processed into the MOLAP store.

The Analysis Services server uses XML for Analysis (XMLA) as its sole protocol.

Client

Clients communicate with Analysis Services, like any other web service, via the Simple Object Access Protocol (SOAP). Client applications can hide XMLA and SOAP details by using the provided data access interfaces to access Analysis Services:

✦ All .NET languages can use ADOMD.NET.

✦ Win32 applications (e.g., C++) can use the OLE DB for OLAP driver (MSOLAP90.DLL).

✦ Other COM-based applications (e.g., VB6, VBA, scripting) can use ADOMD.

While the server will only speak XMLA via TCP/IP, clients have the option of using the HTTP protocol for their communications, if an appropriately configured IIS server is available to translate.

In addition to custom applications, Analysis Services can be accessed by several provided tools, including the following:

✦ Business Intelligence Development Studio, for defining database structure

✦ SQL Server Management Studio, for managing and querying the server

✦ Reporting Services, which can base report definitions on Analysis Services data

✦ Excel features and add-ins, for querying and analyzing data

A wide variety of third-party tools are also available to exploit the features of Analysis Services.

Building a Database

An Analysis Services database is built by identifying the data to include in the database, specifying the relationships between those data, defining dimension structures on those data, and finally building one or more cubes to combine the dimensions and measures. This section describes the overall process with an emphasis on gathering the data needed to define the database. Subsequent sections describe the many facets of dimensions and cubes.

Business Intelligence Development Studio

The process of building an Analysis Services database begins by opening a new Analysis Services project in the Business Intelligence Development Studio. Each project corresponds to a database that will be created on the target server when the project is deployed.

Along with opening an Analysis Services project, it is also possible to directly open an existing database in Business Intelligence Development Studio. While this is a useful feature for examining the configuration of a running server, changes should be made in a project, deployed first to a development server, and deployed to production only after testing. Keep the project and related files in source control.

Be sure to set the target server before attempting to deploy your new database. Right-click on the project in the Solution Explorer and choose Properties. Set the target server in the deployment property page for the configuration(s) of interest (e.g., development vs. production). Taking care with this setup when a project is created will avoid inadvertently creating a database on the wrong server.

Cross-Reference

For more details about working in Business Intelligence Development Studio, see Chapter 6, "Using Management Studio."

Data Sources

Define a data source for each distinct database or other source of data needed for the Analysis Services database. Each data source encapsulates the connection string, authentication, and properties for reading a particular set of data. A data source can be defined on any data for which an OLE DB provider exists, enabling Analysis Services to use many types of data beyond the traditional relational sources.

Start the New Data Source Wizard by right-clicking the Data Sources folder in the Solutions Explorer and selecting the New option. After viewing the optional welcome screen, the "Select how to define a connection" screen appears and presents a list of connections. Select the appropriate connection if it exists.

If the appropriate connection does not exist, bring up the connection manager by clicking the New button and add it. Within the connection manager, choose an appropriate provider, giving preference to native OLE DB providers for best performance. Then enter the server name, authentication information, database name, and any other properties required by the chosen provider. Review entries on the All tab and test the connection before clicking OK to complete the connection creation.

Work through the remaining wizard screens, choosing the appropriate login (impersonation) information for the target environment and finally the name of the data source.

When managing multiple projects in a single solution, basing a data source in one project on information in another project can be useful. For those cases, instead of choosing a connection at the "Select how to define a connection" window, select the option to "Create a data source based on another object." This leads the wizard through the "Data sources from existing objects" page. This page offers two alternatives:

✦ "Creating a data source based on an existing data source" minimizes the number of places in which connection information must be edited when it changes.

✦ "Create a data source based on an analysis services project" enables two projects to share data. This functionality is similar to using the Analysis Services OLE DB provider to access an existing database, but in this case the databases can be developed simultaneously without deployment complications.

Data Source View

Whereas a data source describes where to look for tables of data, the data source view specifies which available tables to use and how they relate to each other. The data source view also associates metadata such as friendly names and calculations with those tables and columns.

Creating the Data Source View

Use the following basic steps to create a data source view:

1. Add needed tables and named queries to a data source view.

2. Establish logical primary keys for tables without a primary key.

3. Establish relationships between related tables.

4. Annotate tables/columns with friendly names and calculations.

Begin by creating the data source view via the wizard: Right-click on the Data Source Views folder and select the New option. There are several pages in the wizard:

✦ **Select a Data Source:** Choose one of the data sources to be included in this data source view. If more than one data source is to be included in the data source view, the first data source must be a SQL Server data source.

✦ **Name Matching:** This page will only appear when no foreign keys exist in the source database, providing the option of defining relationships based on a selection of common naming conventions. Matching can also be enabled via the `NameMatchingCriteria` property once the data source view has been created, identifying matches as additional tables added to an existing view.

✦ **Select Tables and Views:** Move tables to be included from the left (available objects) to the right (included objects) pane. To narrow the list of available objects, enter any part of a table name in the Filter box and press the Filter button. To add objects related to included objects, select one or more included objects and press the Add Related Tables button. This same dialog is used as the Add/Remove Tables dialog after the data source view has been created.

✦ **Completing the Wizard:** Specify a name for the data source view.

Once the data source view has been created, more tables can be added by right-clicking in the diagram and choosing Add/Remove Tables. Use this method to include tables from other data sources as well.

Similar to a SQL view, named queries can be defined, which behave as if they were tables. Either right-click on the diagram and choose New Named Query or right-click on a table and choose Replace Table/with New Named Query to bring up a Query Designer to define the contents of the named query. If the resulting named query will be similar to an existing table, it is preferable to replace that table because the Query Designer will default to a query that recreates the replaced table. Using named queries avoids the need to define views in the underlying data sources and allows all metadata to be centralized in a single model.

As tables are added to the data source view, primary keys and unique indexes in the underlying data source are imported as primary keys in the model. Foreign keys and selected name matches (see Name Matching, above) are automatically imported as relationships between tables. For cases where primary keys or relationships are not imported, they must be defined manually.

For tables without primary keys, select one or more columns that define the primary key in a given table, right-click and select Set Logical Primary Key. Once primary keys are in place, any tables without appropriate relationships can be related by dragging and dropping the related columns between tables. If the new relationship is valid, the model will show the new relationship without additional prompting. If errors occur, the Edit Relationship dialog will appear. Resolving the error may be as simple as pressing Reverse to correct the direction of the relationship, as shown in Figure 43-4, or it may take additional effort depending upon the type of error. A common issue when working with multiple data sources is different data types — for example, a key in one database may be a 16-bit integer while another database stores the same information in a 32-bit integer. This situation can be addressed by using a named query to cast the 16-bit integer as its 32-bit equivalent.

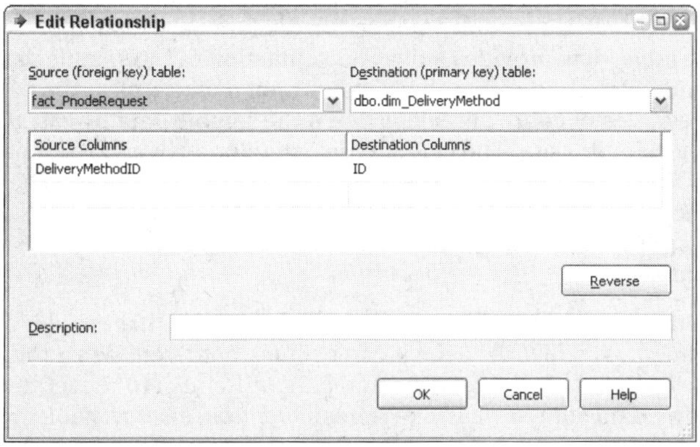

Figure 43-4: The Edit Relationship dialog

The Edit Relationship dialog can also be accessed by double-clicking an existing relationship, by right-clicking the diagram, and from toolbar and menu selections. Be sure to define all relationships, including relationships between different columns of the fact table and the same dimension table (e.g., OrderDate and ShipDate both relate to the Time dimension table), as this enables role-playing dimension functionality when a cube is created.

Managing the Data Source View

As the number of tables participating in the data source view grows, it can become difficult to handle. An excellent way to manage the complexity is by dividing the tables into a number of diagrams. The diagram pane in the upper left corner of the Data Source View page is initially populated with a single <All Tables> diagram. Right-click in the diagram pane and choose the New option to define a new diagram, and then drag and drop tables from the lower-left corner Tables pane to add tables to the new diagram. Alternately, right-click the diagram and use the Show Tables dialog to include tables currently in the <All Tables> diagram. However, don't confuse the Show Tables dialog, which determines the data source view in which tables appear in a given diagram with the Add/Remove Tables dialog, which determines which tables are in the data source view as a whole.

Other tools for managing data source views include the following:

✦ **Tables pane:** All the tables in a data source view are listed in the Tables pane. Click on any table and it will be shown and highlighted in the current diagram (provided the table exists in the current diagram).

✦ **Find Table:** Invoked from toolbar or menu, this dialog lists only tables in the current diagram and allows filtering to speed the search process. Once chosen, the diagram shows and highlights the selected table.

✦ **Locator:** The locator tool allows quick scrolling over the current diagram. Find it at the lower-right corner at the intersection of the scroll bars. Click and drag the locator to move around quickly.

✦ **Switch layout:** Right-click the diagram to toggle between rectangular and diagonal layout. The rectangular layout is table oriented and good for understanding many relationships at once. The diagonal layout is column oriented and thus good for inspecting relationship details.

✦ **Explore data:** Looking at a sample of the data in a table can be very useful when building a data source view. Right-click any table to open the Explore page, which presents four tabbed views. The table view provides a direct examination of the sample data, while the pivot table and pivot chart views allow exploration of patterns in the data. The chart view shows a series of charts, breaking down the sample data by category based on columns in the sample data. The columns selected for analysis are adjustable using the drop-down at the top of the page, as are the basic charting options. The size and type of sample is adjustable from the Sampling Options button on the page's toolbar. After adjusting sampling characteristics, press the Resample button to refresh the currently displayed sample.

The data source view can be thought of as a cache of underlying schemas that enables a responsive modeling environment, and like all cache it can become outdated. When the underlying schema changes, right-click on the diagram and choose Refresh to reflect the latest version of the schema in the data source view. The refresh function, also available from the toolbar and menu, opens the Refresh Data Source View dialog, which lists all the changes affecting the data source view. Before accepting the changes, scan the list for deleted tables, canceling changes if any deleted tables are found. Instead, inspect the underlying schema for renamed and restructured tables to determine how equivalent data can be retrieved, and resolve the conflicts before attempting the refresh again. For example, right-click on a renamed table and choose Replace Table/with Other Table to select the new table. This approach avoids losing relationship and other context information during the refresh.

Refining the Data Source View

One of the strengths of the UDM is that queries against that model do not require an understanding of the underlying table structures and relationships. However, even the table name itself often conveys important semantics to the user. For example, referencing a column as accounting.hr.staff.employee.hourly_rate indicates that this hourly rate is on the accounting server, hr database, staff schema, and employee table, which suggests this hourly rate column contains an employee pay rate and not the hourly charge for equipment rental. Because the source of this data is hidden by the unified dimensional model, these semantics will be lost. The data source view allows the definition of friendly names for every table and column. It also includes a description property for every table, column, and relationship. Friendly names and descriptions allow for the preservation of existing semantics and the addition of others as appropriate.

Best Practice

Make the data source view the place where metadata lives. If a column needs to be renamed to give it context at query time, give it a friendly name in the data source view, rather than rename a measure or dimension attribute—the two names are displayed side-by-side in the data source view and help future modelers understand how data is used. Use description properties for non-obvious notes, capturing the results of research required in building and modifying the model.

Add a friendly name or description to any table or column by selecting the item and updating the corresponding properties in the Properties pane. Similarly, add a description to any relationship by selecting the relationship and updating the Properties pane, or by entering the description from the Edit Relationship dialog. The display of friendly names can be toggled by right-clicking the diagram.

Best Practice

Applications and reports based on Analysis Services data are likely a large change for the target organization. Assign friendly names that correspond to the names commonly used throughout the organization to help speed adoption and understanding.

Many simple calculations are readily included in the data source view as well. As a rule of thumb, place calculations that depend upon a single row of a single table or named query in the data source view, but implement multi-row or multi-table calculations in MDX. Add calculations to named queries by coding them as part of the query. Add calculations to tables by right-clicking the table and choosing New Named Calculation. Enter a name and any expression the underlying data provider can interpret.

Creating a Cube

The data source view forms the basis for creating the cubes, which in turn present data to database users. Running the Cube Wizard with Auto Build enabled generally provides a good first draft of a cube. Begin by right-clicking the Cubes folder and selecting New, and then work through these pages:

✦ **Select Build Method:** Choose "Build the cube using a data source" with Auto Build checked and "Create attributes and hierarchies" selected.

✦ **Select Data Source View:** Highlight the appropriate data source view.

✦ **Detecting Fact and Dimension Tables:** The wizard is preparing defaults for the next page.

✦ **Identify Fact and Dimension Tables:** Adjust which tables contain facts (measures), which contain dimension information, or both. The Tables tab presents this information as a simple checklist, whereas the Diagram tab shows the same information in a color-coded diagram (blue for dimension, yellow for fact, green for both). The time dimension can also be specified here, but specifying time dimension details within the wizard requires detailed knowledge of how the time dimension is configured; most users will want to leave this pull-down blank (time dimensions are covered in the next section).

✦ **Review Shared Dimensions:** Move the dimensions to include in this cube from the left (available dimensions) to the right (cube dimensions) pane. The list includes both existing dimensions and those being added by the wizard. Occasionally the wizard will guess incorrectly about how to combine tables into a dimension — these cases can safely be excluded at this stage and manually added later.

✦ **Select Measures:** Check only the columns that will be useful measures in your cube. The wizard defaults to including everything in a fact table not used in a relationship, so it often includes too many columns. Columns are arranged alphabetically within each fact table being processed. The names of measures can be edited here as well, but the need to edit is usually a sign to revisit friendly name assignments in the data source view.

✦ **Detecting Hierarchies:** The wizard is detecting drill-down paths (hierarchies) within the dimension table columns (attributes) for dimensions being added.

✦ **Review New Dimensions:** Mark the attributes and hierarchies that should be included in the new dimensions. Include items that will make good data categorizations, such as names, codes, and descriptions. Exclude items that don't help in categorizations, such as obscure identifiers or insert dates.

✦ **Completing the Wizard:** Enter a name for the new cube.

Upon completion of the wizard, a new cube and possibly several new dimensions will be created. The number of dimensions created depends upon the number of tables marked as providing dimension information and how many of those dimensions were previously defined.

Dimensions

Recall from the discussion of star schema that dimensions are useful categorizations used to summarize the data of interest, the "group by" attributes that would be in a SQL query. Dimensions created by a wizard generally prove to be good first drafts, but will need refinement before deploying a database to production.

Careful study of the capabilities of a dimension reveal a complex topic, but fortunately the bulk of the work involves relatively simple setup. This section deals first with that core functionality and then expands into more complex topics in "Beyond Basic Dimensions."

Dimension Designer

Open any dimension from the Solution Explorer to use the Dimension Designer, shown in Figure 43-5. This designer presents information in three tabbed views:

✦ **Dimension Structure:** Presents the primary design surface for defining the dimension. Along with the ever-present Solution Explorer and Properties panes, three panes present the dimension's structure: The Data Source View pane (center) shows the portion of the data source view on which the dimension is built. The Attributes pane (lower left) lists each attribute included in the dimension. The Hierarchies and Levels pane (upper left) provides a space to organize attributes into common drill-down paths.

✦ **Translation:** Provides a place to define alternative language versions of both object captions and the data itself.

✦ **Browser :** Displays the dimension's data as last deployed to the target analysis server.

Unlike data sources and data source views, cubes and dimensions must be deployed before their behavior can be observed (e.g., browsing data). The process of deploying a dimension consists of two parts. First, during the build phase, the dimension definition (or changes to the definition as appropriate) is sent to the target analysis server. Examine the progress of the build process in the output window. Second, during the process phase, the Analysis Services server queries underlying data and populates dimension data. Progress of this phase is displayed in the Deployment Progress window, usually positioned as a tab of the Properties window. The Business Intelligence Development Studio attempts to build or process only the changed portions of the project to minimize the time required for deployment.

Figure 43-5: Dimension Designer with AdventureWorks Customer dimension

Attributes and Hierarchies

The Attributes pane is populated with one attribute for each column in the source table(s) the wizard was allowed to create. The key icon denotes the key attribute (Usage property = Key), which corresponds to the primary key in the source data used to relate to the fact table. There must be exactly one key attribute for each dimension.

Once deployed, each attribute not specifically disabled becomes an *attribute hierarchy* for browsing and querying. The attribute hierarchy generally consists of two levels: the All level, which represents all possible values of the attribute, and a level named after the attribute itself that lists each value individually.

The Hierarchies and Levels pane allows the creation of *user hierarchies,* which define common drill-down paths by organizing attributes into multiple levels. For example, Figure 43-5 shows a user hierarchy that will first present the browser with a list of countries, which can be expanded into a list of states, then cities, and so on.

Best Practice

User hierarchies provide drill-down paths for users who will interactively browse the contents of a cube, so it is important to define paths that make sense to the user of the cube, not the designer. Spend time considering how various users think about the data being presented and adapt the design to their perspective(s). Conversely, if a cube is not exposed for interactive use (e.g., only exposing pre-defined views in an application or report), then don't bother with user hierarchies. They only complicate the developer's view of the data.

The browser view is a good place to get a feel for how both types of hierarchies are presented to the users of Analysis Services data. Choose the hierarchy to browse from the drop-down at the top of the view, and then expand nodes at each level to drill into the data. Note the differing icons to distinguish between user and attribute hierarchies while browsing.

The Cube and Dimension wizards will attempt to detect and create user hierarchies if you allow them to try, but their guesses may not match the organization's needs. Drag and drop attributes from the Attributes pane to a hierarchy to modify, or drag an attribute to an empty spot of the Hierarchies and Levels pane to start a new hierarchy.

Likewise, new attributes can be added by dragging columns from the Data Source View pane. If the table containing the column you want to add is not shown, right-click on the pane and use the Show Table options to include the table of interest — once an attribute from a table has been included in the dimension, the default Show Only Used Tables view will show the new table. Of course, any attribute added must relate back to the fact table via the same key attribute, even if that key is a snowflake relationship or two away.

Attribute Source Columns and Ordering

Columns from the data source view are assigned to an attribute's KeyColumns and NameColumn properties to drive which data is retrieved in populating the attribute. During processing, Analysis Services will include both key and name columns in the SELECT DISTINCT it performs against the underlying data to populate the attribute. The KeyColumns assignment determines which items will be included as members in the attribute. The optional NameColumn assignment can give a display value to the key(s) when the key itself is not adequately descriptive. For the majority of attributes, the single key column assigned when the attribute is initially created will suffice. For example, an Address attribute in a customer dimension is likely to be a simple string in the source table with no associated IDs or codes; the default of assigning that single Address column as the KeyColumns value with no NameColumn will suffice.

Some scenarios beyond the simple case include the following:

✦ **Attributes with both and ID/code and a name** — The approach for this case, which is very common for dimension table primary keys (key attributes), depends upon whether the ID or code is commonly understood by those who will query the dimension. If the code is common, leave its NameColumn blank to avoid hiding the code. Instead, model the ID/Code and Name columns as separate attributes. If the ID or code is an internal application or warehouse value, then hide the ID by assigning both the KeyColumns and NameColumn properties on a single attribute.

✦ **ID/Code exists without a corresponding name:** If the ID or code can only take on a few values, derive a column to assign as the NameColumn by adding a Named Calculation in the data source view. If the ID or code has many or unpredictable values, consider adding a new snowflaked dimension table to provide a name.

✦ **Non-Unique keys:** It is important that the KeyColumns assigned will uniquely identify the members of a dimension. For example, a time dimension table might identify months with numbers 1 through 12, which are not unique keys from one year to the next. In this case, it makes sense to include both year and month columns to provide a good key value. Once multiple keys are used, a NameColumn assignment is required, so add a named calculation to the data source view to synthesize a readable name (e.g., Nov 2005) from existing month and year columns.

In the preceding non-unique keys scenario, it might be tempting to use the named calculation results (e.g., Jan 2006, Feb 2006) as the attribute's key column were it not for ordering issues. Numeric year and month data is required to keep the attribute's members in calendar, rather than alphabetic, order. The attribute's OrderBy property enables members to be sorted by either key or name. Alternately, the OrderBy options AttributeKey and AttributeName enable sorting of the current attribute's members based on the key or name of another attribute, providing the other attribute has been defined as a member property of the current attribute. Member properties are described in detail in the next section.

Change the `KeyColumns` property by clicking on the current value and then clicking the ellipsis to launch the DataItem Collection Editor, shown in Figure 43-6. The left pane of the DataItem Collection Editor shows each of the current key members; highlighting a member will display its properties in the right pane. Use the Add or Remove buttons to adjust the number of members. Assign a column to a member by clicking on the source property's current value and clicking the ellipsis to launch the Object Binding dialog, shown in Figure 43-6. Choose Column Binding for the binding type, select the appropriate table, and highlight the desired column.

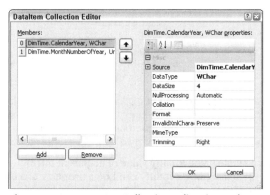

Figure 43-6: DataItem Collection Editor is used to view the members and set their respective properties.

Add or change an attribute's `NameColumn` binding by choosing (new) from the property's drop-down list, which launches directly to the Object Binding Dialog. Choosing (none) from the drop-down will clear the name assignment.

Attribute Relationships

One important way in which Analysis Services achieves query speed is by pre-calculating data summaries. These summaries, or aggregations, are created to correspond to the attributes of a dimension. For example, totals by year or month might be pre-calculated along the time dimension.

> **Note** Carefully review each dimension to ensure that relationships are properly established. The improved performance is worth the effort.

Both the aggregation and query processes can be made more efficient if the relationships between attributes are expressed in the dimension's structure. Consider a simple time dimension with attributes for year, quarter, month, and day, with day relating to the fact table (key attribute). By default, every attribute in a dimension is related directly to the key attribute, resulting in the default relationships shown in Figure 43-7. Aggregations for each non-key level summarize all the day totals. Contrast this to the properly assigned relationships, where aggregations for the month level must reference all the day totals, but the quarters level need only reference the months, and the years only reference the quarters. The larger and more complicated the dimension, the bigger the impact on performance.

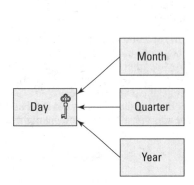
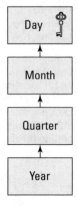

(a) Default attribute relationships   (b) Assigned relationships

Figure 43-7: Attribute relationships

Attributes are related by assigning member properties. Right-click the Attributes pane in the Dimension Designer, choose Show Attributes in Tree, and then expand any attribute to see its member properties. By default, all member properties are found under the attribute corresponding to the primary key of the table from which they are read.

A member property must only take on a single value for any value of its parent attribute. Thus, year can be a member property of quarter, but a county can't be a property of a city because cities sometimes span counties. This is why the default assignment is to the primary key column, as it is true by definition.

Click on a member property to view its associated properties, especially the relationship type. The relationship type can be either of the following:

✦ **Rigid:** Denotes that the attribute values and member property values will have static relationships over time. If those relationships change over time, a processing error will result. It is, however, more efficient than the flexible alternative because Analysis Services can retain aggregations when the dimension is processed. Examples include quarter as a member property of month, and state as a member property of city.

✦ **Flexible:** Used for attribute values and member property values that change in relationship over time. Aggregations are updated when the dimension is processed to allow for changes. For example, department as member property of employee should be flexible to allow for the occasional movement between departments.

Change the relationships of a dimension by expanding attributes and dragging member properties between lists. Dragging an attribute name onto a member property list appears to work as well, but actually adds a new relationship instead of redirecting an existing relationship. Avoid configuring an attribute as a member property more than once unless it is required to allow other functionality, such as calculation or ordering.

These relationships between attributes define a *natural hierarchy*. Unlike the attribute and user hierarchies described earlier, this third type of hierarchy is not directly visible to the user of a dimension. Instead, a natural hierarchy determines how internal aggregation and index structures are built.

Visibility and Organization

Most cubes will have a large number of dimension attributes, which can tend to overwhelm the user. Using familiar names will help, but the simplest way to combat attribute overload is not exposing attributes that will not be useful to the user. Specific strategies include the following:

✦ Delete attributes that are not useful to users. This includes items not well understood and any alternative language information that can be specified in the translation view.

✦ For attributes that need to be modeled but are very infrequently used, consider setting their `AttributeHierarchyVisible` property to False. These attributes will not be available to users browsing cube data, but can still be referenced via MDX queries.

✦ Some attributes can be presented to the user only within a user hierarchy. For example, when interpreting a list of cities without knowing their corresponding country and state information, it may be challenging to tell the difference between Paris, Texas, and Paris, France. For these cases, build the appropriate user hierarchy and set the `AttributeHierarchyVisible` property to `False` for the corresponding attributes.

✦ Attributes that will not be queried but are still needed for member properties, such as columns used only for sorting or calculations, can be fully disabled. Set `AttributeHierarchyEnabled` to `False` and note how the attribute icon is now grayed out. Also set `AttributeHierarchyOptimizedState` to `NotOptimized`, and `AttributeHierarchyOrdered` to `False` so that Analysis Services doesn't spend unnecessary time processing.

Once the list of visible attribute and user hierarchies has been determined, consider organizing dimensions with more than a handful of visible hierarchies into folders. Attributes will organize under the folder name entered into the `AttributeHierarchyDisplayFolder` property, whereas user hierarchies have an equivalent property named `DisplayFolder`. In general, these properties should be left blank for the most frequently used hierarchies in a dimension so that those items will display at the root level.

Best Practice

Well-organized dimensions are essential to gaining acceptance for interactive applications — most users will be overwhelmed by the amount of available attributes. Excluding unused attributes not only helps simplify the user's view of the data, it can greatly speed performance — especially for cubes with substantial calculations because the more attributes, the larger the number of cells each calculation must consider.

Basic Setup Checklist

After creating a basic dimension via either the Dimension or the Cube wizards, the following checklist outlines a first-order refinement. This level of attention is adequate for the majority of circumstances:

✦ Ensure that attribute names are clear and unambiguous in the context of all dimensions in the model. If changes are required, consider modifying names in the data source view and regenerating the dimension to keep all names consistent within the model. Alternately, change the names of attributes and user hierarchy levels directly.

✦ Review any user hierarchies the wizard created and adjust levels as necessary. Add any missing hierarchies. Override default names with useful alternatives.

✦ Delete unneeded attributes and adjust visibility as outlined previously.

✦ Adjust attribute relationships to match the data they will contain.

✦ Review each attribute's source (`KeyColumns` and `NameColumn` properties) and ordering. Make frequent use of the browser view to check the results.

✦ Organize dimensions with many hierarchies into folders.

Changing Data in Dimensions

Proper handling of changes to dimension data can be a complex topic, but it boils down to how the organization would like to track history. If an employee changes her last name is it important to know both the current and previous values? How about address history for a customer? Or changes in credit rating?

Analysis Services will faithfully reflect changes made to the data in a dimension table whenever the dimension is processed. It has no facility to track the history of changes to a dimension beyond the history that is tracked in underlying dimension tables. Following are the four common scenarios for tracking history in dimension tables:

✦ **Slowly Changing Dimension Type 1:** History is not tracked, so any change to dimension data applies across all time. For example, when the customer's credit rating changes from excellent to poor, there will be no way to know when the change occurred or that the rating was ever anything but poor. Such tracking makes it difficult to explain why the customer's purchase order was accepted last quarter without prepayment. Conversely, this simple approach will suffice for many dimensions. When implementing an Analysis Services database on OLTP data instead of a data warehouse, this is usually the only option available, as the OLTP database rarely tracks history.

✦ **Slowly Changing Dimension Type 2:** Every change in the source data is tracked as history by multiple rows in the dimension table. For example, the first time a customer appears in OLTP data, a row is entered into the dimension table for that customer and corresponding fact rows are related to that dimension row. Later, when that customer's information changes in the OLTP data, the existing row for that customer is expired, and a new row is entered into the dimension table with the new attribute data. Future fact rows are then associated with this new dimension table row.

✦ **Slowly Changing Dimension Type 3 :** Combines both type 1 and 2 concepts, whereby history on some but not all changes is tracked based on business rules. Perhaps employee transfers within a division are treated as type 1 changes (just updated), while transfers between divisions are treated as type 2 (a new dimension row is inserted).

✦ **Rapidly Changing Dimension :** Occasionally an attribute (or a few attributes) in a dimension will change rapidly enough to cause a type 2 approach to generate too many records in the dimension table. Such attributes are often related to status or rankings. This approach resolves the combinatorial explosion by breaking the rapidly changing attributes out into a separate dimension tied directly to the fact table. Thus, instead of tracking changes as separate rows in the dimension table, the fact table contains the current ranking or status for each fact row.

While managing dimension change must be handled in the warehouse, the Dimension Wizard can assist in creating a dimension table to support type 2 functionality. Build a dimension without using a data source, and then specify that it will be a changing dimension. The wizard will configure columns to use in maintaining history:

✦ A primary key configured as an IDENTITY column, sometimes called a *surrogate key*, which will be used to relate back to the fact table

✦ An Original_ID, sometimes called an *alternate key*, which is usually the primary key of the source data. For example, it might be an employee ID or a customer ID in the source OLTP table.

✦ A Start_Date to denote the beginning point of a row's effective date range

✦ An End_Date to denote the ending point of a row's effective date range

✦ A status to denote the active or inactive state of the row

The wizard-generated schema assumes that the end date of the currently active row is 12/31/9999, so status is created as a computed column with code like the following:

```
case when [Customer_SCD_End_Date]='12/31/9999'
  then 'Active'
  else 'Inactive' end
```

Once the dimension is configured by the wizard, add additional attributes as needed, and then click on the link in the dimension's Data Source View pane to generate the corresponding schema.

Beyond Regular Dimensions

Dimension concepts described so far in this chapter have focused on the basic functionality common to most types of dimensions. It is somewhat challenging, however, to understand what exactly is meant by the "type" of a dimension. Some sources refer to dimensions as being of only two types: data mining and standard, which encompasses everything else. Each dimension has a type property that assigns values such as Time, Geography, Customer, Accounts, and Regular, which corresponds to everything else not on the list. Furthermore, other characteristics of a dimension such as parent-child organization, write-enabling a dimensions, or linking a dimension from another database, can be thought of as different dimension types.

For clarity, this chapter limits the discussion to standard dimensions, and uses "type" only in the context of the dimension property, but it is important to understand how "type" is overloaded when reading other documents.

Time Dimension

Nearly every cube needs a time dimension, and a great many production cubes exist with poorly implemented time dimensions. Fortunately, the Dimension Wizard will automatically create a time dimension and a corresponding dimension table, and populate the table with data. Right-click on the dimension folder in the Solution Explorer pane and choose New Dimension to start the wizard.

✦ **Select Build Method:** Select "Build the dimension without using a data source," check Use a Dimension Template, and choose Time from the list of templates.

✦ **Define Time Periods:** Choose the date range and periods that should appear in the dimension.

✦ **Select Calendars:** In addition to the standard calendar, choose and configure any other calendars that should appear in the dimension.

✦ **Completing the Wizard:** Modify the name if desired; leave the "Generate schema now" check box unchecked.

Review the structure of the dimension created by the wizard. Note that the dimension's `type` property is set to `Time`, and that each attribute has an appropriate type set as well: days, months, quarters, and so on. Perform the basic checklist outlined above on the dimension design and adjust as necessary. `KeyColumns` and `NameColumn` properties do not require attention, but names assigned to attributes and hierarchies can be adjusted to work for the target audience. Attribute relationships will require refinements. Once the dimension has been adjusted, click the link in the Data Source View pane to create the time dimension table using appropriate naming and location choices.

Time dimensions can be developed from existing dimension tables as well, using either the Cube or Dimension wizards. The challenge in this approach is specifying the attribute type for each of the columns in the time dimension. Using the wizard to generate a similar dimension table can act as a guide when integrating a custom time table.

Assigning the proper attribute types provides documentation, may enable features in applications that use a cube, and are used for some features within Analysis Services, including Business Intelligence calculations.

A *server time dimension* is an alternative to a traditional time dimension that relies on an underlying relational table. The server time dimension is created internally to Analysis Services, and while not as flexible as the traditional approach, it can be a great shortcut for a building a simple cube or quick prototype. To create a server time dimension, start the Dimension Wizard as described above, but leave the Use a Dimension Template box unchecked, and then select Server Time Dimension on the second page of the wizard.

Because server time dimensions to not have an underlying dimension table, they will not appear in the data source view, so the relationship to the fact table(s) cannot be described there. Instead, use the Cube Designer's dimension usage view to establish relationships to selected fact tables (also known as *measure groups*).

Other Dimension Types

In addition to the time dimension, Analysis Services recognizes more than a dozen other dimension types, including Customers, Accounts, and Products. Many of these can be created with templates, similar to the process described for time dimensions. For each dimension type there are many corresponding attribute types to document the role of the attributes within the dimension. Assigning dimension and attribute types is encouraged for both the documentation they provide and the functionality they enable.

Using the available templates to create the dimension, its corresponding table, and the package that loads it is at best an excellent shortcut and at worst a good example.

Parent-Child Dimensions

Most dimensions are organized into hierarchies that have a fixed number of levels, but certain business problems do not lend themselves to a fixed number of levels. For example, a minor organizational change may add a new level to the organization chart. Relational databases solve this problem with self-referential tables. Analysis Services solves this problem using parent-child dimensions.

A self-referential table involves two key columns — for example, an employee ID and a manager ID. To build the organizational chart, start with the president and look for employees that she manages, then look for the employees they manage, and so on. Often this relationship is expressed as a foreign key between the employee ID (the primary key) and the manager ID. When such a relationship exists on the source table, the Dimension Wizard will suggest the appropriate parent-child relationship. In the employee table example, the employee ID attribute will be configured with the `Usage` property set to `Key`, while the manager ID attribute will be configured with a Usage of Parent. Other important properties for configuring a parent-child dimension include the following:

✦ **RootMemberIf:** As set on the parent attribute, this property tells Analysis Services how to identify the top level of the hierarchy. Values include ParentIsBlank (null or zero), ParentIsSelf (parent and key values are the same), ParentIsMissing (parent row not found). The default value is all three, ParentIsBlankSelfOrMissing.

✦ **OrderBy:** The OrderBy of the Parent attribute will organize the hierarchy's display.

✦ **NamingTemplate:** By default, each level in the hierarchy will be named simply Level 01, Level 02, etc. Change this naming by clicking the ellipsis on the parent attribute's NamingTemplate property and specifying a naming pattern in the Level Naming Template dialog. Levels can be given specific names, or a numbered scheme can be specified using an asterisk to denote the level number's location.

✦ **MembersWithData:** As set on the parent attribute, this property controls how non-leaf members with data are displayed. Under the default setting, NonLeafDataVisible, Analysis Services will repeat parent members at the leaf level to display their corresponding data. For example, if you browse a cube using a parent-child employee dimension to display sales volume by salesperson, the sales manager's name will show first at the manager level and then again at the employee level so that it can be associated with the sales the manager made. The alternative setting, NonLeafDataHidden, will not repeat the parent name or show data associated with it. This can be disconcerting in some displays since, as the totals do not change; the sum of the detail rows will not match the total: in the sales manager example, the totals will differ by the sales manager's contribution.

✦ **MembersWithDataCaption:** When MembersWithData is set to NonLeafDataVisible, this parent attribute property instructs Analysis Services how to name the generated leaf members. Left at the default blank, generated leaf members will have the same names as the corresponding parents. Enter any string using an asterisk to represent the parent name to change the default name generation. For example, "* (mgr)" will cause the string " (mgr)" to be suffixed to each sales manager's name.

✦ **UnaryOperatorColumn:** This is a custom rollup function often used with account dimensions, enabling the values associated with different types of accounts to be added or subtracted from the parent totals as needed. Set on the parent attribute, this property identifies a column in the source data table that contains operators to direct how totals are constructed. The column is expected to contain "+" for items that should be added to the total, "-" for subtracted, and "~" to ignore. The column can also contain "*" to multiply a value and the current partial total, or "/" to divide a value by the partial total, but these operators will produce different results depending upon which values are accumulated first. To control the order of operation, a second column can be added as an attribute in the parent-child dimension, given the type of sequence. Blank operators are treated as "+".

Once the parent-child relationship is configured, the parent attribute presents a multi-level view of the dimension's data. In addition, all the other attributes of the dimension are available and behave normally. The basic setup checklist applies to a parent-child dimension, although the name of the parent attribute will likely need to be adjusted within the dimension instead of in the data source view, given the unique usage.

Dimension Refinements

Once a dimension has been built, a large number of properties are available to refine its behavior and that of its attributes. This section details some of the more common and less obvious refinements possible.

Hierarchy (All) Level and Default Member

The (All) level is added to the top of each hierarchy by default, and represents every member in that hierarchy. At query time, the (All) level allows everything in a hierarchy to be included, without listing each member out separately. In fact, any hierarchy not explicitly included in a query is implicitly included using its (All) level. For example, a query that returns products sold by state explicitly is implicitly products sold by state for all years, all months, all customers, etc.

By default, the name of the (All) level will be All, which is quite practical and sufficient for most applications, but it is possible to give the (All) level a different name by setting the dimension property `AttributeAllMemberName` or the user hierarchy property `AllMemberName`. For example, the top level of the employee dimension could be changed to "Everyone."

Regardless of name, the (All) member is also the default member, implicitly included in any query for which that dimension is not explicitly specified. The default member can be changed by setting the dimension's `DefaultMember` property. This property should be set with care. For example, setting the `DefaultMember` for the year attribute to 2005 will cause every query that does not explicitly specify the year to return data for only 2005. Default members can also be set to conflict: Setting the `DefaultMember` for the year to 2005 and the month to August 2004 will cause any query that does not explicitly specify year and month to return no data.

Default members are often set when data included in a cube is not commonly queried. Consider a cube populated with sales transactions that are mostly successful, but sometimes fail due to customer credit or other problems. Nearly everyone that queries the cube will be interested in the volume and amount of successful transactions. Only someone doing failure analysis will want to view other than successful transactions. Thus, setting the status dimension's default member to success would simplify queries for the majority of users.

Another option is to eliminate the (All) level entirely by setting an attribute's `IsAggregatable` property to false. When the (All) level is eliminated, either a `DefaultMember` must be specified or one will be chosen at random at query time. In addition, the attribute can only participate in user hierarchies at the top level.

Grouping Dimension Members

The creation of member groups, or discretization, is the process of taking a many-valued attribute and grouping those values into discrete "buckets" of data. This is a very useful approach for representing a large number of continuous values, such as annual income or commute distance. Enable the feature on an attribute by setting the `DiscretizationBucketCount` property to the number of groups to be created and by choosing a `DiscretizationMethod` from the list. A `DiscretizationMethod` setting of Automatic will result in reasonable groupings for most applications. Automatic allows Analysis Services to choose an algorithm to match the data being grouped. Should the Automatic setting not yield acceptable groupings, try other methods in turn, except `UserDefined`, which is reserved for local cubes. Once the groupings have been created they are not necessarily static—changes to the underlying data may cause new groupings to be calculated during cube processing.

An attribute that is being grouped must not have any member properties—that is, other attributes cannot rely on a discretized attribute as the source of their aggregations. If the attribute to be discretized must participate in the natural hierarchy (e.g., it is the key or greatly impacts performance), consider adding a second dimension attribute based on the same column to provide the grouped view.

Take care to configure the attribute's source columns and ordering because the `OrderBy` property will determine both how the data is examined in creating member groups and the order in which those groups are displayed.

Cubes

A cube brings the elements of the design process together and exposes them to the user, combining data sources, data source views, dimensions, measures, and calculations in a single container. In this sense, the cube *is* the UDM.

A cube can contain data (measures) from many fact tables organized into measure groups. The data to be presented in Analysis Services is generally modeled in as few cubes and databases as is reasonable, with advantages both to the designer and the end user. Users that only need a narrow slice of what is presented in the resulting cube can be accommodated by defining a perspective, rather like an Analysis Service view, exposing only what makes sense to them. From the designer's perspective, limiting the number of cubes and databases keeps the number of linked dimensions and measures to a minimum.

Using the Cube Wizard has been covered in earlier sections, both from the top-down approach (see "Analysis Services Quick Start") using the cube design to generate corresponding relational and Integration Services packages, and from the bottom-up approach (see "Creating a Cube"). Once the cube structure has been created, it is refined using the Cube Designer.

Open any cube from the Solution Explorer to use the Cube Designer, shown in Figure 43-8. The Cube Designer presents information in several tabbed views described in the remainder of this section.

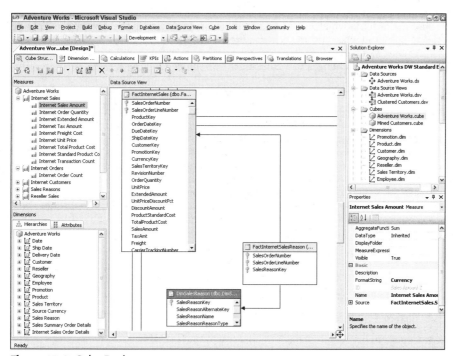

Figure 43-8: Cube Designer

Cube Structure

The cube structure view is the primary design surface for defining a cube. Along with the ever-present Solution Explorer and Properties panes, three panes present the cube's structure:

✦ The Data Source View pane, located in the center of the view, shows some portion of the data source view on which the cube is built. Each table is color-coded: yellow for fact tables, blue for dimensions, and white for neither. Normally, only the portion of the data source view actually involved in the cube is displayed, but more tables can be accessed by selecting Show All Tables or Show Tables from the context menu. Diagrams defined within the data source view can be used as well by selecting the Copy Diagram From option on the context menu. Additionally, the toolbar can be used to toggle between diagram and tree views of the table and relationship data.

✦ The Measures pane, located in the upper left corner of the view, lists all the cube's measures organized by measure group. Both the toolbar and the context menu will toggle between the tree and grid view of measures.

✦ The Dimensions pane, located in the lower left section of the view, lists all dimensions associated with the cube. It has two tabs. The Hierarchies tab shows each dimension and any user hierarchies in that dimension. The Attributes tab shows each dimension and all attributes in that dimension. Each dimension on both tabs has a link to edit that dimension in the Dimension Designer.

Because the order in which measures and dimensions appear in their respective lists determines the order in which users see them presented, the lists can be reordered using either the right-click Move Up/Move Down options or drag-and-drop while in tree view. Like the Dimension Designer, changes to a cube must be deployed before they can be browsed.

Measures

Each measure is based on a column from the data source view and an aggregate function. The aggregate function determines how data is processed from the fact table and how it is summarized. For example, consider a simple fact table with columns of day, store, and sales amount being read into a cube with a sales amount measure, a stores dimension, and a time dimension with year, month, and day attributes. If the aggregate function for the sales amount measure is Sum, rows are read into the cube's leaf level by summing the sales amount for any rows with the same store/day combinations, and then the summarizing to higher levels by adding the sales amount values together. However, if the aggregate function is Min, the smallest value is saved from any duplicate rows, with summarized values derived by finding the minimum value.

Available aggregate functions include the following:

✦ **Sum:** Adds the values of all children

✦ **Min:** Minimum value of children

✦ **Max:** Maximum value of children

✦ **Count:** Count of the corresponding rows in the fact table

✦ **Distinct Count:** Counts unique occurrences of the column value (e.g., Unique Customer Count)

✦ **None:** No aggregation performed. Any value not read directly from the fact table will be null.

✦ **AverageOfChildren:** Averages non-empty children

✦ **FirstChild:** Value of the first child member

✦ **FirstNonEmpty :** Value of the first non-empty child member

✦ **LastChild :** Value of the last child member

✦ **LastNonEmpty:** Value of the last non-empty child member

✦ **ByAccount:** Aggregation varies based on the values in the Account Dimension. The dimension's Type property must be Accounts and one of the dimension's attributes must have the Type property set to AccountType. The column corresponding to AccountType contains defined strings that identify the type of account and thus the aggregation method to Analysis Services.

The best way to add a new measure is to right-click in the Measures pane and choose New Measure. Specify the aggregation function and table/column combination in the New Measure dialog. The new measure will automatically be added to the appropriate measure group. Measure groups are created for each fact table plus any distinct count measure defined. These groups correspond to different SQL queries that are run to retrieve the cube's data.

Beyond measures derived directly from fact tables, calculated measures can be added by the Business Intelligence Wizard and directly via the calculations view.

 Cross-Reference For more information about calculated measures, see Chapter 45, "Programming MDX Queries."

Measures can be presented to the user as grouped in folders by setting the DisplayFolder property to the name of the folder in which the measure should appear. It is also good practice to assign each measure a default format by setting the FormatString property, either by choosing one of the common formats from the list or by directly entering a custom format.

Each cube can have a default measure specified if desired, which provides a measure for queries when no measure is explicitly requested. To set the default measure, select the cube name at the top of the Measures pane tree view, and set the DefaultMeasure property by selecting a measure from the list.

Cube Dimensions

The hierarchies and attributes for each dimension can be either disabled (Enabled and AttributeHierarchyEnabled properties, respectively) or made invisible (Visible and AttributeHierarchyVisible properties, respectively) if appropriate for a particular cube context (see "Visibility and Organization," earlier in the chapter, for example scenarios). Access these settings by selecting the hierarchy or attribute in the Dimensions pane and then adjusting the associated properties. These properties are specific to a dimension's role in the cube and do not change the underlying dimension design.

Dimensions can be added to the cube by right-clicking the Dimensions pane and choosing New Dimension. Once the dimension has been added to the cube, review the dimension usage view to ensure that the dimension is appropriately related to all measure groups.

Dimension Usage

The dimension usage view displays a table showing how each dimension is related to each measure group. With dimensions and measure groups as row and column headers, respectively, each cell of the table defines the relationship between the corresponding dimension/measure group pair. Drop-down lists in the upper left corner allow rows and columns to be hidden to simplify large views.

 New in 2005 Information that would have been separated into individual cubes in Analysis Services 2000 is now easily included in a single cube in 2005. Instead of separate cubes, dimension usage view enables cube dimensions to apply differently to different measure groups.

The Cube Designer creates default relationships based on the data source view relationships, which are quite accurate in most cases, although any linked objects require special review because they are not derived from the data source view. Click on the ellipsis in any table cell to launch the Define Relationship dialog and choose the relationship type. Different relationship types will require different mapping information, as described in the following sections.

No Relationship

For a database with more than one fact table, there will likely be dimensions that don't relate to some measure groups. Signified by gray table cells with no annotation, this setting is expected for measure group/dimension pairs that don't share a meaningful relationship. When a query is run that specifies dimension information unrelated to a given measure, it is ignored by default.

Regular

The regular relationship is a fact table relating directly to a dimension table, ala a star schema. Within the Define Relationship dialog, choose the Granularity attribute as the dimension attribute that relates directly to the measure group, usually the dimension's key attribute. Once the granularity attribute has been chosen, specify the fact table column names that match the granularity attribute's key columns in the relationships grid at the bottom of the dialog.

Choosing to relate a dimension to a measure group via a non-key attribute does work, but it must be considered in the context of the dimension's natural hierarchy (see "Attribute Relationships," earlier in the chapter). Think of the natural hierarchy as a tree with the key attribute at the bottom. Any attribute at or above the related attribute will be related to the measure group and behave as expected. Any attribute below or on a different branch from the related attribute will have "no relationship," as described in the preceding section.

Fact

Fact dimensions are those derived directly from the fact table when a fact table contains both fact and dimension data. No settings are required beyond the relationship type. Only one dimension can have a fact relationship with a given measure group, effectively requiring a single fact dimension per fact table containing all dimension data in that fact table.

Referenced

When dimension tables are connected to a fact table in a snowflake schema, the dimension could be implemented as a single dimension that has a regular relationship with the measure group, or the dimension could be implemented as a regular dimension plus one or more referenced dimensions. A referenced dimension is indirectly related to the measure group through another dimension. The single dimension with a regular relationship is certainly simpler, but if a referenced dimension can be created and used with multiple chains of different regular dimensions (e.g., a Geography dimension used with both Store and Customer dimensions), the referenced option will be more storage and processing efficient. Referenced relationships can chain together dimensions to any depth.

Create the referenced relationship in the Define Relationship dialog by selecting an intermediate dimension by which the referenced dimension relates to the measure group. Then choose the attributes by which the referenced and intermediate dimensions relate. Normally, the Materialize option should be selected for best performance.

Many-to-Many

Relationships discussed so far have all been one-to-many: One store has many sales transactions, one country has many customers. For an example of a many-to-many relationship, consider tracking book sales by book and author, where each book can have many authors and each author can create many books. The many-to-many relationship enables such relationships to be modeled in Analysis Services, but it requires a specific configuration beginning with the data source view (see Figure 43-9). The many-to-many relationship is implemented via an intermediate fact table that lists each pairing of the regular and many-to-many dimensions. For other slightly simpler applications, the regular dimension can be omitted and the intermediate fact table related directly to the fact table.

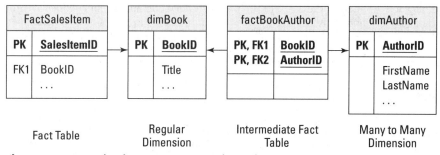

Figure 43-9: Example of a many-to-many relationship

The Define Relationship dialog only requires the name of a measure group created on the intermediate fact table to configure the many-to-many relationship. Other configuration is derived from the data source view.

Many-to-many relationships have the query side effect of generating result sets that don't simply total. Using the book sales example, assume that many of the books sold have multiple authors. A query showing books by author will display a list of numbers whose arithmetic total is greater than the total number of books sold. Often, this will be expected and understood behavior, although some applications will require calculation scripting to gain the desired behavior in all views of the cube.

KPIs

A *Key Performance Indicators (KPI)* is a server-side calculation to define an organization's most important metrics. These metrics, such as net profit, client utilization, or funnel conversion rate, are frequently used in dashboards or other reporting tools for distribution at all levels throughout the organization. Using a KPI to host such a metric helps ensure consistent calculation and presentation.

Within the KPIs view, an individual KPI consists of several components:

✦ The actual value of the metric, entered as an MDX expression that calculates the metric.

✦ The goal for the metric — for example, what does the budget say net profit should be. The goal is entered as an MDX expression that calculates the metric's goal value.

✦ The status for the metric, comparing the actual and goal values. This is entered as an MDX expression that returns values between -1 (very bad) to +1 (very good). A graphic can also be chosen as a suggestion to applications that present KPI data, helping to keep the presentation consistent across applications.

✦ The trend for the metric, showing which direction the metric is headed. Like status, trend is entered as an MDX expression that returns values between -1 and +1, with a suggested graphic.

As KPI definitions are entered, use the toolbar to switch between form (definition) and browser mode to view results. The Calculations Tools pane (lower left) provides cube metadata and the MDX functions list for drag-and drop-creation of MDX expressions. The Templates tab provides templates for some common KPIs.

Actions

Defining actions enables the client to run parameterized commands, including drill-through to detail data, running a Reporting Services report, or executing URLs or command lines. Actions can be specific to any displayed data, including individual cells and dimension members, resulting in more detailed analysis or even integration of the analysis application into a larger data management framework.

Partitions

Partitions are the unit of storage in Analysis Services, storing the data of a measure group. Initially, the Cube Designer creates a single MOLAP partition for each measure group. As discussed in the "Server Architecture" section, MOLAP is the preferred storage mode for most scenarios, but setting partition sizes and aggregations is key to both effective processing and efficient query execution.

Partition Sizing

Cube development normally begins by using a small but representative slice of the data, yet production volumes are frequently quite large, with cubes summarizing a billion rows per quarter and more. A partitioning strategy is needed to manage data through both the relational and Analysis Services databases, beginning with the amount of data to be kept online and the size of the partitions that will hold that data.

The amount of data to be kept online is a trade-off between the desire for access to historical data and the cost of storing that data. Once the retention policy has been determined, there are many possible ways to partition that data into manageable chunks, but almost universally a time-based approach is used, usually keeping either a year's or a month's worth of data in a single partition. For partitions being populated on the front end, the size of the partition is important for the time it takes to process — processing time should be kept to a few hours at most. For partitions being deleted at the back end, the size of the partition is important for the amount of data it removes at one time.

Matching the partition size and retention between the relational database and Analysis Services is a simple and effective approach. As the number of rows imported each day grows, smaller partition sizes (e.g., week or day) may be required to expedite initial processing. As long as the aggregation design is consistent across partitions, Analysis Services will allow smaller partitions to be merged, keeping the overall count at a manageable level.

Best Practice

Take time to consider retention, processing, and partitioning strategies before an application goes into production. Once in place, changes may be very expensive given the large quantities of data involved.

Creating Partitions

The key to accurate partitions is including every data row exactly once. Because it is the combination of all partitions that is reported by the cube, including rows multiple times will inflate the results. A common mistake is to add new partitions while forgetting to delete the default partition created by the Designer; because the new partitions contain one copy of all the source data, and the default partition contains another, cube results are exactly double the true values.

The partition view consists of one collapsible pane for each measure group, each pane containing a grid listing the currently defined partitions for that measure group. Highlighting a grid row will select that partition and display its associated properties in the Properties pane.

Start the process of adding a partition by clicking the New Partition link, which launches a series of Partition Wizard dialogs:

✦ **Specify Source Information:** Choose the appropriate Measure group (the default is the measure group selected when the wizard is launched). If the source table is included as part of the data source view, it will appear in the Available tables list and can be selected there. If the source table is not part of the data source view, choose the appropriate data source from the Look in list and press the Find Tables button to list other tables with the same structure. Optionally, enter a portion of the source table's name in the Filter Tables text box to limit the list of tables returned.

✦ **Restrict Rows:** If the source table contains exactly the rows to be included in the partition, skip this page. If the source table contains more rows than should be included in the partition, select the "Specify query to restrict rows" option, and the Query box will be populated with a fully populated `select` query missing only the `WHERE` clause. Supply the missing constraint(s) in the Query window and press the Check button to validate syntax.

✦ **Processing and Storage Locations:** The defaults will suffice for most situations. If necessary, choose options to balance load across disks and servers.

✦ **Completing the Wizard:** Supply a name for the partition — generally the same name as the measure group suffixed with the partition slice (e.g., `Internet_Orders_2004`). If aggregations have not been defined, define them now. If aggregations have already been defined for another partition, copy these existing aggregations from that partition to ensure consistency across partitions.

Once a partition has been added, the name and source can be edited by clicking in the appropriate cell in the partition grid.

Aggregation Design

The best trade-off between processing time, partition storage, and query performance is defining only aggregations that help answer queries commonly run against a cube. Analysis Services' usage-based optimization tracks queries run against the cube and then designs aggregations to meet that query load. However, representative query history often requires a period of production use, so the Aggregation Design Wizard will create aggregations based on intelligent guesses. The wizard steps through several pages:

✦ **Specify Storage and Caching Options:** Specifies how the individual partition will be stored and updated. These options can be set for most partitions at the cube level, ensuring consistency, and then modified for special cases here. See the section "Data Storage" for details.

✦ **Specify Object Counts:** Accurate row counts for each partition and dimension table drive how aggregations are calculated. Pressing the Count button will provide current row counts. Numbers can be manually entered if the current data source is different from the target design (e.g., a small development data set).

✦ **Set Aggregation Options:** This page actually designs the aggregations. The general approach is to design a modest number of aggregations here, planning on usage-based optimization to provide the long-term aggregation design. The options on the left tell the designer when to stop creating new aggregations, while the graph on the right provides estimated storage versus performance gain.

There are no strict rules, but some general guidelines may help:

• Unless storage is the primary constraint, target an initial performance gain of 10–20 percent. On the most complex cubes this will be difficult to obtain with a reasonable number of aggregations (and associated processing time). On simpler cubes more aggregations can be afforded, but they are already so fast the additional aggregations don't buy much.

• Keep the total number of aggregations under 200 (aggregation count is shown at the bottom, just above the progress bar).

• Look for an obvious knee (flattening of the curve) in the storage/performance graph and stop there.

✦ **Completing the Wizard:** Choose to either save the aggregation design or to save and deploy it.

Best Practice

The best aggregations are usage-based: Collect usage history in the query log and use it to optimize each partition's aggregation design periodically. Query logging must be enabled in each Analysis Server's properties, in the Log\QueryLog section: Set `CreateQueryLogTable` to `true`, define a `QueryLogConnectionString`, and specify a `QueryLogTableName`.

Perspectives

A perspective is a view of a cube that hides items and functionality not relevant to a specific purpose. Perspectives appear as additional cubes to the end user, so each group within the company can have its own "cube," each just a targeted view of the same data.

Add a perspective by either right-clicking or using the toolbar and a new column will appear. Overwrite the default name at the top of the column with a meaningful handle, and then uncheck the items not relevant to the perspective. A default measure can be chosen for the perspective as well—look for the `DefaultMeasure` object type in the second row of the grid.

Data Storage

The data storage strategy chosen for a cube and its components determines not only how the cube will be stored, but also how it can be processed. Storage settings can be set at three different levels, with parent settings determining defaults for the children:

✦ **Cube:** Begin by establishing storage settings at the cube level to set defaults for the entire cube (dimensions, measure groups, and partitions). Access the Cube Storage Settings dialog by choosing a cube in the Cube Designer, and then clicking on ellipsis on the Proactive Caching property of the cube.

✦ **Measure Group:** Used in the unlikely case that storage settings for a particular measure group will differ from cube defaults. Access the Measure Group Storage Settings dialog by either clicking on ellipsis on the measure group's Proactive Caching property in the Cube Designer or by choosing the Storage Settings link in partition view without highlighting a specific partition.

✦ **Object level (specific partition or dimension):** Sets the storage options for a single object. Access the Dimension Storage Settings dialog by clicking the ellipsis on the dimension's Proactive Caching property in the Dimension Designer. Access the Partition Storage Settings dialog by selecting a partition in the partition view and clicking the Storage Settings link. The Partition Storage Settings dialog also appears as the first step of the Aggregation Design Wizard.

Each of the storage settings dialogs are essentially the same, differing only in the scope of the setting's effect. The main page of the dialog contains a slider that selects preconfigured option settings — from the most real-time (far left) to the least real-time (far right). Position the slider and click the Options button to examine the options associated with a particular position. Beyond these few presets, the Storage Options dialog enables a wide range of behaviors.

By default, the pure MOLAP setting is chosen. This setting works well for traditional data warehousing applications because the partitions can be processed by the same procedure that loads large batches of data into the warehouse. Pure MOLAP is also an excellent choice for historical partitions in which data additions and updates are not expected. However, if a partition is built based on frequently changing source data (e.g., directly on OLTP tables), then proactive caching can manage partition updates automatically.

Proactive caching is controlled by the many options on the Storage Options dialog, but these options are all controls on the same basic procedure: Analysis Services is notified each time underlying data is updated, it waits for a pause in the updates, and then begins rebuilding the cache (partition). If an update notification is received before the rebuild completes, the rebuild will be restarted. If the rebuild process takes longer than allowed, the cache will revert to ROLAP (SQL Queries) until the rebuild is complete.

The options that control the rebuild process are located on the Storage Options' General tab (select the Enable Proactive Caching check box to enable updates):

✦ **Silence Interval:** Amount of quiet time since the last update notification before beginning the rebuild process. An appropriate setting depends upon the table usage profile, and should be long enough to identify when a batch of updates has completed.

✦ **Silence Override Interval:** After this amount of time, begin the rebuild even if no silence interval has been detected.

✦ **Latency:** The amount of time from when the first notification is received until queries revert to ROLAP. Essentially, this guarantees that data returned by Analysis Services will never be more than the specified amount of time out of date. Of course, this may represent a significant extra load against the SQL database(s) and server(s) that must service the queries in the interim, depending on the number and complexity of the queries.

✦ **Rebuild Interval:** Causes a cache rebuild even when no update notifications are received. Specifies the time since the last rebuild that a new rebuild will happen. This option can be used independently of data changes (e.g., don't listen for notifications, just rebuild this partition every four hours) or as a backup to update notifications, as update notification may not be guaranteed.

✦ **Bring online immediately:** Causes a newly created cube to come online immediately in ROLAP mode without waiting for the MOLAP build process to complete. Improves availability at the possible expense of extra load on relational database(s) and server(s) that will process the ROLAP queries.

✦ **Enable ROLAP aggregations:** Creates views to support ROLAP aggregations.

✦ **Apply storage settings to dimension:** Only available at the cube or measure group levels, this option applies the same storage settings to all dimensions related to the cube or measure group.

The Notifications tab specifies how Analysis Services will be notified of underlying relational data changes. Notifications options must be set for each object (partition and dimension) individually. These options are only relevant when rebuilds on data change are enabled (i.e., Silence Interval and Silence Override Interval are set).

SQL Server Notifications

SQL Server notifications use trace events to tell Analysis Services when either an insert or an update has occurred in the underlying table. Because event delivery is not guaranteed, this approach is often coupled with periodic rebuilds to ensure that missed events are included on a regular schedule. Enabling trace events requires that Analysis Services connects to SQL Server with an appropriately privileged account.

A partition that relies directly on an underlying table, without the use of query binding or a named query in the data source view, does not require tracking tables be specified. Other partitions will need to have tracking tables specified, listing the underlying tables that when changed indicate the partition is out of date. Dimensions must always list tracking tables.

Client-Initiated Notifications

Client-initiated notification enables a custom application that changes data tables to notify Analysis Services when a table has been changed. The application sends a `NotifyTableChange` command to the server to specify which table has been changed. Otherwise, processing behaves much like SQL Server notification.

Scheduled Polling Notifications

Scheduled polling notification is simple to configure and works for non-SQL Server data sources, but only recognizes when new rows have been added to the table. If update-only transactions are common against a table, combine polling with the periodic rebuild option to incorporate missed updates.

Polling works by running a query that returns a high-water mark from the source table and notices when the mark changes. For example, a partition built on the factSales table with an always increasing primary key SalesID can poll using the following query:

```
SELECT MAX(SalesID) FROM factSales
```

Enable polling by selecting the polling interval and entering the corresponding polling query. Multiple polling queries can be used if the object (e.g., a multi-table dimension) relies on multiple tables for data.

Notification based on polling can help implement incremental updates. Incremental updates become important as partition sizes grow, increasing processing time and resource requirements beyond convenient levels. Incremental processing is based on a query that returns only data added since the partition was last processed. Continuing the preceding example, Analysis Services replaces the first parameter (?) with the last value previously processed and the second parameter with the current polled value:

```
SELECT * FROM factSales WHERE SalesID > COALESCE(?,-1) AND SalesID <= ?
```

The COALESCE function handles the empty table case where no data had been previously processed. Enable incremental updates by selecting the Enable Incremental Updates check box and entering a processing query and tracking table for each polling query.

Data Integrity

Data integrity functionality in Analysis Services addresses inconsistencies that would otherwise cause improper data presentation. Analysis Services views these inconsistencies in two categories:

✦ **Null Processing:** When nulls are encountered in source data. For example, if a measure contains a null, should it be reported as zero or remain a null value?

✦ **Key Errors:** When keys are missing, duplicated, or otherwise don't map between tables. For example, how should a CustomerID in the fact table without a corresponding entry in the customer dimension be handled?

Basing a cube on a traditional data warehouse will help minimize data integrity issues by addressing these problems during the warehouse load.

Best Practice

A key strength of OLAP in general and the UDM in particular is consistent interpretation of data. Data integrity settings and centralized calculations are examples of the many ways that UDM centralizes data interpretation for downstream data consumers. Address these issues in the design of the warehouse and/or UDM to deliver the most useful product. Think of it as building a "data object" complete with information hiding and opportunities for reuse.

Null Processing

How nulls are treated depends upon the NullProcessing property of the object in question.

For measures, the NullProcessing property appears as part of the source definition with four possible values:

✦ **ZeroOrBlank:** The server converts nulls to zero for numeric data items, and blank for string data items.

✦ **Automatic:** Same as ZeroOrBlank.

✦ **Error:** The server will trigger an error and discard the record.

✦ **Preserve:** Stores the null value without change.

A good way to choose between these settings is to consider how an average value should be calculated on the data for a given measure. If the best interpretation is averaging only the non-null values, then `Preserve` will yield that behavior. Otherwise, `ZeroOrBlank` will yield an average that considers null measures as zero.

For dimensions, the `NullProcessing` property can take on an additional value:

✦ **UnknownMember:** Interprets the null value as the unknown member.

The `NullProcessing` property appears in several contexts for dimensions:

✦ Each dimension attribute's NameColumn, if defined, contains `NullProcessing` as part of the source definition. This setting is used when a null name is encountered when building the dimension.

✦ Each dimension attribute's KeyColumns collection contains a `NullProcessing` property for every column in the collection. This setting is used when null key column(s) are encountered when building the dimension.

✦ Each cell on the Dimension Usage tab that relates a measure group and dimension via a regular relationship. The `NullProcessing` property is located on the Advanced (Measure Group Bindings) dialog, and is used when the related column in the fact table is null.

For dimension attributes, the default setting of `Automatic NullProcessing` mostly results in blank members being created. Usually a better setting is `UnknownMember` if nulls are expected or Error if nulls are not expected.

For dimension relationships, the default setting of `Automatic NullProcessing` is actually quite dangerous. As the key column is read as null, it will be converted to 0, which may be a valid key into some dimensions, causing null entries to be assigned to that member. Usually a better setting is `UnknownMember` if nulls are expected, or `Error` if nulls are not expected. Alternately, a dimension member could be created for a 0 key value and assigned a name such as "Invalid" to match the automatic processing behavior.

Unknown Member

Choosing an unknown member option, either as part of null processing or in response to an error, requires the unknown member to be configured for the affected dimension. Once the unknown member is enabled for a dimension, the member will be added to every attribute in the dimension. The `UnknownMember` dimension property can take on three possible settings:

✦ **None:** The unknown member is not enabled for this dimension and any attempt to assign data to the unknown member will result in an error. This is the default setting.

✦ **Visible:** The unknown member is enabled and is visible to queries.

✦ **Hidden:** The unknown member is enabled, but not directly visible in queries. However, the (All) level of the dimension will contain the unknown member's contribution and the MDX `UnknownMember` function can access the unknown member's contribution directly.

The default name of the unknown member is simply "Unknown," which can be changed by entering a value for the dimension's `UnknownMemberName` property.

Error Configuration

For data integrity errors as described above and several others, the `ErrorConfiguration` property specifies how errors will be handled. Initially, the setting for this property will be (default), but choose the (custom) setting from the list and eight properties will appear. The `ErrorConfiguration` properties are available on several objects, but are primarily set for dimensions and measure groups.

The error configuration properties are as follows:

✦ **KeyDuplicate:** Triggered when a duplicate key is seen while building the dimension. The default is `IgnoreError`; other settings are `ReportAndContinue` and `ReportAndStop`. `IgnoreError` will cause all the attribute values to be incorporated into the dimension, but Analysis Services will randomly choose which values to associate with the key. For example, if a product dimension table has two rows for productID 73, one with the name Orange and the other with the name Apple, then both Orange and Apple will appear as members of the product name attribute, but only one of those names will have transactions associated with it. Conversely, if both product names are Apple, then there will be only one Apple in the product name dimensions and a user of the cube will be unable to tell there were any duplicate records.

✦ **KeyErrorAction:** Triggered when a `KeyNotFound` error is encountered. This occurs when a key value cannot be located in its associated table. For measure groups, this happens when the fact table contains a dimension key not found in the dimension table. For snowflaked dimension tables it similarly implies one dimension table referencing a non-existent key in another dimension table. Settings are either `ConvertToUnknown` (the default) or `DiscardRecord`.

✦ **KeyErrorLimit:** The number of key errors allowed before taking the `KeyErrorLimitAction`. The default value of 0 will cause the first error to trigger the `KeyErrorLimitAction`. Set to -1 for no limit.

✦ **KeyErrorLimitAction:** The action triggered by exceeding the `KeyErrorLimit`. Settings are either `StopProcessing` (default) or `StopLogging`. `StopLogging` will continue processing and allow any number of key errors, but will only log the first `KeyErrorLimit` errors.

✦ **KeyErrorLogFile:** File to log all key errors.

✦ **KeyNotFound:** Determines how `KeyNotFound` errors interact with the `KeyErrorLimit`. The default setting of `ReportAndContinue` counts the error against `KeyErrorLimit`, whereas a setting of `IgnoreError` does not count the error against `KeyErrorLimit`. The setting of `ReportAndStop` will log the error and stop processing immediately without regard for any `KeyErrorLimit` or `KeyErrorAction` settings. The `IgnoreError` setting is useful when multiple `KeyNotFound` errors are expected, allowing the expected mapping to an unknown member to occur while counting other types of key errors against the `KeyErrorLimit`.

✦ **NullKeyConvertedToUnknown:** Identical in concept to the `KeyNotFound` property, but for null keys converted to an unknown member (`NullProcessing =UnknownMember`) instead of `KeyNotFound` errors. The default setting is `IgnoreError`.

✦ **NullKeyNotAllowed:** Identical in concept to the `KeyNotFound` property, but for disallowed null keys (`NullProcessing=Error`) instead of `KeyNotFound` errors. The default setting is `ReportAndContinue`.

These same properties can be set as server properties to establish different defaults. They can also be set for a particular processing run to provide special handling for certain data.

Summary

Every organization uses BI whether they realize it or not, because every organization needs to measure what is happening in its business. The only alternative is to make every decision based on intuition instead of data. The quest for BI solutions usually begins with simple queries run against OLTP data and evolves into an inconsistent jumble of numbers. Analysis Services is central to the Microsoft strategy for addressing an organization's need for BI, providing a remedy to the usual chaos of ad hoc data silos.

Analysis Services provides the capability to build fast, consistent, and relevant repositories of data suitable for both end-user and application use. See the other chapters in this section for details on loading, analyzing, querying, and reporting BI data.

✦　　✦　　✦

Data Mining with Analysis Services

CHAPTER

44

Many business questions can be answered directly by querying a database, such as "What is the most popular page on our web-site?" or "Who are our top customers?" Other, often more important, questions require deeper exploration—for example, the most popular paths through the website or common characteristics of top customers. Data mining provides the tools to answer such non-obvious questions.

The term "data mining" has experienced a great deal of misuse. One of my favorite anecdotes is about a marketing person who intended to "mine" data in a spreadsheet by staring at it until inspiration struck. In this book, data mining is not something performed by intuition, direct query, or simple statistics. Instead, it is the algorithmic discovery of non-obvious information from large quantities of data.

Analysis Services implements algorithms to extract information addressing several categories of questions:

✦ **Segmentation:** Groups items with similar characteristics. For example, develop profiles of top customers or spot suspect values on a data entry page.

✦ **Classification:** Places items into categories. For example, determine which customers will respond to a marketing campaign or which e-mails are likely spam.

✦ **Association:** Sometimes called *market basket analysis,* this determines which items tend to occur together. For example, which web pages are normally viewed together on the site or "Customers who bought this book also bought...".

✦ **Estimation:** Estimates a value. For example, estimate revenue from a customer or the life span of a piece of equipment.

✦ **Forecasting:** Predicts what a time series will look like in the future. For example, when will we run out of disk space or what revenue do we expect in the upcoming quarter?

✦ **Sequence Analysis:** Determines what items tend to occur together in a specific order. For example, what are the most common paths through our website? Or in what order are products normally purchased?

These categories are helpful in thinking about what data mining can be used for, but with increased comfort level and experience many other applications are possible.

The Data Mining Process

A traditional use of data mining is to train a data mining model using data for which an outcome is already known and then use that model to predict the outcome of new data as it becomes available. This use of data mining requires that several steps be performed, only some of which happen within Analysis Services:

✦ **Business and Data Understanding:** Understand the questions that are important and the data available to answer those questions. Insights gained must be relevant to business goals to be of use. Data must be of acceptable quality and relevance to obtain reliable answers.

✦ **Prepare Data:** The effort to get data ready for mining can range from simple to painstaking depending upon the situation. Some of the tasks to consider include the following:

- Eliminate rows of low data quality. Here the measure of quality is domain specific, but it may include too small an underlying sample size, values outside of expected norms, or failing any test that proves the row describes an impossible or highly improbable case.

- General cleaning. Eliminate duplicates, invalid values, inconsistent values, scaling, formatting, etc.

- Analysis Services accepts a single primary "case" table, and optionally one or more child "nested" tables. If the source data is spread among several tables, denormalization by creating views or preprocessing will be required.

- Erratic time series data may benefit from smoothing.

- Derived attributes can be useful in the modeling process, typically either calculating a value from other attributes (e.g., Profit=Income-Cost) or simplifying the range of a complex domain (e.g., mapping numeric survey responses to High, Medium, or Low).

Some types of preparation can be accomplished within the Analysis Services data source view using named queries and named calculations. When possible, this is highly recommended as it avoids reprocessing data sets if changes become necessary.

Finally, it is necessary to split the prepared data into two data sets: a training data set that is used to set up the model, and a testing data set that is used to evaluate the model's accuracy. The Integration Services Row Sampling and Percentage Sampling transforms are useful to randomly split data, typically saving 10 to 20 percent of rows for testing.

✦ **Model:** Analysis Services models are built by first defining a data mining structure that specifies the tables to be used as input. Then data mining models (different algorithms) are added to the structure. Finally, all the models within the structure are trained simultaneously using the training data.

✦ **Evaluate:** Evaluating the accuracy and usefulness of the candidate mining models is simplified by Analysis Services' Mining Accuracy Chart. Use the testing data set to understand the expected accuracy of each model and compare it to business needs.

✦ **Deploy:** Integrate prediction queries into applications to predict the outcomes of interest.

For a more detailed description of the data mining process, see `www.crisp-dm.org/`.

While this process is typical of data mining tasks, it does not cover every situation. Occasionally, exploring a data set is an end in itself, providing a better understanding of the data and its relationships. The process in this case may just iterate between prepare/model/evaluate cycles. At the other end of the spectrum, an application may build, train, and query a model to accomplish a task, such as identifying outlier rows in a data set. Regardless of the situation, understanding this typical process will aid in building appropriate adaptations.

Modeling with Analysis Services

Open an Analysis Services project within the Business Intelligence Development Studio to create a data mining structure. When deployed, the Analysis Services project will create an Analysis Services database on the target server.

Begin the modeling process by telling Analysis Services where the training and testing data reside:

✦ Define data source(s) that reference the location of data to be used in modeling.

✦ Create data source views that include all training tables. When nested tables are used, the data source view must show the relationship between the case and nested tables.

For information on creating and managing data sources and data source views, see Chapter 43, "Business Intelligence with Analysis Services."

Data Mining Wizard

The Data Mining Wizard steps through the process of defining a new data mining structure and the first model within that structure. Right-click on the Mining Structures node within the Solution Explorer and choose New Mining Model to start the wizard. The wizard consists of several pages:

✦ **Select Definition Method:** Allows the choice of either relational or cube training data. Choose relational. (See the "OLAP Integration" section in this chapter for differences between relational-based and cube-based mining structures.)

✦ **Select Data Mining Technique:** Choose the algorithm to use in the structure's first mining model. (See the "Algorithms" section in this chapter for common algorithm usage.)

✦ **Select Data Source View:** Choose the data source view containing the training data table(s).

✦ **Specify Table Types:** Choose the case table containing the training data and any associated nested tables. Nested tables always have one-to-many relationships with the case table, such as a list of orders as the case table and associated order line items in the nested table.

✦ **Specify the Training Data:** Categorize columns by their use in the mining structure. When a column is not included in any category, it will be omitted from the structure. Categories are as follows:

- **Key:** Choose the columns that uniquely identify a row in the training data. By default, the primary key shown in the data source view will be marked as the key.

- **Predictable:** Identify all columns the model should be able to predict.

- **Input:** Mark each column that may be used in prediction — generally this includes the predictable columns as well. The Suggest button may aid in selection once the predictable column(s) have been identified by scoring columns by relevance based on a sample of the training data, but take care to avoid inputs with values that are unlikely to occur again as input to a trained model. For example, a customer ID, name, or address might be very effective at training a model, but once the model is built to look for a specific ID or address, it is very unlikely new customers will ever match those values. Conversely, gender and occupation values are very likely to reappear in new customer records.

✦ **Specify Columns' Content and Data Type:** Review and adjust the data type (Boolean, Date, Double, Long, Text) as needed. Review and adjust the content type as well, and pressing the Detect button to calculate continuous versus discrete for numeric data types may help. Available content types include the following:

- **Key:** Contains a value that, either alone or with other keys, uniquely identifies a row in the training table

- **Key Sequence:** Acts as a key and provides order to the rows in a table. It is used to order rows for the sequence clustering algorithm.

- **Key Time:** Acts as a key and provides order to the rows in a table based on a time scale. It is used to order rows for the time series algorithm.

- **Continuous:** Continuous numeric data — often the result of some calculation or measurement, such as age, height, or price.

- **Discrete:** Data that can be thought of as a choice from a list, such as occupation, model, or shipping method

- **Discretized:** Analysis Services will transform a continuous column into a set of discrete buckets, such as ages 0–10, 11–20, and so on. In addition to choosing this option, additional column properties must be set once the wizard is complete. Open the mining structure, select the column, and then set the `DiscretizationBucketCount` and `DiscretizationMethod` properties to direct how the "bucketization" will be performed.

- **Ordered:** Defines an ordering on the training data, but without assigning significance to the values used to order. For example, if values of 5 and 10 are used to order two rows, 10 simply comes after 5; it is not "twice as good" as 5.

- **Cyclical :** Similar to ordered, but begins again defining a cycle in the data, such as day of month or month of quarter. This enables the mining model to account for cycles in the data such as sales peaks at the end of a quarter or annually during the holidays.

✦ **Completing the Wizard:** Provide names for the overall mining structure and the first mining model within that structure. Select Allow Drill Thru to enable the direct examination of training cases from within the data mining viewers.

Once the wizard finishes, the new mining structure with a single mining model is created, and the new structure is opened in the Data Mining Designer. The initial Designer view, mining structure, allows columns to be added or removed from the structure, and column properties, such as `Content` (type) or `DiscretizationMethod`, to be modified.

Mining Models

The mining models view of the Data Mining Designer allows different data mining algorithms to be configured on the data defined by the mining structure. Add new models as follows (see Figure 44-1):

1. Right-click the structure/model matrix pane and choose New Mining Model.

2. Supply a name for the model.

3. Select the desired algorithm.

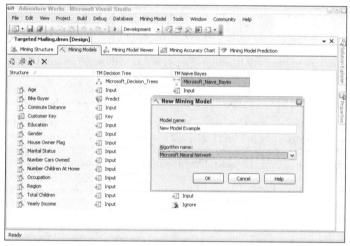

Figure 44-1: Adding a new model to an existing structure

Depending upon the structure definition, not all algorithms will be available—for example, the Sequence Clustering algorithm requires that a Key Sequence column be defined, while the Time Series algorithm requires a Key Time column to be defined. In addition, not every algorithm will use each column in the same way—for example, some algorithms ignore continuous input columns (consider using discretization on these columns).

Each mining model has both properties and algorithm parameters. Select a model (column) to view and change the properties common to all algorithms in the Properties pane, including Name, Description, and AllowDrillThru. Right-click on a model and choose Set Algorithm Parameters to change an algorithm's default settings.

Once both the structure and model definitions are in place, the structure must be deployed to the target server to process and train the models. The process of deploying a model consists of two parts. First, during the build phase, the structure definition (or changes to the definition as appropriate) is sent to the target analysis server. Examine the progress of the build in the output pane. Second, during the process phase, the Analysis Services server queries the training data and trains the models.

Before the first time a project is deployed, set the target server by right-clicking on the project in the Solution Explorer pane containing the mining structure and choosing Properties. Then select the Deployment topic and enter the appropriate server name, adjusting the target database name at the same time (deploying creates an Analysis Services database named by default after the project).

Deploy the structure by choosing Process or Process Mining Structure and All Models from either the Mining Model or context menu. After processing, the Mining Designer will move to the Mining Model Viewer tab, where one or more viewers are available depending upon which models are included in the structure. The algorithm-specific viewers assist in understanding the rules and relationships discovered by the models (see the "Algorithms" section in this chapter).

Model Evaluation

Evaluate the trained models to determine which model predicts the outcome most reliably, and to decide whether the accuracy will be adequate to meet business goals. The mining accuracy chart view provides tools for performing the evaluation.

The charts visible within this view are enabled by supplying data on the Column Mapping tab. First ensure that the mining structure to be evaluated is selected in the left-hand table. Press the Select Case Table button on the right-hand table and choose either the training or test data table to view. The joins between the selected table and the mining structure will map automatically for matching column names, or can be manually mapped by drag-and-drop when a match is not found. Verify that each non-key column in the mining structure participates in a join.

Once the source data has been specified, switch to the Lift Chart tab, and verify that Lift Chart is selected from the Chart Type list box (see Figure 44-2). Because the source data (either training or test) contains the predicted column(s), the lift chart can compare each model's prediction against the actual outcome. The lift chart plots this information on %Correct versus %Population axes, so when 50 percent of the population has been checked, the perfect model will have predicted 50 percent correctly. In fact, the chart automatically includes two useful reference lines: the Ideal Model, which indicates the best possible performance, and the Random Guess, which indicates how often randomly assigned outcomes happen to be correct.

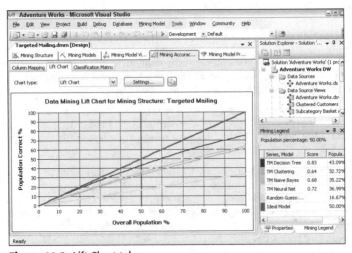

Figure 44-2: Lift Chart tab

It is useful to first view a lift chart using the training data and then again using the test data. Well-constructed models with adequate data will display lines approaching the Ideal Model line, with relatively consistent scores on both data sets. Some common problems include the following:

✦ Models that do well on training data but less well on test data have been poorly trained. Look for the following:

- A non-random split of data into training and test data sets. If the split method used was based on a random algorithm, rerun the split to produce different training and test data sets and try again.

- Input columns are too case specific (e.g., IDs, Names, etc.). Adjust the mining structure to ignore data items containing values that occur in the training data but then never reappear for test or production data.

- Too few rows (cases) in the training data set to accurately characterize the population of cases. Look for additional sources of data for best results. If additional data is not available, better results may be obtained by limiting the special cases considered by an algorithm (e.g., increasing the `MINIMUM_SUPPORT` parameter).

✦ If all models are closer to the Random Guess line than the Ideal Model line, the input data does not correlate with the outcome being predicted.

The profit chart is an extension to the lift chart that aids in calculating the maximum return from marketing campaigns and similar efforts. Press the Settings button to specify the number of prospects, the fixed and per-case cost, and the expected return from a successfully identified case; then choose Profit Chart from the Chart Type list box. The resulting chart describes profit versus Population % included, offering a guide as to how much of the population should be included in the effort either by maximizing profit or locating a point of diminishing returns.

The simplest view of model accuracy is offered by the Classification Matrix tab, which creates one table for each model, with predicted outcomes listed down the left side of the table and actual values across the top, similar to the example shown in Table 44-1. This example shows that for red cases, this model correctly predicted red for 95 and incorrectly predicted blue for 37.

Table 44-1: Example Classification Matrix

Predicted	Red (Actual)	Blue (Actual)
Red	95	21
Blue	37	104

This description of model evaluation, using tools provided by Analysis Services and Business Intelligence Development Studio, has focused on predicting discrete values. When predicting continuous values, the Classification Matrix is not available and the Lift Chart provides a slightly different comparison of actual versus predicted values. In addition, some algorithms, such as Time_Series, do not support the mining accuracy chart view at all.

Regardless of the tools available within the development environment, it is important to perform an evaluation of the trained model using test data held in reserve for that purpose. Then modify the data and model definitions until the results meet the business goals at hand.

Deploying

Several methods are available for interfacing applications with data mining functionality:

✦ Directly constructing XMLA, communicating with Analysis Services via SOAP. This exposes all functionality at the price of in-depth programming.

✦ Analysis Management Objects (AMO) provides an environment for creating and managing mining structures and other metadata, but not for prediction queries.

✦ The Data Mining Extensions (DMX) language provides for most model creation and training tasks, in addition to a robust prediction query capability. DMX can be sent to Analysis Services via the following:

- ADOMD.NET for managed (.NET) languages

- OLE DB for C++ code

- ADO for other languages

DMX is a SQL-like language modified to accommodate mining structures and tasks. For purposes of performing prediction queries against a trained model, the primary language feature is the prediction join. As the following code example shows, the prediction join relates a mining model and a set of data to be predicted (cases). Because the DMX query is issued against the Analysis Services database, the model [TM Decision Tree] can be directly referenced, while the cases must be gathered via an OPENQUERY call against the relational database. The corresponding columns are matched in the ON clause like a standard relational join, and the WHERE and ORDER BY clauses function as expected. DMX also adds a number of mining-specific functions such as the Predict and PredictProbability functions shown here, which return the most likely outcome and the probability of that outcome, respectively. Overall, this example returns a list of IDs, names, and probabilities for prospects that are over 60 percent likely to purchase a bike, sorted by descending probability:

```
SELECT t.ProspectAlternateKey,t.FirstName,t.LastName,
  Predict([TM Decision Tree].[Bike Buyer]),
  PredictProbability([TM Decision Tree].[Bike Buyer]) as Prob
FROM [TM Decision Tree]
PREDICTION JOIN
  OPENQUERY([Adventure Works DW],
    'SELECT
      ProspectAlternateKey, FirstName, LastName, MaritalStatus,
      Gender, YearlyIncome, TotalChildren, NumberChildrenAtHome,
      Education, Occupation, HouseOwnerFlag, NumberCarsOwned, StateProvinceCode
    FROM dbo.ProspectiveBuyer') AS t
ON
  [TM Decision Tree].[Marital Status] = t.MaritalStatus AND
  [TM Decision Tree].Gender = t.Gender AND
  [TM Decision Tree].[Yearly Income] = t.YearlyIncome AND
  [TM Decision Tree].[Total Children] = t.TotalChildren AND
  [TM Decision Tree].[Number Children At Home] = t.NumberChildrenAtHome AND
  [TM Decision Tree].Education = t.Education AND
```

```
    [TM Decision Tree].Occupation = t.Occupation AND
    [TM Decision Tree].[House Owner Flag] = t.HouseOwnerFlag AND
    [TM Decision Tree].[Number Cars Owned] = t.NumberCarsOwned AND
    [TM Decision Tree].Region = t.StateProvinceCode
WHERE PredictProbability([TM Decision Tree].[Bike Buyer]) > 0.60
AND   Predict([TM Decision Tree].[Bike Buyer])=1
ORDER BY PredictProbability([TM Decision Tree].[Bike Buyer]) DESC
```

Another useful form of the prediction join is a singleton query, whereby data is provided directly by the application instead of read from a relational table, as shown in the next example. Because the names exactly match those of the mining model, a NATURAL PREDICTION JOIN is used, not requiring an ON clause. This example returns the probability that the listed case will purchase a bike (i.e., [Bike Buyer]=1):

```
SELECT
   PredictProbability([TM Decision Tree].[Bike Buyer],1)
FROM [TM Decision Tree]
NATURAL PREDICTION JOIN
(SELECT 47 AS [Age], '2-5 Miles' AS [Commute Distance],
   'Graduate Degree' AS [Education], 'M' AS [Gender],
   '1' AS [House Owner Flag], 'M' AS [Marital Status],
   2 AS [Number Cars Owned], 0 AS [Number Children At Home],
   'Professional' AS [Occupation], 'North America' AS [Region],
   0 AS [Total Children], 80000 AS [Yearly Income]) AS t
```

The Business Intelligence Development Studio aids in the construction of DMX queries via the Query Builder within the mining model prediction view. Just like the Mining Accuracy chart, select the model and case table to be queried, or alternately press the singleton button in the toolbar to specify values. Specify SELECT columns and prediction functions in the grid at the bottom. SQL Server Management Studio also offers a DMX query type with metadata panes for drag-and-drop access to mining structure column names and prediction functions.

Numerous prediction functions are available, including the following:

✦ **Predict:** Returns the expected outcome for a predictable column

✦ **PredictProbability:** Returns the probability of the expected outcome, or for a specific case if specified

✦ **PredictSupport:** Returns the number of training cases that the expected outcome is based on, or that a specific case is based on if specified

✦ **PredictHistogram:** Returns a nested table with all possible outcomes for a given case, listing probability, support, and other information for each outcome

✦ **Cluster:** Returns the cluster to which a case is assigned (clustering algorithm specific)

✦ **ClusterProbability:** Returns the probability the case belongs to a given cluster (clustering algorithm specific).

✦ **PredictSequence:** Predicts the next values in a sequence (sequence clustering algorithm specific)

✦ **PredictAssociation:** Predicts associative membership (association algorithm specific)

✦ **PredictTimeSeries:** Predicts future values in a time series (time series algorithm specific)

Algorithms

When working with data mining, it is useful to understand the mining algorithm basics and when to apply each algorithm. Table 44-2 summarizes common algorithm usage for the problem categories presented in this chapter's introduction.

Table 44-2: Common Mining Algorithm Usage

Problem Type	Primary Algorithms
Segmentation	Clustering, Sequence Clustering
Classification	Decision Trees, Naive Bayes, Neural Network, Logistic Regression
Association	Association Rules, Decision Trees
Estimation	Decision Trees, Linear Regression, Logistic Regression, Neural Network
Forecasting	Time Series
Sequence Analysis	Sequence Clustering

These usage guidelines are useful as an orientation, but not every data mining problem falls neatly into one of these types, and other algorithms will work for several of these problem types. Fortunately, with evaluation tools such as the lift chart, it's usually simple to identify which algorithm provides the best results for a given problem.

Decision Trees

This algorithm is the most accurate for many problems. It operates by building a decision tree beginning with the All node, corresponding to all the training cases (see Figure 44-3). Then an attribute is chosen that best splits those cases into groups, and then each of those groups is examined for an attribute that best splits those cases, and so on. The goal is to generate leaf nodes with a single predictable outcome. For example, if the goal is to identify who will purchase a bike, leaf nodes should contain cases that either are bike buyers or not bike buyers, but no combinations (or as close to that goal as possible).

The Decision Tree Viewer shown in Figure 44-3 graphically displays the resulting tree. Age is the first attribute chosen in this example, splitting cases as less than 31, 31 to 38, etc. For the under 31 crowd, Region was chosen to further split the cases, while Number Cars Owned was chosen for the 31 to 38 cases. The Mining Legend pane displays the details of any selected node, including how the cases break out by the predictable variable (in this case, 2,200 buyers and 1,306 non-buyers) both in count and probability.

The Dependency Network Viewer is also available for decision trees, displaying both input and predictable columns as nodes with arrows indicating what predicts what. Move the slider to the bottom to see only the most significant predictions. Click on a node to highlight its relationships.

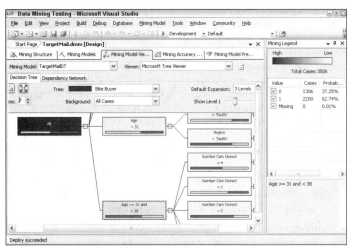

Figure 44-3: Decision Tree Viewer

Linear Regression

The *linear regression algorithm* is implemented as a variant of decision trees and is a good choice for continuous data that relates more or less linearly. The result of the regression is an equation in the form

$$Y = B_0 + A_1{}^*(X_1 + B_1) + A_2{}^*(X_2 + B_2) + \ldots$$

where Y is the column being predicted, X_i are the input columns, and A_i/B_i are constants determined by the regression. Because this algorithm is a special case of decision trees, it shares the same mining viewers. While by definition the Tree Viewer will show a single All node, the Mining Legend pane displays the prediction equation. The equation can be either used directly or queried in the mining model via the Predict function. The Dependency Network Viewer provides a graphical interpretation of the weights used in the equation.

Clustering

The *clustering algorithm* functions by gathering similar cases together into groups called clusters and then iteratively refining the cluster definition until no further improvement can be gained. This approach makes clustering uniquely suited for segmentation/profiling of populations. Several viewers display data from the finished model:

✦ **Cluster Diagram:** This viewer displays each cluster as a shaded node with connecting lines between similar clusters — the darker the line, the more similar the cluster. Move the slider to the bottom to see only lines connecting the most similar clusters. Nodes are shaded darker to represent more cases. By default, the cases are counted from the entire population, but changing the Shading Variable and State pull-downs directs shading to be based on particular variable values (e.g., which clusters contain homeowners).

✦ **Cluster Profile:** Unlike node shading in the Cluster Diagram Viewer, where one variable value can be examined at a time, the Cluster Profiles Viewer shows all variables and clusters in a single matrix. Each cell of the matrix is a graphical representation of that variable's distribution in the given cluster (see Figure 44-4). Discrete variables are shown as stacked bars describing how many cases contain each of the possible variable values. Continuous variables are shown as diamond charts with each diamond centered on the mean (average) value for cases in that cluster, while the top and bottom of the diamond are the mean and -/+ the standard deviation, respectively. Thus the taller the diamond, the less uniform the variable values in that cluster. Click on a cell (chart) to see the full distribution for a cluster/variable combination in the Mining Legend, or hover over a cell for the same information in a tooltip. In Figure 44-4, the tooltip displayed shows the full population's occupation distribution, while the Mining Legend shows Cluster 3's total children distribution.

✦ **Cluster Characteristics:** This view displays the list of characteristics that make up a cluster and the probability that each characteristic will appear.

✦ **Cluster Discrimination:** Similar to the Characteristics Viewer, this shows which characteristics favor one cluster versus another. It also allows the comparison of a cluster to its own complement, clearly showing what is and is not in a given cluster.

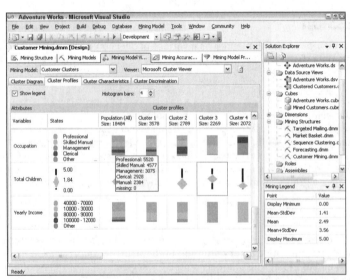

Figure 44-4: Cluster Profiles Viewer

Once a better understanding of the clusters for a given model has been gained, it is often useful to rename each cluster to something more descriptive than the default "Cluster n." From within either the Diagram or Profiles Viewer, right-click on a cluster and choose Rename Cluster to give it a new name.

Sequence Clustering

As the name implies, this algorithm still gathers cases together into clusters, but based on a sequence of events or items rather than case attributes. For example, the sequence of web pages visited during user sessions can be used to define the most common paths through that website.

The nature of this algorithm requires input data with a nested table, whereby the parent row is the session or order (e.g., shopping cart ID) and the nested table contains the sequence of events during that session (e.g., order line items). In addition, the nested table's key column must be marked as a Key Sequence content type in the mining structure.

Once the model is trained, the same four cluster viewers described above are available to describe the characteristics of each. In addition, the State Transition Viewer displays transitions between an item (e.g., web page), with its associated probability. Move the slider to the bottom to see only the most likely transitions. Select a node to highlight the possible transitions from that item to its possible successors. The short arrows that don't connect to a second node denote a state that can be its own successor.

Neural Network

This famous algorithm is generally slower than other alternatives, but often handles more complex situations. The network is built using input, hidden (middle), and output layers of neurons whereby the output of each layer becomes the input of the next layer. Each neuron accepts inputs that are combined using weighted functions that determine the output. Training the network consists of determining the weights for each neuron.

The Neural Network Viewer presents a list of characteristics (variable/value combinations) and how those characteristics favor a given outputs (outcomes). Choose the two outcomes being compared in the Output section at the upper right (see Figure 44-5). Leaving the Input section in the upper-left blank compares characteristics for the entire population, whereas specifying a combination of input values allows a portion of the population to be explored. For example, Figure 44-5 displays the characteristics that affect the buying decisions of adults 32–38 years of age with no children.

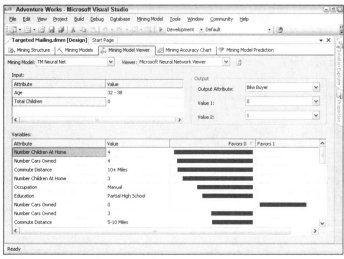

Figure 44-5: Neural Network Viewer

Logistic Regression

Logistic regression is a special case of the neural network algorithm whereby no hidden layer of neurons is built. While logistic regression can be used for many tasks, it is specially suited for estimation problems where linear regression would be a good fit, but because the predicted value is discrete, the linear approach tends to predict values outside the allowed range—for example, predicting probabilities over 100 percent for a certain combination of inputs.

Because it is derived from the neural network algorithm, logistic regression shares the same viewer.

Naive Bayes

Naive Bayes is a very fast algorithm with accuracy that is adequate for many applications. It does not, however, operate on continuous variables. The Naive portion of the name derives from this algorithm's assumption that every input is independent. For example, the probability of a married person purchasing a bike is computed from how often married and bike buyer appear together in the training data without considering any other columns. The probability of a new case is just the normalized product of the individual probabilities.

Several viewers display data from the finished model:

✦ **Dependency Network:** Displays both input and predictable columns as nodes with arrows indicating what predicts what. Move the slider to the bottom to see only the most significant predictions. Click on a node to highlight its relationships.

✦ **Attribute Profile:** Similar in function to the Cluster Profile Viewer, this shows all variables and predictable outcomes in a single matrix. Each cell of the matrix is a graphical representation of that variable's distribution for a given outcome. Click on a cell (chart) to see the full distribution for that outcome/variable combination in the Mining Legend, or hover over a cell for the same information in a tooltip.

✦ **Attribute Characteristics:** This viewer displays the list of characteristics associated with the selected outcome.

✦ **Attribute Discrimination:** Similar to the Characteristics Viewer, but shows which characteristics favor one outcome versus another.

Association Rules

This algorithm operates by finding attributes that appear together in cases with sufficient frequency to be significant. These attribute groupings are called *itemsets,* which are in turn used to build the rules used to generate predictions. While Association Rules can be used for many tasks, it is specially suited to market basket analysis. Generally, data will be prepared for market basket analysis using a nested table, whereby the parent row is transaction (e.g., Order) and the nested table contains the individual items. Three viewers provide insight into a trained model:

✦ **Itemsets:** Displays the list of itemsets discovered in the training data, each with its associated size (number of items in the set) and support (number of training cases in which this set appears). Several controls for filtering the list are provided, including the Filter Itemset text box, which will search for any string entered (e.g., "Region = Europe" will display only itemsets that include that string).

✦ **Rules:** Similar in layout and controls to Itemsets, but lists rules instead of itemsets. Each rule has the form A, B -> C, meaning that cases that contain A and B are likely to contain C (e.g., People who bought pasta and sauce also bought cheese). Each rule is listed with its probability (likelihood of occurrence) and importance (usefulness in performing predictions).

✦ **Dependency Network:** Similar to the Dependency Network used for other algorithms, with nodes representing items in the market basket analysis. Note that nodes have a tendency to predict each other (dual-headed arrows). The slider will hide the less probable (not the less important) associations. Select a node to highlight its related nodes.

Time Series

The Time Series algorithm predicts the future values for a series of continuous data points (for example, web traffic for the next six months given traffic history). Unlike the algorithms already presented, prediction does not require new cases on which to base the prediction, just the number of steps to extend the series into the future. Input data must contain a *time key* to provide the algorithm's time attribute. Time keys can be defined using date, double, or long columns.

Once the algorithm has run, it generates a decision tree for each series being forecast. The decision tree defines one or more regions in the forecast and an equation for each region, which can be reviewed using the Decision Tree Viewer. For example, a node may be labeled `Widget.Sales-4 < 10,000`, which is interpreted as "use the equation in this node when widget sales from four time-steps back is less than 10,000." Selecting a node will display the associated equation in the Mining Legend, and hovering over the node will display the equation as a tooltip. Note the Tree pull-down at the top of the viewer that enables the models for different series to be examined. Each node also displays a diamond chart whose width denotes the variance of the predicted attribute at that node. In other words, the narrower the diamond chart the more accurate the prediction.

The second Time Series Viewer, labeled simply Charts, plots the actual and predicted values of the selected series over time. Choose the series to be plotted from the drop-down list in the upper-right corner of the chart. Use the Abs button to toggle between absolute (series) units and relative (percent change) values. The Show Deviations check box will add error bars to display expected variations on the predicted values, and the Prediction Steps control enables the number of predictions displayed. Drag the mouse to highlight the horizontal portion of interest and then click within the highlighted area to zoom into that region. Undo a zoom with the zoom controls on the toolbar.

Because prediction is not case based, the Mining Accuracy Chart does not function for this algorithm. Instead, keep later periods out of the training data and compare predicted values against the test data's actuals.

OLAP Integration

Data mining can use cube data as input instead of a relational table (see the first page of the Data Mining Wizard), which behaves much the same as described for relational tables, with some important differences:

✦ While a relational table can be included from most any data source, the cube and the mining structure that references it must be defined within the same project.

✦ The case "table" is defined by a single dimension and its related measure groups. When additional data mining attributes are needed, add them via a nested table.

✦ When selecting mining structure keys for a relational table, the usual choice is the primary key of the table. Choose mining structure keys from dimension data at the highest (least granular) level possible. For example, generating a quarterly forecast will require that quarter to be chosen as the key time attribute, not the time dimension's key (which is likely day or hour).

✦ Data and content type defaults will tend to be less reliable for cube data, so review and adjust type properties as needed.

✦ Some dimension attributes based on numeric or date data may appear to the data mining interface with a text data type. A little background is required to understand why this happens: When a dimension is built, it is required to have the Key column property specified. Optionally, a Name column property can also be specified, giving the key values friendly names for the end user (e.g., June 2005 instead of 2005-06-01T00:00:00). However, data mining will use the Name column's data type instead of the Key column's data type, often resulting in unexpected text data types showing up in a mining structure. Sometimes the text data type works fine, but for other cases, especially Key Time or Key Sequence attributes, it can cause the mining structure not to build or to behave incorrectly once built.

Resolving this issue requires either removing the Name column property from the dimension attribute or adding the same column to the dimension a second time without using the Name column property. If a second copy of the attribute is required, it can be marked as not visible to avoid confusing end users.

✦ The portion of cube data to be used for training is defined via the mining structure's cube slice. Adjust this slice to exclude cases that should not be used in training (e.g., discontinued products and future time periods). Consider reserving a portion of the cube data for model evaluation (e.g., train a forecast on 18 of the last 24 months of data and compare actual and forecast values for the final six months).

✦ A Lift Chart cannot be run against cube test data, so model evaluation will either require test data in a relational table, or some strategy that does not rely on the tools of the Mining Accuracy Chart.

Using a cube as a mining data source can be very effective, providing access to what is often large quantities of data for training and testing, and providing the ability to create a dimension or even an entire cube based on the trained model.

Summary

Data Mining provides insights into data well beyond those provided by reporting, and Analysis Services streamlines the mining process. While the data must still be prepared, mining models hide the statistical and algorithmic details of data mining, allowing the modeler to focus on analysis and interpretation.

Beyond one-time insights, trained models can be used in applications to allocate scarce resources, forecast trends, identify suspect data, and a variety of other uses.

✦　　✦　　✦

Programming
MDX Queries

◆ ◆ ◆ ◆

In This Chapter

Cube addressing basics

MDX SELECT statements

Commonly used MDX functions

MDX named sets and calculated members

Adding named sets, calculated members, and business intelligence to cube definitions

◆ ◆ ◆ ◆

MDX, or Multidimensional Expressions, is to Analysis Services what SQL is to the relational database, providing both definition (DDL) and query (DML) capabilities. MDX queries even look somewhat like SQL, but the ideas behind them are dramatically different. Certainly, MDX returns multidimensional cell sets instead of two-dimensional result sets, but more important, MDX does not contain a JOIN statement, as the cube contains explicit relationships between all the data it summarizes. Instead, hierarchically organized dimension data is manipulated in sets to determine both the content and structure of the result.

Learning to write basic MDX queries goes quickly for most students, especially those with other database experience. However, many beginners have a tendency to stall at the basic query level. This learning plateau seems to stem from a lack of understanding of only a dozen or so terms and concepts. These are the same concepts presented at the beginning of this chapter: tuples, sets, the parts of a dimension, and so on.

Avoid getting stalled by attacking MDX in manageable bites:

1. Read the "Basic Select Query" section at the beginning of this chapter, followed by practicing basic queries until you become comfortable with them.

2. Return to and reread "Basic Select Query" carefully until you have the concepts and terminology down cold. These basics will enable you to read the documentation of advanced features in "Advanced Select Query" with confidence. Practice advanced queries.

3. Get started defining sets and calculations within the cube structure by reading the "MDX Scripting" section.

Cross-Reference For background in creating the cubes that MDX queries, see Chapter 43, "Business Intelligence with Analysis Services."

New in 2005 While Analysis Services functionality has been part of the SQL Server product since version 7.0, the 2005 release is a full reimplementation of the product. Many of the underlying concepts carry over from previous versions, but the syntax is substantially expanded and many restrictions have been dropped.

Basic Select Query

Like SQL, the `SELECT` statement in MDX is the means by which data is retrieved from the database. A common MDX form is as follows:

```
SELECT { Set1 } ON COLUMNS, { Set2 } ON ROWS
FROM  Cube
WHERE ( Set3 )
```

This query will return a simple table, with `Set1` and `Set2` defining the column and row headers, `Cube` providing the data, and `Set3` limiting which parts of the cube are summarized in the table.

Cube Addressing

A set is a list of one or more tuples — consider the example cube in Figure 45-1, which has been limited to three dimension hierarchies (Product, Year, Measure) so it can be represented graphically. An MDX query summarizes the individual blocks of the cube, called *cells,* into the geometry specified by the query. Individual cells of the cube are addressed via tuples.

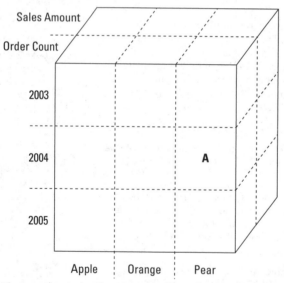

Figure 45-1: A simple cube with three dimension hierarchies

Tuples list entries from every hierarchy providing coordinates in the cube, selecting all the cells where those coordinates intersect. For example, (Pear, 2004, Order Count) addresses the cell marked as "A" in Figure 45-1. Tuples can also address groups of cells using a dimension's All level — for example, (Pear, All Years, Order Count) refers to three cells: the cell marked as "A" and the cells immediately above (Pear, 2003, Order Count) and below (Pear, 2005, Order Count) it. In fact, even when a tuple does not explicitly list a dimension, MDX uses the dimension's default member (usually the All level) to fill in the missing information. Thus, (Sales Amount) is the same as (All Products, All Years, Sales Amount).

Sets are built from tuples, so {(Pear, 2004, Order Count)} is a set of one cell, while {(Apple),(Orange)} consists of 12 cells — all the cells that don't have Pear as the product. Of course, the MDX syntax is a bit more formal than these examples show and practical cubes are more complex, but the addressing concepts remain the same.

Dimension Structure

Each dimension is a subject area that can be used to organize the results of an MDX query. Within a dimension are hierarchies, essentially topics within that subject area. For example, a customer dimension might have hierarchies for city, country, and postal code, describing where a customer lives. Each hierarchy in turn has one or more levels that actually contain the members or dimension data. Members are used to build the sets that form the basis of MDX queries.

Dimension References

Referring to one of the components of a dimension is as simple as stringing together its lineage separated by periods. Here are some examples:

```
[Customer]  -- Customer dimension
[Customer].[Country]                      -- Country hierarchy
[Customer].[Country].[Country]            -- Country level
[Customer].[Country].[Country].&[Germany] -- Germany member
```

While it is technically allowed to omit the square brackets around each identifier, many cube names have embedded spaces and special characters, so it is customary to include them consistently. The ampersand (&) before the member denotes a reference by key — every member can be referenced by either its key or its name, although keys are recommended. In this case, the key and name are the same thing, so [Customer].[Country].[Country].[Germany] refers to the same member. Members from other hierarchies may have more cryptic keys — for example, [Customer].[Customer].[Customer].&[20755] may be equivalent to [Customer].[Customer].[Customer].[Mike White].

In addition to referring to individual members in a dimension, most dimensions also have an [All] level that refers to all the members in that dimension. The default name for this level is [All], but it can be changed by the cube developer. For example, the [All] level for the AdventureWorks Customer dimension is named [All Customers]. The [All] level can be referenced from either the dimension or the hierarchy:

```
[Customer].[All Customers]           -- Customer [All] level from dimension
[Customer].[Country].[All Customers] -- Customer [All] level from hierarchy
```

Tuples and Simple Sets

As outlined earlier in the section "Cube Addressing," tuples are constructed by listing one member from each hierarchy, or if no member is explicitly specified for a particular hierarchy, the default member (usually the [All] level) for that hierarchy is implicitly included in the tuple. Parentheses are used to group the tuple's member list. For example, the following tuple references all the cells that contain Internet sales volume for German customers over all time, all territories, all products, and so on:

```
([Customer].[Country].[Country].&[Germany], [Measures].[Internet Sales Amount])
```

When a simple tuple is specified with only one hierarchy member, the parentheses can be omitted, so all German customers becomes simply [Customer].[Country].[Country].&[Germany].

The simplest way to build a set is by listing one or more tuples inside of braces. For example, using simple tuples without parentheses, the following is a set of French and German customers:

```
{[Customer].[Country].[Country].&[France],
 [Customer].[Country].[Country].&[Germany]}
```

Basic SELECT Statement

Simple sets allow the construction of a basic SELECT statement. The following example query returns Internet sales to French and German customers for calendar years 2003 and 2004:

```
SELECT
{[Customer].[Country].[Country].&[France],
 [Customer].[Country].[Country].&[Germany]} ON COLUMNS,
{[Date].[Calendar Year].[Calendar Year].&[2003],
 [Date].[Calendar Year].[Calendar Year].&[2004]} ON ROWS
FROM [Adventure Works]
WHERE ([Measures].[Internet Sales Amount])
```

Result:

	France	*Germany*
CY 2003	$1,026,324.97	$1,058,405.73
CY 2004	$922,179.04	$1,076,890.77

This example places sets on two axes, rows and columns, which become the row and column headers. The WHERE clause limits the query to only cells containing Internet sales volume; this clause is often called the *slicer*, as it limits the scope of the query to a particular slice of the cube. Think of the slicer as determining how each hierarchy that isn't part of some axis definition will contribute to the query.

Any number of headers can be specified for an axis by including more than one non-default hierarchy in each tuple that builds the axis set. The following example creates two row headers by listing both the Product Line and Sales Reason Type hierarchies in each row tuple:

```
SELECT
{[Customer].[Country].[Country].&[France],
 [Customer].[Country].[Country].&[Germany]} ON COLUMNS,
{([Product].[Product Line].[Product Line].&[S],
    [Sales Reason].[Sales Reason Type].[Sales Reason Type].&[Marketing]),
 ([Product].[Product Line].[Product Line].&[S],
    [Sales Reason].[Sales Reason Type].[Sales Reason Type].&[Promotion]),
 ([Product].[Product Line].[Product Line].&[M],
    [Sales Reason].[Sales Reason Type].[Sales Reason Type].&[Marketing]),
 ([Product].[Product Line].[Product Line].&[M],
    [Sales Reason].[Sales Reason Type].[Sales Reason Type].&[Promotion])
} ON ROWS
FROM [Adventure Works]
WHERE ([Measures].[Internet Sales Amount],
       [Date].[Calendar Year].[Calendar Year].&[2004])
```

Result:

		France	*Germany*
Accessory	Marketing	$962.79	$349.90
Accessory	Promotion	$2,241.84	$2,959.86
Mountain	Marketing	$189.96	$194.97
Mountain	Promotion	$100,209.88	$126,368.03

This hierarchy-to-header mapping provides a way to control the geometry of the result set, but it begets a restriction on creating sets for an axis: The hierarchies specified for tuples in the set must remain consistent for every item in the set. For example, having some of the tuples in the preceding example use the Product Category hierarchy instead of the Product Line hierarchy would not be allowed. Think of inconsistencies between the tuples as causing blank header cells, which MDX doesn't know how to handle.

Another restriction on creating sets for an MDX query is that each hierarchy can appear on only one axis or slicer definition. If the Calendar Year hierarchy is explicitly named in the row definition, it cannot appear again in the slicer. This restriction applies purely to the hierarchy— another hierarchy that contains the calendar year data (e.g., the Calendar hierarchy in AdventureWorks) can appear on one axis while the Calendar Year hierarchy appears elsewhere.

Measures

Measures are the values that the cube is created to present. They are available in MDX as members of the always present Measures dimension. The Measures dimension has no hierarchies or levels, so each measure is referenced directly from the dimension level as `[Measures].[measure name]`. If no measure is specified for a query, the cube's default measure is used.

Generating Sets from Functions

Developing MDX code would quickly get very tedious if every set had to be built by hand. Several functions can be used to generate sets using data within the cube; some of the most popular are listed below. To save space, each example has been constructed such that it provides the row set of this example query:

```
SELECT
{[Measures].[Internet Sales Amount],
 [Measures].[Internet Total Product Cost]} ON COLUMNS,
{ } ON ROWS
FROM [Adventure Works]
```

✦ `.Members`: Lists all of the individual members of either a hierarchy or a level. Used with a level, all the members of that level are listed (e.g., `[Date].[Calendar].[Month].Members` returns all calendar months). When used with a hierarchy, all members from every level are listed (e.g., `[Date].[Calendar].Members` returns every year, semester, quarter, month, and day).

✦ `.Children`: Lists all the children of a given member (e.g., `[Date].[Calendar].[Calendar Quarter].&[2002]&[1].Children` returns all the months in first quarter of 2002).

✦ Descendants(start [,depth [,show]]): Lists the children, grandchildren, and so on, of a member or set of members. Specify start as the member or set of members, depth as either a specific level name or the number of levels below start. By default, if depth is specified, only descendants at that depth are listed; the show flag can alter that behavior by allowing levels above, at, or below to be shown as well — values include SELF, AFTER, BEFORE, BEFORE_AND_AFTER, SELF_AND_AFTER, SELF_AND_BEFORE, SELF_BEFORE_AFTER. Some examples are as follows:

- Descendants([Date].[Calendar].[Calendar Year].&[2003]) lists the year, semesters, quarters, months, and days in 2003.

- Descendants([Date].[Calendar].[Calendar Year].&[2003], [Date].[Calendar].[Month]) lists the months in 2003.

- Descendants([Date].[Calendar].[Calendar Year].&[2003],3, SELF_AND_AFTER) lists the months and days in 2003.

✦ LastPeriods(n, member): Returns the last n periods ending with member (e.g., LastPeriods(12,[Date].[Calendar].[Month].&[2004]&[6]) lists July 2003 through June 2004). If n is negative, future periods are returned beginning with member.

✦ TopCount(set, count [,numeric_expression]): Returns the top n (count) of a set sorted by the numeric_expression (e.g., TopCount([Date].[Calendar].[Month]. Members, 5, [Measures].[Internet Sales Amount]) returns the top five months for Internet sales. See also the similar functions BottomCount, TopPercent, and BottomPercent.

Unlike TopCount and its cousins, most set functions do not involve sorting as part of their function, and instead return a set with members in their default cube order. The Order function can be used to sort a set: Order(set, sort_by [, { ASC | DESC | BASC | BDESC }]). Specify the set to be sorted, the expression to sort by, and optionally the order in which to sort. The ASCending and DESCending options sort within the confines of the hierarchy. For example, sorting months within the AdventureWorks Calendar hierarchy using one of these options, months will move around within a quarter, but will not cross quarter (hierarchy) boundaries. The "break hierarchy" options, BASC and BDESC, will sort without regard to the parent under which a member normally falls.

Generated sets frequently have members for which no measure data are available. These members can be suppressed by prefixing the axis definition with NON EMPTY. The following example shows sales by salesperson for months in 2004; NON EMPTY is used for the column headers because the cube does not contain data for all months in 2004, and NON EMPTY is useful in the row definition because not every employee is a salesperson. In addition, the Order function is used to rank the salespeople by total sales in 2004. Note that the sort_by is a tuple specifying sales for the year of 2004. Had the [Date].[Calendar].[Calendar Year].&[2004] been omitted, the ranking would have instead been sales over all time.

```
SELECT
NON EMPTY {Descendants([Date].[Calendar].[Calendar Year].&[2004], 3)} ON COLUMNS,
NON EMPTY {
  Order(
    [Employee].[Employee].Members,
    ([Date].[Calendar].[Calendar Year].&[2004],
    [Measures].[Reseller Sales Amount]),
    BDESC
  )
} ON ROWS
FROM [Adventure Works]
WHERE ([Measures].[Reseller Sales Amount])
```

The prior query yields the following:

	January 2004	February 2004	...	June 2004
All Employees $3,415,479.07	$1,662,547.32	$2,700,766.80		
Linda C. Mitchell	$117,697.41	$497,155.98		$282,711.04
Jae B. Pak	$219,443.93	$205,602.75		$439,784.05
...	...			
Stephen Y. Jiang	$70,815.36	(null)		$37,652.92
Amy E. Alberts	$323.99	$42,041.96		(null)
Syed E. Abbas	$3,936.02	$1,376.99		$4,197.11

These generated sets all contain a single hierarchy, so how are multiple headers generated? The Crossjoin function will generate the cross-product of any number of sets, resulting in single large set with tuples made in every combination of the source sets. For example, Crossjoin([Product].[Product Line].[Product Line].Members,[Sales Territory].[Sales Territory Country].[Sales Territory Country].Members) will provide two levels of headers listing Product Line and Sales Territory Country. Alternately, the crossjoin operator "*" can be placed between sets to generate the cross-product. Enclosing a list of sets in parentheses separated by commas also has the same effect. This latter construct can be confusing in some contexts. For example,

```
([Customer].[Country].[Country].&[Germany],
{[Date].[Calendar Year].[Calendar Year].&[2003],
 [Date].[Calendar Year].[Calendar Year].&[2004]})
```

looks rather like a tuple, but MDX will implicitly convert the first member (German customers) into a set, and then generate the cross-product, resulting in a set of two tuples.

Using SQL Server Management Studio

The names of objects within a cube can be very long and difficult to type correctly. Fortunately, SQL Server Management Studio provides a convenient drag-and-drop interface for specifying both object names and MDX functions. Begin by opening a new Analysis Services MDX Query, and choose the appropriate Analysis Services database in the toolbar, and the target cube in the upper left-hand corner of the query window. The Metadata tab (see Figure 45-2) is automatically populated with all the measures, dimensions, and so on, for that cube. MDX queries can then be built up by dragging objects onto the script pane or by switching to the Functions tab and similarly dragging function definitions.

Cross-Reference   For more details about working in SQL Server Management Studio, see Chapter 6, "Using Management Studio."

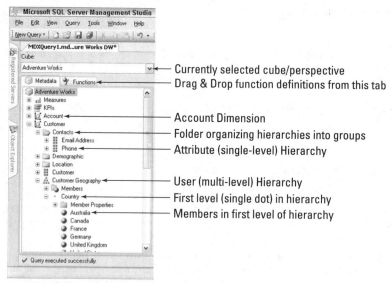

Figure 45-2: SQL Server Management Studio Metadata tab

The developer of a cube may choose to group dimension hierarchies into folders, also shown in Figure 45-2. Folders provide a handy way to organize long lists of hierarchies and have no effect on the structure of the cube or how MDX is written.

Advanced Select Query

Beyond the basic table generation described so far in this chapter, the syntax described here includes the commonly used features:

```
[ WITH <calc | set> [ , <calc | set> ... ] ]
SELECT [ <set> on 0
    [ , <set> on 1 ... ] ]
FROM <cube> | <subcube>
[ WHERE ( <set> ) ]
```

The SELECT statement can return from 0 to 128 axes, with the first five having aliases of ROWS, COLUMNS, PAGES, SECTIONS, and CHAPTERS. Alternately, axis numbers can be specified as AXIS(0), AXIS(1), etc.

Best Practice

As the complexity of a query increases, the need for clarity and documentation increases as well. Break long queries onto several lines and use indentation to organize nested arguments. Add comments about the intent and meaning using "--" or "//" for end of line comments, or /*comment*/ for embedded or multi-line comments.

Subcubes

Specify a subcube in the FROM clause by enclosing another SELECT within parentheses where a cube name would normally appear. This works much like a derived table in SQL, except that whereas a derived table includes only the columns explicitly identified, a subcube includes all hierarchies in the result, except some of the hierarchies will have limited membership. The following example creates a subcube of the top five products and top five months for U.S. Internet sales, and then summarizes order counts by day of the week and subcategory:

```
SELECT
    {[Date].[Day Name].Members} on Columns,
    {[Product].[Subcategory].[Subcategory].Members} ON ROWS
FROM (SELECT
        {TOPCOUNT([Product].[Model Name].[Model Name].Members, 10,
            [Measures].[Internet Sales Amount])} ON COLUMNS,
        {TOPCOUNT([Date].[Calendar].[Month], 5,
            [Measures].[Internet Sales Amount])} ON ROWS
    FROM [Adventure Works]
    WHERE ([Customer].[Country].&[United States]))
WHERE ([Measures].[Internet Order Count])
```

Subcubes are helpful for breaking complex logic down into manageable segments. They can also be helpful building applications when either a consistent view of a changing population or a fixed population with alternate views is desired.

WITH Clause

The WITH clause enables the creation of sets and calculated members. While some of the functionality provided can be performed directly within axis definitions, it is good practice to use sets and members to break logic apart into units that can be more easily constructed and understood.

Best Practice

Sets and calculations can also be defined as part of the cube (see the "MDX Scripting" section that follows). If any item is to be used in more than a handful of queries, create it as part of the cube, making it globally available and adjustable by changes in a single location.

New in 2005

Previous versions of MDX require that the definition of each WITH item be enclosed in single quotes, such as WITH [MySet] AS '...Definition...'. The quotes are no longer required and are omitted from the examples that follow.

Sets

Add a named set to the WITH clause using the syntax set_name AS definition, where set_name is any legal identifier, and definition specifies a set appropriate for use in an axis or WHERE clause. The following example builds three sets to explore the nine-month trends on products with more than a 5 percent growth of sales in 2004:

```
WITH
  SET [ProductList] AS
    Filter( [Product].[Product].[Product].Members,
      ([Date].[Calendar Year].&[2004],
        [Measures].[Internet Ratio to All Products])>0.05
      )
  SET [TimeFrame] AS
    LastPeriods(9,[Date].[Calendar].[Month].&[2004]&[6])
    SET [MeasureList] AS {
      [Measures].[Internet Order Count],
      [Measures].[Internet Sales Amount]
    }
SELECT
  {[MeasureList]*[ProductList]} ON COLUMNS,
  {[TimeFrame]} ON ROWS
FROM [Adventure Works]
```

The prior query yields the following:

	Internet Order Count	...	Internet Order Count	Internet Sales Amount	...	Internet Sales Amount
	Mountain-200 Silver, 38		Mountain-200 Black, 46	Mountain-200 Silver, 38		Mountain-200 Black, 46
October 2003	29	...	29	$67,279.71	...	$66,554.71
November 2003	28		31	$64,959.72		$71,144.69
December 2003	32		42	$74,239.68		$96,389.58
January 2004	28		36	$64,959.72		$82,619.64
February 2004	36		34	$83,519.64		$78,029.66
March 2004	35		33	$81,199.65		$75,734.67
April 2004	45		34	$104,399.55		$78,029.66
May 2004	48		50	$111,359.52		$114,749.50
June 2004	62		44	$143,839.38		$100,979.56

This example uses the Filter function to limit the set of products to those with more than 5 percent of sales. The Filter function has the following general form: Filter(set, condition).

Best Practice

Perhaps the most important query optimization available is limiting the size of sets as early as possible in the query, before crossjoins or calculations are performed.

Calculated Members

Although the syntax of a calculated member is similar to that of a set: member_name as definition, the member name must fit in to an existing hierarchy, as shown in the following example:

```
WITH
  MEMBER [Measures].[GPM After 5% Increase] AS
    ( [Measures].[Internet Sales Amount]*1.05 -
      [Measures].[Internet Total Product Cost] ) /
      [Measures].[Internet Sales Amount], FORMAT_STRING = 'Percent'
  MEMBER [Product].[Subcategory].[Total] AS
      [Product].[Subcategory].[All Products]
SELECT
  {[Measures].[Internet Gross Profit Margin],
   [Measures].[GPM After 5% Increase]} ON 0,
  NON EMPTY{[Product].[Subcategory].[Subcategory].Members,
    [Product].[Subcategory].[Total]} ON 1
FROM [Adventure Works]
WHERE ([Date].[Calendar].[Calendar Year].&[2004])
```

The previous query yields the following:

	Internet Gross Profit Margin	GPM after 5% Increase
Bike Racks	62.60%	67.60%
Bike Stands	62.60%	67.60%
Bottles and Cages	62.60%	67.60%
...	...	
Touring Bikes	37.84%	42.84%
Vests	62.60%	67.60%
Total	41.45%	46.45%

This query examines the current and what-if gross profit margin by product subcategory, including a subcategory "total" across all products. Note how the names are designed to match the other hierarchies used on their query axis. FORMAT_STRING is an optional modifier to set the display format for a calculated member. The source cube contains default formats for each measure, but new measures created by calculation will likely require formatting. [Product].[Subcategory].[Total], like most totals and subtotals, can rely on a parent member (in this case the [All] level) to provide the appropriate value:

```
WITH
  SET [Top20ProductList] AS
    TOPCOUNT([Product].[Product].[Product].Members,
    20,
    ([Date].[Calendar].[Calendar Year].&[2004],
    [Measures].[Internet Order Count]))
```

```
SET [NotTop20ProductList] AS
   Order(
   Filter(
   {[Product].[Product].[Product].Members - [Top20ProductList] },
    NOT IsEmpty([Measures].[Internet Order Count])),
   [Measures].[Internet Order Count],BDESC)
MEMBER [Measures].[Average Top20ProductList Order Count] AS
   AVG([Top20ProductList],[Measures].[Internet Order Count])
MEMBER [Measures].[Difference from Top20 Products] AS
   [Measures].[Internet Order Count] -
   [Measures].[Average Top20ProductList Order Count]
MEMBER [Product].[Product].[Top 20 Products] AS
   AVG([Top20ProductList])
SELECT
   {[Measures].[Internet Order Count],
    [Measures].[Difference from Top20 Products] } ON COLUMNS,
   {[Product].[Product].[Top 20 Products],
    [NotTop20ProductList]} ON ROWS
FROM [Adventure Works]
WHERE ([Date].[Calendar].[Month].&[2004]&[6])
```

Result:

	Internet Order Count	Difference from Top20 Products
Top 20 Products	176	0
Hydration Pack - 70 oz.	76	-100
Mountain-200 Silver, 38	62	-114
...	...	
Touring-3000 Yellow, 54	4	-172
Touring-3000 Yellow, 58	4	-172
Mountain-500 Black, 40	2	-174

This example compares the average June 2004 order count of the top 20 products to the other products ordered that month. A contrived example to be sure, but it demonstrates a number of concepts:

✦ Top20ProductList: Builds a set of the top 20 products based on orders for the entire year of 2004

✦ NotTop20ProductList: Builds the list of everything not in the top 20. The "except" set operator (-) is used to remove the top 20 products from the list of all products. That list is filtered to exclude empty members, which is in turn ordered by order count descending.

✦ Average Top20ProductList Order Count: Calculates the average order count across the set of top 20 products. Similar aggregate functions, including SUM, MIN, MAX, and

MEDIAN, share this syntax: AVG(set [, numeric_expression]). In practice, this calculation would likely be implemented as part of the next calculation, but it's included here to show one calculation depending upon another.

✦ Difference from Top20 Products: Difference between a given product's order count and the top 20 average

✦ Top 20 Products: Created as part of the product hierarchy to get a row to display showing the top-20 average. Because this row will display for a couple of measures, the numeric_expression is omitted so that it will be calculated in the context of the cell being displayed.

Dimension Considerations

There are several things to understand about dimensions and the properties of the cube being queried, as they affect query execution, including the following:

✦ MdxMissingMemberMode: This dimension property, when set to true, causes invalid members specified as part of a query to be ignored without generating an error. For example, if an axis is defined as {[Product].[Product].[Mountain-100 Silver, 38], [Product].[Product].[Banana]} and Banana is not a valid product name, no error will be generated. Instead, the result will list the mountain bike and not the fruit. When MdxMissingMemberMode is set to false, an error is generated for invalid member names. MDX scripts (calculations described within the cube definition) always throw an error for missing members, regardless of this property setting.

✦ IgnoreUnrelatedDimensions: When true, this measure group property tells MDX to ignore dimensions unrelated to a measure being queried. For example, the employee dimension of Adventure Works is not related to the Internet measures because no salesperson is involved with an Internet sale. Thus, the query

```
SELECT {[Measures].[Internet Sales Amount]} ON COLUMNS,
       {[Employee].[Employee].[Employee].Members} ON ROWS
  FROM [Adventure Works]
```

will list every employee with the total Internet sales amount, satisfying both the requirement to list all employees and the requirement to ignore the unrelated employee dimension when evaluating Internet sales. The alternative setting would result in null values being returned for every employee. An IgnoreUnrelatedDimensions setting of true is both the default and the more flexible option, but it requires some care by MDX query writers.

✦ If a default member has been specified for a hierarchy, then results will be limited to that default unless another value for that hierarchy is explicitly listed in the query. For example, if [Date].[Calendar].[Calendar Year].&[2003] is the default member for year, then referencing [Date].[Calendar].[Month].&[2004]&[6] in a query without referencing the calendar year hierarchy will result in no data being returned. To retrieve the June 2004 data, either reference the [All] level of calendar year, or, if the cube developer has suppressed the [All] level, reference the 2004 member of the year hierarchy. Default members are generally avoided, but they can be useful in some situations, and a query writer should be aware of any hierarchy that has a default member.

✦ Autoexists vs. Non Empty: Placing the set `{[Date].[Calendar Year].[Calendar Year].Members * [Date].[Calendar].[Month].Members}` on a query axis will result in listing the year 2001 with the months from 2001, the year 2002 with the months from 2002, etc. Why doesn't the crossjoin result in a true cross-product between the years and months? Analysis Services automatically detects which members of the hierarchies exist with each other, and only returns the valid combinations. This behavior is referred to as *autoexists,* and only functions for hierarchies within a single dimension. `Non Empty` is used to further restrict sets to only those that have corresponding measure values.

MDX Scripting

Sets and calculations like those described in this chapter can be created directly within the cube. Using the Business Intelligence Development Studio, open the Cube Designer for the cube of interest and switch to the Calculations tab.

Cross-Reference   For more information on designing cubes specifically, see Chapter 43, "Business Intelligence with Analysis Services."

The cube contains a single declarative script that describes all the calculations and sets, although by default the designer presents this script as a series of forms (see Figure 45-3). Even if no calculated members or sets exist in the cube, a single `CALCULATE` statement should exist, instructing the cube to populate non-leaf cells within the cube.

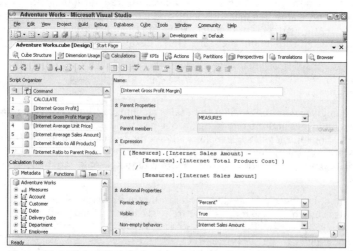

Figure 45-3: Calculations tab of Business Intelligence Development Studio Cube Designer

Calculated Members and Named Sets

Click on an existing calculated member (refer to Figure 45-3) or select New Calculated Member from the toolbar. A form appears with several options:

✦ **Name:** Name of the calculated member, without its parent hierarchy.

✦ **Parent Hierarchy:** Hierarchy to which this member should be added. For measures this will be simply Measures; for other hierarchies, use the built-in navigation to locate the appropriate dimension.hierarchy combination.

✦ **Parent Member:** Only applies to multi-level hierarchies; specify the parent member of the calculated member. Essentially, this specifies the drill-down path in the multi-level hierarchy to reach the calculated member.

✦ **Expression:** The formula that calculates the appropriate member value; equivalent to the expression used for a `WITH MEMBER` definition.

✦ **Format String: :** Optional format string; generally specified for measures.

✦ **Visible:** Calculations are sometimes made not visible when they form the basis for other calculations but are not themselves valuable to the end user.

✦ **Non-empty behavior:** Select one or more measures to determine how to resolve a `NON EMPTY` axis definition. If not specified, the calculated member must be evaluated at every possible cell to determine whether it is empty. If specified, the listed measure(s) will be used to determine whether a cell will be empty.

✦ **Color and Font Expressions:** Display attributes can be changed, providing the client is using software that supports the appropriate display, based on any MDX expression. For example, values within budget could appear in green, whereas those outside of budget could be displayed in red.

Sets are defined in a similar fashion to calculated members, but only the set name and defining expression need to be specified.

Adding Business Intelligence

The Cube Designer's Business Intelligence Wizard can add calculations to a cube from standard templates. Templates include currency conversion, combining values based on a chart of accounts, and time-based calculations such as moving averages and period to date. Each template has individual requirements and purposes documented in Books Online, but time calculations are described here because they are most widely applicable.

Using time intelligence requires a properly configured time dimension, with attribute types assigned, based on a dimension table (not a server dimension). Time intelligence is generally added late in the cube development cycle so all the manually built calculated members are available for creating time-based calculations. Start the wizard by opening the cube of interest in the Cube Designer and selecting Add Business Intelligence from the toolbar. The wizard presents a series of pages:

✦ **Choose Enhancement:** Select Define time intelligence.

✦ **Choose Target Hierarchy and Calculations:** Calculations defined by the wizard will apply to a single time hierarchy. If the cube has multiple roles (e.g., Order vs. Ship date) or calendar types (e.g., Calendar vs. Fiscal), multiple runs of the wizard will be required to create calculations for different target hierarchies. Generally, a multi-level hierarchy is chosen as the target hierarchy.

Choose the target hierarchy at the top of the page, and then choose the calculations to be created for this hierarchy (e.g., Twelve Month Moving Average).

✦ **Define Scope of Calculations:** Choose the measures that will be averaged, summarized, and so on, by the time calculations.

✦ **Completing the Wizard:** Review the changes the wizard will make to the cube.

The wizard adds the following: a named calculation to the data source view in the time table, a new hierarchy in the time dimension to contain the calculated members, and the MDX script that defines the calculated members. Calculation results are accessed by queries that combine the target hierarchy and the hierarchy containing the calculated members. Results will be one of the following: a value when one can be calculated, null when not enough data is available, or "NA" if the calculation does not apply to the cell (e.g., 12-month average calculation in a cell corresponding to one year).

Summary

MDX provides a way to define and query constructs within Analysis Services databases much the way SQL provides those capabilities for relational databases. Unlike SQL, MDX accommodates the multi-dimensional data by specifying sets along multiple axes that specify the geometry of the resulting cell set. Functions are available to generate, order, and filter sets. The WITH keyword can be used to create building blocks for larger and more complex queries.

MDX can also be used as the basis for calculations and sets defined within a cube definition. These MDX scripts are an excellent place to include commonly used calculations and groupings that are then available to any query.

These features combine to create an extraordinarily rich and efficient data query and analysis environment.

✦   ✦   ✦

Authoring Reports with Reporting Services

Reporting Services delivers a powerful toolset for report author-ing. The Report Designer in Visual Studio 2005 provides robust capabilities for developers, while nontechnical users can build and update reports using the Report Builder. This chapter demonstrates how to build reports using Visual Studio 2005.

Building good reports requires an odd and often conflicting set of skills. Reports bridge the gap between nontechnical decision-makers and the database you've worked so hard to make understandable, robust, complete, consistent, and stable. Given this, it is worth stat-ing the result that report developers strive to achieve:

- ✦ Speed and availability

- ✦ Accuracy and timeliness

- ✦ The right amount of detail — not too much, not too little

- ✦ Consistent, organized, and easily interpreted formatting and presentation

This chapter explores the anatomy of a report, demonstrates the steps required to create a report, and covers several additional fea-tures of Reporting Services to satisfy nearly any reporting need.

Anatomy of a Report

A Reporting Services report consists of data sources, data sets, parameters, and the report layout or design. This section describes each of these report components.

Report Definition Language (RDL)

The Report Definition Language (RDL) is an open XML schema used to represent data retrieval and layout information for a report. For example, the RDL schema contains elements that define report data sources, data sets, and parameters to specify the data available within the report. The RDL schema also contains elements to control the report layout and formatting, including the header, body, footer, label, and table elements.

A report definition in Reporting Services is nothing more than an XML file that conforms to the RDL specification. Microsoft provides two tools for creating RDL report definitions so that you don't have to handwrite the XML: Visual Studio 2005 and Report Builder. This chapter focuses on building reports using Visual Studio 2005. The Report Builder tool is part of the Report Manager deployment and provides end users (nontechnical) with the ability to author and update reports.

Cross-Reference

See the next chapter, Chapter 47, "Administering Reports with Reporting Services," for more information on how to configure and deploy reports.

One powerful facet of Reporting Services is the ability to extend the RDL schema. Because the RDL schema is an open schema, it is possible to accommodate advanced or custom scenarios by adding elements and attributes to it. This can be accomplished by hand or programmatically using the classes in the System.XML namespace.

It is also possible to programmatically build, deploy, and execute reports, which means the possibilities are endless when it comes to creating custom report authoring tools, authoring reports on-the-fly, and integrating reports into applications. For example, a developer could use the XmlTextWriter to programmatically create an RDL report definition, and then use the Report Server Web Service to deploy and render the report from within an application. The Report Server Web Service also contains methods to manage nearly all aspects of the report server.

Data Sources

A data source contains the connection information for a database or data file and includes the data source type, connection string, and credentials. A data source is required to retrieve data for a report. It can be defined and stored within a single report, or it can be shared by multiple reports within the project. Like a report, shared data sources can be deployed to the report server. Both shared data sources and report-specific data sources can be modified using the Report Manager or SQL Server Management Studio once deployed to the report server.

Data Source Types

While it is possible to extend Reporting Services by creating a custom data extension, several data source types are available out of the box:

✦ Microsoft SQL Server

✦ Microsoft SQL Server Analysis Services

✦ Oracle

✦ OLE DB (Object Linking and Embedding for Databases)

✦ XML (Extensible Markup Language)

✦ ODBC (Open DataBase Connectivity)

✦ Report Server Model

Common Data Source Connection Strings

To connect to SQL Server 2005, select the Microsoft SQL Server data source type. The following connection string shows an example to connect to the AdventureWorks database on the SQL Server instance named SQL2005 on the local SQL Server machine using Windows Authentication:

```
Data Source=localhost\SQL2005;Initial Catalog=AdventureWorks
```

To connect to Analysis Services 2005, select the Microsoft SQL Server Analysis Services data source type. The following connection string shows an example to connect to the AnalysisServicesDB database on the SQL2005 instance of the local Analysis Services server:

```
Data Source=localhost\sql2005;Initial Catalog=AnalysisServicesDB
```

To connect to an Oracle server, the Oracle client tools must be installed. Select the Oracle data source type and use the following connection string (replace ServerName with the name of the Oracle server).

```
Data Source=ServerName
```

The XML data source type is new in Reporting Services 2005. Use a URL as the connection string to XML resources including a Web Service, an XML file, or an application that returns XML data. To connect to an XML data source, select the XML data type and provide a URL as the connection string. The following example shows a connection string to connect to the Report Server Web Service on the local machine.

```
http://localhost/reportserver$sql2005/reportservice2005.asmx
```

The following connection string shows how to connect to an XML file named StateList.xml located on the local web server:

```
http://localhost/StateList.xml
```

Writing a query for an XML data source is demonstrated in the section "Working with XML Data Sources."

Using Expressions in a Connection String

Connection strings can contain expressions, allowing the connection string to be determined at runtime. For example, the following connection string will connect to the server and database specified by the parameter:

```
="data source=" & Parameters!ServerName.Value & ";initial catalog=" &
Parameters!Database.Value
```

Adding parameters to the report for the server and database enables the user to specify the data source of the report.

Setting Data Source Credentials

The data source credentials can be set to use Windows Authentication, database authentication (such as SQL Server Authentication), or none. The credentials can be stored in the Report Server database, or can be configured to prompt the user for the credentials upon report execution. The best configuration choice depends on your network and security environment.

For more information about configuring data source credentials, see the "Administering Security" section in Chapter 47, "Administering Reports with Reporting Services."

Reporting Services Data Sets

In Reporting Services, a data set refers to the results of a query used to define the data available for the report. A Reporting Services data set is not an ADO.NET data set. A data set can be created using either the Report Wizard or the Data tab in the Report Designer.

A data set requires a data source. When creating a data set, you can either select an existing shared data source, or you can specify a new report-specific data source.

A single report can contain multiple data set definitions, and each data set can access a different data source. This powerful feature means that a report can contain data from multiple databases and XML data sources. The data set command text can contain text SQL statements, stored procedure calls, or XML queries. Data sets can also contain parameters and filters to limit the data returned in the report.

Query Parameters and Report Parameters

Parameters can be used to empower the user to specify the report criteria and control report formatting. Query parameters are included in the data set definition and are used to select or filter data. For example, the parameter @CategoryID can be used to return the subcategories for a selected category, as demonstrated in the following example:

```
Select * From Subcategory Where CategoryID = @CategoryID
```

Query parameters can also be used to specify the values passed to a stored procedure. The following example calls a stored procedure named uspSubcategories that contains a parameter for the CategoryID:

```
EXEC uspSubcategories @CategoryID
```

Report parameters are used to control report formatting and behavior. For example, adding a Boolean parameter named ShowDetails can control the visibility of report items used to display additional details in the report. Parameters can control nearly any design element available in a report. Query parameters can be associated with report parameters using the tabs named Parameters and Filters on the data set's Properties window.

 New in 2005   Reporting Services 2005 allows dynamic grouping (the group criteria for a table can be provided using report parameters).

Many options are available to control the way parameters are rendered on the report. For example, setting the Parameter data type to Boolean will render the parameter as radio buttons, enabling the user to select True or False. Setting the data type to Integer and adding a list of available values will render the parameter as a drop-down list.

New in 2005   Report parameters can now be configured to allow the selection of multiple values. Figure 46-1 shows the result of creating a color parameter with the Multi-value option selected. The values selected by default can also be specified.

Figure 46-1: The ability to select multiple parameter values represents a powerful new feature in Reporting Services 2005.

Three options are available for specifying parameter values and parameter defaults: None, Non-queried, and From Query. Selecting None adds a textbox to the report, enabling the user to enter any value. Providing values using the Non-queried and From Query options adds a drop-down list to the report, enabling the user to select from the available values. The Non-queried option enables the report author to create the parameter values, while the From Query option populates the parameter values from a data set.

Report Content and Layout

Report content and layout is defined using the Layout tab in the Report Designer. Reports contain a header, body, and footer section. Many report items are available to accommodate virtually any report formatting requirement.

New in 2005 It is now possible to develop custom report Items that can be added to the Toolbox and leveraged in reports for functionality beyond the standard report items included with Visual Studio. Custom report Items can be bound to data sets and leverage the sorting, grouping, filtering, and expression evaluation features of the report processing engine.

Table 46-1 contains the report items included with Visual Studio 2005.

Table 46-1: Visual Studio 2005 Report Items

Report Item	Description
Textbox	Adds report content that is not located within a table or matrix. The textbox can contain static text or an expression.
Line, Rectangle	Adds visual separation and formatting to a report.
Image	Places an image in the report. The image source can be Embedded, Project, Database, or the Web. Visual Studio 2005 contains a wizard to make adding images easy.
Table	Renders the details of a data set. The table report item can be bound to a data set and contains many options to control how the data is grouped, sorted, exported, and presented. A report can contain multiple tables, providing the capability to include data from multiple data sets and data sources in a single report.
Matrix	Presents crosstab data from a data set. For example, the matrix report item could show total sales by region and period. Multiple column, row, and detail criteria can be added to the matrix report item. Working with the matrix is very similar to working with the table.
List	The list is bound to a data set. The content of a list is repeated for each row in the data set or for each grouped row if group criteria are specified. The body of the list represents the template for the report items to be displayed.
Chart	This item includes a wide variety of charts. This report item provides much control of the chart type and formatting.
Subreport	Use this item to render a report within a report.

The Report Authoring Process

The report authoring process includes creating a new Reporting Services project using Visual Studio 2005, defining a data source for the report, adding a report to the project, creating a data set to retrieve the report data, and formatting the report content. This section describes the primary tasks required to create a report and contains an example to walk you through the process.

Creating a Reporting Services Project in Visual Studio 2005

Visual Studio 2005 contains the tools required to author and deploy Reporting Services reports. Follow these steps to create a new Reporting Services project:

1. Open Visual Studio 2005.

2. Select File ➪ New ➪ Project to open the New Project dialog window. Alternately, you can click the Create Project link in the Recent Projects section of the Start Page to open the New Project dialog window. By default, the Start Page is displayed when opening Visual Studio 2005. Figure 46-2 shows the New Project dialog window.

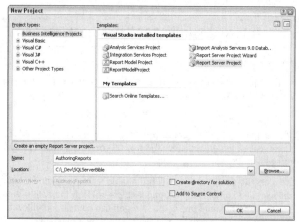

Figure 46-2: Use the New Project dialog window to create a new Reporting Services project.

3. Select the Business Intelligence Projects project type in the Project Types pane on the left side.

4. Select the Report Server Project template in the Templates pane on the right side.

5. Name the project.

6. Specify the location of the project. To create a folder to contain the Solution file with a subfolder containing the report project, check the option to Create Directory for Solution. The value provided for the Solution Name field specifies the name of the solution folder, while the value provided for the Name field specifies the name of the report project. To create the solution and project under a single folder, uncheck the option to Create Directory for Solution.

7. Select OK to create the new Reporting Services project.

Steps to Create a Report

Two methods are available to create a report in Visual Studio 2005: using the report wizard and adding a blank report. The following steps represent the tasks involved to create a report, regardless of the method:

1. Add a report to the report project by selecting Project ⇨ Add New Item. Select the Report Wizard template to have the wizard help you create a report, or select the Report template to create a blank report.

2. Create a data source.

3. Create one or more report data sets.

4. Design the report layout.

5. Add and configure report parameters.

6. Use the Preview tab on the Report Designer to preview the report.

Using the Report Wizard to Create Reports

The Report Wizard is a good way to build a simple report quickly. The Report Wizard will walk you through selecting (or creating) the data source, designing the report query, choosing the report type, adding data fields to the report, choosing the report style, and naming the report. This takes as little as 60 seconds, and when completed you have a report that's ready to run.

If we could satisfy all of our report requirements using the wizard, that would be wonderful. However, this is typically just a starting point. After creating a report using the wizard, the Visual Studio 2005 Report Designer can be used to customize the report.

Authoring a Report from Scratch

Creating a report without using the Report Wizard involves adding the report to your project, specifying one or more data sets, and building the report layout. The following example demonstrates how to build a simple product list report using the AdventureWorks database.

Adding a Blank Report

Follow these steps to create a blank report:

1. Select Project ⇨ Add New Item from the menu.

2. From the Add New Item dialog window, select the Report template.

3. Name the report "Project List."

4. Click Add.

The new empty report is added to your project and opened in the Report Designer. The Report Designer window contains three tabs: Data, Layout, and Preview.

Creating a Shared Data Source

Figure 46-3 shows the Shared Data Source dialog window configured for the AdventureWorks database. Follow these steps to create a new shared data source:

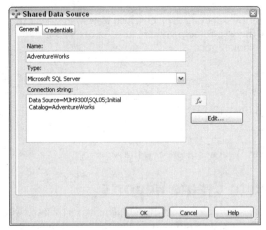

Figure 46-3: Creating a shared data source

1. Select Project ⇨ Add New Item to open the Add New Item dialog window.

2. Select the Data Source template and click Add. The Shared Data Source dialog window will appear.

3. Name the data source "AdventureWorks."

4. Select Microsoft SQL Server from the Type drop-down list.

5. Enter the connection string to the AdventureWorks database. You can click the Edit button to build the connection string.

6. Click OK to add the new data source to the project.

Creating a Data Set

Follow these steps to create a data set to return product information:

1. Select the Data tab in the Report Designer (see Figure 46-4).

2. Select the Dataset drop-down list and click <New Data Set...>.

3. Name the data set "Products."

4. Select the AdventureWorks data source.

5. Select OK. Note that while you can write the SQL query in this dialog window, it is easier to use the familiar Query Designer to write SQL on the Data tab in the Report Designer.

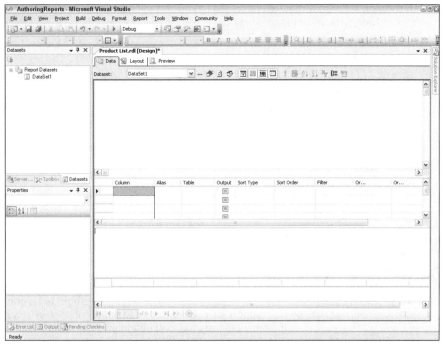

Figure 46-4: The Visual Studio 2005 Report Designer Data tab contains the familiar Advanced Query Designer to help build SQL statements.

6. Enter the following SQL (this SQL statement returns the product information, including the Category and Subcategory names and IDs from the AdventureWorks database):

```
SELECT P.ProductID, P.[Name], P.ProductNumber, P.MakeFlag,
.   P.Color, P.[Size], P.ListPrice, P.StandardCost,
    P.ProductSubcategoryID, SubCat.[Name] AS Subcategory,
    SubCat.ProductCategoryID, Cat.[Name] AS Category
  FROM Production.Product P
    INNER JOIN Production.ProductSubcategory SubCat
      ON P.ProductSubcategoryID = SubCat.ProductSubcategoryID
    INNER JOIN Production.ProductCategory Cat
      ON SubCat.ProductCategoryID = Cat.ProductCategoryID
```

7. Execute the query to verify the SQL, preview the data, and update the list of fields available in the report. You should see the data set representing the list of product, category, and subcategory data that will be available within the report.

Displaying Data in the Report

The results can be displayed in the report using either the list, table, or matrix report items. Working with these items is covered in more depth later in this chapter. To display the results of the data set, follow these steps to add a table to the body of the report, bind it to the data set, and add data fields to the table:

1. Select the Layout tab on the Report Designer, or select Report ➪ View ➪ Layout from the menu.

2. Add a table to the body of the report by dragging a table report item from the Toolbox and dropping it on the report body.

3. Set the `DataSetName` property of the table to the Products data set.

4. Add fields from the data set by dragging fields from the Datasets window and dropping them in the details row of the table. If the Datasets window is not visible, select View ➪ Datasets from the menu.

Previewing the Report

The Product List report now contains a data set that will return products data from the shared AdvenureWorks data source. The report layout consists of a single table to show the contents of the data set for the fields selected. Click the Preview tab to see a preview of the report.

Working with Data

Working with data in Reporting Services 2005 empowers report authors to leverage multiple data sources and data source types. Using parameters and expressions, report authors can empower the report user to control the report content and interact with the report. This section demonstrates how to create data sets using SQL and XML data sources, how to create and use parameters to select and filter data, and how to use expressions.

Working with SQL in the Report Designer

The toolbar in the Report Designer contains a button to toggle between the Generic Query Designer, which contains only the SQL and Results panes, and the Advanced Query Designer which contains the Diagram, Grid, SQL, and Results panes. Figure 46-5 shows the Advanced Query Designer view containing the Products query used earlier in this chapter. Notice that the Datasets window on the left contains the Products data set, including the fields returned by the SQL.

Best Practice

To better leverage SQL Server and minimize report maintenance, create stored procedures and call the stored procedures from the report. For example, the Products data can be returned by a stored procedure named `uspProducts`. Instead of writing the SQL statement in the report, set the command type to `text` and call the stored procedure using the following SQL:

```
EXEC uspProducts
```

Alternatively, you can call a stored procedure by setting the command type to `StoredProcedure` and providing the stored procedure name in the query string. In this case, if the stored procedure contains parameters, you must use the Parameters tab on the Dataset Properties page.

Whether including the SQL statement in the report or calling a stored procedure, query parameters can be used to select and filter data, as described in the next section.

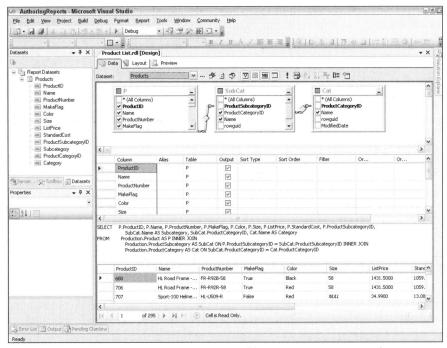

Figure 46-5: The Advanced Query Designer simplifies writing SQL command text.

Using Query Parameters to Select and Filter Data

As discussed earlier, it is possible to use query parameters to select and filter data for the report. For example, the following SQL passes the `CategoryID` and `SubcategoryID` parameters to the `uspProducts` stored procedure:

```
EXEC uspProducts @CategoryID, @SubcategoryID
```

Nested Report Parameters

This example demonstrates how to use parameters in the data set SQL and how to create parameters that are dependent on the selection of other parameters. For example, selecting the Bikes category from the `Category` parameter can populate the Bike subcategories in the `Subcategory` parameter.

To create this nested parameter example, we'll add two data sets to the Product List report created earlier. Both new data sets use the AdventureWorks data source. The first data set, named CategoryList, returns the list of categories using the following SQL:

```
SELECT ProductCategoryID, Name
FROM Production.ProductCategory
ORDER BY Name
```

The second data set, named SubcategoryList, returns the list of subcategories and includes a parameter to select only the subcategories for the selected category. Adding the `OR` condition allows this data set to return all subcategories, enabling other report items to use the data without specifying a CategoryID:

```
SELECT ProductSubcategoryID, ProductCategoryID, Name
  FROM Production.ProductSubcategory
  WHERE (ProductCategoryID = @ProductCategoryID) OR
    (@ProductCategoryID IS NULL)
  ORDER BY Name
```

Update the Products data set with the following SQL to include the new parameters. Again, the OR condition enables the data set to return all products if the user doesn't select any parameters:

```
SELECT P.ProductID, P.[Name], P.ProductNumber, P.MakeFlag,
    P.Color, P.[Size], P.ListPrice, P.StandardCost,
    P.ProductSubcategoryID, SubCat.[Name] AS Subcategory,
    SubCat.ProductCategoryID, Cat.[Name] AS Category
FROM Production.Product P
  INNER JOIN Production.ProductSubcategory SubCat
    ON P.ProductSubcategoryID = SubCat.ProductSubcategoryID
  INNER JOIN Production.ProductCategory Cat
    ON SubCat.ProductCategoryID = Cat.ProductCategoryID
WHERE (P.ProductSubcategoryID = @ProductSubcategoryID
OR @ProductSubcategoryID IS NULL)
    AND (SubCat.ProductCategoryID = @ProductCategoryID
OR @ProductCategoryID IS NULL)
```

Writing the data set SQL to accommodate optional parameters can be very convenient in many situations, but be careful if the data set can possibly return an enormous amount of data. In that case, you may want to require the user to select a parameter before executing the report.

Best Practice

To configure the report parameters, select Report ➪ Report Parameters from the menu. Figure 46-6 shows the Report Parameters dialog window with the ProductSubcategoryID parameter selected.

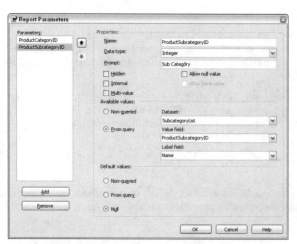

Figure 46-6: The Report Parameters dialog window allows extensive control of report parameters.

Follow these steps to configure the parameters:

1. Select the `ProductCategoryID` parameter.

2. Change the data type to `Integer`.

3. Change the prompt to something user friendly like "Category."

4. Select From Query under Available values. This will populate the available values from the data set specified.

5. Select the CategoryList data set.

6. From the Value Field drop-down list, select ProductCategoryID.

7. From the Label Field drop-down list, select Name.

8. Configure the `ProductSubcategoryID` parameter to match the configuration illustrated in Figure 46-6.

Preview the report. Note that the `Subcategory` parameter is disabled until you select a value from the `Category` parameter. Once you select a category, the `Subcategory` parameter is enabled and contains the list of subcategories for the selected category. Click the View Report button to return only the products within the selected subcategory.

Multi-Value Report Parameters

The previous example demonstrated how to build a report with nested parameters. Let's enhance the report now to enable the user to select multiple values from each parameter and include all products matching the criteria.

Changing the parameters to multi-value parameters requires some minor modifications to the SQL for the SubcategoryList and Products data sets. Specifically, the `Where` clause must change to use the `IN` statement instead of `equals`. In addition, we must remove the capability to return all rows where the parameter is null because the syntax of the parameter value causes invalid SQL when executed. Note, however, that this functionality is not lost, because Reporting Services includes an option to Select All values in a multi-value parameter.

Update the SQL for the CategoryList data set as follows.

```
SELECT ProductSubcategoryID, ProductCategoryID, Name
FROM Production.ProductSubcategory
WHERE ProductCategoryID IN (@ProductCategoryID)
ORDER BY Name
```

Update the Products data set:

```
SELECT P.ProductID, P.[Name], P.ProductNumber, P.MakeFlag,
    P.Color, P.[Size], P.ListPrice, P.StandardCost,
    P.ProductSubcategoryID, SubCat.[Name] AS Subcategory,
    SubCat.ProductCategoryID, Cat.[Name] AS Category
FROM Production.Product P
    INNER JOIN Production.ProductSubcategory SubCat
        ON P.ProductSubcategoryID = SubCat.ProductSubcategoryID
    INNER JOIN Production.ProductCategory Cat
        ON SubCat.ProductCategoryID = Cat.ProductCategoryID
WHERE P.ProductSubcategoryID IN (@ProductSubcategoryID)
    AND SubCat.ProductCategoryID  IN (@ProductCategoryID)
```

Follow these steps to configure the parameters as Multi-value parameters:

1. Select Report ⇨ Report Parameters.

2. Select the `ProductCategoryID` parameter and then select the Multi-value check box.

3. Select the `ProductSubcategoryID` parameter and then select the Multi-value check box.

4. Click OK to save the changes.

Now run the report and select Accessories and Clothing from the `Category` parameter. The `Subcategory` parameter now contains all subcategories for Accessories and Clothing, as shown in Figure 46-7. Select several subcategories and run the report. The report contains all products for the selected subcategories. The report is no longer limited to the selection of a single parameter value.

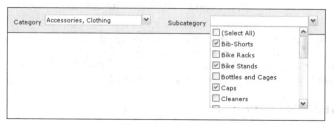

Figure 46-7: This example demonstrates multi-value nested parameters.

Adding Calculated Fields to a Data Set

Once the data set is defined, it is possible to add fields to it and specify an expression for the field value. For example, you could add a field to the Products data set named Margin, and set the expression to calculate it as `ListPrice - StandardCost`. To add a field, follow these steps:

1. Open the Datasets window by selecting View ⇨ Datasets.

2. Right-click on the Products data set and select Add.

3. Name the new field "Margin."

4. Select Calculated Field, and enter the following expression:

   `=Fields!ListPrice.Value - Fields!StandardCost.Value`

5. Select OK and the new field is added to the data set.

Best Practice

While it is possible to achieve the same result by including the calculation in the SQL statement, this approach is very convenient when calling a stored procedure that you don't want to include the calculation in, or you don't have permission to update.

It is also possible to include expressions in the report layout; however, this may require writing and maintaining the expression multiple times within the report. Adding the calculated field to the data set ensures that the expression is defined in one place and simplifies report construction and maintenance.

Working with XML Data Sources

Reporting Services 2005 now provides the capability to use XML as a data source for reports. For example, you can obtain data from an XML Web Service or an XML file and display the data in your report.

The following example demonstrates how to create a report using data from two XML sources: an XML file and a Web Service. The report uses the XML file to populate a `StockSymbol` parameter. The selected stock symbol is passed as a parameter to a Web Service to load current (delayed) information about the selected stock. The following XML file contains the stock symbols and their associated companies:

```
<?xml version="1.0" encoding="utf-8" ?>
<StockSymbols>
  <Symbol Value="AAPL" Name="Apple Computer, Inc. (AAPL)" />
  <Symbol Value="MSFT" Name="Microsoft Corporation (MSFT)" />
  <Symbol Value="ORCL" Name="Oracle Corporation (ORCL)" />
  <Symbol Value="STK"  Name="Storage Technology Corp. (STK)" />
  <Symbol Value="SUNW" Name="Sun Microsystems, Inc (SUNW)" />
</StockSymbols>
```

Follow these steps to create a new data set for the `StockSymbols.xml` file:

1. Create a file named `StockSymbols.xml` containing the Stock Symbols XML code just created, and save it at the root of your web server.

2. Create a new data set named dsStockSymbols.

3. Configure the data source as an XML data source and use the following URL for the connection string:

   ```
   http://localhost/StockSymbols.xml
   ```

4. Use the following code for the data set command text to query the XML file:

   ```
   <Query>
   <ElementPath IgnoreNamespaces="true">
   StockSymbols/Symbol
   </ElementPath>
   </Query>
   ```

5. Set the data source credentials to use Windows Authentication. This is the default when creating a new data source.

6. Execute the query to ensure successful connection and configuration. This also updates the data set definition in the report.

Now create a report parameter named `Symbols` and use the dsStockSymbols data set to populate the values. Follow these steps:

1. Open the Report Parameters dialog window by selecting Report ➪ Report Parameters from the menu.

2. Click Add to create a new parameter.

3. Name the parameter `Symbols`, set the data type to `String`, and set the prompt to something user friendly like "Stock Symbol."

4. Under the Available Values section, select the From Query option.

5. Select the dsStockSymbols data set in the Dataset drop-down list.

6. Select the Value field in the Value Field drop-down list.

7. Select the Name field in the Label Field drop-down list.

8. Click OK to save the new parameter and close the Report Parameters dialog window.

When the report is executed, the user will be prompted to select a stock symbol from the parameter to obtain a quote. Now create a data set to retrieve stock quote information from a Web Service. CDYNE Corporation provides a Web Service to return delayed stock quotes. The GetQuote method of the Web Service retrieves a current stock quote and requires two parameters: StockSymbol and LicenseKey. You will associate the StockSymbol to the StockSymbol parameter just created and hard-code the LicenseKey with a value of 0; the key is provided for testing purposes. Follow these steps to create the Stock Quote data set:

1. Create a new data set named dsStockQuote.

2. Configure the data source as an XML data source and use the following URL for the connection string:

   ```
   http://ws.cdyne.com/delayedstockquote/delayedstockquote.asmx
   ```

3. Use the following code for the data set command text to query the XML Web Service:

   ```
   <Query>
   <Method Namespace="http://ws.cdyne.com/"
   Name="GetQuote" />
   <SoapAction>http://ws.cdyne.com/GetQuote</SoapAction>
   </Query>
   ```

4. On the Parameters tab of the data set properties (click the "..." next to the Dataset drop-down list to open the data set properties), add a parameter named StockSymbol and select the Symbols parameter as the parameter value. Add a second parameter named LicenseKey and set the value to 0 (remove the =). Be aware that the parameter names are case sensitive.

5. Execute the query to ensure successful connection and configuration. This also updates the data set definition in the report.

Add content to the report to display the stock quote results. Preview the report and watch the power of XML unfold beneath your eyes.

Working with Expressions

Expressions are a powerful resource for report authors. For example, expressions can be used to summarize data, perform calculations, format text, and control the report formatting. Figure 46-8 shows the expression editor used to build expressions in Visual Studio 2005.

 New in 2005 The expression editor has been enhanced to improve the expression-building experience for report authors. It now includes a list of available functions and IntelliSense® features to provide statement completion, syntax checking, and inline parameter information.

The expression editor can be opened by selecting <Expression...> from a property value list, by right-clicking on an object and selecting Expression from the context menu, or by selecting the function button labeled "fx" next to a property in a property page. The expression editor contains the expression code window, a category tree, category items, and a description pane. Double-clicking a value in the category items pane or description pane inserts code into the code window.

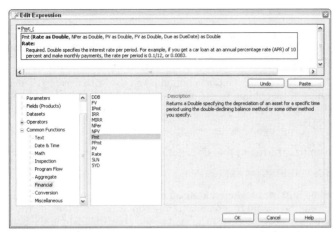

Figure 46-8: The expression editor now contains advanced features such as IntelliSense® and a list of available functions.

Table 46-2 describes the categories available in the expression editor.

Table 46-2: Expression Editor Categories

Constants	Constants are not available for all report items and properties. Depending on the property for which the expression is being written, this category will contain the constant values available for that property. For example, when editing an expression to set the BackgroundColor for a row in a table, the Constants category contains the list of colors available and exposes controls enabling the addition of a custom color.
Globals	The Globals expression category contains functions to access information about the report and the execution of the report, such as ExecutionTime, PageNumber, TotalPages, and UserID.
Parameters	The Parameters expression category contains the list of parameters defined in the report.
Fields	The Fields expression category contains the list of fields for the data set within scope of the selected report item or property. For example, when editing the expression for a cell in a table bound to the Products data set, the Fields expression category will list all of the fields available in the Products data set.
Datasets	The Datasets expression category contains each data set defined in the report. Selecting a data set displays the default aggregation function for each field in the data set. The default aggregation function is dependent on the data type for the field. For example, the default aggregation function of the ListPrice field in the Products data set is Sum(ListPrice). Double-clicking this field adds the following code to the code window: `Sum(Fields!ListPrice.Value, "Products")`
Operators	The Operators expression category contains Arithmetic, Comparison, Concatenation, Logical/Bitwise, and Bit Shift operators to assist with expression syntax and construction.
Common Functions	The Common Functions expression category contains functions for working with Text, Date and Time, Math, Inspection, Program Flow, Aggregate, Financial, and Conversion.

Expression Scope

Aggregate functions enable you to specify the scope for performing a calculation. Scope refers to either the name of a data set or the name of a grouping or data region that contains the report item in which the aggregate function is used.

For example, consider a "Sales by Product" report containing a table with a group named grpProduct. To add a Running Total column to the report that resets the running total on each product, use the following expression:

```
=RunningValue(Fields!LineTotal.Value, Sum, "grpProduct")
```

To add a Running Total column to the report that does not reset by product, use this expression:

```
=RunningValue(Fields!LineTotal.Value, Sum)
```

Expression scope can also be important when adding an expression to a text box. Because the textbox report item cannot be bound to a data set, the expression must include the data set's scope. The following expression calculates the sum of the LineTotal field in the Sales data set:

```
=Sum(Fields!LineTotal.Value, "Sales")
```

Express Yourself with Common Expressions

The following examples demonstrate several common expressions used in reports. Using the following expression as the BackgroundColor property for the detail row in a table will set the background color for the even rows to AliceBlue:

```
=IIf(RowNumber(nothing) mod 2 = 1, "AliceBlue", "White")
```

It's a good idea to include the date and time a report was executed. The following expression produces an output like "Report Executed on Monday, August 15, 2005 at 2:24:33 P.M.":

```
="Report Executed On " & Globals!ExecutionTime.ToLongDateString & " at
" & Globals!ExecutionTime.ToLongTimeString
```

Expressions can be used to format text. The following expression calculates the sum of the LineTotal field in the Sales data set and formats the result as a currency string such as $4,231,205.23:

```
=FormatCurrency(Sum(Fields!LineTotal.Value, "Sales"), 2, true, true,
true)
```

Sometimes it doesn't make sense to show certain report items based on the parameters selected. To toggle the visibility of a report item or even just a cell in a table, use an expression similar to this in the Visibility.Hidden property:

```
=IIf(Parameters!CategoryID.Value = 10, true, false)
```

It is even possible to build the command text for a data set using expressions. The following example expression will only include the Where clause if a value is selected from the parameter named SubcateogryID. The default value for the parameter in this case is -1:

```
="Select * From Products " &
IIf(Parameters!SubcategoryID.Value = -1, "",
" Where ProductSubcategoryID = " & Parameters!SubcategoryID.Value &
")") & " Order By ProductName"
```

Designing the Report Layout

The Report Designer in Visual Studio 2005 contains a rich feature set for designing reports. This section discusses the basics of report design and demonstrates creating a report design, grouping and sorting data, and adding charts to a report.

Design Basics

The Layout tab in the Report Designer contains rich features to make formatting even the most complicated reports possible. The page layout contains three sections: header, body, and footer. Table 46-3 summarizes the behavior and purpose for each section. Designing the report layout is similar to working with Windows Forms. Report items are added by dragging them from the Toolbox onto the report.

Best Practice

Because a report represents the state of a data set at a particular moment in time, it is important to include enough information in the report to answer the "5 Ws" of the report: who, what, when, where, and why? Who ran the report? What criteria were provided to execute the report? When was the report generated? Why does the report exist? Communicating these facts on the report in a consistent manner will eliminate confusion and debate over the report's content.

Table 46-3: Report Sections

Header	By default, content in the header will appear on every page. This is a good place to include the report title to indicate why the report exists. The `PrintOnFirstPage` and `PrintOnLastPage` properties can be used to prevent the header from appearing on the first and last pages.
Body	If the report contains parameters, it's a good idea to add a section to the top or bottom of the body to show the value of the parameters used to execute the report, and perhaps a short description of what the report represents. Adding this detail at the top or bottom of the body will ensure that the information is printed only once, rather than on every page. Designing the report body is a mix between laying out Windows Forms and web forms. When the report runs, the report items will retain their position in the report relative to each other.
Footer	Like the header, the footer also appears on every page by default and can be turned off for the first and last pages. This is a good place to include information about who ran the report, when they ran it, the report version, and page numbering.

Designing the Report Header

To add a report title, follow these steps:

1. Right-click on the left margin of the report and select Page Header to show the page header section. Be aware that once you have added content to a report section, the content is lost if you toggle that section off.

2. Add a text box to the header from the Toolbox.

3. Type the report title and format the text box. You may want the title to be dynamic based on the report content or parameters selected. This can be achieved using an expression. Nearly all visual aspects of the text box permit expressions too.

Designing the Report Footer

The footer should include information such as who ran the report, when the report was executed, and page numbering. This type of information can be added using expressions. Follow these steps to build the footer:

1. Right-click on the left margin of the report and select Page Footer to show the page footer section.

2. Add three text boxes using these expressions:

```
=User!UserID
=Globals!PageNumber & " of " & Globals!TotalPages
=Globals!ExecutionTime
```

3. Add a line above the text boxes to provide visual separation.

Adding and Formatting a Table Report Item

Use the Table report item to render the data from the data set. Follow these steps to add a table showing the data from a data set named Products:

1. Add a table to the body of the report from the Toolbox.

2. Set the `DataSetName` property to the Products data set. When only one data set has been defined, the table will automatically bind to that data set by default. If more than one data set exists, you must set this property manually.

3. Drag fields from the data set to the detail section of the table. Column headers are automatically set based on the field name. Note that dropping fields into the Header and Footer sections of the table will create an expression to either return the value for that field from the first row in the data set, or to calculate the sum of a numeric dataset field.

4. Format the table by adding and deleting columns and setting the numerous formatting options available to control data presentation. Additional tables, lists, images, charts, and various other controls are available to meet your reporting needs.

5. Select the left margin of the table header and set the `RepeatOnNewPage` property to true. This will cause the column headers to appear on every page.

6. Right-click on the left margin of the table footer and select Table Footer to remove the table footer.

Figure 46-9 shows the layout of the report, including the header, table, and footer. Figure 46-10 shows the rendered report.

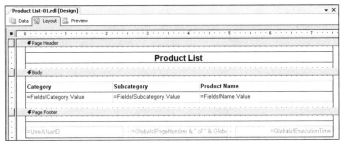

Figure 46-9: Report layout with formatted header, body, and footer

Product List		
Category	Subcategory	Product Name
Components	Road Frames	HL Road Frame - Black, 58
Components	Road Frames	HL Road Frame - Red, 58
Accessories	Helmets	Sport-100 Helmet, Red
Accessories	Helmets	Sport-100 Helmet, Black
Clothing	Socks	Mountain Bike Socks, M
Clothing	Socks	Mountain Bike Socks, L
Accessories	Helmets	Sport-100 Helmet, Blue
Clothing	Caps	AWC Logo Cap
Clothing	Jerseys	Long-Sleeve Logo Jersey, S
Clothing	Jerseys	Long-Sleeve Logo Jersey, M
Clothing	Jerseys	Long-Sleeve Logo Jersey, L
Clothing	Jerseys	Long-Sleeve Logo Jersey, XL
Components	Road Frames	HL Road Frame - Red, 62
Components	Road Frames	HL Road Frame - Red, 44
Components	Road Frames	HL Road Frame - Red, 48
Components	Road Frames	HL Road Frame - Red, 52
Components	Road Frames	HL Road Frame - Red, 56
Components	Road Frames	LL Road Frame - Black, 58
Components	Road Frames	LL Road Frame - Black, 60
Components	Road Frames	LL Road Frame - Black, 62
Components	Road Frames	LL Road Frame - Red, 44
Components	Road Frames	LL Road Frame - Red, 48
Components	Road Frames	LL Road Frame - Red, 52
Components	Road Frames	LL Road Frame - Red, 58

Figure 46-10: Rendered report with formatted header, body, and footer

Adding and Formatting a List Report Item

Using the List report item is an excellent way to include summary data in a report. For example, consider a Product Sales report that contains a table showing the sales detail grouped by Order Date and Order Number. The List report item can be used to add a summary of sales by product to the report. Sorting the list in descending order on the total sales will quickly reveal the top-selling products. Now the report represents two views of the data using the same data set.

To add and format a list as described, follow these steps:

1. Add a List report item to the body of the report from the Toolbox.

2. Open the List Properties page by right-clicking on the List and selecting Properties.

3. Click the Edit Detail Group button to specify the group criteria for the list.

4. Name the group grpProductList.

5. Select the ProductID field in the Group On section.

6. If you want to display a document map in the report for this list, select the ProductName field under the Document Map Label.

7. Click OK to apply the grouping details and return to the List Properties page.

8. Click the Sorting tab and enter the following expression:

```
=Sum(Fields!LineTotal.Value, "grpProductList")
```

9. Set the direction for the sort expression to Descending.

10. Click OK to apply the changes to the List.

11. Now add two text boxes to the List report item using the following expressions for the text box values:

```
=Fields!ProductName.Value
=Sum(Fields!LineTotal.Value, "grpProductList")
```

12. Set the Format property of the text box that calculates the total sales to "C" to display the currency amount.

13. Add additional report items and then format as desired.

14. Preview the report to view the list of products sorted in descending order by the total sales amount.

Using the Table and Matrix Property Pages

Use the Table and Matrix property pages to define behavior such as data set binding, visibility, navigation, filters, sorting (Table only), groups, and data output. Table 46-4 summarizes the options available on each tab of the property pages. While the options vary slightly between the Table and Matrix report items, the process to work with both is very similar.

Table 46-4: Table and Matrix Property Pages

General	Name the table or matrix, bind a data set, set the tooltip text and control page breaks.
Visibility	Control the initial visibility of the item upon report execution. Allow the item visibility to be toggled by another report item.
Navigation	Include a link in the document map, enabling quick navigation within the report to data included in the table or matrix.
Sorting (Table only)	Set the sort order of the details section of the table. This applies only to the Table report item.
Groups	Add and edit group definitions and change the order of the groups.
Filters	Supply filter criteria. Use expressions to apply values from report parameters for filtering.
Data Output	Control the format of exports. Specify whether the report item will be included in exports.

To open the property pages for a Matrix or Table, select a cell within the report item and then right-click the upper-left margin and select Properties from the context menu. The Properties window also contains an icon to open the Properties pages for selected items and contains a drop-down list of all report items, to provide an alternate method of selecting objects.

Grouping and Sorting Data in a Table and Matrix

The Matrix and Table report items offer excellent control of grouping and sorting using the Grouping and Sorting Properties pages. The Grouping and Sorting Properties page shown in Figure 46-11 is used to configure grouping and sorting for both the Matrix and the Table report items.

To open the Grouping and Sorting Properties, you can either right-click the margin of a table row (or the header of a matrix column) and select Edit Group, or you can use the Groups tab of the Table or Matrix Properties page. Use the Grouping and Sorting Properties page to define filters, sorting, visibility, and data output options for the selected group.

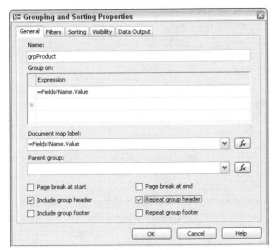

Figure 46-11: The Grouping and Sorting Properties dialog is used for creating and managing groups for the Matrix and Table report items.

The General tab of the Grouping and Sorting Properties page contains the following options to define the group:

✦ **Name:** This name is used when defining the expression scope.

Best Practice

To simplify writing expressions in a table or matrix, it is important to provide a name for each group.

✦ **Group on:** Select the data set fields to group on or build an expression.

✦ **Document map label:** Select the value to include in the document map (optional).

✦ **Parent Group:** This is used to define a recursive hierarchy of data in which all parent-child relationships are represented in the data, such as a company organizational chart.

✦ **Page breack check boxes:** Control page breaks and toggle the header and footer visibility for the group.

The Filters, Sorting, Visibility, and Data Output tabs contain similar functionality to the respective tabs on the Table and Matrix Properties pages described earlier. Defining options on these tabs for a group affects the behavior of the selected group only. Both the Matrix and Table report items can contain multiple groups. To manage the order of the groups and simplify managing the groups, use the Table and Matrix Properties pages as described earlier in this chapter.

The biggest difference between the Matrix and the Table is that the Matrix can contain group definitions for both the columns and the rows, whereas the Table can only contain group definitions for the rows. Once you know how to create and manage group definitions, you are prepared to work with both the Table and the Matrix.

Setting the Sort Order for a Table

Follow these steps to specify the sort order for the details section of a Table report item:

1. Open the Properties window for the Table report item.

2. Select the Sorting tab.

3. Select the fields to sort by in the Expression column and specify the sort direction for each in the Direction column. Use the up and down arrows to change the sort order, and the Delete icon to remove any unwanted sort criteria.

4. Select OK to apply the changes.

This sort criterion controls the default sort order when the report is executed. To add the capability to sort the report at runtime, use the new Interactive Sort feature.

New in 2005
Reporting Services 2005 contains an Interactive Sort feature, enabling the report author to specify the sort criteria for each column. When the report is executed, the columns with Interactive Sorting defined contain a link in the column header, enabling the results to be sorted by the user at runtime.

To define Interactive Sort criteria for a column in a table, follow these steps:

1. Right-click the table header cell for the column to which you want to add sort criteria and select Properties to display the Textbox Properties page.

2. Select the Interactive Sort tab.

3. Click the option to "Add an interactive sort action to this textbox."

4. Select the field to Sort By to specify the sort expression.

5. If the table contains groups, you can also choose the data region or group to sort and set the scope for evaluating the sort expression.

6. Select OK to apply the changes.

Repeat this process for each column you want to allow the user to sort.

Adding Groups to a Table

Follow these steps to group the Products report created earlier in this chapter by category and then by subcategory:

1. Open the Table Properties window and select the Groups tab. Notice that the Group list is currently empty.

2. Click the Add button to create a new group. This opens the Grouping and Sorting Properties window.

3. Name the group "CategoryGroup."

4. In the Expression column of the Group On option, select the Category field.

5. If you want the report to include a document map, enabling the user to quickly navigate within the report using a tree view control, select the Category field for the Document Map Label. It is important to select a field that has a one-to-one mapping to the field used to group on. For example, group on the CategoryID field, and use the Category field for the document map.

6. When creating the top-level group, do not specify a value for the Parent Group.

7. Set the page break, header, and footer visibility, and header and footer repeat behavior for the group using the available check boxes.

8. When creating a group, you must also specify the field by which the group will be sorted. To do so, select the Sorting tab and then select the Category field.

9. Select OK to close the Grouping and Sorting Properties window and return to the Table Properties window. Notice that the Group List now contains the CategoryGroup.

10. To add the Subcategory Group, click the Add button and configure the group as shown in Figure 46-12. Don't forget to set the sort to sort on the subcategory field.

11. Select OK to apply the changes.

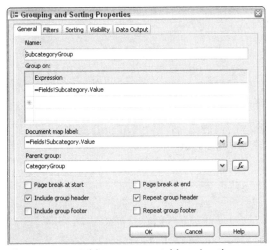

Figure 46-12: Add groups to a table using the Grouping and Sorting Properties window.

Formatting Tables with Groups

After creating the groups for Category and Subcategory, the table contains two new rows for the layout of each group. The left margin of the group rows contains a number to indicate the sequence of the group. To determine the group name, select the left margin and view the Grouping/Sorting property.

Figure 46-13 shows the formatted groups. Figure 46-14 shows the rendered report.

Illustrating Data with Charts

Reporting Services offers extensive chart and graph capabilities to illustrate data. Adding charts to a report is simple. Like all other report items in Reporting Services, most properties of a chart can contain expressions. The Chart Properties page of the Chart report item shown in Figure 46-15 contains tabs to define the chart type and style, the chart data, the legend style and position, 3D effects, and filters.

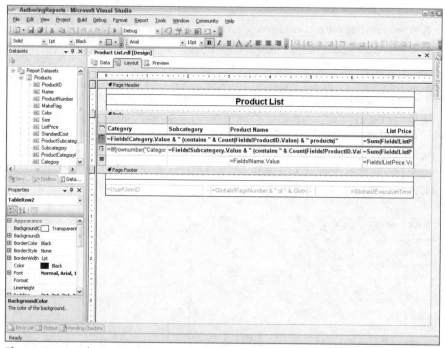

Figure 46-13: Enhance a table layout by adding groups.

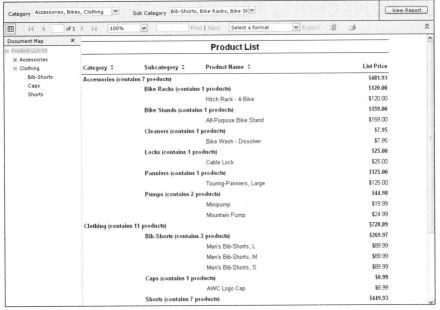

Figure 46-14: Report with grouping and document map

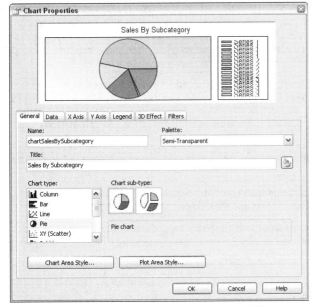

Figure 46-15: Use the Chart Properties page to define and fine-tune charts.

Adding a Pie Chart to a Report

To add a chart to a report, follow these steps:

1. Add a Chart report item to the body of the report from the Toolbox.

2. Right-click the chart and select Properties to open the Chart Properties page.

3. Select the pie chart from the chart types.

4. Enter the chart title.

5. Select the Data tab.

6. Select the data set containing the data for the chart.

7. Click OK to save the changes.

8. Select the chart to display the data, series, and category windows.

9. Drag fields from the data set to the data, series, and category windows. For example, if the data set contains a field for the LineTotal for sales order detail, and the product category, then drop the LineTotal field on the Data fields section and drop the Category field on the Series section. The pie chart will show the total sales by category.

Now preview the report to view the results.

Summary

Reporting Services 2005 delivers abundant features that enable report authors and developers to empower business decision-makers by providing access to interactive reports. The Reporting Services Project in Visual Studio 2005 contains a rich set of tools to make report authoring possible. The Report Wizard provides an easy way to quickly create basic reports. Many advanced features are available to meet nearly any reporting need.

Reports can leverage a wide variety of data sources, and a single report can include data from multiple data sources. Including query parameters and report parameters enables report users to control the selection, sorting, and filtering of report criteria. Expressions can control nearly any aspect of a report, making it possible to perform advanced calculations used to present data within a report.

Visual Studio 2005 contains many new features and enhancements, as highlighted in the following list:

✦ The new XML data source enables reports to contain data from XML files, Web Services, and applications that return XML data.

✦ Group criteria for a table can contain expressions and parameters, enabling reports to contain dynamic groups.

✦ Multi-value report parameters enable the selection of multiple parameter values.

✦ Custom report items can be developed and added to the Toolbox to extend the report items available in a report.

✦ In addition to the list of available functions within a report, the expression editor now contains IntelliSense® to assist with expression syntax, as well as statement completion features.

✦ The new Interactive Sort feature enables a report author to specify sort criteria for columns in a table, which enables the report to be sorted by the user at runtime.

The Report Designer in Visual Studio 2005 includes various report items to format reports. The List, Table, Matrix, and Textbox report items provide great flexibility for displaying data, and the Chart report item enables reports to contain visual representations of the data. In addition to controlling the data within the report, parameters and expressions can be used to control nearly any visual aspect of a report.

The Reporting Services 2005 product delivers an outstanding reporting solution. As a developer, you will be hard-pressed to reach the limits of this technology; and if you do, just extend it to meet your needs. After all, a report is just a collection of XML that complies to the open and extensible standard of RDL. As a business decision-maker, you will find yourself in awe of the convenience, reliability, stability, and performance offered by this technology.

✦   ✦   ✦

Administering Reports with Reporting Services

Reporting Services 2005 contains an ASP.NET web application called the Report Manager. The Report Manager application provides the tools required to administer the report server and deploy items, including reports, shared data sources, and data models. The Report Manager also provides the interface for users to access, manage, and execute reports. The default URL for the Report Manager is http://localhost/reports. Figure 47-1 shows the Report Manager application.

This chapter explains how to deploy reports and administer the report server using the Report Manager application shown in Figure 47-1. It includes three strategies for report deployment, including Visual Studio 2005, the Report Manager, and deploying reports programmatically using the Reporting Services Web Service. This chapter also introduces the Report Builder tool, which enables end users to create their own reports.

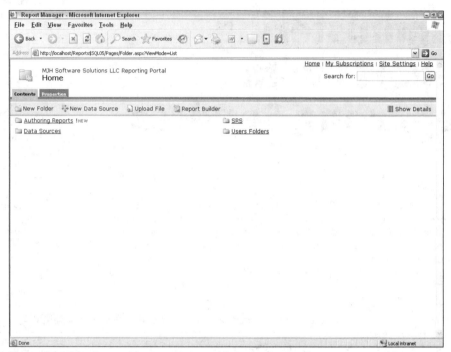

Figure 47-1: The Report Manager comes with Reporting Services 2005. It enables users to access, execute, and manage reports; and enables administrators to deploy reports, and manage security and report server configuration.

Deploying Reporting Services Reports

The last chapter discussed how to author reports using Visual Studio 2005. This section explores the options and strategies to deploy the reports to the report server.

Deploying Reports Using Visual Studio 2005

Deploying reports using Visual Studio 2005 requires some basic configuration of the Reporting Services project. Once configured, reports (and other resources such as data sources and images) can be deployed individually or the entire project can be deployed.

To configure the deployment properties for a Reporting Services project, open the project's Property page by right-clicking on the Reporting Services project and selecting Properties. Figure 47-2 shows the Property page for a Reporting Services project, and Table 47-1 summarizes the deployment properties available for a Reporting Services project.

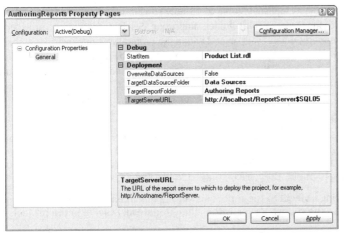

Figure 47-2: Use the settings on the Property page of a Reporting Services project in Visual Studio 2005 to configure the deployment options.

Table 47-1: Reporting Services Project Deployment Properties

OverwriteDataSources	Set this to True if you want to overwrite data sources on the report server with the data sources in the report project. The default value is False, which prevents data sources from being overwritten. This is helpful if the data source used for development is different from the data source used on the report server.
TargetDataSourceFolder	This is the path of the folder to which you wish to deploy shared data sources. Using this parameter enables the definition of a common data source that can be deployed to a common location and used by reports across multiple folders (or projects in development). Using a common shared connection minimizes administration efforts for the Data Source object. Leave this property blank to deploy the shared data source(s) to the folder specified in the `TargetReportFolder` property (not recommended).
TargetReportFolder	This is the path of the folder to which you wish to deploy reports. In Visual Studio 2005, you must create a project for each folder (or subfolder) to which you wish to deploy reports. For example, to simplify deploying reports to two folders named Sales and Customers, set up two Reporting Services projects in Visual Studio 2005 and specify the respective folder name in the `TargetReportFolder` property. You can then move the reports between the projects to control their deployment destination. It is also possible to use the `TargetReportFolder` variable to deploy to subfolders on the report server. For example, setting this value to `Sales/Regional` would create a nice home for your regional sales reports.
TargetServerURL	This is the URL of the report server you wish to deploy to. The default location of your local report server is `http://localhost/ReportServer`. If you named the instance of SQL Server SQL05, the local report server would be `http://localhost/ReportServer$SQL05`.

New in 2005   Reporting Services projects in Visual Studio 2005 now contain properties for the target data source folder and the target report folder. Reporting Services 2000 only provided a `TargetFolder` property, whereby all objects within the project were deployed. Now shared data sources can be deployed to a common folder and shared by reports in multiple folders and subfolders. This minimizes the administration efforts required to maintain Data Source objects on the report server, and simplifies deployment.

Deploying a Single Report or Data Source

Once the deployment properties are configured for a Reporting Services project, a report or data source can be deployed by simply right-clicking on the report and selecting Deploy. The status bar at the bottom of Visual Studio 2005 indicates the deployment progress. If errors are encountered during deployment, they are displayed in the Error List window.

This method of deploying objects to the report server is convenient when you want to update only selected objects on the report server, rather than update all objects in the project.

Deploying a Reporting Services Project

To deploy all objects in the Reporting Services project, ensure that the project deployment properties are correctly configured, and then right-click on the project and select Deploy. Note that the `OverwriteDataSources` project property can be used to prevent overwriting data source objects. This is an important feature because the data source for your reports on the report server will often require different configuration than the data source used for report development.

Deploying Reports Using the Report Manager

While Visual Studio 2005 provides an easy way to deploy reports to the report server, it is not required for report deployment. It is possible to deploy and configure individual Reporting Services objects using the Report Manager. The Report Manager includes features that enable the creation of new folders and data sources, and it provides the capability to upload and update report definitions (.rdl files), report data sources (.rds files), and any other file type you wish to make available on the report server (such as a PDF, Word document, Power Point presentation, Excel file, etc.).

To deploy a report using the Report Manager, follow these steps:

1. Open the Report Manager application in a web browser. The default location for the Report Manager is `http://localhost/reports`.

2. Select the folder to which you want to deploy the report.

3. Click the Upload File button.

4. Enter the path to the file or use the Browse button to find the file.

5. Enter the report name.

6. If you want to overwrite an existing report with the same name, check the option to "Overwrite item" if it exists.

7. Click the OK button to upload the file and return to the contents of the folder. The new report now appears in the list and is marked as New to grab the user's attention.

It's a good idea to execute the report and verify that the data source is valid. You may need to use the Data Sources link on the Properties tab of the report to either select a shared data source or specify a custom data source for the report. You should also review the other links available on the Properties tab to set parameter defaults and configure report execution, history, and security settings.

Deploying Reports Programmatically Using the Reporting Services Web Service

The Reporting Services Web Service exposes methods to deploy reports and enables custom applications to be written to perform such tasks. Remember that the Report Manager is an example of an ASP.NET user interface that leverages the Reporting Services Web Service to manage the report server. All functionality available in the Report Manager is available for your application development pleasure using the Reporting Services Web Service.

To begin developing an application that will use the Reporting Services Web Service, create a project in Visual Studio 2005 and add a web reference to the Reporting Services Web Service. The default location of the Web Service on the local machine is `http://localhost/ReportServer/ReportService.asmx`. After adding this web reference, you will have access to classes that enable your custom application to perform nearly any task on the report server, including deploying and executing reports. The `ReportingService` class OntheWeb Service contains methods that enable the creation (and deletion) of folders, reports, data sources, schedules, and subscriptions, along with many other operations on the report server. It also contains methods to render reports in any of the formats summarized in Table 47-6, later in the chapter.

Configuring Reporting Services Using the Report Manager

The Report Manager is a web application included with SQL Server 2005 Reporting Services. It provides features required to administer the report server and features for end users to access and execute reports. The Report Manager is an ASP.NET user interface built upon the Reporting Services Web Service. The default URL for the Report Manager is `http://localhost/reports`. This section describes how to use the Report Manager application to administer Reporting Services.

Configuring Reporting Services Site Settings

The Site Settings page (shown in Figure 47-3) contains settings to enable user-owned folders, control report history and execution timeout settings, and report execution logging. The page also contains links to configure site security, to create and manage shared schedules, and to manage jobs. To configure the Site Settings for the report server, click the Site Settings link in the header of the Report Manager.

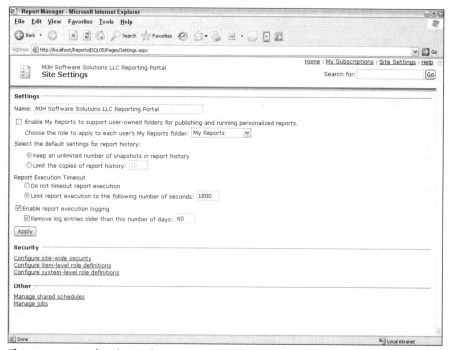

Figure 47-3: Use the Site Settings page in the Report Manager to administer sitewide settings.

Enabling My Reports

By default, the option to enable My Reports is turned off. Turning this feature on enables users to manage a personal folder named My Reports, where they can publish their own reports, create linked reports, and manage their own content. Each user gets his or her own My Reports folder, similar to the My Documents folder in Windows. Reporting Services contains a default role named My Reports to provide appropriate security access for this folder. Later in the chapter you'll see how to customize roles and create new roles, but note that you can specify the role applied to the My Reports folder.

Enabling the My Reports option provides a location where users can save the reports they build using the Report Builder. This new tool available in Reporting Services 2005 enables users to create their own reports based on pre-defined data models.

New in 2005

Reporting Services 2005 contains a Report Builder tool that enables end users to build their own reports. Business decision-makers can use this excellent feature to access and analyze the data and ultimately support timely and more accurate decision-making. At the same time, the complexities related to building reports are minimized. The IT staff designs, develops, and administers Report Builder Models and then exposes the finished Models to information workers.

Configuring Report History Settings

Default behavior for keeping report history can be set to either an unlimited number of snap-shots or a number that you specify. The latter is the default setting, which can be overridden for specific reports if necessary. To override this for a specific report, select the Properties tab on the report, and then select the History link. For the report selected, you can configure the following options:

✦ Allow report history to be created manually (checked by default). To create a snapshot manually, select New Snapshot on the History tab of the report.

✦ Store all report execution snapshots in history (unchecked by default).

✦ Use a report-specific schedule or a shared schedule to add snapshots to report history (unchecked by default).

✦ Select the number of snapshots to keep. If you select Use Default Setting (default), the Site Setting will be applied. Otherwise, you can override the site setting.

Configuring Report Execution Settings

Similar to the default report history setting, the Report Execution Timeout enables you to set the default timeout for the site. The default is set to limit report execution to 1,800 seconds (30 minutes). On the Site Settings page, you can change the time limit or select "Do not time-out report execution." To override this behavior for a specific report, select the Properties tab on the report and select the Execution link. On this page, you can choose to always run the report with the most recent data or you can render the report from a report execution snapshot. You can also control the report execution timeout behavior for the selected report.

If "Enable report execution logging" is checked, a row is written to the ExecutionLog table in the ReportServer database each time a report is executed. While the Report Manager doesn't contain an interface to access this data, it is available; and you can create your own solution if you find it valuable. The Site Settings page also allows you to optionally remove log entries older than a certain number of days.

Administering Security

The security model in Reporting Services leverages Active Directory to grant access to the Report Manager and to items (folders, reports, shared data sources, etc.) within the Report Manager. Security is administered by assigning users or groups to roles. Roles contain selected tasks that enable specific actions within the Report Manager application. Two types of pre-defined roles and tasks exist: system-level and item-level.

System-Level Roles

Two system-level roles are created when the report server is installed: the System Administrator and System User roles. Table 47-2 shows the tasks granted to these roles by default. To change the pre-defined roles or create new roles, select the Configure System-level Role Definitions link on the Site Settings page.

Table 47-2: Default System Roles

Task	System Administrator	System User
Execute report definitions	X	X
Generate events		
Manage jobs	X	
Manage report server properties	X	
Manage report server security	X	
Manage roles	X	
Manage shared schedules	X	
View report server properties		X
View shared schedules		X

The default role definitions can be changed by selecting the role on the System Roles page. If necessary, additional roles can be created by clicking the New Role button on the System Roles page and selecting the tasks permitted for the new role.

Granting System Access to Users and Groups

By default, the BUILTIN\Administrators group is assigned the System Administrator role. Follow these steps to grant system access to additional users or Active Directory groups:

1. Select the Configure Site-wide Security link on the Site Settings page.

2. Click the New Role Assignment button on the System Role Assignments page.

3. Enter the Group or User name — for example, myDomain\jdoe or myDomain\SRSAdminstrators.

4. Select one or more roles to assign to the group or user.

5. Click the OK button to save.

Best Practice

It is important to remain consistent regarding your approach to granting access to the Report Manager and to items within the Report Manager. Consider your environment when choosing how to manage and assign access and whether you grant access to Active Directory groups or to individual users. If you have already taken the effort to create Active Directory groups in your organization, you can most likely leverage your existing groups to administer access to your report server.

For example, if you have an Active Directory group for accounting, you can simply create a new system role assignment for that group to grant all of the accounting members access to the report server. Perhaps you will have an Accounting folder with accounting reports to which only accounting employees should have access. When creating this folder, simply adjust the inherited role assignments to ensure that only the accounting group has access.

Regardless of which strategy you choose (user vs. groups), by maintaining a consistent approach, you will minimize maintenance, research, and troubleshooting efforts in the future.

Item-Level Roles

Item-level roles are used to control the tasks available for managing folders, reports, shared data sources, models, and other resources in the Report Manager application. Table 47-3 describes the default item-level roles created when the report server is installed. To access item-level roles, select the Configure Item-level role definitions link on the Site Settings page. Alternately, select the Security link on the Property tab of any item beneath the root directory in the Report Manager and click the Edit link for an existing assignment or click the New Role Assignment button.

Table 47-3: Default Item-Level Roles

Task	Content Browser	Manager	My Reports	Report Publisher	Builder
Consume reports		X			X
Create linked reports		X	X	X	
Manage all subscriptions		X			
Manage data sources		X	X	X	
Manage folders		X	X	X	
Manage individual subscriptions	X	X	X		X
Manage models		X		X	
Manage report history		X	X		
Manage reports		X	X	X	
Manage resources		X	X	X	
Set security for individual items		X			
View data sources		X	X		
View folders	X	X	X		X
View models	X	X			X
View reports	X	X	X		X
View resources	X	X	X		X

Just as you can create additional system-level roles, you can also create new item-level roles. To create a new item-level role, follow the steps in the next section.

Controlling Item-level Security

By default, every item-level resource inherits the security settings of its parent. If the security settings for an item have not been modified (they still inherit from their parent item), the Security page for that item contains an Edit Item Security button. After modifying the security settings (and breaking the inheritance from the parent item), the Security page for the item contains item-level access to a user or group. You must belong to a System role with the Set Security for Individual Items task to complete these tasks. Follow these steps:

1. Select the Security link on the Properties tab for the item for which you wish to modify security settings.

2. If the item still inherits its security settings from its parent, click the Edit Item Security button. An alert will be displayed indicating that the security is inherited, and that if you continue to edit the item's security, you will break the inheritance. Select OK to continue. Note that you can also delete role assignments that were assigned to the parent.

3. Click the New Role Assignment button.

4. Enter the group or username, e.g., myDomain\accounting.

5. Select one or more roles to assign to the group or user. If you need to view or edit the tasks associated with a role, you can click the role name. You can also create a new role from this page.

6. Click the OK button to save the new role assignment.

Remember that in order for users to access in item-level resource, they must also be granted system-level access. Don't forget to ensure that the users and groups you assign to item-level resources also have been assigned system-level access.

In addition, modifying an item's security will automatically apply the security to all child items that inherit that security. To restore the inherited security for an item that has been customized, click the Revert to Parent Security button. An alert will be displayed confirming that the security settings defined for that item will be replaced by the security settings of its parent.

Working with Linked Reports

A linked report is a shortcut to an actual report. It enables configuration of the report parameters, execution, history, and security independent of the actual report. If the report server is configured to allow user-owned folders for publishing and running personalized reports, users can create a linked report and configure the parameter defaults to suit their specific needs.

Linked reports also provide a powerful way to administer report security and limit the available parameters by user, group, or role. For example, consider a regional sales report with an optional parameter used to execute the report for a selected region. Certain users should be able to execute the report for all regions, while other users should only be able to execute the report for their own region. You can limit access to the actual report to the users (or an Active Directory group) who should be able to view all regions, and then create a linked report for each region and limit access to the linked reports according to the user's privileges. For each linked report, hide the region parameter and set the default value to the desired region. Furthermore, you could create a folder for each region and save the linked reports in these folders. That way, security can be controlled for the folder and multiple linked reports can be saved to the folder, thereby eliminating the need to administer security on each linked report.

Creating Linked Reports

To create a linked report, select the Properties tab on the report to which you wish to create a link and select the Create Linked Report button. Name the new linked report and enter the description and location of the report. Click OK. To administer the parameters, execution, history, and security for the linked report, select the Properties tab on the new linked report. It is also possible to create subscriptions and set up history snapshots for the linked report.

To simplify analysis of dependencies and management of linked reports, it's a good idea to include the actual report name either in the name of the linked report or in the description of the linked report. This way, you can enter the actual report name in the Search criteria (see the Search feature in the header of the Report Manager) and return a list of all linked reports and the actual report.

Leveraging the Power of Subscriptions

The capability to subscribe to reports represents an extremely valuable feature in Reporting Services to automate report delivery. Reporting Services supports both push-and-pull paradigms for report delivery. For example, upon scheduled report execution, a subscription can send an e-mail with an attachment containing the report content (push), with the report content in the body of the e-mail (push), or with a link to the report stored on the report server (pull). Alternatively, reports can be written to a file share where users or other systems can access the report or exported data.

Report subscriptions require that the SQL Server Agent (SQL Server 2005) service is running on the Reporting Services machine. This service executes jobs, monitors SQL Server, fires alerts, and allows automation of some administrative tasks for the report server. Before creating a subscription, ensure that this service is started. In addition, to successfully create a report subscription, the connection credentials for the report data source must be stored.

To begin creating a subscription, select the report you wish to subscribe to and click the New Subscription button in the report control header. Figure 47-4 shows the options available for an e-mail subscription. You can configure options for report delivery, subscription processing and scheduling, and the report parameter values. More information about each of these options is detailed in the next section, which describes how to create data-driven subscriptions, which enables these options to be set using the results from a query.

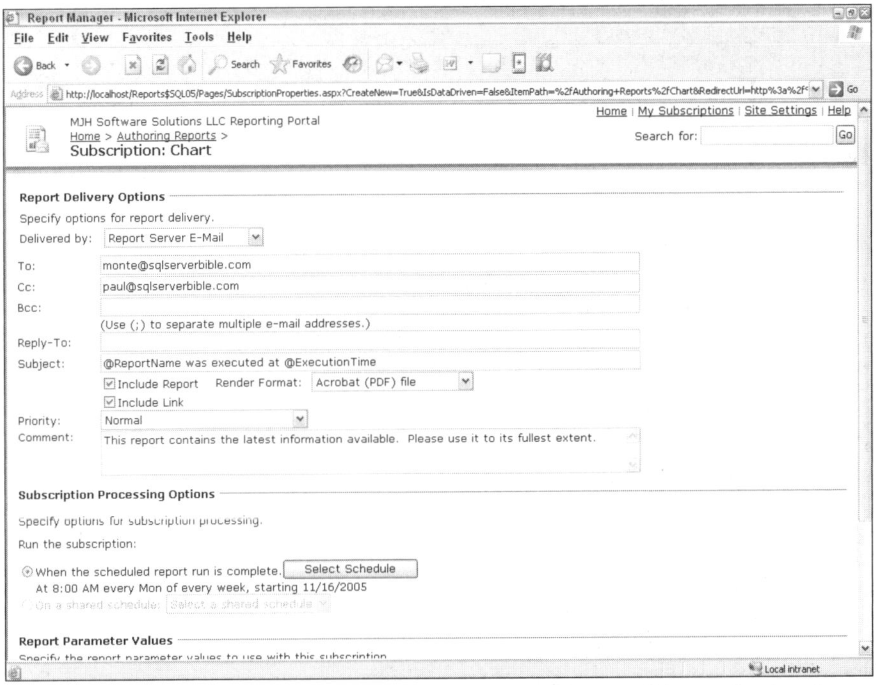

Figure 47-4: Create a report subscription to be delivered by e-mail by configuring these options.

Creating a Data-Driven Subscription

A data-driven subscription enables delivery settings and report parameters to be set dynamically using the results of a query. This is an excellent way to deliver reports and to customize the content of the reports being delivered. For example, instead of creating linked reports for each region as described earlier, a data-driven report could obtain the list of recipients and their corresponding region from a data source and automatically generate and deliver the reports with the appropriate content to each recipient.

To create a data-driven subscription, select the Subscriptions tab on the report you wish to deliver and click the New Data-driven Subscription button. This will guide you through the process of creating a data-driven subscription. Data-driven subscriptions can be delivered by e-mail or written to a file share. In either case, you can specify a data source containing the dynamic data for the report and write a query to return the appropriate data.

Figure 47-5 shows the options available to specify the command or query that returns data for the data-driven subscription. Just like a report, this data can be accessed from a variety of data sources, including Microsoft SQL Server, Oracle, and XML. The values returned in the command or query can be used to execute the report, as shown in Figure 47-6.

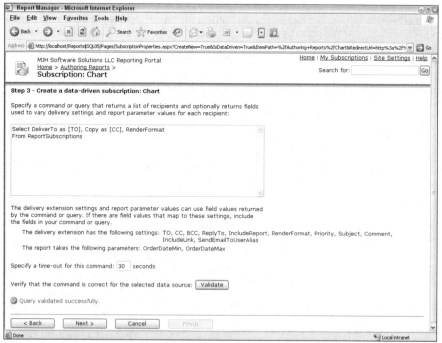

Figure 47-5: Use the Data-Driven Subscription feature to tailor report subscriptions to users based on another data source.

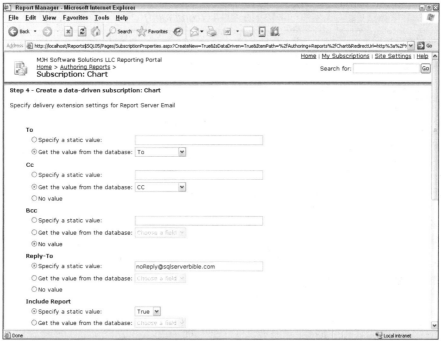

Figure 47-6: To control report execution, provide static values or use values from the database.

In addition to dynamically setting the delivery settings for the report, the query fields can also set values for the report parameters. This powerful feature enables you to dynamically deliver the right report with the right content to the right user. Table 47-4 contains the delivery settings available for an e-mail subscription, and Table 47-5 contains the delivery settings available for a file share subscription.

Table 47-4: Available E-Mail Delivery Settings

Field Name	Description	Sample Value
TO	List of e-mail addresses to which the report will be sent. Separate multiple addresses with semicolons. Required.	myself@xyz.com; myboss@xyz.com
CC	List of e-mail addresses to which the report should be copied. Separate multiple addresses with semicolons. Optional.	mycoworker@xyz.com
BCC	List of e-mail addresses to which the report should be blind copied. Separate multiple addresses with semicolons. Optional.	mysecretinformer@xyz.com

Continued

Table 47-4 *(continued)*

Field Name	Description	Sample Value
ReplyTo	The e-mail address to which replies should be sent. Optional.	reportReplies@xyz.com
IncludeReport	True or False value. Set to True to include the report in the e-mail message. Use RenderFormat to control the format.	True
RenderFormat	The format of the report. See Table 47-6 for the list of valid values. Required when IncludeReport is True.	PDF
Priority	Use High, Normal, or Low to set the priority of the e-mail message.	High
Subject	The subject of the e-mail message.	Daily sales summary
Comment	Text to be included in the body of the e-mail message.	This is the daily sales summary. Please review.
IncludeLink	True or False value. Set to True to include a link in the e-mail body to the report on the report server. Note that this is a link to the actual report with the parameters used to execute the report for this subscription. It is not a link to a snapshot of the report.	True

Table 47-5: Available File Share Delivery Settings

Field Name	Description	Sample Value
FILENAME	The name of the file to be written to the shared folder.	MyReport_1
FILEEXTN	True or False value. When this is True, the file extension will be appended to the filename based on the specified render format.	True
PATH	The UNC path for the shared folder to which the file will be written.	\\computer\sharedFolder
RENDER_FORMAT	The format of the report. See Table 47-6 for the list of valid values.	PDF
USERNAME	The username credential required to access the file share.	myDomain\bobUser
PASSWORD	The password credential required to access the file share.	Bobpasswd
WRITEMODE	Valid values include None, AutoIncrement, and OverWrite.	AutoIncrement

Subscriptions can generate a variety of output formats, as detailed in Table 47-6. This provides great flexibility to accommodate different usage of the output. For example, one user might prefer to receive the report as a PDF because all of the formatting of the report remains intact and the file may be easily distributed, while another user might prefer to receive the report as a comma-delimited file (CSV) so the data can be imported into another system. Both CSV and Excel formats are a good choice if the user wants the data in Excel, although the Excel will attempt to retain the formatting of the report within Excel, while the CSV will simply export the raw data used in the report.

Table 47-6: Available Report Formats

Value	Description
MHTML	Web archive
HTML3.2	Web page for most web browsers (.htm)
HTML4.0	Web page for IE 5.0 or later (.htm)
CSV	CSV (comma delimited)
EXCEL	Excel
PDF	Acrobat (PDF) file
XML	XML file with report data
IMAGE	TIFF file

Data-driven subscriptions allow the same scheduling or trigger options as normal subscriptions. Once you create a data-driven subscription, it will appear in the list of subscriptions on the My Subscriptions page. Use this page to view information about the subscription, including the trigger type, last run date and time, and the subscription's status. You can also edit the subscription from this page.

Summary

Three methods are available to deploy reports to a Reporting Services report server. Each method serves its own purpose and fulfills its placement in the report deployment life cycle. Deploying reports using Visual Studio 2005 provides the capability to deploy an entire project at one time. Using the Report Manager to deploy reports provides greater flexibility over the deployment configuration and enables users and administrators to deploy and manage the report server content without Visual Studio 2005. Alternatively, custom applications can consume the Reporting Services Web Service to automate report deployment.

The Report Manager delivers rich features to place the power of Reporting Services in the hands of end users, while empowering administrators to efficiently and effectively administer the report server. Administrators can easily manage report server content, control security, and automate report delivery using the Report Manager.

✦   ✦   ✦

Analyzing Data with Excel and Data Analyzer

Reporting Services provides a method to create reports that
expose trends, exceptions, and other important aspects of data
stored in SQL Server. Reports can be created with a level of interac-
tivity, but even interactive reports only provide a basic level of data
analysis capabilities.

The advantage of data analysis is the ability to discover trends and
relationships that are not obvious, and to look at data in ways and
combinations not normally performed. Often such analysis is a pre-
lude to, or is done in conjunction with, data mining.

This chapter describes data analysis uses of Microsoft Excel and
Microsoft Data Analyzer. Excel offers PivotTable and PivotChart views
of both relational and multidimensional data, providing a drag-and-
drop approach to viewing data. Excel also offers a data range that provides a spreadsheet window into relational data. Data Analyzer focuses
on multidimensional data, providing both table and graphical views.

Organizational interest in data analysis tends to be focused among a
small population, with the majority of staff satisfied with reports
created by others. Interested staff tend to share the following
characteristics:

✦ They perceive the value of data to their success (or feel hin-
dered by a lack of data).

✦ They have mastered basic office automation skills (e.g., spreadsheet construction).

✦ They have a basic understanding of the data being analyzed
(e.g., know the difference between a product category and a
product line).

Championing data analysis among staff likely to have these characteristics can have a positive impact on the organization, increasing the
availability of data to staff while decreasing the number of reports
needed.

Alternately, data analysis tools can provide a fast report prototyping
tool to nail down requirements before building a complicated report.

Excel PivotTables

The idea of *pivoting* data is to display summaries based on categories that are placed as row and column headers. As categories are dropped onto the header areas, the table quickly reformats itself to display values grouped by all the currently selected category values, as shown in Figure 48-1.

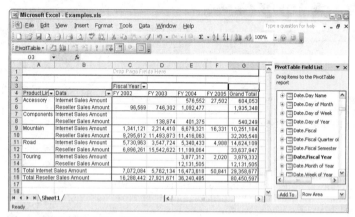

Figure 48-1: Excel PivotTable

Note   The Excel functionality and figures in this chapter are taken from Microsoft Excel 2003. Equivalent functionality is available in Microsoft Excel 2000 and later, although some of the details will differ.

Available data fields are displayed in the PivotTable Field List, ready for dragging onto one of the four table areas:

✦ **Data:** The center of the table that displays data aggregates, such as the sum of Internet Sales shown in Figure 48-1.

✦ **Row headers:** Category data that provides row groupings on the left side of the table (e.g., Country in Figure 48-1).

✦ **Column headers:** Category data that provides column groupings along the top of the table (e.g., Fiscal Year in Figure 48-1).

✦ **Page:** Provides an overall filter for the PivotTable that does not change the layout of the table. This area is unused in Figure 48-1, thus noted by the "Drop Page Fields Here" notation in the table.

In addition to page-wide filters, any field in the row or column headers can select any subset of the current category values. After a bit of practice, generating a desired view in this environment is extremely time efficient, limited mostly by the speed of the underlying data source.

When built against a relational data source, the data displayed is cached within the Excel workbook, so analyzing large data sets results in large workbook file sizes. Using a multidimensional data source (Cube) relies on the speed of the Analysis Services server when running a query for each change to the PivotTable. Working offline with a multidimensional source requires building a local cube file.

Multidimensional Connections

While PivotTables can be created based on lists of data created within Excel, PivotTables using external data are described here, so a connection must be created to that data. Start a new PivotTable by selecting PivotTable and PivotChart Report from the Data menu in Excel. The PivotTable and PivotChart Wizard will step through several pages:

1. Choose External Data as the data source and select either a PivotTable or PivotTable/PivotChart combination.

2. Press the Get Data button to access the Choose Data Source dialog. Within the Choose Data Source dialog, select the OLAP Cubes tab. If the desired cube is already on the list, select it and skip ahead to the Step 3 page.

   a. Add a new cube to the list by choosing <New Data Source> and pressing OK to invoke the New Data Source dialog, shown in Figure 48-2.

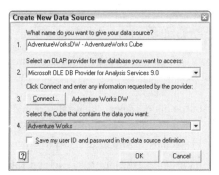

Figure 48-2: Create New Data Source dialog

   b. Enter a name for the data source and choose Microsoft OLE DB Provider for Analysis Services 9.0 as the provider.

Best Practice

Because a data source is specific to an individual cube, it is good practice to identify both the Analysis Services database and the cube as part of the data source name. Optionally, the server or environment can be included for databases that exist in multiple places (e.g., Development-AdventureWorksDW-AdventureWorks Cube).

   c. Press the Connect button to identify the desired server and database via the Multidimensional Connection Wizard.

   d. On the first page of the Multidimensional Connection Wizard (see Figure 48-3), identify the server name. Login information is generally not required because standard Analysis Services connections are made as trusted connections. Alternately, if a local cube file has been created, choose the Cube File option and identify the .CUB file (see Books Online documentation for the MDX statement CREATE GLOBAL CUBE to find details on extracting a local cube file).

   e. On the second page of the Multidimensional Connection Wizard, select the database that contains the cube of interest.

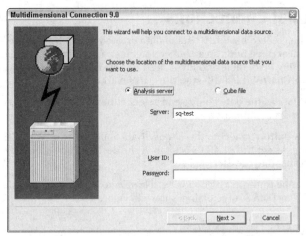

Figure 48-3: Multidimensional Connection dialog

    f. Returning to the Create New Data Source dialog, choose a cube from the drop-down list. Note that cube perspectives are also included in the list of available cubes.

    g. Returning to the Choose Data Source dialog, select the newly created data source and press OK.

    h. Returning to the PivotTable and PivotChart Wizard, press Next to proceed to Step 3.

3. Review the location (worksheet and upper-left corner) for the new PivotTable, and press Finish to complete the wizard.

As you can see from this procedure, Excel collects several pieces of information the first time a cube is accessed, but subsequent PivotTable setups are a quick three-step process. Once the wizard is complete, see the section "PivotTable Construction" later in this chapter for tips on presenting the returned data.

Relational Connection

To receive data from a relational source, use the PivotTable and PivotChart. You can find the wizard under the data menu:

1. Choose External Data as the data source and select either a PivotTable or PivotTable/PivotChart combination.

2. Press the Get Data button to access the Choose Data Source dialog. When the Choose Data Source dialog appears, note the "Use the Query Wizard to create/edit queries" check box at the bottom of the dialog. When this option is checked, a wizard will follow the choice of a data source, stepping through the process of building a query on a single table. When this option is deselected, the Microsoft Query applet follows data source selection, allowing more complicated queries to be built.

3. Once the "Use the Query Wizard to create/edit queries" selection has been made, choose either the Databases tab to start a new query or the Queries tab to begin with a previously saved query. If an existing query is chosen, skip ahead to step 4.

The Databases tab is populated with any relational data sources previously defined in this wizard or defined in the Data Sources (ODBC) applet under Administrative Tools. If the desired database is not in the list, select <New Data Source> to invoke the Create New Data Source dialog. Completing the New Data Source requires a few steps:

    a. Give the data source a name. Because a data source is specific to the database level, data sources are normally named after the database, and optionally the server/environment (e.g., Development-AdventureWorks).

    b. Choose the appropriate driver, e.g., SQL Native Client for a SQL Server database.

    c. Press the Connect button to connect to the desired server and database via the driver-specific setup/login dialog. For example, the SQL Server version is shown in Figure 48-4 and described here. Specify the Server name and login information. Then expand the dialog using the Options button and choose the desired database. Press OK.

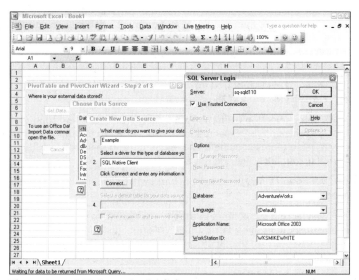

Figure 48-4: SQL Server Login dialog

    d. Returning to the Create New Data Source dialog, optionally choose a default table for the data source. The default table is automatically selected for use each time a data source is used. Press OK.

    e. Returning to the Choose Datasource dialog, highlight the desired data source and Press OK. Either the Query Wizard or the Microsoft Query applet will now run based on the "Use the Query Wizard to create/edit queries" check box at the bottom of the Choose Data Source dialog. See the following corresponding sections for hints about using these tools to create a query.

When control returns to the PivotTable Wizard, the message "Data fields have been retrieved" will be displayed next to the Get Data button.

4. Review the location (worksheet and upper-left corner) for the new PivotTable and press Finish to complete the wizard.

Once the wizard is complete, see the section "PivotTable Construction" for tips on presenting the returned data.

Query Wizard

As described earlier, the Query Wizard runs after a data source has been chosen if the "Use the Query Wizard to create/edit queries" check box is selected. It walks through four pages of query definitions against a single table; no joins or stored procedures can be specified. Instead, the table, columns, filter conditions, and sort order are selected from wizard forms without requiring knowledge of SQL. At the completion of the wizard, options include saving the query for future reuse and editing the query further in Microsoft Query. In addition, canceling the Query Wizard at any point will offer the option of switching to Microsoft Query to complete query construction.

Microsoft Query

Recall from the earlier discussion that the Microsoft Query applet runs after a datasource has been chosen if the "Use the Query Wizard to create/edit queries" check box is not selected. It provides a Microsoft Access-like query-building environment, with regions for graphically including tables and specifying table joins, specifying filter criteria, and previewing query results. Useful actions in this environment include the following:

✦ Press the SQL button in the toolbar to directly enter the query without relying on the graphical interface. This is required for advanced queries, including those using stored procedures, subselects, and `HAVING` clauses.

✦ Use the Add Tables selection from the Tables menu (or equivalent toolbar selection) to invoke the Add Tables dialog. Selected tables are added to the top pane of the Query Designer with default joins specified. Use drag-and-drop to specify additional joins or select and delete join lines that are not appropriate.

✦ The View ➪ Tables and Criteria menu command will toggle the display of the table are criteria panes.

✦ Set criteria by selecting the column in the top row and then entering one or more lines of criteria on subsequent lines. For a single criterion, just enter its value; for pattern matching, use `LIKE 'A%'` to match all entries beginning with A; and for multiple possible values, enter those values on separate lines.

✦ Use the Automatic Query toggle on the Records menu to disable/enable the rerunning of the query after every change. Disabling this option is very helpful for long-running queries. Once disabled, use the Query Now selection to refresh the currently displayed records.

✦ Specify sort order by choosing the Sort item from the Records menu.

PivotTable Construction

Dragging fields between the PivotTable and the PivotTable Field List is the easiest way to add and delete fields from the PivotTable. The currently selected cell must be within the PivotTable to display the PivotTable Field List. Right-click within the PivotTable and choose Hide Field List or Show Field List to toggle list display.

The format of the PivotTable Field List for a relational data source is simply one field per column, whereas multidimensional sources display a list with dimensions on top and measures on the bottom. Measures can only be displayed in the data (center) portion of the PivotTable, whereas dimensions can be placed as a row, column, or page header. Note the difference in icons between dimensions and measures to aid in identification.

Each field placed on the PivotTable is anchored under a field header that includes a drop-down. The drop-down for row and column headers displays a value selection tree that provides several methods for selecting values: Clicking Show All Items will place a single check mark on any unchecked values. Removing a check mark excludes that value from display; a single check mark selects a value for display; and a double check mark indicates that one or more children have been selected for display. Figure 48-5 provides an example of this selection behavior. Child members and double check marks are not available for relational data sources and single-level dimensions.

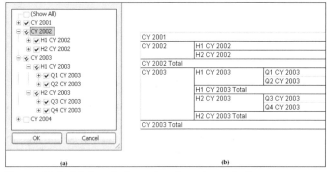

Figure 48-5: (a) Row/column header value selection
(b) Resulting headers

All data (center) area fields display under a single field header named Data, which can be used to remove unwanted data fields by unchecking the unwanted fields in the drop-down.

The drop-downs associated with a page field apply filters across the entire table. For example, Figure 48-6 (a) limits the PivotTable to only displaying items associated with German customers. Multidimensional data sources allow a filter to include multiple value selections, as shown in Figure 48-6 (b).

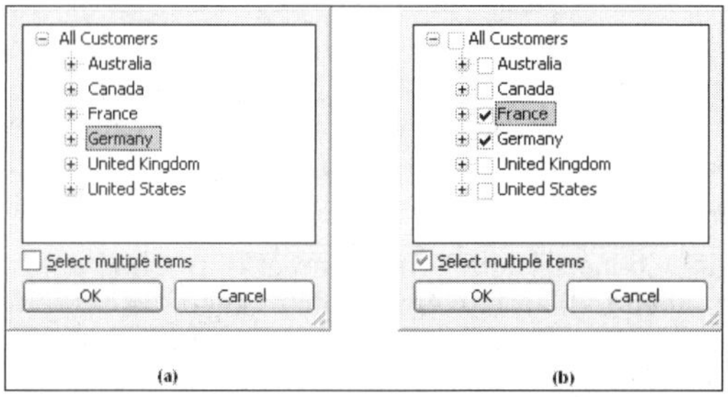

Figure 48-6: Page field filter selection in (a) single and (b) multiple select modes

Following are additional tips for manipulating PivotTables:

✦ For multi-level dimensions, double-clicking an item will toggle the display of its children. Show/hide all the children of a level by right-clicking the field header and choosing the appropriate option under Group and Show Detail.

✦ For PivotTables based on relational data sources, double-clicking a cell in the data area will create a new worksheet that displays each detail row that contributes to the chosen cell.

✦ Double-click the field header (or right-click on a field and choose Field Settings) to access the PivotTable Field dialog. From here several actions are possible:

  • The name displayed for a field can be changed.

  • The number format for data fields can be set. Unlike direct formatting commands, these formats are preserved across table updates.

  • Aggregates displayed can be changed for data fields based on relational sources, such as Min, Max, Average, Sum, Count, etc.

  • Alternative displays for data fields can be chosen by pressing the Options button, such as Running Total, % of Total, etc.

  • Subtotals for row and column header fields can be turned on or off.

  • By pressing the Advanced button for row or column header fields, both sort order and top/bottom display settings can be adjusted.

  • Layout options for row and column headers can be adjusted, included tabular versus. outline layout, totals at top or bottom, page breaks, etc.

✦ Right-click in the PivotTable and choose Table Options to set tablewide options such as the appearance of Grand Totals and various formatting options.

✦ Right-click in the PivotTable and choose Refresh Data to update the PivotTable with the latest data, and the Field List with the latest field names (in case of structure changes to the underlying data source).

✦ On the PivotTable toolbar, choose Format Report from the PivotTable pull-down to access a list of predefined formats for the entire PivotTable. These formats can add a level of polish difficult to obtain by manual formatting changes.

PivotChart Construction

A PivotChart works much like a regular Excel chart, except it is bound to a PivotTable — when the PivotTable changes so does the chart, and vice versa. A PivotChart is automatically created when the PivotChart selection is made in the wizard, or one can be created at any time by right-clicking in the PivotTable and choosing the PivotChart option. By default, the chart is created on a separate tab, but it can be copied and pasted onto another sheet as desired.

While stand-alone PivotTables will often be constructed with a number of row and column headers, tables paired with PivotCharts need to be relatively simple to keep the chart understandable. For example, Figure 48-7 shows a PivotChart based on a single row header (time) and a single column header (data series). Note that while the PivotTable associated with this chart displays all three levels of the time dimension, the PivotChart only draws the bottom level to avoid scaling problems on the chart.

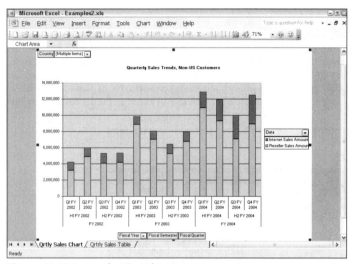

Figure 48-7: A sample PivotChart

The same Field headers display on the PivotChart as the associated PivotTable. Row headers display at the bottom, column headers on the right, and page headers at the top. The header drop-downs allow much of the same configuration from the PivotChart view as from the PivotTable view; and by enabling the PivotTable Field List, the contents of the chart can be changed. Field headers can also be hidden if desired by right-clicking on one of the headers and choosing the Hide PivotChart Field Buttons option. Chart type, options, and formatting are available from the context menu, much the same as a standard Excel chart.

Excel Data Ranges

Excel data ranges are similar to defining a PivotTable based on a relational data source, except the data returned by the query is displayed as a detailed list. This allows the contents of a table, the results of a stored procedure, or any query to be listed in the rows and columns of a spreadsheet. This list of data is referred to as a data range.

Define a new data range by choosing Import External Data ➪ New Database Query from the Data menu in Excel. Then define the query as described in the "Relational Table Connection" section earlier in this chapter.

Once the data range is in place within the worksheet, right-clicking in the data range offers several options, including the following:

✦ **Refresh Data:** Reruns the query and places the latest data in the data range

✦ **Edit Query:** Reopens either the Query Wizard or Microsoft Query to change the content or organization of the data returned

✦ **Data Range Properties:** Offers automatic refresh scheduling, adjustment of layout and format properties, options for applying changes during refresh, etc.

Data Analyzer

Data Analyzer takes a different approach to displaying multidimensional data. Instead of defining row and column headers like a PivotTable, each dimension is displayed in a different window, as shown in Figure 48-8. Once a useful view has been constructed, it can be saved and shared. A collection of such views can provide an analysis workbench, providing both predefined ways of looking at the latest available data and useful starting points for further analysis.

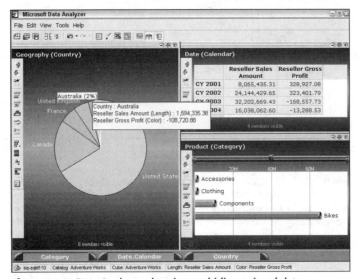

Figure 48-8: Data Analyzer, showing multidimensional data

Each window in a view can display data as a bar chart, pie chart, or grid. Each of these summaries by dimension use either one or two measures. The first, called the *length measure,* is used to determine the length of the bars or the size of the pie slice. The second, called the *color measure,* provides the shade of the bar or pie slice, from red at the smallest through orange and yellow to green as the largest. For example, Figure 48-8 uses Unit Sales as the length measure and Profit as the color measure, as shown by the status bar at the bottom of the page. Exact values for chart displays can be found by hovering over the bar/slice of interest.

Creating a View

Begin creating a new view by choosing "Create a new view" from the Startup dialog, or by choosing New from the File menu. Choose a connection from the Connections page, or press Add to create a new view. When adding a new connection, the Connection Properties dialog shown in Figure 48-9 defines the server/database/cube combination for that view. Create the new connection as follows:

1. Enter the connection name and server.

2. Use the Advanced button to adjust the connection string as needed. Access to Analysis Services 2005 requires that at least the provider be specified as `provider=Msolap.3`.

3. Press the Connect button to connect to the server and repopulate the Catalog (database) and Cube lists.

4. Choose the appropriate Catalog and Cube combination.

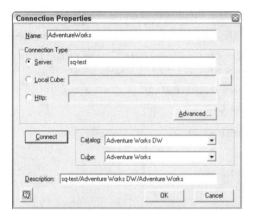

Figure 48-9: Data Analyzer Connection Properties dialog

After defining/selecting a connection, the Dimensions page of the Define View Wizard lists all the dimensions in the selected cube. Choose the dimensions to appear in the new view, remembering that a new window is created for each selected dimension. Finally, on the Measures page of the wizard, choose the measures that will play the length and color roles in the view.

Formatting a View

What defines a useful view varies by application, but generally simpler is better, and simplicity is best achieved by having an objective for each view developed. It's better to develop additional views than to muddy the conclusions a user will draw. Note also that windows can be minimized, holding that dimension's window in ready reserve in the navigation bar across the bottom of the screen. The following list provides additional tips on formatting:

✦ Change the display in a window between bar/pie/grid using the control at the lower left corner of each window.

✦ Drag windows to stack and otherwise arrange their default horizontal tiling.

✦ Right-click on a member within a dimension to find several options:

- **Filter by <name>:** Limits the display in all other windows to data pertaining to the selected member. This is equivalent to left-clicking the member. Only one member from a dimension can be chosen this way, but members from other dimensions can be added to the filter criteria by selecting items from other windows.

- **Remove <name> from filter:** Leaves every member except the chosen one in the filter criteria.

- **Hide <name>:** Removes the member from both the filter criteria and the display.

- **Drill down <name>:** Shows children of the selected member in multi-level dimensions.

✦ The toolbar in each window also provides several useful functions:

- **Drill Up/Down:** Displays the parents or children of the current members
- **Default members:** Resets all filters and hidden members in the current window
- **Filter by All Visible:** Resets all filters but ignores hidden members
- **Hide Members Not in Filter:** Hides filtered out members in the current window
- **Filter by Criteria:** Allows members to be filtered based on the value of any cube measure (e.g., only include stores with less than $10,000 in quarterly sales)
- **Reverse Filter:** Swaps the filtered/unfiltered status of all members
- **Hide Empty:** Hides empty members
- **Length/Color/Name:** Sorts members by the chosen attribute
- **Natural:** Uses the cube sort order
- **Properties:** Allows members to be sorted on any cube measure

Summary

PivotTables and PivotCharts are powerful tools for analyzing data. As features of Excel, they tend to be less intimidating to staff than alternative tools. In addition, many organizations already own Excel, minimizing the investment required. Some companies have even built their entire reporting structure using PivotTables to enable drill-down and non-obvious analysis once the report is delivered.

Data Analyzer is another very useful tool for data analysis. Useful views can be developed and later accessed on demand, enabling a more polished presentation than PivotTables provide.

✦   ✦   ✦

Optimization Strategies

T his book opened with the Information Architecture Principle, which stated that information must be made *readily available*. Optimization theory explains the dependencies between various optimization techniques. This final part puts optimization theory into action with practical optimization strategies.

Schema design—The first layer of optimization theory is the schema, discussed in Chapters 1, 2 and 17. A clean schema that avoids over complexity enables better queries.

Set-based queries—Layer two makes the most use of the Query Optimizer. Part II devotes 10 chapters to writing set-based queries, and Chapter 20, "Kill the Cursor!" takes iterative programming head on.

Indexing—Indexes are the high-performance bridge between the schema and queries, so they depend on the schema design and set-based queries to be effective. Chapter 50 details analyzing query execution plans and tuning indexes.

Concurrency—Locking and blocking can be a cascading performance nightmare, but excellence in schema design, queries, and indexing yields short transaction durations and enables fine-tuning transactions and locks. Concurrency tuning is covered in Chapter 51, "Managing Transactions, Locking, and Blocking."

Advanced Scalability—When the schema through the transactions are all optimized, and the database is providing its best performance, the true hardware requirements are known, and advanced scalability technologies such as table partitioning become effective. Chapter 53 digs into scaling very large databases.

If SQL Server is the box, Part VI is about making the box scream.

Measuring
Performance

◆ ◆ ◆ ◆

In This Chapter

Establishing baselines

Viewing performance data

Defining a Database Performance KPI

◆ ◆ ◆ ◆

The first optimization strategy has to be measuring performance. Without the objective evidence of hard numbers, performance is a subjective feeling, and while a positive perception of performance is a good thing, bottlenecks, trends, and optimizations are best defined by the facts. Optimization theory — the framework for designing high-performance databases — works. Solid measurements are the proof.

Fortunately, some excellent methods are available for measuring SQL Server performance:

- ◆ SQL Server installs several counters within Windows' *Performance Monitor,* which can graph the aggregate performance of SQL Server and other system resources, or save the data in logs for later analysis.

- ◆ *SQL Server Profiler* exposes nearly every event within SQL Server with incredible detail. This tool is a database optimizer's dream.

- ◆ *Dynamic management views* expose many details about resource usage within SQL Server 2005.

- ◆ The Database Engine can return *time and I/O statistics* following any T-SQL command execution.

- ◆ T-SQL batches or stored procedures using GetDate() can easily calculate their overall execution time to three milliseconds accuracy and write the duration to a log table.

Measuring Accuracy

I can't write about performance testing without first mentioning testing for accuracy. One of my pet peeves is the tendency of management to readily spend money for hardware, rarely spend money on database optimization, and never spend money on accuracy testing. If your CIO isn't like this, be thankful.

The process of testing for accuracy involves a series of predictions and explanations. While testing an application or database with 10 rows is a standard joke in IT circles, using a test scenario is the only valid method of proving the accuracy of an application.

A test scenario measures the accuracy of the database by comparing the answers to test queries with the predictable results. A complex query that runs against 27 million rows is difficult to test for accuracy. Contrast that with a test scenario — a carefully crafted set of data that represents all possible data combinations but is small enough (10–50 rows per table) that the correct answer to any query is easily calculated by a human. The test scenario should be implemented in an easily repeatable script, `CreateScenario.sql`, that creates the database and inserts the sample data, much like this book's sample database scripts.

The test script, `TestScenario.sql`, executes the stored procedures and views in the data abstraction layer and compares the result with the known correct result. Ideally, the test scenario database and test script are developed prior to developing the data abstraction layer. The data abstraction layer is then developed to solve for the correct responses to the test script.

Best Practice

The scenario test is any database's most significant test. If the database has not passed a careful scenario test, do not deliver, or accept, a database into production.

Software developer and consultant Scott Ambler is a vocal proponent of test-driven development (TDD). You can read more about Scott's work and TDD at his website: `www.ambysoft.com`.

SQL Data Quality Analyzer is a rule-based application I've developed for measuring the quality of your production SQL Server data. It detects when a row fails to meet a rule and flags the row for review. It then detects when a row conforms to the rule or was manually validated. I invite you to download a copy from `www.SQLServerBible.com` and try it for yourself.

Using Performance Monitor

Performance Monitor, or "perfmon" includes two snap-ins: *System Monitor*, and *Performance Logs and Alerts*. Some servers have it installed in the Administrative Tools menu. It's also found at Control Panel ➪ Administrative Tools ➪ Performance, and it can be launched from SQL Server Profiler's Tools ➪ Performance Monitor menu command.

Note

There's a lot of confusion over the name Performance Monitor. `PerfMon.exe` was an application that shipped with older versions of Windows. The new Performance Monitor is actually an MMC (Microsoft Management Console) application and is more accurately called Performance console, but SQL Server Books Online and SQL Server Profiler call it Performance Monitor, so I will too. For more details about Performance Monitor, see *Windows Administration at the Command Line* by John Meuller (Sybex, 2006).

System Monitor

System Monitor, or "sysmon," is familiar to anyone with experience with Windows server administration. System Monitor graphically displays multiple counters, aggregate but detailed data from the server internals. It looks a bit like a heart EKG monitor for Windows and SQL Server, as shown in Figure 49-1.

The performance counters are added to System Monitor one counter at a time using the plus-symbol button in the toolbar. A performance counter can watch the local server or a remote server, so it isn't necessary to run System Monitor at the SQL Server machine. The counters can be watched as a timed line graph, a histogram bar graph, or a real-time report.

Counters are organized by object and, sometimes, instance. For example, in Figure 49-1, the `SQL Server: Databases` object exposes many counters, including the Transactions/sec counter. This counter can be watched for All Instances (all databases), or as selected instances (the PerfTest database).

Note The SQL Server Database Engine isn't the only server to expose counters to System Monitor. Analysis Services, Reporting Services, .NET, ASP, BizTalk and other servers all add counters to System Monitor.

Typically, a new counter will display as a line at the top or bottom of the graph because the scale needs adjustment. Using the System Monitor Properties dialog, available from the context menu, you can adjust the scale of the graph, the scale of each counter, and the presentation of each counter.

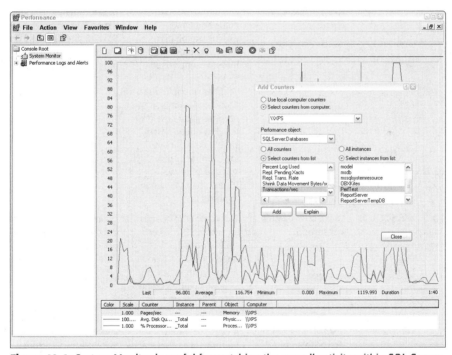

Figure 49-1: System Monitor is useful for watching the overall activity within SQL Server.

Although there are hundreds of possible System Monitor counters, Table 49-1 describes the counters commonly used when investigating a SQL Server installation.

Table 49-1: Key Performance-Monitor Counters

Object	Counter	Description	Usefulness
SQLServer: Buffer Manager	Buffer-cache hit ratio	The percentage of reads found already cached in memory.	SQL Server typically does an excellent job of pre-fetching the data into memory. If the ratio is below 95 percent, more memory will improve performance.
Processor	Percentage of processor time	The total percentage of processor activity.	If CPUs are regularly more than 60 percent active, additional CPU cores or a faster server will increase performance.
SQLServer: SQL Statistics	Batch requests per second	SQL batch activity.	A good indicator of user activity.
Physical Disk	Average disk-queue length	The number of both reads and writes waiting on the disk; an indication of disk throughput; affected by the number of disk spindles on multi-disk RAID configurations. According to Microsoft, the disk-queue length should be less than the number of disk spindles plus two. (Check the scale when applying.)	Disk throughput is a key hardware performance factor. Splitting the database across multiple disk subsystems will improve performance.
SQLServer: SQL Statistics	Failed auto-params per second	The number of queries for which SQL Server could not cache the query execution plan in memory; an indication of poorly written queries (check the scale when applying).	Locating and correcting the queries will improve performance.
SQLServer: Locks	Average wait time (in milliseconds), and lock waits and lock timeouts per second	A cause of serious performance problems; lock waits, the length of the wait, and the number of lock timeouts are all good indicators of the level of locking contention within a database.	If locking issues are detected, the indexing structure and transaction code should be examined.

Object	Counter	Description	Usefulness
SQLServer: User Connections	User connections	The number of current connections.	Indicates potential database activity.
SQLServer: Databases	Transactions per second	The number of current transactions within a database.	A good indicator of database activity.

Additionally, the SQL Server: Wait Statistics counters are useful windows into potential SQL Server bottlenecks.

A complete list of SQL Server counters and their current values can be queried from the `sysdm_os_performance_counters` dynamic management view. This is cool, because you can get the counter data from within Transact-SQL code.

You can create custom counters using T-SQL to pass data from your database code to System Monitor. This can be useful to show the number of transactions processed by a performance test or the number of rows inserted by a data generator. There are ten possible user counters. The following trivial example increments the counter:

```
DECLARE @Counter Int
SET @Counter = 0
While @Counter < 100
  BEGIN
    SET @Counter = @Counter + 1
    EXEC sp_user_counter1 @Counter
    WAITFOR Delay '00:00:02'
  END
```

I use System Monitor to get an overall picture of the health of the server and to get an idea of the types of issues that might be occurring within SQL Server. Using this information, I then move to SQL Server Profiler to target the specific problem.

Best Practice

The configuration of System Monitor, including every counter, can be saved to a configuration file using File ⇨ Save As, and later restored using File ⇨ Open. Using this technique you can export a System Monitor configuration to other servers.

There is one catch: The counter must be monitoring the local server to move from server to server. However, if the counters monitor a remote server, then the configuration will monitor that remote server regardless of where the System Monitor configuration file is opened. Because DBAs are seldom physically at the SQL Server being monitored, this is a problem. If this bothers you as much as it bothers me, e-mail me; one of these days I'm going to write a custom system monitor to fix this and other problems.

Counter Logs

Performance Monitor also includes the Performance Logs and Alerts plug-in, which includes Counter Logs, Trace Alerts, and Alerts. This section focuses on Counter Logs. Counter Logs use the same server counters as System Monitor, but instead of graphically displaying the data in real time, the Counter Logs write the counter data to a log file. This means the data can be analyzed after the fact or even replayed within SQL Server Profiler (more on this cool new feature in the next section).

Counter Logs configurations are listed under the Counter Logs node in Performance Monitor. To see the resulting log files you have to look in the output directory.

To create a new Counter Log, use the Counter Log's context menu and choose New Log Settings. After naming the log, the SQL Server Trace Property dialog (illustrated in Figure 49-2) is used to define the log. Adding an object adds every counter for the object, while adding counters provides a more granular capability to select counters similarly to System Monitor.

Counter Logs can be scheduled to run in the Counter Log Property dialog, or manually started and stopped using the Log's context menu or the start and stop toolbar buttons.

If the Counter Log file was defined as a text file (comma-delimited), you can open it using Excel. Each column is a counter value, and each row is a sample interval.

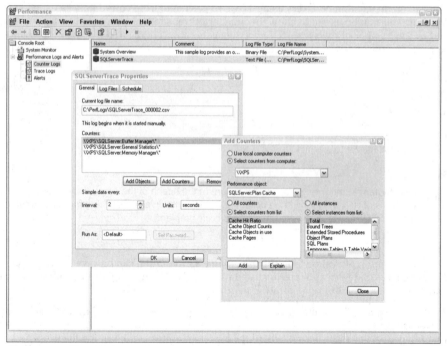

Figure 49-2: The SQLServerTrace Counter Log is configured to write server performance counter data to the C:\PerfLogs directory.

Using SQL Server Profiler

One of my favorite tools, SQL Server Profiler, often just called Profiler, displays copious data about any number of detailed SQL Server events. The activity can be watched on the Profiler Trace Properties window, shown in Figure 49-3, or recorded to a file or table for further analysis. The filters can be set to record all the activity or they can focus on a specific problem.

SQL Server Profiler can be launched from the Tools menu in Management Studio, or from SQL Server 2005's Start menu. Profiler opens to an empty window; you must define a new trace, or open a saved trace file to begin to see any action.

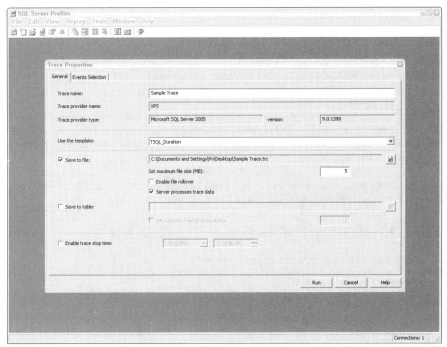

Figure 49-3: This SQL Server Profiler is using the T-SQL Duration template to display the performance times of all T-SQL statements.

Defining a New Trace

When a new trace is created (with the New Trace toolbar button or File ➪ New Trace), a connection is created to a SQL Server and the Trace Properties dialog box (see Figure 49-4) is presented. The Trace Properties General tab sets up the trace (name, file destination, etc.) and the Events Selection tab defines the events and data columns to be recorded, as well as the filter. If the trace is running, the properties may be viewed but not changed. A trace configuration can be saved as a template to make creating new traces easier.

A Profiler trace is primarily viewed interactively, but the data can also be written to a file or a SQL Server table. This is useful for further manual analysis, viewing alongside System Monitor counter data, or importing into Database Engine Tuning Advisor.

When Profiler data is written to a file, SQL Server writes 128KB chunks of data at a time for performance. Conversely, writing data to a table is a series of row inserts that hinders SQL Server's performance.

Best Practice

To save Profiler data for further analysis, use the high-performance file method and a server side trace (discussed later). If you want to analyze the data using T-SQL, save the trace to a file; and after the trace is complete, open the trace file using Profiler and select File ⇨ Save As ⇨ Table.

Selecting Events

The Events Selection tab determines the actions within SQL Server that the Profiler records. Like Performance Monitor, the Profiler can trace numerous key SQL Server events. The default templates of events are useful for getting started.

Note

The Profiler's SQL Batch Completed event is based on an entire batch (separated by a batch terminator), not a single SQL statement. Therefore, the profiler will capture one event's worth of data for even a long batch. Use the SQL Statement Complete event to capture single DML statement events.

If the trace is to be replayed, certain events must be captured. For example, the SQL Batch Start event can be replayed, but SQL Batch Complete cannot.

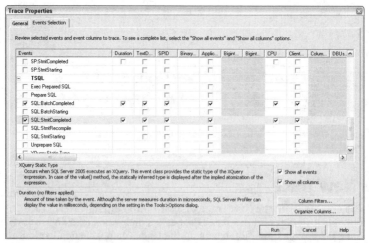

Figure 49-4: The Trace Properties Events Selection page enables you to select the events tracked by the Profiler.

Depending on the events, different data becomes relevant to the trace. The data columns automatically offer the appropriate data. Although the SPID data column appears optional, it's only fooling you — it's mandatory.

Filtering Events

Profiler can capture so much information that it can fill a drive with data. Fortunately, the Profiler Trace Filter (see Figure 49-5) can narrow the scope of your search to the data of interest.

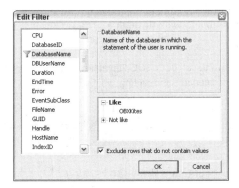

Figure 49-5: The Edit Filter dialog box serves as a `where` clause for the trace, restricting it to certain events only. Here, only events for the OBXKites database will be captured.

The filter uses a combination of `equal` and `like` operators, depending on the data types captured. A frustrating aspect of the filter is that it only works against collected data, and the data collected for some columns may not be what was expected. For example, if you want to filter the trace to only those batches that reference a specific table or column, filtering by object name won't work. Defining a `like` filter using wildcards on the `text data` column, however, will cause the Profiler to select only those batches that include that table name.

Another popular Profiler trace filter is to filter for events with a duration greater than or equal to a specified time, to select all the longer-running batches.

The "Exclude system IDs" check box sets the filter to select only user objects.

Organizing Columns

To add a column to the `group by` (not shown in a figure), select `group by` in the right-hand column before clicking the Add button. Columns can also be escalated to group status by means of the Up button. Any `group by` columns become the first columns in the trace window, and as new events are added to the Trace window those events are automatically added within their group.

Using the Profiler Trace

Once the trace is captured it can be browsed through the Profiler trace window, although a more useful option is to configure the trace to save results to a database table. The data can then be analyzed and manipulated as in any other SQL table.

Once the file is written, you can open the file using SQL Server Profiler and display the trace data. Trace data may be saved to a table for further aggregate analysis using File ⇨ Save As.

SQL Profiler has the ability to replay traces. However, the restrictions on the replay option are such that it's unlikely to be useful for most databases.

Additionally, the entire trace file can be submitted as a workload to the Database Tuning Advisor so that it can tune for multiple queries.

Integrating Performance Monitor Data

System Monitor and Profiler each present their own unique perspective on the state of the server. You can merge the two sets of information and walk through a scenario viewing both perspectives using SQL Server Profiler.

This way cool new feature increases the value of both SQL Server Profiler and System Monitor, and is great for walking through a scenario and seeing what's happening in the server.

To set up the dual-perspective experience, simultaneously capture server performance logs using both Performance Monitor's Counter Logs and SQL Server Profiler. These steps are specific:

1. Configure System Monitor with the exact counters you want to view later. Be sure to get the scale and everything just right. Set up the Counter Log to the exact same configuration.

2. Configure Profiler with the right set of trace events. They must include the start and end time data columns so Profiler can integrate the two logs later. Script the trace to T-SQL code. Close Profiler.

3. Manually start the Counter Log. Execute the T-SQL trace code to start the server-side trace.

4. Exercise the server with the code and load you want to analyze.

5. When the test is complete, stop both the Counter Log and the server-side trace.

6. Open Profiler and open the saved trace file.

7. Use the File ⇨ Import Performance Data menu command to import the Counter Log.

Profiler responds to the import by adding a pane that displays the System Monitor graph, as shown in Figure 49-6. As you select a Profiler event or a time in the System Monitor graph, the two stay in sync. Cool, eh?

To watch these steps visually, download the screencast from www.SQLServerBible.com.

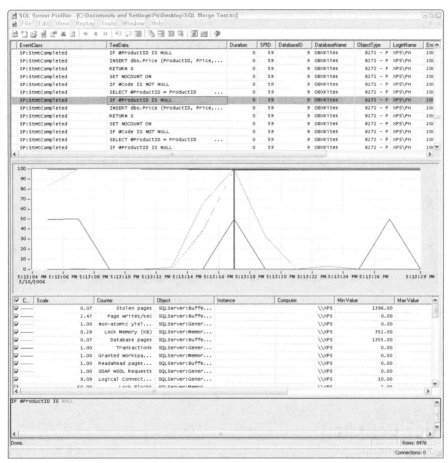

Figure 49-6: SQL Server Profiler can integrate Performance Monitor data and move through the events in sync.

Using SQL Trace

SQL Profiler is usually used interactively, and for ad hoc data gathering this is probably sufficient. However, longer traces can easily generate hundreds of thousands of trace entries or more, which can cause problems at the workstation running the trace. The solution is to log the trace to a file on the server. These high-performance traces cause the least amount of overhead for SQL Server and write in 128KB blocks to the file.

Best Practice

For production systems running server-side traces, writing to a file is the best way to collect performance data with the least overhead to the server.

Server-side traces may be defined and executed using a set of system stored procedures. You could write this yourself, or let SQL Server Profiler create the server-side trace script for you.

Once the trace is set up and tested in SQL Server Profiler, select File ➪ Export ➪ Trace Definition ➪ For SQL Server 2005 to generate a T-SQL script that will launch the server-side trace.

 To find out which traces are running on the server, query the `systraces` dynamic management view. When you look at the results, you'll notice an extra trace. Trace 1 is the "default trace," which gathers data for SQL Server's logs. The default trace can't be stopped.

To stop a server-side trace use the `sp_trace_setstatus` system stored procedure. The first parameter is the `traceid`, and the second parameter specifies the action: 0 = stop the trace, 1 = start the trace, and 2 = close and delete the trace. The sample code uses trace as 2:

```
EXEC sp_trace_setstatus 2, 0
```

Using Transact-SQL

SQL Server includes several means of observing performance data using T-SQL.

Using Dynamic Management Views

Dynamic management views expose the current internal state of SQL Server and supply a wealth of information, most of it very useful for optimization.

Specifically, `sysdm_exec_cached_plans`, `sysdm_exec_query_stats`, `sysdm_exec_query_plan()`, and `sysdm_exec_requests` provide a variety of information about current executions.

Using GetDate()

Calculating the duration of a stored procedure is a trivial problem with T-SQL and is useful for logging production performance data. Setting a `datetime` variable to `GetDate()` at the beginning of the procedure sets up the solution:

```
CREATE PROC PerfTest
AS
SET NoCOunt ON
DECLARE @Duration DATETIME
SET @Duration = GetDate()
--Code
SET @Duration = GetDate() - @Duration
INSERT PerfLog (ProcName, ExecDateTime, Duration)
  VALUES('PerfTest', GetDate(), @Duration)
RETURN
```

Using Statistics

SQL Server can also provide statistics interactively when executing individual queries using Management Studio. Setting statistics on tells SQL Server to pass time and/or I/O statistics with the query results:

```
USE OBXKites
Set statistics io on
SELECT LastName + ' ' + FirstName as Customer, Product.[Name],
Product.code
  FROM dbo.Contact
    JOIN dbo.[Order]
      ON Contact.ContactID = [Order].ContactID
    JOIN dbo.OrderDetail
      ON [Order].OrderID = OrderDetail.OrderID
    JOIN dbo.Product
      ON OrderDetail.ProductID = Product.ProductID
  WHERE Product.Code = '1002'
  ORDER BY LastName, FirstName
Set statistics io off

 Set statistics time on
SELECT LastName + ' ' + FirstName as Customer
  FROM dbo.Contact
  ORDER BY LastName, FirstName
Set statistics time off

go
Set showplan_all on
go
SELECT LastName
  FROM dbo.Contact
go
Set showplan_all off
go

Set showplan_xml on
go
SELECT LastName
  FROM dbo.Contact
go
Set showplan_xml off
go
```

The Database Performance KPI

The Database Performance KPI is a single comprehensive key performance indicator (KPI) that can indicate the overall performance health of the database at a management level over time.

Consistency is critical to the value of any KPI. Establishing a baseline measurement and then repeating the same measurement the exact same way is the only way to identify trends or optimization efforts. The tests should be repeated in regular intervals.

The Database Performance KPI should factor performance data from the clean test environment, actual production performance data, and a scalability performance test. Your DBA team should decide on the specific requirements of the tests and how the results are calculated to produce the Database Performance KPI. I recommend multiplying the baseline measurement of each test to equal ⅓, so their sum, the initial comprehensive metric, is 1, as shown in the spreadsheet and graph in Figure 49-7.

On The Web The Comprehensive Database Performance Metric Excel spreadsheet is available for download from `www.SQLServerBible.com`.

Repeatable Performance Testing

The repeatable performance test measures the overall performance of the database using a repeatable test script and database on a test server platform. Execution times can be gathered using T-SQL variables or SQL Server Profiler.

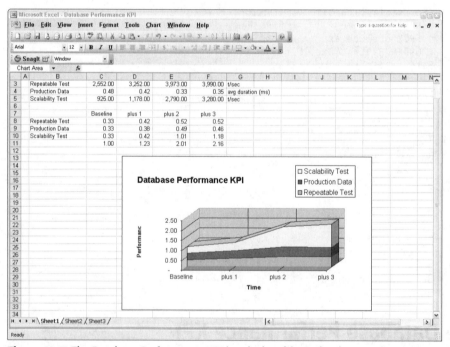

Figure 49-7: The Database Performance KPI is calculated from the three performance tests using Excel.

If your architecture enforces a data abstraction layer, then the test need only execute calls to that layer. If your database uses a more casual client-server model, then you'll need to mix typical queries into the test. If your database uses SOA Web Services, then, of course, calls to the Web Service will also be required. The balance of selects and update operations, and the distribution of tables affected, should be representative of those of the actual client applications and the batch processes.

An initial execution of the repeatable performance test establishes the performance baseline. Each time the test is rerun, the test database is restored and the test script re-executed. The repeatable performance test is most useful for measuring the results of optimization efforts in a clean environment — unaffected by other processes, user load, or data changes.

Numerous factors can affect response-time performance. To objectively determine which factor accounted for which change in performance, it's important to alter only one factor per test, and to measure the response time using a consistent method. Each run of the performance test should begin with the same data, and the server used for testing should be free of other processes, connections, or users.

You may choose to run two tests — one test as a single user and another test for multi-user concurrency — by running several instances of differing tests simultaneously. These could be a mix of read/write, report readers, read queries, and mass updates attempting to simulate the typical load of the production database.

To test the multi-user concurrency script, write a .NET application that makes numerous connections and calls to the database to simulate a heavy user load. The closer the user load is to the number and type of queries generated by the actual active users, the better the test. Keep in mind that not all current users are actually submitting queries at any given second. This test should be able to report the number of transactions the database can support.

To estimate the number of transactions required, I've actually done some observational research (walking around the organization making notes on how many users were performing what type of tasks and how often they performed those tasks).

Production Performance Data

Measuring the actual response time of the data abstraction layer's stored procedures, the Production Performance Test provides information about the user's experience.

Production performance data can be gathered a few different ways:

✦ SQL Server Profiler can gather server-side traces to collect every stored procedure execution time. Traces can be written to a database and analyzed for performance tuning or for the production performance data value. The trace is easy to start and stop, giving you complete freedom to sample performance data during selected times.

✦ Code at the end of every stored procedure can calculate the duration of the stored procedure and write it to a log file for later analysis. Depending on the configuration of the Profiler trace, this method probably yields fewer details than SQL Server Profiler. Depending on the complexity of the logging code, another problem with this method is that it's difficult to turn off if you decide to sample performance data during limited times or days.

✦ The application code can log the duration from the time the user presses the Submit button to the completion of the refresh of the form. Although this gives an accurate picture of the user experience, this method gives the least amount of detail necessary for tuning.

While all of these methods add some overhead to the database, and there are many variables, I believe that SQL Server profiler gives you the best information at the lowest cost.

Scalability Performance Load Testing

A scalability performance load test is a variation of the repeatable performance test. The purpose is to evaluate the scalability and future usability of the database. Load testing evaluates the scalability of the database by measuring its response time at both half of the estimated load and the full estimated load. Data is generated to expand the primary working tables to twice their current production number of rows. The number of concurrent simulated users should also be doubled in the .NET test application. Once the database is expanded, the repeatable performance test is executed.

For SQL Server, the database schema and queries can only be load-tested when the data exceeds the memory capacity of the server by several times. Index behavior is different when SQL Server has the luxury of loading all the required data pages and index pages into memory. If all the pages are in memory, logical reads are the only significant factor. Because physical disk reads are not an issue, performance of the indexes is less significant.

Note   SQL Server is optimized to intelligently cache data in memory, which will affect subsequent tests. Memory can be flushed by stopping and restarting the server, or with the `DBCC DropCleanBuffers` and `DBCC FreeProcCache` commands.

On The Web   For an example of a Database Performance KPI, download the PerfTest database from `www.SQLServerBible.com`.

Summary

Measuring performance is fundamental to both operations and to database tuning and optimization. Your organization needs the Database Performance KPI to understand the overall performance of the database, and optimization efforts require the performance measurement details to identify the problems and correct them. SQL Server Profiler, along with System Monitor and the new dynamic management views, provide rich details about the performance of the database.

Armed with the ability to observe the effects of optimization, the next chapter explores the heart of SQL server — queries and indexes. With the tools to measure and the ability to tune queries and indexes, you're on your way to optimizing a high-performance database.

✦   ✦   ✦

Query Analysis and Index Tuning

The Information Architecture Principle, detailed in Chapter 1, promotes meeting the performance requirement as a key objective for any data store.

Optimization theory tackles that objective and provides a framework for designing high-performance databases by explaining the dependencies between the layers of optimization.

Indexes are right in the middle of the optimization theory layers. They depend on a well-designed normalized schema, and well-written queries. Those two foundations enable good indexing, but without them, it is difficult to design an indexing strategy or get good results from the indexing.

There's no doubt that indexing is vital to a high-performance database. Just keep indexes in perspective; they depend upon the schema and query layers, and they enable concurrency and high-scalability server tuning.

Query analysis and indexing tuning is an area in which SQL Server 2005 excels. SQL Server exposes copious information about the query execution plan, and the indexes are fast, balanced-tree (b-tree) style indexes that are easy to set up and can be finely tuned or almost left on auto-pilot.

A Holistic Approach to Index Tuning

SQL is a declarative language, meaning that the SQL query describes the question and SQL Server decides how to execute the query. This means that much of the optimization is being performed by SQL Server, not the query.

Considering the estimated cost of each logical operation based on the data distribution, available indexes, and hardware capabilities, the Query Optimizer sequences a tree of logical operations to produce the fastest possible overall query execution plan.

Therefore, optimizing queries is largely a matter of providing the right indexes so the Query Optimizer can select the data in the fastest means possible. For a few rare queries, altering the structure of the query can affect performance, but for the majority of production queries, writing the query three different ways will return three similar if not identical query execution plans.

Index tuning is a skill that demands understanding of several interdependent factors. What makes query tuning difficult is that the Query Optimizer is something of a black box; and before you can predict how the black box will behave, you must understand how the following factors relate:

✦ SQL Server pages architecture, physical schema design, and query execution plan logical operators

✦ Data distributions, index statistics, Query Optimizer index selection, and index maintenance

✦ Clustered index design, fill factors, page splits, and index maintenance

✦ Queries, indexes, query execution plans, and the Query Optimizer

✦ Query plan reuse and parameter sniffing

To further complicate things, as a database developer or DBA, you must consider which indexes are best for the entire mix of all production queries, not just one query.

The best advice I can offer is to study these factors and then experiment on your own to continue to learn the complex correlations between your data, your schema, your indexes, and your queries. Indexes may be adjusted without affecting the logical result of any query. DBAs need not fear experimenting with indexes.

Indexing

A book's index aids the reader in finding an answer to a question. The best index is one that is organized so that the reader can quickly go from having a question to finding the relevant text in the book. Database indexes play the same role.

Although indexing can be complex, the goal of indexing is simple: reduce the number of physical page reads.

Index Basics

There are two basic types of indexes. An index that actually sorts the text pages, like a telephone book, is called a *clustered index* because the data itself is clustered into a specific order. This type of index is physically located within the text of the book. Obviously, the text can only be in one sort order. Likewise, SQL Server tables can have only one physical sort order, and that sort order is called the table's clustered index.

A *nonclustered index* is like the index in the back of the book that refers the reader to text pages. Any topic may be easily found in the text by first finding the topic in the book index and then using the index to point to a page in the book. This index is physically outside the main text of the book and is sorted differently than the main text of the book. SQL Server also has nonclustered indexes that sort using different columns than the clustered index.

The columns used in the index are called the index's *key columns*.

Because primary keys are the unique method of identifying any row, indexes and primary keys are intertwined — in fact, a primary key must be indexed, but it can be either a clustered or nonclustered index.

When planning indexes, there's a subtle tension between serving the needs of select queries vs. update queries. While an index may improve query performance, there's a performance cost because when a row is inserted or updated, the indexes must be updated as well. Nonetheless, some indexing is necessary for write operations. The update or delete operation must locate the row prior to performing the write operation, and useful indexes facilitate locating that row, thereby speeding up write operations.

 Cross-Reference Indexes on tables should not be confused with indexed views, an Enterprise Edition denormalization feature that builds a clustered index spanning multiple tables. Misusing indexed views can significantly degrade the performance of operational databases. See Chapter 53, "Scaling Very Large Databases," for more information on index views.

Clustered Indexes

A *clustered index* is a merger of a b-tree and the table's data pages, keeping the data in the same physical order as the index, as shown in Figure 50-1. The leaf node of the b-tree index actually is the data on the data page.

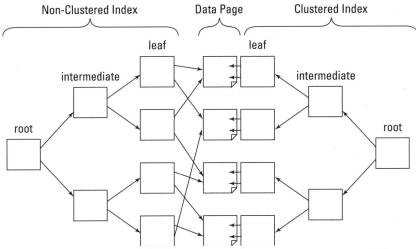

Figure 50-1: A clustered index merges the leaf nodes of the index page with the data page, keeping the data in the same order as the index.

A clustered index can affect performance in one of two ways:

✦ When an index seek operation finds a row using a clustered index, the data is right there. This makes the column used to select the row, probably the primary key, an ideal candidate for a clustered index.

✦ Clustered indexes gather rows with the same or similar values to the smallest possible number of data pages, thus reducing the number of data pages required to retrieve a set a rows. Clustered indexes are therefore excellent for columns that are often used to select a range of rows, such as secondary table foreign keys like `OrderDetail.OrderID`.

Note   Every table has some physical order. For tables without a clustered index, the table is in a *heap* — an unordered list. Instead of being identified by the clustered index key columns, the rows are identified internally using the heap's RowID. The RowID cannot be querie.

Nonclustered Indexes

A *nonclustered* index is a b-tree index that begins at the root node and extends through intermediate nodes to the leaf node. The leaf node then points to the data row in the data page, as illustrated in Figure 50-1. A SQL Server 2005 table may have up to 249 nonclustered indexes, but I've never seen a table that required more than a dozen well-designed indexes.

A nonclustered index may be created on a calculated column. The `quoted_identifier` setting must be on to create or modify indexed views or indexes on calculated columns.

Creating Indexes

Within the Management Studio's Object Explorer, existing indexes under for each table are listed under the Databases ⇨ Tables ⇨ Indexes node. Every index property for new or existing indexes may be managed using the Index Properties page, shown in Figure 50-2. The page is opened for existing indexes by right-clicking on the index and choosing Properties. New indexes are created from the context menu of the Indexes node under the selected table.

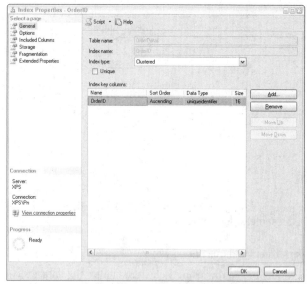

Figure 50-2: Every index option may be set using Management Studio's Index Properties page.

Using Management Studio, indexes are visible as nodes under the table in Object Explorer. Use the Indexes context menu and select New Index to open the New Index form, which contains four pages:

✦ *General* index information includes the index name, type, uniqueness, and key columns.

✦ Index *Options* control the behavior of the index. In addition, an index may be disabled or reenabled.

✦ *Included Columns* are non-key columns used for covering indexes.

✦ The *Storage* page places the index on a selected filegroup.

When opening the properties of an existing index, the Index Properties form also includes two additional pages:

✦ The *Fragmentation* page displays detailed information about the health of the index.

✦ *Extended Properties* are user-defined additional properties.

Changes made in the Index Properties page may be executed immediately using the OK button or scheduled or scripted using the icons at the top of the page.

Indexes are created in code with the `create index` command. The following command creates a clustered index named `IxOrderID` on the `OrderID` foreign key of the `OrderDetail` table:

```
CREATE CLUSTERED INDEX IxOrderID
  ON dbo.OrderDetail (OrderID);
```

To retrieve fascinating index information from T-SQL code, use the following functions and catalog views: `sysindexes`, `sysindex_columns`, `sysstats`, `sysstats_columns`, `sysdm_db_index_physical_stats`, `sysdm_index_operational_stats`, `sysindexkey_property`, and `sysindex_col`.

A clustered index may be created automatically when the primary key is defined.

To remove an index use the `drop index` command with both the table and index name:

```
DROP INDEX OrderDetail.IxOrderID;
```

Cross-Reference

Indexes, once created, do not automatically maintain their efficiency. Updates can fragment the index and affect the index page's fill factor. While this chapter mentions index maintenance, Chapter 37, "Maintaining the Database," details the administrative requirements for index performance.

Composite Indexes

A *composite index* is a clustered or nonclustered index that includes multiple columns. Most indexes are composite indexes. If you use SQL Server Management Studio's Index Properties form, composite indexes are created by adding multiple columns to the index in the General page. When creating a composite index with code, it must be declared in a `create index` DDL statement after the table is created. The following code sample creates a composite clustered index on the `Guide` table in the CHA2 database:

```
CREATE CLUSTERED INDEX IxGuideName
    ON dbo.Guide (LastName, FirstName);
```

The order of the columns in a composite index is important. In order for a search to take advantage of a composite index it must include the index columns from left to right. If the composite index is `lastname`, `firstname`, a search for `firstname` will not use the index, but a search for `lastname`, or `lastname` and `firstname`, will.

Cross-Reference

SQL Server 2005 can index words within columns using Full-Text Search, covered in Chapter 13, "Using Full-Text Search."

Primary Keys

A primary key can be initially defined as a clustered or nonclustered index. However, for the index type to be changed, the primary-key constraint must be dropped and recreated — a painful task if numerous foreign keys are present or the table is replicated.

 Cross-Reference Creating primary keys is covered in Chapter 17, "Implementing the Physical Database Schema."

Covering Indexes

A *covering index* is any index that completely meets the needs of a specific select query. As SQL Server chooses which index to use to locate the data, it's possible that every column needed by the query is present in a nonclustered index; in this case, the relational engine retrieves the data from the index pages and never has to read from the data pages. This significantly reduces I/O by reading from a narrower table that includes more data rows per page, avoiding additional reads from the data pages.

When designing a covering index it's important to realize how the clustered index affects the nonclustered index. Because the nonclustered index must be able to refer to the data pages, it must include the clustered index key columns in their leaf nodes (assuming the table has a clustered index). This effectively includes the clustered index columns at the end of every nonclustered index (even though you don't see them listed as columns in the Index Properties form). For example, if a table has a clustered index on column ContactID, and a nonclustered index on columns LastName and FirstName, then the nonclustered index actually contains the data from columns LastName, FirstName (sorted) and ContactID (unsorted). This fact is important when designing covering indexes.

A covering index may need to include some columns that are not required for the relational engine to identify the rows requested by the query's where clause. These extra, non-key columns don't need to be sorted in the b-tree index — they are included solely for the purpose of returning the columns in the select query.

New in 2005 The downside to covering indexes in previous versions of SQL Server was that every column had to be sorted during updates — even when the column was not used for selecting the row but was included in the index solely for returning data. SQL Server 2005's ability to specify non-key columns improves the update performance of covering indexes by not having to sort the non-key columns, and improves query retrieval performance by reducing the size of the b-tree index.

To specify the non-key, non-searchable columns for nonclustered indexes, use the include option. These non-key columns will not be sorted as part of the index's b-tree structure and are only included in the index's leaf node. This example creates an index that is sorted by OrderNumber, and includes the data from the OrderDate column:

```
CREATE NONCLUSTERED INDEX IxOrderNumber
  ON dbo.[Order] (OrderNumber)
  INCLUDE (OrderDate);
```

Think of included columns as a narrow copy of a wide table that SQL Server automatically keeps in sync with the original table; it doesn't need extra page reads to retrieve the data.

Included columns are not counted in the nonclustered index limitation of 16 key columns and 900 bytes. In fact, up to 1,023 non-key columns may be included in a covering index. In addition, XML, varchar(max), nvarchar(max), and varbinary(max) data type columns may be added as included columns, while they are not permitted as key columns.

A table column may not be dropped if it is an include column in a covering index. The covering index must be dropped before the table's column can be dropped.

Filegroup Location

If the database uses multiple named filegroups, the index may be created on a certain filegroup with the on filegroupname option:

```
CREATE NONCLUSTERED INDEX IndexName
  ON Table (Columns)

  ON filegroupname;
```

This option is useful for spreading the disk I/O throughput for very heavily used databases. For example, if a web page is hit by a zillion users per minute, and the main page uses a query that involves two tables and three indexes, and several disk subsystems are available, then placing each table and index on its own disk subsystem will improve performance. Remember that a clustered index must be in the same location as the table because the clustered index pages and the data pages are merged.

 Cross-Reference The physical location of tables and indexes may be further configured using filegroups and partitioning. For more details on table and index partitioning, refer to Chapter 53, "Scaling Very Large Databases."

Index Options

SQL Server 2005 indexes may have several options, including uniqueness, space allocation, and performance options.

Unique Indexes

A unique index option is more than just an index with a unique constraint; index optimizations are available to unique indexes. A primary key or a unique constraint automatically creates a unique index.

In Management Studio, you create a unique index by checking the Unique option in the General page of the Index Properties form.

In code, you set an index as unique by adding the unique keyword to the index definition, as follows:

```
CREATE UNIQUE INDEX OrderNumber
  ON [Order] (OrderNumber);
```

Index Fill Factor and Pad Index

An index needs a little free space in the tree so that new entries don't require restructuring of the index. When SQL Server needs to insert a new entry into a full page, it splits the page into two pages and writes two half-full pages back to the disk. This causes three performance problems: the page split itself, the new pages are no longer sequential, and less information is on each page so more pages must be read to read the same amount of data.

Because the index is a balanced tree (b-tree), each page must hold at least two rows. The fill factor and the pad index affect both the intermediate pages and the leaf node, as described in Table 50-1.

Table 50-1: Fill Factor and Pad Index

Fill Factor	Intermediate Page(s)	Leaf Node
0	One free entry	100% full
1-99	One free entry or ≤ fill factor if pad index	≤ Fill factor
100	One free entry	100% full

The fill factor only applies to the detail, or leaf, node of the index, unless the `pad index` option is applied to the fill factor. The `pad index` option directs SQL Server to apply the looseness of the fill factor to the intermediate levels of the b-tree as well.

Best Practice

The best fill factor depends on the purpose of the database and the type of clustered index. If the database is primarily for data retrieval, or the primary key is sequential, a high fill factor will pack as much as possible in an index page. If the clustered index is nonsequential (such as a natural primary key), then the table is susceptible to page splits, so use a lower page fill factor and defragment the pages often.

Cross-Reference

The index's fill factor will slowly become useless as the pages fill and split. The maintenance plan must include periodic reindexing to reset the fill factor. Chapter 37, "Maintaining the Database," includes information on how to maintain indexes.

Using Management Studio, the fill factor is set in the Index Properties Options page. In T-SQL code, include the fill factor and index pad options after the `create index` command. The following code example creates the OrderNumber index with 15 percent free space in both the leaf nodes and the intermediate pages:

```
CREATE NONCLUSTERED INDEX IxOrderNumber
  ON dbo.[Order] (OrderNumber)
  WITH FILLFACTOR = 85, PAD_INDEX = ON;
```

New in 2005

Controlling the index locks, building indexes online, and limiting the parallelism of indexes are all new index options in SQL Server 2005. The syntax has been updated for the index options `pad_index`, `fillfactor`, `sort_in_tempdb`, `ignore_dup_key`, `statistics_norecompute`, `drop_existing`. The new syntax requires the explicit = on. The old syntax is still supported for backward compatibility, but will not be supported in future versions.

Limiting Index Locks and Parallelism

The locking behavior of queries using the index may be controlled using the `allow_row_locks` and `allow_page_locks` options. Normally these locks are allowed.

Index Sort Order

SQL Server can create the index as a descending index.

Any query using an order by clause will still be sorted ascending unless the query's order by specifically states desc.

The asc or desc option follows the column name in the create index DDL command.

The Ignore Dup Key Index Option

The ignore duplicate key option doesn't affect the index, but rather how the index affects data modification operations later.

Normally, transactions are atomic, meaning that the entire transaction either succeeds or fails as a logical unit. However, the ignore duplicate key option directs insert transactions to succeed for all rows accepted by the unique index, and to ignore any rows that violate the unique index.

This option does not break the unique index. Duplicates are still kept out of the table, so the consistency of the database is intact, but the atomicity of the transaction is violated. Although this option might make importing a zillion questionable rows easier, I personally don't like any option that weakens the ACID (atomic, consistent, isolated, durable) properties of the database.

The following command is the same as the previous create unique index command, but with the ignore_duplicate_key option:

```
CREATE UNIQUE INDEX OrderNumber
   ON [Order] (OrderNumber)
   WITH IGNORE_DUP_KEY = ON
```

The Drop Existing Index Option

The drop existing option directs SQL Server to drop the current index and rebuild the new index from scratch. This may cause a slight performance improvement over rebuilding every index, if the index being rebuilt is a clustered index and the table also has nonclustered indexes, because rebuilding a clustered index forces a rebuild of any nonclustered indexes.

The Statistics Norecompute Index Option

The SQL Server Query Optimizer depends on data-distribution statistics to determine which index is most significant for the search criteria for a given table. Normally, SQL Server updates these statistics automatically. However, some tables may receive large amounts of data just prior to being queried, and the statistics may be out of date. For situations that require manually initiating the statistics update, the statistics norecompute= on index option disables automatic statistics, but for nearly all indexes this option should be ignored.

Sort in Tempdb

The sort_in_tempdb = on option modifies the index-creation method by forcing it to use tempdb as opposed to memory. If the index is routinely dropped and recreated, this option may shorten the index-creation time. For most indexes, this option is neither required nor important.

Disabling an Index

An index may be temporarily disabled, or taken offline, using the Use Index check box in the Index Properties ➪ Option page. Using T-SQL, to disable an index use the `alter index` DDL command with the `disable` option:

```
ALTER INDEX [IxContact] ON [dbo].[Contact] DISABLE
```

During some intensive data import operations, it's faster to drop the index and recreate it than to update the index with every newly inserted row. The benefit of disabling an index is that the metadata for the index is maintained within the database, rather than depending on the code to recreate the correct index.

Caution   Disabling a clustered index effectively disables the table.

To re-enable an index, use the `alter index... rebuild with` command:

```
ALTER INDEX [PK__Contact__0BC6C43E]
  ON [dbo].[Contact]
  REBUILD WITH
  ( PAD_INDEX  = OFF,
    STATISTICS_NORECOMPUTE  = OFF,
    ALLOW_ROW_LOCKS  = ON,
    ALLOW_PAGE_LOCKS  = ON,
    SORT_IN_TEMPDB = OFF,
    ONLINE = OFF )
```

Creating Base Indexes

Even before tuning, the locations of a few indexes are easy to determine. These base indexes are the first step in building a solid set of indexes. Here are a few things to keep in mind when building these base indexes:

1. Create a clustered index for every table. For primary tables, cluster on the column most likely used to select the row — probably the primary key. For secondary tables that are most commonly retrieved by a set of related rows, create a clustered index for the most important foreign key to group those related rows together.

2. Create nonclustered indexes for the columns of every foreign key, except for the foreign key that was indexed in step 1. Use only the foreign key values as index keys.

3. Create a single-column index for every column expected to be referenced in a where clause, an order by, or a group by.

While this indexing plan is far from perfect, it provides an initial compromise between no indexes and tuned indexes, and a baseline performance measure to compare against future index tuning.

Query Analysis

After the basics of indexes and SQL Server pages, the second skill necessary for tuning indexes is interpreting query execution plans — being able to read a query execution plan and identify the steps the Query Optimizer is taking to solve the query.

Viewing Query Execution Plans

Another of my favorite parts of SQL Server is the Query Editor's display of the query execution plan. You can view either the estimated query execution plan or the actual execution plan. Both are enabled in the toolbar or Query menu.

The logical operations are the same in both the estimated and actual query plans. The actual execution plan can only be viewed after the query executes.

The estimated query plan uses the statistics to estimate the number of rows involved in each logical operation. Besides being able to view the execution plan immediately, this can be important because the number of estimated rows produced by each operations plays a large part in choosing the logical operations.

The query plan is read from right to left, as shown in Figure 50-3. Each logical operation is presented as an icon. The Query Editor isn't just a static display:

✦ Mousing over the logical operation causes a dialog box to appear containing detailed information about the logical operation, including the logical cost and the portion of the query handled by the operation.

✦ Mousing over a connector line presents detailed information about how much data is being moved by that connector.

Plans can also be saved to a plan file (.sqlplan) to be reexamined later.

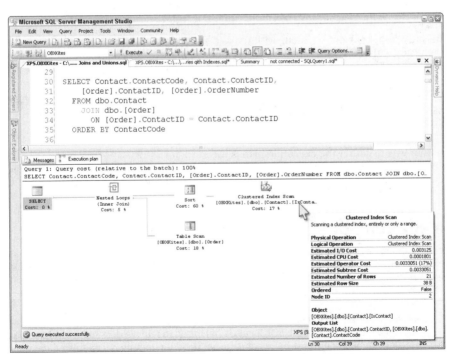

Figure 50-3: Query execution plans show the logical operations SQL Server uses to solve the query.

Using the Showplans

In addition to the graphical execution plan, the Showplan option reveals the execution plan with some additional detail. Showplan comes is three flavors: all, text, and XML.

When showplan is on, SQL Server will return the query execution plan, but won't execute the statement, as show estimated plan would. Set showplan must be the only statement in the batch.

Like show estimated plan, SQL Server will return the showplan query execution plan, but won't execute the statement. For the XML version of showplan, the show actual plan option must be off. In addition, if the query results are set to grid, then the grid will offer a link to open the XML using the browser. The showplan options work as follows:

✦ Showplan_all displays the operators as a result set. It exposes the same information as the graphical execution plan. The executing statement is returned in the first row and every operator is returned as subsequent rows.

✦ Showplan_text is very similar to showplan_all except that the executing statement and the operations are in separate result sets and only the stmt text (first column) is displayed.

✦ Showplan_xml displays more detail than any other method of viewing the execution plan and it offers the benefit of storing and displaying unstructured data, so it can display additional information that may not pertain to all execution plans. For example, in the <Statement> element, Showplan_xml displays the Query Optimizer optimization level, or the reason why the Query Optimizer returned this execution plan.

The showplan_text option, along with the set statistics options, may also be toggled graphically within Query Editor. Use the context menu's Query Options command to open the Query Properties and you can find the showplan options by selecting Execution ⇨ Advanced.

The sysdm_exec_query_plan also displays the same XML query execution plan information, but it takes some digging to supply the required parameter.

Another way to gather the execution plan is the set statistics profile on command, which will execute the query and then supply the same detail as showplan_all with the addition of actual row counts and execution counts. This is the result set equivalent of the show actual execution plan.

Interpreting the Query Execution Plan

Reading query execution plans may seem difficult at first. The graphics are unfamiliar and the detail can be overwhelming. SQL server uses about 60 operators. Some represent specific physical tasks, while most logically represent a collection of hidden tasks. Table 50-2 lists the key operators regarding select queries and indexing.

Best Practice

A common misunderstanding is that seeks are always good and scans are always bad. This is not completely true. Because SQL Server is optimized to retrieve data sequentially, scans are excellent for gathering large blocks of data, but poor at retrieving a few isolated rows. Index seeks are great at retrieving a few rows here and a few rows there, but retrieving a large percentage of a table using index seeks performs extremely poorly compared to a scan.

Table 50-2: Query Execution Plan Operators

Icon	Definition	Description
	Clustered index scan	In a clustered index scan, SQL Server sequentially reads the entire clustered index or a range within the clustered index. SQL Server chooses this operation when the set of rows requested by the `where` clause can be determined as a range within the order of the clustered index, or a large percentage of rows is needed from the table.
	Clustered index seek	In a clustered index seek, SQL Server rapidly navigates the clustered index b-tree to retrieve specific rows. The benefit of the clustered index seek is that when the row(s) are determined all the columns are immediately available.
	Filter	In some situations, SQL Server retrieves all the data from a table and then uses filter operations to select the correct rows. Sometimes the Query Optimizer will use a Filter for performance reasons, but it's more often due to the lack of a useful index.
	Hash match	A hash match is an unordered join method that builds a temp table and iteratively matches with data from another table. A hash match is more efficient if one table is significantly larger than the other table. This is the worst-case join method and is used when no suitable index is available.
	Merge join	The merge join is the fastest method of comparing two tables if both tables are pre-sorted.
	Nested loop	A nested loop iterates through two tables and identifies matches. Typically, nested-loop joins are best when a large index is joined with a small table.
	Nonclustered index scan	In a nonclustered index scan, SQL Server reads through all or part of the index sequentially looking for the data.

Continued

Table 50-2 *(continued)*

Icon	Definition	Description
	Nonclustered index seek	A nonclustered index seek navigates the b-tree index from the root node, through the intermediate node, to the leaf node, and finally to the row. For selecting a few individual rows this can be a very fast operation. The benefit of a nonclustered index seek is that it tends to be narrow (have few columns), so more rows can fit on a page.
		Once the correct row is identified, if all the required columns are found in the index, then the seek is complete because the index covers the needs of the query. Conversely, if additional columns are needed, SQL Server will need to fetch them from the data pages.
	RID lookup	The RID lookup locates rows in the data pages. Typically, a RID lookup works with a nested loop to locate the data pages following a clustered index seek or scan.
	Sort	In some situations SQL Server retrieves all the data from a table and then sorts the data to prepare it for operations to perform the order by. Filters and sorts are slow operations and indicate a lack of useful indexes.
	Spool	In a spool operation, SQL Server has to save off a temporary set of data.
	Table scan	In a table scan, SQL Server sequentially reads the entire table to select the rows that meet the criteria. Depending on the number of rows needed, this might be the fastest method of retrieving the data. For instance, if SQL Server needs to select 80% of the table, then it's far faster to read the entire table sequentially than to seek each row individually. However, if fewer rows are needed and the Query Optimizer still chooses a table scan, it may be because there's no suitable index to use instead of the table scan, the index statistics are wrong, or the table is so small that it doesn't matter.

New in 2005 The Bookmark Lookup logical operation was removed in SQL Server 2005 and replaced with clustered index seek and RID lookup. Previous versions of SQL Server displayed the Bookmark Lookup icon but actually performed the clustered index seek and RID lookup.

Index Tuning

With this understanding of indexes and query execution plans, several performance issues may be identified and corrected using indexes.

Missing Indexes

The most obvious opportunity for improving performance with indexing is creating an index where one was missing. The trick is identifying the need.

SQL Server 2005 exposes index usage statistics via dynamic management views. Specifically, `sysdm_db_index_operational_stats` and `sysdm_index_usage_stats` uncover information about how indexes are being used. In addition, there are four dynamic management views that reveal indexes that the Query Optimizer looked for, but didn't find: `sysdm_missing_index_groups`, `sysdm_missing_index_group_stats`, `sysdm_missing_index_columns`, and `sysdm_missing_index_details`.

The first example uses a simple query in the OBXKites database. The clustered index is on the lastname's soundex code, for retrieval of groups of names by soundex code. This simple query retrieves the data and orders by `ContactCode`:

```
SET STATISTICS TIME ON;
USE Adventureworks;
SELECT WorkOrderID
  FROM Production.WorkOrder
  ORDER BY StartDate;
```

Result (statistics time):

```
SQL Server Execution Times:
   CPU time = 126 ms, elapsed time = 679 ms.
```

The query uses a clustered index scan to read the data, followed by a sort operation to order the data by `StartDate`. The sort operation is the clue that an index is missing.

Creating an index on `StartDate` alters the execution plan:

```
CREATE INDEX WOStartDate ON Production.WorkOrder (StartDate);
```

Rerunning the query shows a significant drop in CPU time, from 126 ms to 63 ms, and the new query execution plan shows only a nonclustered index scan of the new `WOStartDate` index.

A more complex query execution plan still reveals the need for an index:

```
USE OBXKites;
SELECT LastName, FirstName, ProductName
  FROM dbo.Contact
    JOIN dbo.[Order]
      ON Contact.ContactID = [Order].ContactID
```

```
   JOIN dbo.OrderDetail
     ON [Order].OrderID = OrderDetail.OrderID
   JOIN dbo.Product
     ON OrderDetail.ProductID = Product.ProductID
   JOIN dbo.ProductCategory
     ON Product.ProductCategoryID = ProductCategory.ProductCategoryID
  WHERE ProductCategoryName = 'Kite'
  ORDER BY LastName, FirstName;
```

Result (statistics time):

```
SQL Server Execution Times:
   CPU time = 0 ms, elapsed time = 46 ms.
```

The execution time is quick because the database is small. Nevertheless, the query execution plan shows several problems with this query, as shown in Figure 50-4. To highlight one of those problems, a table scan of `OrderDetail` is being joined using a hatch match operation. The hatch match is joining the `OrderDetail` table with the `Product` table. The only index on the `OrderDetail` table in this copy of OBXKites is a nonclustered primary key consisting of the `OrderDetailID` column.

Building a nonclustered index on `ProductID` will begin to solve this problem. With the index in place, the table scan and hatch match are replaced with an index scan and a nested loop. However, the nonclustered index doesn't cover the needs of the query, so an additional data page read is generated, as shown in Figure 50-5.

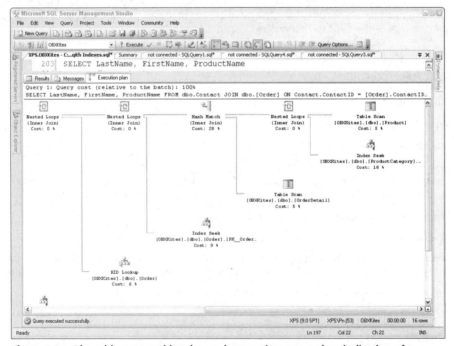

Figure 50-4: The table scan and hatch match operations are a clear indication of a missing index.

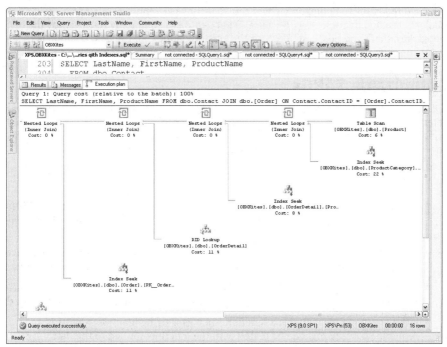

Figure 50-5: The bookmark lookup problem can be seen in the RID lookup operation and the nested loop.

Bookmark Lookup

While not as costly as a missing index, a more common problem is when SQL Server finds the correct rows using the nonclustered index and then has to fetch more columns from the data page — a situation known as a *bookmark lookup*.

Bookmark lookups can be devastating to performance because while the nonclustered index may have grouped the data to a few index pages, the bookmark lookup must now fetch data from numerous data pages.

To compare the database bookmark lookup operation to an actual book, in a bookmark lookup you locate just what you need in the index, but 200 discreet page numbers are listed after the index. Turning to the 200 pages in the text of the book is the time-consuming bookmark lookup (refer to Figure 50-5).

The bookmark lookup is physically performed by retrieving data from the data pages and joining the data with the results from the nonclustered index. In this case, it's a RID lookup operation because there's no clustered index, but it could also be from a clustered index seek or clustered index scan.

To solve this bookmark lookup problem, either add the `OrderDetailID` to the `ProductID` nonclustered index so all the data required by the join is directly available from the nonclustered index, or convert the primary key to the clustered index, which would replace the RID in the nonclustered index with the clustered index keys. Both solutions enable the `ProductID` nonclustered index to completely cover the OrderDetail requirements of the query and eliminate the bookmark lookup. Because OrderDetail is commonly retrieved by the OrderID foreign key, that's the best candidate for the clustered index, so the best solution is to add OrderDetailID to the ProductID index.

Optimizable SARGs

SQL Server's Query Optimizer examines the conditions within the query's where clause to determine which indexes are actually useful. If SQL Server can optimize the where condition using an index, the condition is referred to as a *search argument* or *SARG* for short. However, not every condition is a "sargable" search argument:

✦ Multiple conditions that are ANDed together are SARGs, but ORed conditions are not SARGs.

✦ Negative search conditions (<>, !>, !<, Not Exists, Not In, Not Like) are not optimizable. It's easy to prove that a row exists, but to prove it doesn't exist requires examining every row.

✦ Conditions that begin with wildcards don't use indexes. An index can quickly locate Smith, but must scan every row to find any rows with ith anywhere in the string.

✦ Conditions with expressions are not SQL Server compliant, so these expressions will be broken down with the use of algebra to aide with the procurement of valid input data.

✦ If the where clause includes a function, such as a string function, a table scan is required so every row can be tested with the function applied to the data.

Index Selectivity

Another aspect of index tuning is the selectivity of the index. An index that is very selective has more index values and selects fewer data rows per index value. A primary key or unique index has the highest possible selectivity.

An index with only a few values spread across a large table is less selective. Indexes that are less selective may not even be useful as indexes. A column with three values spread throughout the table is a poor candidate for an index. A bit column has low selectivity and may not even be indexed.

SQL Server uses its internal index statistics to track the selectivity of an index. DBCC Show_ Statistics reports the last date on which the statistics were updated and the basic information about the index statistics, including the usefulness of the index. A low density indicates that the index is very selective. A high density indicates that a given index node points to several table rows and that the index may be less useful, as shown in this code sample:

```
Use CHA2
DBCC Show_Statistics (Customer, IxCustomerName)
```

Result (formatted and abridged; the full listing includes details for every value in the index):

```
Statistics for INDEX 'IxCustomerName'.
                     Rows                        Average
 Updated    Rows  Sampled  Steps  Density  key length
 --------- -----  -------- ------ -------- -----------
 May 1,02   42     42       33     0.0      11.547619
```

```
All density     Average Length  Columns
--------------  --------------  ---------------------------
3.0303031E-2    6.6904764       LastName
2.3809524E-2    11.547619       LastName, FirstName

DBCC execution completed. If DBCC printed error messages,
contact your system administrator.
```

Sometimes changing the order of the key columns can improve the selectivity of an index and improve its performance. Be careful, however, because other queries may depend on the order for their performance.

Reusing Query Execution Plans

As `statistics time` demonstrates, the query-parse and query-compile time can be expensive. Stored query plans are therefore critical to the continued performance of the database. If the query qualifies, the first time it is executed SQL Server attempts to save the query plan in the procedure cache.

While optimizing a query execution plan can be an expensive task, making reuse of a query execution plan a smart thing, there are definitely times when the best course of action is to recompile the query execution plan.

The Query Optimizer chooses the best index and the correct join method based on a prediction of the number of rows each operation will return. This prediction is dependent on two factors: the query parameter and the index statistics.

To illustrate this idea, assume that most of your firm's customers are local—from the area around Victoria Station in London. You have some customers from the rest of the U.K., and a handful of international customers. The query is searching for all customers in London. SQL Server creates an excellent query execution plan that uses a clustered index scan because the majority of rows must be retrieved. The query plan is stored in memory.

Now assume that in the next few minutes, the firm merges with a New York company that is ten times the size, the data has also been merged, and the next query searches for customers in Colorado. The initial query plan is based on the prediction that the parameter will return a large percentage of customers. That plan is now the worst possible plan to locate the two customers from Colorado.

Fortunately, SQL Server makes an educated guess about which plans to recompile based on changing data and parameters. SQL Server keeps statistics on the data spread within tables so that it can tell how rows exists for London, New York, or Colorado Springs.

Statistics are usually set to auto, and SQL Server updates the statistics when enough data is inserted to warrant it. However, at times you might want to turn off auto-statistics, such as when you're about to truncate the table and reload a million rows.

 Cross-Reference You can manually control the statistics using DBCC commands, which are covered in Chapter 37, "Maintaining the Database."

In order to be saved in memory, a query must have parameters—not just a constant, but the `parameter = value` syntax. Fortunately, SQL Server will auto-parameterize the query, replacing literals and constants in the query with parameters, thus allowing the query to be saved.

A more restrictive condition specifies that all table references must the qualified (at least two-part: schema.tablename) for the query plans to be saved.

You can look at the query-plan cache to verify that the query is in fact cached. The procedure cache can be large. While it's not recommended in a production environment, clearing the cache will make checking for a specific query easier:

```
DBCC FREEPROCCACHE
```

To examine the procedure cache, use the syscacheobjects table:

```
SELECT cast(C.sql as Char(35)) as StoredProcedure,
    cacheobjtype,  usecounts as Count
  FROM Master.dbo.syscacheobjects C
  JOIN  Master.dbo.sysdatabases D
    ON C.dbid = C.dbid
  WHERE D.Name = DB_Name()
    AND ObjType = 'Adhoc'
  ORDER BY StoredProcedure
```

Result (abridged):

```
cacheobjtype        Count        StoredProcedure
----------------    -----------  -------------------------------
Compiled Plan       1            INSERT [Lumigent_Profiler]([Pre
Executable Plan     1            SELECT LastName + ' ' + FirstNa
Compiled Plan       1            SELECT LastName + ' ' + FirstNa
Compiled Plan       1            UPDATE msdb.dbo.sysjobschedules
```

Performance depends on a combination of the query, the indexes, and the data. A saved query plan is useful only as long as the data statistics, indexes, and parameters are consistent. When the table or index structure changes, or the data statistics are updated, or a significant amount of data is updated, SQL Server marks the query as unusable and generates a new query plan the next time it is executed.

To efficiently handle memory, query plans are also aged out of the cache, with the most complex queries taking the longest time to be removed.

A Comprehensive Index Strategy

An index strategy deals with the larger problem, and not isolated situations to the detriment of the whole. While doing actual performance audits, the most common index problems (in order) are missing indexes and extra, redundant indexes. This is why it's best to take the time to index on a per-table basis, rather than a per-query basis.

Best Practice

Developing an indexing strategy without a solid data abstraction layer is much more difficult. You'll need to run Profiler for a significant time and capture every query. This is one more reason why no production database should run without a data abstraction layer.

First, identify the procedures and queries that access the table and plot the data using a CRUD (create, retrieve, update, delete) matrix, as show in Table 50-3. This example will analyze an OrderDetail table and examine only three fictitious procedures for simplicity sake.

The abbreviations are as follows: S for selected column, O for order by column, W for a column referenced in the where clause, and G for group by function.

Table 50-3: Table CRUD Usage Analysis

Column	pGetOrder	pCheckQuantity	pShipOrder
OrderDetailID	S		W
OrderID	W	W	
ProductID	S	S	
NonStockProduct	S		
Quantity	S	S	
UnitPrice	S		
ExtendedPrice	S		
ShipRequestDate	S	W	
ShipDate	S		U
ShipComment	S		U

The next step is to design the fewest number of indexes that satisfies the needs for the table. This process will first determine the clustered index and then create indexes for every procedure and query that access the table as shown in the following list and Table 50-4. The numbers in the chart indicate the ordinal position of the column in the index. An included column is listed as I.

Since the OrderDetail table is often selected using the OrderID column, and this column can also be used to gather multiple rows into a single data page, OrderID is the best candidate for the clustered index (CI). The clustered index will consist of one column – the OrderID – so a 1 goes in the ordered row for the clustered index indicating that it's the first column of the clustered index.

The clustered index satisfies the pGetOrder procedure.

Table 50-4: Table Strategic Index Plan

Column	CI	Ix2	Ix1
OrderDetailID			1
OrderID	1	(cl)	(cl)
ProductID		I	
NonStockProduct			
Quantity		I	
UnitPrice			
ExtendedPrice			
ShipRequestDate		1	
ShipDate			
ShipComment			

The pCheckQuantity procedure verifies the quantity on hand prior to shipping. It filters the rows by ShipRequestDate and OrderID. Creating a nonclustered index with ShipRequestDate will index both the ShipRequestDate column and the OrderID column, since the clustered index is present in the leaf node of the nonclustered index. Since the procedure needs only four columns, adding ProductID and Quantity as included column will enable Ix1 to completely cover the needs of the query and significantly improve performance.

The third procedure can be satisfied by adding a nonclustered index, Ix2, with the OrderDetailID column.

Although this example had only three procedures, with a production table, you'll see many more procedures and indexes will be able to overlap several procedures.

Using the Database Engine Tuning Advisor

SQL Server 2005 includes a smart tool that can analyze a single query or a set of queries and recommend indexes and partitions to improve performance, as shown in Figure 50-6.

New in 2005
The Database Engine Tuning Advisor is an upgrade to SQL Server 2000's Index Tuning Wizard. The new advisor also recommends file structure modifications.

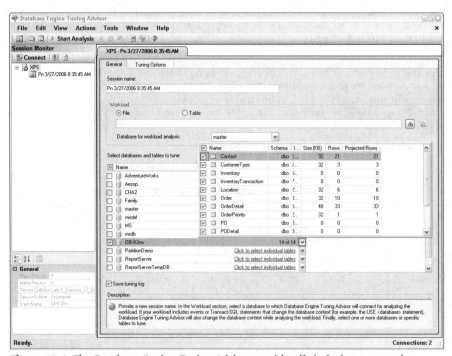

Figure 50-6: The Database Engine Tuning Advisor can identify indexing gaps and recommend solutions.

Best Practice

Use the Database Engine Tuning Advisor to validate and refine the indexing strategy. If the advisor wants to add an index, try to figure out why. An understanding of the data, the queries, and the indexing is too important for the database developer simply to let the tool do all the work.

Summary

The middle layer of optimization theory is indexing. To intelligently create indexes you need to understand not only the technologies — the Query Optimizer, index pages, and indexing options — but also both your schema and your data abstraction layer inside out. This is one problem space where your unique knowledge and skills make a significant difference. The next chapter continues the discussion of performance with strategies to improve database availability.

✦   ✦   ✦

Managing Transactions, Locking, and Blocking

CHAPTER

51

I like food, and I even like grocery shopping, but I'll never figure out why stores don't open more check-out lanes when the line grows long. If they stocked tech magazines instead of gossip rags, it wouldn't be so bad.

Concurrency means contention. As the number of users increases, so will the performance hit as they fight to use the same resources.

Databases are all about transactional integrity, but the nemesis of transactional integrity is concurrency — multiple users simultaneously attempting to retrieve and modify data. While transaction isolation is less of an issue in small databases, in a production database with thousands of users, concurrency competes with transactional integrity.

Here's why: To protect a transaction from other transactions, by default, a transaction that's reading will block a transaction that's writing. Similarly, a transaction that's writing blocks both writing and reading transactions. The more transactions that occur simultaneously, especially long transactions, the more blocking, and the problems grow exponentially as waiting transactions block other transactions for an ever-increasing duration.

That's why concurrency is level four in optimization theory.

A good schema, set-based queries, and a sound indexing strategy all work together for the good of the database, and together they reduce transaction duration. This naturally increases concurrency (the number of users who can share a resource) and sets up the database for the more advanced high-scalability features such as table partitioning.

I can't stress enough that if you have a transaction locking and blocking problem, the best solution is to first solve the schema, query, and indexing problems. This chapter digs deeply into how transactions affect other transactions, explaining the database theory behind transactions, how SQL Server accomplishes transactional integrity, and how to get the best performance while maintaining data integrity.

Transactional Basics

A *transaction* is a sequence of tasks that together constitute a logical unit of work. All the tasks must complete or fail as a single unit. For example, in the case of an inventory movement transaction, the inventory subtraction and addition must both be written to the disk, or neither will be written to the disk.

In SQL Server, every DML operation is a transaction, whether it has a begin transaction or not. For instance, an insert command that inserts 25 rows is a logical unit of work. Each and every one of the 25 rows must be updated. An update to even a single row operates within a transaction so that the data, and all indexes, are updated or rolled back.

To wrap multiple commands within a single transaction, a little code is needed. Two markers — one at the *beginning* of the transaction, and the other at its completion, at which time the transaction is *committed* to disk — define the perimeter of a transaction. If the code detects an error, the transaction can be *rolled back*, or undone. The following three commands appear simple, but a volume of sophistication lies behind them:

✦ begin transaction

✦ commit transaction

✦ rollback transaction

The following example demonstrates a typical transaction. The sequence of work is wrapped inside a begin transaction and a commit transaction. Each task in the sequence is followed by basic error-handling code and aborts the transaction with a rollback transaction command if a problem arises. If the first task (the subtraction from inventory) executes fine, but the second task (the addition to inventory) fails, the rollback transaction will undo the first and second tasks. SQL Server will even roll back the transaction if the plug is pulled halfway through the transaction. This is how an inventory transaction system could handle the inventory move:

```
BEGIN TRANSACTION;
  INSERT InventoryTransaction (InventoryID, Location, Quantity)
    VALUES (101, 'Vault A', -2000);
  IF @@Error <> 0
    BEGIN
      ROLLBACK TRANSACTION;
      RAISERROR('Inventory Transaction Error', 16, 1);
      RETURN;
    END;
  INSERT InventoryTransaction (InventoryID, Location, Quantity)
    VALUES (101, 'Vault 12', 2000);
  IF @@Error <> 0
    BEGIN
      ROLLBACK TRANSACTION;
      RAISERROR(Inventory Transaction Error', 16, 1);
      RETURN;
    END;
COMMIT TRANSACTION;
```

Cross-Reference Program flow control (if, begin, end, and return) and error handling (@@Error and raiserror) are explained in Chapter 18, "Programming with T-SQL."

Transactions can be nested, although as soon as one transaction is rolled back, all pending transactions are rolled back as well.

Attempting to `commit` or `rollback` a transaction if no pending transactions exist will cause an error.

While SQL Server requires an explicit `begin transaction` to initiate a transaction, this behavior can be modified so that every batch assumes a transaction. The following code alone will not update the `Nickname` column in the CHA2 database:

```
USE CHA2;
SET Implicit_Transactions ON;
UPDATE CUSTOMER
  SET Nickname = 'Nicky'
  WHERE CustomerID = 10;
```

Adding a `commit transaction` to the end of the batch commits the transaction, and the update actually takes place:

```
COMMIT TRANSACTION;
```

Note Implicit transaction is the default behavior for Oracle, and the adjustment takes getting used to for Oracle developers moving up to SQL Server.

It is also possible to declare a *save point* within the sequence of tasks and then roll back to that save point only. However, I believe that this mixes program flow of control with transaction handling. If an error makes it necessary to redo a task within the transaction, it's cleaner to handle the error with standard error handling than to jury-rig the transaction handling.

Transactional Integrity

The study of how transactions impact performance must include *transactional integrity*, which refers to the quality of a transaction. There are three types of problems that violate transactional integrity: dirty reads, non-repeatable reads, and phantom rows. Solving these three problems involves enforcing various levels of integrity or *isolation* between the transactions.

The ACID Properties

The quality of a database product is measured by its transactions' adherence to the ACID properties. ACID is an acronym for four interdependent properties: atomicity, consistency, isolation, and durability. Much of the architecture of any modern relational database is founded on these properties. Understanding the ACID properties of a transaction is a prerequisite for understanding SQL Server.

Atomicity

The transaction must be *atomic*, meaning all or nothing. At the end of the transaction, either all of the transaction is successful, or all of the transaction fails. If a partial transaction is written to disk, the atomic property is violated.

Consistency

The transaction must preserve database *consistency*, which means that the database must begin in a state of consistency and return to a state of consistency once the transaction is complete. For the purposes of ACID, consistency means that every row and value must agree with the reality being modeling, and every constraint must be enforced. If the order rows are written to disk but the order detail rows are not written, the consistency between the `Order` and `OrderDetail` tables is violated.

Isolation

Each transaction must be *isolated,* or separated, from the effects of other transactions. Regardless of what any other transaction is doing, a transaction must be able to continue with the exact same data sets it started with. Isolation is the fence between two transactions. A proof of isolation is the ability to replay a serialized set of transactions on the original set of data and always receive the same result.

For example, assume Joe is updating 100 rows. While Joe's transaction is under way, Sue reads one of the rows Joe is working on. If the read takes place, their transactions are not fully isolated from each another. This property is less critical in a read-only database or a database with only a few users.

Durability

The *durability* of a transaction refers to its permanence regardless of system failure. Once a transaction is committed, it stays committed. The Database Engine must be constructed so that even if the data drive melts, the database can be restored up to the last transaction that was committed a split second before the hard drive died.

Transactional Faults

The isolation between transactions can be less than perfect in one of three ways: dirty reads, non-repeatable reads, and phantom rows. These transactional faults can potentially affect the integrity of the transactions.

Dirty Reads

The most egregious fault is a transaction's work being visible to other transactions before the transaction even commits its changes. When a transaction can read another transaction's uncommitted updates, this is called a *dirty read*, illustrated in Figure 51-1.

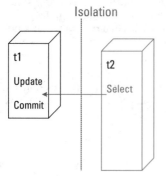

Figure 51-1: A dirty read occurs when transaction two can read uncommitted changes made by transaction one.

To illustrate a dirty-read transactional fault, the following code represents a setup that uses two transactions (transaction one is on the left, and transaction two is on the right). The second transaction will see the first transaction's update before that update is committed:

```
BEGIN TRANSACTION;
SET TRANSACTION ISOLATION LEVEL
  READ COMMITTED;
USE CHA2;

-- Transaction 1
USE CHA2
BEGIN TRANSACTION
  UPDATE Customer
    SET Nickname = 'Transaction Fault'
    WHERE CustomerID = 1;
```

In a separate Query Editor window, as shown in Figure 51-2, execute another transaction in its own connection window. This transaction will set its isolation level to permit dirty reads. (The isolation level must be set here if the dirty read is to be demonstrated. The isolation-level command is explained further in the next section.)

```
-- Transaction 2
                        SET TRANSACTION ISOLATION LEVEL
                          READ UNCOMMITTED
                        USE CHA2
                        SELECT Nickname
                          FROM Customer
                          WHERE CustomerID = 1;
```

Result:

```
                        NickName
                        ---------------------
                        Transaction Fault
```

Transaction one isn't done working with the data set, but transaction two was able to read "Transaction Fault." That's a violation of transactional integrity.

To finish the task, the first window still needs to commit the transaction:

```
-- Transaction 1
COMMIT TRANSACTION
```

Non-Repeatable Reads

A *non-repeatable read* is similar to a dirty read, but a non-repeatable read occurs when a transaction can see the committed updates from another transaction (see Figure 51-3). *True isolation* means that one transaction never affects another transaction. If the isolation is complete, then no data changes from outside the transaction should be seen by the transaction. Reading a row inside a transaction should produce the same results every time. If reading a row twice results in different values, that's a non-repeatable read type of transaction fault.

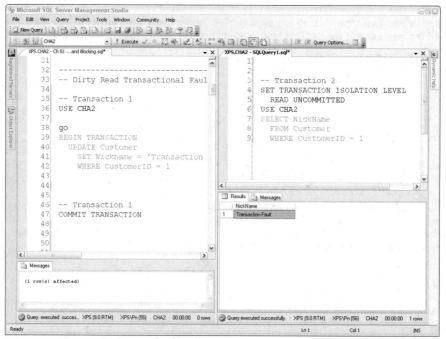

Figure 51-2: Opening multiple Query Editor windows is the best way to experiment with transactions. Here, the transaction in the left window updated the nickname to "Transaction Fault" but did not commit the transaction. The transaction on the right selected the Nickname column and read "Transaction Fault."

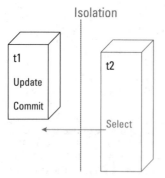

Figure 51-3: When transaction one's committed changes are seen by transaction two, that's a *non-repeatable read* transaction fault.

The following sequence sets up two concurrent transactions. Transaction one opens a transaction and performs a select. The initial value of the nickname for customerid 1 is "Transaction Fault":

```
-- Transaction 1
SET TRANSACTION ISOLATION LEVEL
  READ COMMITTED
BEGIN TRANSACTION
  USE CHA2
  SELECT NickName
    FROM Customer
    WHERE CustomerID = 1;
```

Result:

```
Nickname
----------------------
Transaction Fault
```

With the first transaction still open, another transaction updates the nickname to 'Non-Repeatable Read" and commits the changes.

```
                        -- Transaction 2
                        USE CHA2
                        BEGIN TRANSACTION
                          UPDATE Customer
                        SET Nickname = 'Non-Repeatable Read'
                        WHERE CustomerID = 1;

                        COMMIT TRANSACTION;
```

With transaction two's update committed, transaction one reselects the same row. Transaction one now attempts to reselect the same nickname. If it sees the value updated by transaction two, that will be a non-repeatable read transaction fault:

```
-- Transaction 2
  USE CHA2
  SELECT Nickname
    FROM Customer
    WHERE CustomerID = 1;
```

Result:

```
Nickname
---------------------
Non-Repeatable Read
```

Sure enough, transaction two's read was not repeatable. The second `select` reflected transaction one's `update`. To complete the work, transaction two commits its changes:

```
COMMIT TRANSACTION
```

Phantom Rows

The least severe transactional-integrity fault is a *phantom row*. Like a non-repeatable read, a phantom row occurs when updates from another transaction not only affects the result set's data values, but causes the `select` to return a different set of rows, as shown in Figure 51-4.

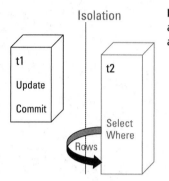

Isolation

Figure 51-4: When the rows returned by a select are altered by another transaction, the phenomenon is called a *phantom row*.

In the following code, transaction one will update a nickname to 'Missy' while transaction two is selecting rows with that nickname value:

```
-- Transaction 2
BEGIN TRANSACTION
  USE CHA2
  SELECT CustomerID, LastName
    FROM Customer
    WHERE NickName = 'Missy';
```

Result:

```
CustomerID  LastName
----------  ----------------
2           Anderson
```

```
-- Transaction 1
USE CHA2
BEGIN TRANSACTION
  UPDATE Customer
    SET Nickname = 'Missy'
    WHERE CustomerID = 1;
```

```
COMMIT TRANSACTION;
```

If the isolation between the transactions is complete, transaction two's result set will contain the same row set as the previous select:

```
-- Transaction 2
  USE CHA2
  SELECT CustomerID, LastName
    FROM Customer
    WHERE Nickname = 'Missy';
```

Result:

```
CustomerID  LastName
----------  ----------------
1           Adams
2           Anderson
```

Adams is a phantom row because it appears for the first time in the second result set because of a change in the data based on another transaction's data modification.

The final line of code in this series closes transaction two's logical transaction:

```
COMMIT TRANSACTION
```

Of these transactional faults, dirty reads are the most dangerous, while non-repeatable reads are less so, and phantom rows are the least dangerous of all.

Isolation Levels

Databases deal with the three transactional faults by establishing isolation between transactions. The level of isolation, or the height of the fence between transactions, can be adjusted to control which transactional faults are permitted. The ANSI SQL-92 committee has specified four isolation levels, listed in Table 51-1.

Table 51-1: ANSI-92 Isolation Levels

Isolation Level	Dirty Read	Non-Repeatable Read	Phantom Row	Write Blocking
	Seeing another transaction's non-committed changes	Seeing another transaction's committed changes	Seeing additional rows selected by where clause as a result of another transaction	The first write is blocked by the second write.
Read Uncommitted (least restrictive)	Possible	Possible	Possible	No
Read Committed (SQL Server default; moderately restrictive)	Prevented	Possible	Possible	No
Repeatable Read	Prevented	Prevented	Possible	No
Serializable (most restrictive)	Prevented	Prevented	Prevented	No
Snapshot	Prevented	Prevented	Possible	Yes
Read Committed Isolation	Prevented	Possible	Possible	Yes

SQL Server implements isolation levels with locks. Because locks affect performance, there's a trade-off between tight transaction isolation and performance. SQL Server's default isolation, read committed, is a balance appropriate for most OLTP projects.

The isolation level can be set for a connection or batch. Alternately, the isolation level for a single DML statement can be set by using table-lock hints in the from clause.

Level 1 – Read Uncommitted

The least restrictive isolation level is *read uncommitted*, which doesn't prevent any of the transactional faults. It's like having no fence at all because it provides no isolation between transactions. Setting the isolation level to read uncommitted is the same as setting SQL Server's locks to no locks. This mode is best for reporting and data-reading applications. Because this mode has just enough locks to prevent data corruption, but not enough to handle row contention, it's not very useful for databases whose data is updated regularly.

Level 2 – Read Committed

Read committed prevents the worst transactional fault, but doesn't bog the system down with excessive lock contention. For this reason, it's the SQL Server default isolation level and an ideal choice for most OTLP projects.

Level 3 – Repeatable Read

By preventing dirty reads and non-repeatable reads, the *repeatable read* isolation level provides increased transaction isolation without the extreme lock contention of serializable isolation.

Level 4 – Serializable

This most restrictive isolation level prevents all transactional faults and passes the serialized-transaction test mentioned in the definition of isolation. This mode is useful for databases for which absolute transactional integrity is more important than performance. Banking, accounting, and high-contention sales databases, such as the stock market, typically use serialized isolation.

Using the serializable isolation level is the same as setting locks to hold locks, which holds even share locks for the length of the transaction. While this setting provides absolute transaction isolation, it can cause serious lock contention and performance delays.

New in 2005 Beyond the ANSI standard isolation levels, SQL Server 2005 has added *snapshot isolation*, which literally makes a copy of the data being updated in its own physical space, completely isolated from any other transactions.

Snapshot Isolation

Snapshot isolation is essentially optimistic locking at the database level. Traditionally, concurrency conflict has been between readers and writers. Snapshot isolation is a completely different twist. It makes a snapshot copy of the data being updated. During the update, readers can continue to read the original data. When the update is committed, it's written back over the original data.

Note Snapshot isolation uses row versioning, which writes copies of the rows to TempDB. This puts an incredible load on TempDB. If you use snapshot isolation, you'll need to locate TempDB's data and transaction log on their own DAS disk subsystems.

Snapshot isolation eliminates writer versus reader contention. Nevertheless, contention isn't really gone — it's shifted to writers conflicting with writers. If a second writer attempts to update a resource that's already being updated, the second resource is blocked.

Read Committed Snapshot

This variation of snapshot isolation behaves the same as read committed but without the writer versus reader contention.

Transaction-Log Architecture

SQL Server's design meets the transactional-integrity ACID properties, largely because of its write-ahead transaction log. The write-ahead transaction log ensures the durability of every transaction.

Transaction Log Sequence

Every data-modification operation goes through the same sequence, in which it writes first to the transaction log and then to the data file. The following sections describe the 12 steps in a transaction.

Database Beginning State

Before the transaction begins, the database is in a consistent state. All indexes are complete and point to the correct row. The data meets all the enforced rules for data integrity. Every foreign key points to a valid primary key.

Some data pages are likely already cached in memory. Additional data pages or index pages are copied into memory as needed. Here are the steps of a transaction:

1. The database is in a consistent state.

Data-Modification Command

The transaction is initiated by a submitted query, batch, or stored procedure, as shown in Figure 51-5.

2. The code issues a `begin transaction` command. Even when the DML command is a stand-alone command without a `begin transaction` and `commit transaction`, it is still handled as a transaction.

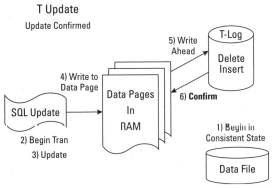

Figure 51-5: The SQL DML commands are performed in memory as part of a transaction.

3. The code issues a single DML insert, update, or delete command, or a series of them.

   To give you an example of the transaction log in action, the following code initiates a transaction and then submits two update commands:

   ```
   USE OBXKites;
   BEGIN TRANSACTION;

   UPDATE Product
     SET ProductDescription = 'Transaction Log Test A',
         DiscontinueDate = '12/31/2003'
     WHERE Code = '1001';

   UPDATE Product
     SET ProductDescription = 'Transaction Log Test B',
         DiscontinueDate = '4/1/2003'
     WHERE Code = '1002';
   ```

   Notice that the transaction has not yet been committed.

4. The query-optimization plan is either generated or pulled from memory. Any required locks are applied and the data modifications, including index updates, page splits, and any other required system operation, are performed in memory.

The following section continues our chronological walk through the process.

Transaction Log Recorded

The most important aspect of the transaction log is that all data modifications are written to it and confirmed prior to being written to the data file, as shown in Figure 51-6.

5. The data modifications are written to the transaction log.

6. The transaction-log DML entries are confirmed. This ensures that the log entries are in fact written to the transaction log.

Best Practice

The write-ahead nature of the transaction log is what makes it critical that the transaction log be stored on a different disk subsystem from the data file. If they are stored separately and either disk subsystem fails, then the database will still be intact and you will be able to recover it to the split second before the failure. Conversely, if they are on the same drive, a drive failure will require you to restore from the last backup.

Transaction Commit

When the sequence of tasks is complete, the commit transaction closes the transaction. Even this task is written to the transaction log, as shown in Figure 51-6.

7. The code closes the transaction:

   ```
   COMMIT TRANSACTION
   ```

ScreenCast

To watch transactions post to the transaction log, watch the Transaction screencast on www.SQLServerBible.com.

T Commit

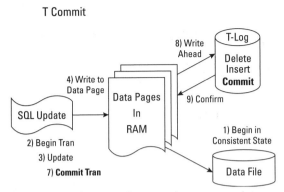

Figure 51-6: The commit transaction command launches another insert into the transaction log.

8. The `commit` entry is written to the transaction log.

9. The transaction-log `commit` entry is confirmed (see Figure 51-7).

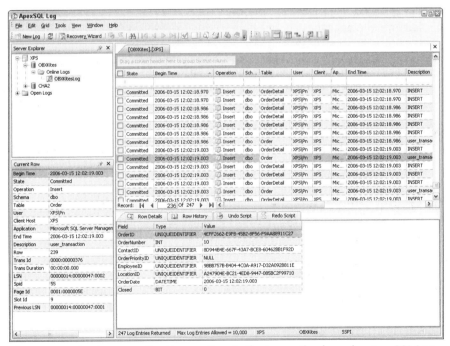

Figure 51-7: Viewing committed transactions in the transaction log using ApexSQL Log, a third-party product

Data-File Update

With the transaction safely stored in the transaction log, the last disk operation writes the data modification to the data file, as shown in Figure 51-8.

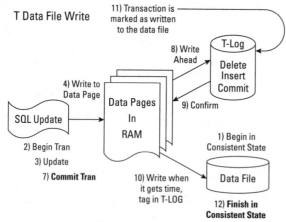

Figure 51-8: As one of the last steps, the data modification is written to the data file.

10. In the background, when a checkpoint occurs (a SQL Server internal event), the lazy writer process writes any dirty (modified) data pages to the data file. It tries to find sequential pages to improve the performance of the write. Even though I've listed it here as step 10, this can happen at nearly anytime during the transaction. SQL Server receives a "write complete" message from Windows.

11. At the conclusion of the background write operation, SQL Server marks the oldest open transaction in the transaction log. All older, committed transactions have been confirmed in the data file and are now confirmed in the transaction log. The DBCC OpenTran command reports the oldest open transaction.

Transaction Complete

The sequence comes full circle and returns the database to a consistent state.

12. The database finishes in a consistent state.

In ancient Hebrew poetry, an *inclusion* is a line or phrase that begins a poem and is repeated at the close of the poem, providing a theme or wrapper for the poem. In the same way, the beginning consistent state and ending consistent state together provide a stable wrapper, or bookends, for the database transaction.

Transaction-Log Rollback

If the transaction is rolled back, the DML operations are reversed in memory, and a transaction-abort entry is made in the log.

Transaction-Log Recovery

The primary benefit of a write-ahead transaction log is that it maintains the atomic transactional property in the case of system failure.

If SQL Server should cease functioning, the transaction log is automatically examined once it recovers, as follows:

✦ If any entries are in the log as DML operations but are not committed, they are rolled back.

To test this feature you must be brave. Begin a transaction and unplug the server before issuing a `commit transaction`. The server must be physically turned off. Simply closing Query Analyzer won't do it; Query Analyzer will request permission to commit the pending transactions, and will roll back the transaction if permission isn't given. If SQL Server is shut down normally, it will wait for any pending tasks to complete before stopping. You have to turn off the server to see the transaction log recover from a failed transaction.

If you have followed the steps outlined previously, and you disable the system just before step 7, the transaction-log entries will be identical to those shown later, in Figure 51-10. SQL Server will recover from the crash very nicely and roll back the unfinished transaction.

✦ If any entries are in the log as DML operations and committed but not marked as written to the data file, they are written to the data file. This feature is nearly impossible to demonstrate.

Understanding SQL Server Locking

SQL Server implements the isolation property with locks that protect a transaction's rows from being affected by another transaction. SQL Server locks are not just a "page lock on" and "page lock off" scheme. These are serious locks. Before they can be controlled, they must be understood.

Within SQL Server, you can informally picture two processes: a query processor and a lock manager. The goal of the lock manager is to maintain transactional integrity as efficiently as possible by creating and dropping locks.

Every lock has the following three properties:

✦ **Granularity:** The size of the lock

✦ **Mode:** The type of lock

✦ **Duration:** The isolation mode of the lock

Locks are not impossible to view, but some tricks will make viewing the current set of locks easier. In addition, lock contention, or the compatibility of various locks to exist or block other locks, can adversely affect performance if it's not understood and controlled.

Lock Granularity

A portion of the data controlled by a lock can vary from only a row to the entire database, as shown in Table 51-2. Several combinations of locks, depending on the lock granularity, could satisfy a locking requirement.

Table 51-2: Lock Granularity

Lock Size	Description
Row Lock	Locks a single row. This is the smallest lock available. SQL Server does not lock columns.
Page Lock	Locks a page, or 8KB. One or more rows may exist on a single page.
Extent Lock	Locks eight pages, or 64KB
Table Lock	Locks the entire table
Database Lock	Locks the entire database. This lock is used primarily during schema changes.
Key Lock	Locks nodes on an index

For best performance, the SQL Server lock manager tries to balance the size of the lock against the number of locks. The struggle is between concurrency (smaller locks allow more transactions to access the data) and performance (fewer locks are faster). To achieve that balance, the lock manager dynamically swaps one set of locks for another set. For example:

1. Twenty-five row locks might be escalated to a single page lock.

2. Then, if 25 more rows are locked that extend over four other pages on the same extent, the page lock and 25 row locks might be escalated to an extent lock because more than 50 percent of the pages on the extent are affected.

3. If enough extents are affected, the entire set of locks might be escalated to a table lock.

Dynamic locking brings significant benefits for SQL Server developers:

✦ It automatically provides the best performance/concurrency balance without custom programming.

✦ The performance of the database is preserved as the database grows and the lock manager continually applies the appropriate lock granularity.

✦ Dynamic locking simplifies administration.

Lock Mode

Locks not only have granularity, or size, but also a mode that determines their purpose. SQL Server has a rich set of lock modes (such as shared, update, exclusive). Failing to understand lock modes will almost guarantee that you develop a poorly performing database.

Lock Contention

The interaction and compatibility of the locks plays a vital role in SQL Server's transactional integrity and performance. Certain lock modes block other lock modes, as detailed in Table 51-3.

Table 51-3: Lock Compatibility

T1 has:	T2 Requests:					
	IS	**S**	**U**	**IX**	**SIX**	**X**
Intent shared (IS)	Yes	Yes	Yes	Yes	Yes	Yes
Shared (S)	Yes	Yes	Yes	No	No	No
Update (U)	Yes	Yes	No	No	No	No
Intent exclusive (IX)	Yes	No	No	Yes	No	No
Shared with intent exclusive (SIX)	Yes	No	No	No	No	No
Exclusive (X)	No	No	No	No	No	No

Shared Lock (S)

By far the most common and most abused lock, a *shared lock* (listed as an "S" in SQL Server) is a simple "read lock." If a transaction gets a shared lock it's saying, "I'm looking at this data." Multiple transactions are typically allowed to view the same data, depending on the isolation mode.

Best Practice

Be careful with shared locks. I believe that misused shared locks are a common cause of update-performance problems. Applications should grab the data in a way that doesn't hold the shared lock. This is one compelling reason to use stored procedures to retrieve data.

Exclusive Lock (X)

An exclusive lock means that the transaction is performing a write to the data. As the name implies, an exclusive lock means that only one transaction may hold an exclusive lock at one time, and that no transactions may view the data during the exclusive lock.

Update Lock (U)

An update lock can be confusing. It's not applied while a transaction is performing an update—that's an exclusive lock. Instead, the update lock means that the transaction is getting ready to perform an exclusive lock and is currently scanning the data to determine the row(s) it wants for that lock. Think of the update lock as a shared lock that's about to morph into an exclusive lock.

To help prevent deadlocks (explained later in this chapter), only one transaction may hold an update lock at a given time.

Intent Locks

An intent lock is a yellow flag or a warning lock that alerts other transactions to the fact that something more is going on. The primary purpose of an intent lock is to improve performance. Because an intent lock is used for all types of locks and for all lock granularities, SQL Server has many types of intent locks. The following is a sampling of the intent locks:

✦ Intent Shared Lock (IS)

✦ Shared with Intent Exclusive Lock (SIX)

✦ Intent Exclusive Lock (IX)

Intent locks serve to stake a claim for a shared or exclusive lock without actually being a shared or exclusive lock. In doing so they solve two performance problems: hierarchical locking and permanent lock block.

Without intent locks, if transaction one holds a shared lock on a row and transaction two wants to grab an exclusive lock on the table, then transaction two would need to check for table locks, extent locks, page locks, row locks, and key locks.

Instead, SQL Server uses intent locks to propagate a lock to higher levels of the data's hierarchical levels. When transaction one gains a row lock, it also places an intent lock on the row's page and table.

The intent locks move the overhead from the checking transaction to the establishing transaction by enabling the transaction gaining the lock to place intent locks on the greater scope of its lock. That one-time write of three locks potentially saves hundreds of searches later as other transactions check for locks.

The intent locks also prevent a serious shared-lock contention problem — what I call "permanent lock block." As long as a transaction has a shared lock, another transaction can't gain an exclusive lock. What would happen if someone grabbed a shared lock every five seconds and held it for 10 seconds while a transaction was waiting for an exclusive lock? The update transaction could theoretically wait forever. However, once the transaction has an intent exclusive lock (IX), no other transaction can grab a shared lock. The intent exclusive lock isn't a full exclusive lock, but it lays claim to gaining an exclusive lock in the future.

Schema Lock (Sch-M, Sch-S)

Schema locks protect the database schema. SQL Server will apply a schema stability (Sch-S) lock during any query to prevent data definition language (DDL) commands.

A schema modification lock (Sch-M) is applied only when SQL Server is adjusting the physical schema. If SQL Server is in the middle of adding a column to a table, the schema lock will prevent any other transactions from viewing or modifying the data during the schema-modification operation.

Lock Duration

The third lock property, lock duration, is determined by the isolation level of the transactions involved — the tighter the isolation, the longer the locks will be held. SQL Server implements all four previously described transaction-isolation levels. An absolute level of isolation (serialization) will create the strictest locks. At the other extreme, a low level of transaction isolation (read uncommitted) will effectively turn off locks, as detailed in Table 51-4.

Table 51-4: Isolation Levels and Lock Duration

Isolation Level	Share-Lock Duration	Exclusive-Lock Duration
Read Uncommitted	None	Held only long enough to prevent physical corruption; otherwise, exclusive locks are neither applied nor honored
Read Committed	Held while the transaction is reading the data	Held until `transaction commit`
Repeatable Read	Held until the transaction is committed	Held until `transaction commit`
Serializable	Held until `transaction commit`	Held until `transaction commit`. The exclusive lock also uses a keylock (also called a range lock) to prevent inserts.
Snapshot Isolation	n/a	n/a

Monitoring Locking and Blocking

Without the ability to see the lock, the various types of locks and their durations may seem like pure theory. Fortunately, SQL Server is a relatively open environment, and it's easy to inspect the current locks.

 New in 2005 The Activity Monitor is an excellent graphical method of viewing and tracking down locking and blocking.

Using Management Studio

With Management Studio, transactions for a selected database can be viewed using the Summary page, which pulls data from the dynamic management views. The transaction related reports include All Transactions, All Blocking Transactions (shown in Figure 51-9), Top Transactions by Age, Top Transactions by Blocked Transaction Count, Top Transactions by Lock Count, Resource Locking by Object, and User Statistics.

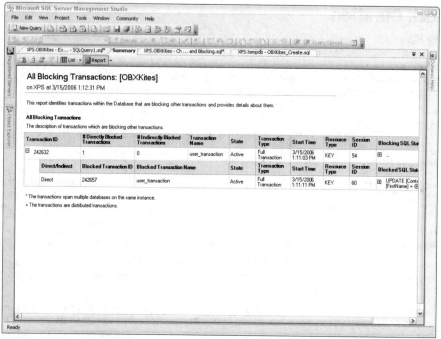

Figure 51-9: Management Studio's Summary page is a quick way to view key transaction locking and blocking information.

Using Activity Monitor

The Activity Monitor (see Figure 51-10) is the tool to use to keep a watch on locks by process or object. It can be manually refreshed or automatically refreshed as often as every five seconds. Activity Monitor can be opened from Object Explorer; select the server ➪ Management ➪ SQL Server Logs.

Using Profiler

You can also use SQL Server Profiler to watch blocked processes using the Error and Warnings: Blocked Process Report event (see Figure 51-11).

Best Practice

Of the many possible methods to monitor locking and blocking, Activity Monitor and Management Studio's Summary page provide the best overall view to determine whether locking and blocking is a problem. To home in on the specific locking and blocking issues, Profiler provides the actual code for the transactions involved.

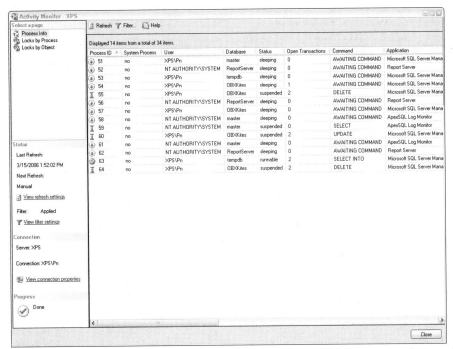

Figure 51-10: Activity Monitor displays a wealth of information about the current locks and any blocking going on.

The catch to using Profiler is that by default this event is configured as off. To enable the event, you have to configure the blocked process threshold setting. In addition, that's an advanced option, which must be first enabled. The following snippet sets the blocking duration to 1 second:

```
sp_configure 'show advanced options', 1;
GO
RECONFIGURE;
GO
sp_configure 'blocked process threshold', 1;
GO
RECONFIGURE;
```

The result is a complete XML-formatted disclosure of the blocked and blocking process (see Figure 51-11). Saving this trace to a file and analyzing it in total is an excellent locking and blocking debugging technique.

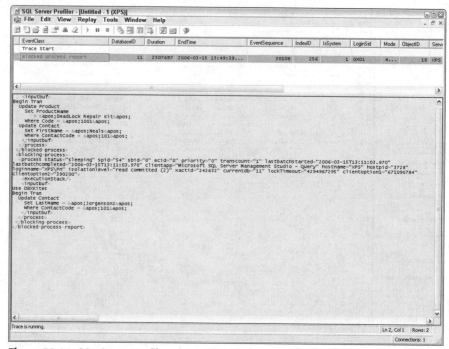

Figure 51-11: SQL Server Profiler can monitor and display the blocked and blocking code in XML.

Controlling SQL Server Locking

If you've written manual locking schemes in other database languages to overcome their locking deficiencies (as I have), you may feel as though you still need to control the locks. Let me assure you that the SQL Server lock manager can be trusted. Nevertheless, SQL Server exposes several methods of controlling locks, which are detailed in this section.

Best Practice

Don't apply lock hints or adjust the isolation level casually—trust the SQL Server lock manager to balance concurrency and transaction integrity. Only after you're positive that the database schema is well tuned and the code is polished should you consider tweaking the lock manager to solve a specific problem. When this is the case, setting select queries to no lock solves most problems.

Setting the Connection Isolation Level

The isolation level determines the duration of the share lock or exclusive lock for the connection. Setting the isolation level affects all queries and all tables for the duration of the connection, or until the isolation level is changed again. The following code sets a tighter-than-default isolation level and prevents non-repeatable reads:

```
SET TRANSACTION ISOLATION LEVEL REPEATABLE READ
```

The valid isolation levels are as follows:

- ✦ read uncommitted
- ✦ read committed
- ✦ repeatable read
- ✦ serializable
- ✦ snapshot

The current isolation level may be verified with the database consistency checker (DBCC):

```
DBCC USEROPTIONS
```

Results (abbreviated):

```
Set Option         Value
-----------------  ------------------
isolation level    repeatable read
```

Isolation levels may also be set on a query and table level by means of locking hints.

Using Database Snapshot Isolation

There are two variations of snapshot isolation: snapshot isolation and read committed snapshot isolation. Snapshot isolation operates like repeatable read isolation without the locking and blocking issues, while read committed snapshot isolation mimics SQL Server's default isolation level of read committed, again without the locking and blocking issues.

While transaction isolation is traditionally set at the connection level, snapshot isolation must be configured at the database level, as it effectively turns on row versioning in the database. Row versioning is the technology that makes a copy of the rows in TempDB for updating. Besides the TempDB load, row versioning also adds a 14-byte row identifier.

Using Snapshot Isolation

The following code turns on snapshot isolation. To alter the database and turn on snapshot isolation, there can no other connections to the database:

```
USE Aesop;

ALTER DATABASE Aesop
SET ALLOW_SNAPSHOT_ISOLATION ON
```

To determine whether snapshot isolation is enabled for the database, query select name, snapshot_isolation_state_desc from sysdatabases;

Transaction one now begins a reading transaction, leaving the transaction open (uncommitted) :USE Aesop

```
SET TRANSACTION ISOLATION LEVEL Snapshot;

BEGIN TRAN
SELECT Title
  FROM FABLE

  WHERE FableID = 2
```

Result:

```
Title
--------
The Bald Knight
```

A second transaction begins an update to the *same* row that the first transaction has open:

```
USE Aesop;
SET TRANSACTION ISOLATION LEVEL Snapshot;

BEGIN TRAN

UPDATE Fable
  SET Title = 'Rocking with Snapshots'
  WHERE FableID = 2;

SELECT * FROM FABLE WHERE FableID = 2
```

Result:

```
Title
--------------------------
Rocking with Snapshots
```

This is pretty amazing. The second transaction was able to update the row even though the first transaction is still open. Going back to the first transaction, it will still see the original data:

```
SELECT Title
  FROM FABLE

  WHERE FableID = 2
```

Result:

```
Title
--------
The Bald Knight
```

Opening up a third of fourth transaction, they would all still see the original value, The Bald Knight.

Even after the second transaction committed the change, the first transaction would still see the original value, but any new transactions would see 'Rocking with Snapshots'.

Using Read Committed Snapshot Isolation

Read committed snapshot isolation is enabled using a similar syntax:

```
ALTER DATABASE Aesop
  SET READ_COMMITTED_SNAPSHOT ON
```

Like snapshot isolation, read committed snapshot isolation uses row versioning to stave off locking and blocking issues. In the previous example, transaction one would see transaction two's update once it was committed.

Because read committed is SQL Server's default transaction isolation level, only the database option is required.

Handling Write Conficts

Transactions that write to the data within a snapshot isolation can be blocked by a previous uncommitted write transaction. This blocking won't cause the new transaction to wait; instead, it will generate an error. Be sure to use `try...catch` to handle these errors, wait a split second, and try again.

Using Locking Hints

Locking hints enable you to make minute adjustments in the locking strategy. While the isolation level affects the entire connection, locking hints are specific to one table within one query (see Table 51-5). The `with (locking hint)` option is placed after the table in the `from` clause of the query. You can specify multiple locking hints by separating them with commas.

Table 51-5: Locking Hints

Locking Hint	Description
ReadUnCommitted	Isolation level. Doesn't apply or honor locks. Same as no lock.
ReadCommitted	Isolation level. Uses the default transaction-isolation level.
RepeatableRead	Isolation level. Holds share and exclusive locks until `commit transaction`.
Serializable	Isolation level. Applies the serializable transaction isolation–level durations to the table, which holds the shared lock until the transaction is complete.
ReadPast	Skips locked rows instead of waiting.
RowLock	Forces row-level locks instead of page, extent, or table locks.
PagLock	Forces the use of page locks instead of a table lock.
TabLock	Automatically escalates row, page, or extent locks to the table-lock granularity.
NoLock	Doesn't apply or honor locks. Same as ReadUnCommitted.
TablockX	Forces an exclusive lock on the table. This prevents any other transaction from working with the table.
HoldLock	Holds the share lock until the `commit transaction`. (Same as Serializable.)
Updlock	Uses an update lock instead of a shared lock and holds the lock. This blocks any other writes to the data between the initial read and a write operation.
XLock	Holds an exclusive lock on the data until the transaction is committed.

The following query uses a locking hint in the from clause of an update query to prevent the lock manager from escalating the granularity of the locks:

```
USE OBXKites
UPDATE Product
  FROM Product WITH (RowLock)
  SET ProductName = ProductName + ' Updated'
```

If a query includes subqueries, don't forget that each query's table references will generate locks and can be controlled by a locking hint.

Index-Level Locking Restrictions

Isolation levels and locking hints are applied from the connection and query perspective. The only way to control locks from the table perspective is to restrict the granularity of locks on a per-index basis. Using the sp_indexoption system stored procedure, rowlocks and/or page-locks may be disabled for a particular index, as follows:

```
sp_indexoption
  'indexname',
  AllowRowlocks or AllowPagelocks,
  1 or 0
```

This is useful for a couple of specific purposes. If a table frequently causes waiting because of page locks, setting allowpagelocks to off will force rowlocks. The decreased scope of the lock will improve concurrency. In addition, if a table is seldom updated but frequently read, then row-level and page-level locks are inappropriate. Allowing only table locks is suitable during the majority of table accesses. For the infrequent update, a table-exclusive lock is not a big issue.

Sp_indexoption is for fine-tuning the data schema; that's why it's on an index level. To restrict the locks on a table's primary key, use sp_help tablename to find the specific name for the primary-key index.

The following commands configure the ProductCategory table as an infrequently updated lookup table. First, sp_help will report the name of the primary key index:

```
sp_help ProductCategory
```

Result (abridged):

```
index                          index           index
name                           description     keys
-----------------------------  -------------   -----------------
PK__ProductCategory__79A81403  nonclustered,   ProductCategoryID
                               unique,
                               primary key
                               located
                               on PRIMARY
```

Having identified the actual name of the primary key, the sp_indexoption system stored procedure can now set the index lock options:

```
EXEC sp_indexoption
  'ProductCategory.PK__ProductCategory__79A81403',
  'AllowRowlocks', FALSE
EXEC sp_indexoption
  'ProductCategory.PK__ProductCategory__79A81403',
  'AllowPagelocks', FALSE
```

Controlling Lock Timeouts

If a transaction is waiting for a lock, it will continue to wait until the lock is available. By default no timeout exists — it can theoretically wait forever.

Fortunately, you can set the lock time using the `set lock_timeout` connection option. Set the option to a number of milliseconds or set it to infinity (the default) by setting it to `-1`. Setting the `lock_timeout` to `0` means that the transaction will instantly give up if any lock contention occurs at all. The application will be very fast, and very ineffective.

The following query sets the lock timeout to two seconds (2,000 milliseconds):

```
SET Lock_Timeout 2000
```

When a transaction does time out while waiting to gain a lock, a 1222 error is raised.

I recommend setting a lock timeout in the connection. The length of the wait you should specify depends on the typical performance of the database. I usually set a five-second timeout.

Best Practice

Evaluating Database Concurrency Performance

It's easy to build a database that doesn't exhibit lock contention and concurrency issues when tested with a handful of users. The real test is when several hundred users are all updating orders.

Multi-user concurrency should be tested during the development process several times. To quote the MCSE exam guide, ". . . don't let the real test be your first test."

Best Practice

Concurrency testing requires a concerted effort. At one level, it can involve everyone available running the same front-end form concurrently. A .NET program that constantly simulates a user viewing data and updating data is also useful. A good test is to run 20 instances of a script that constantly pounds the database and then let the test crew use the application. Performance Monitor (covered in Chapter 49, "Measuring Performance") can watch the number of locks.

Application Locks

SQL Server uses a very sophisticated locking scheme. Sometimes a process or a resource other than data requires locking. For example, a procedure might need to run that would be ill affected if another user started another instance of the same procedure.

Several years ago, I wrote a program that routed cables for nuclear power plant designs. After the geometry of the plant (what's where) was entered and tested, the design engineers entered the cable-source equipment, destination equipment, and type of cable to be used. Once several cables were entered, a procedure wormed each cable through the cable trays so that cables were as short as possible. The procedure also considered cable failsafe routes and separated incompatible cables. While I enjoyed writing that database, if multiple instances of the worm procedure ran simultaneously, each instance attempted to route the cables and the data became fouled. An application lock is the perfect solution to that type of problem.

Application locks open up the whole world of SQL Server locks for custom uses within applications. Instead of using data as a locked resource, application locks use any named user resource declared in the sp_GetAppLock stored procedure.

Application locks must be obtained within a transaction. The lock mode (Shared, Update, Exclusive, IntentExclusive, or IntentShared) may be declared. The return code indicates whether or not the procedure was successful in obtaining the lock, as follows:

✦ 0: Lock was obtained normally

✦ 1: Lock was obtained after another procedure released it

✦ -1: Lock request failed (timeout)

✦ -2: Lock request failed (canceled)

✦ -3: Lock request failed (deadlock)

✦ -999:Lock request failed (other error)

The sp_ReleaseAppLock stored procedure releases the lock. The following code shows how the application lock can be used in a batch or procedure:

```
DECLARE @ShareOK INT
EXEC @ShareOK = sp_GetAppLock
                    @Resource = 'CableWorm',
                    @LockMode = 'Exclusive'
IF @ShareOK < 0
   ...Error handling code

  ... code ...

EXEC sp_ReleaseAppLock @Resource = 'CableWorm'
Go
```

When the application locks are viewed using Enterprise Manager or sp_Lock, the lock appears as an "APP"-type lock. The following is an abbreviated listing of sp_lock executed at the same time as the previous code:

```
Sp_Lock
```

Result:

```
spid  dbid  ObjId  IndId  Type  Resource        Mode  Status
----- ----- ------ ------ ----  --------------  ----- ------
57    8     0      0      APP   Cab11f94c136    X     GRANT
```

Note two minor differences from the way application locks are handled by SQL Server:

✦ Deadlocks are not automatically detected.

✦ If a transaction gets a lock several times, it will have to release that lock the same number of times.

Deadlocks

A deadlock is a special situation that occurs only when transactions with multiple tasks compete for the same data resource. For example:

✦ Transaction one has a lock on data A and needs to lock data B to complete its transaction.

and

✦ Transaction two has a lock on data B and needs to lock data A to complete its transaction.

Each transaction is stuck waiting for the other to release its lock, and neither can complete until the other does. Unless an outside force intercedes, or one of the transactions gives up and quits, this situation could last until the end of time.

In earlier days a deadlock was a serious problem. Fortunately, SQL Server handles deadlocks refreshingly well.

Creating a Deadlock

It's easy to create a deadlock situation in SQL Server using two connections in Management Studio's Query Editor, as illustrated in Figure 51-12. Transaction one and transaction two will simply try to update the same rows but in the opposite order. Using a third window to run pGetLocks will help you monitor the locking situation.

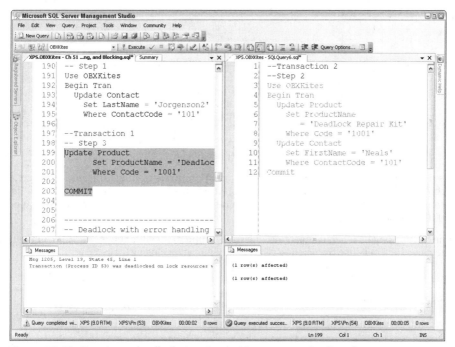

Figure 51-12: Creating a deadlock situation in Management Studio using two connections tiled vertically

To execute the code, you'll need to do the following:

1. Create a second window in Query Editor.

2. Move the code in step 2 to the second window.

3. In the first window, select the code in step 1 and execute it by pressing F5.

4. In the second window, execute step 2.

5. Back in the first window, execute step 3.

6. After a short moment, SQL Server will detect the deadlock and automatically resolve it.

Here's the code:

```
-- Transaction 1
-- Step 1
USE OBXKites
BEGIN TRANSACTION
UPDATE Contact
  SET LastName = 'Jorgenson'
  WHERE ContactCode = '101'
```

Transaction one now has an exclusive lock on ContactCode 101. Transaction two will gain an exclusive lock on ProductCode 1001 and then try to grab an exclusive lock on ContactCode 101, but transaction one already has it locked:

```
-- Transaction 2
-- Step 2
USE OBXKites
BEGIN TRANSACTION
  UPDATE Product
    SET ProductName
      = 'DeadLock Repair Kit'
    WHERE ProductCode = '1001'
  UPDATE Contact
    SET FirstName = 'Neals'
    WHERE ContactCode = '101'
COMMIT TRANSACTION
```

It's not a deadlock yet, because although transaction two is waiting for transaction one, transaction one is not waiting for transaction two. At this point, if transaction one finished its work and issued a commit transaction, the data resource would be freed; transaction two could get its lock on the contact row and be on its way as well.

The trouble begins when transaction one tries to update ProductCode 1001. It can't get an exclusive lock because transaction two already has an exclusive lock:

```
-- Transaction 1
-- Step 3
UPDATE Product
  SET ProductName
    = 'DeadLock Identification Tester'
  WHERE ProductCode = '1001'
COMMIT TRANSACTION
```

Transaction one returns the following friendly error message in about two seconds. The dead-lock can also be viewed using SQL Server Profiler (as shown in Figure 51-13):

```
Server: Msg 1205, Level 13,
  State 50, Line 1
Transaction (Process ID 51) was
  deadlocked on lock resources with
  another process and has been chosen
  as the deadlock victim. Rerun the
  transaction.
```

Transaction two completes as if there's no problem. Result:

```
(1 row(s) affected)
(1 row(s) affected)
```

Automatic Deadlock Detection

As the previous deadlock code demonstrated, SQL Server will automatically detect a dead-lock situation by examining the blocking processes and rolling back the transaction that has performed the least amount of work. A process within SQL Server is constantly checking for cross-blocking locks. The deadlock-detection delay typically ranges from instantaneous to two seconds. The longest I've waited for a deadlock to be detected is about five seconds.

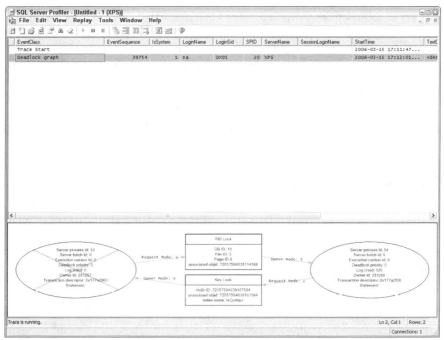

Figure 51-13: SQL Server Profiler can monitor deadlocks using the Locks: Deadlock Graph event and can display the resource conflict that caused the deadlock.

Handling Deadlocks

Once a deadlock occurs, the connection that's selected as the deadlock victim will need to perform the transaction again. Because the work will need to be redone, it's good that the transaction that has completed the least amount of work is the transaction that has to go back to the beginning and try again.

The error code 1205 will need to be trapped by the client application and the transaction should be re-executed. If all goes well, users will not be aware that a deadlock occurred.

Instead of letting SQL Server decide which transaction will be the "deadlock victim," a transaction can volunteer to serve as the deadlock victim. The following code inside a transaction will inform SQL Server that the transaction should be rolled back in case of a deadlock:

```
SET DEADLOCK_PRIORITY LOW
```

Minimizing Deadlocks

Even though deadlocks can be detected, it's better to avoid them altogether. The following practices will help prevent deadlocks:

✦ Keep a transaction short and to the point. Any code that doesn't have to be in the transaction should be left out of it.

✦ Never code a transaction to depend on user input.

✦ Try to write batches and procedures so that they obtain locks in the same order — for example, TableA, then TableB, then TableC. This way, one procedure will wait for the next, and a deadlock will be avoided.

✦ Plan the physical scheme to keep data that might be selected simultaneously close on the data page by normalizing the schema and carefully selecting the clustered indexes. Reducing the spread of the locks will help prevent lock escalation. Smaller locks will help prevent lock contention.

✦ Don't increase the isolation level unless it's necessary. A stricter isolation level will increase the duration of the lock.

Application Locking Design

Aside from SQL Server locks, another locking issue deserves to be addressed. How the front-end application holds locks and deals with multi-user contention is important to both the user's experience and the integrity of the data.

Implementing Optimistic Locking

The two basic means of dealing with multi-user access are *optimistic locking* and *pessimistic locking*. The one you use determines the coding methods of the application.

Optimistic locking assumes that no one else will attempt to change the data while a user is working on the data in a form. Therefore, optimistic locking does not apply locks while a user is working with data in the front-end application. The disadvantage of optimistic locking is that it can result in lost updates.

The pessimistic (or "Murphy") method takes a different approach: If anything can go wrong it will. When a user is working on some data, a pessimistic locking scheme locks that data.

While pessimistic locking may work in small workgroup applications on desktop databases, large client/server applications require higher levels of concurrency. If SQL Server locks are held while a user has data open in a VB or Access form, the application will be unreasonably slow.

The best method is to implement an optimistic locking scheme using minimal SQL Server locks as well as a method for preventing lost updates.

Lost Updates

A lost update occurs when two users edit the same row, complete their edits, and save the data, and the second user's update overwrites the first user's update. For example:

1. Joe opens Product "1001," a 21-inch box kite, in the Visual Basic front-end application. SQL Server applies a shared lock for a split second while retrieving the data for VB.

2. Sue also opens Product "1001" using the front-end application.

3. Joe and Sue both make edits to the box-kite data. Joe rephrases the product description, and Sue fixes the product category.

4. Joe saves the row from VB to SQL Server. The `update` command replaces the old product description with Joe's new description.

5. Sue presses the "save and close" button and her data are sent to SQL Server in an `update` statement. The product category is now fixed, but the old description was in Sue's form, so Joe's new description was overwritten with the old description.

6. Joe discovers the error and complains to the IT vice president during the next round of golf about the unreliability of that new SQL Server–based database.

Because lost updates only occur when two users edit the same row at the same time, the problem might not occur for months. Nonetheless, it's a flaw in the transactional integrity of the database and it needs to be prevented.

Minimizing Lost Updates

If the application is going to use an optimistic locking scheme, try to minimize the chance that a lost update can occur, as well as minimize the effects of a lost update, using the following methods:

✦ Normalize the database so that it has many long, narrow tables. With fewer columns in a row, the chance of a lost update is reduced. For example, the OBXKites database has a separate table for prices. A user can work on product pricing and not interfere with another user working on other product data.

✦ If the `update` statement is being constructed by the front-end application, have it check the controls and send an update for only those columns that are actually changed by the user. This technique alone would prevent the lost update in the previous example of Joe and Sue's updates, and most lost updates in the real world. As an added benefit, it reduces client/server traffic and the workload on SQL Server.

✦ If an optimistic locking scheme is not preventing lost updates, the application is using a "he who writes last, writes best" scheme. Although lost updates may occur, a data-audit trail can minimize the effect by exposing updates to the same row within minutes, and tracking the data changes.

Preventing Lost Updates

A stronger solution to the lost update problem than just minimizing the effect is to block lost updates using the rowversion method. The rowversion data type, previously known as a timestamp in earlier versions of SQL Server, automatically provides a new value every time the row is updated. By comparing the rowversion value retrieved during the row select and the rowversion value at the time of update, it's trivial for code to detect a lost update.

The rowversion method can be used in select and update statements by adding the rowversion value in the where clause of the update statement.

The following sequence demonstrates the rowversion technique using two user updates. Both users begin by opening the 21-inch box kite in the front-end application. Both select statements retrieve the RowVersion column and ProductName:

```
SELECT RowVersion, ProductName
  FROM Product
  WHERE ProductCode = '1001'
```

Result:

```
RowVersion              ProductName
------------------      -------------------------
0x0000000000000077 Basic Box Kite 21 inch
```

Both front-end applications can grab the data and populate the form. Joe edits the ProductName to "Joe's Update." When Joe is ready to update the database, the "save and close" button executes the following SQL statement:

```
UPDATE Product
  SET ProductName = 'Joe''s Update'
  WHERE ProductCode = '1001'
    AND RowVersion = 0x0000000000000077
```

Once SQL Server has processed Joe's update, it automatically updates the RowVersion value as well. Checking the row again, Joe sees that his edit took effect:

```
SELECT RowVersion, ProductName
  FROM Product
  WHERE ProductCode = '1001'
```

Result:

```
RowVersion              ProductName
------------------      -------------------------
0x00000000000000B9 Joe's Update
```

If the update procedure checks to see whether any rows were affected, it can detect that Joe's edit was accepted:

```
SELECT @@ROWCOUNT
```

Result:

```
1
```

Although the RowVersion column's value was changed, Sue's front-end application isn't aware of the new value. When Sue attempts to save her edit, the update statement won't find any rows meeting that criterion:

```
UPDATE Product
  SET ProductName = 'Sue''s Update'
  WHERE ProductCode = '1001'
    AND RowVersion = 0x0000000000000077
```

If the update procedure checks to see whether any rows were affected, it can detect that Sue's edit was ignored:

```
SELECT @@ROWCOUNT
```

Result:

```
0
```

This method can also be incorporated into applications driven by stored procedures. The fetch or get stored procedure returns the rowversion along with the rest of the data for the row. When the VB application is ready to update and calls the update stored procedure, it includes the rowversion as one of the required parameters. The update stored procedure can then check the rowversion and raise an error if the two don't match. If the method is sophisticated, the stored procedure or the front-end application can check the audit trail to see whether or not the columns updated would cause a lost update or report back the last user in the error message.

Transaction Performance Strategies

Transaction integrity theory can seem daunting at first and SQL Server has numerous tools to control transaction isolation. If the database is low usage or primarily read-only, transaction locking and blocking won't be a problem, but for heavy-usage OLTP databases you'll want to apply the theory and working knowledge from this chapter using these strategies. Because locking and blocking comprise the fourth optimization strategy, ensure that strategy one through three are covered before tackling locking and blocking:

1. Begin with the optimization theory: Start with a clean simplified schema to reduce the number of unnecessary joins and reduce the amount of code used to shuttle data from bucket to bucket.

2. Use efficient set-based code, rather than painfully slow iterative cursors or loops.

3. Use a solid indexing strategy to eliminate unnecessary table scans and to speed transactions.

To identify locking problems, using the Activity Monitor or SQL Profiler.

To reduce the severity of a locking problem, do the following:

✦ Evaluate and test using the read committed snapshot isolation level. Depending on your error handling and hardware capabilities, snapshot isolation can significantly reduce concurrency contention.

✦ Check the transaction-isolation level and make sure it's not any higher than required.

✦ Make sure transactions begin and commit quickly. Redesign any transaction that includes a cursor. Move any code that isn't necessary to the transaction out of the transaction.

✦ If two procedures are deadlocking, make sure they lock the resource in the same order.

✦ Make sure client applications are fetching access the database through the data abstraction layer.

✦ Consider forcing page locks with the (`rowlock`) hint to prevent the locks from escalating.

Summary

A transaction is a logical unit of work. Although the default SQL Server transaction isolation level works well for most applications, there are several means of manipulating and controlling the locks. To develop a serious SQL Server application, your understanding of the ACID database principles, SQL Server's transaction log, and locking will contribute to the quality, performance, and reliability of the database.

The next chapter adds the optimization strategy of high availability — moving beyond backup and restore to always there.

✦   ✦   ✦

Providing High Availability

◆ ◆ ◆ ◆

In This Chapter

Configuring a warm
standby server with
Enterprise Manager or
SQL Server Agent

Understanding failover
clusters and availability

◆ ◆ ◆ ◆

The *availability* of a database refers to the overall reliability of the system. The Information Architecture Principle, discussed in Chapter 1, lays the foundation for availability in the phrase "readily available." Defining readily available varies by the organization and the data. A database that's highly available is one that rarely goes down. For some databases, being down for an hour is not a problem; for others, 30 seconds of downtime is a catastrophe. Organization requirements, budget constraints, and other resources will dictate the proper solution.

A plan for maintaining availability is executed at three distinct cascading levels:

1. Maintaining the primary database's availability

2. Providing a near-instant substitute, or secondary, database

3. Recovering from a lost database

Several methods of increasing availability are unrelated to SQL Server proper. The quality and redundancy of the hardware, the quality of the electrical power, preventive maintenance of the machines and replacement of the hard drives, the security of the server room — all of these contribute to the availability of the primary database. The first line of availability defense is quality hardware.

If a database is lost because of hardware failure, the third level of availability is executed and the database must be recovered according to the methods detailed in Chapter 36, "Recovery Planning." Even in the best of circumstances, recovering a database requires several minutes to an hour, and a more likely scenario is half a day to rebuild a server and recover the data. Moreover, some data might be lost, depending on the recovery plan.

Advanced availability, the ability to handle a failure and switch to another server, is the layer between quality hardware and a last-resort recovery operation, and is often the difference between several hours of downtime and a few seconds.

Best Practice

Before implementing the middle layer of advanced availability, ensure that the primary server layer is well thought out and that the disaster recovery planning is complete. Money spent on implementing a software solution, if the primary computer's drives provide no redundancy, is wasted money.

SQL Server 2005 with Service Pack 1 provides three options for advanced availability: log shipping, failover clustering, and database mirroring.

Cross-Reference   Some IT shops have implemented transactional replication to keep a backup server in sync with the primary server. The advantage of this method is that each transaction is individually moved to the backup server. The disadvantage is that any software developed to use replication as a redundant option implies a number of database design considerations. Replication is covered in Chapter 39, "Replicating Data."

Availability Testing

A database that's unavailable isn't very useful. The availability test is a simulation of the database restore process assuming the worst. The measurement is the time required to restore the most current production data to a test server and prove that the client applications work.

Warm-Standby Availability

Warm-standby refers to a database that has a copy set up on separate hardware. A warm-standby solution can be achieved with log shipping. Log shipping involves periodically restoring a transaction log backup from the primary server to a warm-standby server, making that server ready to recover at a moment's notice. In case of a failure, the recovery server and the most recent transaction-log backups are ready to go. Because of this, log shipping can be implemented without exotic hardware and is significantly cheaper. However, log shipping has a few drawbacks:

✦ When the primary server fails, any transactions made since the last time the log was shipped to the warm-standby server will be lost. For this reason, log shipping is usually set to occur every few minutes.

✦ The switch is not transparent. Some code must be executed on the warm-standby server, and front-end application connections must redirect the data source and reconnect to the warm standby server. Sample code to illustrate this is provided later in this chapter.

✦ An Integration Services job must be created and periodically run to move user logins from the primary server to the warm-standby server.

✦ Once the primary server is repaired, returning to the original configuration requires manual DBA intervention.

If these issues are acceptable, log shipping to a warm-standby server can be an excellent safeguard against downtime.

Ideally, the primary server and the warm-standby server should be in different locations so that a disaster in one location will not affect the other. In addition, log shipping can place a large demand on a network every few minutes while the transaction logs are being moved. If the two servers can be connected with a private high-speed network, log shipping can take place without affecting other network users and the bandwidth they require.

Log Shipping

The high-end edition of SQL Server includes a Log Shipping Wizard (integrated into the Database Maintenance Plan Wizard) that creates a maintenance plan to back up, copy, and restore the transaction log from the primary server to the warm-standby server every few minutes.

The Servers

Log shipping normally involves three SQL Servers: a primary server, a warm-standby server, and a monitor server.

✦ The *primary server* is the main server to which clients normally connect. This server should be a high-quality server with redundant disk drives.

✦ The *warm-standby server* is the backup server, otherwise known as the *secondary server*. If the source server fails, it becomes the primary server. This server should be capable of meeting the minimum performance requirements during a short-term crisis.

✦ The *monitor server* polls both the primary server and the warm-standby server by keeping track of what files have been sent where, generating an alert when the two are out of sync. A single monitor server can monitor multiple log shipping configurations.

The monitor server can be an instance on the destination server, but locating the monitor server on the source server would be a self-defeating plan. If the source server physically failed, the monitor server would also fail and the destination server would not receive a signal to go live. The best practice is to assign a monitor server to its own hardware.

Best Practice

Each primary-server database can have only one log-shipping plan, and each plan can ship only one database. However, a plan may ship to multiple destination servers.

Configuring Log Shipping with Enterprise Manager

Log shipping can be configured by using one of two methods: either by using Management Studio or by using system stored procedures. With either method of configuration, disk space will need to be created and shared. Both the primary and all the secondary servers need to be able to read and write into that directory share. The following steps create a log shipping configuration using SQL Server Management Studio:

1. In the Object Explorer on the primary server in SQL Server Management Studio, right-click on the database that will be log shipping and look at the database properties.

2. On the Transaction Log Shipping page, check the box that Enables transaction log shipping.

3. Configure the backup settings by clicking the Backup Setting button. Enter either the network share or the local directory that is shared. This is the location where transaction logs are stored before being copied to the secondary server.

Tip

A network share that is not located on the primary server will better protect the database in case of a hardware failure on the primary server.

4. Enter an amount of time after which the transaction log files should be deleted. For example, if the files should be deleted after one day, then the Delete Files Older Than option should equal one day.

5. Enter an amount of time that the server should wait to send an alert if no new transaction log files are found. For example, if the server has not seen a transaction log backup in the past three hours, then the alert If No Backup Occurs Within option should be set to three hours.

Note   The longer the length of the alert time, the higher the risk. With a long alert setting, a transaction log backup failure will result in a larger amount of data loss.

6. Schedule the job that will back up the transaction log by setting the job's name, time, and frequency. A shorter duration between transaction log backups will minimize the amount of data that could be lost.

Tip   Make sure that the only transaction log backup that occurs is scheduled through the Transaction Log Shipping page. Otherwise, not all the data changes will be propagated to the secondary servers.

7. Add the secondary servers to the transaction log configuration by clicking the Add button under the secondary instance's window. Multiple secondary instances can be added here by repeating steps 7 through 14.

8. On the secondary database screen, connect to the server that will be the secondary server and enter the database name for the secondary database. If the database is not there it will be created.

9. Initialize the secondary database by selecting either the option to have log shipping start with a backup it will create when you are completed or the option to have it use the last known backup. If you select to use the last backup that was created, the name of the directory in which the backup is located will need to be supplied. There is also the option of not initializing at all.

10. The Copy Files tab designates where the backup files and the transaction log files will be copied. This tab also has a setting that enables files to be deleted after a designated time.

It's a good idea to have the files copied to the secondary server of a third location. This ensures that the files are available in case of a problem with the hardware on the primary database.

Best Practice

11. On the Copy Files tab, set when the files are to be copied through the job.

12. On the Restore Transaction Logs tab, choose either no recovery mode or standby mode. Standby will allow access to the secondary server for read-only operations. If the standby mode is selected, the option to have the user connection killed during the transaction log restore is available. The no recovery mode option will not allow any database access to the secondary database.

13. On the Restore Transaction Log tab, the option for delaying a restore and alerting is available as well. This configuration option enables all the transaction logs to be held until the end of the business day or to apply the transaction logs as soon as they are received.

14. The option for more granularities on restores and when they are applied are set in the job on the Restore Transaction Logs tab.

15. Click OK to complete the secondary database setup, and return to the database's Properties tab.

16. Once the secondary database setups have been completed, a monitor server can be configured on the database's Properties tab. In addition, the option of scripting the setup is available.

Tip   If your log shipping has a number of non-default options, scripting your changes makes it easier to ensure that each time it is done the configuration stays the same.

17. Once you click OK on the Properties tab, the Save Log Shipping Configuration dialog box sets up the log shipping.

To remove log shipping, open the database properties and click on the Transaction Log Shipping page. Clear the Log Shipping check box and then click OK.

Monitoring Log Shipping

To monitor log shipping, several tables and stored procedures can be used. The information that can be retrieved from these sources includes the database name, last backup, last restore, time since last restore, and whether the alerts are enabled.

The following is a list of the tables that can be used to monitor log shipping:

✦ log_shipping_monitor_alert

✦ log_shipping_monitor_error_detail

✦ log_shipping_monitor_history_detail

✦ log_shipping_monitor_primary

✦ log_shipping_monitor_secondary

These tables exist in the MSDB database (because log shipping is mainly executed by a collection of jobs) on all the servers that are involved in the log shipping configuration.

The following is a list of stored procedures that can be used to monitor log shipping. They exist on all the servers in the master database that are involved in the log shipping configuration:

✦ sp_help_log_shipping_monitor_primary

✦ sp_help_log_shipping_monitor_secondary

✦ sp_help_log_shipping_alert_job

✦ sp_help_log_shipping_primary_database

✦ sp_help_log_shipping_primary_secondary

✦ sp_help_log_shipping_secondary_database

✦ sp_help_log_shipping_secondary_primary

Also helpful is a transaction log shipping report that monitors the log shipping. This report is found under Reports on the summary page of the server.

Switching Roles

Log shipping enables the capability to manually switch roles. This action can be performed for maintenance or in the case of a disaster. Depending on the cause of the disaster and its severity, the likely first step is to execute the transaction log backup job on the primary server. If the disaster is data corruption, then you should not execute this step — to ensure that bad data does not make it over to the secondary server.

To transfer to the secondary server, you first need to copy the transaction log files either using a SQL Agent job or copying them manually. Once copied, the transaction logs need to be restored in sequential order to the secondary server. The last transaction log is restored using the WITH RECOVERY option to close any open transactions and bring the SQL Server up in an updateable state. Ideally, these steps should be executed and documented prior to needing to failover to the secondary server.

Configuring a Read-Only Standby Query Server

In SQL Server 2005, log shipping configuration changes are much easier than in earlier versions of SQL Server. To change a secondary database that is read-only to allow reads is very simple. A log-shipped database can reduce the load of an over-active primary server, by transferring reads to the secondary server. To accomplish this action simply follow these steps:

1. In SQL Server Management Studio, right-click on the database to access the database's properties.

2. Click on the Transaction Log Shipping page to access the transaction log shipping information.

3. Edit the properties of the log shipping secondary node by clicking on the ellipsis (. . .).

4. Change the restore option on the transaction log's Restore tab and click OK.

5. Click OK on the Transaction Log page and the Log Shipping Configuration dialog will execute the changes and display the status.

From that point on, any data access that needs read access and not write access can access the secondary node, relieving the primary database server of reads.

Shipping the Users

Neither the log shipping in SQL Server Management Studio nor the stored procedures synchronize the server logins between the primary server and the warm-standby server. If the warm-standby server becomes the current live server but no one can log in, then it will be the same to the users as if the server were down. It's important, therefore, to move the user logins from the primary server to the warm-standby server. The best way to do that is to create an Integration Services job that connects to each server and transfers the users. If you are routinely adding several users, you may want to schedule this job to run several times per day; otherwise, once daily should suffice.

Returning to the Original Primary Server

Once the primary server has been repaired and is ready to return to service, the following steps reinitialize the primary server during a period when users are not connected:

1. Use Integration Services job to move all the user logins from the warm-standby server to the primary server.

2. Transfer the database from the warm-standby server to the primary server using either a full backup and restore or a detach and attach.

Failover Servers and Clustering

The best method to achieve high-availability recovery is to implement failover servers by clustering. A cluster enables multiple servers (the number of server depends on the OS) to appear as a single virtual SQL Server. The user connects to the virtual SQL Server and is unaware of which physical server is processing the request.

A SQL Server cluster is not a network load balancing cluster, which provides scalability for web servers. SQL Server clusters provide redundancy, not scalability. Clusters do not balance the SQL load.

This method requires Windows 2003 clusters and a shared disk subsystem. Each server requires a connection (usually SCSI or optical) to the shared disk subsystem. Because both servers use the same disk subsystem, they share the same transaction log and data file; however, only one server at a time owns the file resource. The cluster also uses a high-speed network dedicated to the clustering servers (usually optical), which serves as the heartbeat. Hardware manufacturers make specific models and configurations for clustering, and an OEM (Original Equipment Manufacturer)–specific version of Windows 2000 Server must be purchased with the hardware. Using failover servers and clustering costs several times more than using a warm-standby server.

Each server in the cluster may be active or passive. An active/passive cluster is referred to as a *single-instance cluster*. A cluster with multiple active servers (at least one database per server) is a *multiple-instance cluster*. If an active server fails, a designated passive server automatically becomes active and takes over from the shared transaction log and data file. From the user's perspective a failover looks just like a failed connection. Many applications are designed to see this; when they do, they wait a few seconds and try to reconnect. Applications that are developed this way can present the user with a transparent failover.

Best Practice

If you are planning to implement failover clusters, I recommend the SQL Server 2005 Resource Kit, which contains five chapters on high availability; it's also a good idea to read as many white papers as possible from your hardware vendor. A visit to an IT shop running clustering using the proposed equipment would be time well spent. If your hardware vendor won't supply a list of suitable referral sites, keep shopping.

Failover SQL Server Installs

In many ways, a failover clustering install is not different from a normal SQL Server install. One of the reasons for this is because clustering is an operation of the operating systems. To configure a SQL Server cluster, the operating system must first be set up as a cluster system. Once this has been completed, the operating system configuration has a virtual server name. SQL Server is installed on the virtual operating system with another virtual server name and IP. Figure 52-1 shows the layout of the physical servers and the virtual servers.

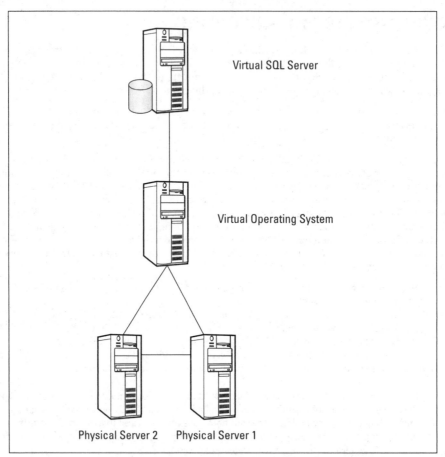

Figure 52-1: Users connect to the virtual SQL Server, which is then passed to the active physical SQL Server through the cluster.

Configuring

Once the operating system has been clustered, the SQL Server install can begin. SQL Server clustering is available in Enterprise Edition. Before starting, ensure that the account logged in on the server can add NT users to NT groups. The following steps walk through the SQL Server Enterprise install of clustering:

1. Start the Enterprise Edition of the installer. The installer will recognize that the operating system has been clustered. Continue through a normal install until you reach the Microsoft SQL Server Setup dialog screen that asks which services you would like to install.

2. When you select the SQL Server Database Server option, check Create a SQL Server Failover Cluster. Select any other options that are required in the install, such as notification services or integration services. Then click Next.

3. The option of a default instance or named instance is not available. Select your option and click next.

4. This screen requires a virtual server name. This is the name of the server that will be distributed to connect to the cluster. Click Next.

5. This screen requires that the virtual SQL Server has its own IP address. Enter the IP address, click add, and then click OK.

6. The next screen will require you to assign the SQL Server to a valid disk cluster. Select the appropriate disk cluster and click Next.

Best Practice

The cluster on the operating system level uses a *quorum drive*. This drive is used to store all the configurations of the cluster nodes and the current owner of the resources (files). It is a best practice not to place your SQL resources on the quorum drive.

7. The Cluster Node Configuration screen is where you add nodes to the cluster. Add the secondary node and click Next.

8. Enter the account name and password under which the SQL Server and related services will run.

9. Assign the groups or accounts that will control the resources. The account that you are logged in to at the time of the install needs to be able to assign users to groups. Click Next. The rest of the install at this point is just like the standard install.

Best Practice

Once clustering has been installed, let the operating system manage the stopping and starting of all the services. I would not recommend starting or stopping any of the SQL Server services via SQL Server Management Studio.

Best Practice

When you install service packs, make sure that you read the information on how to do the installs on clustered systems. Many of them allow you to install the service pack on the secondary node prior to failing the server over to the second node as the resource owner. This will then give you the time to install the service pack on the primary node while the secondary node answers all query requests.

After the install has completed, make sure that time is spent failing between the nodes of the cluster to ensure that the cluster has been installed correctly. Database activity can now resume as normal by connecting to the virtual name that was assigned in step 4. Clustering sounds much more advanced than it is, and with recent improvements in Windows 2000 and Windows 2003, management and installation gets easier with each iteration.

Database Mirroring

The solution that resides between clustering and log shipping is the very exciting capability to mirror a database from the primary server to a secondary server and switch from the primary to the secondary almost seamlessly. A third server, called the *witness,* watches both the primary server and secondary server and then notifies the secondary server to activate if the primary server goes down.

What makes database mirroring such a cool and flexible feature is that it does not depend on specific hardware or the distance between nodes. Database mirroring is the combination of failover clustering without the expensive hardware, and log shipping without all the manual intervention. For added redundancy, database mirroring can be used in combination with log shipping and clustering.

New in 2005 One of the most anticipated new SQL Server 2005 features is database mirroring. Database mirroring requires the installation of SQL Server 2005 Service Pack 1, however. This feature was not available in the original release without trace flag 14000 enabled.

Prerequisites

Like transaction log shipping, database mirroring relies on the transaction logs to keep the mirror data current. Because of this, the database that is going to be mirrored must be in *full recovery mode*.

Each database that is going to participate in database mirroring needs to have database endpoints configured. This is done manually through T-SQL or by using the wizard on the mirroring page. The configuration section demonstrates the wizard; however, the command used to create these manually is the Create Endpoint syntax.

The database that is going to be mirrored should be on each server before the configuration steps are taken. The best way to do this is to back up the principal server and then restore it on the mirror. When the database is restored, it should be done in *no recovery mode*. This will ensure that the endpoints are set up correctly and that the data is ready to be mirrored as soon as the few steps have completed.

Configuring

To configure database mirroring, follow these steps:

1. In the Object Explorer, right-click on the principal database and select the database's Properties.

2. Click on the Mirroring page.

3. Start the Security Wizard. This configures the database endpoints after you click the Configure Security button.

4. Click through the customary welcome screen.

5. Indicate whether you want to use a witness server. This configuration uses a witness server. By using a witness server, the security endpoints are stored on all systems other than the witness server.

6. Click to store the security on the witness as well. Click Next.

7. Set the port number and name the endpoint. Check the Encrypt box to ensure that all the data is kept in a secure manner. Click Next.

8. Set the mirror server up by selecting the name from the drop-down. If the server name is not in the drop-down options, click Connect to add it. You can adjust the port number here, as well as the mirror's endpoint name.

9. Complete the same information for the witness server. If the witness server is a second instance on either the principal or the mirror, the port numbers must be different. Click Next.

10. If, for security considerations, separate accounts need to be used on the separate servers, enter them here and click Next.

11. The Verify and Create screen appears. Once it has completed, a dialog box will appear asking whether database mirroring should be started. In this case, click Start Mirroring.

Tip
To remove database mirroring, return to the Mirroring page under the properties of the database in the Object Explorer. Simply click Remove Mirroring.

Architecting the Environment

The solutions described in this chapter may not work for everyone, but many of these solutions can be combined to create an environment that meets all the business needs. With the combination of high-availability systems, SQL Server 2005 scales horizontally better in SQL Server 2005 than in any previous editions of SQL Server.

Figure 52-2 illustrates how database mirroring, transaction log shipping, and failover clustering can be combined to create a highly redundant system with failover capabilities and a server that can be used as an online data store (a holding area before data goes into a data warehouse). The server in Chicago can be the witness to the cluster servers in Los Angeles and New York. This keeps production servers up and serving requests. The transaction log shipping keeps the online data store up-to-date with data so the data warehouse can be updated.

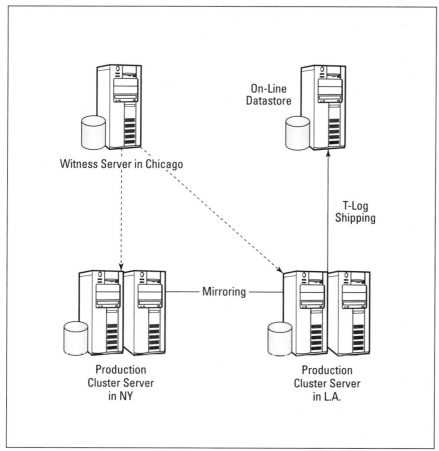

Figure 52-2: Database mirroring uses a witness to check the pulse of the mirrored databases.

Summary

Availability is paramount to the success of most database projects, and is becoming increasingly important in regard to business requirements. Log shipping, failover clusters, and database mirroring are all high-end techniques to provide a stable database environment for the users.

Log shipping backs up the log every few minutes and restores it on the warm-standby server with a no restore option so the warm-standby server is ready to go live at a moment's notice. However, log shipping requires manual intervention. Therefore, log shipping works best when trying to offload processes from a production server and up-to-the-second data is not required.

Failover clusters configure multiple servers that share a single disk subsystem into a single virtual server, which provides a seamless switch from one physical server to another in case of a server fault. The only downfall to failover clusters either active/active or active/passive is the resulting loss of connection to running queries. However, a well-designed application will wait 10 seconds and retry the connection before returning an error, which gives the end user the impression that the server was just slow and did not have a hardware failure.

Database mirroring can be the next best thing for geographical load balancing and disaster planning. Consider a database server in San Francisco damaged in an earthquake. A database server that has been mirrored in Omaha can pick up the load without any loss of business processes.

A cousin to availability is scalability — the capability of a server to handle increasing numbers of users and data. The next chapter provides a framework for understanding scalability, and offers practical techniques to improve the scalability of your projects.

✦   ✦   ✦

Scaling Very Large Databases

I n years past I've enjoyed gardening. One year I had four rows of corn, a 10-foot-square mountain of fresh peas, and about a dozen other vegetables. The watermelon vines nearly took over the back-yard. The process was easy. I spent one Saturday tilling and planting and then a relaxing half an hour a day weeding or harvesting as the crops came in. Voila! We had fresh veggies for supper.

When driving cross-country from North Carolina to Colorado, I drove for hours through the heartland and saw nothing but corn.

The contrast between managing my quarter-acre family garden and the statewide mega-farms of Kansas illustrates scalability perfectly. Each scale of problem needs its own set of solutions.

Moving from a small scale to a large scale can be addressed by *scaling out* or by *scaling up*.

Scaling out applies more of the same solution. Scaling out the agriculture analogy would apply more of my manual gardening techniques to the farm by bringing in a thousand helping hands to attempt to plant, weed, and harvest manually.

To compare, scaling up brings more sophistication to the solution. A combine is a farmer's way of scaling up. Moving from a tiller to a tractor is scaling up.

Another point from the farm analogy is to use the right-sized solution for the problem. Bringing in a combine for a family garden just won't work.

To contrast availability with scalability, availability is agreeing with your neighbor that if either of your combines breaks down, you'll help each other out. Think of it as a failover plan for your combine.

For web servers, scaling out means adding more servers to the web farm. SQL Server doesn't work that way; you typically can't add another database server (except perhaps in some replicated topologies). Therefore, for the purposes of this chapter, I'll define scaling out SQL Server as adding more hardware to handle an increased load without modifying the database. Applying the advanced scalability features of SQL Server 2005 is scaling up.

Optimization Theory and Scalability

Designing a database that will scale requires more than just turning on a cool new technology or adding a *storage area network (SAN)*. Optimization theory explains the dependencies between optimization techniques, and these advanced techniques are dependent on the underlying layers.

The most scalable database will be one with a simplified schema, well-crafted set-based code, excellent indexing, and minimal concurrency conflicts. When these four levels are all optimized, you can then focus on the advanced scalability technologies. That's why advanced scalability tuning is the top level of optimization theory.

If your manager thinks he can improve database performance by buying a SAN and turning on an Enterprise Edition scalability feature while bypassing optimization theory's foundational layers, he'll throw money away. I've seen databases limp on eight-way servers with a SAN that I believe would have run great on a four-way server with local disk subsystems — if only management would have invested in the layers of optimization theory. The application would perform better today and be more scalable in the future if management would invest in cleaning up the schema and in refactoring the iterative code rather than just running the slow database on a faster box and writing new wrappers around the old database schema.

Scaling Out the Platform

Assuming that the database has been optimized with optimization theory levels 1–4, here are my personal suggestions for designing a scalable hardware platform:

✦ Dedicate the server to SQL Server. Don't use the server for file or printer services, and no exchange, and no IIS.

✦ Balance the performance of the CPUs, memory, and disk subsystems, but add more memory than you think is needed, because SQL Server can use memory to reduce the load from the CPU and disk subsystems. I recommend maxing out the physical memory limitations of the server and using an edition of Windows Server that will support the memory; always buy the fastest memory available.

✦ The scalability bottleneck is typically the disk subsystem throughput. If you can use a SAN for your disk subsystem, do so. A properly configured SAN will scale further than local disk subsystems. SANs offer four significant benefits. They spread the files across several disk spindles. They use a high-speed fiber optic connection. They typically include a very large RAM buffer to absorb bursts of traffic. And SANs can usually perform a hardware level snapshot backup and restore.

The downside is that SANs cost 40–50 times as much as local disk space, and they are very difficult to configure and tune, so encourage the SAN administrator to focus on the database requirements and carefully configure the database LUNs so the database isn't lost in the organization's common file traffic. This can be very difficult to do, especially when file server and database traffic are combined on the same SAN.

✦ Use log shipping or replication to create a read-only reporting database.

 Cross-Reference   Replication is explained in Chapter 39, "Replicating Data," and log shipping and database mirroring are discussed in Chapter 52, "Providing High Availability."

✦ Consider using a solid-state RAM drive for tempdb or the Windows swap file.

Scalability and Business Processes

Issues of scale, and how different levels of volume require different levels of sophistication, apply to other areas of an organization as well. Receiving payments and processing orders come to mind. As data professionals, we need to be attuned to how data moves within an organization.

On a small scale, voice communication is workable. As the organization grows, face-to-face communication isn't viable, and e-mail or SharePoint become the standard tool of communication. These too eventually fail as the organization begins to lose communication in the hundreds of e-mails.

As IT developers, we tend to think of "the user" as a common ubiquitous knowledge worker. They enter data in, and the database saves it and returns it when queried. One look at the one-size-serves-all GUI applications demonstrates this viewpoint.

As organizations grow, it's not the knowledge worker to database flow that is the problem; it's the knowledge worker to knowledge worker flow of the data that's the real issue. Designing applications that incorporate this flow and assist the organization in handling process flow exceptions is the real scalability solution.

If you aren't using a SAN, here are my recommendations for configuring local direct attached storage (DAS). Each DAS disk subsystem has its own disk controller:

✦ Using a large RAID 5 disk array and placing all the files on the array may be easy to configure, but it will cost you performance. The goal of the disk subsystem is more than redundancy. You want to separate different files onto dedicated disks for specific purposes.

✦ When choosing drives, go for throughput. Currently, Ultra 320 SCSI drives offer the fastest throughput, although SATA 2 drives are gaining, and there are some interesting SATA RAID controllers. Spindle speed is the other key factor in throughput. There is a direct correlation between the speed of the spindle and how much data can be read from, or written to, the disk in a millisecond; 15K rpm drives are currently top of the line.

✦ SQL Server is optimized to read and write sequentially from the disk subsystem for both data files and transaction logs, so use RAID 1 (mirrored), which is also optimized for sequential operations, rather than RAID 5, which is better for random access.

✦ The goal for database disk subsystems is not to use the largest disk available, but to use more spindles. Using two 73GB drives is far better than a single 146GB drive.

✦ The transaction log for any database that sees significant updates should be on a dedicated DAS so that the heads can stay near the end of the transaction log without moving to other files. In addition, be sure to put enough memory on the disk controller to buffer a burst of transactions.

✦ SQL Server adds additional threads to handle additional data files, so it's far better to use three data files on three DAS subsystems than a single larger file. Using multiple files to spread the load across multiple drives is better than manually using multiple filegroups to separate tables.

✦ SQL Server 2005's Query Optimizer makes heavy use of `tempdb`. The best disk optimization you can do is to dedicate a DAS to `tempdb` and, of course, another disk to `tempdb`'s transaction log. Placing tempdb on multiple files across multiple DAS disk subsystems is another good idea.

✦ Windows wants to have a quick swap file. Regardless of how much physical memory is in the server, configure a large swap file and place it on a dedicated disk subsystem.

✦ To recap scaling out a non-SAN disk subsystem, Table 53-1 lists one possible configuration of disk subsystems.

Table 53-1: Scaling Non-SAN Disk Subsystems

Logical Drive	Purpose
C:	Windows System and SQL Server executables
D:	Windows Swap file
E:	TempDB Data File
F:	TempDB Transaction Log
G:	Data File
H:	Transaction Log
I: ...	Additional Data Files

Note Common wisdom holds that SANs performs about four times faster than DAS disk subsystems. Using Dr. Jim Gray's research, however, Microsoft Consulting Services recently built a system-24 Tb data warehouse, using 48 SATA drives, and achieved throughputs equal to a SAN (2.2GB per second for sequential reads and 2.0GB for sequential writes) at about 1/40 the cost.

Read more at www.sqlmag.com/Article/ArticleID/49557/sql_server_49557 .html.

Of course, another option for scaling out is moving from Standard Edition to Enterprise Edition to enable more CPU sockets, or moving to a 64-bit edition of SQL Server 2005.

Scaling Up the Solution

The pinnacle of optimization theory's pyramid is advanced scalability tuning. SQL Server 2005 offers several technologies and means of scaling up the sophistication level of the database solution to improve performance:

✦ Service Broker can buffer requests, increasing scalability during peak load times. Service Broker is covered in Chapter 28, "Queuing Data with Service Broker."

✦ The read-committed snapshot isolation level offers high-performance read operations without concurrency conflicts with write operations. Snapshot isolation is discussed in Chapter 51, "Managing Transactions, Locking, and Blocking."

Enterprise Edition adds these potential scalability enhancements:

✦ Partitioned tables and indexes can intelligently spread the data load across multiple files, reducing maintenance overhead while improving both select and update performance.

✦ Indexed views can build clustered indexes on views that effectively denormalize a materialized view.

✦ Online indexing and parallel index operations can improve the performance of the database during maintenance.

This chapter details these Enterprise Edition scalability features.

Partitioned Tables and Indexes

To *partition* a table is to split the table into two or more smaller segments based on a defined range of data. The partitions are most effective when the partition key is a column often used to select a range of data, so that a query has a good chance of addressing only one of the segments. For example:

✦ An organization has representatives in five distinct regions; splitting the order table by region will enable each representative's queries to likely access only that representative's partition.

✦ A manufacturing company partitions a large activity-tracking table into several smaller tables, one for each department, knowing that each of the production applications tends to query a single department's data.

✦ A financial company has a couple of terabytes of historical data and must be able to easily query across current and historical data. However, the majority of current activity deals with only the current data. Segmenting the data by era enables the current-activity queries to access a much smaller table.

New in 2005
SQL Server 2000 has distributed partition views and federated databases, but they are difficult to configure and use. While the theory isn't new, the implementation in this version is. SQL Server 2005's table partitioning is much easier to configure and manage. SQL Server 2000's distributed partition views are still supported for backward compatibility, but you should upgrade them to partitioned tables.

Partitioning tables reduces the sheer size of the clustered and non-clustered b-tree indexes, which provides these scalability benefits:

✦ Inserts and update operations must also insert and update index pages. When a table is partitioned, only the affected partition's indexes are updated.

✦ Index maintenance can be a costly operation. A partition's index will be significantly smaller and will reduce the performance cost of reindexing or defragmenting the index.

✦ Backing up part of a table using Backup Filegroups eases backups.

✦ The smaller index b-tree speeds index seeks.

✦ Perhaps the most significant scalability benefit for a partitioned table is that SQL Server can use parallel CPU operations when working with partitioned tables.

Best Practice The performance benefit of partitioned tables doesn't kick in until the table is extremely large — billion-row tables in terabyte-size databases. In fact, in some testing, partitioned tables actually hurt performance on smaller tables with less than a million rows, so reserve this technology for the big problems. Maybe that's why table partitioning isn't included in Standard Edition.

Creating SQL Server 2005 table partitions is a straightforward four-step process:

1. Create the partition function that will determine how the data will be segmented.

2. Create the partition scheme that assigns partitions to filegroups.

3. Create the table with a non-clustered primary key.

4. Create a clustered index for the table using the partition scheme and partition function.

Partition functions and partition schemes work together to segment the data as illustrated in Figure 53-1.

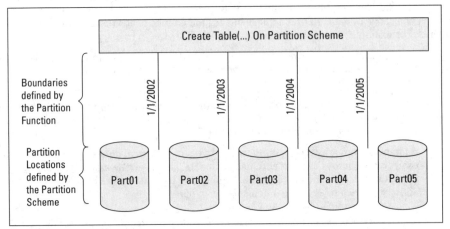

Figure 53-1: The partition function is used by the partition scheme to place the data in separate filegroups.

 On The Web This demo uses the database `PartitionDemo`, which has three filegroups: `Primary`, `Part1`, and `Part2`. You can download the script from `www.SQLServerBible.com`.

Creating the Partition Function

A *partition function* is simply a means to define the boundaries that will separate the partitions.

A table partition can segment the data based on a single column. Even though the table isn't yet defined, the function must know the segmenting column's data type, so the partition function's parameter is the data type that will be used to segment the data. In the following example, the function `fnYears` will accept `datetime` data.

An important aspect of partitions is that they function only as separators; they don't define the upper or lower max ranges of the tables. As a separator, a partition boundary typically defines the upper end of a partition. The data above the highest boundary is considered the *next* partition.

Boundaries, or ranges, are defined as left or right. Left ranges mean that data equal to the boundary is included in the partition to the left of the boundary. A boundary of `'12/31/2004'` would create two partitions. The lower partition would include all data up to and including `'12/31/2004'`, and the right partition would include any data greater than `'12/31/2004'`.

Right ranges mean that data equal to the boundary goes into the next partition. To separate at the new year starting 2005, a right range would set the boundary at `'1/1/2005'`. Any values less than the boundary go into the left, or lower, boundary. Any data with a date equal to or higher than the boundary goes into the next partition. These two functions use `left` and `right` ranges to create the same result:

```
CREATE PARTITION FUNCTION fnyears(DateTime)
AS RANGE LEFT FOR VALUES
('12/31/2001','12/31/2002','12/31/2003','12/31/2004');
```

or

```
CREATE PARTITION FUNCTION fnYearsRT(DateTime)
AS RANGE RIGHT FOR VALUES
('1/1/2002', '1/1/2003', '1/1/2004', '1/1/2005');
```

These functions both create four defined boundaries and a fifth, next, boundary.

Note SQL Server 2005's table partitions are declarative, meaning that the table is segmented by data values. A hash partition segments the data randomly. To simulate a hash partition and randomly spread the data across multiple DAS disk subsystems, define the table using a filegroup and then add multiple files to the filegroup.

There are three catalog views that expose information about partition function: `syspartition_functions`, `syspartition_function_range_values`, and `syspartition_parameters`.

Creating Partition Schemes

The partition schema builds on the partition function to specify the physical locations for the partitions. The physical partition tables may all be located in the same filegroup, or spread over several filegroups. The first example partition schema, named `psYearsAll`, uses the `pfYearsRT` partition function and places all the partitions in the `Primary` filegroup:

```
CREATE PARTITION SCHEME psYearsAll
AS PARTITION pfYearsRT
  ALL TO ([Primary]);
```

To place the table partitions in their own filegroup, omit the `all` keyword and list the filegroups individually:

```
CREATE PARTITION SCHEME psYearsFiles
AS PARTITION pfYearsRT
  TO (Part01, Part02, Part03, Part04, Part05);
```

The partition functions and schemes must be created using T-SQL code, but once they've been created you can view them in Management Studio's Object Explorer under the database Storage node, as shown in Figure 53-2.

To examine information about partition schemes programmatically, query `syspartition_schemes`.

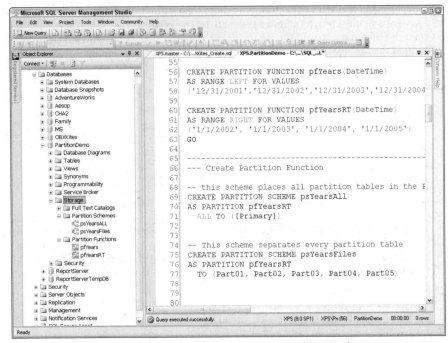

Figure 53-2: The partition configuration can be viewed in Object Explorer.

Creating the Partition Table

Once the partition function and partition schemes are in place, actually creating the table is a piece of cake (pun intended). A partition table must be created with a non-clustered primary key. Then, adding a clustered index to the table actually segments the tables based on the partition scheme, as shown in Figure 53-3. The WorkOrder Table Properties page also displays the partition scheme being used by the table.

Partition functions and partition schemes don't have owners, so when referring to partition schemes or partition functions you don't need to use the four-part name or the schema owner in the name.

The following table is similar to the Adventureworks work order table in the production scheme:

```
CREATE TABLE dboWorkOrder (
  WorkOrderID INT NOT NULL PRIMARY KEY NONCLUSTERED,
  ProductID INT NOT NULL,
  OrderQty INT NOT NULL,
  StockerQty INT NOT NULL,
  ScappedQty INT NOT NULL,
  StartDate DATETIME NOT NULL,
  EndDate DATETIME NOT NULL,
  DueDate DATETIME NOT NULL,
```

```
ScapReason INT NULL,
ModifiedDate DATETIME NOT NULL
);
```

```
CREATE CLUSTERED INDEX ix_WorkORder_DueDate
  ON dbo.WorkOrder (DueDate)
    ON psYearsAll(DueDate);
```

The next script inserts 7,259,100 rows into the WorkOrder table in 2 minutes and 42 seconds as is confirmed by the database Summary page:

```
DECLARE @Counter INT;
SET @Counter = 0;

WHILE @Counter < 100
BEGIN
  SET @Counter = @Counter + 1;
  INSERT dbo.WorkOrder (ProductID, OrderQty, StockedQty, ScrappedQty,
     StartDate, EndDate, DueDate, ScrapReasonID, ModifiedDate)
    SELECT ProductID, OrderQty, StockedQty, ScrappedQty,
        StartDate, EndDate, DueDate, ScrapReasonID, ModifiedDate
     FROM AdventureWorks.Production.WorkOrder;
END;
```

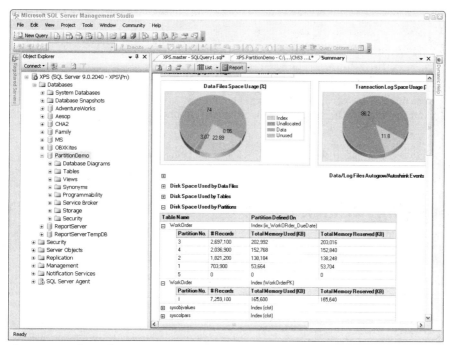

Figure 53-3: The Disk Usage report in Management Studio's Summary page for the PartitionDemo database displays usage information for each partition.

It's possible for multiple partition schemas to share a single partition function. Architecturally, this might make sense if several tables should be partitioned using the same boundaries because this improves the consistency of the partitions. To verify which tables use which partition schemes, based on which partition functions, use the Object Dependencies dialog, shown in Figure 53-4, for the partition function or partition scheme. You can find it using the partition function's context menu.

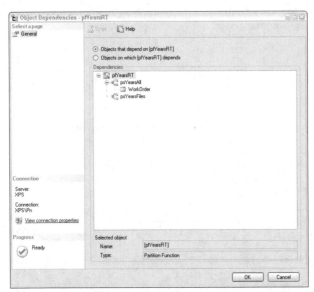

Figure 53-4: As shown in the Object Dependencies dialog, it's clear that the `WorkOrder` table uses the `psYearsAll` partition schema, which uses the `pfyearsRT` partition function.

To see information about how the partitions are being used, look at `syspartitions` and `syspartition_counts`.

Querying Partition Tables

The nice thing about partition tables is that no special code is required to query across multiple underlying partition tables or from only one partition table. The Query Optimizer automatically uses the right tables to retrieve the data.

The `$partition` operator can return the partition table's integer identifier when used with the partition function. The next code snippet counts the number of rows in each partition:

```
SELECT $PARTITION.pfYearsRT(DueDate) AS Partition,
   COUNT(*) AS Count
  FROM WorkOrder
  GROUP BY $PARTITION.pfYearsRT(DueDate)
  ORDER BY Partition;
```

Result:

```
Partition        Count
-----------      -----------
1                703900
2                1821200
3                2697100
4                2036900
```

The next query selects data for one year, so the data should be located in only one partition. Examining the query execution plan in Figure 53-5 reveals that the Query Optimizer used a high-speed clustered index scan on partition ID PtnIds1005:

```sql
SELECT WorkOrderID,ProductID, OrderQty, StockedQty, ScrappedQty
  FROM dbo.WorkOrder
  WHERE year(DueDate) = '2002';
```

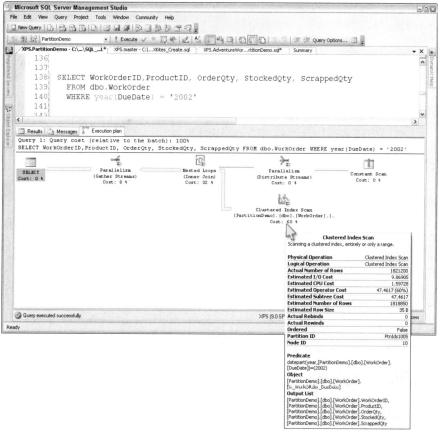

Figure 53-5: The clustered index scan logical operation includes a new property, the Partition ID.

Altering Partition Tables

In order for partition tables to be updated to keep up with changing data, and to enable the performance testing of various partition schemes, they are easily modified. Even though the commands are simple, as you can imagine, modifying the design of partition tables never executes very quickly.

The easiest way to modify the partition table is to drop the existing clustered index constraint and apply a new clustered index that includes the on partition schema clause referring to the new partition scheme and partition function, but this method is overkill in most situations.

Merging Partitions

Merge and split surgically modify the table partition design. The alter partition ... merge range command effectively removes one of the boundaries from the partition function and merges two partitions. For example, to remove the boundary between 2003 and 2004 in the pfYearsRT partition function, and combine the data from 2003 and 2004 into a single partition, use the following alter command:

```
ALTER PARTITION FUNCTION pfYearsRT()
  MERGE RANGE ('1/1/2004');
```

Sure enough, following the merge operation, the previous count-rows-per-partition query now returns three partitions, and scripting the partition function from Object Explorer creates a script with three boundaries in the partition function code.

Note   If multiple tables share the same partition scheme and partition function being modified, then multiple tables will be affected by these changes.

Splitting Partitions

To split an existing single partition, the first step is to designate the filegroup for the new partition in the partition scheme using the alter partition ... next used command. Then the partition function can be modified to specify the new boundary using the alter partition ... split range command to insert a new boundary into the partition function. It's the alter function command that actually performs the work.

This example segments the 2003–2004 work order data into two partitions. The new partition will include only data for July 2004, the last month with data in the Adventureworks table:

```
ALTER PARTITION SCHEME psYearsFiles
  NEXT USED [Primary];

ALTER PARTITION FUNCTION pfYearsRT()
  SPLIT RANGE ('7/1/2004');
```

Switching Tables

Switching tables is the cool ability to move an entire table into a partition space within a partition table, or to remove a single partition so that it becomes a stand-alone table. This is very useful when importing new data, but note a few restrictions:

✦ Every index for the partition table must be a partitioned index.

✦ The new table must have the same columns (excluding identity columns), indexes, and constraints (including foreign keys) as the partition table, except that the new table cannot be partitioned.

✦ The source partition table cannot be the target of a foreign key.

✦ Neither table can be published using replication, or have schema-bound views.

✦ The new table must have Check constraint restricting the data range to the new partition, so SQL Server doesn't have to re-verify the data range.

✦ Both the stand-alone table and the partition position that will receive the stand-alone table must be on the same filegroup.

✦ The receiving partition must be empty.

In essence, switching a table into a partition is rearranging the database metadata to reassign the existing table as a partition, as shown in Figure 53-6. No data is actually moved, which makes table switching nearly instantaneous regardless of the size of the table.

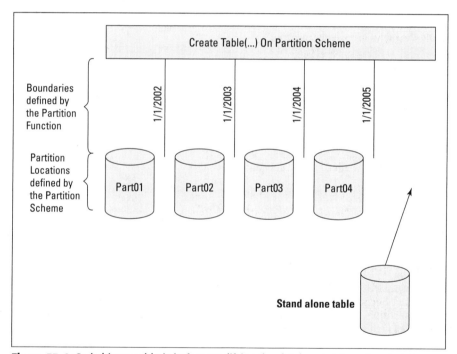

Figure 53-6: Switching a table is in fact modifying the database's internal metadata so an existing stand-alone table becomes one of the partitions.

Prepping the New Table

The WorkOrderNEW table meets these criteria and will hold August 2004 data from Adventureworks:

```
CREATE TABLE dbo.WorkOrderNEW (
  WorkOrderID INT IDENTITY NOT NULL,
  ProductID INT NOT NULL,
  OrderQty INT NOT NULL,
  StockedQty INT NOT NULL,
  ScrappedQty INT NOT NULL,
```

```
StartDate DATETIME NOT NULL,
EndDate DATETIME NOT NULL,
DueDate DATETIME NOT NULL,
ScrapReasonID INT NULL,
ModifiedDate DATETIME NOT NULL
)
ON Part05;
```

Indexes identical to those on the preceding table will be created on the partitioned table:

```
ALTER TABLE dbo.WorkOrderNEW
  ADD CONSTRAINT WorkOrderNEWPK
  PRIMARY KEY NONCLUSTERED (WorkOrderID, DueDate)
go
CREATE CLUSTERED INDEX ix_WorkOrderNEW_DueDate
  ON dbo.WorkOrderNEW (DueDate)
```

Adding the mandatory constraint:

```
ALTER TABLE dbo.WorkOrderNEW
  ADD CONSTRAINT WONewPT
    CHECK (DueDate BETWEEN '8/1/2004' AND '8/31/2004');
```

Now to import the new data from Adventureworks, reusing the January 2004 data:

```
INSERT dbo.WorkOrderNEW (ProductID, OrderQty, StockedQty, ScrappedQty,
    StartDate, EndDate, DueDate, ScrapReasonID, ModifiedDate)
  SELECT
     ProductID, OrderQty, StockedQty, ScrappedQty,
     DATEADD(mm,7,StartDate), DATEADD(mm,7,EndDate),
     DATEADD(mm,7,DueDate), ScrapReasonID, DATEADD(mm,7,ModifiedDate)
  FROM AdventureWorks.Production.WorkOrder
  WHERE DueDate BETWEEN '1/1/2004' and '1/31/2004';
```

The new table now has 3,158 rows.

Prepping the Partition Table

The original partition table, built earlier in this section, has a non-partitioned non-clustered primary key. Because one of the rules of switching into a partitioned table is that every index must be partitioned, the first task for this demo is to drop and rebuild the WorkOrder table's primary key so it will be partitioned:

```
ALTER TABLE dbo.WorkOrder
  DROP CONSTRAINT WorkOrderPK

ALTER TABLE dbo.WorkOrder
  ADD CONSTRAINT WorkOrderPK
  PRIMARY KEY NONCLUSTERED (WorkORderID,DueDate)
    ON psYearsAll(DueDate);
```

Next, the partition table needs an empty partition:

```
ALTER PARTITION SCHEME psYearsFiles
  NEXT USED [Primary]

ALTER PARTITION FUNCTION pfYearsRT()
  SPLIT RANGE ('8/1/2004')
```

Performing the Switch

The `alter table ... switch` command will move the new table into a specific partition. To determine the empty target partition, select the database Summary page ⇨ Disk Usage report:

```
ALTER TABLE WorkOrderNEW
  SWITCH TO WorkOrder PARTITION 5
```

Switching Out

The same technology can be used to switch a partition out of the partition table so that it becomes a stand-alone table. Because no merger is taking place, this is much easier than switching in. The following code takes the oldest partition out of the WorkOrder partition table and reconfigures the database metadata so it becomes its own table:

```
ALTER TABLE
  SWITCH PARITION 1 to WorkOrderArchive
```

Rolling Partitions

With a little imagination, the technology to create and merge existing partitions can be used to create rolling partition designs.

Rolling partitions are useful for time-based partition functions such as using a partition for each month. Each month, the rolling partition expands for a new month. To build a 13-month rolling partition, perform these steps each month:

1. Add a new boundary.

2. Point the boundary to the next used filegroup.

3. Merge the oldest two partitions to keep all the data.

Switching tables into and out of partitions can enhance the rolling partition designs by switching in fully populated staging tables and switching out the tables into an archive location.

Indexing Partitioned Tables

Large tables mean large indexes, so non-clustered indexes can optionally be partitioned.

Creating Partitioned Indexes

Partitioned non-clustered indexes must include the column used by the partition function in the index, and must be created using the same `on` clause as the partitioned clustered index:

```
CREATE INDEX WorkOrder_ProductID
  ON WorkOrder (ProductID, DueDate)
    ON psYearsFiles(DueDate);
```

Maintaining Partitioned Indexes

One of the advantages of partitioned indexes is that they can be individually maintained. The following example rebuilds the newly added fifth partition:

```
ALTER INDEX WorkOrder_ProductID
  ON dbo.WorkOrder
  REBUILD
  PARTITION = 5
```

Because partitioning is only available in Enterprise Edition, online rebuilding of indexes is also available.

Removing Partitioning

To remove the partitioning of any table, drop the clustered index and add a new clustered index without the partitioning ON clause. When dropping the clustered index, you must add the move to option to actually consolidate the data onto the specified filegroup, thus removing the partitioning from the table:

```
DROP INDEX ix_WorkOrder_DueDate
  ON dbo.Workorder
  WITH (MOVE TO [Primary]);
```

Working with Indexed Views

A popular technique to woo performance out of a database is to make a *denormalized* copy of some of the data whereby data is extracted and stored elsewhere, enabling faster reads — for example, data stored in five large tables may be extracted and stored in a single wide table. I once did some extreme denormalization on a project, replacing a query that had a couple of dozen joins with a single table, and reduced the search time from a couple of minutes to about one second. It was OK for that project because the data was read-only. When the queries go against live data, denormalization can be a source of data-integrity problems.

Microsoft provides an alternate to denormalizing the actual data. SQL Server's *indexed views* are actually clustered indexes storing a denormalized set of data, as illustrated in Figure 53-7.

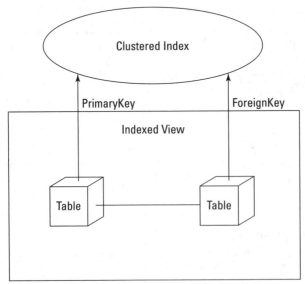

Figure 53-7: Indexed views create a bridge between two tables that might in actuality be a dozen joins apart.

Instead of building tables to denormalize a join, a view can be created that can select the two primary keys from the joined tables. A clustered index created on the view stores the valid data from the primary-key and foreign-key pairs.

While a normal view only stores the SQL select statement and the data isn't materialized until the view is called, an indexed view stores a copy of the data in a clustered index. Clustered indexes merge the data page and the b-tree index leaf to store the actual data in the physical order of the index. The clustered index uses a view as a framework to define the columns to be stored.

Numerous restrictions exist on indexed views, including the following:

✦ The ANSI null and quoted identifier must be enabled when the view is created, and when any connection attempts to modify any data in the base tables.

✦ The index must be a unique clustered index; therefore, the view must produce a unique set of rows without using distinct. This can be a problem because situations that need denormalizing include most many-to-many relationships, which tend to produce duplicate rows in the result set. For this reason, most indexed views only span one-to-many relationships.

✦ The tables in the view must be tables (not nested views) in the local database and must be referenced by means of the two-part name (owner.table).

✦ The view must be created with the option with schema binding.

> **Note**
>
> Because indexed views require schema binding, they can't be mixed with table partition switching or rolling partitions. To switch a table partition, you must drop the indexed view, perform the switch, and then rebuild the indexed view.

As an example of an indexed view being used to denormalize a large query, the following view selects data from the contact to product tables in the OBXKites database:

```
USE OBXKites;

SET ANSI_Nulls ON;
SET ANSI_Padding ON;
SET ANSI_Warnings ON;
SET ArithAbort ON;
SET Concat_Null_Yields_Null ON;
SET Quoted_Identifier ON;
SET Numeric_RoundAbort OFF;

GO

CREATE VIEW vContactOrder
WITH SCHEMABINDING
AS
SELECT c.ContactID, o.OrderID
  FROM dbo.Contact as c
    JOIN dbo.[Order] as o
      ON c.ContactID = o.ContactID;
  GO

CREATE UNIQUE CLUSTERED INDEX ivContactOrder ON vContactOrder
  (ContactID, OrderID);
```

Indexed Views and Queries

When SQL Server's Query Optimizer develops the execution plan for a query, it includes the indexed view's clustered index as one of the indexes it can use for the query, even if the query doesn't explicitly reference the view.

This means that the indexed view's clustered index can serve as a covering index to speed queries. When the Query Optimizer selects the indexed view's clustered index, the query execution plan indicates it with an index scan, as illustrated in Figure 53-8. The following query selects the same data as the indexed view:

```
SELECT Contact.ContactID, OrderID
  FROM dbo.Contact
    JOIN dbo.[Order]
      ON Contact.ContactID = [Order].ContactID
```

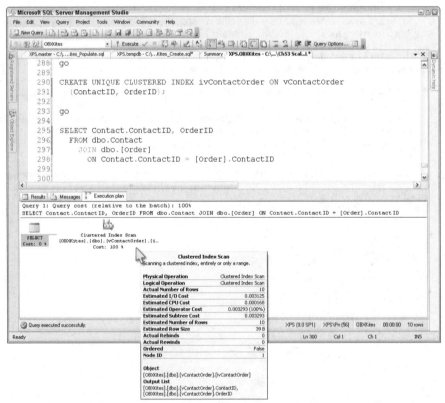

Figure 53-8: The query execution plan performs a clustered index scan to retrieve the data directly, instead of accessing the base tables.

While indexed views are essentially the same as they were in SQL Server 2000, the Query Optimizer can now use indexed views with more types of queries.

Best Practice

Just adding indexed views without fully analyzing how the queries use them will likely hurt performance more than it helps. Updating indexed views entails a serious performance hit, so avoid them for transactional databases. Carefully add them to databases used primarily for reporting, OLAP, or querying, by identifying specific joins that are impeding frequent queries and surgically inserting an indexed-view cluster index.

Updating Indexed Views

As with any denormalized copy of the data, the difficulty is keeping the data current. Indexed views have the same issue. As data in the underlying base tables is updated, the indexed view must be kept in sync. This process is completely transparent to the user and is more of a performance consideration than a programmatic issue.

Summary

Not every database will have to scale to higher magnitudes of capacity, but when a project does grow into the terabytes, SQL Server 2005 provides some advanced technologies to tackle the growth. However, even these advanced technologies are no substitute for optimization theory.

✦　　✦　　✦

Designing High-Performance Data Access Providers

✦   ✦   ✦   ✦

In This Chapter

Data access concepts

Working with data
access objects (DAOs)

Factories

Data providers

✦   ✦   ✦   ✦

Today, nearly all information is stored in a database, with even more information collected on a daily basis. This accumulation of information provides no value without a lens to shape our view. This is where the real value of that information comes into existence. When you provide a view into the data, you can begin to extract meaning and even predict future patterns, directions, or behavior. When information is presented in a meaningful fashion, individuals or applications can make decisions that have an impact on our lives.

Consider, for example, credit reports. As we go about our daily lives purchasing various items with a credit/debit card, making our car and mortgage payments along with our various other bills, this information is stored in databases. Each item on its own does not provide much information, but when a lens such as a credit report is applied to the data, various patterns emerge that help both individuals and institutions make decisions about us — hopefully for the better!

This chapter covers some data access concepts and explores three data access patterns using VB.NET data access objects (DAOs), factories, and providers. Within the Microsoft realm of development, DAO refers to a collection of classes that provide database access optimal for Microsoft Access. For the purposes of this chapter, DAO refers to classes that provide the layer between a client application and the database in a more general sense, i.e., not tied to one database technology.

Best Practice

Use software patterns whenever possible. A *pattern* is a technology that defines a solution to a recurring software problem. This solution typically includes the classes and even the code required for the classes to interact.

Note

Throughout the code samples in this chapter, exception handling is illustrated with the generic `Exception` class in the `Catch` block. In actual implementation, these exceptions should be more specific to the types of errors you are attempting to handle.

Data Access Concepts

Just as various factors drive data access needs, additional factors drive the data access implementation. Good data access matters, and various heuristics or rules can be developed to aid in selecting an appropriate data access pattern.

Why Good Data Access Matters

Ideally, good data access provides a high-performance, flexible, and complete "layer" through which any number of consuming clients can persist, modify, and extract information. This layer should insulate any database knowledge from the client and be as transparent as possible. It should also provide a cohesive and complete collection of exposed functionality for client applications to access. If done well, this data layer can be reusable, easily upgradeable, and maintainable with minimal efforts.

Defining Requirements

Many data access patterns exist and each pattern has inherent strengths and weaknesses when applied to real-world problems.

Some questions to ask before deciding on a data access pattern could include the following:

✦ How often does the schemas change? How often are new ones added? An extensible, maintainable, and deployable friendly pattern can mitigate schema changes.

✦ How often will databases expand and new databases get added? To support this, choose a pattern that is easily extensible and deployable.

✦ How "big" is the data layer? If the need for a large number of data objects exists, then look for a pattern that is easily maintainable.

✦ Will the data layer be shared? Choose a pattern that cleanly encapsulates the data layer objects to improve deployment, extensibility, and maintenance.

✦ Are transactional updates being considered? If so, consider this up front, as it will have an impact on the design. Transactional database interaction from the middle tier is beyond the scope of this chapter and is mentioned only as an additional consideration.

Other questions can clarify the data needs even further. The main point here is to spend some time up front identifying the needs that the data layer will meet and the impact those needs have on the design.

Table 54-1 illustrates some of the criteria that should be considered in choosing the data access layer pattern. This is illustrated for the three patterns discussed in this chapter.

Table 54-1: Data Access Pattern Characteristics

Data Design	Complexity	Maintenance Effort	Reusability	Extensibility	Deployment Friendly
Data Access Objects	low	neutral	low	low	high
Factories	neutral	low	neutral	neutral	high
Data Providers	high	low	high	high	high

With these characteristics in mind, it's time to take a more detailed look at these three patterns.

Data Access Objects

The code samples used in this example are written in VB.NET 2005 and can be found online at www.SQLServerBible.com/files.htm.

As a design pattern, data access objects (DAOs) make use of inheritance and polymorphism to build the data object hierarchy. This general pattern is shown in Figure 54-1.

Note

In the object-oriented world, polymorphism is the ability of classes to provide unique implementations for the same public interface. In practice, this means that two or more classes that present the same interface can be treated the same by the client code.

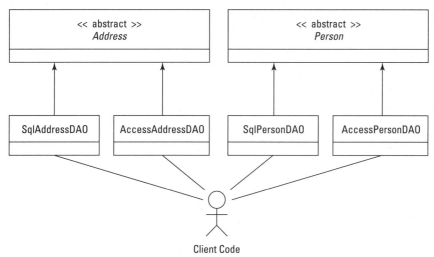

Client Code

Figure 54-1: This DAO example shows how specific implementations are derived and how a client can reference each one.

Note

The Data Access Object (DAO) pattern relies on inheritance to provide the specialized or descendant class with functionality. In this pattern, there is always an abstract base class specific to each type of data object that the developer needs to support. A specialized class is created for each database access object that needs to be supported, and includes the specific SQL for its database. Typically, the name of the class will include the name of the database, e.g., AddressSQLDAO or AddressAccessDAO. Any code that makes use of these objects must initially know what type of DAO to create.

How the DAO Scenario Works

Consider a DAO scenario. The requirement is that Microsoft SQL Server 2005 and Microsoft Access databases must be supported. The determination of what type of data object to instantiate is based on an external flag contained in a configuration file.

The DAO `Address` base class shown in the following code example provides the common functionality for any descendant that supports a specific database. The various member properties will be common. The only real difference is how the data is loaded from the data source.

DAO Address base class

```
Public MustInherit Class Address
' Various private member variables defined (see the
' online code) such as City, State, Street1, Street2 and
' their public property definitions.

   '''-----------------------------------------------------------
   ''' The Load method will be provided by each descendant
   ''' class for the unique data source that is accessed.
   '''-----------------------------------------------------------
   Public MustOverride Sub Load(ByVal strId As String)
End Class
```

The `MustOverride` enforces that any descendent class must provide a `Load` method. The next example shows a descendent class that inherits the `Address` class:

AddressSQLDAO.vb

```
Public Class SqlAddressDAO
   Inherits Address

   ' Declare configuration file key value.
   Private Const SQL_BINDING_INFO As String = "Sql_BindingInfo"

   ' Class variables are inherited from Address base class.

   '''-----------------------------------------------------------
   ''' Override the Load method defined in the Address class.
   '''-----------------------------------------------------------
   Public Overrides Sub Load(ByVal strId As String)
     Dim cmd As SqlCommand = Nothing
     Dim conn As SqlConnection = Nothing
     Dim dr As SqlDataReader = Nothing

     Try
       ' setup the db connection.
         conn = New SqlConnection(PropertyLoader.Instance _
           .GetProperty(SQL_BINDING_INFO))
         conn.Open()

     ' setup and execute the SQL command.
   cmd = New SqlCommand(PropertyLoader.Instance
   .GetProperty("Sql_Address_Select").Replace("%1", strId), conn)

       dr = cmd.ExecuteReader(CommandBehavior.CloseConnection)

       If dr.Read Then
         ' load the member variables from the reader.
       End If
```

```
            Catch ex As Exception
            ' generic error handling for sample.
            Throw (ex)
            Finally
            ' close the variables
            If cmd IsNot Nothing Then cmd.Dispose()
            If conn IsNot Nothing Then conn.Close()
            If dr IsNot Nothing Then dr.Close()
        End Try
    End Sub
End Class
```

VB.NET 2005 introduces the IsNot keyword, which provides a more intuitive reading for conditional logic tests. This functions the same as the previous syntax, Not <variable> Is <value>.

Best Practice

Data objects should access their databases through stored procedures whenever possible. This provides the best insulation from database implementation changes. At the very least, externalize the SQL statements and parameterize them as necessary.

Cross-Reference

Chapter 25, "Creating Extensibility with a Data Abstraction Layer," provides more detailed information about BestPractices related to database access abstraction from code.

With the member variables defined in the abstract parent class, Address, the AddressSqlDAO class only has to initialize its member variables. The AddressAccessDAO class provides the same functionality but contains Microsoft Access–specific connection and SQL code.

Consider the client code in the following example, which makes use of the AddressSqlDAO and AddressAccessDAO classes for gathering information from SQL Server and Access data sources.

TestMain.vb

```
Public Class TestMain
  '''----------------------------------------------------------
''' create a sql and access address dao.
  '''----------------------------------------------------------
Sub Main()
  Try
    ' local variable to hold the generic address reference.
    Dim objAddr As Address

    ' get data from the SQL database & display it.
      objAddr = New SqlAddressDAO
    objAddr.Load("2")
    Call PrintAddress( objAddr )

    ' now get data from the Access database & display it.
      objAddr = New AccessAddressDAO
    objAddr.Load("1")
```

```
    Call PrintAddress( objAddr )
  Catch ex As Exception
    Console.WriteLine(ex.Message)
  End Try
End Sub


  '''-----------------------------------------------------
''' Print out the address information.
  '''-----------------------------------------------------
Private Sub PrintAddress( ByVal objAddr As Address )
  Console.WriteLine(objAddr.Street1)
  Console.WriteLine(objAddr.City)
  ' other attributes get printed in the same way.
End Sub
End Class
```

In looking at how the DAO is actually used, it is evident that both the SQL and Access DAO can have their data accessed in the same way because they derive from `Address`. While polymorphism regarding how the client can view the SQL and Access DAOs exists, it still needs to know what type of data source it's dealing with. As shown in the `TestMain` code, the appropriate DAO is being explicitly created, and this dependency can cause problems when it's time to support another database or make enhancements.

The DAO concept is pretty easy to understand and teach to others. No specialized knowledge is necessary in implementing and supporting this design. It is better suited for small quantities of objects and a couple of data sources, and it can be coded fairly quickly.

The Cons of the DAO Pattern

The client must make the determination of what data source to use. This couples the client pretty heavily to the data access layer. One approach to solve this dependency is to have each ancestor data object provide the following method, creating the appropriate descendants. Note, however, that this is not the best way to abstract data source logic:

```
Public MustInherit Class Address
  '''-----------------------------------------------------
''' Same address functionality as defined above but with
''' the GetInstance() method added to handle data source
''' determination.
  '''-----------------------------------------------------
Public Shared Function GetInstance() As Address
  If PropertyLoader.Instance.GetProperty("UseSql"). _
    Equals("True") Then
    Return New AddressSqlDAO
  Else
    Return New AddressAccessDAO
  End If
End Function

' the other functionality exists as shown above.
End Class
```

While this can be made to work, design faults now exist within the data layer. Business logic, the If test, now resides in the data layer. The second issue is that the ancestor class must now be explicitly aware of any descendants. Yet another drawback involves maintenance. If the conditional logic needs to change, then every single ancestor data object that implements this solution will have to be updated. Furthermore, anytime the supported databases are extended or additional data objects are added, every single ancestor data object has to be updated. It's best to just avoid this approach.

How can the client be insulated from these issues? The factory design pattern can help externalize the GetInstance() business logic into a separate class and hide the database differences from the client code.

Factories

The code samples used in this example are written in VB.NET 2005 and can be found online at www.SQLServerBible.com/files.htm.

A factory provides a central location for object creation. When client code needs a data object, it makes the request from the factory and the factory handles the creation and initialization of the object. In addition to this, a factory may also contain business logic that determines what specific types of objects should be created. In the example shown in Figure 54-2, this is the logic that determines whether to use SQL or Access as the database.

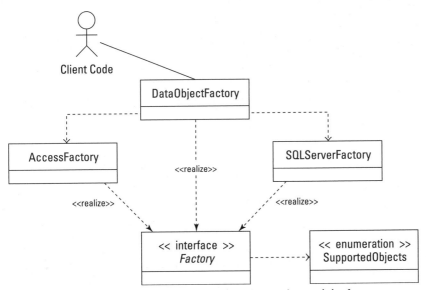

Figure 54-2: Factory example showing the client interaction and the factory dependencies

Note   Factories are pretty straightforward constructs that provide support for client code to defer creation of a class instance to the factory. Factories can also act as the proxy or intermediary for other factories. In Figure 54-2, both of these facets are being implemented with the primary factory, `DataObjectFactory`, containing the logic for determining the specific database, and passing creation requests through to the appropriate database-specific factory.

In this case, the factory pattern helps us to decouple the business logic from the DAOs themselves, as presented in the previous example, and gives the client code a single point of reference when creating new data objects. The benefit is that if the data source logic changes, then that change occurs in one place instead of every DAO base class. This improves maintainability and further aligns the code with general object-oriented design principles.

By organizing the creation of DAO classes into database-specific factories and using them as subfactories, greater encapsulation and cohesion is achieved. Additionally, it becomes easier to add databases by creating the appropriate subfactory and making the necessary changes in the main factory.

The Address DAO code previously presented remains valid when using a factory. The factory consolidates the creation responsibilities into a single entity, as shown in the following code:

Main Factory

```
Public Class DataObjectFactory
   Inherits Factory

   '''------------------------------------------------------------
   ''' delegate the object request to a sub-factory.
   '''------------------------------------------------------------
   Public Shared Shadows Function GetDAO(ByVal typeRequested _
   As Factory.SupportedDAOs) As Object
     Try
        If CBool( PropertyLoader.Instance.GetProperty("UseSql") ) Then
          Return SqlServerFactory.GetDAO(typeRequested)
        Else
          Return AccessFactory.GetDAO(typeRequested)
        End If
     Catch ex As Exception
        ' This is here in case the "UseSql" flag and/or value
        ' is not available.  This value would be set in the
        ' application configuration file.
        Throw New ApplicationException( "Invalid UseSql value." )
     End Try
   End Function
End Class
```

In the preceding code, the main factory determines the data source and delegates the request to the specialized factory.

The following code shows how the example `SqlServerFactory` handles the delegation. The real work takes place within the data-source-specific factory. The `Access` factory functions in a similar fashion.

SqlServerFactory

```
Public Class SqlServerFactory
  Inherits Factory

  '''----------------------------------------------------------
  ''' create the requested DAO object.
  '''----------------------------------------------------------
  Public Shared Shadows Function GetDAO(ByVal typeRequested _
  As Factory.SupportedDAOs) As Object
    Select Case typeRequested
      Case Factory.SupportedDAOs.Address
      Return New AddressSqlDAO
      Case Else
        Return Nothing
    End Select
End Function

End Class
```

The SqlServerFactory knows what specific classes it can instantiate and doesn't have to worry about additional data sources. It is self-contained and complete for SQL objects.

Note In VB.NET, a shared method cannot be overridden in a descendent class; it must be declared 'Shadows' in the overriding signature for the desired effect.

How is a factory used in client code? Take a look at the following example:

MainTester.vb

```
Public Class MainTester
  '''----------------------------------------------------------
  ''' The main method requests a data object from the factory.
  ''' Because the factory returns Objects, the return value
  ''' must be appropriately type cast.
  '''----------------------------------------------------------
Sub Main()
  Try
Dim objAddr As Address

objAddr = CType( SmarterDaoFactory.GetDAO( _
Factory.SupportedDAOs.Address), Address)
objAddr.Load("1")
      Call PrintAddress(objAddr)
    Catch ex As Exception
      Console.WriteLine(ex.Message)
    End Try
End Sub

  '''----------------------------------------------------------
  ''' Print out the address information.
  '''----------------------------------------------------------
```

```
Private Sub PrintAddress( ByVal objAddr As Address )
  Console.WriteLine(objAddr.Street1)
  Console.WriteLine(objAddr.City)
  ' other attributes get printed in the same way.
End Sub
End Class
```

Notice that the creation of a data-source-specific object has been omitted from the client code. Instead, there is a call to the `Factory.GetDAO(...)` method. That method contains the logic for determining which specific database to use, and defers the creation request to that specific (sub) factory. This is definitely a step in the right direction of insulating the client from having to know any details about data source and object creation. The following sections discuss the pros and cons of the factory approach, and then describes how to make data access completely transparent to client code.

The Pros of the Factory Pattern

As previously mentioned, one of the benefits of the factory approach is that the business logic determining the data source exists in one centralized location, e.g., the `SmarterDAOFactory`. The factory handles the request with the assistance of data-source-specific subfactories, so the `SmarterDAOFactory` is acting as a proxy for the database-specific factories. A client that always deals with a single data source could bypass the main factory and make requests from the database-specific factory. In addition to these benefits, by using the factory, maintainability improves, the design is easier to conceptualize, code readability improves, and developers know what objects are supported at design time because .NET's IntelliSense displays the object enumeration values for the factory. Furthermore, this design could work for a larger number of objects and databases than the DAO approach.

The Cons of the Factory Pattern

The downsides associated with using this pattern center on the implementation. The example discussed here was simple enough that the use of subfactories was not really needed. However, in the real world, with a large number of objects and potentially multiple data sources to be included, subfactories become more integral to the solution. In this case, using a main factory as a proxy requires additional coordination with the subfactories when adding new data objects and databases. All subfactories have to be written in such a way that they could handle a request for an unknown data object. Another drawback is that the main factory always needs to present a superset of the objects available. This can cause problems when subfactories do not support the exposed object.

The complete source for the Factory project can be found at www.SQLServerBible.com/files.htm. Included in the source is a `BasicDaoFactory.vb` class that requires the client to supply the type of data source for the requested object. This approach is not recommend for reasons similar to the DAO pattern and is only included for illustrative purposes.

Data Providers

The code samples used in this example are written in VB.NET 2005 and can be found online at www.SQLServerBible.com/files.htm.

What, then, should be done when there is a need for a flexible design that allows updating and even enhancing the behavior of the program without recompiling? What if the data source for the client weren't a traditional database but maybe an XML store? Or even just computed values that were completely stand-alone? What if data access must be completely transparent to consuming code? The data provider pattern addresses these issues and others, including the externalization of the data source logic from the factory construct and the ability to dynamically adjust the data layer's runtime behavior.

 Note The term *data provider* is also used by Microsoft in the ADO.NET space to denote the group of classes that provide access to a specific data source. In this section, the term data provider refers to an individual class that provides transparent access to information typically stored within a database.

 On The Web Typically, configuration files are loaded only once, either at application startup or first access. Sometimes, however, you want to adjust an application's behavior at runtime, without having to restart. In these situations, a property loader that can monitor configuration file changes solves the problem. The `PropertyLoader.vb` class makes a good starting point for this and can be found OntheWebsite. For example, consider a web application running on Internet Information Services (IIS) for which a need arises to modify the runtime behavior. The application is running in a high-availability environment, however, and restarting the server so it can reload its configuration file values is out of the question. By implementing a property loader that monitors for configuration file changes and reloads the configuration file upon change, the application does not need a restart. Any changed values are reloaded and made available to the application during runtime.

A data provider is a client-consumable class that abstracts the data source implementation in a transparent manner. Data providers make use of the bridge pattern and polymorphism for their implementation. Figure 54-3 illustrates the polymorphism and bridge pattern of the data providers from an abstract class perspective. Figure 54-4 provides a contextualized example by having an Address data provider (`DpAddress`) and the necessary support classes.

 Note The bridge pattern provides a design pattern for decoupling an interface from a varying implementation. In practice, this means that the client-consumed class does not change its interface; instead, the implementation behind the interface varies as appropriate to support the given data source. This is also an example of polymorphism because multiple support classes will provide a different implementation while all support the same defined interface(s).

Data Providers

The concrete `DpDeterminer` class, `SqlOrAccessDeterminer`, provides the business logic to identify what database will be interacted with. Because this logic has been encapsulated with configuration values identifying it, it's possible to plug in any class that inherits `DpDeterminer` and change the business logic without forcing a recompile.

The `DataProvider` abstract base class provides the core for the dynamic identification and creation of the data-source-specific implementation as defined by a determiner.

The `DpImplementation` abstract base class provides the first layer of the implementation hierarchy. It provides some common member variables and methods. Specific implementations ultimately derive from this class.

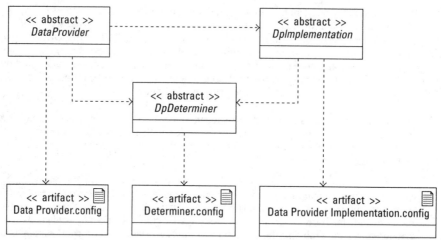

Figure 54-3: This data provider example illustrates the base classes and the required configuration files.

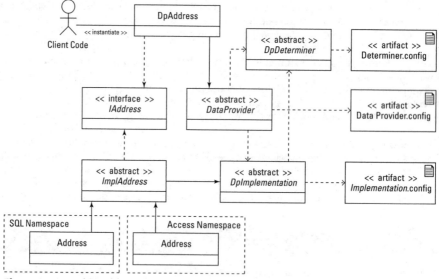

Figure 54-4: In this Address data provider example, the client code references only the DpAddress class.

How a Data Provider Works

The data provider queries the associated determiner and dynamically creates the data-source-specific implementation at runtime. Various configuration files (refer to Figure 54-3) provide the flexibility and information required to create the appropriate class instances at runtime for the determiners and the actual data provider implementations.

The Determiner class plays a critical role in the data provider design because it externalizes and encapsulates the business logic that determines what data source to support and how to connect to it. This contrasts with the tighter coupling of the Factory and DAO designs. A determiner exists on its own and can be swapped out with another determiner as needs change. The sequence diagram shown in Figure 54-5 better illustrates the actual flow. Notice that the SqlOrAccessDeterminer and the Address objects are created by the DataProvider base class. The information required for these objects is contained in the configuration files. Also notice that when the Load(id) call occurs, the database-specific Address object requests database connection information from the SqlOrAccessDeterminer. More important, notice that the client code only interacts with the DpAddress object to load and access properties for the address, so from the client's perspective, the DpAddress appears as any class would — providing methods and properties. The database access remains behind the scenes.

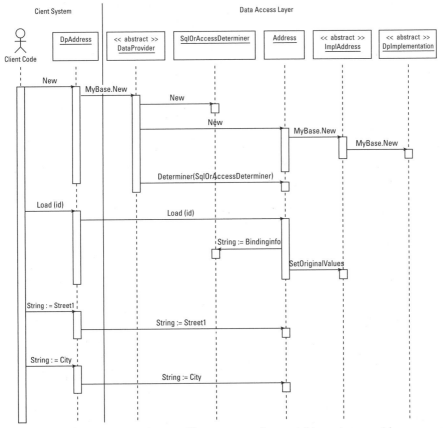

Figure 54-5: This sequence diagram illustrates creating an Address data provider, followed by loading specific address data, and then accessing a couple of fields.

Take a summary look at the `DpDeterminer` base class in the following code, and then an example implementation.

Determiner Base Class

```
Public MustInherit Class DpDeterminer
  Private Const BINDING_INFO_TAG As String = "_BindingInfo"
  Private Const DESCRIPTION_TAG As String = "_Description"

  '''-----------------------------------------------------------
  ''' Constructor.
  '''-----------------------------------------------------------
Public Sub New()
' some initialization omitted.  What really matters
' is the configuration file loading for property
' access...

' the config file exists so load it.
PropertyLoader.Instance.LoadProperties(strPropertyFile)
  End Sub

  '''-----------------------------------------------------------
  ''' The connection / binding information for the current
  ''' data source.
  '''-----------------------------------------------------------
Public ReadOnly Property BindingInfo() As String
Get
Return PropertyLoader.Instance.GetProperty( _
Me.GetType.Name & "_" & Me.DataSource &
BINDING_INFO_TAG)
End Get
End Property

  '''-----------------------------------------------------------
  ''' The data source type for this determiner.
  '''-----------------------------------------------------------
Public MustOverride ReadOnly Property DataSource() As String

  '''-----------------------------------------------------------
  ''' The description for the current data source.
  '''-----------------------------------------------------------
Public ReadOnly Property Description() As String
Get
  Return PropertyLoader.Instance.GetProperty( _
Me.GetType.Name & "_" & Me.DataSource &
DESCRIPTION_TAG)
End Get
  End Property
```

The bulk of this base class returns various configuration file values that are dependent on the type (name) of this determiner. The part of interest is the `MustOverride DataSource()` property. That method, defined in a descendent class, contains the business logic that specifies what type of data source will be accessed. Take a look at the example:

SqlOrAccessDeterminer.vb

```
Public Class SqlOrAccessDeterminer
  Inherits DpDeterminer

  '''-------------------------------------------------------
  ''' Internal business logic to determine what type of data
  ''' source is being dealt with.
  '''-------------------------------------------------------
  Public Overrides ReadOnly Property DataSource() As String
  Get
    With PropertyLoader.Instance
  If CBool(.GetProperty(Me.GetType.Name & "_UseSQL")) Then
    Return .GetProperty(Me.GetType.Name & "_SqlTag")
  Else
  Return .GetProperty(Me.GetType.Name & _
  "_AccessTag")
  End If
      End With
  End Get
  End Property

  End Class
```

Looking over the business logic contained in the SqlOrAccessDeterminer, notice that if "_UseSQL" evaluates to True, then the determiner returns the "SqlTag", indicating that a SQL Server will be used. Otherwise, the "AccessTag" is returned. The key concept here is that the business logic has been completely externalized from the data object creation and now exists on its own. This loose coupling helps to provide increased flexibility in the design.

> **Note** The configuration filenames follow the Microsoft convention of <assemblyName>.dll. config, so when looking through the sample source code, keep in mind that the configuration files will be named that way, e.g., Providers.dll.config or Provider Implementations.dll.config, etc.

The configuration file value referenced by the SqlOrAccessDeterminer looks like this:

ProviderDeterminers.dll.config

```xml
<?xml version="1.0" encoding="utf-8" ?>
<configuration>
<appSettings>

<!-- Determiner settings. -->
<add key="SqlOrAccessDeterminer_UseSQL" value="True" />

<!-- The 'tag' values below are included in building a   -->
<!-- class instance namespace.  i.e        -->
<!-- Providers.Implementations.Sql.Address or      -->
<!-- Providers.Implementations.Access.Address     -->
<add key="SqlOrAccessDeterminer_SqlTag" value="Sql" />
<add key="SqlOrAccessDeterminer_AccessTag" value="Access" />

<!-- Other settings omitted...        -->
</appSettings>
</configuration>
```

By simply changing the "True" value in the "SqlOrAccessDeterminer_UseSQL" key to "False", the database changes and all data providers that utilize this determiner, without having to recompile the application, now use the new database. This is a significant benefit, especially for applications running in environments where downtime is critical.

Tip   When it becomes necessary to create a property loader to manage the application settings, include the functionality to monitor changes to the configuration file. By doing this, any updates can be automatically reloaded and used by the application without the need to restart. The .NET Framework provides support for monitoring files with the FileSystemWatcher class. Using this class, it is possible to determine what file events will be handled and what methods will handle the file events.

Take a look at the configuration file (see the following code listing) for the data providers to gain some insight as to why the single change mentioned above can have such a significant impact on data access:

Providers.dll.config configuration file

```
<?xml version="1.0" encoding="utf-8" ?>
<configuration>
<appSettings>

<!-- Data Provider implementation settings. -->

<!-- Address Data Provider -->
<add key="DpAddress_Determiner"
value="Providers.Determiners.SqlOrAccessDeterminer" />
<add key="DpAddress_Determiner_Assembly"
  Value="ProviderDeterminers" />

<add key="DpAddress_Instance" value="Address" />
<add key="DpAddress_Instance_Assembly"
value="ProviderImplementations" />
<add key="DpAddress_Instance_RootNameSpace"
value="Providers.Implementations" />

</appSettings>
</configuration>
```

The "DpAddress_Determiner" line specifies what determiner this data provider would use when creating the data source implementation, so any changes that affect that determiner's logic would impact all the data providers dependent upon it. Also included in this configuration section are values specifying what assembly to find the determiner in as well as information needed to create an instance of the data provider implementation through reflection. Now that you've seen how a data provider is configured, take a look at the code, starting with the base class DataProvider:

DataProvider.vb class

```
Public MustInherit Class DataProvider
  ' constants and local declarations omitted

  '''-------------------------------------------------------
''' Constructor.
  '''-------------------------------------------------------
```

```
Public Sub New ()
' code to load configuration file...

' create the determiner for this data provider based on
' configuration file values.
With PropertyLoader.Instance
Dim strAssembly As String = .GetProperty( _ Me.GetType.Name &
DETERMINER_ASSEMBLY_TAG)
Dim strClass As String = .GetProperty(Me.GetType.Name _ & DETERMINER_TAG)
' set the Determiner for this data provider.
Determiner = CType(Activate(strAssembly, strClass), _ DpDeterminer)

' using the new Determiner, get the implementation.
strAssembly = .GetProperty(Me.GetType.Name & _ INSTANCE_ASSEMBLY_TAG)
strClass = .GetProperty(Me.GetType.Name & _ INSTANCE_ROOT_NAME_SPACE) &
"." & _ Determiner.DataSource & "." & _ .GetProperty(Me.GetType.Name &
INSTANCE_TAG)

' set the implementation for this data provider.
Implementation = CType(Activate(strAssembly,strClass),_ DpImplementation)
Implementation.Determiner = Determiner
End With
End Sub

    '''------------------------------------------------------------
    ''' Create an instance of the requested class from the
    ''' specified assembly.
    '''------------------------------------------------------------
Private Function Activate(ByVal strAssembly As String, _
ByVal strClassName As String) As Object
' validation code...

' create the instance via reflection and return it.
Dim instanceType As Type = _
System.Reflection.Assembly.Load(strAssembly).GetType( _ strClassName)

Return Activator.CreateInstance(instanceType)
    End Function

' other general support methods omitted.  See the online code.
End Class
```

The constructor attempts to load the configuration file and then begins to dynamically create the class instance it needs. First the determiner associated with this data provider (specified in the configuration file) is created. Next, the specific data source implementation (SQL, Access, etc.), defined by the newly created determiner is created. This code automatically runs whenever a data provider is instantiated. During development, this frees developers from the tedium of creating support classes so that they can focus on the details of the data provider. The Address data provider looks like this:

DpAddress.vb Data Provider

```
Public Class DpAddress
    Inherits DataProvider
    Implements IAddress

    ' all this class does is expose the implementation properties
    ' defined in the IAddress interface.  Keep in mind that this
    ' interface is also implemented in the data source specific
    ' classes.

    '''-----------------------------------------------------------
    ''' Helper method to cast the implementation to the
    ''' appropriate type. 'Implementation' is a property
    ''' defined in the base class DataProvider.
    '''-----------------------------------------------------------
    Protected Function MyImplementation() As IAddress
        Return CType(Implementation, IAddress)
    End Function

    ' here is an example property.

    '''-----------------------------------------------------------
    ''' City value.
    '''-----------------------------------------------------------
    Public Property City() As String Implements Interfaces.IAddress.City
    Get
        Return MyImplementation.City
    End Get
    Set(ByVal Value As String)
        MyImplementation.City = Value
    End Set
    End Property

    ' all the other interface properties are exposed in a
    ' similar fashion.

End Class
```

By inheriting from the `DataProvider` class, the `DpAddress` class has picked up all of the creation functionality. By implementing the `IAddress` interface, the `DpAddress` class has agreed to a public contract defining its capabilities. The only custom method for this class was the `MyImplementation()` method, and this was to type cast the implementation for developer convenience and to pick up the IntelliSense feature of Visual Studio. All in all, this class is pretty lightweight. Now take a look at what makes the data source implementation work, starting with the `DpImplementation.vb` base class (see the following code listing) before looking at a specific implementation.

DpImplementation.vb Base Class

```
Public MustInherit Class DpImplementation

    '''-----------------------------------------------------------
    ''' Determiner property.
    '''-----------------------------------------------------------
```

```vbnet
      Public Property Determiner() As DpDeterminer
' implementation pretty straightforward so it's omitted.
      End Property

      '''--------------------------------------------------------
      ''' Constructor.
      '''--------------------------------------------------------
Public Sub New()
      ' load the appropriate configuration file.
      Dim strFileName As String

strFileName = My.Application.CurrentDirectory & "\" & _
Me.GetType.Module.ScopeName & ".config"

      ' load the property file.
      PropertyLoader.Instance.LoadProperties(strFileName)
End Sub

End Class
```

This implementation class provides the `Determiner` property and local storage and loads the appropriate implementation configuration file. The real work for the create, read, update, and delete (CRUD) functionality lives in the data-source-specific implementations.

New in 2005 VB.NET 2005 introduces the `'My'` keyword, which provides convenient access to common values about the running program and the platform it is on. By using `'My'`, `'Application'`, `'Computer'`, `'User'` and `'WebServices'`, values become significantly easier to access.

Note In previous versions of VB.NET, when a developer needed to determine the current directory, `AppDomain.CurrentDomain.BaseDirectory` was used. This method returned the current directory with a `Path.DirectorySeparatorChar()` appended to the end of the string. The new `My.Application.CurrentDirectory()` property returns the current directory *without* the `Path.DirectorySeparatorChar()` value appended. This will break code that assumed the directory character was present at the end of the path.

Here is the base implementation class for all database-specific classes:

ImplAddress.vb Base Class

```vbnet
      Public MustInherit Class ImplAddress
         Inherits DpImplementation
         Implements IAddress

         Private m_CurrentValues As doAddress
         Private m_OriginalValues As doAddress

         ' this class implements the IAddress interface which
         ' will be common to all data source specific
      ' implementations.

      ' Aside from the data object declarations above, there
      ' is not much special about the class so see the online
```

```
' code for complete details.

'''------------------------------------------------------------
''' Load interface definition.  This must be supplied by the
''' descendent class.
'''------------------------------------------------------------
    Public MustOverride Sub Load(ByVal strId As String)

End Class
```

The `ImplAddress` class provides the general functionality for all Address implementations and defers the data-source-specific work for the data-source-specific implementations. This can be seen in the `Load (...)` declaration. Also notice that the `Load (...)` declaration has been declared with the `MustOverride` attribute, forcing any descendent classes to provide the implementation. The other code to notice here is the `doAddress` data object. This data object holds the state of the `Address` class in an encapsulated fashion, referred to as a *memento*.

Note   A memento supports the capture and externalization of an instance's internal state. This provides a variety of benefits, including serialization of the values to and from a store, easy tracking of the object's state, undo/redo capabilities, easy equality testing, and so on.

Externalize the data provider's state by using a memento. Mementos can be used for persisting and loading an object's state, testing for equality, and testing for actual changes in values, e.g., `IsDirty()` functionality.

Best Practice

On The Web   An abstract class named `DataObject.vb` provides ancestor functionality when creating memento data objects. This abstract class contains reflective methods to clone the object, test for equality, and reset the object's values. This is the base class for the mementos used in the online code.

Take a look at a data source–specific Address example:

Address.vb - SQL Server Implementation

```
'''------------------------------------------------------------
''' This is the SQL implementation.
'''------------------------------------------------------------
Public Class Address
  Inherits ImplAddress

'''------------------------------------------------------------
''' The actual SQL specific implementation for the load()
'''------------------------------------------------------------
  Public Overrides Sub Load(ByVal strId As String)
Dim cmd As SqlCommand = Nothing
Dim conn As SqlConnection = Nothing
Dim dataReader As SqlDataReader = Nothing

Try
  ' setup the database connection using the determiner
```

```
' information.
  conn = New SqlConnection(Me.Determiner.BindingInfo)
  conn.Open()

  ' setup the command.
cmd = New SqlCommand( PropertyLoader.Instance.GetProperty( _
"Sql_Address_Select").Replace("%1", _ strId.ToString), conn)

dataReader = cmd.ExecuteReader( _  CommandBehavior.CloseConnection)

    If dataReader.Read Then
Me.Street1 = MySqlHelper.GetStringValue( _ dataReader, "Street1", "
<no value>")
Me.Street2 = MySqlHelper.GetStringValue( _ dataReader, "Street2", "
<no value>")
' similar code to initialize City, State & Zip...
    End If
    Me.SetOriginalValues()
Catch ex As Exception
  ' Do any special processing here.
  Throw(ex)
Finally
  ' cleanup
  If cmd IsNot Nothing Then cmd.Dispose
  If conn IsNot Nothing Then conn.Close()
  If dataReader IsNot Nothing Then dataReader.Close()
End Try
  End Sub

End Class
```

Because the `Address` class inherits from the `ImplAddress`, it picks up the full interface contract and does not have to worry about defining the property getter/setters for the individual fields. Instead, this class just focuses on the specifics of how to interact with the SQL Server database and populate the appropriate data object. The same is true of the Access `Address` class.

Best Practice

Use interfaces when defining the public contract (API/methods) of the data providers. This forces functional consistency between the client's consumed data object and the data-source-specific implementation of that object. This also enables customers to create their own classes implementing the defined interfaces and plug them into the application.

The client code in the following example utilizes this pattern. Contrast it with both the Factory and DAO code presented earlier.

Data Provider MainTester

```
Public Class MainTester
  '''-------------------------------------------------------------
''' This method tests the address data provider.
  '''-------------------------------------------------------------
```

```
Sub Main()
  Try
  Dim objAddr As New Address

objAddr.Load("1")
      Call PrintAddress(objAddr)
    Catch ex As Exception
      Console.WriteLine(ex.Message)
    End Try
End Sub
End Class
```

This client test code is even slimmer than the factory client code and there is no need to cast the object. In fact, in this client test code, there is no way to know that a database is providing the various class values. If transparency and low client code impact matter, the data provider approach supports these. Compared to the DAO approach, this approach has three lines of code versus the original seven, and presents a more intuitive way to work with the `Address` data object, as this code appears no different than typical code, e.g., `Dim strSomeString As String`.

Pros of the Data Provider Pattern

The data provider pattern can be extremely flexible, enabling either the developer or the client to replace data access classes quickly, and to specify unique determiners per provider, what data providers are supported, and to what data sources they can attach. Because the provider implementation definitions have been externalized, it is quite easy to change the behavior of an application by simply making changes to the configuration file. This is a huge gain because a recompile is not necessary to deploy a new build. Additionally, the ability to override the behavior of the application after deployment is a plus from the support and customer perspective.

Cons of the Data Provider Pattern

When using the data provider pattern, more discipline will be required when setting up external values contained in the configuration file(s), when creating the namespaces for classes, and when organizing the code base. Additionally, this pattern is more involved than the other two patterns discussed, and so requires more time to learn and a more object-oriented background to understand. This additional complexity may not fit all projects or teams.

 The complete source for the Data Providers project can be found OntheWebsite at www.SQLServerBible.com/files.htm. It includes templates to provide a starting point for data provider development.

Summary

Once you have determined that you will be building a data access layer for your application, you should ask yourself key questions about your expected, future, and client-oriented usage to help determine what pattern best fits your needs. Choosing the appropriate pattern can speed up coding and improve extensibility during your development cycle, while also reducing maintenance costs for the life cycle of your data access layer.

Externalizing your SQL queries, database dependencies, and business logic into configuration files, as the data provider pattern does, gives you flexibility to modify an application's behavior at runtime without the need to recompile. You can even support new databases by adding entries to the configuration files and providing the database-specific .NET assemblies — all with no need to recompile the application or even restart it. This ability to dynamically adjust the behavior of your data access layer at runtime and without recompilation benefits environments that require as little downtime as possible.

While three patterns have been explored in this chapter, there are other patterns for data access and variations on the patterns discussed in this chapter. Don't be afraid to explore other data access design options, and ask your elaborating questions when examining them.

Having a flexible, well-encapsulated data access layer can provide numerous benefits to your application during design, implementation, and once deployed.

✦   ✦   ✦

Appendixes

The appendixes provide some look-up information that applies to nearly every chapter - SQL Server specifications, listings of the system views, and details of the book's sample databases. Also, continue to check the book's website for code updates, additional material, and ScreenCasts; www.SQLServerBible.com.

SQL Server 2005 Specifications

Table A-1, starting on the following page, lists the SQL server specifications for SQL Server 2005. Table A-2, which follows, lists its edition features.

Table A-1: SQL Server Specifications

Feature	SQL Server 6.5	SQL Server 7.0	SQL Server 2000	SQL Server 2005
Server Features				
Automatic Configuration	No	Yes	Yes	Yes
Page Size	2KB	8KB	8KB	8KB + extendable
Max Row Size	1,962 bytes	8,060 bytes	8,060 bytes	8,060 bytes
Page-Level Locking	Yes	Yes	Yes	Yes
Row-Level Locking	Insert only	Yes	Yes	Yes
Files Located	Devices	Files and filegroups	Files and filegroups	Files and filegroups
Kerberos and Security Delegation	No	No	Yes	Yes
C2 Security Certification	No	No	Yes	Yes
Bytes Per Character Column	255	8,000	8,000	8,000
Automatic Log Shipping	No	No	Yes	Yes
Index-Computed Column	No	No	Yes	Yes
Max Batch Size	128KB	65,536 * network packet–size bytes	65,536 * network packet–size bytes	65,536 * network packet–size bytes
Bytes Per Text/Image	2GB	2GB	2GB	2GB
Objects in Database	2 billion	2,147,483,647	2,147,483,647	2,147,483,647
Parameters Per Stored Procedure	255	1,024	1,024	1,024
References Per Table	31	253	253	253
Rows Per Table	Limited by available storage	Limited by available storage	Limited by available storage	Limited by available storage
Table Per Database	2 billion	Limited by available storage	Limited by available storage	Limited by available storage
Table Per select Statement	16	256	256	256
Triggers Per Table	3	Limited by number of objects in database	Limited by number of objects in database	Limited by number of objects in database
Bytes Per Key (Index, Foreign, or Primary)	900	900	900	900
Bytes Per Group by or Order by	900	8,060	8,060	8,060

Feature	SQL Server 6.5	SQL Server 7.0	SQL Server 2000	SQL Server 2005
Bytes Per Row	900	8,060	8,060	8,060
Bytes of Source Text Per Stored Procedure	65,025	Batch size or 250MB, whichever is less	Batch size or 250MB, whichever is less	Batch size or 250MB, whichever is less
Columns Per Key (Index, Foreign, or Primary)	16	16	16	16
Columns in Group by or Order by	16	Limited by bytes	Unspecified	Unspecified
Columns Per Table	255	1,024	1,024	1,024
Columns Per select Statement	4,096	4,096	4,096	4,096
Columns Per insert Statement	250	1,024	1,024	1,024
Database Size	1TB	1,048,516TB	1,048,516TB	1,048,516TB
Databases Per Server	32,767	32,767	32,767 (per instance)	32,767 (per instance)
File Groups Per Database	–	256	256	256
Files Per Database	32	32,767	32,767	32,767
Data-File Size	32GB	32TB	32TB	16TB
Log-File Size	32GB	4TB	32TB	2TB
Foreign-Key References Per Table	16	253	253	Unlimited
Identifier Length (Table, Column Names, etc.)	30	128	128	128
XML Indexes	-	-	-	249
Instances Per Computer	1	1	16	16
Locks Per Instance	2,147,483,647	2,147,483,647 or 40 percent of SQL Server memory	2,147,483,647 or 40 percent of SQL Server memory	2,147,483,647 or 40 percent of SQL Server memory (64-bit limited only by memory)
Parallel Query Execution	No	Yes	Yes	Yes
Federated Databases	No	No	Yes	Yes
Indexes Per Table Used in Query Execution	1	Multiple	Multiple	Multiple

Continued

Table A-1 *(continued)*

Feature	SQL Server 6.5	SQL Server 7.0	SQL Server 2000	SQL Server 2005
Administration Features				
Automatic-Data and Log-File Growth	No	Yes	Yes	Yes
Automatic Index Statistics	No	Yes	Yes	Yes
Profiler Tied to Optimizer Events	No	Yes	Yes	Yes
Alert on Performance Conditions	No	Yes	Yes	Yes
Conditional Multistep Agent Jobs	No	Yes	Yes	Yes
Programming Features				
Recursive Triggers	No	Yes	Yes	Yes
Multiple Triggers Per Table Event	No	Yes	Yes	Yes
instead of Triggers	No	No	Yes	Yes
Unicode Character Support	No	Yes	Yes	Yes
User-Defined Function	No	No	Yes	Yes
Indexed Views	No	No	Yes	Yes
Cascading DRI Deletes and Updates	No	No	Yes	Yes
Collation Level	Server	Server	Server, database, table, query	Server, database, table, query
Nested Stored-Procedure Levels	16	32	32	32
Nested Subqueries	16	32	32	32
Nested Trigger Levels	16	32	32	32
XML Support	No	No	Yes	Yes
Replication Features				
Snapshot Replication	Yes	Yes	Yes	Yes
Transactional Replication	Yes	Yes	Yes	Yes
Merge Replication with Conflict Resolution	No	Yes	Yes	Yes
Enterprise Manager/Management Studio Features				
Database Diagram	No	Yes	Yes	Yes
Graphical Table Creation	Yes	Yes	Yes	Yes
Database Designer	No	Yes	Yes	Yes
Query Designer	No	Yes	Yes	Yes

Table A-2: Edition Features

Feature	Mobile	Express	WorkGroup Edition	Standard Edition	Enterprise Edition
Target Audience/ Intended Application	Windows Mobile Smart Client Devices	Embedded within application	Small Workgroups	Mid-size, department, workgroup databases	Very large enterprise databases
Scaling Limitations					
Database Size Limit	2GB	4GB	No limit	No limit	No limit
CPUs Supported (may also be limited by the Windows version)	1	1	2	4	No limit
Memory Supported (also limited by the Windows version)	1GB	1GB	3 GB	Windows Max	Windows Max
64-bit Support	n/a	WOW	WOW	Yes	Yes
Engine Features					
Multiple Instances	No	Yes	Yes	Yes	Yes
Failover Clustering	No	No	No	Yes	Yes
Log Shipping	No	No	No	Yes	Yes
Enhanced Parallelism	No	No	No	No	Yes
Indexed Views	No	No	No	Yes	Yes
Federated Databases	No	No	No	Yes	Yes
Developer Features					
Notification Services	No	No	No	Yes	Yes
Service Broker	No	Yes, subscriber only	Yes	Yes	Yes
Web Services	No	No	No	Yes	Yes
Import/Export	No	No	Yes	Yes	Yes
Replication					
Merge Replication	Yes	Subscriber only	Yes, up to 25 subscribers	Yes	Yes
Transactional Replication		Subscriber only	Yes, up to 5 subscribers	Yes	Yes
Oracle Replication	No	No	No	No	Yes (Oracle Publisher)

Continued

Table A-2 *(continued)*

Feature	Mobile	Express	WorkGroup Edition	Standard Edition	Enterprise Edition
Manageability					
Profiler	No	No	No	Yes	Yes
Management Studio	?	Express Edition download only	Yes	Yes	Yes
Database TuningAdvisor				Yes	Yes
Full-Text Search		No	Yes	Yes	Yes
SQL Agent		No	Yes	Yes	Yes
BI Features					
Report Services		Soon	Yes	Yes	Yes
Report Builder			Yes	Yes	Yes
Report Data Sources		Soon, local only	Local only	Yes	Yes

✦   ✦   ✦

Sample Databases

In addition to Microsoft's Adventureworks sample database, this book draws examples from the following five sample databases, each designed to illustrate a particular design concept or development style:

- ◆ *Cape Hatteras Adventures* is actually two sample databases that together demonstrate upsizing to a relational SQL Server database. Version 1 consists of a simple Access database and an Excel spreadsheet — neither of which is very sophisticated. Version 2 is a typical small- to mid-size SQL Server database employing identity columns and views. It uses an Access project as a front end and publishes data to the Web using the SQL Server Web Publishing Wizard and stored procedures.

- ◆ The *OBXKites* database tracks inventory, customers, and sales for a fictitious kite retailer with four stores in North Carolina's Outer Banks. This database is designed for robust scalability. It employs GUIDs for replication and Unicode for international sales. In various chapters in the book, partitioned views, full auditing features, and Analysis Services cubes are added to the OBXKites database.

- ◆ The *Family* database stores family tree history. While the database has only two tables, `person` and `marriage`, it sports the complexities of a many-to-many self-join and extraction of hierarchical data.

- ◆ Twenty-five of *Aesop's Fables* provide the text for Chapter 13, "Using Full-Text Search."

This appendix documents the required files (Table B-1) and the database schemas for the sample databases.

All the files to create these sample databases, and chapter code files, may be downloaded from www.SQLServerBible.com.

The Sample Database Files

The sample files should be installed into the C:\SQLServerBible directory. The SQL Server sample web applications are coded to look for template files in a certain directory structure. The DTS packages and distributed queries also assume that the Access and Excel files are in that directory.

Table B-1: Sample Database Files

Cape Hatteras Adventures Version 2

C:\SQLServerBible\Sample Databases\CapeHatterasAdventures

CHA2_Create.sql	Script that generates the database for Cape Hatteras Adventures Version 2, including tables, constraints, indexes, views, stored procedures, and user security.
CHA_Convert.sql	Distributed queries that convert data from Access and Excel into the Cape Hatteras Adventures Version 2 database. This script mirrors the DTS package and assumes that the Access and Excel source files are in the C:\SQLServerBible directory.
CHA1_Customers.mdb	Access database of customer list, used prior to SQL Server conversion. Data is imported from this file into the CHA1 SQL Server database.
CHA1_Schdule.xls	Excel spreadsheet of events, tours, and guides, used prior to SQL Server conversion. Data is imported from this file into the CHA1 SQL Server database.
CHA2_Events.xml	Sample XML file.
CHA2_Events.dtd	Sample XML Data Type Definition file.
CHA2.adp	Sample Access front end to the CHA2 database.

OBXKites

C:\SQLServerBible\Sample Databases\OBXKites

OBXKites_Create.sql	Script that generates the database for the OBXKites database, including tables, views, stored procedures, and functions.
OBXKites_Populate.sql	Script that populates the database for the OBXKites database with sample data by calling the stored procedures.
OBXKites_Query.sql	A series of sample test queries with which to test the population of the OBXKites database.

The Family

C:\SQLServerBible\Sample Databases\Family

Family_Create.sql	Script that creates the Family database tables and stored procedures, and populates the database with sample data.
Family_Queries.sql	A set of sample queries against the Family database.

Aesop's Fables

C:\SQLServerBible\Sample Databases\Aesop

Aesop_Create.sql	Script that creates the Aesop database and Fable table and populates the database with 25 of Aesop's fables. This sample database is used with full-text search.
Aesop.adp	Access front end for browsing the fables

Material Specifications

C:\SQLServerBible\Sample Databases\MaterialSpec

MS_Create.sql	Script to create the Material Specification database.
MS_Populate.sql	Script to populate the Material Specification database with sample data from a computer-clone store.

To create one of the sample databases, run the `create` script within Query Analyzer. The script will drop the database if it exists. These scripts make it easy to rebuild the database, so if you want to experiment, go ahead. Because the script drops the database, no connections to the database can exist when the script is run. Enterprise Manager will often keep the connection even if another database is selected. If you encounter an error, chances are good that Enterprise Manager, or a second connection in Query Analyzer, is holding an open connection.

Cape Hatteras Adventures Version 2

The fictitious Cape Hatteras Adventures (CHA) is named for the Cape Hatteras lighthouse in North Carolina, one of the most famous lighthouses and life-saving companies in America. Cape Hatteras is the easternmost point of North Carolina's Outer Banks, known for incredible empty beaches and the graveyard of the Atlantic.

Cape Hatteras Adventures leads wild and sometimes exotic adventures for the rich and famous. From excursions down the gnarly Gauley River in West Virginia to diving for sunken treasure off the Outer Banks to chopping through the Amazon jungle, Cape Hatteras Adventures gets its guests there and brings them back, often alive and well.

The staff and management of CHA are outdoors folks and their inclination to avoid the indoors shows in the effort that's been put into IT. The customer/prospect list is maintained in Access 2000 in a single-table database. It's used primarily for mailings. The real workhorse is an Excel spreadsheet that tracks events, tours, and tour guides in a single flat-file format. In the same page, a second list tracks customers for each event. Although the spreadsheet is not a proper normalized database, it does contain the necessary information to run the business.

QuickBooks handles all financial and billing activities and both the company president and the bookkeeper are very satisfied with that setup. They foresee no need to improve the financial or billing software.

Application Requirements

CHA has grown to the point that it realizes the need for a better scheduling application; however, it desires to "keep the tough work in the rapids and not in the computer." CHA has contracted for the development and maintenance of the database.

All scheduling and booking of tours takes place at the main office in Cape Hatteras, North Carolina. CHA launches tours from multiple sites, or base camps, throughout the world. The base camps generally have no computer access and sometimes no electricity. Guides are dispatched to the base camp with a printed guest list. If it's determined in the future that a base camp may need to be staffed and have access to the schedule online, a web page will be developed at that time.

Each base camp may be responsible for multiple tours. A tour is a prearranged, repeatable experience. Each time the tour is offered, it's referred to as an event. An event will have one lead guide, who is responsible for the safety and enjoyment of the guests. Other guides may also come along as needed.

As CHA brings on more guides with broader skills, the database must track the guides and which tours each one is qualified to lead.

Database Design

The database design uses typical one-to-many relationships between customer type and customer, and from guide to base camp to tour to event. Many-to-many relationships exist between customer and event, guide and tour, and guide and event, as shown in Figure B-1.

Concerning the development style, there is currently no need for multiple database sites, so identity columns will be used for simplicity of design. The primary means of access to the data is through views and direct select statements.

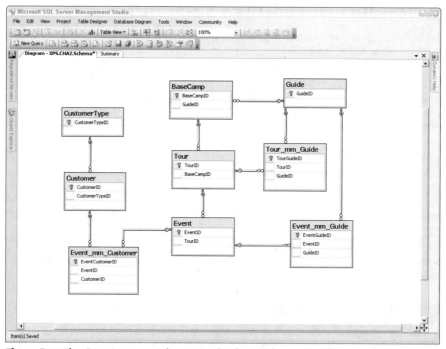

Figure B-1: The Cape Hatteras Adventures database schema

Data Conversion

The `CHA2_Create.sql` script creates an empty database. The data resides in the Access and Excel spreadsheets. Both the `CHA_Conversion` DTS package and the `CHA_Convert.sql` script can extract the data from Access and Excel and load it into SQL Server.

CHA2.adp Front End

Because the Cape Hatteras Adventures staff is comfortable with Access forms and does not require the robustness of a full Visual Basic or .NET application, a simple front end has been developed using Access.adp project technology.

OBX Kites

OBX Kites is a high-quality kite retailer serving kite enthusiasts and vacationers around the Outer Banks, where the winds are so steady the Wright brothers chose the area (Kill Devil Hills) for their historic glider flights and their first powered flights. OBX Kites operates a main store/warehouse and four remote retail locations, and is planning to launch an e-commerce website.

Application Requirements

OBX Kites needs a solid and useful order/inventory/purchase order system with a middle-of-the-road set of features. For simplicity, all contacts are merged into a single table and the contact type is signified by flags. A contact can be a customer, employee, or vendor. Customers have a lookup for customer type, which is referenced in determining the discount. Full details are maintained on customers, with a summer location and the home location. The product/inventory system must handle multiple suppliers per product, price history, multiple inventory items per product, multiple locations, and inventory transactions to track inventory movement.

Database Design

The database design uses standard one-to-many relationships throughout.

The database construction must support replication and Unicode for international customers. For performance and flexibility, the database implements with two filegroups — one for heavy transactions and the other for static read-mostly data.

The database design (see Figure B-2) is a standard inventory, order-processing database.

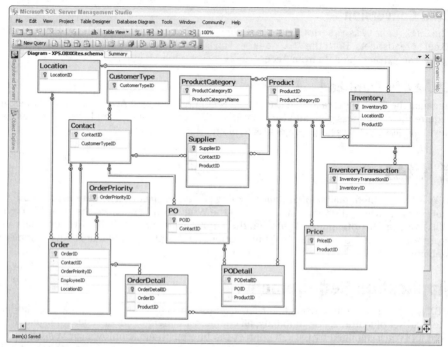

Figure B-2: The OBXKites sample database schema, as shown in Enterprise Manager's Database Designer

The Family

This small database demonstrates multiple hierarchical reflexive relationships for interesting queries and both cursors and queries to navigate the genealogical hierarchy.

Application Requirements

The Family database must store every person in the family, along with genealogical information, including both biological and marital relationships. The database is populated with five generations of a fictitious family for query purposes.

Database Design

The Family database consists of two tables and three relationships, as configured in the Database Designer in Figure B-3. Each person has an optional reflexive MotherID and FatherID foreign key back to the PersonID. The marriage table has a foreign key to the PersonID for the husband and the wife. The primary keys are integer columns for simplicity.

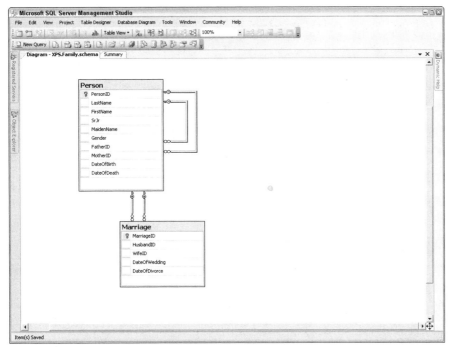

Figure B-3: The Family sample database schema as shown in Enterprise Manager's Database Designer

Aesop's Fables

Aesop's collection of fables is an excellent test bed for string searches and full-text search. The fables are relatively short and familiar, and they're in the public domain.

Application Requirements

The primary purpose of this database is to enable you to experience SQL Server's full-text search. Therefore, the database must include a few character columns, a BLOB or image column, and a BLOC-type column.

Database Design

The database design is very simple — a single table with one fable per row.

✦　　✦　　✦

Index

Index

Continued

Continued

Continued

Continued

Continued

Continued